Using Vis

PHIL FELDMAN
ROGER JENNINGS
BARRY SEYMOUR
BOB EIDSON
PAM PALMER
STEVE GILLMOR
JACK PESSO

PROGRAMMING
S E R I E S

Using Visual Basic 3

Copyright © *1993 by Que®Corporation.*

Library of Congress Catalog No.: 93-62614

ISBN: 1-56529-763-X

95 94   6 5 4

Interpretation of the printing code: the rightmost double-digit number is the year of the book's printing; the rightmost single-digit number, the number of the book's printing. For example, a printing code of 93-1 shows that the first printing of the book occurred in 1993.

Screen reproductions in this book were created with Collage Plus from Inner Media, Inc., Hollis, NH.

Publisher: David P. Ewing

Associate Publisher: Rick Ranucci

Director of Publishing: Michael Miller

Managing Editor: Corinne Walls

Marketing Manager: Ray Robinson

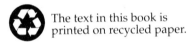

The text in this book is printed on recycled paper.

Trademarks

For Bugg and Michael, who make it all worthwhile.

CREDITS

Publishing Manager
Joseph B. Wikert

Acquisitions Editor
Sarah Browning

Product Development Specialists
Bryan Gambrel
Jay Munro

Production Editor
Michael Cunningham

Editors
Mary Anne Sharbaugh
Linda Seifert
Phil Kitchel
Jodi Jensen
Lori Cates
Susan Moore
Patick Kanouse
Chris Haidri
Thomas Hayes

Technical Editor
Robert W. Karp,
WinResources Computing, Inc.
Eric Bloom

Book Designer
Amy Peppler-Adams

Production Team
Nick Anderson
Angela Bannan
Danielle Bird
Ayrika Bryant
Laurie Casey
Charlotte Clapp
Brook Farling
Michelle Greenwalt
Carla Hall
Heather Kaufman
Bob LaRoche
Caroline Roop
Tina Trettin
Mary Beth Wakefield
Lillian Yates

Indexers
Michael Hughes
Joy Dean Lee
Johnna VanHoose

Composed in Goudy and MCPdigital by Que Corportion

Phil Feldman received his B.A. degree in physics from the University of California in 1968 and did graduate work in computer science at U.C.L.A. For 15 years, he worked at TRW Systems, Inc. where he was a manager of software development on numerous aerospace engineering projects. He has contributed many articles to engineering journals and personal computer magazines. He has authored or coauthored with Tom Rugg more than 20 computer magazines. He has also authored or coauthored with Tom Rugg on more than 20 computer books. Mr. Feldman is managing partner of 32 Plus, Inc., a software development and consulting firm.

Roger Jennings is a consultant specializing in Windows database, word processing, and multimedia applications. He was a member of the beta-test team for Microsoft Access, Word for Windows 2.0, Windows 3.1, Windows for Workgroups, Video for Windows, Visual Basic for DOS, Visual Basic 2.0 and 3.0, and the Microsoft Professional Toolkit for Visual Basic 1.0. He is the author of *Discover Windows 3.1 Multimedia*, *Access for Windows Hot Tips*, and *Using Access 1.1 for Windows*; a contributing author to *Killer Windows Utilities*; and was a technical editor for *Using Word for Windows 2,* Special Edition, and *Using Windows 3.1*, Special Edition, each published by Que Corporation. Roger has more than 25 years of computer-related experience and has presented technical papers on computer hardware and software to the Academy of Sciences of the USSR, the Society of Automotive Engineers, the American Chemical Society, and a wide range of other scientific and technical organizations. He is a principal of OakLeaf Systems, a Northern California software development and consulting firm; you may contact him via CompuServe (ID 70233,2161), the Internet (70233,2161@compuserve.com), or fax (510-839-9422).

Steve Gillmor has written numerous articles and features for a variety of computer and video-related magazines. He has specialized in user-programming and authoring system technologies, both as a writer of software manuals and also as a developer of integrated automation systems for desktop video and graphics. He is currently Director of Southern Digital, Inc., in Charleston, South Carolina, where he consults on computing and video while writing a weekly technology column for the Charleston Post and Courier.

Barry Seymour does business as Marquette Computer Consultants, providing Visual Basic consulting, training, and programming services to clients throughout the San Francisco Bay Area. He has also authored a number of popular shareware programs in Visual Basic, including TaskTracker, a time management/billing application, and Visual Basic Office, an add-on to Visual Basic 2.0 and 3.0 which adds code, filed, clipboard, window, program, and project management functions to the VB programming environment. He is a regular participant in the MSBASIC forum on CompuServe.

Pam Palmer is an independent consultant specializing in the software development and quality assurance areas. She provides training, planning, and development assistance to a wide range of businesses. She is a Certified Microsoft Visual Basic Instructor. She can be contacted via CompuServe (ID 74170, 1526).

ACKNOWLEDGMENTS

It's with much gratitude that I welcome the opportunity to thank those who helped shape this book into the finished product which you now hold. Most certainly, this book represents the cooperative efforts of several talented individuals.

First and foremost, I want to acknowledge my collaborators. Pam Palmer, Barry Seymour, and Bob Eidson each did yeoman's work on several chapters. Steve Gillmor developed the material on the Data Control while Jack Pesso helped write about text displays. These contributors are all Visual Basic programming professionals whose ideas and sample applications are spread throughout the book. Many thanks.

The top-notch staff at Que Corporation did its usual fine job. Special thanks to Jay Munro and Bryan Gambrel for their project development and to Michael Cunningham as head of the editing team. Sarah Browning was the glue that held the crumbling pieces together. Kudos all around.

On a personal note, the support from my family and friends is most appreciated. To Tom Rugg, my longtime collaborator and even longer-time friend, thanks for being a sounding board and for just being. To Gilda and Michael, I know the long days (and nights!) were a strain. You're the greatest. Thanks for everything.

OVERVIEW

TABLE OF CONTENTS

I Getting Started with Visual Basic

II Building Applications

III Designing User Interfaces

V Customizing Applications

VI Interacting with Other Windows Applications

VII Using VB Professional Edition

xxxvii

Introduction

"Programmers have power."

Throughout my career as programming instructor and author, I've said (and written) that statement many times. The power referred to here is the ability to make a computer do exactly what you want.

Never have programmers been more empowered than with Visual Basic. Windows programming used to be the domain of the elite. Writing a Windows application with C or Microsoft's Software Development Kit (SDK) was a time-draining exercise laden with arcane syntax, hard-to-debug code, and constant frustration.

Microsoft's release of Visual Basic a few years ago was not only a much needed breath of fresh air, it was nothing short of an evolutionary step. Suddenly, just the right tools were in the hands of the Windows programmer.

With Visual Basic, if you want to create a window, you simply draw it on the video screen. Using the Toolbox, a few mouse clicks is all you need to put a text box, command button, or other standard control into the window. Like a graphics designer, you simply draw the window and its contents exactly as you want them to appear—in whatever sizes and screen locations you choose. Add a few lines of code to make things work and, almost like magic, you're done. Instead of frustration and delay, creating Windows applications becomes relatively short work, and even fun. The power is back.

Who Should Use This Book

This book gives you the power of Visual Basic. The target reader is anyone who wants to learn Windows programming. No prior Visual Basic experience is assumed. In fact, the first few chapters focus on making the Visual Basic novice comfortable with Windows programming in general, and with the event-driven nature of Visual Basic in particular.

Because Visual Basic exists in the domain of Windows, you need some familiarity with that environment. If you have ever used a Windows application such as word processor or spreadsheet, you already have sufficient experience. If you are new to Windows, take some time to explore how Windows works. Chapter 2, "A Windows Primer," will help.

You should have some prior exposure to elementary programming. Although this book could be used by someone who has never written a line of code, it's best if you know at least a few simple concepts—such as what a variable is, and the difference between numerical and text data.

Any experience you have with the BASIC language will be a big plus. If you have ever programmed at all with GW-BASIC, BASICA, QuickBASIC, QBasic, or any other dialect of BASIC, you are in good stead here. Visual Basic contains many language extensions not found in these earlier versions of BASIC, but Visual Basic's core language is BASIC, pure and simple. If you have not had any exposure to BASIC (or any programming experience at all), it would be a good idea to spend some time with one of the BASIC programming books such as *Using Basic,* 2nd Edition, written by this author and published by Que.

A Word about BASIC and Microsoft

The Microsoft software empire was built on BASIC. The company's first products back in the late 70's and early 80's were BASIC language interpreters for emerging microcomputers such as the Altair, Commodore Pet, Tandy TRS-80, and the IBM PC.

Today, Microsoft Windows is fast becoming (many would say already *is*) the de facto computing environment for IBM PC's and compatibles. Windows is the second best-selling software product of all time, behind only DOS.

It's interesting that, when deciding on what language tool to offer Windows developers, Microsoft bypassed "trendy" languages like C and Pascal. Instead, the company went back to its roots and chose BASIC. This is nothing short of a testimonial to the popularity and flexibility of BASIC—a language that has been going strong and evolving for 30 years. With Visual Basic for Windows, BASIC has come full circle.

What's New in Version 3.0 of Visual Basic

This book covers both the Standard and Professional Editions of Visual Basic, Version 3.0. If you are familiar with the earlier versions of Visual Basic, here are some key new features introduced with Version 3.0. Unless stated otherwise, these features apply to both the Standard and Professional Editions.

- The Data control, which can manipulate existing databases.

- The Access engine that provides the Data control with a link to databases in popular formats such as Paradox, dBASE, FoxPro, and Access.

- An improved OLE (Object Linking and Embedding) control that supports the recent OLE 2.0 standards, including advanced features such as OLE automation and in-place activation.

- Financial functions that provide loan and annuity information.

- MRU (Most Recently Used) project list in the File menu. By selecting a project from this list, you can quickly bring that application into Visual Basic's design environment.

- Pop-up menus.

- The option to Save on Run, which automatically saves your project each time you run it.

- The Common Dialog custom control, which previously was included only in the Professional Edition, is now included with the Standard Edition as well.

- The Outline custom control, which enables you to create hierarchical lists, is provided with the Professional Edition.

An Overview of the Book's Contents

This book is divided into seven parts with 33 total chapters that cover a wide range of Visual Basic topics. The first 31 chapters apply equally to both the Standard and Professional Editions of Visual Basic 3.0. The final two chapters cover features unique to the Professional Edition. The following sections provide an overview for each of the seven parts of the book.

Part I: Getting Started with Visual Basic

This section contains four chapters designed to familiarize the novice Visual Basic user with the programming environment. Chapter 1, "An Overview of Visual Basic," introduces Visual Basic's event-oriented approach to Windows programming.

Chapter 2, "A Windows Primer," brings the inexperienced Windows user up to speed in understanding how Windows works and how Windows programs should behave. This chapter discusses Windows from both a user's perspective and a programmer's point of view.

In Chapter 3, "Test Driving Visual Basic: A Sample Application," you plunge right into developing a working application. Visual Basic is best taught by example. The approach throughout this book is action oriented—plenty to do, no long discourses. If you are a Visual Basic novice, this chapter is especially important. You gain a hands-on feeling for the way Visual Basic works and the things that it can do.

Chapter 4, "Learning the VB Environment," explains the Visual Basic programming environment with step-by-step practice in navigating the menu system, using the Toolbar, getting on-line help, and using the Code editor.

Part II: Building Applications

Now that you have a solid understanding of the programming environment, the five chapters in this section teach you the fundamental techniques of developing applications. You learn how to use the myriad of tools that Visual Basic puts at your disposal. This section explains how you place Toolbox controls on a form, manipulate the Properties window to assign property values to these controls, and use the Code editor to write event procedures, which are the heart and soul of Visual Basic applications. The final chapter in this section explains how to manage the components of a project using the Project window.

Part III: Designing User Interfaces

This section contains three chapters to help you design the visual appearance of your applications. Chapter 10, "Using Dialog Boxes," explains how to create input boxes and message boxes through which the user of an application can provide input or view output, respectively.

Chapter 11, "Displaying Graphics," covers the many ways that Visual Basic can manipulate graphics images. Windows is a visual environment and Visual Basic takes full advantage of this graphical platform to provide you with an extensive set of graphing tools. By manipulating pictures, colors, coordinate systems, and other graphics elements, you can relatively easily give your finished applications the look of professional applications.

Chapter 12, "Displaying Text and Fonts," explains how to create effective text displays so that an application can powerfully convey information to the user. Visual Basic provides tools to select fonts and font attributes, and to display numbers and text strings in easy-to-read formats. Also, this chapter explains how to direct program output to a printer.

Part IV: Using the Programming Language

Chapters 13 through 21 explore the Visual Basic programming language. Although the approach is experiential, the discussion explains each topic thoroughly. These chapters cover such subjects as procedure structure, logic flow, data types, numeric and string functions, object variables, working with the Code editor, debugging, and application testing. Many short program examples demonstrate the ideas.

Part V: Customizing Applications

At this point, you have the fundamental knowledge necessary to develop Visual Basic applications. This section expands your horizons by discussing the finer points of program development. You learn how your applications can respond to any of the user's mouse movements or key presses that you wish to recognize.

Other subjects discussed in this section include the following: building a customized menu system complete with submenus and hotkeys, working with disk files, using the Grid control to display data in ordered rows and columns, creating parent and child windows with the Multiple Document Interface (MDI), and using the Data control to manipulate databases.

Part VI: Interacting with Other Windows Applications

The Windows environment supports multitasking, which means that multiple applications can run simultaneously. As such, your Visual Basic applications can utilize the resources of Windows, manipulate other loaded applications, and share information with them. This section contains three chapters that discuss how your Visual Basic applications can take advantage of this dynamic environment.

Chapter 29, "Manipulating the Windows Environment," concentrates on ways that Visual Basic applications can manipulate the resources of Windows itself. Topics include the use of the Clipboard, sending keystrokes to other applications, using timers to manipulate unattended applications, calling procedures in a Dynamic Link Library (DLL), and using the Common Dialog control to create standardized Windows dialog boxes.

Chapter 30, "Using Dynamic Data Exchange (DDE)," discusses how a Visual Basic application can use DDE to exchange data to "converse" with another Windows application. Visual Basic has a variety of methods, events, and properties which support DDE. You learn how to develop client and server applications, how to establish application links, and how to exchange data.

Chapter 31, "Using Object Linking and Embedding (OLE)," explores the most advanced form of Windows data exchange. OLE extends the capabilities of DDE in that, with OLE, a complete graphical image of data (such as a spreadsheet chart) can be embedded into another application. The updated OLE control lets your Visual Basic applications take advantage of the latest advances in OLE technology.

Part VII: Using VB Professional Edition

The Professional Edition of Visual Basic adds some extra features to the capabilities of the Standard Edition. These extra features include the following: additional custom controls, the Control Development Kit (CDK) for writing customized control files, the Help Compiler for adding a help system to an application, enhanced capabilities of the Data control, and the Crystal Reports and the Crystal Control for writing reports based on information contained in databases.

Covering all these topics in detail is beyond the scope of this book. However, this section contains two chapters that delve into a great many of the features unique to the Professional Edition.

Chapter 32, "Using Custom Controls," explains most of the custom controls provided with the Professional Edition. These controls include Graphs, 3D controls, Spin buttons, Masked Edits, Key Status controls, Picture Clip controls, Gauges, Animated buttons, and the Outline control.

Chapter 33, "Adding a Help System to an Application," explains how to use the Help Compiler. This tool enables you to add a full-featured, Windows-compatible Help system to any Visual Basic application. With such a Help system, the user can browse through the topics, search for particular information, jump to related topics, and look at explanatory graphics.

Conventions Used in This Book

The design of this book uses the following typeface conventions:

- New terms and emphasized words appear in *italics*.

- Text you are asked to type is in **bold**.

- DOS commands, file names, and file paths usually appear in all uppercase characters (for example the SHARE command and the C:\VB\CONSTANT.TXT file).

- Program code lines, keywords, variable names, and other code items appear in a `monospace` font so that they stand out from the rest of the text.

- Tables and figures are numbered for easy reference.

A code instruction that is too long to fit on one physical line in the book must be printed on multiple lines. When that happens, you see a line-continuation icon that indicates that the instruction continues on the following line. This icon appears as a three-dimensional right-facing arrow. When you type such an instruction into the Visual Basic Code editor, continue to type one long line. The following instruction shows the line-continuation icon:

```
Response% = MsgBox("Click when you are ready to proceed",
➥BoxStyle, "Continue")
```

Getting Started with Visual Basic

PART

1

An Overview of Visual Basic

Anew era in BASIC programming is here. As Microsoft Windows becomes the de facto operating system of today's PCs, a programming challenge emerges. How can a programmer develop Windows applications as painlessly as possible?

Enter Visual Basic. This revolutionary programming language from Microsoft was first released in mid-1991. Version 2.0 came a year later, with Version 3.0 following in mid-1993. With Visual Basic, you can write full-fledged Windows applications with relative ease.

Although the syntax of the Visual Basic language parallels that of previous versions of BASIC, Visual Basic represents a conceptually different approach to programming, called *event-driven* programming. An application developed with an event-driven model *responds* to events that happen in the computer environment. Such events include the press of a mouse button or a call from another application running concurrently.

As a Visual Basic programmer, you are something of a designer, architect, and builder. You create the user interfaces for your applications by directly manipulating on-screen objects such as control buttons and dialog boxes. You assign values for the properties of these objects by selecting various characteristics such as colors and fonts from an extensive list.

You don't actually *write* any program code until you define what happens when a particular event occurs. Indeed, one of the great triumphs of Visual Basic is that you can develop complete Windows applications with minimal program instructions.

This chapter serves as an overview of Visual Basic. The main goals are to introduce you to the following subjects:

- Understanding the graphical interface revolution

- Installing Visual Basic

- Introducing event-oriented programming

- Learning the phases of developing an application

- Understanding the opening screen

The Graphical Revolution

The ongoing trend in the PC computing environment is toward more graphical, visual user interfaces. The typical computer user is now accustomed to software applications that feature drop-down menus, a variety of colors and fonts, and multiple windows.

Rather than typing archaic commands from the keyboard, today's users regularly move the mouse pointer onto an appropriate icon or menu option, then click the mouse button to activate a command or initiate a program.

In the current PC market, Microsoft Windows is the epitome of the graphical user interface. Windows applications have a consistent look and feel featuring icons, mouse support, drop-down menus, and resizable windows. (For more on Windows, see Chapter 2, "A Windows Primer.")

Visual computing works because it is intuitive. People are visually oriented and commonly interact with their world by responding to visual clues. The more visual their computing environment, the more natural it feels.

Programming follows suit. The more visual the programming tools are, the easier it is to develop and program applications. By combining graphical design tools with a structured, event-driven language, Visual Basic defines a new level of programming capability known simply as *visual programming*.

 **NOTE** **A Gooey Jargon**

Visual computing has spawned many colorful phrases and terms. Even some "graphical" acronyms have crept into everyday computer jargon. For example, GUI (pronounced "gooey") for Graphical User Interface, and WYSIWYG (pronounced "wizzywig") for What You See Is What You Get.

Visual Basic makes it a snap to create professional-looking user interfaces in your applications. Historically, programming graphics-oriented applications has been difficult. If you have experience with QBasic, QuickBASIC, or GW-BASIC, just consider the complexity of writing a program that includes drop-down menus and dialog boxes. With Visual Basic, you can design such interfaces with a minimal amount of actual programming.

Installing Visual Basic

Visual Basic 3.0 for Windows (see fig. 5.10). comes in two versions: Standard Edition and Professional Edition. Compared to the Standard Edition, the Professional Edition offers additional control objects that you can place in your applications, and some advanced programming features.

NOTE This book covers both the Standard and Professional Editions of Visual Basic 3.0. Most of this book describes Visual Basic from the point of view of the Standard Edition. However, if you have the Professional Edition, all this material still applies.

Indeed, because the Professional Edition simply extends the capabilities of the Standard Edition, this book is equally relevant to users of both editions of Visual Basic. Part VII of this book, beginning with Chapter 32, "Using Custom Controls," covers the features unique to the Professional Edition.

Visual Basic is a Windows application. As such, you install Visual Basic like you do most other Windows software. The following sections explain details of the installation process.

System Requirements

Visual Basic requires that your computer system has the following hardware and software:

- *An IBM-compatible computer, AT or higher.* The computer must have a processor chip compatible with the Intel 80286, 80386, or 80486 chip.

- *A hard disk.* As explained later in the section on installation, you can get by with 3.5M of available disk space, but 10M or more is preferred.

- *A graphics card and video display monitor, EGA or higher.* A VGA display is preferred.

- *A mouse or mouse-compatible pointing device.*

- *1M of RAM.* 2M or more is preferred.

- *MS-DOS 3.1 or PC DOS 3.1 or higher.*

- *Microsoft Windows 3.0 or higher, running in standard or enhanced mode.* Windows 3.1 is preferred.

Because Windows places heavy demands on the resources of a computer system, the more powerful your computer, the faster Visual Basic will perform. Ideally, your system should have at least an 80386SX processor chip, a VGA display, 4M of RAM, and 10M of available hard disk space (before installation) for the Standard Edition of Visual Basic.

First Installation Steps

The next several sections describe the installation of Visual Basic. The directions discuss the installation of both the Standard Edition and the Professional Edition. For the most part, the instructions are the same regardless of which edition you are installing. When there is a difference, however, the directions describe what to do in each case.

To install Visual Basic, follow these steps:

1. Start Windows.

2. Place Visual Basic's Disk 1, labeled "Setup," into your computer's A drive.

   You can also install from your B drive.

3. From Windows Program Manager, open the **F**ile menu and choose the **R**un... option.

   Alternatively, you can select the **R**un... option from the File menu in Windows File Manager.

4. Type **a:setup** (see Figure 1.1).

   If you are installing from the B drive, type **b:setup** instead.

Figure 1.1.

Launching the SETUP program from the Program Manager.

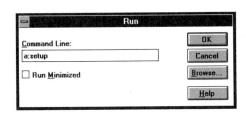

5. Follow the on-screen directions to execute this SETUP program.

   You will be prompted to type your name. (Each time you run Visual Basic, your name appears on-screen as the registered owner.)

   You must also indicate the directory for the Visual Basic files. By default, Visual Basic uses the C:\VB directory. However, you can optionally indicate a different directory name. If necessary, Visual Basic creates the directory name you specify.

Custom Setup

Early in the installation process, the SETUP program asks whether you want a complete installation or a custom installation. For the Standard Edition, the complete installation requires approximately 13M of available hard disk space. The complete installation of the Professional Edition requires approximately 32M of hard disk space.

Unless your hard disk space is at a premium, choose the complete installation. If you do select this option, skip ahead to the section titled "Completing the Installation."

If you need to worry about every megabyte of hard disk space, you can choose the custom installation. Figure 1.2 shows the custom installation screen for the Standard Edition, and Figure 1.3 shows the corresponding screen for the Professional Edition. These figures show the amount of hard disk space required to install each custom component.

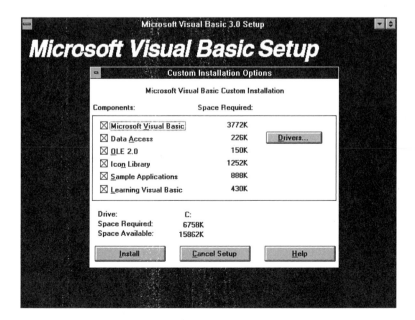

Figure 1.2.

The Custom Installation window for the Standard Edition.

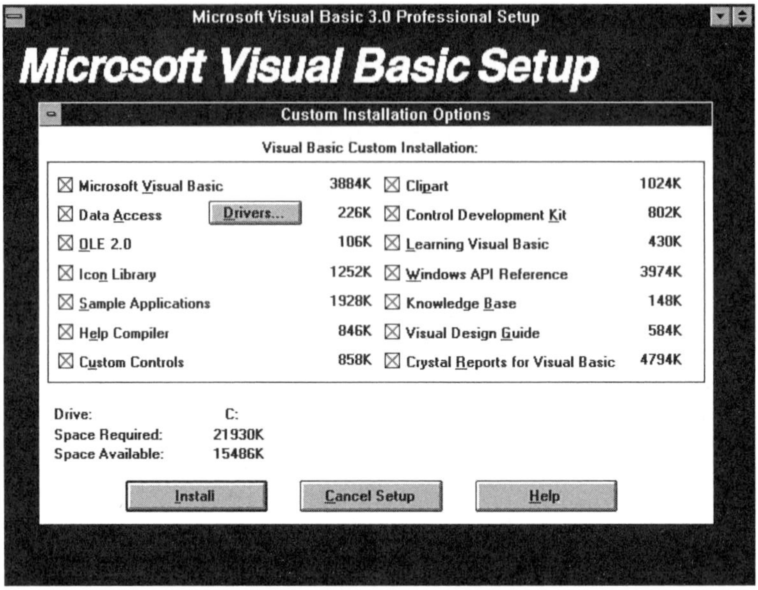

Figure 1.3.

The Custom Installation window for the Professional Edition.

As Figure 1.2 shows, there are six separate installation components you can select when installing the Standard Edition. For the Professional Edition, as shown in Figure 1.3, there are fourteen installation components.

For either edition, you can elect to *not* install a component by clicking its check box. When you deselect an option, the *X* in the check box disappears. Alternatively, you can toggle the *X* off and on by pressing the hot key associated with each option.

The following two sections describe the various components. When each component is listed, its hot key appears in boldface.

Custom Components Available in the Standard and Professional Editions

The six components available in the Standard Edition are also available in the Professional Edition. Here is a synopsis of these components:

Microsoft Visual Basic — The Visual Basic program (VB.EXE) and related support files, including the on-line help facility (VB.HLP) and a text file of predefined constants (CONSTANT.TXT). You must have VB.EXE installed if you want to develop applications. VB.EXE is just under 1M, VB.HLP is almost 3M, and the other files are relatively small. As a result, selecting this option requires almost 4M of hard disk space.

Data **Access**	The Data control (new in Visual Basic 3.0) facilitates the creation of database applications. This option installs software drivers so your Visual Basic applications can access data in various industry-standard formats. Click the Drivers button to select any or all of the following drivers for the Data control: BTrieve, dBASE, FoxPro, ODBC, and Paradox. This option requires approximately 250K of hard disk space. For details about using the Data control, see Chapter 28, "Using the Data Control to Interact with Databases."
OLE 2.0	The OLE control (improved in Visual Basic 3.0) supports Object Linking and Embedding, including advanced features such as OLE Automation. This option installs software libraries that extend the capabilities of the OLE control. Selecting this option uses about 100K of hard disk space. For information about developing OLE applications, see Chapter 31, "Using Object Linking and Embedding (OLE)."
Icon Library	Icons (graphic images) that you can use to enhance the look of your programs. This option requires more than 1M of disk space.
Sample Applications	Several examples of working Visual Basic programs. Besides providing instructive examples of Visual Basic programs, some of these applications are quite useful. For example, with the Icon Editor, you can design, modify, and save graphic icons for use with your applications. This option takes about 1M of hard disk space for the Standard Edition, and about 2M for the Professional Edition.
Learning Visual Basic	An on-screen tutorial about using Visual Basic. This option requires approximately one-half a megabyte.

The minimum installation includes only the Microsoft Visual Basic component. By deselecting the other available options, the installation requires less than 4M of hard disk space. (Actually, after installation is complete, you could delete the VB.HLP file to recover about 3M. Of course, you would not have access to any on-line help, but Visual Basic would run. Be aware that deleting the VB.HLP file is *not* recommended.)

If you choose not to install an option that you later decide to include (or vice versa), you can rerun the SETUP program and select a new installation configuration.

If you are installing the Standard Edition of Visual Basic, you can skip ahead to the section titled "Completing the Installation."

Custom Components Available Only in the Professional Edition

For the Professional Edition of Visual Basic, there are eight more custom components in addition to the components mentioned in the previous section. Here is a synopsis of these components:

Help Compiler	A tool with which you can add a Windows-compatible Help system to your Visual Basic applications. This option requires almost 1M of hard disk space. For more about creating Help facilities, see Chapter 33, "Adding a Help System to an Application."
Custom Controls	The Professional Edition adds over 20 custom controls that facilitate the creation of specialized applications. Select this option to include these customized controls in your Visual Basic environment. Almost 1M of hard disk space is required. For details on working with these custom controls, see Chapter 32, "Using Custom Controls."
Clipart	This option, which requires about 1M of hard disk space, installs approximately 100 graphical bitmap images on your hard disk. You can use these images to embellish the appearance of your applications.
Control Development Kit	A library of specialized routines with which you can create your own custom controls for use with Visual Basic. To take advantage of this kit, you must have advanced Windows programming skills based on the Microsoft Windows Software Development Kit (SDK) and a Windows version of the C programming language. This option requires almost 1M of hard disk space.
Windows API Reference	The Windows API (Application Program Interface) Reference is a library of low-level Windows routines that Visual Basic applications can call to directly interact with the Windows environment. This option, which requires almost 4M of hard disk space, installs into Visual Basic a Help system for the Windows API routines.

Knowledge **B**ase	A series of technical articles that answer frequently asked questions about Visual Basic. This option, which requires about 150K, installs as an extension to the regular Visual Basic Help system.
Visual Design **G**uide	This option, which requires about 600K, provides design tips on creating user interfaces for your Visual Basic applications. Included is a discussion of the de facto Windows standards for menu items and dialog box options. The design guide installs as an extension to the regular Visual Basic Help system.
Crystal **R**eports	A tool for writing reports and creating lists based on information contained in one or more databases. You can use this program separately from Visual Basic or, through the Crystal custom control, you can print reports with program code from within a Visual Basic application. This option requires almost 5M of hard disk space.

Completing the Installation

SETUP continues by loading the various Visual Basic files into the C:\VB directory (or whatever directory you specified for the installation). You are prompted to insert the installation disks into your A (or B) drive. The exact disks you must use depends on whether you chose a complete installation or a customized installation.

After copying the Visual Basic files to your hard disk, you see a screen indicating that installation is complete. Select the option that returns your computer to Windows.

Notice that SETUP creates a new Windows program group for Visual Basic. The group is labeled Visual Basic 3.0 and appears under the Program Manager along with your other Windows program groups (Main, Accessories, Games, etc.).

To start Visual Basic, first double-click the Visual Basic program group. A window opens that shows the Visual Basic icon. (See Figure 1.4.) Depending on the installation options you selected, other icons can appear in the group window. These icons represent support programs and files such as tutorials, Help files, and sample applications. Double-click the Visual Basic icon to start Visual Basic.

Figure 1.4.

The Visual Basic icon.

Understanding the Opening Screen

If you installed the Standard Edition, and chose a complete installation, your screen looks like Figure 1.5. For a complete installation of the Professional Edition, see Figure 1.6. Notice that the most significant difference between these two figures is that the Professional Edition includes many more icons in the Toolbox than the Standard Edition. The Toolbox is located on the left side of the screen. As described later in this chapter, these Toolbox icons represent the control objects that you can place into your applications.

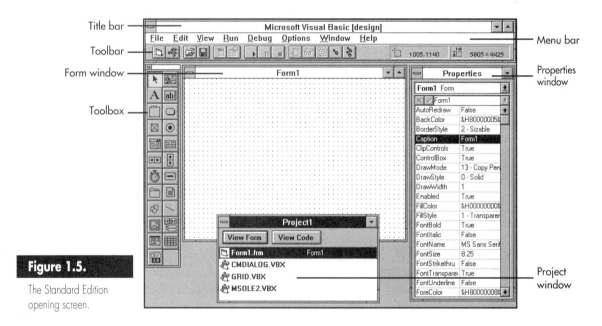

Title bar — Toolbar — Form window — Toolbox — Menu bar — Properties window — Project window

Figure 1.5.

The Standard Edition opening screen.

This chapter provides a brief introduction to the major components of the opening screen. Chapter 4, "Learning the Visual Basic Environment," explores this screen in more detail.

NOTE   **Rearranging the Default Screen**

In Figures 1.5 and 1.6, individual windows have been resized and repositioned so you can easily see each window. When you start Visual Basic, the default screen has some windows protruding over others. This overlapping obscures certain windows. As with most Windows applications, you can resize and reposition Visual Basic's individual windows. If you are unfamiliar with Windows resizing techniques, see Chapter 2, "A Windows Primer."

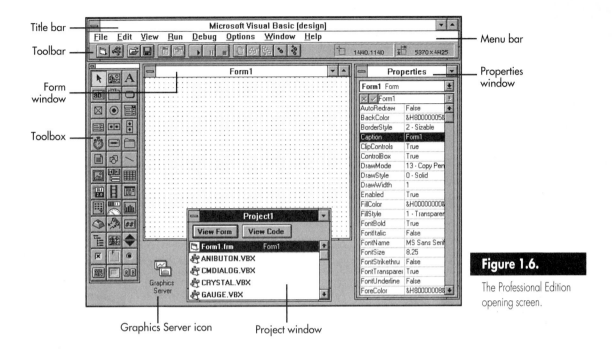

Title bar

Toolbar

Form window

Toolbox

Menu bar

Properties window

Figure 1.6.

The Professional Edition opening screen.

Graphics Server icon

Project window

The opening screen can seem crammed and a bit imposing. Don't dismay. It's true that Visual Basic is a complex product with many features. You become familiar with a whole new terminology and a new approach to programming. However, everything is fairly intuitive and any previous BASIC programming experience you have will help you along.

Here is a brief introduction to the major components of the opening screen:

Title bar	The horizontal bar along the top of the screen. This bar, present in most Windows applications, contains the name of the application. For now, the title bar reads Microsoft Visual Basic [design].
Menu bar	The menu bar is your gateway to Visual Basic's drop-down menu system. Each of the eight main menus opens to a submenu with additional choices. The menu system contains options to manipulate files, edit and debug programs, view particular windows, and get context-sensitive Help, along with many other features.

Form window	This window, located in the center of the screen, is the cornerstone of your application's user interface. When you design an application, you place text boxes, graphic buttons, and other visual objects onto a form. When the application is run, the form is what users see. An application can have several forms.
Toolbar	A row of icons located horizontally near the top of the screen. These icons provide instant access to frequently used commands (that are also available through the menus). Some commands include opening an existing project, running an application, and single-step tracing.
Toolbox	The vertical icon group located on the left side of the screen. The Toolbox provides a set of graphic objects, called *controls*, that you can place onto the forms of your application.
Graphics Server	This icon, that appears only for the Professional Edition, represents some Windows graphics routines that support the Graph custom control. The Graph control is included only with the Professional Edition of Visual Basic. Visual Basic automatically loads the Graphics Server into the Windows environment whenever the Graph custom control is loaded into the Toolbox.
Project window	This window lists the files, forms, and modules that comprise the current application. By clicking a name in this window, you can activate (view) the form or see the program code associated with the form.
Properties window	This window shows the attributes (properties) associated with a selected form or control. By manipulating values displayed in this window, you can modify the attributes of a control. For example, by changing the `BackColor` property, you can specify the background color of the current object.

A Note to Users of the Professional Edition

The first 31 chapters of this book describe Visual Basic and explain how to create applications using the tools and features found in the Standard Edition. As a user of the Professional Edition, you have access to all the Standard Edition features as well as some additional capabilities that are described in the later chapters of this book.

Until Chapter 32, the descriptions and screen shots that involve the Toolbox describe and show the Standard Edition. Your Toolbox, however, contains several additional controls not found in the Standard Edition. If you closely compare the Toolbox icons in Figures 1.5 and 1.6, you'll see that all the icons found in the Standard Edition Toolbox appear in the upper half of the Professional Edition Toolbox.

As such, you can easily use the Professional Edition when following the examples and descriptions in this book. When a particular Toolbox control is described, simply find that icon in your Toolbox. Each individual control found in the Standard Edition, and therefore the Professional Edition, is completely compatible between both editions.

However, you can easily make your Professional Edition Toolbox look exactlylike the Toolbox in the Standard Edition. By doing so, you make this book's description of each control, including its location in your Toolbox, exactly match your configuration. You may prefer this option, especially if you are a novice Visual Basic programmer.

To make your Toolbox look just like the Standard Edition, follow these steps. Start any text editor or word processor that works with text files. (One good choice is the Notepad application that comes with Windows.) Load for editing the file named AUTOLOAD.MAK that you should find in your Visual Basic directory. (This directory is C:\VB for a regular installation of Visual Basic.) In this file, you will see a list of files whose names end with a .VBX file extension. Before modifying the file, create a duplicate (backup) version of AUTOLOAD.MAK, that you can name AUTOLOAD.BAK.

With AUTOLOAD.MAK loaded into the text editor, delete each of the .VBX file names except for CMDIALOG.VBX, GRID.VBX, and MSOLE2.VBX. Place these three file names in alphabetical order if they are not in order already. Do not delete or modify any other lines in the AUTOLOAD.MAK file. Save your modified AUTOLOAD.MAK file in text format. Now exit from the text editor and restart Visual Basic. Your Toolbox will appear just like the Standard Edition Toolbox shown in Figure 1.5.

continues

A Note to Users of the Professional Edition, continued

What you have done is modify the startup file that initializes Visual Basic's default configuration. Each .VBX file name in the AUTOLOAD.MAK file instructs Visual Basic to load the corresponding custom control into the Toolbox. For more about the AUTOLOAD.MAK file, see Chapter 9, "Managing Projects."

When you later want to restore all the Professional Edition custom controls, simply restore the original version of AUTOLOAD.MAK. You can do so by deleting your modified AUTOLOAD.MAK file and renaming your saved AUTOLOAD.BAK file as AUTOLOAD.MAK.

Thinking Like a Visual Basic Programmer

Working with Visual Basic forces you to think about programming with a fresh mind-set. Just as with other programming languages, everything is logical and orderly, but compared to languages such as QuickBASIC or Pascal, Visual Basic adopts a *different kind* of logic and orderliness. The Visual Basic programmer views the working environment in terms of forms, controls, object orientation, event-driven procedures, and methods.

Also, the Visual Basic programmer is part artist and part programmer. You build Visual BASIC applications by literally drawing controls and other graphic objects onto a blank form. This form becomes the application's user interface, what users see when running your program. Indeed, beginning Visual Basic programmers often feel like they are using a Windows paint program rather than a programming language.

The actual coding required to construct the graphical objects on a form is minimal, often nonexistent. That is remarkable to a Basic programmer used to QBASIC, QuickBASIC, or GW-BASIC, because with these earlier versions of BASIC, programming graphical objects is code-intensive and error-prone. With Visual Basic, it's done by interactive trial and error, and involves little more than mouse movements and button clicks.

The following sections explain some of the terminology important in Visual Basic.

Event-Driven Programs

One of the most profound differences between Visual Basic and earlier versions of BASIC is the difference between an event-driven language and a procedural language.

QBasic, QuickBASIC, BASICA, and GW-BASIC are all *procedural* languages. With a procedural language, an application executes by proceeding logically through the program one line at a time. Sure, GOTO instructions and subprogram CALLs can temporarily transfer logic flow so that the sequential order is interrupted, but the essence of a procedural language is that the program is in control, directing the logic flow procedurally through the program from the beginning of the program to the end.

Visual Basic is completely different. Instead of being a procedural language, Visual Basic is *event-driven*. Program instructions execute only when a particular event calls that section of code into action.

Events in a Visual Basic application can come from several sources (see Table 1.1).

Table 1.1. Event sources.

Source of Event	Sample Event(s)
User	Clicking the mouse, pressing a key.
Computer	A specified time period elapses.
Program	A program instruction explicitly activates an event.
Another Program	Another application, running concurrently in Windows, requests data interchange.

Visual Basic automatically executes a Sub procedure when an application event occurs. For example, when users click a command button on the form, Visual Basic executes the associated procedure. In this case, Visual Basic executes the Command1_Click() procedure. Here, Command1 is the control name and Click is the event.

The point is that Visual Basic contains, by default, blank procedure bodies for a myriad of events that the visible components of your application can recognize. Here is where you finally do some actual BASIC coding. You decide which events your program will respond to, and then you write code in the appropriate procedure bodies.

For example, when users click the command button, your application can open a new form, display some information, and request data input. To accomplish this, you write the appropriate BASIC instructions in the Command1_Click() procedure. Should you leave this procedure blank, the application simply will not respond when users click the command button.

NOTE

The Resemblance to BASIC

If you have had experience with any version of BASIC, you won't have much trouble with the language used to write Visual Basic procedures. It's BASIC and any programming you've done puts you in good stead here. Visual Basic contains many language extensions not found in earlier versions of BASIC, but Visual Basic's core language is BASIC, pure and simple.

You can think of an event-driven model as something like a mine field. No, not in the sense of destruction, thank goodness, but in the sense of a series of actions that take place when an event occurs. Consider that an application contains controls. Lurking *behind* these controls is a series of procedures that spring to action when the appropriate triggering mechanism takes place.

Event-driven procedures are not completely unprecedented in procedural versions of BASIC. For example, QBASIC and QuickBASIC have a hint of event-driven procedures in some statements involving error handling (ON ERROR GOTO) and event trapping (ON *event* GOTO). These procedures trap system events and invoke sections of code to respond to these events.

Unlike a program written with a procedural language, an event-driven program does not consist of a set of instructions that executes in an orderly top-to-bottom manner. Instead, an event-driven program consists of several independent procedures. Each procedure is associated with one of the objects defined in the application's user interface.

Object-Oriented Programming

Objects are one of the hot topics in today's programming. In general, an *object* combines programming code and data into a single unit. Once defined, an object takes a life of its own. You no longer need to know how the object was created or how it works; you can simply pass information to the object. Also, you can save an object for use in other programs.

NOTE   **What's All the OOPLA About?**

Object-oriented programming (OOP) is a boon for acronym makers. For example: OOPS (*Ob*ject-*O*riented *Pr*ogram *S*ystem) and OOPLA (*Ob*ject-*O*riented *Pr*ogramming *LA*nguage).

In Visual Basic, the primary objects are *forms* and *controls.* A form defines a window on-screen. Forms (and their controls) are what users actually see when running the application.

A *control* is an object you place onto a form. Each control performs a specific function. Visual Basic includes several predefined controls. Typical Visual Basic controls are the command button, check box, and scroll bar. Each control is represented by an icon in the Toolbox.

You can specify the values of various properties for each object. These properties include size, color, and text caption, to name just a few. These values can be modified while the application runs.

Each Visual Basic object has an associated set of event procedures. As described previously, you choose which events each object recognizes by writing code for the appropriate event procedures. Objects can take on a life of their own. For example, you can pass objects as parameters to various procedures. You can create new objects that are identical (or nearly identical) to other objects.

Forms can be saved as disk files and reused in other applications. Such a saved file includes a description of the form, the controls on the form, the assigned property values, and the associated event procedures. Such "objects" are close to the OOP sense of the term. The object now exists independently of any particular application. In fact, you can load a saved form into other applications.

Methods

In Visual Basic, program statements manipulate an object to perform desired actions. The program statements associated with objects are known as *methods.*

To invoke a method in a Visual Basic instruction, you type the object name, a dot, and then the name of the method. Required or optional arguments come after the method name.

For example, the PRINT statement so familiar to procedural BASIC programmers, is transformed into a method by Visual Basic. Consider the following Visual Basic instruction:

```
Form1.Print "There's a method to this madness"
```

Here, `Print` is a method acting on the `Form1` object. The `Print` method displays text on the form. In this case, the instruction displays `There's a method to this madness` on the form.

Summary

Visual Basic represents a radical departure from the type of programming done by traditional BASIC programmers. Instead of being a procedural language like the earlier versions of BASIC, Visual Basic uses an event-driven program model with objects, properties, and methods.

There are three major steps in the development of a Visual Basic application:

- Draw the controls on the interface.
- Assign values for the properties of the forms and controls.
- Write the event procedures.

You design a user interface by selecting graphic controls from the Toolbox and placing these controls directly onto a form. You assign property values by choosing the values from an on-screen list in the Properties window. Writing actual code is minimized. The program instructions are primarily located inside event procedures.

With an introduction to Visual Basic under your belt, you're ready to start programming an application. However, for those without much Windows experience, the next chapter takes a slight detour by offering a crash course in using Windows. If you are already a Windows user comfortable with running Windows applications, you can skim (or even skip) Chapter 2. In Chapter 3, "Test Driving VB: A Sample Application," you plunge right in to Visual Basic and develop a working application.

A Windows Primer

This chapter provides an overview of Windows. If you are new to Windows, this chapter helps you learn how to manipulate the Windows environment and find out how Windows works. If you are new to Windows programming, this chapter is a guide to how your programs should behave.

As a Visual Basic programmer, you need to be familiar with the standard look and feel of Windows applications for two reasons. First, Visual Basic is itself a Windows application. Second, you will be developing Windows applications and your users will expect those applications to appear and behave like standard Windows applications.

All Windows programs have a consistent look and feel. The programs use windows that can be opened, closed, moved, and resized, and have menus, buttons, list boxes, and other controls you can manipulate with mouse clicks or from the keyboard.

NOTE If you are an experienced Windows user, you can skip this chapter without loss of continuity.

The main goals of this chapter are to:

- Provide a brief history of Windows
- Explain Windows from a user's point of view
- Introduce Windows from a programmer's perspective

A Brief History of Windows

Although Windows was introduced in the mid 1980s, it did not gain substantial market momentum until the release of Windows 3.0 in 1990. A year later, this momentum increased with the subsequent release of Windows 3.1. Today, Windows is the second best-selling software product of all time, behind DOS. Most IBM-compatible PC manufacturers include DOS *and* Windows with their machines.

Windows works with DOS but acts like an operating system in its own right. By adding a software layer on top of DOS, Windows adds graphical computing extensions to DOS.

The popularity of Windows has spurred many software vendors to develop applications written specifically for the Windows environment. All these applications have the same general look and feel. If you know how to navigate the menu structures in one Windows application, you know how to do the same in other Windows applications. Today, almost all the major software applications—including Lotus 1-2-3, Excel, WordPerfect, and Microsoft Word— are available in versions that operate under Microsoft Windows.

Following are some of the main features of Windows:

- A multitasking environment, in which several applications can be run simultaneously

- A consistent look and feel to all applications written specifically for Windows

- A graphical environment manipulated with a mouse (or from the keyboard)

- The capability of transferring data—including scanned images, spreadsheets, and text—from one Windows application to another

- An assortment of accessories and utilities, including a text editor, a drawing program, a word processor, an appointment scheduler, a calculator, and a modem communications program

Windows from a User's Perspective

With Windows, the overriding metaphor is the *electronic desktop*. Just as you organize your real-life desktop with stacks of paper, a calendar, a phone, and a notepad, Windows organizes your computer screen into electronic tools. These electronic tools include software applications such as a word processor and a spreadsheet program. Windows also includes utility tools such as a calendar, calculator, and file organizer.

You can customize your Windows environment by lumping certain applications into specific groups called *program groups*, which are represented on your electronic desktop by individualized icons. By creating various groups of related programs, you can better organize your applications. For example, you might create individual program groups for your business applications, educational programs, and flight simulators.

Understanding the Window

The fundamental object in Windows is, naturally enough, the window. A *window* is a rectangular frame that can contain anything from a complete running application (such as a word processor or spreadsheet program) to a group of icons to a text document. You work with your applications and documents inside these windows.

You can have several windows open simultaneously. Each window can contain a different application, which means that Windows can run multiple applications simultaneously. By switching the focus from window to window, you can work in several applications at one time. For example, you can actively work with a spreadsheet in one window while retrieving stock quotes by modem in another window.

A window that contains a running application is called an *application window*. For example, the Windows Program Manager, Visual Basic, and a spreadsheet program (such as Excel) each run in an application window. The application window is the main window of a program. Many programs, such as Notepad and Write (accessories supplied with Windows), work with a single window.

Inside an application window, you may see inner, or *child*, windows. These interior windows are called document windows. The term *document window* originated with word processing programs that could open several documents simultaneously. Each document was in a separate window inside the application window. Now, the term *document* has a more general meaning. Besides text, a document can also be a graphic image, a group of icons, or even a list of file names. When a document window contains a group of icons, each icon might represent a program. By double-clicking one of the icons, you activate a program.

Figure 2.1 shows a typical Windows screen. Three windows are visible: the Program Manager, the Accessories window, and the Visual Basic window. Within the document windows, icons represent individual programs you can run. In this figure, the mouse pointer is positioned under the Microsoft Visual Basic icon. You can start Visual Basic by moving the mouse pointer to this icon and double-clicking.

Application window

Document window

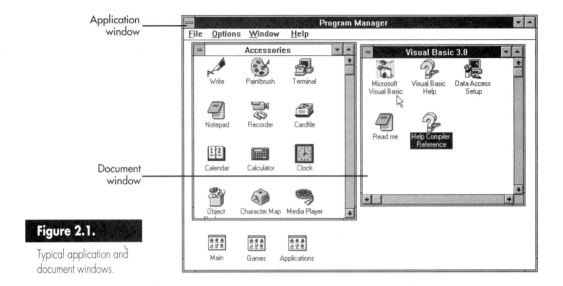

Typical application and document windows.

Learning Mouse Techniques

Although you don't have to use a mouse with Windows, it is the most convenient way to work with icons, windows, and programs. For more information on using the keyboard with Windows, see the section "Using the Keyboard" later in this chapter.

As you move the mouse on your desk or mousepad, the on-screen mouse pointer mimics your hand movements. When you click the mouse button, you tell Windows to perform a desired action, depending on the location of the mouse pointer. For example, you might use the mouse to select commands from a menu, move a sentence from one part of a document to another (in a word processing program), drag an icon from one window to another, or draw objects in a paintbrush program. Table 2.1 explains some common mouse terminology.

Table 2.1. Mouse terminology.

Term	Meaning
Point	By moving the mouse with your hand, you point the mouse arrow on-screen. Depending on the context of the Windows application, the arrow can change shape, highlight text, or manipulate a graphics object.
Pointer	The visible on-screen mouse symbol. Depending on the context of the program and the operation being performed, the symbol might be an arrow, an hourglass figure, or other shape.

Term	Meaning
Click	A mouse can have one, two, or three buttons. (For Windows use, two or more buttons are desirable.) When the pointer is located on a desired item, you click (press and release) a mouse button to select the item. For some applications, clicking different buttons produces different effects. (For example, you select a menu option with the left button and exit the menu by clicking the right button.)
Double-click	By pressing and releasing a mouse button twice in rapid succession, you can immediately activate a menu option or launch an application directly from its icon.
Drag and drop	By pressing and holding the mouse button and moving the pointer across the screen, you can drag an object (such as an icon) across the screen or highlight a block of text. When you release the mouse button, you drop the object at its new location or end the text highlighting.

Clicking and Double-Clicking

Clicking involves moving the mouse arrow to a desired on-screen object and pressing and releasing the left mouse button. Some objects (such as menu items) instantly respond to a single click with some action. Other objects become highlighted, but do not do anything until you click the mouse a second time or press a particular key. Some objects respond only to a double-click (for example, you can start a program by double-clicking its icon). A double-click must be fairly quick, or the program interprets the clicks as two single clicks.

For example, suppose that you are working with a word processing program. You want to open a file. A single click on the File item in the main menu drops down a submenu containing a list of file-related options. The Open... option is one example. A single click on the Open... menu option displays a list of possible files. To select the file you want to open, you either double-click the file name, or click the file name once and then click a button labeled OK.

Dragging and Dropping

By using the dragging and dropping mouse techniques, you can perform actions by moving objects around the screen. For example, with some programs, including the File Manager utility in Windows, you can copy a file by dragging the file name onto the desired disk icon. With a word processor such as Microsoft Word, you can move a block of text by selecting the text and dragging the block to the new location. Objects can be dragged and dropped within a single program or even between different programs.

To drag an object, position the mouse pointer on the item you want to move and then press and hold the mouse button while moving the mouse in the necessary direction. The object follows the pointer. To drop the object, release the mouse button. If you drop an object onto another object that "recognizes" the drop, an action takes place. Otherwise, the dragged object pops back to its original position.

Understanding the Mouse Pointer

As you move the mouse, the pointer moves on-screen. The pointer can change shape in different areas of the screen. The shape determines the type of action that takes place when you click the mouse. Table 2.2 shows the most common pointer shapes and the actions that correspond to these shapes.

Table 2.2. Pointer shapes.

Pointer Shape	Name	Action
↖	Arrow	The default pointer shape. The arrow points to the object being clicked or double-clicked.
⟺	Double arrow	When the pointer is over a window border, the double arrow indicates where you can move the border.
+	Crosshair	This pointer shape manipulates drawing tools in painting or drawing utilities.
I	Insertion point	Resembling a vertical I-beam, this pointer shape shows where the cursor should appear in text-editing applications.
⌛	Hourglass	While the cursor has this shape, Windows is completing a task and the user cannot issue any new commands. When the current task completes, the cursor changes to a different shape to let the user know that a new command can be accepted.

Using the Keyboard

Although the mouse provides the most natural way to use Windows, you can use the keyboard for most Windows tasks. This section briefly describes the most important Windows keys and keystroke combinations.

- *Alt.* Selects the menu bar, if any, for the active window. With the menu bar selected, you can use the left and right arrow keys to select an individual menu on the menu bar. Then press Enter to open the selected menu. Note that many menu option contain an underlined letter. By pressing Alt in conjunction with the key of the underlined letter, you can immediately open the indicated menu.

- *Alt+Esc.* Repeatedly pressing this keystroke combination cycles through the icons contained in all the opened windows. One at a time, each icon becomes highlighted (moving the icon's window to the foreground if necessary). When an application icon is highlighted, you can press Enter to activate that application. Notice that the combination of pressing Alt+Esc to highlight an icon and then pressing Enter is equivalent to double-clicking the icon.

- *Alt+- (hyphen).* Opens the control menu for a document window or document icon.

- *Alt+Spacebar.* Opens the control menu for an application window or a dialog box. As explained later in this chapter in the section "Dialog Boxes," a dialog box either prompts you to supply information needed by a program or simply displays information for you.

- *Tab.* Moves between areas in a dialog box.

- *F1.* Activates the Windows help system.

Working with Windows

As explained later in this chapter, you can manipulate the size and location of visible windows. For example, you can align windows, overlap windows, or reduce windows to small icons. As such, you can organize your electronic desktop as you see fit. Compared with Figure 2.1, Figure 2.2 shows that the Program Manager and Accessories windows have been resized. The Visual Basic window has been reduced to an icon near the lower right corner of the screen.

The icons at the bottom of the screen represent groups of utilities and applications. These program groups can be formed in several ways. When you install Windows, the installation program creates the program groups named Accessories, Main, and Games. Many Windows applications, such as Visual Basic, create their own program groups during installation of the application. Also, with the Windows Program Manager, you can organize and arrange Windows applications into your own program groups.

When you double-click a group icon, you enlarge that group into its own window. Often, the new window contains icons for several programs or utilities. When you double-click one of these icons, you launch (initiate) that program. You can also create groups that contain documents such as spreadsheets or text files.

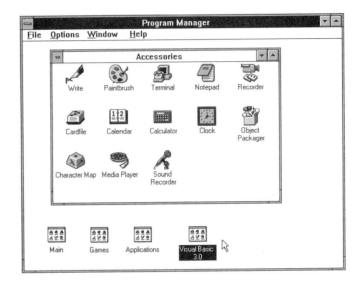

Document icons are linked to specific applications. When you double-click a
document icon, you initiate the host application with the document. For
example, double-clicking a spreadsheet icon might activate the Microsoft Excel
program and load the spreadsheet you selected.

Even on a screen that contains several windows, only one window can be
active at a time. When you click anywhere on a window, that window becomes
active. In Windows jargon, the clicked window has the *focus*. All other windows
are inactive. The active window is the only one that responds to keyboard
input. An active window has a slightly different set of colors than inactive
windows so that you can determine which window has the focus. The title bar
of the active window appears highlighted. Only one application window can
have the focus and only one document window can be active inside the active
application window at any one time. (The title bar of a window is the horizontal strip along the top of the window that contains a name or description for
the window.)

Features of Individual Windows

Individual windows have many common features. Figure 2.3 shows the Visual
Basic group window opened in the Program Manager. Table 2.3 discusses the
window elements shown in Figure 2.3.

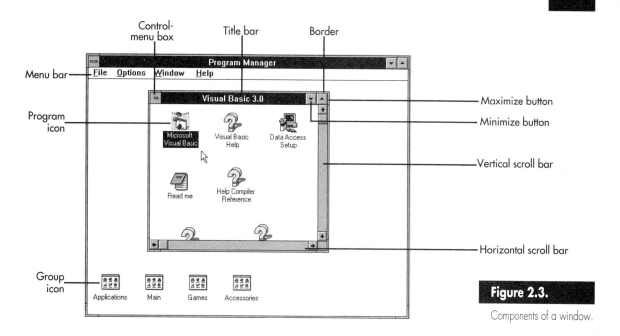

Figure 2.3.

Components of a window.

Table 2.3. The common elements found in windows.

Element	Description
Title bar	The title bar is the strip along the top of each window that contains the title for that window (Program Manager and Visual Basic 3.0 in Figure 2.3).
Border	Besides defining the boundary of a window, the border can be moved with the mouse to resize the window.
Control-menu box	Located at the left end of the title bar, this button opens a control menu from which you can resize, minimize, or close a window.
Minimize button	Located at the right end of the title bar, this button reduces the window to an icon. (The minimize button looks like a triangle pointing down.)
Maximize button	Located next to the minimize button, this button enlarges a window to fill the screen.
Menu bar	The menu bar is the horizontal strip located just below the title bar that contains the titles of the menus supported by that window. Not all windows contain menu bars. Further, the options on various menu bars differ from window to window. The Program Manager contains the menus File, Options, Window, and Help. By clicking a menu title, a drop-down menu appears from which you can select one of the available options. Figure 2.4 shows the Window menu opened from the Program Manager.

continues

Table 2.3. Continued

Element	Description
Scroll bars	When all of a window's contents cannot fit in the window, a scroll bar appears. With a scroll bar, you use the mouse to pan the contents of the window horizontally and vertically. Scroll bars located on a window's right border enable vertical scrolling; scroll bars located on the bottom border enable horizontal scrolling.
Icon	Icons represent windows that have been minimized. By double-clicking an icon, you activate (or restore) the window.

The sections that follow describe what you can do with various parts of a window. The discussions include borders, menus, and scroll bars.

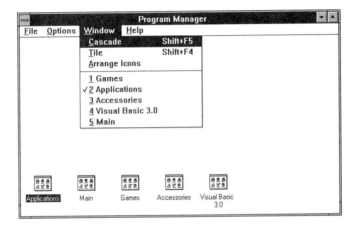

Figure 2.4.

The Program Manager's Window menu.

Borders

Most windows have visible borders. The appearance of a border determines what the window can do. A window can be resized if its border appears as a double line. A window with a single-line border (whether a thick or thin line) cannot be resized.

You can change the height or width of a resizable window by using the mouse. As you move the mouse pointer over the border of a resizable window, the pointer shape changes to a double arrow. The arrows point in the direction you can resize the window.

Figure 2.5 shows the mouse pointer changing shape on the vertical border of a resizable window. When the pointer passes over a vertical border, the shape changes to a horizontal double arrow, indicating that the border can be moved horizontally. Similarly, a horizontal border yields a vertical double arrow, showing that you can move the border vertically. When the pointer passes over the corner of a sizable window, the resulting double arrow points at an angle. Dragging the corner in the indicated direction moves simultaneously the adjoining vertical and horizontal borders.

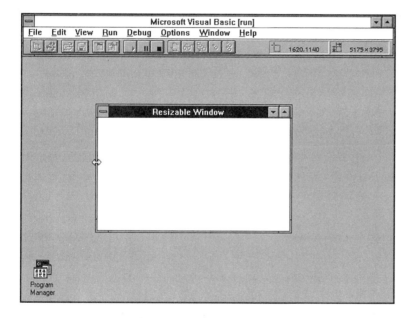

Figure 2.5.

The resizing mouse pointer on a resizable vertical border.

To change the size or shape of a window, move the mouse to the desired border until the pointer changes to a double arrow. Then hold down the mouse button and move the mouse. You will see an outline of the window move with the pointer. When you release the button, the window snaps to fit this new outline. This technique works with application windows and document windows, as long as the windows are resizable.

To move a window without changing its shape, drag the title bar to a new location. When you release the mouse button, the entire window moves to the updated position.

Menus

Menus give you control over a program. A menu appears as a row of words along the top of a window. Each word represents a menu item. A single click on a menu item results in a drop-down list of further choices. Figure 2.6 shows a drop-down menu list from Notepad's **F**ile menu. (Notepad is a text editor supplied with Windows.)

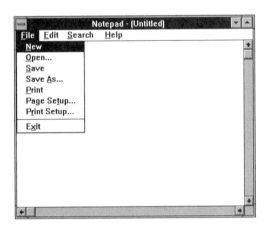

Figure 2.6.

Notepad's **F**ile menu with drop-down menu list.

You select items in a drop-down menu with a single mouse click. Usually, a specific action occurs. Sometimes, the click opens a secondary drop-down menu with a new set of items.

If the name of the menu item ends with an ellipsis (...), a dialog box pops open when you click the menu item. As described later in this chapter, a dialog box prompts you for additional information about the action you are performing. For example, if you click on a menu item named **O**pen... in a word processor, a dialog box opens so that you can indicate the name of the file you want to open.

Menu items often include an access key that enables you to select the menu item from the keyboard. An *access key* is indicated by an underlined letter in a menu item. For example, in the menu item **F**ile, F is the access key.

To use an access key in a main menu item, you must hold down the Alt key and press the indicated access key. For drop-down submenus, the letter key alone (with or without Alt) is sufficient. For example, you can select the **F**ile **O**pen... item by pressing the F key while holding down Alt and then pressing the O key.

NOTE A menu item described in this book with two access keys, such as **F**ile **O**pen..., means that the second item appears on a submenu of the first item. Here, selecting **F**ile on the main menu opens a drop-down menu that contains the **O**pen... option.

If you are working in a word processor, access keys are often much handier than using the mouse because your fingers never leave the keyboard.

Menu items can also have shortcut keys to simplify repetitive tasks. A *shortcut key* is a single key or a keystroke combination that immediately activates the menu item. For example, Notepad enables you to search for a word with the **S**earch **F**ind... menu option. To repeat the search, you can click **S**earch Find **A**gain (or use the access keys Alt+S and then A). However, the shortcut key for this menu option is F3. Pressing F3 has the same effect as using both access keys. If you are doing a repetitive search through a Notepad text file, the F3 key comes in very handy.

> When designing a Windows application with Visual Basic, it's best to provide access keys in your menus. That way, the user can choose between using the mouse or the keyboard. Shortcut keys should be used sparingly.
>
> **T I P**

On some menus, items may appear dim, or grayed out. A dimmed item is not presently available. For example, a word processor might show the **E**dit **C**ut item dimmed if there isn't any text selected for deletion. After you select text, **E**dit **C**ut becomes available.

Control Menus

You access a window's control menu by clicking the control-menu box. This button appears in the top left corner of a window. The control-menu box is a small gray box that contains a horizontal bar. Most windows, but not all, have control menus.

The items in a control menu pertain to the window itself, not to the application. The control window contains commands to move, resize, or close the window, or to switch to another task.

As Figure 2.7 shows, control menus look and work just like application menus. A single click activates the menu items, and some items have access keys and shortcut keys.

NOTE The control button for a document window has a slightly shorter horizontal bar than the control button for an application window. In fact, that is one way you can tell the difference between an application window and a document window. You can see the difference by referring back to Figure 2.1.

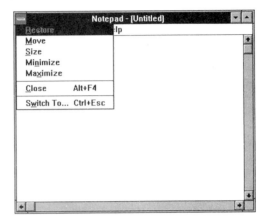

Figure 2.7.

A control menu.

Understanding Information Boxes

Windows programs often use special boxes to display information or to enable the user to provide information. Two such boxes are the dialog box and the message box.

Dialog Boxes

As stated previously, a *dialog box* prompts the user to supply information needed by the program to continue with the application. When you click on a menu item that has an ellipsis (...) at the end of its name, a dialog box opens.

Figure 2.8 shows an example of a file-specification dialog box, the most common type of dialog box. You use this dialog box to choose a file you want to use by selecting the appropriate drive, directory, and file name. The dialog box opens after you choose **O**pen... from a **F**ile menu.

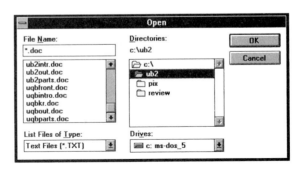

Figure 2.8.

An Open dialog box.

A dialog box remains open until you provide the necessary information and click OK or press Enter, or click the Cancel button, or press Esc. If you select Cancel or press Esc in the present example, the dialog box closes and you abort the File Open request.

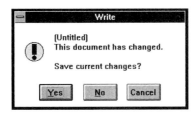

Figure 2.9.

A message box.

Message Boxes

A *message box* pops open when a program needs to inform you about a special situation. Often the message is a warning. For example, Figure 2.9 shows a message box that opens when you try to quit Write (a word processor supplied with Windows) without saving your current document.

The message box remains on-screen until you click one of the continuation options specified inside the box. In the message box shown in Figure 2.9, you can choose one of the following three continuation options: click Yes to save the document before ending the application, click No to end the application without saving the document, or click Cancel (or press Esc) to cancel the quit request, close the dialog box, and resume running the application.

Exploring Controls

Controls are various on-screen objects that you can manipulate with the mouse. Controls are located inside windows. Some controls cause events to occur. With other controls, you can view and edit data. Each type of control responds to mouse clicks in a different way and meets a different need. Figure 2.10 shows a window that has many different types of controls.

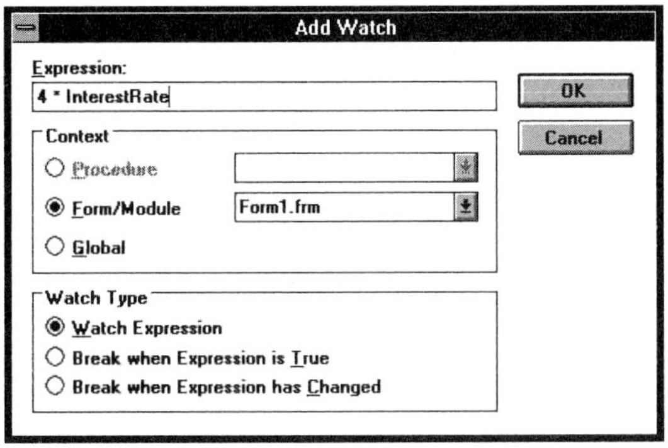

Figure 2.10.

A window with a variety of controls.

The term *control* suggests that these objects can be manipulated. Indeed, the controls respond to user events such as clicking the mouse. For example, you can click an option button or check box to select it, and you can enter text in a text box.

In Windows programs, you find the following controls:

- Buttons
- Text boxes
- Option buttons
- Check boxes
- List boxes
- Pictures and icons

Buttons

Buttons respond to a single mouse click. Generally, a button has a text caption or a picture (or both) to indicate what the button does. To activate a button, you click the mouse pointer on the button. Most buttons look three-dimensional and appear to sink into the screen when activated.

As shown in Figure 2.11, buttons appear in windows, dialog boxes, or special devices such as toolbars. Buttons give you a quick way to operate a program because a single click activates an event. Generally, buttons do not respond to double clicks.

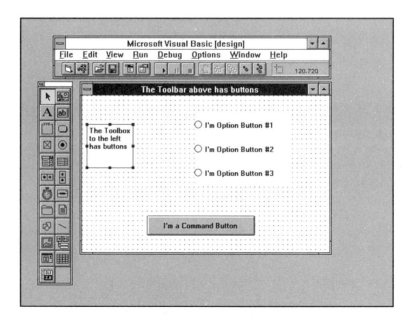

Figure 2.11.

Examples of buttons.

Text Boxes

With a *text box*, you can type information into your application. For example, Figure 2.12 shows a dialog box that opens when you click **S**earch **F**ind… in Windows Notepad. The text box (labeled Fi**n**d What) is where you type the text you want to find.

Figure 2.12.

The Find dialog box
containing a text box
labeled Fi**n**d What.

In a single-line text box, such as the Fi**n**d What text box, you can enter only one line of text. With text editors and word processors that require many lines of text to be entered, a multiline text box is used.

All text boxes respond similarly to user input. You can select, cut, copy, paste, and delete text using a consistent set of mouse or keyboard commands.

Option Buttons

Option buttons typically appear in groups. You select a single option button from the group. Option buttons are also called *radio buttons* because they work like the buttons on a car radio—only one button can be selected at a time. When you click a new button, the previously selected button is deactivated.

Check Boxes

A *check box* appears as a small square. When you click the square, an X appears inside the box. With a check box, you can indicate whether you want a particular program option in effect. Unlike option buttons, you can select none, one, several, or all the boxes in a check box group.

List Boxes

A *list box* provides a list from which you can choose one or more items. For example, to choose a font to display on-screen, a list box might display all the possible font options. You can use the mouse or the keyboard to choose an item from a list box. If the list box contains more items than can be shown in the space reserved for the box, a vertical scroll bar appears on the right side of the box. You can manipulate this scroll bar to view items up and down the list.

Figure 2.13 shows a special kind of list box known as a *drop-down list box*. A drop-down list box occupies only a single line until you click the down-arrow on the right edge of the box. Then the list drops down so that you can view the items and make your choice.

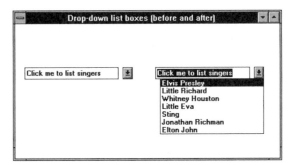

Figure 2.13.

A drop-down list box, before and after.

Pictures and Icons

Pictures and *icons* are graphical controls. Although the main purpose of such controls is to display images, pictures and icons are full-fledged controls because they can respond to mouse events such as clicking and dragging. The Paintbrush application in Windows works as a picture control in the sense that you can draw pictures with the mouse.

Icons are small pictures that represent various objects. For example, the File Manager application in Windows represents disk drives, files, and directories with suitable icons. Windows uses icons also to represent programs that have been minimized. To restore the window of a minimized program, you double-click the icon. Often, icons can be dragged and dropped on other controls as well.

Windows Utilities and Accessories

Windows is a complex product that contains several accessories and utility programs. Here are some highlights:

- *Program Manager.* The central application that executes when you first start Windows. Inside the Program Manager, you can organize your programs and documents into meaningful groups, each represented by a group icon.

- *File Manager.* An accessory program from which you can manipulate the file and directory structures on your hard and floppy disks. You can organize your directory structures and quickly see which files are in which directories. By double-clicking the file name of an application, you can start that application.

- *Control Panel.* An accessory program in the Main group that contains utilities for customizing Windows. For example, you can select colors, fonts, and special drivers, and you can configure supported printers.

- *Clipboard.* The clipboard is a temporary holding location for graphics or text. By copying information to the Windows Clipboard, you can move graphics or text from one application to another or from one part of a document to another.

- *General Utilities.* Windows includes several built-in utilities and accessories, such as a paint and drawing program, a word processor, a calendar, a clock, a modem communications utility, and a few games.

- *Printer Utilities.* Windows supports fonts and graphics printing on laser printers and other graphics printers. The TrueType fonts supplied with Windows 3.1 are scalable and can be displayed on-screen as well as printed to graphics printers supported by Windows.

Multitasking

Windows can run two or more applications concurrently. This capability is called *multitasking.* Most of the time, you merely have several programs waiting in the background while you work on one program in the foreground. Sometimes, however, you may have a background program executing a task while you actively work with another program. For example, a word processor may be printing a document in the background while you are working with a spreadsheet in the foreground.

In reality, Windows does not do true multitasking. Although programs may seem to be running at the same time, they are actually taking turns sharing the computer's central processor. Windows handles the switching between programs so quickly that the programs *appear* to be running simultaneously. However, if you run several programs concurrently—especially programs that do a great deal of work—Windows noticeably slows down.

> To give the focus to a program running in the background, you can click anywhere in the program's application window. If the program is minimized, you can double-click its icon. This enables you to switch quickly between applications. **T I P**

Windows also includes a Task Manager box. The Task Manager displays a list of every running program. Figure 2.14 shows a sample Task Manager box. With the Task Manager, you can switch to another program, end a program, or arrange the windows and icons on your desktop.

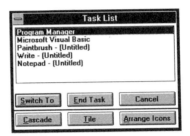

Figure 2.14.

The Task Manager.

You can open the Task Manager in several ways: by double-clicking the desktop, by pressing Ctrl+Esc, or by selecting the **S**witch To item in the control menu. With Task Manager, you can quickly switch to any program running in the Windows environment.

Windows from a Programmer's Perspective

The power and convenience of Windows is nice from a user's point of view, but for programmers, there is a price to pay. Before Visual Basic, writing a full-fledged Windows program was a formidable task.

The complexity of Windows requires that programs cooperate fully with the Windows environment, meaning that programs must manipulate drop-down menus, icons, the size and placement of windows, and other graphical objects. Furthermore, with DDE (Dynamic Data Exchange) and OLE (Object Linking and Embedding), Windows programs must be able to share information and communicate with each other.

Fortunately, Visual Basic shields the programmer from most of this complexity. With Visual Basic, you can design the user interface for an application by selecting graphical objects from a visual toolkit. Standard Windows features, such as resizing and minimizing, are automatically built into your application. Visual Basic includes tools to facilitate DDE and OLE.

For program developers, Windows includes a body of routines known as the *Windows API* (Application Program Interface). Over 500 functions enable the programmer to interact with the Windows environment. These functions control low-level actions, such as drawing visual elements, creating windows and menus, managing system memory, and communicating with the printer and other peripheral devices.

Within Windows, the API functions are located in Dynamic Link Libraries (DLLs). Windows makes the DLLs available to all applications. The libraries are dynamic in the sense that they are dynamically linked on an as-needed basis while a program executes.

Before Visual Basic, access to the Windows API required specialized development tools such as Borland's Turbo C++ or the Microsoft Windows SDK (System Development Kit). The programmer had to write code using the arcane syntax demanded by the Windows API.

For most applications, the built-in features of Visual Basic make it unnecessary to access the Windows API directly. For specialized needs, such as adding sound support to your applications, you can still use the Windows API. Thankfully, Visual Basic has tamed the wild beast of Windows programming.

Summary

Windows provides a set of graphical objects including menus, buttons, movable windows, and icons. You can work with these objects by using the mouse or the keyboard. All programs written for Windows use these graphical objects in a consistent way. This consistency makes learning each new Windows program a simple task. If you know how to use one Windows program, you have a pretty good idea of how to use other Windows programs.

As a budding Visual Basic programmer, you need to understand Windows graphical objects and learn how users expect Windows programs to behave. Visual Basic provides a set of convenient tools that enable you to develop Windows applications with relative ease.

Test Driving Visual Basic: A Sample Application

T he best way to learn Visual Basic is to try it out and get your programming hands dirty, so to speak. This chapter takes you through the steps for creating a simple Visual Basic application.

The purpose here is to give you an understanding of some of the most commonly used Visual Basic techniques. Explanations in this chapter are brief. Rest assured that every topic mentioned here is discussed in detail later in the book. For now, you are trying to develop an intuitive feel for Visual Basic programming.

Visual Basic represents a new approach to programming—the more experience you get, the better you can grasp what Visual Basic is all about. If you have trouble understanding something, move on to the next step and don't let yourself get bogged down in the details. You will have many more chances to explore Visual Basic as you progress through this book.

This chapter explores the following topics:

- Designing a form
- Placing controls on the form
- Setting control properties
- Writing event procedures

■ Saving a project

■ Creating an executable file

The Sample Application: A Number Cruncher

Suppose that you need to write a program that lets the user type two numbers. Then the user can have the program perform one of the following three actions:

> Display the sum of the two numbers

> Display the product of the two numbers

> Quit the program

Although this is a simple program, it demonstrates how Visual Basic works. The following sections describe the steps required to develop such an application.

First, if you haven't yet done so, start Visual Basic. (Chapter 1, "An Overview of Visual Basic," shows you how to install and start Visual Basic.) Notice that the title bar on Visual Basic itself says Microsoft Visual Basic [design]. The word *design* is quite appropriate—in the initial stages of developing an application, you are designing the user interface.

Introducing Forms and Properties

The blank form has a name and a title of Form1. The name of the form is the identifier Visual Basic uses to refer to that form. This concept is similar to a variable name, but here the reference is to a Visual Basic object.

The title of the form, called a *caption* in Visual Basic terminology, is simply the text you place in the form's title bar. By default, Visual Basic uses Form1 as both the name and caption for this form. Don't confuse the name and the caption: they are two similar but different attributes of certain objects.

Name and caption are two examples of an object's properties. In Visual Basic, every object (such as a form) has an associated set of attributes, called *properties*. Other properties of a form include its size, location, and color and determine whether the form is visible. Different kinds of objects have different sets of properties.

Changing the Form's Caption

You use the Properties window to change the caption on the form. First, click somewhere on the form to select it. Then press F4 (or click somewhere on the Properties window) to make the Properties window active. In the Properties window, a list box displays the various properties associated with the form. You can use the scroll bars on the right side of the Properties window to scroll vertically through the various properties.

Click on the Caption property. The settings box near the top of the Properties window shows the current value of the Caption property (Form1). To change the caption, first click on the text Form1 (located in the settings box). Notice that when you move the pointer into the settings box, the pointer shape changes to an insertion point (which looks like the letter I). When you click on the text in the settings box, a cursor in the shape of a vertical line appears. You can use the left- and right-arrow keys to move the cursor within the text. Press Del to delete unwanted characters.

Type the new caption, **A Number Cruncher**, as shown in Figure 3.1. As you type, you can watch the caption change inside the Caption box of the Properties window and on the title bar of the form itself. After typing the complete caption, press Enter to accept the new caption.

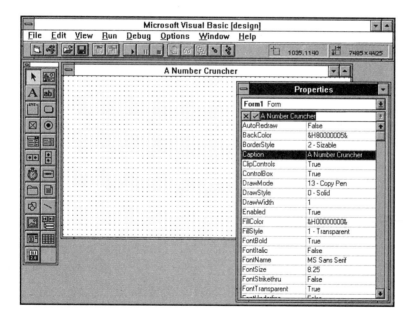

Figure 3.1.

Changing the form's caption.

Adding Text Box Controls

You can now add the desired controls to the form. First, you will create two boxes. When the program is run, the user will type the two input numbers into these boxes.

You use a *text box*, one of several Visual Basic controls, for text input by the user. To activate any control, you must select its icon from the Toolbox located along the left side of the screen. To select an icon, you click the mouse button when the arrow pointer is on the icon. A Text box icon appears as follows:

Click the Text box icon and move the pointer to the form. Notice that the cursor shape changes to a cross hair.

Now, with the pointer anywhere on the blank form, press and hold down the left mouse button. While keeping the button depressed, drag the mouse over an area of the form. As you do so, you see a rectangular frame change shape directly on the form. When you release the mouse button, the control appears on the form in the size and location indicated by the frame. Figure 3.2 shows a text box placed near the upper left corner of the form.

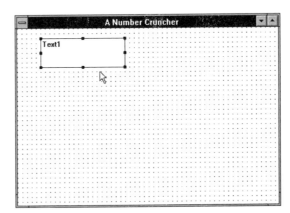

Figure 3.2.

Adding a text box control to the form.

Notice that the text box control has eight little squares along its boundaries. These are sizing handles. To resize a control, click the mouse pointer on a handle and drag the handle. To move the text box control, click inside it and drag the entire control. Experiment with moving the text box and changing its shape. Eventually, place the control so the form appears similar to the one shown in Figure 3.2. Visual Basic displays the name of the control, Text1, inside the control.

In a similar manner, place a second text box to the right of the first. (Click the Text box icon in the Toolbox and then place the control on the form.) Visual Basic names this control Text2. Make this control approximately the same size as the first text box. Don't worry about making the control any exact size or placing it in a precise location. You can modify the size and location later.

Adding Labels

Like a text box, a label is another Visual Basic control. A *label* displays text on the form. The text cannot be changed by the user when the program is run. To place a label on the form, first click the label icon in the Toolbox. Here is the Label icon:

Place the label by using the same technique you used to place the text boxes. (Click on the Label icon, drag the pointer over the form, then resize and move the control as desired.)

Here, you want two label controls, one below each text box. Visual Basic gives the labels default names of Label1 and Label2. Figure 3.3 shows the two labels displayed on the form.

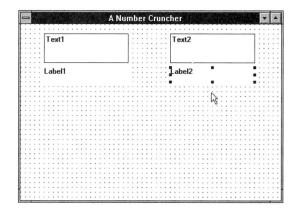

Figure 3.3.

Placing two labels on the form.

Displaying Text Inside the Labels

When the program begins, you want the labels to say Type first number and Type second number instead of the default labels Label1 and Label2.

You can use several methods to display text inside a label. (As you work with Visual Basic, you will find that there are often many ways to do something.) One way involves the same technique you used to change the caption on the form. You simply activate the Properties window and set the Caption property for the label to the desired value.

Try that technique for Label1. First, activate the label by clicking inside it. Then, make the Properties window active by pressing F4 or by clicking the Properties window. Scroll through the list of properties, click the Caption property, and change the value to Type first number by editing the text in the settings box.

A second way to change the text inside a label is to write a procedure that displays the desired text when the program begins. Visual Basic includes a Form_Load procedure that executes when the form is loaded in memory, that is, just before the program displays the form.

To write code for a procedure, you double-click inside the form (but not inside one of the controls located on the form). Visual Basic displays a window in which you can write program code for any system event.

When you double-click the current form, you see the coding window shown in Figure 3.4. The title bar for the Code window says Form1.frm. That means you are working with events recognized at the level of the form, as opposed to the level of a specific control on the form.

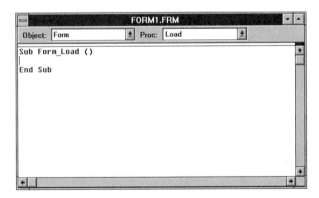

Figure 3.4.

The Code window.

The template appears for a procedure named Form_Load. For now, the procedure consists of two Visual Basic instructions: Sub Form_Load () and End Sub. In a few moments, you will write additional code between these two instructions.

Below the title bar are two boxes labeled Object: and Proc:. If you click the down arrow at the right end of the Object box, Visual Basic drops down a list box showing all the objects defined for the current form. By clicking on one of these listed objects, you can access the code procedures for that object.

If you click the down arrow at the right end of the Proc box, Visual Basic drops down a list box showing all the events recognized by the selected object. You can then click on one of these event names. In this manner, the Proc box lets you write Sub procedures for any event (such as Click) recognized by that object.

 NOTE Sub stands for subprogram. In this context, a *subprogram* is simply a set of program instructions that execute as a group. The subprogram executes when the appropriate system event occurs.

In this case, the default procedure (the procedure that first appears when you open the coding window) is exactly the one you want to write. The Load event occurs when the form is loaded, so this Sub procedure, labeled Form_Load, also activates when the form is loaded.

You want to specify the text inside Label2. That means you must modify the Caption property of the Label2 object. To do so, type the following instruction inside the procedure template:

```
Label2.Caption = "Type second number"
```

Note that the cursor appears as a vertical line inside the procedure template. When you type the instruction, begin by typing a few blank spaces (or pressing the right-arrow key a few times) to indent the line a few characters. Such indentation makes the code for the procedures a bit more attractive and therefore easier to read.

The left side of this assignment instruction specifies the control name (Label2) separated by a dot from the property (Caption). The right side specifies a value for this property which, in this case, is the string value "Type second number".

 NOTE In BASIC terminology, a *string* is a sequence of text characters. You specify a string by enclosing text characters in quotation marks.

In the Form_Load procedure, you should also add instructions that initialize the two text boxes. By default, the program displays Text1 and Text2 inside the two text boxes. You can change things so that when the form loads, the program erases this default text and displays nothing inside the two text boxes. The Text property specifies the text that displays inside a text box. The following instructions erase the text in the two text boxes:

```
Text1.Text = ""
Text2.Text = ""
```

These two instructions cause the program to start without any default text appearing in the two text boxes. (The two double quotation marks on the right side specify a *null string*—that is, a string containing no characters.) After you add these instructions, your final `Form_Load` procedure appears as follows:

```
Sub Form_Load ()
    Label2.Caption = "Type second number"
    Text1.Text = ""
    Text2.Text = ""
End Sub
```

Closing the Code Window

Close the Code window by pressing Alt+F4 or by selecting Close from the drop-down control menu in the Form1.frm window. (You open the control menu by clicking on the little box in the upper left corner of the Code window.) You are then returned to the design environment and you can make additional modifications to the form.

Notice that, even though you modified the `Form_Load` procedure, the caption for the second label still reads `Label2` and the text inside the text boxes read `Text1` and `Text2`, respectively. Although the program instructions in the `Form_Load` procedure modify these values, those instructions do not take effect until you actually run the application later in this chapter.

Preparing for Program Output

Next, create a large label control in the middle of the screen. The program will display the results of the desired calculations inside this label. Because this is the third label you have created on this form, Visual Basic uses the default name of `Label3` for this control. Using the Properties window, change the caption for this label to `Results will be shown here`. Figure 3.5 shows this label in place on the form.

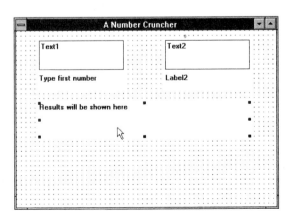

Figure 3.5.

The third label is added.

Adding the Command Buttons

The final design step is to add three command buttons near the bottom edge of the form. A *command button* is a control that triggers an action when the user selects the button. Typically, the user selects a command button by clicking it with the mouse. The Toolbox icon for a command button appears as follows:

In the sample program, three command buttons perform the following tasks:

> Display the sum of the two numbers
>
> Display the product of the two numbers
>
> Quit the program

Add the command button controls to your form. Visual Basic gives the command buttons the default names of Command1, Command2, and Command3.

Setting the *Caption* Properties of the Command Buttons

Now use the Properties window to change the caption displayed on each command button. Specify the Caption properties of the three command buttons as Compute the sum, Compute the product, and Quit, respectively. Figure 3.6 shows the completed form.

```
┌─────────────────────────────────────────────┐
│ ─        A Number Cruncher           ▼ ▲ │
├─────────────────────────────────────────────┤
│                                               │
│    Text1                  Text2               │
│                                               │
│                                               │
│    Type first number       Label2             │
│                                               │
│                                               │
│    Results will be shown here                 │
│                                               │
│                                               │
│                                               │
│  ┌──────────────┐ ┌──────────────────┐ ┌──────┐ │
│  │ Compute the sum │ │ Compute the product │ │ Quit │ │
│  └──────────────┘ └──────────────────┘ └──────┘ │
└─────────────────────────────────────────────┘
```

Figure 3.6.

The command buttons are added to the form.

T I P If you find that one of the command buttons is not long enough to display the entire text of its caption, you can resize the button. To elongate the button, click it and drag the sizing handle on either of the vertical edges of the control.

Writing Code for the Command Buttons

The form is designed, but you still must write the event procedures that define what happens when the user clicks each command button.

For the first button, the application should display the sum of the two numbers the user types in the text boxes. The event associated with the command button is Click. In other words, the Command1_Click procedure defines what happens when the user clicks the first command button.

To activate the Code window for Command1, double-click inside the button. When the Code window opens, the Click procedure (for the Command1 object) displays by default. Type the following instructions inside the procedure block:

```
Value = Val(Text1.Text) + Val(Text2.Text)
Label3.Caption = "The sum is " + Str$(Value)
```

Press Enter at the end of the first instruction to move the cursor to the following line.

In these instructions, Value is an ordinary variable that will store numerical values. Text1.Text and Text2.Text refer, respectively, to the text the user types in the two text boxes. The result of these instructions is that the caption for the third label displays the sum of the two numbers entered by the user.

NOTE These instructions use the Val and Str$ functions, which you encounter in Chapter 17, "Working with Strings."

Similarly, the program instructions required inside the Command2_Click procedure are as follows:

```
Value = Val(Text1.Text) * Val(Text2.Text)
Label3.Caption = "The product is " + Str$(Value)
```

To activate the Code window for the second command button, click the down arrow to the right of the Object box. A drop-down list appears that identifies the controls currently on the form. Click Command2 to activate the Code window for the second command button. Then type the preceding two instructions inside the procedure template.

Finally, the `Command3_Click` procedure must end the program when the third button is pressed. The code for this procedure requires nothing more than an `End` instruction inside the procedure template. (To activate the procedure template, click `Command3` from the drop-down list of the Object box.)

To summarize, here is the code required for the three event procedures:

```
Sub Command1_Click ()
    Value = Val(Text1.Text) + Val(Text2.Text)
    Label3.Caption = "The sum is " + Str$(Value)
End Sub

Sub Command2_Click ()
    Value = Val(Text1.Text) * Val(Text2.Text)
    Label3.Caption = "The product is " + Str$(Value)
End Sub

Sub Command3_Click ()
    End
End Sub
```

After typing the code for the procedures, press Alt+F4 to close the Code window.

Running the Application

Now for the big moment—trying the application to see whether it works. To run the program in the Visual Basic environment, simply click the Run button in the Toolbar. The Run button looks like this:

Notice that when this application starts, the `Form_Load` procedure removes the default text from the two text boxes so that they are blank. Also, the same procedure specifies the text for the second label control (`Type second number`).

To use this program, type a number in each text box. To activate the box for typing, simply click inside the box. (If you prefer to use the keyboard, you can press Tab repeatedly until the cursor appears inside the desired text box.) When the cursor appears inside the box, you can type a number.

After you type a number in each text box, click one of the command buttons. If you select the calculation of the sum or product, you should see a message with the appropriate value displayed inside the label box. Figure 3.7 shows the application displaying the product of 17 and 13. You can try typing new numbers in the text boxes and displaying the sum or product of those numbers.

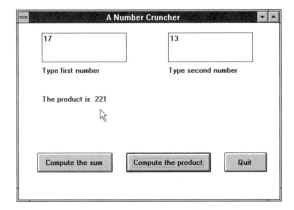

Figure 3.7.

Running the sample application.

NOTE

The Application Runs as a Standard Window

Notice that the form for this application appears like any other window used with Microsoft Windows. The control menu button appears on the left side of the title bar. You can click this button to open the standard window's control menu. Minimize and maximize buttons are located on the right side of the title bar.

Further, you can resize the window by dragging one of the edges of the window. You can move the window by dragging the title bar itself. If you are not familiar with some of these terms or with the techniques for manipulating windows, see Chapter 2, "A Windows Primer."

Click the third command button to end the program. Visual Basic returns to the design environment.

Saving the Project

In Visual Basic terminology, a *project* refers to all the files associated with an application. When you save a project to disk, Visual Basic saves several individual files associated with the project.

For each form on the project, Visual Basic creates a file with the default extension of .FRM. The .FRM file contains information about the size of the form, the controls placed on the form, and the program code for the event procedures associated with the form.

To save the project on disk, Visual Basic uses a file with the default extension of .MAK. This file lists all the .FRM files and other files associated with the project.

To save your sample application, you could select Save Project from Visual Basic's File menu. Instead, for this example, use the alternative method of clicking the Save Project button in the Toolbar. This button appears as follows:

First you are prompted to save the application's form. Visual Basic suggests the default name of FORM1.FRM for this file (see Figure 3.8). Note that the file is saved in the default Visual Basic directory \VB. Click the OK button to save this file.

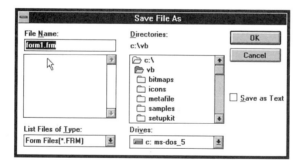

Figure 3.8.

Saving the form file.

Next you are prompted to save the project with the default file name of PROJECT1.MAK. You could accept this name, but instead type the name **CRUNCHER** in the File Name dialog box (see Figure 3.9). Now click the OK button and the file is saved. When saving the file, Visual Basic automatically adds the .MAK extension to the file name.

Now that the project is saved on disk, you can load the application back into the Visual Basic environment during any subsequent work session. You have two ways to load the application: select **O**pen Project from Visual Basic's **F**ile menu, or click the Open Project button on the Toolbar. This button appears as follows:

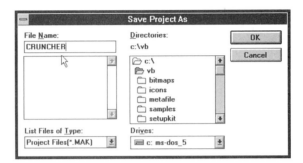

Figure 3.9.

Saving the project.

When you load a saved project, Visual Basic prompts you for the project's file name. In this case, you simply select CRUNCHER.MAK and the application loads into the Visual Basic environment.

Creating an Executable File

Before leaving the sample application, you might want to try creating an executable version of the Number Cruncher. Such a file can be run from Windows outside the Visual Basic environment. You can launch the program from Window's File Manager or directly from the DOS prompt.

To create such a file, open Visual Basic's File menu and select the Make EXE File option. A file selector box appears. Type the name CRUNCHER in the box prompting you for the file name. If you saved the project with the name CRUNCHER, the file name CRUNCHER.EXE appears by default so you don't need to type in the name (see Figure 3.10). Now click OK. When saving the file, Visual Basic automatically adds the .EXE file extension.

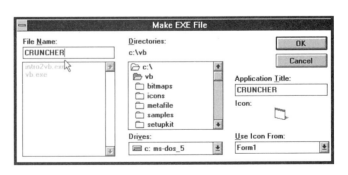

Figure 3.10.

Creating an executable file.

Try executing Number Cruncher directly from DOS. To do so, exit Visual Basic and Windows, returning to the DOS prompt. Make \VB the current directory (that is, your DOS prompt should be C:\VB). Verify that the CRUNCHER.EXE file exists in the directory. (To display a list of files in the directory, type **dir** and press Enter.)

Now, type **CRUNCHER** and press Enter. This starts Windows and launches the Number Cruncher application. Note that the form appears as a standard window containing minimize and maximize buttons. You can move the form, resize it, or reduce it to an icon just as you can most Windows applications. (For details about manipulating windows with Microsoft Windows, see Chapter 2, "A Windows Primer.")

Try reducing the program to an icon. Click on the Minimize button, which is the first button on the right side of the title bar. (The button looks like a triangle pointing down.) Windows reduces the program to an icon labeled A Number Cruncher (see Figure 3.11). To redisplay the program, double-click the icon.

Figure 3.11.

Number Cruncher reduced to an icon.

After you run the program, click the Quit button. The application terminates, leaving Windows in control.

Summary

The sample application in this chapter is a simple one that only touches on the capabilities of Visual Basic. This single-form application uses only a few of the available controls, properties, and triggering events. With Visual Basic, you can design multiple-form applications. Further, the Toolbox contains many additional controls that offer much more functionality than the simple controls used in this example.

However, this sample application does give you an idea of what working with Visual Basic involves. If you have experience programming with QBasic or another one of the procedural BASIC languages, you can see that Visual Basic is a whole new world.

Learning the VB Environment

By this time, you have had some experience with the Visual Basic environment. In the last chapter, you created and ran the Number Cruncher application. As you might know, Visual Basic features a development environment containing many tools and options.

This chapter explores the Visual Basic environment in more detail. The main topics covered in this chapter include the following:

- Using the menu system
- Using the Toolbar buttons
- Working with the code editor
- Loading and running a saved application
- Using the Help system
- Printing a program listing

The Screen Components

One useful way to learn the Visual Basic environment is to examine various windows on the opening screen, which is shown in Figure 4.1. In this figure, some windows have been resized and repositioned so that each window is fully visible.

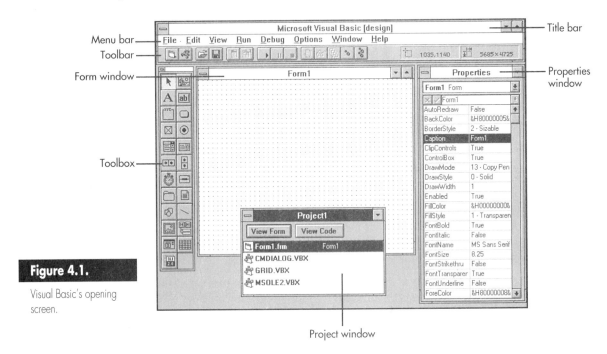

Figure 4.1.

Visual Basic's opening screen.

This chapter examines the screen's windows and other features, starting with the Toolbar.

The Toolbar

The Toolbar consists of a series of buttons, also called icons. Each button represents a frequently used command that is available also from the menu system. By clicking a Toolbar button, you immediately activate the indicated command. For example, instead of opening the File menu and selecting Save Project, you can click the Save Project button in the Toolbar. (You might think of the Toolbar as a collection of shortcut buttons.)

NOTE Today, many major Windows applications have toolbars. By including a toolbar with Visual Basic, Microsoft follows an ongoing trend in Windows software.

Each command on the Toolbar is available also from the menu system, so the method you choose is a matter of personal preference. Most likely, you will find the Toolbar quite convenient. The choice, however, is up to you.

The following list contains a description of each Toolbar button:

Project Tools

Button	Name	Description
	New **F**orm	Adds a new form to the current application. This button is equivalent to choosing the New **F**orm option from the **F**ile menu (Alt+F, then F). For information on developing multiform applications, see Chapter 9, "Managing Projects."
	New **M**odule	Adds a new module to your application. Each module contains program code inde-pendent of specific forms and controls. A module contains the program code not found in event procedures, such as declarations for global con-stants and variables, and user-defined subprograms and functions. You can save modules independently, then reuse them in different applica-tions. For more about multiple modules, see Chapter 9, "Managing Projects." This button is equivalent to choos-ing the New **M**odule option from the **F**ile menu (Alt+F, M).
	Open Project	Loads a previously saved project (application) into the Visual Basic environment. After loading the project, you can then run or modify it. This button is equivalent to choos-ing the **O**pen Project... option from the **F**ile menu (Alt+F, O). For more information on loading an existing project, see "Loading A Sample Application" later in this chapter.

continues

Project Tools

Button	Name	Description
	Save Project	Saves the current project to disk. You used this option in Chapter 3, "Test Driving VB: A Sample Application," when you saved the Number Cruncher application. This button is equivalent to choosing the Save Project option from the File menu (Alt+F, V). For more information on saving and loading projects, see Chapter 9, "Managing Projects."

Special Window Tools

Button	Name	Description
	Menu Design Window	Opens a special window that lets you add a fully functioning menu system to your applica-tion. This button is equivalent to choosing the Menu Design option from the Window menu (Alt+W, M), or pressing the shortcut key, Ctrl+M. For more on creating menus, see Chapter 24, "Designing Custom Menus."
	Properties Window	Activates the Properties window. You use the Properties window to designate various attributes (proper-ties) of a form and the controls placed on the form. If the Properties window becomes hidden behind other windows, pressing this button brings the Properties window to the foreground. This button is equivalent to choosing Properties from the Window menu (Alt+W, O), or pressing the shortcut key, F4.

Mode Switching Tools

Button	Name	Description
	Run	Executes the current application (or resumes a suspended application), and places Visual Basic in the Run mode. This option is equivalent to choosing the Start or Continue option from the Run menu, or pressing the shortcut key, F5.

Mode Switching Tools

Button	Name	Description
II	Break	Suspends and pauses the current application, and places Visual Basic in Break mode. Once suspended the current application is suspended, you can use various debugging tools. You can resume the application by pressing the Run button on the Toolbar, or choosing the **C**ontinue option from the **R**un menu (Alt+R, C), or by pressing F5. The Break button is equivalent to choosing the Brea**k** option on the **R**un menu (Alt+R, K), or pressing Ctrl+Break.
■	Stop	Ends the current application and returns Visual Basic to Design mode. The Stop button is available any time the current application is running (Run mode) or suspended (Break mode). This button is equivalent to choosing the **E**nd option from the **R**un menu (Alt+R, E).

Debugging Tools

Button	Name	Description
🖐	Breakpoint	Designates a line in your program code that, when about to be executed, places Visual Basic in Break mode. This button is equivalent to choosing the **T**oggle Breakpoint option from the **D**ebug menu (Alt+D, T), or pressing the shortcut key, F9.
👓	Instant Watch	While in Break mode, lets you see the current value of any expression selected from your program code. This button is equivalent to choosing the **I**nstant Watch... option from the **D**ebug menu (Alt+D, I), or pressing the shortcut key, Shift+F9.
🗂	Calls	While in Break mode, displays a list of procedures that are pending—that is, the procedures that have not yet completed execution, but have made a call to another procedure. This

continues

Debugging Tools

Button	Name	Description
		button is equivalent to choosing the Calls… option from the **D**ebug menu (Alt+D, C), or pressing the shortcut key, Ctrl+L.
	Single Step	From Break mode, executes the next line of your program, then reenters Break mode. This button is equivalent to choosing the Single Step option from the **D**ebug menu (Alt+D, S), or pressing the shortcut key, F8.
	Procedure Step	Similar to Single Step, except that this mode treats a called procedure as a single step. In other words, when the next single step of your program calls a procedure, Visual Basic executes the entire procedure before reentering Break mode. This button is equivalent to choosing the **P**rocedure Step option from the **D**ebug menu (Alt+D, P), or pressing the shortcut key, Shift+F8.

Menu System

The Visual Basic menu bar offers several options. You can open a menu from the keyboard by holding down the Alt key, then pressing the underlined letter. For example, you can open the **F**ile menu by pressing Alt+F. Alternatively, you can access a menu by clicking the menu name.

Each menu opens to reveal a drop-down submenu. Each submenu option contains an underlined letter. You can activate an option on a submenu by pressing the underlined letter, or by clicking on the option name. For example, you can choose the **O**pen Project… option from the **F**ile menu by pressing the O key.

Many submenu options have also an associated shortcut key. By pressing the shortcut key, you immediately perform the desired command without directly entering the menu system. For example, Ctrl+P is the shortcut key for the **P**rint… option on the **F**ile menu. By pressing Ctrl+P at any time, you can immediately open the dialog box to specify printing options.

The following sections present an overview of the menu system. The attempt here is to demystify the abundance of available options. By gaining an understanding of the available options, you get a general understanding of how Visual Basic works, and how you can utilize it to its full potential.

File Menu

Here's a summary of the menu options available under the File menu:

New Project	Starts a new project. This option prompts you to save all files associated with the current project. It then closes them, and initializes Visual Basic to start a new project.
Open Project...	Loads a previously saved project into Visual Basic. Before loading the specified project, this option prompts you to save any project currently active.
Save Project	Saves the current project to disk. This option saves all forms and modules as separate files, and also creates a Make file (.MAK file). The Make file contains a list of all files that comprise the project. If you have previously saved the project, this option updates the existing files to reflect program changes. If you have not previously saved the project, this option prompts you to provide a project name.
Save Project As...	Prompts you to supply a project name and file formats (binary or text) before saving the current project. You can use this option to save a copy of the current project under a new name.
New Form	Creates and initializes a new form for the current project. An application can have several forms.
New MDI Form	Creates a Multiple Document Interface (MDI) form for your application. An MDI window acts as a *parent* window that can have multiple *child* windows open inside. Only one MDI form can exist in a given application. For more on MDI forms, see Chapter 27, "Creating Multiple Document Interfaces (MDI)."

New **M**odule	Creates a new module for the current project. A module contains program code that exists separately from the event procedures. For example, a module might contain constant and variable declarations, and user-defined subprograms and functions. Procedures and other modules can share code in a given module. You can save a module as a separate file and load it into different projects. Any project can contain multiple modules.
A**d**d File...	Opens a dialog box that prompts you to specify a previously saved file that you want to include in the current application. The included file can be a saved form (.FRM file), module (.BAS file), or custom control (.VBX file). A *custom control* is an additional graphics control placed in the Toolbox. The Professional Edition of Visual Basic includes several custom controls (see Chapter 32, "Using Custom Controls"). The shortcut key for this option is Ctrl+D.
Remove File	Removes a file (form, module, or custom control) from the current project. This option removes the part of the application that has the focus (that is, the active form, module, or custom control). Note that this option does not remove the file from disk, but rather unloads it as a part of the current project. The removed file no longer appears listed in the Project window.
Save File	Saves the active form or module to disk. If you have previously saved the form or module, this option updates the existing file to reflect any program changes. If you have not previously saved the form or module, you are prompted to supply a file name. The shortcut key for this option is Ctrl+S.
Save File **A**s...	Prompts you to supply a file name before saving the active form or module to disk. You can use this option to create a second copy of the active form or module with a different file name. The shortcut key for this option is Ctrl+A.

Load Text…	Loads a previously saved text file into the current project. You can load the file into a user-defined or event procedure, a module, or the Declarations section of a form. You can use this option to load code created outside of Visual Basic, or to load Visual Basic files such as CONSTANT.TXT (the file containing declarations of several useful constants. For more about CONSTANT.TXT, see Chapter 14, "Language Building Blocks.")
Save Text…	Saves the code in the active form or module as a text file. (To save an entire form with the controls and property values, use the Save File **As…** option.) A dialog box opens for you to supply the file name. A text file is saved in ASCII format so that it can be read by word processors and other applications.
Print…	Prints a copy of forms or program code on the system printer. For more about this option, see "Creating Printed Listings" later in this chapter. The shortcut key for this option is Ctrl+P.
Make EXE File…	Saves the current project (forms and modules) to a single file (with an .EXE file extension) as a stand-alone application. This option opens a dialog box that prompts you to supply the file name. Once saved as an .EXE file, the application can be run in the Windows environment independently of Visual Basic. The file VBRUN300.DLL must be present, however, to run an application outside Visual Basic. This file, which contains necessary run time support routines, is supplied with Visual Basic. Microsoft grants you the right to freely distribute VBRUN300.DLL to users who run any stand-alone Visual Basic application.
1, 2, 3, 4	Retains a Most Recently Used (MRU) list of the four most recently opened and saved projects. Using this feature of Visual Basic, you can immediately open one of these saved projects by clicking the project's name in the **F**ile menu, or pressing the corresponding shortcut key (Ctrl+1, Ctrl+2, Ctrl+3, or Ctrl+4). Between succesive work sessions, Visual Basic retains this list in the **F**ile menu. That is, when you restart Visual Basic, the MRU list appears unchanged from your previous work session.

Exit	Lets you exit Visual Basic. This option closes all files and removes Visual Basic from the active Windows environment. If you have not saved recent updates to the current application, you are prompted to save the appropriate program files before ending the Visual Basic session.

Creating Printed Listings

To create a printed listing of the current project, choose the **Print...** option from the **File** menu. The Print dialog box opens (see Figure 4.2).

Figure 4.2.

The Print dialog box.

NOTE Visual Basic directs printed listings to the Windows Print Manager. Once sent to the Print Manager, Windows controls the printing. Make sure that your printer is properly installed with Windows. If your system has more than one printer, make sure that the Windows default printer is set to the active printer. To specify the default printer and to install printers, double-click the Printers icon in the Windows Control Panel utility.

The Print dialog box presents several printing options. You can print forms in two different ways: as the graphical image you see on-screen, or with a text-based description. The graphical image requires a printer capable of producing a graphics image, such as a laser printer. The printed image of a form is a graphical snapshot of the form's on-screen appearance. On the other hand, the text-based description is a text listing of the form's properties and their values, including descriptions of the controls placed on the form.

You can choose also to print the actual Visual Basic program code. This includes a listing of the event procedures, the module-level declarations, and the user-defined procedures.

Using the Print Dialog Box

The following is a brief description of each option in the Print dialog box:

Current	Prints only the active form or module.
All	Prints every form and module in the current application.
	Notice that Current and All are represented by control (radio) buttons. The options, therefore, are mutually exclusive. You must select one option, or the other. To select an option, simply click the appropriate button.
Form	Prints a graphical representation.
Form Text	Prints a text-based representation.
Code	Prints a listing of the program code. The setting of Current or All determines whether the printing is limited to the current form or module, or includes every form and module.

The options Form, Form Text, and Code are represented on-screen with check boxes. These options are not mutually exclusive. You can select one, two, or all three of the options. (You must choose at least one option.) Clicking a check box toggles the option on and off.

When you have the Print dialog box options set correctly, click OK. Visual Basic routes the print job to the Windows Print Manager for printing. If you decide not to print anything, click Cancel to close the Print dialog box.

Edit Menu

Visual Basic includes an editor similar to those found in other Windows applications. In Visual Basic, of course, the primary use of the editor is to write program instructions. To aid programming, the Visual Basic editor includes specialized features (such as automatic syntax checking) when you type an instruction.

The editing cursor appears as a vertical bar. As you type, new text appears at the cursor location. The editor permits full-screen editing. As such, you can move the cursor with the arrow keys or mouse before typing.

When editing, the mouse pointer acts as an *insertion point*. The insertion point has a shape something like a capital I. By moving the mouse, you can position the insertion point anywhere in the current text. When you click the mouse, the cursor jumps immediately to the insertion point. Then, you can type text at the new location.

The editor can work with text blocks. You select a block of text by first moving the cursor to one end of the block. Then, you press Shift and use an arrow key to highlight a text block. The selected block can be moved, copied to the Clipboard, or deleted. You can also paste text already in the Clipboard into your program code.

By default, the editor works in *Insert* mode. So, as you type, any existing text to the right of the cursor moves toward the right to accommodate the new text. By pressing the Ins key, you can toggle the editor between the Insert and Overstrike modes. In *Overstrike* mode, existing text to the right of the cursor is replaced by your new text.

You can access several editing features from the **E**dit menu. The remainder of this section explains the various commands available with the editor. For more information on editing, see Chapter 13, "Using the Editor."

Undo	Reverses the previous editing action. Actions that you can undo include typing a line of code, deleting a block of it, or deleting a control on a form. In these three cases, **Undo** deletes the line of typed code, restores the block of code, or restores the deleted control, respectively. By repeatedly selecting **Undo**, you can successfully cancel the most recent editing actions (up to a maximum of 20 times). **Undo** cannot be used to perform a nonediting action, such as modifying the properties on a form. The shortcut key for Undo is Ctrl+Z.
Redo	Restores the previous Undo action. That is, **Redo** "undoes" the previous **Undo**. This option works with program code only, not with controls on forms. As with **Undo**, you can use **Redo** up to 20 times in succession. The shortcut key for **Redo** is Ctrl+Backspace. (Although Ctrl+Backspace works as a shortcut key, this keystroke combination does not appear listed in the **E**dit menu.)
Cut	Deletes selected text and places it in the Clipboard. The previous contents of the Clipboard are erased. This option works with selected text or control. The shortcut key is Ctrl+X.

Copy	Places a copy of the selected text or control into the clipboard. This option is similar to Cut, except that the selected text or control is not deleted from the application. The shortcut key is Ctrl+C.
Paste	Places a copy of the Clipboard's contents into the current application. If you paste program code, it is placed at the insertion point; if you insert a control, it is placed in the upper left corner of the form. This option does not delete the Clipboard contents, so you can use Paste repeatedly to insert multiple copies of code (or a control) into your application. The shortcut key is Ctrl+V.
Paste Link	Places a copy of the contents of the Clipboard into the current application and simultaneously opens a dynamic link with the Windows application that provided the Clipboard contents. This option is available only when the Clipboard contents come from a Windows application that responds to Dynamic Data Exchange (DDE). For more information on Paste Link and DDE, see Chapter 29, "Using Dynamic Data Exchange (DDE)."
Delete	Deletes the selected text or control. This option is similar to Cut, except that the deleted item is not moved to the Clipboard. The shortcut key is Del.
Find...	Searches the program code for a specified text string. This option opens a dialog box. In the Find dialog box, you specify the search string and the scope of the search (the current procedure or the entire application). The shortcut key is Ctrl+F.
Find Next	Repeats the previous search. This option finds the next occurrence of the previously specified search string. If no search string was previously specified, this option opens the same dialog box as the Find... option. The shortcut key is F3.
Find Previous	Similar to Find Next, this option searches the program code in reverse order. When performing successive searches, you can use this option to find the previous occurrence of the search string. The shortcut key is Shift+F3.

Replace...	Searches the program code for a specified text string, and replaces it with a second specified string. This option opens a dialog box for you to specify the search and replacement strings, as well as such options as the scope of the search, and whether to replace all occurrences of the search string. The shortcut key is Ctrl+R.
Bring to Front	Moves a selected control to the foreground, in front of all other objects. This option works only at design time, and if the selected control is overlapped by other controls. The shortcut key is Ctrl+=.
Send to Back	Moves a selected control to the background, behind all other objects. This option works only at design time, and if the selected control can be overlapped by other controls. The shortcut key is Ctrl+-.
Align to Grid	Moves and resizes the selected control(s) to align with the nearest grid dots on the form. This option has meaning only when automatic control alignment is disabled through the **E**nvironment item in the **O**ptions menu. Otherwise, when placed on the form, each control automatically aligns with the grid. For more information on grid alignment, see "Options Menu" later in this chapter, and Chapter 6, "Using Controls."

View Menu

Various options on the View menu affect what you see in the Visual Basic environment. The available options are primarily concerned with manipulating the Code windows for the Visual Basic editor.

The **C**ode option (shortcut key F7) acts as a gateway to viewing program code. When you select this option, Visual Basic opens the code editor and displays the default procedure for the current form, or the default module. You can now begin making program modifications.

Several other options on the **V**iew menu move the display to other procedures and modules. For example, you can cycle through available procedures, one at a time. For more information about editing program code, see Chapter 13, "Using the Editor."

The final option on the View menu is Toolbar. This option is a toggle that alternately removes and displays the Toolbar. By removing the Toolbar from the visible desktop, you can decrease some screen clutter and reclaim a bit of screen space. You might occasionally find this useful when developing an application that uses a large form, or when running an application. Most of the time, however, you will probably prefer to keep the Toolbar visible.

Run Menu

Although the **R**un menu always presents three options, these vary slightly, depending on whether Visual Basic is in the Design, Break, or Run mode. In this section, you load and execute a sample application included with Visual Basic. During the course of running the program, you can see how the options on the **R**un menu change.

As described earlier in this chapter, the Toolbar contains three buttons (Run, Break, and Stop) that correspond to the three options (**S**tart, **B**reak, and **E**nd, respectively) on the **R**un menu. Whether you click the Toolbar buttons, choose options from the **R**un menu, or press appropriate shortcut keys is a matter of personal taste. Many people find the Toolbar the most convenient option.

Loading a Sample Application

This section guides you through the steps of loading and executing one of the sample applications bundled with Visual Basic. The selected program, called Mouse, demonstrates how Visual Basic can respond to various mouse movements.

To begin, choose the **O**pen Project... option from the **F**ile menu (or use the Open Project Toolbar button). If you previously had an unsaved application loaded in the environment, you now see a message box asking if you want to save the prior application. Select Yes or No.

Visual Basic opens the Open Project dialog box. If you have installed Visual Basic in the normal manner, you should see a subdirectory named samples visible in the **D**irectories box in the middle of the screen. Click samples, then click OK.

The dialog box should now display a list of directory names located under the samples subdirectory (see Figure 4.3). Scroll through the list until the directory named mouse becomes visible. Click mouse, then click OK.

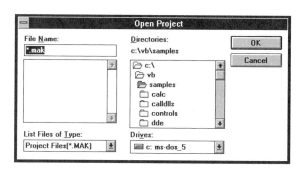

Figure 4.3.

Selecting
C:\VB\SAMPLES in the
Open Project dialog box.

NOTE Figure 4.3 assumes that you have performed a normal installation of Visual Basic onto your computer's C drive. If you have installed Visual Basic in a different drive, you should use the appropriate drive letter when trying the example.

Notice that the file named MOUSE.MAK is now visible in the File Name box (located to the left of the **Directories** box). Click mouse.mak to make the file name appear in the text box in the upper left corner of the dialog box. See Figure 4.4.

Click OK to close the dialog box. Visual Basic loads the new application. Notice that the Project window lists the forms that comprise this application (see Figure 4.5). You can make any of the forms visible by clicking the name of the form, then clicking the View Form button. For more information on the Project window, see Chapter 9, "Managing Projects."

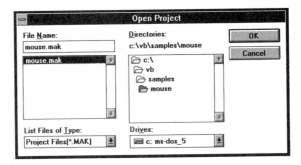

Figure 4.4.

Specifying the
C:\VB\SAMPLES\MOUSE\
MOUSE.MAK file.

Figure 4.5.

The Project window for the
Mouse application.

Running the Sample Application

The project is now loaded, but not yet running. Notice that the title bar for Visual Basic still reads as follows:

```
Microsoft Visual Basic [design]
```

Open the **R**un menu. Although three options are listed, two appear dimmed. The only available option is **S**tart. While in Design mode, **S**tart is the only option you can select from the **R**un menu.

Start the application with any of these three equivalent actions:

- Click the Run button in the Toolbar.
- Choose the **S**tart option from the **R**un menu.
- Press the shortcut key, F5.

A window appears on-screen labeled Mouse Examples. Although nothing seems to be happening on-screen, notice that the program is running. You can verify this by looking at the Visual Basic title bar that now reads as follows:

```
Microsoft Visual Basic [run]
```

Look at the Toolbar. Notice that the Run button appears dimmed. The Break and End buttons, which appeared dimmed in Design mode, however, are now active.

Trying a Scribble

The sample application has several options. Try the Scribble option. First click on the **O**ptions menu at the top of the window. A submenu appears (see Figure 4.6). Choose the **S**cribble option.

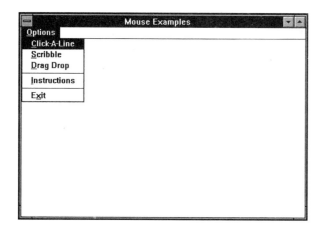

Figure 4.6.

The **O**ptions menu.

A blank form opens titled Scribble. You can create mouse scribbles in this form by pressing and holding a mouse button while dragging the mouse across the form. This produces a line embellished with small circles. Figure 4.7 shows the author's attempt at scribbling the letters VB. Try your own scribbles.

84

Figure 4.7.

Scribbling the letters VB.

Entering Break Mode

Open the **R**un menu. Notice that the first option on the menu has changed to Brea**k**. The other two options are **E**nd (stop execution) and **R**estart (begin execution again).

You can now temporarily suspend execution by entering Break mode. To do so, use any of these three equivalent techniques:

- Click the Break button in the Toolbar.
- Choose Brea**k** from the **R**un menu.
- Press the shortcut key, Ctrl+Break

Try one of the techniques. You notice that the Debug window opens, and the title bar now reads as follows:

```
Microsoft Visual Basic [break]
```

 If the Debug window is not visible, open the **W**indow menu and choose the **D**ebug option.

Program execution has been interrupted. You do most of your debugging in Break mode. In this mode, you have several debugging tools available. For example, you can examine program code, test the values of key variables or expressions, then resume program execution.

Trying the Debug Window

From the Debug window, you can immediately execute any Visual Basic program instruction. In fact, another name for the Debug window is the *Immediate window*. The Immediate window available with two languages, QBasic or QuickBASIC, is similar to Visual Basic's Debug window.

In the Debug window, you can execute any valid single-line Visual Basic instruction by simply typing the instruction and pressing Enter. This is an invaluable debugging tool. By displaying the values of program variables, for example, you can discover exactly how your program is working, and what might have gone wrong. For more information on debugging techniques and using the Debug window, see Chapter 21, "Debugging and Testing."

For now, try some simple experiments with the Debug window. Type **beep**, then press Enter. You should hear a beep from your computer's speaker. This is a valid instruction that causes the speaker to beep.

Try some math. Type **print 2+3**, then press Enter. Visual Basic displays the answer: 5. The print instruction causes Visual Basic to display the result of the ensuing expression. You can abbreviate print with a question mark. Type **? 1/7**, then press Enter. Visual Basic displays the result (see Figure 4.8).

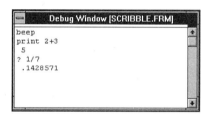

Figure 4.8.

Using the Debug window.

Resuming and Ending Execution

Open the **R**un menu. Notice that the first option has changed again. This time, it reads **C**ontinue. Use this option to resume execution of the program. You can accomplish the same task by clicking the Run button in the Toolbar, or pressing the F5 key.

With the program now running again (note that the title bar indicates the Run mode), you can stop the program with either of these two equivalent actions:

■ Click the End button on the Toolbar.

■ Choose the **E**nd option on the **R**un menu.

The program stops executing, and Visual Basic re-enters the Design mode.

Debug Menu

Visual Basic's **D**ebug menu provides several options that are useful when testing and debugging a program. For information on the available debugging options, see Chapter 21, "Debugging and Testing."

Options Menu

By adjusting the values of various settings available with the **O**ptions menu, you can change the way Visual Basic looks and works. The **O**ptions menu opens to reveal two submenus: Environment... (controls various Visual Basic settings) and **P**roject... (controls the way some options work on the current application). The following sections describe the options available from these two submenus.

The Environment... Submenu

When you select the Environment... submenu, a dialog box opens (see Figure 4.9). This dialog box presents several different default values that you can modify. As you scroll through the available items, you find options for such operations as adjusting the number of characters in a tab stop, verifying whether the code editor checks for valid syntax, modifying the screen colors for various kinds of program statements, and specifying how the grid works.

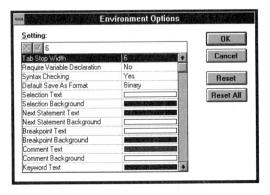

Figure 4.9.

The Environment Options dialog box.

As you work with Visual Basic, you might find that at times you want to modify default values. For example, you might want to change the file format for saved files from the default binary format to text format (which can be read by word processors and outside editors). Also, you might prefer to change the default colors for program code due to color blindness, or simply for aesthetic reasons.

To learn to use this dialog box, try changing the value of the **A**lign to Grid option. To do so, follow these steps:

1. Scroll through the dialog box until the final item (Align to Grid) is visible.

   Note that the default value for this item is Yes.

2. Click the line reading `Align to Grid` to select this option.

When you select an item, it immediately becomes highlighted. Also, the value `Yes` appears in the settings box at the top of the form.

3. To scroll through the available options, click the down arrow to the right of the settings box.

For the **Align** to Grid option, the only possible values are `Yes` and `No`.

4. Click `No` to change the value.

5. Click OK to activate the change.

Alternatively, you can double-click anywhere on the Align to Grid line to toggle the value of this option between `Yes` and `No`.

By changing the **Align** to Grid option to `No`, controls placed on the form do not have to line up with the grid dots. This option affects all controls placed on all forms. Compare this option with **Align** to Grid from the **Edit** menu, which affects only one selected control on a particular form.

Some items from the Environment Options dialog box present several possible choices. For example, you can change the special colors that Visual Basic uses to display various components of program code such as keywords, comments, and selected text. For each component, you can choose one of several choices for the foreground or background color.

Some items require you to type a value. For example, to change the number of characters skipped with each press of the Tab key, first select the Tab Stop Width item. (The default value is 4.) Then, type a new value. Figure 4.10 shows the value of 7 entered in the settings box. Press Enter to accept the value.

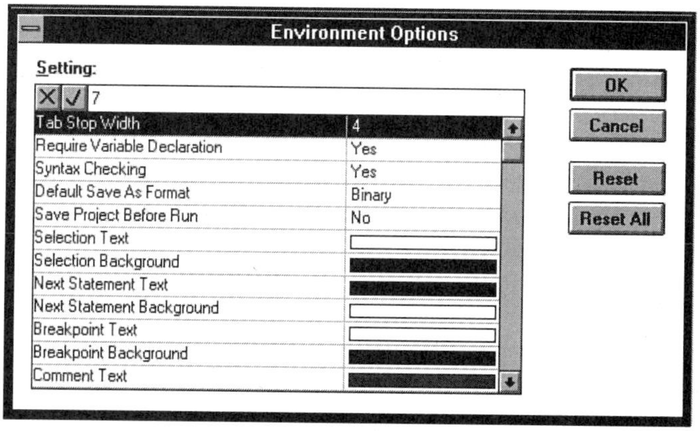

Figure 4.10.

Changing the value of
Tab Stop Width.

The various Environment Options items are discussed throughout this book. For now, you might want to scroll through the list to get an idea of the options available.

By clicking the Reset All button, you can restore the values of all settings to their default values. Try it. Notice how the value of Tab Stop Width returns to the default value of 4. The environment now looks and works just as it did when you first installed Visual Basic.

When you finish making any changes, click OK to accept the new values and close the dialog box.

The Project... Submenu

The **Project**... submenu (of the **O**ptions menu) presents three options of use when working on a particular application.

The Command Line Argument item is useful when developing stand-alone applications invoked outside of Visual Basic. The Start Up Form options specifies the first form that appears for a multiform application. For more information on these options, see Chapter 9, "Managing Projects."

With the Help File option, you can specify a Help file for use in conjunction with your application. Designing a custom Help file requires the Professional Edition of Visual Basic. For more information on designing Help systems, see Chapter 33, "Adding a Help System to an Application."

Window Menu

When you're using Windows, especially when running multiple applications, the desktop screen can become cluttered. Sometimes, icons (and even whole windows) seem to become hopelessly buried under a morass of overlapping windows.

The **W**indow menu provides a quick way to activate and display several windows involved with the Visual Basic environment. You can use this menu to reactivate a previously disabled or minimized window, or simply to "dig out" a buried window.

Not all items in this menu are always available. The availability of an item depends on the current mode (Design, Run, or Break), and which other windows are currently visible. For example, you cannot activate the Properties window while in Run mode. When a menu item appears dimmed, it is not currently available.

When you select one of the options, the selected window moves to the foreground and obtains the focus. You can begin using the window immediately. The following is a brief description of each submenu option available from the Window menu:

Color Palette	Opens a box that displays available color combinations. With this box, you can select foreground and background colors for a wide variety of objects, including forms, texts, and graphics controls. For information on using the color palette, see Chapter 6, "Using Controls."
Debug	Activates the Debug (Immediate window) window. The shortcut key is Ctrl+B.
Menu Design	Activates the Menu Design window from which you add a menu system to an application. For more information on this window, see Chapter 24, "Designing Custom Menus." The shortcut key is Ctrl+M.
Procedures	Opens a dialog box from which you can select any procedurethat you want to view or edit. The shortcut key is F2.
Project	Opens the Project window. For more about this window, see Chapter 9, "Managing Projects."
Properties	Opens the Properties window. For more information on this window, see the next several chapters. The shortcut key is F4.
Toolbox	Opens the Toolbox from which you can select graphics controls to place on a form. For more information on using the Toolbox, see the next several chapters.

Help Menu

Visual Basic offers an extensive full-featured Help system. Some of these features include searching for topics or keywords, cutting and pasting code examples from Help screens to your programs, and using hypertext-type links in which special highlighted words in one Help screen open related screens.

Perhaps the most useful feature of the Help system is that it is context sensitive. When you press F1, a screen opens to provide Help with the current topic. For example, if you are programming in the Code window, press F1 to open a screen with information about the Visual Basic keyword at the cursor location. If the focus is on a form, control, menu item, or error message, press F1 to open a screen describing the current item.

For example, Figure 4.11 shows the Help screen that opens when you press F1 while the focus is on the Form window.

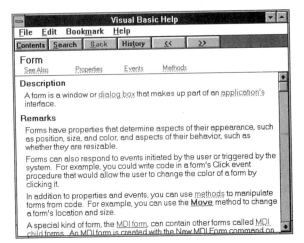

Figure 4.11.

The Help screen describing the Form window.

Help screens function like ordinary windows. Not only can you move a Help window around the desktop, you can resize, maximize, and reduce it to an icon.

In addition to context-sensitive Help, you can access the Help system directly from the **H**elp menu. The following is a brief description of the submenu options available from the **H**elp menu:

Contents	Provides a general Help menu from which you can better specify your Help topic choice. This option is described in the "Using Help" section that follows.
Search for Help on...	Opens a window from which you can select a Help screen by searching through an extensive list of topics. When you click a topic, the appropriate Help screen opens.
Obtaining Technical Support...	Provides information on Visual Basic support services.
Learning Microsoft Visual Basic	Provides an on-screen tutorial on using Visual Basic.

About Microsoft   Displays the released version of Visual Basic
Visual Basic...   and shows Microsoft's copyright announce-
                     ment. The screen shows also information perti-
                     nent to your system, such as the serial number
                     of your copy of Visual Basic, and how much
                     memory you have available.

Using Help

Figure 4.12 shows the screen that opens when you select the Contents option
from the Help menu. On a color monitor, several options display in green text.
These items are links to other Help screens.

Hand-shaped pointer

Figure 4.12.

The main Help screen with
the hand-shaped cursor
visible.

When you move the mouse cursor near a green element on any Help screen,
the mouse's cursor shape changes from an arrow to a small hand with a
pointing index finger. This hand shape means that clicking the mouse opens a
new Help screen explaining the highlighted option. Figure 4.12 shows the hand
cursor pointing to Programming Environment.

When you click most green items, a new Help screen opens describing the
item. The new screen likely contains further links to other items. By examining
successive links, you can explore the Help system. Green items underlined
with a dotted line are glossary terms. When you click a glossary term, a
window opens with its definition. To close this window, click the mouse button
once more or press any key.

Within a given screen, you can move the highlight from green item to green item by repeatedly pressing Tab. Use Shift+Tab to move backward. If you press Enter, the Help screen opens for the currently highlighted item.

The Help system includes help on the Visual Basic keywords that comprise the programming language. This help includes sample program examples as well as descriptions of the keywords.

Besides the features already described, a Help screen has its own menu bar, as well as six help (accelerator) buttons located just below the menu bar.

Using the Help Buttons

The following is a brief description of the buttons found on each Help screen:

Contents	Click this button to display the main Help screen that Figure 4.12 shows. From here, you can restart your quest for help.
Search	Click this button to open a window containing two boxes that can be scrolled. The upper box displays an extensive alphabetic list of Visual Basic topics. (The list is extensive. For example, there are approximately 100 items beginning with A.) You can scroll through this list looking for a topic of interest. When you click a topic, a list of related Help topics appears in the lower box. For example, if you double-click `Colors` in the upper box, the lower box displays `BackColor`, `ForeColor Properties`, `Color Palette`, `QBColor Function`, `RGB Function`, and `Setting Colors`. You then click a topic in the lower box, and click **G**o To to see the appropriate Help screen. You can also search for any topic by typing its name in the list box. The related topics appear in the lower box.
Back	As you open successive Help screens, Visual Basic keeps track of the screens you have viewed. When you click the **B**ack button, Visual Basic redisplays the last screen you viewed. You can back up repeatedly by continually clicking this button.
History	When you click this button, a window opens containing a list of the Help screens you have viewed. By selecting an item from this list and pressing Enter (or by double-clicking the item), you can quickly redisplay any Help screen you viewed in the current session.

Forward (>>)   When you click this button, Visual Basic displays the next Help screen in Visual Basic's sequential order. The symbol for this button appears as two right-pointing chevrons (that is, two "greater than" symbols, Shift+period on most keyboards).

Reverse (<<)   This button is the opposite of Forward. When you click the Reverse button, you see the previous Help screen in Visual Basic's sequential order. The symbol for this button appears as two left-pointing chevrons (that is, two "less than" symbols, Shift+comma on most keyboards).

Using the Help Menu Bar

The menu bar on each Help screen has four options. The following is a brief description of each item:

File   This menu provides several file- and print-related options. With Open..., you can open the Help system for another Visual Basic application. With Print Topic, you can print the contents of the current Help window. With Print Setup..., you can modify the default printer settings, or select a different printer altogether. With Exit, you can quit the Visual Basic Help system.

Edit   This menu provides copying and editing functions. With the Copy option, You can move selected text from a Help window to the Windows clipboard. From there, you can paste the copied text into your Visual Basic program code, or into another Windows application, such as a word processor. With the Annotate... option, you can associate your own comments with any Help screen. Once you add a comment, you see your annotations anytime you reopen that Help window.

Bookmark   With this menu item, you can create a sort of express method to get to any Help screen in the future. When you first select this menu option, only the Define option appears. By selecting Define, you open the Bookmark Define dialog box. From here, you can create a bookmark, which adds the name of the current Help window to the drop-down submenu that opens under Bookmark. By clicking a bookmarked item shown under the Bookmark menu, Visual Basic directly opens the associated Help screen. The Bookmark Define dialog box includes an option to delete previously created bookmarks.

Help   The Help screen contains its own **Help** menu. This item provides assistance on how to use **Help**.

Other Components of the Environment

This chapter focuses on the workings of the Toolbar and the menu system. Three remaining components of the development environment include:

Toolbox   This window contains a set of controls used to build the user-interface for your applications. Controls are graphics objects, such as text boxes, option buttons, and scroll bars.

Properties window   This window specifies the attributes (properties) of the various objects in your application. These objects include forms, and the graphic controls you place on them. By modifying the values in the Properties window, you can customize values for such attributes as colors, fonts, size, location, and captions.

Project window   This window lists the forms, modules, and custom controls that compose an application. Through the Project window, you can access the individual components in your application. For example, you can quickly make visible the program code for any form or module.

In the next several chapters, you learn to build Visual Basic applications from the beginning. You learn also more about the Toolbox and the Properties window. For more information on the Project window, see Chapter 9, "Managing Projects."

Summary

Visual Basic offers a full-featured development environment. The menu system offers commands to save and load files, edit program code, and customize how the environment looks and responds.

The Toolbar provides quick access to some of the most frequently used menu commands. By simply clicking a Toolbar button, you activate a command immediately. For example, there are Toolbar buttons to open a new project, begin program execution, and pause a program into the Break mode.

Visual Basic's full-screen editor has special features to facilitate programming. For example, the editor displays program components such as keywords and comments with special (adjustable) colors. Also, the editor checks the syntax of each program instruction as you type. You can print program listings on a line printer. The Edit menu provides many editing commands.

Online help is available through the Help menu. You can get context-sensitive help by pressing F1 at any time. The Help system responds by displaying information about the current task.

Visual Basic has three fundamental modes of program operation. In Design mode, you construct the user interface and write program code. In Run mode, you execute the application. With Break mode, you temporarily suspend execution. You can use the Debug window to test and debug programs.

Building Applications

PART

II

Understanding Forms, Events, and Properties

W hen designing any Visual Basic application, you should start with the form. The *form* is a window that constitutes the background for the visible part of the application.

For most applications, you place graphical control objects onto the form. Examples of control objects are command buttons and text labels. Many applications use multiple forms.

This chapter discusses the form—the attributes of the form and the various ways in which a form responds to the events that occur while an application is running. The sample applications consist of a single form containing no controls.

The main topics covered in this chapter include:

■ Customizing a form's appearance at design time

■ Understanding the common properties of a form

■ Using the Properties window

■ Writing event procedures

■ Changing property values at run time

■ Saving the form and project as disk files

Understanding the Default Form

When you start a new Visual Basic project, a blank form appears in the middle of the screen. Figure 5.1 shows this default form.

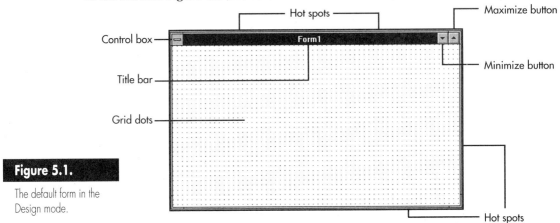

Figure 5.1.

The default form in the Design mode.

The title bar of the form reads Form1. In Visual Basic terminology, Form1 is the *caption* for this form. The *caption* is the text you see in the title bar. Whenever you start a new project, Form1 is the form's default caption.

NOTE As the caption Form1 implies, a project might include multiple forms having captions that indicate numerical order, such as Form2, Form3, and so on. For the next few chapters, the discussion is restricted to single-form applications. For more information on multiple forms, see Chapter 9, "Managing Projects."

Click anywhere inside the form. Notice that the form's title bar is highlighted, appearing in dark blue on most color monitors. Now, click somewhere on Visual Basic's menu bar. Notice that the form's title bar is no longer highlighted. Click again anywhere inside the form to restore the highlight in the title bar. When the form has the focus, the title bar is highlighted.

Notice the rectangular array of dots that make up the interior of the form. These dots comprise the *grid*. As described in Chapter 6, "Using Controls," you can use this grid to align controls, and other items that you place on the form.

You can resize the form and move it around the desktop. For example, to move the form, position the mouse pointer inside the title bar. Then, hold down the left mouse button and drag the title bar to a new location. Release the mouse button. The minimize and maximize buttons are active, as is the control box. Experiment with these effects.

Click the Control box. A standard Windows Control menu opens (see Figure 5.2). Select the **C**lose option. The form closes and disappears from the desktop. Although the form is temporarily invisible, your computer's memory has not removed it.

To recover the form, use the Project window. (If you cannot see the Project window on the desktop, choose the P**r**oject option from Visual Basic's **W**indow menu.) The Project window lists the various files that compose the application you are developing. Notice that the highlight is on Form1.frm (see Figure 5.3). Now, click the button that reads View Form. The form reappears on your desk-top. For more information on the Project window, see Chapter 9, "Managing Projects."

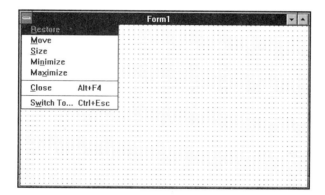

Figure 5.2.

The Control menu.

Running an "Empty" Application

Even a default form has certain built-in attributes. One way to better understand these attributes is to run an *empty* application. To do so, simply begin program execution without first making any design-time modifications to the form.

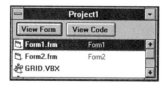

Figure 5.3.

The Project window.

Use one of the following techniques to begin program execution:

- Click the Run button in the Toolbar.
- Choose the **S**tart option from the **R**un menu.
- Press the shortcut key, F5.

Although you have not modified any properties or written any program code, the form acts as a standard window. For example, you can move the form around the desktop by dragging the title bar. Try doing this.

Minimize and Maximize buttons are in the upper right corner of the form. Try clicking these buttons. With the maximize button, you enlarge the form to fill the entire screen. With minimize, you reduce the form to an icon.

 NOTE When you minimize the form, the Debug window might obscure the form's Minimize icon. If necessary, drag the Debug window until you see the form's icon.

Notice that the icon for the minimized form displays the name Form1. When a form is minimized, the name of its icon matches the text displayed in the form's title bar. The minimized Form1 icon resembles this:

With the form minimized, you can see the Debug window that previously was behind the form. You can use the Debug window as a debugging tool in Break mode; this is discussed in previous chapters, and in Chapter 21, "Debugging and Testing."

Double-click the icon to restore the form. Then move the mouse pointer onto the form and click the left mouse button. Nothing special happens. Notice that the mouse pointer retains the standard arrow shape while located inside the form. Later in the chapter, you set some property values and write program code to change the shape of the pointer and to make the form respond to a mouse click.

As with standard windows, you can resize the form. Try it. Move the pointer near one of the form's *hot spots*. These hot spots occur along the border of the form. When you are on a hot spot, the pointer shape changes to a double-sided arrow. By dragging the mouse in one of the arrow directions, you can resize the form (either larger or smaller).

Now, end the program by either clicking the Stop button in the Toolbar or choosing the **E**nd option from the **R**un menu.

Understanding Properties

Visual Basic associates a number of properties with each form. The *properties* are the form's attributes. For example, each form has height, width, screen location, and color attributes. These properties, along with several others, describe the characteristics of the form.

When you begin a new project, Visual Basic assigns a default value for each of the form's properties. By changing the default values of various properties, you can customize how a particular form appears and behaves. Make the Height property larger, and the form becomes taller. Change the MinButton property to False, and the form no longer has a Minimize button—the user is not able to reduce the form to an icon.

You can change the values of a form's properties at design time, or at run time. As described in the next section, you use the Properties window to change values at design time. When you run the application, new values take effect immediately. For example, if you change the BackColor property to blue at design time, the form appears with a blue background when the application is run.

Often, you want to change the value of a property while the program is running. When your program executes an instruction that modifies a property value,the form responds immediately. As explained later in this chapter, such code goes in the event procedures associated with the form.

For example, suppose you plan to display some important information on the form when the user clicks the mouse. By programming an instruction that changes the value of WindowState to 2 inside the Form_Click procedure, the form enlarges to full size when the user clicks the mouse. For more information on the Form_Click procedure, see the section "Responding to Form Events," later in this chapter.

Most property values can be changed at design time or run time. Some property values can be changed, however, at design time only. Such properties are called *read-only*. This phrase means that, at run time, the program code can read the current value of the property, but cannot modify its value. For example, you can modify the value of the BorderStyle property at design time, but you can't change the value while the program is running.

Conversely, some property values can be read or modifed at run time but not at design time. Such properties are *not* found in the Properties window (see the next section). As a result, their values cannot be modified at design time. For example, the CurrentX and CurrentY properties specify horizontal and vertical drawing coordinates. Your code can modify the values of these properties while the application is executing, but you can't specify their values at design time.

The Properties Window

To change property values at design time, you use the Properties window (see Figure 5.4). If the Properties window is not visible, press F4, (or choose the Properties option from Visual Basic's **W**indow menu.)

Title bar

Object box

Settings box

Property list

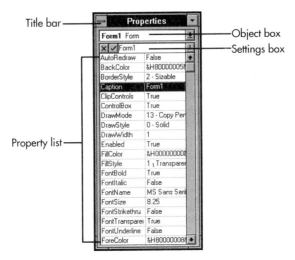

Figure 5.4.

The Properties window.

Click anywhere on the form to give it the focus. Press F4 to bring the Properties window to the foreground. Notice that the form's properties appear in the Properties window.

The main portion of the Properties window consists of a two-column list. All the form's properties are listed in the left column. The values of those properties are in the right column. Using the scroll bar on the right side of the window, scan through the various properties. About 45 different properties are featured. As you develop various applications, you probably find that you frequently modify the values of some of these properties. Other values you seldom, if ever, change.

Title Bar

The Properties window has a title bar with a Control box to the left and a minimize button to the right. You can reduce the Properties window to an icon by clicking the Minimize button. Alternatively, you can close the window completely by choosing the Close option from the Control menu. Remember: if the Properties window is not visible and you want to bring it to the foreground, press F4.

Object Box

The Object box is just under the title bar. The text in the Object box reads Form1 Form. This Object box displays the name of the object that has the focus (Form1), and what type of object it is (Form).

Visual Basic uses Form1 as the default name for the form. The Object box informs you that the properties and values currently displayed in the Properties window belong to the default form.

The *objects* in an application refer to the forms, and the controls that you can place on them. If you click the down arrow to the right of the Object box, a drop-down list appears that specifies the objects on the current form. If you click any name in this list, the Properties window displays values for that object's properties.

Because the form does not contain any controls, there is only one entry in the Object box list—Form1. In later chapters, when you place controls onto forms, you see additional items listed in the Object box.

Settings Box

The Settings box displays the value of the highlighted property. The term *setting* refers to the value of a property. The Settings box not only displays the current value, but enables you to modify it as well.

To highlight a property, use the mouse or arrow keys to scroll through the list of properties, then click your selection. You can move the highlight quickly by holding down Shift+Ctrl while you press a letter key. The highlight moves to the first property that begins with that letter. By repeating this keystroke combination, you can move the highlight to successive properties that begin with the same first letter.

The Shift+Ctrl+letter keystroke combination does not always work. Some Windows applications use Shift+Ctrl+letter keystroke combinations for special purposes. If you have another Windows application loaded in addition to Visual Basic, you might encounter some difficulty.

Modifying Some Property Values

To understand the process of modifying property values, try the following example. In the Properties window, move the highlight to the Caption property. The *caption* of a form is the text that displays in the form's title bar. The current (default) caption is Form1. You can type any new caption. Try typing **Go For It**. Notice that blank spaces can occur within a caption.

As you type, your new text replaces the old contents of the Settings box. Notice that the caption changes not only in the Settings box, but also in the title bar of the form and in the right-hand column of the Properties window.

Notice the two boxes to the left of the Settings box—one box has a check mark (the Enter box), and the other, a large × (the Cancel box). These standard Windows boxes signify acceptance and rejection, respectively. When you're finished typing the new caption, click the Enter box to accept the new value. If you click the Cancel box, Visual Basic does not accept your typed value, and returns the setting back to its previous value.

You don't have to use the check box to finalize a new value. You can press Enter, Tab, or simply click the mouse in another location. If you press Enter, the focus returns to the main part of the Properties window.

Similarly, you don't have to click the Cancel box if you make a mistake while typing a property value. You can also press Escape to restore the setting to its original value.

Try moving the mouse pointer into the Settings box. Notice that the cursor shape changes to an insertion point. By clicking the mouse inside the current text, you indicate the place in which you want to insert characters.

The Caption property is an example of a property that can have any value, and you can type whatever caption you want. Many properties, however, can have only a limited range of valid values.

The MousePointer property, for example, determines the shape of the mouse pointer when you move it over the form. This is an example of a property that you must select from a predefined list.

Follow these steps to select a value for this MousePointer:

1. Click the MousePointer property in the left column of the Properties window.

2. Look at the right edge of the Settings box. You see a combo box containing a boldfaced down arrow. Click this down arrow.

   A list box opens that displays the values that you can use for MousePointer (see Figure 5.5). Notice that this list box has vertical scroll bars. You can scroll the contents of the box, which offers other values.

3. Scroll the list box until you see the value 11 - Hourglass.

4. Click 11 - Hourglass. The value appears in both the Settings box and the right-hand column of the Properties window.

With this setting, the shape of the pointer changes when you move it over the form at run time—it becomes the standard Windows hourglass. Notice, however, that during design time, the pointer does *not* change shape when you move it over the form.

Figure 5.5.

The MousePointer
list box.

You can modify many properties by double-clicking their values in the right-hand column of the Properties window. Try double-clicking the MousePointer value in the right-hand column. The value increases to 12. Continually double-click this value until you cycle back to the value of 11.

Several properties have only two acceptable values: True and False. The value of the ControlBox property, for example, determines whether a Control box appears on the form during run time. The default value is True. If you change the value to False, the user cannot open the Control menu. As a result, the user can't close the form when the application is running.

There are several ways you can change the value of ControlBox to False. One way is to press the F key after highlighting ControlBox in the Properties window. Try it. Notice that False now appears in the Settings box. You can toggle the value between True and False by pressing T and F, alternatively.

Another way is to open the drop-down list box. True and False are the only values that appear. Then, you can select False. A third way is to double-click the value of True that appears in the right-hand column of the Properties window. The value toggles to False. Try these various methods, but leave the final value as False.

Double-Clicking the Property Value

By double-clicking a property value in the right-hand column of the Properties window, you either change the value or prepare the Settings box for this change. Table 5.1 shows the results of double-clicking the various types of properties.

Table 5.1. Results of double-clicking the property values.

Type of Property	Example Property	Result of Double-Click
True/False (Boolean)	ControlBox	True changes to False. False changes to True.
Provided List	MousePointer	The next value in the list is selected.
Text or Numerical Value	Caption	Property combo box receives the focus, so that you can type the new value.
Color Property	BackColor	Color Palette appears.
Picture Property	Icon	A dialog box opens for you to choose the desired picture (or icon) file.

This table reveals some new property types: colors and pictures. For more information on the Color Palette, see "Opening the Color Palette" later in this chapter. For a discussion of the Picture property, see Chapter 8, "Using the Toolbox and the Common Controls."

Rerunning the Application with the New Property Values

Start the updated application to see the effects of the modified property values. First, notice that the form's title bar has the new caption: Go For It (or whatever else you typed for the caption). The Control box (to the left of the title bar) is now gone. The user cannot open the Control menu.

Move the mouse pointer onto the form. The pointer shape changes to the hourglass (see Figure 5.6). When you move the pointer off the form, the hourglass changes back to the standard arrow. The changing pointer shape is the direct result of modifying the value of the MousePointer property.

Click the Minimize button. The form reduces to an icon. Notice that the name of the icon, Go For It, matches the form's caption. The Caption property not only determines the name you see in the title bar, but also the name displayed when the form is minimized.

Double-click the icon to restore the form. Then, choose the End option on the Run menu (or click the Stop icon in the Toolbar) to end the application.

Although this example was extremely simple, it was instructive. By modifying the values of a few properties, you customized a form and began the process of designing an application.

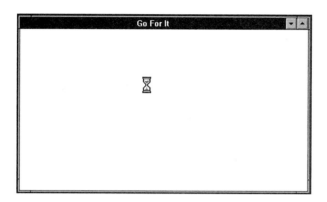

Figure 5.6.

The modified form in action, including the hourglass pointer.

Understanding Common Properties

As you've seen, the Properties window contains several modifiable properties—almost 50 properties are featured! As you become more proficient with Visual Basic, you are most likely to use some properties more often than others. This section examines the most commonly used properties.

BorderStyle

The BorderStyle property determines the appearance of the form's border. This property is more than cosmetic—the border style affects whether the user can resize the form. This property accepts values of 0, 1, 2, or 3. The default value is 2. Table 5.2 shows the effects of the various values.

Table 5.2. The values of BorderStyle.

Value	Style Name	Effect
0	(None)	No border appears. The form does not have Minimize or Maximize buttons, or a Control box. The user cannot move, resize, or minimize the form.
1	Fixed Single	The border does not have hot spots. As a result, the user cannot resize the form, except for minimizing and maximizing.

continues

Table 5.2. Continued

Value	Style Name	Effect
2	Sizable	This is the default value. Resizing is enabled.
3	Fixed Double	The border appears twice as thick as normal. The form can contain the Control box, but it cannot contain Minimize and Maximize buttons. The border does not contain hot spots, so resizing is disabled.

You can change the value of BorderStyle with the Properties window at design time. As mentioned earlier in this chapter, however, you cannot change the value of BorderStyle through program code at run time. (Writing program code is discussed later in this chapter.)

Caption

You have already seen the effects of changing the Caption property. Remember that the value of Caption not only specifies the text in the forms's title bar, but also the name of the icon when the form is minimized.

ControlBox

Earlier in the chapter, you experimented with modifying the value of the ControlBox property. Notice that if the BorderStyle property is set to 0 (no border), the value of ControlBox is immaterial. If BorderStyle has any other value, the value of ControlBox determines whether the Control box is visible.

MinButton and MaxButton

The value of MinButton determines whether the form has a Minimize button. The default value is True. If you set the value to False, the form does not have a Minimize button. Similarly, the value of MaxButton determines whether the form has a Maximize button.

 NOTE If BorderStyle is 0 or 3, the values of MinButton and MaxButton are immaterial because the form cannot display Minimize and Maximize buttons.

Enabled

This property determines whether the form can respond to *any* events. The only valid values are True and False. The default value is True. As you see shortly, you can write program code that makes the form respond to various events. If the Enabled property is set to False, however, you prohibit the form from responding.

You rarely set the value of this property at design time. During run time, however, you might want the form temporarily unresponsive to user-generated events. For example, while you are displaying important information on the form, you don't want the user to be able to minimize it. You can set Enable to False while displaying the information. Then, reset the value to True when the information has been displayed.

Name

The Name property specifies the name of the form. You can use this name in program code when referencing the form object. The default value is Form1. By changing the value of Name to something more descriptive, you make the program code easier to read and debug. For example, in a loan analysis program, you might use Loan as the name of the form. For single-form applications, modifying the Name property is not particularly beneficial. As you create multiform applications, however, more descriptive names go a long way toward making your program code easier to understand. For more information on multiform applications, see Chapter 9, "Managing Projects."

Don't confuse the Name property with the Caption property. The Caption is simply the text that displays in the form's title bar. Name is the identifier used to specify the form in the program code. Some confusion might result as Visual Basic uses the default value of Form1 for both the Caption and Name properties.

Font Properties

The Font properties determine the appearance of text displayed in the form. You can change the type of font, its size, and the special effects, such as italic and boldface. (The Font properties do *not* affect the appearance of the caption in the title bar).

The `FontName` property specifies the font. At design time, you select the font from a displayed list. The values in this list depend on your computer configuration— your video monitor, installed printer, version of Windows, and which Windows fonts you have installed. The default value of `FontName` is normally `MS Sans Serif`.

The `FontSize` property determines the size of the text displayed in the form. Each font recognizes a discrete set of values. For this reason, you should normally adjust the value of `FontName` before you modify the value of `FontSize`.

The `FontBold`, `FontItalic`, `FontStrikethru`, `FontTransparent`, and `FontUnderline` properties each can be set to True or False. The default value is True for `FontBold` and `FontTransparent`. The other properties are False by default. The values of these properties determine the appearance of displayed text. In general, you can combine effects. For example, you can generate boldface, italic text by setting both `FontBold` and `FontItalic` to True.

`FontTransparent` determines whether displayed characters obscure the form's background. When `FontTransparent` is True, you see the form's background behind any displayed text. When `FontTransparent` is False, the newly displayed text obscures the old background.

For more information on fonts, see Chapter 12, "Displaying Text and Fonts."

Size and Location Properties

You can modify the form's size with the `Height` and `Width` properties. Similarly, you can specify the form's on-screen location with the `Left` and `Top` properties. If you modify these properties at design time, the form reflects the changes immediately.

Visual Basic uses an unusual unit to measure the values of these properties— the twip. A *twip* is 1/1440 of an inch. The name stands for *tw*entieth of a *p*oint.

In the printing industry, a *point* is 1/72 of an inch. Common printing font sizes are 10-point and 12-point. (With more than 1000 twips in an inch, a single twip is quite small.)

The Location and Size Coordinates on the Toolbar

By now, you have probably noticed the four numbers at the right-hand edge of the Toolbar (see Figure 5.7). These numbers change as you move and resize the form.

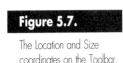

Figure 5.7.

The Location and Size coordinates on the Toolbar.

The number pair to the left specifies the location of the upper left corner of the form relative to the same corner of the screen. The numbers are measured in units referred to as twips. The first number in the pair is the distance in twips from the left edge of the screen to the left edge of the form. The second number is the distance in twips from the top of the screen down to the top edge of the form (notice that larger numbers mean farther *down* the screen.)

Try dragging the form's title bar around the screen. Watch how this pair of numbers changes. If you move the form to the upper left corner of the screen, each number becomes 0.

Now, look at the values of Left and Top in the Properties window. These values reflect the first pair of numbers you see in the Toolbar. As you move the form, the numbers change in the Properties window as well as in the Toolbar.

You can modify the values directly from the Properties window. Change the value of Left, and the form immediately moves horizontally. Change the value of Top, and the form moves vertically.

Similarly, the pair of numbers on the right in the Toolbar indicates the width and height of the form. Again, the unit is twips. These numbers correspond to the Width and Height properties. Try resizing the form and watch the numbers change in both the Toolbar and the Properties window.

 NOTE Twips do not precisely indicate physical distances as measured on-screen. Instead, twips specify printed sizes. The actual size of a twip on your screen depends on your video monitor—its screen size and scanning characteristics.

Changing the Scale Properties

You can change the measurement units from twips to something else. By adjusting the ScaleMode property, you can choose a different standard unit (such as inches or centimeters), or create a customized scale of your own. Table 5.3 shows the eight possible values of ScaleMode.

Table 5.3. Values of *ScaleMode*.

Value	Scale Units
0	Indicates a custom scale
1	Twip (default value)
2	Point (1/72 of an inch)
3	Pixel (smallest unit of screen resolution)

continues

Table 5.3. Continued

Value	Scale Units
4	Character (horizontal = 1/12 inch, vertical = 1/6 inch)
5	Inch
6	Millimeter
7	Centimeter

By changing the values of the ScaleHeight, ScaleWidth, ScaleLeft, and ScaleTop properties, in conjunction with ScaleMode, you can create a custom scale. For more information on scaling, see Chapter 11, "Displaying Graphics."

Icon

The Icon property specifies the form's minimize icon. That is, the value of this property specifies what icon represents the form when it is minimized.

Visual Basic comes with a large library of graphical icons. You can choose one of these icons for the Icon property. You can also create custom icons. The Visual Basic package includes a sample application named ICONWRKS that lets you create customized icons.

Follow these steps to modify the value of the Icon property:

1. Highlight the Icon property in the Properties window (see Figure 5.8).

Figure 5.8.

The Icon property in the Properties window.

2. Click the box on the right-hand edge of the Settings box.

   Notice that this box contains an ellipsis (...). The ellipsis indicates that a dialog box opens.

3. Select the ICONS directory from the Load Icon dialog box (see Figure 5.9).

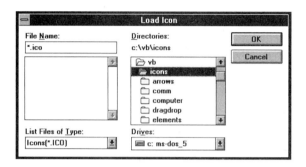

Figure 5.9.

Selecting the
C:\VB\ICONS directory.

If you have a normal installation of Visual Basic, you see the ICONS subdirectory listed under your VB directory. You can select the ICONS subdirectory by double-clicking the name in the **D**irectories list box, or by typing the directory path in the File **N**ame text box.

4. Double-click the INDUSTRY directory.

   You might have to scroll the **D**irectories list box to find the INDUSTRY subdirectory.

5. Double-click PLANE.ICO in the File **N**ame list box. Notice that `plane.ico` appears in the File **N**ame list box (see Figure 5.10).

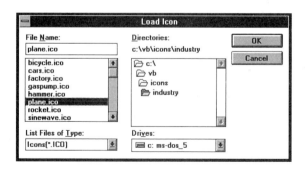

Figure 5.10.

Selecting the
C:\VB\ICONS\INDUSTRY
\PLANE.ICO file.

6. Click the OK button to close the Load Icon dialog box.

You have now selected an icon that resembles an airplane. To verify that the `Icon` property invokes this new icon, click the form's Minimize button. The form's icon should appear as follows:

This icon is just one example of several icons that come with Visual Basic. To see pictures of the included icons, consult the documentation included with Visual Basic.

MousePointer

You have already experimented with the MousePointer property. You can change the pointer to any of 12 different shapes.

Visible

The Visible property is True, by default. If you change the value to False, the form disappears from the desktop. This property is most often changed at run time, usually in multiform applications. By making all forms invisible, except one, you can draw your user's attention to the visible form.

WindowState

The WindowState property determines the appearance of the form at run time. Three values are possible: 0 (the default value—the form appears in normal size), 1 (the form is minimized, shrunk to an icon), and 2 (the form is maximized). If you modify the value at design time, the form's appearance does not change until run time. You usually change the value of WindowState with program code that executes when the program runs.

The Color Properties

A form has two color properties: BackColor and ForeColor. The value of BackColor determines the form's background color. The value of ForeColor determines the color of text and graphics displayed on the form. These colors can be changed at design time with the Properties window, or at run time through program code.

Try changing the background color. Select the BackColor property from the Properties window. Notice that the current value is the hexadecimal number &H80000005&.

Treating Colors as Hexadecimal Numbers

Several methods are available for you to manipulate colors. You don't *have* to work with arcane numbers such as &H80000005& to choose colors. A little later you learn that the Color Palette provides a much simpler way to select colors.

NOTE **Hexadecimal Numbers are Base 16**

The number &H80000005& is expressed in hexadecimal notation. The &H notation at the left of the number indicates that the remaining digits are considered to be in hexadecimal, or base 16. *Hexadecimal numbers* use the digits 0-9 plus the letters A-F. This system is convenient for several computer-related numbers because, unlike base 10 decimal numbers, hexadecimal numbers are based on an exact multiple of 2, that is 16 = 2 * 2 * 2 * 2. The number of bits in a byte is 256 (16 * 16), expressed with the values from 0 to 255. In hexadecimal notation, this number range is &H00 to &HFF.

The ampersand (&) after the number &H80000005& indicates that the number is a *long integer*, which in Visual Basic indicates an integer number larger than 32,767.

For more information on hexadecimal notation and long integers, see Chapter 16, "Working with Numbers."

Visual Basic uses the same scheme as Windows to represent colors with numbers. The foundation of this scheme is an RGB (Red, Green, Blue) numerical representation for colors.

Opening the Color Palette

With the BackColor property highlighted in the Properties window, click the ellipsis on the right side of the Settings box. A Color Palette window opens (see Figure 5.11).

Figure 5.11.

The Color Palette.

From this window, you can choose a color directly. Click a dark blue color, or any other color you want. The corresponding numerical color code is placed in the Settings box.

Now, accept the new value by pressing Enter, clicking the check box, or moving the focus off the Settings box. The form's color changes to blue (or whatever color you selected).

If you don't like any of the colors found in the Color Palette, you can create your own customized colors. In theory, Visual Basic can display over 16 million colors. For more information on creating your own colors, see Chapter 11, "Displaying Graphics."

Responding to Form Events

Although modifying the values of properties goes a long way toward creating a useful application, you really haven't made the form *do* anything yet. When the application runs, the form remains relatively inactive.

Suppose that you want to display a message on the form when the user clicks the mouse. To make the form respond to such an action, you must write program code.

A mouse click is an example of a Visual Basic *event*. A form can respond to several different events defined by Visual Basic. For a form, Visual Basic recognizes more than 20 different events.

Each event has a corresponding event procedure. In an *event procedure*, you write the program code that instructs Visual Basic to perform the desired action when the event occurs. For example, you write a `Form_Click` event procedure to tell Visual Basic what to do when the user clicks the form.

Although Visual Basic does not actually write event procedures for you, it does provide the template for each event procedure; the beginning and ending program lines for each event procedure are built into Visual Basic. You supply the *body* of each procedure—the lines of code that accomplish the desired actions.

Until you supply the procedure body, Visual Basic does not respond to the event. For example, when you run the blank application discussed earlier in this chapter, you can click on the form without anything happening. But once the application includes the body for the `Form_Click` procedure, the form responds to menu clicks according to your program code.

Opening the Code Window

In the following sections, you write an event procedure that displays a message on the form in response to a mouse click. First, double-click anywhere on the form to open the Code window (or choose the Code option from the View menu, or press the F7 shortcut key). The Code window appears as Figure 5.12 shows.

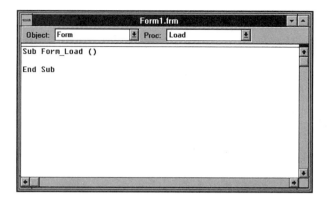

Figure 5.12.

The Code window.

The title bar for the Code window reads Form1.frm. This title is also the file name that Visual Basic uses when you save your form to disk. In Figure 5.12, Form1 is the name of the form. The .FRM file extension indicates that the file stores the description of a form.

The Object Box

Just under the title bar are two list boxes labeled Object: and Proc:. By clicking the down arrow on the right side of the Object box, a list of the objects in Form1 drops down (see Figure 5.13). This list contains the names (general) and Form. The term (general) refers to user-created functions and procedures. (For more information, see Chapter 7, "Writing Event Procedures.") Form is the only specific object in the list because you have not added any control objects to the form. (For more information about controls, see Chapter 8, "Using the Toolbox and the Common Controls.")

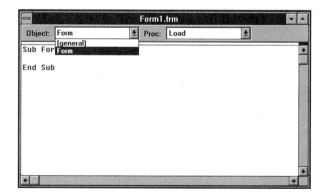

Figure 5.13.

The drop-down Object list.

The Proc Box

Click the down arrow on the right side of the Proc: box. Here, *Proc* is short for *Procedure*. When you click the arrow, a list of events drops down. You can scroll through them. This list enumerates several events. The form can respond to the various events.

By selecting one of these events, you can write the corresponding event procedure. When it runs, the application responds to the event.

As discussed earlier in this chapter, suppose you want the form to display a message when the user clicks the mouse pointer on the form. The name of the desired event procedure is Click.

To activate the Click procedure, highlight the word Click in the drop-down list. You can use the arrow keys to move the highlight. Perhaps the easiest way to highlight Click is to use the conventional Windows shortcut of pressing the C key to move the highlight to the first item that begins with the letter *C*. Your form should resemble the one in Figure 5.14.

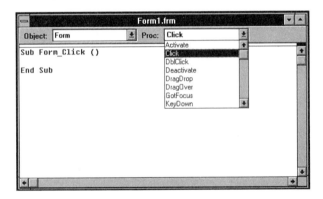

Figure 5.14.

Highlighting **Click** in the Procedures list.

Close the drop-down Procedures list. Several methods are available to do this. Two easy ways are to press Enter, or click the mouse in the Code window.

Understanding the Procedure Template

You see the following program lines in the Code window:

```
Sub Form_Click ()


End Sub
```

These lines constitute the template for the Click event procedure. The word Sub indicates that this procedure is a subprogram as opposed to a function. The name of the procedure, Form_Click, conforms with the Visual Basic convention of the object name (Form) followed by an underscore character, then the name of the event (Click).

This procedure defines what happens when the Click event occurs on the form. The parentheses at the end of the line are part of the required Visual Basic syntax for event procedures. You learn more about writing event procedures in the next several chapters.

Writing the Event Procedure

To write the body of an event procedure, you create program instructions in the blank space between the Sub and End Sub instructions in the procedure template.

Move the mouse pointer over the Code window. Notice that the pointer shape becomes an insertion point. If the text cursor (the blinking vertical bar) is not positioned at the left edge of the blank line between the Sub and End Sub instructions, move the insertion point there, then click.

Press Tab to indent the cursor several spaces, then type the following program line:

```
Print "Please don't click so hard!"
```

Your Code window should now resemble the one in Figure 5.15. When you run the application and click the form, Visual Basic displays a message inside the form.

Figure 5.15.

The Form_Click event procedure.

NOTE

Correcting Typing Errors

When you type program lines, Visual Basic checks that each line conforms to the syntax of the programming language. Visual Basic finds some errors at design time (while you are typing), and others at run time.

If an error occurs, Visual Basic displays a warning box that informs you of a syntax error. The offending word is highlighted in the program code. To close the warning box, click the OK button. You can then correct the program. If you need help determining the error, press F1 to invoke the context-sensitive Help.

You worked with Print instructions in Chapter 3, "Test Driving VB: A Sample Application." Print is an example of a Visual Basic method. A *method* performs an action on an object. In this context, the Print method performs an action (displaying a message) on an object (the form).

Running the Sample Program

Start the application, and move the pointer onto the form. (If you still have the Icon property set to 11, the cursor shape becomes an hourglass icon.)

Now, click the mouse. Visual Basic responds by displaying a message in your form (see Figure 5.16).

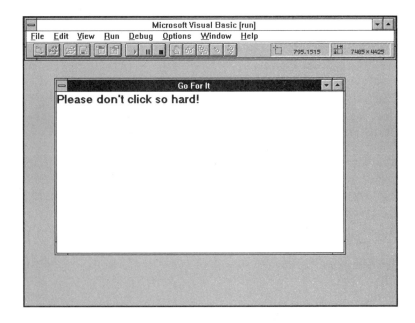

Figure 5.16.

Results from the sample application.

Click again. A duplicate message appears below the first message. You see another copy of the message each time you click the form.

With the `Click` event procedure defined, Visual Basic continually monitors the form during run time in anticipation of the `Click` event. When a mouse click occurs, the event procedure springs to action. This is the event-driven program model at work.

End the application (click the Stop button on the Toolbar, or choose **End** from the **R**un menu). As Visual Basic re-enters the Design mode, notice that the Code window reappears with the `Form_Click` procedure visible.

Changing Properties at Run Time

You can change the properties of a form at run time by adding program instructions to the event procedures. This capability adds noticeable power to your programs.

An instruction that changes a form's property has the following general format:

```
ObjectName.Property = NewValue
```

in which

> `ObjectName` identifies the object whose property value is to be changed;

> `Property` is the name of the property whose value is to be changed;

and

> `NewValue` specifies the new value of `Property`.

The `ObjectName` parameter is optional. If omitted, the property value of the default object is updated.

For example, suppose you want to move the form toward the right every time the user clicks it. The following instruction accomplishes this:

```
Form1.Left = Form1.Left + 200
```

This instruction increases the value of the `Left` property of `Form1` by 200 twips. `Form1` is the object's name. In this case, `Form1` is the default name that Visual Basic uses for the form.

Omitting the Object Name

If you omit the ObjectName parameter, Visual Basic assumes that the instruction modifies the property value of the object for which the event procedure is defined. Consider the following instruction:

```
FontItalic = Not FontItalic
```

This instruction toggles the value of the FontItalic property between True and False. If the value was True before the instruction executes, the value becomes False afterward, and vice versa.

Notice that the instruction does not specify an object name. If the instruction occurs in the Click event procedure for Form1, then Visual Basic assumes that Form1 is the referenced object.

Trying an Example

To see the effect of dynamically modifying properties at run time, add the two previous instructions to the Form_Click procedure. If the Code window is not visible, double-click the form (or press F7), then select the Click procedure from the Proc: list box.

To add the two instructions just before the existing Print instruction, move the insertion point to the beginning of the Print instruction, then click. Now type the two instructions, pressing Enter after you type each one. If necessary, press Tab, or insert some blank characters to align each line at the same indentation. The completed procedure should appear as follows:

```
Sub Form_Click ()
    Form1.Left = Form1.Left + 200
    FontItalic = Not FontItalic
    Print "Please don't click so hard!"
End Sub
```

Now, start the application. Click inside the form. The form jumps 200 twips (about 1/7 of an inch) toward the right. The displayed message appears in italics.

Click the form again. The form moves farther toward the right edge of the screen. The displayed message appears again, but this time it is in plain font.

Click several more times. Each time, the form moves to the right, and the message toggles between italics and plain font. Figure 5.17 shows the form after six clicks.

Stop the application (click the Stop button on the Toolbar, or choose the End option from the Run menu). You can close the Code window by first clicking the Code window's Control box to open the Control menu. Then select the Close option.

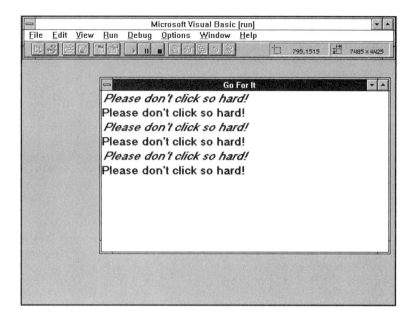

Figure 5.17.

The effects of modifying property values with program code.

Saving the Application on Disk

To save your application on disk, click the Save Project button on the Toolbar (or choose the Save Project option from the **F**ile menu.) The Save File **A**s dialog box opens (see Figure 5.18).

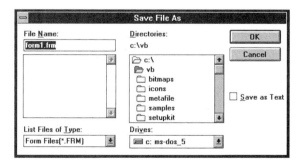

Figure 5.18.

The Save File **A**s dialog box.

The Form File

The file name FORM1.FRM appears in the File **N**ame box. Recall that Form1 is the default name for the form's Name property in the Properties window. The default file name is simply the value of the form's Name property with the .FRM extension added. The **D**irectories box shows the directory path as the C:\VB, the directory where Visual Basic is installed.

If you click the OK button (or press Enter), Visual Basic saves a copy of the form to a disk file named FORM1.FRM located on the C:\VB directory. Instead, you can specify a different path and file name by using the **Directories** and File **N**ame list boxes. You can scroll through the **Directories** box to highlight any directory path you choose. Similarly, you can type an alternate file name and path in the File **N**ame box.

As you develop more applications, make it your practice to give each form a descriptive name. For example, you might name this file GOFORIT.FRM. Also, you should create one or more subdirectories specifically used for storing your programs. You can then save your files to these directories, and keep the C:\VB directory reserved for the Visual Basic program files.

The Project File

After you specify the .FRM file, a second dialog box opens named Save Project As (see Figure 5.19). This box prompts you to save the entire project to a disk file named PROJECT1.MAK.

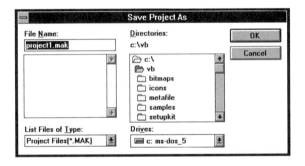

Figure 5.19.

The Save Project **A**s dialog box.

This file, called a *Make* file, lists all the form files, and others, that constitute the entire application. When you load a saved project back into the development environment, Visual Basic uses the Make file to determine the individual files required by the application.

For this simple application, the Make file lists only FORM1.FRM. As you develop multiform applications, however, and create independent modules of program code, the Make files list several other files. For more information on multiform applications and code modules, see Chapter 9, "Managing Projects."

You can use the dialog box to specify your own project name for the Make file. Once again, descriptive names are best. For this project, you might use the name GOFORIT.MAK. Notice that the same root name, GOFORIT, is recommended for both the .FRM and .MAK files. Identical root names are a common practice when a specialized form is developed for a single-form project.

Saving Work During Development

It's a good idea to frequently save your work as you develop a project. That way, if you inadvertently leave Visual Basic, crash Windows, or suffer a computer failure, you always have a relatively recent version of your project's files saved on disk.

> While developing an application, it's a particularly good idea to save your
> work before making each trial run. Although chances of crashing Windows or Visual Basic are always small, such problems are most likely to occur during the running of a nondebugged program. Be safe. Save often.
>
> Visual Basic 3.0 has a new feature that allows you to automatically save your work before making a trial run. To use this feature, open the Environment Options dialog box by choosing the Environment item from the Options menu. The dialog box contains a property titled Save project before run. The default value is No. If you change the value to Yes, Visual Basic automatically saves your work before any run.

T I P

To update existing files, click the Save Project button on the Toolbar (or choose the Save Project option from the File menu). If the files already exist, Visual Basic updates the existing files to reflect your program changes. (The assumption is that you want to save your work in the same files.)

If you have not yet saved the files, either the Save File As or the Save Project As dialog box appears. Of course, if you want to save your updated project under new file names, choose the Save Project As option from the File menu.

Ending a Visual Basic Session

To end a Visual Basic working session, choose the Exit option on the File menu. If you have not saved your work, Visual Basic prompts you with one or more dialog boxes to save your updated form or project.

Summary

The form lets the user set the visual background of an application. A form automatically acts as a standard window that can be moved, resized, minimized to an icon, or maximized to fill the entire screen.

Forms have several predefined properties. By modifying the values of these properties, you can customize how the form looks and acts. You can modify values both at design time with the Properties window, and at run time by writing program code.

At run time, a form can respond to various events. To make the form respond, you write an appropriate event procedure. For example, by placing program code in the `Form_Click` procedure, you can specify what happens when the user clicks the form.

With a fundamental understanding of the form, your next step is to place control objects onto the form. You do this in the next chapter as you begin to build more practical applications.

Using Controls

The backbone of most every Visual Basic application is a form. In the previous chapter, you learned about the attributes of a form and the ways that it responds to events when the application runs.

Almost every practical Visual Basic application uses control objects placed onto the form. Examples of controls are command buttons, list boxes, and scroll bars. The next three chapters discuss controls—what the various controls can do, how you add them onto a form to build an application, and how to write event procedures so that the controls respond appropriately to the user's actions.

This chapter discusses the techniques of working with controls at design time. In Chapter 7, "Writing Event Procedures," you build a working application by writing the program code that makes the application interactive with the user. Chapter 8, "Using the Toolbox and the Frequently Used Controls," is a comprehensive look at the various controls found in the Toolbox. That chapter explains the properties and events associated with each control, and its capabilities.

The main topics covered in this chapter include:

- Adding controls to a form
- Resizing and repositioning a control
- Manipulating controls with the mouse
- Using the grid
- Using the Properties window to assign control properties
- Working with a group of controls

Adding Controls onto a Form

As you've seen with the applications developed in the previous chapters, it's easy to add controls onto a form. You begin by moving the mouse pointer onto the Toolbox and clicking the desired control.

For example, if you want to add a command button to the form, you move the mouse pointer to the Command button icon in the Toolbox. Then, you can utilize either of the two techniques discussed in the following section.

The Two Techniques for Adding Controls

With the pointer on the desired icon in the Toolbox, choose one of these three techniques to place the control onto the form:

- Click the Toolbox icon that represents the desired control. To indicate that it has been selected, the icon appears in a color. Now, move the pointer onto the form. The pointer shape changes to a cross hair while over the form. (Figure 6.1 shows an example of the cross hair over a form.) When the pointer is positioned at one corner of the control's desired location, hold down the left mouse button and begin dragging the pointer across the form. A grayed rectangle appears over the area determined by your mouse movements. This rectangle indicates the control's size and location on the form. When you are satisfied with the control's position, release the mouse button. The control snaps into place on the form.

- A shortcut method is to double-click the Toolbox icon that represents the desired control. A control with the default size immediately appears in the center of the form.

- Hold down the Ctrl key when selecting the control, then create as many controls as needed without having to reselect the control.

An Exercise in Control

The following short exercise familiarizes you with some of the subtleties of adding controls to a form. Start by creating a new project. (If you have any work in progress, you can start a new project by choosing the New Project option from the File menu.) Now follow these steps:

1. Click the List box icon in the Toolbox. (This is the fifth icon down on the right side of the Toolbox).

    Notice that inside the Toolbox, the icon appears highlighted in color (red on most monitors). This highlighting indicates that you have selected the icon.

2. Move the pointer onto the form.

   The pointer shape changes to a cross hair (see Figure 6.1).

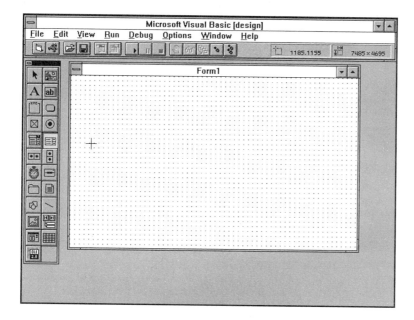

Figure 6.1.

The mouse pointer is a cross hair.

3. With the pointer near the upper left corner of the form, hold down the left mouse button and drag the control's grayed outline around the form. Try dragging the outline off the form; notice that you cannot do so.

4. Drag the outline so that it occupies most of the upper left quarter of the form (see Figure 6.2).

5. Release the mouse button to place the control onto the form.

6. Move the mouse pointer back onto the Toolbox. Double-click the Command button icon (the third icon down on the right side).

   A command button appears instantly in the center of the form. Notice that the caption for the command button reads Command1.

7. Double-click the Command button icon once again.

   A second command button appears on the form, completely covering the first command button. You can tell that this has happened because the caption for the command button now reads Command2 (see Figure 6.3). Temporarily, at least, the second command button obscures the first.

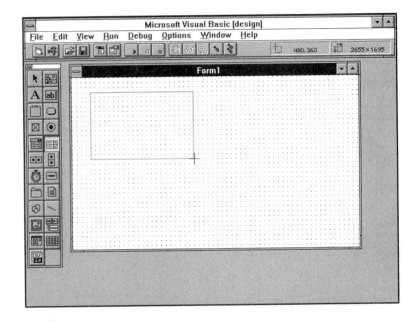

Figure 6.2.

The grayed outline for the List box control.

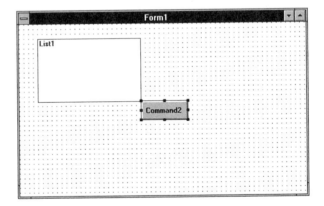

Figure 6.3.

The second command button on top of the first button.

You'll do more with this example shortly.

Resizing and Repositioning a Control

While developing an application, you will frequently want to change the size of various controls and reposition some controls to new locations on the form. Visual Basic makes it easy to alter the location and size of each control on the form.

This capability to conveniently tinker with the layout of a form and its controls is one of the triumphs of Visual Basic. With just a few button clicks and mouse movements, you can relocate the controls and change their size. Customizing the appearance of a form is easy.

To resize or reposition a particular control, it must have the focus. You know that a control has the focus when the control's sizing handles are visible.

To move the focus onto a control, you can use either of the following two techniques:

- Move the mouse pointer onto the control, then click the left mouse button.

- While the focus is on the form or on one of the controls, press Tab one or more times. As you repeatedly press Tab, the focus moves from control to control. Eventually, the focus reaches the desired control.

Once the focus is on a control, you can move the control around the form and change the control's size. You can do this by manipulating the control with the mouse, or by changing some of the control's property values using the Properties window.

Using the Mouse to Manipulate Controls

Return to the sample project to try some of the techniques involved in manipulating controls. Follow these steps:

1. Click the command button in the middle of the form (the control with the caption Command2).

   The command button becomes highlighted. Notice that the sizing handles for the control appear.

2. Move the mouse pointer inside the control. (Make sure the pointer is not directly on one of the sizing handles.) Press and hold down the mouse button.

3. You can now drag the control around the form. Try it.

   As you move the mouse, a gray outline of the control shape moves around the form.

4. Move the gray rectangle near the lower right corner of the form, then release the mouse button.

   The command button snaps to the new location. Notice that the first command button, labeled Command1, is once again visible at the center of the form (see Figure 6.4).

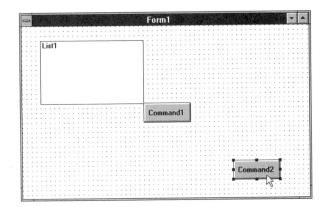

Figure 6.4.

After you relocate the second button, the first command button is again visible.

5. Click the mouse on the command button Command1.

   The focus transfers from the second command button to the first button. Sizing handles appear on the first command button (Command1), but not on the second button (Command2).

To change the size of a control with the mouse, move the mouse pointer onto one of the eight sizing handles. The cursor shape changes to a double-sided arrow. You can then drag the sizing handle in one of the directions indicated by the arrow. The border of the control drags along with the sizing handle. When you release the mouse button, the size of the control changes to reflect the new position of the border.

Figure 6.5 shows the mouse pointer positioned on the sizing handle in the middle of the lower border of Command1. In Figure 6.5, the lower border of this command button has been moved downward. As a result, the control is stretched vertically.

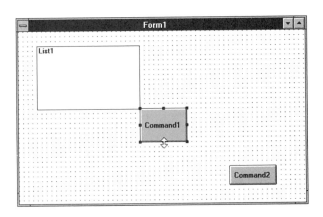

Figure 6.5.

Moving the sizing handles.

By dragging the border up or down, you can resize the control. Try resizing Command1 by dragging the various sizing handles in the directions that are offered.

The Location and Size Coordinates on the Toolbar

As you move or resize a control, notice that the two number pairs on the right side of the Toolbar change to indicate the current position and size of the control. The previous chapter explained that, when the form has the focus, these numerical coordinates indicate the form's location and size relative to the whole screen.

When a control has the focus, these numbers work the same as they did with the form. The size and location of the control, however, are specified relative to the upper left corner of the form. The units are twips. (This concept is explained in the section "Size and Location Properties" in Chapter 5.)

The number pair on the left side of the Toolbar specifies the location of the upper left corner of the control relative to the upper left corner of the form. The first number in the pair is the distance in twips from the left edge of the form to the left edge of the control. The second number is the distance in twips from the top of the form down to top edge of the control. (Remember that larger numbers mean farther *down* the screen.)

Similarly, the pair of numbers on the right side of the Toolbar indicates the width and height of the control. Again, the units are twips.

Repositioning and Resizing with the Properties Window

In addition to manipulating a control with the mouse, you can also relocate and resize a control at design time by adjusting the appropriate properties with the Properties window. To do so, first move the focus to the desired control by clicking it.

Next, bring the Properties window to the foreground (either click anywhere on the Properties window, or press F4). As Table 6.1 shows, four properties affect the location and size of the control. These properties are the same ones you encountered in the previous chapter when working with forms. Here, the properties refer to the size and location of a control relative to the form. Again, the units are twips.

Table 6.1. The Size and Location properties.

Property	Description
Height	Measures the distance from the center of the control's upper border to the center of its lower border. The center of the border is used so that multiple controls with different border widths can easily be aligned.
Width	Measures the distance from the left border of the control to the right border. Again, measurements are taken from the center of each border.
Left	Measures the distance from the left edge of the form to the internal left edge of the control.
Top	Measures the distance from the top edge of the form down to the internal top edge of the control.

Try relocating and resizing Command1 (or any of the controls on the form) by directly modifying the four property values in the Properties window. Remember to highlight the desired control before accessing the Properties window.

Notice that the values shown in the Properties window for the size and location properties match the four numbers displayed on the right side of the Toolbar.

When the Properties window is active, the Object box indicates the active control. For example, if you are working on the first command button, the text in the Object box of the Properties window reads Command1 CommandButton. As you noticed in the previous chapter, this Object box displays the name of the object that has the focus (Command1) and what type of object it is (CommandButton).

NOTE You can click the down arrow on the right side of the Object box to display a drop-down list of all the forms and controls defined for the current form. By clicking a control in this list, you give the selected control the focus and load the control's properties into the Properties window.

Using the Grid

The *grid* is the rectangular array of dots located on the form. Using these dots, you can align the graphics controls you place on a form. The grid is visible during design time, but when you run an application, it disappears. You might have noticed that the corner of each control always aligns directly with one of the dots on the grid. When you move a control or change the control's size, Visual Basic automatically adjusts each corner of the control to snap onto the nearest grid dot.

You can see the effect by moving a control. Try slowly dragging a control around the form. Notice that the control does not move continuously. Instead, it jumps in step increments from one grid dot to the next.

You can control the size of the grid and how the grid works with the Environment Options dialog box. To access this dialog box, choose the **Environment** option from Visual Basic's **O**ptions menu. Scroll through the list of options to reach the grid options at the end of the list.

Figure 6.6 shows the Environment Options dialog box with the highlight on the Grid Width setting. You use this dialog box much as you do the Properties window. You specify the values of the various options in the dialog box just as you specify property values with the Properties window.

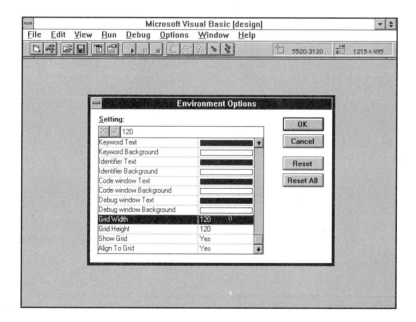

Figure 6.6.

The grid attributes available in the Environment Options dialog box.

The four grid-related attributes that you can adjust with the Environment Options dialog box are as follows:

Grid Width   Specifies the horizontal distance between two grid dots. The units are twips. The default value is 120. If you make the value larger, a more widely dispersed horizontal grid results. Similarly, a smaller value creates a tighter grid.

Grid Height	Specifies the vertical distance between two grid dots. Again, the units are twips with a default value of 120.
Show Grid	You can turn off the grid at design time by changing the value of this attribute from the default value of Yes to No. You do have the option to turn off the grid.
Align to Grid	This attribute specifies whether controls must align exactly on the grid dots. The default value is Yes. By changing the value to No, you can position controls anywhere on the form, even between grid dots. Occasionally, you might want to turn this option off to design a specialized form containing several controls. In such cases, you might want to consider adjusting the size of the grid (usually to a tighter grid) rather than changing the value of this property to No.

T I P Occasionally, you might be designing a form in which you want some controls to always align on the grid dots, while maintaining the freedom to place other controls anywhere on the form. To obtain this flexibility, first turn off the Align to Grid attribute in the Environment Options dialog box. This temporarily removes the restriction of grid alignment for all controls.

Next, you can select any particular control you want to align on the grid. Then, choose the **Align to Grid** option from the **Edit** menu.

As you develop more applications with Visual Basic, the grid becomes almost second nature. Without even thinking about it, you find that you are always taking advantage of the grid to carefully position your controls. As a result, you can almost effortlessly give your applications a polished, professional appearance.

Deleting a Control

At times, you might find that you have placed too many controls on a form. You might want to delete a control. To do so, follow these steps:

1. Select the control you want to delete.

2. Choose the **D**elete option from the **E**dit menu.

Alternatively, you can select the control and then press Del.

The control is removed from the form. Try deleting the Command1 command button from the sample form you've been working on in this chapter. Notice that Visual Basic does not renumber the second command button. Even though there is no longer a command button with the caption (and name) of Command1, Visual Basic maintains the caption (and name) of Command2 for the only remaining command button on the form.

NOTE If you delete a control for which you have already written event procedures, Visual Basic does *not* delete those event procedures from the form's code. Instead, the event procedures for the deleted control are placed in the (General) section of the form. While editing in the Code window, you can still access the orphaned code through the form's General section. Such procedures retain the status of general procedures rather than event procedures.

Of course, with the deleted control no longer present in the application, the relocated event procedures can no longer be activated by system events while the application runs. Such procedures, however, can be directly called by program code placed in other (active) event procedures.

Cutting, Pasting, and Copying a Control

Besides deleting controls, you can manipulate them with the Visual Basic **E**dit menu in many of the same ways you can work with text. In particular, you can cut and paste a control, or make a copy of it. When you cut or copy a control, Visual Basic places a copy of it into the Windows Clipboard. Once a control is in the Clipboard, you can paste a copy of it onto a form.

Although you can use all these control-editing features within the domain of a single form, the power of these features is particularly useful when working among different applications or multiple forms on the same application. For example, you can copy a particular control from one application to another. That way, if you have a control in one application that would be useful in another, you don't have to duplicate your design work. Simply copy the control directly.

Be aware that if you copy or cut and paste a control, no event procedures are copied. To use the same event procedures specified for the control in one application in another new one, you must copy the text of each event procedure in a separate step. When copying a control, however, the property values associated with it are transferred from the original application to the new one.

Table 6.2 explains the details of the Cut, Copy, and Paste operations available from the Edit menu. The second column shows the shortcut key for the operation. By using a shortcut key, you immediately activate the command without having to open the Edit menu.

Table 6.2. Control-editing techniques.

Operation	Shortcut Key	Description
Cut	Ctrl+X	Removes the selected control from the current application and keeps a copy of it in the Clipboard.
Copy	Ctrl+C	Places a copy of the control in the Clipboard without removing it from the current application.
Paste	Ctrl+V	Places a copy of the control in the Clipboard onto the current form. The control is placed in the upper left corner of the form. You can then move or resize the control.

An Example of How to Cut and Paste a Control

To get an idea of how to cut and paste a control, follow these steps:

1. Click the Command2 command button to select it.

2. Open the Edit menu and choose the Cut option.

   The command button is deleted from the form. A copy of the button is placed in the Windows Clipboard.

3. Press Ctrl+V to copy the control from the Clipboard back onto the form.

   The control appears in the upper left corner of the form. You can now resize and reposition the control.

Although this exercise is instructive, the technique is not particularly useful. Essentially, all you've accomplished is moving the command button from one part of the form to another. You don't need to use Cut and **Paste** to accomplish this movement. Instead, you can simply move the control directly around the form. The next section shows you the power of Cut and **Paste** as you copy a control from one application to another.

 **NOTE** If you paste a control onto a form that already contains a copy of it, a conflict arises. Visual Basic does not let multiple controls have the same Name property. Instead, Visual Basic interprets this operation as an attempt to create a control array. When you do such a paste operation, Visual Basic opens a dialog box that asks if you want to create a control array. In Chapter 7, "Writing Event Procedures," you learn to use a control array to group together related controls as a single programming entity.

Copying a Control to Another Application

You use the power of cut-and-paste techniques when you move a control from one application to another. To get an idea of how this works, follow these steps:

1. On the form, click the list box control to select it.

2. Open the **Edit** menu and choose the **Copy** option.

   Behind the scenes, Visual Basic instructs Windows to place a copy of the list box control into the Clipboard.

3. Choose the **New Project** option from the **File** menu.

4. When prompted whether you want to save the form, click **No**.

5. After the blank form for the new project appears, choose the **Paste** option from the **Edit** menu.

Visual Basic pastes a copy of the previous list box onto the new form. Notice that the List1 control has the same size and shape as the original list box from the earlier project.

The control, however, appears in the upper left corner of the new form. Visual Basic does not retain information about the control's specific location on the form when it is placed into the Clipboard.

Assigning Properties to Controls

In the previous chapter, you used the Properties window to assign values to various properties of the form. The technique involves selecting the form, then opening the Properties window and specifying the desired properties.

The technique for specifying the properties of individual controls is the same. The following are the steps involved:

1. Select the desired control.

   Simply click the control. An alternative method is to press the Tab key repeatedly until the desired control is selected. You know that a control is selected when its sizing handles are visible.

2. Activate the Properties window.

   Three methods are available to do this: Click the Properties window (this works, of course, only if part of the Properties window is visible), press F4, or choose the Properties option from the Window menu.

3. Click a property listed in the Properties window and specify a new value in the Settings box.

In the Properties window, the name of the selected control appears in the Object box near the top of the window. For example, Figure 6.7 shows the Properties window opened with the List1 control selected. Notice that the Object box on the Properties window reads List1 ListBox. Here, List1 is the name of the selected control, and ListBox indicates the type of control selected.

Figure 6.7.

The Properties window with the List1 control selected.

For more information on the various properties available with a list box, see Chapter 8, "Using the Toolbox and the Frequently Used Controls."

Working with a Group of Controls

You can move a group of controls as a single unit. For example, this is handy when you have a row of controls you want to move up or down the same distance. By moving the controls as a group, you maintain the relative size and spacing between each control.

To see how this works, start a new project and follow this example:

1. Add four text box controls onto the blank form. (The Text box icon is the second one down on the right side of the Toolbox.) Position these text boxes near, but not touching, the right edge of the form.

2. Place Text1 on top, Text2 under it, followed by Text3, and finally Text4. Leave some space between each text box control. You don't need to align the left or right edges of each text box with the same column of grid dots. Your form should resemble Figure 6.8.

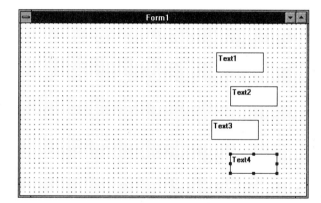

Figure 6.8.

The form with the four text box controls added.

Suppose you now want to relocate several adjacent controls as a single group. You can do this without moving each control individually. To do so, you must first enclose the group of controls in a rectangular frame (a technique similar to that used when marking an area in Windows Paintbrush). As explained in the next section, you can then move the entire frame in a single operation.

An Exercise in Grouping Controls

Try the following steps to move the top three text box controls on your form as a group.

1. Move the mouse to a position above and to the left of Text1.

   To avoid any selection problem, you might want to make sure this position is farther left than the left edge of *any* of the top three text boxes.

2. Press and hold down the left mouse button.

3. Drag the mouse pointer to a position below and to the right of Text3. Be sure the dotted rectangular frame encloses the top three text boxes, but not any part of Text4 (see Figure 6.9).

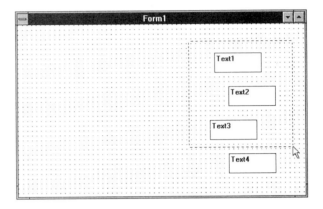

4. Release the mouse button.

    The top three text box controls display grayed sizing handles (see Figure 6.10). You can now move the three enclosed controls as a single group.

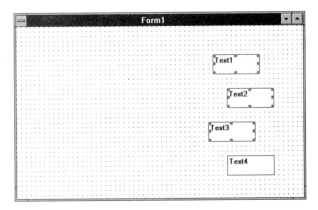

5. Move the mouse pointer onto one of the enclosed controls. Press and hold the left mouse button while you move the pointer around the form.

    A gray outline of each control in the group moves together across the form to reflect your mouse movements.

6. When the controls are positioned as desired, release the mouse button.

The group of controls immediately snaps to the new location.

Figure 6.11 shows the group of controls relocated near the upper left corner of the form.

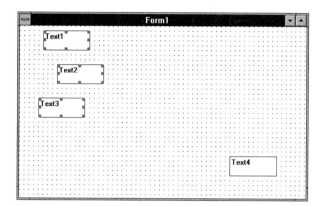

Figure 6.11.

The grouped controls are relocated near the upper left corner of the form.

> While you have controls grouped, you can execute the Cut, Copy, and De- **T I P**
> lete commands from the Edit menu. You can delete also the entire group of
> controls from the form by pressing Del (the shortcut key for choosing the
> **Delete** option from the **Edit** menu).

You can cancel the grouping by clicking the mouse button anywhere outside the grouped controls. The formerly enclosed controls become individual entities again.

Grouping Controls Scattered throughout the Form

The rectangular frame method of grouping controls works well, as long they are all conveniently located in an area of the form in which you can easily enclose them. Occasionally, you might want to group controls that are scattered throughout the form in order to move them as a unit.

You can create a group consisting of any controls on the form as follows: Press and hold the Ctrl key while moving the mouse pointer to each control one at a time. With the pointer on the control, click the mouse button while still holding down the Ctrl key. Repeat this process for each control in the group. Release the Ctrl key only when every control in the group has been selected.

You see gray sizing handles appear on each control in the group after you select its *second* control. Once your entire group is selected, you can move the controls as a single unit.

Setting Properties of Grouped Controls

With a group of controls selected, you can work with the Properties window for the entire group. Press F4 to bring the Properties window to the foreground. The Properties window contains only those properties shared by every selected control.

By specifying a value for any property shown in the Properties window, you indicate that each control in the group should have the specified value for that particular property. By taking advantage of this feature, you need to type only once a property value shared by several controls.

 If the enclosed control group contains different types of controls, the Properties window lists those properties that exist only for every control in the group. By specifying a value for a listed property, you modify the property value for every control in the group.

One common use of this technique is to align a group of controls. For example, you can align the left edge of the three selected text box controls by selecting the group and specifying the Left property in the Properties window. When you do so, each selected control moves so that its left edge is consistent with the Left property.

An Exercise in Setting Properties of Grouped Controls

Follow these steps to see how you can set property values for a group of controls:

1. Select the Text1, Text2, and Text3 controls by dragging a rectangular frame around the controls.

   The sizing handles for the three controls appear grayed.

2. Press F4 to open the Properties window.

   Notice that the left column of the Properties window lists the properties for the text box controls, but you don't see specific values listed on the right side of the Properties window. Also, when you select multiple controls, the Object box in the Properties window is blank.

3. If the Text property is not highlighted in the Properties window, scroll through the list of properties until you find Text. Click Text in the Properties list to highlight that property.

   The Text property specifies the default text that the user sees displayed in the text box.

4. If Text1 is not highlighted in the Settings box of the Properties window, move the mouse pointer to the Settings box, then click.

5. Delete the text in the Settings box and type **There's power in groups**.

   Notice that as you type, the new text appears in the Settings box of the Properties window, and also in the text box control at the top. The text is sufficiently long enough, however, to scroll past the right edge of the text box control.

6. Press Enter to indicate that you have finished typing the new text.

   A copy of the newly typed text immediately appears in all three grouped text boxes. The text, however, scrolls past the right edge of each of the grouped controls.

Aligning Grouped Controls

You can align the grouped controls by specifying the Size and Location properties: Left, Top, Width, and Height.

For example, while the group of controls remains selected, use the Properties window to set the value of the Left property to 2000. The three text boxes immediately align so that their left edges are each 2000 twips from the left border of the form.

Now, set the Width property to 3000. The controls elongate horizontally by an amount sufficient enough to reveal the complete text in each control (see Figure 6.12).

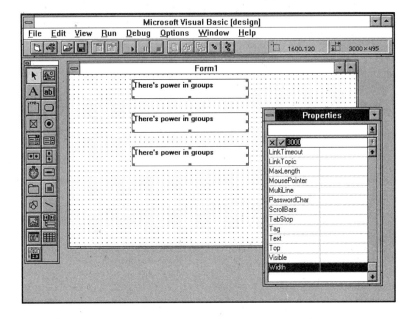

Figure 6.12.

The Text, Left, and Width properties are specified for the grouped controls.

Specifying *BackColor* with the Color Palette

While the group of controls is selected, you can use the Color Palette to choose a background color for the text boxes. To do so, open the Properties window and click the BackColor property.

In the right end of the Settings box, click the ellipsis (three dots). Visual Basic pops open the Color Palette window, which displays several different colors. (Recall that you used the same Color Palette in the previous chapter to select a background color for the entire form.)

You use the Color Palette the same way here. Click one of the colors. Visual Basic places the numerical value that corresponds to your selected color in the Settings box. The background color of the three grouped text boxes changes to the one you chose.

Summary

This chapter shows various ways to manipulate controls at design time. You learned how to add and delete controls, move and resize controls, and use the grid to align. By grouping controls together, you can move them as a unit and specify property values common to each control.

By sticking to the design-time features of working with controls, you did not develop any practical applications in this chapter. After placing controls on a form, the next steps toward a working application are assigning the properties and writing the event procedures that let the application and user interact. In the following chapter, you will build a practical application.

Writing Event Procedures

I n this chapter, you build on what you learned in the preceding two chapters to create a working application. Emphasis here is on the event procedures necessary to make an application work.

The event procedures are the heart and soul of any application. When you write event procedures, you give life to an application—you determine how it responds to anything taking place in its environment.

The application you develop here is a multiline text editor that features cut and paste, and font attributes that can be selected. The core of the application is a text box control which contains the text that is edited. In the course of developing this application, you learn much about a text box—especially its properties and events. (The chapter that follows this chapter explores other Toolbox controls in more detail.)

The main subjects covered in this chapter include:

- Using the Code window
- Modifying property values at run time
- Initializing an application with the Form_Load event
- Naming controls in a consistent manner to facilitate references throughout the program code
- Creating access keys
- Making general declarations and procedures
- Saving a form as a text file
- Using control arrays

Creating Ted—A Text Editor Application

The text editor you develop in this chapter is similar to the Notepad utility that comes with Windows. The application is affectionately known as Ted (*Text editor*). The controls used in the application are a text box, three check boxes, and four command buttons.

To create Ted, start a new project. (Choose the **New** Project option from the **F**ile menu.) In the Toolbox, double-click the Text box icon to place a text box in the center of the form. The sizing handles for the text box should now be visible. If the handles are not visible, click inside the text box, and they appear.

Using the sizing handles, enlarge the text box approximately twice its original width and height. Don't worry about its exact size and location. At this point, it's important only that you have a form containing a text box.

Ted's Text Box Properties

Ted works with the Text, MultiLine, and ScrollBars properties of the text box. Table 7.1 summarizes these properties.

Table 7.1. Some text box properties.

Property	Default Value	Description
Text	Text1	Specifies the text contained in the edit area
MultiLine	False	Specifies whether the text box can display multiple lines
ScrollBars	0 '(none)	Specifies whether the text box contains horizontal or vertical scroll bars (or both)

At this point, Ted consists of a form containing a text box. If you open the Properties window, you can check the default values of the text box properties.

Exploring How a Text Box Works

The various Visual Basic controls have quite a bit of built-in functionality. It's instructive to see what you can do with a text box before you write even one line of program code.

Run the application. The text box reads Text1. The contents of a text box are specified by the value of its Text property. Recall that the default value of the Text property is Text1.

You can delete the contents of the text box. First, move the cursor to its upper left corner. Then, hold down the Del key until all the text is erased.

Try typing into the text box. Continue typing until the text cursor reaches the right edge of the box. Notice that, as you continue typing, the cursor stays at the right edge, and scrolls the previous text to the left to accommodate the newly typed characters.

By repeatedly pressing the left (or right) arrow key, you can move the cursor to the left (or right) edge of the text box, and scroll the previously typed text into view. The Home and End keys move the cursor to the beginning and end of the text, respectively.

Press Enter. Visual Basic beeps, and nothing happens. The value of the MultiLine property is False, so the text box does not display multiple text lines. Thus, pressing Enter does not move the cursor down to the next line.

Selecting Text

You can select a block of characters. To do so, hold down its left button as you drag the mouse over a block of characters. Then, release the button. Another method is to hold down the Shift key as you use the arrow keys to move the cursor. The selected characters appear highlighted in a different color. Press Del. Visual Basic deletes the selected characters from the text box.

Thus far, without typing a single line of code, or modifying a property value, you have already created the beginning of a text editor application.

Understanding Word Wrap

Stop the application. Select the text box by clicking it. Then, open the Properties window (press F4). Find the MultiLine property, and change its value from False to True.

Run the application again. Try typing some text, and watch what happens when you reach the right edge of the text box. The text wraps down to the next line of the text box. Continue typing characters until the box contains several lines.

Notice that the text box automatically implements *word wrap*. That is, the lines break at the boundaries of whole words, not just at the first character which reaches the right edge (see Figure 7.1).

Figure 7.1.

A text box demonstrating word wrap.

Also, you can press Enter at any time to force the cursor down to the next line. If you continue typing past the lower border, the text box automatically scrolls upward to accommodate the new text.

Adding Scroll Bars

Stop the application. Open the Properties window for the text box, and click on the ScrollBars property.

Click the right arrow of the Settings Box to drop down the available choices for this property. The default value is 0 (no scroll bars). Other possible values are 1 (horizontal scroll bars), 2 (vertical scroll bars), and 3 (horizontal and vertical scroll bars). Change the value to 2 (vertical scroll bars).

Run the application once again. Scroll bars appear on the right edge of the text box. Type several lines of text so that the contents of the text box scroll past the bottom edge. Use the scroll bar to move the contents of the text box vertically through the editing area.

Stop the application. As you can see, a multiline text box is the beginning of a text editor. Without writing a single line of code, the text box supports multiple lines, scroll bars, and selected text.

Designing Ted's User Interface

The next step in creating Ted is to design the user interface. You must place the various controls on the form, and set the design-time property values. Figure 7.2 shows the finished interface. As the figure shows, Ted's form contains four command buttons and three check boxes, in addition to the text box.

Using the Toolbox, place four command buttons and three check boxes onto the form. (The check box is the Toolbox icon which resembles a square with an × inside.) Using the Properties window, assign the property values that Table 7.2 shows.

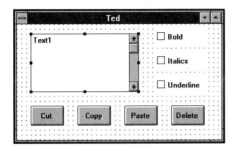

Figure 7.2.

Ted's user interface.

Table 7.2. Design-time property values for Ted.

Object	Property	Value
Form1	Caption	Ted
	Height	3300
	Left	1185
	Top	1440
	Width	5370
	Name	frmTed
Text1	Height	1455
	Left	360
	Top	240
	Width	2775
	Name	txtTed
Command1	Caption	Cut
	Height	495
	Left	360
	Top	2040
	Width	855
	Name	cmdCut
Command2	Caption	Copy
	Height	495
	Left	1560
	Top	2040
	Width	855
	Name	cmdCopy

continues

Table 7.2. Continued

Object	Property	Value
Command3	Caption	Paste
	Height	495
	Left	2760
	Top	2040
	Width	855
	Name	cmdPaste
Command4	Caption	Delete
	Height	495
	Left	3960
	Top	2040
	Width	855
	Name	cmdDelete
Check1	Caption	Bold
	Height	375
	Left	3600
	Top	120
	Width	1215
	Name	chkBold
Check2	Caption	Italics
	Height	375
	Left	3600
	Top	720
	Width	1215
	Name	chkItalics
Check3	Caption	Underline
	Height	375
	Left	3600
	Top	1320
	Width	1215
	Name	chkUnderline

Notice that the Name property for each object begins with a three-letter prefix. The prefix identifies the object type: frm for form, txt for text box, cmd for command button, and chk for check box. After the prefix, the remainder of the name helps to describe the particular object. For example, chkBold is the check box used to indicate whether bold text is desired. This naming convention helps to clearly identify each object in the subsequent code. For more about naming conventions, see Chapter 8, "Using the Toolbox and the Common Controls."

The interface is now designed. Run the application. Click one of the check boxes a few times. Notice that a large × toggles on and off in the check box. If you click a command button, it appears to quickly press into the form. These visual capabilities of check boxes and command buttons are built into the controls.

At this stage, of course, clicking a check box or command button doesn't actually *do* anything. To add such functionality to your applications, you must write program code in the event procedures. You do this next.

Writing Ted's Event Procedures

The following sections examine the various event procedures necessary to make the Ted application work. The approach is incremental: You add more procedures and code as you build the application piece by piece.

The *Form_Load* Procedure

You have undoubtedly noticed that, each time you start the sample application, the contents of the text box read Text1. It is much better if the editing area is blank when the application begins. That way, the user has a clean slate with which to begin editing.

For a text box, the Text property indicates its current contents. By default, Visual Basic uses the original name of the text box as the initial value of the Text property—Text1, in this case. If you haven't done so already, you can open the Properties window, and verify that Text1 is the value of the Text property for txtTed (the text box)."

You can clear the contents of the text box by using the Properties window to change the value of the Text property at design time. This works, but there is another way. You can change the value of the Text property with a program instruction. Just set the value of the Text property to the empty string (" "). The necessary instruction is as follows:

```
txtTed.Text = " "
```

Notice the syntax when referring to a property: the object name (txtTed, in this case) followed by a period, then the name of the property (Text, in this case). The general syntax is as follows:

`object.property.`

The instruction makes sense. In which place, however, do you put such an instruction? As it turns out, the Form_Load event procedure is a natural location.

When you first run an application, Visual Basic loads the form into memory, then displays it on-screen. The process of loading the form generates a Form_Load event. If you place program instructions in the Form_Load event procedure, they execute when the application begins. As a result, the Form_Load procedure is a natural place to initialize an application.

Opening the Code Window

If you have the application currently running, stop the application to return Visual Basic to design mode. You can then use any of the following techniques to open the Code window in preparation for writing program instructions:

- Press F7.
- Choose the **C**ode option from the **V**iew menu.
- Click the View Code button on the Project window. (If the Project window is not visible, choose the **P**roject option from the **W**indow menu.)
- Double-click the form, or any object on it.

As you've seen in previous chapters, the Code window has two boxes labeled Object and Proc. Click the down arrow to the right of the Object box to view its list of objects defined in the application. In this drop-down list, click Form.

Now, click the down arrow to the right of the Proc box. A drop-down list appears containing all the events recognized by the form. Click Load. The Code window now displays the Form_Load event which, for the moment, is nothing but the following procedure stub:

```
Sub Form_Load ()


End Sub
```

NOTE The Form_Load event is the default event for a form. If you double-click the form, the Code window opens with the Form_Load event visible.

Clearing the Text Box

Into the procedure template for `Form_Load`, type the instruction that clears the text box. The following is the result:

```
Sub Form_Load ()
    txtTed.Text = ""        'Blank contents of text box
End Sub
```

Try running the application. Notice that the contents of the text box are now blanked out (see Figure 7.3). Stop the application.

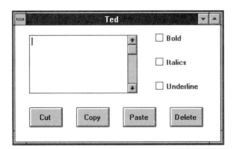

Figure 7.3.

Ted with a blanked-out text box.

Initializing the Font Attributes

Ted supports bold, italic, and underline emphasis in the text box. You can choose some or all of these font attributes at any time.

Visual Basic uses the `FontBold`, `FontItalic`, and `FontUnderline` properties to indicate whether a particular font attribute is active. A value of True means that the text has that attribute, False—the text does not have it.

Suppose that, when Ted begins, you want to turn off all the font attributes. The following instructions do this:

```
txtTed.FontBold = False
txtTed.FontItalic = False
txtTed.FontUnderline = False
```

Add these instructions to the `Form_Load` event procedure.

NOTE By default, the value of only one of these attributes—`FontBold`—is True; the other two are False. (You can verify these values by checking the properties in the Properties window.)

As a result, you don't need to set the values of `FontItalic` and `FontUnderline` to False in the `Form_Load` procedure. Including these instructions, however, doesn't hurt. They clarify that all the special font attributes are off when the application begins.

Initializing the Check Boxes

Each check box indicates whether one of the font attributes is active. The check box displays an × when the corresponding attribute is active. In this case, the box is said to be *checked*. Otherwise, it is blank.

Visual Basic uses the Value property to specify whether the check box is checked. Value is not, however, a True/False property. Rather, Value can be 0 (unchecked), 1 (checked), or 2 (dimmed). The value of 2 creates a gray text box. You can use this value to indicate that the box itself is currently inactive.

The font attributes are not active when Ted begins, so you want each check box to be blank. To blank each check box, add the following instructions to Form_Load:

```
chkBold.Value = 0
chkItalics.Value = 0
chkUnderline.Value = 0
```

The completed Form_Load event procedure is as follows:

```
Sub Form_Load ()
    txtTed.Text = ""          'Blank contents of text box

    txtTed.FontBold = False
    txtTed.FontItalic = False
    txtTed.FontUnderline = False

    chkBold.Value = 0
    chkItalics.Value = 0
    chkUnderline.Value = 0
End Sub
```

Activating the Font Attributes

When the user clicks a check box, you want it to become checked, and the contents of the text box to have the corresponding font attribute. For example, when the user clicks the Italics check box, it should become checked, and the contents of the text box should appear in italics. Furthermore, if the user clicks the Italics check box a second time, it should become unchecked, and the contents of the text box should no longer appear in italics.

You've already seen that, each time you click a check box, Visual Basic automatically toggles it between checked and unchecked. You don't need to write any program code to get that effect.

Using *Not* to Toggle a True/False Property Value

Concerning the font attribute in the text box, you must write program code to toggle the corresponding property value between True and False. For example, when the Underline check box is clicked the first time, you want the value of txtTed.FontUnderline to change from False to True. The next time the check box is clicked, txtTed.FontUnderline should once again become False.

Several ways exist to code such an instruction. The simplest way is probably with the Not operator. The following instruction toggles the value of the FontUnderline property between True and False:

```
txtTed.FontUnderline = Not (txtTed.FontUnderline)
```

For more information on Not, and other Visual Basic operators, see Chapter 14, "Language Building Blocks."

Writing a *Click* Procedure

By placing the Not instruction inside the Click procedure for the Underline check box, you can underline the text inside the text box. Create the following event procedure:

```
Sub chkUnderline_Click ()
    txtTed.FontUnderline = Not (txtTed.FontUnderline)
End Sub
```

This is all you need to implement underlining. Try it. Run the application and type an entry in the text box. Then, click the Underline check box a few times. The check box toggles between checked and unchecked. At the same time, the contents of the text box toggle between underline and normal font. Figure 7.4 shows an example of underlined text.

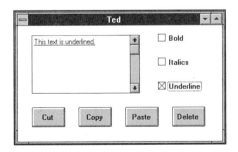

Figure 7.4.

An example of underlined text.

Using the *SetFocus* Method

As long as the Underline box is checked, any new text you type in the edit area appears underlined. Notice, however, that after clicking the Underline check box, the blinking text cursor does not appear inside the text box. To type new text, you must move the pointer inside the text box, and click to reposition the cursor.

In Visual Basic parlance, the term *focus* refers to the active object. When you click a check box, it has the focus. When you see the blinking cursor inside the text box, you know that it has the focus.

For Ted, you would like the focus to move to the text box after a check box is clicked. That way, the user can immediately type new text (or use the arrow keys to move the cursor) without having to first click inside the text box.

Visual Basic provides the `SetFocus` method for just this purpose. Recall from Chapter 5 ("Understanding Forms, Events, and Properties"), that a Visual Basic method specifies a particular action performed on an individual object. In that chapter, you used the `Print` method to display text on a form.

The syntax for a method uses a dot to separate the object that is acted upon, and the action that is taken. The general form is as follows.

```
object.method
```

This syntax tells Visual Basic to apply the action specified by `method` on the object designated by `object`. (Notice that this syntax is similar to the syntax for specifying a property of an object.) The following instruction, for example, uses the `Print` method to display a message on `Form1`.

```
Form1.Print "Here I am."
```

The `SetFocus` method has a simple syntax.

> ```
> object.SetFocus
> ```
> in which
> > `object` is the name of the object that gets the focus.

To move the focus to the text box, therefore, you need only the following instruction:

```
txtTed.SetFocus
```

Stop the application, and add this `SetFocus` instruction to the `chkUnderline` event procedure. The updated event procedure is as follows.

```
Sub chkUnderline_Click ()
    txtTed.FontUnderline = Not (txtTed.FontUnderline)
    txtTed.SetFocus
End Sub
```

Run the application again, and notice what happens when you click the Underline check box a few times. The focus never seems to leave the text box. As a result, you can type new text without having to first click inside the text box.

 NOTE Actually, when you click the check box, the focus moves momentarily to it. The SetFocus method in the Click procedure, however, immediately moves the focus back to the text box.

Writing the *Click* Procedures for the Other Check Boxes

In a similar way, you can create the event procedures for the Bold and Italics check boxes. Stop the application and create the following two event procedures:

```
Sub chkBold_Click ()
    txtTed.FontBold = Not (txtTed.FontBold)
    txtTed.SetFocus
End Sub

Sub chkItalics_Click ()
    txtTed.FontItalic = Not (txtTed.FontItalic)
    txtTed.SetFocus
End Sub
```

This is all you need to make the three check boxes work. Run the application, and click various combinations of the check boxes. Notice that you can activate some or all of the text attributes in any combination. Figure 7.5 shows an example of the bold and italics text attributes.

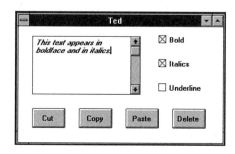

Figure 7.5.

The bold and italics attributes are activated.

Coding the Delete Command Button

Next, you must write the program code to make the command buttons work. The Delete button is a good place to start. When the user clicks this button, the entire contents of the text box should be deleted.

Writing the `Click` procedure for the Delete button is simple. You need only set the `Text` property of the text box to the empty string. The event procedure is as follows:

```
Sub cmdDelete_Click ()
    txtTed.Text = ""
    txtTed.SetFocus
End Sub
```

As with the check boxes, this event procedure uses `SetFocus` also to reactivate the text box after the user clicks the Delete button.

Try running the application. Type something into the text box, then click the Delete button. The entire contents of the text box are erased.

That's one command button successfully programmed. The next step is to program the other three buttons. To do that, you must first understand how Visual Basic treats selected text.

Understanding Selected Text

A text box has built-in capabilities for selecting text. As you learned earlier, the user can select a block of text by moving the pointer into the text box. Next, the user presses and holds the left mouse button while moving the mouse to another location. Then, the user releases the mouse button. The text between the start and end positions becomes selected.

The user can select text also by holding down the Shift key while pressing an arrow key to move the cursor over a region of text. On most monitors, selected text appears highlighted with a different background color.

To help you work with selected text, Visual Basic provides three text box properties: `SelLength`, `SelStart`, and `SelText` (see Table 7.3).

Table 7.3. Properties associated with selected text.

Property	Data Type	Description
SelLength	Numeric	Specifies the number of characters selected. Its value is 0 if no text is selected.
SelStart	Numeric	Specifies the character position at which the selected text begins. A value of 0 indicates the first character.

Property	Data Type	Description
SelText	String	Specifies the selected text. Its value is the empty string if no characters are selected.

Because these properties do not appear in the Properties window, you cannot set their values at design time. However, you can access the properties in your program code. If a text box contains selected text, the value of SelLength indicates how many characters are selected, the value of SelStart indicates the character position of the first selected character, and the value of SelText is a string consisting of the selected characters.

Although you cannot modify these property values at design time, you can modify their values at run time in your program code. For example, by setting SelStart to 5, and SelLength to 3, the text box appears with the sixth, seventh, and eighth characters highlighted.

If you modify the value of SelText, Visual Basic replaces any currently selected text with the newly specified string value. Also, the value of SelLength is automatically set to 0. The result is that the contents of the text box are modified but no text is selected. If the text box does not contain any selected text when an instruction modifies the value of SelText, the newly specified string is inserted at the character position specified by the value of SelStart.

For Ted, you must write program instructions to make the command buttons work correctly. As it turns out, you need only to modify the value of SelText.

Programming the Cut, Copy, and Paste Buttons

The Cut, Copy, and Paste buttons work with selected text. Before writing the event procedures for these buttons, it's important to have a clear understanding of exactly what these buttons should do.

When the user clicks the Cut button, any selected text is deleted from the text box, but held in a temporary memory location. The Copy button places a copy of the selected text into the temporary memory location, but does not alter the selected text in the text box. With either Cut or Copy, the current selected text replaces any previously held in the temporary memory location.

The Paste button pastes any text held in the temporary memory location back into the text box. When Paste is clicked, pasted text held in memory replaces any currently selected in the text box. If it contains no selected text when Paste is clicked, the pasted text is inserted at the current cursor position.

Declaring a Form-Level Variable

To implement the temporary storage location, you can store the cut or copied text in a string variable. Then, when the Paste button is clicked, the stored text can be retrieved from this variable.

Suppose you name this variable ClipText. The variable must be available to all of Ted's event procedures. You can create such a form-level variable by declaring it in the *general declaration* section of the form. Follow these steps:

1. Press F7 to open the Code window.

2. In the Object box, choose (general).

   (general) is the first item in the drop-down list.

3. In the Proc box, choose (declarations).

4. Type the following instruction.

   ```
   Dim ClipText As String
   ```

This instruction declares that ClipText is a variable of the string data type. For more information on the Dim instruction, and variable types, see Chapter 14, "Language Building Blocks."

By placing this instruction in the form's general declarations section, you can read or set the value of ClipText in any of the form's event procedures. For a detailed discussion of the scope of variables, see Chapter 9, "Managing Projects."

Coding the Cut Button

You want to store a copy of the selected text in the ClipText variable when the user clicks the Cut button. You must also delete the selected text from the text box. As it turns out, you can accomplish these objectives with two program instructions that take advantage of the SelText property:

```
ClipText = txtTed.SelText
txtTed.SelText = ""
```

The first instruction places a copy of the selected text into ClipText. If no text is selected, the value of ClipText becomes the empty string. The second instruction deletes any selected text from the text box.

These instructions go in the Click procedure for the Cut button. Create the following event procedure:

```
Sub cmdCut_Click ()
   ClipText = txtTed.SelText
   txtTed.SelText = ""
   txtTed.SetFocus
End Sub
```

By adding the `txtTed.SetFocus` instruction, you move the focus back to the text box when the Cut button is clicked.

Coding the Copy Button

The Copy and Cut buttons are similar. The only difference is that, with Copy, the selected text is not deleted from the text box. The `cmdCopy_Click` procedure is as follows:

```
Sub cmdCopy_Click ()
    ClipText = txtTed.SelText
    txtTed.SetFocus
End Sub
```

Notice that this procedure does not reset the value of the text box's `SelText` property to the empty string. When the user clicks the Copy button, the selected text is copied to `ClipText`, but remains in the text box.

Coding the Paste Button

As explained earlier, when an instruction modifies the value of `SelText`, the string specified in the instruction replaces any text that is currently selected. However, if no text is currently selected, the specified string is simply inserted at the position of the cursor. In both cases, Visual Basic deselects the entire contents of the text box (that is, the value of `SelLength` is set to 0 to indicate that no text is selected).

Therefore, to make the Paste button respond appropriately when clicked, all you need to do is set the value of `SelText` to the current value of `ClipText`:

```
Sub cmdPaste_Click ()
    txtTed.SelText = ClipText
    txtTed.SetFocus
End Sub
```

Running the Ted Application

At this point, Ted is functional. Try running the application, and experimenting with the command buttons. Notice that, if you select some text, then click Cut, you can immediately recover the selected text by clicking Paste. Figure 7.6 shows Ted in use.

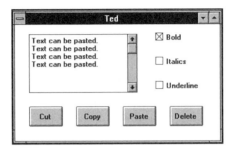

Figure 7.6.

Ted is working.

What happens if you click the Paste button when some text is highlighted in the text box? You find that the contents of ClipText *replace* the currently selected text. This behavior is the Windows standard and is built into the text box. In other words, if you paste when other text is highlighted, the highlighted text is replaced by the pasted text. If you paste when no text is highlighted, however, the pasted text is inserted at the current cursor position.

Disabling Command Buttons

Ted works correctly, and you can stop here. Several possible refinements exist, however, that can make Ted a more polished application. One such embellishment is to disable a command button when its use doesn't make sense.

For example, when ClipText is empty, clicking Paste is meaningless, because there is no stored text to paste. ClipText is empty when the application begins. Also, ClipText becomes empty if you click Cut or Copy when no text is highlighted. The contents of ClipText become the empty string, and there is no text to paste.

Similarly, if the text box has no contents, the Cut, Copy, and Delete buttons cannot produce any meaningful effect. In this situation, however, ClipText *could* contain text, and the Paste button would be meaningful.

The *Enabled* Property

Visual Basic has a way to disable command buttons. The Enabled property of a command button determines whether it responds to any user events. The Enabled property can have the value True or False. When True, the button is enabled, and responds normally to user-generated events, such as a click. True is the default value of Enabled.

When Enabled is False, however, the button does not respond to any user-generated events. The button's caption appears dimmed (or grayed) as a visual cue to the user that the button is disabled.

With Ted, you can take advantage of the Enabled property to disable command buttons in appropriate situations. You need to add program instructions that modify the value of Enabled for the various command buttons, depending on the current context of the text box.

For example, when the application first begins, all four command buttons should be disabled. After all, with no text in the text box, you can't copy, cut, or delete anything. Further, ClipText contains the empty string, so you have nothing to paste either.

Writing the General Procedure *BlankText*

In fact, whenever the contents of the text box become blank, the Cut, Copy, and Delete buttons should be disabled. Also, whenever ClipText is the empty string, the Paste button should be disabled.

You can write a user-defined procedure to disable the command buttons. The program code can invoke this procedure when the application begins, and anytime that the contents of the text box become blank.

Similar to an event procedure, a user-defined Sub procedure begins with Sub, and ends with End Sub. Unlike an event procedure, however, a user-defined one is not triggered by a system event. Instead, a user-defined procedure must be explicitly called by another instruction. You can give a user-defined procedure any name.

Suppose you create a user-defined procedure named BlankText. This procedure disables the Cut, Copy, and Delete buttons. It disables also the Paste button, if ClipText contains the empty string. The following is the BlankText procedure:

```
Sub BlankText ()
   cmdCut.Enabled = False
   cmdCopy.Enabled = False
   cmdDelete.Enabled = False

   If ClipText = "" Then
      cmdPaste.Enabled = False
   Else
      cmdPaste.Enabled = True
   End If
End Sub
```

In which place in the program code do you put such a procedure?

Such procedures go in the form's general section. Visual Basic uses the term *general procedure* to refer to a user-defined procedure.

Follow these steps to add `BlankText` into Ted's program code:

1. Press F7 to open the Code window.

2. In the drop-down list for the Object box, choose (`general`).

3. Choose the **New Procedure...** option from the **View** menu to open the New Procedure dialog box.

4. Type **BlankText** in the Name section.

5. Choose **S**ub.

   Sub is the default option (see Figure 7.7).

6. Click OK, or press Enter.

   Visual Basic provides a template stub for the procedure as follows:

```
Sub BlankText ()

End Sub
```

7. Type the following procedure:

```
Sub BlankText ()
    cmdCut.Enabled = False
    cmdCopy.Enabled = False
    cmdDelete.Enabled = False

    If ClipText = "" Then
        cmdPaste.Enabled = False
    Else
        cmdPaste.Enabled = True
    End If
End Sub
```

You have now created a general procedure named `BlankText`. If you click the down arrow to the right of the Proc box, you see `BlankText` in the list of procedures.

The procedure uses a block `If-Then_Else` instruction to take different actions, depending on the value of `ClipText`. (If you don't understand this block `If` syntax, see Chapter 15, "Program Flow and Decision Making.")

The If instruction tests the contents of ClipText. If ClipText is the empty string (that is, there is no text to paste), the procedure disables the Paste button.

If ClipText does *not* contain the empty string (there is some text to paste), however, the Else clause goes into effect. The instruction in the Else clause enables the Paste button.

Invoking *BlankText* from Event Procedures

BlankText now exists at the form level along with the event procedures. You can invoke BlankText from any event procedure by using Visual Basic's Call instruction as follows:

```
Call BlankText
```

In fact, the Call keyword is optional. All you need to invoke BlankText is the following simple instruction:

```
BlankText
```

For more information on general procedures and Call, see Chapter 18, "Using Procedures: Subs and Functions."

Modifying *Form_Load*

When the application begins, the text box is blank, and the contents of ClipText are empty. You want the four command buttons to be disabled. Now that the BlankText procedure is defined, you can invoke it in the Form_Load event to disable the command buttons.

The following is the revised event procedure. The only modification from the earlier version of Form_Load is the second program instruction which invokes BlankText. Add the BlankText line to make Form_Load appear as follows:

```
Sub Form_Load ()
    txtTed.Text = ""        'Blank contents of text box
    BlankText

    txtTed.FontBold = False
    txtTed.FontItalic = False
    txtTed.FontUnderline = False

    chkBold.Value = 0
    chkItalics.Value = 0
    chkUnderline.Value = 0
End Sub
```

Now, run Ted. The four command buttons all appear dimmed (see Figure 7.8).

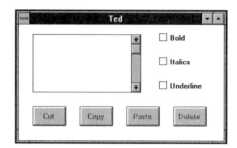

Type some text in the text box. Notice that the command buttons remain disabled. You obviously need to do more programming—whenever there is text in the text box, the Cut, Copy, and Delete buttons should always be enabled. Stop the application.

Enabling the Command Buttons

To enable the command buttons when the user types into the text box, Visual Basic provides the Change event.

The Change event triggers whenever the contents of the text box become modified. For example, typing new characters into, or deleting any from the text box triggers the Change event. Selecting text, however, or simply moving the cursor does not generate a Change event.

The Change event triggers also anytime a program instruction modifies the contents of the text box. The program can modify the contents of the text box by changing the value of its Text property.

Create the following txtTed_Change event procedure:

```
Sub txtTed_Change ()
    If txtTed.Text = "" Then
        BlankText
    Else
        cmdCut.Enabled = True
        cmdCopy.Enabled = True
        cmdDelete.Enabled = True
    End If
End Sub
```

The procedure uses a block If-Then_Else instruction to take different actions, depending on the value of the txtTed.Text property. The If instruction tests whether there is any text in the text box. If it is empty, the procedure calls the BlankText procedure, and terminates.

If the text box contains some text, however, BlankText does not get called. Instead, the Else clause goes into effect. The three instructions in the Else clause enable the Cut, Copy, and Delete command buttons.

Try running the application once again. Notice that as soon as you type something in the text box, the Cut, Copy, and Delete buttons are enabled. Click Delete. The four buttons are once again disabled, thanks to the txtTed_Change event procedure. (You can also delete the text box's contents by selecting all the text and pressing Del, or by moving the cursor to the upper-left corner of the text box, then holding down the Del key until the entire contents of the text box are deleted.)

Verifying the Paste Button

An empty text box is not necessarily a sign that the Paste button should be disabled. The contents of the text box can be empty even though ClipText contains some text.

For example, type several characters in the text box. Select a few characters so that a portion of the text in the box is highlighted. Click Copy to place a copy of the selected text in the ClipText variable.

Now, click Delete to clear the contents of the text box. Notice that the Paste button becomes enabled, while the other three buttons are disabled.

Click Paste to transfer a copy of the saved text into the text box. Notice that doing so enables the remaining command buttons. Paste remains enabled, also. You can, therefore, paste additional copies of the saved text by clicking Paste repeatedly.

Honing the Code for the Cut and Copy Buttons

Ted is close to completion. One more detail with the Cut and Copy buttons, however, requires attention.

Now that you have added code to enable and disable the command buttons, you find that Cut and Copy don't quite work properly. If you cut or copy some text when the Paste button is disabled, it does not become enabled.

Most likely, you saw the effect when verifying the Paste button in the previous section. If not, you can see the effect if you start the application, type into the text box a few lines, then select some of it. Now, click Cut or Copy. Notice that the Paste button does not become enabled. (The Paste button should become enabled, because the cut or copy operation placed text in ClipText.)

To correct this problem, just add the following instruction to the Click procedures for both the Cut and Copy buttons:

```
If ClipText <> "" Then cmdPaste.Enabled = True
```

The <> operator means "not equals." This instruction enables the Paste button when the contents of ClipText are not equal to the empty string.

The following are the updated event procedures:

```
Sub cmdCut_Click ()
   ClipText = txtTed.SelText
   txtTed.SelText = ""
   If ClipText <> "" Then cmdPaste.Enabled = True
   txtTed.SetFocus
End Sub

Sub cmdCopy_Click ()
   ClipText = txtTed.SelText
   If ClipText <> "" Then cmdPaste.Enabled = True
   txtTed.SetFocus
End Sub
```

NOTE You might wonder why the Click procedure for the Cut button doesn't check whether the contents of the text box have become empty. After all, when the entire contents of the text box are highlighted, clicking Cut clears the box. You might expect the cmdCut_Click procedure to call BlankText when the contents of the text box are deleted.

Actually, the necessary code is contained in the Change procedure for the text box. When you select some text, and click the Cut button, a Change event triggers for the text box. The code in the Change event procedure invokes BlankText.

This is one example of a single action triggering multiple events. Here, when you click the Cut button, a Click event occurs for it. The cut, however, changes the text in the text box. Thus, a Change event for the text box occurs, as well.

A Few Comments on Event Procedures

You must understand that, although the form and controls in an application can recognize many possible events, nothing happens unless you place code into the appropriate event procedures.

The situation is analogous to the familiar conundrum: Does a falling tree make a sound if no one's around to hear it? Well, here's the comparison to Visual Basic: Does an event occur if no event procedure is written for it? For example, what happens if you click a command button for which no Click event procedure has been written?

The answer remains rhetorical. The point is that, whether or not you say the event occurred, Visual Basic takes no action unless you place code into the corresponding event procedure.

Viewing the Available Events

You can use the Code window to view all the available events for a form or control. Just open this window when Visual Basic is in Design mode.

For example, in the Ted application, double-click a control (or the form) to open its Code window. Then, click the down arrow to the right of the Proc box. A drop-down list appears which shows all the available events.

Events listed in boldface are those for which you have already written an event procedure. Figure 7.9 shows the Code window and event procedure list for the Cut command button.

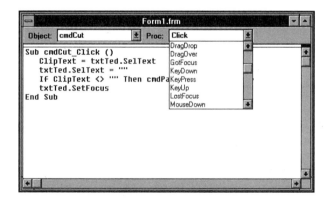

Figure 7.9.

The Code window for the Cut command button.

Viewing the User-Defined Procedures

To see the program code not associated with any event procedure, click the down arrow to the right of the Object box in the Code window. Click (general), the first item in the drop-down list.

Now, click the down arrow to the right of the Proc box. The drop-down list contains the names of the general procedures. For Ted, the only general procedure is BlankText.

Notice that the drop-down list also contains the item (declarations). Click this item to see the form-level declarations. Ted has only one such declaration, shown on the following line:

```
Dim ClipText As String
```

Viewing the Event Procedures

You can cycle through an application's event procedures by repeatedly pressing Ctrl+Up or Ctrl+Down when the Code window is open. With each keystroke, the next coded event procedure (or the general declarations section) scrolls into view.

Viewing a Particular Event Procedure

Another way to view an application's existing event procedures is with the View Procedures dialog box. To do so, open the Code window (press F7), then press F2. Figure 7.10 shows this dialog box for Ted.

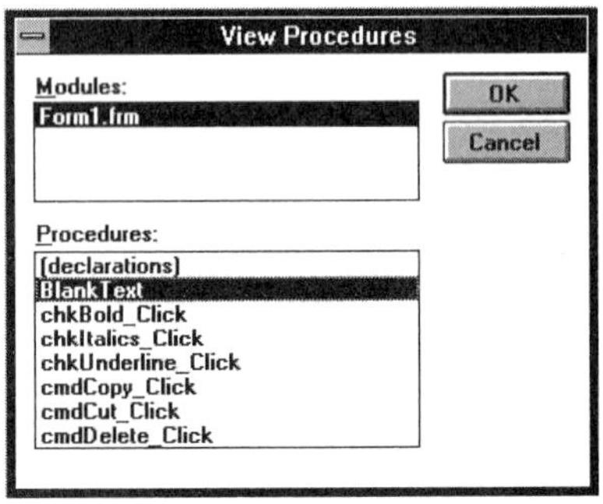

Figure 7.10.

The View Procedures dialog box for the Ted application.

The View Procedures dialog box lists all the event procedures for which program code has been written. To bring any procedure into view, double-click its name. Alternatively, you can select the procedure name from the list by clicking it. Then click OK.

Using Access Keys

Ted is now a fully functional application. The event procedures are complete. That doesn't mean, however, you can't improve on the application.

You can add access keys to the command buttons and check boxes. An *access key* is a key you press in conjunction with the Alt key to immediately activate a particular command button, check box, or other element of an application.

Many Windows applications use access keys, including Visual Basic itself. An access key is conventionally indicated with an underline. All Visual Basic's main menu options use access keys. The File menu, for example, appears with the "F" underlined. As such, you can open the File menu by pressing Alt+F. Similarly, various options in dialog boxes use access keys.

Creating Access Keys in Visual Basic

In a Visual Basic application, you can create an access key for any control which has a Caption property. You need to make only a small modification to the value of each control's Caption property. Put an ampersand (&) in front of the character you want to designate as the access key.

For example, you can make "C" the access key for the Copy button by changing its Caption property to &Copy. Similarly, you can make "B" the access key for the Bold check box by changing its caption to &Bold.

Notice that, once you make "C" the access key for the Copy button, a small problem arises with the Cut button. You can't use the same access key for two different controls, so "C" cannot function this way for Cut. Instead, "t" is a reasonable choice for the Cut button's access key. The caption becomes Cu&t.

Adding Access Keys to Ted

To add access keys to Ted's four command buttons and three check boxes, open the Properties window, and change the Caption properties as Table 7.4 shows.

Table 7.4. Access keys for the Ted application.

Control	Access key	Value of *Caption* property
chkBold	B	&Bold
chkItalics	I	&Italics
chkUnderline	U	&Underline
cmdCut	T	Cu&t
cmdCopy	C	&Copy
cmdPaste	P	&Paste
cmdDelete	D	&Delete

That is all you need to do. Visual Basic takes care of the rest. When you run the application, each access key appears underlined. (The ampersand character is not displayed.) Furthermore, you don't need any additional program code to make the access keys functional.

Run the application. Figure 7.11 shows an example of Ted in use. Notice that each access key appears underlined. If you press Alt in conjunction with one of the access keys, you activate the corresponding command button or check box.

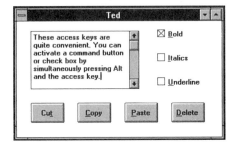

Figure 7.11.

Ted has access keys.

For example, if you press Alt+D, you delete the contents of the text box. The effect is the same as clicking Delete. Further, by pressing Alt+U several times, you toggle underlining on and off—the same as clicking the Underline check box several times in succession.

Ted is now a honed application. Of course, you can always add more functionality. For example, to make Ted a professional text editor, you might add options to save the contents of the text box to a disk file, and load them back into the box. To find out how to do this, see Chapter 25, "Processing Files."

Saving Ted

To save Ted's form as a disk file, choose the Save File **As** option from Visual Basic's **F**ile menu. When the Save File As dialog box opens, save the form as TED.FRM. (If you specify the name as simply TED, Visual Basic automatically adds the .FRM file extension). Be sure the directory path is specified correctly, so that the file is saved in your intended directory.

Figure 7.12 shows the Save File As dialog box. Notice the check box which reads Save as Text. This check box is near the lower right corner of the dialog box. The check box gives you a choice of saving the file in one of two formats: the binary (the default), or text-readable ASCII. If you don't choose this option, the form is saved in a compressed binary format which creates a relatively small file.

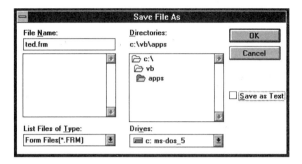

Figure 7.12.

The Save File As
dialog box.

If you click the check box to choose the Text option, the form is saved as a text file. As you see in the next section, saving as a text file enables you to easily view the form's property values and event procedures. The disadvantage is that, compared to a binary file, a text file is somewhat larger.

Choose the **S**ave as Text option. Then, click OK (or press Enter) to save the form as a disk file named TED.FRM.

Next, choose the Sa**v**e Project As option from the **F**ile menu. When the Save Project As dialog box opens, specify TED.MAK as the file name. (If you specify the file name simply as TED, Visual Basic automatically adds the .MAK file extension.) Again, be sure the directory path is specified correctly. For more information on .MAK files, see Chapter 9, "Managing Projects."

Once you have Ted saved on disk, you can later load the application back into Visual Basic with the **O**pen Project option from the File menu.

Working with the Form as a Text File

When you save a form as a text file, you can view it with a word processor or text editor. The file consists of a readable description of the form. The description enumerates each of the controls on the form, including all associated property values, and a complete listing of every general and event procedure. This description provides a concise representation of the form, so it's a valuable debugging aid.

To work with the text description of the form, you must have saved the .FRM file with the **S**ave as Text option. The previous section describes the necessary process to do this.

Viewing TED.FRM

To view the text file, you only need to load it into any word processor or text editor. The text file for TED.FRM is as follows:

```
VERSION 3.00
Begin Form frmTed
    Caption         =    "Ted"
    Height          =    3300
    Left            =    1185
    LinkTopic       =    "Form1"
    ScaleHeight     =    2895
    ScaleWidth      =    5250
    Top             =    1440
    Width           =    5370
    Begin CheckBox chkUnderline
        Caption         =    "&Underline"
        Height          =    375
        Left            =    3600
        TabIndex        =    7
        Top             =    1320
        Width           =    1215
    End
    Begin CheckBox chkItalics
        Caption         =    "&Italics"
        Height          =    375
        Left            =    3600
        TabIndex        =    6
        Top             =    720
        Width           =    1215
    End
    Begin CheckBox chkBold
        Caption         =    "&Bold"
        Height          =    375
        Left            =    3600
        TabIndex        =    5
        Top             =    120
        Width           =    1215
    End
    Begin CommandButton cmdDelete
        Caption         =    "&Delete"
        Height          =    495
```

```
      Left          =    3960
      TabIndex      =    4
      Top           =    2040
      Width         =    855
   End
   Begin CommandButton cmdPaste
      Caption       =    "&Paste"
      Height        =    495
      Left          =    2760
      TabIndex      =    3
      Top           =    2040
      Width         =    855
   End
   Begin CommandButton cmdCopy
      Caption       =    "&Copy"
      Height        =    495
      Left          =    1560
      TabIndex      =    2
      Top           =    2040
      Width         =    855
   End
   Begin CommandButton cmdCut
      Caption       =    "Cu&t"
      Height        =    495
      Left          =    360
      TabIndex      =    1
      Top           =    2040
      Width         =    855
   End
   Begin TextBox txtTed
      Height        =    1455
      Left          =    360
      MultiLine     =    -1   'True
      ScrollBars    =    2    'Vertical
      TabIndex      =    0
      Text          =    "Text1"
      Top           =    240
      Width         =    2775
   End
End
Dim ClipText As String
```

```
Sub BlankText ()
   cmdCut.Enabled = False
   cmdCopy.Enabled = False
   cmdDelete.Enabled = False

   If ClipText = "" Then
      cmdPaste.Enabled = False
   Else
      cmdPaste.Enabled = True
   End If
End Sub

Sub chkBold_Click ()
   txtTed.FontBold = Not (txtTed.FontBold)
   txtTed.SetFocus
End Sub

Sub chkItalics_Click ()
   txtTed.FontItalic = Not (txtTed.FontItalic)
   txtTed.SetFocus
End Sub

Sub chkUnderline_Click ()
   txtTed.FontUnderline = Not (txtTed.FontUnderline)
   txtTed.SetFocus
End Sub

Sub cmdCopy_Click ()
   ClipText = txtTed.SelText
   If ClipText <> "" Then cmdPaste.Enabled = True
   txtTed.SetFocus
End Sub

Sub cmdCut_Click ()
   ClipText = txtTed.SelText
   txtTed.SelText = ""
   If ClipText <> "" Then cmdPaste.Enabled = True
   txtTed.SetFocus
End Sub

Sub cmdDelete_Click ()
   txtTed.Text = ""
   txtTed.SetFocus
```

```
End Sub

Sub cmdPaste_Click ()
    txtTed.SelText = ClipText
    txtTed.SetFocus
End Sub

Sub Form_Load ()
    txtTed.Text = ""          'Blank contents of text box
    BlankText

    txtTed.FontBold = False
    txtTed.FontItalic = False
    txtTed.FontUnderline = False

    chkBold.Value = 0
    chkItalics.Value = 0
    chkUnderline.Value = 0
End Sub

Sub txtTed_Change ()
    If txtTed.Text = "" Then
        BlankText
    Else
        cmdCut.Enabled = True
        cmdCopy.Enabled = True
        cmdDelete.Enabled = True
    End If
End Sub
```

Understanding the Text File

The format of the text file is relatively straightforward. The first line lists the version number of Visual Basic. Then, the design-time property values of the form are listed. Following that, each control is named, along with its property values. The controls are listed in alphabetical order, as are the properties of each.

The listed properties include those of the location (Top, Left, Height, and Width), and any set to nondefault values at design time.

The `TabIndex` property shown for each control specifies the tab order. The tab order determines the sequence in which each control gets the focus if you repeatedly press the Tab key. For more information on `TabIndex` and the tab order, see Chapter 8, "Using the Toolbox and Its Common Controls."

The General Declarations section follows the list of each control's property values. For Ted, the general declarations section consists of the single `Dim` instruction which declares the variable `ClipText`.

Next comes a complete list of the general and event procedures. Notice that, similar to the lists of controls and properties, Visual Basic arranges these procedures in alphabetical order.

Printing the Text File

It's easy to print out a listing of the text file. All you need to do is print the file as you would any other text document. Just use the normal printing capability of the word processor or text editor with which you are viewing the file. In Windows Notepad, for example, you print a file by choosing the **P**rint option from the **F**ile menu.

By printing the file, you get a hard copy archive of the form. If you ever lose the TED.FRM file, you can regenerate the application from the information on the printed listing.

Modifying the Text File

Once you have a form's text file loaded into a word processor or text editor, you can actually modify the description of the form. For example, you can change some property values, or modify an event procedure. You can even add a new control or event procedure.

After you modify the file, you can save the file again under either the old name or a new one. Be sure that the word processor or text editor saves the file in ASCII (text) format, not in any special proprietary format specific to either of these two systems.

When you later load the modified file back into Visual Basic, your modifications are immediately implemented. With this technique, you can "program" Visual Basic applications in your word processor!

Using Control Arrays

Often, a Visual Basic application has several controls of the same type which perform similar functions. For example, Ted has three check boxes which manipulate the font attributes.

Each of Ted's three check boxes has a separate name: `chkBold`, `chkItalics`, and `chkUnderline`. To enable each check box to respond to the `Click` event, you wrote three separate event procedures: `chkBold_Click`, `chkItalics_Click`, and `chkUnderline_Click`.

Visual Basic provides an easier way, however, to work with groups of similar controls: the control array. A *control array* is a group of controls which share the same name. Each member of the control array is called an *element* of the control array. As explained shortly, each individual control in this type of array is distinguished by a separate value for its `Index` property.

A control array always contains controls of the same type. For example, a control array can consist of command buttons, check boxes, or labels. However, you can't have a control array comprised of a command button, a check box, and a label.

Advantages of Control Arrays

With control arrays, you can realize several advantages:

- *Your program code can manipulate a group of controls more efficiently.*

  For example, you can create a program loop which, in a few lines of code, modifies the property values for every element of the control array.

- *Several controls can share the same event procedures.*

  You can write a single event procedure for each type of event. For example, one `Click` procedure is all you need to make *every* element of the control array respond to the `Click` event. In this way, the elements of a control array can share program code.

- *You can add or delete elements of a control array at runtime.*

  Sometimes, you want to add or remove a control while the application is running. By using Visual Basic's `Load` and `UnLoad` statements in program code, you can add or remove elements of a control array at runtime. For more information on loading and unloading elements of a control array, see Chapter 20, "Using Object Variables."

NOTE The only way to add or remove controls at run time is by using a control array. As explained in this section, you must first create the control array at design time. Then, as explained in Chapter 20, you can write program code to add elements to, and remove them from, this array.

Creating a Control Array

You create a control array by assigning the same name to two or more controls which already have been placed on the form. That is, you use the Properties window to assign the same value of the Name property to two or more controls. When you do, Visual Basic pops open a dialog box which asks if you want to create a control array. By clicking Yes, you establish a control array.

As explained in the previous chapter, you can also create a control array by copying and pasting it through Visual Basic's Edit menu.

A third way also exists to create a control array. As explained in the following section, if you assign a value to the Index property of a control, you establish a control array.

Working with the *Index* Property

Your program code needs a way to reference the individual controls in the control array, as its various elements share the same name. That's the job of the Index property.

Each element of a control array has a different Index value. Index values start at 0, and increase incrementally. In other words, Index is 0 for the first element of the control array, 1 for the second element, 2 for the next, and so on.

When working with the Properties window, you might have seen Index in the list of properties. Index has meaning only for control arrays. When onto a form you first place a control, its Index property has no value. When you create a control array, however, to each of its elements Visual Basic assigns a specific value of Index.

You can modify Index values also at design time with the Properties window. In fact, by simply assigning a value to Index for any control, you immediately establish it as belonging to a control array. This is the third way to create a control array, as discussed in the previous section.

In program code, you reference a particular element of a control array by enclosing its Index value in parentheses. For example, suppose you establish a control array consisting of three command buttons named cmdButtons. The Index values for the three controls are 0, 1, and 2. The following instruction assigns a new caption to the third command button:

```
cmdButtons(2).Caption = "My Index is 2"
```

If you are familiar with regular variable arrays in any version of BASIC, you can see that control arrays use a similar syntax. The array name is immediately followed by a set of parentheses. In the parentheses, a numeric value specifies the element of the array. For more information on arrays and their syntax, see Chapter 19, "Using Arrays and Structures."

A Simple Example of a Control Array

The following exercise demonstrates several aspects of control arrays. You create a simple application containing a control array of three command buttons.

Start by creating a new project. Choose the **New Project** option from the **File** menu. Be sure that you have saved Ted before starting the new project. You pay another visit to Ted a bit later in this chapter.

Follow these steps:

1. Double-click the command button icon in the Toolbox to place a command button near the center of the form.

   Visual Basic assigns the default name Command1 to this control.

2. Stretch the control horizontally to approximately twice its initial width. (Don't worry about being exact. You want the command button to be roughly twice its initial width).

3. Move the control near the upper left corner of the form.

4. Add two more command buttons to the form, and stretch each one approximately to the same width as the first. Place these controls in a vertical column below the first control.

   The two new command buttons have the default names Command2 and Command3. Figure 7.13 shows the form at this stage.

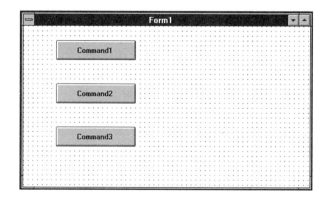

Figure 7.13.

Three command buttons are placed on the form.

5. Click Command1 to select it. Press F4 to open the Properties window. Change the value of the Name property to cmdButtons.

6. Click Command2. Open the Properties window, and change the value of the Name property to cmdButtons.

   Visual Basic pops open a dialog box which asks if you want to create a control array (see Figure 7.14).

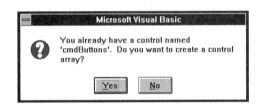

7. Choose the Yes option.

   Notice that, in the Properties window, the Object box reads cmdButtons(1) CommandButton. The parentheses indicate that this control is part of a control array. The 1 inside the parentheses indicates that the value of Index for this control is 1. You can verify this value of Index by searching through the Properties window to find this property, and checking its value. Similarly, if you open the Properties window for the upper-left command button, you see that its Index value is 0.

8. Click Command3. As with the other two command buttons, change the value of its Name property to cmdButtons.

   Index is 2 for this control.

9. In the Properties window, click the down arrow to the right of the Object box.

   Notice that the drop-down list shows the various elements of the control array (see Figure 7.15).

10. Press F7 to open the Code window. Select the Click procedure for cmdButtons.

    Notice that the Sub instruction in the procedure template now appears as follows:

    ```
    Sub cmdButtons_Click (Index As Integer)
    ```

    Ordinarily, the parentheses inside a Click event procedure do not contain any parameters. Here, however, Index As Integer appears inside the parentheses. This phrase specifies Index as a parameter of data type Integer. As a result, when the Click procedure activates, Visual Basic passes Index to the procedure. In the procedure, you can use the Index parameter to determine which element of the control array was clicked.

In this way, a single `Click` event procedure works for all elements of the control array.

Figure 7.15.

The Object list in the Properties window.

11. Create the following event procedure:

```
Sub cmdButtons_Click (Index As Integer)
    cmdButtons(Index).Caption = "You clicked me!"
End Sub
```

Notice how the instruction in the event procedure uses `Index` to modify the caption of the clicked command button.

12. Run the application. When you click any of the three command buttons, its caption changes to `You clicked me!`

13. Stop the application, and reopen the Code window to the `Click` procedure for the command buttons. Modify the right side of the caption instruction as follows:

```
Sub cmdButtons_Click (Index As Integer)
    cmdButtons(Index).Caption = "I'm Index #" & Str$(Index)
End Sub
```

Here, the `Str$` function converts the numeric value of `Index` into a string value. As such, the right side is entirely in string format, as required by the `Caption` property. For more information on `Str$`, and manipulating strings, see Chapter 17, "Working with Strings."

14. Run the application again. When you click one of the command buttons, the new caption displays the `Index` value for the control.

In Figure 7.16, the top two command buttons have been clicked.

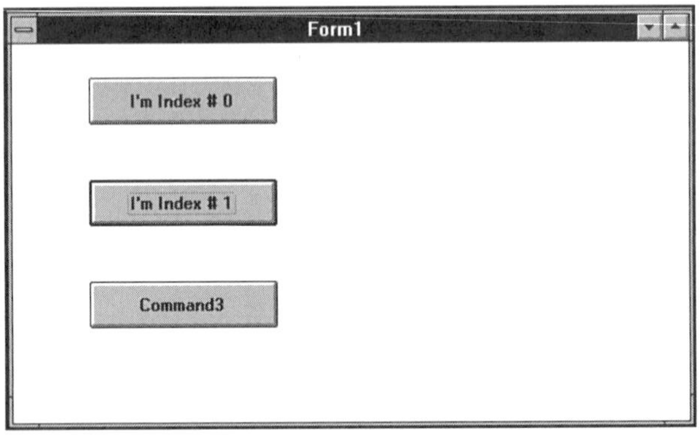

Figure 7.16.

Two command buttons
display their new captions.

Stop the application. Save the form and the project, if you want to.

Using *Index* in Event Procedures

When writing an event procedure for a control array, Visual Basic always adds the Index parameter with the phrase Index As Integer. The As Integer qualification specifies that Index is a parameter which has an integral numeric value.

In the event procedure, you can test the value of Index to determine which element of the control array triggered the event. For example, you might write an instruction, such as

```
If Index = 1 Then Beep
```

This instruction beeps the speaker only if the control with an Index value of 1 triggered the event.

So far, you have worked exclusively with event procedures that normally do not contain any parameters. As you learn throughout the book, some events always contain specialized parameters.

For example, the KeyPress event occurs when the user presses a key while a control has the focus. Consider the KeyPress event for a command button named MyButton. Here, MyButton is not part of a control array. In the Code window, the Sub instruction for this event appears as follows:

```
Sub MyButton_KeyPress (KeyAscii As Integer)
```

KeyAscii has a numeric value which indicates the key that was pressed. If MyButton is a control array, however, the Sub instruction appears as follows:

```
Sub MyButton_KeyPress (Index As Integer, KeyAscii As Integer)
```

In this case, Visual Basic passes both the Index and KeyAscii parameters.

The point here is not to explain KeyPress (for that, see Chapter 23, "Responding to Keyboard Events"), but rather to emphasize that Visual Basic adds the Index parameter to *any* event procedure associated with a control array.

Modifying Ted to Use a Control Array

Recall that the Ted application has three check boxes that manipulate the bold, italic, and underline font attributes. The check boxes have the names chkBold, chkItalics, and chkUnderline respectively.

When designing Ted, you could have created a control array for these three check boxes. In this case, a single Click procedure would manipulate the font attributes for all three buttons.

You can also change the current application to convert the check boxes from ordinary separate controls into a control array. This section shows you how.

First, load Ted back into the Visual Basic environment. To do so, choose the **O**pen Project option from the File menu. When the dialog box pops open, specify the file TED.MAK. Be sure you specify the proper directory path to the file.

If the form is not visible after the file loads, open the Project window. (If the Project window is not visible, choose the P**r**oject option from the **W**indow menu.) To see the form, click the View Form button in the Project window.

Follow these steps to turn the three check boxes into a control array named chkFontStyle.

1. Open the Properties window, and find the check box at the top.

    This check box is currently named chkBold.

2. Change the value of the Name property to chkFontStyle.

3. Open the Properties window for the chkItalics check box.

4. Again, change the value of Name to chkFontStyle.

    You specified the same name as an existing check box, so Visual Basic pops open the dialog box which asks if you want to create a control array.

5. Choose Yes to confirm that you want to create a control array.

6. Open the Properties window for the third check box. As with the other two boxes, change its Name to chkFontStyle.

    You now have a control array named chkFontStyle. If you examine the values of Index in the Properties window, you find that the values are 0, 1, and 2 for the three check boxes moving from top to bottom, respectively.

NOTE You no longer have controls named chkBold, chkItalics, and chkUnderline, so you might wonder about the fate of the Click procedures that you previously defined for them. After all, you no longer can have a chkBold_Click event procedure if you no longer have a chkBold control!

You can verify that the old event procedures no longer exist. Open the Code window, and examine the Object list. The list doesn't even contain the old control names, so their Click procedures are no longer event procedures.

However, Visual Basic does not discard the old procedures; instead, the system moves them to the General Procedures section. As such, they are no longer event procedures, but are similar to the user-defined procedure BlankText. The old procedures cannot be called by system events, but you can write program code to explicitly invoke one of them.

To verify that the procedures are intact, choose (general) in the Object list. Then, drop down the list in the Proc box. You will see the old Click procedures.

The old Click procedures are no longer used in the modified Ted application, so it's a good idea to delete them completely. No harm is done if you don't delete the old procedures—you simply have extraneous program code. To delete these old procedures, open the Code window for each procedure one at a time, and delete each in its entirety.

7. Open the Code window for the chkFontStyle_Click event procedure.

Visual Basic provides the following template for the event procedure. Notice that Index is present as a parameter:

```
Sub chkFontStyle_Click (Index As Integer)
End Sub
```

8. Write the code for the Click event procedure.

You can write a series of If instructions as follows:

```
If Index = 0 Then txtTed.FontBold = Not (txtTed.FontBold)
If Index = 1 Then txtTed.FontItalic = Not (txtTed.FontItalic)
If Index = 2 Then txtTed.FontUnderline = Not (txtTed.FontUnderline)
```

As explained in the next step, another way is to use Visual Basic's `Select Case` statement.

9. Create the following procedure:

```
Sub chkFontStyle_Click (Index As Integer)
    Select Case Index
        Case 0
            txtTed.FontBold = Not (txtTed.FontBold)
        Case 1
            txtTed.FontItalic = Not (txtTed.FontItalic)
        Case 2
            txtTed.FontUnderline = Not (txtTed.FontUnderline)
    End Select
    txtTed.SetFocus
End Sub
```

Here, the `Select Case-End Select` block examines the value of `Index`, and executes the appropriate instruction, depending on the value. For more information on `Select Case`, see Chapter 15, "Program Flow and Decision Making."

10. Open the Code window for the `Form_Load` procedure.

The final three lines of the procedure initialize the `Value` properties for the three check boxes:

```
chkBold.Value = 0
chkItalics.Value = 0
chkUnderline.Value = 0
```

As explained in the next step, these three lines must be modified to use the name of the control array.

11. Modify the final three lines of the procedure as follows:

```
chkFontStyle(0).Value = 0
chkFontStyle(1).Value = 0
chkFontStyle(2).Value = 0
```

NOTE

In `Form_Load`, you can use a loop to initialize the `Value` properties. For example, you can write a `For-Next` loop as follows:

```
For J = 0 To 2
    chkFontStyle(J).Value = 0
Next J
```

Such a loop hints at the power inherent in control arrays. For a control array with only a few elements, there's no particular advantage to writing a loop rather than a series of individual assignment instructions. However, suppose the control array had 20 or more elements. With only a small change in the `For` instruction (`For J = 0 To 20`), the three-instruction loop can still initialize the entire control array.

The capability of manipulating control arrays with loops (and with variable names inside the parentheses) is especially important in applications that add or remove elements of control arrays at run time.

In such applications, you often write program code that must manipulate an unknown number of control array elements. Such code might define a variable named `NumElements` which indicates the highest current `Index` value for the elements of the control array. Then, a `For` loop might be written as follows: `For J = 0 To NumElements`.

That completes the conversion of Ted so that the application uses a control array. Run the modified application. Ted should perform just as it did previously. Use the Save File **As** option from the **File** menu to save Ted with a new file name.

Summary

Similar to gas that lets a car operate, event procedures make a Visual Basic application go. In an event procedure, you place the program instructions that execute when the event triggers. Such instructions often modify various property values to create desired effects on the form.

In this chapter, you created Ted—a functional text editor which implements cut, and paste, and selectable font attributes. By developing Ted, you learned not only about writing event procedures, but employing user-defined procedures, form-level variables, the `Form_Load` event, and the properties of a text box. You learned also how to create an access key by modifying the `Caption` property.

With the Code window, you can view and edit your program code. By using the Object and Proc boxes in this window, you have access to all the instructions in an application, which includes the general (user-defined) and event procedures, and the general declarations.

You can save a form on disk as a text file. By so doing, you can view or print a textual description of an application. The description includes the property values for the form and its controls, and a listing of all the event procedures.

A control array groups together several controls under a common name. Visual Basic uses the Index property to distinguish the individual elements in the control array. For controls that all function in a similar way, this kind of array presents several advantages. For example, the same event procedure activates whenever the event occurs for *any* element of the control array.

Using the Toolbox and the Common Controls

The Toolbox contains a wealth of different controls. By placing these controls on a form, you can design user interfaces which meet the needs of most any application.

Each control has its own set of associated properties and events. Once you place a control on a form, you use the Properties window to assign initial property values for that control. Using the Code window, you write program instructions for the relevant event procedures.

This chapter discusses in depth the frequently used controls—that is, the controls which programmers tend to use the most often. Later chapters cover the more specialized controls found in the Standard Edition of Visual Basic as well as the additional controls included with the Professional Edition.

Examining the Toolbox

Figure 8.1 shows the Toolbox for Visual Basic 3.0, Standard Edition. (If you have the Professional Edition of Visual Basic, your Toolbox contains additional controls.)

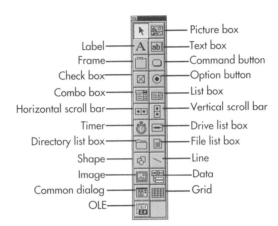

Figure 8.1.

The standard Toolbox controls are marked with callouts.

Table 8.1 summarizes each of the controls found in the Toolbox. The second column shows the default name which Visual Basic assigns to a control of that type. For example, if you place a command button on a form, Visual Basic assigns the default name Command1 to this button. If you add more controls of the same type, Visual Basic increases the numeric count. For example, additional command buttons are named Command2, Command3, and so on.

As explained later in this chapter, you might want to rename the controls in an application to use more descriptive names. The third column shows the standard name prefix for each of the controls. For more information on these prefixes, and naming schemes in general, see "The Name Property," later in this chapter.

The fourth column identifies the chapter which discusses the control in depth. Many controls, of course, are discussed in several places throughout the book. The first 12 controls in this table are the most common ones. These controls are the subject of the remainder of this chapter.

Table 8.1. The Toolbox controls.

Control	Default Name	Name Prefix	Chap. Num.	Description
Picture box	Picture1	pic	8	Provides a rectangular area in which graphics can be displayed.
Label	Label1	lbl	8	Displays text that the user cannot directly modify at run time.
Text box	Text1	txt	8	Displays text that the user can directly modify at run time.

Control	Default Name	Name Prefix	Chap. Num.	Description
Frame	Frame1	fra	8	Provides a rectangular area in which other controls can be placed as a group.
Command button	Command1	cmd	8	Responds to a user click to activate a requested event.
Check box	Check1	chk	8	Displays an × or an empty box to indicate the current state of a True/False option, and responds to a user click to toggle the choice.
Option button	Option1	opt	8	Displays a bullet if an option is selected; this control typically appears in groups to enable the user to choose from mutually exclusive options.
Combo box	Combo1	cbo	8	By combining the features of both a text and a list box, the user can specify data by typing in a value or selecting an appropriate value from a drop-down list.
List box	List1	lst	8	Displays a drop-down list of values, from which the user can select one value.
Horizontal Scroll Bar	HScroll1	hsb	8	Provides a visual mechanism for the user to select a particular value from a continuous range of possible values.
Vertical Scroll Bar	VScroll1	vsb	8	Similar to the Horizontal scroll bar, but with a vertical orientation.

continues

Table 8.1. Continued

Control	Default Name	Name Prefix	Chap. Num.	Description
Timer	Timer1	tmr	8	Triggers an event when a specified time period elapses.
Drive list box	Drive1	drv	25	Provides a list of the PC's available disk drives, enabling the user to select one.
Directory list box	Dir1	dir	25	Provides a list of paths and directories, enabling the user to select a path.
File list box	File1	fil	25	Provides a list of files, enabling the user to select one.
Shape	Shape1	shp	11	Provides a tool for drawing two-dimensional geometric shapes.
Line	Line1	lin	11	Provides a tool for drawing straight lines.
Image	Image1	img	11	Provides a rectangular area in which graphics can be displayed; this control is similar to, but simpler than, a picture box.
Data	Data1	dta	28	Supports databases, including compatibility with commercial products such as Microsoft Access.
Grid	Grid1	grd	26	Displays data in rows and columns.
OLE	OLE1	ole	31	Provides a data link with an external OLE (Object Linking and Embedding) compliant application.

The BOOK Application

To illustrate a practical use of the common controls, this chapter takes you through the process of developing a sample application named BOOK. This application is a Book Reservation system for a fictitious bookstore named "Do It Yourself Bookstore."

The application is an on-screen ordering form designed to record a customer's request for particular books. On this form, an employee of the store can enter the customer's name, selected books, method of payment, delivery date, and other pertinent information. Figure 8.2 shows how the completed application appears when run.

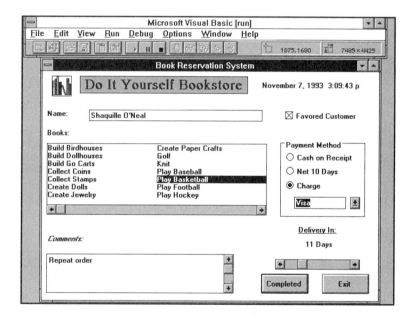

Figure 8.2.

The BOOK application.

The BOOK application uses all of the common controls. As you develop the application, you learn about each of these controls.

Starting to Develop the Application

To start developing the BOOK application, choose the New Project option from the File menu. Click the blank form to select the form. Then press F4 to access the Properties window. Modify the form's property values as Table 8.2 shows.

Table 8.2. Initial property values for *Form1*.

Object	Property	Value
Form1	Caption	Book Reservation System
	Height	6120
	Left	855
	Top	1125
	Width	8760

NOTE This sample application uses a large form. On standard VGA systems (640 by 480 pixel resolution), the form dominates the screen, leaving only room for the Toolbox on the left, and the Toolbar on top.

As you place controls on the form, and assign design-time property values, you often need to access the Properties window. To do this, simply press F4. The Properties window appears superimposed on the form. Remember that to see a particular part of the form, you can move the Properties window around the screen by dragging its title bar.

If you click any part of the form, or place a new control on it, the Properties window becomes temporarily hidden. To bring the window back to the foreground, simply press F4 again.

The Shared Properties

Every control has its own set of properties. You can set values for these properties at design time, with the Properties window, or at run time through the program code. (You can modify certain properties only at design time, and read or write others solely at run time.)

Some properties exist only for particular controls. For example, the Text property of a text box identifies its current text string. It doesn't make sense to think of the Text property of a scroll bar, because a scroll bar has no textual component. Indeed, as discussed in this chapter, the only controls which have a Text property are text, list, and combo boxes.

On the other hand, there is a set of properties shared by all the common controls. For example, the Width property specifies the horizontal width of controls, so it pertains to all of them.

NOTE Using words like "every" and "all" in a Visual Basic context is dangerous. Any time you make an absolute statement, there is likely to be an exception.

Indeed, not *every* common control has a Width property. The Timer control is an exception. As discussed later in this chapter, the Timer is a special type of control with unique characteristics.

This section discusses the properties which are, for the most part, shared by all the common controls.

The *Name* Property

Every control in an application has a unique Name property. Whenever you place a control on a form, Visual Basic assigns the control a default name. That name consists of a base name followed by a number. For example, the first command button you place on a form is given the name Command1. If you place additional command buttons on the form, the default names are Command2, Command3, and so on. The second column in Table 8.1 shows the default name for each control type.

In code, you use a control's name to reference the individual control. For example, the following instruction modifies the Caption property of the command button Command2:

```
Command2.Caption = "What's in a name?"
```

You use a control's name also when referring to one of the control's event procedures. For example, the Click procedure for the second command button is Command2_Click ().

When an instruction uses one of Visual Basic's methods on a control, you designate the control by name. For example, the following instruction uses Visual Basic's Move method to move a command button to the upper left corner of the form:

```
Command2.Move 0, 0
```

In any application, you can simply accept the default names that Visual Basic assigns to the controls (and to the forms). In applications with several controls, however, it's a good idea to modify their names to be more descriptive.

If an application has five command buttons named Command1 to Command5, it's difficult when looking through the code to immediately recognize how each command button operates. Instead, you might want to assign more descriptive names such as OKButton, QuitButton, DeleteButton, and so on. That way, when the control name appears in code, it's quite obvious which command button is being referenced.

Changing a Control Name

To change the name of a control (or a form, for that matter), use the Properties window to modify the value of the control's Name property. Unlike most of the properties discussed in this chapter, you can modify a Name property only at design time, not at run time.

Once you modify a control name, Visual Basic automatically creates templates for the control's event procedures using the new name. For example, if you change the name of Command1 to QuitButton, Visual Basic renames the template for the control's Click procedure from Command1_Click to QuitButton_Click.

NOTE

Be careful about modifying the Name property *after* writing event procedures. If you modify the Name property of a control for which you have already written an event procedure, Visual Basic does *not* rename the existing event procedure. Instead, the old event procedure is placed in the general declaration section of the form, and a stub for the newly named event procedure is created.

For example, suppose you have written a Command1_Click event procedure. Then you change the name of Command1 to QuitButton. The Command1_Click procedure is no longer considered to represent an active event, and is moved to the form's general declaration section. Visual Basic creates a new template (without any program instructions) for the QuitButton_Click event procedure. You must rewrite the program code for the new Click procedure. (You could, of course, cut and paste the instructions from the old procedure into the new one.)

In any case, if you are going to modify the Name properties of controls and forms, you should do so *before* writing any associated event procedures.

Naming Conventions

You can give your controls names up to 40 characters in length. The name can contain letters, digits, and underscore characters, but must begin with a letter. You can't place any blank spaces in a name.

It is generally considered good programming practice to give your forms and controls descriptive names. Doing so helps make the program code easier to read—which is especially important when debugging. The more controls you have in an application, the more this advice is relevant.

Using Name Prefixes

When renaming controls, you are free to use any names. One common renaming scheme uses a three-letter prefix immediately followed by a descriptive
name. The prefix identifies the control type. For example, the prefix for a
command button is cmd. Using this scheme, you might write the name cmdQuit
instead of QuitButton.

The advantages of this scheme are as follows:

■ The prefix immediately identifies the type of control. Anytime you see a
control name in the program code which begins with cmd, for example,
you know that the control is a command button.

■ The prefixes ensure that controls of the same type appear together in the
Code window list. In the object box of the Code window, the controls and
forms of a project are listed alphabetically. By systematically using the
suggested prefixes, the command buttons appear listed together. Similarly, each of the other types of controls is listed in a group. When you
look through the list of controls, you can quickly identify every command
button in the application.

The third column in Table 8.1 shows the prefixes for a naming scheme in
popular use.

The *Height, Width, Left,* and *Top* Properties

The Height, Width, Left, and Top properties determine the size and location of a
control on a form. By default, these properties are measured in twips. You can
specify a different unit of measurement, however, by modifying the ScaleMode
property of the form on which the controls are placed.

The Height and Width properties specify the size of the control. The Left and
Top properties specify its position relative to the form. If the values of Left and
Top are both zero, the control appears in the upper left corner of the form.

 The timer control is a special case. As explained later in this chapter, each timer control has a fixed size. As a result, the timer has
Left and Top properties, but not Height and Width properties.

The *Enabled* and *Visible* Properties

The Enabled and Visible properties regulate the user's run-time access to a
control. Each of these properties can have the value True or False, with True
as the default value.

When the value of Enabled is False, the user cannot access the control at run time. The control appears dimmed or grayed as an indication that it is disabled. When disabled, a control does not respond to any user-generated events, such as a mouse click.

In code, you can set the value of Enabled to False to temporarily disable a control. When you want the user to regain access to it, change the value back to True. For example, suppose that an application has opened a dialog box for the user to provide a file name for data storage. You might temporarily disable a command button used to exit the application until the user types the file name.

The Visible property determines whether the user is able to see the control at run time. When the value of Visible is False for a control, the control is hidden from view. When hidden, a control does not respond to any user-generated events.

 NOTE In general, you should avoid using the Visible property as a way of restricting the user's options. Controls which suddenly disappear, then later reappear, tend to confuse users. They might think that an application, which is working just as you programmed it, is not performing correctly.

The *HelpContextID* Property

The HelpContextID property assigns a special *context number* to each control in an application. The context number identifies the control for a context-sensitive Help system which you can build into the application. For more information on this property, and creating context-sensitive Help systems, see Chapter 33, "Adding a Help System to an Application."

Except for labels and timers, each of the common controls discussed in this chapter has the HelpContextID property.

The *MousePointer* Property

The MousePointer property determines the run time shape of the mouse pointer while it is over the control. For most controls, the default shape is the familiar arrow. For text boxes, however, the default shape is the I-Beam, which signifies the text insertion point.

By setting the value of MousePointer to appropriate numeric values, you can make the pointer take on one of several shapes, including an hourglass, cross hair, I-beam, icon (small square), size arrow, up arrow, or no drop (the no-drop shape is somewhat similar to the international Not symbol—a circle with a diagonal line through it).

The *Parent* Property

Each control has a Parent property. This property identifies the form on which the control appears; it is used most often in multiform applications which pass controls as procedure parameters. For more information on multiform applications, see Chapter 9, "Managing Projects." Chapter 20, "Using Object Variables," discusses the passing of controls and other objects as procedure parameters.

The value of the Parent property can never be modified. Your code, however, can read the value of this property at run time.

The *TabIndex* and *TabStop* Properties

In general, while an application is running, the user can repeatedly press the Tab key to move the focus from one control to the next. The values of each control's TabIndex and TabStop properties determine how this tabbing operates.

At design time, Visual Basic assigns a TabIndex value of 0 to the first control you place on the form. As you add more controls to it, the TabIndex value of each new one increases by one. At run time, pressing Tab moves the focus from one control to another, based on consecutive values of the TabIndex property.

The TabStop property can have a True or False value, with True as the default. When the value of TabStop is set to False for any control, it is bypassed in the Tab order at run time. In other words, the user cannot get access to the control with the Tab key. In such a case, however, the control retains its TabIndex value.

At design time or at run time, you can modify the value of a control's TabIndex and TabStop properties. By doing so, you alter the run-time tab order, which modifies the sequence in which the controls get the focus when the Tab key is pressed.

If you change the value of TabIndex for a control, Visual Basic automatically adjusts this value for the other controls to reflect your modification. Visual Basic ensures that the controls' TabIndex values always range from 0 to $N - 1$, where N is the total number of controls on the form.

Although all controls have a TabIndex property, some of them cannot receive the focus at run time. By definition, the following cannot receive the focus at run time: labels, timers, and disabled or hidden controls. In such cases, the controls retain their TabIndex value, but are bypassed in the tab order at run time. Labels and timers cannot receive the focus, so these two controls do not have a TabStop property.

The *Tag* Property

The Tag property is a string value you can associate with a control. This property is not directly used by Visual Basic, so you are free to assign any string value to a Tag property. You can assign a Tag value at design time, and modify or read it at run time.

One use of Tag is to indicate whether any change has occurred in a control. For example, you might set the design-time Tag of the Command1 command button as "unused." The Click event procedure for the control might contain the following instruction:

```
Command1.Tag = "Clicked"
```

Then in another event procedure, you can test whether the command button has ever been pressed. If so, you can take appropriate action. For example, you can disable the command button with the following instruction:

```
If Command1.Tag = "Clicked" Then Command1.Enabled = False
```

 **NOTE** The Tag property exists because of an historic development. In earlier versions of Visual Basic, the Tag property specified a context-sensitive help tag. As you've seen in this chapter, however, the HelpContextID property now serves that role. In newer versions of Visual Basic, Microsoft chose not to remove the Tag property. As a result, you can now use the Tag property to associate any string value with a control.

Surveying the Common Controls

The previous few sections examined the properties shared by most of the controls. The following sections take a survey look at each of the common controls.

The discussion focuses on the properties and events most relevant to each control. Along the way, you build the BOOK application, adding each type of control.

The Label Control

A label displays a text string which the user cannot directly modify at run time. As the name suggests, a label typically provides a heading, or other annotation, on the form. One common use of a label is to identify a control, such as a text box, which does not have its own Caption property.

Properties of the Label Control

The Caption property determines the text string displayed in the label. At run time, the caption is visible on the form. Although most label captions are short, you can use a caption up to 1K in length.

The Height, Width, Left, and Top properties determine the size and location of the label on the form. With the Alignment property, you can specify how the caption aligns in the label. The value of Alignment can be 0 (left aligned), 1 (right aligned), or 2 (centered). The default value is 0.

Instead of Alignment, you can use the AutoSize property to specify whether Visual Basic automatically resizes a label to fit its caption. The default value is False, which means that the size of the label is fixed. In this case, the tail end of the caption is clipped, and simply not visible, if it extends beyond the label border.

If you change the value of AutoSize to True, Visual Basic automatically adjusts the label's Height and Width properties so that the caption is not surrounded with wasted space. Then you can modify its Left and Top properties to relocate the resized label anywhere on the form.

The WordWrap property is unique to label controls. The value of this property determines how the label resizes when AutoSize is True. When WordWrap is False (the default value), caption text does not wrap. If necessary, the label expands horizontally to encompass the caption text. If WordWrap is True, however, the width of the label remains fixed. If necessary, the caption text wraps to multiple lines, and the label expands vertically to enclose the complete caption.

The BorderStyle, BackStyle, BackColor, and ForeColor properties provide more detail about the label's appearance. The BorderStyle property determines whether a visible border appears around the label. The default value is 0, which indicates that no border appears at run time. By setting the value to 1 (Fixed Single), a thin, black rectangular border appears around the label.

The BackStyle property specifies whether objects behind the label are visible. The default value is 1 (Opaque), which prevents objects behind the label from showing through. If you change the value to 0 (Transparent), any background object, such as a picture, shows through the label.

The BackColor and ForeColor properties specify the colors for the label background and the caption text, respectively. At design time, you can specify values for these properties with the Properties window and the Color Palette. At run time, you must specify these property values with the hexadecimal numbers that correspond to your desired colors.

NOTE Visual Basic provides a file named CONSTANT.TXT which contains predefined constants for several values, including the hexadecimal ones for several colors. For example, after loading CONSTANT.TXT into your application, you can give `Label1` a green background with the following instruction:

```
Label1.BackColor = GREEN
```

For more information on the CONSTANT.TXT file, see Chapter 14, "Language Building Blocks."

The `FontName`, `FontSize`, `FontBold`, `FontItalic`, `FontStrikeThru`, and `FontUnderline` properties specify the appearance of the caption text. The `FontName` and `FontSize` properties determine the typeface and size of the caption text, respectively. At design time, use the Properties window to view a list of fonts available on your system. For more information on specific fonts and type-faces, see Chapter 12, "Displaying Text and Fonts."

NOTE ### Choosing *FontName* and *FontSize*

Under Windows, individual computer systems can have different sets of available screen fonts. Several font sources exist, ranging from Windows itself to various word processors to third-party vendors. When developing Visual Basic applications which can be run on different computers, it's a good idea to limit your choices to the standard fonts and sizes that ship with Windows.

If you specify an unknown `FontName`, Visual Basic tries to substitute the closest match. The result can be fuzzy-looking text, however, and eyestrain for your users. In program code, you can use the `FontCount` and `Fonts` properties to identify the fonts available in the computer system. For more information on these properties, see Chapter 12, "Displaying Text and Fonts."

The `FontBold`, `FontItalic`, `FontStrikeThru`, and `FontUnderline` properties determine various attributes of the caption text. If you set the value of any of these properties to True, the caption text retains that attribute. For example, the following instruction makes the caption text of `Label1` appear in italic:

```
Label1.FontItalic = True
```

By default, the value of `FontBold` is True. The other three properties are False by default.

Adding Labels to the Sample Application

The BOOK application (introduced earlier in the chapter) has seven different labels. Now it's time to start adding the controls. Begin by placing the seven labels on the form. By default, Visual Basic names these labels Label1 through Label7.

Using the Properties window, modify the property values for these labels as Table 8.3 shows. Notice that you modify each label's Name property to create descriptive names. As mentioned earlier in the chapter, the lbl prefix is used for each label name. For example, you change the name of the first label from Label1 to lblTitle.

 Remember that you can access the Properties window for each label by first clicking the label, then pressing F4.

Table 8.3. Label properties for the BOOK application.

Default Name	Property	Value
Label1	Alignment	2 'Center
	BackColor	&H00FFFF00& 'Lt Blue from the palette
	BorderStyle	1 'Fixed Single
	Caption	Do It Yourself Bookstore
	FontName	MS Serif
	FontSize	18
	ForeColor	&H00000080&
	Height	435
	Left	960
	Name	lblTitle
	Top	120
	Width	4320
Label2	Alignment	2 'Center
	AutoSize	True
	Caption	Time Display
	Height	195

continues

Table 8.3. Continued

Default Name	Property	Value
	Left	5640
	Name	lblTime
	Top	240
	Width	1095
Label3	Caption	Name:
	Height	255
	Left	120
	Name	lblName
	Top	960
	Width	735
Label4	Caption	Books:
	Height	255
	Left	120
	Name	lblBooks
	Top	1440
	Width	615
Label5	Caption	Comments:
	FontItalic	True
	Height	255
	Left	120
	Name	lblComment
	Top	4080
	Width	1215
Label6	Alignment	2 'Center
	Caption	Delivery In:
	FontUnderline	True
	Height	255
	Left	6360
	Name	lblDelivery
	Top	3840
	Width	1455

Default Name	Property	Value
Label7	Alignment	2 'Center
	Caption	'set to a blank string
	Height	255
	Left	6120
	Name	lblDate
	Top	4200
	Width	1935

After setting the properties for the seven labels, your form should resemble Figure 8.3.

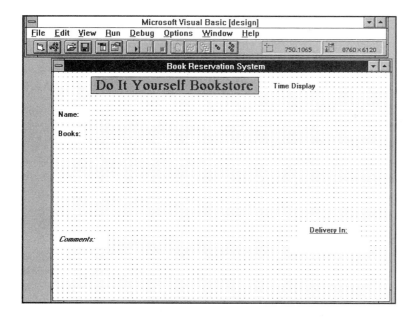

Figure 8.3.

The form for the Book Reservation System with labels added.

Additional Label Properties

Labels have some additional properties. The Index property has meaning if the label appears in a control array. For more information on Index and control arrays, see Chapter 7, "Writing Event Procedures."

The DragIcon and DragMode properties determine the behavior of the label when the control is dragged and dropped. For more information on dragging and dropping, see Chapter 22, "Responding to Mouse Events."

The LinkItem, LinkMode, LinkTimeout, and LinkTopic properties have meaning when the label is part of a Dynamic Data Exchange (DDE) conversation. For more information on these properties, see Chapter 30, "Using Dynamic Data Exchange (DDE)."

Events of the Label Control

Labels usually display headings, so you generally don't write event procedures for label controls. A label can respond, however, to the following events: Change, Click, DblClick, DragDrop, DragOver, LinkClose, LinkError, LinkNotify, LinkOpen, MouseDown, MouseMove, and MouseUp.

The Change event occurs whenever the caption of a label changes. As the user cannot directly modify the caption at run time, this event triggers when a label caption is changed within code. The Click event occurs when the user clicks a label. DblClick occurs when the user double-clicks.

The MouseDown, MouseMove, and MouseUp events respond to mouse activity when the pointer is over the label. For more information on these mouse events, see Chapter 22, "Responding to Mouse Events."

The Link events have meaning in Dynamic Data Exchange applications. For more information on these events, see Chapter 30, "Using Dynamic Data Exchange (DDE)."

The Text Box Control

Similar to a label, the text box control displays text. Unlike a label, however, the text in this type of box *can* be directly modified by the user at run time. The primary purpose of most text boxes is to provide a mechanism for the user to type necessary input while an application is running.

Properties of the Text Box Control

Unlike labels, text boxes don't have the Caption property. Instead, the Text property determines the current string value displayed in a text box. At run time, the user can click on a text box and begin typing text. To reflect the current contents of the text box, Visual Basic automatically updates the value of the text box's Text property.

By default, Visual Basic assigns the name of the text box to the Text property. For example, the default value of the Text property for the first text box is Text1. At design time, you can specify a new value for the Text property.

That value appears in the text box when the application starts. You usually set the `Text` property to an empty string at design time.

You can manipulate the appearance of a text box with the same properties used for labels: `Height`, `Width`, `Left`, and `Top` properties for size and placement; `BackColor` and `ForeColor` for background and text colors; `Alignment` for the text justification; `FontName`, `FontSize`, `FontBold`, `FontItalic`, `FontStrikeThru`, and `FontUnderline` for the text attributes, and `BorderStyle` for a visible border around the box. For text boxes (unlike labels), the default value of `BorderStyle` is `1` (Fixed Single), which produces a thin line around the box.

The `MultiLine` property is unique to the text box. When this property's value is True, and the user-typed text reaches the right border of the text box, it automatically wraps text onto multiple lines. When False (the default value), the text is restricted to a single line.

The `ScrollBars` property determines whether the text box displays scroll bars. The default value is `0`, which means that no scroll bars appear on the text box. Other values are `1` (horizontal scroll bars), `2` (vertical scroll bars), and `3` (both scroll bars). You typically set the value of `ScrollBars` to `2` or `3` when `MultiLine` is True.

The `ScrollBars` property lets you create a text box with a fixed size and position on the form, yet accept sizable text from the user. For example, by setting the value of `ScrollBars` to `1`, the user can type text past the right edge of the control. The text box scrolls horizontally to accommodate every new character. With both vertical scrolling and `MultiLine` enabled, typed text that reaches the right edge of the text box wraps down to the next line.

Adding Text Boxes to the Sample Application

The sample application has two text boxes. One is for the customer name, and the other for comments. The comments text box uses the `MultiLine` and `ScrollBars` properties.

To continue the BOOK application, add the two text boxes to the form. Visual Basic assigns these controls the default names `Text1` and `Text2`. Using the Properties window, assign the property values that Table 8.4 shows.

Table 8.4. Text box properties for the BOOK application.

Default Name	Property	Value
Text1	Height	285
	Left	1200

continues

Table 8.4. Continued

Default Name	Property	Value
	Name	txtName
	Text	(blank) 'set to empty string
	Top	960
	Width	4455
Text2	Height	975
	Left	240
	MultiLine	True
	Name	txtComment
	ScrollBars	2 'Vertical
	Text	(blank) 'set to empty string
	Top	4560
	Width	4815

Figure 8.4 shows how your form should now appear.

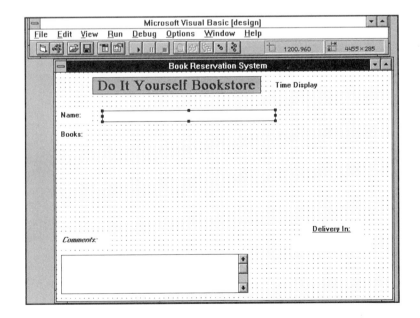

Figure 8.4.

The Book Reservation
System with text boxes.

Unique Properties of Text Boxes

The MaxLength property is unique to text boxes. This property establishes a maximum character length for the Text property of the text box. If the user tries to type additional text, or if the code attempts to assign a longer value than permitted, the excess characters are truncated. The default value is 0, which signifies that no maximum text length is established.

The MaxLength property is useful when you expect the user to type a fixed number of characters in a text box. For example, suppose the user is to input a postal ZIP code. Then you could set MaxLength to 5. If the user tries to type more than five characters, Visual Basic beeps the speaker, and doesn't accept the additional input.

Another unique property of a text box is PasswordChar. This property masks the contents of a text box, so that one particular character (usually an asterisk) displays instead of the one actually typed. The value of this property is the string character used for the mask. The value of the text box's Text property is *not* affected by the value of PasswordChar.

The final property unique to text boxes is HideSelection. When the focus on the text box is lost, this property determines whether its selected text remains highlighted. The default value is True, which specifies that selected text is deselected when the text box loses the focus. If you set the value of HideSelection to False, however, selected text remains highlighted, regardless of which control has the focus.

Other Properties of Text Boxes

By default, when the mouse pointer is over a text box, the pointer shape changes to the I-Beam. By clicking the left mouse button, the I-Beam acts as a text insertion point—the text cursor moves to the location of the I-Beam. You can use the MousePointer property of the text box to change the pointer shape.

As in other controls, the Index property is pertinent if the text box is part of a control array (see Chapter 7, "Writing Event Procedures").

With the SelLength, SelStart, and SelText properties, you manipulate which text is selected (highlighted) in the text box. These properties are not available in the Properties window at design time. You can use these properties only in program code at run time.

The SelLength, SelStart, and SelText properties are especially useful when the text box interacts with the Windows Clipboard. For more information on the Clipboard, see Chapter 29, "Manipulating the Windows Environment."

The DragIcon, DragMode, LinkItem, LinkMode, LinkTimeout, and LinkTopic properties operate for the text box control just as they do for the label control described previously.

Events of the Text Box Control

The main event for text boxes is the Change event. This event occurs anytime the value of the Text property is modified. The change can come when the user types text, or when the program code modifies the value of the Text property.

The Change event procedure has many uses. Often, the contents of a text box are linked to a variable or to a particular property value in another control.

For example, suppose an ordering application for a clothes manufacturer has a text box designed for the user to indicate the number of shirts to be purchased. A label displays the total cost of the order. The code for the text box's Change event can determine the size of the order from the box's Text property. The number ordered is multiplied by the unit cost to determine the price of the entire order. To display the total cost in the label, you update its Caption property. All this code can be placed in the text box's Change procedure.

The GotFocus and LostFocus events trigger when the text box gets the focus or loses it, respectively. For a text box, GotFocus occurs when the user tabs to or clicks in it. LostFocus occurs when the user tabs away from the text box, or clicks another control. You see a blinking cursor in the text box when it has the focus.

Text boxes respond to KeyDown, KeyUp, and KeyPress events. These events occur when the user presses a key while the text box has the focus. For more about these events, see Chapter 23, "Responding to Keyboard Events."

In addition, text boxes support the DragDrop and DropOver events discussed in Chapter 22, "Responding to Mouse Events," and the DDE-related Link events discussed in Chapter 30, "Using Dynamic Data Exchange (DDE)."

The Picture Box Control

A picture box acts as a container for a graphics image. The image can be a bitmap, icon, or metafile stored in a disk file. Also, a picture box can display output from graphics methods such as Line and Circle as well as text created with the Print method. Further, a picture box can contain other controls, such as option buttons, and shape and line controls.

Properties of the Picture Box Control

When a picture box displays an image, the Picture property specifies the name of the graphics file. The picture box can display graphics files in bitmap, icon, or metafile format. Such file names typically have .BMP, .ICO, and .WMF extensions, respectively.

At design time, you use the Properties window to set the value of Picture to the desired graphics file. At run time, you set a value for Picture with the LoadPicture function. For example, the following instruction loads a bitmap file into the Picture1 control:

```
Picture1.Picture = LoadPicture("C:\WINDOWS\CARS.BMP")
```

 NOTE When you assign Picture at design time, a copy of the image is saved with the form. As a result, you can run the saved .FRM file on any computer, even one without the original graphics file. The desired image is going to be there. If you compile the application to an executable (.EXE file), the image is included. (For more information on creating executable files, see Chapter 9, "Managing Projects.")

On the other hand, if you set Picture at run time with the LoadPicture function, the application must have access to the graphics file to display the image. If you compile the application to an executable file, the image is not stored in the .EXE file. To successfully display the image, the graphics file must be available in the host computer at run time.

A trade-off is involved here. By assigning Picture at design time, you no longer need access to the original graphics file. The sizes of the saved .FRM and .EXE files, however, are relatively large. If you assign Picture at run time, the graphics file must be present, but the sizes of the saved .FRM and .EXE files are substantially smaller.

The BackColor property specifies the background color of the control. ForeColor specifies the color of any text displayed in the control in connection with the Print method. Text attributes can be set also with the FontName, FontSize, FontBold, FontItalic, FontStrikeThru, and FontUnderline properties.

The picture box has a FontTransparent property. If the value of FontTransparent is True, the contents of the picture box show through the text. If False, the text obscures any background graphics.

By default, the extra portions of the graphics image are clipped if it is larger than the picture box. If you set the value of the AutoSize property to True, however, the picture box automatically resizes to display the entire image.

The BorderStyle and MousePointer properties are available to specify a border, or to change the shape of the pointer when the mouse is over the picture box.

Adding a Picture Box to the Sample Application

For the sample application, a picture box displays the logo of Do It Yourself Bookstore. This logo depicts several books on a shelf. The file containing the logo ships with Visual Basic as an .ICO file.

To add the logo to the application, follow these steps:

1. Place a picture box on the form.

2. Using the Properties window, assign the property values that Table 8.5 shows.

Table 8.5. Picture box properties for the BOOK application.

Default Name	Property	Value
Picture1	AutoSize	True
	Left	240
	Name	picLogo
	Top	120

3. Double-click the Picture property in the Properties window.

   The Load Picture dialog box pops open.

4. Specify the C:\VB\ICONS\WRITING\BOOKS03.ICO file.

   (Your system might have the BOOKS03.ICO file stored in a different directory. If so, use the Windows File Manager to search for this file, then specify the appropriate file path in the Properties window.)

Your form should now resemble Figure 8.5. Notice the picture box with the book logo in the upper left corner of the figure.

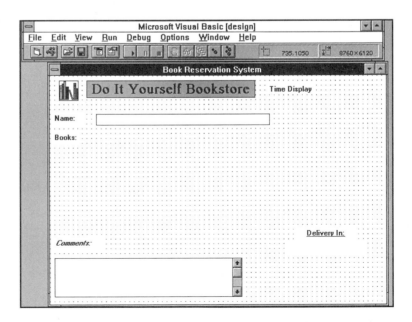

Figure 8.5.

The Book Reservation System with the picture box.

Additional Properties of a Picture Box

The `Align` property is unique to the picture box. When the value of this property is `0` (the default), the picture box appears on the form at the location determined by its `Height`, `Width`, `Left`, and `Top` properties.

When `Align` is `1`, however, the picture box moves to the top of the form, and expands horizontally over its entire width. Similarly, when `Align` is `2`, the picture box moves to the bottom of the form, and expands horizontally. You typically use `Align` to create a picture box which acts as a toolbar at the top of the form, or a status bar at the bottom.

The `hWnd` and `hDC` properties identify the picture box and its device context to the Windows environment. These properties are used in specialized situations with applications that make direct function calls to Windows. For more information on directly interacting with Windows, see Chapter 29, "Manipulating the Windows Environment."

The `Index`, `Tag`, `DragIcon`, `DragMode`, `LinkItem`, `LinkMode`, `LinkTimeout`, and `LinkTopic` properties work as discussed previously in this chapter.

The picture box has several properties that are used when the control acts as a container for graphics. The `AutoRedraw` property determines whether the graphics image is redrawn when the picture box has been temporarily hidden by another window, and subsequently re-exposed. Similarly, the `ClipControls` property determines whether graphics methods used in a picture box are entirely repainted, or just the newly exposed regions.

The `ScaleHeight`, `ScaleWidth`, `ScaleLeft`, `ScaleTop`, and `ScaleMode` properties determine the measuring units and drawing style inside a picture box. You can use these properties to create a custom coordinate system, or measure in units other than twips.

The `CurrentX` and `CurrentY` properties specify the current horizontal and vertical coordinates of the drawing pen. These properties specify where in the control the next drawing method begins. These properties are not available from the Properties window at design time but can be referenced in program code at run time.

The `DrawMode` property indicates the type of drawing tool used when creating graphics with the Visual Basic drawing controls, such as Shape and Line, or the graphics methods, such as `Circle`. The `DrawStyle` and `DrawWidth` properties specify the style and width of the drawn line, respectively. When two-dimensional shapes are created, the `FillColor` and `FillStyle` properties specify the color and pattern used inside the shape, respectively.

For more information on creating graphics, and related properties, see Chapter 11, "Displaying Graphics."

Events of the Picture Box Control

The Paint event is unique to picture boxes. (Paint is defined for forms, but not for any other control.) The Paint event triggers when part or all of a picture box is reexposed after it is hidden by another window. If the value of AutoRedraw is set to True, repainting and redrawing are automatic, so you usually don't need to write code for any Paint events.

Another event unique to picture boxes (and forms) is Resize. This event occurs whenever the size of the picture box changes.

For picture boxes, the Change event occurs whenever the Picture property changes (or a DDE link is updated).

Although this happens infrequently, a picture box can respond to the following events: Click, DblClick, GotFocus, LostFocus, MouseDown, MouseMove, MouseUp, KeyDown, KeyUp, KeyPress, DragDrop, DragOver, LinkClose, LinkError, LinkNotify, and LinkOpen.

A limitation to using the Click and DblClick events with picture boxes exists— the picture box does not respond with any visual cue when clicked. (Note that many other controls do offer visual cues. For example, a command button appears pushed when clicked.) Of course, you can add code to a Click or DblClick event to change the Picture property when a picture box is clicked.

 NOTE The Professional Edition of Visual Basic comes with several custom controls which are designed to display graphics and otherwise provide visual cues when clicked (or when other events occur). For more information about such controls, see Chapter 32, "Using Custom Controls."

The Frame Control

The Frame control acts as a container for other controls, typically option buttons or check boxes. When option buttons are placed in a frame, those buttons are mutually exclusive. If one such button is selected by the user, Visual Basic automatically deselects the others in the frame.

To group controls in a frame, you must first place the frame onto the form. Then you place the controls inside the frame. As such, you cannot place a control inside a frame by double-clicking the control icon in the Toolbox.

Instead, you must click the control icon in the Toolbox, then move the mouse pointer into the frame. Press the left mouse button, and drag the pointer over a region of the frame. Then release the button.

Once you have controls placed in a frame, they are fixed relative to it. If you move the frame, the controls move with it. When you place a control inside a frame, the control's `Left` and `Top` properties are specified relative to the upper left corner of the frame.

The Properties of the Frame Control

A frame appears as a rectangular border with a caption near the top. The `Caption` property specifies the caption text. Although most captions are short, you can have one up to 255 characters (any excess characters are truncated). The caption appears along the top border of the frame, beginning near its upper left corner.

A frame also has `BackColor`, `ForeColor`, `FontName`, `FontSize`, `FontBold`, `FontItalic`, `FontStrikeThru`, and `FontUnderline` properties. The `DragIcon` and `DragMode` properties affect dragging and dropping the frame, and the `hWnd` property tracks it for the Windows environment.

As with a picture box, a frame has a `ClipControls` property. This property determines what happens when a frame is covered by another window, and subsequently re-exposed. If the value of `ClipControls` is True (the default), the entire frame is repainted when the control is re-exposed. If False, only the affected portion of the frame is repainted. If you place graphics in a frame, set the value of `ClipControls` to False—this generally saves execution time.

Adding a Frame to the Sample Application

For the sample application, the user indicates the payment method by clicking the appropriate option button. The option buttons are grouped in a frame control. In this section, you add the frame to the application. (Another section, later in the chapter, discusses adding the option buttons.)

Place a frame onto the form. The default name for the frame is `Frame1`. Using the Properties window, assign the property values that Table 8.6 shows.

Table 8.6. Frame properties for the BOOK application.

Default Name	Property	Value
Frame1	Caption	Payment Method
	Height	1935
	Left	6120
	Name	fraPayment
	Top	1680
	Width	2175

Figure 8.6 shows the form after the frame control is added.

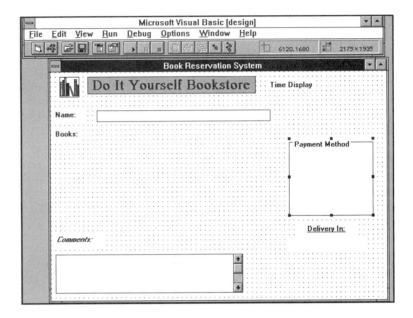

Figure 8.6.

The Book Reservation
System with the frame.

Events of the Frame Control

A frame acts as a container for other controls, so the frame itself does not respond to many events. Instead, action in a frame is usually centered in one of the enclosed controls.

The frame does, however, support the following events: Click, DblClick, DragDrop, DragOver, MouseDown, MouseUp, and MouseMove. By writing code for the DragDrop and DragOver events, you allow the user to drag and drop the frame to a new location on the form.

The Option Button Control

An option button appears as a little circle with a text description alongside it. When the option is selected, a black dot appears in the circle. When it is not selected, no dot appears. An option button displays a choice which the user can select at run time. By clicking the option button, the user toggles the dot on or off.

Typically, several option buttons are grouped together to represent mutually exclusive choices. One button in the group is always selected. When the user selects a different one in the group, Visual Basic automatically deselects the previously selected button.

In Windows applications, dialog boxes often present a group of option buttons to display multiple choices. The user must select one choice. For example, Visual Basic's Print dialog box uses two option buttons for you to specify whether you want to print the Current Form or All Forms.

All option buttons you place directly on a form are considered part of a single group. You can select only one such option button at any time. As mentioned, you can group option buttons by placing them in a frame. All option buttons placed in a frame are considered to be one separate group. A form can have several frames, with each one housing a group of option buttons.

Generally, you display a group of option buttons vertically. At run time, Visual Basic selects the first option button you placed in the group (you can change this default in your program code). As a rule, you should place option buttons from the top down, with the uppermost button representing the one the user most likely selects.

The Properties of the Option Button Control

You can specify the state of an option button with the Value property. When Value is set to True, the button is selected. When Value is False, the button is deselected. Keep in mind that anytime you set a button's Value property to True, Visual Basic automatically sets Value to False for the other option buttons in the group.

Use the Caption property to specify the text title that appears alongside the button. The caption can contain as many as 255 characters, with additional ones truncated. The title can appear either to the left or right of the button, as determined by the value of the Alignment property. The default value is 0, which specifies that the title appears to the right of the button. If you change the value of Alignment to 1, the text appears to the left.

Option buttons also have the standard appearance properties: BackColor, ForeColor, FontName, FontSize, FontBold, FontItalic, FontStrikeThru, and FontUnderline. The DragIcon, DragMode, and hWnd properties also are available.

Adding Option Buttons to the Sample Application

With option buttons, the user of the BOOK application can select a payment method. The available payment options are Cash, Bill later (net 10 days), and Charge.

Place three option buttons into the frame. You must individually drag each button from the Toolbox onto the frame. Visual Basic assigns Option1, Option2, and Option3 as the default names for these buttons. Using the Properties window, assign the property values that Table 8.7 shows.

Table 8.7. Option button properties for the BOOK application.

Default Name	Property	Value
Option1	Caption	Cash on Receipt
	Height	375
	Left	150
	Name	optCash
	Top	250
	Value	True
	Width	2000
Option2	Caption	Net 10 Days
	Height	375
	Left	150
	Name	optNet
	Top	600
	Width	2000
Option3	Caption	Charge
	Height	375
	Left	150
	Name	optCharge
	Top	960
	Width	2000

Figure 8.7 shows the form after the option buttons are added.

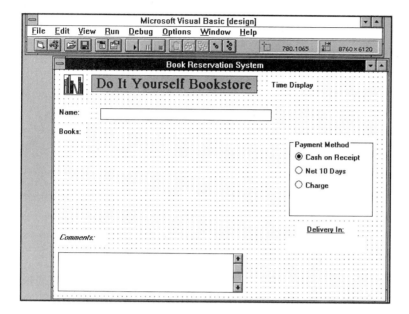

Figure 8.7.

The sample application
with the option buttons in
place.

Option Button Events

Option buttons respond to the following events: Click, DblClick, GotFocus, LostFocus, KeyDown, KeyPress, KeyUp, DragDrop, DragOver, MouseDown, MouseMove, and MouseUp.

For option buttons, you most often use Click procedures to respond when the user clicks one of the buttons. As described later in this chapter, the sample application uses Click events for the option buttons to set property values for other controls.

The Check Box Control

A check box is similar to an option button in that the user can make a choice by selecting an option. A check box appears as a little square with a text caption alongside it. When a check box is selected, an X appears inside the square. When the check box is deselected, the square appears empty.

The major functional difference between check boxes and option buttons is that check boxes do not present mutually exclusive choices. When grouped, the user can select any, all, or none of the check boxes. For example, a text editor can contain check boxes for Italic, Bold, and Underline. The user can select these options in any combination, including none of the options and all of the options.

Properties of the Check Box Control

Similar to an option button, the state of a check box is represented with the `Value` property. `Value` works differently, however, with a check box than it does with an option button. For a check box, `Value` can be 0, 1, or 2. When `Value` is 0 (the default), the check box is deselected, and the square appears empty. When `Value` is 1, the check box is selected, and an ✕ appears inside the square. When `Value` is 2, the control appears gray or dimmed. You can set `Value` to 2 to signal the user that the option presented in the check box is not currently available.

Other than the difference in the `Value` property, a check box has the same set of properties as does an option button: `Alignment`, `BackColor`, `Caption`, `DragIcon`, `DragMode`, `FontBold`, `FontItalic`, `FontName`, `FontSize`, `FontStrikeThru`, `FontUnderline`, `ForeColor`, and `hWnd`.

Adding a Check Box to the Sample Application

Regular customers of the Do It Yourself Bookstore have favored customer status. Such customers can charge purchases to a company charge account, and get faster delivery. The form for the BOOK application includes a check box which indicates whether the customer making the current purchase has favored status.

Place a check box onto the form. The default name for this control is `Check1`. Using the Properties window, assign the property values that Table 8.8 shows.

Table 8.8. Check box properties for the BOOK application.

Default Name	Property	Value
Check1	Caption	Favored Customer
	Height	255
	Left	6240
	Name	chkFavored
	Top	960
	Value	1 'Checked
	Width	1935

Figure 8.8 shows the form after the check box is added.

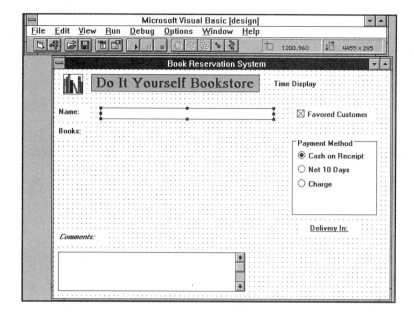

Figure 8.8.

The Book Reservation System with the Favored Customer check box.

Check Box Events

As with option buttons, the primary event used with check boxes is Click.
Unlike an option button, a check box does not respond to a DblClick event.
With that exception, check boxes and option buttons respond to the same
additional events: DragDrop, DragOver, GotFocus, LostFocus, KeyDown, KeyPress,
KeyUp, MouseDown, MouseMove, and MouseUp.

Controls for Both the List Box and Combo Box

A list box displays a list of items from which the user makes a selection. To
select one of the items, the user clicks it. The user also can press the up and
down arrow keys to move the highlight from one item to another. Usually, a
list box is more appropriate than a group of option buttons when the number
of items is four or more.

A combo box combines the attributes of both a text and a list box. This control
contains an edit area in which the user can type data, as well as a list box
which displays a list of items. You typically use a combo box when the user

must supply a piece of information, and the application can suggest some possible values. The user can either select an item from the list, or type a value in the edit area. The currently selected item in the list appears in the edit area of the combo box.

List and combo boxes automatically add scroll bars if the number of list items exceeds the size of the control. At run time, the user can maneuver through the list of items using the scroll bars.

Visual Basic provides three different styles of combo boxes: simple combo, drop-down combo, and drop-down list. The simple combo box displays an edit area with an attached list box immediately below.

The drop-down combo box first appears as a text edit area, with a down arrow to the right. The list portion stays hidden until the user clicks the down arrow to drop the list portion. The user can either select a value (from the list), or type one into the edit area.

The drop-down list style turns the combo box into a drop-down list box. At run time, the control appears as the drop-down combo box. The user can click the down arrow to see the list drop. The difference is that the edit area in a drop-down list box is disabled. The user can only select one of the list's items, and cannot type a value into the edit area. This area, however, does display the item currently selected in the list.

Figure 8.9 shows an example of a list box on the left, and a simple combo box on the right. Each box lists the same six cards in a baseball card collection. The combo box includes an edit area in which the user can type in a value. The list box presents only fixed options.

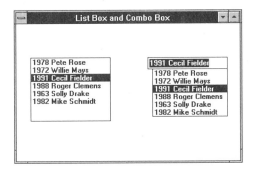

Figure 8.9.

Sample list box and combo box.

Choosing between a List Box or a Combo Box

To choose between either type of box, a list or a combo box, ask yourself how much form space is available for the control, and what features it must provide. The following are some questions that can help you decide:

■ How much space is available for the list?

A drop-down combo box initially requires only a single line of space on the form. As such, combo boxes are space efficient. (Of course, the box expands when the user drops down the list portion.) Initially, a list box requires more space to accommodate its items.

■ Do you want the user to be able to type a choice instead of just selecting from a list?

If the user might have to type a value not available from the list, a combo box is, of course, your only option. Keep in mind that many users adept at typing prefer to keep their hands on the keyboard. Such users prefer to type items, even when their desired item appears in the list. The combo box is the only option that provides this flexibility.

■ Do you want a multicolumn list?

A list box can display items in a multiple-column format with horizontal scrolling. Combo boxes cannot display multicolumn lists.

■ Does the user need to choose more than one item from the list?

A list box can support multiple items selected simultaneously. Using a combo box, the user can select only one item from the list portion. Figure 8.10 shows a list box with four names selected at once.

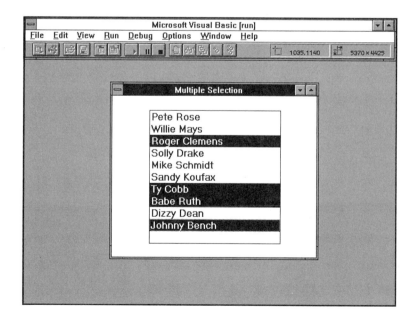

Figure 8.10.

A list box with four names selected simultaneously.

Methods for Both the List Boxes and Combo Boxes

When discussing both the list and combo boxes, it's important to mention the special methods used with these controls. With the AddItem and RemoveItem methods, you add and remove items from the list portion of these controls, respectively.

You cannot add list items at design time. Instead, you must use the AddItem method in program code at run time. For most applications, you want the list items loaded when the application starts. To do so, you use AddItem instructions in the Form_Load procedure.

 **NOTE** As explained in the next chapter, Visual Basic triggers the Form_Load procedure when an application begins. As such, you can place program code in this procedure to initialize the form, variables, and property values not set at design time. For controls for both list and combo boxes, you often place AddItem instructions in the Form_Load procedure.

The syntax for the AddItem method is as follows:

```
List1.AddItem "January"
List1.AddItem "February"
List1.AddItem "March"
List1.AddItem "April"
```

Here, List1 is the name of a list box control. These instructions populate the list box with the names of the first four months. Each successive instruction adds a new item to the end of the current list.

You can place an item in the middle of the current list by including an optional parameter at the end of the instruction. This parameter has an integer value, and specifies the place in the list at which the new item should be inserted. For example, the following instruction inserts a new item between February and March:

```
List1.AddItem "Here I am", 2
```

Visual Basic considers the first item in the list to have an index value of 0. As specified in this instruction, index 2, therefore, indicates that the new item becomes the third one in the list. When you place a new item in the list, Visual Basic automatically adjusts the other items to accommodate the insertion.

To remove an item from a list, use the RemoveItem method. The syntax specifies the index number of the item you want to remove. For example, the following instruction removes the fourth item (index number 3) from the list portion of a combo box Combo1:

```
Combo1.RemoveItem 3
```

You can remove all items in a list with the `Clear` method. For example, the following instruction removes all items from the list box `List1`:

```
List1.Clear
```

Properties of the Controls for Both the List Boxes and Combo Boxes

The `Sorted` property is unique to both list and combo boxes. When `Sorted` is True, Visual Basic sorts list items alphabetically. When `Sorted` is False (the default), list items appear in the order specified with the `AddItem` instructions.

List and Combo boxes support the following properties: `BackColor`, `DragIcon`, `DragMode`, `FontName`, `FontSize`, `FontBold`, `FontItalic`, `FontStrikeThru`, `FontUnderline`, `ForeColor`, and `hWnd`.

The `ListIndex`, `List`, `ListCount`, `NewIndex`, and `ItemData` properties help with list management. These property values are available only at run time.

The `ListIndex` property specifies the index number for the currently selected item. If the list has no items, the value of this property is `-1`. The `List` property acts as a string array which specifies the actual contents of a list item. For example, the value of `Combo1.List(2)` is the third list item in the combo box `Combo1`.

The `ListCount` property indicates the total number of items stored in a list. The `NewIndex` property specifies the index number of the item most recently added to the list.

The final List property is `ItemData`. This property is set up as an array containing the same number of values as the `List` property. With `ItemData`, you can assign a specialized tracking number that corresponds to each list item. For example, you could use `ItemData` to store the number of employees in each department listed for a large company.

For combo boxes, the `Text` property specifies the text in the edit area. For list boxes, the `Text` property specifies the currently selected item.

Specialized List Box Properties

List boxes have four properties not available with combo boxes: `Selected`, `TopIndex`, `Columns`, and `MultiSelect`. The `Columns` and `MultiSelect` properties are available at run time in program code and at design time in the Properties window. The `Selected` and `TopIndex` properties are available only at run time.

For any list, the Selected property specifies whether a given list item is selected. If Selected is True, the item is selected. If Selected is False, the item is not currently selected. The property uses an array syntax. For example, the following instruction specifies that the first item in the List1 list box should be selected:

```
List1.Selected(0) = True
```

The TopIndex property specifies the index number of the item you want to appear at the top of the list.

A list box can display items in multiple columns. The value of the Columns property determines how many columns are displayed and how scrolling works. If the value of Columns is 0 (the default), the list box has a single column, and vertical scrolling is enabled.

If the value of Columns is 1 or more, the value indicates the number of columns displayed. In these cases, horizontal scrolling is enabled.

A list box can let the user select more than one item from the list. The value of the MultiSelect property determines the multiselection capability. When MultiSelect is 0 (the default), multiple selection is disabled. When MultiSelect is 1, you can select multiple items by clicking each desired item individually. When MultiSelect is 2, multiple items can be selected in groups.

Specialized Combo Box Properties

The following properties exist for a combo box, but not for a list box: Style, SelLength, SelStart, and SelText.

Recall that Visual Basic supports three types of combo boxes. You use the Style property to designate which of the three a combo box should be. The value 0 (the default) designates a drop-down combo box. This style has an edit area and a drop-down list. The value 1 specifies a simple combo box that has an edit area and a list which remains displayed. Finally, the value 2 designates a drop-down list. This form turns the combo box into a drop-down list box.

When Style is 0 or 1, the user can select from the list, or type a value in the edit area. When Style is 2, the edit area is disabled for typing, and the user must choose an item from the supplied list.

The SelLength, SelStart, and SelText properties work with selected text in the same way for both combo and text boxes.

Adding Both a List Box and Combo Box to the Sample Application

The sample application contains a list box to hold the available book titles, and a combo box placed in the frame to hold the charge account possibilities.

To add these controls to the sample application, follow these steps:

1. Place a list box control on the form. Visual Basic assigns the default name List1 to this control.

2. Place a combo box inside the frame. The default name for this control is Combo1.

3. Using the Properties window, assign the property values that Table 8.9 shows.

Table 8.9. Properties for both list boxes and combo boxes for the BOOK application.

Default Name	Property	Value
List1	Columns	2
	Height	1785
	Left	120
	MultiSelect	2 'Extended
	Name	lstBooks
	Sorted	True
	Top	1800
	Width	5655
Combo1	Enabled	False
	Height	300
	Left	360
	Name	cboCharge
	Text	Bookstore
	Top	1440
	Width	1695

At this point, the lists for both the list and combo boxes do not contain any items. As explained later in the chapter, you add program code to supply these lists at run time.

The form for the application should now resemble Figure 8.11.

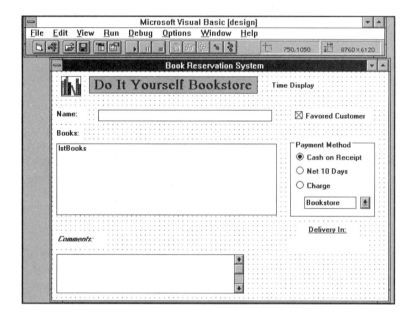

Figure 8.11.

The Book Reservation System with both a list and a combo box added.

Events of Both the List Boxes and Combo Boxes

Both a list and a combo box respond to the following events: `Click`, `DblClick`, `DragDrop`, `DragOver`, `GotFocus`, `LostFocus`, `KeyDown`, `KeyUp`, and `KeyPress`.

The list box also responds to `MouseDown`, `MouseUp`, and `MouseMove` events.

The combo box responds to a `Change` event, which occurs whenever the user types anything in the edit area (or the contents of the edit area are modified in code). The `DropDown` event is unique to combo boxes. This event occurs when the arrow to the right of the edit area is clicked to drop down the list portion of the control.

Scroll Bar Controls

Scroll bars are familiar to users of Windows applications. Windows itself supplies scroll bars so that the user can specify such settings as the cursor blink rate in the Window Control Panel. Scroll bars are most frequently employed to let the user move window contents to bring into view a portion temporarily outside the visible region.

In Visual Basic, scroll bar controls consist of a bar with arrows at each end. Between these arrows is a square scroll box. The scroll box slides along the scroll shaft between the two arrows. You can create both horizontal and vertical scroll bars.

A scroll bar control can be employed as a user input device to specify a value within a prescribed range. By moving the scroll box between the two arrows, the user can specify a value in an intuitive, visual manner. The scroll bar acts as a sliding input device, somewhat similar to the analog slides on professional audio equipment.

 **NOTE** Don't confuse a scroll bar control with the scroll bars that Visual Basic automatically adds to other controls. A scroll bar control is just that—a full-fledged control that you can select from the Toolbox and place directly on a form. By contrast, Visual Basic sometimes adds scroll bars to other controls. For example, when the display of the control's contents requires more space than that allocated for the list box, it has a scroll bar.

To work with a scroll bar control, you must understand the parts of the bar, and their purposes. The scroll box on the scroll shaft indicates the current value specified by the bar. When the user clicks the arrow at either end of the scroll bar, the scroll box moves an incremental unit toward that arrow. When the user clicks the scroll shaft somewhere between an arrow and the scroll box, it moves a larger incremental unit toward the click position. Furthermore, with the mouse, the user can directly drag the scroll box along the shaft.

Properties of the Scroll Bars

For any scroll bar, you must determine the range of values that the control can designate. Scroll bars always specify integer numbers. The smallest permissible value is -32,768, and the largest, 32,767.

The Min and Max properties are unique to scroll bars. Min specifies the smallest value that the scroll bar can represent, while Max specifies the largest. For example, if a scroll bar indicates a temperature scale in degrees Fahrenheit, you might set Min to 32, and Max to 212. The default values for Min and Max are 0 and 32,767, respectively.

For scroll bars, the Value property specifies the current value represented by the scroll bar. The position of the scroll box along the scroll shaft graphically reflects where Value lies between Min and Max. If the user moves the scroll box, the Value property adjusts appropriately. Similarly, if you modify Value in program code, Visual Basic moves the scroll box to the appropriate position.

The SmallChange property indicates how much Value changes when the user clicks one of the arrows at the end of the scroll bar. Similarly, LargeChange indicates how much Value changes when the user clicks the scroll shaft between the scroll box and one of the arrows. The default value for both properties is 1.

You can set values for the scroll bar properties at design time, or in program code. For the temperature example mentioned in this section, here is the program code you might use to initialize a vertical scroll bar named VScroll1:

```
VScroll1.Min = 32
VScroll1.Max = 212
VScroll1.SmallChange = 1
VScroll1.LargeChange = 212
VScroll1.Value = 100
```

Scroll bar controls have the following properties: DragIcon, DragMode, hWnd, MousePointer, and Tag.

Adding a Scroll Bar to the Sample Application

The BOOK application has a horizontal scroll bar used to specify the number of delivery days. When the user specifies a value with this scroll bar, the text in the delivery days label is updated to reflect the chosen value.

Place a horizontal scroll bar on the form. The default name for this control is HScroll1. Using the Properties window, assign the property values that Table 8.10 shows.

Table 8.10. Horizontal scroll bar properties for the BOOK application.

Default Name	Property	Value
HScroll1	Height	300
	LargeChange	5
	Left	6000
	Max	45
	Min	1
	Name	hsbDelivery
	Top	4680
	Value	45
	Width	2175

Figure 8.12 shows how the form looks with the addition of the scroll bar.

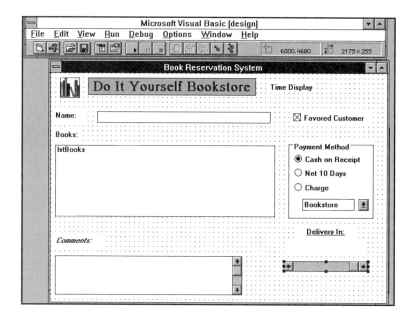

Figure 8.12.

The Book Reservation
System with a scroll bar.

Events of the Scroll Bars

The Change event occurs whenever the Value property changes. This
happens when the user manipulates the scroll bar with the mouse, or
when program code modifies the Value property.

The Scroll event is unique to scroll bars. This event triggers while the
user drags the scroll box along the shaft. The difference between the
Change and Scroll events is that Change occurs once when the scroll bar
Value is updated, while Scroll occurs continuously, as long as the user
drags the scroll box. As a result, you can use Scroll to continuously
update the property values in other controls that must be coordinated
with the scroll bar.

Scroll bars respond also to the following events: DragDrop, DragOver,
GotFocus, KeyDown, KeyPress, KeyUp, and LostFocus.

The Timer Control

The timer control acts similar to an alarm clock. You specify a time
interval. When the interval elapses, the control generates a Timer event.

One frequent use of the timer control is to add a visible clock to your form. The clock can continuously update and display the current time.

Timers have many other uses. For example, you can periodically back up files when a specified time interval elapses. A quiz program might give the user 15 seconds to answer a question. When 15 seconds is up, the application can take appropriate action.

Windows limits the number of timers to 16. That's not a practical concern, however, as Visual Basic applications rarely use more than a single timer control.

A timer control is unlike any other control. At design time, the control has a fixed size which you cannot change. It doesn't matter where on a form you put a timer because, at run time, it is always invisible. Also, the user cannot directly access the control.

The sole purpose of a timer control is to trigger a Timer event at regular intervals.

Properties of the Timer Control

Timers have few properties. Width and Height properties do not exist because the control has a fixed size at design time, and is invisible at run time. Consequently, timers do not have any appearance properties.

You can set the Left and Top properties to position the control at design time. It doesn't matter, however, in which place on the form you put the control. As a result, you generally move it to an out-of-the-way spot that doesn't interfere with the ongoing placement of the other controls.

The Interval property, unique to timers, specifies the time interval that must elapse before the Timer event triggers. You specify the value of Timer in milliseconds. The value can range from 0 to 65,535 milliseconds. Notice that the maximum value specifies a time period of a little more than a minute. (You can't use timers to specify long time intervals.) If you set the value of Interval to 0 (the default), the timer is disabled. The following instruction specifies that the time interval for the timer Timer1 should be one second:

```
Timer1.Interval = 1000    '1000 milliseconds equals 1 second
```

If the value of the Enabled property is True, the timer control triggers the Timer event when the specified time interval elapses. If the value of Enabled is False, the timer is disabled, and no Timer event can occur. The default value of Enabled is True.

Adding a Timer Control to the Sample Application

The BOOK application uses a timer to update the display of the correct time. Place a timer control on the form. The default name for this control is Timer1. Using the Properties window, assign the property values that Table 8.11 shows.

Table 8.11. Timer properties for the BOOK application.

Default Name	Property	Value
Timer1	Enabled	True
	Interval	1000
	Left	8040
	Name	tmrTime
	Top	120

Figure 8.13 shows how the form now appears.

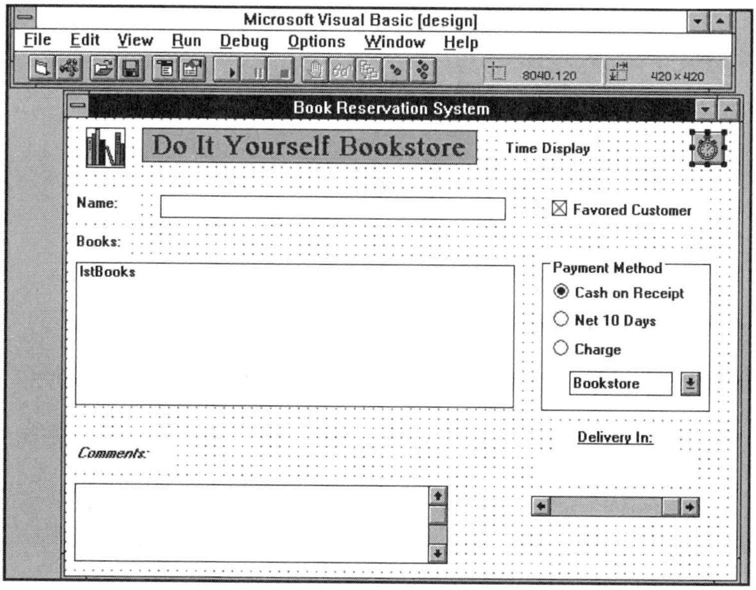

Figure 8.13.

The Book Reservation System with a timer added.

Event for the Timer Control

`Timer` is the only event which the timer control supports. This event triggers when the specified time period elapses. Notice that if you don't disable a timer, the `Timer` event occurs repeatedly. The countdown for the next time interval begins immediately after the previous time period elapses.

The Command Button Control

The final common control is the command button. You have already used command buttons in several applications presented in earlier chapters.

Typically, a command button represents a task that activates when the user clicks the button. When clicked, a command button seems to press into the form, and back out again. For this reason, command buttons are sometimes called "push buttons."

The user can activate a command button by clicking it. Alternatively, when the command button has the focus, the user can press Enter or the space bar.

Properties of the Command Buttons

The `Caption` property of a command button specifies the text which the user sees displayed in the button. If you include the ampersand character (&) as part of the caption, the character following the ampersand appears underlined in the command button. The user can activate that command button by pressing and holding the Alt key, then pressing the key corresponding to the underlined character. Such an underlined key is known as an *access key*.

 You can create an access key for any control that has a `Caption` property. Other such controls include check boxes and option buttons. For simplicity, the BOOK application does not use access keys. You can easily add access keys, however, by modifying the `Caption` properties of the various controls.

For example, suppose you set the `Caption` property for a command button to be "&Calcuate Results". The caption inside the command button appears as Calcuate Results. The user can select this command button by pressing Alt+C.

The `Default` and `Cancel` properties are unique to command buttons. If you set the value of `Default` to True for a command button, that button activates whenever the user presses Enter. The effect is the same as clicking the button.

The default button appears with an outline that is darker than the other command buttons. One common use of the Default property is to create an OK button for a form. To create such a button, just specify its `Caption` property as `OK`, and set its `Default` property to True.

Similarly, the `Cancel` property determines which command button activates if the user presses Esc. If you set the value of a command button's `Cancel` property to True, that button activates whenever the user presses Esc. Be careful when you use this property. Visual Basic does not provide any visual cue to indicate which command button, if any, has the `Cancel` property. The primary purpose of this property is to create a command button labeled `Cancel` that activates when the user presses Esc. Keep in mind that if you set the `Cancel` property to True for some other button, the user might not understand what happened when the Esc key was pressed.

The initial values of `Default` and `Cancel` are False for every command button. Only one command button can have a `Default` value of True. If you set `Default` to True for one command button, Visual Basic automatically sets the `Default` to False for every other command button. Similarly, only one command button can have a `Cancel` value of True.

The `Value` property for a command button indicates whether the button is selected. True means yes, and False means no. If you set `Value` to True in program code, the command button's `Click` event activates.

Command buttons have the standard size and appearance properties, as well as the following ones: `BackColor`, `DragIcon`, `DragMode`, `FontName`, `FontSize`, `FontBold`, `FontItalic`, `FontStrikeThru`, and `FontUnderline`. `hWnd` is also available.

Adding Command Buttons to the Application

The sample application uses two command buttons. The first, labeled `Completed`, indicates that the order form has been satisfactorily filled out, and the application should process the book order.

The second command button, labeled `Exit`, terminates the application.

Place two command buttons on the form. The default names for these controls are `Command1` and `Command2`. Using the Properties window, assign the property values that Table 8.12 shows.

Table 8.12. Command button properties for the BOOK application.

Default Name	Property	Value
Command1	Caption	Completed
	Left	5640

continues

Table 8.12. Continued

Default Name	Property	Value
	Default	True
	Name	cmdCompleted
	Top	5040
Command2	Caption	Exit
	Left	7200
	Name	cmdExit
	Top	5040

The form for the sample application is now complete. Save the form as BOOK.FRM. To do so, choose the Save File **As** option from the **F**ile menu. Then specify the file name as BOOK. Visual Basic automatically adds the .FRM extension.

Figure 8.14 shows how the completed form appears at design time.

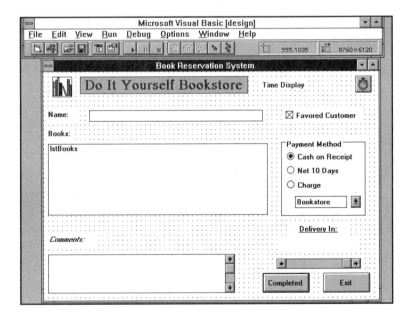

Figure 8.14.

The completed Book Reservation System form.

Events of the Command Button Control

The primary event for a command button is the Click event. This event activates whenever the user clicks the command button or, alternatively, whenever the user presses Enter (or the space bar) when the command button has the focus.

The other events recognized by a command button are DragDrop, DragOver, GotFocus, LostFocus, KeyDown, KeyUp, KeyPress, MouseDown, MouseUp, and MouseMove.

The Importance of *TabIndex* and *TabStop*

As mentioned earlier in the chapter, the tab order of all the controls in an application is determined by the values of their TabIndex properties. Recall that the tab order refers to the sequence in which each control gets the focus as the Tab key is pressed.

For applications that require the user to type information in different places on the form, the tab order can be important. Keep in mind that some users prefer to run an application without using the mouse. Such users are likely to be touch typists, comfortable with their fingers on the keyboard.

You can check the tab order of the controls on a form without using the Properties window to examine the TabIndex values. Simply press Tab repeatedly, and watch the focus move from one control to the next. Try this tabbing with the BOOK application. As you press Tab repeatedly, you see the focus move from one control to another in the order that each was placed on the form.

Once a form is designed, you might want to change the values of TabIndex to update the tab order. These two ordering schemes are the most commonly used:

- *Reading order.* Set the tab order from left to right, then up and down (or vice versa). With this scheme, the focus moves in a logical, natural order through adjacent controls.

- *Order of importance.* Set tabbing to move from one control to another in the order the user would most likely want. That is, controls in which input is likely to be typed are early in the tab order. Controls not likely to be utilized appear later in the order.

For the BOOK application, the user must first type the customer's name. The Name text box, therefore, should be first in the Tab order. You might want to reassign TabIndex values as Table 8.13 shows. This step is not necessary. Adjusting the tab order, however, does make the application easier to manipulate for keyboard specialists.

Table 8.13. Recommended tab order for the BOOK application.

Control	Value of *TabIndex*
txtName	0
chkFavored	1
lstBooks	2
optCash	3
optNet	4
optCharge	5
cboCharge	6
hsbDelivery	7
cmdCompleted	8
cmdExit	9

The BOOK application has twenty controls with TabIndex values ranging from 0 to 19. Remember that anytime you change TabIndex for one control, Visual Basic automatically adjusts the TabIndex values for the others. The adjustment consists of adding or subtracting 1 to or from the value of some of the other controls' TabIndex properties so that each control ends up with a unique TabIndex value, and the relative tab ordering of the other controls is preserved.

If you assign the TabIndex values that Table 8.13 shows, the remaining controls stay in the tab order, but occur later in the chain. As explained earlier in the chapter, you can skip a control in the run-time tab order by setting the value of its TabStop property to False.

Writing Program Code for the Sample Application

So far, you have designed the form for the sample application. The next step is to write the program code that makes the application work properly.

 NOTE At this stage in your Visual Basic programming career, you might not understand all the instructions contained in the following event procedures. Some of the functions and statements might be new to you. Be aware that all the statements and functions are explained throughout the course of this book.

By trying the sample application, and writing these procedures, you can get a general idea of how the application works. Even if you don't try the application, you can still look at the program instructions. In later chapters, you learn all the details of how these instructions work.

Defining the Form-Level Variables

You use some variables throughout the application. As explained in the previous chapter, you place such variables in the general declarations section of the form. By doing so, you can use these variables in any of the event procedures associated with the form.

To access the Code window for the form, double-click anywhere on the form (be sure the pointer is directly on the form, not in one of the controls). The Code window opens. In the object box of the form window, select (general). In the procedure box, select (declarations).

Type in the following variable declarations:

```
Dim Customer As String     'Customer's name
Dim Books As String        'Books ordered
Dim Pay As String          'Payment method
Dim Deliv As String        'Delivery date
```

These lines declare the string variables used throughout the application. For more information on declaring variables, see Chapter 14, "Language Building Blocks."

Writing the *Form_Load* Procedure

The application requires some initialization at start-up. For example, the list box for the book titles must contain the actual list of available books. The Time and Date labels must be initialized.

When you first start an application, Visual Basic loads the default form into memory, then displays the form. The process of loading the form triggers the event called Form_Load. By writing program code for this event, you assign property values, and do other program initialization before the user interacts with the form. For more information on Form_Load and other start-up events, see Chapter 9, "Managing Projects."

To create the `Form_Load` event procedure, open the Code window, and select `Form` from the object list box. Select `Load` in the procedure list box. Now type the following instructions:

```
Sub Form_Load ()
    lblTime.Caption = Format$(Now, "mmmm d, yyyy    h:nn:ss a/p")
    lblDate.Caption = Str$(hsbDelivery.Value) + " Days"
    lstBooks.AddItem "Create Paper Crafts"
    lstBooks.AddItem "Create Jewelry"
    lstBooks.AddItem "Create Dolls"
    lstBooks.AddItem "Build Dollhouses"
    lstBooks.AddItem "Build Birdhouses"
    lstBooks.AddItem "Build Go Carts"
    lstBooks.AddItem "Sew"
    lstBooks.AddItem "Knit"
    lstBooks.AddItem "Weave"
    lstBooks.AddItem "Collect Stamps"
    lstBooks.AddItem "Collect Coins"
    lstBooks.AddItem "Sail"
    lstBooks.AddItem "Golf"
    lstBooks.AddItem "Play Tennis"
    lstBooks.AddItem "Play Baseball"
    lstBooks.AddItem "Play Basketball"
    lstBooks.AddItem "Play Football"
    lstBooks.AddItem "Play Hockey"
    cboCharge.AddItem "Visa"
    cboCharge.AddItem "MasterCard"
    cboCharge.AddItem "Amer. Express"
    cboCharge.AddItem "Discover"
    cboCharge.AddItem "Bookstore"
End Sub
```

The first instructions in this procedure set the captions for the Time and Date labels. The `Format$` and `Str$` functions convert numbers into string values. These functions are necessary because the `Caption` property is always a string value. For more information on strings and these functions, see Chapter 17, "Working with Strings."

The remaining instructions use the `AddItem` method to add items to the list and combo boxes.

Writing the Event Procedures for the Controls

You must now write the event procedures associated with the various controls. These procedures do the detailed work of the application.

The *chkFavored* Check Box

The application has a check box labeled Favored Customer. In the code, this check box is named chkFavored.

A favored customer can get delivery in less than five days, and can charge purchases directly to the Bookstore account. Customers who don't enjoy this favored status must wait at least five days for delivery, and cannot charge directly to the store.

The user clicks the check box to toggle between favored and nonfavored status. As a result, the chkFavored_Click event procedure contains the program code related to the customer status.

In the object list of the Code window, choose chkFavored. Choose the Click event from the procedure list. Visual Basic now opens a template for the chkFavored_Click event procedure. The completed procedure is as follows:

```
Sub chkFavored_Click ()
    If chkFavored.Value = 1 Then        'Favored customer
        cboCharge.AddItem "Bookstore"
        hsbDelivery.Min = 1             'Minimum scroll bar value
    Else                                'Non-favored customer
        cboCharge.RemoveItem 4
        hsbDelivery.Min = 5
        cboCharge.Text = ""
    End If
End Sub
```

The Value property of the check box determines whether the customer is favored. Based on that property, the procedure adds or removes the Charge account options, and changes the minimum value for the delivery scroll bar.

The Option Buttons for Selecting a Payment Method

The Payment section of the form contains three option buttons. The first two are for cash payment and net 10 days, respectively. When one of these options is selected, the user should not have access to the Charge combo box.

The third option button is for charge payment. When this button is selected, the Charge combo box must be activated. Access to the Charge combo box can be regulated with the Enabled property of the cboCharge control.

Create the following three event procedures:

```
Sub optCash_Click ()
    cboCharge.Enabled = False
End Sub

Sub optNet_Click ()
    cboCharge.Enabled = False
End Sub

Sub optCharge_Click ()
    cboCharge.Enabled = True
End Sub
```

The Delivery Scroll Bar

The user can move the scroll bar to specify the delivery period. The following two event procedures update the caption of the Date label to indicate the current setting on the scroll bar.

```
Sub hsbDelivery_Change ()
    hsbDelivery_Scroll        'Invokes the Scroll event procedure
End Sub

Sub hsbDelivery_Scroll ()
    lblDate.Caption = Str$(hsbDelivery.Value) + " Days"
End Sub
```

These two procedures work together to continuously update the lblDate caption as the user moves the scroll bar.

The Timer Control

The Timer event occurs once a second. (Recall that the value of the timer's Interval property was set to 1000 at design time.) As a result, Visual Basic generates a call to the tmrTime.Timer event procedure every second. The code in this procedure must update the Timer label to display the current time. The result is, essentially, a digital clock.

The Timer event procedure is as follows:

```
Sub tmrTime_Timer ()
    lblTime.Caption = Format$(Now, "mmmm d, yyyy  h:nn:ss a/p")
End Sub
```

In this procedure, the Now function uses the computer's internal clock to return the current date and time. The Format$ function converts the information to string format. For more information on manipulating date and time text formats, see Chapter 17, "Working with Strings."

The Command Buttons

When an order has been entered on the form, the user clicks the command button labeled Completed. Alternatively, the user can simply press Enter because the Default property of this command button is set to True.

In a full-fledged practical implementation of this application, the program would probably save the order information on a disk file. Here, the BOOK application opens a message box to display the order information.

The code for the cmdCompleted event procedure is as follows:

```
Sub cmdCompleted_Click ()
    Dim N As Integer        'Loop counter
    Dim CRLF As String      'Carriage return, line feed

    CRLF = Chr$(13) + Chr$(10)
    Books = ""
    Customer = txtName.Text + " has ordered:" + CRLF + CRLF

    For N = 0 To (lstBooks.ListCount - 1)
        If lstBooks.Selected(N) = True Then
            Books = Books + "How To " + lstBooks.List(N) + CRLF
        End If
    Next N

    Deliv = CRLF + "To be delivered on "
    Deliv = Deliv + Format$(Now + Val(lblDate.Caption), "mmmm d, yyyy") +
    ➥CRLF

    If optCash.Value = True Then
            Pay = CRLF + "To be paid with cash." + CRLF
        ElseIf optNet.Value = True Then
            Pay = CRLF + "To be billed Net 10 days." + CRLF
        ElseIf optCharge.Value = True Then
            Pay = CRLF + "To be charged to the " + cboCharge.Text + "
            ➥account." + CRLF
    End If

    MsgBox Customer + Books + Pay + Deliv, 64
End Sub
```

The *CRLF* variable uses the Chr$ function to specify a carriage return and a line feed. For more information on the Chr$ function, see Chapter 17, "Working with Strings." The next instruction initializes the variable *Books* to an empty string. Later, the contents of *Books* are the list of books ordered by the customer. The subsequent instruction gets the customer's name from the Text property of the Name text box, and creates the first part of the message that is displayed in the message box.

The next five lines compose a For-Next loop. This loop uses the selected items from the list box to construct the Books string. These selected items are the books which the customer ordered. The phrase "How To" is added to each book title.

The Deliv string represents the delivery date. The property lblDate.Caption reads the number of days until delivery in string form. The Val function converts this string to a number which is then added to the current date to create the final delivery date. Again, the Now function returns the current date and time. For more information on Val, see Chapter 17, "Working with Strings."

 NOTE The computation of Deliv involves conversion between string and numeric formats. Further, the Now function returns values in a data type known as Variant. For more information on Variants, and how these conversions work, see Chapters 14 and 17.

The next seven lines compose a block If-Then instruction, which assigns the selected payment option to the Pay string variable. This code block inserts also the charge account information, if the user selects the charge option. For a discussion of If-Then instructions, see Chapter 15, "Program Flow and Decision Making."

Finally, the procedure uses a MsgBox instruction to display the completed book order in a message box. For more information on message boxes and the MsgBox instruction, see Chapter 10, "Using Dialog Boxes."

The event procedure for the Exit command button is simple:

```
Sub cmdExit_Click ()
    End
End Sub
```

The End instruction terminates the application, and returns Visual Basic to design mode.

Running the BOOK Application

Before running the application, resave the form now that you have added the event procedures. Use the **S**ave File option from the **F**ile menu. Then using the Sav**e** Project As option on the **F**ile menu, save the project as BOOK.MAK.

Try running the BOOK application to see how the form works. You can experiment with the various options, such as the Favored Customer check box, the charge options, and the delivery date scroll bar. When you have specified all the order information, click the Completed command button (or press Enter). A message box pops open showing the completed order. Figure 8.15 shows a sample customer order.

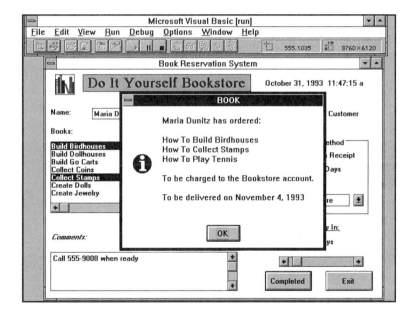

Figure 8.15.

The message box for a completed customer order.

Summary

You design the user interface for an application by placing controls onto a form. The Toolbox contains the various available controls.

This chapter introduced the controls that you are likely to use most often. These common controls are: label, text box, picture box, frame, option button, check box, list box, combo box, horizontal scroll bar, vertical scroll bar, timer, and command button. Each control has an associated set of properties and events.

The Toolbox also contains several specialized controls not covered in this chapter. These controls are discussed in later chapters.

Once you place a control on the form, assign initial values to its properties by using the Properties window. Later, in program code, you can read property values and assign new ones as appropriate. Each control also has a set of event procedures to which it responds.

You created the BOOK application, a book ordering system custom-designed for the Do It Yourself Bookstore. This application demonstrates most of the common controls in a practical setting.

Managing Projects

When you save an application in the design environment, Visual Basic creates a project file for the application. Each project file has the .MAK extension. A project file lists all the various files that comprise the application.

In essence, a Visual Basic *project* consists of its collection of component files. These component files include the forms and code modules that constitute the application.

This chapter discusses how you develop and manage a project. The main topics are as follows:

- Using the Project window
- Using the File menu
- Working with form (.FRM) and module (.BAS) files
- Managing Project (.MAK) files
- Using AUTOLOAD.MAK
- Understanding the scope of procedures and variables
- Developing multiple-form applications
- Creating an executable version (.EXE file) of an application

Understanding the Anatomy of a Project

From Visual Basic's point of view, a project consists of several files. When you save a project, Visual Basic keeps a record of the individual component files. As explained later in this chapter, such a project "record" is saved in a special project file which has the .MAK extension.

Table 9.1 shows the types of files that comprise a project. The extension name of the file indicates the file type. Forms, for example, are saved with the .FRM file extension.

Table 9.1. Component files of a project.

File Type	Extension	Description
Form	.FRM	Each form is saved as a separate file.
Code module	.BAS	Each code module is saved as a separate file.
Custom control	.VBX	Each custom control is saved in a separate file and added to the Toolbox.
Binary data	.FRX	An .FRX file stores specialized data needed when a property value specifies an icon or picture at design time.

The following sections describe each of the four file types in more detail.

Forms (.FRM)

Applications can have multiple forms. In a multiple-form application, your program code can control which forms are visible and which are hidden at any one time. For more about multiple-form applications, see the section titled "Working with Multiple Forms" later in this chapter.

Each form is saved as a separate file. The .FRM file contains a description of the form's appearance, including a description of all the controls placed on the form. The design-time property values are stored in the file also. Furthermore, the file contains the code for all the event procedures, general procedures, and variable declarations defined at the form level.

Visual Basic's File menu contains several options used to add and delete forms from an application. Table 9.2 summarizes these options.

Table 9.2. File Menu options useful for managing forms.

Option	Description
New Form	Creates a new form and adds it to the application. The newly added form initializes with the default property values.
Save File	Saves the active form to a disk file. If the form was saved previously, this option updates the existing file to reflect any modifications made at design time. If the form was not saved previously, you are prompted to supply a file name. (Note: As explained later, this option can also be used to save code modules to disk files.)
Save File As	Prompts you to supply a file name before saving the active form to disk. You can use this option to save a second copy of the active form under a different file name. (You can also use this option to save code modules.)
Add File...	Adds a previously saved form to the current application. This option opens a dialog box that prompts you to specify the file name. If you specify a .FRM file, the previously saved form is added to the application. (You can also use this option to add previously saved code modules and custom controls to the application.)
Remove File	Removes a form from the design-time environment. If you place the focus on a form and then choose this option, the form is removed from the application. This option does not remove the file from disk, but rather removes the association of the file with the current project. (You can also use this option to remove a code module or a custom control from the application.)

Code Modules (.BAS)

A code module contains the program code that exists independently from any particular form. A code module can contain declarations of variables and constants. Also, you can define general procedures in a code module. A *general procedure* is a Function or Sub that you create. For example, you might write a Sub procedure named GetTotal that sums the values of several arrays to compute the total monthly sales of a department store.

Unlike event procedures, general procedures don't activate due to system events. Instead, a general procedure is invoked only when explicitly called by a program instruction.

To create a new code module, choose the New **M**odule option from the **F**ile menu. The default name for the first module placed in an application is Module1.bas. When a code module has the working focus, you can save the module to a disk file with the **S**ave File or Save File **A**s options from the **F**ile menu.

To add a previously saved module to your application, choose the A**d**d File option and specify the desired .BAS file. You can remove a code module from the design-time environment with the **R**emove File option.

Custom Controls (.VBX)

A *custom control* is a control that can be added to your Toolbox to provide extra functionality. Like the standard controls, each custom control has its own set of properties and events. Many third-party vendors market specialized custom controls which you can purchase and add to your Visual Basic environment.

A custom control is saved with a .VBX file extension. The Standard Edition of Visual Basic includes three custom controls: GRID.VBX, MSOLE2.VBX, and CMDIALOG.VBX. The Professional Edition of Visual Basic adds many more custom controls.

To add a custom control to your environment, choose the A**d**d File option from the **F**ile menu. When the File Selection dialog box opens, specify the desired .VBX file. Visual Basic adds the custom control to your Toolbox. You can then use the custom control when developing the current application. You can remove a custom control from the Toolbox with the **R**emove File option.

If you want to add a permanent custom control to your environment, specify the .VBX file in your AUTOLOAD.MAK file. For more about AUTOLOAD.MAK, see the section titled "Understanding the AUTOLOAD.MAK File" later in this chapter.

Binary Data Files (.FRX)

Some applications require associated data files. If you specify the Icon property of a form or the Picture property for a Picture Box control, for example, Visual Basic must access the necessary graphics information from a stored graphics file.

When a property value requires such data, Visual Basic saves the required data in a special binary data file. Visual Basic creates one such data file per form. The single file holds all the binary data needed for that form. For the file name, Visual Basic uses the root name of the form with the .FRX extension.

In general, you don't have to worry about managing .FRX files. Visual Basic takes care of the details. However, if you copy application files to different directories, be sure you copy the .FRX files, if any, along with the other files.

Opening and Saving Projects

The File menu contains four options used for managing projects. Table 9.3 summarizes these options.

Table 9.3. File menu options useful for managing projects.	
Option	**Description**
New Project	Starts a new project. This option prompts you to save all files associated with any current project. It then closes the prior application and initializes Visual Basic to start a new project.
Open Project...	Loads a previously saved project into Visual Basic. Before loading the specified project, this option prompts you to save any project currently active.
Save Project	Saves the current project to disk. This option saves all forms and modules as separate files and creates a project file with the .MAK extension. If the project was saved previously, this option updates the existing files to reflect current modifications, if any. If the project was not saved previously, this option prompts you to provide a project name.
Save Project As...	Prompts you to supply a project name before saving the current project. You can use this option to save a copy of the current project under a new name.

When you save a project, Visual Basic creates a project file with the .MAK extension. This project file lists all the files that comprise the project. For more about project files, see the section titled "Understanding .MAK Files" later in this chapter.

A Few Words about Variable Declaration and Program Scope

The program code for an application is scattered throughout the forms and the code modules. Generally, program code can be categorized into two types of instructions: declarations and executable instructions.

■ *Declarations.* These instructions declare the variables, arrays, data types, and constants used in the application. The keywords used in declarations are `Dim`, `ReDim`, `Static`, `Global`, `Const`, and `Type`. Declarations can be placed in the general declarations section of any form or module, and can also be placed in an event or general procedure.

■ *Executable instructions.* These instructions comprise the largest part of the program code. As opposed to declarations, executable instructions actually *do* something. That is, an executable instruction takes a specific action according to the statements, functions, or methods contained in the instruction. Every executable instruction must occur within a procedure—either within an event procedure associated with a form, or within a general procedure defined at the form or module level.

Table 9.4 shows a few examples of declarations and executable instructions.

Table 9.4. Sample instructions.

Declarations	Executable Instructions
`Dim MyCost As Single`	`MyCost = RetailPrice * 0.65`
`Global StdColor&`	`Command1.Caption = "Click me"`
`Const NUMCLIENTS = 150`	`MsgBox MyMsg`

The *scope* of a variable refers to the portions of the application which can access that variable. Procedures also have scope. The following sections briefly describe the scope of procedures and variables.

 NOTE For additional information about variables, declarations, and procedures, see Chapter 14, "Language Building Blocks," and Chapter 18, "Using Procedures: Subs and Functions."

Scope of Procedures

As mentioned previously, an executable instruction always occurs in a procedure. The procedure may be an event procedure or a general procedure defined as a `Sub` or `Function`. Each event procedure is attached to a specific form. As a result, the scope of an event procedure is limited to the form in which the event procedure is defined.

When an event triggers, Visual Basic associates the event with the form on which the event occurred. Visual Basic then activates the appropriate event procedure defined within that form. For this reason, within the same application, two different forms can each have an event procedure with the same name. For example, every form in an application can define a separate event procedure named `Form_Click`. There's no conflict because when a `Click` event occurs on a form, Visual Basic activates the `Form_Click` event procedure defined for that form.

General procedures, on the other hand, can be defined in the general section of any form or code module. If defined at the form level, only instructions within that form can call the general procedure. A general procedure defined at the form level is not accessible to instructions in other forms nor to the general procedures of any code module.

However, a general procedure placed in the general section of a code module is accessible throughout the application. Such a procedure can be invoked by any instruction anywhere in the application.

Scope of Declarations

You declare variables, arrays, and constants with `Dim`, `ReDim`, `Static`, `Global`, and `Const` statements. For more information about these statements, see Chapter 14, "Language Building Blocks." Once declared, the variable, array, or constant has a particular scope.

Determining the scope of variables is more complicated, however, than determining the scope of procedures. That's because the scope of a variable depends not only on where the declaration occurs, but also on the keyword used to make the declaration.

Declarations can appear at the module, form, or procedure level. When declared in a procedure (either general procedure or event procedure), the variable is accessible only within that procedure. Such variables are said to have *local* scope. When the procedure terminates, the variable and its value are lost. No instruction anywhere outside that particular procedure can access and use the variable. However, should the procedure become active again, the variable becomes redeclared and once again becomes available to the instructions within that procedure.

Variables declared in the general declarations section of a form have scope throughout the form. That is, all the event procedures and general procedures throughout that particular form have access to the variable. However, instructions inside other forms and in the general procedures of a code module do *not* have access to the variable.

The scope of variables declared at the module level depends on the keyword used to make the declaration. When a variable is declared with `Dim` in the general declarations section of a module, the variable has scope throughout the module. The general procedures within that code module can access the variable. However, instructions in other code modules and in form-level procedures do *not* have access to the variable.

To declare a variable with scope throughout the application, use the Global keyword rather than Dim. The declaration goes in the general declarations section of a module. For example:

```
Global MyTitle As String
```

If you place this declaration in the Declarations section of any module, you make MyTitle available to every procedure in every form and code module. When a variable can be accessed by any instruction in the application, the variable is said to have *global* scope.

Working with Multiple Forms

Visual Basic applications are not limited to a single form. Indeed, as your applications become more sophisticated, you frequently will develop applications comprised of multiple forms. For example, an application written for an automobile parts supply might have one form for the user to specify the desired part, another form to indicate where the part can be found and its price, and a third form showing how to install the part.

As explained in the following sections, you have the flexibility to make all of an application's forms visible simultaneously. Alternatively, the program code can load and unload forms as required by the application.

By default, if you display several forms at one time, the user can manipulate the forms with the same techniques used in most Windows applications. For example, clicking a form gives that form the focus. Each form can be moved around the desktop, minimized, and resized. However, by setting certain property values and by using particular methods associated with forms, you can restrict the user's options in manipulating the forms.

Adding Forms at Design Time

At design time, you can have all the forms in the application loaded simultaneously. You can then customize each form individually. For each form, you add the controls, set the property values, and write the event procedures.

When you begin a new project, Visual Basic displays a form of the default size and location. The initial name for this form is Form1. As you add additional forms, Visual Basic assigns the default names Form2, Form3, and so on.

Two ways exist to add a new form to your application at design time:

■ Click the New Form button in the Toolbar.

The New Form icon is the leftmost button in the Toolbar.

■ Choose the New Form option from the File menu.

Accessing Forms at Design Time

New forms have the same size and screen location as Form1. As a result, a recently added form can completely obscure a previous form. When working with multiple forms, you often need to bring one of the obscured forms to the foreground and give that form the focus.

If you can see any part of your target form on the desktop, click anywhere on the form. The form gets the focus and moves to the foreground. Once a form has the design-time focus, you can add controls, use the Properties window to set property values, and use the Code window to write event procedures and other program code.

If you cannot see the form, use the Project window to give the form the focus. Either double-click the name of the form in the Project window, or click the form name and click the View Form button. In either case, the indicated form moves to the foreground. (If the Project window is not visible, you can access it by choosing the Project option from the Window menu.)

At design time, you frequently need to work with one form exclusively for a period of time. If you minimize the other forms by clicking their minimize buttons, the desktop becomes less cluttered. This action will help you to focus your attention on a particular form.

T I P

As an alternative to minimizing a form, you can close a form by opening its Control menu and choosing the Close option. This action completely removes the form from the desktop. To recover the form, select the form's name in the Project window and click the View Form button.

Working with Multiple Forms at Run Time

At run time, the program code can manipulate individual forms to make a form visible or invisible. Visual Basic distinguishes between loading a form and showing a form. *Loading* a form means placing the form in memory. *Showing* a form means actually displaying the loaded form.

A `Load` instruction places a form into memory. The companion instruction, `Unload`, removes a form from memory. You use the `Show` method to display a loaded form and the `Hide` method to remove the form from view. (As explained shortly, the `Show` method will also load the form if the form is not in memory.) The following sections describe loading and showing in more detail.

The *Load* Statement

Use the `Load` statement to load a form into memory.

> `Load formname`
>
> where
>
> > `formname` is the name of the form you want to load.

For example, the following instruction loads `Form3` into memory:

`Load Form3`

Visual Basic loads a form with property values set to their design-time values. At the end of the loading process, Visual Basic calls the `Form_Load` event procedure. The `Form_Load` event is discussed later in this chapter.

As long as a form is loaded, you can modify the form's property values in the program code. The form does not have to be visible.

Visual Basic automatically takes care of loading a form when your code makes any reference to the form. If, for example, you assign a new value to a property of an unloaded form, Visual Basic automatically loads the form before assigning the new property value.

The *Show* Method

Use `Show` to display a loaded form. `Show` is not a statement, but rather a Visual Basic method. The following is the syntax for `Show`.

> `formname.Show modestyle`
>
> where
>
> > `formname` is the name of the form to show,
>
> and
>
> > `modestyle` indicates whether the form is modal.
>
> The `formname` and `modestyle` parameters are optional.

For example, the following instruction shows `Form2`:

```
Form2.Show
```

Automatic Loading of Forms

Before a form can be shown, the form must be loaded into memory. However, if the form is not in memory, Visual Basic loads the form before executing the `Show` method. For this reason, you don't have to execute a `Load` statement before using the `Show` method.

 **NOTE** Any code reference to a form loads the form if it is not already loaded. The reference might be a `Show` method, or the resetting of a property value in code. As a result, you never have to use explicit `Load` instructions.

The main reason to use `Load` is to improve the execution time when eventually showing a form. With the form already loaded, the time to display the form is minimized. In multiple-form applications, you can load all the forms when the application begins. Then when you want to show a form, the response time is optimized because Visual Basic doesn't have to load the form first.

If you leave off the name of the form, Visual Basic shows the form associated with the current form-level code. For example, the instruction `Show` (without any other parameters) displays `Form2` if the instruction occurs anywhere in the form-level code for `Form2`.

Creating Modal Forms

The *modestyle* parameter, when present, determines whether the form is modal. A *modal* form retains the focus until the form is hidden or unloaded. The user cannot divert the focus away from a modal form by clicking any other form. Further, Visual Basic does not execute the instructions that follow `Show` until a modal form is hidden or unloaded.

To make a form modal, include the *modestyle* parameter. Use the value of 1 for *modestyle*. For example, the following instruction shows `MyForm` and makes the form modal:

```
MyForm.Show 1
```

Modal forms still respond to form-level events. For example, a command button on a modal form responds to the button's `Click` event. That's how you typically continue the application after displaying a modal form. For example, a modal form might include a command button labeled `Cancel` or `OK`. The `Click` procedure for this command button could hide the form or just make the form nonmodal so that the user could access other forms.

To make a form nonmodal, change the value of modestyle to 0. For example:

```
MyForm.Show 0
```

The main reason to make a form modal is to concentrate the user's attention on the form. The form might display some important information such as an error message.

Forms are nonmodal by default. If you don't include the *modestyle* parameter with the Show method, the form is nonmodal. For more about modality, see Chapter 10, "Using Dialog Boxes."

The *Hide* Method

Hide is the opposite of Show. Use Hide to make a form invisible.

> *formname*.Hide
>
> where
>
> > *formname* is the name of the form to hide.
>
> The *formname* parameter is optional.

For example, the following instruction hides MyForm:

```
MyForm.Hide
```

Hide does not unload the form. Hiding a form sets the Visible property of the form to False and makes the form's controls inaccessible to the user. However, your program code can still assign property values associated with the form and its controls.

If you don't specify the form name, Visual Basic hides the form associated with the current form-level code.

The *Unload* Statement

Use the Unload statement to unload a form from memory.

> Unload *formname*
>
> where
> > *formname* is the name of the form you want to unload.

For example, the following instruction unloads Form3 from memory:

```
Unload Form3
```

When a form is unloaded, run-time property values assigned to the form or its controls become lost. Should you later reload the form, Visual Basic reverts to the property values specified with the Properties window at design time.

Unloading a form reclaims for the system the memory used to store the form. It's important to understand, however, that only the memory used to store the visible portion of the form is recovered. The program code associated with the form always remains in memory.

DuckSoup—A Sample Application with Multiple Forms

DuckSoup is a whimsical application that demonstrates multiple forms. The application contains three forms: frmHuey, frmDewey, and frmLouie. Each form contains a single command button. By clicking the various buttons, the user can make forms trade places on-screen, and make forms invisible and then visible once again.

Creating the Huey Form

To create DuckSoup, start a new project. Place a command button on the form. Using the Properties window, set the property values shown in Table 9.5.

Table 9.5. Design-time property values for *Form1*.

Object	Property	Value
Form1	Name	frmHuey
	Caption	Huey
	Height	4470
	Left	1035
	Top	1680
	Width	4950
	Icon	C:\VB\ICONS\MISC\FACE03.ICO
Command1	Caption	Show Everyone
	Height	495
	Left	1560
	Top	1680
	Width	1695

Notice that you change the name of the form from Form1 to frmHuey. The name for the command button, however, is not changed from the default value of Command1.

The value of the Icon property specifies the icon Visual Basic uses to represent the minimized form. The icon file FACE03.ICO depicts a smiling face. It's possible that, on your system, this file is in a different subdirectory than the directory shown in Table 9.5. If so, specify the appropriate path when you assign the value of Icon. For more about specifying the Icon property, see Chapter 5, "Understanding Forms, Events, and Properties."

Creating the Dewey Form

Choose the New Form option from the File menu to add a second form (Form2) to the application. Place a command button on this form. Assign the property values shown in Table 9.6.

Table 9.6. Design-time property values for *Form2*.

Object	Property	Value
Form2	Name	frmDewey
	Caption	Dewey
	Height	2775
	Icon	C:\VB\ICONS\MISC\FACE01.ICO
	Left	2715
	Top	1305
	Width	6720
Command1	Caption	Change places with Louie
	Height	495
	Left	1920
	Top	840
	Width	2775

Creating the Louie Form

Add a third form (Form3) and place a command button on this form also. Assign the property values shown in Table 9.7.

Table 9.7. Design-time property values for *Form3*.

Object	Property	Value
Form3	Name	frmLouie
	Caption	Louie
	Height	2775
	Icon	C:\VB\ICONS\MISC\FACE02.ICO
	Left	2715
	Top	4260
	Width	6720
Command1	Caption	Hide with Dewey
	Height	495
	Left	1920
	Top	840
	Width	2775

Figure 9.1 shows how the three forms appear at design time. Notice that the Huey form is partially obscured behind the other two forms.

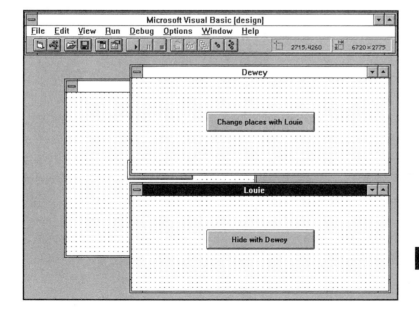

Figure 9.1.

The DuckSoup application at design time.

Writing the Event Procedures

When the application begins, only the Huey form is visible. Huey contains a command button labeled Show Everyone. When you click this button, you want to make the other two forms visible.

To make the other forms visible, use the Show method. The code goes in the Click procedure for the command button. Open the Code window for frmHuey and create the following event procedure:

```
Sub Command1_Click ()
    frmDewey.Show
    frmLouie.Show
End Sub
```

As explained earlier in the chapter, you don't need to include Load instructions to load frmDewey and frmLouie. The Show method loads the appropriate form before showing it.

The command button on the Dewey form causes the Dewey and Louie forms to switch places on-screen. The switching is accomplished by swapping the values of the Top properties for Dewey and Louie. Open the Code window for frmDewey and create the following Click procedure:

```
Sub Command1_Click ()
    ' Switch the values of Top for Dewey and Louie
    Dim HoldDeweyTop As Integer
    HoldDeweyTop = frmDewey.Top
    frmDewey.Top = frmLouie.Top
    frmLouie.Top = HoldDeweyTop
End Sub
```

Clicking Louie's command button causes Dewey and Louie to hide, leaving only Huey's form visible. The Hide method does the trick. Open the Code window for frmLouie and create the following Click procedure:

```
Sub Command1_Click ()
    frmDewey.Hide
    frmLouie.Hide
End Sub
```

Avoiding Name Conflicts

Notice that each command button retains the same default name: Command1. Although the three buttons have the same name, no conflict arises when activating a Click event. Every control and its event procedures are attached to a particular form. When one of the buttons is clicked, Visual Basic identifies the associated form and activates the proper event procedure.

Of course, within the context of a single form, every control that is not part of a control array must have a unique name. You cannot have, for example, two different Command1_Click procedures associated with any single form. But it's okay for an application to have several different Command1_Click procedures, provided each such procedure is defined on a separate form.

TIP

Although two controls in different forms can have the same name, it's good programming practice to give *every* control in an application a unique name. That way, you avoid multiple event procedures with the same name—such as the three different Command1_Click procedures in DuckSoup. Your reward for this renaming is an easier debugging life. Furthermore, when modifying your code, you avoid potential confusion about which event procedure applies to which control.

For DuckSoup, you might give each command button a unique name. Appropriate names might be HueyButton, DeweyButton, and LouieButton. With these names, each of the three Click procedures has a unique name: HueyButton_Click, DeweyButton_Click, and LouieButton_Click.

Running DuckSoup

When you first run DuckSoup, only the Huey form is visible (see Figure 9.2). Click Huey's button, and the other two forms come into view. The Huey form becomes partially obscured. See Figure 9.3.

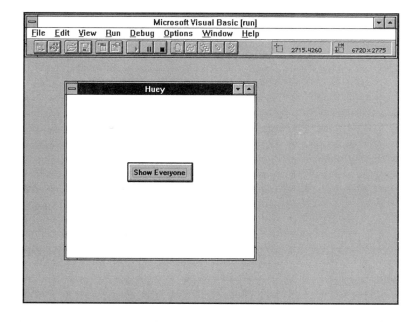

Figure 9.2.

DuckSoup starts with only Huey.

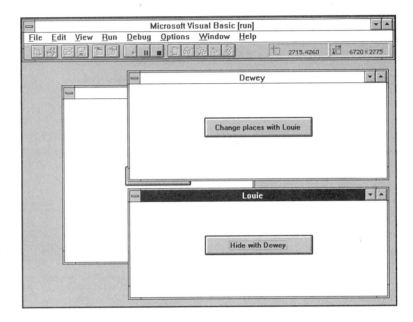

Clicking Huey's button makes all three forms visible.

Now, click Dewey's button to make Dewey and Louie change places on the desktop. See Figure 9.4. Click Dewey's button again. Dewey and Louie are back to their original positions.

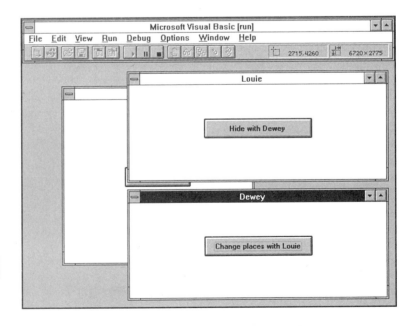

Dewey and Louie have exchanged positions.

By clicking Louie's button, you make Dewey and Louie invisible. Only Huey remains. The screen once again looks like Figure 9.2.

Experiment with moving the forms around the screen. Resize, minimize, and maximize the forms. When you click Dewey's button, Dewey and Louie exchange places. More properly, the values of the Top properties of the two forms are swapped. If you want, you can modify the code to swap the Left property values as well.

When you minimize a form, its icon appears on the desktop. Huey, Dewey, and Louie each have different icon files: FACE03.ICO, FACE01.ICO, and FACE02.ICO, respectively. These three files depict slightly different versions of the smiley face character. Figure 9.5 shows Huey and Dewey minimized. Recall from Chapter 5, "Understanding Forms, Events, and Properties," that the name displayed with a minimized icon is the form's caption.

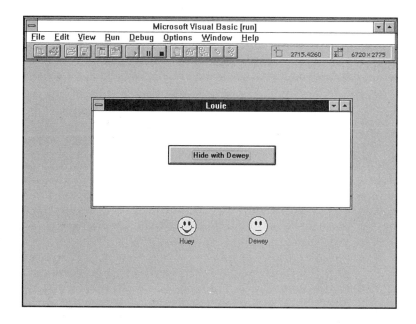

Figure 9.5.

Huey and Dewey are minimized.

Saving DuckSoup

To save DuckSoup, stop the application and return to design mode. When saving DuckSoup on disk, you must save each form as a separate .FRM file.

Click the Huey form to select it. Choose the Save File **As** option from the **File** menu and save the form as HUEY.FRM. Similarly, save the Dewey form as DEWEY.FRM and the Louie form as LOUIE.FRM. Finally, use the Save Project As option from the File menu to save the project as DUCKSOUP.MAK.

For a further discussion of .MAK project files, see the section titled "Understanding .MAK Files" later in this chapter.

Creating an Executable Version of an Application

One of Visual Basic's most attractive features is that you can create an executable version of any application. An *executable file* is a file that can be run directly from Windows. Executable files don't require the presence of Visual Basic. Executable files are stored on disk with a file extension of .EXE.

Advantages of Executable Files

Compared to running an application from Visual Basic's development environment, an executable version has the following advantages:

- *You can distribute your application on disk or electronically (by modem).* Others can run your application directly from Windows without the need for Visual Basic. Commercial applications are usually sold as executable files. If you develop applications commercially, you will likely create executable versions of your applications.

- *An executable file is in binary form.* When you compile your code into an executable file, Visual Basic creates the .EXE file in binary format. Users of your application cannot view the program code. This protects your proprietary interests because the source code is safeguarded.

- *An executable file amalgamates all the individual components of an application into one self-contained file.* An application comprised of multiple forms, modules, and picture files is saved to a single .EXE file. The fact that the application is on a single file facilitates the transfer of the application from one disk to another.

Creating an .EXE File

You can create an executable version of an application directly from the Visual Basic development environment. With the application loaded and Visual Basic in design mode, choose the Make EXE File option from the File menu. A dialog box opens, similar to the one shown in Figure 9.6.

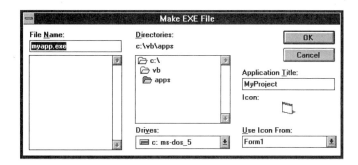

Figure 9.6.

The Make EXE File dialog box.

In the File **N**ame box, you specify the name for the executable file. Generally, you use the base name of the project followed by an extension of .EXE. However, you can use any file name that you want. With the **D**rives and **D**irectories list boxes, you can specify the path in which you want Visual Basic to save the executable file.

Near the lower right corner of the Make EXE File dialog box, a picture of the application's icon appears. The displayed icon is used by Windows to represent the application on the desktop. As you can see in Figure 9.6, the default icon for an .EXE file is the same icon Visual Basic uses to represent forms.

If, however, you specified the Icon property for the Start Up form, that icon appears instead. (As explained later in this chapter, the *Start Up form* is the form that first appears when the application begins.) Furthermore, if the application has multiple forms with different icons, you can drop down the **U**se Icon From list box to select an icon associated with any of the application's forms. This list box is in the lower right corner of the dialog box, just below the displayed icon.

In the Application Title box, you specify a title for the application. On the Windows desktop, this title displays alongside the icon. The icon and title appear inside the program group and when the application is minimized. As with other Windows applications, you can launch the application by double-clicking its icon inside the program group.

Try creating an executable version of the DuckSoup application. Load DuckSoup into the Visual Basic development environment. Then choose the Ma**k**e EXE File option from the **F**ile menu. The Make EXE File dialog box opens. Specify a file name of DUCKSOUP.EXE. (Most likely, this file name already appears in the File Name box, and you can just click the OK button to accept this file name.)

Notice that Huey's icon is the default icon for DuckSoup. Click the down arrow at the right end of the Use Icon From list box. See Figure 9.7. You can choose the icon from any one of DuckSoup's three forms to be the Windows icon for the entire application.

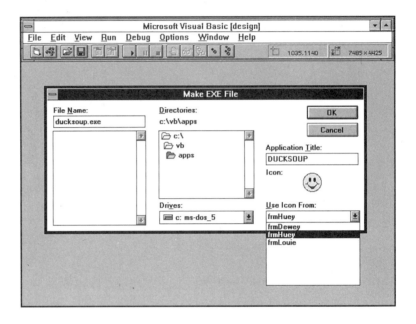

Figure 9.7.

Creating an executable
file for DuckSoup.

Click the OK button. Visual Basic creates an executable version of DuckSoup with the file name DUCKSOUP.EXE.

Using the VBRUN300.DLL File

It's not quite correct to say that the executable version of your application can be run independently under Windows. A special support file named VBRUN300.DLL must also be present in your user's system. This file is a *dynamic link library* (DLL). The DLL contains necessary run-time support routines.

The file comes with Visual Basic. When you install Visual Basic, the installation program places this file in your Windows directory, most likely in the C:\WINDOWS\SYSTEM directory.

Microsoft grants you, as a registered owner of Visual Basic, the rights to freely copy and distribute this file. You owe no royalties or other compensation to Microsoft.

If you distribute your executable files to others, you must also distribute copies of VBRUN300.DLL. No matter how many executable files are on a user's system, only a single copy of VBRUN300.DLL needs to be present. The user should save the file in the C:\WINDOWS, C:\WINDOWS\SYSTEM, or another directory accessible to Windows.

Upgrading Applications Created with Earlier Versions of Visual Basic

With each new release of Visual Basic, Microsoft has supplied an upgraded VBRUN file. The first release of Visual Basic came with VBRUN100.DLL, version 2.0 came with VBRUN200.DLL, and now Visual Basic 3.0 comes with VBRUN300.DLL. When you install Visual Basic 3.0 on your system, the installation program searches for an earlier version of the VBRUN file and, if one is found, replaces this file with VBRUN300.DLL.

In general, VBRUN300.DLL will successfully run .EXE programs created with Visual Basic 2.0 or 1.0. Also, in some cases, .EXE programs created with Visual Basic 3.0 will run with VBRUN200.DLL or VBRUN100.DLL.

For complete confidence that everything is compatible, upgrade your users' executable programs and VBRUN files to version 3.0 if at all possible. If your users are running programs created with an earlier version of Visual Basic, create new .EXE files using Visual Basic 3.0. Then distribute the upgraded .EXE files as well as VBRUN300.DLL.

 Besides the VBRUN300.DLL file, you also must distribute the appropriate .VBX file for any custom control used in your application.

Running an Executable File

After you create an .EXE file, you (and all who receive the file) can treat the file as you treat any other Windows application. You can install the program into an existing program group or create a new program group for the file. Furthermore, you can launch the program with the Run option from the Windows Program Manager or from the File Manager.

Understanding .MAK Files

When you save a project in the development environment, Visual Basic creates a .MAK (pronounced "make") file. The .MAK file for the DuckSoup application, for example, is DUCKSOUP.MAK.

Visual Basic saves a .MAK file as a text file in ASCII format. As such, you can load the .MAK file into a text editor or word processor. Once loaded, you can view and modify the file.

The .MAK file contains a description of the project. This description includes a list of the .FRM and .BAS files that comprise the project, as well as other initialization information. When you load an existing project into the development environment, Visual Basic reads the .MAK file to determine the initial configuration of the project.

The following sections describe the .MAK file in greater detail.

A Sample .MAK File

The following is the .MAK file for DuckSoup. (On your system, the directory paths and other components of this file may vary.)

```
FRMHUEY.FRM
FRMDEWEY.FRM
FRMLOUIE.FRM
CMDIALOG.VBX
GRID.VBX
MSOLE2.VBX
ProjWinSize=74,385,252,206
ProjWinShow=2
IconForm="frmHuey"
Title="DUCKSOUP"
ExeName="DUCKSOUP.EXE"
```

The file begins with the names of the three .FRM files. The .VBX files are the three custom controls supplied with the Standard Edition of Visual Basic. The other components of this file are described in the following section.

Items in a .MAK File

Table 9.8 specifies the items that may appear in a .MAK file.

Table 9.8. Components of a .MAK file.

Item	Description
filename.FRM	Specifies a form to load into the project. The first form listed in the file becomes the startup form.
filename.BAS	Specifies a module to load into the project.
filename.VBX	Specifies a custom control to place in the Toolbox.

Item	Description
ProjWinSize= *top,left,width,height*	Specifies the initial position and size of the project window. Only the *top* parameter is mandatory.
ProjWinShow=*value*	Specifies whether the project window is displayed at initialization. *value* can be 0 (hidden), 1 (minimized), or 2 (visible).
Command=*strexpr*	If this item is present, *strexpr* specifies a string expression passed as the command line argument.
IconForm=*frmname*	If this item is present, *frmname* specifies the name of the form whose icon should be used for the executable file.
HelpFile=*filename*	If this item is present, *filename* specifies the file to use for the application's Windows help file.
Title=*strexpr*	*strexpr* specifies the application's default title to appear in the Make EXE File dialog box.
EXEName=*filename*	Specifies the default file name to use for the application's executable file in the Make EXE File dialog box.
Path=*pathname*	If this item is present, *pathname* specifies the path name set in the Make EXE File dialog box.

Modifying the .MAK File

As explained previously, Visual Basic saves .MAK files in ASCII text format. By loading a .MAK file into a text editor or word processor, you can modify the contents of the file. When you resave the modified .MAK file, your changes go into effect the next time you load the application into Visual Basic. Make sure that you save the file in ASCII text format.

Normally you don't need to modify a .MAK file because you can accomplish most modifications while working directly in Visual Basic. For example, you can modify the values of ProjWinSize and ProjWinShow in a .MAK file in order to customize how the Project window appears when the application is loaded. However, if you resize the project window in Visual Basic, and then resave the project, you get the same effect.

You can add new .FRM and .BAS files into the .MAK file. In that way, you can add new forms and modules to the application. Similarly, you can delete .FRM and .BAS files to remove forms and modules from the application. Of course, you can duplicate these effects with the **A**dd File and **R**emove File options from the **F**ile menu.

> **T I P** If you are not using any custom controls in a particular application, you can remove the .VBX files from the .MAK file. That way, your Toolbox appears less cluttered.

Understanding the AUTOLOAD.MAK File

Visual Basic has a special .MAK file named AUTOLOAD.MAK. When you start a new project, Visual Basic uses this file to configure the initial design-time environment. In particular, any files listed in AUTOLOAD.MAK are loaded into the development environment.

By default, the AUTOLOAD.MAK file for Visual Basic's Standard Edition specifies the three custom controls CMDIALOG.VBX, GRID.VBX, and MSOLE2.VBX. As a result, Visual Basic adds the common dialog, grid, and Object Linking and Embedding tools into the Toolbox. If you prefer, you can customize your Toolbox by removing any or all of these file names from AUTOLOAD.MAK. Also, you can modify `ProjWinSize` and `ProjWinShow` to customize the initial appearance of the Project window.

> **T I P** If you routinely develop applications that always use a particular saved form or code module, include the .FRM or .BAS file name in the AUTOLOAD.MAK file. This way, every time you start a new project, the specified form or code module is already present.

Understanding How Visual Basic Starts Running an Application

When you run an application, the first thing you typically see is the application's form. Usually, the form has associated event procedures. As you interact with the application, the various event procedures activate and the application proceeds to its conclusion.

As simple as that sounds, Visual Basic actually takes many steps when beginning an application. Before displaying the start-up form, Visual Basic invokes the following five different event procedures in the order listed:

```
Form_Load
Form_Resize
Form_Activate
Form_GotFocus
Form_Paint
```

As you can see by the procedure names, each of these event procedures is associated with the form. If you write code for one (or more) of these procedures, the event (or events) occurs when the program is first run. Of course, if you don't place code in any of these procedures, nothing happens when Visual Basic tries to activate these events.

Keep in mind that each of these events can, and often does, occur during the normal execution of the application. For example, the Resize event triggers any time the user modifies the size of the form. It's a special feature of an application's initialization process that Visual Basic calls these five event procedures at program start-up.

The following sections briefly describe these five events.

Form_Load

A Load event occurs when Visual Basic loads a form into memory. Remember that, as described earlier in the chapter, loading a form is not the same as displaying a form. The form must be loaded into memory before it can be displayed on-screen.

The most common uses of Form_Load are to initialize form-level variable values and to assign property values to the form (and its controls) at run time. If you prefer, you can set some or all of the application's property values with program code rather than with the Properties window. By placing such code in the Form_Load event procedure, the property values are assigned before the user sees the form.

Form_Resize

The Resize event occurs when the size of the form changes. The form's size can change when the user moves one of the form's borders or when the program code modifies the value of one of the form's size properties.

The most common use of this event is to reposition and/or resize the form's controls—graphic and text. Suppose your form has a label placed in the center of the form. The user now resizes the form. In Form_Resize, you can place code that calculates the new center of the form and repositions the label accordingly.

Form_Activate

The Activate event is used mostly in multiform applications. The event occurs when the user changes the focus from another form to the current form (or to one of the controls on the current form). The current form must be visible for the Activate event to occur. That is, Activate does *not* occur when a form is loaded except, of course, as part of the start-up process when an application is initialized.

Activate occurs only within the domain of the Visual Basic application. That is, Activate triggers when another form has the focus and the user (or the program code) changes the focus to the current form. If the user temporarily moves the focus to a separate Windows application running concurrently and then moves the focus back to the Visual Basic application, the Activate event is not triggered.

Form_GotFocus

The GotFocus event is defined not only for forms, but for most controls as well. Form_GotFocus triggers when the form gets the focus through the user's actions or through the SetFocus method in program code. Keep in mind, however, that a form cannot get the focus unless all the visible controls on the form are disabled. If a form contains *any* enabled control, the form itself cannot receive the focus. Instead, one of the controls on the form gets the focus. As such, Form_GotFocus is seldom programmed because the event does not usually occur in the normal execution of most applications.

Form_Paint

Before discussing the Paint event, a brief discussion of the AutoRedraw property of a form is in order. AutoRedraw is a Boolean (True/False) property. You can set its value in either the Properties window or with program code.

When AutoRedraw for a form is True, Visual Basic keeps a bit-mapped graphics representation of the entire form in memory. When all or part of the form is covered up and then later exposed, Visual Basic automatically redraws the visual screen image from the saved bit map. The redrawing process is convenient, certainly, but can be slow and memory-intensive. (Keep in mind that, if you develop applications for use by others, their machines may not be as fast or powerful as yours. Consider testing your applications on as wide a variety of computers as possible.)

When AutoRedraw for a form is False (the default value), a newly uncovered form, or part of a form, is not automatically redrawn. Instead, the program code must contain instructions that explicitly redraw the desired parts of a form.

That's where the Paint event comes into play. Form_Paint triggers when part or all of a form becomes uncovered. If AutoRedraw is False, you can place the instructions to redraw the form inside this event procedure.

When AutoRedraw is True, however, the redrawing of the form is automatic. Visual Basic does not trigger the Paint event. For more about AutoRedraw and the Paint event, see Chapter 11, "Displaying Graphics."

Using the Project Window

While working in design mode, the Project window maintains a current list of all the files associated with the project. As you add, delete, rename, and create new files, the Project window updates the file list. You may see three types of files listed in the Project window:

- .FRM files. These are the forms that comprise the project.

- .BAS files. These are the code modules.

- .VBX files. These are the custom controls added to the Toolbox.

Figure 9.8 shows the Project window as it appears when you start a new project with the Standard Edition of Visual Basic.

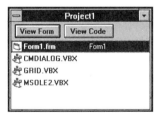

Figure 9.8.

The default Project window.

Opening the Project Window

You can manipulate the Project window like other windows. For example, you can resize the Project window, move it around the desktop, minimize it, and close it.

Sometimes you want to work with the Project window but the window is closed or hidden behind other windows. At any time, you can open the Project window and bring it to the foreground by choosing the Project option from the **W**indow menu.

Working with the Project Window

When applications have multiple forms, various forms can be minimized or hidden behind other windows. You can use the Project window to bring any form to the foreground. Simply double-click the form name in the Project window. Alternatively, you can highlight the name of the form and click the View Form button.

To open the Code window for any form or module, highlight the name of the form or module in the Project window and click the View Code button.

Demonstrating the Project Window

The following short exercise demonstrates various aspects of working with the Project window. Start a new project. If the Project window is not visible, choose the Project option from the Window menu. The Project window should appear as shown in Figure 9.8.

Open the File menu and choose the New Form option. Visual Basic opens a new form named Form2. Choose the New Form option once again to open a third form named Form3.

Choose New Module from the File menu to open the Code window for a new code module. Visual Basic gives this module the default name Module1.bas.

Take a look at the Project window (see Figure 9.9). The three forms and the code module are listed. Notice that the title bar of the Project window displays the default name for the project: Project1.

Figure 9.9.

The Project window with three forms and a code module.

You can view any of the forms by highlighting the form name in the Project window and clicking the View Form button. You can open the Code window for any form (or code module) by highlighting the form (or module name) and clicking the View Code button. (Notice that, if you highlight Module1.bas, the View Form button becomes disabled.)

Using the Project window, double-click Form2.frm to bring Form2 into view. Open the Properties window (press F4) and change the value of the form's Name property to MyForm. Reopen the Project window. Notice that the window reflects the change in the form name.

Highlight Module1.bas in the Project window and click the View Code button. The Code window opens for the code module. Now choose the Save File **As** option from the **F**ile menu to save the code module with a different name. Rename the module MyCode.bas.

Choose the Sav**e** Project As option from the **F**ile menu to save the project. Name the project MyApp. (When the dialog boxes open and ask if you want to save the changes to the various forms, click the *No* option.) When saving the project file, Visual Basic automatically adds the .MAK extension. The project's file name becomes MYAPP.MAK.

Reopen the Project window. As Figure 9.10 shows, the window reflects the updates to the project. Notice that the title bar now reads MYAPP.MAK. In the Project window, the MyForm.frm and MYCODE.BAS entries reflect their updated names.

Figure 9.10.

The Project window reflects the updated project files.

Notice in the Project window that some form, module, project, and custom control names appear in all uppercase, while other names appear with a mixture of upper- and lowercase. Visual Basic uses all uppercase to indicate that the file corresponding to that form, module, project, or custom control has already been saved on disk with that name. Names containing some lowercase letters indicate that no corresponding file has yet been saved on disk.

Setting the Project Options

If you choose the **P**roject option from Visual Basic's **O**ptions menu, a dialog box named Project Options opens (see Figure 9.11). This dialog box presents three parameters that you can set.

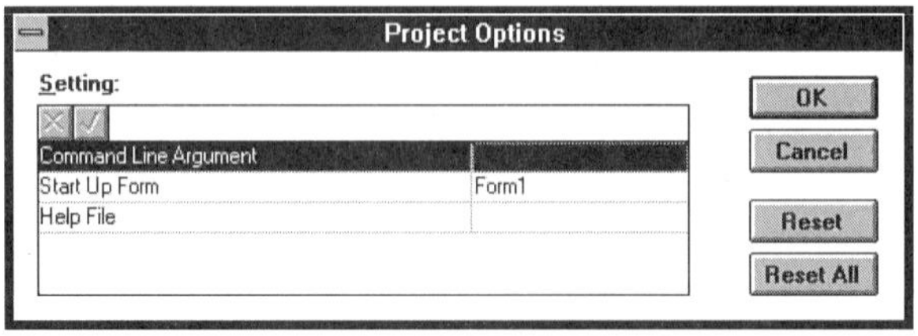

Figure 9.11.

The Project Options dialog box.

Table 9.9 summarizes the contents of the Project Options dialog box.

Table 9.9. Items in the Project Options dialog box.

Item	Description
Command Line Argument	Specifies an optional argument passed to the application when the application is launched from the DOS prompt.
Start Up Form	Specifies the form that displays when a multiple-form application is run; can also specify the user-defined procedure `SubMain`.
Help File	Specifies the name of the application's Help file.

You use the Help File item when you want to link a file containing Help text to your application. For more about Help files, see Chapter 33, "Adding a Help System to an Application."

The following sections describe the Command Line Argument and Start Up Form options.

Starting an Application from the DOS Prompt

Once you have a project saved as a .MAK file, you can launch the application from the DOS prompt. To do so, type the following command:

```
vb /run makefile
```

Here, *makefile* is the name of the project's .MAK file. You can leave off the .MAK extension when specifying *makefile*. If, for example, you have a project stored on disk as MYAPP.MAK, you can launch the project with the following command at the DOS prompt:

```
vb /run myapp
```

Doing so activates Windows, starts Visual Basic, loads the MYAPP.MAK file to initialize the project, and begins executing the application.

Adding a Command Line Parameter

When launching a program from the DOS prompt, you can pass a command line argument to the application. To do so, add an optional /cmd clause to the DOS command:

```
vb /run makefile /cmd parameter
```

Here, *parameter* is a string value passed to the application. The code in the Visual Basic application receives the parameter through Visual Basic's Command$ function. By testing the value of Command$, the program code can determine what parameter, if any, was specified.

Suppose, for example, that an application requires the user to specify the password Watergate in order to successfully launch the program from the DOS prompt. The program code can test for this password by using Command$ as follows:

```
If Command$ = "Watergate" Then...
```

The Command function is the companion function to Command$. Whereas Command$ returns a value of type String, Command returns a value of type Variant.

While working with Visual Basic in design mode, you can simulate a command line argument as you're developing the application. To do so, choose the **P**roject item from the **O**ptions menu. When the Project Options dialog box opens, specify a value for the Command Line Argument item. By so doing, the Command and Command$ functions return your specified value when you run the application. In this way, you can test how your application will respond to various command-line parameters that the user might specify when the completed application is launched from outside of Visual Basic.

Using a Command-Line Parameter with an Executable File

If you create an executable version of your application, the user can specify command-line parameters when launching the application from the DOS prompt. For example, suppose you create an executable file of an application named MYAPP. The file name is MYAPP.EXE.

At the DOS prompt, anything the user types after the name of the application is passed to the application. For example, the user could specify the required password as follows:

```
myapp Watergate
```

This command, typed at the DOS prompt, launches the executable file MYAPP.EXE. In the program code, the Command$ function returns the value Watergate.

> **NOTE** If the user does not type any command-line parameter, the `Command$` function returns the empty string. In code, you can determine whether any command line argument was specified by testing for the empty string: `If Command$ = " " Then...`

Specifying the Start Up Form

By default, when you start an application, Visual Basic displays `Form1` (or whatever name you have given to the original form). Normally, that's exactly what you want. However, in an application containing multiple forms, you may prefer that Visual Basic display one of the other forms when the application begins.

To specify which form displays when an application initializes, modify the value of the Start Up Form item in the Project Options dialog box. To do so, move the highlight to the Start Up Form option. Click the down arrow to the right of the Setting box. Visual Basic drops down a list of the project's forms. Figure 9.12 shows the list for a project with three forms.

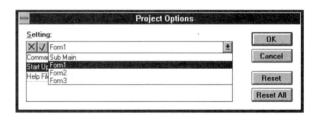

Figure 9.12.

Choosing a Start Up Form.

Select one of the items in the list by clicking the item. Click OK to close the dialog box. If you now run the application, the first form displayed is the form you designated to be the start-up form.

Understanding *Sub Main*

Look again at the drop-down list of forms in Figure 9.12. Notice the item labeled `Sub Main`. If you select this item, the application begins by executing a user-defined general procedure named `Main`. No form displays at start-up. Instead, the application begins by executing the instructions of the `Main` procedure.

`Main` must be defined in a code module as a general procedure. As described earlier in this chapter, a general procedure is not an event procedure, but rather a procedure that you create to be invoked directly by program instructions. For more information about general procedures, see Chapter 18, "Using Procedures: Subs and Functions."

Only one procedure named Sub Main can exist in any given project. If your project uses several code modules, only one of the modules can contain a Sub named Main.

If you choose Sub Main for the setting of the Start Up Form option, the code you place in Main is responsible for controlling the application. In particular, if a form is to be displayed later, instructions inside Sub Main must load and show the form.

Creating a Formless Application

You can create an application without any forms at all! Of course, an application without any forms cannot contain any controls. It follows that an application without any forms or controls cannot have any event procedures.

If an application has no forms, you must designate Sub Main to be the Start Up item. The Main procedure can then call other procedures. Often, the entire application consists only of Sub Main.

Formless applications can be useful in performing routine maintenance tasks. For example, an inventory control application might open a file containing a list of the company's inventory. The application might update the record of each item to show which items are in stock on the current date, save the amended file, and then exit. Such an application does not require any user interaction and, therefore, no forms.

To try a simple example of a formless application, follow these steps:

1. Choose **New** Project from the **File** menu to start a new project.

2. Remove Form1 from the project.

   To do so, click the form and then choose the **R**emove File option from the File menu. Notice that the form is no longer listed in the Project window.

3. Choose the New **M**odule option from the **File** menu to add a code module to the application.

   The default name for this code module is Module1.bas. Visual Basic displays the Code window for this module.

4. In the Code window, type **Sub Main** and press Enter.

   Visual Basic creates a template for the procedure consisting of a Sub Main () instruction and an End Sub instruction.

5. Type the following procedure:

```
Sub Main ()
   Beep
End Sub
```

6. Choose **P**roject from the **O**ptions menu to open the Project Options dialog box (see Figure 9.13).

   Notice that Visual Basic presets the value of the Start Up Form item to Sub Main. Because the application has no forms, Sub Main is the only possible value.

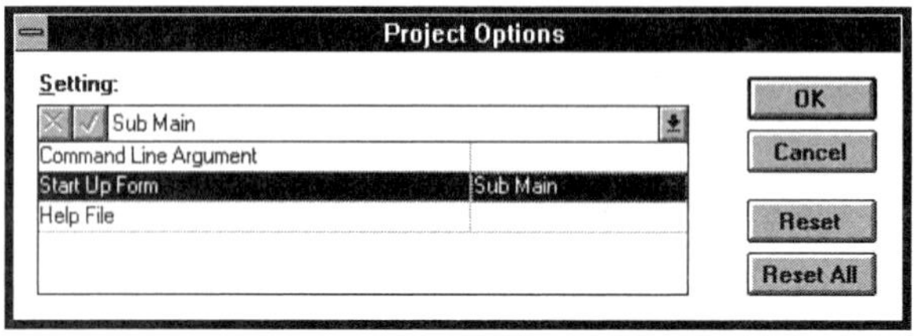

Figure 9.13.

Sub Main is selected as the Start Up Form item.

7. Click OK to close the dialog box.

8. Run the application.

The application beeps once and stops. Although quite simple, the project does demonstrate a formless application that uses Sub Main.

Summary

A project consists of a group of files. Each form in a project is saved with the .FRM extension, and each code module is saved with the .BAS extension. The project itself is saved as a .MAK file. The .MAK file lists the various files that comprise the application. The .MAK file also specifies certain initialization information, such as the size and on-screen location of the Project window.

Visual Basic provides several tools to help manage projects. With the Project window, you can quickly view any form or code module. The File menu provides several options for creating, adding, and deleting forms and modules.

Projects can have any number of forms. In multiple-form applications, you can show and hide individual forms as the needs of the project demand. You can use the Start Up Form item in the Project Options dialog box to specify which form first appears when the application begins. You can also designate that, when the application begins, a special procedure named Sub Main gets control instead of any form.

You can create an executable version of any application. By creating an .EXE file, the application can be run directly from Windows without the need for Visual Basic.

Designing User Interfaces

PART

III

Using Dialog Boxes

In many applications, you want the user to provide a small amount of input—perhaps a file name, a numeric value, or someone's name. The application's main window sometimes has a text box set up to receive such input from the user.

Often, however, the main window is not designed to accept the information. If this is the case, your application can pop open a new window over the main one. The new window, called an *input box,* prompts the user for the desired information. The input box contains any of three boxes for data input: text, list, or combo. After inputting the data, the user clicks OK to close the input box and to resume the main part of the application.

An input box is one example of a *dialog box.* Another type of a dialog box is the *message box.* A message box pops open solely to display some information—perhaps an error message or some explanatory text. The message box usually contains an OK button which the user clicks after reading the information. The click closes the message box and resumes the main application.

Windows applications often use message boxes. For example, Windows uses a message box when you select Exit Windows from the Program Manager's File menu. A message box pops open to warn you that you are about to end Windows. This message solicits your confirmation.

Your Visual Basic applications are likely to use dialog boxes quite frequently. A dialog box is nothing more than a customized form. Therefore, you can create dialog boxes by adding new forms to an application. If you are willing to forgo some customization, however, Visual Basic provides built-in statements and functions that create standard dialog boxes quickly and easily.

This chapter explains how to create and use dialog boxes. The main topics covered in this chapter include:

- Using the `InputBox$` function to create an input box
- Using the `MsgBox` function and `MsgBox` statement to display a message box
- Designing a customized dialog box
- Using sample applications which demonstrate dialog boxes

The *InputBox$* Function

Many applications require that the user type a data value before they can proceed. Such required input often occurs near the beginning of an application. For example, an application that manipulates an employer's personnel records can request that the user type the name of an employee. The program then might display the worker's salary history.

Such required input can also occur in the middle of, or throughout, the application. Consider a program that simulates a poker game. The program repeatedly asks you how much you want to wager.

Many applications require that you design customized forms so the user can type data values. Typically, you use a text box control to accept the user's input. If your program needs a single line of text from the user, however, Visual Basic's `InputBox$` function provides a quick and easy alternative to creating a custom form.

The `InputBox$` function opens a modal input box that displays a message, two command buttons, and a text box into which the user can type a single line. Recall that *modal* means that the input box retains exclusive focus. Until the user closes the input box, no other part of the application responds to clicks, or to any other event. Therefore, you use `InputBox$` when your program requires that the user provide some necessary data before continuing the application.

Understanding the Syntax of the *InputBox$* Function

The syntax for the `InputBox$` function is as follows:

```
InputBox$(promptstr, titlestr, defaultstr, left, top)
```

in which

promptstr is a string expression that specifies the message that ap
pears in the dialog box;

titlestr is a string expression that specifies the text that appears in
the dialog box's title bar;

defaultstr is a string expression that specifies the initial text placed in
the text box;

left is an integer expression that specifies the distance from the left
edge of the screen to the same place on the border of the dialog box;

and

top is an integer expression that specifies the distance from the top of
the screen down to the same place on the border of the dialog box.

The *titlestr*, *defaultstr*, *left*, and *top* parameters are all optional.

The `InputBox$` function returns the string value typed by the user. Usually,
`InputBox$` occurs in the following type of instruction:

`Response$ = InputBox$(prompt$)`

The `InputBox$` function appears on the right side of the equal sign. The function assigns the text typed by the user to the variable on the left side.

For example, `Response$ = InputBox$("Where were you born?")` produces the
dialog box that Figure 10.1 shows.

Figure 10.1.

An example of
InputBox$.

An input box always contains a title bar with a control box at the left; the
prompting message (`Where were you born?`, in this case); OK and Cancel
buttons; and a text box near the bottom.

Specifying the Prompt String

The only required parameter is *promptstr*. This parameter specifies the prompting message displayed in the input box. The prompting message must be a string expression, which can be a string literal enclosed in quotation marks, or a variable containing string information. For more information on string expressions, see Chapter 17, "Working with Strings."

The prompting message can contain as many as 255 characters. Visual Basic automatically breaks up lengthy messages into multiple lines.

Typing the Input Text

The user can type any single line of text into the text box. Clicking OK or pressing Enter closes the input box and assigns the entered text string to the variable Response$. Clicking Cancel or pressing Esc closes the input box and assigns the null string (no characters) to the variable Response$.

 NOTE If the user clicks OK without typing anything in the text box, InputBox$ returns the null string. This response is the same as if the user clicked Cancel.

Specifying the Optional Parameters

After the first parameter, the remaining ones are optional.

The second parameter, *titlestr*, specifies the text displayed in the title bar. If you omit this parameter, as in Figure 10.1, the title bar is blank.

The third parameter, *defaultstr*, specifies initial text to display in the text box. You use this parameter when your program can anticipate the most likely response the user makes. The user can choose this default text by simply clicking OK. Of course, the user can modify the default text before clicking OK.

Consider the following program fragment:

```
Prompt$ = "What is your favorite Windows programming language?"
Title$ = "Computer Questionnaire"
Default$ = "Visual Basic"
Response$ = InputBox$(Prompt$, Title$, Default$)
```

Figure 10.2 shows the resulting input box. Notice that it includes a text title and a default value in the text box.

Figure 10.2.

An example of InputBox$ with optional parameters.

You can skip over one of the optional parameters. If you do, however, you must use a comma as a separator. For example, you can write the final instruction from the preceding program fragment without specifying a title bar in this way:

```
Response$ = InputBox$(Prompt$, , Default$)
```

This instruction specifies default text for the text box, but does not display anything in the title bar.

The final two optional parameters specify the location of the input box on-screen. You must specify both of these parameters, or omit them. Although you can specify on-screen the position of the input box, you have no control over its size, or in which place Visual Basic displays the prompt message in relation to the text box. You pay this small price in flexibility for the simpler functionality that InputBox$ gives you.

Retrieving Numeric Input

The InputBox$ always returns a string value. You can use InputBox$ to solicit a numeric value. Although the user can type a number, Visual Basic returns the value as a string. As explained in Chapter 17, "Working with Strings," you can use Visual Basic's Val function to convert this text string to a numeric value.

Using the *InputBox* Function with Variant Variables

In addition to the InputBox$ function, Visual Basic includes a companion function, InputBox, which returns a value of type Variant. Recall that a variable of the Variant data type can store both numeric and string information. Except for the dollar sign omitted from the end of the function name, the syntax for InputBox is exactly the same as InputBox$. For more information on Variant variables and the Variant data type, see Chapter 14, "Language Building Blocks."

The *MsgBox* Function

The MsgBox statement pops open a dialog box containing a message. This type of dialog box is called a *message box* because its primary purpose is to display a message. Unlike InputBox$, the dialog box opened by MsgBox does not accept text input from the user.

Each message box created by MsgBox contains one or more command buttons. By default, OK is the only command button. With optional parameters in the MsgBox function, however, you can include other buttons or an illustrative icon.

The message box is modal. To close this box, the user must click one of the command buttons in it.

Although the MsgBox function does not return any text, the function does return a numeric value. This value indicates which button the user selected when closing the message box.

Message boxes are most often used to display short messages, and to obtain quick feedback from the user. For example, suppose your user tries to exit a program without saving some open files. Your program might open a dialog box to ask the user whether the open files should be saved. Figure 10.3 shows a sample message box created with MsgBox.

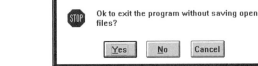

Figure 10.3.

A sample message box.

Understanding the Syntax of the *MsgBox* Function

The syntax of the MsgBox function is as follows:

```
MsgBox(msgstr, options, titlestr)
```

in which

    msgstr is a string expression that specifies the message displayed in the message box;

options is a numeric expression that specifies the buttons, icon, and other attributes of the message box,

and

titlestr is a string expression that specifies the text displayed in the title bar of the message box.

The *options* and *titlestr* parameters are optional.

The only required parameter is *msgstr*. This parameter specifies the message displayed in the message box. The string expression can contain as many as 1,024 characters. If necessary, Visual Basic automatically breaks up a lengthy message string into multiple lines.

Specifying the *options* Parameter

The *options* parameter specifies the appearance of the message box. The value of this parameter controls the following four options:

- Which group of command buttons the message box displays
- Which icon is present (if any)
- Which button is the default
- Whether the message box is modal to all loaded applications (or just to the current one)

Visual Basic associates a specific integer number with each of these options. You select the options you want, add the numbers, and use the result as the value of the *options* parameter.

Using the CONSTANT.TXT File

The CONSTANT.TXT file supplied with Visual Basic defines several constants, each with a descriptive name. This file assigns an integer (or long integer) value to each constant.

For example, CONSTANT.TXT assigns the constant MB_YESNO (which stands for *Message Box, Yes No*) the value 4. As indicated in Table 10.1, when the *options* parameter has this value, the message box contains command buttons labeled Yes and No.

Once you have CONSTANT.TXT loaded into an application, you can use constant names in the program code. The result is that your programs are easier to read and to understand. As an example of using a constant, the following program line uses MB_YESNO in a MsgBox instruction:

```
Response% = MsgBox(Message$, Options%)
```

The sample application at the end of this chapter demonstrates how to load and use the CONSTANT.TXT file. For more information on constants and CONSTANT.TXT, see Chapter 14, "Language Building Blocks."

Specifying the Button Group

Table 10.1 summarizes the six sets of buttons you can use with the MsgBox function. If you don't specify a button group, Visual Basic displays only the OK button in the message box.

Table 10.1. Button groups used with *MsgBox.*

Value	CONSTANT.TXT Name	Meaning
0	MB_OK	Display only an OK button
1	MB_OKCANCEL	Display OK and Cancel buttons
2	MB_ABORTRETRYIGNORE	Display Abort, Retry, and Ignore buttons
3	MB_YESNOCANCEL	Display Yes, No, and Cancel buttons
4	MB_YESNO	Display Yes and No buttons
5	MB_RETRYCANCEL	Display Retry and Cancel buttons

Specifying the Default Button

Each group of buttons has a default. The MsgBox function returns the value of the default button if the user presses Enter (instead of clicking one of the buttons). If the value of *options* does not specify otherwise, the button to the extreme left is the default. (Normally, this button is the one you want as the default button.) As Table 10.2 shows, however, you can specify any button as the default.

Table 10.2. The default button.

Value	CONSTANT.TXT Name	Default
0	MB_DEFBUTTON1	First button
1	MB_DEFBUTTON2	Second button
2	MB_DEFBUTTON3	Third button

Displaying an Icon

By having Visual Basic display one of the four available icons in the message box, you help the user quickly understand the type of message displayed. For example, the question mark icon informs the user that the dialog box is asking a question. Table 10.3 summarizes the four available icons.

Table 10.3. The icons available with *MsgBox*.

Value	CONSTANT.TXT Name	Meaning
0		No icon
16	MB_ICONSTOP	Displays a red STOP sign
32	MB_ICONQUESTION	Displays a green question mark
48	MB_ICONEXCLAMATION	Displays a yellow exclamation point
64	MB_ICONINFORMATION	Displays an *i* inside a blue circle

Changing the Modality

The message box is automatically modal to the application. Therefore, no other part of the application responds to any event until the user closes the message box. As Table 10.4 shows, you can make the message box modal also to the entire Windows desktop. If you do, all other loaded applications stop and wait for the user to clear the message box. Table 10.4 shows the two values for this modality option.

Value	CONSTANT.TXT Name	Meaning
0	MB_APPLMODAL	Modal to the current application
4096	MB_SYSTEMMODAL	Modal to all loaded applications

Table 10.4. The modality values.

Combining Effects

You can combine numeric values to produce various effects. Use only one number, however, from each group. For example, consider the following program fragment:

```
Message$ = "Exiting now will delete files"
Options% = 305
Response% = MsgBox(Message$, Options%)
```

Figure 10.4 shows the resulting message box. Notice that the value of Options% is 305, which equals 1 (OK and Cancel buttons) + 48 (Exclamation Point icon) + 256 (second button default). If the user presses Enter, the second button (Cancel) is selected.

Figure 10.4.

A sample message box.

With the CONSTANT.TXT file loaded, you can specify the value of Options% more descriptively as follows:

```
Options% = MB_OKCANCEL + MB_ICONEXCLAMATION + MB_DEFBUTTON2
```

Adding a Title

The third parameter, *titlestr*, specifies the text to include in the title bar of the dialog box. For example, the following instruction displays the message box that Figure 10.5 shows. Notice that Continue appears in the title bar of the message box.

```
Response% = MsgBox("Click when ready to proceed", 64, "Continue")
```

If you don't include the *titlestr* parameter, Visual Basic displays the name of the project in the title bar. For example, if you don't specify *titlestr* and you saved the project as TAXFORM.MAK, the title bar displays TAXFORM.

Returning the Value of the Selected Button

When the user selects a button, the message box closes and the MsgBox function returns a numeric value from 1 to 7. This value indicates the selected button. Table 10.5 shows the values returned by MsgBox.

Value	CONSTANT.TXT Name	Meaning
1	IDOK	User selected the OK button
2	IDCANCEL	User selected the Cancel button
3	IDABORT	User selected the Abort button
4	IDRETRY	User selected the Retry button
5	IDIGNORE	User selected the Ignore button
6	IDYES	User selected the Yes button
7	IDNO	User selected the No button

Table 10.5. Values returned by the *MsgBox* function.

Most of the time, the user selects a button by clicking it. If the user presses Enter, the system selects the default button. If the user presses Esc and there is a Cancel button in the message box, the system selects the Cancel button.

To illustrate, consider the following instruction presented earlier in this chapter:

```
Response% = MsgBox(Message$, Options%)
```

If the user clicks OK, the value of Response% becomes 1. Similarly, if the user clicks Cancel, the value of Response% becomes 2.

The *MsgBox* Statement

The MsgBox statement works similarly to the MsgBox function. The difference is that the MsgBox statement does not return information about which button the user selects.

The syntax of the MsgBox statement parallels that of the MsgBox function. You place the MsgBox statement, however, on a line by itself—you don't use this statement on the right side of an assignment instruction. The general syntax is as follows:

```
MsgBox msgstr, options, titlestr
```

Notice that the parentheses are gone. As is the case for the MsgBox function, the *options* and *titlestr* parameters are optional. The following is an example of the simplest form of the MsgBox statement:

```
MsgBox "Top of the morning to you"
```

This instruction produces the message box that Figure 10.6 shows.

Figure 10.6.

An example created with the MsgBox statement.

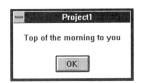

You can display the same set of buttons and icons with the MsgBox statement as you can with the MsgBox function. The *options* parameter can have the same values with the statement as with the function.

The statement does not provide information about which of the buttons the user selects, so you rarely include any others (except the OK button). If you do include other buttons, the message box closes, regardless of which one the user selects.

You can add both an icon and a custom title by providing values for the two optional parameters. For example, here is the preceding instruction with an exclamation point icon and a title bar:

```
MsgBox "Top of the morning to you", 48, "Greetings"
```

Figure 10.7 shows the result.

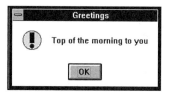

Figure 10.7.

The MsgBox statement with optional parameters.

The DIALOGBX Example— No Forms Allowed

The following sample application, called DIALOGBX, uses both input and message boxes. With an InputBox$ function, the program requests that you enter your name. Then, the program uses a MsgBox statement to greet you. Finally, with a MsgBox function, you are asked whether you want to continue.

This project demonstrates an interesting technique—writing an application that does not use any forms or graphics controls. The user sees only the dialog boxes generated by InputBox$ and MsgBox.

The program consists of a single code module. The active code for the module consists of a Sub Main procedure. As described in Chapter 9, "Managing Projects," Visual Basic looks for the Sub Main procedure as a start up module whenever an application does not have any forms.

Creating DIALOGBX

Follow these steps to create the DIALOGBX application:

1. Start a new project (choose the **New Project** option from the **File** menu).

2. Choose the New **Module** option from the **File** menu.

   This step creates a code module with the default name of MODULE1.BAS.

3. Activate the code module for MODULE1.BAS. (Note: This step is not necessary if the Code window for MODULE1.BAS is currently open, with the Module1.bas title bar highlighted.)

   To do so, open the Project window (choose the **Project** option from the **Window** menu). In the Project window, click MODULE1.BAS to highlight that item. Then, click the View Code button in the Project window.

4. Load Visual Basic's CONSTANT.TXT file into MODULE1.BAS.

   To do so, choose the Load Text...option from the **File** menu. The Load Text dialog box opens. Find the file named CONSTANT.TXT; it should be visible in the File Name list box. (If not, you must search through your directory files to find CONSTANT.TXT.) Double-click CONSTANT.TXT (alternatively, you can click the file name once to highlight it, then click Merge).

5. Type the `Sub Main` procedure into the General Declarations section of MODULE1.BAS.

The module currently consists of a copy of CONSTANT.TXT. Scroll to the end of the module and type the following procedure:

```
Sub Main ()
    Dim NewLine As String
    Dim ThreeLines As String
    Dim YourName As String
    Dim Message As String
    Dim Reply As Integer
    Dim BoxStyle As Integer

    NewLine = Chr$(10)
    ThreeLines = NewLine & NewLine & NewLine

    Do
        YourName = InputBox$("What's your name?", "Name please")

        Message = "Welcome aboard:" & ThreeLines & YourName
        BoxStyle = MB_ICONEXCLAMATION
        MsgBox Message, BoxStyle, "Hello"

        BoxStyle = MB_YESNOCANCEL + MB_ICONQUESTION
        Reply = MsgBox("Greet another?", BoxStyle, "What do you say?")
    Loop While Reply = IDYES
    End
End Sub
```

6. Save the module as DIALOGBX.BAS.

To do so, choose the Save File **As**... option from the **File** menu. When the Save File As dialog box opens, type the file name as DIALOGBX.BAS, then click OK.

7. Make `Sub Main` the start up form.

This step causes `Sub Main` to execute when the application begins (as opposed to the application loading a form and waiting for event procedures to occur). To do this step, choose the **P**roject...item from the **O**ptions menu. Click the Start Up Form option, moving the text `Form1` to the Settings box. Click the down arrow to the right of the Settings box to open a drop-down list. Choose `Sub Main` from this list (see Figure 10.8). Click OK to close the dialog box.

Figure 10.8.

Designating **Sub Main** as the start up form.

8. Remove `Form1` from the Project.

   This project does not use any forms, so you can remove `Form1` (currently blank) from the project. To do so, open the Project window and click FORM1.FRM. This gives `Form1` the focus. Now, open the **F**ile menu and choose the **R**emove File option.

9. Save the Project as DIALOGBX.MAK.

   To do so, choose the Sav**e** Project As option from the **F**ile menu. When the Save Project As dialog box opens, specify the project name as DIALOGBX.MAK.

Running DIALOGBX

The application begins by displaying an input box that prompts you to enter your name. Figure 10.9 shows this input box with the name `Rumplestiltskin` entered. After typing your name, click OK to continue.

Figure 10.9.

The Name please input box.

The input box closes, and a message box opens (see Figure 10.10). This box greets Rumplestiltskin by name, and includes an exclamation point icon. Click OK to continue.

The first message box closes and a second one opens (see Figure 10.11). This new box displays the question mark icon, and asks whether another user wants to be greeted. If you click either the No or Cancel button, the application ends. If you click the Yes button, however, the message box closes and the program recycles by reopening the original input box.

How DIALOGBX Works

Sub Main contains a Do-Loop structure that executes repeatedly, as long as the user requests that additional people be greeted. For more information on loops, see Chapter 15, "Program Flow and Decision Making."

The InputBox$ function opens an input box. It contains a text box in which you type a name. When you close the input box, the variable YourName contains a copy of the text string that you typed.

The program now displays a message box using the MsgBox statement. The variable Message contains the text displayed in the message box. Notice how the value of Message is constructed using the NewLine and ThreeLines variables. NewLine consists of the special character, Chr$(10), which creates a line feed. ThreeLines consists of three line feeds. The ampersand (&) is a string operator that joins individual strings to create a longer one.

By embedding three line feeds in Message, you format the displayed text in the message box. A line break appears after Welcome Aboard: and three blank lines occur before the name is displayed. For more information on working with the ampersand operator, the Chr$ function, and manipulating string data in general, see Chapter 17, "Working with Strings."

The program code assigns the value of the constant MB_ICONEXCLAMATION to the variable BoxStyle. This constant is one of several defined in the CONSTANT.TXT file. The CONSTANT.TXT file assigns the value 64 to the constant MB_ICONINFORMATION. This value corresponds to the correct value for the information icon. For more information on CONSTANT.TXT, see Chapter 14, "Language Building Blocks."

Then, BoxStyle specifies the displayed icon in the MsgBox instruction which follows. Notice that the MsgBox instruction uses the third parameter to specify a caption which reads Hello.

The program code then assigns a new value to BoxStyle in preparation for the MsgBox function. Notice here that the value of BoxStyle consists of adding together two constants: one to display the Yes, No, and Cancel buttons, and the other—the question mark icon.

The MsgBox function asks the user whether the program should greet another person. The function returns the value of the selected button, which the program assigns to the variable Reply. Then, the Loop instruction checks whether Reply has the value corresponding to the Yes button. If so, the program continues going through the loop. If not, the program terminates.

Creating Customized Dialog Boxes

Although InputBox$ and MsgBox work well for creating standard input and message boxes, you might want to design a custom dialog box for a particular application. You might want to do this for many reasons. Perhaps you want the dialog box to display a picture, contain more than one input box, or not be modal.

You create customized dialog boxes by designing forms that contain the graphics controls and properties you require. You can load and hide these custom dialog boxes as required by your application.

When used in a general sense, the terms "dialog box" and "form" become hard to differentiate. After all, most forms display information, and sometimes request it from the user. At times, a form can have attributes of either an input or message box, or both.

Custom Dialog Boxes—An Example

Consider a practical example of an application built around dialog boxes. This project, called Loan, computes the payment required to pay back a loan. You might use Loan when contemplating a loan for a home, car, computer, or other major purchase. By comparing loan terms and your payments, you are better equipped to determine the best loan for your situation.

For houses, cars, and most other purchases that might require consumer loans, you make payments monthly. Besides monthly payments, Loan can calculate quarterly and yearly payments.

Loan assumes that all payments (except possibly the last) are equal. You provide the amount of the loan, the annual interest rate, the term of the loan (in years), and whether the payment schedule is monthly, quarterly, or annually. Loan computes the amount of each payment.

A Sample Run

When you start Loan, you first see a customized dialog box. You provide the loan information using this dialog box. At its top are three text boxes. In these boxes, you input the loan principal (the amount borrowed), the interest rate, and the length of the loan (in years).

You specify the payment schedule by clicking one of the three option buttons. These buttons represent monthly, quarterly, and yearly payments.

To see the computed payment, click the command button to the far left. This button has the label Calculate Payment. Loan responds with a message box showing the amount of each payment. To end Loan, you click the command button to the far right labeled Quit.

Figure 10.12 shows the input dialog box filled with sample loan data.

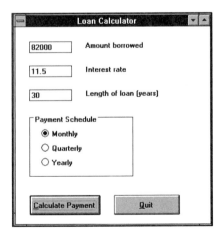

Figure 10.12.

Sample loan information is input.

When you click the Calculate Payment button, Loan responds with the message box that Figure 10.13 shows. As the box indicates, the monthly payment for the sample loan is $812.04.

Figure 10.13.

Output from the Loan application.

Creating the Loan Project

The Loan project consists of one form containing several controls. You create a user-defined function, named LoanPay, which you place in the Declarations section at the form level. The following sections explain how to draw the interface and write the event procedures.

Drawing the Interface

Start a new project with a blank form which you will turn into a customized dialog box. Using the toolbox, place the following controls on the form: three text boxes, three labels, one frame, three option buttons (in the frame), and two command buttons.

> *Before* you put option buttons in the frame, make sure you place the frame on the form. If you try to place a frame over the option buttons, it obscures them.

Use the Properties window to assign the properties that Table 10.6 shows.

Table 10.6. Design-time properties.

Control	Property	Value
Form1	Caption	Loan Calculator
	Left	630
	Top	1140
	Width	5115
	Height	5325

Table 10.6. Continued

Control	Property	Value
Text1	Name	txtPrincipal
	Left	360
	Top	360
	Width	1095
	Height	285
Text2	Name	txtIntRate
	Left	360
	Top	960
	Width	1095
	Height	285
Text3	Name	txtTerm
	Left	360
	Top	1560
	Width	1095
	Height	285
Label1	Caption	Amount Borrowed
	Left	1800
	Top	360
	Width	2055
	Height	255
Label2	Caption	Interest Rate
	Left	1800
	Top	960
	Width	1215
	Height	255

Control	Property	Value
Label3	Caption	Length of Loan (years)
	Left	1800
	Top	1560
	Width	1935
	Height	255
Frame1	Caption	Payment Schedule
	Left	360
	Top	2160
	Width	2655
	Height	1575
Option1	Caption	Monthly
	Name	optMonthly
	Left	300
	Top	360
	Width	1215
	Height	255
Option2	Caption	Quarterly
	Name	optQuarterly
	Left	300
	Top	720
	Width	1335
	Height	255
Option3	Caption	Yearly
	Name	optYearly
	Left	300

Table 10.6. Continued

Control	Property	Value
	Top	1080
	Width	1095
	Height	255
Command1	Caption	Calculate Payment
	Name	cmdCalcPayment
	Left	360
	Top	4200
	Width	1815
	Height	495
Command2	Caption	Quit
	Name	cmdQuit
	Left	2520
	Top	4200
	Width	1695
	Height	495

Writing the Code

Open the Code window (press F7). Select the (general) section from the Object drop-down list box. Then, choose (declarations) from the Proc drop-down list box. Type the following code:

```
Dim Prin As Currency     'Principal
Dim Payment As Currency
Dim Term As Integer, TotalNumPay As Integer
Dim NumPayPerYear As Integer
Dim IRate As Double      'Interest Rate
Dim AdjustedRate As Double, Factor As Double
```

```
Function LoanPay (Prin, IRate, Term, NumPayPerYear) As Currency
    TotalNumPay = Term * NumPayPerYear
    AdjustedRate = Log(1# + IRate / 100 / NumPayPerYear)
    Factor = Exp(-TotalNumPay * AdjustedRate)
    LoanPay = Prin * IRate / 100 / NumPayPerYear / (1# - Factor)
End Function
```

The LoanPay function returns the loan payment as a function of the following: the principal (amount borrowed), the interest rate, term (length of the loan), and the number of payments per year.

The main work of the program occurs when the user clicks the Calculate Payment command button. In the program, this button has the name cmdCalcPayment. Create the following Click event procedure:

```
Sub cmdCalcPayment_Click ()
    'Get loan data from text boxes
    Prin = Val(txtPrincipal.Text)       'Amount borrowed
    IRate = Val(txtIntRate.Text)        'Interest rate
    Term = Val(txtTerm.Text)            'Length of loan (years)

    'Get number of payments per year
    If optMonthly Then NumPayPerYear = 12
    If optQuarterly Then NumPayPerYear = 4
    If optYearly Then NumPayPerYear = 1

    'Calculate size of each payment
    Payment = LoanPay(Prin, IRate, Term, NumPayPerYear)

    'Display Results
    Pay$ = Format$(Payment, "Currency")    'String form of Payment
    Message$ = "Payment is " & Pay$
    MsgBox Message$, , "Loan Payment"
End Sub
```

Finally, create the Click event procedure for the second command button. Clicking this button ends the program, so the necessary event procedure is simple:

```
Sub cmdQuit_Click ()
    End
End Sub
```

How Loan Works

The following section describes how the programming instructions in the Loan project work. If you are not familiar with some of the language keywords, the discussion includes references to the various chapters that discuss these words.

Declaring the Variables

The Dim instructions declare the variables used in the program and assign to them the data types. Currency is a Visual Basic data type specifically designed for variables storing financial data. For more information on Dim and the Currency data type, see Chapter 14, "Language Building Blocks."

The *LoanPay* Function

LoanPay is a user-defined function. This function calculates the loan payment as a function of the loan specifications. The calculations involved in this function are derived from financial formulas. Note that the function returns a value of the Currency data type. Along with the Dim instructions, this function goes in the (general) section at the form level. The cmdCalcPayment_Click event procedure calls LoanPay.

Reading the Data in the Text Boxes

The Click procedure for the cmdCalcPayment command button begins with three instructions that read the input values in the text boxes. The Val function used in these instructions converts the string information from the text boxes into numeric values. For more information on Val, see Chapter 17, "Working with Strings."

Reading the Option Buttons

Next, the three If instructions read the option buttons and set the value of NumPayPerYear accordingly. These instructions work with Boolean (True/False) values. For example, optMonthly has the value True if the Monthly option button is on, and False if it is off. Option buttons work as a group. At any time, therefore, only one button from optMonthly, optQuarterly, and optYearly is on. In other words, *only one* of the three If instructions is True.

Notice that each If instruction has an implied "is true" phrase. For example, the instruction If optMonthly Then...is equivalent to saying "if the value of optMonthly is true, then..." For more information on If and testing for True/False conditions, see Chapter 15, "Program Flow and Decision Making."

Calculating the Payment

After the If instructions, the next executable instruction invokes the LoanPay function. The program stores the returned value in the variable named Payment.

Formatting the Output

Finally, the value of Payment must be expressed as a string value in a format suitable for display. Visual Basic's Format$ function does this. Notice the term "Currency" that appears in the function call. This term is one of Visual Basic's predefined format names. As its name implies, Currency formats financial data in standard business format: a dollar sign in front, a comma after every three digits, and two digits to the right of the decimal point. Then, the program assigns the formatted string to the string variable Pay$. For more information on Format$, see Chapter 17, "Working with Strings."

The variable Message$ stores the string message, then the MsgBox instruction displays the string. Notice that the assignment instruction for Message$ uses the ampersand (&) as the string concatenation operator. As explained in the DIALOGBX example, this operator joins two string expressions to create a larger one. For more information on concatenating strings and using the & operator, see Chapter 17, "Working with Strings."

Summary

Dialog boxes provide a mechanism for displaying and receiving information. The three general types of dialog boxes include a message box, which displays information; an input box, which provides a way for the user to type text input; and a customized dialog box, which you can design to handle special needs, such as inputting two or more values at one time.

Visual Basic provides the InputBox$ function to create standard input boxes. The MsgBox statement and MsgBox function produce standard message boxes. The dialog boxes created by InputBox$ and MsgBox are modal. The user cannot activate any other part of the application until closing the dialog box.

By designing your own forms, you can create customized dialog boxes that fit particular situations. These forms need not be modal.

Displaying Graphics

E ffective graphics can enhance almost any application by providing easy-to-view output, user-friendliness, style, and animation. Being a graphical environment, Windows fully supports the manipulation of graphics images. As a "citizen" of the Windows environment, Visual Basic takes advantage of this graphical platform to provide you with an extensive set of graphing tools.

The net result is that you can create and manipulate graphics images with astonishing ease. Your finished applications can have the look of professional commercial applications.

This chapter discusses graphics from several perspectives. The main topics include:

- Using the Line and Shape graphic controls
- Drawing points, lines, and two-dimensional shapes with the graphics methods at run time
- Displaying pictures and icons
- Using colors
- Understanding the trade-offs between persistent graphics and memory usage
- Working with standard and customized coordinate systems
- Using `Paint` events
- Creating simple animation

NOTE In Windows, and therefore in Visual Basic, the distinction between graphics and text is less well defined than in DOS-based programming languages. Except for the text-based controls such as list boxes, labels, and text boxes, Visual Basic treats text as just another type of graphics image. This chapter, however, discusses the "traditional" graphics of lines, shapes, circles, and picture images. For more about displaying text, see Chapter 12, "Displaying Text and Fonts."

Introduction to Graphics

In Visual Basic applications, you create graphics with the following three types of tools:

Line and Shape controls	These controls, available from the Toolbox, create straight lines and two-dimensional shapes such as boxes and rectangles. As you develop the user interface for an application, you can use these controls at design time to enhance the application's appearance. The Line and Shape controls work on forms, picture boxes, and frames.
The graphics methods	The graphics methods, such as PSet, Line, and Circle, appear in your program code. With these methods, you can draw points, lines, and two-dimensional shapes at run time. The graphics methods work on forms and picture boxes.
Pictures and icons	The effective use of pictures and icons can enhance any application. Such graphics images are stored in disk files. You can display pictures and icons in forms, picture boxes, and image controls.

During the course of this chapter, you learn how to use each of these tools to create effective graphics.

Understanding Graphic Containers

Whenever you draw a graphics image, whether a single point or a fancy picture, you draw the graphic inside a container. In Visual Basic parlance, a *container* is simply an object that holds other objects.

The primary containers for graphics are forms and picture boxes. Anytime you draw a graphic in Visual Basic, you specify (either explicitly or implicitly), the container that holds that graphic.

Once drawn, the graphic is bound inside its container. If you move or resize the container, the graphic remains confined inside its container.

For example, suppose you draw some graphics on a form. If you move the form, the graphics move as well. The graphics always keep the same proportional relationship to the form. If you resize the form to a smaller size, you can cut off some of the graphics from view. The graphics will not "spill over" outside the form's new boundary.

The container concept is prevalent at all levels in Visual Basic. For example, consider a graphics image drawn inside a picture box control. The picture box is the container for the graphics. The form is the container for the picture box. Finally, the Screen object is the container for the form.

NOTE The Screen object has several properties that you can use to reference individual forms and to specify characteristics of the video display. For example, your program code can determine the height and width of the entire video screen by examining the values of Screen.Height and Screen.Width, respectively. For more information about using the Screen object to determine available fonts, see Chapter 12, "Displaying Text and Fonts."

Introducing Coordinate Systems

If you're going to draw a graphic, you must have a way to specify exactly where that graphic should appear. The purpose of a coordinate system is to provide you with a mechanism for doing just that.

Inside a container, a location is specified by an x-coordinate and a y-coordinate. The x-coordinate specifies the horizontal position with a numerical value. Similarly, the y-coordinate specifies the vertical position with a number.

By convention, the upper left corner of a container is designated to have an x-coordinate of 0 and a y-coordinate of 0. X-values increase toward the right and y-values increase toward the bottom of the container.

Coordinates are often specified as a number pair in parentheses, with the x-coordinate first. For example, the point (200, 350) lies 200 units to the right of the upper left corner, and 350 units below that corner. See Figure 11.1.

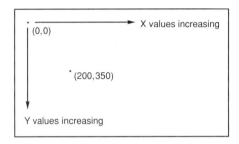

Figure 11.1.

A standard coordinate system.

The point here is that each container has its own local coordinate system. For example, no matter where a picture box is located within a form, and no matter where the form is located on-screen, the coordinates of the upper left corner of that picture box are (0, 0). Move the picture box and the upper left corner is still at location (0, 0).

So, to specify a drawing location, you specify the container *and* the coordinates within that container. Later in this chapter you learn how to manipulate the measuring units of a coordinate system and also how you can customize a coordinate system.

Working with Colors

Windows supports the full color capability of today's PC equipment. Your Visual Basic applications can tap these color resources to produce spectacular looking applications.

If you could take out a powerful magnifying glass and examine your video screen, you would see what appears to be a dense grid of dots. Each dot can be one of several possible colors. By specifying the color of each dot, you create a visual image. With standard VGA resolution, the screen consists of more than 300,000 dots.

In computing terminology, these dots are called pixels. A *pixel* ("picture element") is the smallest screen area that can be assigned an individual color.

Now, if your program code has to display the color for each pixel one at a time, you're going to be old and gray before you finish writing your first serious graphics application. Visual Basic provides several functions, techniques, and methods so that you can specify colors for a group of pixels at once. For example, with the `Circle` method, you can draw a circle of any size in a specified color.

Foreground and Background Colors

When discussing graphics, the terms *foreground color* and *background color* become important. If you think about these terms, however, the distinction between the foreground and the background is a bit vague.

After all, the video screen is simply a grid of pixels with each pixel having a particular color. Technically speaking, you can't say that one pixel is in the foreground and another pixel is in the background. It's like trying to decide if a zebra is black with white stripes or white with black stripes.

Nevertheless, programmers do speak of foreground and background colors. In practice, most graphics consist of images drawn on a uniform background. In this light, you can distinguish between foreground and background colors as follows:

- The *foreground color* is the color of the drawn object. For example, you draw a red circle by turning each pixel of the circle into red. In this case, red is the foreground color.

- The *background color*, naturally enough, is the color of all the background pixels. When you start a new project, the default form has a white background.

For forms and for most controls, the ForeColor property specifies the foreground color and the BackColor property specifies the background color.

Specifying a Color Value

Visual Basic identifies each available color with a unique numerical value. Standard VGA equipment can display 256 different colors simultaneously. However, there are more than 16 million different colors available! That's a lot of colors. Fortunately, Visual Basic provides several ways to specify these color values without requiring you to have a photographic memory.

There are several situations where you need to specify a color. At design time, you often choose a color as a property value. For example, in previous chapters, you used the Properties window to specify the value of a form's BackColor property.

At run time, your program code frequently must specify colors. For example, the graphics methods accept a color parameter so that you can specify the foreground color for the drawn image.

There are four techniques for specifying a color value in your program code:

- Specify the numerical value explicitly as a hexadecimal number.

- Use a constant in the CONSTANT.TXT file.

■ Use the RGB function.

■ Use the QBColor function.

The following sections briefly explain each of these techniques.

Specifying the Numeric Value Explicitly

The simplest way to specify a color is to write its numerical value explicitly. However, unless you have an incredible penchant for remembering large arcane numbers, you're not likely to use this technique.

Recall from Chapter 5, "Understanding Forms, Events, and Properties," that color values are usually expressed as large hexadecimal values. You can see examples of these numbers if you open the Properties window and examine the values for the form's ForeColor and BackColor properties. With the Color Palette, you can choose specific colors and watch the numerical values for the properties change. (The Color Palette is explained throughout the earlier chapters.)

For example, the color code value for bright pink is &H00FF00FF&. In your program code, the following instruction specifies that the background color of MyForm should be bright pink:

```
MyForm.BackColor = &HFF00FF&
```

Using CONSTANT.TXT

Visual Basic's CONSTANT.TXT file defines several constants associated with colors. With these constants, you can specify a color value with a descriptive name. For example, with CONSTANT.TXT loaded into your application, you can specify a green background as follows:

```
MyForm.BackColor = GREEN
```

CONSTANT.TXT is introduced in Chapter 8, "Using the Toolbox and Its Common Controls," and is discussed in depth in Chapter 14, "Language Building Blocks."

Using the *RGB* Function

Screen colors are often called *RGB colors*. That's because each color is a blend of the three primary screen colors: *Red, Green,* and *Blue*. The resulting color depends on the intensity level of each of the primary colors.

Visual Basic's RGB function returns the hexadecimal (long integer) value that corresponds to an RGB color. You specify the intensity level for each of the three primary colors. Each intensity level can range from a value of 0 (exclude that primary color) to 255 (strongest possible intensity).

```
RGB(red, green, blue)
```

in which

    red specifies the intensity of red,

    green specifies the intensity of green,

and

    blue specifies the intensity of blue.

For example, `RGB(128, 128, 128)` specifies a moderate amount of each primary color. The result is gray. `RGB(220, 120, 20)` specifies a strong red component, moderate green component, and weak blue component.

The following instruction makes the background color of the form named `MyForm` the richest possible green:

```
MyForm.BackColor = RGB(0, 255, 0)
```

Using the *QBColor* Function

The QuickBasic and QBasic languages have 16 predefined colors. (These DOS-based versions of BASIC have been around for many years and are still in use today.) With Visual Basic's `QBColor` function, you can designate one of these 16 colors with a numeric argument from `0` to `15`.

```
QBColor(colorval)
```

in which

    colorval specifies a color with an integer value in the range from `0` to `15`.

Table 11.1 shows the relationship between the `colorval` parameter and the resulting RGB color.

Table 11.1. The *QBColor* function.

Value of *colorval*	Resulting color
0	Black
1	Blue
2	Green

continues

Table 11.1. Continued	
Value of *colorval*	**Resulting color**
3	Cyan
4	Red
5	Magenta
6	Yellow
7	White
8	Gray
9	Light blue
10	Light green
11	Light cyan
12	Light red
13	Light magenta
14	Light yellow
15	Bright white

To make `MyForm`'s background green, you can use the `QBColor` function as follows:

```
MyForm.BackColor = QBColor(2)
```

Introducing Persistent Graphics and the *AutoRedraw* Property

In the coursep of running most Windows applications, individual windows become temporarily obscured and then later re-exposed. Your Visual Basic applications are no exception.

A form or picture box can become momentarily concealed in a number of ways. For example, a dialog box might pop open, a form can be resized and minimized, or you might move one window temporarily over another. When several applications are running simultaneously, it's normal for one application to temporarily cover up another application.

Whenever a window is re-exposed, the contents of that window must be redrawn. As it turns out, Windows automatically handles this redrawing process for everything except graphics drawn at run time with the graphics methods.

When a form or picture box container is covered and then re-exposed, you usually want that container to appear just as it did before being covered. If the graphics in the container automatically regenerate themselves, such graphics are called *persistent graphics*.

Forms and picture boxes have an AutoRedraw property. By default, the value for this property is False. However, if you set a container's AutoRedraw property to True, Visual Basic automatically creates persistent graphics for that container.

When AutoRedraw is True, Visual Basic taxes the memory resources of your computer. As discussed later in this chapter, many tradeoffs come into play involving persistent graphics, AutoRedraw, memory usage, and application performance.

To reiterate, AutoRedraw affects only the graphics drawn with the graphics methods such as PSet and Circle. Whether AutoRedraw is True or False, Windows automatically regenerates the controls and pictures you place in a form or picture box.

Device Independence versus Resource Allocation

One of the nice features about Visual Basic graphics is device independence. If you have experience programming in DOS-based versions of BASIC such as QuickBASIC and QBasic, you know the complications involved in writing graphical applications. Your program code must specify the desired graphics screen mode, determine whether the host computer has a compatible video board installed, and then create the actual graphics.

Windows, on the other hand, standardizes the video environment. Because your Visual Basic applications run in this standard environment, your program code is spared from having to determine the hardware configuration of the host computer. This device-independent nature means that your applications tend to run smoothly on any system running Windows.

However, Windows is resource-hungry. The functionality and flexibility of Windows comes at the cost of less memory available for your application. Also, there is some performance degradation due to the Windows overhead in managing the graphical environment.

Using the Line and Shape Controls

With the Line and Shape controls, you can draw straight lines and various two-dimensional shapes. These controls are available from the Toolbox. You can place line and shape controls on a form, picture box, or frame.

The primary use of line and shape is to enhance a form's visual appearance. Usually, you place these controls on a form or picture box at design time and keep the controls fixed (relative to their container) while the program runs. As with all controls, line and shape controls have a Name property. At run time, your program code can reference line and shape controls and their properties.

However, compared to most of the other controls in the Toolbox, line and shape controls have limited functionality. Here are some of their limitations:

- *Line and shape controls have no events.* As a result, the controls can't respond to system or user-generated events at run time.

- *Line and shape controls have a limited set of properties and methods.* Although you rarely do so in practice, you can modify their property values at run time to create various visual effects.

- *Line and shape controls cannot receive the focus at run time.* The controls have no TabIndex property. At run time, the user cannot access the controls with the mouse or keyboard.

A line or shape control is not affected by the value of its container's AutoRedraw property. A line or shape persists even if its container's AutoRedraw property is False.

The following sections describe in detail how you use the line and shape controls.

The Line Control

A Line control displays a straight line. The line can be horizontal, vertical, or diagonal. At design time, a line control has two sizing handles, one handle at each end of the line. By moving these handles anywhere on the form (or other container holding the line control), you can create a line of any length, location, and angular orientation.

A few well-placed lines can greatly enhance a form's appearance. For example, Figure 11.2 shows a survey form that contains some line controls mixed in with the labels and check boxes.

Line controls have thirteen properties: BorderColor, BorderStyle, BorderWidth, DrawMode, Index, Name, Parent, Tag, Visible, X1, X2, Y1, and Y2. You can set values for these properties at design time and also modify their values in program code at run time. (The Parent property is an exception. This property is not available at design time, but can be read at run time.) The following sections describe the most important of these properties.

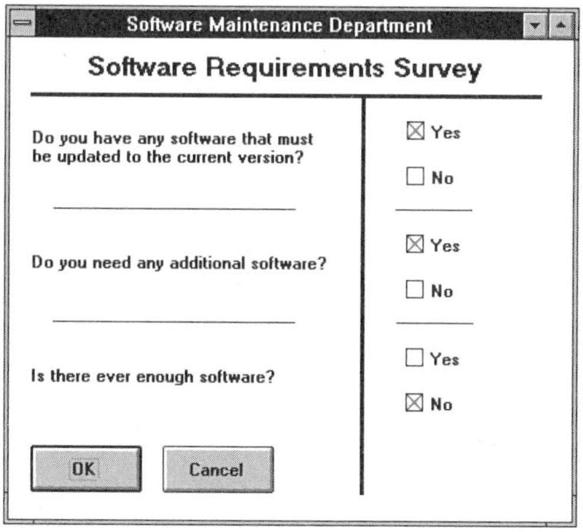

Figure 11.2.

A form containing some line controls.

The *Name* Property

By default, Visual Basic names the first line control on a form as Line1. Subsequent lines are named Line2, Line3, and so on. At design time, you can modify a default name by changing the value of the control's Name property.

Location Properties—*X1, Y1, X2, Y2*

The X1, Y1, X2, and Y2 properties determine the location of the line relative to its container. Line controls are the only controls that have these properties. (Line controls do not have the Left, Top, Height, and Width properties supported by most other controls.)

The values of X1 and Y1 specify, respectively, the horizontal and vertical coordinates at one end of the line. Similarly, X2 and Y2 specify the coordinates at the other end of the line. Remember that unless you have modified the container's Scale-related properties, the values of Y1 and Y2 increase downward toward the bottom of the container. If X1 and Y1 are both 0, one end of the line is at the upper left corner of the container.

Line controls do not support the Move method. If you want to move a line at run time, your program code can modify the values of X1, Y1, X2, or Y2 as appropriate. For example, the following instructions move one end of a line control named Line1 350 twips to the right and 200 twips upward:

```
Line1.X2 = Line1.X2 + 350
Line1.Y2 = Line1.Y2 - 200
```

(For more about the Move method, see "Moving Pictures at Run Time" later in this chapter.)

The *BorderWidth* Property

The BorderWidth property determines the thickness of the drawn line. The default value is 1, which specifies the minimum line thickness. To get wider lines, you can increase the value up to a maximum of 8192.

The *BorderColor* Property

The BorderColor property determines the color of the drawn line. The default value is the standard Windows drawing color, normally black. At design time, you can select the value of BorderColor from the Color Palette. At run time, you can modify a line control's color by changing the value of this property in program code.

In program code, you can assign any numerical value that represents a color to the value of BorderColor. The easiest way to do this is with the RGB function or the QBColor function. For example, the following instruction changes the color of the Line3 control on MyForm to green:

```
MyForm.Line3.BorderColor = QBColor(2)    'green
```

Notice that this instruction specifies the form and the control. If you omit the form designation, Visual Basic assumes the current form.

Alternatively, if CONSTANT.TXT is loaded in the application, you can assign the value of BorderColor with one of the color constants from that file.

The *BorderStyle* Property

A drawn line does not have to be solid. By modifying the value of the BorderStyle property, you can draw a line in one of several styles. Table 11.2 shows the various styles that correspond to the values of BorderStyle. The settings in this table are valid for both the line control and the shape control.

Table 11.2. Values of *BorderStyle* for line and shape controls.

Value of *BorderStyle*	Drawing Style
0	Transparent
1	Solid (the default style)
2	Dashed

Value of *BorderStyle*	Drawing Style
3	Dotted
4	Dash-dot
5	Dash-dot-dot
6	Inside solid

BorderStyle values of 1 and 6 each produce solid lines. The distinction between these values is not important for the line control but it is meaningful for shapes. For more on this topic, see "The Shape Control" later in this chapter.

The values of BorderWidth and BorderStyle are not independent. If BorderWidth is greater than the default value of 1, the resulting line is solid regardless of the value of BorderStyle. In fact, if BorderWidth is greater than 1, and BorderStyle has a value other than 1 or 6, Visual Basic automatically resets the value of BorderStyle back to the default value of 1.

The *DrawMode* Property

You can think of Visual Basic drawing each line with a pen. By default, this pen draws the line in the color specified by BorderColor. However, if you modify the value of DrawMode, you can make the pen produce specialized drawing characteristics. The color of each point in the drawn line depends on the pen color *and* the color of the background pixel on which each point in the line is to be drawn.

For example, the default value of DrawMode is 13. This represents the simplest situation—each point in the line is just the pen color. If DrawMode is 4, Visual Basic applies the Not operator to the pen's color code. The result is a line of the "opposite" pen color. If DrawMode is 6, Visual Basic applies Not to the color code of the pixel to be drawn upon. The resulting color is the "opposite" of the background color.

Other values of DrawMode are more interesting. For example, if DrawMode is 15, Visual Basic combines the color codes for the pen color and the current color of the pixel to be drawn upon. The resulting color code specifies the actual drawing color.

If DrawMode is 7, Visual Basic applies the Xor operator to the color codes of the pen and the background pixel. When a line is drawn twice with this setting, the second drawing restores the background exactly as it existed before the first drawing. This effect is known as *Xor animation*.

In all, Visual Basic supports 16 different values of DrawMode.

The *Visible* Property

As with other controls, the Visible property determines whether the line control is visible at run time. A value of True (the default) makes the line visible, False makes the line invisible.

NOTE The value of Visible affects only run-time visibility. If you set Visible to False with the Properties window, the control remains visible at design time.

The Shape Control

A Shape control displays a two-dimensional enclosed figure. Six different geometric shapes can be drawn. At design time, a shape control has the conventional six sizing handles that appear with most controls. By moving a shape's handles, you can stretch the shape to any desired size.

Figure 11.3 shows an example of each of the different shapes you can draw with the shape control. In this figure, each shape is drawn with different property values. As explained in the following sections, you can adjust these property values to produce a variety of visual effects.

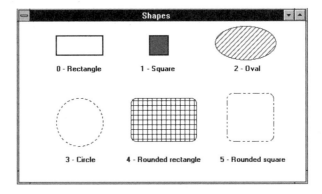

Figure 11.3.

Six examples of the shape control.

NOTE Although each shape drawn with a Shape control produces an enclosed two-dimensional figure, you cannot use the resulting shapes as containers for other graphics.

With the exceptions of the X1, Y1, X2, and Y2 properties, shape controls have the same properties as line controls. In addition, shape controls have the

BackColor, BackStyle, FillColor, FillStyle, Left, Top, Height, Width, and Shape properties. The following sections describe the differences between the Shape control properties and the Line control properties.

The *Shape* Property

The value of the Shape property determines which of the six possible shapes the Shape control displays. In Figure 11.3, the value of the Shape property is indicated below each of the six shapes. Table 11.3 lists the possible shapes.

Table 11.3. Values of the *Shape* property.	
Value of *Shape* Property	**Resulting shape**
0	Rectangle
1	Square
2	Oval
3	Circle
4	Rectangle with rounded corners
5	Square with rounded corners

The default value of Shape is 0, which produces a rectangle.

Location Properties—*Left, Top, Height,* and *Width*

Like most controls, a Shape control supports the Left, Top, Height, and Width properties. The values of Left and Top specify the control's location relative to its container.

Unlike the line control, you can use the Move method at run time to move a shape control inside its container. If you do, Visual Basic adjusts the values of Left and Top as necessary.

The *Name* Property

By default, Visual Basic names the first shape control on a form as Shape1. Subsequent shape controls are named Shape2, Shape3, and so on.

Border Properties

The BorderColor, BorderWidth, and BorderStyle properties affect the perimeter of the drawn shape. For the most part, these properties work for shape controls as they do for line controls. The values of BorderStyle presented in Table 11.2 are valid for shapes as well as lines.

When the value of BorderWidth is greater than 1, you need to define whether the height and width of the control include the border and exactly where the border begins and the interior area ends.

As it turns out, if the value of BorderWidth is 5 or less, Visual Basic measures the control's height and width from the center of the border. The center of the border doesn't change as long as BorderWidth stays within this range.

However, if BorderWidth has a value greater than 5, the border grows inward (toward the center of the shape) as the border width gets larger. The control's height and width are measured from the outside of the border.

The *BackColor* Property

The BackColor property determines the color of the shape's enclosed area. You can assign a value for this property as you do for other color properties: with the Color Palette at design time, with a color code constant, or with the RGB or QBColor functions at run time.

The *BackStyle* Property

The BackStyle property specifies whether the background behind the shape control is visible. The default value is 1 (Opaque), which means that the color specified by the BackColor property obscures anything from showing through the shape.

If you change the value of BackStyle to 0 (Transparent), the background shows through the shape. This background may be a solid color or may contain graphics such as a picture. When BackStyle is set to transparent, the value of BackColor is irrelevant.

The *FillColor* and *FillStyle* Properties

The FillColor property specifies the color used to fill the shape's enclosed area. As with only color properties, you can assign a value for this property with the Color Palette at design time, with a color code constant, or with the RGB or QBColor functions at run time.

The FillStyle property determines the manner in which the color is applied.

Table 11.4 shows the eight possible values of FillStyle and their resulting effects.

Table 11.4. *FillStyle* effects.

Value of *FillStyle*	Resulting Effect
0	Solid fill
1	Transparent
2	Horizontal lines
3	Vertical lines
4	Upward diagonal (lines go up toward the left)
5	Downward diagonal (lines go down toward the left)
6	Cross-hatched with horizontal & vertical lines
7	Cross hatched with diagonal lines

When FillStyle is 1, the default value, the background shows through and the value of FillColor is irrelevant. When FillStyle is 0, a solid color fills the shape. In this case, the effect is the same as when the BackStyle property is set to opaque.

The other values of FillStyle produce a pattern inside the shape. In Figure 11.3, the value of FillStyle is 5 for the Oval.

Using the Graphics Methods

Visual Basic provides five methods for drawing graphics images at run time. The containers for these graphics methods can be forms or picture box controls but not image controls. Table 11.5 summarizes the five methods.

Table 11.5. Summary of graphics methods.

Method	Description
Cls	Clears the current graphics in the container
PSet	Sets the color of an individual graphic point
Point	Returns the color of a designated point
Line	Draws lines, rectangles, and filled-in boxes
Circle	Draws arcs, circles and ellipses

The graphics methods also work on the `Printer` object. As such, you can display graphics on suitable printers. For more about using printers to display text and graphics, see Chapter 12, "Displaying Text and Fonts."

Before discussing the specifics of how each graphics method works, some introductory discussion is in order. The following topics are discussed next:

- Comparing the graphics methods and the line and shape controls
- Understanding the `Paint` and `Resize` events
- Using the `Refresh` method
- Working with coordinate systems

Comparing the Graphics Methods with the Line and Shape Controls

With the graphics methods, you can draw points, lines, arcs, and certain enclosed shapes. There is some duplication in the effects that you can create with the graphics methods as compared to the line and shape controls. For example, the Shape control and the `Circle` method can each draw circles.

Like all other methods, you can only use the `Line` and `Circle` methods in your program code. The results do not appear until the application is run and the relevant instructions execute. As a result, you never see the effects of the graphics methods at design time. In general, you use the graphics controls when you can create the graphics effects you want at design time.

The graphics methods provide visual effects that you cannot achieve with the line and shape controls. For example, with the graphics methods, you can paint an individual pixel and draw partial arcs. Also, you can draw graphics that appear behind all the form's controls.

On the other hand, the Shape control can draw some shapes that the graphics methods cannot duplicate. For example, the rounded rectangle cannot be (easily) drawn with the graphics methods.

Working with the *Paint* and *Resize* Events

The graphics methods work inside picture boxes and directly on forms. When the value of the container's `AutoRedraw` property is False, the graphics do not persist if another object temporarily obscures the graphic. However, if `AutoRedraw` is True, Visual Basic automatically redraws any necessary graphics.

The `Paint` event occurs for a form (or picture box) when all or part of the form (or picture box) becomes exposed. Such "re-exposure" can occur when the container is moved or resized, or when another window covering the container moves away.

As a result, you frequently use the graphics methods inside the container's `Paint` event. That way, you can redraw the necessary graphics when the container's `AutoRedraw` property is False. Recall that, when `AutoRedraw` is True, Visual Basic does not generate a `Paint` event because the graphics are redrawn automatically.

The `Resize` event occurs in a form or picture box anytime the size of the control changes. This change can result from the user's direct interaction or by instructions in the program code. When `AutoRedraw` is False, Visual Basic automatically calls a `Paint` event after the `Resize` event terminates.

Using the *Refresh* Method

The `Refresh` method causes Visual Basic to immediately redraw a form or control, even when the value of its `AutoRedraw` property is True. For example, the following instruction refreshes the picture box named `MyPicture`:

```
MyPicture.Refresh
```

One by-product of using the `Refresh` method on a form or picture box is that Visual Basic also calls the `Paint` procedure for that control. As a result, many Visual Basic programmers use the `Refresh` method inside `Resize` event procedures to redraw graphics generated from the control's `Paint` event procedure.

Syntax for the Graphics Methods

As with any Visual Basic method, the syntax for the graphics methods includes the object on which the method acts. For example, the following instruction uses the `Cls` method on a picture box named `Picture2`:

```
Picture2.Cls
```

However, you can omit the object in an instruction that invokes a graphics method. For example, `Cls` is a valid instruction all by itself.

When the object is omitted, Visual Basic applies the method to the current form. You must be careful that this result is what you want. For example, if you want to clear the contents of the current picture box, you can't use `Cls` without specifying the picture box. If you do, the result is a cleared form.

In any case, it's good programming practice to always include the object name when using one of the graphics methods. That way, your program code is easier to read and debug.

Some Words about Coordinate Systems

When using the graphics methods, the location of each graphics pixel is identified by two values: an x- (horizontal) coordinate and a y- (vertical) coordinate. As explained earlier in the chapter, such coordinates often are specified as an x,y pair and enclosed in parentheses. For example, (130, 89) identifies the pixel at x-coordinate 130 and y-coordinate 89. Notice that when two coordinate pairs have the same first value, the two pixels are on the same vertical line; when the second values are the same, the two pixels are on the same horizontal line.

By default, location (0, 0) identifies the pixel at the upper left corner of the container. Remember that the container can be a form or a picture box. The x-coordinates increase moving horizontally to the right, and y-coordinates increase moving vertically down.

If you are familiar with mathematical graphs, you are probably accustomed to graphs with origins in the lower left corner and y values increasing upward. The origin in the upper left corner is a computing tradition, and traditions die hard.

The default measuring units are *twips*. A twip is 1/1440 of an inch. So a graphics pixel point at (1440, 0) is 1 inch to the right of the upper left corner.

Keep in mind, however, that twips really measure graphics distances when the object is printed. On two different monitors, the exact distance can vary somewhat between two points specified with the same pairs of coordinates. The size of the difference depends on the specifications of the monitor and the operation of the host computer's graphic card. If you're curious, try drawing some graphics to determine on your monitor how close 1440 twips is to one inch.

Visual Basic provides several properties that allow you to customize the graphics scale and coordinate system for any container. For example, you can specify that the lower left corner of the container is at position (0, 0) and y-coordinates increase as you move up the screen. Also, you can change the measuring units from twips to something else. The "something else" can be inches, pixels, other standard units, or even a customized scale that you create.

For more about redefining the coordinate system, see "Customizing the Coordinate System" later in this chapter. For the time being, the examples in this chapter use the standard coordinate system.

Specifying Coordinates

Most of the graphics methods require one or more coordinate pairs as parameters. In general, there are three ways you can specify a coordinate pair:

- Absolute coordinates
- LPR (Last Point Referenced)
- Relative coordinates

Absolute Coordinates

The simplest way to designate a pixel location is to specify the x,y-coordinates explicitly.

For example, the PSet method draws a point at a specified location. Using absolute coordinates, the following instruction draws on MyForm a point at x-coordinate 214 and y-coordinate 89:

```
MyForm.PSet (214, 89)
```

LPR (Last Point Referenced)

For each container, Visual Basic keeps track of where the last point was displayed. The position of this last point is called the *LPR* (Last Point Referenced).

The Line and Circle methods accept the LPR as a default coordinate point. For example, one form of the Line instruction accepts only a destination parameter. A line is then drawn from the current LPR to this destination point. After the line is drawn, the destination point becomes the new LPR.

Each form and picture box has CurrentX and CurrentY properties. The values of these properties specify the current location of the LPR. You cannot set values for CurrentX and CurrentY at design time, but your program code can read and modify their values at run time. As various graphics instructions execute, Visual Basic automatically adjusts the values of CurrentX and CurrentY.

Relative Coordinates

A third option, available only with the PSet, Line, and Circle methods, is to specify coordinates as a displacement from the LPR. Such coordinates are called *relative* coordinates. You use the keyword Step to specify relative coordinates. Here is a typical example:

```
MyForm.PSet Step (-240, 98)
```

This instruction directs Visual Basic to draw a point 240 twips to the left and 98 twips below the LPR. If the LPR happens to be at (370, 100), the new point plots at (130, 198). Notice that relative coordinates can be positive or negative. Positive x-values are to the right and negative x-values to the left. Positive y-values are down and negative y-values are up.

Drawing Simple Shapes

The following methods produce points, lines, and circles:

- PSet (single points)
- Line (straight lines)
- Circle (circles)

For the time being, the discussion focuses on the simplest forms of these methods. The graphics are drawn in the default color, which is black images on a form's white background. Later in this chapter, you see how to add optional parameters that produce color graphics and create fancier shapes such as rectangles and pie slices.

Plotting Points—The *PSet* Method

The PSet method draws a single point at a given screen location. You may specify the coordinates of the point in absolute or relative terms.

```
container.PSet (x-coord, y-coord)          'Absolute syntax
```

or

```
container.PSet Step(x-coord, y-coord)      'Relative syntax
```

where

   container specifies the name of the form or picture box where the point is to be drawn,

   x-coord specifies the x-coordinate of the point,

and

   y-coord specifies the y-coordinate.

The *container* parameter is optional.

The first syntax, without Step, indicates that the coordinates are in absolute form. For example, the following instruction plots on Form1 the point at x-coordinate 321 and y-coordinate 103:

```
Form1.PSet (321, 103)
```

The second syntax, with `Step`, indicates that the coordinates are in relative form. For example, the following instruction turns on the pixel 200 pixels to the right of the LPR and 180 pixels below the LPR:

```
PSet Step (200, 180)
```

Using the *DrawWidth* Property

Want to test your eyesight? Start a new project with a blank form. Create the following `Form_Click` event procedure:

```
Sub Form_Click ()
   Form1.PSet (3500, 2000)
End Sub
```

The default form has a width of approximately 7000 twips and a height of approximately 4000 twips. So the `PSet` instruction in this procedure draws a point roughly near the center of the form.

Run the application and click the blank form. Visual Basic draws a single point near the form's center. If you can't see the point, don't worry. Good eyesight is mandatory.

To make sure you get the point (pun intended), stop the application. With the Properties window, change the value of the form's `DrawWidth` property to `10`. Run the application again. You won't have trouble seeing the enlarged point now.

For any of the graphics methods, the `DrawWidth` property specifies the size of the drawn line. That is, for `Line` or `Circle`, the value of `DrawWidth` specifies the width of the resulting line and the width of the circle's perimeter, respectively. For `PSet`, the value of `DrawWidth` determines the size of the drawn point.

The default value of `DrawWidth` is `1`. With this setting, the resulting graphics are `1` pixel wide.

`DrawWidth` is a property of the container. The value of `DrawWidth` determines the width of all graphics drawn inside the container.

For any container, you can modify the value of `DrawWidth` at design time or in your program code. If you change the value of `DrawWidth` at run time, you affect the size of subsequent graphics, but nothing happens to previously drawn graphics.

Drawing Straight Lines—The *Line* Method

The Line method draws a straight line. The line can be short, long, horizontal, vertical, or at any angle. You just specify the two end points, and Visual Basic does the rest.

---

container.Line *startpoint* - *endpoint*

where

  container specifies the name of the form or picture box where the line is to be drawn,

  startpoint is the *x,y* location of the starting point of the line,

and

  endpoint is the *x,y* location of the end point of the line.

The *container* parameter is optional. The *startpoint* parameter is also optional, but the *endpoint* parameter is mandatory. If you omit *startpoint*, the line begins at the LPR.

For example, the following instruction draws a line from the point (1000, 300) to the point (2100, 800):

```
Form1.Line (1000, 300)-(2100, 800)
```

 NOTE As with any graphics method, you can specify the coordinates with variables, constants, expressions, and even functions. For example, this instruction is perfectly acceptable:

```
Form1.Line (StartX, 40)-(Form1.CurrentX * 2, Sqr(Ydistance))
```

Drawing a Mountain of Lines

The following event procedure shows Line in action. When you click the form, the procedure draws the simple "mountain" shape shown in Figure 11.4.

```
Sub Form_Click ()
   Dim Xbottom As Integer
   For Xbottom = 500 To 7000 Step 250
      Form1.Line (3750, 250)-(Xbottom, 3700)
   Next Xbottom
End Sub
```

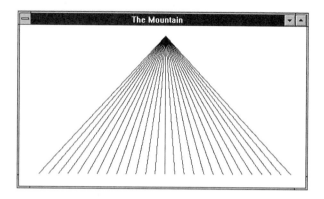

Figure 11.4.

The "mountain" drawn with the **Line** method.

In the mountain figure, all the lines start at x-coordinate 3750 and y-coordinate 250. This point, located near the upper center of the form, is the top of the mountain. The For-Next loop variable Xbottom controls the x-coordinate at the bottom of the mountain. Notice how Xbottom changes values to draw the various lines in the mountain.

Specifying Line Coordinates

In a Line instruction, you can specify the beginning and ending points in absolute coordinates (without Step) or in relative coordinates (with Step).

To specify a relative coordinate, you can use Step with *startpoint*, *endpoint*, or both parameters.

Here are some examples of instructions that use relative coordinates:

```
Picture1.Line Step(100, -300)-(650, 700)
```

The line begins at the point 100 pixels to the right and 300 pixels above the LPR. The line ends at the point with absolute coordinates (650, 700):

```
Picture1.Line (Xval, Yval)-Step(500, 400)
```

The line begins at the point specified by the absolute coordinates (Xval, Yval). This point becomes the LPR. The line ends at the point 500 twips to the right and 400 twips below the first point. The end point becomes the LPR:

```
Picture1.Line Step (-100, 200)-Step(605, 850)
```

The line begins 100 twips to the left and 200 pixels below the LPR. This starting point becomes the LPR. The line ends at the point 605 twips to the right and 850 pixels below the starting point. The end point becomes the LPR.

The last two instructions demonstrate how relative coordinates work with the *endpoint* parameter. When Step appears with the *endpoint* parameter, the LPR when determining the end point is simply the first point in the line.

The starting point parameter is optional in a `Line` instruction. For example:

```
Form1.Line -(800, 1200)
```

This instruction draws a line from the LPR to absolute location (800, 1200). When you omit the *startpoint* parameter, the line begins at the LPR. It's just as though you specified the starting point with the parameter `Step(0, 0)`. Another way to say the same thing is that the line begins at the position specified by the current values of `CurrentX` and `CurrentY`.

One last example:

```
Form1.Line -Step(1440, 0)
```

This instruction draws a horizontal line beginning at the LPR and extending 1440 twips (one inch) to the right.

Using the *DrawStyle* Property

Normally, the graphics methods produce solid lines. By modifying the value of the `DrawStyle` property, you can produce stylized lines. Table 11.6 shows the various available line styles.

Table 11.6. Line styles.

Value of *DrawStyle*	Line Style
0	Solid
1	Dashed
2	Dotted
3	Dash-dot
4	Dash-dot-dot
5	Transparent
6	Inside solid

As with the `DrawWidth` property, `DrawStyle` is a property of the container. The value of `DrawStyle` determines the line style for all graphics drawn inside the container.

The default value of `DrawStyle` is 0. With this setting, the resulting graphics are opaque. Drawing with the Transparent style creates an invisible line. The background remains visible.

Figure 11.5 shows the effect of `DrawStyle` on the mountain you created with the `Line` method. In this figure, dashed lines are drawn instead of solid lines.

To generate the dashed lines, open the Properties window for the form and change the value of DrawStyle to 1. The instructions in the Form_Click procedure do not change.

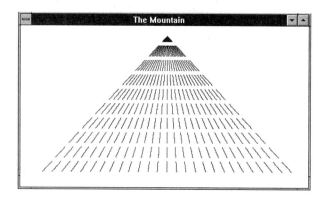

Figure 11.5.

Dashing the mountain.

For any container, you can modify the value of DrawStyle at design time or in your program code. Like DrawWidth, if you change the value of DrawStyle at run time, you affect the size of subsequent graphics. However, nothing happens to previously drawn graphics.

DrawStyle and DrawWidth are not independent. You can generate stylized lines only when the value of DrawWidth is 1. If you set the value of DrawWidth larger than 1, Visual Basic generates solid lines even if DrawStyle has a value in the range from 1 to 4.

Drawing Circles—The *Circle* Method

The Circle method draws circles. (It's hard to argue with that!) For now, the discussion considers only the simplest form of Circle, which draws a complete circle in the default color. Later in the chapter, you see how optional parameters can produce ellipses, arcs, and pie-shaped wedges.

For example, the following instruction draws a circle centered at absolute location (750, 600) with a radius of 300 twips:

```
Picture1.Circle (750, 600), 300
```

The *xcenter* and *ycenter* parameters specify the location of the circle's center. As usual, you can use absolute coordinates (without Step) or relative coordinates (with Step).

A circle is a curved line whose points are all the same distance from a single point called the *center*. The *radius* of a circle is the distance between any point on the curved line and the single point in the center. With the *radius* parameter, you specify the radius length (in twips) of the circle you want Visual Basic to draw.

```
container.Circle (xcenter, ycenter), radius          'Absolute syntax

or

container.Circle Step (xcenter, ycenter), radius     'Relative syntax

where
```

    `container` specifies the name of the form or picture box where the circle is to be drawn,

    `xcenter` is the x coordinate of the circle's center,

    `ycenter` is the y coordinate of the circle's center,

and

    `radius` specifies the radius of the circle.

The `container` parameter is optional.

The following `Form_Click` event procedure demonstrates the `Circle` method by drawing the five-circle symbol of the Olympic games:

```
Sub Form_Click ()
    Dim Radius As Integer
    Dim X As Integer
    Radius = 950

    For X = 1200 To 6000 Step 2400
        Form1.Circle (X, 1500), Radius    'Draw top 3 circles
    Next X
    For X = 2400 To 4800 Step 2400
        Form1.Circle (X, 2500), Radius    'Draw bottom 2 circles
    Next X
End Sub
```

Figure 11.6 shows the result.

Clearing the Container—The *Cls* Method

The `Cls` method removes all run-time graphics in a container.

```
container.Cls
```

where

> *container* specifies the name of the form, picture box, or image control to be cleared.

The *container* parameter is optional.

For example, the following instruction clears the contents of the form named MyForm:

```
MyForm.Cls
```

Only graphics created at run time are cleared. Whatever you place in the container at design time, such as line and shape controls, are not cleared by Cls.

Cls does not clear graphics drawn while the value of AutoRedraw was True. Even if you subsequently change AutoRedraw to False before using Cls, anything drawn while AutoRedraw was True remains.

Cls clears text as well as graphics. Text displayed with the Print method is erased. For more about the Print method and displaying text, see Chapter 12, "Displaying Text and Fonts."

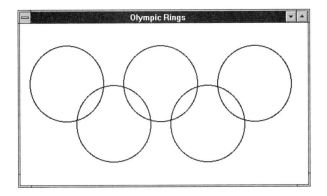

Figure 11.6.

The Olympic symbol drawn with the **Circle** method.

NOTE The name Cls is a mnemonic for *Clear* screen. This name is a throwback to earlier versions of BASIC, such as QBasic, where the Cls statement erased the contents of the entire screen.

Setting the Container's Color and Fill Properties

The graphics methods respond to their container's ForeColor, BackColor, FillColor, and FillStyle properties. By setting values for these properties at design time, or in the program code, you create various graphics effects.

As explained earlier in this chapter, the ForeColor property of a form or picture box specifies the default color for the subsequent graphics drawn in that container. BackColor specifies the background color. For example, the following instructions establish for Form1 a default color scheme of red graphics drawn on a gray background:

```
Form1.ForeColor = QBColor(4)     'Red
Form1.BackColor = QBColor(8)     'Gray
```

The FillColor and FillStyle properties work for the graphics methods just as they do for the line and shape controls. See "The FillColor and FillStyle Properties" earlier in this chapter. (Table 11.4 indicates the effects created by different values of FillStyle.) Of course, these properties are meaningful for the graphics methods only when you draw an enclosed shape.

For example, if you use the Properties window to set the value of Form1's FillColor property to blue, the interior of any circle you draw is blue.

Figure 11.7 shows the Olympic rings drawn with cross-hatching. To create this effect, use the Properties window to set the value of the form's FillStyle property to 6. Use the same Form_Click procedure that generated the original Olympic rings figure.

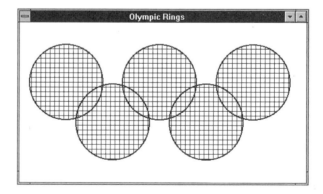

Figure 11.7.

Cross-hatched Olympic rings.

Setting the Foreground Color When Drawing

You can specify a drawing color with the graphics methods. By so doing, you temporarily override the value of ForeColor.

The PSet, Line, and Circle methods accept an optional parameter that specifies the drawing color Visual Basic should use when executing that instruction.

```
container.PSet (x-coord, y-coord), color

container.Line startpoint - endpoint, color

container.Circle (xcenter, ycenter), radius, color
```

where

   color specifies the drawing color.

(The container, x-coord, y-coord, startpoint, endpoint, xcenter, ycenter, and radius parameters work as explained previously.)

You specify the color parameter with a long-integer value that represents one of the RGB color values. If you have CONSTANT.TXT loaded, you can use one of the constants in that file to specify a color. For example, the following instruction draws a horizontal magenta line 500 twips in length:

```
Form1.Line (2000, 1000) - Step (500, 0), MAGENTA
```

You can also use the RGB or QBColor functions to specify a color parameter. For example, the following instruction draws a light red circle:

```
Form1.Circle (3000, 1000), 750, QBColor(12)    'light red
```

By using a color parameter with one of the graphics methods, you specify the drawing color for that current instruction only. That is, Visual Basic ignores the value of ForeColor when executing a graphics method including a color parameter. However, once the instruction executes and draws the graphic, the value of ForeColor remains in effect for subsequent graphics drawn without a color parameter.

Drawing Rectangles, Arcs, and Ellipses

The Line and Circle methods accept optional parameters that enable you to draw rectangles, arcs, ellipses, and wedges.

Drawing Rectangles with *Line*

To draw a rectangle, use the optional B parameter with the Line method. (The B is an abbreviation for *Box*.) With BF rather than just B, the rectangle fills with color.)

```
container.Line startpoint - endpoint, color, B
```

or

```
container.Line startpoint - endpoint, color, BF
```

where

B draws a rectangle,

and

BF draws a box and paints the interior a solid color.

The `container`, `startpoint`, `endpoint`, and `color` parameters have been explained previously.

When drawing a rectangle, the `startpoint` and `endpoint` parameters establish the location of the diagonally opposite corners.

You can paint the interior of the rectangle by using *BF* rather than *B*. (*BF* stands for *Box Filled*.) The interior color is the same color used to draw the rectangle's boundary. You can specify this color by including the `color` parameter.

If you don't specify a value of `color`, Visual Basic uses the current values of `FillColor` and `FillStyle` to determine the appearance of the rectangle's interior. Recall that the default value of `FillStyle` is Transparent, which produces a rectangle drawn over the container's background.

The following `Click` procedure demonstrates the `Line` method by drawing some simple lines and rectangles. Because it's hard to show color in a black-and-white book, the `color` parameter is not used with the `Line` methods:

```
Sub Form_Click ()
   Dim Delta As Integer
   Delta = 750
   Form1.DrawWidth = 2

   Form1.Line (500, 500)-(1250, 500)
   Form1.Line -Step(Delta, Delta)
   Form1.Line -Step(Delta, -Delta)
   Form1.Line -Step(Delta, 0)          'Completes a "flying V"


   Form1.Line (4000, 500)-(6500, 1250), , B         'Draws rectangle
   Form1.Line (500, 2000)-Step(4 * Delta, Delta), , BF   'Filled rectangle
```

```
Form1.FillStyle = 3                  'Vertical lines
Form1.Line (4000, 2000)-(6500, 2750), , B    'Rectangle with vertical
                                      stripes
End Sub
```

Notice how the final two `Line` instructions use two consecutive commas to omit the *color* parameter.

To try the effect yourself, type the `Form_Click` procedure. Run the application and click anywhere on the form. Figure 11.8 shows the result.

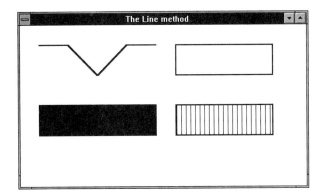

Figure 11.8.

Lines and rectangles drawn with the **Line** method.

Drawing Arcs, Ellipses, and Wedges with the *Circle* Method

You can add three optional parameters (*start*, *end*, and *aspect*) to the end of a `Circle` method. With these parameters, you can draw not only a circle but also a partial circle, partial ellipse, complete ellipse, or a pie-shaped wedge. (An ellipse is a squashed-in circle resembling the outline of a football.)

container.Circle (*xcenter*, *ycenter*), *radius*, *color*, *start*, *end*, *aspect*

where

container, *xcenter*, *ycenter*, *radius*, and *color* have been explained previously,

start specifies the beginning point of an arc as an angle in radians,

end specifies the ending point of an arc as an angle in radians,

and

aspect specifies the aspect ratio of the x-radius to the y-radius.

The `Circle` method can contain eight parameters! That may seem imposing, but actually you can quickly learn the syntax of `Circle`. Remember, with `Circle`, you need to specify only the *xcenter*, *ycenter*, and *radius* parameters. The other five parameters are optional.

Creating an Arc

Use *start* and *end* to draw a partial circle (that is, an arc). The *start* and *end* parameters identify each terminus of the arc as an angle in radians (not degrees) from the horizontal. Each angle must be in the range from –2π to +2π. The angles are located in the conventional geometric manner with 0 to the right, 0.5π straight up, π to the left, and 1.5π straight down.

 **NOTE** A complete circle contains 2π radians (that is, 2π radians equals 360 degrees. As a result, π is approximately 3.14). Visual Basic uses radians instead of degrees because radians are more convenient for mathematical computations. For more about angular measurements and π, see Chapter 16, "Working with Numbers." In that chapter, Figure 16.1 shows the relationship between radians and degrees.

Visual Basic draws each arc counterclockwise. Consider the drawing "pen" to be raised above the container and moving in a circle with the prescribed center and radius. The pen sweeps counterclockwise. When the *start* angle is reached, the pen "drops" to the container and begins drawing. When the *end* angle is reached, the pen "lifts" from the container to complete the desired arc. If you specify either *start* or *end*, but not both, the absent parameter defaults to a value of zero.

If *start* or *end* is negative, Visual Basic draws a straight line from the respective terminus of the arc to the center of the circle. Thus, by making both parameters negative, you generate a pie-shaped wedge. To locate an arc, the minus sign is stripped from the parameter to form a positive number (that is, the absolute value of the parameter determines the location angle).

Creating an Ellipse

By adjusting *aspect*, you create an ellipse (or partial arc of an ellipse), rather than a true circle. When drawing an ellipse, the *radius* parameter specifies the length of the major (larger) axis of the ellipse. When *aspect* is less than 1, *radius* is the x-radius, and the ellipse has a larger x-radius than y-radius. When *aspect* is greater than 1, *radius* is the y-radius, and the ellipse has a larger y-radius than x-radius.

When *aspect* is 1 (the default value), the ellipse becomes a true circle. If *aspect* is negative, the results are unpredictable, but no fatal error occurs. You have to experiment with your particular hardware to determine appropriate values of aspect for your desired circles and ellipses.

When a complete circle or ellipse is drawn, the LPR becomes the center of the circle or ellipse. When an arc is drawn, the LPR becomes the center that the circle or ellipse would have if the arc were completed.

Demonstrating the *Circle* Method

The following Form_Click procedure demonstrates many features of the Circle method:

```
Sub Form_Click ()
    Dim MyRadius As Integer
    Dim Pi As Double

    MyRadius = 700
    Pi = 4 * Atn(1)    'Calculates the value of Pi

    DrawWidth = 2

    Circle (1500, 1000), MyRadius                     'Shape A
    Circle (3750, 1000), MyRadius, , Pi / 10, Pi / 2  'Shape B
    Circle (6000, 1000), MyRadius, , Pi / 2, Pi / 10  'Shape C

    Circle (1500, 3000), MyRadius, , -Pi / 10, -Pi / 2 'Shape D
    Circle (3750, 3000), MyRadius, , , , .2            'Shape E
    Circle (6000, 3000), MyRadius, , , , 2             'Shape F
End Sub
```

Notice that, for variety's sake, the *container* parameter does not appear in any of the graphics instructions in this procedure. Remember that, when you omit the container parameter, the graphics instructions refer to the current form by default. Figure 11.9 shows the result of running this procedure.

The shape in the upper left corner is a complete circle. The two additional shapes in the top row are partial circles that demonstrate the flip-flopping of the *start* and *end* parameters. The leftmost shape in the bottom row is a pie-shaped wedge created with negative values for *start* and *end*. The remaining two shapes demonstrate how changing *aspect* creates different ellipses.

Using the *Point* Method

The Point method returns the color code of a specified point.

```
container.Point(x-coord, y-coord)
```
where

    `container` specifies the name of the form or picture box,

    `x-coord` specifies the x-coordinate relative to the container,
and

    `y-coord` specifies the y-coordinate relative to the container.

The returned value is the numerical color code value of the referenced point. If the specified point is outside the boundaries of the container, `Point` returns a value of `-1`.

The `Point` method works for forms and picture boxes. `Point` has the syntax of a method but acts more like a function.

For example, the following instruction assigns to `Hue&` the color of a point inside the picture box named `MyPicture`. The point is at location (65, 30) in the picture box:

```
Hue& = MyPicture.Point(65, 30)
```

You can use `Point` to specify the `color` parameter in various graphing instructions. For example, the following instruction turns the point at location (2000, 1000) in `Form1` into the same color as the point at (500, 750):

```
Form1.PSet (2000, 1000), Point(500, 750)
```

Similarly, the following instruction sets the `ForeColor` property to the color of the point at (1000, 1000):

```
Form1.ForeColor = Form1.Point(1000, 1000)
```

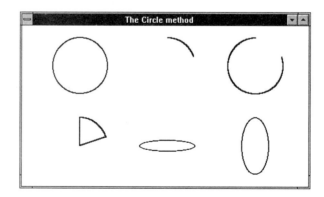

Figure 11.9.

Arcs, ellipses, and wedges drawn with the `Circle` method.

Keeping Track of the LPR

As mentioned earlier in the chapter, Visual Basic maintains the coordinates of the LPR for each form and picture box. You can use the `CurrentX` and `CurrentY` properties to determine the current LPR for each container. For example, the following instruction draws a circle in the picture box named `Picture2`. The circle is centered on the current LPR and has a radius specified by the variable `MyRadius`:

```
Picture2.Circle (Picture2.CurrentX, Picture2. CurrentY), MyRadius
```

When you use one of the graphics methods, Visual Basic updates the container's LPR as specified in Table 11.7.

Table 11.7. LPR as a result of the graphics methods.

Graphics Method	Resulting LPR
PSet	At the drawn point
Line	At the end point of the line or rectangle
Circle	At the center of the circle
Cls	At the container's upper left corner, point (0, 0)

Redefining the Coordinate System— The Scale Properties

Let's face it. The coordinate system used by Visual Basic is somewhat arbitrary and unnatural. You might prefer a coordinate system that's more natural to certain applications. For example, you might like the y-values to increase as you move up the container rather than down the container. Maybe you would like the measuring units to be something other than twips.

The following sections explain the various Scale properties and the `Scale` method. With these tools, you can customize both the measuring units and the coordinate system.

The *ScaleHeight* and *ScaleWidth* Properties

The `Height` and `Width` properties specify the size of a form or picture box. However, the total height and width of a container is not quite the same as the height and width of the container's drawing area.

For example, consider a form. The Height property measures the total height of the form. This height includes the title bar and the widths of the horizontal borders. Similarly, the Width property measures the total width, which includes the widths of the vertical boundaries.

The actual drawing area, however, lies in the form's interior. This drawing area lies inside all the external borders.

To measure the available drawing area, Visual Basic uses the ScaleHeight and ScaleWidth properties. See Figure 11.10.

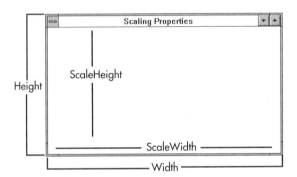

Figure 11.10.

A form's scaling properties.

The default form is 7485 twips wide and 4425 high. You can verify these values by starting a new project and opening the Properties window. The values of the form's Width and Height properties are 7485 and 4425, respectively. Examine the default values of ScaleWidth and ScaleHeight. The values are 7365 and 4020, respectively.

NOTE The default height and width of forms may vary depending on the video hardware used in your computer system. The values given in this section are for VGA systems with standard-sized video monitors. The values on your system may be different.

Determining Graphing Locations with *ScaleHeight* and *ScaleWidth*

You can use ScaleWidth and ScaleHeight in your program code to accurately determine graphing locations. For example, the following instruction plots a point in the center of Form1 regardless of how the form may have been resized:

```
Form1.PSet (Form1.ScaleWidth / 2, Form1.ScaleHeight / 2)
```

Also, your code can determine the exact boundaries of the drawing area with the ScaleWidth and ScaleHeight properties. Figure 11.11 shows the coordinates of the four corners of a container. In this figure, consider the four dots to be located in the exact corners of the drawing area.

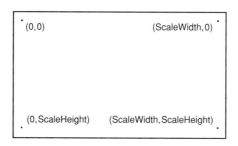

Figure 11.11.

The boundaries of the drawing area.

Creating Customized Scales with *ScaleHeight* and *ScaleWidth*

You can create a customized scale within a form or picture box. To do so, you modify the values of the container's ScaleHeight and ScaleWidth properties. The modification can be done at design time or with program code at run time.

For example, if you execute the following instruction, the horizontal coordinates of Picture1's drawing area range from 0 to 500:

```
Picture1.ScaleWidth = 500
```

This instruction does not affect the size of the picture box on-screen, nor the picture box's location on-screen. What happens is that the right-hand border of the drawing area now has an x-coordinate of 500 while the left-hand border remains at x = 0.

If you make ScaleWidth positive, the x-coordinate values increase as you move toward the right. When ScaleWidth is negative, the x-values decrease from left to right. In both cases, the x-coordinate of the left boundary remains at 0. As a result, when ScaleWidth is negative, the x-values go from 0 at the left boundary to negative values as you move toward the right.

Similarly, you can modify the value of ScaleHeight to customize the vertical scale. When you set ScaleHeight to a positive value, the y-coordinate values increase as you move down the container. If you make ScaleHeight negative, the coordinates decrease as you move downward. The y-coordinate of the upper boundary remains at 0.

A customized scale can be quite convenient. For example, a standard VGA screen has a resolution of 640 pixels by 480 pixels. Within the Picture1 picture box, you can model this resolution with the following instructions:

```
Picture1.ScaleWidth = 640
```

```
Picture1.ScaleHeight = 480
```

Now, regardless of the form's physical size on-screen, references to the form's x,y-coordinates mimic drawing on a full VGA screen.

 NOTE The values of Height and Width are always measured in twips. No matter what scale or measuring units you specify with ScaleHeight and ScaleWidth, the measuring scale for the Height and Width properties remains unaffected.

Using the *ScaleLeft* and *ScaleTop* Properties

As explained in the previous section, modifying ScaleHeight and ScaleWidth leaves the upper boundary at y = 0 and the left boundary at x = 0.

You can change the values of the boundary coordinates with the ScaleLeft and ScaleHeight properties. For example, by setting ScaleLeft to 500 and ScaleTop to 750, the coordinates of the upper left corner of the container become (500, 750).

By using ScaleLeft and ScaleTop in conjunction with ScaleHeight and ScaleWidth, you can completely designate a customized coordinate system. For example, suppose you want the lower-left corner of Form1 to be at location (0, 0) and the upper right corner at (100, 100). Notice that this scale has y-coordinates increasing as you move upward.

The following instructions do the trick:

```
Form1.ScaleWidth = 100
Form1.ScaleHeight = -100
Form1.ScaleLeft = 0
Form1.ScaleTop = 100
```

Figure 11.12 shows the result.

Figure 11.12.

A customized coordinate system.

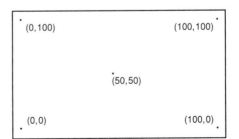

Using the *Scale* Method to Customize a Coordinate System

At run time, you can create a customized coordinate system with a single instruction. Use the `Scale` method.

```
container.Scale (Xleft, Ytop)-(Xright, Ybottom)
```

where

   `container` specifies the name of a form or picture box,

   `Xleft,Ytop` specify the horizontal and vertical coordinate values of the container's upper left corner,

and

   `Xright,Ybottom` specify the coordinate values of the lower right corner.

Using the `Scale` method is natural and efficient anytime you want to change the coordinate system in your program code (as opposed to design time).

For example, the following instruction creates the same coordinate system established with Figure 11.12:

```
Form1.Scale (0, 100)-(100, 0)
```

When you execute a `Scale` instruction, Visual Basic automatically updates the values of `ScaleHeight`, `ScaleWidth`, `ScaleLeft`, and `ScaleTop` appropriately.

In a `Scale` instruction, you can specify the coordinates as single-precision numbers. This allows you to create fractional scales. For example, the following scale ranges from +.1 to -.1, horizontally and vertically:

```
Form1.Scale (-.1, .1)-(.1, -.1)
```

If you execute `Scale` without specifying any coordinate values, Visual Basic restores the coordinate system to the default scale. The upper left corner once again has location (0, 0) and the measuring units are twips. For example, the following instruction restores `Picture1`'s default scale:

```
Picture1.Scale
```

Adjusting the Measuring Units with *ScaleMode*

Another way to modify the coordinate system is to use measuring units other than twips. To do so, modify the value of the container's `ScaleMode` property.

You can modify this property at design time or with program instructions at run time.

As Table 11.8 shows, you can choose standardized units other than twips, or you can choose to specify a customized scale.

Table 11.8. Values of the *ScaleMode* property.	
Value of *ScaleMode*	**Measuring Units**
0	Indicates a custom scale has been specified
1	Twips (the default value)
2	Point (One point equals 20 twips, 72 points per inch)
3	Pixel (Smallest displayable monitor dot; this value is hardware dependent and reported by Windows to Visual Basic)
4	Character (Horizontally, one character equals 120 twips. Vertically, one character equals 240 twips.)
5	Inches
6	Millimeters
7	Centimeters

When you modify the value of a container's ScaleMode property, you don't change the size of the container or its location on-screen. All you do is change the scale that describes how many units Visual Basic equates to a given distance on-screen. The coordinates of the upper left corner remain at (0, 0) unless you previously customized the scale.

You can see the effect of modifying ScaleMode at design time. Start a new project and open the Properties window. The default values of ScaleWidth and ScaleHeight are 7365 and 4020, respectively. (Remember that these values may be different on your computer.) Because there are 1440 twips to an inch, the values of ScaleHeight and ScaleWidth correspond to a drawing area in the form approximately 5 inches wide and 3 inches high.

To see the exact dimensions in inches, change the value of ScaleMode to 5. This setting uses inches rather than twips as the measuring units. Examine the new values of ScaleWidth and ScaleHeight. These properties are now measured in inches. You should see that ScaleWidth is 5.115 inches (approximately 5) and ScaleHeight is 2.792 inches (approximately 3). By continually choosing new values for ScaleMode, you can watch the ScaleWidth and ScaleHeight values change appropriately.

The ScaleMode value of 0 means that a custom scale is in effect. Anytime you modify the value of ScaleWidth, ScaleHeight, ScaleTop, or ScaleLeft (or use the Scale method), Visual Basic automatically sets the value of ScaleMode to 0.

When you change ScaleMode to a positive value, Visual Basic sets the values of both ScaleTop and ScaleLeft to 0. Visual Basic also modifies the values of ScaleWidth and ScaleHeight to reflect the new measuring units. (You demonstrated this effect with the Properties window.) Additionally, Visual Basic updates the values of CurrentX and CurrentY to specify the LPR correctly in the new coordinate system.

Drawing Out of Bounds

When using the graphics methods, drawing is confined within the borders of the container. To illustrate this principle, start a new project. Using the Properties window, specify the value of the form's Height property to be 7485. Then create the following Form_Click event procedure:

```
Sub Form_Click ()
    Dim Pi As Double
    Dim Xcenter As Integer, Ycenter As Integer
    Dim MyRadius As Integer

    Pi = Atn(1)
    Form1.DrawWidth = 2
    Form1.Caption = "Concentric Circles"

    Form1.Cls    'Clear form of existing graphics, if any

    Xcenter = ScaleWidth / 2
    Ycenter = ScaleHeight / 2

    For MyRadius = 100 To 1500 Step 100
        Form1.Circle (Xcenter, Ycenter), MyRadius
    Next MyRadius
End Sub
```

Run the application and click the blank form. The result is a series of concentric circles. See Figure 11.13.

Stop the application. Save the form as BULLSEYE.FRM and the project as BULLSEYE.MAK. Increase the upper limit on the For loop as follows:

```
For MyRadius = 100 To 3000 Step 100
```

Now, when you run the application again and click the form, the concentric circles go beyond the form's borders. See Figure 11.14.

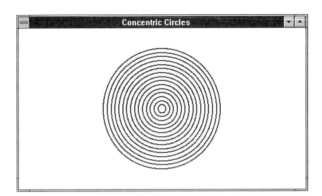

Figure 11.13.

A set of concentric circles.

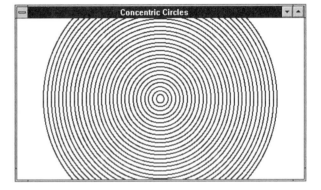

Figure 11.14.

Circles drawn out of
bounds.

When you draw graphics outside the container's borders, the extralimital
points are lost. No run time error occurs, however. The lost graphics are said
to be *cropped*.

Try enlarging the form in an attempt to expose some of the cropped graphics.
It doesn't work. The graphics are lost, not hiding in waiting. However, as
discussed in the upcoming sections, you can use the AutoRedraw property to
enable the automatic redrawing of lost graphics.

Understanding Persistent Graphics

Out of bounds graphics are important in the Windows environment because
various windows can obscure the graphics drawn in a form or picture box. For
example, a dialog box can pop open, covering up some displayed graphics.
Also, the user may move one window over another, and then re-expose the
covered window. Furthermore, resizing and minimizing a form can temporarily
obscure graphics drawn inside the form.

Of course, Windows contains much built-in functionality to manage the graphical environment. As it turns out, Windows handles the redrawing of the window and its controls, including the line and shape controls. However, your program code must handle what happens to graphics drawn with the graphics methods.

Generally speaking, when a container is covered and then re-exposed, you want the graphics image to be redrawn as it looked originally. Such graphics are said to be *persistent graphics*.

As explained in the following sections, Visual Basic provides several options for creating persistent graphics. Many trade-offs are involved.

For example, to implement persistent graphics, Visual Basic must store a bitmapped image of each window. That can place a considerable drain on your system's memory resources.

Using the *AutoRedraw* Property of Forms

The simplest way to create persistent graphics for a form is to set the form's AutoRedraw property to True. Visual Basic stores a bitmapped image of the form in memory. Then, whenever any part of the form must be reconstructed, Visual Basic generates the necessary graphics from the stored bitmap.

To see how AutoRedraw works, go back to the original BULLSEYE.MAK application (in which the upper limit on MyRadius is 1500). Notice that the default value of the form's AutoRedraw property is False. (You can verify this value with the Properties window.)

Run the application and click the form to draw the circles. Resize the form by moving the lower border and the right-hand border to cover up part of the bullseye. See Figure 11.15.

Now move the borders back to re-expose the covered portion of the graphic. Notice that the covered graphics are erased. See Figure 11.16. Because AutoRedraw was False, the graphics did not persist.

Stop the application, open the Properties window, and set the value of AutoRedraw to True. Try running the same experiment. This time, Visual Basic redraws the lost graphics when you re-expose the covered areas.

When the value of AutoRedraw is True, Visual Basic stores a complete image of the form in memory. This image includes any extralimital points that you draw "out of bounds." When you enlarge the form to full size, the extralimital points appear even if they were never visible in the first place.

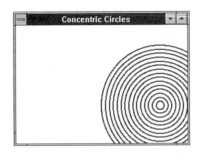

Figure 11.15.

The form is resized to cover up some of the bullseye.

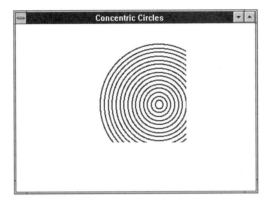

Figure 11.16.

Re-exposing the covered graphics.

CAUTION

If `AutoRedraw` is False, don't use the graphics methods in the `Form_Load` procedure in order to initialize a form's appearance. Remember that `Form_Load` executes before the form is first displayed. If you draw graphics in `Form_Load`, those graphics do not appear when Visual Basic subsequently executes `Form_Show` to display the form. That's because the graphics are drawn when the form is invisible, and run-time graphics don't persist. You can correct this problem by placing the graphics methods in the `Form_Paint` procedure, or by leaving the methods in `Form_Load` and setting `AutoRedraw` to True.

Using the Paint Event

Because persistent graphics are generally desirable, it's tempting to set `AutoRedraw` to True for every form. That way, the graphics always persist.

However, programming life is not so simple. The memory required to store a form's bitmap is considerable.

One alternative is to leave `AutoRedraw` False and write code to redraw the graphics whenever any part of the form is uncovered. You often put such code in the `Form_Paint` event procedure.

Visual Basic triggers the form's `Paint` event whenever any part of the form becomes uncovered. Recall, from Chapter 9, that Visual Basic executes the `Paint` event as part of an application's startup process. Furthermore, as long as `AutoRedraw` is False, the `Resize` event automatically invokes `Paint`.

For all these reasons, the `Paint` event is the natural place to draw graphics when `AutoRedraw` is False. The advantage of using `Paint` (rather than setting `AutoRedraw` to True) is the memory savings that you realize.

T I P

The cleanest way to use `Paint` is to have the procedure regenerate *all* of the form's dynamic graphics. After all, when `Paint` gets control, the form may have been totally obscured or only partially obscured. If `Paint` regenerates everything, the form is guaranteed to appear intact. Most programmers use a `Cls` instruction at the beginning of the `Paint` procedure to clear any partial graphics images which might be present when `Paint` triggers. The code in the procedure then redraws all the run-time graphics.

You can experiment with `Paint` by transferring the instructions from BULLSEYE's `Form_Click` procedure into the `Form_Paint` procedure. (To do so, you can use the Cut and Paste commands from the Edit menu.) If necessary, set `AutoRedraw` to False (the default value) and run the application. Experiment with enlarging, resizing, minimizing, and moving the form. The graphics will persist.

Using the *Refresh* Method

When `AutoRedraw` is True, Visual Basic generates a complete bitmap before any part of the image is displayed. The redrawn graphics do not appear until the bitmap is complete and the CPU is not tied up processing other events. Your program may experience noticeable delays. This is another reason why you should consider *not* setting `AutoRedraw` to True.

However, you can use the `Refresh` method to speed things up. For example, the following instruction refreshes `Form1`:

```
Form1.Refresh
```

This instruction forces Visual Basic to redraw `Form1` immediately. On screen, you see the graphics image reconstructing point by point. The `Refresh` method acts the same whether the value of AutoRedraw is True or False.

NOTE The Refresh method is valid, not only for forms, but also for any visible control. You can refresh any object immediately. For example, the following instruction refreshes the first frame on Form3:

```
Form3.Frame1.Refresh
```

Modifying *AutoRedraw* at Run Time

When you change the value of AutoRedraw at run time, you affect which graphics persist and which graphics become lost. Graphics persist if they were drawn with the graphics methods while AutoRedraw was True. Anything drawn while AutoRedraw was False becomes lost when the graphics are covered.

For example, suppose you set AutoRedraw to True for a picture box. You draw some graphics in the picture box. Your code then sets AutoRedraw to False and you draw more graphics.

Suppose further, that another window covers the picture box, thus obscuring all the graphics. The covering window then moves away to re-expose the picture box. (Or, instead of a covering window, suppose you execute a Cls method on the picture box.) In any case, the graphics you drew before modifying AutoRedraw persist. However, the graphics you drew when AutoRedraw was False become lost.

Another way to think about this effect is that each graphic has its own attached AutoRedraw value. The value is assigned when the graphics methods execute. Throughout execution, this associated AutoRedraw value stays with the graphic, regardless of how many times the value of the container's AutoRedraw property changes.

T I P You can take advantage of dynamically modifying AutoRedraw in order to create background graphics in a form or picture box. For example, suppose you want to create a background grid on which you will draw a series of graphics images. Set the container's AutoRedraw property to True and draw the background grid. Then set AutoRedraw to False. You can now draw a series of graphics using the Cls method between each drawing. When Cls executes, the background grid persists but the individual graphics images clear in preparation for the next drawing.

Persistent Graphics on Picture Boxes

The AutoRedraw property and the Paint event are supported by picture boxes as well as forms. However, there is an important difference between the way AutoRedraw works for forms and picture boxes.

When AutoRedraw is True for a form, Visual Basic generates a bitmap which includes any out-of-bounds graphics. In general, the bitmap contains an image which can fill the entire screen. As such, when you enlarge the form, you see any hidden graphics. This feature requires a great deal of memory but it's necessary if you expect to draw out-of-bound graphics on a form which may become enlarged.

On the other hand, graphics on a picture box are confined to the size of the box. If you draw out-of-bound graphics on a picture box, the extralimital graphics are always lost. That's true whether AutoRedraw is True or False. As a result, persistent graphics on a picture box are always less taxing on memory than persistent graphics on a form.

> Here's a technique to conserve memory and still enjoy persistent graphics. **T I P**
> Place a picture box on any form which will contain graphics. For the picture
> box, set AutoRedraw to True. Leave AutoRedraw False for the form. Draw the
> graphics in the picture box. If you want, you can enlarge the picture box to
> fill the entire form.

The point is that, when AutoRedraw is True for a form, the bitmap stores an image the size of the whole screen. On the other hand, when AutoRedraw is True for a picture box, the bitmap is confined to the size of the box (which may be as large as the containing form).

Layering

When constructing screen images, Visual Basic places the visual components on three different screen layers. You can think of these layers lying on top of each other: the topmost layer is closest to you and the lowest layer is deep inside the graphic monitor. As shown in Table 11.9, Visual Basic places different types of objects on different layers.

Table 11.9. The three graphic layers.

Layer	Components
Lowest	Graphics produced by PSet, Circle, and the other graphics methods
Middle	Label, Line, and shape controls
Topmost	Other toolbox controls such as command buttons and combo boxes

Anything drawn in a lower layer becomes obscured by an object drawn at the same screen position in a higher layer. This is true even when the object in the lower layer is drawn after the obscuring object.

Figure 11.17 shows a screen drawn with objects in the three layers. The two command buttons were placed at design time. These buttons exist on the topmost layer. The two rounded rectangles were created at design time with the shape control. These shapes are in the middle layer. Finally, the concentric circles were drawn with the Circle method at run time. These circles are in the lowest layer. Notice that the circles are obscured by the other objects even though the circles were drawn last.

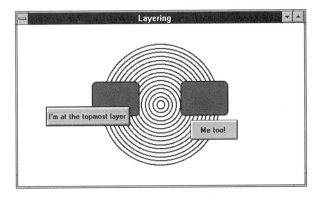

Figure 11.17.

A demonstration of layering.

Keep layering in mind when you design a form or picture box. If you plan to create a number of graphic objects which might overlap each other, layering can become important.

Displaying Pictures

You display pictures in containers. A picture is stored in a disk file and then loaded into a Visual Basic application. Visual Basic can work with the following three different kinds of picture files:

Bitmaps

Bitmaps store graphics images as a series of pixels. That is, the data in the file specifies the colors for the pixel pattern. A bitmapped image is always rectangular, but it can be any size in both the horizontal and vertical directions. Bitmap files are usually stored on disk with a .BMP or .DIB (Device Independent Bitmap) file extension. With Windows Paintbrush, you can create bitmap files that you import into Visual Basic applications. Windows comes with a library of several .BMP files.

Icons

Icons are bitmaps confined to a region of 32 pixels by 32 pixels. Icons are usually saved with the file extension .ICO. Visual Basic contains a library of several hundred icons. Also, you can create custom .ICO files with the IconWorks sample application that ships with both the Standard and Professional editions of Visual Basic.

Windows Metafiles

Unlike a bitmap, a metafile specifies a graphics image with a series of color "pen-stroke" commands. As such, the information in the file describes how the appropriately colored pen should move to create the image. This is sometimes called *vector graphics*. Windows Metafiles are usually saved with the file extension .WMF. The Professional Edition of Visual Basic includes several .WMF files.

You can display pictures in containers that have the Picture property. These containers consist of Forms, Picture Boxes, and image controls.

When loading a picture into a container, Visual Basic aligns the upper left corner of the picture with the upper left corner of the container. The picture fills the container horizontally toward the right and vertically toward the bottom. If the container is too small for the picture, the picture is cropped on the right edge and/or the bottom edge.

Working with Picture Boxes

To load a picture into a picture box control, you assign the name of the picture file to the `Picture` property of the picture box. You learned this technique in Chapter 8, "Using the Toolbox and Its Common Controls."

Remember that, at design time, you use the Properties window to set the value of the `Picture` property to the desired graphic file. When you double click the `Picture` property in the Properties window, the Load Picture dialog box pops open for you to specify the file name.

Using the *LoadPicture* Function

At run time, you use the `LoadPicture` function to assign a value to Picture. For example, the following instruction loads a bitmap file into the `Picture1` control:

```
Picture1.Picture = LoadPicture("C:\WINDOWS\LEAVES.BMP")
```

You can copy a picture from one picture box to another. For example, the following instruction makes `Picture2` display the same graphic as `Picture1`:

```
Picture2.Picture = Picture1.Picture
```

To delete a picture from a Picture Box, set the value of its `Picture` property to the null string. For example,

```
Picture1.Picture = ""    'Clear contents of picture box
```

The *AutoSize* Property

One special property of picture boxes is `AutoSize`. When the value of this property is True, the picture box automatically resizes to fit the size of the picture. The box can resize larger or smaller, as necessary.

When `Autosize` is False (the default value), no such automatic resizing takes place. If the picture is larger than the box, the picture is cropped by the boundaries of the box.

Figure 11.18 shows the effect of the `AutoSize` parameter. The figure shows three picture boxes. At design time, the value of the `Picture` property for each picture box is set to C:\WINDOWS\ARCHES.BMP. This specifies a bitmap file that ships with Windows. (Note: You may have this .BMP file in a different directory. If so, specify the proper directory path when assigning the `Picture` properties.)

For the leftmost picture box, `AutoSize` is set to True. Here the box resizes to exactly fit the size of the picture. For the remaining two picture boxes, `AutoSize` is False. The center box is smaller than the picture and the picture gets cropped. The rightmost box is larger than the picture so the picture box extends beyond the picture.

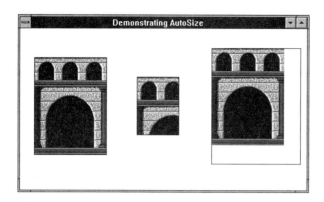

Figure 11.18.

Demonstrating AutoSize
with three picture boxes.

Working with Image Controls

The Image control on the Toolbox is designed for displaying pictures. Compared to a Picture box control, an Image control has many fewer properties, events, and methods.

The default name for the first image control you place on a form is Image1. Subsequent image controls are named Image2, Image3, and so on.

Displaying Pictures in an Image Control

To display a picture in an image control, assign a file name to its Picture property, just as you do with a picture box. You can load the picture at design time with the Properties window or at run time with the LoadPicture function. For example, the following instruction loads a bitmap file into the Image1 control:

```
Image1.Picture = LoadPicture("C:\WINDOWS\LEAVES.BMP")
```

Behavior of Image Controls

When displaying pictures, image controls differ from picture boxes in two important ways:

■ Image controls do not have an AutoSize property.

Instead, image controls *always* act as though automatic resizing is in effect. That is, whenever you load a picture into an image control, the control resizes to fit the size of the picture.

■ Image controls have a Stretch property.

The *Stretch* Property

The Stretch property is unique to image controls. The default value of Stretch is False. As just explained, when Stretch is False, the control resizes to fit a picture being loaded.

If you resize an image control once a picture is already loaded, the effect is similar to that of picture boxes. That is, if you make the control smaller, you crop off part of the picture. If you enlarge the control, the picture remains at its original size fixed at the upper left corner of the control. You can resize an image control at design time by moving the control's sizing handles, or at run time by modifying the values of the control's Height and Width properties.

If you set Stretch to True, the control's resizing behavior is much different. The loaded picture resizes to fit the new size of the control. That is, the picture and the control expand or shrink together. You can take advantage of this effect to elongate or narrow a picture horizontally, vertically, or both. You not only can make a picture larger or smaller, but you can stretch the picture to make it "fatter" or "skinnier."

For example, Figure 11.19 shows three image controls that each contain the arches bitmap shown in the Figure 11.18. The image controls have been resized to stretch the picture in various ways.

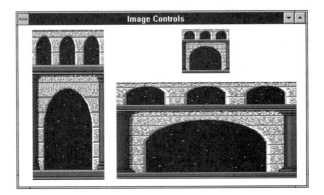

Figure 11.19.

Stretching image controls.

Comparing Picture Boxes and Image Controls

Image controls and picture boxes can both act as containers for picture files. However, the similarity ends there. As explained in this section, picture boxes offer much more functionality than image controls.

If you just want to display a picture, the image control is generally a better choice than a picture box. Compared to picture boxes, image controls use less memory and other system resources. Furthermore, when moving controls on-screen or when re-exposing a previously covered picture, Visual Basic regenerates pictures in image controls faster than pictures in picture boxes.

However, image controls cannot act as containers for anything except picture files. You can't place other controls or run-time graphics into image controls. That is, image controls do not support the graphics methods such as `PSet` and `Circle`. Accordingly, image controls do not have the `AutoRedraw`, `CurrentX`, and `CurrentY` properties.

Furthermore, image controls do not support the `Paint` event. When an image control is covered by another window and then re-exposed, Windows automatically regenerates the control and any picture it may contain.

Picture boxes, on the other hand, offer much more flexibility than image controls. You can place other controls in a picture box as well as draw run-time graphics. As you'll learn in the next chapter, you can also display text inside a picture box. Picture boxes have a full range of properties, events, and methods. These include the `AutoRedraw` property, the `Paint` event, and the graphics methods. As such, picture boxes are often considered to be "forms within a form."

Moving Pictures at Run Time

You can dynamically move a picture within a form by loading the picture into an image or picture box container and then moving the container with program instructions. If you modify the values of the container's `Left` and `Top` properties, the picture moves accordingly. For example, the following instructions move an image control named `MyImage` 500 twips to the right and 250 twips upward.

```
MyImage.Left = MyImage.Left + 500
MyImage.Top = MyImage.Top - 250
```

Visual Basic provides the `Move` method to simplify moving a form or control with a single instruction. You can also change the size of the moved object.

If you omit the *object* parameter, the current form moves. Notice that only the *left* parameter is mandatory.

For example, the following instruction moves the upper left corner of a picture box to location (300, 400):

```
MyPicture.Move 300, 400
```

This next instruction moves the picture box to a location 500 twips to the right and 750 twips downward from its current location:

```
MyPicture.Move Picture1.Left + 500, Picture1.Top + 750
```

> ```
> object.Move left,right,top,width,height
> ```
> where
>> `object` is the name of the form or control to be moved,
>>
>> `left, right` are the horizontal and vertical coordinates for the object's upper left corner after the move,
>
> and
>> `width, height` are the final values for the object's width and height respectively.
>
> The `object` parameter is optional. Also, the `top`, `width`, and `height` parameters are optional.

The following instruction doubles the height and width of the picture box:

```
MyPicture.Move Picture1.Left, Picture1.Top, 2 * Picture1.Width, 2 *
➡Picture1.Height
```

After the `Move` method relocates or resizes the object, Visual Basic updates the values of the object's `Left`, `Top`, `Width`, and `Height` parameters accordingly.

Creating Simple Animation

You can achieve simple animation by using a program loop to move an object repeatedly. To see how this type of animation works, try the following experiment. Start a new project and place two image controls anywhere on the form.

Create the following `Form_Load` event procedure:

```
Sub Form_Load ()
   Form1.Caption = "Click form to see animation"

   Image1.Move 600, 240
   Image1.Picture = LoadPicture("C:\WINDOWS\ARCHES.BMP")

   Image2.Move 5000, 1920
   Image2.Picture = LoadPicture("C:\VB\ICONS\MISC\MISC26.ICO")
End Sub
```

This procedure loads a picture into each image control. The first picture is the Arches bitmap you used earlier in this chapter. The second picture is an icon representing a woman..

If you installed Visual Basic in the standard way, these picture files should be in the directories indicated in the `LoadPicture` instructions. If your files are in different subdirectories, substitute the correct directory paths in the LoadPicture instructions.

Notice how this procedure uses the Move method to correctly position the two image controls on the form.

Now create the following Form_Click event procedure:

```
Sub Form_Click ()
    Dim Delta As Integer
    Delta = 4      'Change value to adjust movement rate

    Do
        Image2.Move Image2.Left - Delta
    Loop Until Image2.Left < 1320

End Sub
```

This procedure uses the Move method to incrementally move the icon of the woman. Each time the Move instruction executes, the image control moves a small distance to the left. The value of Delta specifies, in twips, the incremental distance.

Run the application. At first the woman appears outside the arch. See Figure 11.20. Click anywhere on the form and the woman "walks" until she is under the arch. See Figure 11.21.

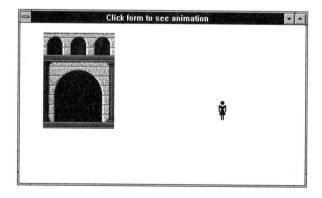

Figure 11.20.

The woman is outside the arch.

The speed and smoothness of the animation depend on the value of Delta. When Delta is larger, the picture moves faster but with a jerkier motion. Reduce the value of Delta and you get a smoother, slower movement.

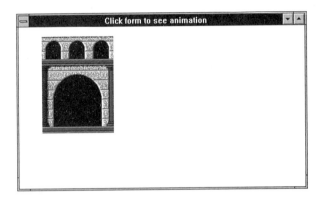

Click form to see animation

Figure 11.21.

The woman has walked under the arch.

NOTE The animated movement of an image control tends to cause flicker in the moving picture. On the other hand, pictures in picture box controls tend to move without this flicker. To see the difference, modify the application to use two picture boxes rather than the two image controls.

To do so, replace the two image controls with two picture boxes at design time. In the program code, change each occurrence of Image1 to Picture1. Similarly, change Image2 to Picture2. Specify AutoResize to be True for both picture boxes. When you run this modified application, the flicker should be gone (or at least greatly reduced).

Summary

Visual Basic provides an assortment of graphics tools. You can display bitmaps and other pictures inside forms, picture boxes, and image controls. With an image control, you can stretch the picture to create an elongated or shrunken picture. By moving a picture around a form, you produce animated effects.

With line and shape controls, you can place lines and two-dimensional shapes on a form at design time. As such, you can customize the form's appearance to create attractive user interfaces.

The graphics methods such as PSet, Line, and Circle enable you to dynamically draw graphics while your application is running. You can draw points, lines, boxes, and ellipses with instructions in your program code.

The graphics tools fully support color and pattern fills. In general, Windows manages the graphic environment to ensure that your graphic objects persist when temporarily covered by other windows. However, Windows guarantees persistent graphics only for objects created at design time. With the AutoRedraw property of forms and picture boxes, you can guarantee the persistence of dynamic graphics that you create at run time.

Displaying Text and Fonts

For most applications, displaying text is critical. By combining graphics with effective text displays, you can create polished applications that convey information in imaginative and forceful ways. In fact, how well you display results often determines the impact of an application.

The Windows environment has dramatically changed the way program information is displayed. Visual Basic takes advantage of Windows to provide numerous display tools. These tools include selecting fonts and font attributes, as well as displaying numbers and text strings in easy-to-read formats. Consequently, Visual Basic owes much of its popularity to the flexibility that programmers enjoy when presenting, printing, and manipulating text.

This chapter explores how you display text on-screen and on the printer. Here are the main topics presented:

- Treating text as graphical objects
- Using the Print method
- Determining text dimensions with the TextHeight and TextWidth properties
- Working with various fonts and the font attributes
- Using the Printer object to send output to the printer

Displaying Graphical Text on Visual Basic Objects

In previous chapters, you learned several different ways to display text strings. One way is by assigning values to certain properties. For example, by setting the Caption property of a form or label, you specify, respectively, the text that appears in the title bar of the form or inside the label. With the List property, you can specify the string items that appear inside a list box. There are many other examples of properties specified with text strings.

Another way to display text is with parameters in various statements and functions. For example, you can create a message box that displays a certain text string by specifying the string as a parameter in a MsgBox statement. To illustrate, the following instruction pops open a message box that warns the user to reconsider a particular action:

```
MsgBox "I suggest you think more about this situation."
```

Visual Basic also lets you display text strings on four types of objects: forms, picture boxes, the Debug window, and the printer. To do so, you use the Print method.

Visual Basic treats text strings displayed with the Print method as graphical images—just like images created with the Line or Circle methods. For this reason, text strings displayed with Print are often referred to as *graphical text*. (For more information about Line, Circle, and the other graphics methods, see Chapter 11, "Displaying Graphics.")

Although most of the Print concepts presented in the next several sections apply to all four types of objects, the ensuing discussion concentrates on forms and picture boxes. For more information about sending output to the printer, see "Using the Printer" later in this chapter.

A text string displayed with Print is a graphical image in the sense that, once the text is displayed, Visual Basic no longer has any link to the individual characters that comprise the string. The text string is a picture, like any other picture drawn with the graphics methods.

The string is *not* stored anywhere in memory as a sequence of characters with each character specified by an ANSI value. Notice that other string items, such as the List property of a list box or the caption for a label, *are* stored in memory as a sequence of ANSI values.

Graphical text displayed with Print is subject to the same graphics properties of the container displaying the text. For example, the values of CurrentX and CurrentY specify where the text string begins. Also, the AutoRedraw property of the container determines whether graphical text persists when the container is temporarily covered and then re-exposed.

Using the *Print* Method

You use the `Print` method to display graphical text. `Print` displays both string and numeric values.

> `object.Print expressionlist punctuation`
>
> where
>
> > `object` specifies the object on which the text is to be displayed,
>
> > `expressionlist` is a list of expressions separated by commas and semicolons,
>
> and
>
> > `punctuation` is either a comma or a semicolon.
>
> The `object`, `expressionlist` and `punctuation` parameters are all optional.

Specifying the *Print* Object

The `object` parameter specifies where the text is displayed. The parameter can have one of four values: the name of a form, the name of a picture box, `Debug`, or `Printer`. The latter two values display text in the Debug window and on the printer, respectively.

For example, the following instruction displays a text string on the form named `MyForm`:

```
MyForm.Print "You're in good form."
```

The following instruction prints the same message on the printer:

```
Printer.Print "You're in good form."
```

If you omit the `object` parameter, Visual Basic displays the text on the current form. For example:

```
Print "You're in good form."
```

When displaying text on a form, the text becomes part of the form's background. As such, the displayed text appears behind any controls on the form. For this reason, you usually don't use `Print` to display text on the main form of an application. However, you often create secondary forms solely for the purpose of displaying text messages. Such secondary forms do not contain controls but are, essentially, customized dialog boxes.

Appearance of Displayed Text

On a form or picture box, the displayed text appears in the font, size, and color specified by various properties of the form or picture box. As described later in this chapter, you can set values for these properties to create a wide variety of text effects.

By default, text displayed with `Print` appears in a font and size determined by your computer's hardware and software. Most important are your version of Windows and whether you changed font defaults with the Windows Control Panel utility. Most likely, your default font is *proportional*, which means that individual characters have different widths. For example, in a proportional font, a *W* is wider than a *J*.

As discussed later in this chapter, Visual Basic provides several techniques for determining the actual width and height of text strings. For now, be aware that the font you see on-screen is probably proportional. As such, two text strings containing the same number of characters are unlikely to occupy the same physical width on-screen.

Specifying the Expression List

Each expression in *expressionlist* must be in numeric or string form and can consist of a literal, constant, variable, property value, function, or a more general construct combining two or more individual components with appropriate operators. In all cases, each individual expression in your expression list must reduce to a single value, which is then displayed. Here are six simple `Print` instructions:

```
Print "Hello, my friend"      'String literal

Print X&                      'Numeric variable

Print Sales!(Factory%)        'Numeric array element

Print Label3.Caption          'Property value

Print 4.6 * Sqr(Area#)        'Mathematical expression

Print Left$(LastName$, 10)    'String function
```

Use `Print` by itself (without *expressionlist*) to force a carriage return. This causes the cursor to reposition itself at the left edge of the next lower print line ("lower" in the sense that it is toward the bottom of the container). Another way to say this is that the value of `CurrentX` is set to 0 and `CurrentY` is increased by the height of the most recently displayed text string. If `CurrentX` is already 0, `Print` (by itself) creates a blank line.

The use of a semicolon or comma for punctuation is explained later in this chapter in "The Semicolon Delimiter" and "The Comma Delimiter and Print Zones."

NOTE

Using ? for Printing

For compatibility with earlier versions of Basic, Visual Basic recognizes the question mark (?) as an abbreviation for the keyword Print. However, the editor immediately makes the conversion. For example, if you type the instruction ? MyValue#, when you press Enter the editor converts the instruction to

```
Print MyValue#
```

String *Print* Formats

Print displays a string value straightforwardly. The string is treated as a graphic image and displayed in a single line. Remember that, with proportional fonts, the on-screen widths of individual characters can vary. If you display text past the right edge of a form or picture box, the text is clipped. Text displayed with Print does not word wrap to the next lower line.

Print works with string literals and variables. For example:

```
Message$ = "There is no"
Print Message$           'Print contents of variable
Print "place like home." 'Print a string literal
```

The output on the default form is

```
There is no
place like home.
```

Notice that, in a Print instruction, a string literal must be enclosed in quotation marks.

Numeric *Print* Formats

When displaying numbers, Print uses special formats:

- Every number displays with a trailing space.

- Negative numbers have a leading minus sign (-).

- Positive numbers (and zero) have a leading space.

The displayed degree of precision depends on the numeric format.

Integer and Long Integer

The following code fragment shows how `Print` displays integer and long integer variables:

```
ExampleInt% = -123
ExampleLng& = 12345678
Print ExampleInt%
Print ExampleLng&
```

The output demonstrates the leading space in front of the positive (long integer) value:

```
-123
 12345678
```

Single-Precision

`Print` displays single-precision values in fixed-point format, if possible, or in exponential format otherwise. Fixed-point format uses only the digits and, if necessary, a decimal point and a minus sign. The maximum degree of precision is seven digits.

The following code fragment demonstrates how `Print` formats some single-precision numbers using fixed-point representation:

```
Example1! = 2.5 * 4
Example2! = 1 / 1000
Example3! = -1 / 3
Example4! = 100000 / 3
Example5! = 123 + .456
Print Example1!
Print Example2!
Print Example3!
Print Example4!
Print Example5!
Print 1 / 7
```

The output looks like this:

```
 10
 .001
-.3333333
 33333.33
 123.456
 .1428571
```

Notice that the fixed-point display uses up to seven digits of precision. As a result, the largest possible value is 9999999 and the smallest possible (positive) value is .0000001.

To display values outside these limits, `Print` resorts to exponential format. Again, the maximum degree of precision is 7 digits. But the exponential indicator, E, can set the decimal point through the full range of single-precision numbers (approximately –3.0E-38 to 3.0E+38).

The following code fragment demonstrates exponential format:

```
Example1! = 10 ^ 8          '10 * 10 * 10 *  10 * 10 * 10 * 10 * 10
Example2! = Example1! / 3
Example3! = 1 / Example1!
Example4! = -1.234 * Example3! * Example3!
Print Example1!
Print Example2!
Print Example3!
Print Example4!
```

Here is the output:

```
 1E+08
 3.333333E+07
 1E-08
-1.234E-16
```

Double-Precision

For double-precision values, `Print` extends the fixed-point format up to 16 digits. Unlike earlier versions of Basic, the exponential indicator is E for double-precision as well as single-precision. Consider the following code fragment:

```
A# = 1# / 3#
B# = 10# ^ 20#
C# = -A# / B#
D# = 1.23456789# * 1000000000    '9 zeroes in second number
E# = D# * 1000000000             '9 zeroes in second number
Print A#
Print B#
Print C#
Print D#
Print E#
Print 1# / 7#
```

Notice how the pound sign (#) is used on numeric literals to specify full double-precision accuracy. The output is

```
 .3333333333333333
 1E+20
-3.333333333333333E-21
 1234567890
 1.23456789E+18
 .1428571428571428
```

Currency

Print displays Currency values as fixed-point numbers with up to 15 digits to the left of the decimal point and up to 4 digits to the right. The Currency type does not accept an exponential indicator—numbers larger than 15 digits produce Overflow errors.

The following code fragment demonstrates how Print works with Currency values:

```
A@ = 1@ / 3@
B@ = 10@ ^ 5@
C@ = -B@ / A@
Print A@
Print B@
Print C@
```

The "at" sign (@) on numeric literals indicates the Currency data type. The output is:

```
 .3333
 100000
-300030.003
```

Multiple Expressions

You can Print multiple values on one screen line by placing two or more elements in *expressionlist*. The amount of blank space displayed between each element depends on the delimiter used to separate the elements in the Print instruction.

The Semicolon Delimiter

If a semicolon separates the two items, no blank spaces are inserted and the items are juxtaposed. Notice the semicolon in the second line of the following code fragment:

```
MyString$ = "This is a note"
Print MyString$; "worthy achievement"
```

The `Print` instruction causes the following output:

```
This is a noteworthy achievement
```

You must be careful with numeric output. Recall that numbers automatically print with a trailing blank space. Positive numbers and zero display with a leading blank space; negative numbers have a leading minus sign.

The following code fragment demonstrates how these conventions can either help or annoy you when you display multiple expressions with one `Print` instruction:

```
Rem Demonstrate numeric formatting
HighTemp% = 47
LowTemp%  = -12
Print "The high today was"; HighTemp%; "degrees"
Print "and the low was"; LowTemp%; "degrees."
```

The output is as follows:

```
The high today was 47 degrees
and the low was-12 degrees.
```

For a positive number such as the value of `HighTemp%`, the blank space before and after the number produce a nicely formatted line. However, for a negative number such as the value of `LowTemp%`, the blank space before the number is replaced by a minus sign, which appears immediately next to the preceding text expression.

The Space Delimiter

You can also separate multiple items in *expressionlist* with one or more blank spaces. However, the editor inserts semicolons between the items. For example, if you type the following line:

```
Print "I see" 76 "trombones"
```

the editor converts the line to this:

```
Print "I see"; 76; "trombones"
```

The output is

```
I see 76 trombones
```

The Comma Delimiter and *Print* Zones

A Print instruction can align output into predefined fields or zones.

Picture each potential line of screen output divided into zones. Each zone is 14 characters wide. For proportional fonts, the width of a single character is considered to be the average width of all the characters in the font.

By separating the elements of *expressionlist* with commas, you display the items of *expressionlist* in successive zones. Consider this instruction:

```
Print "Zone1", "Zone2", "Zone3"
```

The result is the following zoned output:

```
Zone1         Zone2         Zone3
```

Numbers still display with the usual leading and trailing spaces. One convenient use of comma separators is to display simple tables with a Print instruction, as the following code fragment demonstrates:

```
Rem Demonstrate Print zones
Print , "Position", "Batting Ave."
Print
Print "Rose", "First Base", .347
Print "DiMaggio", "Center", .287
Print "Ruth", "Right Field", .301
Print "Uecker", "Catcher", .106
```

The result is the following aligned table:

```
              Position      Batting Ave.

Rose          First Base    .347
DiMaggio      Center        .287
Ruth          Right Field   .301
Uecker        Catcher       .106
```

Notice how the beginning comma in the first Print instruction forces Position to print in the second print zone.

If a particular item is longer than 14 average-width characters, an item can display past the boundary of the print zone. In such cases, a comma tabs the next item to the beginning of the subsequent print zone. You must be careful not to ruin your table's alignment. The Format$ and Tab functions, discussed shortly, can correct such problems.

Trailing Punctuation

If you terminate a Print instruction with a semicolon or a comma, you suppress the final carriage return (CurrentX does not reset to 0) and the value of CurrentY remains unchanged.

A final semicolon resets the value of CurrentX to the position immediately after the last printed item. A subsequent Print instruction resumes printing from this point. For example, the following code fragment produces only one line of output:

```
Print "A stitch in time saves";
Print 9
```

The result is:

```
A stitch in time saves 9
```

A trailing comma on a Print instruction tabs the cursor to the beginning of the next print zone. A subsequent Print instruction resumes printing from that point.

Evaluating Expressions in a *Print* Instruction

You can evaluate expressions in a Print instruction. As a simple example, consider the following instruction:

```
Print "The answer is"; 20 / 2
```

Visual Basic displays the following result:

```
The answer is 10
```

The *Tab* and *Spc* Functions

Tab and Spc provide additional control over the horizontal cursor position. The two functions can be used only as part of the expression list with the Print method (or in the expression list of a Print# statement). Print# is used to write data on a sequential file. For more about Print#, see Chapter 25, "Processing Files."

```
Tab(column)
```

where

    column is an integer expression.

Tab advances CurrentX to reflect the column position specified by the *column* parameter. The leftmost column on a line is considered to be column number 1 and subsequent column numbers increase toward the right.

For the purposes of using Tab, you can consider the container receiving the text to be divided into fixed-width columns. The width of each column is the average width of all characters of the displayed font.

If CurrentX points to a position beyond the character position specified by *column*, printing occurs on the next lower line at the position specified by *column*.

You can use Tab to display aligned columnar output at tab positions of your choosing. For example, suppose that you keep track of clients' names in an array called ClientName$ and billable hours in an array called BillHours%. The following code fragment displays a summary table:

```
Print "#"; Tab(6); "Client Name" Tab(35); "Billable Hours"
Print
For J% = 1 To NumClients%
    Print J%; Tab(6); ClientName$(J%); Tab(35); BillHours%(J%)
Next J%
```

Spc displays a given number of blank spaces.

Spc(*numspaces*)

where

numspaces is an integer expression in the range from 0 to 32,767.

Consider the following example:

```
Print "Heave"; Spc(20); "Ho"
```

This displays the following output (with 20 embedded blank spaces):

```
Heave                   Ho
```

If either Tab or Spc occurs at the end of the expression list in a Print instruction, the value of CurrentX remains at the end of the line (that is, no carriage return is issued). In essence, an implied semicolon follows each Spc or Tab function, regardless of whether you explicitly include the semicolon.

For example, consider this code fragment:

```
For Num% = 1 To 7
    Picture2.Print Num%; Spc(Num%)
Next Num%
Print "Done"
```

The result is this single line of output on the picture box named `Picture2`:

```
1   2   3   4     5     6       7         Done
```

Notice that the number of blank spaces between successive digits successively increases by one.

> **NOTE**
>
> ## Formatting Text with the Format$ Function
>
> Sometimes `Print` does not provide sufficient formatting. With the `Format$` function, you can specify a format string for enhanced control over your output. Here are just a few of the things you can do with `Format$`: align columns of numbers on the decimal point, place a dollar sign before numbers, display dates and times in various conventional formats, display any number in scientific notation, restrict the number of displayed decimal digits, and display part of a string.
>
> As an example of `Format$`, the instruction
>
> ```
> Print Format$(123.456789, "###.##")
> ```
>
> produces the following output:
>
> ```
> 123.46
> ```
>
> With `Format$`, you can specify customized format strings such as `"##.###"` in the previous example or you can use one of several predefined format names such as `Percent`, `Long Date`, and `Scientific`.
>
> For more information about `Format$`, see Chapter 17, "Working with Strings."

Positioning Text in Forms and Picture Boxes

As with the graphic methods discussed in the previous chapter, you can use the `CurrentX` and `CurrentY` properties of a form or picture box to position text output. Text displayed with a `Print` instruction appears at the location specified by the values of the container's `CurrentX` and `CurrentY` properties.

The `CurrentX` and `CurrentY` properties for a form or picture box work well with the `ScaleWidth` and `ScaleHeight` properties. For example, the following experiment shows how you can position text in the center of a form.

Start a new project. Using the Properties window, set the value of Form1's AutoRedraw property to True. Then create the following Resize event procedure for the form:

```
Sub Form_Resize ()
    Dim Message As String

    Cls     'Clear the contents of the form
    Message = "I'm the center of attention"
    CurrentX = ScaleWidth / 2
    CurrentY = ScaleHeight / 2
    Print Message$
End Sub
```

This procedure sets CurrentX and CurrentY to point to the center of the form's drawing area. When you run the application, the message appears with the top of the first character at the center of the form. (Recall that Visual Basic executes the Resize event during program startup.) See Figure 12.1.

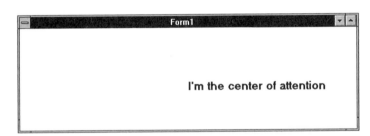

Figure 12.1.

Displaying the text message on the form.

Resize the form several times. The message always displays with the top of the first character at the center of the form's drawing area. Figure 12.2 shows an example of a resized form.

Notice that, if you resize the form to a small enough width, the text message is clipped at the right-hand end of the form. See Figure 12.3. Remember that Visual Basic treats graphical text as any other graphic image. As such, graphical text is subject to the same clipping effects and AutoRedraw effects explained for graphic images in the previous chapter.

Using the *TextHeight* and *TextWidth* Methods

Of course, the previous experiment doesn't really position the text in the center of the form. Only the top of the first character is positioned in the center of the form.

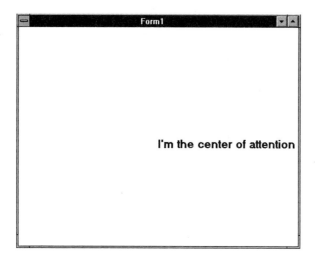

Figure 12.2.

Resizing the form.

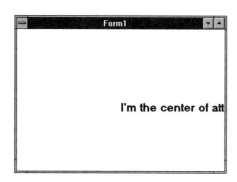

Figure 12.3.

Clipping the end of the
text message.

To help position text accurately, Visual Basic provides the TextHeight and
TextWidth methods. These methods calculate the height and width, respectively, that a text string would have when displayed with the Print method.

TextHeight and TextWidth return the height and width that *stringexpr* would
have when displayed with the current font and size as specified by the object's
FontName and FontSize properties.

Values returned by TextHeight and TextWidth are in units of the object's
ScaleMode property. Recall (from the previous chapter) that the default unit
is twips.

To truly display text in the center of an object, you can use TextWidth and
TextHeight to calculate adjustments to CurrentX and CurrentY. For example, the
following amended Resize procedure truly displays the text message in the
center of the form:

object.TextHeight(*stringexpr*)

object.TextWidth(*stringexpr*)

where

object is the name of a form, the name of a picture box, or the Printer object,

and

stringexpr specifies the string expression for which the height or width is desired.

The object parameter is optional.

```
Sub Form_Resize ()
    Dim Message As String

    Cls
    Message = "I'm the center of attention"

    CurrentX = ScaleWidth / 2 - TextWidth(Message) / 2
    CurrentY = ScaleHeight / 2 - TextHeight(Message) / 2
    Print Message$
End Sub
```

Figure 12.4 shows how the amended procedure displays the message in the center of the form.

Figure 12.4.

Text displayed in the center of the form.

The value returned by TextHeight includes the standard "separating" space above and below the text string. You can take advantage of this to reposition text several lines down the object. For example, the following instruction positions CurrentY for Picture1 three lines further down:

```
Picture1.CurrentY = Picture1.CurrentY + 3 * TextHeight(Message)
```

The TextHeight and TextWidth properties are available only at run time.

Working with Fonts

The term *font* refers to a character style that determines the overall appearance of text characters. Windows includes a standard set of fonts. Additional fonts are available from several vendors. The fonts available on your system depend on your version of Windows and the various hardware and software that you have installed.

Most Windows fonts are proportional. Another name for proportional is *variable pitch*. In a *variable-pitch* font, there is a variance in character widths. Some characters are wider than others. For example, the letter *M* is somewhat wider (takes up more horizontal space) than the letter *I*.

Windows divides fonts into two general types: screen fonts and printer fonts. As the names imply, screen fonts are used for text displayed on the video screen whereas printer fonts are used to print text on the printer.

Determining Available Fonts

You can determine the fonts available on your system with the Fonts and FontCount properties. These properties are available for the Screen object and the Printer object to determine video fonts and printer fonts, respectively.

The FontCount property is read-only at run time. In program code, Screen.FontCount returns the number of available fonts for displaying text on forms and picture boxes. The number returned by Screen.FontCount depends on your system's video hardware and installed software.

The Fonts property is also read-only at run time. This property uses an index value to return the name of one of the available fonts. For example, Screen.Fonts(5) returns the name of the font with an index value of 5. Actually, Screen.Fonts(5) returns the name of the sixth font because index values start with 0.

You can use the Fonts and FontCount properties to see a list of the fonts on your system. To do so, start a new project and create the following Form_Click procedure:

```
Sub Form_Click ()
   Dim Index As Integer
   For Index = 0 To Screen.FontCount - 1
      Print Screen.Fonts(Index)
   Next Index
End Sub
```

Notice that the loop index runs from 0 to (`FontCount` - 1). Because the index starts at 0, the last font specified in the Fonts array has an index value of (`FontCount` - 1).

Start the application. Click anywhere on the form to see a list of the screen fonts available on your system. Figure 12.5 shows the result produced on the author's computer system.

Figure 12.5.

Displaying a list of the available screen fonts.

If you change the two occurrences of `Screen` to `Printer` in the `Form_Click` procedure, the output becomes a list of the printer fonts available on your system.

Changing Fonts

You can change fonts by modifying the value of the `FontName` property. The `FontName` property is defined not only for forms, picture boxes, and the printer, but also for the controls that display text. Such controls include command buttons, list boxes, labels, check boxes, text boxes, and many other controls.

For any object, the default value of `FontName` is determined by the system configuration. For each computer, the video display driver and printer driver affect the default fonts for screen objects and the printer, respectively.

You can modify the value of FontName at design time or with program code. In code, place the font name in quotation marks on the right side of an assignment instruction. For example, the following instruction changes the default font for a picture box to "Roman":

```
Picture1.FontName = "Roman"
```

If you omit an object in such an instruction, the current form is assumed. For example, the following instruction specifies the font for the current form:

```
FontName = "Roman"
```

When you change the value of FontName for a control at run time, any on-screen text displayed in that control changes immediately to the new font. A better way to say this is that any text displayed as a result of a property value is immediately affected by modifying the value of FontName for that control.

For example, suppose you have a label named Label1. You set the Caption property for this label at design-time to display some text. When you run the application, Visual Basic displays the text with the default font. If your code modifies the FontName property for this label, the text changes inside the label to reflect the new font.

Because fonts change at run time when FontName is modified, it follows that you can't simultaneously display multiple fonts inside a control.

However, the situation is different when you use the Print method to display text on a form, picture box, or the printer. One of the advantages of printing directly on these objects is that you can display mixed fonts.

Because text strings displayed with Print are graphical objects, such strings are not altered by changing the value of FontName. For example, when your code modifies FontName for a form, you don't affect the fonts for any previously displayed strings. However, any subsequent strings you display with Print will be in the new font.

As an example of mixing fonts on a form, you can modify the previous Form_Click procedure to show the list of available screen fonts using the actual font to display each font name. All you need to do is add an instruction to modify FontName right after the For instruction. Here is the modified procedure:

```
Sub Form_Click ()
    Dim Index As Integer
    For Index = 0 To Screen.FontCount - 1
        FontName = Screen.Fonts(Index)     'Change font
        Print Screen.Fonts(Index)
    Next Index
End Sub
```

When you run the application and click the form, you see a list of the font names using the actual font to display each name. Figure 12.6 shows the result.

Figure 12.6.

Mixing fonts on a form.

Changing the Font Size

Each font can be displayed in various sizes. With the FontSize property, you can specify the font size for the current font. Sizes are measured in points where one inch equals 72 points. (Because there are 1440 twips per inch, it follows that there are 20 twips per point.)

The FontSize property applies to the same objects as FontName. You can modify the value of FontSize at design time through the Properties window or at run time with program code.

Most fonts can be displayed in a discrete fixed number of point sizes. Windows does support some scalable fonts that can be coverted to any point size. You can use the Properties window to see the available font sizes for a specified font. To do so, open the Properties window and set the value of FontName to the desired font. Select the FontSize property. Click the down arrow to the right of the settings box and Visual Basic drops down a list of the available sizes for the specified font.

If you set FontSize at run time to a value not defined for the particular font, Visual Basic substitutes the closest available font size. You can demonstrate this effect as follows. Start a new project and create the following Click procedure for the form:

```
Sub Form_Click ()
    Dim PtSize As Integer
    For PtSize = 8 To 24 Step 2
        FontSize = PtSize
        Print "This text is"; FontSize; "point"
    Next PtSize
End Sub
```

This procedure sets the font size from 8 points to 24 points in increments of two points. Run the application and click the form. Figure 12.7 shows the result. Notice that the actual point sizes as assigned by FontSize do not always correspond exactly with the values of PtSize.

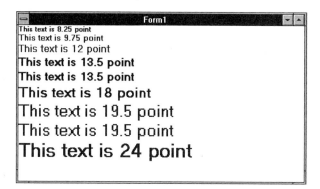

Figure 12.7.

Output demonstrating font sizes.

Assigning the Boolean Font Properties

Besides FontName and FontSize, Visual Basic has several other properties which affect the appearance of displayed text. Table 12.1 lists these properties and the resulting effects.

Table 12.1. Font properties with True/False values.

Property	Effect
FontBold	Displays text in a darker (boldfaced) style
FontItalic	Displays italicized text
FontStrikethru	Displays text with a line through the middle
FontUnderline	Displays underlined text
FontTransparent	Indicates whether background text and graphics are visible behind the displayed text

Like FontName and FontSize, the properties listed in Table 12.1 are defined for forms, picture boxes, the Printer object, as well as for controls that display text specified with property values.

Each of the properties in Table 12.1 can have a value of True or False. For forms and picture boxes, FontBold and FontTransparent are True by default. The other properties are False by default. You can change these properties at design time or at run time.

As long as your hardware and software support it, you can combine the font-related property values in most any combination. For example, it's possible with most fonts to create characters that are boldfaced, italicized, and underlined.

To see an example of how you can use the Font properties to create various effects, start a new project and create the following Form_Click procedure:

```
Sub Form_Click ()
    Dim Message As String

    Message = "These characters are normal"
    FontBold = False
    FontItalic = False
    FontUnderline = False
    FontStrikethru = False
    Print Message
    Print

    Message = "These characters are boldfaced"
    FontBold = True
    Print Message
    Print

    FontItalic = True
    Message = Message + ", italicized"
    Print Message
    Print

    FontUnderline = True
    Message = Message + ", underlined"
    Print Message
    Print

    FontStrikethru = True
    Message = Message + ", struck through"
    Print Message
End Sub
```

Run the application and click the form. Figure 12.8 shows the result.

By modifying the value of FontTransparent for a form or picture box, you can specify whether text displayed with Print shows through the background graphics and background text.

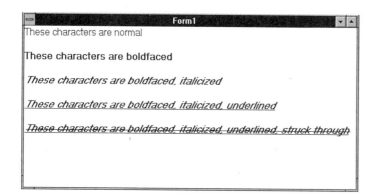

Form1
These characters are normal
These characters are boldfaced
These characters are boldfaced, italicized
These characters are boldfaced, italicized, underlined
These characters are boldfaced, italicized, underlined, struck through

Figure 12.8.

Creating various font attributes.

To demonstrate the effect of the FontTransparent property, start a new project and add a picture box to the form. Using the Properties window, set the AutoSize property and the AutoRedraw properties of the picture box to True. Set the picture box's Picture property to C:\WINDOWS\MARBLE.BMP. (Note: The MARBLE.BMP file may be in a different directory on your system. If so, use the appropriate directory path for your system.)

Now create the following Form_Click procedure:

```
Sub Form_Load ()
    Picture1.Print
    Picture1.Print
    Picture1.FontTransparent = False
    Picture1.Print "FontTransparent is False"

    Picture1.Print
    Picture1.Print

    Picture1.FontTransparent = True
    Picture1.Print "FontTransparent is True"
End Sub
```

Run the application. Figure 12.9 shows the result. Notice that when FontTransparent is True, the background graphics image on the picture box shows through the text displayed with the Print method.

Using the Printer

In Visual Basic code, you access the printer with the predefined Printer object. For example, the following instruction prints a text message on the printer:

```
Printer.Print "This will show up on the printer."
```

In the Windows environment, it's Windows, not each individual application, that handles printer output. That's why Visual Basic provides the Printer object. The Printer object acts as a liaison between an application and Windows. Because Visual Basic methods work only on objects, Visual Basic needs a predefined object for printing. As explained throughout this section, the Printer object accepts several methods and properties with which you can control printed output.

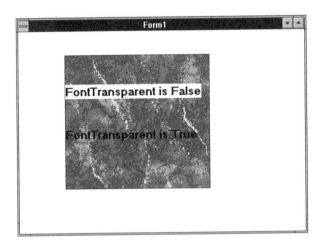

Figure 12.9.

Demonstrating the FontTransparent property.

The Printer object directs printed output to the default printer as specified in the Windows environment. As such, Visual Basic uses the printer you define when you install Windows. If you buy a new printer, or have several printers on your system, you can redefine the default printer with the Windows Control Panel utility. Of course, to achieve graphic effects, your printer must be capable of graphics mode.

Visual Basic treats the printer as a graphics object in much the same manner as a form can be considered a graphics object. Essentially, the Printer object acts as a form on which you can display text and graphics. Using the graphics methods such as Line and Circle, the Print method, and several methods unique to the Printer object, you compose a page containing text and graphics. Only when the page is completed do you issue a command that causes Windows to actually print the page.

Printer Coordinate Systems

As a graphical object, the Printer object uses a coordinate system much like a form. The Printer object has the same scale-related properties as a form, namely `ScaleHeight`, `ScaleWidth`, `ScaleLeft`, `ScaleTop`, and `ScaleMode`. With the `Scale` method, you can redefine the `Printer` object's coordinate system.

You can think of a printed page as a form. In this context, the scale-related properties refer to the coordinate system of the page. For more about these scaling properties, see Chapter 11, "Displaying Graphics."

A page, like a form, has `Height` and `Width` properties. However, unlike a form, the height and width of a printed page cannot be modified. That is, the `Height` and `Width` properties for the `Printer` object are not available at design time. These two properties can be read, but not modified, at run time.

In order to position text and graphics on a printed page, the `Printer` object uses an x,y coordinate system just like a form. By default, the upper left corner of a page is at x = 0 and y = 0. (You can modify these defaults by assigning new values to the `ScaleLeft` and `ScaleTop` properties.) The coordinates of the bottom right corner of a page can be determined by reading the values of the `Printer` object's `ScaleHeight` and `ScaleWidth` properties.

When you execute a method on the `Printer` object, the resulting text or graphics appear at the coordinates specified in the method instruction, or at the present print position. The `Printer` object's `CurrentX` and `CurrentY` properties determine this present print position. At run time, you can read the values of `CurrentX` and `CurrentY` to determine the current print position. Also, you can modify their values to specify a new print position. The measuring unit is twips, unless you change this default by modifying the value of the `Printer` object's `ScaleMode` property.

For example, the following code fragment prints the letter *X* near the center of the page:

```
Printer.CurrentX = ScaleWidth / 2
Printer.CurrentY = ScaleHeight / 2
Printer.Print "X"
```

The Page Orientation of Printing

The `Printer` object is *page oriented*. When constructing the text and graphics on a printed page, Visual Basic calculates all the dots that comprise the page. Only later are the results sent to the printer. The effect is that you have considerable control over how each individual page appears.

Visual Basic works one page at a time. Using many of the same graphics methods available for a form, you construct the appearance of a printed page. The `Printer` methods include `Line`, `Circle`, `TextHeight`, and `TextWidth`, as well as the `Print` method.

With the `Page` property, unique to the `Printer` object, Visual Basic keeps track of the page number for each printed page. The first page is number 1.

Each time a new page is generated, Visual Basic increments the value of this property by 1. You can read the value of `Page` at run time but cannot modify its value.

You end the current page and create a new page with the `NewPage` method. A `Printer.NewPage` instruction increments the value of the Page property. `CurrentX` and `CurrentY` are both reset to `0` and you can begin creating a new page of text and graphics.

It's important to understand that `NewPage` does not actually send any output to the printer. Rather, `NewPage` forces Visual Basic to save the image of the current page in memory and begin a new blank page.

The following code fragment starts a new page and prints a heading which includes the current page number:

```
Printer.NewPage
Printer.Print "This is page number"; Printer.Page
```

To actually initiate printing, use the `EndDoc` method:

```
Printer.EndDoc
```

This instruction tells Windows that the current document is complete and ready for printing. Visual Basic sends all the pages stored in memory to the Windows printer driver. Also, if any `Printer` methods have been executed since the most recent `NewPage` method, Visual Basic sends along the current page as well. The `EndDoc` method resets the value of the `Page` property to `1`.

Font Properties of the *Printer* Object

You can manipulate printer fonts much as you manipulate fonts on-screen objects. The `Printer` object supports the same font-related properties as a form: `Fonts`, `FontCount`, `FontName`, `FontSize`, `FontBold`, `FontItalic`, `FontUnderline`, `FontTransparent`, and `FontStrikethru`.

Remember, to determine the available printer fonts, use the Fonts property of the `Printer` object. For example, the following code fragment prints a text message in each of the available printer fonts:

```
For Num% = 0 To (Printer.FontCount - 1)
    Printer.FontName = Printer.Fonts(Num%)
    Printer.Print "This font is "; Printer.FontName
Next Num%
```

The `ForeColor` property specifies the color of printed text. However, most printers do not support multicolor output and the results of setting this property vary from printer to printer.

Summary of the *Printer* Methods

The Printer object supports nine methods, which are summarized in Table 12.2.

Table 12.2. Methods supported by the Printer object.

Method	Description
Print	Displays text output on the current page
PSet	Draws a point (pixel) on the current page
Line	Draws a line or rectangle on the current page
Circle	Draws a circle on the current page
Scale	Defines the coordinate system for printed pages
NewPage	Ends the current page and starts a new page
EndDoc	Sends output to the Window printer driver for printing
TextHeight	Determines the height a text string would have if printed
TextWidth	Determines the width a text string would have if printed

Printing a Form

To print a complete image of a form, use the PrintForm method. Here is the general syntax:

formname . PrintForm

The *formname* parameter specifies the name of the form you wish to print. This parameter is optional. If you omit *formname*, Visual Basic prints the current form.

PrintForm sends a complete bitmap image of the form to the printer. This image includes all the controls placed on the form, as well as all bitmapped graphics images placed on the form at design time. If the form's AutoRedraw property is True, the printed output includes graphics and text created at run time with Circle, Print, and other graphics methods.

You can take advantage of PrintForm to design customized output forms. For example, you can create a letterhead containing the company logo. On this letterhead, label controls hold text that should print on the form. When you need the printed form, your application can modify the Caption properties of the labels to update the text. To print the form, you execute the PrintForm method. By saving the application, you can modify the form and conveniently create new printed forms any time.

Notice that the `PrintForm` method works for individual forms, not for the `Printer` object. When you execute a `PrintForm` method, Visual Basic immediately sends an image of the form to the Windows printer driver.

Displaying Text in the Debug Window

At run time, you can display text in the Debug window by using the `Print` method on the predefined `Debug` object. For example, the following instruction displays a picture box's current font size in the Debug window:

```
Debug.Print "Font size is"; Picture1.FontSize
```

`Print` is the only method defined for the `Debug` object. For more about the Debug window in general and displaying text in the Debug window in particular, see Chapter 21, "Debugging and Testing."

Summary

With Visual Basic, you can display text in several ways. The `Print` method displays text and numeric strings on forms and picture boxes. `Print` offers several special features, such as automatic tabbing, with which you can customize the appearance of your output.

With the `Printer` object, you can use the `Print` method to display text on the printer. The `Printer` object has several methods and properties that you can use to control the appearance of a printed page.

The font properties of forms, picture boxes, and the `Printer` object specify the font, font size, and appearance attributes of text strings. Such text is *graphical text* in that Visual Basic treats the resulting output as a graphic image. Graphical text is subject to the `CurrentX` and `CurrentY` properties, as well as to the graphics properties such as `AutoRedraw`.

Text strings displayed in controls such as labels and command buttons are specified through property values of the control. For example, several controls have a `Caption` property. List boxes and text boxes have a `Text` property. By modifying font properties of the individual controls, you can affect the appearance of text strings displayed in these controls.

Using the Programming Language

P A R T

IV

Using the Editor

Visual Basic's Code window provides a text editor uniquely suited for the Visual Basic environment. Program code is scattered throughout a Visual Basic project—in the controls, forms, and modules—so the Code window provides you with the power to navigate quickly through this robust environment. The Code window performs also syntax checking on each line of code as you write it, and automatically formats your text, as well. Figure 13.1 shows a typical Code window.

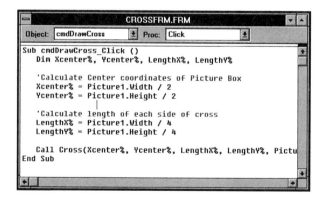

Figure 13.1.

The Code window.

Generally speaking, you can access easily the code you want. For example, to edit a procedure used with a form or control, simply double-click the form or control, and the associated Code window pops open. The event-driven nature of Visual Basic means that code can exist throughout the controls, forms, and modules.

A Quick Overview of the Types of Visual Basic Code

Unlike more traditional programming environments, such as QBasic, program code in Visual Basic is not in a single block. Rather, the code is located in modules and forms throughout the project. Three categories of code include:

- Functions
- Subprograms
- Declarations

Functions

Functions are program procedures that return a value. As such, function references usually occur in an equation of some sort, or are used with a method. Typically, a function call can occur anywhere a literal value would be legal. When executing an instruction that contains a function call, Visual Basic invokes the function to determine the appropriate value. Functions might or might not perform other actions. When a function finishes, however, it always returns a value to the calling procedure.

The value returned by a function can have any Visual Basic data type, most often a numeric or string data type. For example, you might write a function named Volume! that computes the volume of a sphere given its radius. You can invoke this function with an instruction similar to the following:

```
Result! = Volume!(Radius!)
```

When this instruction executes, Result! is assigned the value of the volume of a sphere that has a radius specified by the current value of Radius!.

You also might write a string function named Reverse$ that reverses the order of the characters in the string argument.

Subs

Subprograms, or Sub in Visual Basic terminology, do not return a value, but they do perform actions. Essentially, a Sub acts as does a user-defined statement. You cannot call a Sub as part of an equation, or in an expression that requires a data value (as you do for a function), because a Sub does not return a value. For example, you can invoke a Sub named UnloadDialogBox by simply placing its name on a line by itself, such as:

```
MsgBox "Click OK to unload the dialog box."
UnloadDialogBox
MsgBox "Dialog Box Unloaded."
```

 For more information on user-defined Subs and functions, and how to use features of the Visual Basic editor when developing such procedures, see Chapter 18, "Using Procedures: Subs and Functions."

Declarations

Declarations don't perform actions; in fact, they are not executable instructions. Rather, you use a declaration to define constants, variables, and function calls.

For example, you might have a specific value that is used frequently throughout a program. If the value never changes, and you want it available to every form and module throughout your program, you can create a global constant using the Global Const statement. In the declarations section of a form, declare a variable if you want it to hold information that is available to all the form's procedures. Declarations also include references to functions in external DLLs or to the Windows API. Visual Basic can access external functions with the Declare statement.

As Table 13.1 shows, Visual Basic has four types of declarations. Each type has a different scope throughout the application.

Table 13.1. Types of declarations.

Type	Scope
Local	Current procedure only
Form-level	All procedures associated with the given form
Module-level	Throughout the code module
Global	Throughout the entire application

Global declarations define constants, variables, and functions visible and available to all code throughout the program.

You can embed code in a control, or declare it as a *procedure* (a Sub or function) in a form or module file. As such, writing Visual Basic programs is both easier and more complicated than writing procedural BASIC programs with a language such as QBasic. It's easier because you can get to the underlying code by simply double-clicking a control or form; it's more complicated because it is often difficult to track down a specific coding error, if you don't know exactly in which place to look. Tools in the Code window and the **D**ebug menu can help you solve these problems.

The Code Editor Window

You open a *Code* editor *window*, often called simply a *Code window*, to create or edit declarations or procedures. To open a Code window, use one of the following techniques:

- ■ Choose the **C**ode option from the **V**iew menu. (Alternatively, you can press the shortcut key, F7.)

  A Visual Basic Code window pops open containing one of the event procedures for the form. The opened event procedure is `Form_Click`, if you have defined that procedure, or `Form_Load`, otherwise.

- ■ Double-click a blank area of a form.

  This technique produces the same result as choosing the **C**ode option from the **V**iew menu. The Visual Basic Code window pops open loaded with one of the form's event procedures.

- ■ Double-click the surface of a control object.

  A Code window opens containing an event procedure for the control object. The specific event procedure varies with each type of control object, most often you see the `Click` or `Change` event loaded in the Code window.

- ■ Select the form in the Project window, then click the View Code button.

  The Code editor window for the general declarations of the form pops open. This is a convenient method of getting to the *(declarations)* area. The Code window contains an event procedure for the form (or one of its controls), however, if you have already clicked the surface of one of the two. The idea is that when you click or double-click a form or control object, the editor assumes that you want to work with the event-handling procedures.

- ■ Select the Ne**w** Procedure option of the **V**iew menu and enter the name of the procedure in the New Procedure dialog box.

  You frequently use this technique to create user-defined `Sub`s and functions.

- ■ Type `Sub` *SubName* or `Function` *FuncName* while you are editing code. Here `SubName` or `FuncName` refers to a procedure name that you create.

  Visual Basic immediately pops open a template for the new procedure.

NOTE You might be wondering why (declarations) is enclosed in parentheses. The parentheses cause (declarations) to come first in the list.

The ASCII value of the open parenthesis character is 40, which is less than that for A. (declarations) always comes first in the list because Windows automatically sorts list box contents by their ASCII code.

The same is true for (general), used later in this chapter.

Parts of the Code Window

The Code window has a number of features common to Windows: resizable borders; minimize, maximize, and restore buttons, and a Control-menu box. Horizontal and vertical scroll bars let you move through the text in the window. Figure 13.2 shows the various parts of the Code window.

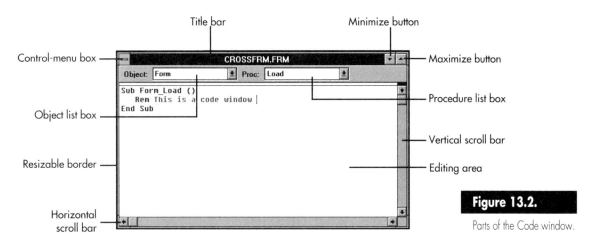

Figure 13.2.

Parts of the Code window.

The Code window does not have a menu of its own. Instead, this window responds to menu events generated in Visual Basic's main menu. Each module and form in the project has a Code window, and any or all of these Code windows can be opened at any given time. Only the active Code window responds, however, to menu commands from the main menu.

When Visual Basic displays a Code window, a default object and a default procedure associated with it are displayed in the editing area. For example, if you double-click on the first form of an application, the default object is Form1, and the default procedure is Click or Load (Click, if you have written code for that event procedure; Load, otherwise).

The top of a Code window contains two pull-down list boxes: the *Object list* and the *Procedure list*. You can use these list boxes to open any other procedure. To open the code for a specific procedure associated with a particular object, select the object from the Object list, then select the procedure from the Procedure list.

The Object List

When you are editing code associated with a form, the Object list contains the name of the form as well as the names of all the controls on it. As such, you can access the code attached to those objects. Additionally, the Object list contains a (general) declaration that provides you with access to form-level declarations and procedures. These general procedures are not associated with any particular control.

For example, if you're working with Form1, which contains the controls Command1, Command2 and Command3, you see five entries in the Object list—one for the form, one for each of the three command buttons, and the (general) section. To view this Object list, click the down arrow on the right side of the Object box. Select the desired control from the pull-down list by clicking on the control's name.

The Procedure List

After you've selected the desired object, you can view any of the procedures associated with it in the Procedure list. For example, if you select a particular command button in the Object list, the Procedure list shows you all the event procedures associated with that button. (If you select the (general) section in the Object list, you can access form- or module-level declarations and procedures that are not directly related to a particular control.)

When you edit code in a module, only the (general) section appears in the Object list because modules don't have associated controls. Similar to a form, the (general) section in a module gives access to module-level declarations and procedures.

Controls and Associated Code

As you know, each type of control can respond to a given number of events. A predefined procedure for each of these events is always present in each control. Table 13.2 shows a partial list of controls: one event to which the control can respond, and the name of the associated event-handling procedure.

Table 13.2. A few controls and their event-handling procedures.			
Control Name	**Control Type**	**Event**	**Procedure**
Command1	CommandButton	Click	Command1_Click
List1	ListBox	Change	List1_Change
Picture3	PictureBox	DblClick	Picture3_DblClick

As you can see, there's a definite pattern here. The name for an event procedure consists of the object's name, followed by an underscore character, then the corresponding event.

If you change the name of the control, or the event procedure, your code loses its association with the control event. For example, suppose that you write code for the Command1_Click procedure. You then rename the command button as btn1. The Command1_Click procedure is now listed in the (general) section of the form, because there is no longer any control named Command1. The new procedure btn1_Click is empty. For this reason, when creating an application, you should finalize the names for all your controls before you start writing the code associated with them.

 NOTE If you do change the name of a control, you can use the cut and paste features of the editor to copy code from the (general) section to the new event procedure.

The View Procedures Window

Another way to navigate through any procedure is by using the View Procedures window. Press F2 to open this window. Figure 13.3 shows the View Procedures window for a typical project. As you can see, this window contains two list boxes. The higher list box displays all the modules and forms defined in your project. The lower list box shows all the procedures associated with the module or form currently highlighted in the higher list box.

To edit the code for any procedure, first select a module or form from the higher list box. Then, select the desired procedure from the lower list box. (You can either double-click on the procedure desired, or highlight the procedure, then click the OK button.) A Code window opens for your selected procedure.

For more information on editing procedures with the code editor, see Chapter 18, "Using Procedures: Subs and Functions."

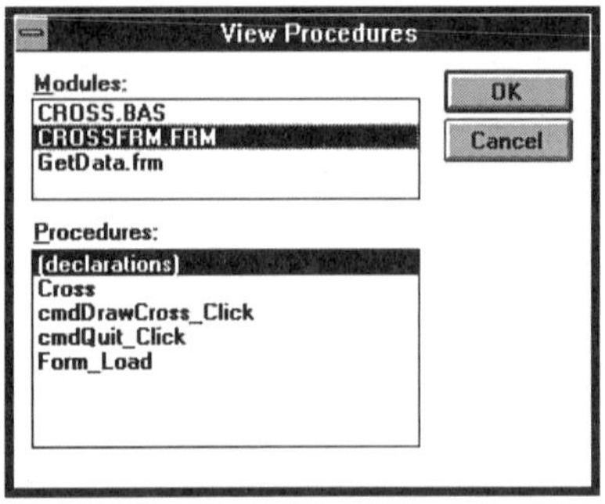

Figure 13.3.

The View Procedures
window.

Fundamental Editing Techniques

When you edit code in a Code window, the editing cursor appears as a vertical bar. As you type, new text appears at the cursor location. The editor supports full-screen editing. As such, you can move the cursor with the arrow keys before typing.

When editing, the mouse pointer acts as an *insertion point*. The insertion point has a shape which resembles a capital *I*. By moving the mouse, you can place the insertion point anywhere on the editing window. When you click the mouse, the cursor jumps immediately to the insertion point. You can then type text at the new location.

The editor can work with text blocks. You select a block of text by first moving the cursor to one end of the block. Then, you press and hold Shift while using an arrow key to highlight a text block. (Alternatively, you can select a block of text by holding down the left mouse button as you drag the mouse pointer over the block.) You can move the selected block, copy it to the Clipboard, or delete it. You can paste text already in the Clipboard into your program code.

By default, the editor works in the *Insert* mode. So that as you type, any existing text to the right of the cursor moves in the same direction to accommodate the newly typed text. By pressing the Ins key, you can toggle the editor between the Insert and Overstrike modes. In *Overstrike* mode, existing text to the right of the cursor is replaced by your newly typed text.

Using the Edit Menu

The Edit menu offers several text-editing features. The following list contains the various text-editing commands available from the Edit menu, and explains how they function.

Undo   Reverses the previous editing action. Actions that you can undo include typing a line of code, and deleting a block of it. In these two cases, Undo deletes the line of typed code, or restores the block of deleted code, respectively. By repeatedly selecting Undo, you can successively cancel the most recent editing actions (up to a maximum of 20 times). Undo becomes unavailable if you perform a nonediting action, such as modifying the properties on a form. The shortcut key for this option is Ctrl+Z.

Redo   Restores the previous Undo action as long as no other editing action occurred since the last Undo. That is, Redo alters your text according to what you previously "undid." As with Undo, you can use Redo up to 20 times in succession. The shortcut key for Redo is Ctrl+Backspace.

Cut   Deletes selected text, and places it in the Clipboard. The previous contents of the Clipboard are erased. The shortcut key is Ctrl+X.

Copy   Places a copy of the selected text into the Clipboard. This option is similar to Cut, except that the selected text is not deleted from the application. The shortcut key is Ctrl+C.

Paste   Places a copy of the Clipboard's contents into the current application. Program code is placed at the insertion point. This option does not delete the Clipboard contents, so you can use Paste repeatedly to insert multiple copies of code into your application. The shortcut key is Ctrl+V.

Paste Link   Places a copy of the contents of the Clipboard into the current application, and simultaneously opens a dynamic link with the Windows application that provided the Clipboard contents. This option is available only when the Clipboard contents come from a Windows application that responds to Dynamic Data Exchange (DDE). For more information on this Paste Link, and DDE, see Chapter 30, "Using Dynamic Data Exchange (DDE)."

Delete   Deletes the selected text. This option is similar to Cut, except that the contents of the Clipboard are unaffected. The shortcut key is Del.

Find...   Searches the program code for a specified text string. This option opens a dialog box. In the dialog box, you specify the search string, and the scope of the search (the current procedure or the entire application). The shortcut key is Ctrl+F. For more information on text searching, see "Using Find" later in this chapter.

Find **N**ext	Repeats the previous search. This option finds the next occurrence of the previously specified search string. If no search string was previously specified, this option opens the same dialog box as the **F**ind…option. The shortcut key is F3.
Find Previous	Similar to Find Next, this option searches the program code in reverse order. When performing successive searches, you can use this option to find the previous occurrence of the search string. The shortcut key is Shift+F3.
Replace…	Searches the program code for a specified text string, and replaces the found text with a second specified string. This option opens a dialog box so you can specify the search and replacement strings, the scope of the search, and whether to replace all occurrences of the search string. The shortcut key is Ctrl+R. For more information on text replacing, see "Using Replace" later in this chapter.

NOTE Many commands available on the **E**dit menu support the editing of graphics controls, as well as text. For example, you can use the **D**elete command on the **E**dit menu to delete a control from a form, as well as a block of text. For more information on the complete use of the commands in the **E**dit menu, see Chapter 4, "Learning the VB Environment."

Entering Code

Writing code is an exact science in any programming language. The syntax must be just right, the logic has to make sense, and the spelling must be perfect.

Further, some stylistic guidelines make programs easier with which to work. Code should be indented, so that blocks of code are distinguished. Comments should stand out for better readability.

Fortunately, Visual Basic's Code window has a number of features that automatically handle many of these requirements.

Syntax Checking

When you type a line of code, Visual Basic keeps it in a temporary storage location known as a *line buffer*. When you press Enter or move the cursor off the line, Visual Basic considers the line complete and immediately *parses* it.

You might recall parsing sentences and determining their parts of speech from your grade school English classes. Visual Basic does the same thing to each line of code. In effect, Visual Basic requires that each instruction you type is a complete sentence that fully obeys the syntax of the language.

If your line contains Visual Basic keywords, the parser tests the completed line for compliance with the specific syntax rules associated with those keywords. If a discrepancy occurs, you get an error message.

When you invoke a built-in function, the editor checks to make sure that the right number of parameters are passed, and that they are the correct type.

Error Messages

If your typed line contains an error that the parser can detect, you see a message box containing a terse description of what the parser believes is wrong. For example, if you do not enter a required argument for a function, you see the message that Figure 13.4 shows. The character at (or immediately following) the point at which the error was detected is highlighted.

Figure 13.4.

A typical error message.

If the message box hides the error, you can move the box by dragging its title bar. To get an explanation of the error, press F1 while the message box is displayed. Usually, the help you receive is no more enlightening than the message.

Leaving an Error Uncorrected

After getting an error message, you can move the cursor off the offending line without correcting the error. You do not receive another error message. As such, you can make temporary changes on a line, and abandon it, even if the line does not conform to proper syntax. The assumption is that you correct the line sooner or later. If you make a change, and leave the line, Visual Basic checks it again. If you run a program that contains an illegal line, however, the application halts, and an error message is displayed.

Disabling Syntax Checking

Syntax checking is optional. You can disable syntax checking by choosing the Environment items from the Options menu. When the Environment Options dialog box opens, change the value of the Syntax Checking property from the default value of Yes to No.

Disabling syntax checking can be helpful if you are typing a long block of code that you intend to edit later. For the most part, however, you want to leave syntax checking enabled.

Run-time Errors

Errors that are not detected by the interpreter during code entry, but are encountered during runtime, are referred to as *run-time errors*. Run-time errors often result from variable type conflicts, such as substituting a string variable for an argument that must be numeric, trying to use elements of an array outside its declared bounds, or using an incorrect calling syntax for Windows API or third-party DLL functions. When the interpreter encounters an error in run mode, you see the same type of message box that was displayed when an error was detected during code entry.

When a run-time error occurs, Visual Basic enters break mode. The editor displays a Code window with the error message box. The location of the error is highlighted in the code. You can correct the error and, in most cases, select the Continue option on the Run menu to continue operation from the point of the error.

You can use the Debug window to inspect and change the values of variables. For example, to see the value of the variable NumClients, type **Print NumClients**. To change the value, you could type a conventional assignment expression, such as NumClients = 45.

If the error involves a problem that affects more than one section of your code, such as wrongly declaring an array, you might not be able to continue program execution after you correct the declaration. In such a case, Visual Basic warns you that you must restart the application.

Autoformatting and Color Coding

One obvious feature of the code editor is that Visual Basic automatically formats your typed code. The Code window makes sure that there is only one space between words, numbers, and mathematical operators. Visual Basic remembers also the last capitalization you typed for variable, procedure, form, and control names. If you alter the capitalization of a variable when you type a new line, Visual Basic adjusts all other occurrences of the same variable name to conform with the new version.

Keywords and comments are color coded for easy recognition. By default, comments are displayed with green text, and keywords with blue. Normal text appears as black. You can alter these color defaults by using the Options Environment menu.

Indenting Your Code

For easy readability, you should indent code in control structures, such as For-Next loops, Select-Case statements, and similar constructs. Indenting your code creates an outline format that not only makes your code easier to read, but also less subject to bugs.

> If your indentation becomes so deep that you must horizontally scroll your text to enter your code, consider this a sign that your procedure is overly complex, and should be broken into subprocedures. A general rule is that a single Visual Basic procedure should not exceed 100 lines of code.
>
> **T I P**

The Code window helps here, too. Each new line of typed code begins at the same indentation as the previous one. You can indent also an entire block of text by selecting it, and pressing the Tab key. To shift a block of text to the left, select the text, press and hold the Shift key, and press Tab. This feature makes it easy to keep your indenting consistent, so program control structures are easy to identify.

> By default, Visual Basic indents four character positions each time you press Tab. You can adjust the number of positions that Tab indents by modifying the value of the Tab Stop Width property in the Environment Options dialog box. To access this dialog box, choose the Environment item from the Options menu. Then, modify the value of the Tab Stop Width property from four to your new specification.
>
> **T I P**

Understanding Find and Replace

Visual Basic's capability to find and replace text is specially tailored to the unique needs of its programming environment. Procedures and declarations are scattered throughout the program in modules, controls, and forms. If you are searching for a specific word or phrase, the scope of your search is important.

Using Find

You open the Find dialog box by selecting Find from the Edit menu. Figure 13.5 shows the Find dialog box.

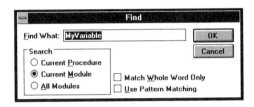

Figure 13.5.

The Find dialog box.

The Find command in Visual Basic is case-insensitive. This means that you can enter in the Find What: box the text you want to find without worrying about capitalization.

The Option buttons in the Search frame let you determine the scope of your search. If you click Current **P**rocedure, your search is limited to the Sub or function you are currently editing. The Current **M**odule option tells Visual Basic to search the entire code module. (An entire form is searched if you are editing code in it.) The **A**ll Modules option searches all forms and modules throughout the project.

If you check Match **W**hole Word Only, your search locates matching text only when a space occurs on each side of the text. Thus, if you are searching for the word *file*, your search does not stop on FileOpen_Click.

The **U**se Pattern Matching option lets you find text that is similar to the Search text entered. This powerful feature lets you use the wild-card characters * and ? in your Search text. Similar to their uses for DOS filenames, the question mark substitutes for any single character, and the asterisk for any string of them.

Table 13.3 illustrates various examples of Search text that uses wild-card characters for pattern matching, and shows the types of text each search might locate.

Table 13.3. Search results with pattern matching.		
Search Text	**Valid Finds**	**Invalid Finds**
Form?	Form1	Form47
	Form2	FormName
	FormA	
Step??A	Step21A	Step1A
	Step01A	StepStopperA
	StepAAA	StepA
Proc*	Proc	Probe
	ProcA	Proxy
	Procedure	Proac
	Proc_Launch	
in*l	Insubstantial	Interlink
	Internal	Int()
	Integral	
	Inl	

Using Replace

The Replace dialog box, which Figure 13.6 shows, works similar to the Find
dialog box. The obvious difference is that you can enter also replacement text.

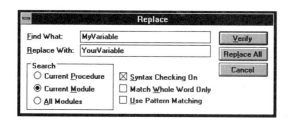

Figure 13.6.

The Replace dialog box.

When you replace text, you have some new factors to consider. First, you can
specify whether you want to verify each replacement by clicking the Verify or
Replace All buttons. This can be especially important if your search scope
includes the current module or the entire project (all modules).

You have to decide also whether you want syntax checking enabled during the Replace process. If syntax checking is enabled, and a replacement results in a syntax error, the search notifies you of the error, stops, and opens the Code window to the offending line.

In most cases, you want syntax checking enabled. There might be occasions, however, when you want to accept the changes, and deal with the syntax errors later. As mentioned previously, Visual Basic checks for syntax errors before running your program, so they don't escape unnoticed.

Importing and Exporting Text

Visual Basic gives you the capability of loading ASCII text files into code modules or forms. Use the **Load Text** option from the **File** menu to load ASCII text files.

You can use this option to load the CONSTANT.TXT file into your program code. CONSTANT.TXT is a text file which consists of several global constant declarations. The file is included as part of the Visual Basic package. For more information on CONSTANT.TXT, and how to load this file, see Chapter 14, "Language Building Blocks."

Figure 13.7 shows the standard Load Text dialog box that lets you select the text file desired.

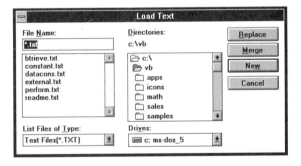

Figure 13.7.

The Load Text dialog box.

Click the **R**eplace button to replace all code in the current Code window with the imported text. Click **M**erge to add the text at the insertion point, or Ne**w** to open a new module to load the text there.

Writing a New Code Procedure

To open a Code window, double-click on the form or control with which the new procedure is to be associated. If the new procedure is at the module level, however, double-click the module's name in the Project window instead.

The procedure which you are creating for an existing form or control already has a name, such as Command1_Click or List1_Change. If you are creating a new procedure in a module or form, however, choose the New Procedure option from the View menu. A dialog box prompts you for the name of the procedure, and an Option button lets you specify whether the new procedure is a Sub or a function. The Code window then creates the new procedure, and you're ready to begin.

Editing Existing Code

To edit existing code in a control or form, simply double-click the object to open a Code window. Use the Procedure list to find the procedure you want, if more than one is defined for the object. You can use also the View Procedures window described earlier in this chapter to edit your desired procedure.

Using Multiple Editor Windows

A unique quality of the Visual Basic editor is that you can have virtually an unlimited number of Editor windows open simultaneously, as long as each one is associated with a different form or module. As you create new forms, the Editor windows are the same size, and generally positioned directly on top of one another, so multiple windows are not always apparent.

You can resize and relocate the window for each form independently, so that its title bar remains visible. You can then give the focus to the desired form window by clicking its title bar, or clicking another spot on the window's visible surface.

Unfortunately, you can have only one window per form or module open at one time. If you are creating the code for an event procedure relating to one form or control object, you cannot open simultaneously a window for an event procedure relating to another object on the same form. You can open simultaneously, however, two Code windows relating to event procedures associated with different forms.

T I P **Using Temporary Modules to Facilitate Code Development**

You can use temporary modules as a repository for procedure code when you are writing complex applications, especially those with nested procedures. You can have as many Module Editor windows open at one time as you want. Each temporary module should contain only one procedure to which you want simultaneous access. Call the procedure in the module from the template for the event:

```
Sub ObjectName_EventName
    Call ModuleProc
End Sub
```

With this technique, you can refer quickly to the module code as you write other form procedures. When you finish writing and testing your code, you can move it back into your form procedure, replacing the `Call` instruction with the code. Then, select the **R**emove File option from the **F**ile menu to delete the module from your application.

Keeping code in a module is a convenient way of saving a backup copy of your original procedure code when you intend to make substantial changes.

Although you can have only one Code editor window active at any time, you can split the window into two panes. With split panes, you can edit quickly two different procedures, or two separate locations in the same procedure. To split a window, follow these steps:

1. Place the cursor on the small black bar in the upper-right corner of the Code editor window. The bar is just above the vertical scroll bar's top arrow.

   When the pointer is on the black bar, the cursor shape changes to a small black double arrow.

2. Press and hold the left mouse button, and drag the black bar halfway down the window. Then, release the button.

   You now have two individual panes in which to edit. The higher pane is always present, as evidenced by the line that appears just under the title bar of the window.

3. Click the surface of either pane to select it for editing. If you click the surface of the higher pane, then click the `Proc:` pull-down combo box, you can select an event procedure to edit.

   The template for your selected event procedure appears.

4. When you finish using the higher pane, you can minimize its presence by moving the black bar back to its original position at the top of the window.

Split-pane Code windows are useful when you create or edit two procedures that interact with one another. In such cases, you usually want to view simultaneously the code in both procedures.

When using split panes, you probably want to enlarge the Code editor window to full-screen size by clicking the window's Maximize button. By clicking this button again, you can return the Code editor window to normal size.

Summary

You use the Code window to create and edit Visual Basic code. A Code window contains the editing pane, and the Object and Procedure lists.

A Code window responds to options chosen from the main menu system. In particular, the **Edit** menu provides several editing features such as Cut and Paste. The View Procedure dialog box lets you quickly and easily navigate among existing procedures.

Visual Basic has three categories of code: functions, subprograms, and declarations. A function performs events and returns a value. A Sub performs events, but does not return a value. Declaration code defines types, constants, and variables at the level of the procedure, the form, the module, or globally.

The Code window automatically performs code formatting and syntax checking. Search and Replace functions are provided that let you carry out variable search scopes, pattern matching, and automatic text replacing. ASCII text files can be imported or exported to disk files.

Language Building Blocks

This chapter begins an examination of the Visual Basic programming language. By this time, you have written several applications. You already have a solid foundation for understanding how the Visual Basic language works. The next several chapters provide an in-depth exploration of various programming topics—explaining what you can and cannot do with the program language. The emphasis is on programming techniques and tips.

If you have prior experience with any version of the BASIC language, you have a good start on mastering Visual Basic's programming language. The event-driven nature of Visual Basic is new to former QBasic, QuickBASIC, and GW-BASIC programmers. Visual Basic also has several language extensions not found in other versions of BASIC. Any experience you might have had with BASIC programming, however, can only help you to learn the aspects of the Visual Basic language.

This chapter examines Visual Basic's fundamental building blocks—the various pieces that you join together to write applications—and just how these pieces fit together. The following key concepts are presented:

- Program structure
- Data types (numbers, strings, and variants)
- Data holders (variables, arrays, and constants)
- Expressions and operators
- Comments

The Macroscopic Perspective

Suppose, for a moment, that you knew nothing about programming. Imagine looking for the first time at Visual Basic program code. The first thing you might notice is that the program (each individual procedure) consists of a series of lines (of text characters). In a Visual Basic program, each line is one of the following:

- A single instruction (or a group of instructions)
- A label

Visual Basic Instructions

An *instruction* is similar to a Visual Basic "sentence." Each instruction orders the computer to perform a particular task, such as calculating an arithmetic quantity, reading from (or writing to) a disk file, assigning a value to a variable, changing a property of a form or control, printing a result, or drawing graphics.

The following are two examples of Visual Basic instructions:

```
MsgBox "Calculation complete"

Print "A stitch in time saves nine."
```

Every Visual Basic instruction begins with a statement or a method. A *statement* is a reserved word (occasionally two or three reserved words) that specifies the particular action that the instruction performs. The statement in an instruction acts as does the verb in a sentence. In the first instruction, MsgBox is a statement. Other examples of statements are Beep, Get, and For-Next.

A Statement about Statements

In this book, the term *statement* can have a slightly different meaning than what you find in other references. Actually, besides the meaning given here, other sources often attribute other meanings to the term *statement*. Most commonly, other books use "statement" to include what this book refers to as "statement" and "instruction."

A *method* is a reserved word that acts on a particular object. Similar to a statement, a method specifies an action. In the second instruction, Print is a method. When no object explicitly is stated in an instruction, the current form is the default object. This instruction prints (displays) its text message on the current form.

NOTE Programmers with prior BASIC experience might recognize that some keywords defined as statements in earlier versions of BASIC have become methods in Visual Basic—namely `Circle`, `Cls`, `Line`, `Print`, and `Pset`.

To specify the object on which the method acts, you separate the two with a period. The following instruction, for example, displays a text message on the current form's second picture box:

```
Picture2.Print "A picture is worth a thousand words."
```

Visual Basic includes approximately thirty methods. Each method works with a particular set of objects. In addition to `Print`, some other methods are `Move`, `Show`, `Cls`, and `Line`.

Two exceptions exist to the rule that all instructions begin with a statement or a method. First, consider this typical assignment instruction (which assigns a value to the variable `Score%`):

```
Score% = 21
```

Where is the statement (or any reserved word)? The answer is that you also can write this instruction with the optional statement `Let`:

```
Let Score% = 21
```

Both instructions do exactly the same thing. The first form simply has an implied `Let` at the beginning of the instruction. If the `Let` is implied, then this exception really conforms to the general rule after all.

Second, the `Call` statement is optional in instructions that invoke user-defined procedures. As with `Let`, the reserved word `Call` is implied when it's not used. For example, the following instruction invokes a user-defined procedure named `DoIt` and passes the parameter `MyVal` to that procedure.

```
DoIt MyVal
```

When the `Call` statement is implied, as in the previous instruction, the procedure name is followed by any parameters. When `Call` appears, the parameters are enclosed in parentheses. For example, the following instruction is equivalent to the previous instruction.

```
Call DoIt(MyVal)
```

`Let` is discussed later in this chapter. For more information on `Call`, see Chapter 18, "Using Procedures: Subs and Functions."

Some statements and methods, such as Beep, End, and Cls, are instructions all by themselves. Most instructions, however, contain a statement or method, *and* additional (optional or required) information. The extra information can be expressions, parameters, or other keywords. The MsgBox and Print instructions just given are examples that contain additional information.

Every Visual Basic instruction must follow the syntax rules associated with the relevant statement. If not, a syntax error occurs.

> **NOTE** **Trying Code Examples**
>
> This chapter contains sample instructions and small program fragments. Several instructions utilize the Print method to display results. Most Print instructions in this chapter do not explicitly indicate the print destination with an object name in front of the Print keyword. (A typical instruction, for example, might simply be Print "Hello", not an instruction with a Print object such as Picture1.Print "Hello".)
>
> To try the examples in this chapter, your code must designate in which place the results appear. You can indicate this destination in several ways. The two simplest approaches are to display results directly on the default form, or in the Debug window.
>
> To display results directly on the form, open the Form_Click procedure. Use the code fragment from this chapter (often a single instruction) as the body of the procedure. Then, start execution of the application, and click the default form. The result appears directly on the form.
>
> The second method is to display results in the Debug window. To do this, start an application without entering any code, then break execution (press Ctrl-Break, or click the Break icon on the toolbar). The Debug window appears. You now can type code fragments directly into the Debug window. Print instructions display results directly in the Debug window.

Placing Multiple Instructions on a Line

You usually place each instruction on its own line. You can, however, have more than one instruction on a line. To do so, just place a colon between instructions. The following is an example of a multiple-instruction line:

```
Xvalue% = 18: Yvalue% = 31: Zvalue% = -5
```

This line contains three individual instructions. Rather than typing this line, you can write three individual lines with one instruction on each:

```
Xvalue% = 18
Yvalue% = 31
Zvalue% = -5
```

 NOTE No distinct advantage or disadvantage exists to writing the instructions on three lines instead of one. It's a matter of individual programming style.

Entering Program Instructions

Visual Basic limits a line to 255 characters. You cannot continue an instruction on the succeeding line. As you type, if the line reaches the right edge of the Code window, Visual Basic scrolls the window so that you can continue typing.

Line Numbers

Following the lead of structured BASIC languages, such as QBasic and QuickBASIC, line numbers are rarely used in Visual Basic. Early versions of BASIC (such as GW-BASIC and BASICA) required that every line begin with a number, such as

```
100 Xvalue% = 18
```

The line number, itself, is an outmoded technique. Visual Basic contains more flexible programming tools—notably, alphanumeric labels and block structures—that make line numbers obsolete. The Visual Basic program examples in this book generally do not contain line numbers. For more information on line numbers, see Chapter 15, "Program Flow and Decision Making."

Labels

A *label* identifies a program line. (This use of label has nothing to do with the Label control in the toolbox.) A label serves as a "highway marker," identifying a location in the program code. That way, if one instruction needs to divert program flow to a particular line in the procedure, the label identifies the target line.

You can use a label at the beginning of a line containing one or more instructions. In this case, a label is a kind of "alphanumeric line number." Alternatively, a label can stand alone as a complete line.

A label consists of a letter followed, optionally, by a combination of letters, digits, and periods. The label ends with a colon. A label can be from 1 to 40 characters long, not counting the terminating colon. A few examples of valid labels are as follows:

```
SumRoutine:
```

```
A:
```

```
BobAndCarol:
```

```
modified09.18.90:
```

For more information on labels, see Chapter 15, "Program Flow and Decision Making."

Introduction to Data Types

Most programs manipulate data in one way or another. As you have seen, all program data consists of the following two primary types:

- *Numbers*—arithmetic data
- *Strings*—text (character) data

The simplest way to specify a data value is to write it explicitly. In the following Print instruction, for example, the value 21 is written explicitly:

```
Print 21
```

Rather than writing data values explicitly, you can store and manipulate them with variables. In the following instructions, for example, the data value for the Print instruction is stored in the variable MyAge%:

```
MyAge% = 21
Print MyAge%
```

When you write a data value explicitly, it is said to be specified by a *literal*. In the instruction Print 21, 21 is a literal because the value is specified with explicit numbers (that is, literally), not with a variable name, such as MyAge%.

 NOTE Some reference sources use the term *constant* rather than the term *literal*. Throughout this book, however, the term *literal* refers to data values written explicitly.

Numeric Literals

Numeric literals look quite natural—similar to the way most people write numbers. You need a decimal point only if the number has a fractional part (that is, the number is not a whole integer). Negative numbers must begin with a minus sign. For positive numbers, the leading plus sign is usually omitted, but you can include it.

Consider the following program fragment:

```
Print 458
Print -23.499
Print 0
Print .000012
```

The output reflects the values in the original instructions:

```
 458
-23.499
 0
 .000012
```

Notice that, for positive numbers and zero, Visual Basic leaves one blank space in front of the displayed number. This blank space is where the (implied) plus sign would be.

One thing you cannot do is place commas within large numbers. `MyNumber! = 25,128.14`, for example, is not recognized by Visual Basic. Also, you cannot embed a blank space anywhere in a numeric literal.

NOTE

Exponential Notation

When numbers become extremely large or small, you need a specialized notation to express them conveniently. To say the least, literals such as .0000000000000389 and 4589100000 are awkward.

To express such numbers, Visual Basic uses *exponential notation,* also called *scientific notation.* The literals 3.89E–14 and 4.5891E+09 specify the two numbers given in the previous paragraph. This notation is computer shorthand for the more common mathematical notations, 3.89×10^{-14} and 4.5891×10^{9}.

To interpret exponential notation, move the decimal point the number of places indicated by the exponent after the *E.* Move the decimal point to the right for positive exponents, and left for negative ones. (You might need to pad the number with zeroes to complete the alignment.)

2.89E+05, for example, is 289,000; –1.67E–06 is –0.00000167.

String Literals

A *string* is a sequence of text characters treated as a single value. To express a string literal, place a double quotation mark (not an apostrophe, which is sometimes called the single quote) at each end of the text. These paired double quotation marks are called *delimiters* because they mark the beginning and end of the string.

Consider this instruction:

```
Print "Things are looking up"
```

The resulting output is an reflection of the string literal with the quotation marks removed:

```
Things are looking up
```

Data Holders: Variables, Constants, Arrays, and Records

Data holders store data for subsequent use. Visual Basic has four kinds of data holders: variables, constants, arrays, and records. Each is appropriate for specific sorts of tasks (see Table 14.1).

Table 14.1. Data holders.

Name	Type of Data Held
Variable	A single value that can change
Constant	A single value that remains fixed
Array	Multiple values of the same data type
Record	Multiple values of different data types

Variables and constants are *scalar* data holders, which means that they store only one data value at a time. Arrays and records are *structured*, or *compound* data holders, which means they can store multiple values simultaneously.

Understanding Variables

A *variable* is simply a name you give to an area of memory in which a data value is stored. When you need to retrieve that data, or modify its value, you can refer to the memory location by the variable's name. In a financial program, for example, the variable BankBalance! might hold the value of the current balance in your checking account. As the program runs, the value stored in `BankBalance!` might change several times.

Naming Variables

You are free to give variables meaningful, descriptive names. As you design your programs, think about what each variable represents, and choose an appropriately informative name.

Visual Basic does insist that you adhere to the following rules when choosing a variable name:

1. The first character must be a letter.

2. Succeeding characters can be letters, digits, or underscores.

3. The final character can be one of the type-declaration characters (%, &, !, #, @, and $).

4. The name is restricted to a 40-character maximum.

5. A variable name cannot be a reserved word, although a reserved word can be embedded in a variable name. For example, you cannot use `Input` as a variable name because `Input` is the name of a statement and function predefined in Visual Basic. However, `MyInput` is an acceptable variable name. For a list of most of Visual Basic's reserved words, see the Keyword Reference in the back of the book.

Remember that Visual Basic considers upper- and lowercase letters equivalent in variable names. The names `MyAge%`, `MYAGE%`, and `Myage%` all refer to the same variable. As you type a procedure, Visual Basic changes *all* occurrences of a variable name to reflect the capitalization you last used.

Table 14.2 shows some acceptable and unacceptable variable names.

Table 14.2. Example variable names.

Name	Status	Comment
MyAge	OK	No data type suffix
MyAge%	OK	Uses data type suffix (see next section of this chapter)
X	OK	Single-letter variable names acceptable
123Graph	Error	Variable names must begin with a letter
Tax_Rate	OK	Underscore characters acceptable
Figure7.4	Error	Periods not acceptable
Bob&Ray	Error	An ampersand can only be at the end (as a data type suffix)
Name	Error	Name is a reserved word
MyName	OK	Name is okay if embedded

T I P **Tips for Naming Variables**

Well-chosen variable names enhance any program. When variable names are meaningful, you have an easier time understanding what is going on in a particular application. After all, the more understandable your programs are, the easier it is for you to make modifications and track errors.

Be creative with variable naming. You can mix upper- and lowercase letters in the variable name. Some examples of good, clear variable names are `Salary!`, `LastName$`, and `InvoiceNumber%`.

All of us try shortcuts in our lives, and programming is no exception. Sometimes in the rush to get an application working, or in the hope of saving some typing time, you might use short nondescriptive variable names, such as `X`, `A5`, or `JJ%`. You often can rationalize using these names by thinking, "Hey, my memory is good; I'll remember what these variables mean." Six months later, you're likely to stare quizzically at your previous work, and throw up your hands in disgust.

Avoid short (and shortsighted) nondescriptive names. After you get in the habit of using descriptive, meaningful variable names, you actually can program faster with them.

Don't go overboard, however, and make your variable names ridiculously long. In your quest for meaningful variable names, you might get carried away with some multisyllabic tongue twisters. You should never need such monstrosities as

```
NextCharacterInTheUsersInputString$
```

or

```
TeamScoreAtTheEndOfRegulation%
```

Such variable names are counterproductive and make your programs cumbersome and awkward to read.

The Eight Fundamental Data Types

Besides choosing a name, you must make another important decision for each variable: the type of data that the variable can store.

As mentioned earlier, the two primary data types are numbers and strings. Visual Basic, however, is even more specific. Actually, eight fundamental data types exist: five different numeric types, two string (text) types, and a combination data type (see Figure 14.1). Except for the combination data type (discussed shortly), an individual variable can store only data of its assigned data type. An integer variable, for example, can store only an integer number, not a string, or a single-precision number.

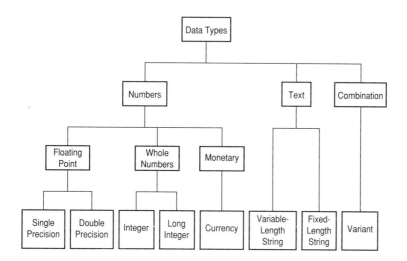

Figure 14.1.

The eight fundamental data types.

Numeric Data Types

Take a closer look at the five numeric data types:

1. *Integer (also called short integer or regular integer).* Integers are whole numbers (numbers without fractional components). Integer values specify items that can be counted discretely. An integer variable, for example, can designate the number of runs scored in a baseball game, the number of times through a programming loop, or the number of orders processed by a shipping department. As explained later in this chapter, integers can represent also Boolean (True or False) values. Integers can be negative, zero, or positive. The range of the integer data type is from –32,768 to +32,767.

2. *Long integer.* Long integers extend the integer data type to a wider range of whole numbers. A long integer variable can store values from –2,147,483,648 to +2,147,483,647.

3. *Single-precision data types.* Many numbers do not lend themselves to the integer or long integer data types. A number might, for example, have a fractional part, such as 89.22, or be too large, such as 1.34E+15. The single-precision data type handles these kinds of numbers. The range of single-precision numerical data is from (approximately) –3.4E+38 to +3.4E+38.

   The price you pay for using single precision is that, in general, the computer cannot represent these numbers exactly—only approximately. The approximation, for most purposes, is close enough. Single-precision numbers are accurate to the first seven digits. The fraction *one-third*, for example, actually is .3333333333333 (with an endless string of threes). In Visual Basic, however, the single-precision accuracy of one-third is .3333333 (exactly seven digits). In practice, you usually do not need to be concerned with possible inaccuracies resulting from single-precision calculations. Only the heaviest number-crunching programs are susceptible to significant errors.

4. *Double-precision numerical.* Just as a long integer extends the domain of integer, double precision extends the domain of single precision. Double-precision variables can store numbers ranging from approximately –1.8D+308 to +1.8D+308. Double-precision numbers are accurate to 15 or 16 digits. In Visual Basic, the fraction one-third is now accurate to .3333333333333333 (16 digits).

The exponential indicator for double-precision literals is D rather than E. The D indicates that the number should be interpreted as double-precision rather than single-precision.

5. *Currency.* This data type (new to QBasic and GW-BASIC programmers) is designed specifically to store financial information. Currency values are in a fixed-point format, with up to 15 digits to the left of the decimal point, and four digits to the right. The range of numbers is from –922,337,203,685,477.5808 to +922,337,203,685,477.5807.

Currency values avoid potential errors that can occur when manipulating large monetary values. The problem is that the binary representation used to store decimal fractions in Single or Double format is not exact. Complex calculations involving Single or Double numbers representing dollars and cents can create rounding errors. The Currency type, however, represents numbers within its data range exactly, avoiding this type of rounding problem. Currency values are stored as 19-digit integers that are scaled by a factor of 10,000. As a result, all calculations are done with integer-type arithmetic, which is not susceptible to rounding errors.

String Data Types

Two string data types exist:

1. *Variable-length string.* Most string variables are variable-length. As the name suggests, the key feature of a variable-length string variable is that the stored string can be any length. Well, almost any length. The range is from a null (zero-length) string ("") to a medium-length string (such as Zippety doo-dah, Zippety Aaay) to a string of the maximum length of (approximately) 65,500 characters.

Variable length string variables can store only one data string at a time, but the length of this string can change frequently, as the program runs. The following code fragment, for example, reassigns the value of the variable-length string variable MyString$ from a short string to a much longer one:

```
MyString$ = "I'm not long"
Print MyString$
MyString$ = "Hey, you made me considerably l-o-n-g-e-r now"
Print MyString$
```

The output is

```
I'm not long
Hey, you made me considerably l-o-n-g-e-r now
```

All string variables in BASICA and GW-BASIC are variable-length strings.

2. *Fixed-length string.* As the name implies, a fixed-length string variable stores a string value of a predetermined length. For each such variable, you declare the fixed length to be from 0 to a maximum of 32,767 characters. A program can change the value stored in a fixed-length string variable, but the length of the stored string cannot change. The fixed-length string data type does not exist in BASICA or GW-BASIC.

The Combination Data Type

In addition to Currency, Visual Basic has another data type not found in QBasic and GW-BASIC—the *Variant.*

Variant. A Variant variable is similar to a chameleon—such a variable can store data of any other type. The stored value can be numeric, string, or date/time information. If required by the context of an instruction, Visual Basic automatically converts a value stored in a Variant variable to the necessary data type. Consider the following code fragment:

```
MyValue = "35"       'String data stored in Variant variable
Print 2 * MyValue    'Data in MyValue is converted to numeric
```

The output is 70. Note that if MyValue were a string variable, the Print instruction would generate a Type mismatch error. Variant variables convert data types automatically. Variant is the default data type for variables.

Comparing Data Types

Inherent trade-offs exist among the various data types. For numeric variables (Integer, Long integer, Single-precision, Double-precision, and Currency), the following three trade-offs come into play:

- Use of computer memory
- Speed of program execution
- Accuracy of calculation

When storing numeric data in memory, Visual Basic converts numbers into a special binary representation. The amount of computer memory needed to store each variable depends only on its data type, not on the actual value stored (except for Variant variables, which can fluctuate in size). Even when the value of the variable changes, the amount of memory needed for the variable remains constant. Table 14.3 shows how much memory Visual Basic uses for each numeric variable type.

Table 14.3. Memory required to store numeric values.	
Data Type	**Memory Required**
Integer	2 bytes (16 bits)
Long integer	4 bytes (32 bits)
Single-precision	4 bytes (32 bits)
Double-precision	8 bytes (64 bits)
Currency	8 bytes (64 bits)

As Table 14.3 shows, you can save substantial memory if you use integer variables as much as possible.

Calculations are faster with integer variables than with any other data type. Double-precision calculations consume the largest amount of time. The more you use integer variables rather than other data types, the faster your programs run.

As mentioned previously, integer and long integer variables also win in the accuracy contest. Currency values also are more precise than single- or double-precision. Double-precision, though still approximate, is more accurate than single-precision.

The conclusion is simple: Use the simplest data type capable of expressing the numbers involved. Use integer if possible. By using Variant variables, Visual Basic generally stores a numeric value in the simplest possible data type.

Most of your string variables are variable-length. The fixed-length string type is appropriate for special situations, such as records (see Chapter 25, "Processing Files").

Introducing Variant Variables

Each Variant variable actually stores two pieces of information: a value, and a code number indicating its data type.

When using Variant variables, you don't need to worry about how Visual Basic represents the data in the variables internally. All conversions occur automatically.

A Variant variable (usually) stores a numeric value with the simplest numeric type that represents the number (Integer is the simplest). As you see in Chapter 16, "Working With Numbers," you can force a Variant to use any numeric format with special conversion functions.

Variants can actually store nine different types of values. That is, the code number stored with each Variant can have nine different values. Using the VarType function, you can determine the type of data stored in a Variant. Table 14.4 shows the values returned by VarType for a Variant variable named MyValue.

 NOTE To determine the value stored in a Variant, you can display the value returned by the VarType function. If a Variant variable is named MyValue, for example, the following instruction displays a number from 0 to 8, which indicates the type of data stored in MyValue:

```
Print VarType(MyValue)
```

Table 14.4. Variant data types.

Result of *VarType(MyValue)*	Variant data type
0	Empty
1	Null
2	Integer
3	Long
4	Single
5	Double
6	Currency
7	Date/Time
8	String

The *Empty* Value

Table 14.4 shows two special data types: Empty and Null. A Variant contains the value Empty until a program instruction assigns a value to the variable. Empty is a special value unto itself, and is not equivalent to the numeric value 0, or a null string (""). If you use a Variant containing the Empty value in a numeric context, however, Visual Basic treats the value as 0.

The *Null* Value

Null, similar to Empty, is another special value. Don't confuse this Null value with the null string (""). Null is a keyword in the Visual Basic language that you can directly assign to a Variant variable:

```
MyValue = Null
```

The Null value has special properties. When a Variant variable containing Null appears in any expression, it evaluates to Null automatically. In an instruction, such as MyValue = *expression,* if *expression* contains any Variant with a Null value, MyValue is assigned also this value.

You can use Null to test for error conditions in an application. By assigning the Null value to Variant variables that do not yet have known values, you can determine if the application tries to use one of the variables with an unknown value. If so, the Null value propagates to the variables that store the results. Variant variables are explored in more depth in the next several chapters.

Date and Time Values

As Table 14.4 shows, Variant variables also can store date and time information. You can manipulate dates and times as both serial quantities (number of days elapsed since a given date), and as string-like values expressed with notation, such as 7/11/93 5:29am. Within the Variant variables, Visual Basic handles the format conversions automatically.

Do you have any idea how many days you have been alive? As a simple example of manipulating dates and times with Variant variables, the following program fragment displays a message box which tells you just how many days have elapsed since your birth date:

```
BirthDate = DateSerial(1950, 1, 30)   'Year, Month, Day
DaysAlive = Now - BirthDate
MsgBox "Number of days alive is " & DaysAlive
```

Here, BirthDate and DaysAlive are Variant variables. The DateSerial function returns the number of days that have elapsed since Jan 1, 100 (quite a long time ago!) to the date entered in the function. When you try the example, type the year, month, and day of your birthdate in the DateSerial function. The Now function returns the number of elapsed days from that ancient date to the current moment. The DateSerial and Now functions both return Variant values of type 7 (date/time). By subtracting BirthDate from Now, the DaysAlive variable stores the desired result.

All that remains is to display the answer. The program fragment uses a message box to display the result. The MsgBox statement requires a string argument. The ampersand (&) operator used in the example MsgBox instruction joins two strings together. For more information on this operator, known as the *concatenation* operator, see the following section, "String Operators," in this chapter.

Notice how Visual Basic takes the date and time information stored in the `DaysAlive` variable, and converts the value to the string form required by `MsgBox`. This shows the power of Variant variables.

The message box displays the result as a large number with a fractional component, something similar to the following:

```
Number of days alive is 15787.3505324074
```

Visual Basic contains several statements and functions which manipulate date and time information. For more information on this topic, refer back to Chapter 11, "Displaying Text and Fonts."

Giving Variables a Data Type

Each variable you create has one of the eight data types. The process of associating a data type with a variable is known as *variable typing* (assigning a data "type," not "typing" on the keyboard).

You can assign a data type to a variable in four different ways:

1. *Use a type-declaration suffix character.*

   By appending one of the type-declaration suffixes to a variable name, you designate the data type for that variable. Table 14.5 lists the available suffixes.

Table 14.5. Variable suffixes.

Suffix	Variable Type	Example Variable Name
%	Integer	Index%
&	Long	Population&
!	Single	Area!
#	Double	AtomicWeight#
@	Currency	MyDebt@
$	String	FullName$

Variant does not have a type-declaration suffix.

2. *Use an **As** clause.*

   The statements `Dim`, `ReDim`, `Global`, and `Static` optionally can include a clause of the following form:

   varname As *type*

   in which *varname* is the name of a variable, and *type* specifies the data type.

   `As` clause typing is discussed in "Declaring Variables" later in the chapter.

3. *Use a `Deftype` instruction.*

   The statements `DefInt`, `DefLng`, `DefSng`, `DefDbl`, `DefCur`, `DefStr`, and `DefVar` (Integer, Long, Single, Double, Currency, String, and Variant) declare that variables beginning with particular letters have a specified data type. These instructions are explained in "Wholesale Variable Typing—`Deftype`," later in the chapter.

4. *Do nothing!*

   When none of the three previous conditions apply, the variable type becomes Variant automatically. If you name a variable `Cost`, for example, `Cost` becomes a variable of type Variant.

Variable-Typing Conflicts

In Visual Basic, unlike most other versions of BASIC, you cannot have two variables with the same root name, but different suffixes. `Price!` and `Price$`, for example, cannot coexist in the same procedure. If you violate this rule, a `Duplicate definition` error occurs.

Declaring Variables—*Dim*

You do not need a special instruction to create a variable. You can use a new variable at any time. When a variable name first appears, Visual Basic creates the variable automatically, and assigns it a default value (0 for a numeric variable, the null string ("") for a String variable, and `Empty` for a Variant). Visual Basic assumes that all new variables without a suffix are Variant, provided that no DefType instruction is in effect and that no Dim instruction (described in the following paragraphs) declares the variable.

You can make your programs more understandable and professional-looking, however, if you use the `Dim` instruction to declare each variable. By declaring it with `Dim`, you specify that the variable exists within the program. `Dim` instructions can indicate also the data type of the variable. (The `As` *type* clause is optional.)

```
Dim varname As type, varname As type ...
```

in which

> *varname* is the name of an ordinary variable,

and

> *type* declares the data type of *varname*.

The following instruction, for example, declares that the variable Cost has the data type Currency:

```
Dim Cost As Currency
```

Scope of *Dim* Declarations

Dim declarations can appear at the module, form, or procedure level. When using Dim inside a procedure, the declared variables are defined only within the procedure. Although you can place Dim instructions anywhere within a procedure, it's good programming practice to put them at the beginning of the procedure (along with a comment that explains what each variable does).

At the form level, you place Dim instructions in the Declarations section. The declared variables then exist throughout the form. Similarly, module-level declarations have scope throughout the module.

 NOTE **Dim and Arrays**

Programmers with previous BASIC experience are accustomed to Dim declaring arrays. Visual Basic uses Dim also to declare arrays, but extends its use to declaring ordinary variables. For details on declaring arrays with Dim, see Chapter 19, "Using Arrays and Structures."

Using the *As* Clause

The optional As clause specifies the data type of *varname*. To use the As clause, *varname* must not contain any type-declaration suffix. The *type* parameter can be any of the terms that Table 14.6 lists.

Table 14.6. *As* clause *type* declarations.

Type	Variable type
Integer	Integer
Long	Long integer
Single	Single-precision
Double	Double-precision
Currency	Currency
String	Variable-length string
String * num	Fixed-length string of length num
Variant	Variant

When declaring more than one variable of the same data type with a single Dim instruction, you must include a separate As clause for each variable, such as

```
Dim Population As Long, Num_Houses As Long
```

You can define a variable with a type-declarations suffix, providing you omit the As clause, such as

```
Dim MyName$
```

Programmers are divided on the issue of whether to declare variables with suffixes, or to use As clauses. The trend today is toward using As clauses. The following is a typical example of the modern programming style:

```
Sub Command1_Click ()
Dim Years_Service As Integer
Dim Salary As Currency
.
.
```

You might, however, prefer the following style:

```
Sub Command1_Click ()
Dim Years_Service%
Dim Salary@
.
.
```

If you declare a variable without specifying either a suffix or an As clause, it has the default data type (Variant unless a Deftype declaration is in effect). For example:

```
Dim Price
```

This instruction and the following one are equivalent:

```
Dim Price As Variant
```

Your program can refer to a variable with the appropriate type suffix after declaring it with an As clause. Consider the following instruction:

```
Dim CompanyName As String
```

CompanyName and CompanyName$ now refer to the same variable.

Declaring Global Variables

To declare that a variable exists throughout all the modules of a program, use the Global keyword rather than Dim. Such a global declaration can appear only in the Declarations section of a code module.

By placing the following, for example, in the Declarations section of any module, you make Title available to all procedures in every module:

```
Global Title As String
```

 NOTE In addition to Dim and Global, Visual Basic has another statement that declares variables: Static. Use Static at the procedure level to declare variables that retain their values throughout multiple calls to the procedure. For more information on Static, see Chapter 19, "Using Arrays and Structures."

Forcing Variable Declarations

Using an Option Explicit instruction, you force all variables to be declared, and lessen program bugs due to typing mistakes.

Suppose your program declares NumParts to be an Integer variable. If you accidentally spell the variable NumPart (omitting the final s) once inside your program, no syntax or logic error occurs. Visual Basic uses the default value of 0 for NumPart when your program needs the value stored in NumParts. Erroneous results are inevitable.

By placing the following instruction in the Declarations section of a form or module, you require that all variables be declared within that form or module:

```
Option Explicit
```

If you try to use an undeclared variable, the Variable not defined error occurs. Use Option Explicit to protect against undeclared variables getting into your programs. It is a worthwhile step toward good programming habits.

To have Visual Basic automatically include an `Option Explicit` instruction in each module of your program, follow these steps:

1. Select **Environments...** from the **O**ptions menu.
2. Specify `Yes` for the value of the Require Variable Declaration option.

Wholesale Variable Typing—*Deftype*

As you have seen, Visual Basic treats any variables without a type-declaration suffix as a Variant variable. With a `Deftype` instruction, you can change this default to one of the other data types.

The seven `Deftype` instructions have a similar appearance.

```
DefInt letterranges

DefLng letterranges

DefSng letterranges

DefDbl letterranges

DefCur letterranges

DefStr letterranges

DefVar letterranges
```

in which

      letterranges specifies a range of letters.

Each `Deftype` instruction corresponds to a particular data type (see Table 14.7).

Table 14.7 Data types of *Deftype* statements.

Statement	Data Type
DefInt	Integer
DefLng	Long
DefSng	Single
DefDbl	Double
DefCur	Currency
DefStr	String
DefVar	Variant

A `Deftype` instruction changes the default data type for all variables that begin with a letter included in the *letterranges* parameter. (`Deftype` instructions also affect array and user-defined function names.)

The following instruction, for example, declares that all variables beginning with the letter *C* are of type Integer:

```
DefInt C
```

After this instruction, variables named `C`, `Cost`, and `CheckDeposit` would all be type Integer.

`Deftype` instructions are put in the Declarations section of a form or module. At the form level, `Deftype` affects only the variables defined within the form. At the module level, the instruction affects all variables defined within the module.

The *letterranges* parameter is either an individual letter from A to Z, or a letter range indicated by two letters separated with a hyphen. Lower- and uppercase letters are considered equivalent. You can specify multiple ranges in a single instruction. To do this, separate ranges with commas. The following are some examples of `Deftype` instructions:

```
DefDbl A, Q-T
```

```
DefStr a-z
```

```
DefInt C-F, R, T, W-Z
```

`Deftype` instructions do not affect variables declared with a `Dim` instruction, or a type suffix (`%`, `&`, `!`, `#`, `@`, or `$`). A suffix on a variable or a `Dim` declaration overrides any default data type established with `Deftype`.

`Deftype` instructions are most useful when all (or most) of the variables within a form or module have the same data type. It is then convenient to change the default data type from `Variant` to another type (usually `Integer` or `String`).

Introduction to Constants

Constants, or more formally, *symbolic constants*, are similar to variables. Constants and variables both have unique names and store data values. The difference is that the value stored in a constant never changes, but one stored in a variable can. By using constants rather than literal data values, you make your programs easier to understand, and simpler to debug. Use a `Const` instruction to define constants.

```
Const constname = expr, constname = expr ...
```

in which

constname is the user-defined name for the constant,

and

expr is an arithmetic or string expression defining the value for the constant.

A single Const instruction can define one or more constants. If more than one constname is defined, use a comma between each definition.

The following instruction, for example, defines the constant NORMAL_TEMP with the value of 98.6:

```
Const NORMAL_TEMP = 98.6
```

Constant names, by convention, are usually expressed with all uppercase letters. This is not a requirement, however, and you freely can mix upper- and lowercase letters in a constant name. Normal_Temp, for example, is a perfectly valid constant name. Names within the program are not case-sensitive— NORMAL_TEMP and Normal_Temp refer to the same constant.

Each constname must conform to the same rules as a variable name. You can append a type-declaration suffix (%, &, !, #, @, or $) to a constant name; however, unlike a suffix used with a variable name, this suffix actually is not part of the name. Suppose that you define a constant named PASSING_GRADE%, as follows:

```
Const PASSING_GRADE% = 65
```

In the body of your program, you don't need the % suffix to refer to PASSING_GRADE%. The following instruction, for example, works just as well:

```
If Score% >= PASSING_GRADE Then MsgBox "You passed!"
```

The data type of a constant is set by the type-declaration suffix used in constname. If you don't use such a suffix, however, expr determines the data type.

If expr is a string expression, a string constant results. When expr is numeric, the constant assumes the simplest numeric type that can represent the value of expr (Integer is the simplest, followed by Long, Single, Double, and Currency). Constants cannot be of type Variant. Constants also are not affected by Deftype instructions, such as DefInt and DefStr.

Some restrictions exist on the expressions that you can use to define the value of each constant. For a string constant, expr can be only a string literal surrounded by double quotation marks. For example:

```
Const Salutation$ = "To Whom It May Concern"
```

For a numeric constant, *expr* can consist of the following elements:

- Literals, such as 438 or 53.44

- Other constants defined previously

- Arithmetic operators, such as + or /. The exponentiation operator (^), however, cannot be used. (The arithmetic operators are discussed later in this chapter.)

- Logical operators, such as And or Not. The logical operators are discussed in Chapter 15, "Program Flow and Decision Making."

expr cannot contain any variables or functions (such as the square root function Sqr).

The following are some examples of Const declarations:

```
Const CONVERSION_FACTOR = 454
```

```
Const TITLE = "Grand Poobah"
```

```
Const MAX_WEIGHT = 538.5
```

```
Const MIN_WEIGHT = MAX_WEIGHT - 200
```

Scope of Constants

The scope of a constant follows the same rules as does a regular variable. If the Const instruction appears inside a procedure, the constant exists only within that procedure. By placing the Const instruction in the Declarations section of the form or module, the constant exists throughout either one.

To make a constant exist throughout all the forms and modules of an application, you use a special form of the Const instruction. Include the keyword Global, and place the Const instruction in the Declarations section of any module. For example:

```
Global Const NUM_EMPLOYEES = 482
```

Advantages of Constants

By assigning well-chosen descriptive names to constants, you make your programs much easier to understand. An appropriate constant name is much easier to read than a cryptic numeric literal. Compare the following two instructions:

```
Profit! = Principal! * 8.5

Profit! = Principal! * INTEREST_RATE
```

When confronted by the first example, you might wonder what the number 8.5 means. The second example makes the meaning of the number clear. In the Declarations section of the form or module, or in the current procedure, use a `Const` instruction to set the actual value of `INTEREST_RATE`:

```
Const INTEREST_RATE = 8.5
```

By using constants, you easily can make wholesale changes. Suppose that a particular literal appears several times in a specific program. By giving such a literal a declared constant name, you later can modify its value throughout the program simply by changing the value of the constant in the `Const` instruction once.

A report-generating program, for example, might use the constant `LINES_PER_PAGE` several times to control the maximum number of lines printed on one report page. If you need to adjust this control number, the only modification required is one change to the definition of `LINES_PER_PAGE` in the `Const` instruction.

Built-In Constants

Visual Basic has a few constants built into the language. The most important of these constants are True and False. You can use these constants to assign values for certain properties. For example:

```
Command1.Visible = False
```

This instruction sets the Visible property of the command button to False. As a result, the command button becomes hidden.

Internally, Visual Basic represents True and False with the integer values -1 and 0, respectively. To verify these values, try this instruction:

```
Print True, False
```

The result is

```
-1              0
```

True and False are predefined, so you do not need to declare them. Visual Basic treats True and False as if they were defined with the following instruction:

```
Global Const True = -1, False = 0
```

The CONSTANT.TXT File

Visual Basic includes a special text file named CONSTANT.TXT. This file consists of a multitude of `Global Const` declarations. The defined constants include property values, color codes, keyboard codes, and many other quantities. Comments throughout the file explain the meaning of the constants. The following includes a few of the constants that you can use to set the shape of the mouse pointer. (For more information on changing the shape of the mouse pointer, see Chapter 22, "Responding to Mouse Events.")

```
Global Const ARROW = 1           ' 1 - Arrow
Global Const CROSSHAIR = 2       ' 2 - Cross
Global Const IBEAM = 3           ' 3 - I-Beam
Global Const ICON_POINTER = 4    ' 4 - Icon
```

To use all or part of the CONSTANT.TXT file in an application, follow these steps:

1. Open a new code module by choosing the New **M**odule option from Visual Basic's **F**ile menu.

2. Choose **L**oad Text... from the **F**ile menu.

3. Select the file CONSTANT.TXT in the VB directory.

These steps load CONSTANT.TXT into the Declarations section of a new module. In your application, you can keep the entire file, or edit it to leave only the declarations you need. The constants are defined with `Global Const` instructions, so you can place the file at the module level only, not at the form or procedure level.

Introduction to Arrays

Arrays are "super variables." As you have seen, ordinary variables store only a single value. An ordinary variable can be of any data type, but can store only a single data value (of the appropriate type).

An array, by contrast, houses multiple data values. A single array is a collection of values, each having the same data type. An array is similar to a set of ordinary variables.

Every array, similar to an ordinary variable, has a name you create. These names follow the same naming conventions as ordinary variable names, including an optional suffix that identifies the data type of all the values in the array.

Each individual array value is called an *element* of the array. Distinct elements of the array are referenced by an *index number* (sometimes called a *subscript*).

With arrays, you easily can manage large groups of related data. Suppose that a company has 100 employees. The personnel department assigns each worker an employee number. The company has 100 employees, so these numbers range from 1 to 100. The salary of each employee is stored in an array called `Salary!`. To display the salary of employee number 73, for example, you use the following instruction:

```
Print Salary!(73)
```

Notice that you enclose the index number in parentheses after the array name. The parentheses tell Visual Basic that this is an array rather than an ordinary variable.

Arrays can also contain string values. You might, for example, create an array called `WorkerName$` that contains the names of all the employees. Then, you can store the name of employee number 73 with an instruction, such as

```
WorkerName$(73) = "Joanna B. Nimble"
```

To declare an array in a program, you use a `Dim` instruction that defines the name of the array, the number of elements contained in it, and the data type. Chapter 19, "Using Arrays and Structures," discusses the details of creating, managing, and utilizing arrays.

Another Look at Assignment Instructions

You assign a value to a variable or property directly with the equal sign. Following are two typical assignment instructions:

```
MyTemp = 98.6
```

```
Command1.Caption = "Click me"
```

The Optional *Let*

You can optionally begin any assignment instruction with the keyword `Let`. You can, for example, write the previous two instructions in this way:

```
Let MyTemp = 98.6
```

```
Let Command1.Caption = "Click me"
```

Both styles (with or without `Let`) carry out the same directive. (`Let` is a vestige from early versions of the BASIC language, which required `Let` in assignment instructions.)

Programmers sometimes refer to assignment instructions as Let *instructions*. Today, Visual Basic programmers almost universally omit the Let keyword from assignment instructions.

The Right Side of Assignment Instructions

The right side of an assignment instruction can consist of a general expression as well as a data literal. The following is a closer look at how assignment instructions work:

```
varname = expr
```
or
```
object.property = expr
```
in which

   varname is a variable or property whose value is to be assigned;

   object is the name of form or control defined in the application;

   property is the name of a Property recognized by the object;

and

   expr is an expression that provides the value to assign to varname.

Two operations are carried out when an assignment instruction executes:

1. The value of expr is calculated.

2. This value is assigned to varname.

The proper way to interpret this assignment instruction is "assign the value of expr to the variable named varname."

Think of the equal sign in an assignment instruction as meaning "is now assigned the value of." The instruction

```
NumItems% = 29 * NumBoxes%
```

therefore means that "the variable NumItems% is now assigned the result obtained by multiplying 29 by the value of NumBoxes%."

That is the reason the following instruction makes computing sense, even though it expresses a mathematical impossibility.

```
X% = X% + 1
```

?

The preceding instruction says that "the new value of the variable X% becomes the old value of the variable X% plus 1."

Except when Variant variables are involved, the general data type of *varname* and *expr* must correspond—if the variable on the left side of an assignment instruction is numeric, the expression on the right side must be numeric, also. Similarly, if the variable is a string, the expression must be a string, also.

Specific numeric data types do not, however, have to correspond. If the variable is one of the five numeric data types (Integer, Long, Single, Double, or Currency), the expression on the right side can be any of the five data types. The following instruction, for example, is acceptable:

```
MyAge% = BigNum!
```

Visual Basic converts the single-precision value in BigNum! to an integer value for MyAge% automatically.

Variant variables are even more elastic. As discussed earlier in this chapter, Visual Basic can convert between string and numeric data stored in Variant variables. (For more information on numeric data type conversion, see Chapter 16, "Working with Numbers.")

Expressions and Operators

An *expression* specifies a single data value. Expressions occur frequently in Visual Basic instructions. One common place for an expression is the right side of an assignment instruction. Expressions, however, occur in many other contexts: as parameters in function calls, as values to display with Print and other statements, and so on.

An expression can be a single literal (such as 38.66 or "Hello out there"), a variable (MyValue%), an array element (Sales!(150)), a function (Sqr(1.88)), or a combination of these elements formed with suitable operators (Sqr(1.88 / MyValue%) + 38.66).

Every valid expression, whether simple or complex, evaluates to a single numeric or string value. If the variable X has the value 2, and Y has the value 5, then the value of the expression X + Y is 7.

Although the expression must evaluate to a single value, it can contain more than one part. When an expression contains two or more parts, some sort of *operator* combines the parts to create the single value. An operator manipulates one or more operands to create a value. Each *operand*, itself, is a data value or expression. In the present example, X and Y are operands, and the plus sign (+) is an operator. Most Visual Basic operators are special symbols (such as + and >), but some operators are keywords (such as Not and Mod).

In general, when Visual Basic requires a single value, you can substitute an expression.

Types of Operators

Visual Basic has five categories of operators. As Table 14.8 shows, these operators work with data of all types: from arithmetic values to string values to specialized values. The following sections introduce the various operators.

Table 14.8. Operator categories.

Category	Description
Arithmetic	Manipulates numbers
String	Manipulates strings
Relational	Compares numbers or strings
Logical	Manipulates Boolean (True or False) values
Special	Performs specialized comparisons

Arithmetic Operators

Table 14.9 shows the arithmetic operators. The operand abbreviations I, L, S, D, and C stand for the five arithmetic data types: Integer, Long integer, Single-precision, Double-precision, and Currency.

Table 14.9. Arithmetic operators.

Symbol	Name	Operand Types	Example	Result
+	Addition	I, L, S, D, C	1.5 + 4.9	6.4
-	Subtraction	I, L, S, D, C	3.4 - 1.2	2.2
*	Multiplication	I, L, S, D, C	1.5 * 2.2	3.3
/	Division	I, L, S, D, C	4.5 / 2.5	1.8
^	Exponentiation	I, L, S, D, C	3 ^ 2	9
-	Negation	I, L, S, D, C	-21	-21
\	Integer division	I, L	6 \ 4	1
Mod	Remainder	I, L	6 Mod 4	2

You can freely mix numeric data types in an arithmetic expression. Visual Basic uses the simplest data type capable of expressing the result. `Print 2.5 * 0.4` produces 1, for example, and `Print 9 / 8` produces 1.125.

Addition and subtraction use the customary plus (+) and minus (-) signs, respectively.

```
Print 25.6 + 14
Print 100 - 38
```

The result is

```
39.6
62
```

Multiplication and division use the asterisk (*) and "division" signs (/), respectively:

```
Print 1.5 * 7
Print 9 / 2
```

The results are

```
10.5
4.5
```

Exponentiation is the process of raising one number to a power. For example, the expression 2^3 means 2 raised to the power of 3. In Visual Basic, this operation is written 2 ^ 3. On most keyboards, the exponential operator (^) is Shift-6.

The operands in an exponential expression do not have to be integers. For example:

```
Print 3.4 ^ 1.29
```

The result is

```
4.848505
```

Two arithmetic operations that might be new to you are *integer division* and *remaindering*. The integer division operator is the backslash (\ ), and the remaindering operator is the keyword MOD.

Integer division is the process of dividing one whole number by another. Only the whole number portion of the answer survives. Any remainder is discarded. If you attempt integer division with a single- or double-precision operand, the operand first is rounded to the nearest whole number.

The following program demonstrates the difference between regular division and integer division:

```
Print 14 / 5      'Regular division
Print 14 \ 5      'Integer division
```

The result is

```
2.8
2
```

Notice that the result of the integer division is to "throw away" the fractional part (0.8) of the regular division answer, not to round it to the nearest whole number. If rounded, the answer would be 3 rather than 2. When one or both operands are single- or double-precision numbers, they first are rounded to the nearest whole number before the integer division proceeds.

Remaindering is a close cousin to integer division. The Mod operator extracts the remainder after dividing by a modulus or divisor. Another way to look at remaindering is that the Mod operator returns the part "thrown away" during integer division. If you're unfamiliar with modular arithmetic, think of the schoolhouse mnemonic "goes into." For example, 4 "goes into" 11 twice, with 3 remaining; or more properly, 11 modulo 4 is 3. The following is how this looks in Visual Basic:

```
Print 11 \ 4        'Integer division quotient
Print 11 Mod 4      'Integer division remainder
```

The outcome is

```
2
3
```

String Operators

The plus sign also works with string operands. Rather than adding the strings in an arithmetic sense, the plus sign merges the text of two strings into one composite string. This process is known as *concatenation*. The text of one string is juxtaposed with the text of another to form one new string. The following program demonstrates the technique:

```
FirstPart$ = "Coca"
LastPart$ = "Cola"
FullName$ = FirstPart$ + LastPart$
Print FullName$
Print "Pepsi" + LastPart$
```

The output is

```
CocaCola
PepsiCola
```

NOTE An interesting situation arises when you concatenate a Variant variable that contains string information with one that contains numeric information.

Suppose you have one Variant variable storing a numeric value. A second Variant variable stores a string value that can be interpreted as a number (for example, the string value "123" can be interpreted as the number 123). If you concatenate the two variables with the plus sign, Visual Basic converts the string value (in the second variable) to a number, then adds the value in the first variable to produce a numeric result.

To avoid ambiguity with the plus sign acting as the addition operator as well as the concatenation operator, Visual Basic defines also the ampersand (&) exclusively as a concatenation operator. Both operands must be strings (or Variants with string values) when the ampersand denotes concatenation. You can write the previous code fragment, for example, as follows:

```
FirstPart$ = "Coca"
LastPart$ = "Cola"
FullName$ = FirstPart$ & LastPart$
Print FullName$
Print "Pepsi" & LastPart$
```

The result is the same as in the previous program.

It is a good idea to get in the habit of using the ampersand for string concatenation, and the plus sign for numeric addition. This way, you avoid possible ambiguities, and create code that is easier to maintain.

Relational Operators

The *relational operators* compare two values to produce a True or False result. This chapter simply introduces the operators (see Table 14.10). For more information on using the relational operators, see Chapter 15, "Program Flow and Decision Making."

Table 14.10. Relational operators.

Symbol	Name	Operand Types	Example
=	Equals	All	4 = 4
<>	Not equal	All	"Dog" <> "Cat"
>	Greater than	All	8 > 5
<	Less than	All	3 < 6
>=	Greater than or equal to	All	9 >= 9
<=	Less than or equal to	All	"Hi" <= "Ho"

Each example in the last column of the table is True. Notice that relational operators work on strings as well as numbers.

The most common use of relational operators is to create testing expressions for decision instructions, such as If-Then. The following is an example of an instruction:

```
If OurScore% > TheirScore% Then MsgBox "We won."
```

Chapter 15, "Program Flow and Decision Making," discusses both If-Then and relational operators with respect to conditional testing.

Logical Operators

The logical operators (as in mathematical "logic") manipulate *Boolean* operands to produce Boolean results. (The term "Boolean" comes from George Boole, a prominent 19th-century British mathematician.) A Boolean operand is simply a True or False value.

Internally, Visual Basic represents True and False with arithmetic integers: 0 for False, and -1 for True. See Chapter 16, "Working with Numbers," for more information on this topic.

Table 14.11 presents the six logical operators, and their official-sounding names. All the logical operators are keywords rather than symbols.

Table 14.11. Logical operators.

Operator	Meaning
Not	Complement (logical negation)
And	Conjunction
Or	Disjunction (inclusive or)
Xor	Exclusive or
Eqv	Equivalence
Imp	Implication

Special Operators

For specialized comparisons, Visual Basic includes two special operators: Is and Like.

The Is operator compares two object variables, and returns a True or False result. (For more information on this operator, see Chapter 20, "Using Object Variables.")

The Like operator compares a string value with a pattern, and returns a True or False result. The pattern can contain wild-card characters. You can, for example, compare a string, such as "MYFILE.BAS," to the pattern "*.BAS" to determine whether the string value is any file name with a .BAS extension. (For more information on Like, see Chapter 17, "Working with Strings.")

Operator Precedence

The sample expressions thus far discussed have had two operands, and one operator. What happens when an expression contains more than one operator? How does Visual Basic resolve the value of such expressions?

Consider this instruction:

```
Print 4 + 3 * 2
```

What is the result—14 or 10? Do you see the problem? The answer is 14 if you add 4 and 3 before multiplying by 2 (4 plus 3 is 7, then 7 times 2 is 14). The answer is 10, however, if you add 4 to the product of 3 times 2 (3 times 2 is 6, then 4 plus 6 is 10). So what answer does Visual Basic produce? Visual Basic returns 10. Why?

When multiple operators occur in an expression, certain operations are carried out before others. Some operators have *precedence* over others. Table 14.12 shows the hierarchy of operations. Each line in the table represents one level of precedence, from highest precedence at the top of the table, to lowest at the bottom.

When expressions contain two or more operators, higher precedence operations occur sooner. The expression 4 + 3 * 2 resolves to 10, because multiplication has higher precedence than addition (in Table 14.12, multiplication is at level 3, whereas addition is at level 6). In this expression, the multiplication is performed before the addition—3 is first multiplied by 2 to yield 6, then 4 is added to 6 to finally produce 10.

When multiple operators occur at the same level of precedence, Visual Basic resolves the expression by proceeding from left to right. The expression 9 - 4 - 2 yields 3, because 4 is first subtracted from 9 to get 5, then 2 is subtracted to produce the final answer of 3. (Notice that the result is 7, if the second subtraction is done first.)

Level	Operator(s)	Name
	Table 14.12. Operator precedence.	
1	^	Exponentiation
2	-	Negation
3	*, /	Multiplication and division
4	\	Integer division
5	Mod	Modulo arithmetic
6	+, -	Addition and subtraction
7	=, >, <, < >, >=, <=	Relational operators
8	Not	Logical negation
9	And	Conjunction
10	Or	Inclusive or
11	Xor	Exclusive or
12	Eqv	Equivalence
13	Imp	Implication

Using Parentheses in Expressions

You can use parentheses in expressions to override the standard operator precedence. When an expression contains parentheses, Visual Basic first evaluates terms inside of them. Then, terms outside of the parentheses are evaluated. In the example of the previous `Print` instruction, this is how you instruct Visual Basic to perform the addition first:

```
Print (4 + 3) * 2
```

Now, the result is

```
14
```

The parentheses force Visual Basic to evaluate 4 + 3 before multiplying this result by 2.

For more complicated expressions, you can *nest* parentheses inside each other. Deeper-nested parentheses evaluate first. For example:

```
Print (24 - (3 * 5)) / 2
```

The result is

```
4.5
```

In this example, Visual Basic first evaluates the expression in the deepest-nested parentheses. The first calculation, therefore, is 3 times 5, which is 15. Then, this value of 15 is subtracted from 24 to get 9. Finally, 9 is divided by 2 to yield the answer, 4.5.

Parentheses are not restricted to mathematical expressions. They can be used also in relational, string, and logical expressions:

```
If (Cost! > 99.95) Or ((Form% = 39) And (Status$ = "VIP")) ...
```

Even when operator precedence is not an issue, you should use parentheses liberally to clarify your expressions.

Program Comments

In general, Visual Basic programs are quite readable. Most keywords, such as If, Print, Visible, and Form, are English words with natural meanings, or easy-to-decipher abbreviations. Unlike other languages, such as C or assembler, Visual Basic seldom requires obscure syntax.

Beginning programmers often overlook the substantial benefits of program comments. Experienced programmers recognize that many subtleties occur in the final code. The cumulative effect of several instructions cannot be easily grasped by someone scanning your program for the first time—that is, unless you place comments in your programs.

In Visual Basic, a *comment* is a remark added to a program. Such remarks usually supply factual data (the date when the program was written, for example), clarify fine points, or just explain what's happening inside the program code.

The sole purpose of a comment is to provide information for you or another person who might need to see or modify your program. When running a program, Visual Basic ignores all comments.

You can place comments in your programs in two ways: the Rem statement, or the single quotation mark or apostrophe (').

Using the *Rem* Statement

The keyword Rem identifies the remainder of the line as a comment. (Rem is short for Remark.)

```
Rem remark
```

in which

> remark is any sequence of characters.

In a loan amortization program, for example, you might document what happens when the user clicks a command button marked "Do loan":

```
Sub Command1_Click ()
Rem Get the principal and interest rate, calculate the payment.
.
.
.
```

You can place a Rem instruction on a line with other instructions. Everything following the Rem, however, is part of the comment. Be careful to avoid this trap:

```
Client$ = "ABC Plumbing": Rem Get discount: Rate! = 23.14
```

This line *does* assign the string value "ABC Plumbing" to Client$. The Rem instruction, however, makes the remainder of the line a remark. Visual Basic does not even read the rest of the line, so it never sees the colon. It, therefore, does not change the value of Rate!.

Using the Apostrophe

The single quotation mark (or apostrophe) is a substitute for the Rem keyword. An apostrophe signals that the remainder of the line is a comment. You can place an apostrophe at the beginning of a line (the whole line becomes a comment), or at some other point in it.

The apostrophe often is used to place a comment on the same line with other instructions. Unlike Rem, you do not need a colon to separate the apostrophe from the other instructions on the same line. For example:

```
Deg.C! = ((Deg.F! - 32) * 5) / 9     'Fahrenheit to Centigrade
```

The one exception to the apostrophe initiating a comment is when it appears inside a string literal, simply as part of the literal. For example:

```
MsgBox "Randy's Donut Shop"
```

This instruction displays Randy's Donut Shop. The apostrophe does not indicate a comment, but rather is part of the string literal.

Tips on Using Comments

The following are some tips for using comments:

Use meaningful comments liberally. These comments obviously go a long way toward making any program more readable. You enhance the self-documentation of your programs by adding comments to your code. This practice facilitates the chores of troubleshooting, or modifying the programs, which you or someone else might have to do later. Experienced programmers know that well-placed comments help in understanding and working with a program.

In a work environment, you might experience pressures, such as meeting deadlines. You sometimes are tempted to forgo comments in the name of expediency. Invariably, though, you need that code (or part of it), later. You might find yourself spending a few puzzling moments glaring at the enigmatic program that was so clear several months ago. You learn one of programming's most sobering lessons the first time you have to rewrite an application because you cannot decipher your previous work.

In fact, the following maxim is worth highlighting:

Every minute spent writing comments will save at least ten minutes later on.

Consider the time you spend writing comments an investment. Your dividends come later, in the forms of saved time, and avoided frustration.

In your zeal to provide comments, however, you can go overboard. Don't fall into the trap of commenting every line. Simple instructions with informative variable names require no comments:

```
NumChecks% = NumChecks% + 1    'increment NumChecks% by 1
Print NumChecks%               'display the number of checks
```

The comments on the preceding two lines do nothing more than restate what is obvious from the instructions themselves. Such comments are frivolous, and actually detract from the program's readability. Comments should add to the reader's understanding. When each line is understood easily, you might want to insert a comment every 10 or so lines to explain what is being accomplished in that section of the code.

Summary

This chapter examined the structure of—and the building blocks (or components) that fit together to form—Visual Basic programs. Each Visual Basic procedure consists of a series of lines, with each line serving as a single instruction, a group of instructions, or a label.

Visual Basic manipulates data of two fundamental types—numbers and text (strings). Numbers are further divided into the Integer, Long integer, Single-precision, Double-precision, and Currency data types. Strings can be Variable-length or Fixed-length. Variant variables can store data of any type, and convert automatically values among the various data types.

Variables, which can have any data type, store a single data value. You can modify the value of a variable with an assignment instruction. Arrays are similar to composite variables, storing multiple data items.

Visual Basic has several operators, including arithmetic, string, relational, and logical. Using the operators, you can form expressions to represent almost any quantity. When they appear in an expression, operands can consist of literals, variables, and parenthetical subexpressions. All expressions, however, resolve to a single value.

Comments enhance any program's readability. Appropriate comments make a program easier to understand, and help in tracking errors.

Program Flow and Decision Making

*P*rogram flow (or *logic flow*) refers to the order in which the instructions of a Sub or Function execute. Generally, program flow proceeds line-by-line, from the top of the procedure to the bottom.

This sequential "top-down" program flow is straightforward and easy to understand. Many practical procedures execute in this systematic sequence.

A limit exists, however, to what you can accomplish with such simple, linear sequencing. Frequently, the need arises to redirect program flow. From one point in a particular procedure, you might want to transfer execution to a location a few lines away, or perhaps a hundred lines later. This redirection usually involves some sort of decision making, or testing.

This chapter examines the following ways in which you can alter program flow from the normal sequential execution order:

- Unconditional branching (GoTo)
- Conditional branching (On-GoTo)
- Ending execution (End)
- Conditional testing (If-Then, Select Case)
- Looping (For-Next, While-Wend, Do-Loop)

NOTE ## What Happens When a Procedure Terminates?

What happens to program flow when a procedure terminates? That depends on the type of procedure, and how it gained control in the first place.

When an event procedure terminates, program flow suspends until a subsequent event invokes another procedure. (The new event, however, might reinvoke the just-terminated procedure.)

Non-event procedures are Sub or Function ones explicitly called from another procedure. When a non-event procedure terminates, control returns to the one which invoked the Sub or Function. Program flow continues at (or just after) the invoking instruction.

Branching

Branching is the direct transfer from one line in your procedure to another line. Suppose one line contains an instruction that causes Visual Basic to jump immediately to another line within the same procedure. In Visual Basic terminology, the former line *branches* to the latter one.

Branching comes in the following two forms:

Unconditional branching   Program control transfers to a specific line in all cases.

Conditional branching   Program control transfers to one of several lines, depending on the value of a testing expression.

Labels and Line Numbers

If you want a program instruction to branch to another line, you need a way to indicate the new location! In order to divert execution to a particular program line, you must name (specify) the target line. Visual Basic provides two such ways—*line labels* and *line numbers*. By placing a line label or number at the beginning of a line, you give it a named identity which can be referenced by a branching instruction.

NOTE **Line Labels and Label Controls**

Don't confuse a line label with the label control. A *line label* is a name that designates a line location within the code of a program. The *label control* is one of the visual controls available from the Visual Basic toolbox. In this chapter, the term "label" refers only to "line label," not the label control.

Labels

As mentioned in the previous chapter, a *line label* begins with a letter, and ends with a colon. The following are some valid labels:

```
CalculateSum:
```

```
Call123:
```

```
Fred:
```

Each label you use in a form or module must be unique. For example, at the form level, you cannot use the same label name twice—even if it is used in two different event procedures. This restriction applies to the event procedures associated both directly with the form, as well as with the controls placed on it. You cannot duplicate also a label name within a given procedure.

A label can contain as many as 40 characters. Upper and lowercase letters are not distinguished in labels; thus, `MyLabel:`, `mylabel:`, and `MYLABEL:` are equivalent.

A label can appear at the beginning of a line containing one or more instructions. In this case, when execution is diverted to the label, the program executes immediately the instructions on that line.

Alternatively, a label can stand alone on a line. When you divert execution to such a label, the program immediately executes the first subsequent line which contains instructions.

Line Numbers

A *line number* is a special form of a line label. A line number consists exclusively of digits that form an integer number from 0 up to the number formed by forty 9's. Unlike a line label, you do not need a colon after the number. The following are two examples of numbered lines:

```
100 MsgBox "This line has a line number"
```

```
4001 A& = 10: B& = 6: C& = 29
```

In contrast to BASICA, GW-BASIC, and older BASIC interpreters, line numbers in Visual Basic do not specify the execution order of program lines. Instead, a line number simply gives an identity to its line—a way to refer to it explicitly. You can, for example, place line number 500 between line numbers 1000 and 2000.

As with line labels, you can use a particular line number only once within a given form or module. Line numbers are entirely optional; you can include them as you see fit. If you do use line numbers, you can number every line, or only certain ones. If you are a former BASICA or GW-BASIC programmer converting to Visual Basic, you quickly get used to programming without line numbers.

Modern programming practice favors labels over line numbers, because an alphanumeric name conveys more information than a colorless line number. Create meaningful label names, such as GraphRoutine or GetUserInput, so that your programs are easier to read and understand.

Although line numbers are discouraged in general, Visual Basic actually *requires* them when you use certain error-tracking program features. The Erl function, for example, indicates line numbers at which program errors occur. Erl does not, however, report line numbers larger than 65,529. For more information on Erl, and error-handling routines, see Chapter 21, "Debugging and Testing."

Although line numbers can be as many as forty digits long, you should avoid making them larger than 65,529. That way, if you ever use Erl in an error-handling routine, all the line numbers are within the range that Erl can report. Limiting line numbers to 65,529 is not much of a programming hardship. You do not, in practice, use line numbers often.

NOTE | **An Historical Note**

BASICA, GW-BASIC, and other BASIC interpreters require that each program line begin with a line number. The numeric value of each line number with these interpreters indicates the proper sequence of the program lines. BASICA and GW-BASIC realign program lines, if necessary, in ascending order from the smallest to the largest line number.

Visual Basic does not reorder this way. Line numbers can appear in any numeric order. (Visual Basic supports line numbers for compatibility with BASICA, and other versions of BASIC.) QBasic and QuickBASIC users are already accustomed to writing programs without line numbers. Most programs written in the Visual Basic environment do not use line numbers.

Unconditional Branching with *GoTo*

Use GoTo for unconditional branches. You can specify the destination with a label, or a line number.

```
GoTo label

or

GoTo linenum
```

in which

    label is a label defined in the same procedure,

and

    linenum is any line number in it.

The destination must exist, or the Label not defined fatal error occurs. To get a feel for GoTo, try the following example:

```
Sub Form_Click ()
    Print "I am"
    GoTo Message
    Print "not"
Message:
    Print "happy"
End Sub
```

Running Program Examples in This Chapter

Most program examples in this chapter consist of short Form_Click procedures. For simplicity, many examples use the Print method to display results directly on the default form.

To try one of the examples, type the Form_Click procedure as shown. Then, run the program. A blank form appears on-screen. Simply click the mouse while the pointer is on the blank form. The click activates the code contained in the Form_Click procedure.

To terminate the program, select **End** from the **Run** menu, or click the Stop icon on the toolbar. Visual Basic returns to the design (programming) mode with the Form_Click procedure visible. You now can modify the instructions in the Form_Click procedure to try another example.

The following is the result that appears on the form:

```
I am
happy
```

The `Print "not"` line never got a chance to execute. The `GoTo` instruction transferred control directly to the `Message` label. The program, therefore, continues with the final `Print` instruction immediately following the `Message` label.

Notice that, in a `GoTo` instruction, the label name does not include a trailing colon. In the present example, the instruction `GoTo Message` does not include a colon after the label `Message`. The actual label, however, must be followed by a colon.

When using line numbers rather than labels, you cannot use a variable for the `linenum` parameter. That is, if `Target` is an integer variable, the following instruction is *not* legal (even if the value of `Target` corresponds to a valid line number):

```
GoTo Target
```

This line results in a syntax error. This situation causes an error because Visual Basic must resolve all `GoTo` references before any program runs. The value of the variable can't be determined until the instruction executes. Thus, if a variable is permitted as the `linenum` parameter, Visual Basic cannot resolve the reference until the program runs.

Using `GoTo`, you can branch to any location in the current procedure: to a previous or subsequent line, or even to the same line. You cannot, however, branch to a line within another `Sub` or `Function` procedure.

Within a procedure, you should only branch to another line at the same level. Avoid branching to or from a multiline `If` construct, `For` loop, or similar structure. Use `GoTo` to control logic flow only within such structures. (These structures are explained later in this chapter.)

Haphazard `GoTo` instructions create programs with logic flow branching in all directions. Experienced programmers, therefore, usually avoid using `GoTo`. Such "spaghetti logic" is difficult to read, and hard to debug.

Conditional Branching with *On-GoTo*

The `On-GoTo` instruction extends the `GoTo` concept. With `On-GoTo`, you branch to one of a specified set of lines, according to the value of a numeric expression.

```
On numexpr GoTo labellist
```

or

```
On numexpr GoTo linenumlist
```

in which

    numexpr is a general numeric expression which evaluates to a value between 0 and 255;

    labellist is a list of one or more labels separated by commas,

and

    linenumlist is a list of one or more line numbers separated by commas.

The value of the numeric expression determines which line in the label list (or line number list) executes next. Branching occurs to the corresponding line in the list—to the first listed line if *numexpr* is one, the second listed line if *numexpr* is two, and so on.

If *numexpr* is 0, or greater than the number of lines in the list, execution simply continues with the instruction immediately after the On-GoTo. If *numexpr* is negative, or greater than 255, your program terminates with the Illegal function call error.

The following is an example of On-GoTo:

```
On NumSingers% GoTo Solo, Duet, Trio, Quartet
```

The value of NumSingers% determines the line that executes next. If NumSingers% equals 1, the program branches to the label Solo:, and continues from there. If NumSingers% equals 2, the program goes to the label Duet:. If NumSingers% equals 3, the program branches to the label Trio:. If NumSingers% equals 4, the branch is to Quartet:.

If NumSingers% is 0, or greater than 4 (but not greater than 255), the program continues with the line that immediately follows the On-GoTo instruction. If NumSingers% is negative or greater than 255, the Illegal function call error occurs.

The same destination can appear in your line number list or label list more than once. For example, the following instruction branches to the label Home, if MyValue% is 1, 3, or 5:

```
On MyValue% GoTo Home, Office, Home, School, Home, Store
```

As the preceding examples show, the numeric expression simply is a variable. You can, however, use any general expression. The following is an example of a more complicated expression:

```
On ((MyScore% - 23) / Average%) GoTo First, Second, Third
```

The numeric expression should resolve to an integer number. To determine the line branched to, a fractional value is rounded to the nearest whole integer.

T I P You can mix labels and line numbers in the same list.

On-GoTo has limited use, because the programming situation must be just right for this instruction to be practical. It's not often that your program has a point from which you want to branch different line numbers, depending on a numeric expression with possible values of 1, 2, 3, and so on.

Similar to GoTo, the On-GoTo statement is outmoded. Visual Basic's Select statement, and multiline If statements (discussed later in this chapter), provide more flexible, modern tools for conditional branching.

Ending Program Execution

The most abrupt way to alter program flow is to terminate your program. To do so, use the End instruction:

```
End
```

The End instruction is equivalent to clicking the Stop icon on the toolbar, or selecting the End option from the **R**un menu. The program stops execution. Any open files are closed, and the values of all variables are cleared. If you are running the program from Visual Basic (as opposed to running an .EXE version of the program from Windows), you return to the design environment.

 NOTE No restriction exists on the number of End instructions you can have in a single procedure, or throughout your program.

You commonly use End in an event procedure that must respond to the user's request to terminate the program. To terminate an application when the user clicks a command button labeled Quit, for example, place an End instruction in the Click procedure associated with that button.

Unlike End, which terminates program execution completely, the Stop instruction suspends execution temporarily. Once suspended, you can use the Debug window, and later resume execution. For more information on Stop, see Chapter 21, "Debugging and Testing."

Conditional Testing

Decision making is a perpetual programming theme. A *logic juncture* is a place in your program in which the subsequent execution path can go different ways. The program chooses the path based on the evaluation of a *test condition.*

Depending on the type of test condition, Visual Basic offers two flexible program structures. The If structure tests for True and False conditions, and the Select Case structure tests for values within specified ranges.

Testing with the *If* Instruction

If tests whether an expression is True or False, and directs logic flow accordingly. With a block If instruction, you can perform successive True and False tests.

The If instruction has many forms, but they all can be classified into two categories: single-line If and multiline If.

Single-Line *If*

The following are the two classic If-Then-Else single-line forms:

```
If condition Then thenclause
```
or
```
If condition Then thenclause Else elseclause
```
in which

   condition is any expression that evaluates to True or False,

   thenclause is the action to perform if condition is True,

and

   elseclause is the action to perform if condition is False.

The Else elseclause phrase is optional.

The following is an example of a procedure containing the simplest form of the If-Then instruction:

```
Sub Form_Click ()
    Dim Temp As Single
    Temp = Val(InputBox$("What is the temperature?"))
    If Temp > 100 Then MsgBox "It is hot"
    Print "So long for now"
End Sub
```

For now, don't worry if you aren't familiar with the Val function. (Val converts the string returned by the InputBox$ function into a numeric value. For more information on Val, see Chapter 17, "Working with Strings.")

Try the program. If you reply with a number larger than 100 when prompted for the temperature, the program responds by opening a box that displays the following message:

```
It is hot
```

When you click the OK button to close the message box, the program responds by displaying the following message on the form:

```
So long for now
```

If you reply with a number of 100 or lower, the program displays So long for now immediately, without ever opening the It is hot message box.

The program opens a box which displays the message It is hot only if the value of the variable Temp is greater than 100. (Remember that the > character is a relational operator meaning "greater than." Relational operators are introduced in Chapter 14, "Language Building Blocks," and are discussed again later in this chapter.)

When the test condition of an If-Then instruction is False, Visual Basic disregards the part of the instruction after Then. The program moves to the next program line immediately.

Adding an *Else* Clause to *If-Then*

Suppose that you want to execute two different instructions: one if the test condition is True, and another if it is False. A second form of the If-Then statement adds an Else clause solely for this purpose.

To demonstrate the form containing an Else clause, change the If-Then instruction so that the new procedure resembles this.

```
Sub Form_Click ()
    Dim Temp As Integer
    Temp = Val(InputBox$("What is the temperature?"))
```

```
    If Temp > 100 Then MsgBox "It is hot" Else MsgBox "Not too bad"
    Print "So long for now"
End Sub
```

If you input a temperature value greater than 100, the result is the same as before. If you input a value of 100 or less, however, the program opens a box in which the Not too bad message appears.

By adding an Else clause to an If-Then instruction, you specify what to do when the testing condition is False (the Else part), as well as when it is True (the Then part). Figure 15.1 illustrates this concept.

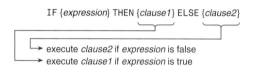

Figure 15.1.

The If-Then-Else Instruction.

Then and *Else* Clauses

The Then and Else clauses can take many different forms. For starters, each clause can be any single Visual Basic instruction. To give you an idea, the following are a few sample instructions:

```
If A = B Then MsgBox "Same" Else MsgBox "Different"

If A = B Then GoTo Identical Else GoTo Unequal

If A = B Then Beep

If A = B Then Profit = 20 Else Profit = Cost * Discount
```

The Then or Else clause can also contain multiple instructions. Simply separate each instruction with a colon. For example:

```
If Score > 500 Then Rate = 3.5: Num = 29: Winner$ = "Debby"
```

This instruction tests whether the value of the variable Score is greater than 500. If so, then the values of Rate, Num, and Winner$ are assigned the values 3.5, 29, and "Debby", respectively. If the value of Score is less than or equal to 500, control passes directly to the next line without assigning values to any of the three variables.

GoTo is one of the most common statements to place in a Then or Else clause. This way, you can branch to different lines, depending on the result of a testing expression. For example:

```
If Age% > 20 Then GoTo Adult
```

If the value of Age% is greater than 20, the program directly proceeds to the label Adult:. Several instructions can be written between If, and the Adult: label. Those instructions execute if the value of Age% is 20 or less.

Visual Basic provides a shortened form of the If instruction when GoTo is used with a line number in a Then or Else clause. In such cases, you can omit the Then or GoTo keywords. The following three instructions, for example, are equivalent:

```
If Age% > 20 Then GoTo 500

If Age% > 20 GoTo 500

If Age% > 20 Then 500
```

When the destination is a line label rather than a line number, however, you cannot use this shortened form. In such cases, the GoTo keyword must appear along with the Then or Else.

Table 15.1 summarizes the various forms of Then and Else clauses that you can use in an If instruction.

Table 15.1. Syntax forms for *Then* and *Else* clauses.

Syntax	Action taken
instructions	instructions are one or more Visual Basic directives separated with colons. After the instructions execute, control passes to the line following the If instruction.
GoTo label	label is a valid line label. Control passes to the line designated by the label. In such a clause, the Then or Else keyword is optional.
GoTo linenum	linenum is a valid line number. Control passes to the line designated by the line number. In such a clause, the Then or Else keyword is optional.
linenum	linenum is a valid line number. Control passes to the line designated by the line number. In such a case (when the GoTo keyword is omitted), the Then or Else keyword must appear.

Types of Testing Expressions

In an If instruction, the testing condition must be a *Boolean expression*, which simply means an expression that evaluates to True or False.

Boolean Expressions Are Really Just Numbers   T I P

Internally, Visual Basic needs a way to represent Boolean values; that is, a way to represent True and False. Visual Basic uses simple integer numbers: 0 for False, and -1 for True. Boolean expressions, therefore, are really just special cases of numeric expressions.

When Visual Basic evaluates a Boolean expression, False becomes 0, and True becomes -1. (When converting a number to a Boolean value, 0 becomes False, and any nonzero number becomes True.) You can demonstrate this conversion with the following short test:

```
NumItems% = 0
If NumItems% Then MsgBox "Nonzero" Else MsgBox "Zero"
```

In the If instruction, the variable NumItems% is itself a Boolean expression. This example opens a dialog box displaying the message Zero, which demonstrates that 0 is treated as False. Now, change the assignment instruction so that the value of NumItems% has any nonzero value. For example:

```
NumItems% = 22
```

The example now displays Nonzero, because the Boolean expression has become True.

Another way to see the arithmetic conversion is to try the following instruction:

```
Print 129 > 45
```

Does that instruction appear odd? What do you think the output is? Try it. Then, try `Print 45 > 129`.

Most often, the expression is a relational one. Such expressions use the equality and inequality operators to form natural conditional tests. A few examples are as follows:

```
If Num% < 0 Then MsgBox "Number is negative"

If Num% <= 0 Then MsgBox "Number is not positive"

If Animal$ = "Dog" Then MsgBox "It's a pooch"

If (MyScore + HerScore) > YourScore Then MsgBox "You lose"
```

The first example uses the "less than" operator (<) to test the value of the variable Num%. The second example is different from the first one in a subtle way, namely the "less than or equal to" operator (<=). Notice that the first and second lines both display their messages when Num% is negative. Neither line displays a message when Num% is positive. The difference arises when Num% is exactly zero. The second line displays its message, but the first does not.

The third example demonstrates that testing expressions can be string as well as numeric. In this example, the "equals" operator (=) tests whether the string stored in Animal$ is Dog. If so, the line displays the message: It's a pooch. In relational expressions, the equal sign really means "equals" (as opposed to the equal sign in assignment instructions which means "is assigned the value"). Also, notice that the expression is True only when there is an exact match. If Animal$ has the value DOG (all caps), the result is False. Dog and DOG are *not* identical strings.

The final example shows an expression involving parentheses. In this example, the values of MyScore and HerScore are added together. Then, this sum is compared with the value in YourScore to decide whether the expression is True or False.

NOTE

If Testing with Control Variables

Visual Basic supports a special form of If instruction that can test whether a graphics control in your application is a particular control type. This form of If uses the TypeOf keyword, the Is keyword, and control variables. The following instruction, for example, tests whether the control variable MyControl is a text box:

```
If TypeOf MyControl Is TextBox Then Result$ = "Done"
```

Chapter 20, "Using Object Variables," discusses control variables and the TypeOf keyword.

The Relational Operators

Visual Basic provides six relational operators for use in testing expressions. The operators are mentioned briefly in the previous chapter, and appear again in Table 15.2.

Table 15.2. Relational Operators.		
Symbol	**Name**	**Example**
=	Equals	4 = (3 + 1)
<>	Not equal	"Dog" <> "Cat"

Symbol	Name	Example
>	Greater than	`8 > 5`
<	Less than	`3 < 6`
>=	Greater than or equals	`9 >= 9`
<=	Less than or equals	`"Hi" <= "Ho"`

Each example in the third column of the table is True.

NOTE

Relational Operators Work on Strings

Relational operators work on strings as well as numbers. One string "equals" another only if both strings are the same length and they contain the exact same sequence of characters. But how can one string be "greater than" or "less than" another? How does the last example in Table 15.2 work?

Every string character has an associated numeric value from 0 to 255. These values conform to an established code known as ANSI (American National Standards Institute). In ANSI, for example, an *A* is 65 and an *** (asterisk) is 42. (Chapter 17, "Working with Strings," discusses ANSI, and Appendix B lists all the ANSI values.)

Using ANSI, you can compare two strings character by character. The details are explained in Chapter 17; however, the essence of the method is: characters at the same position in each string are compared (first character with first character, second with second, and so on). As soon as one pair of characters is different, the comparison stops. The ANSI values of the two characters (in the pair) are compared. One character must have a larger ANSI value than the other. The string containing the "larger" character is considered to be the "larger" of the two.

Consider the last example in Table 15.2 which compares `"Hi"` with `"Ho"`. Both strings have H as their first character. The second character in each string, however, is different. The ANSI value of i is 105, and o has a value of 111. o, therefore, is larger than i, and `"Ho"` is larger than `"Hi"`.

If one string is longer than the other, the same rules apply on a character-by-character basis. For example, `"Don"` is larger than `"Dance"` because o has a larger ANSI value than a (even though `"Dance"` has more characters than `"Don"`). However, if the shorter string appears intact at the beginning of the longer string, the longer string is considered to be larger. For example, `"Dock"` is larger than `"Do"`.

Compound Testing Expressions

Sometimes you need to test two or more conditions. Suppose that you want to assign the value Perfect to Result$ only if *both* of the following conditions are True:

■ The value of Score% is 300

■ The value of Game$ is "Bowling"

You can use the following instruction:

```
If (Score% = 300) And (Game$ = "Bowling") Then Result$ = "Perfect"
```

This instruction uses a compound expression for the test. Note that the two conditions are combined with the logical operator And. Both conditions must be True in order for Visual Basic to assign the value Perfect to the variable Result$. If only one condition is True (or if neither condition is True), the test fails, and program flow proceeds directly to the next line.

The parentheses in this sample If instruction are not required, but they make the line easy to read and understand. In similar instructions, most programmers recommend that you use parentheses for clarity.

The Logical Operators

The sample If instruction uses And to combine the two conditions. And is one of Visual Basic's six logical operators. The logical operators combine Boolean expressions to create one large Boolean expression. (Remember that a Boolean expression is one that can be evaluated to True or False.)

The most common logical operators are And, Or, and Not. They work as follows:

And	Combines two expressions; each expression must be True for the entire expression to be True.
Or	Combines two expressions; either expression (or both expressions) must be True for the entire expression to be True.
Not	Negates a single expression.

The following is an example of Not:

```
If Not (Score% = 300) Then Result$ = "Could do better"
```

Visual Basic has three other logical operators: Xor, Eqv, and Imp. They work as follows:

Xor	Combines two expressions; one (but not both) must be True for the entire expression to be True.
Eqv	Combines two expression; both must be either True or False for the entire expression to be True. (Eqv is the "opposite" of Xor.)

Imp   Combines two expressions; the entire expression is True, except when the first expression is True, and the second, False.

Figure 15.2 shows the results returned by all logical operators. In the figure, A and B represent Boolean operands which have a value of T (True) or F (False). The figure has four lines, because four possible "truth configurations" for the two combined expressions exist.

OPERAND VALUE		VALUE OF LOGICAL OPERATION					
A	B	Not A	A And B	A Or B	A Xor B	A Eqv B	A Imp B
T	T	F	T	T	F	T	T
T	F	F	F	T	T	F	F
F	T	T	F	T	T	F	T
F	F	T	F	F	F	T	T

Figure 15.2.

Results of logical operators.

Nested *If* Instructions

You can nest If instructions to two or more levels. The following is the basic form:

```
If condition1 Then If condition2 Then clause
```

With Else clauses, the form resembles the following:

```
If cond1 Then If cond2 Then clause1 Else clause2 Else clause3
```

Nested If's provide another way to write compound tests. Once again, this is a sample If instruction that appeared earlier in this chapter. The instruction contains a compound testing expression.

```
If (Score% = 300) And (Game$ = "Bowling") Then Result$ = "Perfect"
```

With nested If's, the following instruction is equivalent:

```
If Score% = 300 Then If Game$ = "Bowling" Then Result$ = "Perfect"
```

T I P   Avoid nesting If instructions in a single program line. Such instructions become confusing quickly; furthermore, things get even more muddled when nested If instructions contain Else clauses.

Multiline *If*

You can extend If instructions from a single line to a multiple-line block. A block structure creates more understandable program instructions when one of the following situations occurs:

- The *thenclause* or *elseclause* contains two or more instructions

- If instructions are nested

- An If instruction extends past one line

You should only use a single-line If instruction when the *thenclause* and *elseclause* each contain only one instruction, and the entire If instruction easily fits into one line. In these cases, the If instruction is easily understandable. In other cases, break the single-line If instruction into a multiline block.

The single-line If form is never mandatory. You always can write any If-Then-Else instruction using the multiline form.

The following is the syntax of the multiline If:

```
If condition Then
    {instructions}
ElseIf condition Then
    {instructions}
ElseIf condition Then
    {instructions} …
Else
    {instructions}
End If
```

in which

   condition is a Boolean expression (any expression that evaluates to True or False),

and

   instructions is a block of one or more instructions placed on separate program lines.

ElseIf blocks are optional. You can use as many as you need. Furthermore, the Else block is optional, also.

The following is a simple example of a multiline If:

```
If Amount > 100.0 Then
   NumLargeChecks% = NumLargeChecks% + 1
   MsgBox "Another large check"
Else
   NumSmallChecks% = NumSmallChecks% + 1
   MsgBox "Just a small check"
End If
```

The first line on the multiline If always begins with an If clause, and terminates with the Then keyword. Nothing can follow Then on this first line; that's how Visual Basic differentiates a multiline If structure from the single-line If.

The last line is always End If. Notice that a space separates the two keywords End and If.

You can use any number of ElseIf clauses. Notice that ElseIf is one keyword; there is no internal space. Only one Else clause can appear.

Clauses evaluate sequentially. Visual Basic first checks the initial If clause. If True (nonzero), the first set of instructions executes (that is, the group of instructions following the Then), and program flow continues with the line after End If. If False (zero), each ElseIf clause is tested, one at a time.

As soon as one ElseIf clause is True, the associated set of instructions executes, and program flow continues with the line after End If.

If every ElseIf clause is False, or if there are no ElseIf clauses, the instructions associated with the Else clause execute. If no Else clause appears, program flow resumes at the line after End If.

The Else and ElseIf clauses are optional.

Each set of *instructions* can be one or more Visual Basic instructions. When you use multiple instructions, place each instruction on a separate line to create an instruction block. Any such instruction can be another multiline If structure; you can nest If structures to any level you want.

The following is an example of a block If structure that demonstrates the use of ElseIf clauses. This program fragment evaluates the value of MyNumber%, and displays an appropriate message.

```
If MyNumber% = 0 Then
    MsgBox "Zero"
ElseIf MyNumber% = 1 Then
    Total% = Total% + 1
    MsgBox "One"
ElseIf MyNumber% >= 2 Then
    Total% = Total% + 2
```

```
    MsgBox "Greater than one"
Else
    MsgBox "Negative"
End If
```

When writing multiline structures such as nested If blocks, take advantage of indentation to clarify the block structure. In the sample program fragments presented here, notice how indentation makes the components of the block structure apparent.

Testing with *Select Case*

The Select Case structure tests whether the value of an expression falls within predetermined ranges, whereas the If structure tests for True and False conditions. Use Select Case to execute instructions conditionally, depending on the value of a test expression.

```
Select Case expression
    Case testlist
        {instructions}
    Case testlist
        {instructions} …
    Case Else
        {instructions}
End Select Case
```

in which

expression is any general numeric or string expression;

testlist is one or more test ranges, separated by commas,

and

instructions is a block of one or more instructions placed on separate program lines.

Case blocks are optional. You can have as many as you need. Furthermore, the Case Else block also is optional.

The following is an example of Select Case:

```
Select Case Age%
    Case 1 To 12
        MsgBox "Child"
        NumChildren% = NumChildren% + 1
    Case 13 To 19
```

```
        MsgBox "Teenager"
        NumTeens% = NumTeens% + 1
    Case Is > 19
        MsgBox "Adult"
        NumAdults% = NumAdults% + 1
    Case Else
        MsgBox "Impossible"
End Select
```

The testing expression can be numeric or string. The value of *expression* is tested against the ranges in the various test lists. The *expression* and the test expressions in each *testlist* must agree in type—either all numeric or all string.

Each *testlist* specifies a range of values against which the value of expression is compared. *testlist* has the following three general forms:

testexpr1 To *testexpr2*	The test is True if the value of *expression* lies within the range from *testexpr1* to *testexpr2*.
Is *rel*-optestexp	*rrel-op* is one of the six relational operators: =, >, <, <>, >=, <=. The test is True if the value of *expression* satisfies the relational expression.
testexpr	The test is True if the value of *expression* equals that of *testexpr*.

The expressions *testexpr*, *testexpr1*, and *testexpr2* are any expressions that agree in type (string or numeric) with the *expression* on the Select Case line. Table 15.3 shows some sample test ranges.

Table 15.3. Sample test ranges.

Type	Example
Relational	Case Is >= 39
Equality	Case Is = 21.6
Equality (implied "=")	Case 21.6
Explicit range	Case -7 To 7
Multiple	Case Is <> 14, Is < 101

Notice that *testlist* consists of two or more test ranges separated by commas. A multiple test evaluates to True if any of the individual tests are True.

Select Case evaluates each Case clause sequentially, looking for a match. The first time *expression* is within one of the ranges specified by a *testlist*, the associated *instructions* block executes. Then, control passes to the line following the End Select.

If every Case test is False, the instruction block following the Case Else executes. If no Case Else clause is present, program flow passes to the line following End Select.

Any meaningful Select Case structure contains at least one Case test. If you write a Select Case structure containing no Case test, however, no error occurs. In such a situation, program flow passes to the line following End Select.

Select Case enables you to replace multiple If constructions with more elegant, understandable instructions. Use Select Case liberally. When you're contemplating convoluted If tests, you should use Select Case instead to make your programs more understandable.

The following program fragment displays information about the first character of a test string. The test string is stored in the variable MyString$. (The expression Left$(MyString$, 1) returns the first character of MyString$. For more information, see Chapter 17, "Working with Strings.")

```
Select Case Left$(MyString$, 1)
    Case ""
      MsgBox "Null String"
    Case "A", "E", "I", "O", "U", "a", "e", "i", "o", "u"
      MsgBox "Vowel"
    Case "A" To "Z", "a" To "z"
      MsgBox "Consonant"
    Case "0" To "9"
      MsgBox "Numeric Digit"
    Case Else
      MsgBox "Special Character"
End Select
```

Notice how this example works when MyString$ begins with a letter. If the letter is a vowel, the second Case clause is True. Even though the third Case clause includes all letters (and therefore the vowels), the vowels are intercepted earlier by the second Case clause.

Looping

A *loop* is any group of instructions that executes repeatedly. The following Form_Load event procedure, for example, contains a loop:

```
Sub Form_Load ()
   Show
   MsgBox "Click to begin beeping"
   Print "Now beeping incessantly"
DoBeeps:
   Beep
   GoTo DoBeeps
   Print "How can I get here?"
End Sub
```

To try this example, create a program consisting entirely of this Form_Load procedure. Start the application. The Form_Load procedure obtains control. The Show method first displays a blank form. The MsgBox instruction opens a dialog box that indicates that beeping begins when you click the box. When you click the box (or press Enter), the dialog box closes, and the message Now beeping incessantly appears on the form.

The loop begins with the label DoBeeps: in the fifth line. The end of the loop is the Goto instruction in the seventh line. This is an example of an *endless loop*, because there is no programmed way for the loop and the beeping to stop. The Print instruction in the final line (just above the End Sub) can never execute. To stop the program, press Ctrl+Break.

A useful loop must have a way to end. A loop with an ending mechanism is called a *controlled loop*. A controlled loop executes until a predetermined condition is satisfied. Some form of controlled loop occurs in most nontrivial programs.

Visual Basic provides three special structures for the programming of controlled loops:

- For-Next
- While-Wend
- Do-Loop

The characteristics of each structure are similar, yet different. When programming a controlled loop, you choose among For-Next, While-Wend, and Do-Loop. As Figure 15.3 shows, your choice generally depends on the answers to the following two questions:

- Do you know how many times you must go through the loop before it begins?
- Must the loop execute at least one time?

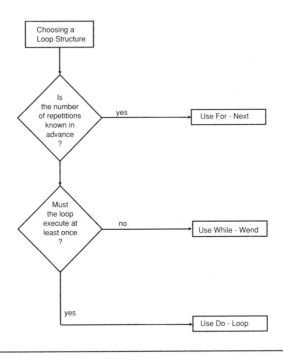

Figure 15.3.

Selecting the appropriate
loop structure.

Using *For-Next* Loops

A For-Next loop uses a numeric variable to control the number of repetitions.
This special variable is called a *counter variable* or *control variable*.

An Example of *For-Next*

The following procedure displays a table of the squares of the numbers from 0
to 6. (The square of a number is simply the number multiplied by itself.) This
kind of task is perfect for a For-Next loop:

```
Sub ShowSquares ()
    Rem - Display Squares of Numbers
    Print "Number", "Square"
    For Number% = 0 To 6
        Square% = Number% * Number%
        Print Number%, Square%
    Next Number%
    Print "End of table"
End Sub
```

Note on Running the Example Programs

To run this example, create a general procedure with the name of ShowSquares. To do so, select **View** from the main Visual Basic menu, then choose **N**ew Procedure from the View submenu. Type the name of the procedure (ShowSquares, in this example) in the dialog box. Close the box by pressing Enter, or clicking OK. Now, type the procedure.

To complete the application, call ShowSquares when a Click event occurs on the form. To do this, create a Form_Click procedure, which does nothing more than call ShowSquares, namely:

```
Sub Form_Click ()
    Call ShowSquares
End Sub
```

Now, when you run the application, simply click anywhere on the blank form. The Click event triggers the Form_Click procedure that, in this case, calls ShowSquares.

Treat other examples in the remainder of this chapter similarly. Just create the general procedures as indicated, and invoke them using a Form_Click event procedure.

The following is the output from ShowSquares:

```
Number       Square
0            0
1            1
2            4
3            9
4            16
5            25
6            36
End of table
```

In this For-Next loop, Number% is the counter variable. The value of Number% changes each time through the loop. The For instruction sets the first value of Number% to 0, and the final value to 6.

The line beginning with Next marks the end of the loop. In a For-Next loop, all the instructions between the For and Next are referred to as the body of the loop.

The body of a loop can have any number of instructions. Most loops are short, though loops with more than thirty instructions occur occassionally. In this example, the body of our modest loop is the two instructions between the For and Next ones.

The value of a counter variable by default increases by one each time through a For-Next loop. In this example, Number% eventually reaches 6. The body of the loop still executes, because Number% has equalled, but not exceeded, the final value of the loop.

The Next instruction then increases the value of Number% to 7. Now, when control returns back to the For instruction, the value of Number% is finally greater than the maximum loop value of 6. This signals that the loop is over. The program then proceeds to the first line after the Next instruction.

The *Step* Clause

By adding a Step clause to the end of the For instruction, you can alter the increment for the counter variable. The following is the ShowSquares procedure with the For instruction now modified to include a Step clause:

```
Sub ShowSquares ()
    Rem - Display Squares of Numbers
    Print "Number", "Square"
    For Number% = 0 To 6 Step 2
        Square% = Number% * Number%
        Print Number%, Square%
    Next Number%
    Print "End of table"
End Sub
```

The output now becomes

```
Number        Square
  0             0
  2             4
  4             16
  6             36
End of table
```

Each time through the loop, the Step clause specifies an increment of 2. As a result, Number% becomes successively 0, 2, 4, and 6.

With certain increments, you might not hit exactly the final value of the loop. Suppose that you write the For instruction as follows:

```
For Number% = 0 To 6 Step 4
```

The successive values of Number% increase by 4 (0, 4, 8...). Number%, therefore, never becomes 6, the designated final value of the loop. In such a case, the loop terminates whenever the counter variable becomes greater than the final value. In this example, the body of the loop executes only for Number% equal to 0 and 4.

You can specify negative increments. When the increment is negative, the counter variable decreases through the loop each time. For a proper "negative" loop, specify the final value of the counter variable to be smaller than the initial value.

Bypassing the Loop

Visual Basic bypasses a For-Next altogether if one of these two conditions is met:

- The starting loop value is greater than its final value when the Step increment is positive.

- The starting loop value is smaller than its final value when the Step increment is negative.

Try changing the For instruction as follows:

```
For Number% = 5 To 2
```

This instruction specifies that the starting value of the loop (5) is less than the final value (2). The default increment is 1 because no Step clause appears. Visual Basic "realizes" that you cannot count upward from 5 and reach 2! The loop, therefore, doesn't execute. The program output becomes

```
Number        Square
End of table
```

Syntax of For-Next

That concludes an intuitive introduction to For-Next loops. To more formally specify such loops, the following section presents the general syntax of For-Next:

```
For countervar = start To end Step increment
    .
    .        'body of loop
    .
Next countervar
```

in which

    countervar is a numeric variable acting as the counter variable;

continues

continued

    `start` specifies the initial value of *countervar*;

    `end` specifies the final value of *countervar*;

    `increment` specifies how much to increase *countervar* each time through the loop,

and

    `body of loop` is a block of Visual Basic instructions.

The `Step` *increment* clause is optional. Also, *countervar* can be omitted in the `Next` instruction.

Using Variables in a *For* Instruction

You can specify loop limits and `Step` increments with variables or with entire expressions. The following `For` instructions, for example, are all acceptable:

```
For Number% = 2 To Final%

For Number% = First% To Last%

For Number% = First% To Last% Step Increment%

For Number% = First% To Last% Step (Last% - First%) / 10

For Number% = (Value1% - Value2%) To 100
```

By using variables, a program can have different loop boundaries from run to run. The following is the `ShowSquares` procedure modified to ask the user for the loop boundaries. When prompted, you type values for the first and last entries in the table.

```
Sub ShowSquares ()
   Rem - Display Squares of Numbers (Get Limits From User)
   First% = Val(InputBox$("Please specify the first value"))
   Last% = Val(InputBox$("Please specify the last value"))
   Print "Number", "Square"
   For Number% = First% to Last%
      Square% = Number% * Number%
      Print Number%, Square%
   Next Number%
   Print "End of table"
End Sub
```

Notice how the For instruction now specifies the loop limits with the variables First% and Last%. The user supplies the values for First% and Last% by using the two InputBox$ functions.

Excluding the Counter Variable in a *Next* Instruction

In a Next instruction, the counter variable is optional; that is, you can write the Next instruction as simply:

```
Next
```

When you leave out the counter variable, the Next instruction automatically matches with the For one. It's good practice, however, to always include the counter variable in Next instructions. That way, you make the looping variables perfectly clear.

When two or more loops are nested, and the counter variables are included, Next instructions are much easier to understand. Another section, later in this chapter, discusses nested loops.

Placing a Loop in a Single Line

You can specify an entire For-Next loop in one program line. You don't have to isolate the loop components into separate lines. Simply use colons to separate the individual instructions. (The body of the loop must be relatively small for a single-line loop to be feasible.) For example:

```
For Item% = 1 To LastItem%: Print Item%: Next Item%
```

In order to execute a loop in the Debug window, you must type the loop on a single line. For more information on the Debug window, see Chapter 21, "Debugging and Testing."

Using the Counter Variable

The *counter variable* can be any numeric type. Usually, counter variables are type Integer (or Long). The following loop works fine, however, with a single-precision counter variable named Value!:

```
For Value! = 1 To 4
   Print Value!
Next Value!
```

The output is what you would expect:

```
1
2
3
4
```

Sometimes you need the counter variable to be Single, Double, or Currency. Suppose that the loop increment has a fractional value:

```
For Counter! = 0 To 1 Step 1 / 4
   Print Counter!
Next Counter!
```

The output now contains fractional numbers:

```
0
.25
.5
.75
1
```

If possible, use Integer (or Long) variables for your counter variables. Avoid Single or Double variables for two reasons. First, loops with integer counter variables execute faster than those with noninteger counter variables. Second, mathematical errors can occur when counter variables, or Step increments, are single- or double-precision. Remember that Visual Basic cannot represent most single- and double-precision numbers exactly, only approximately. Accuracy errors can cause the loop to execute an incorrect number of times when it contains a fractional Step clause (or fractional loop limits).

Nesting *For* Loops

You can nest For-Next loops to any level. Many practical programming projects take advantage of nested loops. When nesting loops, be sure that each loop uses a unique counter variable.

Innermost loops execute the fastest. This means that the Next instructions for nested loops must occur in order, from the deepest nested loop to the outermost one, respectively.

As an example of nested loops, the following procedure displays a multiplication table:

```
Sub MulTable ()     'Demonstrate nested loops
   Max% = 4             'Maximum value in table
   Print "Value 1", "Value 2", "Product"
```

```
    For A% = 1 To Max%
        For B% = A% To Max%
            Product% = A% * B%
            Print A%, B%, Product%
        Next B%
        Print
    Next A%
End Sub
```

The output resembles this:

Value 1	Value 2	Product
1	1	1
1	2	2
1	3	3
1	4	4
2	2	4
2	3	6
2	4	8
3	3	9
3	4	12
4	4	16

The second For instruction begins an inner loop, while the outer loop is still active. The counter variables for the outer and inner loops are A% and B%, respectively. Note how the second For instruction uses A% (the counter variable from the outer loop) as the lower limit of the inner loop. That is the reason "Value 1" in the output table increases each time the inner loop restarts.

You can edit the second program line to change the value of Max%. By doing so, you can create larger (or smaller) multiplication tables.

When nesting For loops, if you omit the counter variable in Next instructions, each Next pairs with the most recently opened For. For program clarity and easier troubleshooting, however, it's a good idea to always include the counter variable in each Next.

NOTE **Indenting Loops**

Be liberal when indenting the body of the loop. This is not a requirement of Visual Basic, but merely common sense. Consistent indentation makes programs easier to read. The result is programs that are easier to understand, and troubleshoot.

The style used in this book places the For and Next keywords for each loop at the same indentation level. The body of the loop is indented three spaces. In nested For-Next loops, each level is successively indented three more spaces.

Using Multiple Counter Variables in a *Next* Instruction

When nested loops end at the same logical program line, you can specify more than one counter variable with a single Next instruction. In such a Next instruction, separate the counter variables with commas. The following is an example:

```
For A% = 1 To 3
   For B% = 5 To 7
      For C% = 10 To 12
         Print A% * B% * C%
Next C%, B%, A%
```

Many programmers feel, however, that the use of multiple counter variables in a single Next instruction generally makes the code somewhat more difficult to read, and understand.

Common Traps in *For* Loops

The following are four "Don'ts" when working with For-Next loops.

- ■ *Don't redefine the control variable inside the loop.* Never explicitly change the value of the counter variable inside the body of the loop. This is asking for problems. Beware of the common ways you might fall into this trap:

  Using the counter variable on the left side of an assignment instruction

  Making the counter variable the value requested from the user in a TextBox control, or InputBox$ function

  Reusing the same counter variable in a nested loop

  If you ever find yourself redefining a control variable inside a loop, throw some water on your face, then rethink your logic. A better way is bound to exist.

- ■ *Don't depend on the value of the control variable outside the loop.* It's best to think of the counter variable as undefined after the loop terminates. You can reuse the counter variable in another place—often in a subsequent loop. Don't assume, however, that the counter variable has any particular value after the loop terminates.

- ■ *Don't branch into or out of loops.* It's okay to use GoTo instructions that branch within the body of a loop, but don't branch into a loop from outside. If you do, the limits of the loop are not defined properly, and it might run indefinitely.

■ *Don't use more than one **Next** for each control variable—pair each **For** instruction with a single **Next**.*

Terminating Loops with the *Exit For* Statement

You sometimes might want to terminate a loop before the final value of the counter variable is reached. To do this, use the `Exit For` statement. Execution resumes just after the `Next` statement.

Consider the following example of `Exit For`. Suppose that you want to display the names contained in the array `EmployeeName$`. The array is dimensioned from 1 to 500. The exact number of employees is unknown, but it is less than 500. The array, therefore, contains names from element 1 up to some (un- known) array element. The remainder of the array values are just null strings.

The following loop displays the names. `Exit For` terminates the loop when the first null string is detected. (The subsequent discussion of `While-Wend` loops shows a more elegant way to solve this problem.)

```
For Counter% = 1 To 500
    If EmployeeName$(Counter%) = "" Then
        Exit For          'prematurely branches out of the loop
    Else
        Print EmployeeName$(Counter%)
Next Counter%
```

Using *While-Wend* Loops

`While-Wend` loops are controlled by a *condition* rather than a counter variable. Think of the condition as a `True` or `False` test placed at the top of the loop. The body of the loop continues to execute as long as the condition remains `True`.

```
While boolexpr
    .
    .         'body of loop
    .
Wend
```

in which

  boolexpr specifies the condition as a Boolean (True or False) expression,

and

  body of loop is any group of Visual Basic instructions.

The Boolean expression typically is a relational one that Visual Basic evaluates to True or False automatically. Such relational expressions are similar to the True or False ones you encountered as If instruction tests, earlier in this chapter.

The following are two examples of While conditions:

```
While TermX% < 100                        'relational expression

While (Day$ = "Mon") Or (Day$ = "Tue")    'compound logical
```

To terminate the body of the loop, use the Wend statement. In nested While-Wend loops, each Wend matches the most recently activated While.

Before entering the body of a While-Wend loop for the first time, Visual Basic evaluates the condition in your While instruction. If False, Visual Basic by-passes the loop entirely, and execution continues on the line immediately following Wend.

If the condition is True, the body of the loop executes. Control then returns to the While instruction, and the condition is reevaluated. As long as the condition remains True, the loop continues to execute.

Instructions within it obviously must do something to affect the testing condition, or the loop is in danger of executing forever. Usually, the body of the loop modifies one or more variables that occur in the testing expression.

As an example of While-Wend, consider the following procedure that mimics a launching countdown:

```
Sub CountDown ()
    Rem Demonstrate While-Wend
    Dim TimeLeft As Integer
    TimeLeft = 5
    While TimeLeft >= 1          'Boolean condition
        Print TimeLeft
        TimeLeft = TimeLeft - 1
    Wend
    Print "Blast off"
End Sub
```

The output of CountDown is

```
5
4
3
2
1
Blast off
```

The two instructions between the While and Wend contain the body of the loop. Notice how the instruction immediately preceding the Wend decrements the value of TimeLeft with each pass through the loop. The condition in the While instruction is True, as long as TimeLeft has a value greater than or equal to 1.

As with For-Next loops, While-Wend loops can be nested to any level. You can write simple While-Wend loops on a single line by separating the instructions with colons.

The previous section on For-Next loops discussed the programming problem of displaying employee names in an array dimensioned from 1 to 500. The following is a solution using a While-Wend loop and a compound testing condition. The test for the end of the array is assimilated into the While condition with a logical And operator.

```
Counter% = 1
While (EmployeeName$(Counter%) <> "") And (Counter% <= 500)
    Print EmployeeName$(Counter%)
    Counter% = Counter% + 1
Wend
```

Using *Do-Loop* Loops

Do-Loop offers you the flexibility to create loops that extend the capabilities of While-Wend loops. Similar to While-Wend, Do-Loop uses a condition to control the loop. Do-Loop, however, is more flexible than While-Wend, because you can place the condition at the beginning of the loop, or at the end. Additionally, a Do-Loop loop can be exited without the condition being met if the End DO statement is met. The End DO statement will be discussed at length latter in the chapter.

Top-test form:

```
Do While boolexpr
    .
    .          'body of loop
    .
Loop
```

or

continues

continued

```
Do Until boolexpr
        .
        .      'body of loop
        .
Loop
```

in which

    boolexpr specifies the condition as a Boolean (True or False) expression,

and

    body of loop is any group of Visual Basic instructions.

Bottom-test form:

```
Do
        .
        .      'body of loop
        .
Loop While boolexpr
```

or

```
Do
        .
        .      'body of loop
        .
Loop Until boolexpr
```

in which

    boolexpr specifies the condition as a Boolean (True or False) expression,

and

    body of loop is any group of Visual Basic instructions.

Notice that for both the top-test and bottom-test forms, the loop begins with a Do statement, and ends with a Loop statement.

Each testing condition must begin with While or Until. With While, the loop continues if the condition is True, but terminates if it is False. Until has the opposite effect: the loop continues if the condition is False, and terminates if it is True. Table 15.4 summarizes the effect of the While and Until keywords.

Table 15.4. Use of *While* and *Until* in Do-Loops.

	Value of Testing Condition	
Keyword	**True**	**False**
While	Continue loop	Terminate loop
Until	Terminate loop	Continue loop

The top-test form of a Do loop is similar to a While-Wend loop. In fact, the following two loop constructions are equivalent:

```
Do While boolexpr
    .
    .          'body of loop
    .
Loop
```

```
While boolexpr
    .
    .          'body of loop
    .
Wend
```

A bottom-test Do loop must execute the loop body at least once. Such loops often terminate with an Until condition. The following loop, for example, asks repeatedly for a number from the user, then displays an appropriate message. When the user types **0**, the loop terminates. (For information on the Val function, see Chapter 17, "Working with Strings."):

```
Do
    Number! = Val(InputBox$("Type a number"))
    If Number! > 0 Then MsgBox "You're being positive"
    If Number! < 0 Then MsgBox "You're so negative"
Loop Until Number! = 0
```

When reviewing the above example, note that if you enter a negative number, the words "You're being negative" are displayed, if you enter a positive number, the words "Your're being positive" are displayed, and lastly, as previously mentioned, if you enter a zero, you will exit the loop.

The following example illustrates how the While and Until clauses can be used to perform the same task. As will become evident, the decision of when to use While or Until, is more a matter of personal preference and style than necessity.

```
x = 1
Print "The While loop example: ";
Do
  Print x;
   x = x + 1
Loop while x <= 5

Print
Print "The Until loop example: ";
x = 1
Do
  Print x;
   x = x + 1
Loop Until x > 5
```

The output of the above program example is:

```
The While loop example: 1 2 3 4 5
The Until loop example: 1 2 3 4 5
```

The While portion of the above example continues to loop as long as the value of x is less than or equal to 5. The Until portion of the example continues to reiterate until x has a value greater than 5.

The following example is the same as the previous example, except that the initial values of x were changed from 1 to 6, which is greater than the upper limit of the loop. Because the test is at the bottom however, the statements within the loop will always be executed at least once. Therefore, each loop will print the number 6 before exiting. This modified example is shown below:

```
x = 6
Print "The While loop example: ";
Do
  Print x;
   x = x + 1
Loop while x <= 5

Print
Print "The Until loop example: ";
x = 6
Do
  Print x;
   x = x + 1
Loop Until x > 5
```

The output of the above program example is:

```
The While loop example: 6
The Until loop example: 6
```

In the next example shown below, the initial values of x are set back to 1 but the While and Until conditions were moved from the bottom of the loop to the top (after the key word Do):

```
x = 1
Print "The While loop example: ";
Do while x <= 5
  Print x;
  x = x + 1
Loop

Print
Print "The Until loop example: ";
x = 1
Do Until x > 5
  Print x;
  x = x + 1
Loop
```

When the above example is executed, the output will be exactly the same as in the first example. Why?

```
The While loop example: 1 2 3 4 5
The Until loop example: 1 2 3 4 5
```

The output will be the same as the first example because once you are in the loop, whether the test is at the bottom of the current reiteration or the top of the next reiteration does not matter—the loop will be exited before the statements are re-executed.

The *Exit Do* Statement

As discussed earlier in the chapter you can prematurely exit a For-Next loop with an Exit For instruction. Similarly, you can prematurely exit a Do-Loop block with an Exit Do instruction. When an Exit Do statement is executed, control is passed to the instruction immediately following the Loop statement.

An example program illustrating the use of the Exit Do statement follows.

```
Do While (1 = 1)

  var1 = Val(InputBox$("Enter the first number to be added"))
  If var1 = 0 Then
    Exit Do
  End If
  var2 = Val(InputBox$("Enter the second number to be added"))
  print var1;" plus ";var2;" equals ";var1 + var2
Loop
```

In the above `Exit Do` statement example, the user is asked to enter two numbers. Once entered, the two values are added together and the answer is displayed.

From a technical perspective, this program has two interesting points. First, the condition being tested is `1 = 1`; by definition, this condition will always produce a True result, thus causing an endless loop. Second, if the user enters a zero as the first number value, the `Exit Do` command will be executed and the loop will be ended. This technique of creating an endless Do loop which contains programming logic that executes an `Exit Do` statement is a very commonly used programming technique.

Even though the endless loop technique is very commonly used by many professional programmers, other professional programmers feel that the `Exit Do` statement should only be used as a last resort and the preceding programming example should be written as follows:

```
Do

  var1 = Val(InputBox$("Enter the first number to be added"))
  If var1 <> 0 Then
    var2 = Val(InputBox$("Enter the second number to be added"))
    print var1;" plus ";var2;" equals ";var1 + var2
  endif
Loop Until var1 = 0
```

The program shown above will run exactly the same as the `Exit Do` programming example, but allows the loop to end naturally without the use of the `Exit Do` statement. The programming technique that you choose to use is strictly a matter of your preference and programming style.

Nested *Do-Loop* Statements

Also like `For-Next` loops, `Do-Loop` loops can be nested as shown in the following example:

```
Outer = 1
Do While Outer <= 5
  Inner = 1
  Do While Inner <= Outer
    Print "*";
    Inner = Inner + 1
  Loop
  Print
  Outer = Outer + 1
Loop
```

When reviewing this program, note that the inner loop is run to completion during each reiteration of the outer loop. The output produced by the above programming example is shown below.

```
*
**
***
****
*****
```

In the second nested loop example, the stars have been replaced with the word "in" and the word "out" has been added to the second print statement to further illustrate the nested loop process:

```
Outer = 1
Do While Outer <= 5
  Inner = 1
  Do While Inner <= Outer
    Print "in ";
    Inner = Inner + 1
  Loop
  Print "out"
  Outer = Outer + 1
Loop
```

The output of the preceding program is:

```
In Out
In In Out
In In In Out
In In In In Out
In In In In In Out
```

Summary

Normal program flow progresses line-by-line down a procedure. You often need, however, to alter this sequential order.

The most straightforward way to alter program flow is with a branch. A branch is the direct transfer from one location in your procedure to another. With GoTo, you can make an unconditional branch. On-GoTo provides conditional branching: you branch to one of several instructions, depending on the value of a particular expression.

Programs frequently need to make decisions. Often, a condition is tested, and the program takes different actions, depending on the result of the test. If-Then-Else instructions and Select Case blocks provide versatile tools for conditional testing.

Loops are instruction blocks which execute repetitively. Loops are one of the most common and useful programming structures. Many programming tasks involve repetitive calculations for which a loop is ideally suited.

A controlled loop executes a limited number of times. Visual Basic has special statements for three kinds of controlled loops: For-Next—when the loop should be executed a specified number of times; While-Wend—when the loop should be executed as long as a condition remains True, and Do-Loop—when the loop should be executed as long as a condition remains True, or until it becomes True.

Working with Numbers

M ost Visual Basic applications manipulate data. After all, when you program routine tasks (such as assigning values to variables, calculating numeric quantities, or displaying results), you are manipulating data. In one way or another, nearly all programming topics relate to data manipulation.

This chapter explores various ways of manipulating numbers. The following topics are covered in this chapter:

- Using Visual Basic's numeric functions
- Generating random numbers
- Converting values from one numeric data type to another
- Manipulating integers at the bit level

Using the Numeric Functions and Statements

A *numeric expression* is any expression that evaluates to a single numeric value. The expression can contain any combination of literals, variables, constants, array elements, and function calls. The final value can have any of the five numeric data types: Integer, Long, Single, Double, or Currency.

Using Suffixes on Variable Names

In this chapter, numeric variable names frequently include type-declaration suffixes. Sample variable names are `Cost!`, `Salary@`, and `NumItems%`. For the short examples in this chapter, the suffixes provide a convenient way to draw attention to the data type of the variable. In actual programming practice, variable names often do not include the suffixes. Data types of variables, however, are regularly specified with `Dim` instructions, such as `Dim Cost As Single, Salary As Currency`.

Table 16.1 shows a few examples of numeric expressions:

Table 16.1. Sample numeric expressions.

Numeric expression	Comment
435	Simple numeric literal
(Cost! * NumItems%) / 12.2	Expression with variables
Salary@(Employee%)	Simple array reference
Sqr(Side1# - Side2#)	Expression containing a function call

A Note to Non-Mathematicians

The numeric functions and statements obviously are mathematical in nature. Many programmers are not math wizards, and don't intend to write programs that perform fancy mathematical manipulation. You can do just fine developing a host of practical applications that require no more math than the simple arithmetic provided by the addition, subtraction, multiplication, and division operators (+, -, *, and /).

If you expect your programs to utilize only simple arithmetic, feel free to skim the following material. You can always review it later, if needed.

As Table 16.2 shows, Visual Basic provides a host of numeric functions and statements.

Table 16.2. Mathematical functions and statements.

Trigonometric

Name	Type	Description
Sin	Function	Sine of an angle
Cos	Function	Cosine of an angle
Tan	Function	Tangent of an angle
Atn	Function	Arctangent of a number

Logarithmic

Name	Type	Description
Exp	Function	Exponential
Log	Function	Natural logarithm

Conversion

Name	Type	Description
CCur	Function	Convert a number to currency
CInt	Function	Convert a number to integer
CLng	Function	Convert a number to long integer
CSng	Function	Convert a number to single precision
CDbl	Function	Convert a number to double precision

Rounding

Name	Type	Description
Fix	Function	Truncate to integer
Int	Function	Round to lower integer

Random Numbers

Name	Type	Description
Randomize	Statement	Seed random-number generator
Rnd	Function	Generate a random number

continues

Table 16.2. Continued

Arithmetic

Name	Type	Description
Abs	Function	Absolute value
Sgn	Function	Sign of a number
Sqr	Function	Square root

Financial—Annuities

Name	Type	Description
Pmt	Function	Amount of payments
IPmt	Function	Interest payment
PPmt	Function	Principal payment
FV	Function	Future value
PV	Function	Present value
NPer	Function	Number of periods
Rate	Function	Interest rate per period

Financial—Business Investment

Name	Type	Description
NPV	Function	Net present value
IRR	Function	Interest rate of return
MIRR	Function	Modified interest rate of return

Financial—Depreciation

Name	Type	Description
SLN	Function	Straight-line method
DDB	Function	Double-declining balance method
SYD	Function	Sum-of-years' digits method

NOTE

Trying Code Examples

This chapter contains small program fragments that utilize the Print method to display results. The Print instructions in this chapter do not explicitly indicate a Print object. (For example, a typical Print instruction in this chapter is Print "Hello", not Form1.Print "Hello".)

To try the examples in this chapter (and succeeding chapters), your code must designate in which place the results appear. You can indicate this destination in several ways. The two simplest approaches are to display results directly on the default form, or in the Debug window.

To display results directly on the form, write code for the Form_Click procedure. Use the code fragment from this chapter as the body of the procedure. Begin execution of the application, then click the default form. The displayed result appears directly on the form.

The second method is to display results in the Debug window. To do this, start an application without entering any code. Break execution (press Ctrl+Break, or click the Break button on the Toolbar). The Debug window appears. You now can type code fragments directly in the Debug window. Print instructions display results in the Debug window.

To use the Debug window, however, you must type loops and other control structures on a single line. Consider the following simple loop:

```
For J% = 1 To 3
 Print J%
Next J%
```

In the Debug window, you must type this loop on a single line, using colons to separate the individual instructions:

```
For J% = 1 To 3: Print J%: Next J%
```

Try the examples that interest you. You can experiment by changing any of the values. Experience always is the best teacher.

Using the Trigonometric Functions

The trigonometric functions Sin, Cos, and Tan return, respectively, the sine, cosine, and tangent of an angle. Visual Basic includes also the Atn function, which returns the arctangent (or inverse tangent) of a number.

Sin(*angle*)

Cos(*angle*)

Tan(*angle*)

Atn(*numexpr*)

in which

> *angle* specifies an angle in radians, and

> *numexpr* is a numeric expression.

The trigonometric functions specify angles in radians which are mathematically more convenient than degrees. One radian is approximately 57.3 degrees. A complete circle contains 2π radians (2π radians equal 360 degrees; as a result, π is approximately 3.14). Figure 16.1 shows the mapping between radians and degrees.

The value of *angle* can be positive, negative, or zero. The Sin and Cos functions always return values between -1.0 and +1.0. The Tan function return values ranging from large negative numbers to large positive ones.

The arctangent of *numexpr* is the angle whose tangent has the value of *numexpr*. Atn, therefore, is the inverse function of Tan. The result of the Atn function is an angle expressed in radians. This angle is confined to the range from $-\pi/2$ to $+\pi/2$.

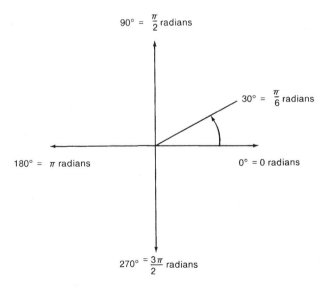

Figure 16.1.

Specifying angles in radians and degrees.

Each of the four trigonometric functions calculates results in single precision when the function argument is Integer, Single, or Currency. If the function argument is Long or Double, the calculated result is double precision.

Using Atn to Find the Value of π

T I P

Many trigonmetric programs need to work with the value of π. The Atn function provides a convenient way to restore the value of π in a variable. The following paragraph explains how to do this.

The tangent of $(\pi/4)$ is exactly 1. This means that the arctangent of 1 is $\pi/4$. The following program fragment demonstrates how to calculate π to single- and double-precision accuracy. The program stores the values in the variables Pi! and Pi#, and displays the results.

```
'PiSing! = 4 * ATm(1)

PiDoub#  = 4# * Atn(1)

Print PiSing!

Print PiDoubl#
```

The following is the output:

```
3.141593

3.1415926535899799
```

Note that Atn(1#) returns a double-precision result. A latter section of this chapter discusses the technique of placing a type suffix (in this example, the pound sign) at the end of a numeric literal.

If you have a program that uses the value of π frequently, consider defining a variable, or constant, set to the value of π. You might, for example, place the following constant declaration in the Declaration section of a module:

```
Global Const Pi# - 3.14159265358979
```

The constant Pi# then becomes available to code throughout the application.

Using the Logarithmic Functions

The Log function returns the natural logarithm. Exp, the inverse function to Log, returns the exponential.

```
Log(numexpr)

Exp(numexpr)
```

in which

    numexpr is a numeric expression.

For the `Log` function, *numexpr* must be positive, or an `Illegal function call` error occurs. (Mathematically, a logarithm is undefined for a negative argument.)

For the `Exp` function, *numexpr* can be positive, negative, or zero. The largest permissible value of *numexpr* depends on the numeric data type of the argument. If *numexpr* is double precision, the upper limit of *numexpr* is 709. If *numexpr* is single precision, currency, integer, or long integer, the upper limit is 88. (A value of *numexpr* that exceeds the limit creates numeric overflow. The reason is that, mathematically, the exponential returns a value larger than the maximum value for that data type.)

When the function argument is Integer, Single, or Currency, `Log` and `Exp` calculate results in single precision. If the function argument is Long or Double, the function is calculated in double precision.

`Log` and `Exp` are based on the natural logarithms, also called logarithms to the base e. The mathematical constant e has a value of approximately 2.71828. You can see Visual Basic's value of e in single- and double-precision accuracy with the following experiment:

```
Print Exp(1)
Print Exp(1#)
```

The result is

```
2.718282
2.71828182845905
```

You might want to do some calculations using logarithms to the base 10, sometimes called *common logarithms*. The following instruction uses the `Log` function to calculate the common logarithm of X!:

```
ComLog! = Log(X!) / Log(10)
```

You can duplicate the exponential function with the exponential operator ^ (the caret). Mathematically, `Exp(X)` is eX (e raised to the power of X). Another way to express this in Visual Basic is `Exp(1) ^ X`. Consider the following program fragment:

```
X! = 4.9
Print Exp(X!)
Print Exp(1) ^ X!
```

The following is the output:

```
134.2898
134.2898
```

Use `10 ^ X` to calculate the base 10 exponential of X (10 raised to the X power).

Using the Conversion Functions

Visual Basic has several functions that convert a number from one numeric type to another (such as, from Single to Integer). The conversion functions are CInt, CLng, CSng, CDbl, and CCur.

CInt, CLng, CSng, CDbl, and CCur convert a numeric expression in any format to the equivalent number in a specified numeric format.

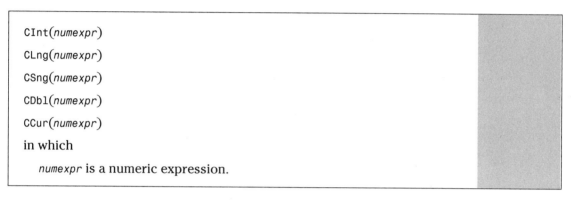

CInt(*numexpr*)

CLng(*numexpr*)

CSng(*numexpr*)

CDbl(*numexpr*)

CCur(*numexpr*)

in which

numexpr is a numeric expression.

CInt converts to Integer. The value of *numexpr* must be in the range from -32,768 to +32,767. If *numexpr* contains a fractional part, CInt rounds to the closest integer. If *numexpr* has a fractional part of exactly .5, CInt rounds to the closest even integer.

CLng converts to Long. The value of *numexpr* must be in the range from -2,147483,648 to 2,147,483,647. The rounding of a fractional number works the same as the CInt conversion.

CSng converts to Single. The value of *numexpr* must be in the range from (approximately) -3.4E+38 to +3.4E+38.

CDbl converts to Double. The value of *numexpr* must be in the range from (approximately) -1.7D+308 to +1.7D+308.

CCur converts to Currency. The value of *numexpr* must be in the range from (approximately) -922337203685477 to +922337203685477.

Table 16.3 shows the results of some conversion instructions.

Table 16.3. Sample commands using the conversion functions.

Instruction	Result
Print CInt(-1.8)	-2
Print CInt(29.4)	29

continues

Table 16.3. Continued

Instruction	Result
Print CInt(29.8)	30
Print CLng(48324.5)	48324
Print CLng(48325.5)	48326
Print CSng(1.23456789#)	1.234568
Print CSng(1 / 7)	.1428571
X! = 1 / 7:Print CDbl(X!)	.142857149243355
Print CDbl(1# / 7)	.142857142857143
Print CCur(100 / 3)	33.3333

In Table 16.3, compare the results of the two CDbl examples with the final CSng example. Although CDbl calculates to 15 digits of precision, only the first seven digits are accurate. The variable X! has only single-precision accuracy, and CDbl cannot convert a single-precision expression to double-precision accuracy. The expression (1# / 7), however, produces double-precision accuracy. CDbl, therefore, processes this expression with full precision.

You do not need conversion functions when you assign a numeric expression to a variable. Consider the following instructions:

```
MyInt% = CInt(1234.5 * 4)
MyLng& = CLng(15 ^ 7)
MySng! = CSng(23.8# / 9)
MyDbl# = CDbl(38.23 * 14.7)
MyCur@ = CCur(95.82 * .085)
```

In each case, you get the same result by omitting the conversion function. The assignment of a numeric expression to a numeric variable forces the appropriate type conversion. No conversion function is necessary. (Another section later in this chapter discusses numeric type conversion, and the use of suffixes on numeric literals. You see how the type conversion functions can prevent certain overflow errors.)

In Visual Basic programs, most numeric data type conversion takes place automatically. Rest assured that unless you are doing sophisticated mathematical computation, your numeric results usually are correct when you simply write your mathematical expressions without using any conversion functions.

Using the Rounding Functions

In addition to `CInt` and `CLng`, Visual Basic has two other functions that convert a numeric expression into a whole number.

`Fix(`*numexpr*`)`

`Int(`*numexpr*`)`

in which

   numexpr is a numeric expression.

`Fix` simply strips off the fractional part of *numexpr*. This is called *truncation*. `Fix(8.9)` is 8, and `Fix(-8.9)` is -8.

`Int` returns the largest whole number that is less than, or equal to, the value of *numexpr*. This is called *rounding down* or *flooring*. `Int(8.9)` is 8 and `Int(-8.9)` is -9.

Recall that `CInt` and `CLng` return the whole number closest to *numexpr*. Rounding can be up or down, as appropriate. `CInt(4.2)` is 4, and `CInt(4.8)` is 5.

`Fix` and `Int` are similar functions. Each returns the same value when *numexpr* is zero or positive. When *numexpr* is negative, however, the functions produce different results.

Unlike `CInt` and `CLng`, `Fix` and `Int` can work with values outside the range of Visual Basic's integer and long integer numbers. Although `Fix` and `Int` return whole numbers, the results have single- or double-precision accuracy. If *numexpr* is single precision, `Fix` and `Int` return a result of type Single. If *numexpr* is double precision, `Fix` and `Int` return a result of type Double. `Print Fix(123456.7)` and `Print Int(123456.7)`, for example, return `123456`. Contrast that with `Print CInt(123456.7)`, which causes an overflow error, because `123456.7` is too large for Visual Basic's Integer data type.

The following `Sub` procedure, `RoundDemo`, demonstrates the differences among values returned by `CInt`, `Fix`, and `Int`:

```
Sub RoundDemo ()
   Dim X As Single
   Rem Demonstrate the rounding functions
   Print "X", "CInt(X)", "Fix(X)", "Int(X)"
   For X = -2.8 TO 2.8 Step 1.4
      Print X, CInt(X), Fix(X), Int(X)
   Next X
End Sub
```

The following is the output from RoundDemo:

X	CInt(X)	Fix(X)	Int(X)
-2.8	-3	-2	-3
-1.4	-1	-1	-2
0	0	0	0
1.4	1	1	1
2.8	3	2	2

Using Random Numbers

The Rnd function returns a double-precision *random* number with a value between 0 and 1. A random number is simply an unpredictable number that cannot be predetermined. (The Rnd function has an optional argument, *numexpr*.)

Rnd

or

Rnd(numexpr)

in which

numexpr is a numeric expression.

You can specify the type of random number that Rnd returns by including the optional *numexpr* parameter. The effects of various values of *numexpr* are explained shortly with regard to the explanation of Table 16.4.

Many scientific simulations, and game-playing programs, use random numbers regularly. As a simple example, the following instruction tosses a simulated coin:

```
If Rnd > .5 Then Print "Heads" Else Print "Tails"
```

Rnd returns values that are not truly random, but rather computed by a numeric formula. Such numbers are said to be *pseudorandom* because they simulate random numbers. The formula used to calculate the pseudorandom numbers is predefined within Visual Basic.

The formula, however, does depend on an initial starting value, called a *seed*. By default, Visual Basic provides the same seed each time you begin an application. Unless you reseed the random-number generator, Rnd produces the same sequence of random numbers each time you run an application.

To reseed the random-number formula, Visual Basic provides the Randomize statement. Notice that the *seed* parameter, which is optional, is *not* enclosed in parentheses.

```
Randomize seed
```

or

```
Randomize
```

in which

   seed is a numeric expression.

In an application that uses random numbers, you typically execute one `Randomize` instruction before calling the `Rnd` function. In order to change the random-number sequence each time you run a particular application, you must alter the value of *seed* with each run. Visual Basic's `Timer` function provides a handy way to seed the random number generator unpredictably. (`Timer` is a special function that returns the number of elapsed seconds since midnight. For more information on `Timer`, see Chapter 29, "Manipulating the Windows Environment.")

Visual Basic uses the value returned by `Timer` as the seed, if you use a `Randomize` instruction without the *seed* parameter. The effect is the same as the following instruction:

```
Randomize Timer
```

`Rnd` operates differently, depending on the value of the *numexpr* argument (see Table 16.4).

Table 16.4. The operation of *Rnd* function.

Value of argument	Action performed
numexpr > 0	Returns the next random number in the current sequence.
numexpr omitted	Produces the same effect as *numexpr* > 0.
numexpr = 0	Returns the previous random number.
numexpr < 0	Reseeds the random-number generator using numexpr, and returns the first number of the new sequence.

The following loop demonstrates the type of random numbers returned by `Rnd`:

```
Randomize
For J% = 1 To 5
   Print Rnd
Next J%
```

The following is typical output from this loop, although your results differ because these are random numbers:

```
.9970131
.1807917
.3427377
.1339383
.6167209
```

Notice that Rnd always returns a decimal fraction between 0 and 1. You can also generate random integers using Rnd and Int. The following formula produces a random integer in the range from *lowinteger* to *highinteger*:

```
Int((highinteger - lowinteger + 1) * Rnd + lowinteger)
```

The expression Int(26 * Rnd + 10), for example, produces a random integer in the range from 10 to 35.

To illustrate this technique, the following procedure calculates and displays five random rolls of two dice.

```
Sub DiceRoll ()
    Dim Roll As Integer, Die1 As Integer, Die2 As Integer
    Rem (Roll dice 5 times)
    Randomize
    For Roll = 1 To 5
        Die1 = Int(6 * Rnd + 1)
        Die2 = Int(6 * Rnd + 1)
        Print "Roll"; Roll; "is"; Die1 + Die2
    Next Roll
End Sub
```

The following results by DiceRoll are typical. (Again, your results will differ because of the Randomize instruction.)

```
Roll 1 is 8
Roll 2 is 12
Roll 3 is 7
Roll 4 is 10
Roll 5 is 4
```

Using the Arithmetic Functions

Visual Basic includes three miscellaneous numeric functions —Abs, Sgn, and Sqr.

```
Abs(numexpr)

Sgn(numexpr)

Sqr(numexpr)
```

in which

numexpr is a numeric expression.

The Abs function returns the absolute value of numexpr. The absolute value of a number is its magnitude, without regard to sign. For example, the absolute value of -21.7, and +21.7, are each 21.7.

Many calculations require that you find the difference between two numbers, regardless of which number is larger. Suppose that you have two variables named A! and B!. You want to set Diff! to the positive difference between A! and B!. You don't know, however, whether A! or B! has the larger value. You could use the following cumbersome If instruction:

```
If A! > B! Then Diff! = A! - B! Else Diff! = B! - A!
```

A better way exists, however, to do this. To calculate the positive difference, use Abs, as follows:

```
Diff! = Abs(A! - B!)
```

The Sgn function returns the sign of numexpr, not to be confused with the trigonometric Sin function discussed previously. As Table 16.5 shows, the Sgn function returns -1, 0, or +1, depending on the value of numexpr.

Table 16.5. The *Sgn* function.

Value of *numexpr*	Result of *Sgn (numexpr)*
Positive (> 0)	1
Zero (= 0)	0
Negative (< 0)	−1

The Sqr function returns the square root of numexpr. Visual Basic does not let you use negative arguments; the value of numexpr must be greater than or equal to 0.

NOTE **Calculating Square Roots**

Mathematically, the square root of a number is equivalent to raising the number to the one-half (.5) power. The following two instructions, therefore, return the same result:

```
MyRoot! = Sqr(MyNumber!)

MyRoot! = MyNumber! ^ 0.5
```

Most programmers find that the Sqr form is easier to read in program code. (Visual Basic executes the Sqr form faster. When you want to calculate a square root, use the Sqr function rather than an expression containing the .5 exponent.)

Using the Financial Functions

Version 3.0 of Visual Basic introduces several new functions useful in financial calculations. These functions fall into three categories:

- Annuities
- Business investment
- Depreciation

NOTE The financial functions are located in a file named MSAFINX.DLL. If you distribute any applications that use the financial functions, you must distribute this file as well. Microsoft grants you the right to distribute MSAFINX.DLL free of charge. Install the file in the user's Windows SYSTEM directory, normally C:\WINDOWS\SYSTEM.

The following sections discuss these financial functions.

Annuities

An *annuity* is a series of cash payments made at periodic intervals. For the purposes of the financial functions, there are two types of annuities: a loan (where you borrow a lump sum of money and pay it off over time), and an investment (where you make periodic payments into a fund and eventually receive back a lump sum).

The payments are made at regular intervals and are assumed to be for a fixed amount. For most annuities, the interval is monthly. However, you can specify quarterly, annual, or any other period you choose. The interest rate remains fixed during the length of the annuity.

A particular annuity is characterized by the following components: amount of each payment, total number of periods (payments), interest rate per period, present value, and future value. The various annuity functions let you compute one of these components (or a related component) as a function of the others:

Function	Value returned
Pmt	Amount of each payment
PPmt	Amount paid to principal in a specific period
IPmt	Amount paid to interest in a specific period
FV	Future value (at the end) of the annuity
PV	Present value (at the beginning) of the annuity
NPer	Total number of periods (payments)
Rate	Interest rate per period

```
Pmt(intrate, numper, pv, fv, flag)

PPmt(intrate, period, numper, pv, fv, flag)

IPmt(intrate, period, numper, pv, fv, flag)

FV(intrate, numper, payment, pv, flag)

PV(intrate, numper, payment, fv, flag)

NPer(intrate, payment, pv, fv, flag)

Rate(numper, payment, pv, fv, flag, seedrate)
```

in which

    intrate is the interest rate per period,

    numper is the total number of periods,

    pv is the present value of the annuity,

    fv is the future value of the annuity,

    flag indicates whether the payments are made at the beginning or the end of the period,

continues

continued

> *period* specifies a specific payment period,
>
> and
>
> *seedrate* is a first approximation of the expected interest rate.

Understanding the Parameters in the Annuity Functions

The *numper* parameter is the total number of payments. For a five year annuity with monthly payments, the value of *numper* is 60 (5 years times 12 payments per year). *intrate* is the interest per payment period. For example, if the APR (annual percentage rate) of an annuity is 9 percent, the value of *intrate* is .09/12, which equals .0075. Notice that the APR itself is expressed as a decimal—9 percent equals .09.

The present and future values vary according to the type of annuity. For a loan, the present value is the amount borrowed (the principal) and the future value is 0. For an investment, the present value is 0 and the future value is the total accumulated value (including interest) after the last payment is made.

Normally, the value of either *pv* or *fv* is 0. However, this is not required. For example, you can borrow $10,000 and pay back half of it over the length of the loan. In this case, the value of *pv* is 10000 while the value of *fv* is 5000.

The *flag* parameter indicates when each payment is made. A value of 0 indicates that payments are made at the end of each period, while a value of 1 specifies that payments are made at the beginning of each period.

Calculating a Loan Payment

Consider an automobile loan of $15,000. Suppose the APR is 8 percent, and the loan payments are monthly over five years. Each payment is due at the beginning of a period. The following program fragment computes the amount of each payment:

```
NumPer% = 5 * 12    'Number of periods (5 years, monthly)
IR! = .08 / 12      'Interest rate per period
PresV@ = 15000      'Present value (principal) of loan
FutV@ = 0           'End value
Flag% = 0           'Payments at end of each period

Payment@ = Pmt(IR!, NumPer%, PresV@, FutV@, Flag%)
Print "Monthly payment is"; Payment@
```

The result is

```
Monthly payment is -304.1459
```

Notice that the calculated payment is negative, meaning that the payment is paid (as for a loan), not received (as for an investment).

Determining Principal and Interest

For each payment made to a loan annuity, a portion goes to paying off the principal and a portion goes to paying interest. The PPmt and IPmt functions compute the principal and interest portions, respectively. The *period* parameter specifies the specific period in the range from 1 to the value of *numper*.

For example, you can compute the amount paid to principal and to interest in the tenth period of the sample car loan, as follows:

```
NumPer% = 5 * 12    'Number of periods (5 years, monthly)
IR! = .08 / 12      'Interest rate per period
PresV@ = 15000      'Present value (principal) of loan
FutV@ = 0           'End value
Flag% = 0           'Payments at end of each period
Period% = 10        'Compute for tenth period

Principal@ = PPmt(IR!, Period%, NumPer%, PresV@, FutV@, Flag%)
Interest@ = IPmt(IR!, Period%, NumPer%, PresV@, FutV@, Flag%)
Print "Principal payment is "; Principal@
Print "Interest payment is "; Interest@
```

The result is

```
Principal payment is -216.7264
Interest payment is -87.4195
```

Notice that the sum of the principal and interest payments is –304.1459, the amount of each payment as calculated previously with the Pmt function.

Calculating Future and Present Values

The FV and PV functions return, respectively, the future and present values of an annuity. For example, suppose you put $100 a month into a trust fund. The APR is 7.5 percent. What will this annuity be worth in ten years? The following program fragment determines the answer.

```
NumPer% = 10 * 12   'Number of periods (10 years, monthly)
IR! = .075 / 12     'Interest rate per period
Payment@ = -100     'Amount of each payment
PresV@ = 0          'Present (initial) value of the trust
Flag% = 0           'Payments at end of each period
FutVal@ = FV(IR!, NumPer%, Payment@, PresV@, Flag%)
```

```
Print "Trust will be worth"; FutVal@
```

The output is

```
Trust will be worth 17793.0343
```

Determining the Number of Periods

The NPer function calculates the number of payments in an annuity. You can use this function when you want to determine how many payments you must make for an annuity to reach a certain value.

For example, suppose you can afford to pay $150 per month into a college education fund. If your savings institution offers an APR of 7 percent, how long will it take for the annuity to be worth the $15,000 you desire? The following instruction calculates the answer.

```
Print NPer(.07 / 12, -150, 0, 15000, 0)
```

The answer is 79 months, about 6 1/2.

Calculating the Interest Rate

The Rate function returns the interest rate. This function requires a first estimate of the answer as one of the parameters. That's because the function calculates its result by performing successive iterations. Typically, a good first approximation for the value of *seedrate* is .1.

Sometimes Rate fails to calculate an answer. If this happens, try the function again using a different value of *seedrate*.

Business Investment

Visual Basic includes three financial functions that calculate a business investment: NPV (net present value), IRR (interest rate of return), and MIRR (modified interest rate of return).

These functions assume a business which undergoes periodic cash flows. The periods are at equal time intervals. However, unlike annuities, the cash flow for each period can be any amount—negative or positive.

You express the cash flows as elements in an array. A positive value indicates a receipt (positive cash flow) while a negative value indicates a payment (negative cash flow). The array must contain at least one positive and one negative value.

Here is the syntax for the business investment functions:

```
NPV(discrate, cashflow())

IRR(cashflow(), seedrate)

MIRR(cashflow(), financerate, investrate)
```

in which

discrate is the discount (interest) rate per period, expressed as a decimal,

cashflow is an array of the cash flow values,

seedrate is an approximate value of the interest rate of return,

financerate is the interest rate for payments (negative cash flows), expressed as a decimal,

and

investrate is the interest rate for reinvested cash (positive cash flows), expressed as a decimal.

Using the *NPV* Function

As an example of using NPV, consider that you have a business which posts monthly accounting balances. Suppose you start the business with an up-front investment of $50,000. As the business gets off the ground, the next four monthly cash flows are –$2,000, $500, $800, and $1,500.

The following program fragment returns the net present value of the business after these four months, assuming an interest rate of return of 5 percent.

```
Static CashFlow(4)
IR! = .05      'Interest Rate for a period
CashFlow(0) = -50000   'Initial investment
CashFlow(1) = -2000    'First month's loss
CashFlow(2) = 500      'Business
CashFlow(3) = 800      '   starts turning
CashFlow(4) = 1500     '     a profit

NetPV@ = NPV(IR!, CashFlow())   'Calculate net present value
```

Using the *IRR* and *MIRR* Functions

The IRR function calculates the interest rate for a business investment. The returned value is based on the payments and receipts posted at periodic intervals, as expressed in the *cashflow* array. Like Rate, the IRR function computes the answer by iteration. You must supply a value for *seedrate*, which represents a first approximation to the answer.

The MIRR function returns a modified investment rate of return. This function allows for the payments and receipts (negative and positive values in the *cashflow* array, respectively), to be financed at different interest rates.

Depreciation

Visual Basic includes three financial functions which calculate the depreciation of an asset by different formulas: SLN (straight-line method), DDB (double-declining balance method), and SYD (sum-of-years' digits method).

Here is the syntax for these functions:

```
SLN(startval, endval, life)

DDB(startval, endval, life, period)

SYD(startval, endval, life, period)
```

in which

   startval is the initial value (cost) of the asset,

   endval is the final (salvage) value of the asset,

   life is the total length of time over which the asset is depreciated,

and

   period is the specific time period for which the depreciation is calculated.

Typically, an asset is depreciated until it has no value. In such cases, the value of *startval* is the initial cost of the asset and the value of *endval* is 0.

Values for *life* and *period* must be expressed in the same units. The value of *period* can range from 1 to the value of *life*. For example, if *life* is expressed in years, you can calculate the depreciation for any specific year.

Suppose you have an asset which cost $10,000. You plan to fully depreciate this asset over a span of five years. The following program fragment computes the amount of the first year's depreciation using each of the three methods.

```
Cost@ = 10000      'Initial value of asset
EndVal@ = 0        'Asset will be fully depreciated
Lifetime% = 5      'Number of years asset is depreciated
Period% = 1        'Year for which the depreciation is calculated

Print "First Year's Depreciation"
Print
Print "Straight-line"; SLN(Cost@, EndVal@, Lifetime%)
Print "Double-decline"; DDB(Cost@, EndVal@, Lifetime%, Period%)
Print "Sum of years"; SYD(Cost@, EndVal@, Lifetime%, Period%)
```

The output is

```
First Year's Depreciation
Straight-line 2000
Double-decline 4000
Sum of years  3333.33333333333
```

Notice that the straight-line (SLN) method depreciates an asset by a fixed amount each period. The DDB and SYD methods use accelerated depreciation, in which the amount of depreciation is larger in the earlier periods than in the later ones.

Type Conversion

Table 16.6 reviews Visual Basic's seven data types. Every variable is one of these seven data types.

Table 16.6. The seven data types.

Data types	Sample variable name
Variable-length string	MyName$
Fixed-length string	TodayDate$
Integer	MyAge%
Long integer	NumPeople&
Single precision	Price!
Double precision	Mass#
Currency	Cost@

NOTE

The Variant Data Type

Throughout the ensuing discussion, variables of data type `Variant` are not treated as a special case. Indeed, `Variant` variables can assume any one of the seven data types listed in Table 16.6. Any Variant variable containing numeric data of a particular type behaves similar to any of that type's numeric variables. For example, a Variant variable containing integer data behaves like a variable of type Integer. For more information on the Variant data type, see Chapter 14, "Language Building Blocks."

Mixing Data Types

When you assign a value to a variable, Visual Basic checks that the value matches the data of the variable. If a mismatch occurs, Visual Basic tries to convert the value of the data to match the data type of the variable. This process, in which Visual Basic converts a value of one data type into another, is known as *type conversion*.

You can freely assign a string value to a variable of either string data type. You also can freely assign any numeric value to a variable of any numeric type. If necessary, Visual Basic makes the required type conversion.

The following instructions, for example, are perfectly legal:

```
MyAge% = 39.9999

Tax! = 23456

Value# = Cost&
```

For each of these instructions, Visual Basic converts the numeric value on the right side of the equation into the data type required by the variable on the left. When numeric variables are involved, the type conversion is called *numeric type conversion*. This chapter explores several more examples a little later. (For more information on string type conversion, see Chapter 17, "Working with Strings.")

Strings and numbers, however, share the incompatible nature of water and oil: You just cannot mix them. If you try to assign string data to a numeric variable or numeric data to a string variable, program errors occur. Each of the following instructions causes a run time error (`Type mismatch`):

```
MyAge% = "Too much"
YourAge& = BigNumber$
MySize$ = YourSize!
YourSize$ = 38
```

Numeric Type Conversion

The subsequent sections explain how Visual Basic can convert a numeric value from one data type to another in the following two situations:

- When assigning a value to a variable
- When evaluating a numeric expression

Type Conversion during Variable Assignment

When you assign a value to a numeric variable, Visual Basic converts that value to the data type of the variable, if necessary. If the numeric conversion occurs, Visual Basic uses the following rules:

1. Rounding occurs when you assign a number with a fractional part to an Integer or Long variable. For example:

   ```
   MyNum% = 34.84
   BigNum! = -53411.2
   Value& = BigNum!
   Print MyNum%
   Print Value&
   ```

   results in

   ```
    35
   -53411
   ```

   A fractional number is rounded (up or down) to the closest whole number. If the number ends in exactly .5, Visual Basic rounds (up or down) to the closest even integer.

2. Rounding occurs when you assign a value of more than seven significant digits to a single-precision value. For example:

   ```
   Debt@ = 123456789
   MyDebt! = Debt@
   TestNum# = 8.7654321D+20
   Test! = TestNum#
   Print MyDebt!
   Print Test!
   ```

results in

```
1.234568E+08
8.765432E+20
```

(In the literal assigned to TestNum#, the D is the exponential indicator for double-precision numbers; the number on the right of the equal sign has double-precision accuracy. For more information, see Chapter 14, "Language Building Blocks.")

3. An Overflow error occurs if you try to assign a value outside the acceptable range of the variable. The following instructions, for example, are illegal:

```
MyNum% = 63111.5
MyNum! = 4.563D+75
```

The first instruction is illegal because the rounded value is too large for an integer variable (not because 63111.5 has a fractional part). Remember that an integer variable cannot be larger than 32,767. The second instruction is illegal because the value of the double-precision literal is too large for a single-precision number (not because a double-precision literal is assigned to a single-precision variable).

4. Loss of precision can occur when you assign a single-precision value to a double-precision variable. Only the first seven digits (rounded) of the result are valid. For example:

```
MyNum! = .11
YourNum# = MyNum!
Print YourNum#
```

results in

```
.109999999403954
```

The digits after the sequence of nines are inaccurate.

Type Conversion During Expression Evaluation

As Visual Basic performs each operation, during the evaluation of an arithmetic expression, the operands must be at the same level of precision. If necessary, Visual Basic converts operands to the same level of precision.

The following is a simple example:

```
TotalCost! = Num% * UnitCost!
```

The expression Num% * UnitCost! multiplies an integer value (Num%) and a single-precision value (UnitCost!). The result is assigned to a single-precision variable (`TotalCost!`). To perform the multiplication, Visual Basic needs both operands at the same level of precision. Before multiplying, therefore, Visual Basic converts the value of `Num%` to single precision automatically.

Why doesn't Visual Basic convert `UnitCost!` to integer instead? Visual Basic converts the operand which is less precise to the data type of the more precise operand. More specifically, the operand whose data type accommodates the smaller range of values is converted to the data type of the operand whose data type accepts the larger range. Table 16.7 shows the range order of numeric data types.

Table 16.7. The range order of numeric data types.

Data Type	Range
Double precision	Largest range
Single precision	
Currency	
Long integer	
Integer	Smallest range

The following two problems can arise during the evaluation of expressions:

- Loss of accuracy
- Overflow

Loss of Accuracy

Consider the following code fragment:

```
A% = 5
B! = 1.5
C# = 1000
Temp! = A% / B!
Print Temp! * C#
Print A% / B! * C#
```

Look closely at the two `Print` instructions. They essentially compute and display the same quantity, because `Temp!` in the first instruction is equivalent to the expression `A% / B!` that occurs in the second.

The two `Print` instructions, however, do not produce the same result. The following is the output:

```
3333.33325386047
3333.33333333333
```

Notice that both results display as double-precision numbers (with 15 digits). Only the second number, however, has double-precision accuracy. (The first number is inaccurate after the string of threes.)

To understand why, look at the fourth line of the program fragment. The variable Temp! is single precision, so Visual Basic computes the expression on the right side to single-precision accuracy (to seven digits of precision). In the subsequent Print instruction, the value of Temp! is multiplied by the double-precision quantity C#. The net result is a double-precision value (15 digits) with only single-precision accuracy (seven digits). This is the reason you see the nonsignificant digits (25386047) after the third decimal place.

The second Print instruction is similar, but different. Here, Visual Basic recognizes that the presence of a double-precision operand (C#) requires the entire expression to have double-precision accuracy. The values of A% and B!, therefore, are converted to double precision during the expression evaluation. As a result, the final value has full double-precision accuracy.

Overflow

The following instruction generates an overflow error:

```
MyNum! = 2 * 25000
```

The two operands—2 and 25000—are integer numbers within the range of the Integer data type. Visual Basic, therefore, performs the multiplication expecting an integer result. The outcome (50,000), however, is too large for the Integer data type, and overflow occurs. (Recall from Chapter 14, "Language Building Blocks," that the maximum positive value for an integer number is 32,767.)

You can avoid this overflow error by using one of the type conversion functions (discussed earlier in this chapter). You could, for example, rewrite the instruction as follows:

```
MyNum! = CLng(2) * 25000
```

Now the instruction works fine. In this modified instruction, the CLng function converts the regular integer 2 to a long integer, thus avoiding the integer overflow. Note that CSng, CDbl, or CCur each would work, also.

Don't, however, make this mistake:

```
MyNum! = CLng(2 * 25000)
```

The expression inside the parentheses causes integer overflow before CLng has a chance to act.

The following section discusses another way to prevent such overflow errors.

Numeric Conversion with the Variant Data Type

Variant variables containing numeric data are subject to the same type conversion rules as regular numeric variables. When an expression contains a Variant variable, its data is evaluated the same as data in a numeric variable. Overflow, rounding, or loss of accuracy can occur.

When the left side of an assignment instruction contains a Variant variable, however, it adopts the most efficient numeric data type capable of expressing the right side of the instruction.

Explicitly Setting the Data Type of a Variant Variable

You occasionally might want to ensure that a Variant variable stores its numeric data with a particular data type. To guarantee the most precise calculations in a financial program, for example, you might want all Variant variables to store numbers with the Currency data type. You can do this by using the CCur function.

For example, if Fee is a Variant variable, RatePerHour is Single, and BillingHours is Integer, the following instruction ensures that Fee contains data of type Currency.

```
Fee = CCur(RatePerHour * BillingHours)
```

Special Variant Values: Empty and Null

Until your program explicitly assigns a data value to a Variant variable, it contains the special data value called *Empty*. If a Variant variable containing Empty appears as part of a numeric expression, Visual Basic treats the Empty value as 0 (zero) for the purpose of evaluating the expression.

On the other hand, the special data value Null indicates that a Variant variable contains no valid data. Null is a reserved word which you can assign to the value of a Variant variable. For example:

```
Fee = Null    'Fee is of type Variant
```

Unlike Empty which is interpreted to have a value of 0, Null does not correspond to any numeric value. If an expression contains a Variant variable with a Null value, the final value of the expression is also Null. This causes an error if the final value is stored in a regular (non-Variant) Variant variable.

Null indicates that a Variant variable *intentionally* does not contain valid data, while Empty means that a Variant variable has not yet been assigned *any* other value. (For more information on the Empty and Null data values, see Chapter 14, "Language Building Blocks.")

Testing the Numeric Data Type of a Variant Variable

You can test a Variant variable to see if it contains data that can be interpreted as a numeric value. To do this, use the IsNumeric function.

IsNumeric(*variantexpr*)

in which

   variantexpr is any expression evaluating to a Variant value.

The IsNumeric function returns True if *variantexpr* can be converted to a numeric value, and False otherwise. The expressions that can be interpreted as a numeric value include Variant types 0 (Empty), 2 (Integer), 3 (Long), 4 (Single), 5 (Double), 6 (Currency), 7 (Date), and 8 (String). The String type returns True only if the string value can be interpreted as a number. (For more information on the Empty data value, see Chapter 14, "Language Building Blocks.")

The IsNumeric function is handy when evaluating input provided by the user. Suppose that your program prompts the user to type a value, then stores this input value in a Variant variable named UserInput. You expect the value to be numeric, but it's always a good idea to check. If the user's input is processed in a Sub procedure named Evaluate, you can use the following instruction to test whether the value is proper:

```
If IsNumeric(UserInput) Then Call Evaluate(UserInput)
```

Using Type-Declaration Characters on Numeric Literals

You can attach a type-declaration suffix to a numeric literal. This suffix specifies its data type. Table 16.8 shows some examples.

Table 16.8. Examples of numeric literals.

Literal	Data Type
2	Integer
2&	Long integer
2!	Single precision

Literal	Data Type
2#	Double precision
2@	Currency
1.5	Single precision
1.5#	Double precision
1.5@	Currency

The following instruction avoids the overflow error mentioned previously:

```
MyNum! = 2@ * 25000
```

2@ is now of type Currency, and the multiplication by 25000 has Currency precision. The result, 50,000, is well within the range of Currency. Note that 2&, 2! or 2# works as well as 2@.

When you type program lines, the Visual Basic editor sometimes converts a literal you type to an alternate form containing a type-declaration suffix. Type the following line, for example:

```
Two! = 2.0
```

When you press Enter, the editor converts the line as follows:

```
Two! = 2#
```

Table 16.9 shows some examples of how the editor reformats certain numeric literals.

Table 16.9. Examples of numeric literal conversion.

You type this...	Editor gives you this...
-14.0	-14#
1.23456789987654321	1.23456789987654
9876543210	9876543210#
1.3D+05	130000#
0.4	.4
1.2e20	1.2E+20
476%	476

Manipulating Integers at the Bit Level

Visual Basic stores regular integers (Integer data type) in two memory bytes. A memory byte consists of 8 bits, so the representation of an integer uses 16 bits altogether.

A 16-bit pattern can be interpreted as four hexadecimal digits, each hex digit consisting of four bits. The decimal number 19,150, for example, has the hexadecimal value of 4ACE. Translating to bit patterns, 4ACE becomes 0100 1010 1100 1110. In other words, Visual Basic stores the decimal value of 19,150 as the 16-bit number 0100101011001110.

Every integer value is represented as a *signed* (positive or negative) 16-bit number. The high order bit (to the far left) indicates the sign of the number: 0 for a positive number, 1 for a negative one.

So if the bit to the far left is 0, the number is positive (or zero). The remaining 15 bits express the value from 0 to 32,767.

If the bit to the far left is 1, the number is negative. Visual Basic uses an inverse ordering for the negative numbers: 1 followed by 15 zeroes represents the smallest negative number (-32768), whereas 1 followed by 15 more ones represents the largest negative number (-1).

Long integer values are signed 32-bit numbers which require four memory bytes to store. Such values can be expressed with 8 hexadecimal digits.

Logical Operations on Integers

The logical operators (And, Or, Xor, Not, Imp, Eqv) manipulate integer values at the bit level. In a logical expression, Visual Basic reduces each operand to a bit pattern, and performs the logical operation on each pair of corresponding bits.

The expression 23 And 25, for example, is equivalent to Anding the bit pattern 0000 0000 0001 0111 together with 0000 0000 0001 1001. The result is 0000 0000 0001 0001, which has the value 17. You can demonstrate this technique by trying the instruction **Print 23 And 25** using the Debug window. Visual Basic displays the result: 17.

If one operand is of type Long, and the other of type Integer, Visual Basic converts the Integer operand to a Long integer before performing the evaluation. Figure 16.2 shows another example of evaluating a logical expression.

Bit-Masking

You sometimes need to know whether particular bits in a data value are 1 or 0. Bit-mapped graphics represent a screen image as a series of bit values, for example. The smallest screen dot, called a *pixel*, is either *on* (bit value = 1) or *off* (bit value = 0). To determine whether a particular pixel is on, you might need to know the value in one bit of a variable.

Evaluate (Not A%) Xor (B% Imp C%) where A% = -312, B% = &HAF73, C% = 1482	
A% = -312 = & HFEC8 =	1 1 1 1 1 1 1 0 1 1 0 0 1 0 0 0
Not A%	0 0 0 0 0 0 0 1 0 0 1 1 0 1 1 1
B% = & HAF73 = C% = 1 4 8 2 = &H05CA =	1 0 1 0 1 1 1 1 0 1 1 1 0 0 1 1 0 0 0 0 0 1 0 1 1 1 0 0 1 0 1 0
B% Imp C% =	0 1 0 1 0 1 0 1 1 1 0 0 1 1 1 0
Not A% = B% Imp C% =	0 0 0 0 0 0 0 1 0 0 1 1 0 1 1 1 0 1 0 1 0 1 0 1 1 1 0 0 1 1 1 0
Result =	0 1 0 1 0 1 0 0 1 1 1 1 1 0 0 1
0 1 0 1 0 1 0 0 1 1 1 1 1 0 0 1 = & H54F9 = 21753	

Figure 16.2.

Evaluating a logical expression.

Some of Visual Basic's event procedures communicate results with bit patterns. Various keyboard procedures, for example, represent the state of the keyboard (which keys have been pressed or released) with a parameter of data type Integer. To ascertain the state of the keyboard with these procedures, you must decipher the value of particular bits in the parameter.

Consider the KeyDown event, for example. When used with a Text box control, the following is a typical Sub heading:

```
Sub Text1_KeyDown (KeyCode As Integer, Shift as Integer)
```

This procedure is invoked when the user presses a key while the Text1 text box control has the focus. The Shift parameter indicates the state of the Shift, Ctrl, and Alt key when the event occurs. Shift consists of 16 bits altogether because it is an Integer parameter.

Now, suppose that you want to determine the state of the Alt key in particular. For the KeyDown event, the third bit from the right end indicates the state of the Alt key.

The task is to isolate this particular bit without regard to the value of the other 15 bits. One technique that solves this problem is known as *bit masking*. A *bit mask* is a specific number (bit configuration) that, when combined with the target value using the appropriate logical operator, masks the undesired bits.

Consider the bit mask 0000 0000 0000 0100, for example. All 16 bits are 0 with the exception of the third bit from the right end, which is 1. If you And this bit mask with *any* 16-bit target configuration, all bits except the third from the right end always are zero (because 0 Anded with anything produces 0). The third bit from the right end becomes 1 only if the corresponding target bit contains a 1.

In other words, the result consists of 15 zero bits plus the third bit from the right end which has the same value as the third bit in the same position in the target configuration. Except for this bit, the other 15 bits have been masked.

Here, the bit mask consists of the hex digits 0004, which can be represented as &H4 in Visual Basic. To use this bit mask, write the following instruction:

```
Alt_State% = &H4 And Shift
```

Alt_State% has the value 4 (the Alt key was pressed), or 0 (the Alt key was not pressed). If you want to write a section of code that executes when the Alt key is pressed, you can now write a testing instruction, such as If Alt_State% = 4 Then....

NOTE Using Predefined Bit Mask Constants

Visual Basic's CONSTANT.TXT file contains several predefined constant declarations. This file includes the constant ALT_MASK which is preassigned to have the value &H4. If you load CONSTANT.TXT into the declarations section of your application's program module, you can utilize the constant name in your test instructions. You can write the following instruction, for example:

```
Alt_State% = ALT_MASK And Shift
```

This instruction is easier to understand than writing the literal value &H4 on the right side. (For more information on CONSTANT.TXT, see Chapter 14, "Language Building Blocks.")

Bit masks can map a single bit as well as a group of them. The bit mask 0000 0000 0000 1111, for example, masks the four bits at the right end of a 16-bit integer value. In hexadecimal notation, this bit mask is &HF. If you AND this bit mask with a target integer, the result is greater than 0, providing that at least one of the four bits at the right end of the target is on.

Similarly, you can construct other bit masks that mask any particular bit configuration.

Summary

Numeric functions solve mathematical problems. Visual Basic has functions for arithmetic, trigonometry, logarithms, rounding, and random numbers.

Numeric expressions can contain numbers with different data types. When evaluating expressions, Visual Basic converts parts of a numeric expression from one data type to another, (for example, from Single to Integer), if necessary. Your final results occasionally lose some accuracy during this process.

With an understanding of how Visual Basic treats numbers, the next step is to explore how it handles text. That's the subject of Chapter 17, "Working with Strings."

Working with Strings

In the previous chapter, you learned about the manipulation of numbers. Now, it's time to turn your attention to data contained in strings (text).

String manipulation is an important topic in Visual Basic programming for one simple reason: Most communication between a program and the user is done with text strings. Graphics controls, such as text boxes and labels, display only text; message boxes and input boxes communicate with the user strictly through text data.

Although numbers obviously are important for calculations and storing information, numeric data must generally be converted to and from strings when displaying results, or accepting user input.

Visual Basic provides great flexibility in manipulating string data. The language includes several predefined string functions which provide many alternatives for converting data between strings and numbers.

This chapter covers the following topics:

- Using Visual Basic's string functions
- Forming string expressions
- Comparing strings
- String type conversion
- Working with strings stored in Variant variables

Fundamental String Concepts

Before discussing the string functions, you need to understand the following fundamental concepts of string manipulation:

- Length of a string
- The null string
- Joining strings
- Forming string expressions

Length of a String

Every data string has a *length*. This length is simply the number of text characters (including blank spaces and punctuation) that compose the string. The string `Hello` has a length of five, for example. The string `Paris, Texas` has a length of 12 (including the comma and blank space). The maximum-length string is 65,535 characters (64K).

A *string variable* also has a length. The length of a string variable is the length of the data string currently stored in the variable.

 NOTE Memory overhead is required for string storage. This overhead is part of the memory allocated to any string. As a result, the maximum-length string is somewhat less than 65,535 characters. In practice, string lengths rarely approach anything close to the theoretical maximum.

The Null String

A string can have a length of zero. Such a string is called a *null string*. You form a null string by placing two quotation marks together. For example:

```
MyText$ = ""
```

`MyText$` has a length of `0` (the null string) because of the two quotation marks.

Don't confuse the null string with one consisting of a single blank space, which has a length of `1`. When you *display* the null string with a `Print` or `MsgBox` instruction, you do not get any characters at all (not even a blank space). Note the following example:

```
Part1$ = "check"
Part2$ = "book"
```

```
Middle$ = ""            'null string
Print Part1$; Middle$; Part2$
Middle$ = " "           'one blank space
Print Part1$; Middle$; Part2$
```

The result is

```
checkbook
check book
```

Also, don't confuse the null string with the Null value of a Variant variable. Null is a special value (neither string nor numeric) that you can assign only to Variant variables. For more information on Null, see Chapter 14, "Language Building Blocks."

Joining Strings

Recall from Chapter 14 that you use either the plus (+) or ampersand (&) operator to join two strings. This process, called concatenation, forms a new string that comprises the first string immediately followed by the second.

When you concatenate two strings together, the length of the result is the sum of the lengths of the two operand strings. For example, consider this program fragment:

```
FirstPart$ = "Don't rock"
Result$ = FirstPart$ & "the boat."
MsgBox Result$
```

The output is

```
Don't rockthe boat.
```

Concatenation does not do any formatting, trimming, or padding with blank characters. In the preceding example, to add a blank space between rock and the, you must change the program. The following is one solution (with the second line changed):

```
FirstPart$ = "Don't rock"
Result$ = FirstPart$ & " the boat."    'blank space before the
MsgBox Result$
```

Now, the output is more readable:

```
Don't rock the boat.
```

T I P   When concatenating strings, use the ampersand operator rather than the plus. That way, you avoid possible ambiguity with the plus sign as the operator for numeric addition, and make your code more understandable.

String Expressions

You can form string expressions as well as numeric ones. The term *string expression* refers to any expression that evaluates to a single string value.

A string expression can be as simple as a single variable name or as complex as a combination of string literals, variables, functions, and the ampersand or plus signs. Table 17.1 shows some examples of string expressions.

Table 17.1. Sample string expressions.

Expression	Comment
`"Bart and Homer"`	Single literal
`Title$`	Single variable
`Left$(Title$, 3)`	String function
`"Mortimer" & LastName$`	Combination expression

Using the String Functions and Statements

As Table 17.2 shows, Visual Basic provides several built-in functions and statements that manipulate strings.

Table 17.2. String functions and statements.

Finding String Length

Name	Type	Description
`Len`	Function	Returns length of string

Converting Case

Name	Type	Description
LCase$, LCase	Function	Converts string to lowercase
UCase$, UCase	Function	Converts string to uppercase

Returning a Substring

Name	Type	Description
Left$, Left	Function	Returns characters at far left
Right$, Right	Function	Returns characters at far right
Mid$, Mid	Function	Returns substring
LTrim$, LTrim	Function	Strips blanks from left of string
RTrim$, RTrim	Function	Strips blanks from right of string
Trim$, Trim	Function	Strips blanks from both ends of string

Converting to and from ANSI

Name	Type	Description
Asc	Function	Returns ANSI (or ASCII) value of a character
Chr$, Chr	Function	Returns character from ANSI value

Converting between Strings and Numbers

Name	Type	Description
Val	Function	Converts string to number
Str$, Str	Function	Converts number to string form
Hex$, Hex	Function	Converts number to hex string
Oct$, Oct	Function	Converts number to octal string
CInt	Function	Converts string to Integer number
CLng	Function	Converts string to Long number
CSng	Function	Converts string to Single number
CDbl	Function	Converts string to Double number
CCur	Function	Converts string to Currency number

continues

Table 17.2. Continued

Converting Data Values to Formatted Strings

Name	Type	Description
Format$, Format	Function	Formats data values to strings

Searching for Substrings

Name	Type	Description
InStr	Function	Searches for substrings

Generating Strings

Name	Type	Description
String$, String	Function	Constructs a string of identical characters
Space$, Space	Function	Constructs a string of blank spaces

Comparing Strings

Name	Type	Description
StrComp	Function	Compares two strings
Option Compare	Statement	Sets comparison mode

Modifying a String Variable

Name	Type	Description
LSet	Statement	Left-justifies a string
RSet	Statement	Right-justifies a string
Mid$	Statement	Merges one string with another

All these functions and statements work with strings. Consider the functions listed on the left side of the table. Some functions return numeric values, and others return string values. The functions that return string values have a dollar sign at the end of the function name. Functions that return numeric values do not end with a dollar sign. However, the functions that return numeric values take string arguments.

The functions that end with a dollar sign can be expressed also without it. Such functions are shown in pairs on the same row of the table. The form without the dollar sign returns a Variant value. The LCase$ function, for example, returns a string value suitable for storing in a variable of type String. The LCase function returns a value suitable for storing in a Variant variable. For more information on manipulating string values in Variant variables, see "Using Strings with Variant Variables," later in this chapter.

Finding String Length

You can use Len to find the length of a string.

```
Len(string)
```
in which

```
    string is a string expression.
```

Consider the following program fragment:

```
NullString$=""          'The double quotes form a null string
Print Len(NullString$)
MyName$ = "Phil Feldman"
Print Len(MyName$)
Print Len("You had to be there")
```

The output is

```
0
12
19
```

Converting Case

You can use LCase$ and UCase$ to convert strings to lower- or uppercase.

LCase$(*strexpr*)

UCase$(*strexpr*)

in which

> *strexpr* is a general string expression.

The LCase$ function returns a copy of *strexpr* that has all uppercase letters converted to lowercase. Nonalphabetic characters, such as digits and punctuation symbols, remain unchanged. Similarly, UCase$ converts all the lowercase letters of *strexpr* to uppercase.

The following is a Sub procedure that shows LCase$ and UCase$ in action:

```
Sub TryCase ()
    Test$ = "Learning Visual Basic is as easy as 1-2-3."
    Print Test$
    Print LCase$(Test$)
    Print UCase$(Test$)
End Sub
```

The output is

```
Learning Visual Basic is as easy as 1-2-3.
learning visual basic is as easy as 1-2-3.
LEARNING VISUAL BASIC IS AS EASY AS 1-2-3.
```

UCase$ is handy when you need to test a user's response. Suppose your program requires that the user be familiar with a special password to access sensitive information. If the user types the correct password, the program displays the information. Suppose that "Big Deal" is the password, and you don't care how the user capitalizes it. The following procedure tests your user's response with one If instruction:

```
Sub TestPassword ()
    Password$ = "BIG DEAL"    'Password defined with all caps
    Response$ = InputBox$("Please type the password to continue")
    If UCase$(Response$) = Password$ Then
        Rem  Display the sensitive info here
    Else
        MsgBox ("Sorry, you entered the wrong password")
    End If
End Sub
```

At this point, the sensitive information displays if the user's response is `Big Deal`, `BIG DEAL`, `big deal`, or even `bIg DeAl`. You do not need to test for the various capitalizations individually. For another method of programming such string comparisons, see the discussion on the `Option Compare` statement, later in this chapter.

> To return Variant values rather than strings, use the `UCase` and `LCase` functions, which work similarly to `UCase$` and `LCase$`, respectively.
>
> **T I P**

Returning a Substring

The `Left$`, `Right$`, and `Mid$` functions return a portion of a string. A portion of a larger string is referred to as a *substring*. `water`, for example, is a substring of `Clearwater`.

To use `Left$`, `Right$`, or `Mid$`, you must specify the length of the desired substring (the number of characters you want returned), and its beginning position in the original string. (The *stringlength* parameter for `Mid$` is optional.)

```
Left$(string, stringlength)

Right$(string, stringlength)

Mid$(string, startposition)
```
or
```
Mid$(string, startposition, stringlength)
```
in which

    string is a string expression;

    stringlength specifies the length of the substring to return,

and

    startposition specifies the position in *string* in which the substring starts.

The *Left$* and *Right$* Functions

Left$ returns a substring copied from the characters to the far left in *string*. Similarly, Right$ extracts the characters to the far right in *string*. The *stringlength* parameter must be in the range from 0 to 65,535. If *stringlength* is zero, a null string is returned. If *stringlength* is greater than the length of *string*, the entire *string* is returned.

The following is a simple example of Left$ and Right$:

```
Test$ = "Bill says hello to Hillary"
Print Left$(Test$, 15)    'leftmost 15 characters of Test$
Print Right$(Test$, 16)   'rightmost 16 characters of Test$
```

The output is as follows:

```
Bill says hello
hello to Hillary
```

The Left and Right functions return values of type Variant. For example:

```
Dim StateAbbr        'Declare variable of type Variant
StateName$ = "California"
StateAbbr = Left(StateName$, 3)
```

The *Mid$* Function

The Mid$ function extracts a substring from *string*. The *stringlength* and *startposition* parameters must be in the range from 1 to 65,535.

Mid$ returns a substring that begins at *startposition* and has a length of *stringlength* characters. If *startposition* is 6 and *stringlength* is 4, for example, Mid$ returns the sixth through ninth characters of *string*.

The following example should clarify the way Mid$ works:

```
Test$ = "Every good boy does fine"
Print Mid$(Test$, 7, 8)       'characters 7,8,9,10,11,12,13,14
Print Mid$(Test$, 12, 3)      'characters 12,13,14
Print Mid$(Test$, 12)         'characters 12 to end of string
Print Mid$(Test$ & " work in school", 12, 18)
```

The output is

```
good boy
boy
boy does fine
boy does fine work
```

Notice that Mid$ has two forms: with and without the *stringlength* parameter. If you omit *stringlength*, Mid$ returns all characters from *startposition* to the end of *string*. You get the same effect in the three-parameter form when *string* contains less than *stringlength* characters from *startposition* to the end of *string*.

In the preceding example, the first, second, and fourth lines use the three-parameter form of Mid$. The third line uses the two-parameter form.

If *startposition* is greater than the length of *string*, Mid$ simply returns a null string.

The Mid function (with no dollar sign) returns a value of type Variant.

The *LTrim$*, *RTrim$*, and *Trim$* Functions

LTrim$ and RTrim$ strip blanks from the left and right sides of a string, respectively. Trim$ strips blanks from both ends of a string.

LTrim$(*strexpr*)

RTrim$(*strexpr*)

Trim$(*strexpr*)

in which

   strexpr is a general string expression.

If a picture box named Picture1 is defined, for example, the following Print method displays Goodnight left-justified, within the picture box frame. The leading blanks in Message$ are removed:

```
Message$ = "        Goodnight"
Picture1.Print LTrim$(Message$)
```

LTrim$ often is used to create message strings that display numeric values. This commonly occurs when displaying numeric output with MsgBox statements. For additional information on this topic, see "Converting Strings to Numbers" later in this chapter.

The LTrim, RTrim, and Trim functions complement the LTrim$, RTrim$, and Trim$ functions, respectively. The difference is that LTrim, RTrim, and Trim return values of type Variant, while the functions ending with the dollar sign return string values.

Converting Strings to ASCII and ANSI

Every string character has an associated numeric value from 0 to 255. These values conform to a special code known as ANSI (American National Standards Institute). The uppercase letter "A" has an ANSI value of 65, for example. The lowercase letter "a" is 9. A blank space is 32. Appendix B lists all the ANSI values and the associated characters.

The functions Asc and Chr$ convert between string characters and numeric ANSI values—Asc returns the ANSI value for a given string character, and Chr$ returns the string character corresponding to a given ANSI value.

 NOTE The Asc function is named in reference to the ASCII character set. The ASCII set was a precursor to the ANSI set. For more about ASCII and ANSI, see the upcoming section titled "Understanding the ANSI and ASCII Character Sets."

Asc(*strexpr*)

Chr$(*ANSIcode*)

in which

 strexpr is a string expression,

and

 ANSIcode is an ANSI code value in the range from 0 to 255.

Notice that Chr$ ends with a dollar sign, but Asc does not. Chr$ is a string function that takes a numeric argument, but returns a string value. Asc, on the other hand, takes a string argument (including a Variant of type String), but returns a numeric value.

Asc returns the ANSI value of the first character in the *strexpr* argument. If *strexpr* is a null string, a runtime error occurs (Illegal function call). Chr$ complements Asc, and returns the single-character string that corresponds to the value of *ANSIcode*. Chr$(65) returns A, for example. The following is an example of Asc in action:

```
Print Asc("A")
Print Asc("Apples")
Print Asc("2")
Motto$ = "23 Skidoo"
Print Asc(Motto$)
```

The result is

```
65
65
50
50
```

Chr$ enables you to display characters that are included in the ANSI character set, but not directly available from the keyboard. Suppose that you want to display the cents symbol, ¢, as part of an output string. The ANSI value for the cents symbol is 162. The following program fragment uses Chr$(162) to display the cents symbol as part of a message string:

```
Message$ = "Bubble gum costs 25" & Chr$(162)
MsgBox Message$
```

The following result appears in the Message Box:

```
Bubble gum costs 25¢
```

> The Chr function (without a dollar sign) returns a single-character value of type Variant.
>
> **T I P**

Understanding the ANSI and ASCII Character Sets

Users of QBasic and other versions of BASIC might be familiar with a numbered character set similar to ANSI—namely the ASCII character set (American Standard Code for Information Interchange). The original ASCII character set was limited to numeric values in the range from 1 to 127. Later, an Extended ASCII character set added values from 128 to 255.

Visual Basic's ANSI character set is a superset of the original ASCII character set; values from 1 to 127 define the same characters in both ASCII and ANSI. The characters associated with the values from 128 to 255, however, differ between ANSI and Extended ASCII (although many characters appear in each set at different numeric values).

The name of Visual Basic's Asc function suggests the historical link between ASCII and ANSI. Earlier versions of the BASIC language contained the ASC function that returned the ASCII code of a character string. Visual Basic retained this Asc name, although Ans or Ansi would be more accurate. To get an idea of the characters included in the ANSI character set, see Appendix B.

Not all numeric values correlate to an ANSI character that can be displayed. Some values produce special effects. For example, `Chr$(9)` produces a Tab, and `Chr$(10)`, a line feed. Not all character values technically defined in the ANSI set are supported by Windows. Each numeric value in the twenties, for example, does not result in any printable character or special effect. (For more information, see Appendix B.)

Creating Linefeeds

`Chr$` frequently is used to add linefeeds and carriage returns to message strings. This way, a message box or multiline text box can display multiple lines of output. The ANSI values of 13 and 10 are special *characters* that correspond to the carriage return and line feed, respectively. You can define a form-level string variable called `NewLine` as follows:

```
NewLine = Chr$(13) & Chr$(10)
```

`NewLine` can be concatenated with other strings to form a single string that contains linefeeds. For example:

```
MailAddress$ = "Occupant" & NewLine
MailAddress$ = MailAddress$ & "235 Lover's Lane" & NewLine
MailAddress$ = MailAddress$ & "Aleutian Islands, Alaska"
MsgBox MailAddress$
```

The message box displays multiline output as follows:

```
Occupant
235 Lover's Lane
Aleutian Islands, Alaska
```

Converting Strings to Numbers

Frequently, your Visual Basic applications need to treat a numeric quantity (such as the value of a variable) as a string. In such a case, you want to convert a number into a string. At other times, you need the capability to do the opposite—to interpret a string as a number.

In many practical applications, values displayed to, and input read from, the user are done with strings. As a result, conversion between numbers and strings comes into play in the following two common situations:

■ When the user types string data containing numeric values into a text box, in response to an `InputBox$` function, or similar mechanism, your program must convert the numeric part of the string into numeric form for processing by the program.

■ When the program displays string output containing numeric data in a text box, MsgBox statement, or similar mechanism, your program must convert the data into string form to create a message string suitable for display.

As explained in the following sections, Visual Basic includes several functions that enable you to convert between numbers and strings. Variant variables also can convert automatically between numbers and strings.

Using the *Str$* and *Val* Functions

The Str$ and Val functions convert between strings and numeric values.

Str$(*numexpr*)

Val(*stringexpr*)

in which

    numexpr is a general numeric expression,

and

    stringexpr is a string expression.

Str$ converts *numexpr* into string form. The first character of the resultant string contains the sign of the number. If *numexpr* is negative, this first character is a minus sign. If *numexpr* is zero or positive, Str$ makes the first character a blank space (indicating an implied plus sign). The following is an example:

```
Number! = 1.8
Num$ = Str$(Number!)
Print "XXXXX"
Print Num$
Print Len(Num$)
```

The output is

```
XXXXX
 1.8
4
```

The Str$ function converts the number 1.8 into the string " 1.8" (with a blank space before the 1.) The output confirms the leading space, and shows the string length of Num$ as 4. (The 4 characters are the leading space, plus the three characters in 1.8.) The Str function (no dollar sign) returns a value of type Variant.

Converting numbers into strings enables you to manipulate numbers with the various string functions, and often makes it easier to format output. The following program fragment, for example, displays a dividend check amount surrounded by 3 dashes on each side. The code uses Print to display the results in a picture box named Picture1.

```
Dividend@ = 458.62
Amount$ = Str$(Dividend@)          'Convert Dividend@ to string
NewAmount$ = LTrim$(Amount$)
' Note: Above line strips the leading blank from Amount$
Picture1.Print "Check amount is --"; NewAmount$; "--"
```

The output is as follows:

```
Check amount is --458.62--
```

The point of this exercise is that if the Print instruction uses Dividend@ or Amount$ rather than NewAmount$, the output contains an annoying blank just before the number (The blank jeopardizes the security intended with the hyphens by leaving a space where another digit could be added to the check amount):

```
Check amount is -- 458.62--
```

The Val function complements Str$, and converts a string to a numeric value. Val works by examining *stringexpr* from left to right until the first character, which cannot be interpreted as part of a number, occurs. (Blank spaces are ignored.) Val("76 trombones"), for example, returns 76.

If the first nonblank character of *stringexpr* is non-numeric, Val returns the value of 0. Table 17.3 shows examples of the Val function.

Table 17.3. Results of the *Val* function.

String	*Val*(String)	Comment
"43.21"	43.21	Val converts the string to the number.
"28,631,409"	28	Val does not *understand* commas; conversion stops at the first comma.
" 14"	14	Leading blanks are ignored.
"-19"	−19	Negative numbers are acknowledged.
"- 1 9"	−19	Internal blanks are ignored.
"Twelve"	0	Val returns 0 when the string is non-numeric.
"$23.44"	0	Val does not recognize the dollar sign as part of a numeric string.
"Lotus123"	0	Val does not find embedded numbers. The L immediately signals a non-numeric string.

Val returns a double-precision numeric value. When Val appears on the right side of an instruction assigning a value to a variable, Visual Basic converts the returned value to the data type of the variable.

Variant variables do not need Val because Visual Basic converts between strings and numbers automatically. For more information on this topic, see "Using Strings in Variant Variables," later in this chapter.

Converting Numbers to Hexadecimal and Octal Strings

Similar to binary numbers, hexadecimal and octal numbers are specialized numbering systems appropriate for manipulating memory addresses and byte values. Two specialized functions, Hex$ and Oct$, convert regular decimal numbers into hexadecimal and octal strings, respectively. The Hex and Oct functions convert regular decimal numbers into Variants. Hex$(2766), for example, returns the string ACE.

Using the Type-Conversion Functions

Chapter 16, "Working with Numbers," introduced the type-conversion functions that convert values from one numeric data type into another. CDbl, for example, converts to double-precision. These type-conversion functions work also with string arguments. CDbl("17"), for example, returns the numeric value 17 in double-precision form.

With reference to converting a string argument to a number, there is a difference between Val and these type-conversion functions. If the string argument cannot be interpreted as a number, Val returns 0, but the type-conversion functions produce the Type mismatch error.

Consider the following program fragment:

```
Test1$ = "100"
Test2$ = "One-hundred"
Print Val(Test1$)
Print CCur(Test1$)
Print Val(Test2$)
Print CCur(Test2$)
```

The result is

```
100
100
0
```

Then, `CCur(Test2$)` produces a `Type mismatch` error because the input string contains letters that cannot be interpreted as a string representation of a numeric value. Notice that `Val(Test2$)` produces `0`, a result that represents a failure to interpret the string as a numeric value.

Formatting Strings with *Format$*

Besides `Str$`, Visual Basic has another function that converts numeric data to string form—the `Format$` function. `Format$` is a flexible function that can format not only numeric data, but also dates, times, and other strings. With `Format$`, you can optionally specify a formatting string that indicates the way in which the output string should appear. The `Format` function (no dollar sign) returns a value of type Variant.

`Format$(`*expr*`)`

or

`Format$(`*expr*`, `*formatexpr*`)`

in which

   expr is a string or numeric expression to be formatted,

and

   formatexpr is a string expression that specifies how *expr* is to be formatted.

If you omit the *formatexpr* argument, and *expr* is a numeric expression, the `Format$` function converts the number to a string. The result is similar to using the `Str$` function, except that, if the number is positive, the value returned by `Format$` does not have a leading blank space. If *expr* is a string expression, and you omit *formatexpr*, the `Format$` function simply returns the value of *expr*.

`Format$` permits a myriad of possible formatting strings. The following sections provide some examples of the available formats. For more information, consult the Microsoft documentation, or Visual Basic's online Help system.

T I P   When used in conjunction with `Print`, the `Format$` function provides capabilities similar to the `PRINT USING` instruction from QBasic and QuickBASIC. `Format$`, however, contains many more options than `PRINT USING`.

Formatting Numeric Values with *Format$*

The best way to understand `Format$` is to study how it is used in some examples. Consider the following instruction:

```
Print Format$(4 / 3, "#.###")
```

Visual Basic displays the following output:

```
1.333
```

In the format string, the character # specifies that a digit should appear in this position (if the expression has a digit in that place).

Notice that the expression to be formatted is numeric, while the format is specified with a string. You can use variables within the `Format$` function, such as `Format$(MyNum!, MyFormat$)`.

Table 17.4 shows the special characters used in the numeric formatting strings.

Table 17.4. Numeric formatting characters.

Character	Meaning
#	Displays a digit (0 through 9) if one exists in the position occupied by the # symbol. Otherwise, displays nothing.
0	Displays a digit (0 through 9) if one exists in the position occupied by the 0 symbol. Otherwise, displays a zero.
.	Displays a period at the specified position.
,	Displays a comma between every three consecutive digits to the left of the decimal point.
%	Multiplies the expression by 100, and displays the percent sign at the position specified.
E+, E-, e+, e-	Specifies scientific format.
Other	Most other characters appear verbatim. The dollar sign $ in the format string, for example, displays as such in the formatted output.

Suppose that `MyNum!` = 1234.5. Table 17.5 shows the formatted strings produced by `Format$(MyNum!, MyForm$)` and `Format$(-MyNum!, MyForm$)` for various examples of `MyForm$`.

Table 17.5. Examples of the *Format$* function.

MyForm$	*MyNum!*	*-MyNum!*
"#.###"	1234.5	-1234.5
"###,#.##"	1,234.5	-1,234.5
"0.000"	1234.500	-1234.500
"0%"	123450%	-123450%
"$0.00"	$1234.50	-$1234.50
"0.00E+00"	1.23E+03	-1.23E+03

Multipart Format Strings

The format string can be expressed in two or three parts, with each separated by a semicolon. In the two-part form, the first format applies if the number is positive, and the second, if it is negative. In the three-part form, the second part applies if the number is zero.

One common use of the two-part form is to express financial numbers differently, depending on whether the numbers are positive or negative. The format "$0.00;($0.00)", for example, expresses a positive number normally, but encloses a negative number in parentheses. The number 1234.5 displays as $1234.50, for example, while –1234.5 appears as ($1234.50).

Predefined Formats

Format$ defines some predetermined format names that can be used for the format string. Acceptable names include Currency, Fixed, Standard, Percent, Scientific, and True/False. Format(1234.5, "Currency"), for example, yields $1,234.50.

Formatting Dates and Times with *Format$*

In Visual Basic, numbers can represent date and time information. Such dates and times are stored as serial numbers in floating point form (Single or Double). Visual Basic includes several special formatting characters that represent date and time information.

day, month, and year formats, for example, can be expressed with the special characters d, m, and y. The string "dd" means to display the day (of the month) as a two-digit number between 01 and 31. The string "ddd" means to display the day as a three-character abbreviation for the day of the week (Sun-Sat). Other day formats exist, as well as several different ones for month, year, and for time information.

The format string `"m/d/y"` displays information in the form month/day/year. A sample result is `10/13/84`.

Several predefined formats exist for date and time information. These formats include `"Long Date"`, `"Short Date"`, `"Long Time"`, and `"Short Time"`.

Formatting Strings with *Format$*

`Format$` also can format a target string under the control of a format string. Table 17.6 shows special characters available for formatting strings.

Character	Meaning
Table 17.6. String formatting characters used with *Format$*.	
&	Displays the character found in this position. If no character is present, nothing appears.
@	Displays the character found in this position. If no character is present, a blank space appears.
<	Displays alphabetic characters in lowercase.
>	Displays alphabetic characters in uppercase. `Format$("Upper Class", ">")`, for example, returns UPPER CLASS.

The following program fragment demonstrates the formatting of string data.

```
Print Format$("Hello", "@ Mary Lou")
Print Format$("and ", "&Ladies &&&&Gentlemen")
Print Format$("Big Deal", "<")
Print Format$("Goodbye", ">")
```

The result is

```
Hello Mary Lou
Ladies and Gentlemen
big deal
GOODBYE
```

Searching for a Substring

Many string-processing programs need to search a large string (or several different strings) to see if a particular substring is present. A program that handles full names of employees, for example, might need to find everyone with the last name Smith.

The InStr function searches a string for a specified substring, and returns the position in which it is found. Visual Basic has three forms of the InStr function. (The *startposition* and *comparemode* parameters are optional.)

InStr(*targetstr*, *substr*)

or

InStr(*startposition*, *targetstr*, *substr*)

or

InStr(*startposition*, *targetstr*, *substr*, *comparemode*)

in which

    startposition specifies the character position in which the search begins;

    targetstr is the string that is searched;

    substr is the string for which the search is undertaken;

and

    comparemode specifies the string-comparison method.

InStr searches the target string from left to right for the first occurrence of *substr*. In the two-parameter form of InStr (without the *startposition* parameter), the search begins at the first character of the target string. In the three- or four-parameter form (with *startposition*), you can specify at which character in the target string you want the search to begin.

InStr returns a numeric value. This value indicates whether a match is found, then specifies its location. A value of 0 means that no match was found (or a special condition has occurred, see Table 17.7). A positive value indicates the position in *targetstr* in which the substring begins. Table 17.7 shows how to interpret a value returned by InStr.

Table 17.7. The results of *InStr*.

Condition	Result of *InStr*
Match is found	Position in which the match occurs
No match is found	0
startposition greater than Len(*targetstr*)	0
targetstr is null ("")	0
substr is null	Value of *startposition*, if given; otherwise 1

For example:

```
Target$ = "The one and only one"
Print InStr(Target$, "one")
Print InStr(7, Target$, "one")
```

The output is

```
5
18
```

Comparison Modes

The *comparemode* parameter, if present, specifies whether the search method should be case-sensitive. The value of *comparemode* is 0 or 1.

If *comparemode* is 0, the search is case-sensitive. That means that an uppercase letter does not match its lowercase counterpart. Uppercase A, for example, does not match lowercase a.

If *comparemode* is 1, the search is not case-sensitive; an uppercase letter matches its lowercase counterpart. Uppercase A, for example, matches lowercase a.

If you omit *comparemode*, Visual Basic uses the default comparison mode of the current module. That mode is case-sensitive (equivalent to *comparemode* = 0), unless you change the default with an Option Compare instruction. For more information on Option Compare, see "Comparing Strings" later in this chapter.

Logical Testing for Substrings

Notice that the Instr function returns a nonzero value if the substring is found, and 0 if it is not in the target string. You can write If tests involving Instr without using a relational operator, because Visual Basic treats 0 as False, and any nonzero value as True. For example:

```
If Instr(Target$, SubString$) Then
    Print "Substring$ does occur in Target$"
Else
    Print "Substring$ does not occur in Target$"
End If
```

The If instruction in this example is equivalent to the following:

```
If Instr(Target$, SubString$) <> 0 Then...
```

Generating Strings of Repeated Characters

The String$ function generates a specified number of identical characters.

String$(*strlength*, *ANSIcode*)

or

String$(*strlength*, *strexpr*)

in which

    strlength specifies the length of the string to return;

    ANSIcode specifies the ANSI code (0 to 255) of the repeating character;

and

    strexpr is a string expression whose first character specifies the repeating one.

The ANSI code for the plus sign, for example, is 43, thus String$(8, 43) creates a string of eight plus signs. String$ often is used to embellish output, as in the following example:

```
Plus$ = String$(8, 43)
Message$ = Plus$ & " Today's News " & Plus$
MsgBox Message$
```

The output in the message box is as follows:

```
++++++++ Today's News ++++++++
```

Notice that the repeating character can be specified with an explicit ANSI value, or with a string expression; the second argument for String$ can be a numerical ANSI code, or a string. The following is the previous program fragment using the latter form of String$:

```
Plus$ = String$(8, "+")
Message$ = Plus$ & " Today's News " & Plus$
MsgBox Message$
```

Both versions of String$ return the identical string of eight plus signs. The String function (no dollar sign) returns a value of type Variant. When the repeating character is a blank space, a special function is available.

Space$(*numspaces*)

in which

    numspaces specifies the number of spaces to return in the range from 0 to 65,535.

The ANSI code for a blank space is 32, so the function Space$(*numspaces*) returns the same string as String$(*strlength*, 32), assuming that the values of *numspaces* and *strlength* are the same. The Space function (no dollar sign) returns a value of type Variant.

Modifying a String Variable

The Mid$ statement replaces part of a string variable's value with another specified string. (The *length* parameter is optional.)

Mid$(*strvar*, *position*, *length*) = *strexpr*

or

Mid$(*strvar*, *position*) = *strexpr*

in which

    strvar is a string variable whose contents are to be modified;

    position is an Integer (or Long) expression specifying the position in *strvar* in which the replacement begins;

continues

continued

>   *length* is an Integer (or Long) expression specifying the number of characters to be replaced;

and

>   *strexpr* is a general string expression specifying the replacement string.

Consider the following instruction:

```
Mid$(Check$, 7, 4) = "highway"
```

This instruction replaces the seventh through tenth characters of `Check$` with the string `"high"`.

When the length of *strexpr* is greater than the value of *length* (as in the preceding example), only the first length characters are replaced.

If you omit the optional *length* parameter, all of *strexpr* is substituted into *strvar*. The original length of *strvar*, however, is never modified by `Mid$`. The replacement of characters terminates at the final character position of *strvar*. If the position is beyond the end of *strvar*, an `Illegal function call` error occurs.

Each of the position and length arguments must have a value between 1 and (approximately) 65,535. Table 17.9 shows various examples of `Mid$` in use. In each case, the initial value of `Test$` is `"Days of wine and roses."`

Table 17.9. Example of *Mid$* instructions.

Instruction	Final value of *Test$*
`Mid$(Test$, 9) = "soda"`	Days of soda and roses.
`Mid$(Test$, 9, 4) = "sodapop"`	Days of soda and roses.
`Mid$(Test$, 14) = "not"`	Days of wine, not roses.
`Mid$(Test$, 18) = "carnations."`	Days of wine and carnations.

Don't confuse the `Mid$` statement discussed here with the `Mid$` function covered earlier in this chapter. The `Mid$` statement replaces text within an existing string variable. The `Mid$` function returns text extracted from a string variable. (You can write the `Mid$` statement simply as `Mid`, without the dollar sign. Both forms produce identical results.)

The `LSet` and `RSet` statements left-justify and right-justify, respectively, a string expression within a given string variable.

LSet *strvar* = *strexpr*

RSet *strvar* = *strexpr*

in which

    strvar is a string variable,

and

    strexpr is a general string expression.

LSet and RSet assign the value of *strexpr* to the variable *strvar*. The length of *strvar* does not change. If the length of *strexpr* is less than the length of *strvar*, blank spaces pad the remaining character positions. If the length of *strexpr* is greater than that of *strvar*, the extra characters are truncated.

LSet and RSet can format columnar output. The following program fragment, for example, right-justifies three strings in successive 15-character fields:

```
Field1$ = Space$(15): Field2$ = Field1$:  Field3$ = Field1$
RSet Field1$ = "Gilda"
RSet Field2$ = "Jeanette"
RSet Field3$ = "Mary"
Print Field1$; Field2$; Field3$
RSet Field1$ = "Phil"
RSet Field2$ = "Jim"
RSet Field3$ = "Jesse"
Print Field1$; Field2$; Field3$
```

The output consists of three right-justified columns:

```
    Gilda       Jeanette     Mary

     Phil            Jim    Jesse
```

LSet can be used also to assign one record variable to another. For more information on the use of LSet with record variables, see Chapter 25, "Processing Files."

Comparing Strings

In Chapter 15, "Program Flow and Decision Making," you saw that the relational operators can compare two strings as well as two numbers. You can write an If instruction that compares strings, such as the following:

```
If MyName$ > "Joe" Then . . .
```

just as you can write If's that compare numbers, such as

```
If MyAge% > 32 Then . . .
```

When examining two strings, Visual Basic compares the ANSI values of corresponding characters. The ranking order of the two strings depends on the first character position in which the two differ. The higher ANSI value determines the "larger" string. The longer string is considered "larger" when it begins with the identical characters of a shorter string. Two strings are equal only if each is the same length, and both consist of the identical sequence of characters. Each of the following expressions, for example, is True:

```
"upper" > "Upper"
```

```
"Apples" <> "Oranges"
```

```
"Foot" < "Football"
```

```
"Chocolate cake" < "Chocolate ice cream"
```

```
("Big" & "Deal") = "BigDeal"
```

```
"3" >= "3"
```

```
"36" > "3245"
```

Using the *StrComp* Function

You can compare two strings with the StrComp function. (The *comparemode* parameter is optional.)

StrComp(*strexpr1*, *strexpr2*)

or

StrComp(*strexpr1*, *strexpr2*, *comparemode*)

in which

    strexpr1 and *strexpr2* are general string expressions,

and

    comparemode specifies the string-comparison method.

StrComp returns a value that indicates whether *strexpr1* and *strexpr2* are identical. If they are not, the value indicates which string is larger. The value returned is of type Variant. Table 17.10 shows values returned by the StrComp function.

Table 17.10. Values returned by the *StrComp* function.

Result	Value Returned
strexpr1 < *strexpr2*	-1
strexpr1 = *strexpr2*	0
strexpr1 > *strexpr2*	1

The *comparemode* parameter, if present, specifies whether the comparison should be case-sensitive. This parameter works the same as the *comparemode* parameter used with the Instr function. When comparemode is 0, the comparison is case-sensitive (A <> a). When comparemode is 1, the comparison is not case-sensitive (A = a).

Comparing Strings with the *Like* Operator

Using the Like operator, you can compare two strings, as well as one against a string pattern. The result of the comparison is True (-1) or False (0).

In its simplest form, Like compares two strings. The following two instructions are equivalent:

```
If MyName$ = "Me" Then Print "It's me."

If MyName$ Like "Me" Then Print "It's me."
```

The real power and flexibility of Like, however, comes when you use a string pattern. The general form is as follows:

strexpr Like *pattern*

in which

    strexpr is a string expression,

and

    pattern is a string expression that specifies a string pattern that can include special characters.

The *pattern* operand can include the DOS wild-card characters (? and *) as well as other special characters. In Table 17.11, which shows pattern-matching characters, the term *charlist* refers to a group of one or more characters.

Table 17.11. Special pattern-matching characters.

Character	Match
?	Any one character
*	Any group of characters
#	Any one digit (0 through 9)
[*charlist*]	Any one character in *charlist*
[!*charlist*]	Any one character not in *charlist*

The following expressions, for example, are all True:

```
"Top" Like "T?p"
"Top" Like "T*"
"76 trombones" Like "## trombones"
"bill" Like "b[aeiu]ll"
"bill" Like "b[!abcdefg]ll
```

In Table 17.11, the brackets enclose a list of one or more characters. The match is successful if any of the characters in the list match the corresponding character in *strexpr*. If an exclamation point (!) precedes the list, the match is successful only if a character *not* in the list matches the corresponding one in *strexpr*.

In *charlist*, you can specify a character range by separating its lower- and uppercase characters with a hyphen. [a-z], for example, specifies any of the lowercase letters. You even can include multiple ranges by simply juxtaposing them (without any delimiting character). [a-zA-z], for example, specifies any alphabetic character.

Table 17.12 shows examples of True and False results obtained with pattern matching. In this table, the expression Test$ Like Pattern$ is examined for various values of Test$ and Pattern$.

Table 17.12. Results of the expression *Test$ Like Pattern$*.

Pattern$	*Test$* yields True	*Test$* yields False
"?B?"	"ABC", "1B2", "BBB"	"abc", "AB", "12B"
"*.BAT"	"DO.BAT", "WIN.BAT"	"DINGBAT", "DO.CAT"

Pattern$	Test$ yields True	Test$ yields False
"#.##*"	"1.23", "2.00 Tax"	"1.2", "2 Tax"
"#[ABC]"	"4A", "9B", "0C"	"A4", "23B", "3D"
"#[A-Z]"	"4A", "3D", "9Y"	"A4", "23B", "4$"
"#[!ABC]"	"3D", "6Y", "4H"	"4A", "23H", "AZ"

Changing the Comparison Mode with Option Compare

By default, string comparisons are case-sensitive. This means that a lowercase letter does *not* match its uppercase counterpart. In fact, a glance at the ANSI character set (Appendix B) reveals that every lowercase letter has a larger ANSI value than every uppercase letter.

You can change the default comparison mode with the Option Compare statement. The statement has two forms:

```
Option Compare Text

or

Option Compare Binary
```

Using an Option Compare Text instruction, you specify that comparisons are no longer case-sensitive. After this instruction, a lowercase letter is considered equal to its uppercase counterpart. With Option Compare Binary, you restore the default mode of case-sensitive comparisons.

> If the country setting in the Windows WIN.INI file is not set to United States, an Option Compare Text instruction can change the relative order of character values.

An Option Compare instruction cannot appear in a Sub or Function procedure. You must use Option Compare in the General declarations section at the form or module level.

An `Option Compare` instruction affects comparisons made with the `StrComp` and `Like` operators, string searches made with `InStr`, as well as string expressions formed with the relational operators. If in an `Instr` or `StrComp` instruction the *comparemode* parameter appears, however, it overrides the comparison mode established with `Option Compare`. Table 17.13 shows the effect of `Option Compare` on some sample string expressions. In this table, every expression is True.

Table 17.13. Effects of *Option Compare* instructions.	
Option Compare **Binary**	*Option Compare* **Text**
StrComp("a", "A") = 1	StrComp("a", "A") = 0
InStr("aA", "A") = 2	InStr("aA", "A") = 1
"ABC" Like "?B?"	"ABC" Like "?b?"
"upper" > "Upper"	"upper" = "Upper"

Remember the `TestPassword` procedure presented earlier in this chapter? In that procedure, the `UCase$` function provides a way to test whether a user's text input matches a password defined in uppercase letters. The following instruction enacts the test:

```
If UCase$(Response$) = Password$ Then ...
```

With an `Option Compare Text` instruction in effect, that same test can be expressed more simply as follows:

```
If Response$ = Password$ Then ...
```

Using Strings with Variant Variables

Variables of type Variant can work flexibly with both string and numeric data. Recall from Chapter 14, "Language Building Blocks," that Variant variables can convert back and forth between string and numeric values.

The following code fragment, for example, demonstrates that Variant variables smoothly handle string-numeric conversions:

```
Dim Test1, Test2            'Declare Variant variables
Test1 = "123"               'Test1 now holds string information
MyNum% = Test1              'Numeric conversion is done automatically
Print MyNum%, 2 * Test1
Test2 = 23.4                'Test2 now holds numeric information
Print Left$(Test2, 2)       'Data in Test2 is converted to string
```

The output is

```
 123        246
23
```

You can use the VarType function to determine whether the data in a Variant variable is of type String. If the Variant contains a string value, the function returns 8. When placed at the end of the previous code fragment, for example, the instruction Print VarType(Test1) returns 8. This value indicates that the current data stored in Test1 is a string.

The Advantages and Disadvantages of Variants

The fact that Variant variables can manipulate both string and numeric data, and convert easily back and forth, is something of a mixed blessing. On one hand, by using Variant variables, you can write code with a minimum number of functions and expressions. The MyNum$ = Test1 instruction in the previous code fragment, for example, bypasses the need for the Val function entirely. On the other hand, when the data stored in Variant variables frequently is changing between numeric and string values, code can be hard to interpret and debug. Logical errors in the coding might not manifest themselves readily because the Variant variables can so adeptly handle type conversion.

When using Variant variables, be sure to liberally document your code with comments. This is good advice for any kind of programming.　**T I P**

Using Variants with String Functions

The string functions work with Variant variables. You freely can use these variables when forming the string expressions used as arguments in string functions. If the data in a Variant variable is numeric, but the variable appears in an expression whose context requires string information, Visual Basic converts the Variant data to string form automatically. In the previous code fragment, for example, the instruction Print Left$(Test2, 2) converts the numeric data stored in the Variant Test2 before applying the Left$ function.

You also can write each string function that ends with a dollar sign without it. The form without the dollar sign returns a Variant value of type String. For example, the Left$ function returns a string, while Left returns a Variant (of type String).

NOTE The data stored in a Variant variable can be set to the special value `Null`. Don't confuse this `Null` value with a null string (the latter is a string value of zero length). `Null` indicates that the data in a Variant is missing, or unknown. When a Variant containing the value `Null` is used as an argument in a function that returns a Variant, the value returned is always `Null`. For more information on `Null`, see Chapter 14, "Language Building Blocks."

Converting Between Fixed-Length and Variable-Length Strings

Variable-length string variables are elastic. As the name implies, you can assign any string (including a fixed-length one) to such a variable. The length of the variable expands or contracts as necessary.

You also can assign any string value to a fixed-length string variable. Type conversion occurs as follows:

- If the length of the variable is greater than that of the string, the extra positions to the far right of the variable become blank spaces.

- If the length of the variable is less than that of the string, Visual Basic truncates the value of the string, keeping only the portion to the far left of it.

The following program fragment demonstrates this conversion:

```
MyName$ =  "Rumplestiltskin"   'MyName$ is variable-length
Dim YourName As String * 6     'YourName is fixed-length
YourName = MyName$             'Truncation occurs
Print YourName
YourName = "Al"                'Blank padding occurs
Print YourName; "XXX"
MyName$ = "Al"                 'Variable-length reassignment
Print MyName$; "XXX"
```

The following is the output:

```
Rumple
Al    XXX
AlXXX
```

Notice the four blank spaces in the middle line of the output. The (fixed-length) string variable `YourName` consists of six characters (the two letters "Al" followed by four blank spaces).

Summary

Manipulation of strings is fundamental to Visual Basic programming. Many controls, such as text and list boxes, and labels, work exclusively with strings. Message and input boxes require strings for communication with the user. You must convert data back and forth between numbers and strings frequently.

The length of a string simply is the number of characters in it. Every string character has an associated numeric value from 0 to 255. These values compose the ANSI character code. With ANSI, you can compare strings, and determine which one is larger. This lets you use strings as well as numbers in relational expressions.

The string functions make complex manipulations easy. Visual Basic includes functions that find a string length (Len); convert ANSI values to strings (Chr$); find a substring (Mid$); compare strings (StrComp$); format strings (Format$); and convert a string to a number (Val).

Variant variables can store string or numeric data. Values stored in Variants convert between numeric and string forms automatically, depending on the context in which the Variants appear. The string functions (that end with a dollar sign) have a companion form (without a dollar sign) that returns a Variant value.

Using Procedures: Subs and Functions

D ivide and conquer. This maxim has been the guiding force behind a myriad of achievements—from putting a man on the moon to waging war to creating a movie epic. The idea is simple: Tackle a large-scale task by partitioning it into a group of subtasks. It's much easier to complete a collection of smaller tasks than a large one.

This step-by-step approach applies also when you work on Visual Basic projects. A complex programming job can seem bewildering, almost impossible. When you concentrate on breaking the whole project into a collection of smaller ones, however, the job suddenly seems achievable.

The idea of breaking a large program into isolated chunks is one of the cornerstones of modern *structured programming*. With Visual Basic, you can create your own program units—called *user-defined procedures* or *general procedures*. Such procedures can be as simple or as complex as you like. They can be invoked also from other parts of your program code—including the event and other user-defined procedures.

You are familiar with the principles of creating and using event procedures. As you know, these procedures are the heart and soul of Visual Basic's event-driven program model. At times, you might find your event procedures becoming too long (more than 40 program lines or so), or several of them need the same action performed. If either of these situations applies, consider "off-loading" some of the program work to user-defined procedures. This chapter shows you how to do this.

Introducing General Procedures

Essentially, general procedures provide a technique for defining your own statements, methods, and functions to supplement those built into Visual Basic.

As you know, an event procedure activates when a particular event occurs in the application. By contrast, a general procedure activates *only* when explicitly called from a program instruction. The call can come from an instruction in either a general or event procedure (or even the same general procedure).

Visual Basic supports two kinds of general procedures:

- *Sub* (sometimes called a *subprogram*). A Sub is similar to a user-defined statement or method.

- *User-defined function.* The name is self-explanatory. A user-defined function adds a new one to the body of built-in functions predefined in Visual Basic.

General procedures enjoy special status in a programming project. The following are the four main features of procedures; these concepts are discussed throughout this chapter:

- *A general procedure can be defined at the form or module level.* At the form level, a general procedure is defined in the General Declarations section of a form. The procedure has scope throughout the form. That is, the procedure can be called from any event or general procedure in the form. Form-level general procedures are saved as part of the form's .FRM file.

  At the module level, a general procedure is defined in the General Declarations section of a code module. Such a procedure has scope throughout the application—including all forms and code modules that compose it. Module-level general procedures are saved as part of the code module's .BAS file.

- *General procedures are isolated from other program components.* Similar to event procedures, Visual Basic maintains general procedures in the editor environment as items that can be individually tested, and edited.

- *General procedures use local variables.* Variables established in a procedure have scope only within it. Such variables are "invisible" to program code outside the procedure. If in a code module, or a general or event procedure, a variable coincidentally has the same name as another one in a particular general procedure, the two variables are distinct entities. Local variables maintain the autonomy of a procedure.

- *General procedures can pass parameter values back and forth to the calling instruction.* Such parameters can be variables, expressions, controls, or even forms. Each call to a procedure can pass different values to it.

Using Sub Procedures

A Sub procedure is a block of instructions that begins with a Sub statement, and ends with an End Sub statement. Use a Call instruction to invoke the Sub procedure. Before delving into the formal syntax for Sub and Call instructions, an example might help to clarify.

The Cross Application

Visual Basic provides the Circle method to draw circles, and the Line method to draw lines and rectangles. Suppose you want a Cross method that draws crosses. Well, Visual Basic doesn't provide such a method. So, write your own!

The Cross application might consist of a form with two command buttons. When you click the first command button, labeled Draw Crosses, Visual Basic draws a figure consisting of several crosses directly on the form. When you click the second command button, labeled Quit, the application terminates.

The application consists of a single form with a Click event procedure defined for each command button. A general procedure, named Sub Cross, is defined at the form level. The Click procedure for the Draw Crosses command button calls the Sub Cross procedure several times to draw the desired pattern of crosses.

Creating the Cross Application

Follow these steps to create the Cross application:

1. Start a new project by choosing the New Project option from Visual Basic's File menu.

2. Create a form containing two command buttons. Assign properties to the form, as Table 18.1 shows.

Table 18.1. Design-time properties for the Cross application.

Control	Property	Value
Form1	Caption	Crosses
	Left	1275
	Top	1140
	Width	7605
	Height	5505

continues

Table 18.1. Continued

Control	Property	Value
Command1	Caption	&Draw Crosses
	Name	cmdDrawCross
	Left	840
	Top	4320
	Width	3375
	Height	495
Command2	Caption	&Quit
	Name	cmdQuit
	Left	5040
	Top	4320
	Width	1815
	Height	495

3. Create the following Click event procedure for the first command button:

```
Sub cmdDrawCross_Click ()
    Dim Xcenter%, Ycenter%, LengthX%, LengthY%

    LengthX% = 600          'Modify these values
    LengthY% = 300          'to see the effect

    Call Cross(4000, 2000, 3000, 1500)          ' Call #1

    For Xcenter% = 2500 To 5500 Step 3000
        For Ycenter% = 1250 To 2750 Step 1500
            Call Cross(Xcenter%, Ycenter%, LengthX%, LengthY%)   'Call #2
        Next Ycenter%
    Next Xcenter%
End Sub
```

4. Create the following Click event procedure for the second command button:

```
Sub cmdQuit_Click ()
    End
End Sub
```

Follow these steps to create a user-defined procedure named Cross. This is a Sub procedure associated with the form.

1. Choose the **New Procedure…** option from the **View** menu.

   The New Procedure dialog box opens (see Figure 18.1).

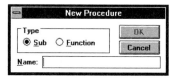

2. Type Cross in the Name input box, but don't press Enter.

3. If not already selected, click the option button labeled **S**ub (see Figure 18.2).

4. Click OK (or press Enter) to close the New Procedure dialog box.

   Visual Basic pops open a window with a template for the Cross procedure (see Figure 18.3).

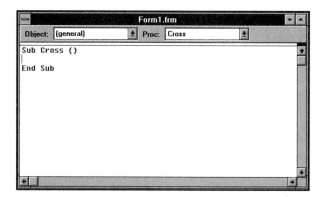

The template includes the `Sub` and `End Sub` statements. Notice that the first line, `Sub Cross ()`, includes an empty set of parentheses. When you type the body of the procedure, you must specify its parameters inside these parentheses.

5. Specify `Sub Cross` by typing the following procedure:

```
Sub Cross (X%, Y%, LengthX%, LengthY%)
    '    X%, Y% specify the center of the cross
    '    LengthX% specifies the horizontal line length from the center
    '    LengthY% specifies the vertical line length from the center
    Line (X%, Y%)-Step(LengthX%, 0)
    Line (X%, Y%)-Step(-LengthX%, 0)
    Line (X%, Y%)-Step(0, LengthY%)
    Line (X%, Y%)-Step(0, -LengthY%)
End Sub
```

The Cross application is now complete. Save the form as CROSS.FRM and the project as CROSS.MAK.

Running the Cross Application

Try running the Cross application. Click the command button labeled Draw Crosses. Figure 18.4 shows the result.

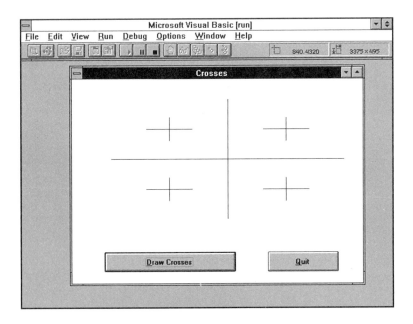

Figure 18.4.

The pattern of crosses produced by the Cross application.

Examining the *Cross* Procedure

Look at the Cross procedure, especially the Sub declaration:

```
Sub Cross (X%, Y%, LengthX%, LengthY%)
```

This Sub instruction defines Cross to be a Sub procedure with four parameters. Here, each parameter is an integer variable. These specified variables communicate values to and from the calling instruction (and the procedure or code block containing it). Parameters specified as part of the definition of a general procedure are called *formal parameters*.

Examine the Line instructions that compose the Cross procedure. You see that the procedure draws a cross centered at coordinates X%,Y%. Two horizontal lines are drawn from the center—one toward the left and another toward the right. Each of these two lines has a length specified by LengthX%. Similarly, two vertical lines are drawn from the center—one upward, and the other downward. Each of these two lines has a length of LengthY%.

Now, look at the cmdDrawCross_Click event procedure. This procedure contains two instructions that invoke the Cross procedure:

```
Call Cross(4000, 2000, 3000, 1500)                'Call #1

Call Cross(Xcenter%, Ycenter%, LengthX%, LengthY%) 'Call #2
```

Each of these two Call instructions passes a value to the corresponding formal parameters. For example, the first Call instruction passes the values 4000, 2000, 3000, and 1500 to the variables X%, Y%, LengthX%, and LengthY%, respectively. These variables are located inside the Cross procedure.

In a Call instruction, each passed value is known as an *actual parameter* (see Figure 18.5).

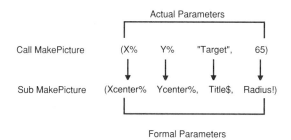

Figure 18.5.

Actual and formal parameters.

Notice that the actual parameters can be literals or variables. The first Call instruction uses literals, the second one uses values specified by variables.

Actual parameters can consist also of expressions. For example, the following instruction works well:

```
Call Cross(1000, 1200, LengthX% + 200, LengthY% * 2)
```

Parameter passing is covered in depth, later in this chapter. At that time, you learn how to pass other data types (including arrays, records, controls, and forms), and how a procedure can pass values back to the calling instruction.

Using User-Defined Functions

A *user-defined function* is similar to a Sub procedure, with one major difference: both user-defined and built-in functions return a value .

After you define a function, you invoke it the same way you do for Visual Basic's built-in functions. That is, you can specify the function name in expressions, as arguments in statements or other functions, or in any other place you can use a built-in function.

A user-defined function consists of a block of instructions that begins with a Function statement and ends with an End Function. You can place any number of instructions in the Function-End Function block.

Writing a User-Defined Function

Consider an example. The built-in function Sqr returns the square root of its argument. The instruction Print Sqr(16) displays 4 because this number is the square root of 16.

Suppose that you want a function called Square that returns the square of its argument. (The *square* of a number is the number multiplied by itself.) You can define Square with the following Function-End Function block:

```
Function Square! (NumValue!)
   Square! = NumValue! * NumValue!
End Function
```

With Square now defined, the instruction Print Square!(4) returns 16 because this number is the square of 4.

Notice that the Square! function uses the single-precision type-declaration suffix (!) on both the name of the function (Square!) and the formal parameter (NumValue!).

Every function returns a value, so you must designate a data type for the function itself. In this case, Square! indicates that the function returns a single-precision result. The parameter NumValue! indicates that the actual parameter passed to the function must be a single-precision number or variable, also.

Similar to variable names, the data type of a function is considered to be Variant, unless the function name ends with a type-declaration suffix (or a DefType instruction is in effect). If the function is named Square (no suffix), therefore, the default data type is Variant, not single-precision.

NOTE As explained later in this chapter, you can use an As *type* clause at the end of the instruction of a Function to define its data type. With this clause, no type-declaration suffix should appear after the function name.

Within every user-defined function, an assignment instruction must specify the resulting value returned by the function. The left side of this assignment instruction consists simply of the name of the function.

Introducing a String Function—*Mirror$*

Square! is a rather simple function. The body of Square! consists of nothing more than the single assignment instruction that specifies the resulting value. You can write complicated functions that require many instructions to define.

The following is a slightly more complicated function:

```
Function Mirror$ (Test$)
   Dim Temp$, Char%
   Temp$ = ""
   For Char% = Len(Test$) To 1 Step -1
      Temp$ = Temp$ + Mid$(Test$, Char%, 1)
   Next Char%
   Mirror$ = Temp$
End Function
```

Mirror$ is a string function. You pass Mirror$ a string argument, and Mirror$ returns the reverse string. That is, if you pass the value NATURES to Mirror$, it returns SERUTAN. If you pass Hello out there, this is returned to you: ereht tuo olleH.

Similar to general procedures, user-defined functions employ local variables. A variable declared in a function has meaning only within that function. A variable with the same name in a general or event procedure, or code module, is another entity.

The Esrever Application

What is meant by *Esrever*? It is simply "Reverse" spelled backward, or actually "reversE" spelled backward. The Esrever application uses the Mirror$ function to instantly display the reverse image of any text string that you type. For example, if you type "stop," the application displays "pots."

The Esrever application consists of a form with a text box and a label. As you type inside the text box, the label caption displays the text in reverse. The text is instantly updated in the label, so that it always displays the reverse image of the text you are currently typing into the text box.

The only event procedure is a Change procedure for the text box. In the text box, whenever the text changes, the Change event procedure displays its reverse image in the label. The general function Mirror$ is defined at the form level, and called from the Change procedure.

Creating the Esrever Application

Follow these steps to create the Esrever application:

1. Start a new project by choosing the New Project option from Visual Basic's File menu.

2. Create a form containing a text box and a label. Assign properties for the form as Table 18.2 shows.

Table 18.2. Design-time properties for the Esrever application.

Control	Property	Value	
Form1	Caption	Esrever	
	Left	1005	
	Top	1215	
	Width	7485	
	Height	4425	
Text1	Caption	(blank)	'erase the default contents
	Name	cmdText	
	Left	720	
	Top	360	
	Width	6135	
	Height	975	
Label1	Caption	(blank)	'erase the default contents
	Name	cmdLabel	
	Left	720	
	Top	1920	
	Width	6135	
	Height	975	

3. Create the following Change event procedure for the text box:

```
Sub cmdText_Change ()
    Dim StringVal$
    StringVal$ = cmdText.Text
    cmdLabel.Caption = Mirror$(StringVal$)
End Sub
```

Now, you must place the Mirror$ function into the application. You can open the New Procedure dialog box, as you did previously when adding the Sub Cross procedure to the Cross application. This opens the dialog box that Figure 18.1 shows. You then choose the option button labeled Function. Type Mirror$ as the Name, then click OK to begin typing the function.

Instead of opening the New Procedure dialog box, follow these steps:

1. With the Code window displaying the General Declarations section for the form, type **Function Mirror$**, then press Enter.

   Visual Basic displays a template procedure for the function, just as if you had used the New Procedure dialog box (see Figure 18.6).

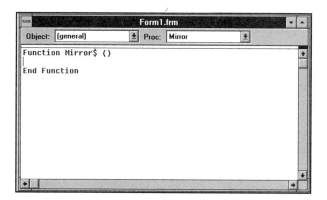

Figure 18.6.

The template for the Mirror$ function.

NOTE When you type general procedures into your applications, you can choose between using the New Procedure dialog box, or simply typing the first line of the procedure. In either case, Visual Basic displays a template for the procedure so that you can type the full procedure block.

2. Type the `Mirror$` function as follows:

```
Function Mirror$ (Test$)
    Dim Temp$, Char%
    Temp$ = " "
    For Char% = Len(Test$) To 1 Step -1
        Temp$ = Temp$ + Mid$(Test$, Char%, 1)
    Next Char%
    Mirror$ = Temp$
End Function
```

The `Esrever` application is now complete. Save the form as ESREVER.FRM, and the project as ESREVER.MAK.

Looking for Palindromes with the Esrever Application

Run the `Esrever` application. Type whatever you want into the text box. You see the text displayed in reverse in the label below the box. The reverse text is immediately updated whenever you make any modification to the text.

You can use this application as a fun way to test for palindromes. A *palindrome* is a word or phrase which reads the same forward and backward. The word "bib" is a simple example of a palindrome. Other examples are "peep" and "radar."

Even whole phrases and sentences can be palindromes, providing that you aren't concerned about punctuation, capitalization, and the spaces between words. Consider "A Toyota." That works. An example of a palindromic sentence is "Madam, I'm Adam." Figure 18.7 shows the `Esrever` application with a famous palindrome typed into the text box.

Examining the Esrever Application

Take a look at the `cmdText_Change` event procedure. The variable `StringVal$` holds the text string passed to the `Mirror$` function. In the event procedure, the instruction `StringVal$ = cmdText.Text` assigns to `StringVal$` the current value of the Text property of the text box. The next instruction, `cmdLabel.Caption = Mirror$(StringVal$)`, assigns the value of the reverse string returned by `Mirror$` to the label's Caption property.

Using Procedures

Procedures now have been introduced. The upcoming sections of this chapter explain in detail how you use procedures. Among other topics, you learn the complete syntax for Sub and Function definitions, how to pass parameters by reference and by value, and how to use Call to invoke Sub procedures.

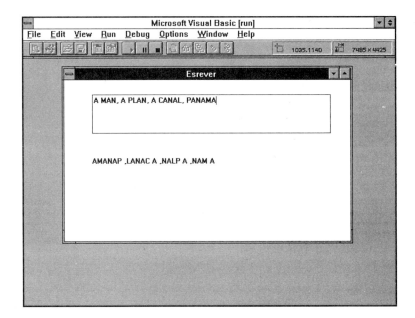

Figure 18.7.

The "Panama" palindrome typed in the Esrever application.

Defining a *Sub* Procedure

The following is a Sub procedure definition in skeletal form:

```
[Static] [Private] Sub subname [(paramlist)]
      [instructions]
[Exit Sub]
      [instructions]
End Sub
```

in which

subname is the name of the Sub procedure;

paramlist is the list of formal parameters,

and

instructions is a block of Visual Basic instructions.

The square brackets ([ ]) denote an optional item. As such, the following items are all optional in a Sub procedure definition: the Static keyword, the Private keyword, the list of parameters, the Exit Sub instruction, and the block of instructions.

The `Sub` procedure name is unique. If the procedure is defined in a code module, the name should not be used for any variable or any other procedure defined in the application. If the `Sub` procedure is defined at the form level, the name should be unique throughout that form.

The name follows the standard rules for Visual Basic variable and procedure names. The maximum number of characters is 40. `Sub` procedure names do not convey any data type. In fact, *subname* cannot have a type-declaration suffix.

The parameter list, if present, consists of a comma-delimited list of the formal parameters. Each formal parameter can be a simple variable, an array, a variable with a user-defined (record) data type, a control, or a form.

The following is the syntax for *paramlist* when no arrays or records are involved. (Discussion on passing arrays and records is deferred until later in the chapter.)

formalparam [As *type*] [, *formalparam* [As *type*]]...

in which

formalparam is the name of a formal parameter,

and

type identifies the data type of the formal parameter.

The square brackets denote an optional item. *type* can be any one of the following keywords: `Integer`, `Long`, `Single`, `Double`, `Currency`, `String`, `Variant`, or an object data type. The `String` type is always a variable-length string.

For example, the following `Sub` procedure definition uses two formal parameters (an integer and a string):

```
Sub ShowName (NumTimes As Integer, LastName As String)
```

Each formal parameter must have an assigned data type. If you don't use an `As` clause, the data type is specified in one of two ways:

- A type-declaration suffix in the formal parameter

- A default data type specified by an active `Deftype` declaration

For example, you could write the preceding `Sub` procedure declaration as follows:

```
Sub ShowName (NumTimes%, LastName$)
```

Some programmers prefer the type-declaration suffixes; others prefer the As clause. You can use either.

In the Sub procedure, *instructions* is any number of valid instructions with the following restriction: You cannot nest a function or Sub procedure declaration inside another procedure. In other words, *instructions* cannot include a Sub-End Sub or Function-End Function block.

The Sub and End Sub statements delineate the beginning and end, respectively, of the Sub procedure. When execution flows into the End Sub statement, the Sub procedure ends, and control returns to the point at which the Sub was called.

Static

The Static keyword specifies that all variables local to the Sub procedure are *static*. Static variables retain their values between successive calls. Without Static, the local variables are reinitialized each time the Sub procedure is called.

For example, consider this program fragment, which calls a Sub procedure named MeAgain from within a For-Next loop:

```
For Counter% = 1 To 3
    Call MeAgain
Next Counter%
```

The following is the Sub procedure definition for MeAgain:

```
Static Sub MeAgain
    Dim NumCalls As Integer
    NumCalls = NumCalls + 1
    Print "You called me again--this is call number"; NumCalls
End Sub
```

The output is as follows:

```
You called me again--this is call number 1
You called me again--this is call number 2
You called me again--this is call number 3
```

The Static declaration in the MeAgain Sub procedure causes the value of NumCalls to be preserved between calls. Remove the Static keyword, so that the Sub procedure declaration is simply Sub MeAgain. Now, the output becomes:

```
You called me again--this is call number 1
You called me again--this is call number 1
You called me again--this is call number 1
```

The *Private* Keyword

By default, general procedures defined at the form level are available throughout the form. General procedures defined at the module level are available throughout the application, including other modules.

By using the Private keyword (on the line with Sub), procedures defined on the module level are available only to others in the same module. Procedures in other modules cannot invoke the Private procedure.

One common situation for using Private occurs when a large application consists of an amalgamation of modules developed by different programmers. By using Private procedures, the risk of name conflicts is minimized.

Private is not necessary with procedures defined at the form level because such procedures are available only within the form. You cannot make a procedure defined at the form level available outside of the form. Instead, you must move such a procedure to a code module.

The *Exit Sub* Statement

An Exit Sub statement creates an early exit from the Sub procedure. When Visual Basic encounters Exit Sub, the procedure terminates immediately. Program execution transfers back to the calling location at the instruction immediately succeeding the one that called the Sub procedure.

The following Sub procedure uses an Exit Sub:

```
Sub ShowFirstAndLast (Value$)
   If Len(Value$) < 2 Then
      Print "Your string is less than 2 characters"
      Exit Sub
   End If
   Print "First character is: "; Left$(Value$, 1)
   Print " Last character is: "; Right$(Value$, 1)
End Sub
```

In general, you should try to avoid Exit Sub instructions. They tend to create "clumsy" code which makes your procedures more difficult to understand. Most of the time, you can write procedures which avoid premature exits.

Occasionally, you might find that an Exit Sub instruction is convenient, and a boon to creating straightforward code. The ShowFirstAndLast procedure is such an example.

Keep in mind that your goal is always to create efficient programs which are easy to understand and debug. In that endeavor, if a feature of the language helps, by all means take advantage of it—even though the feature might have a reputation for creating "clumsy" code.

Calling a *Sub* Procedure

Use a `Call` instruction to invoke a `Sub` procedure. `Call` has a form that can be either explicit or implicit.

```
Call subname (argumentlist)   'Explicit form
```

or

```
   subname argumentlist       'Implicit form
```

in which

   subname is the name of the `Sub` procedure,

and

   argumentlist is a list of the arguments (actual parameters).

In either the explicit or implicit form, *argumentlist* is optional.

The procedure name must be the same one used to define the `Sub` procedure in the `Sub-End Sub` definition. The argument list, if present, is a comma-delimited list of the arguments passed to the `Sub` procedure. Each argument can be a variable, or an expression. For example, consider the following `Sub` procedure declaration:

```
Sub StarSearch (LastName$, Age%, Weight!)
```

Each of the following instructions is a valid call to `StarSearch`:

```
Call StarSearch("Fonda", 44, 145.5)
```

```
Call StarSearch(Actor$, 39 - 10, Heft!)
```

```
Call StarSearch(UCase$(First$ + Last$), CInt(Age!), 159.5)
```

Notice how the last example uses the built-in functions `UCase$` and `CInt` to form expressions used as arguments.

The implicit form omits the `Call` keyword. Simply specifying the `Sub` procedure name is sufficient to invoke the `Sub` procedure.

When you invoke a `Sub` procedure without `Call`, do not place parentheses around the argument list. For example, using the implicit form, the three previous calls to `StarSearch` appear as follows:

```
StarSearch "Fonda", 44, 145.5
```

```
StarSearch Actor$, 39 - 10, Heft!
```

```
StarSearch UCase$(First$ + Last$), CInt(Age!), 159.5
```

In the debate between Call and no Call, the preferred form is (arguably) the explicit form (with Call and parentheses around arguments), rather than the implicit form (with no Call and no parentheses around arguments). Sub procedure calls are easier to identify when Call is present.

You may call a Sub procedure from an event procedure, another user-defined Sub procedure, a user-defined function, or even from within the same Sub procedure. The latter is known as a *recursive* call. Recursion is discussed later in this chapter.

When a Call instruction occurs, Visual Basic first looks for the Sub among the general procedures associated with the current form. If the procedure is not found, the search expands to the current module. If the procedure is still not found, Visual Basic searches all the code modules associated with the project.

The search can expand to all code modules, so each procedure in any code module must have a unique name. Notice, however, that the search never expands to other forms associated with the application. That's the reason you can have two procedures in an application with the same name—as long as they are at the form-level *in different forms*. After all, each form has event procedures with the same name.

Defining a Function

The following is a skeletal look at a user-defined function:

```
[Static] [Private] Function funcname [(paramlist)] [As type]
      [instructions]
[Exit Function]
funcname = expr
      [instructions]
End Function
```

in which

   funcname is the name of the user-defined function;

   paramlist is the list of formal parameters;

   type specifies the data type of the function's returned value;

   instructions is a block of Visual Basic instructions,

and

   expr is any general expression that has a value of the same data type as funcname.

The square brackets denote optional items.

As with a Sub procedure name, *funcname* is a unique name associated with the function. You cannot give any other procedure the same name. Also, you cannot give a variable (within the function's scope) the same name.

> Use meaningful function names, as you do when selecting variable names. **T I P**
> Choosing function names which are descriptive makes your programs
> easier to understand and debug.

Unlike a Sub procedure name, however, *funcname* establishes a data type for the value returned by the function. The same rules used to designate the data type of a variable apply to user-defined functions:

- Use a type-declaration suffix (%, &, !, #, @, or $) on *funcname*.
- Use a Deftype instruction to establish a default data type for *funcname*.
- Don't use anything. The data type defaults to Variant.

Also, you can use an As *type* clause after the name of the function to specify its data type. *type* can be any of the primary data types: Integer, Long, Single, Double, Variant, Currency, or String.

For example, either of the following function definitions specifies that the Square function returns a single-precision value. (The parameter passed to the function is of type Integer.)

```
Function Square! (Value%)
```

```
Function Square (Value%) As Single
```

User-defined functions and Sub procedures are quite similar. For user-defined functions, the *paramlist*, *instructions*, Static and Private keywords work exactly as they do with Sub procedures. An Exit Function instruction in a user-defined function is analogous to the Exit Sub instruction used in Sub procedures.

The main difference, of course, is that a function assigns a value to the name of the function itself. To have your function return a value properly, you must execute (in the function block) an assignment instruction with the name of the function on the left side. If *funcname* has a type-declaration suffix, don't forget to use the same suffix in the assignment instruction.

In the assignment instruction, only the root name of the function is on the left side. That is, do not include any parenthetical arguments after the function name. The right side of the assignment instruction can be any general expression consistent with the data type of *funcname*.

If no such assignment instruction executes, the function returns a default value (0 for numeric functions, the null string for string functions, Empty for Variant functions).

Your function can contain more than one assignment instruction that assigns a value to *funcname*. When the function terminates, the returned value comes from the assignment executed most recently.

For example, the following function returns the string value "Between", "Boundary", or "Outside", depending on whether the value of Target! is between, equal to, or outside the two boundary values Bound1! and Bound2!.

```
Function ShowLocation$ (Target!, Bound1!, Bound2!)
   Select Case Sgn(Bound1! - Target!) * Sgn(Target! - Bound2!)
      Case Is > 0
         ShowLocation$ = "Between"
      Case Is < 0
         ShowLocation$ = "Outside"
      Case Else
         ShowLocation$ = "Boundary"
   End Select
End Function
```

Invoking a Function

You invoke a user-defined function in the same way you do for one of Visual Basic's regular built-in functions. You can use the name of the function in an expression. You can place the function name in any place a variable of the same data type might go. Most commonly, functions are invoked on the right side of assignment instructions.

For example, each of the following instructions invokes the ShowLocation$ function:

```
Print ShowLocation$(Age!, 13, 18)

Abbrev$ = Left$(ShowLocation$(Goal!, High!, Low!), 2)

If ShowLocation$(A!, B!, C!) = "Outside" Then MsgBox "Unbounded"
```

As with Sub procedures, you can invoke a function from a Sub or event procedure, from another function, or even from within the function itself.

Passing Parameters

For both Sub procedures and functions, there are two fundamental rules of parameter passing:

■ The number of arguments in *argumentlist* and of formal parameters in *paramlist* must both be the same.

■ The data type of each argument and its corresponding formal parameter must match.

Suppose you declare a Sub procedure with three formal parameters, as follows:

```
Sub MySub (SmallNum%, BigNum#, Word$)
```

Each of the following calls is illegal:

```
Call MySub(MyNum%, YourNum#)              'Not enough arguments

Call MySub(NumA%, NumB#, Title$, NumC!)   'Too many arguments

Call MySub(MyNum%, YourNum#, HerNum!)     'HerNum! is not string
```

Passing by Reference

Parameters pass between a procedure and the calling instruction along a two-way street. In the examples so far, data has passed from the calling instruction to the procedure. Through the parameter list, however, a Sub procedure or function can pass values back to the calling instruction, as well.

Recall that the parameter list in the procedure declaration designates the formal parameters. Each formal parameter establishes a variable name that is local to that particular procedure.

Recall also that an actual parameter passed to the procedure is either

■ A variable name

■ A literal, constant, or expression

In the former case only, the actual parameter passes by reference. This means that Visual Basic passes the address of the variable to the procedure. Inside the procedure, the corresponding formal parameter is also assigned this same address.

As a result, any modifications to the value of the formal parameter occur at the same address that the calling program associates with the actual parameter. The procedure, therefore, effectively passes a value back to the calling instruction. That is, when program control passes back to the calling instruction, the actual parameter retains the value assigned to the corresponding formal parameter in the procedure.

Consider the following program fragment which invokes a Sub procedure named MySub. In the Call instruction, the variables X% and Y! are passed by reference.

```
X% = 10
Y! = 25.5
Print "Before Call: X% ="; X%; Spc(5); "Y! ="; Y!
Call MySub(X%, Y!)       'Variables passed by reference
Print " After Call: X% ="; X%; Spc(5); "Y! ="; Y!
```

The `MySub` procedure is as follows:

```
Sub MySub (A%, B!)
    Print "MySub: A% ="; A%; Spc(5); "B! ="; B!
    A% = 50
    B! = 13.8
    Print "MySub: A% ="; A%; Spc(5); "B! ="; B!
End Sub
```

The following is the output from this program fragment. Notice how the `Sub` procedure effectively changes the values of `X%` and `Y!` in the calling routine:

```
Before Call: X% = 10      Y! = 25.5
MySub: A% = 10      B! = 25.5
MySub: A% = 50      B! = 13.8
 After Call: X% = 50      Y! = 13.8
```

Passing by Value

When an actual parameter is a literal, a constant, or an expression, parameter passing is by value. Visual Basic passes the value of the parameter, rather than the address.

To simulate true passing by value, Visual Basic uses the following steps to pass a copy of the expression:

1. The value of the expression is calculated.

2. The result is stored in a temporary memory location.

3. The address of this temporary location is passed to the procedure.

If the procedure modifies the value, the change occurs only in the temporary location. As a result, no variables in the calling routine change.

To force Visual Basic to pass a variable by value, you can enclose the variable in parentheses. This makes the argument an expression. In this case, any modifications to the parameter occur only in the copy of the variable. The original variable remains unmodified.

For example, consider the program fragment which a modified version of the previous program fragment employed to demonstrate passing by reference:

```
X% = 10
Y! = 25.5
Print "Before Call: X% ="; X%; Spc(5); "Y! ="; Y!
Call MySub(10, (Y!))         'Arguments passed by value
Print " After Call: X% ="; X%; Spc(5); "Y! ="; Y!
```

The Sub procedure MySub remains unchanged from the previous example:

```
Sub MySub (A%, B!)
   Print "MySub: A% ="; A%; Spc(5); "B! ="; B!
   A% = 50
   B! = 13.8
   Print "MySub: A% ="; A%; Spc(5); "B! ="; B!
End Sub
```

Look at the output. In the Call instruction, parentheses are placed around the actual parameter Y%. That forces Visual Basic to pass Y% by value, rather than by reference. Notice that, after calling the Sub procedure, the values of X% and Y! do not change.

```
Before Call: X% = 10     Y! = 25.5
MySub: A% = 10      B! = 25.5
MySub: A% = 50      B! = 13.8
 After Call: X% = 10     Y! = 25.5
```

You can pass a parameter also by value with the ByVal keyword. You place ByVal before the formal parameter in the procedure declaration. For example, you can write the Sub procedure declaration for MySub as follows:

```
Sub MySub (ByVal A%, ByVal B As Single)
```

Now, the two parameters are always passed to the procedure by value.

Passing a String

A fixed-length string cannot be a formal parameter in a procedure declaration. Any such string parameter must be variable-length. Consider these function declarations:

```
Function Char%(Target$)                'OK--variable length

Function Char%(Target As String)       'OK--variable length

Function Char%(Target As String * 20)  'Illegal--fixed length
```

When you invoke a Sub procedure or function, variable-length strings work well as actual parameters (arguments).

Passing an Array

You can pass an entire array. Use the array name followed by an empty set of parentheses. The corresponding formal parameter also has an empty set of parentheses.

Do not `Dim` the array in the procedure. You can use the `LBound` and `UBound` functions to determine the lower and upper bounds of the array (for more information on `LBound` and `UBound`, see Chapter 19, "Using Arrays and Structures"). For example:

```
Dim Sales% (1 To 8, 0 To 10)
   .
   .
   .
Print "Total Sales ="; SumArray%(Sales%()) 'Note empty ()
End
```

The `SumArray` function is as follows:

```
Function SumArray% (A%())
   Dim Total%, FirstDim%, SecondDim%
   Total% = 0
   For FirstDim% = LBound(A%, 1) To UBound(A%, 1)
      For SecondDim% = LBound(A%, 2) To UBound(A%, 2)
         Total% = Total% + A%(FirstDim%, SecondDim%)
      Next SecondDim%
   Next FirstDim%
   SumArray% = Total%
End Function
```

To pass an individual array element, place the appropriate subscripts inside the parentheses. For example, the following instruction calls a `Sub` procedure, and passes a single array element:

```
Call ShowValue(MyArray(23))     'Single array element
```

Passing a Record

Follow these steps to pass an entire record:

1. Define the record type with a `Type-End Type` block in the Declarations section of the form (or module) in which the calling instruction occurs. For example:

   ```
   Type BaseballPlayer
      FullName As String * 40
      BattingAverage As Single
      HomeRuns As Integer
   End Type
   ```

2. Use a `Dim` instruction to give a variable your user-defined type:

   ```
   Dim Mantle As BaseballPlayer
   ```

3. When you invoke the procedure, pass your declared variable:

```
Call GetStats(Mantle)
```

4. In the procedure declaration, give the formal parameter your record type:

```
Sub GetStats (Person As BaseballPlayer)
```

To pass an individual record element, use the element descriptor when you invoke a procedure:

```
Call HitTotal(Mantle.HomeRuns)
```

Passing Properties of Controls and Forms

You frequently write applications that pass properties of controls and forms. For example, you might want to pass the Caption properties of an application's forms to a procedure which lists the active forms. Perhaps you want to pass the Top, Left, and other position coordinates of some controls to a procedure which computes the available physical screen space to display a graphics image.

Recall the Esrever application discussed earlier in this chapter. This application defined a function named Mirror$. Mirror$ accepts a string argument, and returns its reverse string. Recall the Function declaration for Mirror$:

```
Function Mirror$ (Test$)
```

In the Esrever application, the cmdText_Change event procedure contained the following two program instructions:

```
StringVal$ = cmdText.Text
cmdLabel.Caption = Mirror$(StringVal$)
```

Notice that StringVal$ is assigned the Text property of the cmdText text box control. Then, StringVal$ is used as the actual parameter passed to the Mirror$ function.

Effectively, StringVal$ is a temporary variable. You might have wondered why cmdText.Text was not directly used as the actual parameter. In other words, why not consolidate those two program lines into the following single instruction:

```
cmdLabel.Caption = Mirror$(cmdText.Text)
```

Essentially, the StringVal$ variable contains a *copy* of the property value. Then, it's okay to pass the copy by reference.

You *can* use the property value as an actual parameter, if you declare the formal parameter to be passed by value. As you learned earlier in this chapter, you can force passing by value with the ByVal keyword in the procedure declaration.

Using ByVal, you can change the function declaration for Mirror$ as follows:

```
Function Mirror$ (ByVal Test$)
```

Now, the instruction cmdLabel.Caption = Mirror$(cmdText.Text) works well.

Passing Objects—Controls and Forms

Not only can you pass the properties of forms and controls, you can also pass the objects themselves. In that way, you can write general procedures which work with the properties and attributes of whatever control or form is passed to the general procedures.

To pass a control or form, you must declare the formal parameter representing the passed object to have one of the control or form data types. Visual Basic supports a variety of such data types, including the general ones, Control and Form, and specific types for each control object. Examples of the specific control types are ComboBox, PictureBox, and Label.

To determine the specific object type for any control, create a control of the desired type on a form. Do this with Visual Basic in design mode. Then, with the focus on the control, open the Properties window. The object type for the control appears next to its name, near the top edge of the Properties window. For example, Figure 18.8 shows the Property window open for a command button named Command1. The object type is CommandButton.

As an example of passing controls, reconsider the Cross application introduced earlier in this chapter. Recall that this application uses a general procedure named Cross, which employs the Line method to draw a cross shape of a form.

The Cross procedure, introduced earlier, is reproduced as follows (comment lines have been removed):

```
Sub Cross (X%, Y%, LengthX%, LengthY%)
    Line (X%, Y%)-Step(LengthX%, 0)
    Line (X%, Y%)-Step(-LengthX%, 0)
    Line (X%, Y%)-Step(0, LengthY%)
    Line (X%, Y%)-Step(0, -LengthY%)
End Sub
```

Line is a method which generally uses the syntax containing the object on which the lines should be drawn. In the Cross procedure, the object name doesn't appear. This means that by default the lines are drawn on the current form.

Suppose that you want the Cross procedure to draw lines on a picture box rather than a form. The application might contain several picture boxes. You want to pass to the Cross procedure the picture box on which the lines should be drawn. You can do so by modifying the procedure as follows:

```
Sub Cross (X%, Y%, LengthX%, LengthY%, ThePicture As PictureBox)
    ThePicture.Line (X%, Y%)-Step(LengthX%, 0)
    ThePicture.Line (X%, Y%)-Step(-LengthX%, 0)
    ThePicture.Line (X%, Y%)-Step(0, LengthY%)
    ThePicture.Line (X%, Y%)-Step(0, -LengthY%)
End Sub
```

Here, PictureBox is the object type for picture boxes. The formal parameter ThePicture is assigned the name of the picture box passed to the procedure. Notice that the Line methods now include ThePicture as the object on which the lines should be drawn.

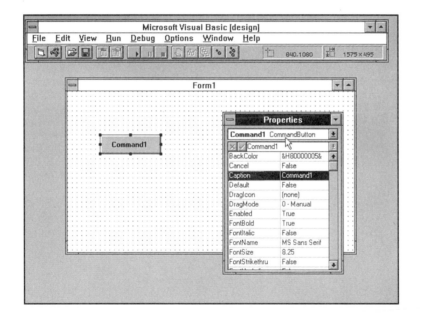

Figure 18.8.

The Properties window for Command1 CommandButton.

To try the new procedure, modify the form in the Cross application to contain one or more picture boxes. You can make the picture boxes any size, and place them anywhere on the form. Then, you can create a new Click event procedure for the DrawCross command button as follows:

```
Sub cmdDrawCross_Click ()
    Dim Xcenter%, Ycenter%, LengthX%, LengthY%
```

```
'Calculate Center coordinates of Picture Box
Xcenter% = Picture1.Width / 2
Ycenter% = Picture1.Height / 2

'Calculate length of each side of cross
LengthX% = Picture1.Width / 4
LengthY% = Picture1.Height / 4

Call Cross(Xcenter%, Ycenter%, LengthX%, LengthY%, Picture1)
End Sub
```

This Click procedure calculates the center of the first picture box using its Width and Height properties. The procedure uses the same properties to calculate the length of each arm of the cross. Finally, the Call instruction invokes Cross, and passes not only the location and dimensions of the desired cross, but also the name of the picture box control—Picture1.

Figure 18.9 shows an example of the modified Cross application. In the figure, the DrawCrosses command button has been clicked to create the cross inside the picture box.

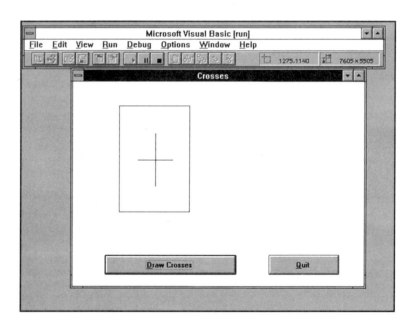

Figure 18.9.

The modified Cross application containing a picture box.

You can experiment with this application by creating additional picture boxes on the form. You can also modify the Click procedure to call Cross several times, each time drawing a cross in a different picture box.

For more information on objects and object variables, see Chapter 20, "Using Object Variables."

Using Static Variables—the *Static* Instruction

In a procedure, use a Static instruction to designate particular variables as static. The value of a static variable remains preserved between successive invocations of the procedure.

 The Static instruction is valid only at the procedure level. You cannot use Static instructions in the General Declarations section of a form or code module.

Static *varname* As *type*, *varname* As *type*...

in which

    varname is a simple variable name, or an array followed by empty parentheses ( ),

and

    type specifies the variable's data type.

The As *type* clause is optional.

A Static instruction is most commonly used when you want some, but not all, variables inside a procedure to retain their values between calls. You cannot use the Static keyword in the Sub or Function declaration because that would make *all* variables static. Instead, use the Static instruction to isolate the particular static variables. In effect, you use the Static instruction to declare particular static variables in otherwise nonstatic procedures.

In the As *type* clause, *type* can be Integer, Long, Single, Double, Currency, String (fixed- or variable-length), Variant, a user-defined type specified with a Type-End Type block, or an object type. For more information on object types, see Chapter 20, "Using Object Variables."

You can use the Static instruction (instead of Dim) to explicitly declare variables. When declaring fixed-size arrays in nonstatic procedures, you *must* use Static rather than Dim.

The following instructions show two examples of `Static` declarations:

```
Static MyVar As Double, FullName$

Static ChessBoard%(1 To 8, 1 To 8)
```

Using Recursive Procedures

A procedure is recursive if in the course of its execution, the procedure makes a call to itself. If the call occurs inside the procedure, the situation is known as direct recursion.

In other cases, a chain of calls may be involved. For example, one procedure calls another procedure which then makes a call back to the original procedure. Of course, longer chains are possible. Anytime the original procedure is called through a procedure chain, the situation is known as indirect recursion.

Visual Basic supports recursive procedures. You must think twice, however, before using recursion. This process can present some difficulties.

Trade-Offs of Recursion

Recursive programming is elegant, but often difficult to understand. This difficulty can lead to future headaches when such an application needs modification. Every application that can be written with recursion can be created also without it. You, therefore, face trade-offs when deciding whether to use this type of programming (see Table 18.3).

Table 18.3. Recursion versus nonrecursion.

Feature	Recursion	Nonrecursion
Clarity of programming	Poor	Good
Compactness of program	Good	Fair
Computational efficiency	Fair	Good

Some problems have naturally recursive definitions. These problems lend themselves to effective recursive solutions. Examples of such problems are binary tree searching, and quick sorting.

A Recursion Example

One of the classic examples of recursion is factorials. For those who need a math refresher, the factorial of a positive whole number is the product of all the whole numbers from one up to the number. For example, the factorial of 4 is 24 (1 * 2 * 3 * 4 = 24). The factorial of 0, by definition, is 1.

A factorial can be defined recursively. The factorial of a positive whole number N is simply N times the factorial of ($N–1$).

The following is a function that recursively computes the factorial of any non-negative whole number:

```
Function Factorial# (N%)
   If N% > 1 Then
      Factorial# = N% * Factorial#(N% - 1)
   Else
      Factorial# = 1
   End If
End Function
```

Many books present such a function to illustrate recursion. Often overlooked is the fact that you can easily write a nonrecursive function to calculate factorials. Consider this:

```
Function Factorial# (N%)
   Dim Value#, Counter%
   Value# = 1!
   If N% > 0 Then
      For Counter% = 1 To N%
         Value# = Value# * Counter%
      Next Counter%
   End If
   Factorial# = Value#
End Function
```

Which function is easier to understand? Both functions are fairly simple, so you might not have much basis for choosing. For most people, the nonrecursive algorithm is clearer.

Consider recursion in terms of a speed comparison. The recursive algorithm runs about ten percent slower.

The criteria for using recursion boil down to two considerations. Use this method if the program is significantly easier to write with recursion, and economy of program length is realized. Otherwise, use a nonrecursive algorithm.

Editing *Sub* Procedures and Functions

Various techniques are presented here for managing procedures with the Visual Basic Code editor:

- To create a new procedure:

  1. With the Code window active, choose the **New Procedures** option from the **View** menu.

     The New Procedure dialog box opens. Refer back to Figure 18.1.

  2. In the Name input box, type the name for your procedure, but don't press Enter.

  3. Click the option button labeled **Sub** or **Function**, as appropriate.

  4. Click OK (or press Enter) to close the New Procedure dialog box.

     Visual Basic pops open a Code window with a template for the new procedure.

     You are now set for editing, and can begin typing the procedure.

T I P There is a shortcut for creating a new procedure. While the Code window is open, you can simply type either **Sub**, or **Function**, followed by the name of the procedure. This shortcut replaces choosing the New Procedures option from the View menu.

- To save a procedure:

  Simply save the form with which the procedure is associated. For a module-level procedure, save the module. Visual Basic does not save procedures as independent disk files.

- To view a list of the procedures in a given application:

  While the Code window is active, press F2. The View Procedures dialog box opens, showing all the procedures associated with the application. The modules are listed in the upper half of the dialog box, the procedures in the lower half of the box. Figure 18.10 shows this dialog box for the Cross application presented in this chapter.

- To view and edit a procedure:

  1. Press F2 to open the View Procedures dialog box.

2. Highlight the desired procedure by clicking its name. (Alternatively, you can use the arrow keys to highlight the desired procedure.)

3. Click OK, or press Enter.

Visual Basic displays the procedure in an Edit window. You can now edit the procedure.

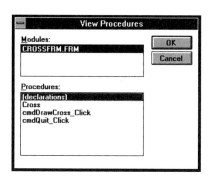

Figure 18.10.

The View Procedures dialog box.

- To cycle through procedures:

  While a procedure is displayed in the Code window, press Ctrl+Down to cycle to the next procedure. Alternatively, you can press PgDn repeatedly until the next procedure pops into view, or you can choose the Next Procedure option from the View menu.

  To cycle backward through the procedures, press Ctrl+Up or PgUp, or choose the Previous Procedure option from the View menu.

- To delete a procedure from your application:

  1. Highlight the entire text of the procedure, including the Sub and End Sub instructions (or the Function and End Function instructions).

  2. Press Del, or choose Delete from the Edit menu.

- To split the Code window into two panes:

  You can split the Code window into horizontal panes. This permits you to view one part of your application's code while writing some for a procedure in another part of your application. The Code window contains a *split bar* with a thin, horizontal black line just above the vertical scroll bar.

By dragging the split bar, you can divide the screen into two horizontal panes. The vertical size of the panes is determined by how far you drag the mouse. Figure 18.11 shows a screen split into two panes, with the pointer aimed at the split bar. To toggle the focus between the two panes, press F6.

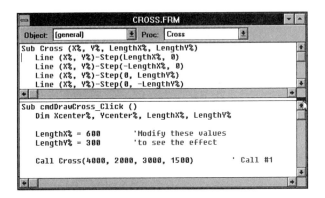

Figure 18.11.

A split Code window.

■ To add an existing code module to an application:

You can share program code among applications by adding to the current application an existing code module. Code modules are normally saved with the .BAS extension; forms are normally saved with the .FRM extension. To add an existing module saved on disk to the current application, follow these steps:

1. Choose the Add File option from the File menu.

2. Specify the file name in the dialog box which opens.

3. Click OK.

■ To delete a code module or form from an application:

1. Choose the Project option from the Window menu.

2. Highlight the code module (.BAS extension) or form (.FRM) you want to remove.

3. Choose the Remove File option from the File menu.

Summary

With user-defined procedures, you can add statements and functions to those predefined by Visual Basic. A Sub procedure is a sort of customized statement or method; a user-defined function is a sort of customized function.

General procedures are programming islands. From any location in your program code, you can invoke the procedure. When the procedure terminates, program execution resumes at the calling instruction. You invoke a Sub procedure with a Call instruction. To invoke a user-defined function, you include its name in an expression—just as you do for one of Visual Basic's predefined functions.

The Visual Basic editor maintains procedures as independent entities. In a procedure, local variables provide autonomy with respect to the "outside world" of the code modules, and user-defined and event procedures.

A procedure can communicate with the calling instruction by passing needed parameters. A user-defined function returns a value in the same way that a regular, predefined function does.

One advantage of procedures is that you don't have to continually write a block of instructions. You write the block once, making it a Sub or function. Then, you invoke the procedure, as needed.

Perhaps the most significant advantage of procedures is that they provide a primary tool for tackling major programming projects. Large-scale programs are best handled by modular programming. You divide the large task into several smaller ones. To create the code for the final application, you write several smaller procedures that you amalgamate together into the final application.

Using Arrays and Structures

Ordinary variables store only a single value. Such variables are quite useful, but ultimately limiting. Many programming projects require the storage and manipulation of large amounts of information.

Suppose, for example, that you want to write an inventory control program for an automobile parts company. You might need to deal with thousands of different parts. You obviously cannot manipulate such large amounts of data with ordinary variables.

To handle such sizable data requirements, you need *arrays*. Arrays are like super variables, storing multiple data values under a single name. Arrays were introduced in Chapter 14, "Language Building Blocks," and are explored in depth in this chapter. The *record,* or user-defined data type, is also introduced.

NOTE In Visual Basic, you can create not only arrays of data values, but also specialized arrays such as control arrays and arrays of forms and objects. Specialized arrays are covered throughout this book in the chapters devoted to those topics. This chapter focuses on arrays of "ordinary" data values.

Working with Arrays

In most of the program examples so far, the variables have been simple variables—"simple" because each variable stores a single value. In the following instructions, for example, the variables Month1$, Month2$, and Month3$ are separate variables that store separate values:

```
Month1$ = "January"
Month2$ = "February"
Month3$ = "March"
```

Simple variables can be numeric, string, or Variant. Of course, the value of a variable might change during the execution of a program. At all times, however, each simple variable "houses" a single data value.

Arrays change all that. *Arrays*—or more properly, *array variables*—consist of several data values maintained under a common name. With arrays, you can easily manipulate large amounts of related data. With only a few program lines, you can recalculate hundreds of data values or display a large table. This chapter shows you how.

Just as with ordinary variables, every array has a name that you create. Array names follow the same conventions as ordinary variables, including the optional %, &, !, #, @, or $ suffix that identifies the data type of the array. Once you give an array a data type, every element of an array conforms to that data type.

As with ordinary variables, arrays can have the data type Variant. In such a case, the individual elements of the array can contain the different kinds of data supported by Variants: numbers, strings, and date/time values.

The distinguishing feature of an array is the *subscript* (or *index number*) that immediately follows the name. Consider the following instruction:

```
Value! = Cost!(30)
```

Here, Cost! is an array. The subscript, 30 in this example, is enclosed in parentheses. The parentheses "tell" Visual Basic that this is an array rather than an ordinary variable.

The value of the subscript identifies a single element of the whole array. For example, the collection of month names can be written as an array, as in the following:

```
MonthName$(1) = "January"
MonthName$(2) = "February"
MonthName$(3) = "March"
```

Here you have an array named `MonthName$`, which is a string array because the name ends with a dollar sign. Each individual element of `MonthName$` contains a string value. The first element of the array, `MonthName$(1)`, has the value `January`. The second element, `MonthName$(2)`, has the value `February`.

 NOTE Sharp-eyed readers may note a potential ambiguity in the instruction `Value! = Cost!(30)`. Suppose `Cost!` is a user-defined function rather than an array variable. Then this instruction invokes the function `Cost!` with a parameter value of 30. To resolve this potential ambiguity, you must declare each array. That way, Visual Basic can distinguish between arrays and function references. As discussed soon, you declare an array with `Dim` or another similar instruction.

An array subscript is always enclosed in parentheses placed immediately after the array name. The subscript can be an explicit number, a variable, or even an expression that evaluates to a number. See Table 19.1 for some examples.

Table 19.1. Sample array subscripts.

Array Element	Type of Subscript
`MonthName$(2)`	Explicit number
`Salary!(Employee%)`	Variable name
`Cost#(23 + J%)`	Simple expression
`Cost#((J% - 1) * 3)`	Expression containing parentheses

Subscript values must be whole numbers. Visual Basic rounds numbers that are not whole to the nearest integer. If, for example, `Salary!` is an array containing the salaries of a company's employees, `Salary!(433.2)` references employee number 433 and `Salary!(228.8)` references employee number 229.

A Sample Program with Arrays

The following program demonstrates that a few simple For-Next loops can manipulate a lot of data.

Suppose you own Ace Accordion Supply. Your 1993 monthly sales figures have finally arrived. The sales data is stored in a text file named YEARDATA.TXT. The file is saved on your drive C in the \SALES directory. In other words, the complete file specification (path and file name) is C:\SALES\YEARDATA.TXT. The following is the text of the data file:

```
Jan, Feb, Mar, Apr, May, Jun, July, Aug, Sep, Oct, Nov, Dec
28, 21, 14, 32, 25, 26, 20, 16, 23, 19, 29, 26
```

To follow along with the ensuing program example, create the YEARDATA.TXT data file on your system. You can use a text editor such as Windows Notepad to type the text of the two-line file. Also, create the C:\SALES directory and save YEARDATA.TXT in that directory.

The first line of the file contains the abbreviated names for each month. A comma separates consecutive entries. The second line contains the number of accordions sold (by month). Again, a comma separates consecutive entries.

Creating the ACE Application

Complete the following steps to create a program, called ACE, that lists the monthly sales and computes the yearly total:

1. Create a form containing a picture box and two command buttons. Assign properties for these controls as shown in Table 19.2.

Table 19.2. Design-time properties for ACE.

Control	Property	Value
Form1	Caption	Ace Accordion Supply
	Height	5085
	Left	1035
	Top	1140
	Width	7485\
Picture1	Height	4095
	Left	480

Table 19.2. Continued

Control	Property	Value
	Top	240
	Width	4215
Command1	Caption	&Show Report
	Height	615
	Left	5040
	Name	cmdShowReport
	Top	1200
	Width	2175
Command2	Caption	&Quit
	Height	615
	Left	5040
	Name	cmdQuit
	Top	2520
	Width	2175

2. Place the following two array-declaration instructions in the General Declarations section at the form level:

```
Dim MonthName(12) As String    'Name for each month
Dim NumSold(12) As Integer     'Number sold per month
```

3. Create the following Click event procedure for the first command button:

```
Sub cmdShowReport_Click ()
    Dim J As Integer            'Array index
    Dim Total As Integer        'Total number sold
    '
    '   Read data from data file
    Open "C:\SALES\YEARDATA.TXT" For Input As #7
    For J = 1 To 12
        Input #7, MonthName(J)  'Read string data for each month
    Next J
    For J = 1 To 12
```

```
      Input #7, NumSold(J)      'Read number sold each month
   Next J
   Close #7                     'Close data file
   '
   '  Display Report Heading
   Picture1.Print "Ace Accordion Supply - 1993 Sales"
   Picture1.Print
   Picture1.Print "Month", "Number Sold"    'Display table heading
   '
   For J = 1 To 12
      Picture1.Print MonthName(J), NumSold(J)  'Display monthly data
   Next J
   Picture1.Print
   '
   Total = 0
   For J = 1 To 12
      Total = Total + NumSold(J)   'Calculate yearly sales total
   Next J
   Picture1.Print "Yearly total = "; Total
End Sub
```

4. Create the following Click event procedure for the second command button:

```
Sub cmdQuit_Click ()
   End
End Sub
```

5. Save the form as ACE.FRM and the project as ACE.MAK.

Running the Ace Application

Run the application. Figure 19.1 shows the output that displays after you click the Show Report command button. The application displays the 1993 sales data in the picture box.

Understanding How ACE Works

By examining the program code, you get a good introduction to the use of array variables. First, consider the two Dim instructions in the General Declarations section of the form.

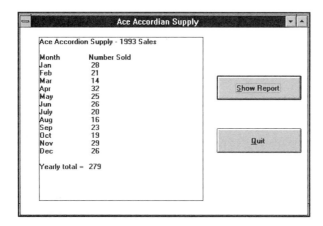

Figure 19.1.

Running the ACE
application.

You are already familiar with the use of `Dim` instructions to declare ordinary variables. The two `Dim` instructions in this program example declare array variables. The instructions tell Visual Basic the names and sizes of the arrays that are used in the application. Because the instructions occur at the form level, these arrays are recognized in the procedures and functions associated with the form and the controls placed on the form.

The details of `Dim` are discussed later in this chapter. For now, realize that these `Dim` instructions inform Visual Basic that the project uses two arrays:

- A string array named `MonthName`
- An integer array named `NumSold`

Each of these arrays contains 12 elements. `Dim` only establishes the names and dimensions of the arrays. You still must get data values into the individual array elements.

NOTE The arrays in this program example actually contain 13 elements, not 12. That's because, by default, Visual Basic includes an array element with a subscript of 0. As explained later in this chapter, you can change this default so that array elements with a subscript of 0 are not present.

The active part of the program code occurs in the `cmdShowReport_Click` event procedure. This is the event procedure that activates when the user clicks the upper command button.

The data file YEARDATA.TXT contains the data values that will be stored in the array elements. The `Open` instruction establishes a link (data channel #7 in this case) between the application and the disk file. Two `For-Next` loops read the data values from the file and copy the values into the arrays.

In each loop, an `Input #7` instruction does the actual reading. The first loop reads the 12 data strings expressing the abbreviations for the names of the months. The second loop reads the 12 monthly sales figures (28 accordions sold in January, 21 sold in February, and so on). After all the relevant data in the file is read, the `Close` instruction terminates the active link between the disk file and the application.

> **NOTE**
>
> In any program using arrays, you must get the necessary data values into the array elements. The three most common techniques to accomplish this are requesting the data from the user at run time, reading the data from a disk file, and storing the data values as part of the program code.
>
> Note that Visual Basic does not support the READ and DATA statements found in QBasic and earlier versions of Basic. (These statements facilitated the storage and retrieval of data values directly in the program code.) As a result, in Visual Basic the data for large arrays is often contained in one or more disk files that are read during run time.
>
> The ACE application demonstrates the techniques of opening a disk file and using `Input` instructions to read data from the disk file into the array elements. The AREACODE application presented later in this chapter further explores reading array data values from text files.

Notice how these two simple loops read all the data values. That's the power of array subscripting. After these loops execute, each array contains 12 data values in preparation for the rest of the program. In the `NumSold` array, for example, `NumSold(1)` is 28, `NumSold(2)` is 21, and so on.

The program now displays the output in the form of a two-column table. With the `Print` method, the program displays results in the picture box.

After displaying the heading for the table, the ensuing `For-Next` loop displays the monthly sales figures. These values are nothing more than the data values picked up from the YEARDATA.TXT file. But again, notice how easily a simple loop can display a whole array full of data.

Finally, the program calculates `Total`, the total sales over the whole year. The ultimate value of `Total` is the sum of the monthly sales figures. That is, `Total` should be the sum of all the elements of the `NumSold` array:

```
NumSold(1) + NumSold(2) + ... + NumSold(12)
```

Again, a simple loop is the answer. The final `For-Next` loop calculates the value of `Total`. When the loop finishes, `Total` contains the desired sum, which is displayed with the `Print` method.

The cmdQuit_Click event procedure consists entirely of an End instruction. When the user clicks the lower command button, the application terminates.

The ACE application demonstrates the power of arrays. With a few simple loops, you can easily manipulate array elements. Notice how the For-Next counter variable (J in this application) is often used as an array subscript. This practice is commonplace in programs with arrays.

Loops and arrays naturally work well together. Loop counter variables increment sequentially, which is exactly how array elements are subscripted.

Dimensioning Arrays with *Dim*

As the two instructions in the General Declarations section of ACE.MAK demonstrate, you use Dim to declare arrays at the form level. Dim permits an extended syntax with several options. For now, consider only the simple form of the Dim instruction. (Extensions to the syntax of Dim are explained later in this chapter.)

NOTE This section discusses Dim instructions used for array declarations. As you saw in earlier chapters, you can also use Dim to declare ordinary variables. Furthermore, as you will see later in this chapter, you can also declare arrays with the Global and Static instructions.

The simple form of the Dim instruction (for array declarations) accomplishes four tasks:

- Establishes the name of the array
- Establishes the data type of the array
- Specifies the number of elements in the array
- Initializes the value of each element of the array; numeric array elements become zero, string array elements become the null string, and Variants become the special value Empty.

The following is the syntax of the simple form of the Dim instruction:

```
Dim arrayname(subscriptrange) As type
```

where

   arrayname is the name for the array,

   subscriptrange specifies the index range for the elements in the array,

continues

continued

and

type declares the data type of `arrayname`.

The As `type` clause is optional.

NOTE All Arrays Must Be Declared

With Visual Basic, you must declare *every* array, including small arrays with less than 10 elements. This is a departure from QBasic, QuickBASIC, and other procedural versions of Basic that permit small arrays to be used without being declared.

Specifying the *As* Clause

The optional As clause specifies the data type of `varname`. To use the As clause, `arrayname` must not contain a type-declaration suffix. The `type` parameter must be one of the terms listed in Table 19.3. In this table, *num* is being used as a placeholder name to represent an expression that can hold many values.

Table 19.3. *As* clause data declarations.

Term	Variable Type
Integer	Integer
Long	Long integer
Single	Single-precision
Double	Double-precision
Currency	Currency
String	Variable-length string
String * *num*	Fixed-length string of length *num*
Variant	Variant
user-defined	User-defined

The user-defined data type, or *record*, is discussed later in this chapter.

Omitting the *As* Clause

If you omit the As clause, array names follow the same conventions as variable names. In particular, a data type suffix (!, #, %, &, @, or $) establishes the data type for each element of the array. (Recall that every element of an array must be the same data type.) If you don't use a suffix on the array name, the data type defaults to Variant.

Defining the Subscript Range

The *subscriptrange* parameter establishes the lowest and highest values allowed for the array subscript. Two forms of the *subscriptrange* parameter exist: a single value or two values separated by the keyword To.

In the former case, the single value of *subscriptrange* establishes the highest permissible value of the array subscript. Visual Basic automatically considers the lowest legal subscript value to be 0 (not 1). For example, the instruction

```
Dim NumVotes(10) As Integer
```

establishes an integer array named NumVotes, which has 11 elements: NumVotes(0), NumVotes(1), ... , NumVotes(10).

In the latter case (with the To keyword), the *subscriptrange* parameter directly specifies the lowest and highest permissible values of the subscript. The lowest value does not have to be 0 or 1. For example, the following instruction declares the integer array CheckNum to have 51 elements ranging from a subscript of 100 to a subscript of 150:

```
Dim CheckNum(100 To 150) As Integer
```

By using the To clause, you can specify any value for the lowest and highest subscript values. Negative values are acceptable. In all cases, however, the lowest subscript value (the number before the To) must always be lower in value than the highest subscript value (the number after the To).

Declaring Multiple Arrays

A single Dim instruction can declare two or more arrays. In these cases, use a comma to separate the array names. Table 19.4 shows some sample Dim instructions.

Table 19.4. Sample *Dim* instructions.

Instruction	Description
`Dim Client(200) As String`	String array with 201 elements: Client(0) to Client(200)
`Dim Profit!(1975 To 1993)`	Single-precision array with 19 elements: Profit!(1975) to Profit!(1993)
`Dim Shares(-40 To 15) As Long`	Long integer array with 56 elements: Shares(-40) to Shares(15)
`Dim Tax(30), Cost(30)`	Two Variant arrays, each with 31 elements
`Dim A%(45), B%(34), C$(21)`	Three arrays: (1) An integer array with 46 elements: A%(0) to A%(45) (2) Another integer array with 35 elements: B%(0) to B%(34). (3) A string array with 22 elements: C$(0) to C$(21)

Where to Put *Dim* Instructions

A `Dim` instruction can appear anywhere before the first use of the array. When possible, however, you should place all your `Dim` instructions together near the beginning of the program. That way, you can quickly identify the names and sizes of all the program's arrays.

Changing the Base Subscript—*Option Base*

An `Option Base` instruction changes the default lower array subscript from zero to one.

```
Option Base basesub
```

where

   basesub specifies the lowest array subscript for subsequent `Dim`, `Global`, and `Static` instructions.

The only valid values for *basesub* are 0 (zero) and 1.

Consider the following program fragment:

```
Option Base 1
Dim MyArray(200) As Double
```

The first line changes the default lower array bound from zero to one. As a result, the Dim instruction creates an array with elements from MyArray(1) to MyArray(200).

You may be wondering what's so important about saving a single array element when you change the default lower subscript from 0 to 1. Not much, really. After all, even if an array has a zero subscript, you don't have to use the zeroth element. Changing the base from 0 to 1 does conserve a small amount of memory storage. This becomes important when you use multiple-dimensional arrays (discussed later in this chapter).

Using Variables and Constants as Array Dimensions

So far, the sample Dim instructions specify the number of array elements with numeric literals. You can use variable names and constants also, however.

Variables and constants provide a convenient way to alter array boundaries between successive runs of a program. Suppose, for example, that you have an application that displays the results of your track club's road races. The program code dimensions arrays as follows:

```
Dim LastName$(300), FirstName$(300)
Dim Age(300) As Integer
Dim Weight(300) As Single
Dim RaceTime(300) As Single
```

A more flexible solution is to use a variable name such as the following:

```
Dim MaxRunners As Integer
MaxRunners = 300
Dim LastName$(MaxRunners), FirstName$(MaxRunners)
Dim Age(MaxRunners) As Integer
Dim Weight(MaxRunners) As Single
Dim RaceTime(MaxRunners) As Single
```

Not only is the variable name MaxRunners% easier to understand than the literal 300, you only need to modify the single line that assigns a value to MaxRunners% (instead of modifying all the Dim instructions) if you need to enlarge the number 300 when your track club membership grows.

You can use this same technique with constants as well as variables. For example, the first line of the preceding program fragment might establish MaxRunners as a constant, as follows:

```
Const MaxRunners = 300
```

Whether MaxRunners is a constant or a variable makes for a subtle distinction in the way memory for the array is allocated. This distinction is discussed in the section titled "Fixed and Dynamic Allocation" later in this chapter.

You can ask the user to supply the array boundaries. For example, you might assign a value to MaxRunners with this instruction:

```
MaxRunners = Val(InputBox$("How many runners in the race"))
```

Remember that in Dim instructions you can use variable and constant names (as well as literals) for the subscript limits.

Scope of Array Declarations

Arrays declared with Dim (and other) instructions have the same scope as ordinary variables declared at the same level. The following rules apply to both:

- When a Dim instruction declares an array in the Declarations section of a code module, the array is available throughout the entire module.

- When a Dim instruction declares an array in the Declarations section of a form, the array is available in all procedures associated with the form.

- When you declare an array inside a procedure, the array is available only within that procedure. As explained in upcoming sections, you cannot declare an array with Dim inside a procedure unless the whole procedure is declared to be static. However, you can always declare an array inside a procedure with Static.

Declaring Arrays with *Static* and *Global* Instructions

Besides Dim, you can use Static and Global instructions to declare arrays. The syntax is exactly as it is with Dim, except that the keyword Static or Global replaces the keyword Dim. For example, the following instructions are valid:

```
Static MyArray(55) As Double

Static YearlySales@(1985 To 1993)

Global TwoD(NumRows, NumColumns)
```

As the following sections explain, the choice of the `Dim`, `Static`, or `Global` keyword affects the attributes and scope of the declared array.

Creating Static Arrays

An array declared with the `Static` statement becomes, naturally enough, a *static array*. As a result, the elements in the array retain their values throughout the execution of the program.

Most importantly, by using `Static` inside a procedure to declare an array, the elements in the array retain their previous values each time you invoke the procedure. Notice that you cannot declare an array inside a procedure with `Dim` unless the whole procedure has been declared to be static. In a static procedure, an array declared with `Dim` automatically becomes a static array.

Of course, as you saw in the previous chapter, you can use the `Static` keyword in the procedure declaration itself to make all variables in the procedure retain their values. For example, consider the following code fragment:

```
Static Sub GetTotal ()
   Dim MyArray(10)

   .

   .
```

Here, the entire procedure is static, so `MyArray` is static even though the array is declared with the `Dim` instruction. Similarly, in the following nonstatic procedure, `MyArray` is static because the array is declared with the `Static` keyword:

```
Sub GetTotal ()
   Static MyArray(10)

   .

   .
```

Comparing the *Static* Keyword and the *Static* Statement

When you declare a procedure with the `Static` keyword, as in `Static Sub GetTotal ()`, the memory storage for the arrays (and other variables) defined within the procedure is allocated once, just before the program executes. The values of the array elements (and the other variables) remain intact throughout the program execution.

For a nonstatic procedure (declared without the Static keyword), you can't use Dim to declare arrays. However, you can still use Dim to declare oridinary variables. The memory storage for the variables declared with Dim instructions is reallocated each time the procedure is invoked. With each termination of the procedure, the memory space is returned to the system and any values stored in the variables are lost.

Declaring Fixed-Sized Arrays in Nonstatic Procedures

Inside a nonstatic procedure, you must declare a fixed-size array with the Static keyword. As mentioned earlier, you cannot use Dim. The previous example, repeated here, illustrates this technique:

```
Sub GetTotal ()
    Static MyArray(10)

        .

        .
```

Notice, however, that the following program fragment generates an error message:

```
Sub GetTotal ()
    Dim MyArray(10)

        .

        .
```

However, in static procedures (declared with the Static keyword), you can declare fixed-size arrays with either the Static or Dim statement.

Creating Global Arrays

Arrays declared with the Global statement are available to every procedure in the project. "Every procedure" means just that: all procedures in every form and every module.

Recall that Global instructions can occur only in the Declarations section of a code module. You cannot use Global at the form or procedure level.

Table Lookup—A Sample Program with Arrays

Suppose you want to write a program that asks the user for a telephone area code. After the user enters the area code, the program responds with the name of the state or province associated with that area code. For example, if the user enters the number 213, the program displays California.

Imagine that your job requires you to respond with a state name when given an area code number. If you didn't have a computer, you would most likely tackle this task by first finding a list or table of all the area codes and the corresponding states. Then, when anyone asked about a particular area code, you would scan your list for that code. If you found a match, you would respond with the corresponding state name. If you didn't find a match, you would reply that there is no such area code on your list.

This general technique is known as *table lookup.* You look through a table to find a specific entry. When you find it, you get the corresponding information from an adjacent "column" of the table.

Using the AREACODE Application

The AREACODE application does precisely the same table lookup. The data is read from a text file. The user types an area code into a text box, and the application displays the state (or province) name in a second text box.

In Figure 19.2, the user typed the area code 207. The application responded with the appropriate state name: Maine.

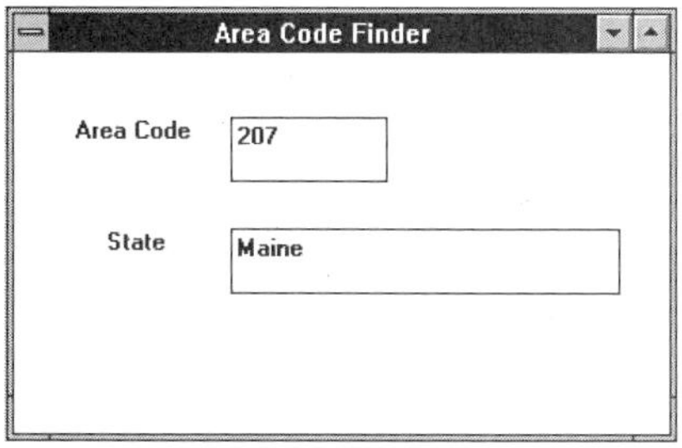

Figure 19.2.

Running the AREACODE application.

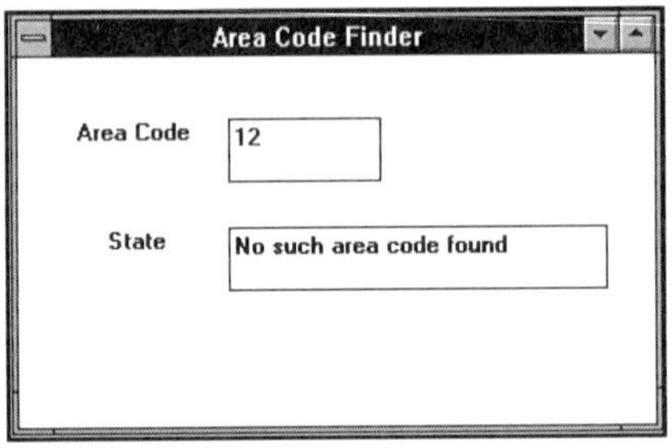

Figure 19.3.

An invalid area code is
entered.

In Figure 19.3, the user has not typed a valid area code. The application
responds with an appropriate message.

Creating the Data File

The AREACODE application reads the area code and state data from a text file
named AREACODE.TXT. The following is a listing of that file:

```
201, New Jersey
202, D.C.
203, Connecticut
204, Manitoba
205, Alabama
206, Washington
207, Maine
208, Idaho
209, California
212, New York
213, California
214, Texas
```

Of course, this list represents only a small portion of the total area codes. Due
to space limitations in this book, the file list is kept relatively short. If you try
this example, you can expand the file to include as many area codes as you
want. In the file, you don't have to place the entries in numerical order. As long
as each state name appears next to its area code, the application works fine,
regardless of the area code ordering.

Designing the Form

To construct the AREACODE application, create a form containing two text
boxes and two labels. Assign properties for these controls as shown in
Table 19.5.

Table 19.5. Design-time properties for AREACODE.MAK.

Control	Property	Value
Form1	Caption	Area Code Finder
	Height	3270
	Left	1365
	Top	1140
	Width	5190
Text1	Name	txtAreaCode
	Height	495
	Left	1680
	Top	480
	Width	1215
Text2	Name	txtStateName
	Height	495
	Left	1680
	Top	1320
	Width	3015
Label1	Caption	Area Code
	Height	375
	Left	480
	Top	480
	Width	975
Label2	Caption	State
	Height	495
	Left	720
	Top	1320
	Width	855

Writing the Program Code

The program consists of two event procedures and some form-level declarations. To start, place the following three Dim instructions in the General Declarations section at the form level:

```
Dim AreaCode(150) As Integer
Dim StateName(150) As String
Dim NumEntries As Integer
```

The first two Dim instructions declare the arrays that hold the area codes and state names, respectively. Each array holds 151 elements with index values ranging from 0 to 150.

Create the Form_Load event procedure as follows:

```
Sub Form_Load ()
    'Read data from disk file into arrays
    Open "c:\vbs\areacode.txt" For Input As #9
    NumEntries = 0
    Do
        NumEntries = NumEntries + 1
        Input #9, AreaCode(NumEntries), StateName(NumEntries)
    Loop Until EOF(9)
    '
    'Blank out initial values in the text boxes
    txtAreaCode.Text = ""
    txtStateName.Text = ""
End Sub
```

Finally, create the txtAreaCode_Change event procedure as follows:

```
Sub txtAreaCode_Change ()
    'Find state name corresponding to area code
    Dim Message As String    'Text message displayed to user
    Dim J As Integer         'Index variable for For-Next loops
    Message = "No such area code found"
    For J = 1 To NumEntries
        If Val(txtAreaCode.Text) = AreaCode(J) Then
            Message = StateName(J)
        End If
    Next J
    txtStateName.Text = Message
End Sub
```

Understanding How the Application Works

When you run the application, the `Form_Load` procedure immediately activates. This procedure opens the data file and assigns data channel number 9 to the link between the data file and the application. Be aware that, in the `Open` instruction, you can modify the path to the data file to specify the directory in which you have saved the data file.

The `Do-Loop` block reads the area codes and state names into the `AreaCode` and `StateName` arrays, respectively. The `EOF` function tests whether the previous `Input` instruction read the last data in the file. If so, `EOF` returns True and the loop terminates. If not, `EOF` returns False and the loop continues for another iteration. The variable `Entries` increments by one each time through the loop. When the loop terminates, the value of `Entries` equals the number of area codes and state names stored in the respective arrays.

Table 19.6 shows how the area codes and state names are stored in the `AreaCode` and `StateName` arrays.

Table 19.6. Partial contents of the area code and state name arrays.

Element Number	Area Code	State Name
1	201	New Jersey
2	202	D.C.
3	203	Connecticut
4	204	Manitoba
5	205	Alabama

The `Form_Load` procedure ends by blanking out the initial text in the two text boxes.

The main work of the application occurs in the `txtAreaCode_Change` event procedure. This procedure activates when the user modifies the text in the area code text box.

The string variable `Message` stores the response that the user eventually sees. At first, `Message` is set to report that a match is not found. If a match is subsequently found, `Message` is updated appropriately.

The application expects the user to enter an area code in the `txtAreaCode` text box. The entered text is treated by Visual Basic as a string value. The `Val` function converts this string value to the actual numerical value.

The For-Next loop searches through the area codes in the AreaCode array attempting to match the entered area code. When the loop finds a match (in the If instruction), the index variable J contains the number of the matching element from the AreaCode array. At this point, Message is assigned the proper state name from the StateName array. Notice that the same index value of J points to the proper corresponding value in the StateName array. That's table lookup in action.

When the For-Next loop finishes, the application displays the response by assigning the value of Message to the Text property of the txtStateName text box. Notice that Message contains the appropriate message whether or not a match was found. If a match was found, Message contains the matching state name; if no match was found, Message contains the no match message originally set before the For-Next loop.

The application continues to process each request by the user. The program responds any time the user modifies the value in the txtAreaCode text box.

To terminate the program, click the Stop button in the Toolbar (or select the End option from the Run menu).

Using Multidimensional Arrays

So far, the sample arrays have been one-dimensional—a list of values. For example, the array Salary!(Employee%) contains salary information as a function of an employee number. One-dimensional arrays use only a single subscript to span all the values of the array.

Suppose, however, that you have data in the form of a table (a spreadsheet, for example). Such data has a two-dimensional, row-and-column structure.

Using Two-Dimensional Arrays

Visual Basic supports two-dimensional arrays to represent two-dimensional data. You need two subscripts to specify an element of a two-dimensional array: one subscript for the row number and one subscript for the column number. Use a comma to separate the two subscripts.

For example, a chessboard can be considered a two-dimensional array. Figure 19.4 shows a chess game in progress. Each square of the 8-by-8 board has a row number from 1 to 8 and a column number from 1 to 8.

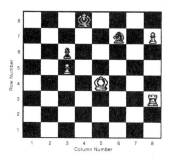

Figure 19.4.

A chess game in progress.

For the chessboard, a two-dimensional array named `Piece` contains the name of the chess piece currently occupying each square. The following instructions represent the board shown in Figure 19.4:

```
Dim Piece(8, 8) As String
For Row% = 1 To 8
   For Column% = 1 To 8
      Piece(Column%, Row%) = "None"
   Next Column%
Next Row%
Piece(3, 5) = "White Pawn"
Piece(8, 7) = "White Pawn"
Piece(8, 3) = "White Rook"
Piece(5, 4) = "White King"
Piece(3, 6) = "Black Pawn"
Piece(6, 7) = "Black Knight"
Piece(4, 8) = "Black King"
```

The first line dimensions the `Piece` array with a `Dim` instruction. The array is designated to be two-dimensional by the use of two subscripts. This `Dim` instruction tells Visual Basic the following information:

- `Piece` is a two-dimensional string array.

- The first dimension has subscript values ranging from 0 to 8.

- The second dimension has subscript values ranging from 0 to 8.

Notice that each dimension actually spans nine values (because the lowest value in each dimension is 0, not 1). There are 81 (9 by 9) total elements in the `Piece` array.

In this program fragment, two nested `For-Next` loops initialize the value of each array element with the string value `None`. Notice how nested loops quickly reference an entire two-dimensional array.

The remaining lines assign specific string values to the array elements that represent squares containing pieces. In each array reference, the first subscript is a column number and the second subscript is a row number. For example, `Piece(3, 5)` refers to the piece at column 3 and row 5.

Just as with one-dimensional arrays, you can use the `To` parameter to specify the subscript range of a two-dimensional array. For example, the following instruction declares that the two-dimensional string array `Title$` has index ranges from 10 to 25 and 30 to 64:

```
Dim Title$(10 To 25, 30 To 64)
```

Extending Arrays to Higher Dimensions

Arrays are not limited to two dimensions. Visual Basic allows arrays with as many as 60 dimensions! In practice, arrays with more than three dimensions are rare. The maximum number of elements per dimension is 32,768. To declare a multidimensional array, just specify the array bounds with a `Dim` instruction.

For example, the following instruction specifies a three-dimensional array of type `Currency`:

```
Dim Profit(6,15,12) As Currency
```

This array might represent the profits of a department store chain as a function of the individual store, the department, and the month. For example, `Profit(2,8,11)` refers to the profit from store #2 (the Miami store, for instance), department #8 (maybe cosmetics), in the 11th month (November).

Determining Array Bounds with *LBound* and *UBound*

The `LBound` and `UBound` functions provide a convenient way to determine the lower and upper bounds of an array.

```
LBound(arrayname, dimension)

UBound(arrayname, dimension)
```

where

   `arrayname` is the name of the array,

and

   `dimension` is an integer expression specifying one of the dimensions of the array.

The `dimension` parameter is optional.

The value of `dimension` can range from 1 to the number of dimensions in the array (with a maximum of 60). For example, suppose that you create a three-dimensional array with the following `Dim` instruction:

```
Dim My3DArray(50, -10 To 18, 1 To 4) As Integer
```

Table 19.7 shows the values displayed by various calls to the `LBound` and `UBound` functions.

Table 19.7. Values returned by *LBound* and *UBound*.

Function Call	Returned Value
LBound(My3DArray, 1)	0
LBound(My3DArray, 2)	-10
LBound(My3DArray, 3)	1
UBound(My3DArray, 1)	50
UBound(My3DArray, 2)	18
UBound(My3DArray, 3)	4

If you omit the dimension parameter, Visual Basic uses 1 by default. Therefore, you need only the *arrayname* parameter for one-dimensional arrays. Consider this program fragment:

```
Dim Velocity#(-30 To 89)
Print LBound(Velocity#)
Print UBound(Velocity#)
```

The output is the following:

```
-30
 89
```

Using User-Defined Data Types

One shortcoming of arrays is that every element of an array must have the same data type. Sometimes you want to assemble diverse data types under a common name.

Visual Basic includes the *user-defined data type*. Other names for the user-defined data type are *record* and *structure*. Records give you a free hand to custom design an individualized data type for a particular application. (One common use of records is in the manipulation of random-access disk files. See Chapter 25, "Processing Files.")

Like an array, a record is a structured data type made up of multiple elements. Unlike an array, elements of a record can be different data types.

NOTE Although every element of an ordinary array must have the same data type, arrays of type Variant permit flexible data types to occur in the same array. As a result, in many programming situations, arrays of type Variant can be used instead of user-defined data types.

Variant arrays have two main advantages over user-defined data types. First, a Variant array can be dynamic so that you can change the size of the array during run time. Second, you can change the data type stored in each array element anytime during program execution.

The one main advantage of user-defined data types is memory conservation. The memory required to store the data is always less with a user-defined data type than with a Variant array.

Use a Type-End Type block structure to define each customized data type. Suppose, for example, that you are writing a payroll application. For each employee, you need to work with his or her name, company ID number, and salary. The following `Type` block establishes a user-defined data type called `Employee`:

```
Type Employee
    FullName As String * 35
    IDNumber As Integer
    Salary As Currency
End Type
```

`Employee` is a record made up of three pieces of information: `FullName`, which stores the employee's name; `IDNumber`, which stores the employee's identification number; and `Salary`, which stores the employee's salary.

Before continuing with this example, following is a more detailed look at `Type-End Type` blocks.

Defining a Record

A `Type-End Type` block must occur in the Declarations section of a code module. User-defined data types have a global scope. You cannot place a `Type-End Type` block in a form module.

Place the `Type` instruction on the first line of the block and the `End Type` instruction on the last line. Between those two lines, each component of the record appears on a separate line.

```
Type recordname
    elementname As type
    elementname As type
    elementname As type
End Type
```

where

 `recordname` is the name for the data type,

 `elementname` is the name for each component of the record,

and

 `type` specifies the data type of the corresponding `elementname`.

You define the names for *recordname* and *elementname*. The normal variable-naming conventions apply, except that you cannot use the type-declaration suffixes (%, &, !, #, @, or $).

Notice that *recordname* gives a name to the data type itself, not to a variable having this data type. In the payroll example, Employee is the name of the data type. No actual variable having this data type has been created yet.

The *type* parameter must be one of the data types listed in Table 19.8.

Table 19.8. Data types in record declarations.

Type	Description
Integer	Integer
Long	Long integer
Single	Single-precision
Double	Double-precision
Currency	Currency
Variant	Variant
String	Variable-length string
String * *num*	Fixed-length string of length *num*
user-defined type	Record (another record type)

Notice that strings can be variable-length or fixed-length. type cannot be an array name. However, type can be another record name. That is, one component of a record can be another entire record of a different type.

Although type cannot be an array name, you can declare a static array (fixed array size) as a component of a record. For example, the following Type-End Type block contains an array with 12 elements:

```
Type Client
    FullName As String * 35
    PhoneNum As String * 15
    MonthlyFee(12) As Currency
End Type
```

Any array declaration appearing in a Type-End Type block must be a static array—that is, an array that uses literal numbers or constants to specify the number of array elements. Arrays declared with the To keyword are permitted. For example, the following declaration is acceptable:

```
MonthlyFee(1 To 12) As Currency
```

However, you cannot use a dynamic array—that is, an array in which a variable name specifies the number of array elements. For example, the following declaration is not acceptable (assuming that NumMonths is a variable, not a constant):

```
MonthlyFee(NumMonths) As Currency
```

The requirement for static arrays arises from the restriction that the total memory size for any user-defined data type must be determinable before the program executes and remain fixed throughout the program execution.

Declaring Variables of a Record Type

After you define a record with Type, use Dim (or Global, ReDim, or Static) to declare a variable as having that data type. For example, the following instruction declares Boss to be a variable of the user-defined data type Employee:

```
Dim Boss As Employee
```

Arrays of records are permissible. The following instruction declares Salesmen to be an array of 75 elements. Each element of the array has the user-defined data type Employee.

```
Dim Salesmen(1 To 75) As Employee
```

Specifying Components of a Record Variable

You isolate individual components of a record variable by separating the root from the element name with a period. For example, the following program fragment assigns values to the three components of Boss:

```
Boss.FullName = "George M. Honcho"
Boss.IDNumber = 122
Boss.Salary = 3530.50
```

Similarly, you can define the 34th element of the Salesmen array as follows:

```
Salesmen(34).FullName = "Ed Closer"
Salesmen(34).IDNumber = 399
Salesmen(34).Salary = 2650.75
```

Placing *Type* Blocks in Program Code

Visual Basic restricts Type declarations to the General Declarations section at the module level. However, once the Type declaration occurs at the module level, you can declare a variable of that type anywhere else in the application—in the General Declarations section, at the form level, or in a Sub or Function procedure.

Nesting Records

You can nest records by defining the component of one record to have the data type of another record. When records are nested, you must use two or more periods to create a path down to the desired element.

Consider an application named NESTREC. Suppose the following Type blocks occur in the Declarations section of a module:

```
Type Employee                 'Define Employee record
    FullName As String * 35
    IDNumber As Integer
    Salary As Single
End Type


Type Committee                'Define record
    ProjectName As String * 30  ' -This component is a string.
    Chairman As Employee        ' -This component is a record.
    Treasurer As Employee       ' -This component is a record.
    Budget As Single            ' -This component is a number.
End Type
```

Now suppose the following code fragment occurs within an event procedure:

```
Dim President As Employee       ' ------------------------
Dim Salesman As Employee        ' Give variables record type.
Dim UrbanRenewal As Committee   ' ------------------------


President.FullName = "Whitney Crabtree"
President.IDNumber = 1000
President.Salary = 823.18


UrbanRenewal.Chairman = President   'Assign a record to a record.


Print UrbanRenewal.Chairman.FullName   ' ------------------
Print UrbanRenewal.Chairman.IDNumber   ' - Note nested paths -
Print UrbanRenewal.Chairman.Salary     ' ------------------
End
```

The `Print` instructions display the following output:

```
Whitney Crabtree
 1000
 823.18
```

Notice that the record type `Committee` has two components that are themselves records of the type `Employee`. After the `Dim` instructions, the next three lines assign values to the record variable `President` using the descriptors `President.FullName`, `President.IDNumber`, and `President.Salary`.

The next line assigns the entire `President` record to the `Chairman` component of the `UrbanRenewal` record. The point is that this one instruction transfers all three components of `President`. As proof, the `Print` instructions use the nested path structure to display the transferred values.

Fixed and Dynamic Allocation

The memory location of a stored variable can be allocated by Visual Basic either when you start the program or while the program is running (executing). The former is called *fixed* (or *static*) *allocation*, and the latter, *dynamic allocation*. The trade-offs involve flexibility versus efficiency.

Dynamic allocation is flexible because storage is allocated and deallocated while the program runs. If a dynamic variable is no longer needed, the memory can be freed for another use.

Fixed allocation, on the other hand, is less flexible but more efficient. Fixed variables are allocated to memory locations before the program runs and remain so allocated throughout the execution of the program. This is efficient because, before the program begins, Visual Basic resolves the necessary addresses. As a result, the machine language instructions produced by Visual Basic already contain the appropriate addresses.

Notice that for fixed allocation, Visual Basic must be able to determine the variable's exact size before the program runs. The exact size is always known for any simple variable or record.

For a string variable, Visual Basic uses a reference, or pointer, to where the string value stored. The pointer itself has a fixed size and occupies a fixed memory location. As such, fixed allocation works for the pointer. The value stored in this pointer specifies the memory location containing the actual string data. When the string value changes during program execution, the value in the pointer changes. However, the size of the pointer and the pointer's memory location remain fixed.

Array Allocation

The way you allocate arrays is important because a large array can require considerable memory.

By default, Visual Basic uses fixed allocation for any array that you dimension with literal subscripts (or constants defined with `Const` instructions) and dynamic allocation for any array that you dimension with variables. Consider the following examples:

```
Dim MonthlyProfit!(1 To 12)      'Literal subscript


Const MaxItems = 520
Dim Invoices%(MaxItems)          'Constant subscript


Dim Salary!(NumEmployees%)       'Variable subscript
```

Notice that Visual Basic has no choice but to use dynamic allocation when an array is dimensioned with a variable subscript. Fixed allocation is impossible because the value of the variable (and therefore the size of the array) is not known until the program runs.

Declaring Dynamic Arrays

For some applications, you want to change the size of the array during run time. With a `ReDim` instruction (explained later), you can dynamically modify the array bounds while the application executes.

Sometimes, you don't know the size of an array when the program begins. You know that the array needs to be present, but the size of the array depends on a condition that occurs at run time. Usually, this condition is input from the user.

For example, a program that grades school tests might use several arrays, each dimensioned to the size of the number of students. But the number of students can vary widely—from 35 for a single classroom, to 500 for an entire school, to 10,000 or more for a school district. The user inputs the number of students, and the program should dimension the arrays accordingly.

 **NOTE**   **Don't Waste Memory**

You could dimension the arrays of a program with fixed sizes large enough to satisfy any possible practical application. The program can then simply ignore the unneeded array elements. However, this approach wastes memory and is needlessly inefficient. By using Visual Basic's dynamic array allocation, you can dimension (and redimension) arrays to precise sizes at run time.

By creating a dynamic array, you can modify the dimensioning one or more times while the program runs. To declare a dynamic array, you use a `Dim`, `Global`, or `Static` instruction, but you don't specify any dimensioning. You simply declare the array with an empty set of parentheses. For example, the following instruction declares `Score` to be a dynamic array:

```
Dim Score() As Integer
```

As with any array declaration, you use `Global` to give the dynamic array global scope, `Dim` at the module level for module-level scope, or `Static` inside a procedure for local scope.

Allocating a Dynamic Array with *ReDim*

Use the `ReDim` statement to allocate a dynamic array that has previously been declared with empty parentheses.

`ReDim` *arrayname*(*subscriptrange*)

where

    arrayname is the name of an array,

and

    subscriptrange specifies the dimensions for the array.

For example, having declared the `Score` array as dynamic, the following instruction declares `Score` to be a two-dimensional array:

```
ReDim Score(20, 40)
```

`ReDim` is an executable instruction that takes effect at run time. Therefore, `ReDim` instructions must appear inside `Sub` and `Function` procedures (including event procedures).

You can specify the array bounds with variables and constants as well as numeric literals, as in the following example:

```
ReDim Score(NumStudents, NumProblems)
```

Eight is the maximum number of array dimensions that you can specify.

Reallocating a Dynamic Array with *ReDim*

You can redimension a dynamic array several times by repeatedly executing ReDim instructions. Here is the simplest syntax for the ReDim instruction:

```
ReDim arrayname(subscriptrange)
```

When *arrayname* is the name of a currently dimensioned array, ReDim deallocates the old array and reallocates the array with the new dimensions. All the old array values are lost during this process. New array values reinitialize to 0 (for numeric arrays), null strings (for variable-length string arrays), ANSI 0 characters (for fixed-length string arrays), and Empty values (for Variant arrays).

ReDim can change the size of each dimension but cannot change the number of dimensions. For example, the following is a typical use of ReDim:

```
Dim MyArray() As Single    'Dynamic array declared at module-level
.
.

ReDim MyArray(30, 20, 10)  'Array allocation inside a procedure
.

.
ReDim MyArray(50, 25, 12)  'Array is redimensioned
```

This works because MyArray! has three dimensions in both ReDim instructions. However, change the second ReDim instruction to ReDim MyArray(5000), and the result is a Wrong number of dimensions error.

The syntax for the ReDim instruction permits the optional Preserve keyword:

```
ReDim Preserve arrayname(subscriptrange)
```

With the Preserve keyword, the existing array values can be retained when the array is redimensioned. However, with Preserve, only the last array dimension can change size without losing any array values. For a single-dimension array, *all* the existing array values can be retained because that single dimension is the last and only dimension. For a multiple-dimension array, however, only the far right array dimension can change size while retaining the contents of the array.

For example, the following program fragment redimensions MyArray while preserving the array contents:

```
.
.

ReDim MyArray(50, 25, 12)  'Dynamic array is redimensioned
.

.
ReDim Preserve MyArray(50, 25, 15)  'Array values are retained
```

Erasing Arrays—the *Erase* Instruction

An Erase instruction affects designated arrays; the effect depends on whether the arrays are declared with fixed or dynamic allocation.

```
Erase arraylist
```

where

arraylist is a list of array names separated by commas.

If arrayname refers to a fixed array:

- Each element is reinitialized (elements of numeric arrays are reset to 0, elements of variable-length string arrays are reset to the null string, elements of fixed-length string arrays are set to ANSI 0, and elements of Variant arrays are reset to the Empty value).

- Each element in an array of records is reset as if it were a separate variable.

  The effect is simply to reset the value of every array element to a default value.

If arrayname refers to a dynamic array, the array is deallocated. This frees the memory used by the array.

The following program fragment reinitializes a static array:

```
Static MyArray(1000) As Integer   'Static array
MyArray(500) = 18

Print MyArray(500)
Erase MyArray                      'Reset all elements to 0
Print MyArray(500)
```

The output is the following:

```
18
0
```

When working with arrays, remember that Visual Basic requires considerable memory resources to store large arrays (especially large, multidimensional arrays). For example, Visual Basic needs more than 15,000 bytes of memory to store the following array:

```
Dim Salary(300, 12) As Single
```

(Because of the 0 subscript, the Salary array is actually 301 elements by 13 elements. This is 3,913 elements total: 301 times 13. Each single-precision element requires four memory bytes. So the total memory requirement is 15,652 bytes: 3,913 times 4.)

When working with dynamic arrays, use the Erase instruction to "erase" an array from memory. The array elements become permanently lost. However, Visual Basic can now use the array's previous memory space for other purposes, such as dimensioning a new array. It's a good idea to erase a dynamic array when the program no longer needs to use the array.

When you specify one or more arrays in an Erase instruction, use only the root names of the arrays, with no parentheses or subscripts. For example, the following instruction erases previously dimensioned arrays named Price! and Client%:

```
Erase Price!, Client%
```

Declaring a Dynamic Array with *ReDim*

You can use ReDim inside a procedure to initially declare a dynamic array. That is, you don't declare the array at the module level with a Dim or Global instruction using empty parentheses. Instead, you declare the array for the first time with a ReDim instruction inside a procedure.

In such a case, the scope of the array is limited to the procedure containing the ReDim instruction. The syntax for this use of ReDim corresponds to that of the Dim instruction:

```
ReDim arrayname(subscriptrange) As type,
    arrayname(subscriptrange) As type ...
```

where

   arrayname is the name of an array,

   subscriptrange specifies the new dimensions for the array,

and

   type declares the data type of *arrayname*.

The As *type* clause is optional.

The advantage of declaring arrays for the first time with ReDim is that the arrays can have up to 60 dimensions. Dynamic arrays declared at the module level are limited to 8 dimensions. (Of course, it's quite rare to use arrays with more than 3 dimensions.) The disadvantage is that the scope of the arrays is confined to the local procedure.

Tips for Saving Array Space

Here are some tips on optimizing array space to conserve memory:

- Use dynamic arrays.

- Turn variable-length string arrays into fixed-length string arrays.

- Make array dimensions smaller. This might sound trite, but perhaps your arrays are larger than necessary.

- Use a more economical data type if possible—integer rather than long integer, single-precision rather than double-precision.

Passing Arrays and Records to Procedures

The previous chapter discussed user-defined procedures. You learned in that chapter how to pass variables as arguments to such procedures. Besides ordinary variables, you can also pass arrays and records to your Sub and Function procedures. The following sections explain these techniques.

Passing an Array

To pass an entire array to a user-defined procedure, use the array name followed by an empty set of parentheses. The corresponding formal parameter within the procedure also has an empty set of parentheses.

Inside the procedure, do not dimension the array. That is, don't use Dim, Static, ReDim, or Global to redefine the array. You can use the LBound and UBound functions to determine the lower and upper bounds of the array.

Suppose, for example, that you create the following `Form_Load` procedure that declares a two-dimensional array named `Sales`. This procedure calls the user-defined `SumArray` function:

```
Sub Form_Load ()
   Static Sales(1 To 8, 0 To 10) As Integer

      .
      .     'These lines specify values for the elements of the Sales array.
      .

   Print "Total Sales ="; SumArray(Sales())    'Note empty ()
End Sub
```

The SumArray function appears as follows:

```
Function SumArray (A() As Integer) As Integer
   Dim Total, FirstDim, SecondDim As Integer
   Total = 0
   For FirstDim = LBound(A, 1) To UBound(A, 1)
      For SecondDim = LBound(A, 2) To UBound(A, 2)
         Total = Total + A(FirstDim, SecondDim)
      Next SecondDim
   Next FirstDim
   SumArray = Total
End Function
```

Notice that `A()` with an empty set of parentheses appears in the formal parameter list in the first line of the function. The empty set of parentheses identifies the argument as an entire array.

To pass an individual array element, place the appropriate subscripts within the parentheses. For example, the following instruction calls a `Sub` procedure named `ShowValue` and passes a single array element:

```
Call ShowValue(MyArray(23))        'Single array element
```

Passing a Record

Follow these steps to pass an entire record:

1. Define the record type with a `Type-End Type` block declared in the Declarations section of a code module, as in the following example:

```
Type BaseballPlayer
   FullName as String * 40
   BattingAverage as Single
   HomeRuns as Integer
End Type
```

2. Use a `Dim` (or `Static`, `ReDim`, or `Global`) instruction to give a variable your user-defined type, as in the following example:

```
Dim Mantle As BaseballPlayer
```

3. When you invoke the procedure, pass your declared variable:

```
Call GetStats(Mantle)
```

4. In the procedure declaration, give the formal parameter your record type:

```
Sub GetStats(Person As BaseballPlayer)
```

To pass an individual record element, use the element descriptor when you invoke a procedure:

```
Call HitTotal(Mantle.HomeRuns)
```

Summary

The array is your primary tool for managing large amounts of related data. Arrays are like super variables that store multiple elements under a common array name. You refer to the individual array elements with a subscript or subscripts. Arrays can be single- or multidimensional.

Arrays and loops work well together. Inside a loop, the loop's counter variable is often used as a subscript in array references. A simple `For-Next` loop can manipulate all the data in a huge array.

Arrays can be declared with `Dim`, `Static`, `Global`, and `ReDim` instructions. The scope of an array depends on where the array declaration occurs; the scope can be throughout a code module, at the form level, or local to an individual procedure. Array allocation can be `fixed` or dynamic.

You can customize your own structured data type with a record, or user-defined data type. A record can group components of different data types under a common name.

Using Object Variables

Visual Basic applications consist of objects. Some of these are objects that you create, such as forms and controls. Other objects, such as Screen and Debug, are predefined by Visual Basic.

Object variables, as the name suggests, are variables that represent objects. In the program code of your applications, you can use object variables to manipulate existing objects at run time, and even to create new instances of forms. This chapter shows you the techniques involved.

The main topics covered in this chapter include:

- Understanding objects
- Introducing the predefined objects
- Creating new instances of objects
- Grouping objects
- Working with object variables
- Understanding the scope of objects

Understanding Objects

Visual Basic is said to be *object-oriented*. In today's programming vernacular, the terms *object* and *object-orientation* are heard quite often. Obviously, the use of objects is an important programming topic. It's important to understand how objects work and what you can do with them.

The modern concept of program objects is that they are dynamic entities containing data and program code. Objects have not only a physical, visible dimension, but also attributes and associated procedures. The latter elements characterize what the object can do, and how it responds to its environment.

For example, suppose you create an application that contains a command button named btnDoIt. The button has a host of associated properties, such as Left and Text. It has a set of methods, such as Move and Refresh, to which it responds. And you can create a number of event procedures, such as btnDoIt_Click, which describe how the button behaves when Click and other events occur. btnDoIt is, therefore, an example of a Visual Basic object.

Object Variables

Objects are interesting theoretically, but they're not particularly useful until object variables enter the picture. An *object variable* is what its name implies— a variable which refers to an object. Contrast that with an ordinary variable which refers to a single data value.

With Visual Basic, you can declare variables that have objects as data types. In the current example, you might create a variable named MyButton whose data type is not Integer, String, or even Variant, but rather btnDoIt.

In this case, MyButton can refer to a specific object and manipulate it, but that's only the beginning. Suppose you assign another variable, named YourButton, to another command button with the btnDoIt data type. With these object variables, you can manipulate the referenced objects in a number of ways: By modifying the property values of the objects, passing the object variables to procedures, comparing one object variable to another, or grouping objects into arrays, to mention a few.

It is even more interesting when object variables reference forms. With form variables, you can create new instances of the form at run time. You can then modify each individual instance of the form to have new property values. You can also eliminate individual forms.

Throughout this chapter, you learn to use object variables in a number of ways to create sophisticated program effects. Objects and object variables are powerful programming tools.

A Sample Application Using Object Variables

This quick sample application demonstrates object variables in action. It uses object variables to create multiple instances of a form.

Start a new project. Double-click the command button icon in the Toolbox to place a command button near the center of the form. The default name for the command button is Command1. The default name for the form is Form1.

Using the Properties window, specify the Caption for Command1 as Click me. Specify the Caption for Form1 as Original Form.

Create the following Click procedure for Command1:

```
Sub Command1_Click ()
    Dim Fm As Form1

    Set Fm = New Form1
    Fm.Show
    FormNumber = FormNumber + 1
    Fm.Caption = "This is copy number " & FormNumber
    Fm.Move Left, Top + (Height \ 10)
End Sub
```

Now, choose the New Module command from the File menu to add a code module to the application. Place the following Global instruction in the General Declarations section of the module:

```
Global FormNumber As Integer
```

This Global declaration defines a variable named FormNumber which exists throughout the application, even in all the forms that it creates.

Running the Application

Run the application. When you click the command button, a second instance (copy) of the form appears. This new form has a caption which reads This is copy number 1. Click the command button on this new form. Another copy of the form appears. Figure 20.1 shows the screen after several copies of the form are created.

Notice that each form is a distinct object. You can click any of the forms to give it the focus, move the form, or resize it. If you click the command button of any form, the application creates another separate instance of it.

Understanding How the Application Works

Consider the Dim declaration in the Click procedure:

```
Dim Fm As Form1
```

Notice that Form1 appears here as an object data type. This means that the variable Fm refers to objects which are copies of the specific object Form1.

To actually create a new form, the procedure uses a Set instruction, which acts as an assignment instruction for objects:

```
Set Fm = New Form1
```

Here, the object variable Fm is assigned a new copy of Form1. Now, the remaining instructions in the procedure can use Fm to manipulate this newly created copy of the form.

This example serves as an introduction to object variables. The techniques used in this example are explained in detail throughout this chapter.

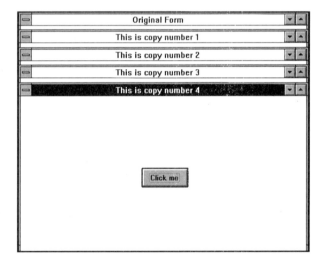

Figure 20.1.

Creating several copies of
Form1.

Declaring an Object Variable

You declare an object variable much as you declare an ordinary one. The Dim, ReDim, Static, and Global statements all can be used to declare object variables. The difference between declaring an object variable and an ordinary one is that, with an object variable, the declaring instruction must include an As *objecttype* clause in which *objecttype* specifies one of several valid object data types.

For example, you already used the following instruction in the sample application to declare Fm as an object variable of the type Form1:

```
Dim Fm As Form1
```

The syntax for the Dim instruction when used to declare an object variable is as follows:

```
Dim varname As New objecttype
```

in which

    varname is a variable name (without a type-declaration suffix),

and

    objecttype specifies an object data type.

The New keyword specifies that, if one doesn't exist, an actual instance of the object should be created when the object variable is used in subsequent instructions. The New keyword is optional.

The various object types and the use of the New keyword are explained in the following sections.

Object Data Types

Visual Basic has two different classes of object data types: *generic* and *specific*. As the names imply, generic object types refer to more than one type of object, whereas a specific type designates a particular one.

Generic Object Types

The three generic object types are Form, Control, and MDIForm. The Form type can refer to any form in the application, including MDI parent and child forms. The Control type can refer to any control in the application, but not to forms. Finally, the MDIForm type can refer only to the MDI form in the application (assuming, of course, that the application uses an MDI form).

 **NOTE**   Visual Basic 3.0 permits only a single MDI (parent) form in an application. As such, the MDIForm generic object type is superfluous because it can only refer to a single type of form. (The specific object type for the MDI form can always be used instead.) Visual Basic supports the generic MDIForm, however, in anticipation that future releases of Visual Basic might support the use of multiple MDI (parent) forms.

Consider the following two instructions:

```
Dim Fm As Form

Dim Ctl As Control
```

Fm is an object variable which can subsequently be assigned to refer to any form in the application. Similarly, Ctl can refer to any control.

Specific Object Types

A specific object type refers to a smaller subset of objects than does a generic type. As the following sections explain, there is a difference between specific form object types and specific control object types.

Specific Form Object Types

For each form created at design time, an application has a corresponding specific form object type. The name of each specific form object type is the same as the Name property of the corresponding form.

For example, a single-form application has only one specific form object type. If the application uses the default name for the form, namely Form1, then it is the name of the specific object type. In the sample application, the following declaration appeared in the Form_Click procedure:

```
Dim Fm As Form1
```

With this declaration, Fm can refer only to the original Form1, or to any new instance of it.

If you change the Name property of the form, say to frmMyForm, then the only available specific object type becomes frmMyForm.

In multiple-form applications, a separate specific object type exists for each form created at design time. A variable declared with one of these object types can represent only objects of that specific form, not of the other form types.

For example, suppose an application defines Form1, Form2, and Form3 at design time. Consider the following declaration of Fm:

```
Dim Fm As Form2
```

Fm can now refer to any instance of Form2, but not to any of Form1 or Form3.

If you use the following generic object type, however, Fm can refer to any instance of any form:

```
Dim Fm As Form
```

Specific Control Object Types

A specific object type exists for each type of control. The following are the specific object types for Visual Basic's built-in controls:

CheckBox	Frame	OptionButton
ComboBox	HScrollBar	PictureBox
CommandButton	Image	Shape
DirListBox	Label	TextBox
DriveListBox	Line	Timer
FileListBox	ListBox	VScrollBar
	Menu	

Suppose you declare MyCtrl as follows:

```
Dim MyCtrl As OptionButton
```

MyCrtl can now refer to any option button in the application, but not to any other type of control.

Although you have specific object types for forms created at design time, for controls made at this time, Visual Basic does not support these same object types. That is, a data type such as Option1 or Option2 is not permitted. Specific control object types always refer to a class of controls (such as OptionButton), not to individual control types created at design time (such as Option1).

 NOTE The Standard Edition of Visual Basic includes three custom controls: CMDIALOG.VBX, GRID.VBX, and MSOLE2.VBX. The Professional Edition has many additional custom controls. Also, third-party vendors sell additional custom controls. You can determine the specific object type for any custom control by using the Properties window, as explained shortly.

Visual Basic has a specific control object type for each of the controls, including the custom ones. (Recall that, when you add a custom control to the Visual Basic environment, you see it listed in the Project window. Also, an icon for the control appears in the Toolbox.)

To determine the object data type for any control (including a custom control), use the Toolbox to place a copy of it on the form. Select the control, then open the Properties window. The object box in the Properties window lists the Name for the control followed by its object type.

For example, Figure 20.2 shows the Properties window opened for a Grid custom control. Note that the object box reads Grid1 Grid. Here, Grid is the specific control object type, while Grid1 specifies the Name property of the particular control placed on the form.

Generic or Specific: Choosing Which Type to Use

You might wonder why Visual Basic has both specific and generic object types. At first thought, generic object types seem to offer more flexibility because they can refer to a larger class of objects than specific object types.

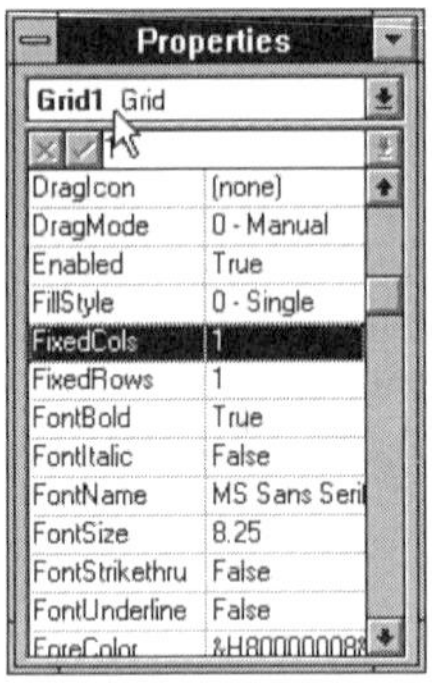

Figure 20.2.

The object box of the Properties window.

In fact, you should use specific object variables whenever feasible. The reasons are improved performance, and less chance of logic errors.

A generic object variable does afford flexibility. For example, suppose an object variable might refer to more than one type of control at different times during execution. You have no choice but to use a generic control variable. Also, generic object variables are appropriate when you don't know, at design time, what specific objects the variable must reference. For example, suppose an application wants to modify the caption of every visible form at some point during run time. You can use a generic form variable which gets set, one at a time, to each visible form.

However, this flexibility for generic object variables comes at a price. At run time, every time a generic variable is referenced in the program code, Visual Basic must determine references to the appropriate properties and methods. This is an inherently slow process which degrades the performance of the application.

By contrast, references for specific object variables can be made once, just before execution begins. This is quite efficient, as no performance degradation occurs at run time.

Whenever possible, therefore, use specific object variables.

Declaring Object Variable with *ReDim,* *Static,* and *Global*

In addition to Dim instructions, you can use ReDim, Static, and Global statements to declare object variables. The syntax is the same as for a Dim instruction except, of course, you use ReDim, Static, or Global instead of Dim.

Just as with an ordinary variable, the scope of an object variable is determined by which keyword you use to declare the variable and where in the code the declaration occurs. These factors also determine the lifetime of the variable. *Lifetime* refers to the length of time the variable exists when the application is run.

The following sections explain the scope and lifetime of object variables.

Scope of Object Variables

The scope of object variables is the same as that of ordinary ones. Recall that the scope of a variable refers to which parts of the program code can actively reference the variable.

If you declare an object variable in a procedure (with Dim, ReDim, or Static), it has local scope. That is, the variable is known only within that particular procedure.

If (with Dim) in the Declarations section of a form or module you declare an object variable, it has scope throughout that form or module.

If (with Global) in the Declarations section of a code module you declare an object variable, however, it has scope throughout the entire application.

Lifetime of Object Variables

An object variable declared with Dim or ReDim in a procedure exists only while the procedure executes. When the procedure terminates, the object variable becomes undefined. If the procedure is reactivated later, the variable is re-created.

An object variable exists for the entire execution of an application in the following two situations:

- The object variable is declared with Global or Dim in the Declarations section of a code module.

- The object variable is declared with Static in a general procedure of a code module.

When in a form module (as opposed to a code module) a form object variable is declared, its lifetime is tied to that of the specific instance of the form. A form object variable exists only as long as does the form in the following situations:

- The object variable is declared with Dim in the Declarations section of a form.

- The object variable is declared with Static inside a procedure defined in the form module.

Using *Set* to Assign Object Variables

The Set instruction acts similar to an assignment instruction for object variables. With Set, you can assign an object variable to a particular object.

For example, consider the following program fragment:

```
Dim MyBtn As CommandButton
Set MyBtn = Form2!Command1
     .
     .
     .
Set MyBtn = Form1!Command1
```

The Dim instruction declares MyBtn to be a specific control object variable that can refer to any command button. At this point, MyBtn does not refer to any particular control.

The first Set instruction assigns MyBtn to refer to the command button named Command1 on Form2. Later, the second Set instruction makes MyBtn refer to the command button named Command1 on Form1.

For a Set instruction to be valid, the object variable must be previously declared with a Dim (ReDim, Static, or Global) instruction.

Creating Instances with the *New* Keyword

You can create additional instances of forms with the New keyword. As explained in the following sections, New works with both Set and Dim instructions.

Using *New* with *Set* Instructions

The sample application presented earlier in the chapter used the keyword New in a Set instruction to create new forms. In that application, the following instructions appeared inside a Click procedure:

```
Dim Fm As Form1
Set Fm = New Form1
Fm.Show
```

With the inclusion of the New keyword, the Set instruction creates a new instance of the form Form1. This is quite a powerful technique. Here, object variables actually create new objects during run time.

In Set instructions, the New keyword is permitted only with specific form variables. You cannot use New to create instances of controls or of generic forms.

Although using Set with New creates a new instance of the form, the Set instruction does not make the form visible. As this code fragment shows, the Show method applied to Fm makes the form appear on-screen.

NOTE

Using the Exclamation Pointer Operator

Recall the use of the exclamation point operator to identify specific controls on forms. Here, the notation Form2!Command1 is a reference to the control Command1 on Form2. Similarly, Form3!Command2 refers to the control Command2 on Form3.

Although not recommended, you can use a period instead of an exclamation point in these contexts. The period is allowed for compatiblity with code written for earlier versions of Visual Basic. In Visual Basic 1.0, the period was the only operator that could reference specific controls on forms.

When writing new applications, you should use the explanation point operator when referencing controls on forms. That way, you avoid any possible ambiguity or confusion involving controls and properties which might have the same name. The situation is compounded by the possibility that new property names may emerge in future releases of Visual Basic.

For example, suppose you name a control Verify and use the notation Form1.Verify to refer to this control on Form1. A future release of Visual Basic might support a property named Verify. If so, the notation Form1.Verify refers to the Verify property, not to the Verify control. Your program code won't work correctly with the new release.

If a control and property have the same name, the period operator refers to the property while the explanation point operator refers to the control. (The period can refer to the control only when the control name is distinct from any property names.) As such, when referring to controls on forms, it's best to use the explanation point.

When Visual Basic creates a new instance of a form, it has all the design-time attributes of the original one. The properties and event procedures associated with the new form are exactly the same as those made for the original one during program design. For example, the size and screen location of the newly created form are those of the original prototype.

NOTE Set with New does not make the newly created form visible, or even load it into memory. To load the form into memory, you must implicitly reference the form, or explicitly use a Load instruction. Here, the Fm.Show instruction references the new form. Before executing the Show method, therefore, Visual Basic loads the form Fm into memory.

Consider the following program fragment:

```
Dim Fm As Form1
Set Fm = New Form1     'First instance of form
Fm.Show
Fm.Caption = "You can't fool me"

Set Fm = New Form1     'Second instance of form
Fm.Show
```

Notice that this code fragment creates a new form instance, then modifies the caption of the newly displayed form. However, the caption on the second form instance reverts back to the caption of the original Form1 at design time. No matter how you modify any specific instance of a form, a new one is a copy of the original.

Using *New* with *Dim* Instructions

You can also use New with Dim instructions that declare specific form objects. In this case, Visual Basic automatically checks whether an instance of the form exists whenever the form variable appears in subsequent code. If an instance does not exist, Visual Basic creates a fresh one. The effect is just as though you had used the Set instruction with New.

For example, instead of the following code fragment discussed previously,

```
Dim Fm As Form1
Set Fm = New Form1     'Create new instance of form
Fm.Show
```

you can produce the same effect with this fragment (notice there is no Set instruction):

```
Dim Fm As New Form1
Fm.Show
```

When the Show method executes, Visual Basic creates a new instance of the form, just as though a Set instruction took place.

A subtle difference exists between using New with Dim, and New with Set. When a Set instruction with New occurs, Visual Basic always creates a new form instance, even if the object variable already refers to an existing one.

When you use New with Dim, however, Visual Basic checks if the object variable refers to an existing instance when a reference to the form occurs. Visual Basic creates a new instance *only* if the object variable does not already refer to an existing instance.

This feature of creating a new instance when necessary is known as *auto-instantiation*. By using New with Dim, you guarantee that an instance of the form exists whenever you use a specific form object variable.

Severing Links Between Object Variables and Objects

Object variables refer to objects. The variables themselves are not objects. As such, when an object variable no longer exists, the object itself can remain in the application.

For example, suppose that you use a Set instruction with New in an event procedure to create a new form instance. Assume that the form object variable was declared in the event procedure. Thus, the form object variable has scope only within that procedure. When the Set instruction executes, Visual Basic adds a new form instance to the application.

Now consider what happens when the event procedure terminates. The form object variable no longer exists because the variable had only local scope. However, the newly created form continues to exist.

If the event procedure is reactivated, the form object variable is re-created. However, there is no longer any link between this new variable and any existing forms. When the Set instruction executes, Visual Basic creates a new instance of the form.

Creating Side Effects with *Set*

When you use Set to assign an object variable to an object, Visual Basic establishes a direct link between the two. The object variable refers directly to the object, not to a copy of it. Such a link is referred to as a *reference* link.

Suppose you then use the object variable to modify a property value of the object. The change occurs on the object itself. If the same object is referenced by a second object variable, the property value changes for that object variable also. Such an indirect change is called a *side effect*. Side effects are by-products of links by reference.

To illustrate a side effect, consider the following code fragment:

```
Dim MyFrm As Form1, YourFrm As Form1, TestStr As String
Set MyFrm = New Form1      'Create new instance of Form1
Set YourFrm = MyFrm        'Equate object variables to same form
MyFrm.Caption = "We're in good form"
TestStr = YourFrm.Caption
```

The point is that `TestStr` has the value `We're in good form`, even though `YourFrm.Caption` was never explicitly assigned this value. `MyFrm` and `YourFrm` refer to the same object, so any change in the property of the object is reflected in the referencing variables. When `MyFrm.Caption` was assigned a new value, `YourFrm.Caption` also changed as a side effect.

Using Implicit Form Variables

If object variables were new to you before reading this chapter, you're in for a little surprise. You have been using object variables all along—implicit form object variables, that is!

Whenever you create a new form, Visual Basic automatically declares for it a global object variable. This variable is a specific form variable. In single-form applications, the global form variable has the name `Form1`.

The implicit form object variable is what you have been using when you write program code that modifies form property values, or otherwise references the form. For example, consider the following instructions:

```
Form1.BackColor = MAGENTA        'Set property value

Form1.Print "I'm in rare form"   'Use Print method

Unload Form1                     'Statement parameter
```

In these instructions, each `Form1` reference is to the implicit form variable called `Form1`.

If you change the `Name` property of a form at design time, Visual Basic changes the name of the implicit form variable accordingly. In multiple-form applications, Visual Basic implicitly declares a form object variable for each new form.

For example, suppose you create, at design time, a new form in an application. You name the form `MyForm`. Effectively, Visual Basic creates a global declaration as follows:

```
Global MyForm As MyForm
```

Of course, you never actually see this declaration. Throughout the program code, however, you can use `MyForm` in any context in which Visual Basic is expecting the name of a form.

Testing the Type of Object Variable with *TypeOf*

You can use a special form of the `If-Then-Else` instruction to test whether an object variable refers to a particular type of object.

In such tests, the testing condition can be specified by a clause of the following kind.

```
TypeOf objectvar Is objecttype
```

in which

> *objectvar* is an object variable,

and

> *objecttype* is any generic or specific object type.

For example, the following instruction tests whether `Fm` refers to an object of type `Form1`.

```
If TypeOf Fm Is Form1 Then Print "Yes it is"
```

You can use `TypeOf` clauses with `ElseIf` clauses in multiline `If` structures. For example:

```
If TypeOf MyCtrlVar Is ListBox Then
    .
    'execute list box processing here
    .
ElseIf TypeOf MyCtrlVar Is ComboBox Then
    .
    'execute combo box processing here
    .
ElseIf TypeOf MyCtrlVar Is TextBox Then
    .
    'execute textbox processing here
    .
End If
```

Some limitations exist to the use of TypeOf. First, TypeOf cannot be used with compound test conditions. For example, the following instruction results in an error:

```
If (TypeOf MyCtrlVar Is TextBox) Or (Result < 50) Then...
```

Secondly, the keyword Not cannot be used with TypeOf. For example, the following instruction is not permitted:

```
If Not(TypeOf MyCtrlVar Is PictureBox) Then Print "No Picture"
```

Instead, to test for the Not condition, you can use a dummy instruction block and an Else clause as follows:

```
If TypeOf MyCtrlVar Is PictureBox Then
    'Dummy statement block
Else
    Print "No Picture"
End If
```

Finally, TypeOf cannot be used with Select Case-End Select structures. Select Case works with numeric and text expressions. TypeOf works with True or False conditional tests.

Testing with *Is*

In an If instruction, you can test whether two object variables refer to the same object. Use the Is operator to form the comparison. For example, the following code fragment tests whether two form object variables refer to the same form:

```
Dim MyFrm As Form1
Dim YourForm As Form
Set YourForm = MyFrm
If MyFrm Is YourFrm Then Print "Yes, they are the same form
```

NOTE The Is operator used in TypeOf clauses, and for comparing two object variables, has no relation to the Is keyword employed to specify ranges with Select Case. For more information on Select Case, see Chapter 15, "Program Flow and Decision Making."

Using the Keyword *Nothing*

Visual Basic uses the keyword Nothing to refer to the contents of an object variable that is not assigned any particular object. When you first declare an object variable, it has the value Nothing.

With the Set instruction, you can assign an object variable to Nothing, for example:

```
Set MyFrm = Nothing
```

Such an instruction removes any association MyFrm has with any existing object. If you no longer need an object variable to refer to an object, it's a good idea to set the variable to Nothing. That way, Visual Basic can release the memory, and other system resources used by the object variable. Note, however, you only need to assign form-level and global object variables to Nothing. Object variables local to the procedure are automatically set to Nothing when the procedure terminates.

You can test for Nothing with the Is keyword just as you can for other object types. For example:

```
If MyFrm Is Nothing Then Print "What happened?"
```

System Objects

Visual Basic has five system objects: App, Clipboard, Debug, Printer, and Screen. These are global objects which are predefined by Visual Basic. You don't need to explicitly declare these objects; they are automatically available in any application.

Each of these objects has specific properties and methods. You can read or assign most of the property values at run time. As explained in the following sections, you can use these objects to control the way an application interacts with the Windows environment.

The *App* Object

The App object houses information about the application's name, path, and associated files. Table 20.1 shows the five properties associated with the App object.

Table 20.1. Properties of the App Object.

Property	Meaning
EXEName	Identifies, in string format, the root name (without a file extension) of the application's executable file. In the developmental environment, specifies the name of the project. Accessible only at run time, its value can be read but not modified.
Path	Specifies, in string format, the file path to the application. When the application is run from the developmental environment, the path is to the project; for an executable file, the path is to the .EXE file. Accessible only at run time, its value can be read but not modified.
Title	Specifies, in string format, the title of the application as the Windows Task Manager shows.
HelpFile	Specifies, in string format, the name of the application's Help file, if any.
PrevInstance	Indicates whether a previous instance of the application is currently running. The value is True or False. Accessible only at run time, its value can be read but not modified.

NOTE The HelpFile property is available only with the Professional Edition of Visual Basic. With the Professional Edition, you can add Windows-compatible Help files to your applications. For more information on creating Help Files, see Chapter 33, "Adding a Help System to an Application."

The EXEName and Path properties are useful in Visual Basic applications that interact with other Windows programs. In sophisticated applications, you can use the App properties as string variables for Windows DLL (Dynamic Link Library) calls that interact with the Windows environment.

The ShowApp Application

The following application, named ShowApp, provides a quick demonstration of the App object. To create ShowApp, start a new project, and follow these steps:

1. Double-click the Command button icon in the Toolbox.

   A command button of the default size appears in the center of the form.

2. Using the Properties window, specify the Caption for the command button to be Show App.

3. Create the following `Click` event procedure for the command button:

```
Sub Command1_Click ()
    Print "Program Name is "; App.EXEName
    Print "Path is "; App.Path
    Print "Title is "; App.Title
End Sub
```

4. Save the form as SHOWAPP.FRM and the project as SHOWAPP.MAK.

You can save the files in any directory.

Now, run the application. Click the command button. On the form, the application displays information about its name, and the path to the project file (see Figure 20.3). As you can see from the `Command1_Click` event procedure, the displayed information is obtained from various properties of the `App` object. Note that, in the computer system used to generate the figure, the application is saved in the directory C:\VB\DEMOS. Your path is likely to be different.

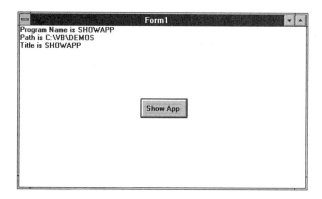

Figure 20.3.

Demonstrating the **App** object.

The *Debug* Object

The `Debug` object has one purpose—to permit the display of information on the Debug window at run time. The `Debug` object has no properties, and only a single associated method, namely `Print`.

You can demonstrate the `Debug` object by modifying the `Command1_Click` procedure in the ShowApp application to appear as follows:

```
Sub Command1_Click ()
    Debug.Print "Program Name is "; App.EXEName
    Debug.Print "Path is "; App.Path
    Debug.Print "Title is "; App.Title
End Sub
```

Now, when you run the application, the displayed information appears on the Debug window, not on the form. If you can't see the Debug window when you try the application, choose the **D**ebug option from the **W**indow menu.

The *Clipboard* Object

The Clipboard system object provides a running Visual Basic application with direct access to the Windows Clipboard. The Clipboard object has no properties, but does have six associated methods as Table 20.2 shows.

Table 20.2. Clipboard methods.

Method	Use
SetText	Send text data to the Clipboard
GetText	Get text data from the Clipboard
Clear	Clear contents of the Clipboard
GetData	Get picture data from the Clipboard
SetData	Send picture to the Clipboard
GetFormat	Determine whether Clipboard has data of a particular format

For more information on accessing the Windows Clipboard in Visual Basic applications, see Chapter 29, "Manipulating the Windows Environment."

The *Printer* Object

With the Printer object, you can control the system printer directly from your Visual Basic applications. With Printer, you can print text and graphics, and control many of the printer's operating features. The Printer object always refers to the default system printer, as specified in the Window Control Panel.

The Printer object has several associated properties: CurrentX, CurrentY, DrawMode, DrawStyle, DrawWidth, FillColor, FillStyle, FontBold, FontCount, FontItalic, FontName, Fonts, FontSize, FontStrikeThru, FontTransparency, FontUnderline, ForeColor, hDc, Height, Page, ScaleHeight, ScaleLeft, ScaleMode, ScaleTop, ScaleWidth, TwipsPerPixelX, TwipsPerPixelY, Width.

Most of these properties have self-explanatory names. The properties are available only at run time. For most of the properties, you can both read the current value and assign a new one. As an example of Printer, the following code fragment specifies that the next printed text should appear in italic, at the left edge of the page, 2,000 twips from the top:

```
Printer.CurrentX = 0          'Print position at left edge of paper
Printer.CurrentY = 2000       'Print position 2000 twips from top
Printer.FontItalic = True     'Print in italics
```

Printer has nine associated methods: Circle, EndDoc, Line, NewPage, Print, PSet, Scale, TextHeight, and TextWidth. Notice that the graphics methods such as Circle, Line, and Pset permit the drawing of graphics on suitable printers.

Of course, Print is the method used most often with Printer. By attaching the Printer keyword to Print instructions, printed output goes to the printer rather than to the form, for example:

```
Print "This sentence appears on the form."
Printer.Print "While this sentence appears on the printer."
```

The *Screen* Object

The Screen object references the entire video screen. Screen has no methods, but it does have the following nine properties: ActiveControl, ActiveForm, FontCount, Fonts, Height, MousePointer, TwipsPerPixelX, TwipsPerPixelY, and Width.

You often use Screen to manipulate the size and placement of forms. For example, by reading the values of Screen.Height and Screen.Width, you can ascertain the screen dimensions and determine whether a particular layout of multiple forms is feasible. Also, you can use the Screen.MousePointer property to specify the shape of the cursor, even when it is outside the active forms.

Working with Collections

Visual Basic provides access to all the forms in an application through an array-type mechanism known as the *Forms Collection*. A similar mechanism, called the *Controls Collection*, provides access to all the controls on each form in an application.

Understanding the Forms Collection

For each application, there is one Forms Collection. Visual Basic automatically declares this collection globally with the predefined word Forms.

The Forms Collection contains only loaded form instances. This is an important point because applications frequently load and unload forms as processing continues.

`Forms` has a single read-only property named `Count`. The `Count` property indicates the number of currently loaded form instances. As such, the value of `Forms.Count` constantly changes as forms are loaded and unloaded.

In some ways, `Forms` acts similar to an array. Most importantly, you can refer to specific form instances with the following syntax:

```
Forms(index)
```

in which

> *index* is a numeric expression.

`Forms` is a *zero-based* collection. As such, the first form in the collection has an index value of `0`. Each subsequent form increments by one the value of *index*, until it reaches the value of (`Count` - `1`).

The first form in the collection, therefore, is referenced as `Forms(0)`. However, `Forms.Count` for this array returns the value `1`.

The second form is `Forms(1)`. Here, `Forms.Count` is 2. The final form in the collection has an index value of `Forms.Count` - `1`.

The order of the forms in the Forms Collection is completely unpredictable. As forms are loaded and unloaded, the location of a particular one in the collection can change unpredictably. However, the index values for all forms in the collection always ranges from `0` to `Forms.Count` - `1`.

The Forms Collection has an array-like syntax, so you frequently use `Forms` in loops. For example, the following code fragment displays the captions of all loaded forms in the Debug window:

```
For FrmNum% = 0 to (Forms.Count - 1)
    Debug.Print Forms(FrmNum%).Caption
Next FrmNum%
```

Similarly, you can modify the captions of the loaded forms as follows:

```
For FrmNum% = 0 to (Forms.Count - 1)
    Forms(FrmNum%).Caption = "Form number " & FrmNum%
Next FrmNum%
```

You can also use `Set` to assign a particular form instance to a form object variable. For example,

```
Dim MyFrmVar As Form
Set MyFrmVar = Forms(3)
```

One thing you cannot do, however, is pass `Forms` as a parameter to a procedure.

Understanding the Controls Collection

Similar to the Forms Collection, Visual Basic provides a Controls Collection for each form in an application. The keyword is `Controls`.

Similar to `Forms`, `Controls` has a `Count` property and an index argument. For example, `Controls.Count` indicates the number of loaded controls on the current form. `Controls(0)` refers to the first control in the collection. The final control in the collection has an index value of `Controls.Count - 1`. Just as with the Forms Collection, the order of the controls in a `Control` collection is unpredictable.

To specify the form that a specific Controls Collection refers to, `Controls` uses an optional form name and a period before the word `Controls`. For example, `Form3.Controls(0)` specifies the first control in the Controls Collection for `Form3`. If you omit a form reference, such as `Controls(2)`, you are specifying the `Controls` Collection for the current form. To reference the `Controls` Collection for a different form, use the explicit form reference.

If you specify the form name, you can omit the word `Controls`. In such a case, you place the index argument that goes with `Controls` around the form name instead. For example, the following instructions are identical:

```
Form2.Controls(indxNum%).Caption = "The Object of my affection"

Form2(indxNum%).Caption "The Object of my affections"
```

Using Arrays of Objects

Visual Basic permits arrays of object data types. With `Dim`, `ReDim`, `Static`, and `Global`, you can declare such arrays in a manner similar to the way you do so for those of ordinary variables. As the following sections explain, you can create arrays of form objects and of control objects.

Using Arrays of Forms

When creating an array of forms, you can use a generic or specific form data type in the `As` clause. The following are some sample declarations:

```
Dim LotsOfForms(30) As frmActPayable    'Specific form object type

Dim MyForms(20) As Form                 'Generic form data type

Global YourForms() As Form              'Dynamic array of generic forms
```

The final example demonstrates a dynamic array of generic form variables (no dimensions in the parentheses). In procedures, you can use the ReDim instruction to dynamically declare a specific size for the array. For more information on dynamic arrays, see Chapter 19, "Using Arrays and Structures."

You can also use the New keyword in an array declaration. For arrays of forms, New works just as it does when declaring a form variable. That is, Visual Basic creates a new instance of the form when the program code references each new element of the array. The following is a sample declaration of an array of forms containing New:

```
Dim Surveys(100) As New frmSurveyType
```

You can use array elements in your program code just as you use ordinary form variables. Often, you utilize arrays of forms in loops. The following is an example:

```
Dim Ctr As Integer
Dim Survey(100) As New frmSurveyType
For Ctr = 1 To NumEmployees
    Survey(Ctr).Caption = "Employee number " & Ctr
Next Ctr
```

Using Arrays of Controls

You can declare arrays of controls. The elements of such an array can be any controls in the application, not just those attached to a particular form.

You can create generic and specific arrays of controls. For example, the following instruction declares an array which can reference all the controls in an application:

```
Dim CtrlArray(100) As Control
```

One use of a generic array of controls is to manage the placement of controls on a form. Each control in the application can be assigned an element in the array. You can then use looping structures to check, for example, that no two arrays overlap. This technique is especially useful if your application adds and deletes controls at run time.

Specific arrays of controls can reference only controls of the declared type. For example, the following declaration specifies that elements in the Pix array can only be picture boxes:

```
Global Pix() As PictureBox
```

Here, Pix also happens to be a dynamic array. With ReDim instructions, you can dynamically adjust the array bounds at run time.

Arrays of controls cannot use the New keyword. When the code specifies a specific element in an array of controls, the referenced control must already exist.

Understanding the Difference Between Arrays of Controls and Control Arrays

Arrays of controls and control arrays are not the same. The concepts are similar, so it's easy to become confused. After all, syntax such as Pix(8) can be referring to a control array, or an array of controls.

A control array is created at design time by giving two or more controls on a form the same Name property. When you do so, Visual Basic pops open a dialog box asking if you want to create a control array. By confirming that you do, Visual Basic assigns a separate value of the Index property for each element of the control array. You can modify these values of Index by using the Properties window at design time. A control array thus becomes a group of controls, all of the same type, with each individual one having a unique Index value.

Once the control array is created, its elements can be referenced in code with an index argument in parentheses. For example, suppose, at design time, you create a control array of list boxes with the name LBox. You can then refer to, say, the second element of the control array as LBox(1). (The first element has an Index value of 0, so the second has an Index of 1.)

With Load and Unload instructions, you can load and unload elements of a control array at run time. If you unload an element of a control array, the Index value for that control no longer refers to an existing one (that is, the control is removed from memory). In essence, you can create a gap in the sequential order of Index values. For more information on control arrays, see Chapter 7, "Writing Event Procedures."

By contrast, you explicitly create an array of controls with a Dim, ReDim, Static, or Global instruction in program code. As with any array, Visual Basic routinely maintains a contiguous order in its elements. You can't create a gap in the ordering of an array of controls in the same way that you can in the Index values of a control array.

However, you *can* change the number of elements in an array of controls. You do so by using the ReDim instruction to dynamically reallocate the storage space for the array at run time. You cannot however, remove elements individually. The elements in an array of controls are always contiguous.

To summarize, the following table compares control arrrays to arrays of controls:

Control Arrays	Arrays of Controls
Created at design time	Created at run time
Have associated property values	Don't have associated property values
Can Load & Unload elements at run time	Can use ReDim to dynamically change the number of elements

Passing Object Variables to Procedures

Object variables can be passed, as arguments, to procedures. Such arguments can be either generic object variables or specific ones.

An object variable is always passed by reference, which means that the passed variable *points* to the actual object, not to a copy of it. As a result, the called procedure can use the formal parameter to modify the properties of the object.

Compatibility of Formal and Actual Parameters

To pass an object variable to a procedure, you must declare the procedure's formal parameter with an object type compatible with the actual parameter. If the formal parameter is a generic object (form or control), than you can pass either a specific object variable or a generic one (compatible with form or control, of course). However, if the formal parameter is specific, then the passed object variable must also be specific.

For the purposes of passing an actual parameter, the object variable's declared data type is what matters, not the object type of variable's current value. For example, suppose you declare a procedure as follows:

```
SubMoveImage (imgCtl As Image)
```

Now, you can pass any object variable to this procedure, as long as it is declared to be of type Image. However, you cannot pass an object variable declared generically as Control, even if the current contents of the passed variable are of type Image.

An Example of Passing Object Variables

Consider the following user-defined procedure named FlipFlop:

```
Sub FlipFlop (SourceA As Control, SourceB As Control)
   Dim TempCapt As String
   TempCapt = SourceA.Caption        'Store copy of Caption A
   SourceA.Caption = SourceB.Caption
   SourceB.Caption = TempCapt
End Sub
```

This procedure switches the Caption properties of two controls. The formal parameters are two generic control variables, SourceA and SourceB. If you pass two object variables to FlipFlop, the procedure switches their captions. Notice that the two passed objects can be different types of controls, as long as each control has a Caption property.

Here's a quick application that uses FlipFlop to switch the captions on a label and a command button. To try the application, start a new project. Place a label control (default name Label1) and a command button (default name Command1) on the form. Using the Properties window, assign the property values that Table 20.3 shows.

Table 20.3. Design-time properties for the *FlipFlop* application.

Object	Property	Value
Form1	Caption	FlipFlop
Label1	Caption	I started as a label
	Left	2520
	Top	840
	Height	495
	Width	2895
Command1	Caption	I started as a command button
	Left	1800
	Top	2040
	Height	495
	Width	4455

Now, type FlipFlop as a user-defined procedure in the General Declarations section of the form. Then, create the following Click event procedure for the command button:

```
Sub Command1_Click ()
    Dim cmdButton As CommandButton
    Dim lbl As Label

    Set cmdButton = Command1
    Set lbl = Label1

    Call FlipFlop(cmdButton, lbl)

End Sub
```

You're now ready to try the application. When you run FlipFlop, the initial form appears as Figure 20.4 shows. If you click the command button, the labels for the two controls change places (see Figure 20.5).

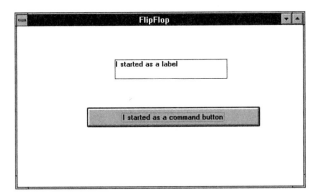

Figure 20.4.

The FlipFlop application when first run.

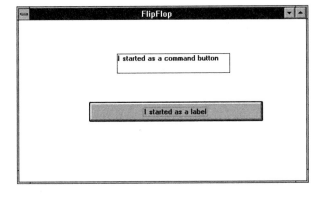

Figure 20.5.

The captions on the controls have traded places.

Notice that the Click procedure declares the object variables cmdButton and lbl as specific control variables of type CommandButton and Label, respectively. These object variables are then assigned to the Command1 and Label1 controls.

After they are assigned, the object variables are passed as actual parameters to the FlipFlop procedure. FlipFlop uses the generic control variables SourceA and SourceB as formal parameters. The actual parameters are controls (not forms), so this works well.

You can expand this application by adding several controls to the form. You can then pass to FlipFlop object variables representing any two controls.

Using the Keyword Me

As you've seen, you can use form object variables to create new instances of forms. Visual Basic creates a new instance of a form whenever you execute a Set instruction containing the New keyword; for example, Set MyFrm = New Form1. (As explained previously in this chapter, another way to create new form instances is to use New with Dim to produce an auto-instantiating form variable.)

When Visual Basic creates new instances of a form, they are distinct from all others. When first created, the new instance has the same property values, declarations, and code events as the prototype form at design time. Once the new instance exists, however, its property values can be modified by the program code. Such modifications affect only the new instance. Visual Basic manages separate property lists for each instance of a form.

Me as a Specific Form Variable

To refer to the currently active instance of a form, Visual Basic predefines Me as a special keyword. Me acts similar to a specific form variable. You can use Me anywhere you use a specific form variable: in Set instructions, as an argument in procedure calls, as part of statements expecting a form argument (Unload Me, for example), and in comparison clauses with the Is operator. In multiple-form applications, Me references the form instance associated with the currently executing code.

NOTE The ActiveForm property of the Screen object specifies the currently active form. As a result, Screen.ActiveForm and Me usually (but not always) refer to the same form. The difference arises when an event happens on a nonactive form. The most likely situation is when a Timer event occurs on a form which does not have the focus. In that situation, Screen.ActiveForm refers to the active (visible) form, and Me—to the form with the Timer control.

The *Me* Application

The following multiform application demonstrates the use of Me. By clicking a command button in any form, you can change its caption. The Click event for the command button passes Me to a user-defined procedure which modifies the form's caption.

To try the application, start a new project. Place two command buttons on the form. Using the Properties window, assign the property values that Table 20.4 shows.

Table 20.4. Design-time properties for *Me* application.

Object	Property	Value
Command1	Caption	Create new forms
	Left	960
	Top	1920
	Height	495
	Width	2295
Command2	Caption	Change form's caption
	Left	4200
	Top	1920
	Height	495
	Width	2295

In the General Declarations section of the form, create the following user-defined Sub procedure named ChangeCaption:

```
Sub ChangeCaption (FormName As Form)
   FormName.Caption = "I've got a new Caption"
End Sub
```

Notice that this procedure accepts any form object variable, then modifies the caption for that form.

Of the two command buttons, when you click the one to the left, the application creates three new instances of Form1. The following is the Command1_Click procedure:

```
Sub Command1_Click ()
   Dim NewForm As Form1
   Dim Idx As Integer

   For Idx = 1 To 3
      Set NewForm = New Form1   'Create new form instance
```

```
        NewForm.Show                'Make new instance visible
        NewForm.Top = NewForm.Top + (400 * Idx) 'Move downward
    Next Idx
End Sub
```

Notice that, to have all form instances visible, each new one moves slightly downward from the previous ones.

When you click the second command button, the caption for that form changes. The following is the Command2_Click event procedure:

```
Sub Command2_Click ()
    Call ChangeCaption(Me)
End Sub
```

This Click procedure simply calls ChangeCaption while passing the Me argument.

Running the *Me* Application

Try running the application. At first, all you see is the single form Form1 with its design-time attributes. The form has two command buttons (see Figure 20.6).

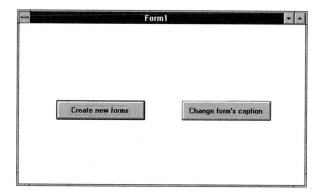

Figure 20.6.

The Me application when first started.

Now, click the command button to the left labeled Create new forms. The Command1_Click procedure creates three new instances of Form1. Each instance has the default caption Form1 (see Figure 20.7).

At this point, you can click the caption of any form to bring it to the foreground. When you click the command button to the far right on any form, its caption changes to I've got a new Caption. You can change the caption on none, some, or all of the forms. Figure 20.8 shows the captions changed on two of the forms.

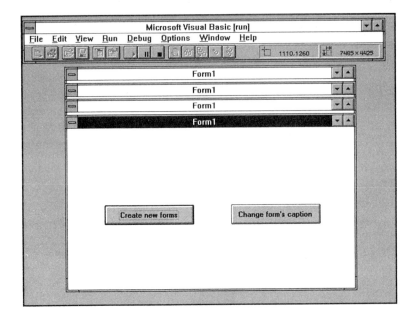

Figure 20.7.

Four instances of **Form1**
now exist.

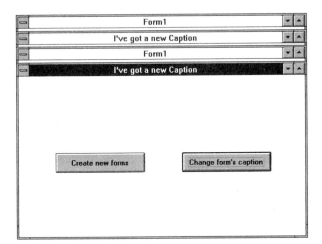

Figure 20.8.

The captions of two
instances have been
modified.

How *Me* Works

The application works because, when the Command2_Click procedure passes Me
to ChangeCaption, Me refers to the current form. Notice that if you change
Command2_Click as follows, the application does not work correctly:

```
Sub Command2_Click ()
    Call ChangeCaption(Form1)
End Sub
```

Here, the argument `Form1` refers to the original instance of the form. With this modification, the caption changes on the *original* form when you click `Command2` on *any* form.

Summary

Applications consist of several types of objects. There are user-defined objects, such as forms and controls. Also, Visual Basic predefines system objects, such as `Screen` and `Clipboard`.

Object variables can reference the objects in an application. Such variables provide extensive run-time flexibility in creating, manipulating, and eliminating the objects in an application.

Each object variable has a form or control object type. You declare an object variable with `Dim` (`ReDim`, `Static`, or `Global`) instructions that specify its object data type. The object types can be generic (such as `Form` or `Control`) or specific (such as `Form1` or `PictureBox`).

Visual Basic provides several keywords and program instructions for object variables. Use `Set` to assign an object variable to an object. When used in reference to specific form variables, the `New` keyword creates new instances of specific forms. `TypeOf` and `Is` facilitate comparison testing of object variables.

Object variables have a scope and a lifetime as do regular variables do. You can pass object variables as procedure arguments, and create arrays of object variables.

For each application, Visual Basic predefines groups of objects called *collections*. The Forms Collection lets you manipulate any form in an application. Similarly, for each form, the Controls Collection provides access to the controls.

Debugging and Error Handling

T he programming process is prone to error. No matter how carefully you plan a new project, and type in the program code, you're going to find that often a complex application doesn't quite work right at first. Bugs come with the programming territory.

Fortunately, Visual Basic has many tools to help you debug programs, and deal with errors. In this chapter, you learn about the debugging and testing features available from the **D**ebug menu—tools for tracing a program, and setting watch expressions. Also, the chapter covers error trapping. By writing an error-handler, your program can anticipate certain errors, and recover gracefully when they occur.

Interactive Debugging and Testing

Every programmer, beginner or expert, makes mistakes. That's why debugging and testing are integral parts of developing any application. In fact, you can gauge programmers' experience by their attitude toward testing and debugging. Experienced programmers realize that for any program to work properly, thorough testing is essential.

Some programmers despise testing and shun debugging. They'd rather spend endless hours in the design and planning stages. By the time they actually type their programs, they feel confident that no bugs could have crept in.

Programmers at the other extreme say to themselves, "Let me just type something approximately close to what I need. I can fix the errors later." These programmers tend to produce sloppy, jumbled programs that are needlessly difficult to debug.

A middle ground between these two extremes, of course, is preferable.

The sloppy-program trap is easy to fall into! Visual Basic's interactive nature, and impressive debugging tools, might lead you to think that you can readily debug your way out of any mess. The following are some of the debugging techniques that you can utilize when troubleshooting:

- Display the values of variables or expressions after you stop your program (`Print` from the Debug window)

- Execute your program one line at a time (**D**ebug menu)

- Determine the location of nonspecific error messages (`On Error GoTo`)

- Repeatedly suspend and resume execution (Breakpoints, Watchpoints, `Stop`, Ctrl+Break)

- Trace your program's logic flow (**D**ebug menu)

The examples in this chapter are deliberately short and contain conspicuous errors. Most of your difficult problem-solving tasks occur in larger programs in which the errors are not so apparent. However, the main goals here are to show errors and demonstrate debugging techniques. This is done with short, to-the-point examples, which are the best teaching methods.

A Debugging Philosophy

To write successful programs, you must perform the interrelated actions of testing and debugging:

- *Testing* refers to the actions that determine whether the program code runs correctly.

- *Debugging* is the subsequent activity of finding and removing the errors, or bugs.

Sometimes a test run shows clearly that an application has coding errors. The testing part can be easy, but the debugging process might be much more difficult. In a sense, testing and debugging never end. Every time you run a program, you're testing.

Programmers (cautious programmers, anyway) often say that every nontrivial program has a bug waiting to be found. Then, when the bug is found and fixed, another remains. Figure 21.1 depicts the process of programming a project from beginning to end. As the figure lightheartedly demonstrates, you never really reach the end.

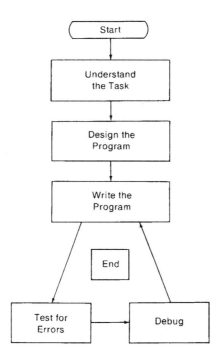

Figure 21.1.

The programming process.

The following are some principles of a sound debugging philosophy:

- *Assume that your code has errors.* No one is perfect, nor does anyone write faultless code all the time. Expect to find errors. Exposing the errors—all of them—is your purpose in testing and debugging. Enjoy the detective work.

- *No single test run can prove that an application is bug-free.* Plan to run many test cases, and to use a variety of test data. A program that runs to completion and produces expected results is a good sign, but that's only the beginning of testing.

- *Try to make your programs fail during testing.* Don't rely on "friendly" data when you test. If the program is destined to be used by others who must supply data, try all kinds of unreasonable values. Your users might type almost anything when prompted for input. Your goal should be a "bullet-proof" application—one that cannot "crash" (produce a Visual Basic error message), or generate an incorrect result, no matter what users try.

■ *While developing the application, test frequently.* After coding a new procedure, or writing just a few new lines, test immediately. It's best to work with small chunks of text. If you make numerous program changes or additions before testing, you're making your work more difficult than necessary.

■ *Use sound programming style.* Modularize your code as much as possible. The event-driven nature of Visual Basic encourages such practices. As explained in Chapter 18, "Using Procedures: Subs and Functions," make each of your Sub and Function procedures short, and to the point. Break a large procedure into two or more smaller ones. Several smaller components are easier to understand, program, test, and debug than a larger one.

NOTE

The First "Bug"

"Bug" and "debug" are well-known terms in the programming vernacular. A *bug* is an error or problem in a program. When an application doesn't work correctly, programmers say the code has a "bug." The process of finding and correcting the bug is called *debugging the program*, or simply *debugging*.

Did you ever wonder how the colorful terms "bug" and "debug" originated?

When computers were in their infancy, some of their operators were having hardware problems. The setting was the late 1940s at an East Coast naval installation. The computers, which were less powerful than the PC on your desk, were vacuum tube devices that required warehouse-sized rooms.

A computer was malfunctioning, and the operators went to take a look. They found a dead moth lodged in one of the electric circuits. Apparently, the moth was killed from either the heat of the vacuum tubes, or contact with one of the exposed circuits. When they removed the moth, the computer resumed functioning normally. By eliminating the bug, the operators solved the problem. Thus, the earliest "bug" was, in fact, a real insect!

This first "debugging" was actually the correction of a hardware problem. This term, however, has gradually evolved to mean the elimination of programming (software) errors.

Dealing with Run-time Errors

Errors are a fact of programming life. All programmers make mistakes, so don't feel bad when the inevitable errors occur. Recognize that errors are bound to happen, learn from them, and continue with your programming tasks.

Understanding Run-time Errors

Errors that you don't discover until you run a program are called *run-time* errors. Three fundamental types of run-time errors can occur:

- *Syntax errors.* A syntax error occurs when an instruction doesn't follow the rules of Visual Basic. For example, you might spell a keyword incorrectly; use improper punctuation; combine keywords in an illegal way, or not provide enough parameters to a built-in function. In any of these cases, the instruction is meaningless, and Visual Basic cannot even *attempt* to execute it. The editor catches some syntax errors as you type. Remaining syntax errors are caught when you actually run the program.

- *Execution errors.* An execution error occurs when Visual Basic cannot perform a program instruction. The action requested by the instruction is impossible, even though its syntax is adequate. For example, you might divide a number by zero—a mathematically illegal operation. When an execution error occurs, Visual Basic enters Break mode and suspends execution. It highlights the offending line in the program, and displays an error message. In general, the error message quickly points out the problem (although sometimes the cause of the problem is not obvious).

- *Logic errors.* A logic error occurs when a program runs to completion, but the results are just not right. All the instructions have legal syntax, and Visual Basic executes the program, and terminates normally. As far as Visual Basic is concerned, everything went well. However, the program just doesn't produce correct results. Logic errors are the most difficult ones to debug. Fortunately, Visual Basic's special debugging features are most helpful with these types of errors.

Recognizing Run-time Errors

This section presents a very simple example of each type of run-time error. In practical applications, of course, your errors are bound to occur in more complex programs.

An Example of a Syntax Error

Syntax errors usually are the result of simple typing mistakes. When a syntax error occurs, Visual Basic stops running the application, and points out the faulty line.

Try the following experiment. Start a new application, and type the following `Form_Resize` event procedure. Type the third line exactly as the following program fragment shows, with `Print` incorrectly spelled as `Prnt`:

```
Sub Form_Resize ()
    Print "Hello"
    Prnt "Goodbye"
End Sub
```

Notice that nothing special happens when you type the incorrect line. This is an example of a syntax error that is not caught by Visual Basic until you actually try to run the program.

Now, run the program. Visual Basic immediately finds the syntax error. As Figure 21.2 shows, the screen shifts back to the Code window and a message box pops open. In the box is a message indicating that a syntax error is present. The offending word, Prnt, is highlighted in your program code. Click OK, or press Enter to close the message box. You can now edit Prnt to read Print.

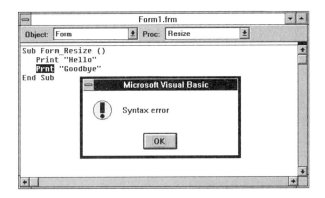

Figure 21.2.

A syntax error occurs.

Visual Basic insists that you follow its rules. You might think that, given the sophistication of Visual Basic, the editor might be able to "figure out" that Prnt should be Print. After all, Prnt is very close to Print. Prnt, however, is indecipherable to Visual Basic, and a syntax error results.

An Example of an Execution Error

When an execution error occurs, Visual Basic suspends your program, and displays an explanatory error message. As an experiment, start a new application, and type the following Form_Load procedure:

```
Sub Form_Load ()
    Dim NumHits As Integer, NumAB As Integer
    Dim Msg As String
```

```
FindBatAve:
   NumHits = Val(InputBox$("Number of hits?"))
   NumAB = Val(InputBox$("Number of times at bat?"))
   Msg = "Batting average is " & NumHits / NumAB
   MsgBox Msg
   GoTo FindBatAve
End Sub
```

This procedure computes baseball batting averages. (A batting average is the total of a baseball player's hits divided by the number of times at bat.) The code uses several input and one message box to get data from the user, and display the results. The code loops so that multiple batting averages can be computed.

Suppose you want to use this application to calculate the following three batting averages:

■ A player had 128 hits in 523 at bats for an entire season.

■ A player had 27 hits in 79 at bats in one month.

■ A player had 8 hits in 30 at bats in one week.

Now suppose you make a mistake when typing the input values, inadvertently entering 0 at bats during the third calculation. Table 21.1 shows the program results. In this table, the first two columns represent values you type in response to the input box prompts. The third column shows the message displayed in the resultant box.

Table 21.1. Results of batting average calculations.

Hits	At Bats	Message box display
128	523	Batting average is .2447419
27	79	Batting average is .3417721
8	0	(Error message)

The first calculation results in a batting average of .2447419. In baseball terminology, batting averages are rounded to three digits. Thus, the first batting average is .245. The second batting average is .3417721, or .342 when rounded to three digits.

When you try the third calculation, a problem develops. You inadvertently enter 0 rather than 30 for the number of times at bat. This means that the value of the variable NumAB becomes 0. In the line assigning a value for Msg, Visual Basic tries to divide by zero, which is an illegal mathematical operation.

What happens? Visual Basic enters Break mode and displays the Code window. As Figure 21.3 shows, a message box pops open to indicate a Division by zero error. Visual Basic highlights the line in your program that caused the error. You can now click OK, or press Enter to clear the error message box. Then, restart the program by pressing Shift+F5 (or selecting **R**estart from the **R**un menu, or clicking the Run icon in the Toolbar).

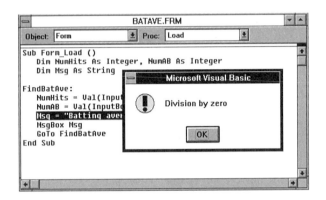

Figure 21.3.

A Division by zero execution error.

An Example of a Logic Error

As with most errors, the Logic kind often result from simple typing mistakes. Consider the following short user-defined procedure named ShowCost. This procedure contains a logic error:

```
Sub ShowCost ()
    Dim NumItems As Integer, UnitCost As Currency

    NumItems = 50
    UnitCost = 6.95
    Print "Total Cost ="; UnitCost / NumItems
End Sub
```

The following is the output produced by the Print instruction:

```
Total cost = .139
```

That answer can't be correct. The total cost is less than the that of one item. The error is fairly obvious—the Print instruction divided by NumItems when multiplication was indicated. That is, in the program code, the division operator (/) should be replaced by the one for multiplication (*).

The program has no syntax or execution errors. It has only a logic error. The procedure executes to completion, but the result is just not correct.

More often than not, logic errors result from typing mistakes that don't produce syntax or execution problems. When you find that a program has a logic error, the first thing to do is carefully check your typing. Make sure your program code reads as you intended.

General Debugging Tips

The following are some general tips for debugging the less obvious types of errors—the execution and logic ones that don't have evident causes.

- *Start by looking for the obvious.* Most errors result from obvious, not subtle, causes. Examine your test for simple mistakes, such as careless typing errors. Examples of common errors include improperly nesting parentheses, and interchanging the less than (<) and greater than (>) operators.

  Obvious errors often are the hardest ones to find because you can't believe you make such ridiculous mistakes. Take heart, all programmers make them.

- *Reasonable-looking output can be wrong.* Usually, incorrect output is so wrong that it seems to leap out at you. Beware, however, of reasonable-looking output. The worst kind of error causes slightly incorrect results, which can lead you to carelessly assume that everything is working correctly. Be suspicious.

- *Verify that the Visual Basic programming language works as you expect.* You might have an incorrect assumption about how a Visual Basic statement, function, method, or event procedure works. Log, for example, works with natural, not common, logarithms. Double-clicking the mouse triggers a Click as well as a DblClick event. Use this book and your Visual Basic documentation for confirmation.

- *Make sure that your algorithms are correct.* An *algorithm* is simply a step-by-step procedure for solving a problem. If you use algorithms from books and magazines, be skeptical of what you read. Printed algorithms and program listings contain errors more often than you might think. Look for a second source, if possible. (It's even possible that, despite painstaking editing, a programming error could be lurking somewhere in this book.)

■ *Learn Visual Basic's debugging features and techniques.* They're explained throughout this chapter.

Debugging Execution Errors

The following is a situation familiar to all programmers: Your application aborts with an explanatory error message, and a highlight on the offending line. But you can't figure out what's wrong. What do you do now?

This question has many answers, depending on what the error message is and what the program line contains. The following are some actions to try, and tips about a few of the more common error messages:

■ *Look again for typing errors.* This cannot be stressed enough: Examine your test for simple errors first—and the most common simple errors occur in your typing. Check that variable names are spelled correctly, and that operators are accurate.

■ *Print the current values of your main variables.* When your application aborts with an error message, you can use Visual Basic's Debug window to display (Print) the values of variables and expressions. This technique is discussed later in this chapter.

■ *Split up multi-instruction program lines.* If you get a Subscript out of range error message for a line containing half a dozen subscript references spread over several instructions, you won't know which one is the culprit. On a separate program line, put each instruction, or split a long one into smaller components.

■ *Search other parts of the program that manipulate the same variables.* If Visual Basic indicates a program line is doing something illegal, the problem often stems from a previous line that erroneously computed the value of a variable. For global variables, you might need to check other procedures. The following error messages are frequently caused by incorrect manipulation of a variable elsewhere in the program:

```
Illegal function call

Subscript out of range

Division by zero
```

■ *Create error-handlers.* With On Error GoTo instructions, you can branch to special routines which can process and recover from error situations. Error-handling is discussed later in this chapter.

Debugging with the Debug Window

One of the best advantages of Visual Basic's interactive environment is that, after your program stops with an error message, you can perform your detective work from the Debug window. Most importantly, you can display the values of essential variables, expressions, and property values to help determine what went wrong.

When in Break mode, Visual Basic retains the current values of all the variables and property values. By issuing Print instructions from the Debug window, you can display the value of any variable, array element, or property.

Ways to Enter Break Mode

During program development and testing, the Debug window is available whenever Visual Basic is in Break mode. You can enter Break mode using several methods. You can force a running application to enter Break mode with any of these actions:

- Press Ctrl+Break while an application is running

- Choose Break from the Run menu while an application is running

- Click the Break icon on the Toolbar while an application is running

Visual Basic automatically enters Break mode when one of the following conditions occurs:

- A run-time error

- Program execution reaches a preset breakpoint

- The value of a watchpoint expression changes or reaches a preset value

- Visual Basic encounters a Stop instruction

Each of these conditions is explained in this chapter.

Viewing the Debug Window

When in Break mode, you can bring the Debug window to the foreground in one of the following two ways:

- Click a visible portion of the Debug window

- Press Ctrl+B

- Choose the Debug option from the Window menu

For example, suppose your program aborts with the following error message:

```
Illegal function call
```

The highlight is on a program line that reads

```
Length! = Sqr(Area!)
```

Apparently the Sqr function fails because something is wrong with the value of Area!. To find out, just activate the Debug window, type the instruction Print Area!, and press Enter. Visual Basic then displays the current value of Area!.

You'll probably discover that Area! has a negative value. If so, that's the problem. Visual Basic's Sqr function works only with positive arguments (or zero).

Of course, if you do find that the value of Area! is negative, that's only the beginning of the whole solution. Now, you must find out how the value of Area! was calculated. If Area! was manipulated several times before the line in which the error occurred, you need to backtrack to determine how the value of Area! erroneously became negative. More Print commands should narrow the problem.

Typing Instructions in the Debug Window

The Debug window executes instructions one line at a time. After typing a line, when you press Enter, Visual Basic immediately executes the instructions on that line. You can re-execute any visible line in the Debug window by moving the cursor to the line, and pressing Enter.

Sometimes, you need to place several instructions on a single line to use the Debug window effectively. This occurs most often when you want to execute a loop.

For example, suppose you want to display all the elements in an array named ClientName$. The array has eight elements. As Figure 21.4 shows, you can type the following line to get the desired results:

```
For J = 1 To 8: Print J; ClientName$(J): Next J
```

You can use the Debug window for more than just Print instructions. For example, you can assign specific values to variables, or make explicit calls to procedures.

When in Break mode, the title bar of the Debug window shows the current form and the procedure which Visual Basic was executing. With Print, you can display the values of any variables local to that procedure, form-level variables, or any global variables. You can't display the values of any variables local to other procedures or other forms.

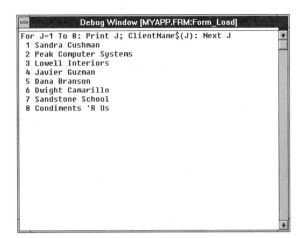

```
Debug Window [MYAPP.FRM:Form_Load]
For J=1 To 8: Print J; ClientName$(J): Next J
 1 Sandra Cushman
 2 Peak Computer Systems
 3 Lowell Interiors
 4 Javier Guzman
 5 Dana Branson
 6 Dwight Camarillo
 7 Sandstone School
 8 Condiments 'R Us
```

Figure 21.4.

Typing a loop in the
Debug window.

NOTE If you have `Option Explicit` in effect, you cannot type undeclared
variable names in the Debug window. In the current example, for
instance, `J` must be declared in the program code. If you plan to
work with the Debug window, you might want to temporarily turn
`Option Explicit` off. You can do so by commenting out the Option
Explicit instructions in the Declarations sections of your forms.
You will then have to rerun the application before using the Debug
Window. For more information on `Option Explicit`, and requiring
variable declarations, see "Debugging Logic Errors", later in this
chapter.

Using the Debug Window with Applications that Are Running

You can place explicit instructions in your program code that display messages directly to the Debug window. As a result, you can display the values of
any variables while the application executes. Later, in Break mode, you can
examine the Debug window to see what was displayed.

To display values in the Debug window, use Visual Basic's predefined `Debug`
object in conjunction with the `Print` method. For example, the following
instruction displays the value of the variable `TotalSales`:

```
Debug.Print "TotalSales ="; TotalSales
```

For more information on the `Debug` object, refer back to Chapter 20, "Using
Object Variables."

Interrupting a Program with Ctrl+Break

When working in the development environment, you can suspend execution at any time while your program is running. Just press Ctrl+Break (or choose Break from the Run menu, or click the Break icon in the Toolbar). Visual Basic enters Break mode, displays the Code window for the current procedure, and highlights the line that was executing at that moment. You can now use the Debug window to test the values of variables and expressions.

Resuming a Program

With the Debug window in Break mode, you can display the values of key variables with Print. But here's the clincher: you can resume execution of your program from the point at which it was interrupted. Simply choose the Continue option from the Run menu. The hot key for Continue is F5.

This is quite a powerful debugging technique. You can interrupt execution, display variable values, then resume the program from the place in which the interruption occurred.

Breaking and resuming is useful when a program seems to be executing for an unduly long time. Often the problem is an endless loop. If your application seems to be running interminably, without producing any results, press Ctrl+Break, and use the Debug window for debugging.

NOTE **Sometimes You Cannot Continue after Editing Your Program**

After interrupting your program with Ctrl+Break, you can issue instructions in the Debug window, then resume execution with the Continue command. Sometimes, however, Continue does not work.

If you edit an instruction that results in Visual Basic being incapable of continuing your program, a dialog box opens to inform you of this. You then have a choice of going ahead with the modification, or leaving the program intact so that you can continue execution.

Debugging Logic Errors

Suppose you have written an application, cleared all the syntax errors, and eliminated any in the executing process. The program, however, doesn't do what you intended. It runs to completion, but the results appear wrong. You have a dreaded *logic error*. Now what?

- Again, examine your test for typing errors.

- Break the program at key places, and display the values of important variables.

- Search for variable conflicts. Don't use two different variables with very similar names, such as `Sale` and `Sales`. Make sure that you spell a variable name consistently throughout the program.

- Don't overwork a global variable by making it perform double duty. Suppose one procedure uses a particular variable. Another procedure subsequently uses the same variable name during an independent calculation. The first procedure then regains control, and needs the variable's old value—but it is no longer valid. Sometimes you might simply forget that perhaps the value of a particular variable is needed later in the execution.

- Verify that Visual Basic's statements, functions, methods, and event procedures work the way you think they do.

- Redesign troublesome parts of the program. Create more user-defined `Subs` and `Functions` to isolate program chunks into smaller units.

- Use the special debugging features found on the **D**ebug menu and the Toolbar. The next section discusses these features.

T I P

A good way to avoid mistyping the names of existing variables is to use the `Option Explicit` instruction. It forces every variable to be explicitly declared in a `Dim`, `ReDim`, `Static`, or `Global` instruction. Option Explicit instructions must be placed in the Declarations section of forms or modules, not inside individual procedures.

You can have Visual Basic automatically add `Option Explicit` to your applications by selecting the **E**nvironments item from the **O**ptions menu, then specifying `Yes` as the value of the Require Variable Declaration option. For more information on `Option Explicit`, see Chapter 14, "Language Building Blocks."

Introducing the Debug Menu

The nerve center of Visual Basic's debugging capabilities is the **Debug** menu. The following three terms are central to Visual Basic's debugging terminology:

- *Trace*—a line-by-line examination of your program's logic flow.

- *Breakpoint*—a designated program line in which you want execution to halt temporarily. When the program line is about to execute, Visual Basic enters Break mode.

- *Watchpoint*—An expression whose value you want to monitor. When the value of the expression changes, or reaches a specified value, Visual Basic enters Break mode.

The last five buttons on the Toolbar quickly activate some of the debugging options available from the Debug window (see Figure 21.5).

Figure 21.5.

The Toolbar's debugging tools.

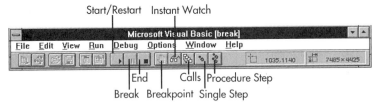

Tracing a Program

Tracing reveals the logic flow of a program. You can request that Visual Basic pause after executing each line of your application. When paused, the Code window for the current procedure opens, and the next line to be executed appears highlighted. The following are the two types of tracing:

- *Single Step.* Executes the highlighted line of the program. When finished, Visual Basic pauses and highlights the next line to be executed. To single step, you can press F8, click the Single Step icon on the Toolbar, or choose **S**ingle Step from the **D**ebug menu.

- *Procedure Step.* Similar to single step, except that each call to a procedure executes as a single step. To procedure step, press Shift+F8, click the Procedure Step icon on the Toolbar, or choose **P**rocedure Step from the **D**ebug menu.

When you single step, each instruction that is executable does so, in turn. As each procedure is called, the Code window opens to show the program code for that procedure. Visual Basic highlights the next instruction to execute by surrounding it with a rectangular frame.

The Debug window is available for use at any time. One common debugging technique is to single step through a program while displaying the values of key variables in the Debug window. Single-stepping is especially useful when debugging troublesome loop structures.

> Remember that while tracing, you can resize either window—the Code or the Debug, or both, to make them visible simultaneously. **T I P**

Figure 21.6 shows how a typical screen might appear while single-stepping. Notice the highlight on the current program instruction.

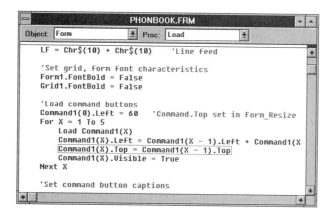

```
PHONBOOK.FRM
Object: Form          Proc: Load

LF = Chr$(10) + Chr$(10)      'Line feed

'Set grid, form font characteristics
Form1.FontBold = False
Grid1.FontBold = False

'Load command buttons
Command1(0).Left = 60    'Command.Top set in Form_Resize
For X = 1 To 5
    Load Command1(X)
    Command1(X).Left = Command1(X - 1).Left + Command1(X
    Command1(X).Top = Command1(X - 1).Top
    Command1(X).Visible = True
Next X

'Set command button captions
```

Figure 21.6.

Tracing a program.

Setting Breakpoints

For many programmers, breakpoints are the best debugging allies. A breakpoint is a specified program line on which you want to suspend execution. When Visual Basic reaches the breakpoint line, execution halts, and the system enters Break mode.

By setting breakpoints, you can halt execution at strategic locations. After the program suspends at a breakpoint, you can set new options from the **Debug** menu, or use the Debug window to display the values of variables and expressions.

To set a breakpoint:

1. Place the procedure containing the target line in the Code window.

2. Move the cursor to the target line.

3. Select **T**oggle Breakpoint from the **D**ebug menu. You can click also the Breakpoint button on the Toolbar, or simply press F9.

Visual Basic shows the breakpoint by highlighting the line in red or reverse video.

Follow the identical procedure to remove a breakpoint. As the name implies, Toggle Breakpoint alternately sets and removes an individual breakpoint.

You can set several breakpoints simultaneously. To remove all the breakpoints in one step, select Clear All Breakpoints from the **D**ebug menu.

NOTE **Changing Visual Basic's Color Scheme**

You can change the default color that Visual Basic uses to highlight breakpoint lines. Choose the **E**nvironment item from the **O**ptions menu. The Environment Options dialog box opens. You can now select the colors used by Visual Basic for breakpoints, program comments, keywords, and other program elements.

Watching a Program

Watchpoints are similar to breakpoints in that program execution suspends when a specified condition occurs. With a watchpoint, you can cause Visual Basic to enter Break mode when the value of a specified expression reaches a predetermined amount.

Specifying a Watch Expression

To specify the expression you want to watch, you use the Add Watch dialog box. To open this box, choose the **A**dd Watch option on the **D**ebug menu. You can access the dialog box before running the application, or anytime Visual Basic is in Break mode.

Figure 21.7 shows an example of the Add Watch dialog box.

The watch expression you specify in the dialog box can be any meaningful item from your program code. It can be a variable, a property value, a function call, or an expression combining several of these elements with suitable operators. Before choosing **A**dd Watch, if you highlight in your program code an expression, Visual Basic displays it as the default watch expression.

In the Context frame of the dialog box, you specify the scope of the variables used in the watch expression. The scope can be procedure level, form/module level, or global.

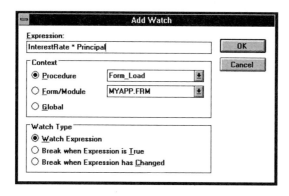

Figure 21.7.

The Add Watch dialog box.

The Watch Type frame offers three option buttons. For now, consider the Watch Expression option as Figure 21.7 shows. The remaining two options are covered shortly.

Viewing the Watch Pane

When you click OK on the Add Watch dialog box, Visual Basic adds a Watch pane to the Debug window. This pane shows the watch expression, and its current value. At the left end of the Watch pane is an icon that depicts a pair of eyeglasses (see Figure 21.8).

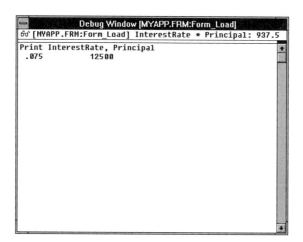

Figure 21.8.

Debug window containing a Watch pane.

Now, as you execute the application, and re-enter Break mode, you can watch the value of the expression change in the Debug window.

You can specify more than one watch expression. If you do, the Watch pane displays updated values for all the watch expressions.

Editing and Deleting a Watch Expression

You can edit a watch expression with the Watch dialog box. Choose the **Edit** Watch option on the **D**ebug menu to access this dialog box (or press the shortcut key, Ctrl+W). Figure 21.9 shows an example of the Edit Watch dialog box.

To work with any watch expression, use the arrow keys to highlight the expression. You can then click the desired Command button to make changes to (or erase) the expression: Edit to edit it; Delete to remove it, or Add to specify a new one. By clicking Delete All, you remove all the watch expressions at once.

Using Watchpoints

Using a watchpoint, you can have Visual Basic suspend program execution when the value of a watch expression changes, or reaches a specified amount. As such, you create a kind of dynamic breakpoint. To specify a watchpoint, select the appropriate option from the Watch Type frame in the Add Watch dialog box (refer back to Figure 21.7).

By choosing the Break when Expression has Changed option, Visual Basic executes the application until the value of the watch expression changes. At that point, execution suspends. Visual Basic opens the Code window, and highlights the line that caused the expression to change (or the line immediately following). The Watch pane in the Debug window shows the new value of the watch expression. With this option, the icon on the Watch pane is an open hand with a triangle.

The Break when Expression is True option executes the application until the value of the watch expression becomes True. (Remember that, for a numeric expression, True is any nonzero value.) The icon on the watch pane now appears as an open hand with an equal sign.

Using Instant Watch

The final watch option is Instant Watch. This option can be used in Break mode to quickly display the value of any expression. As such, Instant Watch is similar to displaying the value of an expression with the Debug window in Break mode.

To use Instant Watch, you highlight the watch expression directly in your program code. Watch expressions might contain several variables and operators, and be a single variable name or property, or anything in between. The highlighted expression can, and usually is, part of a larger Visual Basic instruction.

You then select Instant Watch in any of the following three ways: press Shift+F9, choose Instant Watch from the Debug menu, or click the Instant Watch icon in the Toolbar.

As Figure 21.10 shows, Visual Basic pops open the Instant Watch dialog box that displays the watch expression and its current value. (The figure uses a typical type of expression that might be used as a watch expression.) You can close the dialog box by pressing Esc, or clicking the Cancel button. You also have the option of adding another watch expression by clicking the Add Watch button.

Figure 21.10.

The Instant Watch dialog box.

Using Calls

When in Break mode, the Calls dialog box provides a special way of looking at the execution of your program. This dialog box shows which modules and procedures are involved in the chain of execution at the time it is suspended. Figure 21.11 shows an example of Calls.

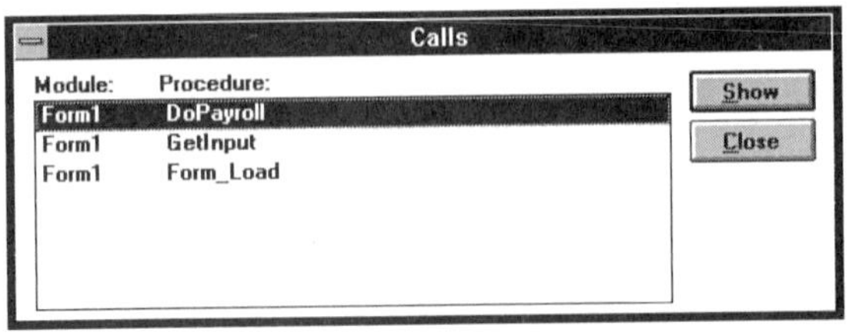

Figure 21.11.

The Calls dialog box.

You can use any of the following three techniques to access the Calls dialog box: press Ctrl+L, choose the **Calls** option on the **D**ebug menu, or click the Calls icon on the Toolbar.

You might find Calls a valuable debugging tool as your applications become more complex. In such applications, you can frequently have one procedure explicitly calling another.

Called procedures can, in turn, invoke other ones. Such a chain of procedures is known as nested procedure calls. Notice that, for the subsequent instruction in the original procedure to execute, this process must be completed for every nested procedure in the chain.

If a bug crops up in one of these procedures, tracing the execution path can be tedious and time-consuming. The Calls dialog box can help by visually displaying the nested procedure chain.

By clicking Show, a procedure highlighted in the dialog box can be listed. This lets you focus on suspected problems without the time-consuming effort required to trace the program execution manually.

The Calls dialog box shows nested procedures in LIFO ("Last In, First Out") order. That is, the earliest active procedure is placed on the bottom of the list; the most recently called procedure appears at the top.

Other Debugging Tools

Besides the major debugging tools already discussed, Visual Basic has some additional debugging features. This section presents the following three debugging aids:

- Selecting the next instruction to execute
- Showing the next instruction to execute
- Using the Stop instruction

Using the Set Next Statement

While tracing a program, or anytime in Break mode, you can designate which instruction executes next. Use the Set Next Statement option on the **D**ebug menu. Rather than execute any instructions, this option simply moves the highlight. When you resume execution with F5, F8, or one of the continuation options from the **D**ebug menu, or Toolbar, the newly highlighted instruction executes first. The effect is similar to a GoTo.

Follow the next four steps to try a Set **N**ext Statement:

1. Pause a program with the highlight on a particular instruction.

2. Move the cursor to whatever instruction you want to execute next. (The instruction must be in the same procedure.)

3. Open the **D**ebug menu (Alt+D).

4. Select the Set **N**ext Statement option.

The highlight (the framing rectangle) moves to your selected instruction. Now, press F5 to resume execution at this new instruction.

Using Show Next Statement

When the Code window is not visible, you can use the Sho**w** Next Statement option from the **D**ebug menu to see which instruction executes next. The Code window opens with the highlight on the instruction which executes when you resume the program. You can then press F5 to resume execution at the highlighted instruction, or use the Set **N**ext Statement option to move the highlight.

Using *Stop*

Visual Basic provides the Stop instruction as a way to set a breakpoint directly in the program code. When Visual Basic encounters a Stop instruction, execution suspends with the highlight on it.

You can now use the Debug window, set options with the **D**ebug menu, or do anything normally associated with suspended programs. As usual, you can resume the program by pressing F5, or selecting the **C**ontinue option from the **R**un menu (or from the Toolbar). Essentially, Stop is similar to a breakpoint set at the Stop instruction itself.

The Stop instruction has one large advantage over setting breakpoints with the **D**ebug menu. While developing an application, you can save the program code between work sessions. The Stop instructions are saved along with the rest of the program code. As a result, the Stop breakpoints are retained from one work session to the next. Any breakpoints you set from the **D**ebug menu are lost as soon as you exit Visual Basic.

A Summary of Debugging Tools

Tables 21.2 through 21.6 summarize Visual Basic's debugging tools.

Table 21.2. Commands that control execution.

Action	Menu	Hot Key
Run/Start	Run	F5
Restart	Run	Shift+F5
Continue	Run	F5
End	Run	
Suspend Execution		Ctrl+Break
Set Next Statement	Debug	
Show Next Statement	Debug	

Table 21.3. Tracing commands.

Action	Menu	Hot Key
Single Step	Debug	F8
Procedure Step	Debug	Shift+F8

Table 21.4. Breakpoint commands.

Action	Menu	Hot Key
Toggle Breakpoint	Debug	F9
Clear All Breakpoints	Debug	

Table 21.5. Watch commands.

Action	Menu	Hot Key
Add Watch	Debug	
Edit Watch	Debug	Ctrl+W
Instant Watch	Debug	Shift+F9

Table 21.6. Viewing commands.

Action	Menu	Hot Key
Activate Debug Window	Window	Ctrl+B
Calls	Debug	Ctrl+L

Error Handling and Error Trapping

Normally, a run-time error terminates your application. If you are running from the development environment (as opposed to running an .EXE file), Visual Basic displays a pertinent error message and enters Break mode. From there, you can use the Debug window and the various techniques mentioned earlier in this chapter to track down what happened.

There is an alternative, however, for dealing with run-time errors. Visual Basic provides *error trapping*. Error trapping lets your application intercept an error, and pass control to an error-handling routine. That is, when an error occurs, instead of terminating your application, program control simply passes to your error handler. An *error handler* is a user-written block of program lines embedded in a procedure. When a program error occurs inside a procedure containing an error handler, execution branches directly to it.

With error trapping, you can do the following:

- Pass control to an error handler when an error occurs
- Determine which line caused the error
- Determine what error occurred
- Correct the problem, or prompt the user for information
- Resume execution at any place in the procedure

Using Error Trapping

Error trapping is most valuable in the following situations:

- You anticipate that certain errors might occur during execution of an application, especially when you know what it should do when one of these errors materializes.

- An error-producing bug has you baffled. With error trapping as a debugging tool, you can trap the error, and branch to a special routine that helps you diagnose the problem.

- You write applications that request others to input data. Your users occasionally might type faulty data that causes errors. (This situation is common with coworkers in a job environment.) Error trapping lets you intercept possible program errors. With the error handler, you can correct the problem and continue execution. Often, such remedial action involves prompting the user for new (or corrected) input data.

If nothing else, an error handler provides graceful program termination. If you cannot fix the problem that caused the error, at least you can display informative messages before the application terminates.

Table 21.7 shows the keywords involved with error trapping.

Table 21.7. Error-handling statements and functions.

Keyword	Action
On Error GoTo	Enables error trapping, and specifies the first line of the error handler
Resume	Branches to a designated line when the error handler finishes
Err function	Returns an error code for logic errors
Erl function	Returns the line causing the error
Err statement	Sets a value for the error code
Error statement	Simulates or creates an error
Error$ function	Returns the error message corresponding to an error code

Visual Basic's error-trapping methodology is a bit primitive. The techniques are inherited from QBasic and other procedural versions of the BASIC language. Branch designations and error locations use line numbers and GoTo clauses. "Primitive," however, does not mean "ineffective." Error trapping is a potent tool.

Enabling Error Trapping

The heart of Visual Basic's error trapping is the `On Error` instruction. Three forms exist:

```
On Error GoTo linenum
```
or
```
On Error GoTo label
```
or
```
On Error Resume Next
```
in which

linenum is the line number on which the error handler begins,

and

label is the line label in which the error handler begins.

The `GoTo` forms of `On Error` do two things:

- Enable error trapping; no error trap occurs until an `On Error GoTo` instruction executes.
- Specify which line gets control when an error occurs.

An error handler is always local to a particular procedure. As such, `label` or `linenum` must refer to a line in the same procedure containing the `On Error GoTo` instruction. That is, an `On Error GoTo` instruction cannot attempt to branch to a line in a different `Sub` or `Function` procedure. However, a single procedure can contain more than one `On Error GoTo` instruction; there is no limit on how many procedures can contain such instructions.

The TRAPERR Application

The following application, TRAPERR, shows the skeletal technique of using an error handler. The application consists of a single `Form_Resize` event procedure:

```
Sub Form_Resize ()
    'The World's simplest Error Handler
    Dim NiceTry As Single
```

```
Rem On Error GoTo ErrorHandler      'Remove Rem to try handler

NiceTry = 1 / 0
MsgBox "No way to get here"
End

ErrorHandler:
    MsgBox "I think you made a boo-boo"
    End

End Sub
```

Notice that the On Error GoTo is inactive because the line begins with Rem.

When you run this application, the assignment instruction causes a run-time error because division by zero is an illegal operation. Visual Basic aborts the application and displays the error message box that Figure 21.12 shows.

Figure 21.12.

Error message box when On Error GoTo is disabled.

Now, remove the Rem at the beginning of the On Error GoTo instruction. This line now activates the error-handling routine. If a program error occurs, control branches directly to the error handler at the line beginning with the ErrorHandler: label.

Try running the application. As Figure 21.13 shows, you now see the message box created by the MsgBox instruction inside the ErrorHandler routine.

Figure 21.13.

Message box when On Error GoTo is enabled.

Notice that, this time, the application does not display the Division by zero error message. When the assignment instruction tries to divide by zero, Visual Basic intercepts the impending error, and branches directly to the error handler. In the handler, the MsgBox instruction displays the "boo-boo" message.

After clicking OK to close the message box, the End instruction ends the application.

In any procedure, you can have multiple error handlers and On Error GoTo instructions. The most recently executed On Error GoTo designates the active error handler. Only one error handler, of course, can be active at any time. When a procedure terminates, its error handlers are automatically disabled.

Using *On Error GoTo 0*

If your application uses line numbers, you cannot place an error handler at line number 0 because the instruction On Error GoTo 0 has special significance.

An On Error GoTo 0 instruction turns off error trapping in the procedure. A subsequent error then halts the application in the usual way. In other words, use the instruction On Error GoTo 0 to turn off error trapping that has previously been turned on.

 NOTE   On Error GoTo 0 does not specify line 0 as the beginning of an error handler, even if the procedure contains a line numbered 0.

The *On Error Resume Next* Instruction

You can have execution continue uninterrupted when an error occurs. To do so, use the following special form of the On Error instruction:

```
On Error Resume Next
```

Now, when an error occurs, Visual Basic simply continues executing the instructions in the procedure. As explained later in this chapter, your subsequent code can use the Err function to find out if any error occurred, and if so, what it was. When debugging a procedure, some programmers use this instruction to force execution past known errors.

Understanding Error Handlers

An error handler is simply a group of lines placed somewhere in a procedure. You can use error handlers in both user-defined and event procedures. Visual Basic does not support automatically branching directly to a user-defined procedure when an error is trapped. Of course, the code in an error handler can explicitly invoke a user-defined procedure.

Returning from an Error Handler

Most error handlers include one or more Resume instructions. With Resume, an error handler returns control to the body of the procedure. The following are the five different forms of the Resume instruction:

```
Resume              'Standard form

Resume 0            'Zero form

Resume Next         'Next form

Resume linenum      'Line number form

Resume label        'Label form
```

in which

  linenum is a line number in the same procedure,

and

  label is a line label in the same procedure.

The form of a Resume instruction determines the place in which execution continues (see Table 21.8).

Table 21.8. Forms of the *Resume* instruction.

Instruction	Return Location
Resume	At the line that caused the error
Resume 0	At the line that caused the error (same as Resume)
Resume Next	At the instruction immediately following the one that caused the error
Resume *linenum*	At the line designated by *linenum*
Resume *label*	At the line designated by *label*

To demonstrate how Resume works, here's the previous TRAPERR application modified to add a Resume Next instruction at the end of the error handler:

```
Sub Form_Resize ()
    'The World's simplest Error Handler
    Dim NiceTry As Single
```

```
On Error GoTo ErrorHandler

NiceTry = 1 / 0
MsgBox "No way to get here"
End

ErrorHandler:
    MsgBox "I think you made a boo-boo"
    Resume Next

End Sub
```

Now, when the error is trapped, the handler returns control to the line immediately following the assignment instruction that caused the error. As a result, the application now displays two message boxes. The first box displays the following message:

```
I think you made a boo-boo
```

The second box displays this message:

```
No way to get here
```

In a `Resume` instruction, `linenum` or `label` must refer to a line in the same procedure as the error handler.

It's possible to activate an error handler located in one procedure, while program control is in another. Suppose a procedure containing an error handler has executed an `On Error` instruction to enable the error handler. Then, that procedure makes an explicit call to a second procedure. While executing this procedure, the error defined in the first procedure occurs. Visual Basic returns control to the error handler in the original procedure. Notice that, in this case, the first procedure never terminated, but had merely transferred program control temporarily to the second one. If the error handler in such a case has a `Resume 0` instruction (or `Resume` without any parameters), execution continues just after the line that called the second procedure.

`Resume` instructions are valid only when error handling is active (`On Error` is in effect). A run-time error (`Resume without error`) occurs if you execute a `Resume` instruction when error handling is not enabled. Furthermore, your application cannot simply run out of instructions in an error handler without a `Resume`. This mistake causes a run-time error (`No Resume`). However, you can use `Exit Sub` or `Exit Function` in an error handler to terminate the procedure.

Writing an Error Handler

Within an error handler, you generally want to accomplish the following:

- Determine the error and which line caused it
- Display diagnostic messages
- Correct the problem
- Resume execution, if feasible

The built-in functions Err and Erl provide information often useful for your error handler.

Using the *Err* and *Erl* Functions

The Err and Erl functions enable your error handler to determine the type of error that occurred, and which program line caused it.

Err returns the code of the error that invoked the error handler. The code is a long integer number.

Visual Basic defines more than 200 error codes. Table 21.9 shows just a few of the values that the Err function can return, and the errors they indicate. For a complete list of the Err error codes, see your Visual Basic documentation, or the online help.

Table 21.9. Partial list of values returned by the *Err* function.

Error code	Error message
5	Illegal function call
6	Overflow
7	Out of memory
10	Duplicate definition
11	Division by zero
19	No Resume
35	Sub or Function not defined
61	Disk full
68	Device unavailable

Erl returns the line number at which the error occurred. If the error occurs in a line without a line number, Erl returns the number of the last executed line that had a line number. If the procedure has not executed any numbered lines before the error, Erl returns 0.

Keep in mind that Erl works only with line numbers, not with labels. This throwback to earlier versions of the Basic language requires you to number all program lines if you want Erl to return the most accurate information.

Using the *Err* Statement

You can assign a particular value to the Err function by using the Err statement.

```
Err = errorcode
```

in which

    errorcode is an integer between 0 and 32,767.

A common use of the Err statement is to create specialized error codes defined only in the application. If you look through the list of Err error codes predefined by Visual Basic, you find that there are several gaps. Many numbers do not correspond with any error. You can use any of these available numbers to define an error code specifically for the application.

For example, suppose you are writing a timed quiz application. You notice that error code 495 is not predefined by Visual Basic. If the user does not reply within 20 seconds, you can assign error code 495 by using the following instruction:

```
Err = 495     'No reply
```

Subsequently, in an error handler, or in the normal program code, you can use the Err function to determine what error occurred. When the Err function returns 495, you know that your user has failed to respond.

You can use the Err statement also to set the value of Err to 0. If you do, Visual Basic acts as though an error did not occur.

Simulating Errors

Use an Error instruction to simulate errors or to create your individualized error codes.

> Error *errorcode*
>
> in which
>
> > *errorcode* is a long integer expression that specifies an error code in the range from 0 to 32,767.

If errorcode is one of the error codes predefined by Visual Basic, the Error instruction causes your application to behave as though the error occurred. Control passes to the error handler from which the Err function returns the value of errorcode. If you have no error handler, Visual Basic displays the normal message associated with that error, and terminates your application.

For example, the following instruction simulates a Division by zero error:

```
Error 11      '11 is the Err code for Division by zero
```

With Error, you can induce different errors while testing and developing an application. You can find out whether or not your error handler recovers adequately.

In addition to the Err statement, the Error statement is suitable for defining your own codes. Just use an errorcode value not defined by Visual Basic. When the Error instruction passes control to the error handler, you can use its Err function inside the handler to test for the value of errorcode and take appropriate action.

If your application has no error handler, an Error instruction that uses an invalid errorcode halts your application, and displays the message User-defined error.

User-defined error codes provide a way to test for special conditions or dangerous data. You can intercept potential errors, and handle the problem in an error handler.

For example, here is the skeletal form of a procedure that asks the user to type in a password. If the user types the proper password (Swordfish), the application displays confidential information. If the typed password is invalid, application control passes to an error handler. The application defines Error 254, which is not an error number used by Visual Basic:

```
On Error GoTo ErrorHandler

    .

    .

Password$ = InputBox$("What is the authorizing password")
If Password$ <> "Swordfish" Then Error 254
MsgBox "Click to see the Strategic Plan Briefing"

    .

    .

End     'of application
```

```
ErrorHandler:
    Select Case Err
    Case 254
        MsgBox "Unauthorized request"
        Rem If possible, correct the problem here
            .
        Resume Next
    Case Else
        Rem Check for other errors here
        .
    End Select
Rem  End of error handler
```

Using the *Error$* and *Error* Functions

The Error$ function returns the text of the error message corresponding to a given error code.

Error$(*errorcode*)

in which

    errorcode is an integer number between 1 and 32,767.

The *errorcode* argument is optional.

For example, the following instruction displays the error message corresponding to error code 11:

```
MsgBox Error$(11)
```

Error$ returns a sting value. The corresponding function, Error, returns a Variant (of type string). Here's an example of Error:

```
Dim MyMessage as Variant
MyMessage = Error(11)
```

If errorcode is not one of the error codes predefined in Visual Basic, the value returned is User-defined error.

If you omit the errorcode argument, the function returns the string message corresponding to the most recent error.

Philosophy of Error Handlers

Error handlers can be simple or complex. Use them to anticipate possible problems and to recover smoothly, especially in workplace environments.

In polished applications, most errors come from user mistakes. The likely culprits are faulty data supplied by users and silly mistakes with equipment, such as placing the wrong disk in a disk drive, or not turning on the printer.

User-supplied numeric data often is a source of errors. Bad data typed by users can lead to errors such as Division by zero. You might write an error handler that checks for Division by zero (among other possibilities). If that's the problem, you can redisplay the user's input, and ask whether the information is correct. If the information is incorrect, branch back to the place in which the data was entered, and start over.

Disk drive errors are common when users must place into a drive a disk, and enter a file name saved on it. Users can use the wrong disk or drive, forget to place the disk in the drive, or supply an invalid file name. You can check for all these errors, and recover without causing the application to crash.

Error handlers often have a series of If instructions or a Select Case block. The handler checks for various anticipated errors by using Err and Erl, and executes individualized instructions that deal with each type of error.

The following is an example of such an error handler:

```
ErrorHandler:
    Print
    Print "Error number"; Err; " has occurred at line"; Erl
    Select Case Err
        Case 11
            Print "You have divided by zero."
            Print "Please rerun the program with new values."
            MsgBox "Click OK to end program"
            End
        Case 61
            Print "The disk is full."
            Print "The program will continue without writing to disk."
            MsgBox "Click OK to continue"
            Resume Next
        Case 68
            Print "The printer is probably not on or is out of paper."
            MsgBox "Check the printer and then click OK."
            Resume
        Case Else
```

```
    Print "An unanticipated error has occurred."
    Print "So long for now -- Stopping the program."
    MsgBox "Click OK to end program"
    End
  End Select
```

At the least, your error handler can display diagnostic information, and solicit the user to notify you. For example:

```
MyErrorHandler:
  Print " An unanticipated program error has occurred."
  Print
  Print "Please report the following information to"
  Print "Jill Programmer, Bldg. R8, Extension 389"
  Print
  Print "Error number"; Err; " in line"; Erl
  Print
  Print "     --Thank you"
  Print "       Jill"
  Stop
```

Summary

Experienced programmers realize that testing and debugging are necessary for successful programming. As a general rule, nontrivial programs contain bugs that must be found, and eliminated. Many programmers dislike testing and debugging. Actually, these processes can be fun. Much depends on your state of mind. After all, most people enjoy solving puzzles, and acting as "detectives".

Three kinds of errors can occur in programs:

■ *Syntax errors*, which are incorrectly worded instructions that don't make sense to Visual Basic

■ *Execution errors*, which cause diagnostic messages as the result of (correctly worded) instructions that Visual Basic just cannot execute successfully

■ *Logic errors*, which occur when your program runs to completion, but yields incorrect results

Fortunately, Visual Basic provides several debugging features and techniques. The most important ones include the capability to suspend program execution, perform detective work with the Debug window, then resume the program.

With breakpoints, you can suspend a program at any line. You can display the values of crucial variables and expressions from the Debug window. You can also reassign the value of any variable. With watchpoints, you can have Visual Basic enter Break mode when the value of a specified expression reaches a particular amount.

Tracing provides a way to observe the logic flow of your program. You can see the order in which each instruction executes. While tracing, you can suspend execution, and use the Debug window.

Most programming errors stem from simple mistakes rather than obscure bugs. Search for the obvious before the subtle. By far, the most likely source of any error is a simple typing mistake. When errors occur, double- and triple-check your typing.

With an error trap, your applications can take measures to intercept, and recover from run-time errors. One use of this technique is "bulletproofing". You can anticipate possible errors caused by users entering faulty input, or mishandling hardware, such as the printer or disk drives. An error handler can smoothly rescue the application from these types of problems.

Occasionally, you can get stuck tracking down an elusive bug. If so, leave the situation for a while. Take a break, and do something relaxing, such as walking or napping. It's amazing how some nagging bugs are swiftly found after a rejuvenating break.

Customizing
Applications

PART

V

Responding to Mouse Events

T he mouse and Windows go hand in hand. Using Windows without a mouse (or a similar pointing device) is the same as running a race without shoes—it's just not natural.

Mouse events are crucial for controlling Windows and its applications. The mouse is a simple device, and quite easy to use. However, behind the scenes, much is happening. Windows constantly monitors and evaluates the movements and clicks of a mouse, and the state of its buttons.

Users expect Windows applications to support the mouse. Your Visual Basic applications should follow suit.

As a programmer, however, detecting clicks and double-clicks is just the beginning of making your applications mouse-compatible. You must make your applications responsive to other events of the mouse, such as the press or release of one of its buttons. You might need to detect which form or control the pointer is over, and to which place an object is being dragged. Fortunately, Visual Basic provides a number of events that respond to various mouse actions.

The main topics covered in this chapter include:

- ■ Responding to clicks and double-clicks
- ■ Understanding the MouseDown, MouseUp, and MouseMove events
- ■ Dragging and dropping

The *Click* and *DblClick* Events

The most common mouse actions are clicking and double-clicking. Forms and controls respond to these actions through the Click and DblClick events, respectively. Throughout the sample applications in this book, you have already seen how these two event procedures can help obtain user input.

Forms respond to the Click and DblClick events. Most controls do, as well, but there are some exceptions. For example, command buttons do not have a DblClick event. Lines and shapes don't have any events, so you can't associate any mouse events with those controls.

NOTE To distinguish between a double-click and two rapid single clicks, Windows maintains a fixed-time interval. When two successive clicks occur, Windows compares the elapsed time between them with this stored time interval. If the elapsed time is less than this interval, Windows recognizes a double-click; otherwise, Windows interprets the clicks as two single ones. The user can modify this stored time interval from the Windows Control Panel anytime that Windows is running.

Table 22.1 summarizes which controls respond to the Click and DblClick events.

Table 22.1. Controls supporting the *Click* and *DblClick* events.

Event(s)	Supported Controls
Click & DblClick	Combo box, File list box, Frame, Grid, Image, Label, List box, OLE, Option button, Picture box, Text box
Click only	Check box, Command button, Directory list box
Neither	Data, Drive list box, Line, Horizontal scroll bar, Vertical scroll bar, Shape, Timer

Programming *Click* and *DblClick* Events

You are already familiar with programming Click and DblClick events. In previous chapters, many sample applications use Click and DblClick event procedures in conjunction with on-screen objects, such as forms, command buttons, and labels.

In later chapters, you will learn about additional Toolbox controls that support the Click and DblClick events. (For example, Chapter 25, "Processing Files," discusses Click events in relation to the File list box control and the Directory list box control.)

Click and DblClick event procedures work in a similar fashion for all the controls that support the events. You should, therefore, have no problem writing Click and DblClick procedures for each control you encounter.

Comparing the *Change* and *Click* Events

Some controls support a Change event, but not Click or DblClick. Examples are the Drive list box, and the Horizontal and Vertical scroll bar controls. The Change event occurs when the contents of a control are modified, either through user action, or as a result of program code.

Often, the change occurs because of a mouse action. For example, in a Drive list box, the user can click the name of a drive to change the selected one. Sometimes the change occurs because a program instruction modifies a property value associated with a control. For example, the program can change the Caption property of a Label.

The point here is that, although a click or double-click can trigger the Change event, it is not strictly a mouse event. No Click or DblClick procedure is necessary in conjunction with a Change event.

The Combo (drop-down list) box supports Change, Click, and DblClick events. On first consideration, Click and Change seem to be the same, but they're separate events. The Change event refers only to the text portion of the Combo box; the Click event refers only to the drop-down list portion.

The *MouseDown*, *MouseUp*, and *MouseMove* Events

Besides Click and DblClick, there are three additional mouse event procedures associated with a form or control: MouseDown, MouseUp, and MouseMove. As Table 22.2 shows, these three events monitor the state of the buttons of the mouse as well as its position and motion.

Table 22.2. Mouse event procedures.	
Event Name	**Triggering Mechanism**
MouseDown	Pressing any mouse button
MouseUp	Releasing a mouse button
MouseMove	Moving the mouse pointer

Similar to Click and DblClick, you associate these three mouse events with a particular form or graphics control. The events respond when mouse activity occurs on that form or control.

When mouse activity occurs on a control, the events associated with the form do not respond. For mouse events on a form to respond to activity of the mouse, the mouse pointer must be directly on the form, not on an attached control.

Controls that Support *MouseUp, MouseDown, MouseMove*

The purpose of the MouseUp, MouseDown, and MouseMove events is to support drag-and-drop operations and other operations unique to the mouse. Consequently, most controls support these mouse events, but some controls do not.

For example, scroll bar controls do not support these mouse events. The reason is that these controls have the Scroll event which triggers when the user drags the box on the scroll bar. If scroll bars supported the mouse events, there would be a conflict between the Scroll event and the mouse events. Also, shape and line controls don't support any events, so they obviously don't supprt the mouse events.

MDI forms do not support any mouse events (including Click). The reason is that actions (such as drawing), and mouse operations (such as drag and drop) should occur in the child windows contained in the MDI form.

Form, picture, and image controls respond to all mouse events. As such, you can create graphics applications that dynamically display the current mouse position and support the dragging and dropping of items into and out of these controls.

List boxes support all mouse events also. As a result, you can program a list box to respond to drag-and-drop events for the items in the list.

Response Order of Mouse Events

Whenever you click, the four mouse button-related events occur in a specific order: MouseDown, MouseUp, Click, and, if you double-clicked, DblClick.

These four events do not always have to occur together, but if they do, they always happen in the same order. For example, suppose while the pointer is on a picture control the user presses a button on the mouse. Then, the user moves it away from this control without releasing the button. In this case, the picture control receives a MouseDown event, but it doesn't get MouseUp or Click.

Demonstrating Mouse Events

Consider this sample application which contains a quick demonstration of the mouse events covered so far. Experiment by starting a new project. You don't need to place any controls on the form. Simply write the following event procedures for the form's Click, DblClick, MouseDown, MouseMove, and MouseUp events:

```
Sub Form_Click ()
    Print "Click"
End Sub

Sub Form_DblClick ()
    Print "DblClick"
End Sub

Sub Form_MouseDown (Button As Integer, Shift As Integer, X As Single,
➡Y As Single)
    Cls
    Print "MouseDown"
End Sub

Sub Form_MouseMove (Button As Integer, Shift As Integer, X As Single,
➡Y As Single)
    Form1.Caption = "X: " & X & "  Y:" & Y
End Sub

Sub Form_MouseUp (Button As Integer, Shift As Integer, X As Single,
➡Y As Single)
    Print "MouseUp"
End Sub
```

Notice that each event (except MouseMove) displays its procedure name on the form. That way, you can see all the mouse events in action as they occur. The MouseMove event modifies the caption of the form to display the current x,y coordinates of the mouse pointer. The MouseDown event also issues a Cls instruction that clears the information currently displayed from the form.

Start the application, and experiment with different mouse activities to see how the various events behave. You can clearly see what is happening. For example, as you move the mouse around the form, you see the pointer's coordinates continually updated in the form's caption. Click the mouse, and observe the generated events. On the form, press a button of the mouse. Then, move it off the form, and release the button. You see a MouseDown and a MouseUp event, but not Click.

Try clicking twice in rapid succession. As Figure 22.1 shows, you produce the following events: MouseDown, MouseUp, Click, DblClick, and a second MouseUp. In the figure, the mouse pointer is shown at the x,y location displayed in the form's caption.

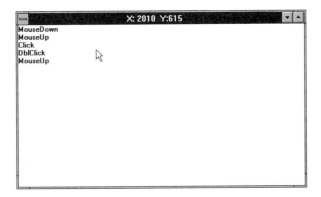

Figure 22.1.

Result of a double-click.

Capturing the Mouse

Remember that, at any time, only the form or control that the pointer is on can receive a mouse event. This form or control is said to have *captured* the mouse.

This principle of capture is consistent with the fundamental philosophy of the mouse as an instrument by which the user manipulates screen objects. When you pick up a spoon you have to put your hand on it first, then you grasp and lift. Similarly, when you select an on-screen object to move, you first put on it the mouse pointer, then you press the button, and drag.

If the mouse moves over a control, therefore, the form under it does not receive a mouse event. Only when the mouse pointer moves directly over the form does Visual Basic generate Form_MouseMove events.

Demonstrating *MouseMove*

Try another quick mouse demonstration. Start a new project, and place two picture controls (Picture1 and Picture2) onto the form. Place the pictures controls side by side, but leave some room between them.

Create code for each Picture control's MouseMove event as follows:

```
Sub Picture1_MouseMove (Button As Integer, Shift As Integer, X As Single,
➥Y As Single)
    Form1.Caption = "X:" & X & "  Y:" & Y
End Sub

Sub Picture2_MouseMove (Button As Integer, Shift As Integer, X As Single,
➥Y As Single)
    Form1.Caption = "X:" & X & "  Y:" & Y
End Sub
```

The active instruction in each procedure is the same. This instruction modifies the form's Caption property so that the caption displays the X and Y coordinates of the mouse's current pointer position.

Now, run the application. Move the mouse pointer around the form and the picture controls. As you move the mouse over Picture1, the form's caption displays the X and Y coordinates of the mouse pointer relative to Picture1. Similarly, when you move the mouse over Picture2, the pointer coordinates relative to this picture control appear in the caption.

However, when you move the pointer between the two pictures, or elsewhere on the form, the application does not update Form1.Caption. The reason is that only the picture controls (and not the form) have code that responds to the mouse event.

When the mouse pointer moves off the pictures, Form1 "captures" the mouse. The application does not contain code for the form, so nothing happens when the pointer is outside the pictures.

If you put the same line of code into Form1_MouseMove that appears in the MouseMove events for the picture controls, the caption updates when the mouse is on the form. In this case, the X and Y coordinates displayed in the caption are relative to the form itself (see Figure 22.2).

Mouse Event Arguments

Besides indicating the current mouse position, the MouseDown, MouseUp, and MouseMove events can also determine which mouse button has been pressed, and which member of a control array is capturing the mouse at any given time.

This information is passed through the arguments built into the event procedures.

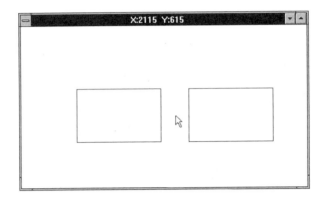

Figure 22.2.

The form's caption displays the pointer coordinates.

All three mouse events share the same arguments:

```
Sub Form_MouseEvent (Button, Shift, X, Y)
```

or

```
Sub Control_MouseEvent (Index, Button, Shift, X, Y)
```

in which

MouseEvent is one of the three mouse-related events: MouseDown, MouseUp, or MouseMove;

Control is the name of a Visual Basic control which supports the mouse events;

Button indicates which mouse button is pressed, if any;

Shift specifies the state of the Shift, Ctrl, and Alt keys when the mouse event occurs,

X and Y refer to the x,y coordinates of the mouse pointer relative to the form or control;

and

Index specifies the index number of the control if it is part of a control array.

Index appears only when a control array is in effect. All arguments are of data type Integer, except X and Y, which are of type Single.

The following sections explain the MouseDown, MouseUp, and MouseMove events in more detail.

The *MouseDown* Event

The MouseDown procedure has a four- and a five-parameter form. Four arguments exist when a control is independent, and five when it is a member of a control array:

```
Sub Form_MouseDown (Button As Integer, Shift As Integer, X As Single,
Y As Single)
```

or

```
Sub CtrlName_MouseDown (Button As Integer, Shift As Integer, X As
Single, Y As Single)
```

or

```
Sub CtrlName_MouseDown (Index As Integer, Button As Integer, Shift As
Integer, X As Single, Y As Single)
```

in which

    CtrlName specifies the control over which the mouse activity is monitored;

    Index specifies the control index if *CtrlName* is part of a control array;

    Button specifies which mouse button was pressed;

    Shift specifies whether Ctrl, Alt and/or Shift key was pressed when the mouse button was clicked,

and

    X and Y specify the location of the pointer when the mouse button was pressed.

The Index As Integer clause appears only when a control array is in effect.

In a MouseDown event procedure, the Button argument indicates which mouse button, if any, was pressed when the event occurs. The value of this argument is represented as a bit pattern, with specific bits corresponding to the different mouse buttons: left button (bit 0), right button (bit 1), and middle button (bit 2).

As a result, when the left mouse button is pressed, Button has the value 1. When the right button is pressed, Button is 2. Finally, when the middle button is pressed (assuming of course, that the mouse has a middle one), Button is 4.

NOTE The value of Button is always 1, 2, or 4 when the mouse event is triggered by the user. Notice that the MouseDown and MouseUp events cannot detect the simultaneous pressing of more than one mouse button. However, Button can be 0, indicating no mouse button was pressed, when the mouse event is triggered by an explicit call from another instruction in the program code.

The Shift argument indicates the state of the Ctrl, Alt, and Shift keys at the time of the MouseDown event. The values of the argument are also represented by a bit pattern. The value for Shift is 1, the value for Ctrl is 2, and the value for the Alt is 4. Unlike the Button parameter, Shift can indicate the status of multiple buttons at one time. As Table 22.3 shows, Shift can have any value from 0 to 7.

NOTE At the present time, the value of Shift must be between 0 and 7. However, Microsoft suggests masking off the extra (high-order) bits of the Shift argument, so that only the first 3 bits are used. This recommendation accommodates future Visual Basic releases, in which additional bits might be used to indicate other keys.

To mask the Shift argument, you just need to And it with the active bits. As Table 22.3 shows, only bits 0, 1, and 2 are of interest, so Shift needs to be masked with those bits (or the bit pattern 00000111, which corresponds to the value 7).

To mask the bits, before testing the value of Shift, insert the following line of code:

```
Shift = Shift And 7
```

This instruction maintains the Shift bits that correspond to values from 0 to 7. Any other high-order bits are cleared.

For more information on bit masking, see the section titled "CONSTANT.TXT" later in this chapter.

Table 22.3. Interpreting the *Shift* argument.

Shift	Shift key	Ctrl key	Alt key
0	Up	Up	Up
1	Pressed	Up	Up

Shift	Shift key	Ctrl key	Alt key
2	Up	Pressed	Up
3	Pressed	Pressed	Up
4	Up	Up	Pressed
5	Pressed	Up	Pressed
6	Up	Pressed	Pressed
7	Pressed	Pressed	Pressed

Finally, the X and Y arguments specify the exact coordinates on the control or form on which the mouse button was pressed. X and Y are expressed in terms of the coordinate system of the object, as determined by the ScaleHeight, ScaleWidth, ScaleLeft, and ScaleTop properties.

The *MouseUp* Event

MouseUp is the companion event to MouseDown. Whereas MouseDown occurs when the user presses one of the mouse buttons, MouseUp occurs when the user releases one of them. The procedures for both events have the same arguments:

```
Sub Form_MouseUp (Button As Integer, Shift As Integer, X As Single,
➥Y As Single)

or

Sub CtrlName_MouseUp (Button As Integer, Shift As Integer, X As
➥Single,
Y As Single)

or

Sub CtrlName_MouseUp (Index As Integer, Button As Integer, Shift As
Integer, X As Single, Y As Single)
```

When the user clicks the mouse, a MouseUp occurs after MouseDown, but before the Click event.

The *MouseMove* Event

A MouseMove event occurs whenever the user moves the mouse. As a result, this event occurs continually as the mouse pointer moves across on-screen objects. The MouseMove event has the same syntax and arguments as do MouseUp and MouseDown.

```
Sub Form_MouseMove (Button As Integer, Shift As Integer, X As Single,
➥Y As Single)
```

or

```
Sub CtrlName_MouseMove (Button As Integer, Shift As Integer, X As
➥Single, Y As Single)
```

or

```
Sub CtrlName_MouseMove (Index As Integer, Button As Integer, Shift As
➥Integer, X As Single, Y As Single)
```

 NOTE Actually, Visual Basic cannot trigger the MouseMove event *continually*. Perhaps *frequently* is a better word. The speed at which the user moves the mouse determines how many MouseMove events occur within a given segment of screen space. As a programmer, you cannot predict exactly how many MouseMove events occur for a given rate of mouse movement. The frequency of MouseMove events depends on the hardware and software in the user's computer.

Although MouseUp and MouseDown use the same arguments as the MouseMove event, it returns more complete information about the state of the mouse buttons than do the other two. Unlike MouseDown and MouseUp, the Button argument in the MouseMove event indicates the state of every mouse button. As Table 22.4 shows, the Button argument indicates whether some, all, or none of the buttons are pressed.

Table 22.4. Interpreting the *Button* argument.

Button	Left button	Right button	Middle button
0	Up	Up	Up
1	Down	Up	Up
2	Up	Down	Up
3	Down	Down	Up
4	Up	Up	Down
5	Down	Up	Down
6	Up	Down	Down
7	Down	Down	Down

CONSTANT.TXT

The CONSTANT.TXT file contains predefined constants that you can use as bit masks for the Button and Shift arguments. The following shows the constants relating directly to the state of the mouse buttons and the Ctrl, Alt, and Shift keys:

```
' Shift parameter masks
Global Const SHIFT_MASK = 1
Global Const CTRL_MASK = 2
Global Const ALT_MASK = 4

' Button parameter masks
Global Const LEFT_BUTTON = 1
Global Const RIGHT_BUTTON = 2
Global Const MIDDLE_BUTTON = 4
```

You can use these constants to mask certain bits in your program code. For example, the following If instruction is True if the left mouse button is pressed, False if it is not pressed:

```
If (Button And LEFT_BUTTON) Then ...
```

Other Considerations

As mentioned earlier in this chapter, MouseDown, MouseUp, Click, and DblClick always happen in this same order. They do not, however, always happen together. For example, a Click event can occur without a DblClick, and a MouseDown can happen without a MouseUp.

Be aware that one mouse event can "trip up" another one. Click and DblClick are the most likely culprits. For example, suppose a picture control has event procedures for both Click and DblClick. The Click event happens first, so if this event procedure generates a dialog box or some other time-consuming action, the code in the DblClick procedure can encounter interference.

Most of the time, such conflicts can be avoided by careful interface design. If a control is supposed to respond to the DblClick event, don't place code in the Click event that would interfere with the other's code.

The *MousePointer* and *DragIcon* Properties

The MousePointer and DragIcon properties enable you to change the shape of the mouse pointer during various mouse operations. Changing these properties gives the user visual cues. These cues not only help the user understand what's happening, but also what possible actions can be taken.

The *MousePointer* Property

Although the MousePointer property is associated with a form, control, or screen, it is related to mouse events. You can set the MousePointer property to one of 13 different values. Each value results in the mouse pointer taking on a particular shape. Table 22.5 shows the possible values of MousePointer, and the corresponding pointer shapes.

Table 22.5. *MousePointer* values.

Value	Cursor
0	(Default value) Shape determined by the control
1	Standard arrow
2	Cross hair
3	I-beam (the text insertion point)
4	Icon (a small square within another one)
5	Sizing arrow (four-pointed arrow pointing north, south, east, and west)
6	Sizing NE-SW arrow (double arrow pointing northeast and southwest)
7	Sizing N-S arrow (double arrow pointing north and south)
8	Sizing NW-SE arrow (double arrow pointing northwest and southeast)
9	Sizing W-E arrow (double arrow pointing west and east)
10	Up arrow
11	Hourglass (the wait indicator)
12	No drop symbol

Probably, the most commonly used value of MousePointer is 11, which turns the mouse pointer into the Windows hourglass shape. This shape is used in Windows to inform the user to wait until the application completes some current activity.

Other commonly used values include 10, which converts the MousePointer into an up arrow, and 2 (the cross-hair pointer), which is often used to indicate a drawing position.

The *DragIcon* Property

The DragIcon property relates to objects that can be dragged and dropped. This property has a direct bearing on the appearance of the mouse pointer during drag-and-drop events.

By setting the DragIcon property of a control, you can designate a particular icon to represent the control while it is dragged. If you leave the DragIcon property of a control at the default value, a box of the same size and shape as the control represents it during dragging. You see how to set the DragIcon property later in this chapter.

Using Mouse Events

The mouse has many uses in Windows applications. For example, with a mouse, the user can control a program by navigating menus, clicking buttons, or by resizing, minimizing, or maximizing windows. The mouse is invaluable also for drawing, manipulating graphics, and performing drag-and-drop operations.

Throughout this book, you've seen many examples of using the mouse in program control—for example, clicking command buttons and list boxes. The remainder of this chapter examines in depth the event procedures that offer you more detailed control of the mouse.

Drawing and Graphics—the MouseDemo Application

The mouse is indispensable for drawing and graphics applications. It becomes an extension of the artist's hand. In this regard, Windows' capability to track the mouse's movements and button states is crucial.

This section presents a simple application that demonstrates Visual Basic's capability to respond to mouse events. The MouseDemo application visually indicates mouse activity on a form. If a button is pressed while the user moves the mouse, the program draws a dot on the form at the current mouse location. MouseDemo uses the MouseDown, MouseMove, and MouseUp events to determine what the user is currently doing with the mouse.

Assigning the Property Values for MouseDemo

To begin developing the MouseDemo application, start a new project. Assign the property values to the form as Table 22.6 shows.

Table 22.6. Form property values for the MouseDemo application.

Property	Value	Comment
Name	frmDemo	
Caption	Mouse Demo	
ScaleMode	3	Measures in pixels
FillStyle	0	Creates solid dots
DrawWidth	3	Creates larger dots (default value is 1)

Creating the Event Procedures for MouseDemo

Next, create the Form_MouseMove procedure. This procedure draws the on-screen dots with the PSet method. This event procedure repeatedly activates while the user moves the mouse across the form:

```
Sub Form_MouseMove (Button As Integer, Shift As Integer, X As Single,
➥Y As Single)
   If Button <> 0 Then PSet (X, Y)
End Sub
```

This event procedure is pretty straightforward. If Button is not equal to zero, a mouse button is being pressed. In such a case, the MouseMove event draws a single point at the current mouse location. The X and Y coordinates specify this location.

You can also change the shape of the mouse pointer while the user draws on the form. To do so, modify the form's MousePointer property with MouseDown and MouseUp procedures:

```
Sub Form_MouseDown (Button As Integer, Shift As Integer, X As Single,
➥Y As Single)
   frmDemo.MousePointer = 2  'Change pointer to cross hair
End Sub

Sub Form_MouseUp (Button As Integer, Shift As Integer, X As Single,
➥Y As Single)
   frmDemo.MousePointer = 0    'Restore normal pointer shape
End Sub
```

Understanding How MouseDemo Works

The sequence of events that occurs when you run MouseDemo is as follows: When you press any mouse button, the pointer shape changes to a cross hair. As you move the mouse over the form, you repeatedly generate Form_MouseMove events. Each one draws a dot on the form at the current pointer location. When you release the mouse button, the pointer changes back to the default arrow, and the drawing of dots stops.

Try running MouseDemo. Press and hold one of its buttons as you move the mouse across the form. The result is a form peppered with little dots. Each dot represents the activation of a MouseMove event (see Figure 22.3).

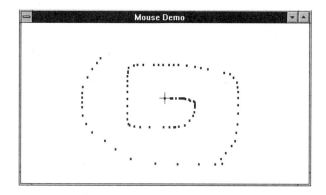

Figure 22.3.

A sample run of the MouseDemo application.

The MouseDemo application provides an excellent picture of what's happening behind the scenes in Windows and Visual Basic applications. Windows generates only a limited number of MouseMove events as the mouse travels around the form. In fact, you'll notice that the faster you move the mouse, the fewer points you see drawn.

MouseDemo is, of course, somewhat limited as a drawing program. However, there are many ways you can embellish the line-drawing capability of MouseDemo. For example, you can save the X and Y coordinates returned by

each previous occurrence of Form_MouseMove. Then, you can draw a line between the saved X and Y coordinates, and those generated by the current
occurrence of Form_MouseMove. The following is an example of such a revised
procedure:

```
Sub Form_MouseMove (Button As Integer, Shift As Integer, X As Single,
➥Y As Single)
    Static OldX As Single, OldY As Single
    If Button <> 0 Then Line (OldX, OldY)-(X, Y)
    OldX = X
    OldY = Y
End Sub
```

With this modification, MouseDemo draws a solid line as you move the mouse.

Dragging and Dropping

Drag and drop refer to the techniques of using the mouse to move a control
around the screen, and placing it onto another on-screen object. Visual Basic
treats drag and drop as events. You *drag* a control by moving the pointer onto
the control, pressing and holding a mouse button, then moving the control
with the mouse. You can drag an object onto various on-screen controls, or
even onto other forms. You *drop* the control at its updated location by releasing the mouse button.

Drag and drop is made possible by the object-oriented nature of the Windows
user environment. Visual Basic fully supports drag-and-drop operations.

When discussing drag-and-drop operations, it's important to understand that
there are two objects involved: the *source object* (the object that is dragged),
and the *destination object* (a control or form) which receives the source object
when it's dropped.

Drag-and-drop objects can be forms or controls. Controls can be dragged and
dropped. Further, a control can recognize when another object is dragged
over it. Forms, however, can only detect and receive dragged objects. Although you can move forms around the screen, they cannot be dropped onto
other objects to trigger program events.

The code that controls the drag-and-drop process occurs in two different
places:

- The *source object* contains the code that starts, stops, or cancels
  dragging.

- The *destination object* contains the code for the drop event, and any
  resulting program events triggered by it.

Drag-and-Drop Events

Managing the drag-and-drop process requires one Visual Basic method and two control events: the Drag method, and the DragOver and DragDrop events.

The Drag method goes in the MouseDown event for the source control. This method can begin or cancel dragging, and also create a drop.

The DragOver event occurs in the destination object when a dragged object is moved over it. The DragDrop event is also located in the destination object, and occurs when the source object has been dropped on it.

The following is the syntax for the Drag method:

```
CtrlName.Drag action
```

in which

   CtrlName is the name of the control that is dragged,

and

   action specifies the type of drag action to take.

The action parameter is optional.

The action parameter can have three values, as Table 22.7 shows.

Table 22.7. Values for the *Action* parameter.

Value	Result
0	Cancel dragging
1	Start dragging the control (default value)
2	Drop the control

If you omit the action parameter, Visual Basic begins dragging. The effect is the same as if you specified that action has the value 1.

Writing Code for Drag-and-Drop Events

To enable the user to drag a control, you place code in its MouseDown event. For example, suppose you have a form that contains a picture box named Picture1. When the user presses the mouse button with the pointer over the picture box, the `Picture1_MouseDown` event occurs. If the event procedure executes the instruction `Picture1.Drag 1` (or simply `Picture1.Drag`), the user can begin dragging the picture box.

NOTE You can cancel dragging with a `Picture1.Drag 0` instruction.

As the user drags an object, it doesn't actually move on-screen. Rather, an image of the object moves in response to the mouse movements. When the user releases the mouse button, a `MouseUp` event occurs. In the `MouseUp` event procedure, the instruction `Picture1.Drag 2` ends dragging, and drops the control. When the object is dropped, the destination object (the form or control receiving the dropped control) executes its `DragDrop` event.

Nothing really happens to the dragged control until the `DragDrop` event occurs—the work actually takes place in the control's `DragDrop` procedure. Here you can program the events that are to take place when the source object is dropped onto the destination object. The syntax for the `DragDrop` event is as follows:

```
Sub Form_DragDrop (Source As Control, X As Single, Y As Single)

or

Sub MDIForm_DragDrop (Source As Control, X As Single, Y As Single)

or

Sub CtlName CtrlName_DragDrop (Source As Control, X As Single,
➡Y As Single)

or

Sub CtrlName_DragDrop (Index As Integer, Source As Control,
➡X As Single, Y As Single)
```

in which

   `Index` is the index number for a control array,

   `Source` is an object variable that identifies the control that is dragged,

and

   `X` and `Y` are the coordinates of the drop point.

The `Index As Integer` argument appears only when *CtrlName* is a control array.

For example, the following is the event procedure for a form that moves a dropped control to the drop location:

```
Sub Form_DragDrop (Source As Control, X as Single, Y as Single)
    Source.Move X,Y
End Sub
```

As this event procedure shows, you typically use the Move method to relocate the object. However, that's just the beginning of what you can do with drag and drop. The DragDrop event procedure can also save a file, launch a program, or do anything else that you can accomplish with program code.

If you want a specific picture to represent a control that is being dragged, you can set its DragIcon property to display any icon you choose. When the control is dragged, a transparent monochrome version of the icon is displayed. The DragIcon property is discussed in more detail later in this chapter.

The *PicDrag* Application

The PicDrag application demonstrates dragging an icon around a form. What actually occurs is that you place the icon in a Picture box control, then drag the picture box around the form.

To begin this application, start a new project. Create a Picture box control on the form. Place this control about a third of the way both vertically down the form, and horizontally to the right.

Using the Properties window, set the BorderStyle property of the picture box to 0. As a result, the picture box has no visible border. Set the Autosize property for the picture box to True. This setting makes the size of the picture box automatically adjust to that of the icon.

To put the icon in the picture box, you assign a value to the Picture property of the picture box. To do so, double-click the Picture… list item in the Properties window. The Load Picture dialog box appears. This dialog box displays the available bitmap (*.BMP), icon (*.ICO), and metafile (*.WMF) files that you can assign to a picture box. The Load Picture dialog box works similar to a standard file specification dialog box.

 Visual Basic includes several icon files. The Microsoft documentation includes a picture of each of the available icons. Visual Basic's icon library has plenty of icons from which you can choose.

For this project, an icon of a plane is appropriate. The C:\VB\ICONS\ INDUSTRY\PLANE.ICO file consists of such an icon. Specify this file name in the dialog box. Once you use the dialog box to select any desired file, the image in it is assigned to the picture control.

NOTE If your C:\VB\ICONS directory is on another drive, or in a different directory path, fill in the correct pathname when specifying the Picture property.

Create the following MouseDown and MouseUp procedures for Picture1:

```
Sub Picture1_MouseDown (Button As Integer, Shift As Integer, X As Single,
➡Y As Single)
    Picture1.Drag 1    'Begin dragging
End Sub

Sub Picture1_MouseUp (Button As Integer, Shift As Integer, X As Single,
➡Y As Single)
    Picture1.Drag 2    'Drop
End Sub
```

Programming the *DragDrop* Event

The form must respond when the picture box is dropped. To do this, program the form's DragDrop event to receive the dropped picture box:

```
Sub Form_DragDrop (Source As Control, X As Single, Y As Single)
    Source.Move X, Y
End Sub
```

As mentioned before, the DragDrop event has three parameters: the control that is dropped, and the X and Y coordinates of the mouse at drop time. The Move method enables the DragDrop event to move the dropped control to the location in which the drop occurs.

Try running the application. Move the mouse pointer over the plane icon. Press the left mouse button, and drag the plane around the form.

What actually happens is that you see a grayed rectangular outline of the picture box move while you drag. The original plane icon remains stationary.

When you release the mouse button, the plane icon jumps to the new location. Figure 22.4 shows the form while the picture is dragged toward the right and downward from its original location. Figure 22.5 shows the form when the drop occurs (that is, when the mouse button is released).

Specifying the Drop Location

As you run the application, you might immediately notice one minor problem when the drop occurs—the Picture1 control does not land in the place exactly indicated by the grayed outline. Instead, the icon ends up slightly downward and to the right of it.

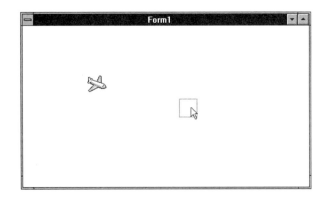

Figure 22.4.

The plane is dragged down and to the right.

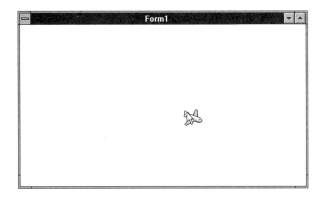

Figure 22.5.

The plane is dropped.

The problem arises because of an inconsistency in locating the mouse pointer relative to the picture control. As you drag Picture1, the tip of the mouse pointer is near the center of the grayed outline (see Figure 22.4). The pointer location represents the exact position of the mouse on Picture1 when the MouseDown event occurred.

However, when the DragDrop event produces a drop, the Left and Top properties of Picture1 are set to the current coordinates of the mouse pointer on the form. The result is that the picture doesn't snap down in the exact place you want. Instead, the picture ends up slightly below, and to the right.

The solution is to store the mouse's X and Y coordinates when the MouseDown event occurs for the picture box. When Picture1 is dropped onto the form, subtract the stored numbers from the form's current x,y mouse coordinates. After this slight adjustment, the picture drops onto the exact place the user expects.

To make this change, store the X and Y mouse coordinates so that both the control and the form can access their values. One solution is to declare the form-level variables DragX and DragY. Place the following instruction in the General Declarations section of the form:

```
Dim DragX as Single, DragY as Single
```

Now, modify the MouseDown and DragDrop events as follows:

```
Sub Picture1_MouseDown (Button As Integer, Shift As Integer, X As Single,
➥Y As Single)
   DragX = X
   DragY = Y
   Picture1.Drag 1     'Begin dragging
End Sub

Sub Form_DragDrop (Source As Control, X As Single, Y As Single)
    Source.Move X - DragX, Y - DragY
End Sub
```

By utilizing the DragX and DragY variables, you can adjust the position of the dropped control so it lands exactly on the drop location.

Using the *DragIcon* Property

As you've seen, when you drag Picture1 in the PicDrag application, a gray rectangle shows the current location of the control. This rectangle is the same size as the picture box. By assigning the DragIcon property of Picture1, you can represent the dragged control with a custom icon rather than a grayed rectangle.

The Form_Load procedure is a natural place to set both the Picture and DragIcon properties of Picture1. (Recall that the Form_Load procedure occurs when the application starts.) The following is an appropriate Form_Load procedure:

```
Sub Form_Load ()
   Picture1.DragIcon = Picture1.Picture
End Sub
```

This procedure assigns to the DragIcon property of the picture box the same icon stored in its Picture property. As a result, the drag icon and the icon in the picture box are identical. This helps identify the control as it is dragged.

Once you assign the DragIcon property, the specified image (in a monochromatic form) represents the object as it is dragged. Figure 22.6 depicts the drag icon with the same plane icon used in the picture box.

Notice that with a DragIcon assigned, the mouse pointer becomes invisible during the dragging of an object. In effect, the drag icon becomes the mouse pointer.

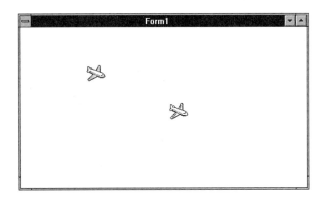

Figure 22.6.

The plane is used as a drag icon.

The *DragOver* Event

As you've seen, the DragIcon property represents the object that is dragged. You can also use the DragIcon property to visually inform the user that a control is being dragged over a location (or another control) that won't accept a drop.

You do this by placing code in the destination object's DragOver event. The DragOver event occurs in a form or control when another object is dragged over it.

The following is the syntax of the DragOver event:

```
Sub CtrlName_DragOver (Source As Control, X As Single, Y As Single,
➡State As Integer)
```

or

```
Sub CtrlName_DragOver (Index As Integer, Source As Control, X As
Single, Y As Single, State As Integer)
```

in which

   Index specifies the control index if *CtrlName* is part of a control array;

   CtrlName specifies the form or control that is dragged over;

   Source specifies the control that is dragged;

   X and Y specify the location of the mouse pointer within the control that is dragged over;

and

   State specifies the situation of the dragged object in relation to the destination object.

The Index As Integer parameter appears only when *CtrlName* is part of a control array.

Again, Source refers to the control that is dragged, and X, Y are the mouse coordinates at the time of the DragOver event.

The *State* Parameter

The State parameter in the DragOver event enables you to determine whether the dragged object is entering or leaving the destination control. Table 22.8 lists the various possible values of State.

Table 22.8. Values of the *State* parameter.

Value of *State*	Meaning
0	Dragged object has just entered the destination object.
1	Dragged object has just left the destination object.
2	Dragged object is inside the destination object.

The information provided by State is particularly useful when you change a dragged control's DragIcon property, so that you can visually alert the user when dropping is prohibited.

Demonstrating the *DragOver* Event

A few simple modifications to the PicDrag application demonstrates the DragOver event. First, use the Properties window to specify the Caption property of the form as DragDrop Demo.

Now, add a second picture box to the form. Visual Basic assigns the default name of Picture2 to this new picture box. Resize Picture2 so that it is a square (or approximately a square) about one-quarter the size of the form. Position the control near the lower right corner of the form.

Picture2 represents an area of the form on which Picture1 cannot be dropped. When the application runs, you need a way to visually indicate this restriction to the user. One approach is to change the icon to a stop sign when it is dragged over the second picture box. In code, you do this by modifying the DragIcon property of Picture1 in the DragOver event procedure for Picture2.

The following is the DragOver event procedure for Picture2:

```
Sub Picture2_DragOver (Source As Control, X As Single, Y As Single,
➥State As Integer)
    Select Case State
```

```
    Case 0     'arriving
        Picture1.DragIcon =
LoadPicture("C:\VB\ICONS\TRAFFIC\TRFFC14.ICO")
    Case 1     'leaving
        Picture1.DragIcon = Picture1.Picture
    Case 2     'moving over
               'no action required
    End Select
End Sub
```

As you can see, the source control's drag icon changes to a stop sign (TRFFC14.ICO in Visual Basic's icon library) when the dragged control enters Picture2. The icon changes back to a plane when the control is dragged from of Picture2.

TRFFC14.ICO is a stop sign. This icon is a natural choice to warn the user that the dragged object temporarily cannot be dropped. (Of course, you can choose any icon.)

Figure 22.7 shows how the plane icon for Picture1 changes to a black-and-white stop sign when Picture1 is dragged over Picture2.

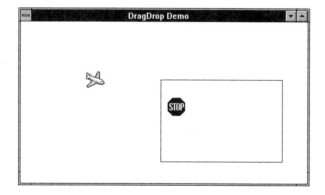

Figure 22.7.

The dragged icon changes to a stop sign.

Notice that the code does not prevent the user from dropping Picture1 onto Picture2. However, there is no code in Picture2's DragDrop event procedure, so nothing happens if the user does this.

If you drop Picture1 onto Picture2, the DragIcon property of Picture1 changes to the stop sign image. As a result, if you drag Picture1 a second time, its icon becomes the stop sign rather than the plane. To restore the plane as the drag icon, modify the Picture1_MouseDown event procedure to look as follows:

```
Sub Picture1_MouseDown (Button As Integer, Shift As Integer, X As Single,
⇥Y As Single)
   DragX = X
   DragY = Y
   Picture1.DragIcon = Picture1.Picture    'add this instruction
   Picture1.Drag 1    'Begin dragging
End Sub
```

This example application enables the user to move a picture control to a new location. However, that's only the beginning of what drag -and- drop can do. For example, you can write an application that deletes a file when the user drops its icon onto a picture of a trash can. Another possibility is an application that permits the user to drop a file icon onto a symbol for a graphics viewer utility or a text editor. For a graphics file, the viewer displays the stored image; for a text file, the editor loads the file in preparation for editing.

The *DragMode* Property—Automatic Dragging

One final aspect of drag and drop is the DragMode property. Controls that can be dragged have the DragMode property. This property has two possible values, 0 and 1. If DragMode equals 1, the control automatically enters the drag mode, (that is, it begins dragging) when the MouseDown event occurs.

If DragMode equals 0 (the default value), dragging is manual. As such, dragging does not automatically begin when the user clicks the control. To start dragging, you must execute the Drag method in the control's Mousedown event.

The DragMode property permits extended control over dragging operations. With automatic dragging, the user can drag the control at any time. With manual dragging, the user can drag it only when explicitly permitted by the program code.

You can set the DragMode property either in the Properties window, or in code. You set the DragMode property in code with instructions, such as Picture1.DragMode = 0, or Picture1.DragMode = 1.

If you have a control array, or several controls that use drag-and-drop operations, consider setting the DragMode property of each to 1 (automatic). By doing so, you might save the need for several Drag method instructions. Notice that you still must assign DragIcon properties if your application uses them, and that a DragDrop procedure must still be present in any destination controls.

Summary

Mouse events permeate Visual Basic applications. The `Click` and `DblClick` events are common to almost every control. The `MouseDown`, `MouseUp`, and `MouseMove` events are useful for responding to mouse actions on a more dynamic level. These events also enable you to monitor and respond to the location of the pointer, and the state of the mouse buttons.

The drag-and-drop capabilities of Windows are fully supported by Visual Basic. The `Drag` method and the `DragOver` and `DragDrop` events make it possible to include drag-and-drop functionality in your applications.

Responding to Keyboard Events

Your Visual Basic applications must respond to what the user does at the keyboard. Although the mouse is certainly important for navigating Windows applications, the keyboard remains the main input tool, especially for text data.

For most applications, you won't do much programming to process keystrokes. Visual Basic has considerable keyboard functionality built into the forms and controls. For example: text boxes accept and display typed text; command buttons respond to access keys; list boxes can be navigated with the arrow and letter keys, and the Tab key moves the focus around an application's controls.

These are only a few examples of Visual Basic's keyboard responsiveness. As a programmer, you get these features without having to write a single line of code.

Some applications, however, require special handling of the keyboard. For example, a tutorial application might need to display a screen of new information anytime the user presses, say, the F5 key. An arcade game must respond quickly to different keystrokes.

Visual Basic lets you take charge of the keyboard through a variety of events and control properties.

The following are the main topics discussed in this chapter:

- Understanding the KeyPress, KeyUp, and KeyDown events
- Capturing keystrokes on forms and controls
- Sending keystrokes to other applications
- Writing keyboard event procedures

The Main KeyBoard Events

As an application executes, the form or control with the focus responds to keystrokes. For example, in a form containing several text boxes, only the one which has the focus displays the characters that the user types.

Visual Basic defines three special keyboard events—KeyPress, KeyDown, and KeyUp. These events are the basis of customized keyboard handling. By writing procedures for these events, you can make a form or control respond in a specific way to particular keystrokes.

KeyPress

The form and most controls have a KeyPress event procedure. This event triggers whenever the user presses an ASCII key. An *ASCII key* is a key corresponding to a printable character. However, some other special keys can also trigger the event.

In a KeyPress event procedure, you can place code to make your application take specific action in response to the triggering keystroke. The event procedure automatically passes information about what key was pressed. As a result, you can write event procedures that check which key was pressed, and take appropriate actions, depending on the keystroke.

The syntax for the KeyPress event is as follows:

```
Sub Form_KeyPress (KeyAscii As Integer)
```

or

```
Sub CtrlName_KeyPress (Index As Integer, KeyAscii As Integer)
```

in which

CtrlName is the name of the control that has the focus,

KeyAscii is the (numeric) ASCII code of the pressed key,

and

> Index specifies the control index when *CtrlName* is a control array.
>
> The Index As Integer clause appears only when a control array is in effect.

Keys that Activate *KeyPress*

Table 23.1 lists the keys that trigger the KeyPress event. The table shows the value of KeyAscii for each triggering keystroke. For printable characters, such as the letter and number keys, the value of KeyAscii is the same as the character's ANSI code. See Appendix B for a table of the ANSI characters and codes.

Table 23.1. Keystrokes that cause a *KeyPress* event.

Keystroke	Value of *KeyAscii*
Printable keyboard character	Corresponding ANSI code
Ctrl+A through Ctrl+Z	1 - 26
Backspace	8
Tab	9
Ctrl+Enter	10
Enter	13
Ctrl+Backspace	127

Passing Keystrokes to the Active Control

When the KeyPress event terminates, the keystroke is still passed to the active control. For example, suppose a form has a single text box named Text1, and an event procedure named Text1_KeyPress. Further, suppose that the user presses the 3 key when the text box has the focus. First, the KeyPress event triggers, and the event procedure activates. When the procedure terminates, the key is passed to the text box. A 3 appears in the text box, as though the KeyPress procedure never happened.

However, in the Keypress procedure, you can affect the passed keystroke by modifying the value of KeyAscii. To do so, just use an assignment instruction, such as KeyAscii = 65. By modifying the value of KeyAscii, you pass the altered keystroke to the control. You can take advantage of this technique to intercept keystrokes, and change their values.

For example, suppose you want only uppercase letters entered in a text box. In the KeyPress procedure for this box, you can examine the value of KeyAscii. If the pressed key corresponds to a lowercase letter, you can modify KeyAscii to use the value of the corresponding uppercase one. When the event procedure terminates, the uppercase letter (not the originally typed lowercase one) gets passed to the text box.

KeyUp and *KeyDown*

The KeyPress event does not capture several special keys, such as the Function keys (F1 through F12), navigation keys (PgUp, PgDn, Home, End, and arrow keys), and keyboard modifiers (Ctrl, Alt, or Shift). Instead, you can use the KeyUp or KeyDown (or both) events to trap such keystrokes.

The KeyDown event for a control (or form) occurs when any key is pressed and that control (or form) has the focus. Similarly, a KeyUp event occurs when a key is released.

KeyUp and KeyDown provide you with more detailed keyboard control than does KeyPress. As described shortly, in addition to reporting the triggering key, KeyUp and KeyDown give information on the general state of the keyboard.

The following is the syntax for KeyDown and KeyUp:

```
Sub Form_KeyDown (KeyCode As Integer, Shift As Integer)
```

or

```
Sub CtrlName_KeyDown (Index As Integer, KeyCode As Integer,
➥Shift As Integer)
```

and

```
Sub Form_KeyUp (KeyCode As Integer, Shift As Integer)
```

or

```
Sub CtrlName_KeyUp (Index As Integer, KeyCode As Integer,
➥Shift As Integer)
```

in which

    CtrlName is the name of the control that has the focus,

    KeyCode is the key's scan code,

> Shift indicates the state of the Ctrl, Alt, and Shift keys when the event occurs,
>
> and
>
> Index specifies the control index when *CtrlName* is a control array.
>
> The Index As Integer clause appears only when a control array is in effect.

The KeyCode parameter works somewhat differently than does the KeyAscii parameter for the KeyPress event. For each physical key on the keyboard, including the Shift, arrow keys, and other special ones, Visual Basic assigns a unique number known as the key's *scan code*.

It's important to understand that the scan code identifies the physical key, not the character that it generates. Also, when keystroke combinations are pressed, such as Ctrl+A, multiple events are generated. For example, if the user presses the A key, KeyCode is 65 (the scan code for the A key). However, if the user presses Shift+A, two KeyDown events occur. For one event, KeyCode is 16 (the Shift key). For the second event, KeyCode is 65 (the A key).

NOTE   The scan code for each keyboard key can be found in Visual Basic's CONSTANT.TXT file.

The Shift parameter indicates the status of the Ctrl, Alt, and Shift keys at the time of the event. When the Shift key is pressed, the Shift parameter is 1. The Ctrl key has the value 2, and the Alt key is 4. Some, all, or none of the keys can be pressed. The value of Shift is the sum of the individual key parameters. Thus, if both Ctrl and Alt are pressed, but not the Shift key, the value of the Shift parameter is 6. If none of these special keys is pressed, Shift is 0.

KeyUp and KeyDown can trap any keystroke, including, but not limited to, the keys which KeyPress can catch. Typically, you use KeyPress to trap character-based keys, and KeyUp and KeyDown for noncharacter keys. Thus, KeyUp and KeyDown are generally used for navigation and control, while KeyPress is employed for the evaluation of alphanumeric input typed by the user.

Sequence of Keyboard Events

You should keep in mind one important point about the KeyPress, KeyDown, and KeyUp events—*they cannot occur separately.* As you might imagine, anytime a KeyDown event occurs, KeyUp almost certainly follows. Further, KeyPress is also generated (for most keystrokes).

The three events occur together, and always in the same order: KeyDown, KeyPress, and KeyUp.

The ShowKeys Application

The ShowKeys application visually demonstrates the keyboard events. The application uses only a form (no controls), and several event procedures. When you press keys, ShowKeys displays information about the generated events directly on the form.

To create ShowKeys, start a new project. Create the following event procedures:

```
Sub Form_KeyDown (KeyCode As Integer, Shift As Integer)
    Print "KeyDown — KeyCode is"; KeyCode; Tab(30);
    Print "Shift parameter is"; Shift
End Sub

Sub Form_KeyPress (KeyAscii As Integer)
    Print "KeyPress returned KeyAscii value of " & KeyAscii;
    Print ", which translates to character ["; Chr$(KeyAscii); "]"
    End Sub

Sub Form_KeyUp (KeyCode As Integer, Shift As Integer)
    Print "KeyUp — KeyCode is"; KeyCode; Tab(30);
    Print "Shift parameter is"; Shift
    Print
End Sub
```

In addition, create this Form_DblClick event procedure that contains a Cls instruction:

```
Sub Form_DblClick ()
    Cls
End Sub
```

Using the Properties window, set the form's Caption to Show Keys. Also, set the AutoRedraw property to True (so you won't lose the displayed text if another window temporarily covers the form).

Now, run the application. Try pressing some keys to see the results. You can double-click the form to clear the displayed messages. Figure 23.1 shows a sample run.

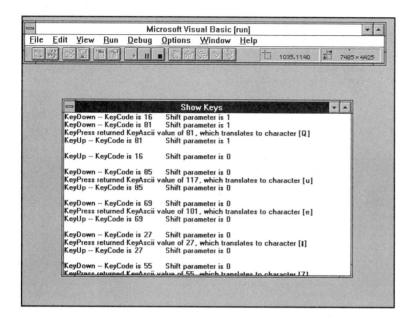

Figure 23.1.

The form responds to keyboard events.

As you can see, the order of the keyboard events is logical: KeyDown, KeyPress, then KeyUp. You can see how KeyPress responds to alphanumeric keys, such as *A*, *Z*, *a*, *1*, and *9*. KeyPress also responds to the Tab and Enter keys. When arrow or control keys are pressed, however, only the KeyUp and KeyDown events respond.

 You can use the ShowKeys application to learn the values of KeyAscii and KeyCode for any key.

The *KeyPreview* Property

In the ShowKeys application, the Form_KeyPress, Form_KeyUp, and Form_KeyDown events occur because there are no controls on the form. If it had any, the control which had the focus would receive the KeyPress, KeyUp, and KeyDown events rather than the form.

If you want the form to capture and process keyboard events *before* individual controls receive them, you can set its KeyPreview property to True. When KeyPreview is True, the form receives the keyboard events before the active control does. When KeyPreview is False (the default), the active control receives all keyboard events instead of the form.

To demonstrate `KeyPreview`, add a text box control to the form for the ShowKeys application. With the Properties window, set the `Text` property of the text box to a blank string. Set the size and location properties of the text box as Table 23.2 shows.

Table 23.2. Properties of *Text1*.	
Property	**Value**
Left	960
Height	1335
Top	1080
Width	2175

Now, try running the application again. Press some keys. Notice that the keystrokes appear in the text box, but nothing displays on the form. It no longer captures the keystrokes. The reason is that the only control in the application, `Text1`, always has the focus. So the form-centered events (`Form_KeyPress`, `Form_KeyUp`, and `Form_KeyDown`) never occur.

End the application. Access the Properties window, and set the form's `KeyPreview` property to True. Then, run the application again.

This time *both* the form and the text box respond to each keystroke. The text box responds because it has the focus; the form does so because `KeyPreview` is set to True. Figure 23.2 shows the result when `This is Text1` is typed from the keyboard.

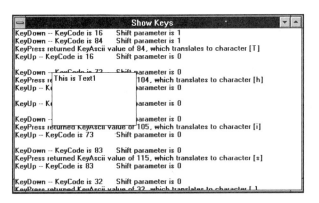

When `KeyPreview` is True for a form, you have several options. You can use the form's keyboard event procedures to simply pass the event to the currently active control, to modify the keystroke, or even to discard it entirely.

For example, in the Form_KeyPress event procedure, you can modify the value of KeyAscii. When the procedure terminates, the modified keystroke is sent to the active control. Similarly, you can modify the value of KeyCode in the Form_KeyUp event procedure.

To discard a keystroke, set the KeyAscii or KeyCode value to zero. The effect is as though no key was ever pressed.

You can try this technique in the current application. Modify the Form1_KeyPress procedure to add the instruction KeyAscii = 0. Similarly, add KeyCode = 0 to the Form_KeyUp procedure. The following are the updated event procedures:

```
Sub Form_KeyPress (KeyAscii As Integer)
   Print "KeyPress returned KeyAscii value of " & KeyAscii;
   Print ", which translates to character ["; Chr$(KeyAscii); "]"
   KeyAscii = 0    'Cancels keystroke
   End Sub

Sub Form_KeyUp (KeyCode As Integer, Shift As Integer)
   Print "KeyUp — KeyCode is"; KeyCode; Tab(30);
   Print "Shift parameter is"; Shift
   Print
   KeyCode = 0       'Cancels keystroke
End Sub
```

Try running the application once again. You find that the form responds to the keystrokes, but the text box does not.

Keyboard Constants

Predefined constants for the scan codes are available in Visual Basic's CONSTANT.TXT file. Recall that the scan code for each key equates to the KeyCode parameter for the KeyUp and KeyDown events. The following is how the beginning of the Key Code section of the CONSTANT.TXT file should appear:

```
' Key Codes
Global Const KEY_LBUTTON = &H1
Global Const KEY_RBUTTON = &H2
Global Const KEY_CANCEL = &H3
Global Const KEY_MBUTTON = &H4     ' NOT contiguous with L & RBUTTON
Global Const KEY_BACK = &H8
Global Const KEY_TAB = &H9
Global Const KEY_CLEAR = &HC
Global Const KEY_RETURN = &HD
Global Const KEY_SHIFT = &H10
Global Const KEY_CONTROL = &H11
```

If your application has to recognize a lot of keystrokes, you can benefit from placing CONSTANT.TXT (or at least the key code section of the file) in a global code module. Then, you can use these constants to test for particular keystrokes.

For example, suppose you want to test whether the Tab key was pressed in a KeyDown event procedure. You want the speaker to beep if this condition exists. With the CONSTANT.TXT file loaded in a code module, the following instruction accomplishes this:

```
If (KeyCode And KEY_TAB) Then Beep
```

The *SendKeys* Statement

With the SendKeys statement, your Visual Basic application can send a keystroke to another Windows application. The effect is as though the other application received keystrokes entered at the keyboard.

The following is the syntax for SendKeys:

```
SendKeys keystring, waitstate
```

in which

    keystring is a string expression which specifies the keystrokes to send,

and

    waitstate specifies whether the target application must process the keystrokes before control returns to the Visual Basic program.

waitstate is an optional parameter.

The *keystring* and *waitstring* Parameters

For alphanumeric keys, the *keystring* parameter is simply a text string of the desired keystrokes. In other words, to send printable characters, just use the characters themselves. For example, the following instruction sends the characters produced by pressing the A, C, and E keys:

```
SendKeys "ACE"
```

For nonprintable keystrokes, *keystring* can contain special text codes. Many of these codes are a descriptive keyword enclosed in braces. For example, the F3 key is {F3}, the Tab key is {TAB}, and the Enter key is {ENTER}. For a complete description of the *keystring* "language," see Microsoft's Visual Basic documentation.

The *waitstring* parameter can be expressed as a Boolean value. If True, the Visual Basic application waits until the target application processes the keystrokes. If False (or omitted), the Visual Basic application sends the keystrokes, but immediately continues executing.

A Sample Program That Uses SendKeys

Consider a quick experiment that demonstrates SendKeys. With a simple event procedure, you can open the Windows Notepad utility and load in the Windows WIN.INI file to be edited.

Start a new project and create the following event procedure:

```
Sub Form_Click ()
    Dummy% = Shell("NOTEPAD.EXE", 1)
    SendKeys "%FO C:\WINDOWS\WIN.INI {ENTER}", True
End Sub
```

Now, run the application and click the form. You see Notepad open in its own window. The WIN.INI file loads into the Notepad, ready to be edited.

Here, the Shell function launches Notepad, and gives it the focus. The SendKeys instruction then sends to Notepad the keystrokes necessary to load in the WIN.INI file. The percent sign is the *keystring* shorthand for the Alt key. As such, the string %FO represents Alt+F followed by the O key. These keystrokes open the Notepad's File menu and choose the Open option.

Notice that *waitstate* is True. As a result, the Visual Basic application suspends until the Notepad application is opened. To close Notepad, open its File menu, and choose the Exit option. You can then end the Visual Basic application.

The Flying Fickle Finger of Fate

To help you further understand some of the techniques and subtleties of keyboard processing, the remainder of this chapter develops two sample applications. The first one is a fun example of keyboard handling called The Flying Fickle Finger of Fate. This application also demonstrates the use of a control array.

In this application, a pointing hand moves around the screen in response to various keystrokes. Figure 23.3 shows the application when first started. You can alter the hand in different ways: change the path of its movement, adjust its speed, point it in different directions, and return it to the "launching pad." This application is an example of the coding techniques used in arcade games.

Figure 23.3.

The Flying Fickle Finger of Fate in position to be launched.

Developing the Interface

To create The Flying Fickle Finger of Fate, start a new project. With the Properties window, set the form's Caption property to Flying Fickle Finger of Fate. Set the KeyPreview property to True.

Add a single picture box control. With the Properties window, set its Name property to picHand, its AutoSize property to True, and its BorderStyle property to 0 (no border). Place the control near the top edge of the form, centered horizontally.

Creating the Control Array

The next step is to create a control array consisting of four Image controls. These serve as a storage location for the four hand images (pointing left, right, up, and down) used in the application. When the application actually runs, these Image controls are invisible.

To create the control array, first place one image control near the left border of the form, below the level of the picture box. Using the Properties window, set the Name property of this image control to imgSource.

Now, add three additional image controls to the form. Line up the added controls horizontally and to the right of the first image control. Set the Name property of each new image control to imgSource, the same name you used for the first image. When Visual Basic asks if you want to create a control array, answer Yes.

NOTE Several ways exist to create a control array. For example, instead of the technique described in this section, you can use the **E**dit menu to **C**opy the first Image control, then **P**aste three additional ones. For more information about creating control arrays, see Chapter 7, "Writing Event Procedures."

When you have the four image controls established as a control array and lined up horizontally, set their `Index` property values from `0` to `3`, moving left to right. Also, set each of the image controls' `Visible` and `Stretch` properties to False.

Assigning the Icons

The next step is to assign pictures to the image controls. This application uses four pictures of the pointing hand. Each one shows the hand pointing in a different direction. Appropriate pictures are found in the Arrows section of the Visual Basic icon library.

You assign a picture to an image control by using the Properties window to set its `Picture` property. With the focus on the image control to the far left, `imgSource(0)`, open the Properties window, and double-click the `Picture` property. This opens the Load Picture dialog box. Using this dialog box, assign the icon file C:\VB\ICONS\ARROWS\POINT05.ICO. This file depicts a hand pointing upward. When you close the dialog box, you should see this hand icon in the image control to the far left.

In a similar manner, assign the POINT03.ICO file to `imgSource(1)`, the POINT02.ICO file to `imgSource(2)`, and the POINT04.ICO file to `imgSource(3)`. Each of these files depicts a hand: the first points downward, the second—to the left, and the third—to the right, respectively. The resulting form should resemble Figure 23.4.

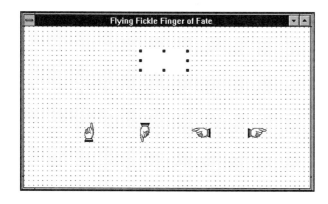

Figure 23.4.

The `picHand` and `imgSource` controls at design time.

NOTE You can use any set of icons or pictures you want when developing this application. However, icons are preferable because they have transparent backgrounds. The Arrows section of the Visual Basic icon library contains several examples which do nicely here. However, any icon or icons will suffice. With an icon editor, you can even rotate an existing icon to create new ones that point in the different directions required for this application.

Writing the Code

The goal of the application is to have the hand image move in response to the arrow keys. For example, if the user presses the right-arrow key, the hand should move toward the right. If the direction of movement changes, the image should also change to point in the new direction. By pressing the middle key on the keypad (5), the hand should return to the initial position.

Defining Constants

To write the program, start by placing the following constants in the general declarations section of the form:

```
'Indexes for imgSource control array
Const UP_HAND = 0
Const DOWN_HAND = 1
Const LEFT_HAND = 2
Const RIGHT_HAND = 3
```

These constants correspond to the indexes of the invisible imgSource() control array. The constants help make more readable the instructions that assign images to picHand.

Next, add constants that specify the scan codes for the arrow keys on the keypad:

```
'Scan codes for the KeyPad keys
Const Key_Center = 12
Const Key_UpRight = 33
Const Key_DownRight = 34
Const Key_DownLeft = 35
Const Key_UpLeft = 36
Const Key_Left = 37
Const Key_Up = 38
Const Key_Right = 39
Const Key_Down = 40
```

These scan codes represent the values of the `KeyCode` parameter used in the `KeyDown` procedure. (You can obtain the values used in these constants from the CONSTANT.TXT file.)

Initializing the Application

The `Form_Resize` event is a good place to set up the hand icon because Visual Basic executes a `Form_Resize` event as part of the start-up process for any application. This event procedure assigns the upward pointing hand, `imgSource(0)`, to the `picHand` control. The procedure centers the picture on the bottom edge of the form:

```
Sub Form_Resize ()
    picHand.Picture = imgSource(UP_HAND).Picture
    picHand.Left = (ScaleWidth - picHand.Width) / 2
    picHand.Top = ScaleHeight - picHand.Height
End Sub
```

Notice the use of the `UP_HAND` constant. As mentioned, such constants make the code easier to understand.

Writing the *KeyDown* Procedure

The final step is to write the code which responds to the user's keystrokes. Whenever the user presses a key, the `KeyDown` procedure activates. Therefore, it is the active procedure for this application.

While there's a considerable amount of code in this procedure, most of it is repetitious and straightforward. The basic concept is actually very simple— move the picture, and change it in response to each `KeyDown` event, if necessary. Again, notice the use of constants to create more readable code.

```
Sub Form_KeyDown (KeyCode As Integer, Shift As Integer)
    Dim Distance As Integer
    Distance = 45       '# of twips to move with each keystroke

    Select Case KeyCode
        Case Key_Center    'Back to the launching pad!
            picHand.Picture = imgSource(UP_HAND).Picture
            picHand.Left = (ScaleWidth - picHand.Width) / 2
            picHand.Top = ScaleHeight - picHand.Height

        Case Key_UpLeft
            picHand.Picture = imgSource(UP_HAND).Picture
            picHand.Left = picHand.Left - Distance
            picHand.Top = picHand.Top - Distance
```

```
      Case Key_Left
         picHand.Picture = imgSource(LEFT_HAND).Picture
         picHand.Left = picHand.Left - Distance

      Case Key_DownLeft
         picHand.Picture = imgSource(DOWN_HAND).Picture
         picHand.Left = picHand.Left - Distance
         picHand.Top = picHand.Top + Distance

      Case Key_Down
         picHand.Picture = imgSource(DOWN_HAND).Picture
         picHand.Top = picHand.Top + Distance

      Case Key_DownRight
         picHand.Picture = imgSource(DOWN_HAND).Picture
         picHand.Left = picHand.Left + Distance
         picHand.Top = picHand.Top + Distance

      Case Key_Right
         picHand.Picture = imgSource(RIGHT_HAND).Picture
         picHand.Left = picHand.Left + Distance

      Case Key_UpRight
         picHand.Picture = imgSource(UP_HAND).Picture
         picHand.Left = picHand.Left + Distance
         picHand.Top = picHand.Top - Distance

      Case Key_Up
         picHand.Picture = imgSource(UP_HAND).Picture
         picHand.Top = picHand.Top - Distance
   End Select
End Sub
```

Running the Application

Try running the application. The result is a fickle finger of fate that flies any-where on the form when you steer it by pressing the keypad arrow keys. You can even fly the finger "out of radar range" by guiding the picture temporarily off the form.

At any time, you can return the image to the bottom center of the form by pressing key 5 on the numeric keypad (with NumLock off), or by resizing the form. Figure 23.5 shows the finger in flight.

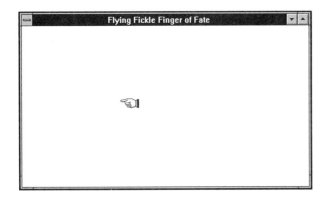

Figure 23.5.

The Fickle Finger of Fate in flight!

Adding Speed Control

You can add additional functionality to the application by allowing special keys to act as accelerators. If the user presses an accelerator key, the picture moves a longer distance, which makes the hand appear to move faster.

One convenient way to implement this option is to take advantage of the Shift argument built into the KeyDown event procedure. With the Shift argument, you can test for the Shift, Ctrl, and Alt keys. By changing the value of the variable Distance according to which special key was pressed, you can make Shift, Ctrl, and Alt act as accelerator keys.

To implement this option, first locate the following instruction near the beginning of the KeyDown procedure:

```
Distance = 45     '# of twips to move with each keystroke
```

Now, replace that instruction with the following block of code:

```
    Select Case Shift      'Determine if accelerator is pressed
       Case 0              'No speed up key was pressed
          Distance = 45    'Standard speed
       Case 1              'Shift key pressed
          Distance = 90    'Fast speed
       Case 2              'Ctrl key pressed
          Distance = 180   'Faster speed
       Case 4              'Alt key pressed
          Distance = 260   'Fastest speed
    End Select
```

Run the application again. Try pressing the Shift, Ctrl, or Alt keys to see the effects.

The GridControl Application

The final application in this chapter is a more practical example of using the KeyDown, KeyPress and KeyUp events. This example uses a spreadsheet-like array of cells, and a text box. Each cell contains text data which can be updated. With only the keyboard, the user can navigate the focus from cell to cell, and update the contents of any one of them.

This application uses the Grid control. Chapter 26, "Using the Grid Control," covers grid controls in detail. Here, the sample application uses a grid on a basic level to demonstrate keyboard event-handling techniques.

A grid control consists of rows and columns of cells which can contain text or pictures. As Figure 23.6 shows, a typical grid resembles a spreadsheet (and works similarly, too).

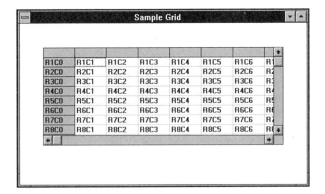

Figure 23.6.

A sample grid.

Using the Grid Control

When the grid has the focus in a running application, the control automatically responds to arrow keys. That is, you can use the arrow keys to move from cell to cell in the grid. No special coding is required.

However, you can't edit directly the text in a grid cell. An application with a grid needs a separate text box control for text editing. As you can imagine, users might get quite irked if they had to leave the keyboard, and use the mouse to click the text box when they want to edit text in a grid cell.

Visual Basic's keyboard events provide an elegant solution to this problem. Using its KeyUp and KeyDown events, the grid can automatically pass control to the text box when the user types in a letter or number.

Further, the same events in the text box control can automatically update the grid contents when the user presses Enter. Similarly, the grid can cancel the update if the user presses Escape. The result is two controls—a grid and a text box—which work in tandem, responding quickly and intuitively to the user's typed input. No mouse required!

Creating the Project

To create the GridControl application, start a new project. Make sure that your toolbox contains the Grid control. The icon for the Grid control resembles the following:

 NOTE   The Grid is a custom control. As such, the control is not automatically built into Visual Basic, but available from add-on files. The files for the Grid control come with all editions of Visual Basic. When you install Visual Basic, the system puts the Grid control in the toolbox.

If your toolbox does not contain the Grid control, you deselected custom control options when installing Visual Basic, or modified the AUTOLOAD.MAK file.

If your toolbox does not have the Grid control, use the following steps to add it:

1. Choose the **Ad**d File option from Visual Basic's **F**ile menu.

   The Add File dialog box opens.

2. Locate, and specify the GRID.VBX file.

   Most likely you find this FILE in the Windows SYSTEM directory. The complete file path is probably C:\WINDOWS\SYSTEM\GRID.VBX

3. Click OK to close the dialog box.

Adding the Controls

Using the toolbox, place two controls—a text box and a grid—onto the form. Visual Basic names these controls Text1 and Grid1, respectively. Using the Properties window, assign to these controls the property values that Table 23.3 shows.

Table 23.3. Property Values for *Text1* and *Grid1*.

Control	Property	Value
Text1	Top	120
	Left	600
	Height	375
	Width	5295
Grid1	Left	600
	Top	600

Set the Caption property for the form to Grid Control. Your form should resemble Figure 23.7.

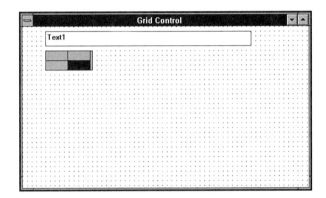

Writing the Form's Event Procedures

The Form_Load event procedure handles the sizing of the Grid control, blanking out the initial contents of the text box, and filling the grid with dummy data:

```
Sub Form_Load ()
   Dim TB As String, LF As String
   Dim Temp As String, X As Integer
   Dim Rowz As Integer, Colz As Integer

   TB = Chr$(9)              'Tab
   LF = Chr$(10) + Chr$(10)  'Line feed
```

```
      'Set the number of rows and columns for the grid
      Grid1.FixedRows = 1
      Grid1.FixedCols = 1
      Grid1.Rows = 2
      Grid1.Cols = 2

      Text1.Text = ""    'Blank out text box

      'Fill the grid with dummy data in R1C1 format
      For Rowz = 1 To 10
         Temp = ""
         For Colz = 0 To 7
            Temp = Temp & "R" & Rowz & "C" & Colz
            If Colz < 7 Then Temp = Temp & TB
         Next Colz
         Grid1.AddItem Temp, Rowz
      Next Rowz
      Grid1.Rows = 11

      'Set the width of each grid column for display
      For X = 0 To Grid1.Cols - 1
         Grid1.ColWidth(X) = 800
      Next X

      'Move focus to row1, column 1 and place cell contents in text box
      Grid1.Row = 1
      Grid1.Col = 1
      Text1.Text = Grid1.Text
End Sub
```

The Form_Resize event procedure ensures that the grid control always fills the form:

```
Sub Form_Resize ()
   Grid1.Width = ScaleWidth - (Grid1.Left * 2)
   Grid1.Height = ScaleHeight - Grid1.Top - Text1.Height
End Sub
```

Creating the Mouse Events

Although this application can be run entirely from the keyboard, you should put in a few mouse events to make the interface even more intuitive. If the user clicks a grid cell, you want the text box to be updated with the contents of the indicated cell. If the user double-clicks a cell, you want also to move the focus to the text box for editing.

The following are the necessary event procedures. The active body of each one only consists of a single line of code:

```
Sub Grid1_Click ()
    Text1.Text = Grid1.Text
End Sub

Sub Grid1_DblClick ()
    Text1.SetFocus
End Sub
```

Responding to Keyboard Events

Now, code the keyboard events. The first (and simplest) procedure is to make sure that the text box is updated if the user changes to a new cell with the arrow keys:

```
Sub Grid1_KeyUp (KeyCode As Integer, Shift As Integer)
    Text1.Text = Grid1.Text
End Sub
```

There are no keystroke evaluations here. Whenever any key is pressed while the focus is on the grid, the contents of the text box should be updated.

Notice that KeyUp is used rather than KeyDown. By using KeyUp, the user can smoothly skim over a number of cells by holding down an arrow key. The text box doesn't update until the key is released.

Coding the *Grid1_KeyPress* Event

Now comes the heart of the matter. The grid control's KeyPress event must evaluate every keystroke the grid receives. In particular, there are three types of keystrokes you want to capture: the Escape key, the Enter key, and the alphanumeric keys.

By pressing Escape, the user signals that the grid cell is edited. The user wants the program to place the contents of the grid cell into the text box. Pressing Enter signals that the user wants to edit the contents of the grid cell. Thus, the focus must shift to the text box. If an alphanumeric key is pressed, the user is simply editing the contents of the grid cell.

Trapping Enter or Escape is as simple as evaluating the value of KeyAscii. If it's 27 (Escape), the application updates the text box with the contents of the cell; if it's 13 (Enter), the application shifts the focus to the text box.

If the keystroke is neither Enter nor Escape, the application converts the value of KeyAscii into the corresponding character, and evaluates it with the Like operator. If the character is a letter or a number, the assumption is that the user is entering data. In this case, the program places the character into the text box, and transfers the focus to it for additional editing.

The following is the program code for the grid control's KeyPress event procedure:

```
Sub Grid1_KeyPress (KeyAscii As Integer)
    Dim X As Integer, Char As String

    Select Case KeyAscii
    Case 27   'Escape key was pressed
        Text1.Text = Grid1.Text

    Case 13   'Enter key was pressed
        Text1.SetFocus
        X = DoEvents()
        Text1.SelStart = Len(Text1.Text)

    Case Else   'Check if key is a letter or digit
        Char = Chr$(KeyAscii)
        If Char Like "[a-z]" Or Char Like "[A-Z]" Or Char Like "#" Then
            'it's a letter or digit
            Text1.Text = Char
            Text1.SetFocus
            Text1.SelStart = 1
            KeyAscii = 0
            X = DoEvents()   'Let Text1_GotFocus execute
            Text1.SelStart = Len(Text1.Text)
                'moves insertion point past character just pasted into Text1
        Else
            'do nothing (the grid automatically responds
            'correctly to arrow keys and other special keys
        End If
    End Select
End Sub
```

As mentioned earlier in the chapter, the KeyPress event does not respond to (most) non-ASCII keys. As a result, the application doesn't have to filter out special keystrokes, such as the arrow keys. For such keystrokes, the KeyPress event simply doesn't occur.

Selecting the Text in the Text Box

In the code for Grid1_KeyPress, notice what happens when an alphanumeric key is pressed. The character becomes the entire contents of the text box (Text1.Text = Char), the focus is shifted to it, and its SelStart property is set to 1.

A text box normally selects all of its contents when it receives the focus. Therefore, setting SelStart to the end of the string guards against losing that first character the user types. The DoEvents() instruction lets the Text1_GotFocus event occur before the Grid1_KeyPress procedure places the insertion point just beyond the newly typed character.

The following is the GotFocus event procedure for the text box:

```
Sub Text1_GotFocus ()
   Text1.SelStart = 0
   Text1.SelLength = Len(Text1.Text)
End Sub
```

Coding the *KeyPress* Event for the Text Box

Finally, consider the KeyPress event for the text box, in which the user input is actually evaluated.

The procedure needs only to check whether the user pressed the Enter or Escape key. If the user presses Enter, the grid is updated with the contents of the text box. Its contents are restored to the original text in the grid cell if the user presses Escape.

The following is the KeyPress procedure for the text box:

```
Sub Text1_KeyPress (KeyAscii As Integer)
   Select Case KeyAscii
      Case 13    'Enter key
         Grid1.Text = Text1.Text
         Grid1.SetFocus
         KeyAscii = 0
      Case 27    'Escape key
         Text1.Text = Grid1.Text
         Grid1.SetFocus
         KeyAscii = 0
   End Select
End Sub
```

For both the Enter and Escape keys, KeyAscii is set to 0. Recall that when Text1_KeyPress terminates, the triggering keystroke is passed to the text box. By setting KeyAscii to 0, the Escape and Enter keys are not passed to the box. This ensures that no beeps or other special characters are transmitted to it.

For *all* keys besides Enter and Escape, the Text1_KeyPress procedure does nothing. More specifically, the value of KeyAscii is not modified. As a result, every key besides Enter and Escape is passed to the text box. (Of course, a text box control automatically knows how to handle keyboard input.)

Running the Application

Try running the application. Using the arrow keys, navigate around the grid. Experiment with updating the contents of various cells, and pressing the Enter and Escape keys.

In Figure 23.8, the user has moved the focus to the cell in the second column and row, then typed **TEST!**. This application demonstrates how KeyPress events and the KeyAscii parameter can make the grid/text box combination powerful, and easy to use.

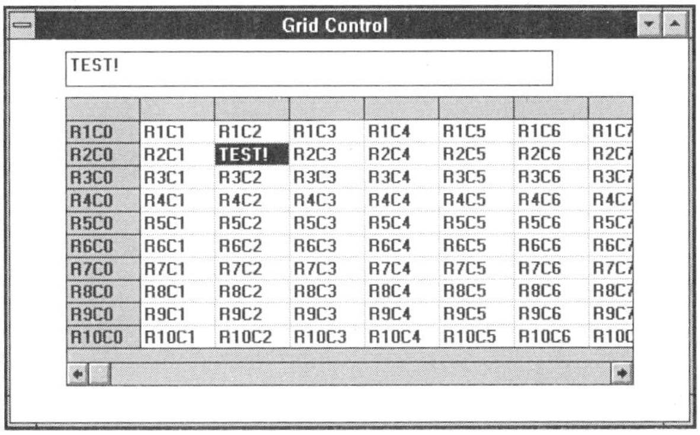

Figure 23.8.

The GridControl application in action.

Summary

Visual Basic fully supports keyboard handling. Using the KeyPress event, you can write event procedures which respond when the user presses an ASCII-related key. The KeyAscii parameter represents the ASCII (ANSI) code for the key pressed.

The KeyUp and KeyDown events provide additional keyboard control. These procedures can detect *any* pressed key, and also return information about the state of the Shift, Ctrl, and Alt keys.

The three keyboard events occur together, and in the same order: `KeyDown`, `KeyPress`, and `KeyUp`.

A form receives and processes all keyboard events when no controls are present. If a form has one or more controls, the one that is currently active processes keyboard events. However, if a form's `KeyPreview` property is set to True at design time, *both* the form and the active control respond to keyboard events.

The `Flying Fickle Finger of Fate` application demonstrated techniques of capturing and using keyboard events to move a Picture box control around a form. The `GridControl` application showed how to embed practical code in the keyboard event procedures of several controls.

Designing Custom Menus

S imple applications require only a few types of controls. Check boxes, option buttons, and command buttons may be all you need for your user to select various options. As your applications become more complex and multiple windows become involved, however, this approach is not practical. In a complex program offering many options, the user needs a convenient way to indicate selections.

The solution is *menus*. With a menu system, most commercial Windows applications provide an easy way for the user to make choices. As a veteran (or almost veteran) of Windows, you have used menus many times. Visual Basic itself has several drop-down menus from which you can select to perform tasks, such as saving a project, changing screen colors, or setting debug options.

To add menus to your applications, Visual Basic includes a tool called the *Menu Design window*. You easily can create a hierarchical menu system that complies with Microsoft's guidelines for Windows' menus. By adding a menu system to a project, you give your finished product the look and feel of a "real" Windows application.

In this chapter, you learn how to do the following:

■ Create a basic menu system using the Menu Design window

■ Create cascading menus

■ Program application responses to menu selections

■ Create Pop-up menus

■ Implement the Microsoft Windows Interface Design Guidelines for menus

■ Become familiar with Windows standard menus

Using the Menu Design Window

Visual Basic treats menus as controls. Just as with controls available from the Toolbox, menu controls—called *items* or *options*—have properties with assignable values. To open the Menu Design window, you can use any of the following techniques (see Figure 24.1):

- Click the Menu Design button on the Toolbar.
- Select Menu Design from Visual Basic's Window menu.
- Press the Ctrl+M shortcut key combination.

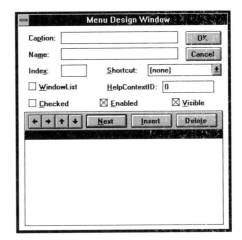

 NOTE   If your application uses multiple forms, be sure to select (activate) the form on which the menu should appear before you open the Menu Design window.

Available Tools

To create a menu, you use the tools available in the Menu Design window. Table 24.1 provides an overview of these tools:

Table 24.1. Tools and features of the Menu Design window.

Tool	Description
Caption	Enables you to specify the text you want to appear on the menu. The value you specify for the Caption, for example, is the menu title that the user sees when running your application. (Many Windows applications have a **F**ile menu.) To create such a menu in your application, type **File** as the Caption. When the Menu Design window opens, the cursor appears in the Caption text box, and you can begin typing the caption immediately.
Name	Enables you to specify a Name for each menu option. This name is the control name recognized throughout your program code. Microsoft recommends that you name menu controls with the standard prefix mnu. You can name an Options menu mnuOptions, for example.
Index	Enables you to specify the position of the menu control in a control array. Menu options, like other controls, optionally can be grouped into control arrays. If you don't specify a value for Index, the menu option is not part of a control array. A menu control array is necessary if your application adds a new instance of a menu control during run time.
Shortcut	Enables you to specify a function key or keystroke combination that allows the user to access a menu command without opening the menu. You can open the Menu Design window, for example, by pressing the Ctrl+M shortcut key. By specifying shortcut keys, the user of your application can access menu options quickly. Many experienced users and touch typists prefer to activate menu options using shortcut keys.
Window List	Enables you to create a menu that lists the open windows in a Multiple Document Interface (MDI) application. For further discussion of Window List, see Chapter 27, "Creating Multiple Document Interfaces (MDI)."
HelpContextID	Enables you to create a context-sensitive Help system with your application. For more information, see Chapter 33, "Adding a Help System to an Application."
Checked	Enables you to place a check mark to the left of a menu option. The Checked property typically indicates whether a menu choice is on or off. The default value is unchecked; if checked, the menu option is on. Most applications don't turn on check marks at design time but rather activate the check marks when the user selects various menu options at run time.

continues

Table 24.1. Continued

Tool	Description
Enabled	Enables you to indicate whether a menu option is available. The default value for the Enabled property is True, which means that the menu option can be selected at run time. When the menu option is False, it appears dimmed or gray and is not available to the user.
Visible	Enables you to indicate whether a menu option is available. The Visible property differs from the Enabled property because when Visible is unchecked, the menu option doesn't appear at all. You commonly use the Visible property when a group of menu options are linked to a particular user action. An application, for example, may not offer certain menu options until the user opens a data file. By making options invisible, you focus your user's attention on the relevant options. The default setting of Visible, however, is checked.
OK button	Click this button to close the Menu Design window. Click the OK button when you complete your menu design rather than after you create each individual menu option.
Cancel button	Click this button to close the Menu Design window without updating recent changes.

Menu Outline

The Menu outline is the large boxed area in the lower half of the Menu Design window. The Menu outline enables you to view and manipulate the order of your menus.

When you create a menu system, think of your menus as an outline. The menu options on the title bar correspond to the first level in your outline. A File menu, for example, typically is at the first level. The choices under the File Menu are second-level options.

The Menu outline contains the following buttons:

Arrow buttons	Enable you to change the level of a menu option and modify the place in which the menu option fits in the outline. You can have up to four submenu levels for each main menu.
Next button	Enables you to move the highlight to the next item in the Outline window or, if positioned at the end of the menus, to add a new menu option.

| Insert button | Enables you to insert a new menu option above the presently highlighted menu option. |
| Delete button | Enables you to remove the selected menu option. |

Creating a Menu Application

With an understanding of the components of the Menu Design window, you are ready to create your first menu. This section takes you through the process of creating a simple menu program using the different tools in the Menu Design window.

The sample application, named GREETER, greets the user with a personalized message. The user can specify through a menu system the name of the person being greeted, the salutation, and various properties of the message, such as the font and color. The application uses a single form saved as GREETER.FRM. It has two labels: one label for the salutation (greeting) and one label for the name of the person being greeted.

To begin the sample application, follow these steps:

1. Select New Project from the File menu to begin a fresh project.

2. Place two label controls on the form: Label1 and Label2.

3. Using the Properties window, assign the property values shown in Table 24.2.

Table 24.2. Properties of *Label1* and *Label2*.

Control	Property	Value
Form1	Caption	The Greeter
Label1	BackStyle	Transparent
	Caption	Welcome to
	Name	lblSalute
	Height	1335
	Left	240
	Top	960
	Width	1935
Label2	BackStyle	Transparent
	Caption	You
	Name	lblPerson
	Height	1335
	Left	2640
	Top	960
	Width	2535

The form should look similar to the form that appears in Figure 24.2. After these steps are completed, you are ready to create the menu.

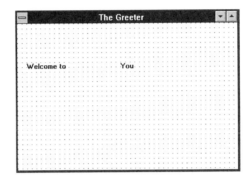

Figure 24.2.

The initial form for the GREETER application.

Creating a Main Menu Option

To create the menu, you have to create menu controls. The Toolbox does not contain a Menu control. Instead, you use the Menu Design window.

After you have created the basic form with the labels, you are ready to create the Options menu for the GREETER application. Follow these steps:

1. Click the form to make the form window active.

2. Open the Menu Design window in one of the following three ways: click the Menu Design button on the Toolbar, select the **M**enu Design option from Visual Basic's **W**indow menu, or press Ctrl+M. The Menu Design window appears.

    You are now ready to specify values for the properties of the first menu option. Notice that a blinking cursor appears in the Caption text box. You will start by specifying a value for Caption and then proceed to specify values for the other properties.

T I P   If you access Visual Basic's **W**indow menu and the **M**enu Design option is dimmed, the form window probably is not active. Click the form window again to ensure that the form is selected.

3. Type **Options** in the Caption text box.

    Notice that Options appears at the top-left of the Menu outline. *Options* is the menu title that will appear on the left end of the menu bar of the application. (A Caption can contain internal blank spaces.)

Specifying an Access Key

In most commercial Windows applications, including Visual Basic, usually each menu title contains one underlined letter. This underlined letter specifies the *access key* for that menu option.

By pressing Alt and the access key simultaneously, the user can activate the menu option quickly. The access key enables keyboard users to take action without needing to fumble for the mouse and manipulate the pointer. Keyboard access is important to maximize typing speed for individuals who are touch typists and perform data entry.

The access key typically is the first letter of each menu option. If a conflict arises because two menu options have the same first letter, however, any other letter in the menu caption can be designated as the access key.

You use the ampersand character (&) in Visual Basic to specify an access key. When you type the Caption for a menu option, type an ampersand just before the letter that corresponds to the access key. The caption &File, for example, makes **F** the access key, and the caption Fo&rmat makes **r** the access key. When the caption appears on the application's menu, the access key is underlined. The ampersand character does not appear on-screen.

 NOTE In this book, all access keys are denoted as bold characters rather than underlined characters.

To specify an access key for the **O**ptions menu in the sample application, follow these steps:

1. Position the cursor in the Caption text box, and press Home to move it to the first letter of Options.

2. Press **&**.

   The caption now reads &Options. The ampersand symbol indicates that the succeeding character (**O** in this case) is the access key. The **O** will appear on the menu underlined.

Specifying the Control Name

When you add a menu option with the Menu Design window, you are creating a control like those selected from the Toolbox. As with other controls, a menu option needs a name so that it can be referenced in the program code. You assign a name to a menu control with the Name property.

To specify the name for the menu control, follow these steps:

1. Move the cursor to the Name text box by pressing Tab, clicking the Name text box, or pressing Alt+M.

2. To specify the control name for the menu option, type **mnuOptions**.

   A menu control name must adhere to the same rules as other control names: the name must begin with a letter; contain only letters, numbers, and the underscore character (_); and must not exceed 40 characters. Microsoft recommends that you name menu controls with the prefix mnu, followed by the caption. This procedure makes it easy to remember control names.

> Control names cannot contain internal spaces. If your caption contains internal spaces, do not include the spaces in the control name. Instead, use the underscore character in the name to represent each space, or omit the spaces entirely.

3. To close the Menu Design window, click OK.

The form now has a menu bar containing the single menu option titled **Op-**tions. Notice that the menu title appears with the access key (**O**) underlined. The ampersand does not appear on-screen (see Figure 24.3).

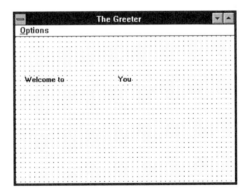

Figure 24.3.

The **O**ptions menu.

Creating a Drop-Down Menu

With the main menu title in place, you can create the *drop-down* (sometimes called *pull-down*) menu that opens when the user clicks the menu title. The drop-down menu presents the user with several options.

NOTE Microsoft suggests that Windows applications not contain stand-alone main menu titles. A drop-down menu should appear each time the user clicks an option in the main menu bar. The idea is that the user should select one of the main menus, see a drop-down menu of available choices, and then select an option from the drop-down menu to take a specific action. Because the user can accidently click one of the main menu options, those options should never take action.

You can design menus for your applications the way you want; however, recognize that adherence to the Microsoft conventions gives your applications the look and feel users expect.

To create a drop-down menu, follow these steps:

1. Open the Menu Design window.

2. Press Enter or click the Next button. The cursor is positioned in the Caption text box, and you are ready to create a new menu option.

3. Type **&Background** for the caption.

4. Press Tab and type **mnuOptBackground** in the Name text box.

   This name consists of the prefix mnu, an abbreviated form of the main menu name Opt, and the caption for the current menu option **Background**. By following this naming convention, you easily can identify the place in the Menu outline for any menu control name that appears in your code. Excessively long control names are not required.

5. Click the right-arrow button to indent **Background** in the Menu outline.

Background is now the first item on the drop-down menu that opens when the user selects the **O**ptions menu. Notice that in the Menu outline, &Background appears indented.

Understanding Indentation

For each menu option, the indentation level in the Menu outline indicates the level of that menu option. Menu options at the same indentation level represent options that appear on the same menu.

The following is the Menu outline structure at one stage in the development of the sample application. (In order to demonstrate various menu creation techniques, as you build the application, this structure will exist in several different forms.)

```
&Message
....&Text
....&Greeting
&Options
....&Background
........&White
........Light &Blue
........Light &Gray
....&Style
........&Plain
........&Fancy
........&Modern
```

With this application, the drop-down **Options** menu consists of two menu options: **Background** and **Style**. The **Style** submenu contains the options **Plain**, **Fancy**, and **Modern**.

Creating Cascading Menus

Using a *cascading menu* or *submenu structure*, a user can branch through a selection of choices to narrow down the desired options. In the sample application, for example, the user can select **Options**, then choose to alter the background, and finally select the desired color.

To create a cascading menu, use the arrow buttons to indent each menu option one further level from the level of the previous menu. Then press Enter or click the Next button.

To create the cascading menu for the color selection, follow these steps:

1. To create a new menu option, click the Next button.

2. Type **Light &Blue** for the caption and **mnuOptBackgroundBlue** for the name.

   Notice that the caption contains a space, but no space appears in the name. The name contains the prefix (mnu), an abbreviation of the main menu caption (Opt), the drop-down menu caption (Background), and a shortened form of the caption of this item (Blue).

3. Click the right-arrow button to indent this option one level further than the indentation level for **Background**.

4. Create two more options at this menu level. Type **Light &Gray** and the name **mnuOptBackgroundGray** for the first caption. Type **&White** and the name **mnuOptBackgroundWhite** for the second caption.

You have now completed the cascading menu for the selection of the background color. To complete this application's **O**ptions menu, you need to add two more options: **S**tyle and **B**order. To add the Style and Border items to the **O**ptions menu, follow these steps:

1. Type **&Style** for the caption and **mnuOptStyle** for the name.

2. Click the left-arrow button and press Enter to move this menu option to the **B**ackground indention level.

3. Type **&Plain** for the caption **mnuOptStylePlain**. Click the right-arrow button and press Enter to make this option a cascading menu option under Style.

4. Type **&Fancy** for the caption and **mnuOptStyleFancy** for the name. Press Enter.

5. Type **&Modern** for the caption and **mnuOptStyleModern** for the name. Press Enter.

6. Type **Bor&der** for the caption and **mnuOptBorder** for the name. To move this option to the same level as **B**ackground and **S**tyle, click the left-arrow button.

   Click OK to exit the Menu Design window.

> **D** is the access key for Bor**d**er. You should not select *B* because that letter is the access key for the **B**ackground option. If two menu options share the same access key, the application recognizes the second one on the menu.
>
> **T I P**

The **O**ptions menu for the sample application is complete. Figure 24.4 shows the menu outline as it should appear in the Menu Design window.

Running the Application

At this stage, you have created the **O**ptions Menu. Now you can run the partially completed application.

1. Press F5 to run the application.

   The menu bar that contains the **O**ptions menu appears under the title bar of your window.

2. Select the **O**ptions menu.

   Notice that Visual Basic places right-facing arrows on the menu options that contain submenus (**B**ackground and **S**tyle in this case).

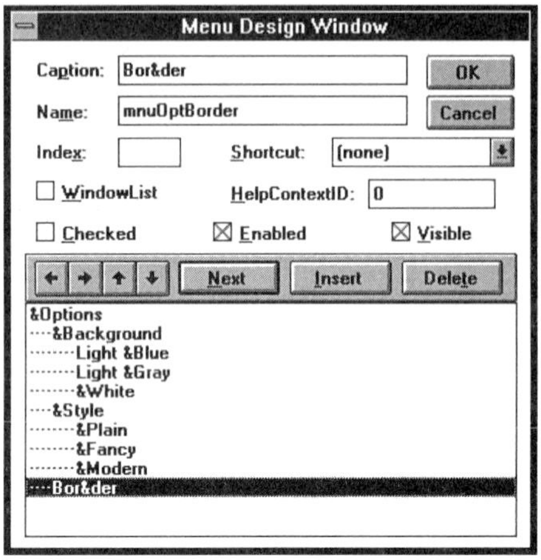

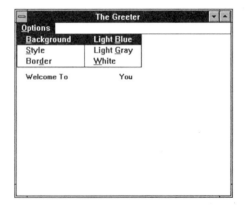

Figure 24.4.

The menu outline for the
Options menu.

3. Select **B**ackground to open a cascading menu that displays the three
   color options (see Figure 24.5).

Figure 24.5.

The **O**ptions **B**ackground
menu.

4. Select the color you want.

   The menu option appears highlighted, and then the menu closes. However, the form does not change color. You designed the look of the menu
   system, but you must add programming code to make each menu option
   operate the way you want. You learn how to add the code later in the
   chapter.

5. Stop the application for now.

Designing a Menu Structure

You can create a maximum of four sublevels in a menu (see Figure 24.6). Using menu levels, you can design a menu structure that leads your user through a decision tree one step at a time.

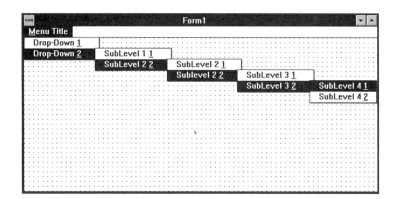

Figure 24.6.

The submenu structure.

Be aware, however, that a complex multilevel menu structure may not be your best choice. Always keep ease-of-use in mind. Design your application to be as user-friendly as possible. The following are some factors to consider when designing menus:

- *Consider menu toggles instead of sub-menus.* If you are contemplating a submenu that contains exactly two items, you may want to use a single, toggled menu option instead of a submenu. Determine whether the items represent two states of the same option. If so, you can use a single *toggle* menu option. A toggle item utilizes a check mark to the left of the caption. The check mark indicates whether the toggle item is on or off. For more about menu toggles, see the section titled "Using the Checked Property" later in this chapter.

- *Replace crowded menus with dialog boxes.* Menus that contain too many items can bewilder a user. From a user's perspective, the menu appears crowded and the desired choices are difficult to determine. In such cases, consider a dialog box with option buttons or check boxes rather than a menu with complex sublevels. Figure 24.7 shows an example dialog box you can use in the sample application if the number of options increases.

- *Decide when to use cascading menus.* You should only use cascading menus when the choices are interdependent. In the sample application, the **B**ackground and **S**tyle menus represent a good example of interdependent options. The user can choose only one background color and only one style. When choices are independent rather than interdependent, a dialog box is recommended.

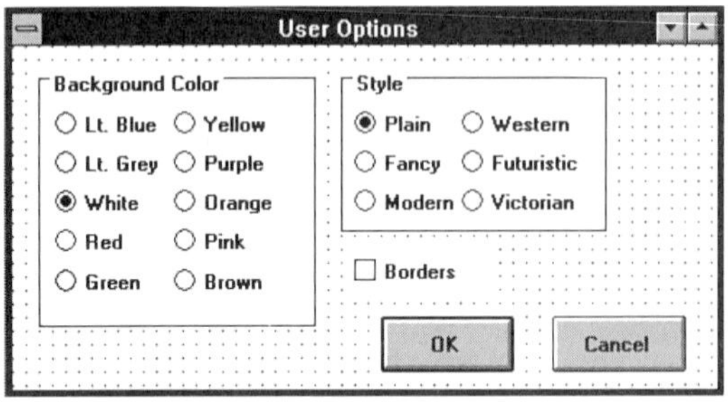

Figure 24.7.

A sample User Options
dialog box.

■ *Organize choices logically.* The relative location of menus and the location
of items within those menus affects the time and effort necessary for the
user to locate the desired task. You want your menu structure to allow
the user to quickly decide where a menu option is located without
searching through several menus to find it.

Editing a Menu

You can easily modify the organization of your menus. Visual Basic provides
simple ways to move menu options, delete unwanted items, and insert new
menu options.

Moving Menu Options

You sometimes will create a menu and realize that you positioned a menu
option in the wrong place.

Consider the **O**ptions **B**ackground menu of the sample application. The colors
are organized alphabetically. Nothing is wrong with this organization; in fact,
the user can scan an alphabetic list quickly. For this application, however,
White is the default background. Placing a default selection at the top of a
menu list is often beneficial because it allows the user to see what is selected
and then scan the other options. To move White to the top of the **B**ackground
menu, follow these steps:

1. Open the Menu Design window.

2. Click &White in the Menu outline to select it.

3. Click the up-arrow button two times. Notice how &White moves up the
   outline to a position above Light &Blue.

To move a menu option down in the list, click the down-arrow button rather
than the up-arrow button.

Deleting Menu Options

When working on a menu, you may decide that you don't need one of the menu options you created. Visual Basic provides the Delete button on the Menu Design window to remove unwanted menu options.

To remove the **B**order option from the **S**tyle menu in the sample application, follow these steps:

1. Click the **B**order menu option in the Menu outline.

2. Click the Delete button.

   The Border option is removed from the menu.

Adding Additional Menus Options

When working on an application, you often will want to add other menu options to meet user needs. With the Menu Design window, you can add new menu options at any menu level.

For example, the sample application currently has but one main menu item—an **O**ptions menu. This menu provides ways to change the appearance of the form. Suppose you want to add another main menu item with which the user can change the text of a message displayed on the form.

The following steps show you how to add a new main menu item to the menu bar. This menu, named **M**essage, opens to reveal a drop-down menu which contains **T**ext and **G**reeting items. When the application is run, the user selects the **T**ext option to type the name of the person being greeted and selects the **G**reeting option to specify the salutation. You can add the new menu by following these steps:

1. In the Menu Design window, click &Options in the Menu outline.

2. Click the Insert button three times—to insert three spaces in the Menu outline.

3. Click the Caption text box—to position the cursor in the Caption text box.

4. Type **&Message** for the caption and **mnuMessage** for the name, then press Enter to create the menu.

5. Type **&Text** for the caption and **mnuMessageText** for the name of the second menu option.

6. Click the right-arrow button and then press Enter to make this item a submenu option under the Message menu.

7. Type **&Greeting** for the caption and **mnuMessageGreeting** for the name to create the third menu option.

8. Click the right-arrow button to move this option to the same indentation level as &Text.

9. Click OK to close the Menu Design window.

You can now click the Message menu to open the new submenu.

Adding Separator Bars

If a menu contains many items, you can break up the list into operational categories by using *separator bars*. A separator bar is a horizontal line placed between menu options.

The Visual Basic Edit menu, for example, contains 14 items. This menu contains horizontal lines that divide the options into groups of related choices.

To add a separator bar to a menu, you create a special menu option with a hyphen (-) as the caption. The sample application does not contain crowded menus; however, to practice this technique, add a separator bar between the Text and Greeting items. To do this, follow these steps:

1. Open the Menu Design window (press Ctrl+M).

2. In the Menu outline, select the &Greeting menu option.

3. Insert a space for the separator bar by clicking the Insert button.

4. Position the cursor in the Caption text box, by clicking the text box. Type - (hyphen) for the caption and **mnuMessageSepBar1** for the name; press Enter (see Figure 24.8).

Figure 24.8.

Adding a separator bar.

Using an Ellipsis to Indicate a Dialog Box

You have used several devices for providing visual indicators in your menus, such as the small arrows to the right of menu options that invoke cascading menus, and separator bars that break up long menus. The next technique adds an indicator for each menu option that opens to a dialog box.

In Windows applications, an ellipsis (...) after a menu option indicates that a dialog box opens when that menu option is selected. In Visual Basic, you can add an ellipsis as part of the Caption of a menu option to indicate a dialog box.

In the sample application, because the **Text** option on the Message menu enables the user to input the name of a person, a dialog box must open when the user selects **Text**. To add an ellipsis to a Caption, follow these steps:

1. In the Menu outline, click the &Text menu option.

2. Click the Caption text box and press End to move the cursor to the end of the caption. Type ... (ellipsis). The caption is now &Text....

3. Click OK to close the Menu Design window.

The menu bar now contains two menus: **Message** and **Options**. Notice that **Message** precedes **Options**. The Message menu shows the **Text** menu option and **Greeting** menu option appearing with a separator bar between them. The **Text** option includes an ellipsis indicating that a dialog box appears when you select **Text** (see Figure 24.9).

Polishing the Appearance of Menus

Experienced users appreciate quick ways of accessing the common functions, and all users like to know which menu options are active and which are available. You want your applications to meet your users' expectations. In addition to what you have already learned, Visual Basic provides four more tools that enable you to polish the look and feel of menu applications:

- Shortcut keys
- Check marks
- Enabled property
- Visible property

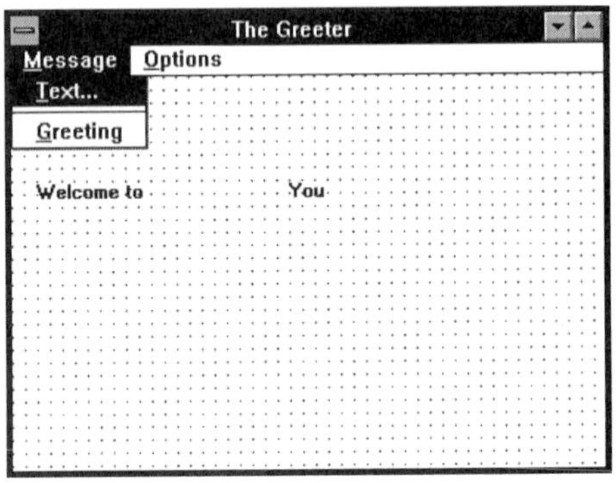

Figure 24.9.

The **M**essage menu.

The following sections examine these tools.

Adding a Shortcut

A *shortcut key* is a keystroke combination that provides instant access to a menu option. A shortcut is faster than an access key because, with a shortcut key, the user doesn't have to open the menu. A shortcut key is sometimes referred to as a *quick-key* combination. Visual Basic enables you to assign several possible shortcut keys.

You don't want to provide a shortcut combination for every menu option. The objective of a shortcut key is to provide quick access to those menu options that will be used most frequently. If every menu option has a shortcut key, the user will probably forget most of the shortcuts. You must first decide which items in your menu system will get frequent use.

Every time the sample application is run, the name of the person greeted must be entered in the Text menu option. To save time in accessing the Text menu option, you can assign a quick key to it by following these steps:

1. Open the Menu Design window.

2. In the Menu outline, click the &Text menu option.

3. Click the Shortcut box (or the list arrow) to pull down the list of possible shortcut keys, as shown in Figure 24.10.

Figure 24.10.

The Shortcut List.

4. Locate Ctrl+T using the scroll bar (if necessary) and click Ctrl+T to select it.

   Notice that in the Menu outline, Ctrl+T appears to the right of the &Text menu option.

5. Click the OK button to close the Menu Design window.

   The shortcut key appears to the right of the Text menu option on the Message menu.

When the user presses a shortcut key, Visual Basic executes the code attached to the corresponding menu option. At this point, you have not yet attached code to a menu option. You do this later in this chapter.

Visual Basic offers many possible keys and keystroke combinations as possible shortcut keys. These include the function keys, the Ctrl key used in combination with several different keys, and the Shift key used in combination with the function keys.

When selecting a shortcut key from the drop-down list box, Visual Basic does not highlight or otherwise indicate the previously selected keystrokes. Visual Basic does, however, check for duplication when you click the OK button. If the shortcut key you choose is already assigned, you get a message box like the one shown in Figure 24.11.

If you get a shortcut error duplication message, click OK or press Enter to close the message box. Repeat the preceding steps to choose an alternative shortcut. To deselect a shortcut key for a menu option, repeat the steps above and select (none).

Figure 24.11.

A sample error message
indicating duplicate
shortcut keys.

Using the *Checked* Property

You can indicate active menu options with a check mark to the left of selected
items. When you design an application, you determine the initial setting of
each check mark property. The sample application, for example, starts with a
white background and with no style settings (that is, a plain style). You can
indicate that these are the default settings by placing check marks next to the
White menu option and the **P**lain menu option. To activate check marks, follow
these steps:

1. Open the Menu Design window.

2. In the Menu outline, click the &White menu option.

3. Click the Checked box. An *X* appears in the check box.

4. In the Menu outline, click the &Plain menu option.

5. Click the Checked box.

6. Click OK to close the Menu Design window.

When you now select the **O**ptions **B**ackground menu, a check mark appears
next to the **W**hite menu option (see Figure 24.12).

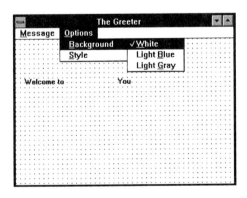

Figure 24.12.

An example of the
Checked property.

At this point, you have used check marks to indicate the defaults when the
user first runs the application. While the application runs, the user may

change the background color. As explained later in this chapter, you must then alter the check mark property accordingly with program code.

Using the *Enabled* Property

Like the Checked property, the Enabled property can control the user's access to any particular menu option while the application executes. By default, a menu option is active and can be selected by the user.

Sometimes you want to deny the user access to a particular menu option. This technique is used in Visual Basic itself. For example, the menu design option cannot be selected from the Window menu if the form doesn't have the focus.

When an item cannot be selected, it is disabled by setting the Enabled property to False. The menu option appears dimmed (or gray). A dimmed menu option informs the user that the option exists within the application, but it is not available currently. Clicking a dimmed item highlights it briefly before the highlight returns to the top item of the menu.

Using the Enabled check box in the Menu Design window, you can assign the initial state for the Enabled property of each menu option. When a menu option is enabled, an X appears in the Enabled check box. By default, each menu option is enabled.

For the sample application, assume that the Modern style can be selected only when the Background color is Light Gray. When the application starts, the White background is the default. The Modern style, therefore, is not available and should be disabled by default. To disable the Modern style, follow these steps:

1. Open the Menu Design window.

2. Click the &Modern menu option in the Menu outline.

3. Click the Enabled check box to unselect it as indicated by the X being removed.

4. Click OK to close the Menu Design window.

When you now select the **O**ptions **S**tyle menu, the **M**odern menu option is dimmed (see Figure 24.13).

To dim an entire drop-down menu, you don't have to change the Enabled property for each item in the menu. Just deselect the Enabled property of the menu title, and the user is unable to access any of the items on that particular submenu.

T I P

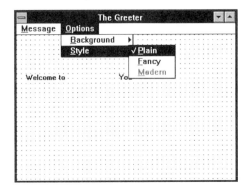

Figure 24.13.

A disabled menu option.

Using the *Visible* Property

Like the Enabled property, you can use the Visible property to deny the user access to particular menu options. If you turn off the Visible property for a particular menu option, that item is removed from the menu. The user will not know that the menu option exists.

Suppose that you want to remove the Fancy menu option when the selected color is White. To do this, follow these steps:

1. Open the Menu Design window.

2. Click the &Fancy menu option in the Menu outline.

3. Click the Visible check box to unselect it. The X disappears.

4. Click OK to close the Menu Design window.

When you select the Options Style menu, notice that the Fancy menu option does not appear. With the Fancy option's Visible property set to false, the Modern option has shifted up on the menu so that it appears below Plain (see Figure 24.14).

Coding Menu Options

In the sample application thus far, you have only created the menu structure. If you run the application and select a menu option, the menu activates but nothing else happens. To make the application work correctly, you need to add program code.

For menu options, the Click procedure defines what happens when the user clicks a menu option with the mouse, uses the access keys, or uses a shortcut key to select a menu option. To make an application respond appropriately to the selection of a menu option, you must write program code for the associated Click procedure.

NOTE

Use the Visible Property Carefully

If your application contains menu options that become visible and invisible at different times during operation, users may become confused. New users tend to appreciate an application that looks and operates the same way every time. Microsoft recommends in the Windows guidelines that you do not use the Visible property to control access to menu options. Instead, Microsoft recommends the Enabled property for controlling which menu options your user can access.

Microsoft's guidelines, however, are only recommendations. Many applications *do* use the Visible property to control access. Using the Visible property to control access to an entire drop-down menu is quite reasonable.

When designing an application, your paramount consideration should be ease-of-use. Use Visible selectively; you don't want to detract from your application by making the user worry about where missing menu options are located.

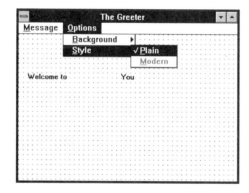

Figure 24.14.

An example of the Visible property set to False.

Coding a menu option is similar to coding the other Visual Basic controls. You must access the Code window for each menu option and insert your code. Be sure that the program maintains a true visual representation of your application by updating the Checked, Enabled, and Visible properties in your code.

Accessing the Code Window

To program any menu option, you first must access the Code window for that option. You can access the Code window in one of three ways: click View Code in the Project window, double-click the menu option on the selected form, or select **C**ode from the **V**iew menu.

To access the Code window from the Project window, follow these steps:

1. Select **P**roject from the **W**indow menu or click the Project window.

2. Select the form name (GREETER.FRM) in the Project window.

3. Click the View Code button. The Code window appears with the general declarations in view.

4. To view a list of all the objects, click the Object List access-arrow.

   As you scroll through the list, a number of objects that start with the prefix mnu appear. These are the menu options (see Figure 24.15).

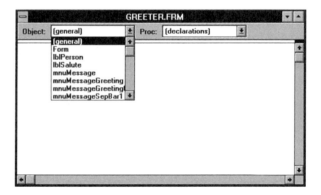

Figure 24.15.

The Code window Object list.

5. Click mnuOptBackgroundBlue. The Code window for the mnuOptBackgroundBlue_Click procedure appears.

6. Close the Code window.

You also can access the Code window directly from the form. Double-click the menu option to bring up the Code window. If the menu option does not contain submenus, you can single-click the menu option to access the Code window.

To access the Code window for the Light **B**lue menu option dircectly from the form, follow these steps:

1. Click on the form to give the form the focus.

2. Click the **O**ptions menu.

3. Click the **B**ackground submenu.

4. Click Light **B**lue.

The Code window for the `Click` procedure appears (see Figure 24.16). The cursor is blinking at the beginning of the second line waiting for you to add code.

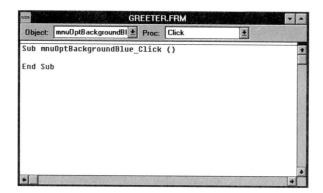

Figure 24.16.

The Light Blue menu Code window.

Adding Code for Menu Procedures

Menus basically have two types of code procedures: those that take specific action and those that open a dialog box. The code procedure for the light blue background option takes action. The user chooses a color and expects the color to change. It does not require verification with a dialog box.

Changing the Background Color

To change the background color of a form at run time, you adjust the form's `Backcolor` property. Open the Code window, and type the following `Click` procedure:

```
Sub mnuOptBackgroundBlue_Click ()
    Form1.BackColor = &HFFFFC0
End Sub
```

This procedure modifies the `BackColor` property of the two labels as well as the `BackColor` property of the form. All three controls are set to a background color of light blue.

Run the application, select **B**ackground from the **O**ptions menu, and then select Light **B**lue. The background color of the form and the two labels changes to a light blue color. Stop the application.

Now create similar procedures for the other two colors: white and light gray. One convenient method is to copy the assignment instruction from the `mnuOptBackgroundBlue_Click` procedure to the Clipboard, and then paste the instruction into the other code procedures. Finally, modify the pasted code to specify the appropriate color values.

The following are the completed procedures for the other two colors:

```
Sub mnuOptBackgroundWhite_Click ()
    Form1.BackColor = &HFFFFFF
End Sub

Sub mnuOptBackgroundGray_Click ()
    Form1.BackColor = &H00E0E0E0
End Sub
```

T I P   In these procedures, the colors are specified with hexadecimal values. To determine these values, you can select the form, change the value of `Backcolor` in the Properties window using the color palette, and then copy the hexadecimal value for each desired color. You can also change colors in other ways. You can, for example, use a `QBColor` instruction, the `RGB` function, or load CONSTANT.TXT in a separate module and use the predefined color constants in the assignment instructions.

Testing the Application

At this point, you can run the application to see the **O**ptions **B**ackground submenu at work. To see the colors change, use the **O**ptions **B**ackground submenu to select colors one at a time. When you are finished testing the different colors, you can stop the application.

Programming the Style Menu

You need `Click` procedures for each menu option of the **S**tyle menu. These procedures activate when the user clicks on the **P**lain, **F**ancy, or **M**odern items. The `Click` procedures set the font color and font style for the label messages.

When you create your application, the default color for text is Black and the default FontName is MS Sans Serif. When you decide to alter the default font, you should consider what fonts are available. If Windows cannot locate the selected font, it will try to find a close substitute, which may create a different effect than you intended.

When you first install Windows, two different sets of fonts may be included with the system. The standard Windows fonts are Courier, MS Sans Serif, MS Serif, Symbol, Modern, Roman, and Script. If you have the basic TrueType font collection, these fonts are also available: Arial, New Courier, Times New Roman, Symbol, Wingdings.

When you create your application, the fonts that are installed on your system will be shown in the FontName property list, with the FontSize property list showing the point sizes for the selected font. For this application, the defaults will be referenced as Plain, Fancy (referring to the Script font), and Modern (using the Modern font).

Create the following Click procedures for the Plain, Fancy, and Modern menu options:

```
Sub mnuOptStylePlain_Click ()
    lblGreeting.ForeColor = &H80000008
    lblGreeting.FontName = "MS Sans Serif"
    lblGreeting.FontSize = 8.25
    lblPerson.ForeColor = &H80000008
    lblPerson.FontName = "MS Sans Serif"
    lblPerson.FontSize = 8.25
End Sub

Sub mnuOptStyleFancy_Click ()
    lblGreeting.ForeColor = &H800000
    lblGreeting.FontName = "Script"
    lblGreeting.FontSize = 24
    lblPerson.ForeColor = &H800000
    lblPerson.FontName = "Script"
    lblPerson.FontSize = 24
End Sub

Sub mnuOptStyleModern_Click ()
    lblSalute.ForeColor = &H80
    lblSalute.FontName = "Modern"
    lblSalute.FontSize = 18
    lblperson.ForeColor = &H80
    lblperson.FontName = "Modern"
    lblperson.FontSize = 18
End Sub
```

You cannot, at this moment, experiment with these procedures by running the application. Fancy is currently an invisible menu option, and **Modern** is disabled. Later in this chapter, in the section titled "Programming the Additional Properties," you will add the code to activate these menu choices.

Adding Code to Access a Dialog Box

When using this application, the user must type the name of the person being greeted. The natural way for the user to input this name is in a dialog box. Rather than create a separate form for this question, the InputBox$ command can be used to create the appropriate dialog box. This dialog box opens when the user selects the **Message Text** menu option.

When the user provides a name in the dialog box, the program must update the Caption of the label lblPerson. Create the following Click procedure:

```
Sub mnuMessageText_Click ()
    Msg$ = "Enter the name of the person you wish to greet."
    Title$ = "Name Please"
    DefVal$ = "You"
    lblPerson.Caption = InputBox(Msg$, Title$, DefVal$)
End Sub
```

You can now test the application. Follow these steps:

1. Run the application.

2. Select **Text** from the **Message** menu.

   The menu closes, and an input box appears and prompts you to enter the name of the person that the application will greet (see Figure 24.17).

Figure 24.17.

The Name Please dialog box.

3. Type a name in the input box and click OK.

   The caption changes on the label in the middle of the form.

4. Stop the application. You need to add additional code for the Fancy and Modern options to work, as discussed in the next section.

Programming the Additional Properties

In the last section, you added code to change the settings for the application, but when you ran the application you may have noticed that the check mark and the Enabled and Visible properties never changed.

When designing the menu structure for this application, you used the Checked, Enabled, and Visible properties to initialize the visual appearance of the menus. You now need to add procedures that change these properties at run time, according to the options the user selects.

The *Checked* Property

The first thing you may have noticed when making the test runs of this application, regardless of the color selected, is that a check mark remains next to the White menu option. You can change the Checked property of a menu option with code.

When considering whether to use the Checked property, you must determine what type of menu option you have. If you have an option that toggles between two states, modifying the Checked property is appropriate.

In the sample application, the user can toggle the message greeting on or off. When Greeting is selected, the message Welcome to appears on the form, and a check mark appears next to the **M**essage **G**reeting menu option. When Greeting is deselected, no greeting message appears on the form, and the check mark does not appear. To toggle the check mark correctly, enter the following code to the mnuMessageGreeting_Click procedure:

```
Sub mnuMessageGreeting_Click ()
   mnuMessageGreeting.Checked = Not mnuMessageGreeting.Checked
   If mnuMessageGreeting.Checked = True Then
      lblGreeting.Caption = "Welcome to"
   Else
      lblGreeting.Caption = ""
   End If
End Sub
```

You need to indicate that a greeting is present when the application starts. Follow these steps to place a check mark next to the **G**reeting menu option:

1. Open the Menu Design window.

2. Click &Greeting in the outline.

3. Click the Checked box.

4. Click the OK button to close the Menu Design window.

5. Run the application.

6. Select **G**reeting from the **M**essage menu two or three times.

   Watch the check mark toggle on and off, and the message Welcome to appear and disappear from the form.

The Greeting option is an example of an independent menu option. Its status doesn't depend on the status of any other option on the menu. This is not the case, however, with the **B**ackground and **S**tyle submenus on the **O**ptions menu. This application can only display one background color and one font style. These options are interdependent, and their event procedures are more complex than that for the Greeting option.

When you turn on one of the Background or Style options, you must turn the other options off. Add the following code to the indicated procedures:

1. Add to the mnuOptBackgroundWhite_Click procedure:

```
mnuOptBackgroundWhite.Checked = True
mnuOptBackgroundBlue.Checked = False
mnuOptBackgroundGray.Checked = False
```

2. Add to the mnuOptBackgroundBlue_Click procedure:

```
mnuOptBackgroundWhite.Checked = False
mnuOptBackgroundBlue.Checked = True
mnuOptBackgroundGray.Checked = False
```

3. Add to the mnuOptBackgroundGray_Click procedure:

```
mnuOptBackgroundWhite.Checked = False
mnuOptBackgroundBlue.Checked = False
mnuOptBackgroundGray.Checked = True
```

4. Run the application.

5. Change the background color to light blue.

6. Select the **O**ptions **B**ackground menu again to see the check mark that now appears next to the Light **B**lue menu option.

To set the Checked properties for the font styles, modify the Click procedures for the **S**tyle menu options. The following are the updated procedures:

```
Sub mnuOptStylePlain_Click ()
   mnuOptStylePlain.Checked = True
   mnuOptStyleFancy.Checked = False
   mnuOptStyleModern.Checked = False
   lblGreeting.ForeColor = &H80000008
   lblGreeting.FontName = "MS Sans Serif"
   lblGreeting.FontSize = 8.25
   lblPerson.ForeColor = &H80000008
   lblPerson.FontName = "MS Sans Serif"
   lblPerson.FontSize = 8.25
End Sub

Sub mnuOptStyleFancy_Click ()
   mnuOptStylePlain.Checked = False
   mnuOptStyleFancy.Checked = True
   mnuOptStyleModern.Checked = False
   lblGreeting.ForeColor = &H800000
   lblGreeting.FontName = "Script"
   lblGreeting.FontSize = 24
   lblPerson.ForeColor = &H800000
   lblPerson.FontName = "Script"
   lblPerson.FontSize = 24
End Sub

Sub mnuOptStyleModern_Click ()
   mnuOptStylePlain.Checked = False
   mnuOptStyleFancy.Checked = False
   mnuOptStyleModern.Checked = True
   lblGreeting.ForeColor = &H80
   lblGreeting.FontName = "Modern"
   lblGreeting.FontSize = 18
   lblperson.ForeColor = &H80
   lblperson.FontName = "Modern"
   lblperson.FontSize = 18
End Sub
```

The *Enabled* Property

In this application, the **M**odern style can be selected only when the background color is gray. When the application begins, the **M**odern menu option is disabled (dimmed) because the default background color is white.

To enable the **M**odern style menu option when the user selects the gray background, you must modify code in the event procedures. However, setting the `Enabled` property to True for the Modern menu option is only part of the task. You also must disable the **M**odern menu option when the background color is changed from gray to either white or blue. Furthermore, the program also should automatically change the **M**odern style to **P**lain when the gray background is changed to another color. The remainder of this section discusses the necessary procedure modifications:

In the `mnuOptBackgroundGray_Click` procedure, add the following instruction to the beginning of the code in order to enable the Gray menu option:

```
mnuOptStyleModern.Enabled = True
```

To disable the **M**odern style menu option and activate the **P**lain style when the user changes the background color to blue or white, add the following two instructions at the beginning of both the `mnuOptBackgroundWhite_Click` and `mnuOptBackgroundBlue_Click` procedures:

```
If mnuOptStyleModern.Checked Then mnuOptStylePlain_Click
mnuOptStyleModern.Enabled = False
```

Notice that the first instruction invokes the **P**lain menu option directly from the program code.

Run the application. Select Light **G**ray from the **O**ptions **B**ackground menu. Notice that the **M**odern style is now available. Select the **M**odern style.

Now select Light **B**lue from the **O**ptions **B**ackground menu. The background color changes to light blue and the font style returns to **P**lain. Access the **O**ptions **S**tyle menu, and notice that the **M**odern option is dimmed again.

The *Visible* Property

The **F**ancy menu option also is dependent on the selected background color. The difference here is that rather than being disabled, the **F**ancy menu option is invisible.

Coding an invisible menu option is similar to coding a disabled menu option, except you modify the `Visible` property rather than the `Enabled` property.

The **F**ancy menu option for this application can be chosen only when the background color is light blue or light gray.

In both the `mnuOptBackgroundGray_Click` and `mnuOptBackgroundBlue_Click` procedures, add the following instruction at the beginning of the code to make the **F**ancy menu option visible:

```
mnuOptStyleFancy.Visible = True
```

To make the **Fancy** menu option invisible and change the font style to **P**lain when the user changes the background color to white, add the following two instructions at the beginning of the `mnuOptBackgroundWhite_Click` procedure:

```
If mnuOptStyleFancy.Checked Then mnuOptStylePlain_Click
mnuOptStyleFancy.Visible = False
```

Run the application again. Select Light **G**ray from the **O**ptions **B**ackground menu. Now access the **O**ptions **S**tyle menu. Notice that the **Fancy** menu option is now visible.

Select **Fancy**. Now select **W**hite from the **O**ptions **B**ackground menu. The background color changes and the style changes back to **P**lain. Access the **O**ptions **S**tyle menu. The **Fancy** menu option is once again invisible.

> The sample application utilizes various menu tools. For demonstration purposes, the Enabled and Visible properties were both used on the same menu. When developing practical applications, you should avoid using Enabled and Visible to control the access to two items on the same submenu because doing so is likely to confuse your users.
>
> **T I P**

Creating a Menu Control Array

An additional menu tool is the *menu control array*. Menu control arrays are just as easy to create and as useful as other control arrays. To demonstrate menu control arrays, you will add a new submenu to the **M**essage **G**reeting menu option.

With this submenu, the user can change the greeting message from "Welcome to" to one of these four messages: "Hello," "Good Morning," "Good Afternoon," or "Good Evening." To change the greeting message, follow these steps:

1. Select **G**reeting from the **M**essage menu.

    The Code window opens showing the `mnuMessageGreeting_Click` procedure.

2. Delete all the code between the `Sub` and `End Sub` instructions.

3. Close the Code window.

4. Open the Menu Design window.

5. In the Menu outline, click `&Options`.

6. Click the Insert button three times to prepare for three new menu options.

7. Click the Caption text box.

8. Type **&Welcome to** for the caption, press Tab and type **mnuMessageGreetingChoice** for the name.

9. Press Tab to move to the Index text box and type **0**.

   This establishes the menu control array.

10. Click the Checked box.

11. Click the right-arrow button twice to place the new menu as a submenu option of the Greeting menu.

12. Press Enter.

13. Create a menu option with a Caption of &Hello and a Name of mnuMessageGreetingChoice.

14. Tab to the Index text box and enter the value **1**.

15. Click the right-arrow button twice to put the menu on the same indentation level as &Welcome to, and then press Enter.

16. Create a menu option with a Caption of &Good ?? and a Name of mnuMessageGreetingChoice.

17. Tab to the Index text box and enter the value **2**.

18. Click the right-arrow button twice, and then press Enter.

19. Click &Greeting in the outline window.

20. Click the Checked box to deselect the check mark. The *X* disappears from the check box.

21. Click OK.

The **Message Greeting** menu now looks like Figure 24.18.

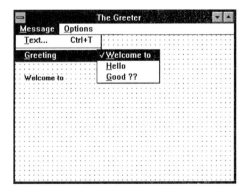

The advantage of a control array with menu options is that you can write a single procedure that specifies the actions for all the items of a submenu. As a result, the program minimizes the amount of duplicate code and makes debugging much easier. As with any control array, you can use the menu control array to add menu options to an application during run time.

Completing the Sample Application

You need to add the code to the sample application to change the label caption for each menu choice and get the system time for the last option. Notice that instead of having three places to add code, there is only the mnuMessageGreetingChoice_Click event, plus the initial settings in the Form_Load event. To complete the sample application, write the following two procedures:

```
Sub mnuMessageGreetingChoice_Click (Index As Integer)
    Select Case Index
        Case 0
            lblGreeting.Caption = "Welcome to"
            mnuMessageGreetingChoice(0).Checked = True
            mnuMessageGreetingChoice(1).Checked = False
            mnuMessageGreetingChoice(2).Checked = False
        Case 1
            lblGreeting.Caption = "Hello"
            mnuMessageGreetingChoice(0).Checked = False
            mnuMessageGreetingChoice(1).Checked = True
            mnuMessageGreetingChoice(2).Checked = False
        Case 2
            lblGreeting.Caption = mnuMessageGreetingChoice(2).Caption
            mnuMessageGreetingChoice(0).Checked = False
            mnuMessageGreetingChoice(1).Checked = False
            mnuMessageGreetingChoice(2).Checked = True
    End Select
End Sub

Sub Form_Load ()
    If Val(Time$) > 0 And Val(Time$) < 12 Then
        mnuMessageGreetingChoice(2).Caption = "Good Morning"
    ElseIf Val(Time$) >= 12 And Val(Time$) < 18 Then
        mnuMessageGreetingChoice(2).Caption = "Good Afternoon"
    Else
        mnuMessageGreetingChoice(2).Caption = "Good Evening"
    End If
End Sub
```

Notice that the `Form_Load` procedure uses `Time$` to determine the time of day and then, for Case 2, assigns the appropriate caption in the menu control array. As a result, when the user opens the **M**essage Greeting menu, the bottom option reads `Good Morning`, `Good Afternoon`, or `Good Evening`.

Adding Pop-up Menus

In addition to creating drop-down menus, you may want to include *pop-up menus*. A pop-up menu is a menu that is not attached to the menu bar. It is sometimes referred to as a floating menu. Pop-up menus normally are programmed to appear by clicking the right mouse button; the menu appears under the mouse pointer.

Pop-up menus can be used to display context-sensitive menus for particular controls or hold commonly used menu options. It is acceptable to repeat items from other menus. Microsoft recommends that pop-up menus not be used to change settings for a particular control. It is very easy to click the right mouse button once, highlight a choice, and click again without even realizing it; you can perform this entire sequence in a few seconds.

With Version 3.0, Visual Basic provides the `PopupMenu` method to make displaying pop-up menus easy. As the following sections explain, you create a pop-up menu by first setting up the menu with the Menu Design window. You then set the main menu's `Visible` property to False. Finally, you program the `MouseUp` (or other) event procedure for the form that should receive the pop-up menu. With `PopupMenu`, you can also specify the menu's placement relative to the mouse pointer.

Setting Up the Pop-up Menu Contents

The first step in implementing pop-up menus is to create the menu outline using the Menu Design window. The main menu option needs to have the `Visible` property set to False so that it will not show up on the menu bar.

In the sample application, you can reset all the window settings and provide a quicker access for the **T**ext option by using another menu control array for easier coding. To create the pop-up menu for these two options, follow these steps:

1. Click the form to select it.

2. Open the Menu Design window.

3. Select the **M**odern menu option in the Menu outline.

4. Press Enter to get a new menu option.

5. Enter **PopUp** as the caption and **mnuPopUp** as the Name.

6. Click the left arrow button twice to put this menu at the top level (left-most indentation position).

7. Click the Visible check box to unselect it. The *X* disappears.

8. Press Enter to get another menu option.

9. Enter **Reset** as the Caption, **mnuPop** as the Name, and **0** as the Index.

10. Click the right arrow button to indent this submenu one level. Press Enter.

11. Enter **Text...** as the Caption, **mnuPop** as the Name, and **1** as the Index.

12. Click OK to close the Menu Design window.

    This action creates the menu structure for the pop-up menu. Notice that the menu is not shown on the menu bar.

Using the *PopupMenu* Method

In program code, you use the PopupMenu method to display pop-up menus. Here is the syntax for the PopupMenu method.

---

*formname.*PopupMenu *menuname, centerval, X, Y*

in which

   formname is the name of the form on which the pop-up menu should appear;

   menuname is the name of the pop-up menu which will be displayed;

   centerval is an integer value which specifies how the pop-up menu is centered;

and

   X and *Y* refer to the X and Y coordinates of the pop-up menu relative to the form.

The *formname* is optional. If you omit this parameter, the current form is assumed. Also, the *centerval, X,* and *Y* parameters are all optional.

If you omit the *X* and *Y* parameters, the pop-up menu appears at the current position of the mouse pointer. The *centerval* parameter, if present, determines how the pop-up menu is aligned relative to *X* and *Y*. When *centerval* is 0 (the default), the left border of the pop-up menu is at *X*. When centerval is 8, the right border is at *X*. Finally, when centerval is 4, the pop-up menu appears centered at *X*.

For example, the following instruction displays a pop-up menu named MyPop whose right border is at the current mouse position:

```
PopupMenu MyPop, 8
```

Writing the Code for the Pop-up Menu

For the GREETER application, after the pop-up menu is created using the Menu Design window, you need to write code to display the pop-up menu when the user clicks the right mouse button. You could have the menu appear after a left click, but users expect to use the left mouse button to take specific action, not to call a pop-up menu. In Windows, a pop-up menu is normally called with a right click.

To program for a right click, use the MouseUp event. You need to write code that tests (after the user releases the mouse button) whether the left or right mouse button was used—and have it take action only when the right mouse button was used.

For the sample application, the pop-up menu can be called from anywhere on the form. To deliver a consistent appearance to the user, this will require some duplicate code in the MouseUp events and in the form and labels. For the sample application, you must add the following lines of code to the MouseUp event for the Form, lblPerson, and lblSalute:

```
If Button = 2 Then    'right mouse button is clicked
    PopupMenu mnuPopUp, 4
End If
```

Notice that the PopupMenu instruction centers the pop-up menu at the location of the mouse pointer.

Once the access to the pop-up menu is provided, you must implement the options on the menu. To make this easier, you set up a menu control array called mnuPop.

The first menu option resets all the form settings to their initial state. The second item repeats the operation provided by the mnuMessageText_Click event. In this case, your program code can simply invoke the other event. To set up the operation of the pop-up menu, enter the following code for the Click event for mnuPop():

```
Sub mnuPop_Click (Index As Integer)
    Select Case Index
        Case 0    'Reset all menus to defaults
            lblGreeting.Caption = "Welcome to"
            lblPerson.Caption = "You"
            mnuOptStylePlain_Click    'Invoke Click procedure
```

```
            mnuOptStylePlain.Visible = True
            mnuOptStyleFancy.Visible = False
            mnuOptStyleModern.Visible = True
            mnuOptStyleModern.Enabled = False
            mnuOptBackgroundWhite.Checked = True
            mnuOptBackgroundBlue.Checked = False
            mnuOptBackgroundGray.Checked = False
            Form1.BackColor = &HFFFFFF
            Form1.lblGreeting.BackColor = &HFFFFFF
            Form1.lblPerson.BackColor = &HFFFFFF
            mnuOptStylePlain.Checked = True
            mnuOptStyleFancy.Checked = False
            mnuOptStyleModern.Checked = False
        Case 1
            mnuMessageText_Click
    End Select
End Sub
```

Follow these steps to test your pop-up menu:

1. Run your application.

2. Click the right-hand mouse button anywhere on the form.

   The pop-up menu appears where your mouse pointer is located on the form, as shown in Figure 24.19.

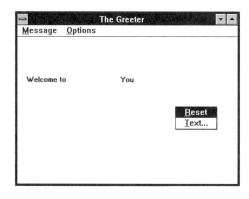

Figure 24.19.

A pop-up menu, appearing at the location of the mouse pointer.

3. Click **Text**... with the left-hand mouse button.

   The Name Please dialog box appears.

4. Enter your name and press Enter.

   The form shows your name.

5. Click anywhere on the form with the right mouse button to display the pop-up menu.

6. Click the Reset option on the pop-up menu.

   The form shows the original "You" response.

7. Experiment with selecting various Background and Style options from the regular menu system.

8. Click the right mouse button to display the pop-up menu once again.

9. Select the Reset option to restore the default appearance of the form.

10. Stop the application.

11. Save the form as GREETER.FRM and the project as GREETER.MAK.

Understanding Standard Menus in Windows Applications

After you have learned to create your own menus, you may want to give some consideration to your users' expectations. Windows users expect your application to operate like other Windows applications.

Microsoft publishes recommendations for the design of Windows applications to help your application conform to the users' expectations. The primary reference manual is a document called "Microsoft Windows Interface Guidelines." In addition to referencing the use of cascading menus, access keys, and quick keys, these guidelines recommend some standard menus for Windows applications.

Standard menus contribute towards Windows applications sharing the same look and feel. Users come to expect certain available options from particular menus.

Four standard menus exist: Control, File, Edit, and Help. Chapter 2, "A Windows Primer," touches on the standardization of menus from the user's point of view. The remainder of this chapter discusses these standard menus from an application developer's point of view.

The Control Menu

The Control menu opens when the user clicks the Control menu button in the upper-left corner of a window (or alternatively, presses the shortcut key Alt+Space). Figure 24.20 shows a standard Control menu. To manipulate the window, the Control menu provides the **Restore, Move, Size, Minimize,** and **Maximize** options. **Close** and **Switch** To are the other two menu options. **Switch** To opens the Task List that enables you to switch from the active task to another running application.

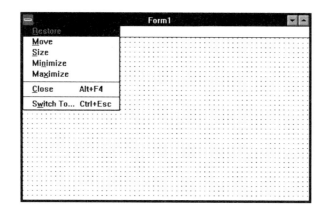

Figure 24.20.

A standard **C**ontrol menu.

For applications you develop with Visual Basic, you don't need to worry about programming the Control menu. The Control menu is a standard feature of Windows and Visual Basic. Your Visual Basic forms include a fully functioning Control menu automatically.

The File Menu

The **File** menu is standard for any application that works with disk files. If your application involves file input and output, you should provide a File menu. Figure 24.21 shows a standard File menu.

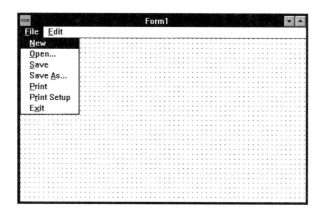

Figure 24.21.

A standard **F**ile menu.

A standard **F**ile menu contains seven items; New, **O**pen..., **S**ave, Save **A**s..., Print, **P**rint Setup, and Exit. Table 24.3 contains descriptions of each option in a standard File menu.

Table 24.3. Standard options on a File menu.

Option	Description
New	Creates a new file. The Visual Basic File menu, for example, offers options to create a new project. The New captions often contain an ellipsis to indicate that a dialog box opens when the option is selected.
Open...	Activates a previously saved file. A dialog box opens from which the user can select the file from a list. With the Common Dialog control, you can easily create this standard dialog box in your Visual Basic applications. (For more information on the Commond Dialog control, see Chapter 29, "Manipulating the Windows Environment.") (Although not a standard, the shortcut combination Ctrl+O is used frequently.)
Save	Saves the current data as a disk file. If a version of the file is already saved on disk (with the current file name), this option updates the disk file. If no file name has yet been established, the Save As... dialog box opens. (Although not a standard, the shortcut combination Ctrl+S is used frequently).
Save As...	Saves the current file with a new file name. Use this option to save a file for the first time or to create a second version of an existing file with a new file name.
Print	Prints the current version of the file. This option may open a dialog box for setting print options (such as the number of copies or the page range to print). The common dialog box tool in the Professional Edition of Visual Basic facilitates the creation of print dialog boxes. (Although not a standard, the shortcut combination Ctrl+P is used frequently.)
Print Setup	Enables you to set options for the printer.
Exit	Terminates the current application. This option should be the last option on the File menu, usually separated from the other menu options with a separator bar.

The Edit Menu

The Edit menu provides six standard options that enable you to edit text. The six standard menu options are Undo, Cut, Copy, Paste, Paste Link, and Links. Figure 24.22 shows a standard Edit menu.

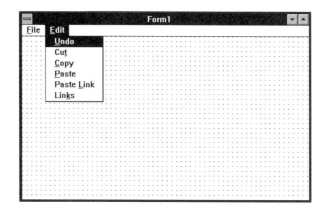

Figure 24.22.

A standard **E**dit menu.

Table 24.4 describes the six options in a standard Edit menu.

Table 24.4. Standard options on an Edit menu.

Option	Description
Undo	Removes the effect of the previous editing operation. The standard shortcut is Ctrl+Z. This shortcut is new with Microsoft Windows 3.1. (In earlier versions of Windows, the shortcut is Ctrl+Backspace.)
Cut	Moves text (or other data) from the application to the Windows Clipboard. The user highlights text, accesses the Edit menu, and selects Cut. The text disappears from the highlighted location and is placed in the Clipboard. In Visual Basic, the `Clipboard.SetText` method moves text to the Clipboard. The standard shortcut is Ctrl+X. This shortcut is new with Windows 3.1. (In prior versions of Windows, the shortcut is Shift+Delete.)
Copy	Places a copy of highlighted text (or other data) on the Clipboard. Unlike the Cut option, the data is not deleted from the source. The standard shortcut, new for Windows 3.1, is Ctrl+C. (In prior versions of Windows, the shortcut is Ctrl+Insert.)
Paste	Transfers the contents of the Clipboard to the application. The data appears at the current cursor position. In Visual Basic, the

continues

Table 24.4. Continued

Option	Description
	Clipboard.SetText method retrieves text from the Clipboard. The standard shortcut is Ctrl+V. (In prior versions of Windows, the shortcut is Shift+Insert.)
Paste Link, Links	These options permit the dynamic linking of information between two open Windows applications simultaneously.

The Help Menu

The **Help** menu provides an on-line Help system. This menu option should appear at the far right of the menu bar. The standard shortcut key is F1. The Help menu usually contains **Contents**, **S**earch for Help On..., How to Use Help..., and **A**bout the application. The Professional Edition of Visual Basic provides tools for creating a Help system. (For more information, see Chapter 33, "Adding a Help System to an Application.")

Summary

Visual Basic includes a special tool for the creation of a menu system: the Menu Design window. By using this window, you easily can create an hierarchical menu system with cascading menus, check marks, separator bars, and dimmed options.

Visual Basic treats menu options as controls. As such, event procedures specify the actions to take when a menu option is selected. With menu control arrays, you can save repetitive coding for related submenu options.

Menu controls have several properties, including Caption, Name, Enabled, Checked, and Visible. By manipulating these properties in program code, you can enable and disable menu options, toggle checkmarks next to menu options, and hide or restore menus from view.

A new feature of Visual Basic 3.0 is the ability to create pop-up menus. With the PopupMenu method, you can display popup menus on a form in response to the user's mouse clicks.

Microsoft publishes guidelines for Windows applications. These guidelines specify the menus and submenus contained in a standard menu system. Besides the Control menu, the standard menu options are File, Edit, and Help.

Processing Files

Many Visual Basic applications work with external files. After all, the most common way for an application to save information is to write it to a data file. Similarly, many applications read required information from an appropriate data file. This chapter shows you how to work with files.

The chapter is divided into three main sections. The first section covers the three file controls found in the Visual Basic Toolbox: the File list box, Directory list box, and the Drive list box. Using these controls, you can build standard Windows-like dialog boxes for the selection and specification of files.

The second section covers the Visual Basic statements and functions that emulate DOS-type file commands. With these statements and functions, you can manipulate files and directories. For example, you can create a new directory. You can also copy files from one directory to another.

Finally, the chapter covers the three types of data files supported by Visual Basic: sequential, random-access, and binary. The discussion focuses on how to use these types of files, and the advantages and disadvantages of each.

Using the File Controls

The three file controls in the Toolbox are the File list box, Directory list box, and Drive list box. Using these controls, you can display lists of files, directories, and disk drives.

Each of the three file controls works similar to the standard list box control. In fact, the file controls share several of the properties associated with ordinary list boxes, including, the List, ListCount, and ListIndex properties.

The Toolbox icons for the file controls depict a page of paper, a folder, and a disk drive (see Figure 25.1).

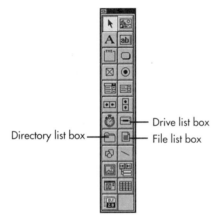

Directory list box ——— Drive list box
File list box

The File list box displays a list of files. A user can select a file with a mouse click or a keystroke. The Directory list box displays the available directories on each disk drive. The user can change directories with a few mouse clicks or keystrokes. Using the Drive list box, the user can specify any available disk drive.

The File and Directory list boxes have built-in scroll bars which enable the user to move up and down through the lists. The Drive list box provides a drop-down list box.

By navigating the file controls in an application, the user can select disk drives, directories and files. As explained in this chapter, the controls share interrelated properties. With a minimum of program code, you can synchronize the control to work together.

The file controls provide a common interface seen in many Windows applications. Figure 25.2 shows a standard Windows-like dialog box used to open a file. Using the file controls, you can create such dialog boxes with relative ease.

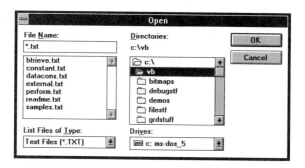

Figure 25.2.

An Open File dialog box.

NOTE Visual Basic includes the Common Dialog custom control. This control can create, among other things, a standard dialog box for the selection of a file. With Visual Basic 2.0, the Common Dialog control was included only with the Professional Edition. However, for Visual Basic 3.0, The Common Dialog control is included in both the Standard and Professional Editions. For more information on the Common Dialog control, see Chapter 29, "Manipulating the Windows Environment."

The design of Visual Basic's file controls conforms to the standards used in most Windows programs. As a result, users of your applications should instantly understand how to use dialog boxes created with the file controls.

The File List Box Control

At design time, Visual Basic assigns a default name of File1 to the first File list box you place on a form. Subsequent list boxes have default names of File2, File3, and so on. Using the Properties window, you can set property values as you do for other controls. Figure 25.3 shows how a File list box might appear at run time.

The File list box control behaves very similar to the standard list box control. The ListCount property indicates how many files are in the list, and ListIndex specifies the index of the currently selected list item. List property returns the items in the list. Further, the File list box has the standard display properties which let you set font, color, location, and size.

In addition to the standard properties of list boxes, the File list box has several specialized properties. By setting or reading (or doing both to) the values of these properties, you can create file management routines in your program code. The following sections discuss the properties specific to the File list box.

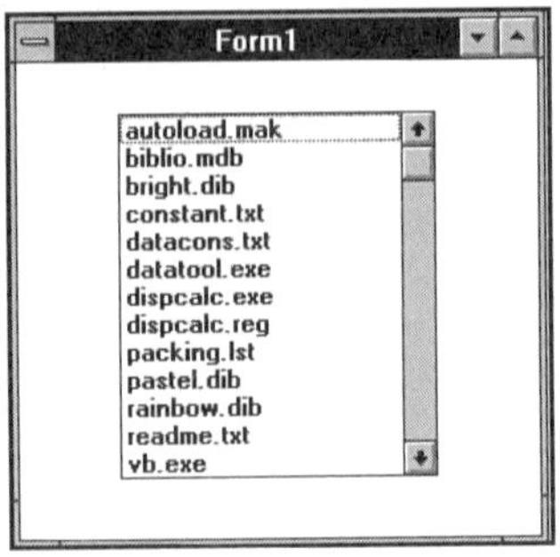

Figure 25.3.

A typical File list box at run time.

The *Pattern* and *Path* Properties

Using the Pattern and Path properties of the File list box, you can specify and determine which files it displays. Both properties have string values. The value of Pattern can be modified at design time and at run time. Path, however, can be modified only in program code at run time.

The Path property specifies the current path for the File list box. For example, the following instruction sets the value of Path in File1 to the default Visual Basic directory:

```
File1.Path = "C:\VB"
```

The Pattern property determines which files should be displayed in the File list box. You can use the DOS wild-card characters (* and ?). The default value of this property is "*.*", which results in the File list box displaying all the files in the specified path. The following instruction displays all the module (.BAS) files in the current directory:

```
File1.Pattern = "*.BAS"
```

The Pattern and Path properties can each be read and written at run time. You can change the values of the properties through user-generated events, in code, or by using a combination of the two.

Be aware that Visual Basic does not generate any error if you set the value of the Pattern property to an invalid file name. As such, if the user supplies a pattern, your code should check for invalid characters. However, setting the value of the Path property to a nonexistent directory does generate an error.

The *FileName* Property

When a File list box displays a list of file names, the user can select one of them by clicking the mouse, or using the arrow keys. The FileName property indicates which file is currently selected. The value is specified as a string.

In code, the value of the `FileName` property can be read or written at run time. When read, the value of the `FileName` property returns the DOS file name. By combining the values in the both the `Path` and the `FileName` properties, you can get a complete file specification for the selected file.

When you set the value of `FileName` in program code, you can optionally include drive and directory path information. Several side effects can occur, depending on how much of the file specification you modify. If you simply change the file name, without modifying the path, the newly specified file is selected in the File list box. Any modification to the `FileName` property triggers a `PatternChange` event for the File list box.

If the new value of `FileName` modifies the path, a `PathChange` event occurs in addition to `PatternChange`. In such cases, you can use the `PatternChange` and `PathChange` event procedures to set the `Path` and `Drive` properties of other file controls on the form. As demonstrated with the `FileSelector` application, discussed later in this chapter, this technique can be a powerful method for automating a file-retrieval system.

Attribute-Related Properties

Under DOS, files have the following attributes which you can evaluate, and change:

- *Archive*. Indicates whether a file has been saved since the last time it was modified.

- *Hidden*. Hides the file from normal display listings, such as the DOS DIR command, and the Windows File Manager.

- *Read-only*. Makes the file write-protected; you can read the file, but not save any modifications to it.

- *System*. Indicates a file associated with the operating system. Such files should not be moved, or erased.

- *Normal*. Indicates a normal file.

For each of these five DOS file attributes, the File list box has a corresponding property. These properties are `Archive`, `Hidden`, `ReadOnly`, `System`, and `Normal`. Each property can have a value of True or False.

By setting the values of these properties, you can qualify the file listings displayed in a File list box. For example, if you set `File1.Archive` to False, the `File1` list box does not display any files that have their DOS Archive attribute set.

Normally, a File list box does not display hidden or system files. However, you can list those files for the `File1` control by setting the values of both `File1.Hidden` and `File1.System` to True.

Keep in mind that a File list box displays those files whose property attributes match any of the DOS attribute settings. For example, if `File1.Hidden` and `File1.Archive` are True, and all other property values are False, you see all files that have either the DOS Hidden or System attribute set (or both attributes).

Creating the *FILEATTR* Application

The FILEATTR application uses a File list box and a series of Check boxes to display files with specified attributes. To create the application, start a new project. Place a single File list box on the form. Notice that this box already displays the files in the current directory. Using the Properties window, set the property values for the form and the File list box as 25.1 shows.

Table 25.1. *Form1* and *File1* property values.

Object	Height	Left	Top	Width
Form1	4230	1830	1380	6225
File1	2565	1200	600	2415

Now, place a Check box control near the upper right edge of the form. The default name for this control is `Check1`. Create a control array with four more check boxes, making five controls in all. The `Index` properties of these controls range from `0` to `4`.

For each of the five Check boxes, set the value of its `Left` property to 4500, `Height` to 495, and `Width` to 1215. Set the `Top` and `Caption` properties of the Check boxes as Table 25.2 shows. In this table, the column to the far left is the value of the Check box's `Index` property as the Properties window shows.

Table 25.2. *Top* and *Caption* property values of the *Check1* control array.

Index	Top	Caption
0	120	&Archive
1	840	&Hidden
2	1560	&Normal
3	2280	&Read-Only
4	3000	&System

Writing the *Form_Load* Event Procedures

The application requires only two event procedures. First, create the following
Form1_Load procedure which initializes the values of some properties:

```
Sub Form_Load ()
    File1.Path = "C:\VB"        'Or any other path you wish
    File1.Pattern = "*.*"
    Form1.Caption = "File Attributes for " & File1.Path & "\" &
File1.Pattern

    Rem  Set initial values for file attributes
    File1.Archive = False
    File1.Hidden = False
    File1.Normal = False
    File1.ReadOnly = False
    File1.System = False
End Sub
```

This procedure sets the path and pattern for the displayed files. Here, the path
is the default Visual Basic directory, C:\VB. You can modify this value to
designate any valid file path in your system.

The form's caption is set to indicate the complete file specifications. Finally,
the procedure sets an initial value of False for each of the five file attributes of
the File list box. As a result, the box does not display any file names when the
application begins.

Writing the *Check1_Click* Event Procedure

Click is the only other event procedure for the Check1 control array:

```
Sub Check1_Click (Index As Integer)
    Dim ValToSet As Integer

    ValToSet = Check1(Index).Value   '0 = False, 1 = True

    Select Case Index
        Case 0: File1.Archive = ValToSet
        Case 1: File1.Hidden = ValToSet
        Case 2: File1.Normal = ValToSet
        Case 3: File1.ReadOnly = ValToSet
        Case 4: File1.System = ValToSet
    End Select
End Sub
```

When a Check box is clicked, its `Value` property changes from 0 (unchecked) to 1 (checked), or vice versa. The `ValToSet` variable stores the current setting of the `Value` property. Visual Basic represents False as 0, and can interpret any non-zero value as True. The `ValToSet` variable, therefore, acts as a Boolean variable indicating False (0) or True (1).

The `Index` parameter indicates which Check box in the control array was clicked. The `Select Case` block sets the appropriate File list box attribute based on the index of the clicked control. Once this procedure executes, the contents of the File list box are automatically updated to display those files which match the selected attributes.

Running FILEATTR

Save the form as FILEATTR.FRM and the project as FILEATTR.MAK. Try running the application. At first, no files display in the File list box because all the attributes are set to False. Try clicking some of the Check boxes to update the displayed files. Figure 25.4 shows an example of Normal and Hidden files. (Of course, your list of displayed files is likely to be different than those that the figure shows.)

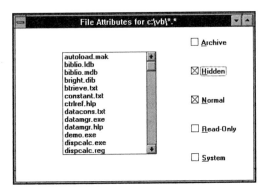

Figure 25.4.

The FILEATTR application with various attributes selected.

You might try setting the value of `File1.Path` to the root directory C:\. The root directory is a good choice for this application because that directory generally contains some hidden/system files which appear when you run the application.

Selecting Multiple Files: The *MultiSelect* Property

A user can select a file in a File list box by clicking a file name. The click causes the name to become highlighted. The highlighted entry is said to be "selected".

In Visual Basic, the value of the Selected property is True for a highlighted entry. By default, only one file name can be selected at a time. You can design applications that permit the selection of multiple file names. The MultiSelect property accomplishes this. Figure 25.5 shows the FILEATTR application running with multiple files selected.

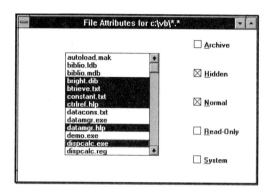

The MultiSelect property works for a File list box as it does for a regular list box. You can assign to the MultiSelect property three possible values: None (0), Simple (1), and Extended (2). The default is none, which means that only one file name can be selected at a time. If another file is selected, the first one is automatically deselected.

You enable simple multiselection in a File list box by setting the value of the MultiSelect property to 1. When a File list box is in simple multiselect mode, a file can be selected or deselected by pressing the spacebar, or clicking its name once. More than one file can remain selected at any given time.

When you set the MultiSelect property to 2, file selection methods become more sophisticated. A single click selects that file, deselecting all others. Multiple adjacent files can be selected by clicking the first file name, then dragging the mouse over the other desired files. You can also click the first file in the group, press the Shift key, then click the last file in the range to be selected. Multiple files that are not adjacent in the list can be selected or deselected with a Ctrl+Click on each file.

The value of the FileName property always contains one file name, so you can't use that property to evaluate multiple file selections. Instead, in a multiple selection environment, you use the Selected property to determine which files were highlighted by the user. This property assigns a True or False value to each item in the list. The property value is expressed much like an array variable—you enclose in parentheses an index value ranging from 0 upwards.

For example, if the first and third files of File1 are selected, then File1.Selected(0) and File1.Selected(2) are True, while File1.Selected(1) is false. This is another example of how the File list box and standard list box controls both work similarly.

By modifying the value of MultiSelect in the FILEATTR application, you can experiment with the different selection modes of a File list box. Using the Properties window, change the value of File1's MultiSelect property, and rerun the application. Try setting the value of MultiSelect to 1, then 2. Remember that the MultiSelect property can only be set at design time, not at run time.

The Directory List Box Control

The Directory list box control displays the directories and paths on the current disk drive. Visual Basic puts a small folder icon to the left of each directory name. The default name for the first Directory list box on a form sis Dir1.

With a Directory list box, a user can navigate and select directories with the mouse or keyboard. If you are in a directory (the current one or its parent directories), the folder icon appears opened. For subdirectories under the current directory, the folder icon appears closed.

Properties and Events of Directory List Boxes

By modifying in code the value of the Path property for a Directory list box, you set its displayed drive and directory. If you set the value of Path to the name of a directory that doesn't exist or is unavailable, Visual Basic generates an error.

A Directory list box generates a Change event when the specified directory changes. The user can change the directory by double-clicking a new one. Also, program instructions can modify the value of Path.

Both the Directory list and the File list boxes have a Path property in which you can begin to synchronize your controls. You can put code in the Change event of a Directory list box to update the Path property of a File list box. Similarly, you can put code in the PathChange and PatternChange events of a File list box to update the value of Path for a Directory list box.

For example, with a single line of code, the following event procedure updates the files displayed in a File list box whenever the directory path changes in a Directory list box:

```
Sub Dir1_Change ()
    File1.Path = Dir1.Path
End Sub
```

Using the *ListIndex* Property

The ListIndex property of a Directory list box works differently than the same property of a regular list box. In a regular or File list box, the value of the ListIndex property indicates the absolute location of the item in the list. The first item in a regular or File list box has a ListIndex value of 0, the second item has ListIndex 1, and so on. If ListIndex has a value of -1, then no item is selected.

A Directory list box, however, operates differently. Negative ListIndex values indicate opened (parent or current) directories, while positive values of this property indicate unopened (child) directories. Figure 25.6 shows a Directory list box. Referring to the figure, the value of ListIndex for the current directory (ICONS) is -1, the immediate parent directory (VB) has a ListIndex value of -2, and so on. The first child subdirectory (ARROWS) has a ListIndex value of 0, the second one (COMM) has a ListIndex value of 1, and so on.

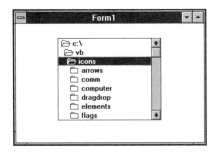

Figure 25.6.

A Directory list box.

Bear in mind that moving the highlight up or down in a Directory list box merely changes the value of the control's ListIndex property. A double-click is required to change the Path of a Directory list box.

The Drive List Box Control

The Drive list box is a drop-down list box containing the names and volume labels of all available disk drives on your system. The default name for the first Drive list box on a form is Drive1. Small icons to the left of each drive name indicate the drive type: floppy or hard disk, network drive, or RAM disk. Figure 25.7 shows an example of a Drive list box.

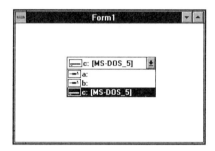

Figure 25.7.

A Drive list box.

Operating a Drive list box is simple. The control first displays only the current drive. By clicking the down arrow, a drop-down list appears which displays all the available drives. Click one of the displayed drives to select it.

When a drive is selected, the value of the Drive property for that Drive list box is updated. The Drive property is a string value which specifies the selected drive. You can specify a value for the Drive property in program code. For example:

```
Drive1.Drive = "B"
```

The control's Drive property need only be represented by a single letter. If to the value of Drive you assign a longer string, Visual Basic uses only its first letter. This comes in handy when you synchronize a Directory list box with a Drive list box. For example, the following instruction works well, even though the value of the Path property for a Directory list box is more than a single letter:

```
Drive1.Drive = Dir1.Path
```

When the value of the Drive property of a Drive list box becomes modified (in code or by the user), a Change event for this box occurs. In this Change procedure, you might modify the value of the Path property for the associated Directory list box. Also, you can update the current DOS drive with a ChDrive statement. ChDrive is discussed in detail later in this chapter.

Making File Controls Work Together

In an application, the three file controls can be synchronized to work together. That way, a user can switch smoothly among drives and directories, and select one or more files. A chain of events must be established for this synchronization to work smoothly. When a property value changes in one control, the others must be notified, and their associated property values must be modified.

For example, suppose an application has three file controls, Drive1, Dir1, and File1. When the drive in Drive1 changes, a Change event for Drive1 triggers. In the Drive1_Change procedure, you can put code which communicates the new drive letter to Dir1. When the Path property of Dir1 changes, the Dir1_Change event can send new path information to File1. The Path property of File1 is then updated. In other words, Drive1 updates Dir1 which, in turn, updates File1. If only Dir1 changes, this chain of events remains intact. Information flows from Dir1 to File1.

Most file selection dialog boxes also include a text box in which the user can quickly type in a complete file specification with drive, path and file name. As the upcoming FileSelector application demonstrates, evaluating the text typed by the user is relatively easy.

The FileSelector Application

Creating the FileSelector application will lead you through the construction of a file selection dialog box that you can utilize in other projects. With this dialog box, a user can change to other drives and directories, and select one or more files. This application demonstrates the basic properties and events of the file controls, and how they are navigated.

You will learn a technique for obtaining a list of selected files from a File list box control. Furthermore, you will write code enabling a user to select a drive, directory, and file (or pattern) by typing directly into a text box control.

Creating the Form at Design Time

To begin the FileSelector, start a new project. Add the following controls onto the form:

- A Drive list box (Drive1)
- A Directory list box (Dir1)

- A File list box (File1)
- A Label (Label1)
- A text box (Text1)
- Two command buttons (Command1 and Command2)

Using the Properties window, position and size the form and controls as Table 25.3 shows. Also, set the values for the Caption properties of the form and the two command buttons as the Table shows. Set the value of Label1's AutoSize property to True.

Table 25.3. Design-time property values for the FileSelector.

Object	Height	Left	Top	Width	Caption
Form1	4470	2340	1350	4695	File Selector
Drive1	315	60	2910	2055	
Dir1	2055	60	660	2055	
File1	2565	2280	660	2175	
Label1	195	60	420	585	
Text1	330	60	60	4395	
Command1	315	1140	3480	975	OK
Command2	315	2280	3480	975	Quit

For Form1, set the value of the BorderStyle property to 3 (Fixed Double). For File1, set the value of the MultiSelect property to 2 (Extended).

The default control names are acceptable, so you don't need to modify the value of Name for any of the controls. Figure 25.8 shows the form with all the design-time property values specified.

Figure 25.8.

The FileSelector application in Design

The *Form_Load* Event Procedure

When the application initializes, the Form_Load procedure specifies default values for several of the controls:

```
Sub Form_Load ()
    Drive1.Drive = CurDir$
    Dir1.Path = CurDir$
    Label1.Caption = Dir1.Path
    File1.Path = CurDir$
    File1.Pattern = "*.*"
    If File1.FileName <> "" Then
        Text1.Text = File1.FileName
    Else
        Text1.Text = File1.Pattern
    End If
End Sub
```

The CurDir$ function returns the current path for the drive in use. For more information on this function, see "The CurDir$ Function", later in this chapter.

The *Drive1_Change* Event Procedure

When the user changes the active disk drive in the Drive list box, the Drive1_Change procedure updates the current path in the Directory list box. The procedure checks for disk drive errors, such as selecting a floppy disk drive when no disk is in it. When an error occurs, a message box displays it, and Drive1.Path is reinitialized to its previous value.

To accomplish these objectives, create the following Drive1_Change procedure:

```
Sub Drive1_Change ()
    Dim Msg As String

    On Error Resume Next

    Screen.MousePointer = 11    'Hourglass mouse pointer
    Dir1.Path = Drive1.Drive
    Screen.MousePointer = 0

    If Err Then    'Dir1 tried to become a bad or unavailable drive
        Msg = "Error " & Err & ": " & Error$ & "."
        MsgBox Msg, 48, "Drive/Directory Error"
        Drive1.Drive = Dir1.Path
```

```
      End If
      On Error GoTo 0
End Sub
```

By setting the value of Dir1.Path to Drive1.Drive, the Directory list box displays the current directory for the selected drive letter. The procedure does not change the current DOS drive because there is no reason to do so. All current drives and directories are maintained by the Visual Basic application, not by DOS itself.

If you change to an unavailable or invalid drive, Drive1 itself does not trigger an error. However, when Dir1 tries to update the path based on the new Drive value, an error occurs. As a result, the appropriate error trapping occurs in the Drive1_Change event procedure. If an error occurs because of changing Dir1, then Drive1.Drive is reset back to Dir1's original drive, and Dir1.Path remains unaltered.

Now, put code into Dir1 so that the control can respond to the change.

The *Dir1_Change* Event Procedure

The following is the Dir1_Change procedure:

```
Sub Dir1_Change ()
    File1.Path = Dir1.Path

    If Len(Dir1.Path) > 3 Then
        Label1.Caption = Dir1.Path + "\" + File1.Pattern
    Else
        Label1.Caption = Dir1.Path + File1.Pattern
    End If

    If File1.FileName <> "" Then
        Text1.Text = File1.FileName
    Else
        Text1.Text = File1.Pattern
    End If
End Sub
```

This procedure sets File1.Path equal to Dir1.Path, thus updating the contents of the File list box appropriately. The remainder of the code in Dir1_Change is cosmetic. The code updates Label1 and Text1 to display the currently selected directory and file, respectively. Once again, notice that there is no need to change the current DOS directory.

The *File1_Click* Event Procedure

The `File1_Click` procedure updates the contents of the text box when the user clicks a file name in the File list box:

```
Sub File1_Click ()
    Text1.Text = File1.FileName
End Sub
```

Getting the Names of Selected Files

In this application, the user selects one or more files in the File list box, then clicks OK. The program code must get the names of the selected files.

To store the names of the selected files, the application uses a form-level string array called `FileList()`. Place the following declaration in the General Declarations section of the form:

```
Dim FileList() As String
```

NOTE If you use the `FileSelector` form as part of other applications, you probably want to declare the `FileList` array global in the Declarations section of a code module. That way, the file list can be referenced by all code modules and forms. This technique works whether one file or many are selected. As a result, you can use the global declaration even if your application design permits only a single selected file (the `MultiSelect` property of `File1` is set to 0).

The *Command1_Click* Event Procedure

Notice that `FileList` is a dynamic array. At run time, the `Command1_Click` procedure appropriately dimensions the `FileList` array, and stores the selected file names in its elements. The `Command1_Click` procedure activates when the user clicks OK:

```
Sub Command1_Click ()
    Dim Ctr As Integer    'Counter
    Dim L As Integer      'List index
    Dim X As Integer      'Loop counter
    Dim Msg As String     'String for message box

    'Redimension the FileList() array and put names of all
```

```
'selected files into the array elements

Ctr = -1
For L = 0 To File1.ListCount - 1
   If File1.Selected(L) = True Then
   Ctr = Ctr + 1
      If Ctr = 0 Then
         ReDim FileList(0)
      Else
         ReDim Preserve FileList(Ctr)
      End If
   FileList(Ctr) = File1.List(L)
   End If
Next L
If Ctr = -1 Then Exit Sub

'Create a message box listing all selected files

Msg = "File(s) Selected:" + Chr$(13)
Msg = Msg + "----------------------" + Chr$(13)

For X = 0 To UBound(FileList)
   Msg = Msg + FileList(X)
   If X < UBound(FileList) Then Msg = Msg + Chr$(13)
Next X
MsgBox Msg, 64, "Files Selected"
End Sub
```

The first For-Next loop redimensions, and then populates the FileList array. The second For-Next loop creates a message box which displays the current contents of the array.

The *File1_DblClick* Event Procedure

If the user double-clicks a file displayed in the File list box, that file should be selected. The following event procedure accomplishes this:

```
Sub File1_DblClick ()
   Command1_Click
End Sub
```

The call to the Click procedure for Command1 activates the code that executes when the user clicks OK.

Using the Text Box

In most Windows applications, file-related dialog boxes offer the user the option of explicitly typing a drive, path, file name, and file pattern. When a file name is typed, it is selected in the File list box. If a pattern is typed, the directory and drive list boxes are updated. Also, the File list box displays the file names which satisfy the pattern.

The FileSelector application uses a text box with which the user can type in an explicit path, file name, or pattern. The coding difficulty lies in interpreting the string typed by the user.

The first step in evaluating the typed string is to use the Like operator, which can help determine if invalid characters have been typed in the text box. The following lines of code, which you will later place in the Text1.KeyPress procedure, determine if the typed string specify a valid path/file name combination:

```
If Text1.Text Like "*[;>]*" Or Text1.Text Like "*[ ,+¦/]*" Then
   Msg = Text1.Text + " is an invalid file name."
   MsgBox Msg, 48, "Bad File Name"  'Display error message
End If
```

These instructions weed out any text containing characters that are not part of a valid file name. For more information on Like, see Chapter 17, "Working with Strings."

The second part of the job is to determine if the file name, path and drive are all valid. To do so, you can simply update the properties of the file controls, and evaluate any errors which might result. A Directory list box generates an error when the application attempts to make the Path property contain an invalid drive or directory. In such a case, the value of Path returns to the previous valid drive and path. If the value of the ListCount property of a File list box is zero, there aren't any files which match the desired name, path, or pattern specification.

For the FileSelector application, an alteration in Drive1 triggers two changes: one in Dir1 and another in File1. When new information is typed in the text box, the flow of events and information is reversed: File1 updates Dir1 which, in turn, changes Drive1. Specifically, the Text1_KeyPress event procedure changes the value of File1.Filename to the newly typed text string. The File1_PathChange event then updates Dir1 and Drive1. If any errors occur, you trap them, and return all values to their previous settings.

The *Text1_KeyPress* Event Procedure

To add the text box functionality to the application, create the following Text1_KeyPress procedure. This procedure contains the code that gains control when the user presses the Enter key:

```
Sub Text1_KeyPress (KeyAscii As Integer)
    Dim Msg As String

    If KeyAscii <> 13 Then Exit Sub    'Check for Enter key
    KeyAscii = 0     'Eliminate unwanted beep

    If Text1.Text = File1.List(File1.ListIndex) Then
        'Filename currently has the focus.
        'Select and Load it.
        File1.Selected(File1.ListIndex) = True
        Command1_Click
        Exit Sub
    End If

    'Evaluate text for unwanted characters using "Like" statement...

    If Text1.Text Like "*[;>]*" Or Text1.Text Like "*[ ,+¦/]*" Then
        Msg = Text1.Text + " is an invalid file name."
        MsgBox Msg, 48, "Bad File Name"  'Display error message
        Text1.Text = File1.FileName
        Text1.SetFocus    'Select text box
        Text1.SelStart = 0
        Text1.SelLength = Len(Text1.Text)
        Exit Sub

    Else    'Change File1.Filename, which starts the
            'chain process in motion...
        On Error Resume Next
        File1.FileName = Text1.Text

        'This will try to change File1.Pattern,
        'Dir1.Path, and Drive1.Drive.

        If Err Then
            Msg = "Error " & Err & ": " + Error$ + "."
            MsgBox Msg, 48, "File Error"
        End If
        'The File controls automatically recover from any error.

        On Error GoTo 0
```

```
      If File1.ListCount > 0 Then
         Text1.Text = File1.FileName
      Else
         Text1.Text = File1.Pattern
      End If

      Text1.SelStart = 0
      Text1.SelLength = Len(Text1.Text)
      Text1.SetFocus
   End If
End Sub
```

The *File1_PathChange* Event Procedure

The File1_PathChange procedure activates when new drive or directory information is sent from Text1_KeyPress:

```
Sub File1_PathChange ()
   If Len(File1.Path) > 3 Then
      Label1.Caption = File1.Path + "\" + File1.Pattern
   Else
      Label1.Caption = File1.Path + File1.Pattern
   End If

   If Dir1.Path <> File1.Path Then Dir1.Path = File1.Path
   If Drive1.Drive <> Left$(File1.Path, 1) Then
      Drive1.Drive = Left$(File1.Path, 1)
   End If
   If File1.ListCount = 0 Then Text1.Text = File1.Pattern
End Sub
```

Consider the following instruction taken from this procedure:

```
If Dir1.Path <> File1.Path Then Dir1.Path = File1.Path
```

On the surface, this If check seems unnecessary because there is no apparent
harm in assigning a property's current value to itself. For this application,
however, there is a danger: if File1.Path changes, Dir1.Path should be assigned a new value *only if* it is different from the current one. Otherwise, the
file controls would repeatedly change each other, resulting in a runaway chain
of procedure calls. An Out of Stack Space error is the final result. The same
warning applies to changing Drive1.Drive in the File1_PathChange event
procedure.

The *File1_PatternChange* Event Procedure

The File1_PatternChange procedure updates the Caption for Label1 to display the current path and pattern. The procedure also updates the contents of the text box, if necessary:

```
Sub File1_PatternChange ()
   'Update label1
   If Len(File1.Path) > 3 Then
      Label1.Caption = File1.Path + "\" + File1.Pattern
   Else
      Label1.Caption = File1.Path + File1.Pattern
   End If

   'Update Text1
   If File1.ListCount = 0 Then
      Text1.Text = File1.Pattern
   Else
      File1.ListIndex = 0
      Text1.Text = File1.FileName
   End If

   Text1.SelStart = 0
   Text1.SelLength = Len(Text1.Text)
   Text1.SetFocus
End Sub
```

This procedure activates every time File1.Filename changes. The procedure always works because the Like operator has already filtered out invalid file name characters.

The *Text1_GotFocus* Event Procedure

When the text box gets the focus, you want to highlight its current text. The Text1_GotFocus accomplishes this:

```
Sub Text1_GotFocus ()
   Text1.SelStart = 0
   Text1.SelLength = Len(Text1.Text)
End Sub
```

The *KeyPress* Event Procedures for *Dir1* and *File1*

The final bit of work is creating `KeyPress` event procedures for `File1` and `Dir1`. These procedures enable the user to change directories and select files with the Enter key:

```
Sub File1_KeyPress (KeyAscii As Integer)
    If KeyAscii = 13 Then
        KeyAscii = 0      'Eliminate beep
        File1_DblClick
    End If
End Sub

Sub Dir1_KeyPress (KeyAscii As Integer)
    If KeyAscii = 13 Then
        KeyAscii = 0 'eliminate beep
        Dir1.Path = Dir1.List(Dir1.ListIndex)
    End If
End Sub
```

Terminating the Application

The `Command2_Click` procedure terminates the application when the user clicks Quit:

```
Sub Command2_Click ()
    End
End Sub
```

Running the FileSelector Application

Try running the application. Use the file controls to change the drive or directory, or to select one or more files. When you do, the controls update themselves automatically, and the File list box displays all the file names that match the current specifications. Figure 25.9 shows the FileSelector application in use.

You can type a file name, path, or pattern into the text box. When you press Enter, the file controls are updated.

Figure 25.9.

The FileSelector
application in Run mode.

When you select one or more files in the File list box, then click OK, the
application pops open a message box which lists them (see Figure 25.10).

Figure 25.10.

The selected files are listed
in a dialog box.

Saving the *FileSelector* Application

Save the form as FILESEL.FRM and the application as FILESEL.MAK. In Chapter
27, "Creating Multiple Document Interfaces (MDI)," the FileSelector form is
used to create a file viewer that can display multiple files.

File and Directory Maintenance in Visual Basic

Visual Basic has seven statements that perform DOS-like commands (see
Table 25.4). Use these statements to do file and directory manipulation
in your program code.

Table 25.4. Visual Basic's DOS-like statements.

Visual Basic Statement	Equivalent DOS Command	DOS Abbreviation	Effect
MkDir	MKDIR	MD	Creates a directory
RmDir	RMDIR	RD	Removes (deletes) a directory
ChDrive	*drive:*		Changes current drive
ChDir	CHDIR	CD	Changes current directory
Kill	ERASE	DEL	Deletes a file
Name	RENAME	REN	Renames a file
FileCopy	COPY		Copies a file

The syntax of these seven statements is straightforward:

```
MkDir pathname

RmDir pathname

ChDrive drive

ChDir pathname

Kill filespec

Name oldfilespec As newfilespec

FileCopy oldfilespec, newfilespec
```

in which

   pathname is a string expression specifying a path;

   drive is a string expression specifying a drive letter,

and

   filespec, *oldfilespec*, and *newfilespec* are string expressions that specify a file.

Using *MkDir, RmDir,* and *ChDir*

In a MkDir, RmDir, or ChDir instruction, the *pathname* parameter can optionally include a drive designator. If you omit the drive in *pathname*, Visual Basic assumes the default drive. Standard DOS path-naming conventions apply.

Notice that *pathname* must be a string. For example, to create a directory called \CLIENTS on your B: drive, you could use

```
MkDir "B:\CLIENTS"      'Note the quotation marks
```

or

```
NewDir$ = "B:\CLIENTS"
MkDir NewDir$           'The path is stored in a string variable
```

but not

```
MkDir B:\CLIENTS        'The path is not a string
```

The *pathname* parameter has a limit of 127 characters. If *pathname* is the null string or it does not designate a valid directory, a run time error occurs (Path not found or Bad file name).

The statements MkDir, RmDir, and ChDir operate similar to their DOS counterparts. Refer to your DOS documentation for additional information.

Using *ChDrive*

In a ChDrive expression, the drive parameter must specify a drive letter valid in the computer system. Visual Basic interprets the first character in the *drive* string as indicating the current drive.

For example, each of the following instructions makes drive D the current one:

```
ChDrive "D"
```

```
ChDrive "dog"
```

```
ChDrive MyDrive$    'assuming the value of MyDrive$ starts with D
```

Using *Kill* and *Name*

In a Kill or Name instruction, the *filespec* parameter can optionally include a drive and path specification. If omitted, the default (or current) path is selected. Again, standard DOS-naming conventions apply. A *filespec* has a 63-character limit. For a Kill instruction, wild-card characters (* and ?) are permitted in a *filespec*.

Using the *Kill* Statement

Kill deletes only files, not directories. Use a RmDir instruction to delete directories.

Be careful when using wild-card characters in a *filespec*. You might accidentally erase more than you intended. If you try to Kill a file that is open, an error occurs. (Opening and closing files are discussed later in this chapter.)

Using the *Name* Statement

Name renames a file. The *oldfilespec* parameter identifies the existing file; *newfilespec* is the new name for the file. When *oldfilespec* and *newfilespec* specify the same path, Name simply renames the file on the same drive. After the Name instruction is carried out, the file exists in the same location on the disk, but with a new name. As such, Name performs the same function in Visual Basic that RENAME does in DOS.

However, Name can do something that the DOS RENAME command cannot. Name can move a file to a different directory on the same drive. (Be careful that you don't confuse directory paths.) For example:

```
Name "\VB\GAMES\PINGPONG.FRM" AS "TENNIS.FRM"
```

This instruction moves the file named PINGPONG.FRM from the \VB\GAMES subdirectory on the current drive to its the default directory. After the move, the file is renamed TENNIS.FRM, and no longer exists in any form on the \VB\GAMES directory. The point is that unless \VB\GAMES is the default directory on the current drive, the file changes directories.

When renaming a file on the same drive, you should include the path with each *filespec* (to avoid ambiguities about the default directory). The current example becomes

```
Name "\VB\GAMES\PINGPONG.BAS" As "\VB\GAMES\TENNIS.BAS"
```

Using the *FileCopy* Statement

The FileCopy statement copies a file. FileCopy works similar to Name, with one difference. With FileCopy, the old file remains intact.

The *oldfilespec* parameter specifies the file to copy; *newfilespec* specifies the new file name. Each file specification can include drive and path, but not wild-card characters.

For example, the following instruction copies a file from drive C to a floppy disk in drive A. The file is renamed in the process:

```
FileCopy "C:\VB\SALES\HOMES.FRM", "A:VBHOMES.FRM"
```

The *FileDateTime* Function

The FileDateTime function returns information about the date and time for a file.

> FileDateTime(*filespec*)
>
> in which
>
> > *filespec* is a string expression that specifies a file name.

The *filespec* string can include a drive and path, but not wild-card characters. FileDateTime returns a value of type Variant. For example:

```
Dim MyFileDtTm As Variant
MyFileDtTm = FileDateTime("C:\VB\SALES\HOMES.FRM")
```

The *GetAttr* Function

The GetAttr function returns information about a file, directory, or volume label.

> GetAttr(*filespec*)
>
> in which
>
> > *filespec* is a string expression that specifies a file, directory, or volume label. No wild-card characters are permitted.

The GetAttr function returns an integer value. By using bit masking on the returned value, you can determine various attributes of the file, directory, or volume label (see Table 25.5).

Attribute	*GetAttr* **Value**	**Constant**
ANormal file	0	ATTR_NORMAL
Read-only file	1	ATTR_READONLY
Hidden file	2	ATTR_HIDDEN
System file	4	ATTR_SYSTEM
Volume label	8	ATTR_VOLUME
MS-DOS directory	16	ATTR_DIRECTORY
Archived file	32	ATTR_ARCHIVE

Table 25.5. Attributes returned by the *GetAttr* function.

The constants in the third column of the table are obtained from Visual Basic's CONSTANT.TXT file. By loading CONSTANT.TXT into your application, you can use these constants to do bit mapping on values returned from the GetAttr function. If you use the And operator with the various constants, you can test for specific attributes. For example:

```
If (GetAttr("C:\DOCS\RESUME.TXT") And ATTR_READONLY Then
    ' File is read only  -  place appropriate code here
Else
    ' File is not read only  -- place appropriate code here
End If
```

If more than one attribute is present in a file, the returned value from GetAttr is the sum of all of them. For example, GetAttr returns 6 for a system file that is hidden.

Reading the archive attribute is often useful. The archive attribute specifies whether a file has been modified since it was last saved on disk.

The *SetAttr* Statement

Using the SetAttr statement, you can specify attributes for a file.

```
SetAttr(filespec, attributes)
```

in which

continues

continued

> *filespec* is a string expression that specifies a file. You can include drive and path information, but no wild-card characters are permitted,

and

> *attributes* is an integer value that indicates the attributes to be set.

The value of attributes specifies the attributes that Table 25.5 shows. However, the volume and directory attributes (values 8 and 16, respectively) are not available. You can combine attribute values to specify multiple attributes with a single instruction. The following are some sample instructions using SetAttr:

```
SetAttr("C:\SALES\HOMES.TXT", ATTR_READONLY)  'Set to read-only

SetAttr("C:\PROGS\SALARY.DOC", 3)   'Hidden and read-only
```

The *CurDir$* Function

The CurDir$ function returns a string that indicates the current path for a specified disk drive. The companion function, CurDir, returns a Variant (of type string).

```
CurDir$(drivename)

CurDir(drivename)
```

in which

> *drivename* is a string expression that specifies a valid disk drive designation.

The *drivename* parameter is optional.

Using the *Dir$* Function

The Dir$ function returns a string that indicates a file or directory matching specified conditions. The companion function, Dir, returns a Variant (of type string).

Dir$(*filespec*, *attributes*)

Dir(*filespec*, *attributes*)

in which

    filespec is a string expression that specifies a path, filename (or both),

and

    attributes is a numeric expression which specifies the types of files to return.

As explained shortly, the *filespec* parameter is sometimes optional. The *attributes* parameter is always optional.

The *attributes* parameter qualifies the directory and file names that the functions can return. As Table 25.6 shows, you can specify file types and other options by setting *attributes* to the appropriate numeric value.

 NOTE You can use the appropriate constants in CONSTANT.TXT to specify the values that Table 25.6 shows. (Table 25.5 lists these constants.)

Table 25.6. Values of the *attributes* parameter.

Value	Description
0	Normal files
2	Hidden files
4	System files
8	Volume label
16	Directory

You can specify combinations by adding the values of the desired attributes. For example, a value of 6 specifies hidden and system files. However, you cannot combine the Volume label option with any other items. If you omit the attributes parameter, the default value is 0 (normal files).

Each call to Dir$ (or Dir) returns a single file name or path. By making repeated calls, you can eventually return all the file names that meet the search criteria. When all names have been returned, the functions produce a null string (zero length).

The first time you call Dir$ (or Dir), you must specify *filespec*. After the first call, you can use Dir$ or Dir (no parameters), to return the subsequent file names that match *filespec* and *attributes*.

As an example, the follow instruction sets the value of HiddenFile$ to a hidden file on the C:\DOS directory:

```
HiddenFile$ = Dir$("C:\DOS", 2)
```

Using Data Files

As a programmer, you face a recurring challenge: getting data into, and saving information created by, your applications. The following shows two of the simplest ways to input data into your applications:

- *Store the data directly in the program.* This is the simplest method. An assignment instruction such as

  ```
  City$ = "Phoenix"
  ```

  stores the data (Phoenix in this case) as part of the program itself.

- *Ask the user for the data.* When the person running the program must supply data, the program can prompt the user to type the data on the keyboard. Your primary tools for this method are both text and InputBox dialog boxes.

These methods work well, but they're only appropriate when the amount of data is relatively small. Suppose you want to write an application that manages a large database, such as your baseball card collection, a mailing list, or the inventory of a hardware store. It's just not feasible to store all the necessary data inside the program or ask the user to supply it when the program runs. Furthermore, the data changes with time, and it needs periodic updating.

The common solution to these problems is to use a data file on disk. The data file can be on either a floppy or a hard disk. Once a data file exists, your program can read directly from the file the data, process it, then write a new (or updated) data file directly to the disk.

By storing data on disk files, independently from the .FRM and .BAS files, you enjoy many tangible benefits:

- Data files can be maintained and updated.

- Large databases can be accessed conveniently.

- Programs are kept intact, and relatively small.

- Files can be shared by several applications.

- Data files created from external sources (such as a word processor or spreadsheet) can be read.

Manipulating Data Files—General Techniques

Visual Basic supports three kinds of data files:

- *Sequential files* store data as ASCII text. Information is read from, and written to the file character by character.

- *Random-access files* store data in special Visual Basic internal formats. Such files require a rigid file structure.

- *Binary files* store data as individual bytes. No file structure exists, and no special internal formats are assumed.

Each file type has certain advantages and disadvantages. In general, sequential files are easy to program and understand, but reading and writing them is relatively slow. Random-access files require more programming complexity, but the I/O operations are relatively fast. Binary files provide maximum flexibility, but impose the greatest demands on the programmer to keep track of the file organization. The remainder of this chapter discusses these trade-offs in detail.

Whether a program uses sequential, random-access, or binary files, some general techniques are common to all three file types. To communicate with a disk file, a program must follow these essential steps:

1. Open the data file. Using the Open statement, you inform Visual Basic of the name and type of the file, and how the program expects to use it.

2. Either read data from, or write it (or do both) to the file. Visual Basic provides a variety of statements to perform I/O operations.

3. Close the data file. With the Close statement, your program terminates I/O operations on the data file.

Using the *Open* Statement

You must establish a communication link before using any disk file. An Open instruction serves several purposes:

- Declares the name and path of the data file
- Establishes the file type, and the I/O mode
- Opens a communications channel between the program and the file
- Associates an integer number with the data file

The remainder of this chapter frequently examines varieties of the Open instruction while discussing the different file types.

Using the *Close* Statement

After your program concludes I/O activity on a data file, use a Close instruction to cancel the communications link. Close terminates the association between the data file on disk and the corresponding file number. The Close statement is explored in detail as each file type is discussed.

Using Files for Database Maintenance

The most common application for both sequential and random-access files is database maintenance. A *database* is simply a collection of related information. For discussion purposes, each database is stored in a separate disk file.

NOTE Here, the term *database* refers to file structures that you design for customized applications. Visual Basic also supports an interface with commercial database packages, such as Microsoft Access. For more information on Visual Basic's data control, and linking to commercial database managers, see Chapter 28, "Using the Data Control to Interact with Databases."

A database consists of a series of *records*. Each record is divided into one or more *fields*. For example, in a personnel list, each employee becomes a record in the database file. The fields for each employee might include name, department, salary, and service date.

Consider a database of your stock investments. Each stock you own is a record. The fields might be the name of the stock, date of purchase, the cost, and the current value.

A Coin Collection—a Sample Database

To provide a common thread in the discussion of various file types, consider a sample database that is a coin collection. Suppose that, as a budding numismatist, you decide to maintain a list of your coin assets in a customized database file.

Each coin is a record in your database. For every coin, you want to record four kinds of information:

- The year the coin was minted
- The category of coin (penny, dime, quarter, and so on)
- The value of the coin
- Any additional pertinent information about the coin

Assume your coin collection consists of three coins. (Okay, you're not Donald Trump yet, but you've got to start somewhere!)

Your database file consists of three records, one for each coin. You can organize the three records in the database that Table 25.7 shows.

Table 25.7. A coin collection database.

Year	Category	Value	Comments
1910	Lincoln penny	$70.00	S mint mark, uncirculated
1916	Mercury dime	$47.25	
1935	Silver dollar	$200.00	Bought at auction for $75

The discussion of both sequential and random-access files in this chapter frequently refers to ways of manipulating this database.

Sequential Files

You write sequential files as ASCII (character) text. This gives the files a degree of portability. Many word-processing programs, and other commercial applications, can read and write ASCII files. Further, the Windows Notepad utility can work with ASCII files, which you can view with the TYPE command from the DOS prompt.

In a record, fields are separated by commas. Record boundaries are maintained automatically. Visual Basic provides several statements to read and write sequential files conveniently. Therefore, programming is relatively easy.

However, sequential files have two main drawbacks:

- You must read records sequentially. Out of 50 records, for example, you want information in the fiftieth. You must first read through 49 of them. This process is relatively slow.

- You cannot read and write a sequential file simultaneously. You must open the file for either reading or writing, and close it before reopening to work in the other mode.

You might think of a sequential file as something similar to a cassette music tape (see Figure 25.11). Individual songs on the tape are similar to records on the file. You must first play through the previous songs to listen to one in the middle of the tape. Similarly, you must first read the previous records to examine one in the middle of the file.

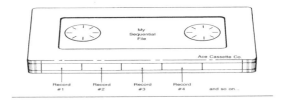

Figure 25.11.

A sequential file is similar to a cassette music tape.

Creating a Sequential File

When creating a sequential file, your program must follow these steps:

1. Open the file as a sequential file for writing.
2. Prepare your data for writing to the file.
3. Use the Write# instruction to write data to the file.
4. Close the file.

The next few sections give an explanation of each step.

Opening the File

The Open statement has many forms. The following is the fundamental syntax used when creating a new sequential file.

```
Open filespec For Output As #filenum
```

in which

   filespec is a string expression that specifies the name (and, optionally, the path) of the new sequential data file,

and

   filenum is an integer expression from 1 to 255 that associates a numeric value with the opened file.

For example, the following instruction creates and opens a sequential file named MYDATA.QUE (on the root directory of the C: drive). A file number of 35 is assigned to this file:

```
Open "C:\MYDATA.QUE" For Output As #35
```

The pound character (#) is optional before the *filenum* parameter. That is, you can also write the previous instruction as follows:

```
Open "C:\MYDATA.QUE" For Output As 35   'No # before file number
```

The phrase For Output tells Visual Basic that this file is a sequential file to which the program writes output. (As you will see later in this chapter, Open accepts other phrases with additional meanings.)

When you open a file For Output, it does not need to already exist. In fact, the file should *not* already exist. Why? The reason is that if the file already exists, Visual Basic completely erases its contents without even a warning. Don't open an existing file For Output unless you intend to create a brand new one.

Make sure Open instructions specify the path and file correctly. You don't want to lose data inadvertently by specifying the wrong file. Of course, it's a good idea to have a backup version of your important files for such emergencies.

The file number (35 in our current example) provides a convenient way to refer to the file in later program instructions. As you will see, when you want to write data to the file, you instruct Visual Basic to write on file number 35, rather than specifying the complete file name. The Open instruction tells Visual Basic exactly what file you mean when you indicate number 35.

Preparing the Data

When you first create a database file, you must somehow get the data into your program. You must decide the best way to enter the data. Several methods exist. You usually use one, or a combination, of the following techniques:

- Enter data explicitly in the program using assignment instructions.
- Use text boxes and other Visual Basic controls to prompt the user for data.
- Read data from other data files or devices.
- Compute data values using various Visual Basic functions.

Writing the Data

When it's ready, write the record to the disk file using the `Write#` instruction. `Write#` works with both strings and numbers.

```
Write #filenum, expressionlist
```

in which

   `filenum` is the file number,

and

   `expressionlist` is a list of expressions separated by commas.

The `expressionlist` parameter is optional.

Each `Write#` instruction writes one record to the file. Each expression in `expressionlist` is the data for one field of the record.

`Write#` does some special formatting. A comma is placed between each item in `expressionlist`. String values are enclosed in quotation marks.

If you omit `expressionlist`, the instruction places a blank line in the file.

Often, you place the `Write#` instruction in a loop that processes all the records in the data file.

Closing the File

After you have written all the records to the file, close it with a Close instruction.

```
Close #filenum
```

in which

>   filenum is an integer expression that specifies the file to close.

>   As with Open instructions, the pound sign (#) is optional.

For example, the following instruction closes file number 35 (which was previously opened for output):

```
Close #35
```

Close terminates the association of the file number with the data file. As a result, the file number becomes available for a subsequent Open instruction. Close also flushes the file buffer, which means that all information written to the file is properly processed.

Creating the Sample Data File MYCOINS.SEQ

Remember the coin collection? The following code fragment creates a new sequential data file called MYCOINS.SEQ and places it in the COINS directory on drive C:

```
Rem Creating Sequential Data File: C:\COINS\MYCOINS.SEQ
Dim Yr%, Category$, Valu!, Comment$
Dim EndFlag as Integer
Open "C:\COINS\MYCOINS.SEQ" For Output As #1

    Do
        '    For each record in file, get data for
        '    Yr%, Category$, Valu!, and Comment$
        Call GetInfo(Yr%, Category$, Valu!, Comment$, EndFlag)
        If EndFlag then Exit Do
        Write #1, Yr%, Category$, Valu!, Comment$
    Loop

    Close #1
    Rem    All Done - C:\COINS\MYCOINS.SEQ is created"
```

The Open instruction declares that the file will be written on drive C:. The \COINS directory must exist, or an error occurs.The Open instruction assigns the file number 1 to the newly opened file.

 NOTE   When specifying a file name in an Open instruction, you generally provide a path as part of the name. If you open a file For Output without specifying a path, Visual Basic places the file in the current directory. Be aware that the file is not placed in the root directory or the Visual Basic directory.

Each data record corresponds to one coin in the collection. Each record contains four fields on the coin: the year it was minted; its category; its value, and any pertinent comments. Two of the fields (year and value) are numeric, and two (category and comment) are string.

The year is a whole number, such as 1976 which is suitable for an integer variable: Yr%. (You can't use the variable name Year% because Year is a reserved word.)

The value is expressed in dollars and cents, such as 47.25 which is suitable for a single-precision variable: Valu!. (Although you could use the variable name Value!, it's best to avoid potential confusion with the Value property of command buttons and other controls.) Furthermore, you can use the Currency data type, but the extra precision required for that type is not necessary here.

The category and comment are stored in the variable-length string variables Category$ and Comment$, respectively.

The Do-Loop block contains a call to a user-defined procedure named GetInfo. This procedure must prompt the user to supply the information for the next coin. The procedure can set up a form with four text boxes, one for each of the four pieces of information. The True/False variable EndFlag indicates if all the data has been entered. The form set up by GetInfo might contain two command buttons. One signals that the typed data is correct, but more info is coming—EndFlag is set to False in this case. The other button signals that the typed data is correct, and no more data is to come—EndFlag is set to True.

For each coin, GetInfo passes back a value for Yr%, Category$, Valu!, and Comment$. Then, the Write #1 instruction writes the record to the data file. Notice that you write all four data fields with a single Write# instruction. The #1 is the same file number you assigned to the file in the Open instruction.

When EndFlag is True, the Exit Do instruction terminates the Do-Loop block. The Close instruction closes the data file.

Examining a Sequential Data File

Suppose you have three coins in your collection. Table 25.8 shows the pertinent data for these coins.

Table 25.8. The coin collection.			
Year	**Category**	**Value**	**Comment**
1910	Lincoln Penny	$70.00	S mint mark, uncirculated
1916	Mercury Dime	$47.25	
1935	Silver Dollar	$200.00	Bought at auction for $75

To create the file MYCOINS.SEQ, you run your program that generates the sequential file for the coin database. Sequential files are standard ASCII text files. Therefore, they are easy to examine. You can view and modify the file with most word processors and text editors.

Try Windows Notepad to see what MYCOINS.SEQ looks like. From the Accessories group in the Windows Program Manager, launch the NotePad application. From NotePad, choose the **O**pen option from the **F**ile menu. Specify the file C:\COINS\MYCOINS.SEQ (or whatever path and name you have used). The contents of the file should resemble the following:

```
1910,"Lincoln Penny",70,"S mint mark, uncirculated"
1916,"Mercury Dime",47.25,""
1935,"Silver Dollar",200,"Bought at auction for $75"
```

The three records (lines) of this file were created with Visual Basic's `Write#` statement. Notice how `Write#` formats the output. `Write#` places a comma between adjacent fields in each record.

String values are enclosed in double quotation marks. This avoids ambiguity if a string value contains an embedded comma. A null string appears as two consecutive quotes—for example, the comment field (final one) of the second record. Numbers do not contain any leading or trailing blanks. This saves disk space by minimizing the file size.

You will soon see that you can read sequential files with `Input#` instructions. `Write#` creates records in the exact form that `Input#` expects.

Appending a Sequential File

Suppose you acquire some new coins. To accommodate your growing collection, you want to adds new records to the end of your existing sequential file MYCOINS.SEQ. The process of adding new records is called *appending* the file.

To append a sequential file, you open it in a special mode called Append. In the Open instruction, use the phrase For Append rather than For Output. For example, the Open instruction for the coin file can appear as follows:

```
Open "C:\COINS\MYCOINS.SEQ" For Append As #1
```

The following are the four steps necessary to append records to an existing sequential data file:

1. Open the file For Append.

2. Prepare your data for writing to the file.

3. Use the Write# instruction to write additional data records at the end of the file.

4. Close the file.

Only the first step differs from the process of creating a new file. Opening a file for Append readies a previously existing one to receive additional records.

If the Open instruction specifies a nonexistent file, one is created just as though it was opened for Output.

Reading a Sequential File

Reading information from a sequential file involves the following steps:

1. Open the file For Input.

2. Use the Input# instruction to read data into variables.

3. Process the data.

4. Close the file.

The first step introduces the third way to open a sequential data file: For Input. (For Output and For Append are the other two ways.) By opening a file for input, you tell Visual Basic that you intend to *read from* the file rather than *write to* it. When you open a file For Input, you can only read records from it. You cannot write any records to the file. For example, the following instruction opens the MYCOINS.SEQ sequential database file for input and specifies 1 as the file number:

```
Open "C:\COINS\MYCOINS.SEQ" For Input As #1
```

Of course, when you open a file for input, it must already exist. If Visual Basic cannot find your specified file, a `File not found` error results.

The *Input#* Statement

After you open a file for input, to read records from it use an `Input#` instruction. `Input#` and `Write#` are complementary statements. `Input#` reads a data record from a file opened for input; `Write#` writes a record to a file opened for output.

`Input#` is designed for reading sequential files created with `Write#`. An `Input#` instruction reverses the process of a `Write#` one.

As with `Write#`, an `Input#` instruction also contains a variable list. `Input#` reads from a sequential file a data record and stores its values in the list's variables.

```
Input #filenum, variablelist
```

in which

   filenum is the file number,

and

   variablelist is a list of variables separated by commas.

To use `Input#`, you must know the number of fields in each record and the type of data in each field. The variables in *variablelist* should match the file data. You guarantee correct matching if the variable list in the `Input#` instruction is exactly the same as the variable list used in the `Write#` instruction that created the file record.

With `Input#`, you can read numeric data into a string variable. However, you cannot read string data into a numeric variable. Of course, Variant variables can handle either type of data.

Even if you need only some of the information in a record, you should read all the fields of the record to make sure that Visual Basic correctly keeps your place in the file.

Usually *variablelist* consists of the same variable names used in the complementary `Write#` instruction that created the file. Such consistency ensures that the data file is read successfully.

Calculating the Total Value of the Coin Collection

Suppose you want to determine the total value of your coin collection. You have three coins: a penny worth $70, a dime worth $47.25, and a Silver Dollar worth $200. The total value should be $317.25.

The following code fragment opens MYCOINS.SEQ for input, reads the data with Input#, and calculates the total value of all the coins in the collection:

```
Dim Yr%, Category$, Valu!, Comment$
Dim TotalValue As Single

Open "C:\COINS\MYCOINS.SEQ" For Input As #1

TotalValue! = 0!
Do Until EOF(1)
    Input #1, Yr%, Category$, Valu!, Comment$
    TotalValue! = TotalValue! + Valu!
Loop

Close #1
MsgBox "Total Value is " & Str$(TotalValue!)
```

Running this program opens a message box that displays the following output:

```
Total value is  $317.25
```

The total is verified!

Notice that the Input# instruction reads all four fields of each record (year, category, value, and comment) even though only Valu! is actually used in the calculations. This follows the practice of making the variable list of the Input# instruction duplicate the one of the Write# instruction which created the file. By matching the variable lists exactly, you make sure that Visual Basic retains the correct place in the file as you read each record.

The *EOF* Function

You might have noticed the EOF function in the previous code fragment. EOF (*End Of F*ile) tests whether the end of a sequential file has been reached.

```
EOF(filenum)
```

in which

    filenum is the file number.

EOF returns a Boolean value: True (1) if the end of file was reached, or False (0) otherwise. This means that you can use EOF with If, Do Until, and While instructions. By using EOF, you don't have to know beforehand how many records are in your data file.

Be sure that you test for EOF before attempting to read past the end of the file. A run time error occurs (Input past end of file) if you try to execute an Input# instruction when the last record has already been read.

Modifying a Sequential Data File

Suppose you want to update some information in your data file. Perhaps the value of a coin changes, and you want to modify the Value field in some of the records.

Updating presents a complication because you can't open a sequential file for reading and writing at the same time. Furthermore, the Output and Append modes let you only add records, not edit existing ones.

The following are three basic solutions to this problem:

■ Open two data files simultaneously—the original file For Input, and a new one For Output. Read each record from the old file into variables. Update the values of these variables as necessary. Then, rewrite the updated record to the new file.

■ Open the original file For Input. Read all the records into arrays. Close the file. Update the data in the arrays as necessary. Open the file again, this time For Output. Write all the data back to the file.

■ Use a word processor or text editor to modify the data file.

The following sections discuss each of the three methods.

Opening Two Files Simultaneously

You can have several files open at the same time. Of course, each file must have a unique file number.

The maximum number of files you can open simultaneously depends on your hardware configuration, and the version of DOS. From DOS, you can use the FILES command in your CONFIG.SYS file to change the default maximum number of opened files. Refer to your DOS documentation for more details.

In a program that opens multiple files, when you need to open a new one, you might not always know which file numbers are already in use. For example, this might occur when files are opened as a result of If tests.

The `FreeFile` function returns the lowest unused file number. The function accepts no parameters, so the syntax is simply

```
FreeFile
```

The `FreeFile` function guarantees to return a *filenum* value that is not currently in use. The following program fragment shows a typical use of `FreeFile`:

```
MyFileNumber% = FreeFile
Open "C:\MYFILE.DTA" For Output As MyFileNumber%
```

One advantage of opening two files, and writing only to the new one, is that the original data file remains intact. This provides a measure of redundancy and safety. You always have the old data file if you make a mistake, or suffer one of those "always at the worst time" system hangups.

Using Arrays

The variable lists in `Input#` and `Write#` instructions can consist of individual array elements. The following code fragment shows how you might update the coin data file using arrays:

```
Rem  Update Coin Values Using Arrays"
Dim Yr%(100), Category$(100), Valu!(100), Comment$(100)
Dim Count As Integer, J As Integer
Open "C:\COINS\MYCOINS.SEQ" For Input As #1

Count = 0
Do Until EOF(1)
   Count = Count + 1
   Input #1, Yr%(Count), Category$(Count), _
           Valu!(Count), Comment$(Count)  'This is one line

   '
   '  Update the array values here
   '
Loop
Close #1

Open "C:\COINS\MYCOINS.SEQ" For Output As #1    'Reopen file for output

For J = 1 To Count
   Write #1, Yr%(J), Category$(J), Valu!(J), Comment$(J)
Next J

Rem   All Done -- C:\COINS\MYCOINS.SEQ updated and rewritten"
Close #1
```

NOTE The `Input #1...` instruction is shown on two physical lines for typographic purposes in this book. When typing this line, remove the underscore character and create one long line.

In this code fragment, four arrays replace the four simple variables. When using this technique, be sure to dimension your arrays sufficiently.

Modifying the File Externally

You can modify your data file with a word processor or text editor. This can be somewhat hazardous to the file formatting. You must be sure to preserve this formatting. Be careful to keep the delimiters intact, and make sure your word processor does not add any extraneous control characters.

Some file modifications are easier to do externally than with a Visual Basic program. As an example, suppose that you want to delete an entire record from your data file.

You can use Windows Notepad. Simply load in the data file, highlight the record to be deleted, then press Del. Save the file, and the job is complete.

Other Sequential File Tools

Visual Basic offers other statements and functions for use with sequential files in special situations. The following sections briefly discuss these other tools with an emphasis on when you might need to use them.

Using the *Line Input#* Statement

`Line Input#` reads an entire record into a single string variable.

```
Line Input #filenum, stringvar
```
in which

   `filenum` is the file number,

and

   `stringvar` is a string variable.

Each record is read in its entirety, including any commas or quotation marks. For example, the first record from MYCOINS.SEQ resembles this:

```
1910,"Lincoln Penny",70,"S mint mark, uncirculated"
```

You might read this record with the following instruction:

```
Line Input #1, MyData$
```

This instruction assigns to MyData$ an exact copy of the entire record, including the quotation marks and commas.

Use Line Input# when a file has either a special or an unknown structure. Perhaps the file was not created with Write#. Or you don't know the exact Write# instruction that was used to create the file. Another possibility is that the number of fields varies from record to record.

In such cases, the programmer is responsible for analyzing the data in *stringvar* appropriately. Depending on the situation, your program might have to search for meaningful delimiters, or break down *stringvar* into usable components.

Reading with the *Input$* and *Input* Functions

Both Input$ and Input read a specified number of characters from the current record. Input$ returns a string while Input returns a Variant (of type string).

```
Input$(numchar, #filenum)

Input(numchar, #filenum)
```

in which

　　numchar is an integer expression that specifies how many characters should be read,

and

　　filenum is the file number.

The pound sign (#) before the file number is optional.

For example, the following instruction reads the next 12 characters from the current record of file number 1 into the string variable NextDozen$:

```
NextDozen$ = Input$(12, #1)
```

Using the *LOF* Function

The LOF function (*Length Of File*) returns the number of bytes (length) of a data file. LOF is handy in certain critical disk-storage situations. One application of LOF is testing whether a file has become too large to save on disk.

```
LOF(filenum)
```

in which

    filenum is the file number of an opened file.

As an example of LOF, the following instruction displays the length of file number 8:

```
MsgBox "Size of file 8 is " & Str$(LOF(8))
```

 NOTE   Visual Basic also has the FileLen function which returns the length of a file (opened or not) as a long integer. The syntax is FileLen(*filespec*) where *filespec* is a string expression that specifies the file name (with or without drive and path).

Using the *Print#* Statement

In addition to using Write#, you can write data to a sequential file using the Print# statement.

```
Print#filenum, expressionlist
```

in which

    filenum is the file number,

and

    expressionlist is a list of expressions separated by commas and semi colons (and optionally ending with either one).

Print# sends to a file some data, much as the Print method displays it on a form. See Chapter 12, "Displaying Text and Fonts," for a detailed discussion of the Print method.

However, Print# generally does not write information in a format suitable for subsequent reading by Input#. The reason is that Print# neither automatically places quotation marks around strings, nor separates fields with commas.

So why would you ever want to use Print#? Actually, you wouldn't if you're writing to files that Input# is going to read later.

There are, however, other reasons to create sequential files. You might want to generate a file destined to be read by people, or go into a word processor, or another application, such as a spreadsheet. Such applications require files designed in specialized formats. Print# supplies this capability.

Setting and Determining the File Position with *Seek* and *Loc*

The Seek statement resets the file position pointer for the next read or write. The Seek and Loc functions return the current position in the file. To use these features, you must consider the file as a sequence of data bytes. The first byte of the file is 1.

The Seek statement sets the file pointer to a specified position.

Seek #*filenum*, *position*

in which

   filenum is the file number of an open file,

and

   position specifies the file position as a byte in the range from 1 to 2,147,483,647.

   The pound sign (#) before the file number is optional.

The Seek function returns the current file position.

Seek(*filenum*)

in which

   filenum is the file number of an opened file.

The Loc function returns the last byte written or read, but in a modified form.

Loc(*filenum*)

in which

> *filenum* is the file number of an opened file.

Loc considers a sequential file to be divided into 128-byte blocks. Loc returns the block number of the file position. For example, if the last byte read from or written to is 287, Loc returns 3 (the byte is inside the third 128-byte block).

By convention, Loc returns 1 (not 0) for a file opened, but not yet read from or written to.

Sequential files usually are not handled byte by byte. Therefore, Seek and Loc are not particularly useful with such files. As you see later in this chapter, however, Seek and Loc become important with random-access and binary files.

Summary of Statements and Functions for Sequential Files

Table 25.9 summarizes the statements and functions available for sequential file processing.

Table 25.9. Sequential file statements and functions.

Keyword	Type	Effect
Open	Statement	Opens a file in specified mode
Close	Statement	Closes a file
Write#	Statement	Writes comma-delimited information
Input#	Statement	Reads comma-delimited information
Print#	Statement	Writes space-delimited information
Input$	Function	Reads given number of characters
Line Input#	Statement	Reads entire record
EOF	Function	Tests for end of file
LOF	Function	Returns size of file
Seek	Statement	Sets file position pointer
Seek	Function	Returns current file position
Loc	Function	Returns current file position

Using Random-Access Files

The second kind of disk data file is the random-access (or simply *random*). Random files meet the needs of large database file applications.

Random files require more complex programming than the sequential ones. Compared to sequential files, however, random files offer these significant advantages:

- Two-way I/O activity. When opened, a random file can be read from and written to.

- Random-access. You can access any record quickly and conveniently.

- Record modification. You can modify individual records without rewriting all the other ones.

As you have seen, you have to read all previous records to get to the one you want to examine in a sequential file. For example, if your application needs only the information in the seventy-fifth record, you must read all the information in the first seventy-four. The deeper into the file the record you want to retrieve is located, the longer it takes to access it.

By contrast, random files are organized in a fashion that more resembles a compact disk player, which can efficiently locate any song on a disk. Random files reference individual records by number. By simply specifying a record number, you can access that record's information quickly. The access time is virtually the same for the first record as for the fiftieth. Random files are the only practical choice for large database applications.

Furthermore, once you read a random file record, you can modify the data. You can rewrite the record directly—no need to close and reopen the file. Appending records is also straightforward.

Random files might seem the best answer for disk database programming. After all, random file records are swiftly read anywhere in the file which can be opened for input and output simultaneously. Why would anyone use sequential files?

Computing, similar to life, is always a series of trade-offs. The following includes some disadvantages—the price you must pay to use random files:

- Rigid file structure. Each record of a random file must have the same configuration: the number of fields, and data type for each one, cannot vary from record to record.

- Lack of portability. You cannot easily read random files with applications, such as word processors, spreadsheets, and text editors. The TYPE command in DOS does not display random files.

- Increased programming effort. For random files, programming is more complex than for sequential ones.

Similar to a sequential file, a random file is a series of records, each one consisting of data fields. Unlike a sequential file, each random file record has a predetermined size that cannot change throughout the file.

Designing a Random-Access File

You might think of a random-access file record as somewhat similar to a survey form—the kind in which you provide data in marked boxes. As Figure 25.12 shows, such forms often provide one box for each data character.

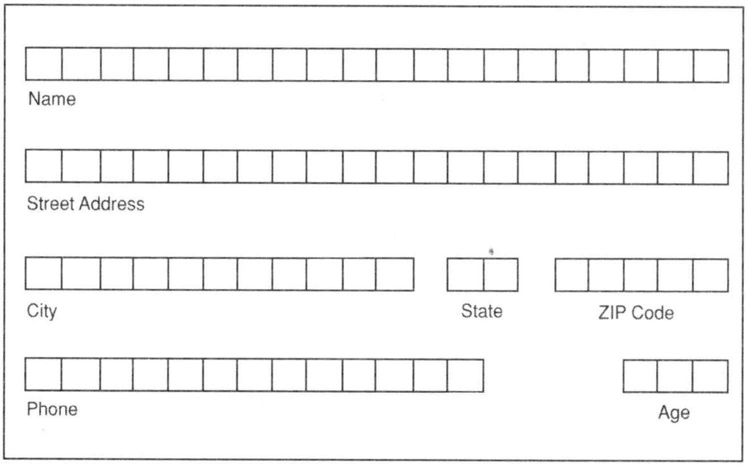

Name

Street Address

City   State   ZIP Code

Phone   Age

Figure. 25.12

A fixed-field data form.

Notice that each field in the form has its own fixed size. The data for one field can require less than the allocated number of characters. You cannot, however, use more characters than allocated. For example, the sample form has a name field of 20 characters. You can enter a name of less than 20 characters, but you can't use more than that number.

This fixed-field size requirement is exactly the situation with random-access files. You must determine a template form for each record. The number of fields, and the size of each, must remain constant throughout the file. You can let each field be any size, but once you specify it, you cannot make a change.

As a result, the size (number of bytes) of each record is constant in a random-access file. That's why Visual Basic can access any record quickly. The reason is that the record size is constant. When a record number is given, the position of the data on the disk is readily computed. For any record in the file, the computer takes essentially the same time to determine the location of the data, find it, then read the information.

Before using a random-access file, you must design the template for each record. Decide how many fields each record has. Then, decide the size of each field. You need to treat text fields differently than you do numeric ones.

Creating Text Fields in a Random-Access File

Determine the maximum number of characters a text field can have. For each record in the file, you allocate that maximum size for the field, whether or not all the characters are actually used.

For example, you can determine that a field reserved for a customer's name should be allocated 30 characters. Whether the actual data is I. M. Sly, Ace Accordion Supply, or Rumplestiltskin Meriweather, that field always occupies 30 bytes (characters) in the data file.

Creating Numeric Fields in a Random-Access File

Random-access files save numbers in the internal binary formats that Visual Basic uses to store numbers in memory. This means that for each numeric field, you designate one of Visual Basic's five numeric types: integer, long integer, single-precision, double-precision, or currency.

Be careful that you choose the numeric type of each field wisely. The numeric type of each field must accommodate every entry for that field. If it contains a number with a fractional component, such as 34.67, that field must be single- or double-precision. For whole numbers, the integer type is limited to 32,767. Use long integer if your values might be larger than 32,767.

Numbers are stored in their binary form. Therefore, the size (in bytes) of each field is determined by the data type (see Table 25.10).

Table 25.10. Size of numeric types.

Number Type	Size (Bytes)
Integer	2
Long integer	4
Single-precision	4
Double-precision	8
Currency	8

For example, a field reserved for a single-precision number is allocated four bytes. Whether the actual data is 10, 28.699, or 6.04E-28, the number is stored in four bytes, just as it can be in the machine's RAM.

A Sample Record

Suppose that you want to design a random file database for the coin collection. Each record (coin) requires four fields: Year, Category, Value, and Comment.

Year is a whole number expressed in four digits, such as 1947. The Integer type is appropriate, so the first field requires two bytes.

Category is a text field. Twenty characters should be enough to describe each coin's category, so the second field is 20 bytes.

Value is a numeric field expressed in dollars and cents, such as 135.50. No coin is worth more than 3000 dollars. Single-precision numbers easily satisfy this data range, so the third field is four bytes long. (The Currency type offers more precision than necessary, and requires twice as much memory storage.)

Comment is a text field. The data for this field varies widely from coin to coin. Fifty characters should be enough, so the length of the fourth field is 50 bytes.

The Comment field typifies the squandering of disk space that can occur with random-access files. For many coins, the Comment field might be short or blank, yet a full 50 bytes is still reserved. This squandering is the price that must be paid to maintain rigid file structure. Typically, a database stored as a random file takes more room on disk than the same database stored as a sequential file.

Figure 25.13 shows the template form for each record of the coin collection database. The total size of each record is fixed at 76 bytes.

Data Type	# Bytes
Integer	2
String *20	20
Single-Precision	4
String *50	50
Total =	76

Figure 25.13.

The random-access record for each coin.

Using a Random-Access File with User-Defined Data Types

The user-defined data type lets you create natural data structures to describe your database records (see Chapter 19, "Using Arrays and Structures").

After you create a user-defined data type, you can designate variables to possess it. These are known as *record* variables.

When you associate a user-defined variable with your database record template, transferring data to and from random files is easy.

Use the following steps to process random files with record variables:

1. Define a record variable matching your database template.

2. Open the file For Random.

3. Use record variables in Get and Put instructions to read and write the data.

4. Close the file.

The following sections examine these four steps.

Defining the Record Variable

Recall from Chapter 19 that you use a Type-End block to create a record (user-defined) data type. For example, the following block creates the data type CoinType which is appropriate for the coin collection database. The ensuing Dim instruction declares the record variable Coin to have the data type CoinType.

```
Type CoinType
    Yr As Integer
    Category As String * 20
    Valu As Single
    Comment As String * 50
End Type

Dim Coin As CoinType
```

Opening the File

You can open a sequential file in Input, Output, or Append mode. By contrast, you always open a random file For Random. The Open instruction adds a Len clause that specifies the length of each record in the file.

```
Open filespec For Random As #filenum Len = recordlength
```

in which

    filespec specifies the name and path of the data file;

    filenum is the file number,

and

recordlength is an integer expression specifying, in bytes, the size of each record.

The pound sign (#) in front of the *filenum* parameter is optional. The For Random and Len clauses are optional, as this section explains.

A single Open instruction opens a random file for any or all I/O activities—reading, writing, and appending.

Suppose that you design a random-access database file for your coin collection. You want to describe each coin (record in the file) with a variable of the user-defined type CoinType. Remember, the size of each record is 76 bytes (2 for the year, 20 for the category, 4 for the value, and 50 for the comments). So 76 is the value for the *recordlength* parameter in the Len clause of the Open instruction.

You name the file MYCOINS.RAN (here the file extension .RAN is used for random files), and it is on a disk in the B: drive. Then, the following instruction opens MYCOINS.RAN as file number 1:

```
Open "B:MYCOINS.RAN" For Random As #1 Len = 76
```

The For Random clause is optional because random-access is the default mode for the Open instruction. This means you can open the coin database file as follows:

```
Open "B:MYCOINS.RAN" As #1 Len = 76
```

However, for clarity, it's a good idea to always include the For Random clause.

As you have seen, the Len clause specifies the length, in bytes, of each random access record. For optimal efficiency, the value in the Len clause should precisely match the record length. Although wasteful of disk space, the value in the Len clause can be larger than the actual record length.

The following tip helps you specify Len clauses in your random-access Open instructions. The Len function calculates the length (number of bytes) of any variable, including a record variable.

Len(*variable*)

in which

variable is any variable.

Notice that this is a second form of the Len function. Chapter 17, "Working With Strings," introduced the alternate form, which returns the number of characters in a string.

It is helpful to use the Len function in the Len clause of the Open instruction. That way, you don't have to know or supply the exact length of the record data type. For example:

```
Open "B:MYCOINS.RAN" For Random as #1 Len = Len(Coin)
```

Remember that the Len clause is optional. If you omit it in an Open instruction, the record length defaults to 128 bytes.

Writing and Reading Records

Use the Put statement to write a random file record.

Put #*filenum*, *recordnum*, *variable*

in which

    filenum is the file number;

    recordnum is a numeric expression (from 1 to 2,147,483,647) specifying the record to be written,

and

    variable specifies the variable containing the data to be written to the file.

The *recordnum* parameter and the pound sign are optional.

The *recordnum* parameter can specify in the file any record: an old one whose data is to be rewritten, or a new one receiving it for the first time. Furthermore, your record numbers don't have to be continuous. For example, you can create record number 15 when only records 1 through 4 have been written previously.

If you omit *recordnum*, the default record number is 1, plus the last record written (using Put) or read. Thus, you can write incrementally, increasing record numbers with successive Put instructions that omit *recordnum*. You can also have a single Put instruction in a loop. When you omit the *recordnum* parameter, use two consecutive commas in the Put instruction. For example, the following instruction writes the next consecutive record to the coin database file, which has been opened as file number 1:

```
Put #1, , Coin
```

variable is usually a variable of the appropriate user-defined data type. However, you can use any variable, as long as its length is not more than that of the record. Visual Basic simply writes all the bytes of the variable.

Before writing a record, you must assign the proper values to each component of your record variable. Recall that Visual Basic record variables use a period notation to identify individual components (see Chapter 19, "Using Arrays and Structures").

The following program fragment demonstrates writing a sample record of the coin database:

```
Coin.Yr = 1910
Coin.Category = "Lincoln Penny"
Coin.Valu = 70.00
Coin.Comment = "S mint mark, uncirculated"

Put #1, 5, Coin            'Write record number 5
```

Use the Get statement to read a record.

```
Get #filenum, recordnum, variable
```

in which

    filenum is the file number;

    recordnum is the record number,

and

    variable specifies the variable to receive the data.

The *recordnum* parameter and the pound sign are optional.

As with Put, *recordnum* can specify any record. If you omit *recordnum*, the default record number is the last record read or written, plus one.

The following instruction reads record number 5 from the coin database into the record variable Coin:

```
Get #1, 5, Coin            'Read record number 5
```

Each component of the record variable Coin now contains the appropriate data.

Closing the Random-Access File

When I/O activity is finished, use the Close statement as usual.

Example of a Random-Access File Program

Suppose that you have the coin database on a random-access file named MYCOINS.RAN. The coin market is favorable, and prices are rising. You decide to update the database file by increasing the value of each coin by 10 percent.

To write such a program, you define CoinType with a Type-End Type block. Place the following instructions in the Declarations section of a code module:

```
TYPE CoinType
Yr As Integer
Category As String * 20
Valu As Single
Comment As String * 50
End Type
```

Now, you can write the active program instructions in this way:

```
Dim Coin As CoinType
Dim RecordNum as Integer
Open "C:\COINS\MYCOINS.RAN" For Random As #5 Len = 76


For RecordNum = 1 To 3              'File has only 3 records
   Get #5, RecordNum, Coin
   Coin.Valu = 1.1 * Coin.Valu      'Increase value by 10%
   Put #5, RecordNum, Coin
NEXT RecordNum


Close #5
```

This code fragment demonstrates one of the great advantages of random files over sequential ones: You can read and write random files without closing and reopening each one.

Furthermore, you can read or write records in any order. For example, you can have RecordNum loop from 3 down to 1, and the program still works well.

Using *Seek* and *Loc* with Random-Access Files

For random files, Seek and Loc deal with record numbers, not bytes.

The Seek statement positions the file pointer at the next record you want to read or write. For example:

```
Seek #9, 23   'Move pointer to the 23rd record of file number 9
```

After this Seek, a Get or Put instruction without a *recordnum* parameter operates on this newly reset file position. For example, after executing the previous instruction, the following instruction writes the Coin information onto record number 23:

```
Put #9, , Coin
```

The Seek function returns the next record to be read or written. The Loc function returns the last record read or written. For example:

```
Dim Msg as String
Get #9, 2, Coin'Read record number 2
Msg = "Last record read was    " & Str$(Loc(9)) & Chr$(13)
Msg = Msg & "Next record to read is" & Str$(Seek(9))
MsgBox Msg
```

The resulting message box displays the following:

```
Last record read was    2
Next record to read is 3
```

Using the *EOF* Function with Random-Access Files

With random files, the EOF function returns True (1) if the most recent Get instruction did not read an entire record. This happens when Get reads beyond the end of the file.

Closing the File

When I/O activity is finished, use a Close instruction as usual.

Summary of Statements and Functions for Random-Access Files

Table 25.11 summarizes the statements and functions that work with random-access files.

Table 25.11. Random-access file statements and functions.

Keyword	Type	Effect
Open	Statement	Opens a file For Random
Close	Statement	Closes a file
Type-End Type	Statement	Defines a record data type
Put	Statement	Writes a record
Get	Statement	Reads a record
EOF	Function	Tests for end of file
LOF	Function	Returns size of file
Seek	Statement	Sets file pointer to desired record
Seek	Function	Returns next record to read or write
Loc	Function	Returns last record read or written

Using Binary Files

In addition to sequential and random-access, Visual Basic offers a third type of data file—the binary.

A binary file is not really a different type of file, but rather a different way of looking at one. At the most elemental level, any file is just a sequence of byte values. You can open any file in binary file mode to read or write such bytes directly. No particular structure is assumed; the entire file is treated as one long sequence of bytes.

When working with such files, you usually need to know how the file data is organized to make any sense of it. Does the data represent text characters, memory maps, bit mappings, numeric formats? Something else?

Binary mode is useful to interpret files created in formats alien to Visual Basic, such as spreadsheets or non-ASCII, word-processing documents. You can read or modify any part of the file, including control characters, end-of-file indicators, or anything else.

A file position pointer is associated with each binary file. At any time the pointer identifies which byte is the next to be read or written. The file bytes are considered to be numbered sequentially: one for the first byte, two for the next, and so on. You can move the pointer anywhere in the file, then read or write as many bytes as you want.

You can both read and write to a file after it is opened in binary mode.

Working with a Binary File

Use the following steps to work with a binary file in a Visual Basic application:

1. Open the file For Binary.

2. Use Get or Put (or both) instructions to read or write data, or to do both.

3. Close the file.

Opening the File

For binary files, the Open instruction simply declares the file as Binary.

For example, the following instruction opens a file residing on the root directory of drive D as file number 3:

```
Open "D:MYFILE.BIN" For Binary As #3
```

A single Open instruction opens a binary file for reading, writing, or appending.

Reading and Writing Data

Use Get to read from the file, and Put to write to it.

```
Get #filenum, startbyte, variable
Put #filenum, startbyte, variable
```

in which

  filenum is the file number;

  startbyte is a numeric expression specifying the byte in the file where I/O begins,

and

  variable is any variable, array element, or record variable to receive or transmit the data values.

The pound sign is optional. As this section explains, the startbyte parameter is optional.

If you omit startbyte, the current file pointer establishes a default value. Successive Get and Put instructions automatically adjust this pointer. Also, you can use Seek to adjust the pointer explicitly.

Get reads the necessary number of bytes required to satisfy the length of *variable* (two bytes for a variable of integer type, eight for a double-precision variable, and so on). If *variable* is a user-defined type, or a fixed-length string, Get simply reads the number of bytes required to satisfy the length of the variable. Its length is considered to be that of the data currently stored in it if *variable* is a variable-length string. Similarly, Put writes the number of bytes equal to the length of *variable*.

The following instruction reads eight bytes from file number 1 into the double-precision variable MyData# (the bytes read are specified as eight because this is how many double-precision variables occupy):

```
Get #1, , MyData#
```

The omission of the second parameter indicates that reading begins from the current position of the file pointer. After the read, the file pointer advances eight bytes.

If you try to read past the end of the file, no error occurs. However, only bytes within the file are read. Bytes past the end of it are "read" as binary 0. The file pointer remains at the end of the file.

The following are some examples of Put instructions:

```
Put #1, 45, MyName$    'Writes string beginning at byte 45

Put #1, , Coin         'Writes coin record at default location
```

Use Put to modify existing data, or write new information past the end of the file.

Closing the File

Close the file in the usual way.

Using the *Seek* Statement

Use the Seek statement to adjust the file pointer. For example, the following instruction sets the pointer position to byte number 50 of file number 3:

```
Seek #3, 50
```

The position can range from 1 to 2,147,483,647.

After you use Seek, a Get or Put instruction without a *startbyte* parameter uses the newly specified file position.

You can Seek to any file position—even one past the end of the file. In such cases, Put appends data, and increases the file size.

Using the *Seek* and *Loc* Functions

With binary files, the Seek and Loc functions return a file position in number of bytes from the beginning of the file. Seek returns the current file pointer, which is always at the next byte to be read or written. Loc returns the last byte read or written.

```
Put #3, 30, MyAge%      'Last byte written is byte number 31
Debug.Print "File pointer is at byte number"; Seek(3)
Debug.Print "Last byte written was number"; Loc(3)
```

The output on the Debug window is

```
File pointer is at byte number 32
Last byte written was number 31
```

Using the *EOF* Function

The EOF function works the same as it does with random files. EOF returns True (1) if a Get statement tries to read past the end of the file.

Summary of Statements and Functions for Binary Files

Table 25.12 summarizes the statements and functions used to process binary files.

Table 25.12. Binary file statements and functions.

Keyword	Type	Effect
Open	Statement	Opens a file For Binary
Close	Statement	Closes a file
Put	Statement	Writes data to the file
Get	Statement	Reads from the file
EOF	Function	Tests for end of file
LOF	Function	Returns the size of the file
Seek	Statement	Sets the file position pointer
Seek	Function	Returns current byte pointer
Loc	Function	Returns pointer to last byte I/O

Opening Files in a Network Environment

Open instructions accept some optional parameters useful when designing file-handling applications for a network environment.

On a network, such as a local area network, two users running independent programs might want to open a specific file at the same time. When working in a network environment, you need control over which files can be shared. You need also to define what privileges (reading and writing) you grant others who use your files.

Visual Basic accommodates network needs with two optional items in the Open instruction: the Access clause, and the *lockmode* parameter. Also, the Lock and Unlock statements provide additional network control.

Declaring Access Permissions in an *Open* Instruction

In an Open instruction, the Access clause and the *lockmode* parameter, both of which are optional, are placed as follows:

```
Open filespec For mode Access accessmode lockmode

As #filenum Len = recordlength
```

in which

   filespec, *mode*, *filenum*, and *recordlength* have the same meanings as described previously in the descriptions of the Open instruction.

   accessmode and *lockmode* are described subsequently in Tables 25.13 and 25.14.

Use the Access *accessmode* clause to declare your intentions on a public file. Table 25.13 shows the three possible values for *accessmode*.

Table 25.13. Access parameters in an *Open* instruction.

accessmode	Meaning
Read	Opens the file for reading only
Write	Opens the file for writing only
Read Write	Opens the file for reading and writing (valid only if mode is Append, Random, or Binary)

For example, the following instruction specifies that you are opening a public file for reading only:

```
Open "C:SALES.DTA" For Input Access Read As #4
```

Use the *lockmode* parameter to specify the type of access other users can have to a file that you open. Table 25.14 shows the possible values of *lockmode*.

Table 25.14. Values for *lockmode* in an *Open* instruction.

lockmode	Meaning
(default)	Only one user can open the file at a time.
Shared	Multiple users can open the file jointly.
Lock Read	No other user can read from the file.
Lock Write	No other user can write to the file.
Lock Read Write	No other user can access the file.

Using the *Lock* and *Unlock* Statements

Use Lock to deny other programs access to an opened file. The companion statement, Unlock, removes the restrictions.

```
Lock #filenum, recordnum

Lock #filenum, start To end

Unlock #filenum, recordnum

Unlock #filenum, start To end
```

in which

   filenum is the file number;

   recordnum is the record or byte to be locked;

   start is the number of the first record or byte to be locked,

and

   end is the number of the last record or byte to be locked.

The pound sign is optional. Also, all information after the *filenum* parameter is optional. Further, you can omit the *start* parameter from the *start* To *end* clause.

Notice that Lock and Unlock instructions each have two syntaxes. The first specifies a single record or byte to be locked. The second specifies a range of either to be locked.

For random-access files, *recordnum*, *start*, and *end* refer to a record number. Record number 1 is the first record of the file. For binary files, the three parameters refer to a byte location with number 1 as the first byte in the file.

Use *recordnum* to specify a single record or byte to be locked or unlocked. Use *start* and *end* to specify a range of records or bytes. If you omit *start*, the default value is 1. If you omit all record arguments, the entire file becomes locked.

The following are some example Lock instructions. The file number parameter is 7, and a binary file is assumed:

```
Lock #7              'Lock the complete file

Lock #7, 49          'Lock only byte 49

Lock #7, 18 To 39    'Lock bytes 18 through 39

Lock #7, To 99       'Lock bytes 1 through 99
```

To remove a lock, Unlock requires the identical parameters used in the companion Lock instruction. You cannot use Unlock to remove only some of the restrictions imposed by Lock.

For example, if you lock records numbered 10 to 25 with a Lock instruction, a subsequent Unlock must also specify this range of numbered records. You can not unlock only the records numbered from, say, 15 to 20.

Using the *FileAttr* Function

The FileAttr function returns the attributes of any opened file.

FileAttr(*filenum*, *attribute*)

in which

    filenum is the file number,

and

    attribute is an integer expression specifying which information to return.

The value of *attribute* can be 1 or 2. When *attribute* is 1, FileAttr returns a number that indicates the mode of the opened file (see Table 25.15).

Table 25.15. Mode values returned by the *FileAttr* function.

Returned Value	File Mode
1	Input
2	Output
4	Random
8	Append
32	Binary

When attribute is 2, FileAttr returns the operating system's internal file number assigned to the opened file. This number is often referred to as the file *handle*.

More on Closing Files

A single Close instruction can close two or more files. To do so, specify all the desired file numbers, separating each with a comma. For example, the following instruction closes files numbered 2, 3, and 8:

```
Close #2, #3, #8
```

Furthermore, Close with no file number arguments closes *all* open files. The Reset statement, which accepts no arguments, has the same effect. End also closes all open files. However, Stop maintains opened files.

After closing a file, the file number previously associated with it becomes available for a subsequent Open instruction. Similarly, after closing a file, you can reopen it with the same or a different file number, as long as the new one doesn't conflict with the number of another opened file.

The following are some examples of instructions that close files:

```
Close #1           'Close file number 1

Close #2, #3       'Close files 2 and 3

Close 2, 3         'Close files 2 and 3 (no pound signs)

Close MyFile%      'Close file specified by variable

Close              'Close all opened files

Reset              'Close all opened files
```

Summary

The Visual Basic Toolbox provides three file-related list box controls: File, Directory, and Drive. Each control operates as a specialized list box with List, ListCount, and ListIndex properties. You can work with the DOS file attributes: Archive, Hidden, and System. By combining these controls on a form, and writing appropriate event procedures, you can create standard Windows-like dialog boxes for the selection and specification of file names.

Visual Basic has several statements that provide DOS-like file and directory management. Some of the operations your programs can carry out include deleting or renaming files, and creating, deleting, or changing subdirectories.

When creating a disk file, you can choose between three different file types: *sequential*, *random-access*, and *binary*. Sequential and random files are organized into a series of primary records, with each one containing a single field, or a number of them. A binary file, by contrast, is treated as a series of data bytes with no assumed structure.

To use any of the three file types, you Open the file, read or write records (or bytes) as appropriate, and finally Close the file.

Sequential files are easy to program. However, reading and writing records are relatively slow. For large databases, random-access files have many advantages. Any record in a random-access file can be read or written quickly. However, programming random-access files is more complicated. Binary files provide great flexibility, but demand that you keep track of both the file organization and the meaning of each data byte.

With the network-related extensions to the Open instruction, you can grant specific permissions to users of the file. For example, you can give users the right to read from a file but not write to the file. Further, you can specify whether multiple users can simultaneously access a file. With Lock, you protect portions of a file from being accessed through a network.

Using the Grid Control

The Grid is a custom control available with both the Standard and Professional Editions of Visual Basic. Using a Grid, you can display text, numbers, and pictures in ordered rows and columns, much like a spreadsheet. You can adjust the height, width, and other display characteristics of grids. You can also manipulate rows and columns individually and in groups.

Chapter 23, "Responding to Keyboard Events", introduced the Grid control with an application named, appropriately enough, GridControl. This chapter explores the Grid control in more detail with a full discussion of the relevant properties, events, and methods. A sample application, called PhoneBook, expands on the sample application developed in Chapter 23.

Introducing the Grid

In a grid, the intersection of a row and a column is called a *cell*. Each cell can hold a data item, either a string value or a picture. (Numerical data is stored in string format.) You identify an individual cell by referring to the row and column in which the cell is located.

A grid automatically responds to user input, allowing the user to move about the grid and to select cells singularly or in groups. A click of the mouse on a cell selects that cell, and clicking and dragging selects a group of cells. You can move the cell-highlight cursor around the grid with the arrow keys, thus changing the active row and column in the grid. You can also set the current row and column, and designate cell regions by modifying property values in program code. Figure 26.1 shows a sample blank grid with the first row selected.

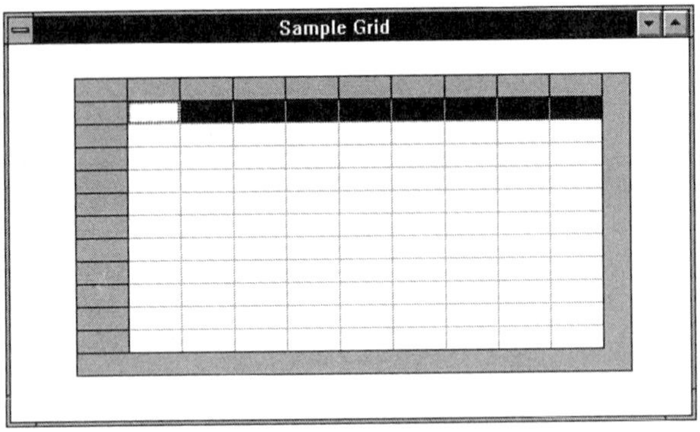

Figure 26.1.

A grid with the first row selected.

Adding the Grid Control to Visual Basic

The Grid control is a custom control. As such, the control is not automatically built into Visual Basic. It is, however, available from add-on files. The files for the Grid control come with both the Standard and Professional Editions of Visual Basic. The normal installation of Visual Basic places the Grid control in the Toolbox.

If your Toolbox does not contain the Grid control, see Chapter 23, "Responding to Keyboard Events." In that chapter, the section titled "Using the Grid Control" explains how to use Visual Basic's File menu to add the Grid control files.

Understanding Basic Grid Characteristics

The grid's Row and Column properties identify the currently active grid cell. You can modify the values of Row and Column in program code. You can read the contents of the current cell from the grid's Text property, and the grid's Clip property references all data in the selected region of the grid. Numeric or text data is always stored in a grid cell as string data.

Internally, the grid manipulates its string data in *tab-delimited format*. If you select a region of a grid and read its Clip property, you get one large string with the data in each cell separated by a Tab character, Chr$(9). Each row of data is separated by a carriage-return (CR) character, Chr$(13). This format facilitates moving data in and out of the grid, either a row at a time or in larger segments.

A tab-delimited format is also handy because many commercial Windows applications support it, including Microsoft Word, WordPerfect, Excel, 1-2-3 for Windows, and Ami Pro. If you save the contents of a grid to a text file, you can read that file with most applications of this type. A Windows spreadsheet program, such as Excel, can automatically convert the data into cells of its own. Windows word processors, such as Ami Pro, leave the tabs and CR characters intact, enabling the user to quickly format the grid information into a text table.

Displaying Pictures

Visual Basic maintains a value of the Picture property for each grid cell. Through the Picture property, you can include picture data in the grid. In code, you can read and write the value of the Picture, which in this context refers to the current cell. You cannot, however, obtain picture data from the Clip property.

You can display both text and picture data in a single cell. If you do, Visual Basic places the picture in the top-left corner of the cell and wraps the string data around the visual image.

Controlling the Grid's Appearance

You can modify the appearance of the grid by setting various grid properties. As explained later in this chapter, you can specify column height and width, column alignment (either left, right, or centered), and a full range of font characteristics. You can also determine whether cells have visible borders, choose a border style for the entire grid, and select from a variety of color options.

Obviously, the Grid control is well suited for applications that work with data in a row-and-column format. The grid is often the best tool for displaying data in tabular format, as well. List boxes are faster and simpler, but they don't offer the capability to work with individual cells of data. Text boxes don't allow consistent formatting of separate, discrete rows and columns.

Because the grid is modeled after the well-known design of spreadsheet packages, the users of your applications have a built-in convenience factor. Most of them will be intuitively familiar with using the grid portion of your applications.

Setting Grid Properties

The Grid supports about 50 properties. Many of these properties are common to other controls. For example, you can set colors, size, position, and font characteristics of the grid with many of the same properties you use for other controls. The properties covered in the following sections are unique to the grid, or work in a specialized way with the grid.

Row, Col, and Text

The Row, Col, and Text properties are at the heart of the grid's functionality. Row and Col specify the row and column of the active grid cell. In other words, the active cell is at the intersection of the row and column specified by Row and Col. Text contains the string contents of the cell specified by Row and Col.

Whenever the user clicks the mouse on a grid cell or presses navigation keys, the active cell changes. Visual Basic updates the values of Row and Col accordingly. Grid rows and columns are numbered, beginning with zero. Row numbering is from the top down, so the uppermost row of a grid is row 0. Column numbering increases toward the right, making column 0 the leftmost column.

Figure 26.2 shows a grid with each cell displaying its row and column number. In this grid, Row is set to 2 (third row counting from 0) and Col is set to 3 (fourth column). The grid's Text property is R2C3; this value appears in the form's caption. Notice that the cell at the location R2C3 appears with a dotted border (although the border may be hard to see in the figure). By default, Visual Basic uses a dotted border to indicate the active cell.

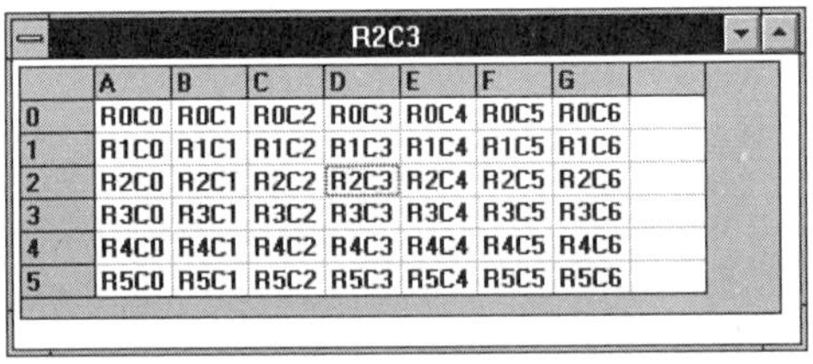

Figure 26.2.

A grid with Row and Col set to 2 and 3, respectively.

You can use program code to modify the Row and Col properties, allowing an application to access grid data one cell at a time. There's no "cell" property; to access the contents of an individual cell, you must first set the grid's Row and Col properties. At that point, the grid's Text property holds the contents of the desired cell.

For example, to get the contents of the third cell in the second row of Grid1, you can use the following code:

```
Grid1.Row = 1
Grid1.Col = 2
Result$ = Grid1.Text
```

Result$ contains the contents of the desired cell. Remember that the topmost row is 0 and leftmost column is 0. That's why the second row is 1 and the third column is 2.

By default, Visual Basic names the first Grid control in an application as Grid1. Subsequent grid controls are named Grid2, Grid3, and so on. You can change a grid name by modifying the grid's Name property.

FixedRow, FixedCol

A grid can have fixed rows and columns. When fixed, a row or column is protected from being selected by the user. The number of fixed rows and columns is specified by the values of the FixedRow and FixedCol properties, respectively. In code, you can both read and write values for these properties.

You typically use fixed rows and columns to construct row and column headings for a grid. By not being able to access a fixed row or column, the user cannot modify the values in these grid cells.

You can specify more than one row or one column as fixed, but fixed rows must start with the topmost row and fixed columns with the leftmost column. Fixed rows start at row 0 and continue down sequentially. You cannot set rows 2 and 4 as fixed, for example. All fixed rows must be contiguous rows starting with row 0. Similarly, fixed columns must be contiguous columns starting with column 0.

Fixed rows and columns appear in gray. You cannot scroll such rows and columns as you can the other rows and columns in a grid. This behavior is similar to the "freezing" panes feature of many commerical spreadsheet programs.

The values of FixedRows and FixedCols indicate the total number of fixed rows and columns, respectively. For example, if FixedCols is 3, then columns 0, 1, and 2 are fixed. Figure 26.3 shows a grid where FixedCols is 1 and FixedRows is 2.

A grid with fixed rows and columns provides a side benefit: the user can change the height of rows and the width of columns with the mouse at run time. To do so, the user clicks and drags on a grid line in the protected row or column.

Figure 26.4 shows the third column being widened. Notice the mouse cursor appears (in the protected row) in the shape of a double arrow. In the figure, the cursor is in the column labeled "Child's Clothes."

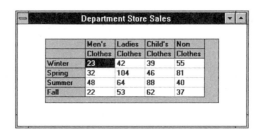

Figure 26.3.

A grid with one fixed column and two fixed rows.

Figure 26.4.

Adjusting the width of a column from within the fixed row of a grid.

You can modify the values of FixedRows and FixedCols in code at run time, but you must always leave at least one row and one column that is not fixed. Visual Basic does not allow you to fix all the rows or all the columns of a grid. By default, a grid has one fixed column and one fixed row.

Rows, Cols

The Rows and Cols properties specify, respectively, the total number of rows and columns in a grid. In program code, you can modify the values of these properties to dynamically change the size of a grid at run time. For example, the following instructions set the grid to have 7 rows and 8 columns:

```
Grid1.Rows = 7
Grid1.Cols = 8
```

 NOTE Don't confuse the Rows and Cols properties with the Row and Col properties. Obviously, these properties have similar names, but they are different. Row and Col specify the active grid cell. Rows and Cols specify the size of the entire grid.

Demonstrating a Basic Grid

The following sample application demonstrates the basic concepts of a grid.
The contents of each cell are set to indicate the row and column occupied by
that cell. As you move the cell cursor around the grid, the application displays
the contents of the cell in the caption of the form.

To create the sample application, start a new project. Double-click the Grid
icon in the Toolbox to add a Grid control to Form1. The grid appears with the
default name of Grid1.

Using the Properties window, set property values as shown in Table 26.1.

Table 26.1. Property values for the sample grid application.

Object	Property	Value
Form1	Height	2500
	Width	6000
Grid1	Left	50
	Top	50
	Height	1850
	Width	5700

Writing the Event Procedures

To set the contents of each grid cell, create the following Form_Load procedure.
(The Form_Load procedure executes when you start the application.) The
procedure also establishes values for several properties not specified at
design time:

```
Sub Form_Load ()
    Dim Temp As String
    Dim R As Integer, C As Integer   'Loop counters for row,column
    Dim TB As String, CR As String

    TB = Chr$(9)    'Tab key
    CR = Chr$(13)   'Enter key


    'Clear and reset the grid
```

```
Grid1.FixedRows = 0
Grid1.FixedCols = 0
Grid1.Rows = 1
Grid1.Cols = 1

'Add the title row to the top of the grid
Temp = TB & "A" & TB & "B" & TB & "C" & TB & "D"
Temp = Temp & TB & "E" & TB & "F" & TB & "G"
Grid1.AddItem Temp
Grid1.RemoveItem 0   'Clear the first (empty) row

'Fill the grid with R#C# data one line at a time
For R = 0 To 5
   Temp = "" & R & TB
   For C = 0 To 6
      Temp = Temp & "R" & R & "C" & C & TB
   Next C
   Grid1.AddItem Temp
Next R

'Reset the number of fixed rows and columns to 1
Grid1.FixedRows = 1
Grid1.FixedCols = 1

'Move to topmost left cell
Grid1.Row = 1
Grid1.Col = 1
Form1.Show
Grid1.SetFocus
End Sub
```

Notice that this procedure uses the following instruction to specify the contents of an entire row of grid cells:

```
Grid1.AddItem Temp
```

AddItem is a method recognized by the Grid control. Temp is a string variable. The string data in Temp contains internal Tab (Chr$(9)) and carriage-return (Chr$(13)) characters. As described earlier in this chapter, each Tab character separates the text in individual cells and each carriage return terminates the text for an entire row.

Similarly, the RemoveItem method removes data from a grid row. AddItem and RemoveItem are discussed in detail later in this chapter.

To complete this first sample application, create the following `RowColChange` event procedure:

```
Sub Grid1_RowColChange ()
    Form1.Caption = Grid1.Text
End Sub
```

The `RowColChange` event, unique to the Grid control, occurs whenever the active grid cell changes. For this application, whenever the cell changes, this procedure displays the contents of the current cell in the form's caption.

Running the Application

Save the form as GRIDEX1.FRM, and save the project as GRIDEX1.MAK. Then run the program. Your form appears like the one in Figure 26.5.

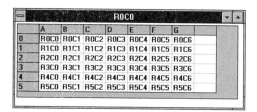

Figure 26.5.

The sample grid application in Run mode.

As you can see, the application places a text string in each cell. For each cell, this string indicates the row and column that the cell occupies. As you move the cell cursor around the grid (either by pressing arrow keys or clicking the mouse), you see the contents of the current cell reflected in the form's caption.

You can also adjust row heights and column widths by clicking and dragging on cell borders in the grayed row or column. Clicking and dragging works because the grid has a fixed row at the top and a fixed column at the left.

One of the shortcomings of the grid becomes apparent with this example: you can't edit the contents of individual cells in the grid. For the user to modify cell contents at run time, you must add an additional control to the application. The best solution is a text box linked to the grid by program code. You learn that technique with the PhoneBook application later in the chapter.

If you haven't done so already, stop the application and return to Design mode.

Selecting Cells

You can work with a group of cells as a single block by selecting a range of cells. As is typical of Windows applications, the selected cells appear highlighted. Cells can be selected by specifying property values at run time. Further, as described shortly, the user can select cells while an application runs.

Selected cells are always in a contiguous rectangular block. As Table 26.2 indicates, Visual Basic designates the selected cells with four properties whose names are fairly self-explanatory. Each property has an integer value.

Table 26.2. Properties used for selected cells.

Property	Meaning
SelStartRow	Uppermost row in the selected block
SelEndRow	Lowermost row in the selected block
SelStartCol	Leftmost column in the selected block
SelEndCol	Rightmost column in the selected block

If you modify the values of these properties in code, the grid highlights these cells. On most monitors, highlighted cells appear in a different color.

For example, add the following instructions to the end of the Form_Load procedure in GRIDEX1:

```
Grid1.SelStartRow = 2
Grid1.SelEndRow = 4
Grid1.SelStartCol = 3
Grid1.SelEndCol = 6
```

These instructions select a region of three rows by four columns, a total of 12 selected cells. Figure 26.6 shows the result of such a cell selection. (Remember that row and column numbering starts with 0. Don't forget to count the fixed rows and columns. For example, a value of 2 for SelStartRow specifies the third row, including the fixed row.)

A grid maintains an active (current) cell whether or not a block of selected cells is present. The active cell can be inside the selected block or independent from it. Notice that, in Figure 26.6, the active cell is in the upper left corner or the grid while the selected block is near the center of the grid.

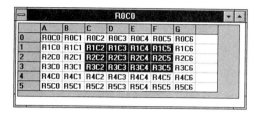

Figure 26.6.

A grid with rows and columns selected.

Enabling the User to Select Cells

At run time, the user can select a region of cells. To do so, the user presses the left mouse button and drags the mouse over a region of the grid. Another method is to hold down the Shift key while pressing the arrow keys.

The highlighting of user-selected cells is built into the Grid control. No special coding is required. You can demonstrate the effect by rerunning the GRIDEX1 application and dragging the mouse pointer over a region of the grid. You also see that, when selecting cells, the current cell remains unchanged.

When the user selects a group of cells, Visual Basic automatically updates the values of the four selection properties. You can read the values of these properties in code to determine the cell block selected by the user.

Understanding the *Clip* Property

The contents of the selected cell region are contained in the grid's Clip property. You can read or write the value of Clip in program code.

The value of Clip is always a single string quantity. Remember that this string contains a Tab character (Chr$(9)) between the contents of each cell and a carriage-return (CR) character (Chr$(13)) after the contents of each row.

Demonstrating Cell Selection

To demonstrate the Clip property, try the following modification to the GRIDEX1 application. This modification adds a SelChange event procedure. A SelChange event occurs whenever the selected region of a grid changes (either by the actions of the user or by modifying the selection properties in code). The event triggers even when only a single cell is selected:

```
Sub Grid1_SelChange ()
    Dim Msg As String
    Dim TB As String, CR As String
```

```
TB = Chr$(9)    'Tab character
CR = Chr$(13)   'Carriage return

If Grid1.Clip = "" Then Exit Sub   'This can't happen

'Prepare a message to show in the message box
Msg = "SelStartRow: " & Grid1.SelStartRow + CR
Msg = Msg + "SelEndRow: " & Grid1.SelEndRow + CR
Msg = Msg + "SelStartCol: " & Grid1.SelStartCol + CR
Msg = Msg + "SelEndCol: " & Grid1.SelEndCol + CR + CR

'Show the contents of Grid1.Clip
Msg = Msg + Grid1.Clip

'Show message box except during Form_Load
If Form1.Visible Then MsgBox Msg, , "Selected Cells"
End Sub
```

When you run the application with this modification, a message box pops up every time you change the cells that are selected. The message box displays the values of the four selection properties as well as the contents of the selected cells. Press Enter or click the OK button to close the message box.

To display the cell contents in tabular format, the procedure uses the grid's Clip property. Figure 26.7 shows the message box which appears when cells R1C0-R3C1 are selected.

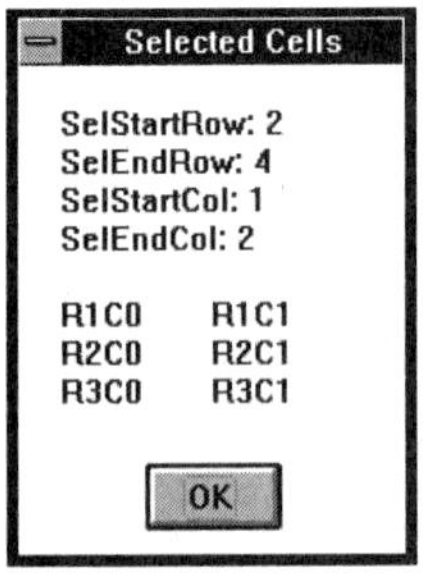

Figure 26.7.

The message box displays information about the selected cells.

Save the modified application as GRIDEX2.

Using the *ColWidth* and *RowHeight* Properties

The ColWidth and RowHeight properties specify a column width and a row height, respectively. You can read or write the values of these properties in program code. These properties are not available in the Properties window at design time. Because each row and column of a grid can have different dimensions, you must include a reference to the desired row or column when using these properties.

The syntax for ColWidth and RowHeight is:

```
grid.ColWidth(column) = size
```

and

```
grid.RowHeight(row) = size
```

in which

   grid specifies the Grid control,

   column specifies the grid column to modify,

   row specifies the grid row to modify,

and

   size is a numeric expression that specifies the row or column size in twips.

For example, to set the width of column 0 in Grid1 to 1000 and the height of row 0 to 750, you can use the following code:

```
Grid1.ColWidth(0) = 1000
Grid1.RowHeight(0) = 750
```

For multiple-form applications, you can also include the name of the form at the beginning of the instruction. For example,

```
Form1!Grid1.ColWidth(2) = 1250
Form3.Grid1.RowHeight(1) = 675
```

 NOTE   Notice that, as always, you can use an exclamation point or period when separating a form name from a control name. The exclamation point is preferred to avoid possible syntax ambiguities in future releases of Visual Basic.

Remember that, if a grid has fixed rows and/or columns, the user can modify the column and/or row sizes at run time. In program code, you can determine any user-modified column or row sizes by reading the values of ColWidth and RowHeight.

There is one technique you might want to experiment with in your programs; try using the value of the form's TextWidth property to obtain the exact width of a text string that is to be stored in a grid cell. You can then use the value determined by TextWidth to set the width for the grid column of the target cell. In this way, you make the column width no larger than necessary. For example, the following instruction sets the column width (of column 2) to be just the right size for the string data stored in MyText$:

```
Grid1.ColWidth(2) = Form1.TextWidth(MyText$)
```

Similarly, you can use the form's TextHeight property to set the height of a grid column. If you use these techniques, make sure the font characteristics of the grid match those of the parent form.

Using the *ColAlignment* and *FixedAlignment* Properties

The ColAlignment and FixedAlignment properties determine text alignment modes within specific grid columns. You can specify left-justified, right-justified, or centered for text entries in any column. The FixedAlignment property specifies the text alignment for fixed columns, and the ColAlignment property specifies the text alignment of columns that are not fixed.

The syntax for FixedAlignment and ColAlignment—which is similar to the syntax for ColWidth—is:

```
grid.FixedAlignment(column) = alignment
```

and

```
grid.ColAlignment(column) = alignment
```

in which

> grid specifies the Grid control,

> column specifies the grid column to be aligned,

and

> alignment is a numeric expression that specifies how the text entries in a column align.

You can set the value of alignment to 0, 1, or 2 to achieve the effects shown in Table 26.3.

Table 26.3. Values of the *alignment* parameter.

Value of *alignment*	Meaning
0	Left-justify text (default value)
1	Right-justify text
2	Center text

For the FixedAlignment property, alignment can also have the value 3. In that case, the text justification of column is determined by the current value of ColAlignment for that column.

For multiple-form applications, you can also include the name of the form at the beginning of the instruction. For example,

```
Form1!Grid1.ColAlignment(MarchCol%) = 2
Form2.Grid1.FixedAlignment(0) = 1
```

To demonstrate the ColAlignment property, add the following Grid1_DblClick event procedure to the GRIDEX2 sample application:

```
Sub Grid1_DblClick ()
   Dim X As Integer

   For X = 1 To Grid1.Cols - 1
      If Grid1.ColAlignment(X) = 2 Then
         Grid1.ColAlignment(X) = 0
      Else
         Grid1.ColAlignment(X) = Grid1.ColAlignment(X) + 1
      End If
   Next X

   Select Case Grid1.ColAlignment(1)
      Case 0: Form1.Caption = "ColAlignment = 0 (Left)"
      Case 1: Form1.Caption = "ColAlignment = 1 (Right)"
      Case 2: Form1.Caption = "ColAlignment = 2 (Center)"
   End Select
End Sub
```

Run the example and widen one of the columns with the mouse so that the upcoming effects are more apparent. Double-click the currently selected cell several times. The ColAlignment property for that column cycles through 0, 1, and 2, which cycles the text alignment through left, right, and centered. The current alignment is displayed in the form's caption. Figure 26.8 shows column C widened and the text centered.

	A	B	C	D	E	F	G	
0	R0C0	R0C1	R0C2	R0C3	R0C4	R0C5	R0C6	
1	R1C0	R1C1	R1C2	R1C3	R1C4	R1C5	R1C6	
2	R2C0	R2C1	R2C2	R2C3	R2C4	R2C5	R2C6	
3	R3C0	R3C1	R3C2	R3C3	R3C4	R3C5	R3C6	
4	R4C0	R4C1	R4C2	R4C3	R4C4	R4C5	R4C6	
5	R5C0	R5C1	R5C2	R5C3	R5C4	R5C5	R5C6	

ColAlignment = 2 (Center)

Figure 26.8.

Demonstrating column alignment.

NOTE When running this sample application, you can avoid the pop-up message box by always double-clicking the currently active cell. (Recall that the message box appears whenever you change the selected text region.)

You can demonstrate the FixedAlignment property by replacing every instance of ColAlignment with FixedAlignment in the DblClick procedure.

The ColAlignment and FixedAlignment properties come in handy when you display both numeric and text data in a single grid. Often you want numbers right-aligned and text left-aligned. For some grids, you use ColAlignment and FixedAlignment to give the column headings in the fixed rows a different alignment than the data in the nonfixed rows.

The ColAlignment and FixedAlignment properties have no effect on pictures displayed in the grid.

Displaying Pictures in a Grid

As mentioned earlier in the chapter, you can display pictures as well as text in grid cells. However, picture data does not show up in the Clip or Text properties. If you put both text and a picture in a cell, the text wraps around the picture.

To load a picture into a cell, set the Row and Col properties of the grid to select the desired cell. Then use the LoadPicture function in conjunction with the Picture property to assign a picture to the grid. For example, you can use the following program code:

```
Grid1.Row = 1
Grid1.Col = 1
Grid1.Picture = LoadPicture("C:\VB\ICONS\COMM\PHONE01.ICO")
```

Keep in mind that the width of the column and the height of the row do not automatically resize to accommodate the picture. You have to set the appropriate sizes in program code. In the case shown here, the picture is an icon. Icons are 32 pixels high and 32 pixels wide, so you can use the following code to set the appropriate dimensions:

```
Grid1.ColWidth(1) = 32 * Screen.TwipsPerPixelX
Grid1.RowHeight(1) = 32 * Screen.TwipsPerPixelY
```

Of course, you want to allow more room in the cell if the cell contains both text and a picture.

Understanding the *TopRow, LeftCol,* and *ScrollBars* Properties

The TopRow, LeftCols, and ScrollBars properties relate to grid navigation. When a grid is so large that it cannot show all of its cells at one time, the grid can set up scroll bars that enable the user to scroll through the cells both horizontally and vertically.

However, scrolling is limited when fixed rows and fixed columns are present. If you scroll horizontally, the fixed columns do not move but the fixed rows scroll along with the other rows. Similarly, if you scroll vertically, the fixed rows do not move, but the fixed columns scroll along with the other columns.

The TopRow property is a numeric value that specifies the first row displayed at the top of the grid (not counting any fixed rows). Because a grid can have more rows than it can display, you can use TopRow in program code to read or set the first visible row. The TopRow property is *not* available in the Properties window at design time. The default value of TopRow is 1.

Similarly, the LeftCol property determines the first column displayed at the left of the grid. Remember that fixed rows and columns are exempt from this sort of manipulation because they are *always* displayed.

For example, suppose that you have a small form containing the Grid control Grid1. The grid currently contains 200 lines (rows) of data. Your program may have a search routine that locates a needed data item in the cell at the intersection of row 148 and column 5. You can then set Grid1.TopRow = 148 and Grid1.LeftCol = 5. If you do, the target cell appears in the top left corner of the grid's display area.

Limitations to *TopRow* and *LeftCol*

TopRow and LeftCol have limitations on their permissible values. You must ensure that sufficient rows exist below the TopRow (and columns to the right of LeftCol) to fill the space occupied by the grid—otherwise an error occurs. For example, suppose that your grid has room to display five rows on a form, but the grid contains 12 lines of data. Then the highest permissible value of TopRow is 8, which displays rows 8 through 12 in the five rows available. Visual Basic generates an error if you attempt to set TopRow to 9 because, in that case, only four grid rows would be available to fill the five visible rows.

Displaying Scroll Bars

As shown in Table 26.4, the ScrollBars property determines whether the grid can display scroll bars. When scrolling is enabled, the grid displays scroll bars when the full range of grid cells cannot fit within the grid boundaries.

Table 26.4. Values of the *ScrollBars* property.

Value of *ScrollBars*	Meaning
0	No scroll bars
1	Horizontal scroll bars
2	Vertical scroll bars
3	Horizontal and vertical scroll bars

For example, the following instruction enables horizontal scroll bars in Grid1:

```
Grid1.ScrollBars = 1
```

The Grid control automatically displays whatever scroll bars are enabled and required. The default value of ScrollBars is 3, enabling both horizontal and vertical scroll bars. When the value of ScrollBars is set to 0, scroll bars do not display in the grid even if more rows and columns of cells exist than the grid can currently display.

Understanding the *HighLight* and *GridLines* Properties

The HighLight and GridLines properties, which are unique to the grid, are purely for the sake of appearance. The HighLight property determines whether selected cells appear highlighted (usually in a different color). When the value of HighLight is True (the default) and the user clicks the grid and drags, the selected cells appear highlighted. (As explained earlier in the chapter, you can also select cells in program code by setting values for the SelStartRow, SelEndRow, SelStartCol, and SelEndCol properties.)

To turn off highlighting, set the value of HighLight to False. For example, the following instruction disables highlighting in Grid2:

```
Grid2.HighLight = False
```

You may want to turn off highlighting in a few situations. For example, you can discourage the user from selecting cells by turning off the visual cues provided by the highlighting. Another reason is that, with highlighting off, selection and deselection occur faster because Windows does not need to redraw the affected region with different cell colors.

The GridLines property determines whether the grid displays a border around the individual cells. When the value is True (the default), a line appears between adjacent cells. When the value is False, no cell borders appear.

Most of the time you retain the cell borders. However, some grids may look better without the cell lines. The decision, of course, is yours. Figure 26.9 shows the grid from the GRIDEX1 example displayed without any cell borders. The following line of code does the trick:

```
Grid1.GridLines = False
```

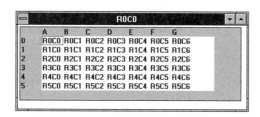

Figure 26.9.

A grid with GridLines set to False.

Using the Grid Events *RowColChange* and *SelChange*

The grid automatically responds to 14 different events. Most of these events occur with other controls besides the Grid. The only events unique to the Grid are RowColChange and SelChange.

The RowColChange event triggers whenever the currently active cell changes to a different cell. The event occurs when the user clicks a new cell or when the program code modifies the Row or Col properties.

The SelChange event occurs whenever the selected region of a grid changes. As the GRIDEX2 sample application demonstrates, the SelChange and RowColChange events often happen together. However, RowColChange does not occur when you programmatically change the selected range without changing the active cell.

Using the *AddItem* and *RemoveItem* Methods

Already, you have used several Grid methods in the sample applications of this chapter. No Visual Basic methods are unique to the Grid. Some methods, however, behave differently with Grids than they do with other controls. This section discusses the two most important grid methods—AddItem and RemoveItem.

As demonstrated by the GRIDEX1 application, the AddItem method places a new row of string data in the grid. If Tab characters exist in the string, the data is placed in separate cells. If more data items than grid columns exist, additional columns are automatically added to the grid.

Because AddItem adds one entire row of string data to the grid, you should not put a carriage-return character (Chr$(13)) at the end of the data string. If you do, the Chr$(13) symbol is considered part of the data string.

The RemoveItem method is similar to AddItem but, as the name suggests, RemoveItem removes a row of data from the grid. Both AddItem and RemoveItem actually change the number of rows in the grid, making the two methods very handy for adding or removing grid data.

The syntax for `Additem` and `RemoveItem` is

`grid.Additem stringdata, row`

and

`grid.RemoveItem row`

in which

    `grid` specifies the Grid control,

    `stringdata` is a tab-delimited string value to add to the grid,

and

    `row` specifies a row in the grid.

For the `AddItem` method, the `row` parameter is optional. If omitted, a new row is added to the end of the current grid.

Understanding the PhoneBook Application

The PhoneBook application provides a more detailed exploration into the workings of the Grid control. Here you build a practical application which displays names, addresses, and phone numbers that you can edit and save.

Using PhoneBook, you can load a file of names and addresses into a grid. Furthermore, you can add, copy, and delete rows in the grid; edit individual cells; and save the contents of the grid back to a file.

Not only do you use the Grid control in constructing this application, you also link the grid to a floating text box. With this text box, which appears over individual cells, you can edit the entry in a grid cell. PhoneBook demonstrates the basic techniques of data file reading and writing. Also, the application uses a control array of command buttons so that the user can select various options.

Figure 26.10 shows a sample of how PhoneBook looks when the application is completed and running. As you can see, PhoneBook even includes a phone icon in the upper left grid cell.

	PhoneBook - PHONFILE.TXT					
	Name	Address	City	State	Zip	Number
1	John Simmons	1289 Foster Ave.	Bakersfield	CA	94322	900/555/1234
2	Aaron Wilford	1819 President's Way	Culver City	CA	94929	213/444/1823
3	Carol Huntington	18 Viennestrauss Blvd	Dearborn	MI	49555	316/234/1000
4	Jonathan Richman	1814 Picasso Rd. #23	Boston	MA	12245	814/338/4567
5	Sarah Greening	23 Bienvenue Dr.	Indianapolis	IN	30405	317/579/2308
6	Robert Stupak	89 Tower St.	Las Vegas	NV	81111	301/998/2300
7	Dave Penguer	415 83rd St.	New York	NY	10019	212/555/1888
8	Miriam Schotley	657 Michael Ln.	Santa Barbara	CA	91515	405/233/1876

Add   Delete   Open   Save   Copy   Exit

Figure 26.10.

An example of the
PhoneBook application.

Constructing the Basic Grid

Start a new project, and add a Grid control (Grid1) and a Text box control
(Text1) to the form (Form1). Add a command button (Command1) to the form.
Move the controls on the form so that none of the controls overlap. Make a
copy of the command button using the **Copy** and **Paste** options from the **Edit**
menu. When prompted by Do you want to create a control array?, choose
Yes. A copy of the Command1 command button appears in the upper left corner
of the form.

NOTE   To copy a control using the **Edit** menu, follow these steps:

1. Click the control in order to select it.

2. Choose the **Copy** option from the **Edit** menu.

3. Choose the **Paste** option from the **Edit** menu. Before it shows
   the new control, Visual Basic displays a dialog box that asks
   whether you want to create a control array.

Now delete the newly created copy of the command button. To do so, select
the new command button. (The button has the value 1 for the Index property.)
Then press Del. The original command button is now the only command
button on the form. (The original button has a value of 0 for Index.) This
technique establishes the single command button as part of a control array
even though, at the moment, the command button is the only member of the
array. Additional array elements are added by program code at run time.

Using the Properties window, set the various property values shown in Table
26.5. (The form's Icon property determines the icon that Visual Basic displays
when the form is minimized.)

Object	Property	Value	
Form1	Caption	PhoneBook	
	Icon	C:\VB\ICONS\COMM\PHONE01.ICO	
	Height	4605	
	Width	6705	
	BackColor	&H00C0C0C0&	(light gray)
Grid1	BorderStyle	0 ' none	
	BackColor	&H00FFFFFF&	(white)
Text1	BorderStyle	0 ' none	
	BackColor	&H0000FFFF&	(yellow)

Table 26.5. Design-time properties for the PhoneBook application.

All other properties for the form and controls are set at run time in the program code.

Writing the *Form_Load* Event Procedure

Most of the initialization for PhoneBook takes place in the Form_Load procedure. A great deal is going on in this Sub: the grid's position and dimensions are set, column headings are specified, and the control array of command buttons is loaded. Quite a bit of code is in the following event procedure, but it's all pretty straightforward:

```
Sub Form_Load ()
    Dim TB As String, LF As String
    Dim X As Integer, C As Integer     'Loop counters
    Dim SetWidth As Integer
    Dim wOffset As Single, hOffset As Single

    TB = Chr$(9)                'Tab character
    LF = Chr$(10) + Chr$(10)    'Line feed

    'Set grid, form font characteristics
    Form1.FontBold = False
    Grid1.FontBold = False

    'Load command buttons
    Command1(0).Left = 60    'Command.Top set in Form_Resize
    For X = 1 To 5
        Load Command1(X)
        Command1(X).Left = Command1(X - 1).Left + Command1(X - 1).Width + 30
        Command1(X).Top = Command1(X - 1).Top
```

```
      Command1(X).Visible = True
Next X

'Set command button captions
Command1(0).Caption = "&Add"
Command1(1).Caption = "&Delete"
Command1(2).Caption = "&Open"
Command1(3).Caption = "&Save"
Command1(4).Caption = "&Copy"
Command1(5).Caption = "E&xit"


'Initialize Grid fixed rows & columns
Grid1.FixedRows = 1
Grid1.FixedCols = 1
Grid1.Rows = 2
Grid1.Cols = 7

Grid1.Row = 0


'Put a picture in the top left corner of the grid
Grid1.Col = 0
Grid1.Picture = Form1.Icon    'Use telephone icon from Form1

'Set Height,Width based on icon size
Grid1.RowHeight(0) = Screen.TwipsPerPixelY * 32
Grid1.ColWidth(0) = Screen.TwipsPerPixelX * 32

'Add column headings and set column widths
'NOTE: Column widths set here are arbitrary.
'       You can modify the widths as desired

Grid1.ColWidth(1) = 1400
Grid1.ColWidth(2) = 2000
Grid1.ColWidth(3) = 1300
Grid1.ColWidth(4) = 500
Grid1.ColWidth(5) = 700
Grid1.ColWidth(6) = 1200

Grid1.Col = 1
Grid1.Text = "Name"
```

```
Grid1.Col = 2
Grid1.Text = "Address"

Grid1.Col = 3
Grid1.Text = "City"

Grid1.Col = 4
Grid1.Text = "State"

Grid1.Col = 5
Grid1.Text = "Zip"

Grid1.Col = 6
Grid1.Text = "Number"

'Insert a row number, then return to row 1, col 1
Grid1.Row = 1
Grid1.Col = 0
Grid1.Text = "1"
Grid1.Col = 1

'Adjust Grid1 width to show all columns
Grid1.Left = 60
Grid1.Top = 60

SetWidth = Screen.TwipsPerPixelX ' allows for borderline around grid
For C = 0 To Grid1.Cols - 1 ' add widths of all columns
    SetWidth = SetWidth + Grid1.ColWidth + (Screen.TwipsPerPixelX * 2)
Next C
Grid1.Width = SetWidth

'Adjust Height, Width of Form1
wOffset = Form1.Width - ScaleWidth
hOffset = Form1.Height - ScaleHeight
Form1.Width = Grid1.Width + (Grid1.Left * 2) + wOffset
Form1.Height = Grid1.Height + hOffset


'Center form on screen
Form1.Left = (Screen.Width - Form1.Width) / 2
Form1.Top = (Screen.Height - Form1.Height) / 2

End Sub
```

Writing the *Form_Resize* Event Procedure

The Form_Resize procedure resets the location and sizes of the grid and of the command buttons in case the user resizes the form. Recall that Visual Basic invokes Form_Resize during the startup of any application. PhoneBook takes advantage of that fact to set the height and width of the grid in the following Form_Resize procedure instead of in Form_Load:

```
Sub Form_Resize ()
    Dim X As Integer      'Loop counter

    'Set grid size
    If Form1.WindowState = 1 Then Exit Sub   'Form was minimized

    For X = 0 To 5
        Command1(X).Top = ScaleHeight - (Command1(0).Height * 1.5)
    Next X

    Grid1.Width = ScaleWidth - (Grid1.Left * 2)
    Grid1.Height = ScaleHeight - Grid1.Top - Command1(0).Height * 2
End Sub
```

Working with the Command Button Array

The Command1() array provides a row of command buttons with which the user can select various options supported by the application. Because Command1 is a control array, a single block of code in the Command1_Click procedure is all that's necessary to control the operation of the various buttons. The completed Command1_Click procedure should appear as follows:

```
Sub Command1_Click (Index As Integer)
    Select Case Index
        Case 0 ' add
            AddGridLine
        Case 1 ' delete
            DeleteGridLine
        Case 2 ' open
            LoadFile
        Case 3 ' Save
            SaveFile
        Case 4 ' Copy Line
            CopyLine
```

```
        Case 5 ' Exit
            Shutdown
    End Select
    Grid1.SetFocus
End Sub
```

AddGridLine, DeleteGridLine, LoadFile, SaveFile, CopyLine, and Shutdown are all user-defined procedures that specify the actions taken when the user clicks one of the command buttons. These procedures are covered later in this chapter.

Form-Level Variable Declarations

PhoneBook utilizes some variables shared between various procedures. Some of these variables are used in saving and restoring the status of the grid, and others are used for file handling and management of the text box.

Because PhoneBook has a single form and no code modules, you can place the shared variables in the Declarations section of the form's code. The necessary declarations are as follows:

```
'Variables for GridStatusSave and GridStatusRestore
Dim SavedStartRow As Integer, SavedEndRow As Integer
Dim SavedStartCol As Integer, SavedEndCol As Integer
Dim SavedTopRow As Integer, SavedLeftCol As Integer
Dim SavedRow As Integer, SavedCol As Integer

'Variable specifying the data file to load
Dim FileName As String

'Variable used for reverse tabbing
Dim Shifting As Integer
```

The *GridStatusSave* and *GridStatusRestore* Procedures

A grid application must often change the grid's row, column, and selected area in order to access target data contained in the grid. When this change happens, the row, column, and selected area set by the user are changed. To ensure that the application operates in a consistent and reliable manner, you must restore the grid's status after such operations; the grid then appears unmodified to the user.

For PhoneBook, the GridStatusSave procedure saves the grid status, and the GridStatusRestore procedure restores the saved status. The parameters saved include the row and column of the current cell, the area of selected cells, and several appearance attributes.

GridStatusSave and GridStatusRestore are both user-defined procedures placed in the General Declarations section of the form. The GridStatusSave procedure is as follows:

```
Sub GridStatusSave ()

    SavedStartRow = Grid1.SelStartRow
    SavedEndRow = Grid1.SelEndRow

    SavedStartCol = Grid1.SelStartCol
    SavedEndCol = Grid1.SelEndCol

    SavedRow = Grid1.Row
    SavedCol = Grid1.Col

    SavedTopRow = Grid1.TopRow
    SavedLeftCol = Grid1.LeftCol

End Sub
```

The following GridStatusRestore procedure uses the same form-level variables found in GridStatusSave:

```
Sub GridStatusRestore ()
    On Error Resume Next
    'Ignore errors generated by
    'setting selected regions
    'outside of grid boundaries.

    Grid1.LeftCol = SavedLeftCol
    Grid1.TopRow = SavedTopRow

    Grid1.SelStartRow = SavedStartRow
    Grid1.SelEndRow = SavedEndRow
    Grid1.SelStartCol = SavedStartCol
    Grid1.SelEndCol = SavedEndCol

    On Error GoTo 0
```

```
'Restore active row & column if possible
If SavedRow <= Grid1.Rows - 1 Then
   Grid1.Row = SavedRow
Else
   Grid1.Row = Grid1.Rows - 1
End If

If SavedCol <= Grid1.Cols - 1 Then
   Grid1.Col = SavedCol
Else
   Grid1.Col = Grid1.Col - 1
End If

End Sub
```

Notice that the second section of GridStatusRestore attempts to restore the previous row and column. However, such restoration may not be possible if a row has been deleted. Although the PhoneBook application doesn't allow for the deletion of columns, other applications you write may do so. You can use GridStatusSave and GridStatusRestore in other applications involving the Grid control.

The *UnSelect* Procedure

The UnSelect procedure is necessary because of a limitation in the Grid control. With program code, you can't unselect every cell using property values. You might want to unselect all cells so that, for example, no cells are highlighted.

Here's the problem. To select a region of cells, you can set SelStartRow, SelEndRow, SelStartCol, and SelEndCol accordingly. To undo a selection, you could set SelStartRow and SelEndRow to the same value and do the same with SelStartCol and SelEndCol. However, that arrangement leaves a selected region consisting of a single cell. You can't unselect *every* cell by modifying the values of these properties in program code.

The solution is to issue a SendKeys instruction that moves the current cell right and then left, as if the user had pressed arrow keys. Remember that, when a region of cells is selected, moving the current cell using the keyboard unselects all selected cells. The purpose of the UnSelect procedure is to simulate such keystrokes. The effect is to unselect all cells while retaining the cursor at the same current cell. For more information about SendKeys, see Chapter 23, "Responding to Keyboard Events."

Place the following procedure in the General Declarations section of the form:

```
Sub UnSelect ()
    'Unselects any selected region of cells
    If Grid1.Visible = False Then Exit Sub

    Grid1.SetFocus

    Select Case Grid1.Col
        Case 1
            SendKeys "{RIGHT}{LEFT}"
        Case Grid1.Cols - 1
            SendKeys "{LEFT}{RIGHT}"
        Case Else
            SendKeys "{LEFT}{RIGHT}"
    End Select
End Sub
```

This procedure is written so that the current cell can be in the rightmost or leftmost column of the grid. UnSelect also allows for the fact that you can't move to column 0 using keystrokes because that column is fixed.

The *AddGridLine* Procedure

You now must develop some of the procedures that produce the necessary results when the user clicks on the various command buttons. The AddGridLine procedure simply adds a row of empty cells to the grid using the AddItem method. This procedure also puts a row number in column 0 of the newly created row. After the row has been added to the grid, the grid display is adjusted to show the new bottom row.

Place the following AddGridLine procedure in the General Declarations section of the form:

```
Sub AddGridLine ()
    Dim Test As Integer
    Dim Dummy As Integer

    GridStatusSave

    UnSelect

    Grid1.Rows = Grid1.Rows + 1    'Add the row
    Grid1.Row = Grid1.Rows - 1     'Move to the new row
    Grid1.Col = 0                  'Insert the row number
```

```
Grid1.Text = Format$(Grid1.Row)

On Error Resume Next
Test = Grid1.Row
Do    'Find the first possible TopRow above the added row
    Grid1.TopRow = Test%
    If Err Then
    Err = 0
    Test% = Test% - 1
    Else
    Exit Do
    End If
Loop
On Error GoTo 0
Dummy = DoEvents()
UnSelect
Grid1.Col = 1

End Sub
```

AddGridLine demonstrates the use of the TopRow property. The procedure searches for the first permissible TopRow setting above the newly added row, and sets the value of TopRow to that setting. As a result, when you add a new line to the grid, the grid display adjusts downward so that the newly added row is the bottommost visible row.

The *DeleteGridLine* Procedure

The DeleteGridLine procedure is the companion procedure to AddGridLine. DeleteGridLine removes the current row. It does not, however, use the RemoveItem method. Normally, RemoveItem would be the way to go, but the PhoneBook application retains the line number of each entry in the phone list. Simply deleting a line results in a gap in the line numbers.

Instead, DeleteGridLine cycles through every physical row below the current row (that is, cycles through higher row numbers). The procedure selects columns one through seven in each of these rows and moves the contents of the grid's Clip (the selected data) up to the previous row. At the end of this process, the last row in the grid is deleted using RemoveItem. The final result is that the current row is removed, and all row numbers are maintained correctly.

Because deleting a row is a permanent sort of thing, a message box requests the user's confirmation before deleting the row.

Here's the `DeleteGridLine` procedure. Like the other user-defined procedures, it goes in the General Declarations section of the form:

```
Sub DeleteGridLine ()
    Dim Msg As String
    Dim Temp As String
    Dim C As Integer
    Dim X As Integer     'Loop counter

    Msg = "Delete line " & Grid1.Row & " from grid?"
    C = MsgBox(Msg, 32 + 4, "Delete Line")
    If C = 7 Then Exit Sub    'User clicked NO.

    Grid1.HighLight = False

    Grid1.SelStartCol = 1    'Don't select the row number
    Grid1.SelEndCol = Grid1.Cols - 1

    For X = Grid1.Row To Grid1.Rows - 2
        Grid1.SelStartRow = X + 1
        Grid1.SelEndRow = X + 1
        Temp = Grid1.Clip
        Grid1.SelStartRow = X
        Grid1.SelEndRow = X
        Grid1.Clip = Temp
    Next X
    Grid1.Rows = Grid1.Rows - 1
    UnSelect
    Grid1.HighLight = True
End Sub
```

`DeleteGridLine` operates on the assumption that the currently selected row is the row to delete. You can easily modify this procedure to accept a row number as a parameter and delete that row.

The *CopyLine* Procedure

The `CopyLine` procedure copies the current row of the grid to a new row at the bottom of the grid. The technique involves selecting the relevant data from the current row (columns 1 through 7), saving the grid's `Clip` data to a temporary variable, adding a new row, and then pasting the saved data into the new row. Because this process happens quickly, the procedure doesn't bother disabling the grid's `HighLight` property.

Place the following `CopyLine` procedure in the form's General Declarations section:

```
Sub CopyLine ()
    Dim Temp As String

    GridStatusSave

    Grid1.SelStartCol = 1
    Grid1.SelEndCol = Grid1.Cols - 1
    Grid1.SelStartRow = Grid1.Row
    Grid1.SelEndRow = Grid1.Row
    Temp = Format$(Grid1.Rows) + Chr$(9) + Grid1.Clip

    Grid1.AddItem Temp

    GridStatusRestore
    Grid1.Row = Grid1.Rows - 1
    Grid1.Col = 1
    UnSelect

End Sub
```

The *ShutDown* Procedure

The `ShutDown` procedure is simple enough. This procedure is called by `Command1_Click` when the user clicks the `Exit` command button (to terminate the application). Place the following `ShutDown` procedure in the General Declarations section of the form:

```
Sub Shutdown ()
    End
End Sub
```

Creating the Floating Text Box

As mentioned earlier in this chapter, the Grid control does not offer the user the capability of directly editing the contents of a cell. In Chapter 23, "Responding to Keyboard Events," the `GridControl` application uses a grid and text box combination so that the user can edit the contents of individual grid cells. In the PhoneBook application, that capability is enhanced by creating a floating text box.

The floating text box is kept invisible until the user wants to edit the contents of a cell. The user signals the desire to edit a cell in a number of ways: double-clicking a cell using the mouse, pressing Enter, or just typing letters or numbers.

When the user edits a cell, PhoneBook places a Text box control directly over the cell and makes the text box visible. The text box has the same size and shape as the cell. The result is that the user appears to be editing directly in the cell, but the editing really takes place in the text box!

The *ShowTextBox* Procedure

Determining the exact size of the text box and where to place it can be tricky. You must take into account the width of the cell column, the thickness of the lines separating each cell, and the top and left edges of the grid itself. The following procedure, called ShowTextBox, is the result of these considerations and goes in the General Declarations section of the form:

```
Sub ShowTextBox ()
    Dim TestX As Integer, TestY As Integer
    Dim C As Integer    'Loop counter

    'Hide the text box and make it two lines tall and wide (for starters)
    Text1.Visible = False
    Text1.Height = Grid1.RowHeight(Grid1.Row) - (Screen.TwipsPerPixelY * 2)
    Text1.Width = Grid1.ColWidth(Grid1.Col) - (Screen.TwipsPerPixelX * 2)

    'Determine the X coordinate of the current cell, figuring in
    ➥Grid1.LeftCol

    'Get the left edge of the grid plus two linewidths...
    TestX = Grid1.Left + Grid1.ColWidth(0) + (Screen.TwipsPerPixelX * 3)

    'Sum all column widths...
    For C = Grid1.LeftCol To Grid1.Col - 1
        TestX = TestX + Grid1.ColWidth + Screen.TwipsPerPixelX
    Next C

    'Determine the Y coordinate of the current cell, figuring in
    ➥Grid1.TopRow

    'Get the top edge of the grid plus two lineheights...
    TestY = Grid1.Top + Grid1.RowHeight(0) + (Screen.TwipsPerPixelY * 2)
```

```
'Sum all column heights...
For C = Grid1.TopRow To Grid1.Row - 1
    TestY = TestY + Grid1.RowHeight + Screen.TwipsPerPixelY
Next C



'Position the text box control
Text1.Left = TestX
Text1.Top = TestY

Text1.ZOrder          'Make sure it's on top!
Text1.Visible = True  'Show it
Text1.SetFocus        'Make it active

End Sub
```

Notice that the Screen properties, TwipsPerPixelX and TwipsPerPixelY, are used throughout ShowTextBox. These Screen properties ensure that the text box (Text1) appears *exactly* within the boundaries of the cell.

The border around the entire grid and the lines separating each cell are each one pixel wide. You must take these one-pixel line widths into account for the grid itself and for each column and row. Text1 has no border style, so the text box fits neatly in the cell being edited. The result is that the text box masquerades as the cell being updated until the editing is completed or canceled.

 NOTE The actual width of a pixel can vary from monitor to monitor, depending on the display resolution of the current Windows video driver. The Screen's TwipsPerPixel properties are used for this reason.

Recognizing Cell Editing

The next task is to create the code for Grid1 so that the Grid control can recognize when the user wants to edit a cell. You must ensure that the user can cancel editing and that standard keyboard navigation rules remain in effect while the user types.

Cell editing begins when any of the following situations occur:

- The user double-clicks a cell.
- The user presses Enter (with the focus on a cell).
- The user starts typing letters or numbers (with the focus on a cell).

On the other hand, cell editing terminates in the following situations:

■ The user presses Enter.

■ The user moves away from the cell using an arrow key.

■ The user clicks on another cell.

Furthermore, cell editing is canceled if the user presses Escape.

Using the Tab Key

The user can navigate the cells in a grid using the arrow keys; this capability is built into the Grid control. However, many Windows-based applications (including Visual Basic), allow the user to move between data fields by pressing the Tab key.

To enable the user to use the Tab key for grid navigation and to recognize when the user wants to begin editing, you can utilize the grid's KeyPress and KeyDown event procedures.

Here is the code for the Grid1_KeyPress procedure:

```
Sub Grid1_KeyPress (KeyAscii As Integer)
   Dim Char As String

   Select Case KeyAscii
   Case 27  'Escape key was pressed
      ' Text1.Text = Grid1.Text  -- Add this if desired

   Case 9    'Tab: move to next column
      If Shifting Then  'Keydown event captured a shift key.
            'Move Left
        If Grid1.Col > 1 Then
           Grid1.Col = Grid1.Col - 1
        End If
      Else 'No shift key.  Move right.
        If Grid1.Col < (Grid1.Cols - 1) Then
           Grid1.Col = Grid1.Col + 1
        End If
      End If
      UnSelect

   Case Else
      If KeyAscii = 13 Then  'Show Text1 with full text
         Text1.Text = Grid1.Text
```

```
           Text1.SelStart = Len(Text1.Text)
      Else   'Send char to Text1, then show it
           Char = Chr$(KeyAscii)
           Text1.Text = Char
           Text1.SelStart = 1
      End If
      ShowTextBox
      KeyAscii = 0
   End Select
End Sub
```

Notice how the KeyPress procedure uses the form-level variable Shifting to determine whether the Shift key is being pressed. The value of Shifting is set in the Grid1_KeyDown event procedure. Here is the necessary code:

```
Sub Grid1_KeyDown (KeyCode As Integer, Shift As Integer)
   Text1.Visible = False    'just in case...
   If Shift = 1 Then Shifting = True Else Shifting = False
End Sub
```

The Text Box Event Procedures

When the user is not editing a cell's contents, the floating text box displays the contents of the current grid cell. The simplest way to keep the contents of the text box up to date is to use the grid's RowColChange event procedure.

Whenever the current grid cell changes, the event procedure loads the contents of the current grid cell into the Text property of the text box. Here is the Grid1_RowColChange event procedure:

```
Sub Grid1_RowColChange ()
    Text1.Text = Grid1.Text
End Sub
```

The floating text box requires some code in order for it to determine when editing ends and how to respond when it does. Remember the keystroke guidelines: pressing Escape cancels editing, and pressing Enter, Tab, or an arrow key completes editing.

The necessary code goes in the Text1_KeyPress event procedure as follows:

```
Sub Text1_KeyPress (KeyAscii As Integer)
   Select Case KeyAscii
      Case 13, 9    'Enter or Tab
      Grid1.Text = Text1.Text
      Text1.Visible = False
```

```
      Grid1.SetFocus
      If KeyAscii = 9 And Grid1.Col < Grid1.Cols - 1 Then
          If Shifting Then    'Keydown event captured a Shift key.
                        'Move Left
              If Grid1.Col > 1 Then
                  Grid1.Col = Grid1.Col - 1
              End If
          Else    'No Shift key.  Move right.
              If Grid1.Col < (Grid1.Cols - 1) Then
                  Grid1.Col = Grid1.Col + 1
              End If
          End If
          UnSelect
      End If
      KeyAscii = 0
      Case 27    'Escape
      KeyAscii = 0
      Text1.Visible = False
      Grid1.SetFocus
    End Select
End Sub
```

The Text1_KeyPress procedure responds to the Escape, Tab, and Enter keys. The text box, however, must also respond correctly when the user presses the up-arrow or down-arrow keys, events that KeyPress does not recognize.

However, the KeyDown event can recognize the arrow keys. That's where the code to respond to the arrow keys goes. Here is the Text1_KeyDown event procedure.

The KeyDown event can recognize the arrow keys. The code to respond to the arrow keys goes in the KeyDown procedure. Here is the Text1_KeyDown event procedure for this application:

```
Sub Text1_KeyDown (KeyCode As Integer, Shift As Integer)
    If Shift = 1 Then
        Shifting = True
    Else
        Shifting = False
    End If

    Select Case KeyCode
    Case 38 ' up
        Text1_KeyPress 13    'Simulate Enter key
        SendKeys "{UP}"
```

```
Case 40 ' down
    Text1_KeyPress 13    'Simulate Enter key
    SendKeys "{DOWN}"

End Select

End Sub
```

Double-Clicking a Grid Cell

The user double-clicking a grid cell is a signal to begin editing the cell. The
Grid1_DblClick event procedure initiates cell editing by sending the Enter key
to the grid's KeyPress event:

```
Sub Grid1_DblClick ()
   If Grid1.Row > 0 And Grid1.Col > 0 Then Grid1_KeyPress 13
End Sub
```

Hiding the Text Box

If the user clicks the mouse, editing is over. In this case, the text box must
again become invisible. Here's the Grid1_MouseDown procedure:

```
Sub Grid1_MouseDown (Button As Integer, Shift As Integer, X As Single,
➥Y As Single)
   Text1.Visible = False
End Sub
```

Writing and Reading the Data File

At this point, you can try running PhoneBook. The application starts with an
empty grid, as shown in Figure 26.11.

Notice the phone icon displayed in the upper left corner. This icon is an
example of a grid cell containing picture data. (The icon is copied from the
data in the Form1.Icon property. Recall that the form's Icon property specifies
the icon which appears when the form is minimized.)

You can add rows, edit individual cells, and delete grid rows. Try entering
some data to see how the floating text box works. Notice that you seem to be
typing the data directly into the grid cell.

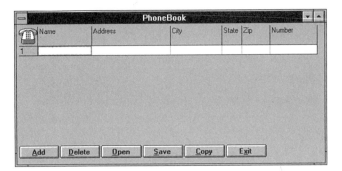

Figure 26.11.

The PhoneBook
application with blank
data fields.

The application, however, does not yet contain any code to save or load data
files. (The Open and Save command buttons are not operational.) That's where
the user-defined SaveFile and LoadFile procedures come into play. Before
typing these procedures, click the Exit command button to terminate the
application and return Visual Basic to Design mode.

The *SaveFile* Procedure

The SaveFile procedure places a copy of the grid data into a text file and saves
that file on disk. Although the code for SaveFile may appear complex, in
reality, the procedure is divided into three sections that are fairly easy to
understand.

First, if no file name had been previously specified by the user, the procedure
asks the user for a file name. The file is saved with this file name. To get the file
name, SaveFile uses the InputBox function. (Other choices would be to use a
customized dialog box or the Common Dialog custom control, but InputBox is
used here for simplicity.) Be aware that SaveFile does little error checking
here. If a file specification error occurs, the user is alerted and the application
terminates. The form-level variable FileName holds the specified file name
without the path.

Second, SaveFile must determine the data to save and prepare that data to be
written to a file. SaveFile accomplishes this step by selecting all the rows and
columns of the grid and copying the Grid1.Clip property to a temporary string
variable named Contents.

Third, SaveFile must actually write the data in Contents to the disk file. Here,
the Print# statement is used. For more about Print# and the techniques of
saving data in disk files, see Chapter 25, "Processing Files."

The following code is for the SaveFile procedure. Place this procedure in the
General Declarations section of the form:

```
Sub SaveFile ()
   Dim Contents As String, Msg As String

   'Get a filename using the InputBox function.
   If FileName = "" Then    'Get a filename
      P$ = "Enter filename to save to:"  'prompt
      T$ = "Save File"                   'title
      D$ = "PHONBOOK.TXT"                'default name
      FileName = UCase$(InputBox(P$, T$, D$))
      If FileName = "" Then Exit Sub     'user canceled
   End If

   Form1.Caption = "PhoneBook - " & FileName

   'Prep grid, screen for activity
   Screen.MousePointer = 11   'hourglass
   Grid1.HighLight = False
   GridStatusSave
   UnSelect

   'Select grid data (minus row numbers) and
   'copy grid contents (Grid1.Clip) into temp variable
   Grid1.SelStartRow = 1
   Grid1.SelEndRow = Grid1.Rows - 1
   Grid1.FixedCols = 0
   Grid1.SelStartCol = 0
   Grid1.SelEndCol = Grid1.Cols - 1
   Contents = Grid1.Clip
   Grid1.FixedCols = 1

   On Error GoTo SaveFileError

   'Open and write the file
   Open App.Path + "\" + FileName For Output As #1
   Print #1, Contents  'Write variable contents to saved file
   Close #1
   On Error GoTo 0

   GridStatusRestore
   Grid1.Visible = True
   UnSelect
   Grid1.HighLight = True
```

```
    Screen.MousePointer = 0

Exit Sub

SaveFileError:
    Msg$ = "Error " & Err & " saving " + FileName + ": " + Error$ + "."
    MsgBox Msg, 48
    Close
    Screen.MousePointer = 0
    Exit Sub

End Sub
```

The *LoadFile* Procedure

The LoadFile procedure reads the contents of a disk file and places the data into the grid. LoadFile only works correctly with data files previously saved with SaveFile. (You can load other data files into the grid with LoadFile, but if the Tab and carriage-return characters aren't properly formatted in the data file, the resulting grid display won't make much sense.)

SaveFile copied the grid data by assigning Grid1.Clip to the string variable Contents. The proper Chr$(9) and Chr$(13) characters (Tab and CR, respectively) are automatically included in Grid1.Clip. As a result, the Contents variable and the disk file are properly formatted.

LoadFile uses an input box to request from the user the name of the file containing the stored data. The data in the file is read one line at a time; each line of data is appended to the grid using the AddItem method. The tabs, which separate the data value for each cell, are already embedded in the data read from the disk.

The following code is the LoadFile procedure and, once again, must be placed in the General Declarations section of the form:

```
Sub LoadFile ()
    Dim Ctr As Integer
    Dim Msg As String

    'Get the file name
    P$ = "Enter filename to load:"     'prompt
    T$ = "Load File"                   'title
    D$ = "PHONBOOK.TXT"                'default file name
    NewFileName = UCase$(InputBox(P$, T$, D$))
```

```
If NewFileName = "" Then Exit Sub 'user canceled

Screen.MousePointer = 11
Grid1.HighLight = False
UnSelect

'Remove every row except row 0 (column headings)
Grid1.FixedRows = 0
Grid1.Rows = 1



'Read file one line at a time and add to grid

If InStr(NewFileName, "\") = 0 Then  'Assume current dir
    FullFileName = App.Path & "\" & NewFileName
Else
    FullFileName = NewFileName
End If

On Error GoTo LoadFileError

If Dir(FullFileName) <> "" Then        'Check if file exists.
    Open FullFileName For Input As #1  'If it does, open it.

    Screen.MousePointer = 11

    Ctr = 1                     'Initialize the line counter
    Do While Not EOF(1)         'Read file data until you're done
        Line Input #1, TextLine 'Get complete line.
        Grid1.AddItem TextLine  'Add it to the grid at the proper line
        Ctr = Ctr + 1           'Increment the line counter
    Loop
    Close 1
    Screen.MousePointer = 0
Else
    MsgBox "File " & FullFileName & " not found.", 48
End If

'Reset fixed rows to 1, and move to the
'top left corner of the grid
Grid1.FixedRows = 1
Grid1.Row = 1
Grid1.Col = 1
```

```
    Grid1.HighLight = True
    Grid1.SetFocus

    FileName = NewFileName    'Update form-level variable
    Form1.Caption = "PhoneBook - " + FileName 'Update form caption
    On Error GoTo 0

Exit Sub

LoadFileError:
    Msg = "Error " & Err & " Loading " & NewFileName
    Msg = Msg & ": " & Error$ & "."
    MsgBox Msg, 48
    Close
    Exit Sub
End Sub
```

Putting PhoneBook to Work

PhoneBook is complete! Save the form as PHONEBK.FRM and the project as PHONEBK.MAK.

PhoneBook has quite a bit of code, but the final result is a practical, database-like application. You can use PhoneBook to keep a record of your personal contacts. You might store different name lists in different disk files. For example, you might keep one data file of your business contacts and another file of your friends and relatives.

Summary

The Grid control can quickly and conveniently display tabular data in a form familiar to spreadsheet users. The Grid's Row and Col properties can be read or set to highlight an individual cell. The SelStartRow, SelEndRow, SelStartCol, and SelEndCol properties work with regions of cells. With the Text property, you can obtain the contents of a single cell, and the Clip property provides the data in the grid's selected region.

A grid can display both text and pictures. Text data is internally represented with a Tab (Chr$(9)) separating the data in adjoining cells and a carriage return (Chr$(13)) terminating each row. This internal data arrangement provides a convenient mechanism for inserting and extracting data to and from the grid.

A grid also has a number of display-related properties that you can set or read at run time. These properties include column width, row height, `TopRow`, and `LeftCol`. The value of the `HighLight` property determines whether selected cells appear highlighted, and the value of the `GridLines` property determines whether cell borders appear.

Creating Multiple Document Interfaces (MDI)

With Visual Basic's Multiple Document Interface (MDI), you can create applications that have the multitasking orientation of Windows. An MDI application features a single parent form that contains one or more child forms. You can manipulate the child forms like ordinary forms, except that child forms always stay within the boundaries of the parent form.

Most of the major commercial Windows applications include MDI functionality. Examples are Windows word processors such as Microsoft Word and WordPerfect, and Windows spreadsheets such as Excel and Lotus 1-2-3. These applications are document-oriented. You can simultaneously open several documents (child windows) in the main parent window.

With Word, for example, you can open several documents simultaneously and transfer text from one document to another. In fact, MDI was originally conceived as a way for word processing programs to work with multiple documents. MDI functionality has since been expanded into many new areas and uses.

Windows includes several MDI programs and utilities. The Windows File Manager is a multiple-document application, as is SysEdit, the multiple-document text editor used to check out your computer's configuration. However, the Windows MDI application with which you're probably most familiar is the Program Manager. Each Program Manager group is displayed as a child window within the main window.

This chapter explains the various components of an MDI application and tells how MDI applications behave. The main topics discussed in this chapter are as follows:

- Understanding MDI parent forms and their characteristics
- Working with MDI child forms
- Creating multiple instances of a child form
- Using a form array to manage child forms
- Arranging child forms with the Arrange method
- Using menus in MDI applications

You also create MultiView, a Visual Basic application that enables you to simultaneously view and edit multiple bitmap files. Each bitmap file is loaded as a child window into a parent form.

Understanding an MDI Application

An MDI application in Visual Basic consists of a single parent form and a number of child forms contained within the parent. The parent form acts as a background window for the child forms. As mentioned previously, MDI applications have a parent form and a number of child forms. Each child form is bounded by the parent.

 NOTE MDI applications can also have regular forms. Unlike child forms, regular forms are not restricted inside the borders of the MDI parent. Regular forms behave the same in MDI applications as they do in standard applications.

Using MDI Forms

The parent form is a unique type of form in Visual Basic. You can only have one MDI parent form in any application.

An MDI parent form can contain child forms. The only controls you can place on a parent form are those controls that have the Align property. In the Standard Edition of Visual Basic, the Picture box is the only control that has the Align property. (The Professional Edition of Visual Basic has several custom controls, such as the 3DPanel control, which have the Align property.)

The Picture box is a *container* control that, by definition, can contain other controls. An MDI parent form must align its container controls at the top or bottom of its client area, always leaving a clear rectangular field within the parent. The MDI form's child windows are placed and manipulated in this rectangular field.

You cannot place non-Align controls directly on a parent form. Instead, you place a picture box (or other container control) on the parent form and then place other controls into the picture box. By placing other controls in a picture box, you can build a toolbar or status bar in an MDI parent. Generally, in MDI applications, the program functionality resides in the child forms, not in the parent.

The *Arrange* Method

In code, an MDI parent form can arrange its child windows using the Arrange method. Child windows can be tiled or cascaded. When *tiled*, the child windows are arranged and resized so that there is no overlapping. Child windows can be tiled horizontally or vertically.

When *cascaded*, the child windows are overlapped consecutively. Each successive child window is placed slightly below and to the right of the previous child.

Demonstrating the *Arrange* Method

You can observe tiling and cascading with the SysEdit application that comes with Windows. Follow these steps:

1. Open the Windows Program Manager and choose the **R**un option from the **F**ile menu.

2. In the Run dialog box, type **SYSEDIT** and press Enter.

   The SysEdit application opens and loads four system text files: CONFIG.SYS, AUTOEXEC.BAT, SYSTEM.INI, and WIN.INI. (This application lets you edit the contents of these files. However, be advised not to do so unless you are confident in your changes. Careless edits to these files can adversely affect the performance of your computer including a strong likelihood of system crashes.)

3. Choose the **T**ile option from the **W**indow menu. The four child windows are tiled. Figure 27.1 shows the result.

4. Choose the **C**ascade option from the **W**indow menu. The child windows are cascaded (see Figure 27.2).

5. Close SysEdit by choosing the Exit option from its **F**ile menu.

   If you made some accidental edits to the system files, select No when prompted if you want to save your changes.

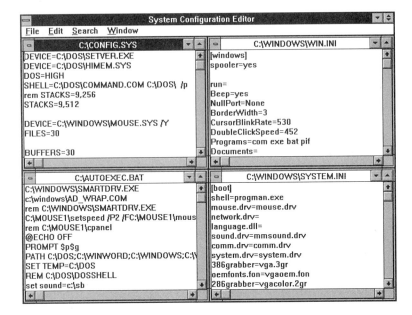

Figure 27.1.

SysEdit with tiled windows.

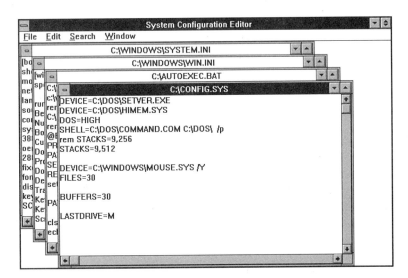

Figure 27.2.

SysEdit with cascaded windows.

Arranging Icons

In an MDI parent application, you can minimize the child windows to icons. You can use Visual Basic's Arrange method to neatly arrange the icons along the bottom edge of the parent's client area. Figure 27.3 shows the SysEdit application with neatly arranged icons.

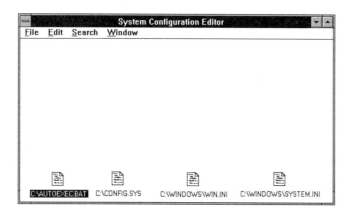

Building an MDI Application

You build an MDI application just like you build any other application: add forms and controls using the File menu and the toolbox, and then write program code with the Code editor.

However, the presence of child windows means that you have to think about MDI applications a bit differently than you do other applications. If you plan on having multiple instances of the same child form in the parent form, you must write code that manages all the child forms. If different types of child forms exist, your code must allow for each form to have its individual functionality within the context of the parent form.

Adding an MDI Form to a Project

To get some experience with MDI applications, start a new project. To add an MDI parent form to an application, you use Visual Basic's menu system. Choose the New MDI Form option from the File menu. The MDI parent form appears. The caption on the parent form reads MDIForm1. If you check the Properties window, you see that the default name for this parent form is also MDIForm1.

The regular form, Form1, is still present. Figure 27.4 shows the budding project at design time. Form1 and MDIForm1 are present.

Open Visual Basic's File menu once again. Notice that the New MDI Form option is now dimmed. You can have only a single MDI parent in any application. After an MDI parent is present, you cannot add another parent form to your project.

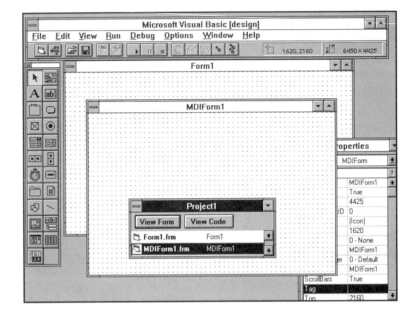

Figure 27.4.

A new project with a
regular form and an MDI
parent form.

Depending on the Windows color scheme that you have selected with the
Window Control Panel, you may notice that the color of the client area of the
MDI form does not match the color of regular forms. Instead, the client
area of the MDI parent form matches the Windows settings for application
workspaces. As such, the default background color of your MDI parent form
can be different than the background color of regular forms.

NOTE   To see the background color difference between MDI parent forms
and regular forms, you may have to use the Windows Control Panel
to adjust the Windows color scheme. Try selecting a color scheme
other than the Windows default.

Creating a Child Window

To designate any regular form as a child form, all you need to do is set the
form's MDIChild property to True. To try setting the property, click anywhere
on Form1 (not on MDIForm1) to give Form1 the focus. Then press F4 to open the
Properties window. Set the value of the MDIChild property to True.

You won't see any change in Form1 at design time. You can freely move the
form around the desktop, resize the form, use the toolbox to add any controls,
create a menu system, and write event procedures. When you run the application, however, the child form is contained within the parent.

Try running the application. The two forms appear together, with the child Form1 in the parent MDIForm1 (see Figure 27.5).

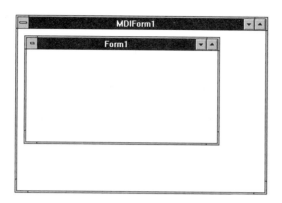

Figure 27.5.

The new MDI project at run time.

Try moving and resizing Form1. You cannot move the form outside of the parent. Minimize Form1. The icon appears within the parent. Notice that the icon for an MDI form is slightly different than the icon for a regular form. You can also observe MDI form icons in the Project window.

Now maximize Form1. The child form expands to fill the entire client area of MDIForm1. Notice that the caption of the child form combines with the caption of the parent form. The combined caption is displayed in the title bar for the parent form and, in this case, appears as follows:

```
MDIForm1 - [Form1]
```

You can minimize, maximize, restore, and move a child form just like a regular form, but only within the borders of the parent form.

Try minimizing the parent form. The icon for the parent form appears on the desktop. The child form disappears from view. The single icon represents all the child forms as well as the parent form. When you restore the parent, the child form reappears as well.

Understanding Scroll Bars

As you have seen, child forms are restricted to the area within the parent. However, if you move a child form (or resize the parent) so that part of the child form is outside the boundaries of the parent, scroll bars appear on the parent. Using these scroll bars, you can move the visible portion of the parent's client area to eventually reveal the entire parent window. The scroll bars ensure that you can access each child form in its entirety.

You can demonstrate scroll bars using the sample application. With the application still running, move the child form to the boundaries of the parent. Figure 27.6 shows the parent form's scroll bars.

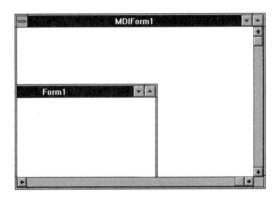

Figure 27.6.

The parent form with scroll bars.

Unlike the ScrollBars property for the grid and text box, the ScrollBars property of an MDI parent form has only two values: True and False. When True (the default value), scroll bars appear when any part of a child form is beyond the parent's borders. You can prevent scroll bars from appearing by setting the ScrollBars property of the parent form to False. You can modify the value of ScrollBars at design time or by using program code.

Using the *Arrange* Method

In the program code of MDI applications, you can use the Arrange method to tile, cascade, and arrange the icons of child forms. The Arrange method applies only to MDI parent forms.

mdiform.Arrange *arrangemode*

in which

    mdiform is the name of the MDI parent form,

and

    arrangemode specifies the desired arrangement.

The value of *arrangemode* is an integer from 0 to 3 (see Table 27.1).

Table 27.1. Values for the *arrangemode* parameter.

arrangemode	CONSTANT.TXT constant	Meaning
0	CASCADE	Cascade child forms
1	TILE_HORIZONTAL	Tile child forms horizontally
2	TILE_VERTICAL	Tile child forms vertically
3	ARRANGE_ICONS	Neatly align icons

For example, the following instruction cascades the child forms of the parent form MDIForm1:

```
MDIForm1.Arrange 0      'Cascade child forms
```

By loading the CONSTANT.TXT file into an application, you can use a constant from the second column of Table 27.1 as the *arrangemode* parameter. For example, the following instruction arranges the icons:

```
MDIForm1.Arrange ARRANGE_ICONS
```

Using the *ActiveForm* Property

When an MDI application has several child forms, the program code can use the parent form's ActiveForm property to identify which child form has the focus. As it's name implies, this property works something like the ActiveControl property for regular forms.

The ActiveForm property is available only at run time. You can read the value of the property to determine the active form. You cannot, however, set the value in an attempt to change the active child form.

The primary uses of ActiveForm are to access the child's properties and to invoke methods on the child forms. For example, the following instruction sets the value of MyTitle$ to the value of the active form's Caption property:

```
MyTitle$ = Form1.ActiveForm.Caption
```

Similarly, the following instruction displays a message in the active child form:

```
Form1.ActiveForm.Print "The focus is on me"
```

Adding Menus to MDI Applications

As mentioned earlier in the chapter, you can work with a child form at design time much as you work with any form in a non-MDI application. For example, you can add controls, set property values, and write code.

You can also add menus to both the parent and child forms. At run time, however, MDI applications handle menus in a specialized way. Whenever a child form with a menu becomes active, the child's menu appears in the parent's menu bar. If the parent form has a menu bar, those menus are visible only when no child forms are loaded or when the active child does not have its own menus.

When developing applications, the fact that a parent window adopts the menu of the active child can be an advantage and a disadvantage. When you have different child forms with different functionalities, it's convenient to have the main parent menu adjust to reflect the options available with the active child.

On the other hand, if you have a parent menu item that you always want available, you must place this item in every child's menu. You typically place the code called from such menus into a global code module.

One helpful menu feature in MDI applications is the `WindowList` menu property. To enable this property for a menu item at design time, check the Window List box in the Menu Design window.

By setting the value of the `WindowList` property to True in one of the form's menus, you create a menu that lists all the captions of the existing child windows. When this menu is open, the user can quickly switch to any available child window by clicking the appropriate caption name displayed in the menu. You typically use this option with a menu named Window. Program Manager is an example of an application with such a Window menu.

Studying the Characteristics of Child Forms

As explained previously, all you need to do to make a form into an MDI child form is to set the value of the form's `MDIChild` property to True. You set this value at design time using the Properties window. At design time, child forms look and behave like any other form. Most notably, child forms are not restricted within the boundaries of the parent form.

At run time, you cannot load and show an MDI child form without the parent. If you `Load` or `Show` a child form, the parent is automatically loaded and/or shown as well (assuming that the parent was not previously loaded and shown).

You can demonstrate this process by going back to the sample application consisting of the parent `MDIForm1` and the child `Form1`. Choose the **P**roject item from Visual Basic's **O**ptions menu to open the Project Options dialog box. Notice that the Start Up Form option specifies `Form1`.

When you run the application, Form1 loads, but because Form1 is an MDI child, Visual Basic also loads and shows the parent MDIForm1. Now, from the Project Options dialog box, change the Start Up Form to MDIForm1. Rerun the application. In this case, only the parent form loads. As explained later in this chapter, you must use program code to load and display the child forms.

In an MDI application, Visual Basic determines the initial size and placement of each child window when the form loads. You can, however, write code to change the initial placement. By default, each child window is cascaded in the parent window as the child windows load.

By definition, you cannot hide MDI child forms. You can minimize or unload them at any time, however. In addition, child forms cannot be modal. Regular (non-MDI) forms, however, can be loaded or shown modally in an application that has parent and child forms.

Using a Form Array

Many MDI applications employ multiple instances of the same kind of child form. The Windows File Manager is a typical example. When you choose the **New** Window option from the **Window** menu, the File Manager opens a second copy of the file-management window. This new window instance behaves just like the original window. By opening two such windows, you can work with different files and directories in each window.

As explained in Chapter 20, "Using Object Variables," Visual Basic applications can create multiple instances of a source form. Each instance has the same property values and program code as the source. As a result, each instance acts the same.

You can demonstrate multiple form instances in the current example by creating a Form_DblClick event procedure for Form1. First, using the Project Options dialog box, change the Start Up Form back to Form1. Open the code window for Form1. (If Form1 is not visible, use the Project window to open the Code window.)

Create the following event procedure for Form1:

```
Sub Form_DblClick
    Dim F As New Form1
    F.Show
End Sub
```

Run the application and double-click any child form a few times. A new child form pops into existence each time you double-click. Figure 27.7 shows the application with a total of four instances of Form1.

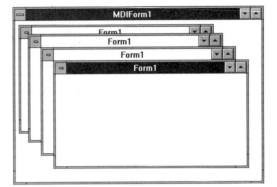

Figure 27.7.

The MDI sample
application with multiple
instances of `Form1`
loaded.

Although this event procedure produces quick results, multiple form instances are not beneficial unless you have a way to reference each child window individually. The best solution is a *form array*.

The form array technique involves defining a dynamic array of forms and an associated data array. The data array contains matching indexes that keep track of the forms. You can use form arrays with any type of form, but the technique is especially useful with MDI child forms. For more information about using form arrays, see the MultiView application later in this chapter.

Using the Me Keyword

As explained in Chapter 20, in the code for multiform applications, you can use the `Me` keyword to specify the current form. For example, the following instruction modifies the caption of the current form, which can be a child form in an MDI application:

```
Me.Caption = "I'm the only one with this caption!"
```

If you have multiple instances of a child form in an MDI application, the child forms are all based on a single source form. When the program code needs to reference the current form, use the `Me` keyword rather than the name of the source form. That way, you can ensure that the referenced form is indeed the currently active form.

You can test the `Me` keyword using the current sample application. Create the following `Form_Resize` event procedure for `Form1`:

```
Sub Form_Resize
    Me.Caption = "Width = " & Me.Width & "; Height = " & Me.Height
End Sub
```

Run the application and launch a few instances of Form1 by double-clicking any form two or three times. As you resize one of the child forms, you see its caption change to display its new dimensions. Figure 27.8 shows the result.

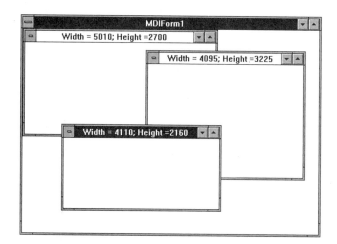

Figure 27.8.

Using the Me keyword in Form_Resize.

Creating the MultiView Application

MultiView is an MDI application with which you can simultaneously view multiple bitmap files. You can tile, cascade, or minimize all the child windows. Furthermore, with Windows Paintbrush, you can edit the picture in any window.

MultiView uses the form from the FileSelector application created in Chapter 25, "Processing Files." Figure 27.9 shows the full running version of MultiView.

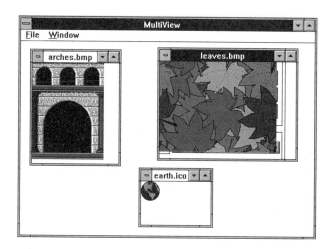

Figure 27.9.

The MultiView application.

MultiView includes three forms and a code module. The MDI parent form, MDIForm1, contains a child form named ViewerType. The ViewerType form contains an Image control that is used to display the pictures. The third form, FileOpen, is taken from the FileSelector application in Chapter 25, "Processing Files." As explained shortly, FileOpen is modified somewhat for this application. The code module is named MULTVIEW.BAS. This module contains the necessary global declarations.

Creating the Project

For this project, begin by creating a new subdirectory on your hard disk. Name the subdirectory MULTVIEW. You can place the subdirectory in any path (for example, C:\VB\MULTVIEW).

Copy the FileSelector form that you created in Chapter 25 to this new directory. (The file for the form was named FILESEL.FRM in Chapter 25). Rename the file in the MULTVIEW directory as FILEOPEN.FRM.

Start a new Visual Basic project. Using the Properties window, set the value of Form1's Name property to ViewerType. Also, set the value of its MDIChild property to True. Place an Image control on the form. The default name for this control is Image1. Save the ViewerType form as VIEWER.FRM in the MULTVIEW directory.

Create the MDI parent form by choosing the New MDI Form option from the File menu. The default name for this form is MDIForm1. (In the application, that name is retained.) Choose the **P**roject item from Visual Basic's **O**ptions menu to open the Project Options dialog box. Specify the Start Up Form as MDIForm1. Click the OK button to close the dialog box. Then, using Visual Basic's **F**ile menu, save the form as MDIFORM1.FRM in the MULTVIEW directory.

To add a code module to the project, choose the New **M**odule option from the File menu. Save the new module as MULTVIEW.BAS in the MULTVIEW directory. You place code in this module later in the chapter.

The next step is to add the FileOpen form to the project. Choose the A**d**d File option on the **F**ile menu. Select FILEOPEN.FRM in the MULTVIEW directory. (You just copied FILEOPEN.FRM into the MULTVIEW directory. The original version of the form was the FILESEL.FRM file developed in Chapter 25.) Later in this chapter, you make some modifications to the form's program code in order to work with MultiView.

Save the project by choosing the Sav**e** Project As option from the File menu. Save the project as MULTVIEW.MAK in the MULTVIEW directory.

You now have all the parts of the MultiView application in place. The following sections step you through the creation of the application.

NOTE As you follow the upcoming instructions to create MultiView, you add menus and controls and write program code in a methodical, linear fashion. In some cases, the program code for an event procedure invokes a Function or Sub that you have not yet created. If you see a procedure name in these instructions that you don't yet recognize, don't worry. The procedure will show up soon.

Creating the Code Module MULTVIEW.BAS

The larger code segments for the MultiView application are contained in the code module MULTVIEW.BAS. This module contains several user-defined procedures that accomplish most of the application's major operations: getting file names, loading files, loading a single image, and managing the viewer windows. The module also contains the application's global declarations.

Global Declarations

Place the following dynamic array declarations in the General Declarations section of the code module:

```
Global FileList() As String
Global Viewer() As New ViewerType
Global ViewerLoaded() As Integer
```

FileList, Viewer, and ViewerLoaded are each dynamic arrays that are redimensioned as the code executes. Understanding what these arrays do is the key to understanding how the MultiView application works.

With Multiview, a user can simultaneously view multiple graphical files by loading each file into a separate MDI child window. To do so, the program must maintain an internal list of file names to load and must also track the status of each loaded window.

The FileList array holds the list of the file names that the user wants to load. The user specifies the desired file names using the File Selector dialog box. This dialog box appears when the user chooses the Open option from the File menu.

MultiView manages the child viewer windows with the aid of a form array technique mentioned earlier in this chapter. The following declaration declares Viewer to be a form array of type ViewerType:

```
Global Viewer() As New ViewerType
```

The New keyword indicates that each array element is a new instance of the ViewerType form. For more information about objects and instances, see Chapter 20, "Using Object Variables."

In subsequent code, you can treat the Viewer array like any other dynamic array. For example, you can redimension Viewer with Redim or ReDim Preserve, and you can refer to each form instance by it's array index.

The following loop, for instance, creates four viewer windows. The ReDim Preserve instruction maintains the data in the existing array elements:

```
For X% = 0 to 3
    If X% = 0 then
        Redim Viewer(0)
    Else
        ReDim Preserve Viewer(X%)
    End If
    Viewer(X%).Tag = Format$(X%)   'Store the index in the form's tag.
Next X%
```

Notice that the index of each form is stored as a string in the form's Tag property. Maintaining the index is necessary because the form itself cannot identify it's own index number.

Another way to add new picture forms one at a time is with Redim Preserve and the UBound function. For example, the following code can add a new form to the global Viewer form array whenever the user wants to load a new picture:

```
NewCount% = UBound(Viewer)+1   'Get next array element
ReDim Preserve Viewer(NewCount%)
Viewer(NewCount%).Tag = Format$(NewCount%)
```

Each of these examples adds additional instances of the ViewerType form to the application without destroying the existing members of the Viewer array that already exist.

You can refer to an individual form in the array with it's index. For example, the following instruction minimizes the fourth Viewer window:

```
Viewer(3).WindowState = 1    'Minimized.
```

(The Viewer array is implemented with the default base 0, which means that the first array element has an index of zero and the fourth element has an index of 3.)

A form can be unloaded from a form array. As a result, you can get "gaps" in the active array elements. The array itself contains no information about where these gaps are. When using a form array to manage child windows, an additional array is usually needed to track the load status of each window. In MultiView, the ViewerLoaded array serves this purpose.

The value of each element of `ViewerLoaded` is True or False, indicating whether the corresponding form is loaded. The index number of each element in `ViewerLoaded` matches the index number of the corresponding form in the `Viewer` array.

LoadFiles

You must now create a number of user-defined procedures in the code module. The first procedure, `LoadFiles`, is at the heart of MultiView's operation. This procedure obtains a list of files to load and creates a new MDI child window to display each one. The procedure then loads each picture into it's newly created `Viewer` window. `LoadFiles` calls a number of other procedures that are described later in this chapter. Now create the following `LoadFiles` procedure:

```
Sub LoadFiles ()
   Dim Idx As Integer, FNameVal As Integer, X As Integer

   FNameVal = GetFileNames() 'Function call to populate global FileList()
                              Array
   If FNameVal = False Then  'Function failed.
      MsgBox "File Load Canceled.", 48  'This is optional.
      Exit Sub
   End If


   'If you get this far you obtained file names.
   'Load a viewer for each new file name.

   Screen.MousePointer = 11   'Hourglass
   For X = 0 To UBound(FileList)
      Idx = GetFreeIndex()
      LoadImage Idx, FileList(X)
   Next X
   Screen.MousePointer = 0     'Restore normal pointer shape
End Sub
```

GetFileNames

`GetFileNames` is a function called by `LoadFiles`. The function returns True or False indicating whether the user selected any files to load. `GetFileNames` uses the File Selector dialog box to obtain a list of files to load. This list is stored in the global array `FileList`. Place the following code in the MULTVIEW.BAS module:

```
Function GetFileNames () As Integer
   Dim TopVal As Integer

   GetFileNames = False   'Set default function value
   Erase FileList         'Clear contents of global array

   'Set up File Open dialog box
   Load FileOpen
   FileOpen.Text1.Text = "*.BMP"
   FileOpen.File1.Pattern = "*.BMP"
   FileOpen.Dir1.Path = App.Path
   FileOpen.Show 1    '1 = modal

   'Upon closure of FileOpen, check the FileList array
   'to see if user canceled.

   On Error Resume Next
   TopVal = UBound(FileList)  'Causes an error if FileList() was not
                                       filled
   Select Case Err
      Case 9    'Subscript out of range.  This is expected.
         Exit Function  'Function returns False (indicating failure).
      Case 0    'No error.  Do nothing
      Case Else 'Unknown error. Report & get out.
         MsgBox "Error " & Err & " getting filename(s): " & Error$, 48
         Exit Function
   End Select
   On Error GoTo 0

   'If get this far, one or more file names were loaded
   'into the globally available array FileList().

   'Set the function result to True and end function.

   GetFileNames = True
End Function
```

The GetFileNames function returns True if one or more files were selected, and
it returns False if no files were selected. The FileOpen form (from Chapter 25)
requires some modification to work with MultiView in general and this function in particular. Those modifications are described shortly.

GetFreeIndex

As described earlier, the `Viewer` form array holds the multiple instances of the `ViewerType` window. Because the unloading of a form has no effect on the `Viewer` array, the application uses the `ViewerLoaded` array to indicate whether a window is actually loaded.

For example, suppose the user has loaded four pictures. The `Viewer` array contains elements 0 through 3. The user now unloads one of the viewers, say `Viewer(2)`. The result is a gap in the `Viewer` array at index 2. When the user wants to load the next picture, the program determines whether any gaps among the array indexes are available before adding another form element to the `Viewer` array. The job of the `GetFreeIndex` function is to search for any gap elements and return the lowest available free index.

Whenever a `Viewer` form is unloaded, the code in its `Form_Unload` procedure assigns False to the corresponding value in the `ViewerLoaded` array. When `GetFreeIndex` is called, one of the following three things happens depending on the available indexes in the `Viewer` array:

■ If no windows are loaded in the `Viewer` array, `GetFreeIndex` initializes the `Viewer` and `ViewerLoaded` arrays to contain a single element with an index of zero.

■ If all forms in the `Viewer` array are still loaded, `GetFreeIndex` adds a new `Viewer` window and returns the index value of the new array element.

■ If the `Viewer` array contains a gap element, `GetFreeIndex` sets the corresponding element of the `ViewerLoaded` array to True and returns that element's index value.

The following code is for the `GetFreeIndex` function:

```
Function GetFreeIndex () As Integer
    Dim ViewerCount As Integer, Idx As Integer

    'Returns an available index number from the Viewer() form array.

    'Check all entries in the ViewerLoaded() array to see if any of the
    'viewers were unloaded. If they were, that 'slot' is available.


    '1. Check to see if any Viewers are loaded at all!
    On Error Resume Next
    ViewerCount = UBound(Viewer)     'Local variable
    If Err = 9 Then
        'No viewers have been loaded--the array is empty.
        'Initialize the array and return Index 0.
```

```
      ReDim Viewer(0)
      ReDim ViewerLoaded(0)
      ViewerLoaded(0) = True
      GetFreeIndex = 0
      On Error GoTo 0
      Exit Function    '<<<<<<<------ Function exits here
   End If
   On Error GoTo 0


   '2. If you get this far the Viewer() array has already
   '   been initialized.  Find the first 'open' slot.

   For Idx = 0 To ViewerCount
      If ViewerLoaded(Idx) = False Then   'This index number is available!
         GetFreeIndex = Idx
         ViewerLoaded(Idx) = True
         Exit Function    '<<<<<<<------ Function exits here
      End If
   Next Idx

   'If you get this far, all index 'slots' are occupied.
   'Load a new instance of Viewer().

   ReDim Preserve ViewerLoaded(ViewerCount + 1)  'Add a viewer Boolean
   ViewerLoaded(ViewerCount + 1) = True

   ReDim Preserve Viewer(ViewerCount + 1)    'Add a viewer form
   Viewer(ViewerCount + 1).Tag = Format$(ViewerCount + 1)
            'Above line puts viewer's index in it's tag.

   GetFreeIndex = UBound(Viewer)   'Return the new viewer's index
End Function
```

LoadImage

At this point, the module contains procedures that obtain a list of file names and load a Viewer form for each file. The remaining task is to place the picture for each file into its Viewer window. The LoadImage procedure performs this duty.

To use LoadImage, you must pass it the full path and file name of the picture file to be loaded. This procedure also needs the proper array index so that the Viewer array can be updated appropriately.

The LoadImage procedure separates the path and file name, loads the picture into the requested Viewer form, and puts the trimmed file name into the form's caption. If an error occurs while loading the picture, the Viewer form is unloaded. The following code is for the LoadImage function:

```
Sub LoadImage (Index As Integer, FileName As String)
    Dim X As Integer, TrimmedName As String

    'The filename provided includes both path and filename.
    'Trim the path from filename
    For X = Len(FileName) To 1 Step -1
        If Mid$(FileName, X, 1) = "\" Then
            TrimmedName = Mid$(FileName, X + 1)
            Exit For
        End If
    Next X

    'Trap for picture loading errors
    On Error Resume Next
    Viewer(Index).Visible = True
    Viewer(Index).Image1.Picture = LoadPicture(FileName)

    If Err = 0 Then    'Picture loaded OK
        Viewer(Index).Image1.Tag = FileName
        Viewer(Index).Caption = TrimmedName
        Viewer(Index).FileEdit.Caption = "&Edit " + TrimmedName
        Viewer(Index).Refresh

    Else  'Error loading picture: Unload this Viewer and set ViewerLoaded()
          value
        MsgBox "Error " & Err & " loading " + FileName + ":   " + Error$, 48
        Viewer(Index).Visible = False
        ViewerLoaded(Index) = False
    End If
    On Error GoTo 0
End Sub
```

Notice that you can't name this procedure LoadPicture because that's a reserved word in Visual Basic.

Forms and Modules

Now you're ready to write code for the project's three forms: MDIForm1, FileOpen, and ViewerType. You write new code for the MDIForm1 and ViewerType event procedures and also make some modifications to the code for FileOpen. (Recall that the FileOpen form comes from the FileSelector application in Chapter 25.)

The *MDIForm1* Parent Form: Design and Code

MDIForm1 is the parent form for the project. This form's job is to contain the child viewer forms and provide the fundamental menu for opening files and exiting the program. (Remember that, when an application is running, the parent form's menu is not available when a loaded child form has a menu. In these cases, the menu of the currently active child form replaces the menu of the parent.)

Click anywhere on the MDIForm1 to make the form active. Open the Properties window and change the caption to MultiView. Open the Menu Design Window (press Ctrl+M) and create the menu depicted in Table 27.2.

Table 27.2. The menu structure for *MDIForm1*.

Menu Caption	Name
&File	FileMain
&Open	FileOpen
E&xit	FileExit

For more information about creating menus, see Chapter 24, "Designing Custom Menus."

As with Visual Basic's Menu Design window, the indentations in Table 27.2 indicate the level of the menu item. Notice the use of the ampersand character (&) in each menu caption to create an accelerator key for that menu item.

Here's the code for the parent form's load procedure:

```
Sub MDIForm_Load ()
    MDIForm1.Width = Screen.Width * .8
    MDIForm1.Height = Screen.Height * .7
    MDIForm1.Left = (Screen.Width - MDIForm1.Width) / 2
    MDIForm1.Top = (Screen.Height - MDIForm1.Height) / 2
End Sub
```

The two menu items that require code are the **O**pen and **E**xit options in the **F**ile menu. Here are the two required `Click` procedures:

```
Sub FileOpen_Click ()
    LoadFiles    'Calls the LoadFiles procedure
End Sub

Sub FileExit_Click ()
    End
End Sub
```

This code is all you need for the parent form. Not much code is required for `MDIForm1` because most of the parent's behavior is built into Visual Basic, including support for child windows. As discussed later in this chapter, additional functionality is coded into the menus of the child windows.

Notice that the Declarations section of `MDIForm1` is empty. All the application's required declarations are defined globally in the code module MULTVIEW.BAS.

The *FileOpen* Form: Some Required Modifications

Recall that the `FileOpen` form was copied from the FileSelector application presented in Chapter 25. As written, the form is designed for stand-alone operation, but this design is not suitable here. Some code changes are necessary so that the form works properly in the context of an MDI application. Only a few small changes are needed, but they're vital.

Property Value Reassignments

You must first modify a few simple property values. Using the Properties window, change the value of the form's `Name` property from `Form1` to `FileOpen`. Then change the caption of the second (rightmost) command button from `Quit` to `Cancel`.

Form-Level Declarations

The General Declarations section of the form defines the `FileList` array. You must remove this declaration because the array is now defined globally in the code module MULTVIEW.BAS. The name of the array remains `FileList` in the MultiView application. As a result, the existing code in `FileOpen` correctly references the array. Just remove the declaration completely from the form-level of `FileOpen`.

Updating the *Form_Load* Procedure

You must add some new code to the `Form_Load` procedure in order to position the form during loading. The updated procedure is as follows:

```
Sub Form_Load ()
   Drive1.Drive = CurDir$
   Dir1.Path = CurDir$
   Label1.Caption = Dir1.Path
   File1.Path = CurDir$
   File1.Pattern = "*.*"
   If File1.FileName <> "" Then
      Text1.Text = File1.FileName
   Else
      Text1.Text = File1.Pattern
   End If
   Me.Left = (Screen.Width - Me.Width) / 2
   Me.Top = (Screen.Height - Me.Height) / 2
End Sub
```

The new instructions are the Me.Left and Me.Top assignments near the end of the procedure.

Notice that the Form_Load procedure sets the Drive, Directory, and File list boxes to reflect the current path and a generic *.* pattern. This arrangement does not present any problem. Recall from the GetFileNames procedure (in the code module), that the FileOpen form is first loaded and then set to the current directory.

Updating *File1_PatternChange*

You must modify one instruction in File1_PatternChange. When the GetFileNames procedure changes the pattern of the File list box, the File1_PatternChange procedure activates. This action, however, occurs after the FileOpen form is loaded but before the form is shown. As a result, in this situation, File1_PatternChange should no longer be able to set the focus to the text box in the FileOpen form.

The final instruction in File1_PatternChange is as follows:

```
Text1.Setfocus
```

Change it to this instruction:

```
If Text1.Visible Then Text1.SetFocus
```

The following is the complete code for File1_PatternChange, including the noted revision:

```
Sub File1_PatternChange ()
   'Update label1
   If Len(File1.Path) > 3 Then
      Label1.Caption = File1.Path + "\" + File1.Pattern
   Else
```

```
    Label1.Caption = File1.Path + File1.Pattern
  End If

  'Update Text1
  If File1.ListCount = 0 Then
     Text1.Text = File1.Pattern
  Else
     File1.ListIndex = 0
     Text1.Text = File1.FileName
  End If

  Text1.SelStart = 0
  Text1.SelLength = Len(Text1.Text)
  If Text1.Visible Then Text1.SetFocus
End Sub
```

Updating *Command1_Click*

The user clicks the left-most command button (Command1) after selecting
multiple file names. This button is labeled OK. For this application, the
Command1_Click procedure must add a complete path name to the values stored
in the FileList array. Also, this procedure must unload the FileOpen form after
the user selects the files.

Here is the amended Command1_Click procedure. Modified instructions are
commented (NEW) in the following code:

```
Sub Command1_Click ()
  Dim Ctr As Integer      'Counter
  Dim L As Integer        'List index
  Dim X As Integer        'Loop counter
  Dim Msg As String       'String for message box
  Dim PathNam As String   'Path name from Dir1        (NEW)


  'Put names of all selected files
  'into the FileList() array

  PathNam = Dir1.Path                              '(NEW)
  If Len(Dir1.Path) > 3 Then PathNam = PathNam + "\"  '(NEW)

  Ctr = -1
  For L = 0 To File1.ListCount - 1
     If File1.Selected(L) = True Then
     Ctr = Ctr + 1
```

```
           If Ctr = 0 Then
               ReDim FileList(0)
           Else
               ReDim Preserve FileList(Ctr)
           End If
        FileList(Ctr) = PathNam + File1.List(L)      '(NEW)
        End If
    Next L
    If Ctr = -1 Then Exit Sub

    Unload FileOpen                                    '(NEW)

    'Create a message box listing all selected files

    Msg = "File(s) Selected:" + Chr$(13)
    Msg = Msg + "-----------------------" + Chr$(13)

    For X = 0 To UBound(FileList)
       Msg = Msg + FileList(X)
       If X < UBound(FileList) Then Msg = Msg + Chr$(13)
    Next X
    MsgBox Msg, 64, "Files Selected"
End Sub
```

Updating *Command2_Click*

The rightmost command button is now labeled Cancel. In the original form, this button quits the application. In MultiView, the button is clicked when the user changes gears and decides not to specify any file names. The button unloads the FileOpen form with no files selected.

The modified procedure is as follows:

```
Sub Command2_Click ()
   Erase FileList   'Clears the array, signals "no load"
   Unload FileOpen
End Sub
```

The *ViewerType* Form: Form Design

The final form, ViewerType, never actually loads during runtime. ViewerType is the template form object from which all instances of the Viewer form array are derived. Each child form takes its code, characteristics, and behavior from the ViewerType template.

As described earlier in the chapter, you should already have changed the form name to `ViewerType` and set its `MDIChild` property to True. This setting for the `MDIChild` property ensures that all instances of the `ViewerType` form are children of `MDIForm1`.

Using the Menu Design window, create the menu structure shown in Table 27.3. For the Window menu item, check the Window List box in the Menu Design window. By checking this box, a list of the loaded files appears below the other menu options when the Window menu is open. The user can choose any file for viewing by clicking the desired file name in the list of menu options.

Table 27.3. The menu structure for *ViewerType*.

Menu Caption	Name
&File	FileMain
&Open	FileOpen
&Edit [???]	FileEdit
-	FileSep
E&xit	FileExit
&Window	WindowMain
&Cascade	WindowArrange (Index 0)
Tile &Horizontal	WindowArrange (Index 1)
Tile &Vertical	WindowArrange (Index 2)
&Arrange Icons	WindowArrange (Index 3)
&Minimize All	WindowMinAll

Keep several things in mind as you design this menu. The File menu contains a `FileEdit` item with the caption `&Edit [???]`. The `LoadImage` procedure (in the MULTVIEW.BAS code module) uses this menu item to display the name of the currently active graphics file. In that procedure, the `[???]` part of the menu caption is replaced by the name of the graphics file.

Notice the `WindowArrange` menu array under the `WindowMain` menu. This menu item behaves just like a control array. The workings of the `WindowArrange` menu array are explained later in the chapter during the discussion of the `WindowArrange_Click` procedure.

The *ViewerType* Form: Code Modules

At this point, the controls and appearance of `ViewerType` are all in place. Now it's time to write the code procedures.

Form Procedures

First, there are three small but important procedures: `Form_Load`, `Form_Resize`,
and `Form_QueryUnload`. `Form_Load` positions the `Image1` control correctly, and
`Form_Resize` makes sure the Image control always fills the Viewer's client area.
Here are those two event procedures.

```
Sub Form_Load ()
    Image1.Left = 0
    Image1.Top = 0
    Image1.BorderStyle = 0
End Sub

Sub Form_Resize ()
    Image1.Width = ScaleWidth
    Image1.Height = ScaleHeight
End Sub
```

The `Form_QueryUnload` procedure is important because it updates the global
`ViewerLoaded` array when the current Viewer is unloaded. The Viewer's index
comes from its `Tag` property. The `ViewerLoaded` array element for that Viewer is
then set to False.

```
Sub Form_QueryUnload (Cancel As Integer, UnloadMode As Integer)
    Dim Idx As Integer
    Idx = Val(Me.Tag)
    ViewerLoaded(Idx) = False
End Sub
```

Control Procedures

`Image1` is the only control on the `ViewerType` form. In this control's `Dbl_Click`
procedure, which is as follows, you put code to maximize the current window
if the user double-clicks the image:

```
Sub Image1_DblClick ()
    Me.WindowState = 2    'Maximized
End Sub
```

`Me` is used in applications where there may be more than one instance of a
form loaded. If instead, you used the instruction `ViewerType.Wi`

Notice the use of the `Me` keyword. `Me` is used in applications in which more than
one instance of a form may be loaded. If instead, you use the instruction
`ViewerType.WindowsState = 2`, the application tries to load `ViewerType` and then
assigns the value to it's `WindowState` property. With `Me`, the `Dbl_Click` procedure
ensures that the window to be maximized is always the current window.

The File Menu

You must write `Click` procedures for the menu items. The following `FileExit_Click` procedure is certainly straightforward:

```
Sub FileExit_Click ()
    End
End Sub
```

Thanks to the `LoadFiles` procedure defined earlier in the MULTVIEW.BAS code module, the following `FileOpen_Click` procedure can simply call `LoadFiles`:

```
Sub FileOpen_Click ()
    LoadFiles
End Sub
```

A special feature of MultiView is that the user can edit any displayed bitmap file with Windows Paintbrush. To do so, the user clicks the desired Viewer window and then chooses the **Edit** option from the application's **File** menu.

The code in `FileEdit_Click` gets the full path and file name for the file and then launches Paintbrush with Visual Basic's `Shell` function. Notice how the following procedure uses the parent's `ActiveForm` property to determine which Viewer currently has the focus:

```
Sub FileEdit_Click ()
    Dim Idx As Integer, X As Integer
    Dim FileToEdit As String

    'Launches Windows Paintbrush to edit the current bitmap

    Idx = Val(MDIForm1.ActiveForm.Tag)
    FileToEdit = Viewer(Idx).Image1.Tag

    Screen.MousePointer = 11    'Hourglass
    X = Shell("PBRUSH.EXE " + FileToEdit, 1)
    Screen.MousePointer = 0     'Normal pointer shape
End Sub
```

Recall from the `LoadImage` procedure that the full path and file name of each viewed picture file is stored in the `Image1.Tag` property.

The Window Menu

Two items in the Window menu of `ViewerType` use the `Arrange` method to have `MDIForm1` arrange its child windows. The first menu item, `WindowArrange`, is itself a control array (of menu items). This array utilizes it's own `Index` property to determine the appropriate argument for the `Arrange` method. Create the following `Click` procedure for the `WindowArrange` menu item.

```
Sub WindowArrange_Click (Index As Integer)

   'Arrange forms or icons according to the value of Index
   ' 0    Cascade all non-minimized child forms.
   ' 1    Tile all non-minimized child forms horizontally.
   ' 2    Tile all non-minimized child forms vertically.
   ' 3    Arrange icons of minimized child forms.

   MDIForm1.Arrange Index
End Sub
```

The second menu item, WindowMinAll, can minimize or restore all the child
windows. When the menu item reads Mimimize All, this option minimizes all
forms and changes the menu item to read Restore All. Similarly, when the
menu item reads Restore All, this option restores all the minimized forms and
changes the menu item back to Minimize All.

The WindowMinAll_Click procedure does the minimizing and restoring. To
determine which action to take, the procedure examines its own menu caption. The form's WindowState property is used to do the actual minimizing and
restoring. The procedure also updates the menu caption appropriately. Here is
the WindowMinAll_Click procedure:

```
Sub WindowMinAll_Click ()
   Dim NewWindowState As Integer, NewCaption As String
   Dim FrmNum As Integer

   '1. Determine whether to minimize or restore all child
   '    windows by checking the menu item caption.

   If WindowMinAll.Caption = "Minimize &All" Then
      NewCaption = "Restore &All"
      NewWindowState = 1    'Minimize

   ElseIf WindowMinAll.Caption = "Restore &All" Then
      NewCaption = "Minimize &All"
      NewWindowState = 0    'Restore
   End If


   '2. Set all windows to the desired windowstate and
   '    update the caption of their WindowMinAll menu items.
```

```
For FrmNum = 0 To Forms.Count - 1 'Cycle through all the project forms
    If TypeOf Forms(FrmNum) Is MDIForm Then
    'Do nothing. You don't want to minimize the parent form.
    Else
    Forms(FrmNum).WindowState = NewWindowState
    Forms(FrmNum).WindowMinAll.Caption = NewCaption
    End If
  Next FrmNum
End Sub
```

Notice the use of the `Forms` Collection in the `WindowMinAll_Click` procedure. As explained in Chapter 20, "Using Object Variables," the `Forms` Collection is a virtual form array containing all the forms in the project. You can cycle through the forms in the Collection to determine the various characteristics of each form. You can't treat the `Forms` Collection as an array, however, by trying to `Dim`, `ReDim`, or `ReDim Preserve` the Collection.

One more thing remains to point out about `WindowMinAll_Click`. The `WindowMinAll.Caption` property is updated for every child when the value of its `WindowState` property changes. Remember that, when a child window is active, the menu of the child replaces the parent's menu in the MDI form. As a result, no matter what window is active, its `WindowMinAll.Caption` property must correctly indicate the last action taken by `WindowMinAll_Click`.

Running MultiView

Before running MultiView, save the individual forms and the code module. Then save the project as MULTVIEW.MAK.

When you first start MultiView, you see only the parent form `MDIForm1`. The form's menu bar contains only a single menu option: **File**. If you choose **File**, a submenu pops down with **O**pen and **E**xit options (see Figure 27.10).

Remember that the `MDIForm1` menu is visible only because no child windows are loaded. As soon you load a child, the parent's menu is replaced by the menu of the child.

To view files, choose the **O**pen option on the File menu. The File Selector dialog box appears. Use this dialog box to select one or more file names. Figure 27.11 shows the File Selector dialog box with several files selected.

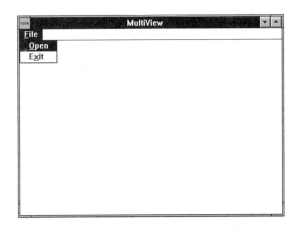

Figure 27.10.

MultiView at startup with no Viewers loaded and the parent window's **F**ile menu opened.

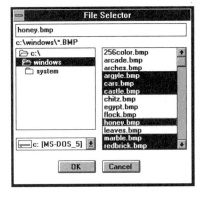

Figure 27.11.

Several files are selected in the File Selector dialog box.

 NOTE Your hard disk undoubtedly contains several files that you can load into the Viewer. Use bitmap files (*.BMP), icons (*.ICO), and Windows metafiles (*.WMF). You can probably find such files in your Windows directory and in various subdirectories of Visual Basic. Likely paths are C:\WINDOWS, C:\VB\BITMAPS, and C:\VB\METAFILES.

After you make your selections and click the OK button (or you just double-click a file name), a Files Selected dialog box displays the list of your selected files. Click OK to close this dialog box. The File Selector dialog box is also unloaded. A Viewer window then loads for every selected file, and the corresponding picture is loaded into the Viewer window.

To arrange the Viewer windows, click the application's **W**indow menu and select the desired option. Figure 27.12 shows MultiView with all the Viewer windows tiled.

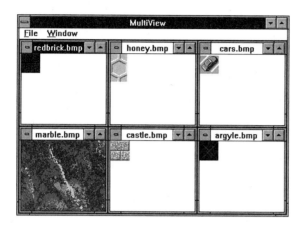

Figure 27.12.

MultiView with Viewers
loaded and tiled.

When you open the **W**indow menu, the captions for all the loaded Viewer windows appear at the bottom of the menu options list. They appear there because you checked the Window List box in the Menu Design Window when you designed the menu system. As a result, you can click directly on one of the file names listed in the File menu to switch to any loaded Viewer window.

To edit a viewed picture, choose the **E**dit option from the **F**ile menu. Windows Paintbrush opens with the picture loaded. You can edit the picture and save the file.

Summary

MDI (Multiple Document Interface) applications use multiple child windows inside a parent window. Child windows are opened, closed, resized, and moved all within the boundaries of the parent.

Visual Basic supports multiple instances of regular forms. The technique applies with MDI child windows as well. You can use a form array to create multiple instances of a template form. In MDI applications, you often load such instances as child windows in a parent. To keep track of all the loaded windows, you can use a second array containing corresponding indexes.

The MultiView sample application uses MDI child windows to create a viewer capable of displaying multiple files at one time. The application supports arranging the child windows inside the parent and selecting a bitmap file for editing with Paintbrush.

Using the Data Control to Interact with Databases

Visual Basic 3.0 adds new tools that let you display, edit, and update data from a variety of existing databases, including Microsoft Access, Microsoft FoxPro, Paradox, Btrieve, and dBASE formats. Visual Basic now includes the database engine from Microsoft Access. As such, Visual Basic includes considerable database functionality, and is particularly compatible with Microsoft Access.

The Data control (new in Visual Basic 3.0) attaches to an existing database, providing a link between your application and your data. Various controls, such as labels, images, text boxes, check boxes, and picture boxes, can be made data-aware by binding (connecting) to the Data Control. In this way, a Visual Basic application can communicate with a database. For example, the Text property of a bound text box control can link with a string field in the database.

You can easily navigate through data with little or no programming by clicking the Data control buttons to move from one record to another. Of course, you can also add commands to control your database access at run time.

This chapter explores the following topics:

- ■ Using the Data control
- ■ Binding data-aware controls
- ■ Adding code to use data controls at run time

■ Putting data into controls that are not data-aware

■ Using multiple tables and queries

■ Using the Data Manager

■ Working with Microsoft Access, and Access-compatible databases

■ Understanding the Professional Edition extensions

To demonstrate several data techniques, you create an Access-compatible database, and develop a sample application that manipulates it.

Understanding Databases

A *database* is a collection of data related to a particular topic or purpose. This collection is further organized into *tables*, which present information on a particular subject in the familiar column (field) and row (record) format. For example, if a database contains information about your business, individual tables might categorize the data as products, customers, suppliers, and employees.

Each *field* in a table is a specific category of information. For example, typical fields in a Customer table include Name, Address, Phone Number, and so on. A *record* stores all the information about one particular individual—for example: John Q. Public's Name, Address, Phone Number, etc. The table consists of a collection of records.

You obtain a specific data value at the intersection of a field and record. For example, John's address is located in the Address field of the John record.

You can search among records to find out if the data values for a field have a particular value. To do so, you use a *query*, which is in essence a question you ask about the data in your database.

You can speed up your search for data by creating an *index* on one or more fields. An index links the data in a field to the general database. For example, a phone number index for the Customer field might contain the phone numbers in numerical order. For each phone number, the index includes a pointer to the corresponding record in the general database. Should you want to query the database for a particular phone number, it's much faster to search through the phone number index than to search the entire database.

A table can have none, one, or more indexes, but if the table grows too large, it's useful to create a *primary key* index. A primary index contains an entry in each field of the primary key, and allows no duplicates. You must have a primary key to *join* two tables, as you'll do later in the chapter.

The Sample Application: Building the Database

To develop the sample application, you first need to create a database. To do so, you will use the Data Manager utility. Both the Standard and Professional Editions of Visual Basic include this utility.

With the Data Manager, you can create databases in Microsoft Access format. That is, databases you create with the Data Manager can be imported into Microsoft Access. Similarly, databases created with Microsoft Access can be manipulated with Visual Basic's Data Manager.

This section takes you through the steps of using the Data Manager to create the sample database. The database will contain one table, several fields, and an index.

NOTE For a standard installation of Visual Basic, the Data Manager is stored on disk as C:\VB\DATAMGR.EXE. (The Microsoft documentation states that the file is stored as C:\VB\SAMPLES\DATAMGR.EXE, but that seems to be in error.) As an executable (.EXE) file, you can launch the Data Manager from the Windows Program Manager when Visual Basic is not active. However, as explained in this section, you can activate the Data Manager directly from the Visual Basic menu system.

Starting the Data Manager and Creating the Database

However, to avoid potential file sharing conflicts, it's best to run SHARE. The program is supplied with DOS, and runs as a TSR (Terminate and Stay Resident) program. You must run SHARE before invoking Windows. To run SHARE.EXE, you can type the command **SHARE** from the DOS prompt. However, a simpler method is to have your AUTOEXEC.BAT file automatically run SHARE every time you boot your system. To do so, place the following line in your AUTOEXEC.BAT file: `C:\DOS\SHARE.EXE`.

> The DOS program SHARE.EXE must be running for the Data Manager to access a database while any project is loaded in the Visual Basic environment. SHARE permits data and file sharing among applications. You don't need to run SHARE if you close any Visual Basic project before working with the Data Manager.

To use the Data Manager, start Visual Basic. Then, choose the Data Manager option from the Window menu. When the Data Manager window appears, open the File menu, and choose New Database. Then, choose either the Access 1.0 or Access 1.1 file format from the submenu (see Figure 28.1).

The Access 1.1 file format is a recent improvement to the older 1.0 format. Among other improvements, the 1.1 format extends the maximum database size, adds connectivity features, and increases file security. Databases created in 1.0 format can be converted to 1.1 format with the latest version of Microsoft Access.

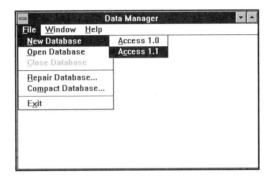

Figure 28.1.

Creating a new database
with the Data Manager.

When the New Database dialog box opens, type **country** in the File Name text box. The path is C:\VB, assuming that you installed Visual Basic (and therefore DATAMGR.EXE) in the default directory. If you wish, you may specify a different directory path when typing the file name. If you do, you must modify the subsequent C:\VB code references to reflect your specified path.

In the dialog box, click OK. The database is created, and saved as a disk file. The file extension MDB is automatically added to the file name.

Using the Tables Window

After you click OK, the Data Manager opens the Database window, and displays the Tables window. Click the New button. The Create New Table dialog box opens. In the text box, type the table name **Country** (see Figure 28.2). (In this figure, the Tables window is maximized to fill the Data Manager's window in its entirety. Notice that the caption reads `Data Manager - [Database: COUNTRY.MDB]`.)

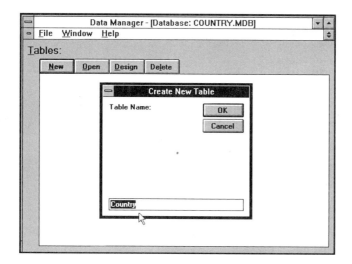

Figure 28.2.

Creating a new table.

Click OK to accept the new table name, then close the Create New Table dialog box. The Table Design window now appears (see Figure 28.3).

Figure 28.3.

The Table Design window.

Click the Add button in the Fields grid to display the Add Field dialog box. In the Field Name text box, type **Country Name**. Click the down arrow to the right of the Field Type combo box. A drop-down list opens to enable the selection of the field's data type. Scroll down the list, and click the Text type. By selecting Text, you indicate that the Country Name field contains text (string) data.

In the Field Size box, type **20**. As such, the data for this field is limited to 20 characters of text. Figure 28.4 shows the completed data entry for this first field.

Figure 28.4.

Completing the data entry
for the first field.

Using the data in Table 28.1, repeat the steps in the previous paragraph to specify the remaining fields in the database. Figure 28.5 shows the Table Design window when all the fields have been added.

Table 28.1. Country table design data for the COUNTRY database.

Field Name	Field Type	Field Size (for text fields only)
Capital Name	Text	20
Population	Long Integer	
Flag	Binary	
Comments	Memo	

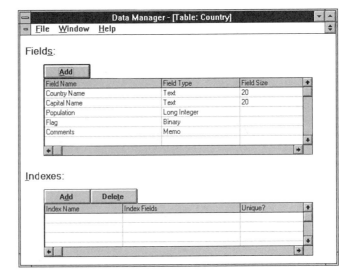

Figure 28.5.

All the fields are specified.

As you see, you can add additional fields to a database table with the Data Manager. However, you cannot rename, modify, or delete the fields individually. If you make any mistakes, you must delete the entire table, and start over. Later in this chapter, you will see how you add a field to this table. You will also learn how to create another table in the COUNTRY database.

Creating an Index

The next step is to create an index for the Country table. Click the Add button in the Indexes portion of the Table Design window to display the Add Index dialog box. The Fields in Table list box displays three of the five fields: Capital Name, Country Name, and Population. The other two fields are not displayed because memo and binary fields cannot be indexed.

Type **CntryName** in the Index Name text box. In the Fields in Table list box, click Country Name to select it (see Figure 28.6). Click the Add (Asc) button to create an ascending (Asc) index. The Country Name field is now removed from the Fields in Table list box, and placed in Fields in Index.

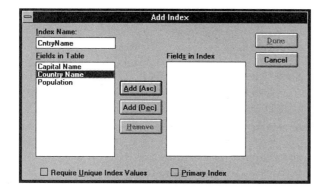

Figure 28.6.

Adding an index for the Country Name field.

Click the Primary Index check box in the lower right portion of the dialog box. Click Done to create the index.

Adding Data to the Database

The design of your database is complete and ready for adding some actual data. First, close the Table Design window. To do so, click the pull-down Control menu button in the window's upper left corner. When the Control menu appears, choose Close. The Database window reappears.

Click the Open button to display the Table Access window. Then, click the Add button to put in the data in Table 28.2. Figure 28.7 shows the data record entered for Canada, the first country in the database.

Figure 28.7.

The data for Canada is entered.

Data Manager - [C:\VB\COUNTRY.MDB : COUNTRY]
File   Window   Help
Add   Update   Delete   Find   Refresh

Field Name:	Value:
COUNTRY	Canada
CAPITAL NAME:	Ottawa
POPULATION:	25652000
FLAG:	
COMMENTS:	

Editing Record

Table 28.2. Table data for COUNTRY database.

Country Name	Capital Name	Population
Canada	Ottawa	25652000
France	Paris	55632000
Germany	Berlin	78420000
Great Britain	London	57142000
Mexico	Mexico City	81163000
Russia	Moscow	284500000
Spain	Madrid	38900000
United States	Washington, D.C.	241078000

After entering each data record, click Update. When the Commit Changes dialog box opens, click Yes to save the data record.

NOTE You also can trigger the Save sequence by navigating with the arrow controls at the bottom of the display. Instead of clicking Update, click an arrow button to move away from the current record. When you do, the Data Manager opens the Commit Changes dialog box.

Creating the Flag Field

The Flag field is a binary data field in which you can store bit-mapped graphics. You use this field to display an icon of each country's flag. You can add the data for the Flag field while you are inputting the data for the other fields, or after the other entries are complete. The following instructions assume that you have already entered the data for the other fields.

Click the arrow to the far left at the bottom of the window. The Canada record comes into view. To add the flag icon image for a country, double-click in the blank Flag field. The Enter Picture FilName dialog box opens. For the Canadian flag, type the appropriate path and file name as Table 28.3 shows, and click OK. Figure 28.8 shows Canada's flag icon added to the database.

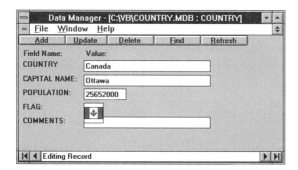

Figure 28.8.

Adding Canada's flag icon to the database.

Click the right-arrow button to move to the next record. When the Commit Changes dialog box opens, click Yes. The France record opens so that you can add the country's flag icon. In a similar manner, you can step through each record, and add the applicable flag icon.

The file specifications that Table 28.3 shows assume a normal installation of Visual Basic. If your icon files are in another directory, specify the appropriate path, instead.

Table 28.3. Flag field data for COUNTRY database.

Country Name	File Specification for Flag Field
Canada	C:\VB\ICONS\FLAGS\FLGCAN.ICO
France	C:\VB\ICONS\FLAGS\FLGFRAN.ICO
Germany	C:\VB\ICONS\FLAGS\FLGGERM.ICO

continues

Table 28.3. Continued

Country Name	File Specification for Flag Field
Great Britain	C:\VB\ICONS\FLAGS\FLGUK.ICO
Mexico	C:\VB\ICONS\FLAGS\FLGMEX.ICO
Russia	C:\VB\ICONS\FLAGS\FLGRUS.ICO
Spain	C:\VB\ICONS\FLAGS\FLGSPAIN.ICO
United States	C:\VB\ICONS\FLAGS\FLGUSA02.ICO

Closing the Data Manager

The database is now complete. Open the Data Manager's File menu. Choose the Exit option to terminate the Data Manager application.

The Data Control

The Data control is the link between Visual Basic and a database. The control lets you access data for the most part without writing code. Once you've attached a Data control to a database, you then bind data-aware controls to the Data control. The data-aware controls display the contents of the fields of each record as you navigate with the Data control. If you make changes in a bound control, the updates are saved as you move to another record.

You place a Data control on a form just as you place any other—by double-clicking the Toolbox icon, or by selecting the icon and sizing the control directly on the form. Visual Basic gives the default name of Data1 to the first Data control you place on a form. Subsequent Data controls are named Data2, Data3, and so on.

Start a new project, and add a Data control to the form. Click the control to select it, then open the Properties window. Notice that the name Data1 appears in the Object box. Select the DatabaseName property, then click the ellipsis (...) button on the right edge of the Settings box. The Database Name dialog box opens for you to choose a database. (You can open the dialog box in one step by double-clicking the DatabaseName property.)

In the dialog box, select the COUNTRY.MDB file, then click OK. Notice that the full path and name of the database is now displayed in the Properties window (see Figure 28.9).

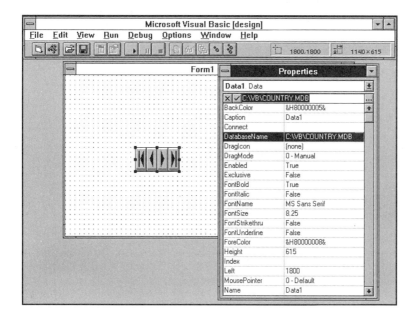

Figure 28.9.

The Properties window for
Data1.

 NOTE You can also set the Connect property, which specifies the type of database, as well as additional properties, such as a database password. No Connect setting is needed to open Microsoft Access databases, such as the COUNTRY.MDB database you created with the Data Manager.

With the DatabaseName property now set, Visual Basic is prepared to access the database file, and populate (or fill) the RecordSource property list. The RecordSource property specifies the underlying data source of the records which the bound controls on the form can access and display.

Scroll through the Properties window, and double-click the RecordSource property; you hear the hard disk engage as Visual Basic determines what tables or QueryDefs exist in the database. In this case, there is only one, the Country table, which becomes visible in the Settings box. If you have multiple tables, you can select one by clicking the down arrow next to the Settings box. Then, click your choice. Double-clicking the RecordSource property repeatedly enables you to cycle through the tables in the database.

 NOTE A QueryDef is an object that contains a description of a query, and can be created using Microsoft Access or the Professional Edition of Visual Basic. You can't create a QueryDef using the Data Manager or Visual Basic's Standard Edition. The sample application presented in this chapter can be created with either edition of Visual Basic.

Several other Data control properties exist, including `Exclusive`, `Options`, and `ReadOnly`. These properties enable you to control access to the database in multiuser situations. You can define who can have access when, and for how long.

Bound Controls

When the database is opened by the Data control, it creates a dynamic set of records called a `Dynaset` object which, similar to a table, has information in records and fields. The difference is that a `Dynaset` can also be the result of a query that joins more than one table. You can use the `Dynaset` to add, modify, and delete records from the underlying table or tables.

The set of records created in the `Dynaset` object are represented by the `Recordset` property of a Data control. You can access this information through controls on your application's form. To do so, you bind (attach) data-aware controls to the Data control. A bound control can display the data contained in a field of the current record, let the user edit the value, and save the modified data back to the underlying database.

A bound control is said to be *data-aware* because it links to the Data control. You can bind five types of controls: Labels, Images, Text boxes, Check boxes, and Picture boxes. To bind a control, you set appropriate property values. Visual Basic 3.0 defines the following new "binding" properties for each of the five data-aware controls:

- The `DataSource` property
- The `DataField` property
- The `DataChanged` property

The value of the `DataSource` property specifies the Data control being bound to. After adding a data-aware control to your form, you bring up the Properties Window, then select the `DataSource` property. As with the `RecordSource` property, you can double-click to cycle through the available Data controls. Alternatively, you can select a Data control from the drop-down Settings list. Visual Basic then examines the recordset as defined by the Data control, and determines what fields are available for binding. To complete the process, you select the `DataField` property, then click the down arrow in the Settings box. Finally, select a field from the drop-down list.

You don't have to bind a control in the order just explained. You can choose the `DataField` property first, but you need to know the name of the field.

Then, you type it in. You can set the `DatabaseName`, `RecordSource` and `DataField` properties at both design time and run time. However, the `DataSource` property can only be set at design time.

The `DataChanged` property is available only at run time. It indicates whether data in the bound control has been modified. When a Data control moves to a new record, Visual Basic sets the value of this property to False. If the program or user modifies the data, Visual Basic sets the value of `DataChanged` to True. When the Data control moves to a new record, Visual Basic updates the data in the underlying database only if the value of `DataChanged` is True. Your program code can set this property value to False to prevent Visual Basic from modifying the data in the database.

Building the Sample Application

In the next several sections, you develop a sample application named COUNTRY.MAK. This application uses a Data control and various bound controls to manipulate the COUNTRY.MDB database you created earlier in the chapter. With COUNTRY.MAK, you can display and navigate through all the information you stored about each country, including the text data and the flag icon graphics. When the application is complete, you will be able to edit individual fields, add and delete records, and even integrate data from another table. In this section, you'll get things working without writing a single line of program code. Later in the chapter, you'll add code to create a robust, interactive program.

You should now have a form containing a single Data control. If not, start a new project, and add a Data control onto the form. Using the Properties window, set the property values that Table 28.4 shows.

Table 28.4. Design-time property values for the *Form* and *Data* controls.

Control	Property	Value
Form1	Caption	Country Database Demo
	Left	1005
	Top	1155
	Width	7485
	Height	5085

continues

Table 28.4. Continued		
Control	**Property**	**Value**
Data1	Caption	Countries
	DatabaseName	C:\VB\COUNTRY.MDB
	Exclusive	False
	Height	375
	Left	600
	Options	0
	ReadOnly	False
	RecordSource	Country
	Top	3960
	Width	3495

The Exclusive, Options, and ReadOnly properties of the Data1 control are set to their default values.

Adding Bound Controls

Add four text boxes and an Image control onto the form. These are the data-aware (bound) controls that become associated with various fields in the database. Assign the property values that Table 28.5 shows.

T I P The four text boxes and the Image control are all bound to the same Data1 control. You can quickly specify the appropriate property value for each of the five controls by using multiple selection. After placing the controls, click the upper left corner of the form. Drag the elastic selector box until it includes all the data-aware controls, but not the Data control itself. Press F4 to open the Properties window, then double-click the DataSource property. Choose Data1 (the only Data control on the form) to assign that property value for all five data-aware controls.

Table 28.5. Design-time properties for bound controls.

Control	Property	Value
Text1	DataField	Country Name
	DataSource	Data1
	Height	285
	Left	1680
	Top	240
	Width	1335
Text2	DataField	Capital Name
	DataSource	Data1
	Height	285
	Left	5400
	Top	720
	Width	1575
Text3	DataField	Population
	DataSource	Data1
	Height	285
	Left	5760
	Top	240
	Width	1215
Text4	DataField	Comments
	DataSource	Data1
	Height	1095
	Left	600
	MultiLine	True
	ScrollBars	2 'Vertical
	TabIndex	0
	Top	2160
	Width	2775

continues

Table 28.5. Continued

Control	Property	Value
Image1	DataField	Flag
	DataSource	Data1
	Height	1575
	Left	5160
	Stretch	'True
	Top	1800
	Width	1815

The Text4 text box permits the user to add comments. This text box is unique in that the MultiLine property is set to -1 (True), with a vertical scrollbar added to handle text that extends beyond the bottom of the control. The value of its TabIndex property is set to 0 so that this text box has the focus when the application is first run.

The Image control displays the flag icons. This control's Stretch property is set to -1 (True), so that the small flag icons that are included with Visual Basic can be enlarged in the application. (Recall that Image controls do not have the AutoSize property that Picture controls do. This property enables a Picture control to alter its size to exactly match any bit-mapped graphics. On the other hand, Image controls display much faster than do Picture controls.)

Adding Labels

Add five labels to the form. These labels identify the bound fields. Assign the property values that Table 28.6 shows.

Table 28.6. Design-time properties for labels.

Control	Property	Value
Label1	Alignment	2 'Center
	Caption	Country
	Height	255
	Left	720
	Top	240
	Width	855

Control	Property	Value
Label2	Alignment	2 'Center
	Caption	Capital
	Height	255
	Left	4440
	Top	720
	Width	855
Label3	Caption	Population
	Height	255
	Left	4560
	Top	240
	Width	975
Label4	Alignment	2 'Center
	Caption	Comments
	Height	255
	Left	1440
	Top	3480
	Width	975
Label5	Alignment	2 'Center
	Caption	Flag
	Height	255
	Left	5760
	Top	3240
	Width	735

Save the form as COUNTRY.FRM, and the project as COUNTRY.MAK.
Now you're ready to see the Data control in action.

Running the Application

Start the application. When COUNTRY runs, the Country Name, Capital Name,
Population, Flag, and Comments data of the first record in COUNTRY.MDB
(Canada) display on the form (see Figure 28.10).

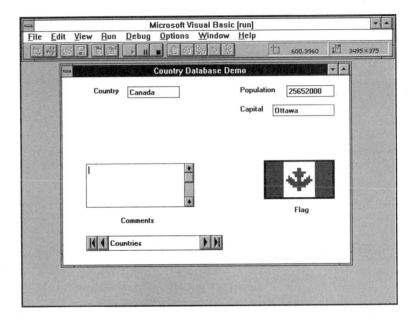

Figure 28.10.

Starting the COUNTRY
application.

Click the arrow buttons on the Data control to move through the records of
the database; you can move to the next, previous, first, and last records. When
you are satisfied that all the information you entered earlier is now accessible,
return to the first record (Canada) by clicking the arrow button to the far left.

At the moment, the Comments field is blank. The reason is that you didn't
enter any information in this field when you created the database. Notice that
the cursor is blinking in the Comments field. That makes sense because the
Text4 control (Comments) has a TabIndex value of 0. So, Text4 gets the focus
when the application begins.

Add some text to describe Canada, the first country in the database (see
Figure 28.11). As you continue typing, the text wraps at the edge of the control,
and scrolls down as you reach the bottom of the text box.

You can cut, copy, and paste text by using the keyboard Control+key alter-
nates: Ctrl+X, Ctrl+C, and Ctrl+V, respectively. Notice that by simply setting
the MultiLine and ScrollBar properties of the text box, you have a full-featured,
mini-text editor tied into your database.

You might be wondering whether the application should have a Save button.
The answer is that you don't need one. The capability to save a record is built
into the Data control's functionality. Just click any of the arrow buttons to
move off the current record, and its contents are saved. You can confirm
this by navigating back to the Canada record, and checking whether your
comments have been preserved.

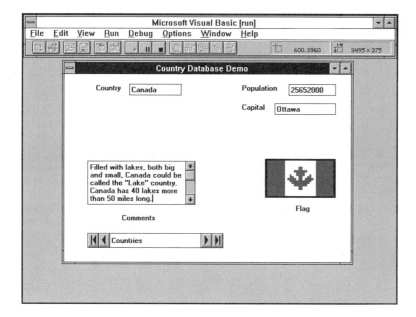

Figure 28.11.

Adding comments to the
Canada record.

You can edit any of the other fields in much the same way as you do Comments. Just click a data field to give it the focus. You might change Russia's name to the Commonwealth of Independent States, or perhaps refer to the country using another name.

The only control whose contents you can't edit—at run time—is the Image control which displays the flag icons. Stop the application, and return to design mode. Next, you add some code that improves on the application's picture-adding capability.

Improving the Image Control

Recall that when you originally added the flag images to the database, you had to double-click the Flag field, then type the complete path and file name in the dialog box. Now, you add program code that makes editing the Flag icon at run time easy. The code uses a Common Dialog control to create a standardized file selection dialog box for the specification of a flag's icon file.

Using the Toolbox, place a Common Dialog control on the form for the COUNTRY application. The default name for the control is CMDialog1. Similar to a Timer, a Common Dialog control automatically resizes itself, and is invisible at run time. Click the Common Dialog control to make sure it is selected. Using the Properties window, assign the property values that Table 28.7 shows.

NOTE The Common Dialog control provides a standard set of dialog boxes for common Windows operations, such as selecting a file or choosing fonts. For more information on Common Dialog, see Chapter 29, "Manipulating the Windows Environment," and Chapter 32, "Using Custom Controls."

Common Dialog is a custom control which should appear in your Toolbox. (If not, use the **Add** File option from the **File** menu to append the file C:\WINDOWS\SYSTEM\CMDIALOG.VBX to your project.) The file is included with both the Standard and Professional Editions of Visual Basic.

Table 28.7. Design-time properties for Common Dialog.

Control	Property	Value
CMDialog1	Left	3960
	Name	CMD1
	Top	2520

Open the Code window and create the following `Image1_DblClick` event procedure:

```
Sub Image1_Click ()
    CMD1.Filter = "Bitmaps (*.bmp)¦*.bmp¦Icons (*.ico)¦*.ico¦
    ➥Metafiles (*.wmf)¦*.wmf¦All Files (*.*)¦*.*"
    CMD1.DialogTitle = "Select a Picture File to Load"
    CMD1.FilterIndex = 2    'Sets default filter to *.ico
    CMD1.Action = 1         'Sets dialog type to Open File
    If CMD1.Filename <> "" Then
        Image1.Picture = LoadPicture(CMD1.Filename)
    End If
End Sub
```

Now, you can run the program, and edit the Flag graphics field by double-clicking any flag icon. The common dialog springs to action, opening a file selection dialog box named "Select a Picture File to Load." Using this dialog box, you can access the C:\VB\ICONS\FLAGS directory, and choose an icon file. By default, the `FilterIndex` property is set to "Icons," but you can change this value to any of the other graphics formats. Moving to another record saves the image to the database.

Using Code with Data Controls

The Data control and its bound controls handle all the work of navigating through, editing, and saving records of your database. However, to add a new record, or delete an outdated one, you must write code for the Data control.

You can duplicate the functionality of Data control without having to use its arrow buttons. You can confirm this by setting the value of Data1's Visible property to False, and adding a command button for each of the four arrow buttons. Then, add code to the appropriate button for each navigational command. For example, to move to the next record, the code would read:

```
Data1.Recordset.MoveNext
```

The *Recordset* Property

The *recordset* is the current set of records, created when the Data control is attached to a database using the DatabaseName, RecordSource, and Connect (if needed) properties. The Recordset property is a reference to the data control's underlying Dynaset object. A Dynaset is a dynamic set of records. You can use the Dynaset to add, change, and delete records from the underlying table(s). A recordset has all the same properties and methods as the Dynaset; the MoveNext method is one example. Other methods you subsequently learn about include

- MoveFirst, MoveLast, and MovePrevious
- Edit
- AddNew
- Update
- Delete
- FindFirst, FindLast, FindNext, and FindPrevious

The Move methods (MoveFirst, MoveLast, and MovePrevious) correspond to the rest of the Data control's arrow button actions. They move to the First, Last, or Previous record of the recordset to change the *current record*.

The Edit method opens the current record for editing by duplicating it on the copy buffer. This method is most often used in conjunction with the recordset's LockEdits property to enable changes to the current record while preventing other users from making alterations. The AddNew method sets all fields in the buffer to Null, in preparation for creating a new record. The current record becomes this cleared-out record. After using AddNew or Edit, the Update method saves the data from the buffer to the database, replacing the current record. As you've seen, using one of the Data control arrow buttons automatically invokes Update when you move off the current record. The Delete and Find methods are discussed shortly.

Adding a New Record

To enable the user to add a new record in the COUNTRY application, add a command button to the form. Set the property values that Table 28.8 shows.

Table 28.8. Design-time properties for New command button.

Control	Property	Value
Command1	Caption	New
	Height	495
	Left	4920
	Top	3840
	Width	975

Create the following Click event procedure for this first command button:

```
Sub Command1_Click ()
    Data1.Recordset.AddNew
    Text1.SetFocus
End Sub
```

Running the Application

Run the program, then click the New button. The current record's fields are cleared from the bound controls. Then, a new record is added to the end of the recordset. The Text1.Setfocus method places the cursor in the Country Name text box. Enter the data for a new country in the appropriate fields, as Table 28.9 shows.

Table 28.9. New country record data.

Control Name	Value
Country Name	Japan
Capital Name	Tokyo
Population	123778000
Flag	C:\VB\ICONS\FLAGS\FLGJAPAN.ICO

Your form should resemble that in Figure 28.12. To move to the last record, click the arrow button to the far right on the Data Control. The new record is saved, and is now a new member of your database's family of nations.

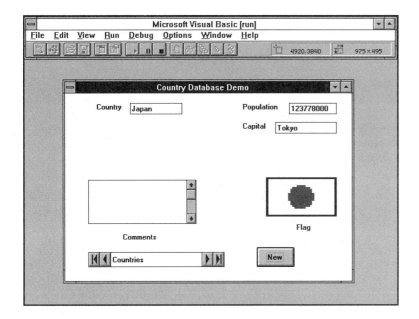

Figure 28.12.

Japan joins the Country database.

Deleting an Existing Record

You can now add a new record. (You've always been able to edit and update existing records with the functionality built into the Data control.) To delete a record, you need to add a new button, and write additional program code.

Return to design mode. Add a second command button to the form, and assign the property values that Table 28.10 shows.

Table 28.10. Design-time properties for Delete command button.

Control	Property	Value
Command2	Caption	Delete
	Height	495
	Left	6240
	Top	3840
	Width	855

Create the following Click event procedure for the second command button:

```
Sub Command2_Click ()
    Dim MSGBOX_TYPE As Integer
    Dim Msg As String
    MSGBOX_TYPE = 17      'Stop icon, OK & Cancel buttons

    Msg = "Are you sure you want to delete" & Chr$(10)
    Msg = Msg & Text1.Text
    If MsgBox(Msg, MSGBOX_TYPE, "Delete Record?") <> 1 Then Exit Sub

    Data1.Recordset.Delete
    Data1.Recordset.MoveNext
    If Data1.Recordset.EOF Then Data1.Recordset.MovePrevious
End Sub
```

Running the Application

Run the sample application. Move to the record you just entered—Japan. Click Delete; a message box asks you to confirm that you want to delete the current record (see Figure 28.13). If you click OK, the record is deleted, and the previous one becomes current. To leave the Japan record intact, click Cancel.

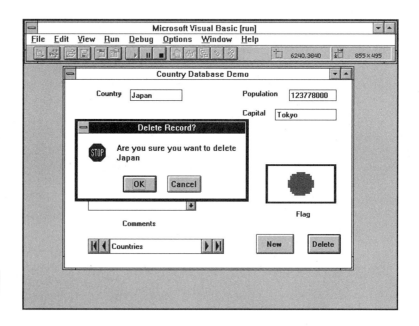

Figure 28.13.

Deleting a record.

How the Delete Button Works

The Delete method works by setting the recordset's current record to Null, and removing the current record from its underlying table(s). However, the deleted record remains current; it becomes invalid. Any references to it produce an error. That might not be a problem here. However, as you'll see, sometimes you need to refer to the current record to do other things in your code. It's always a good idea, therefore, to use the MoveNext method to go to a new current record.

The *EOF* Property

Another way exists to position the current record so that it is invalid: move past the last previously defined record, or before the first one. You cannot do this with the Data control. However, it is possible to do so using code.

You can check for these conditions with the *BOF* and *EOF* properties, which refer to the Beginning Of File, and End Of File, respectively. In this example, if you delete the Japan data, you are erasing the last record. As a result, the MoveNext method moves the position of the current record past the last one in the recordset. The EOF condition now becomes True, and the code uses the MovePrevious method to return to a valid current record.

The MsgBox instructions are added to warn the user about the destructive delete operation that is about to be made. Once the Delete method is applied, the user cannot "undo" the operation, unless the code uses the *Transactions* property and the *Rollback* method. These are discussed later in this chapter.

Working with Unbound Controls

Now that you have mastered the art of the Data and bound controls, you might want to add other familiar controls, such as List and Combo boxes to the features offered by your form. Microsoft recommends obtaining additional data-aware controls from third-party developers. However, you can accomplish quite a lot if you follow some basic rules.

The next task is to add a list box, and fill it with the names of all the countries in your database.

The *Refresh* Method

As you learned earlier, you can set the DatabaseName and RecordSource properties in code at run time. When working with the Data control at run time, you need to use the Refresh method to open the database, and build or reconstruct the Dynaset in the control's Recordset property. The Refresh method also has the side effect of making the first record current in the recordset, as if the MoveFirst method had occurred.

Once the recordset is filled, you can access the individual fields of the current record in code. Form_Load is an appropriate procedure to contain instructions that fill the list box with data.

If the application is running, return to design mode. Place a List box control on the form, and assign the property values that Table 28.11 shows.

Table 28.11. Design-time properties for the List box control.

Control	Property	Value
List1	Height	1200
	Left	1680
	Top	600
	Width	1575

Open the Code window, and create the following Form_Load event procedure:

```
Sub Form_Load ()
    Data1.DatabaseName = "C:\VB\COUNTRY.MDB"
    Data1.RecordSource = "Country"

    Data1.Refresh     'Open database & recordset

    Do While Not Data1.Recordset.EOF
        If Not IsNull(Data1.Recordset(0)) Then    'If not empty, then
            List1.AddItem Data1.Recordset(0)         'add to the list
        End If
        Data1.Recordset.MoveNext     'Move to next record
    Loop
    Data1.Refresh                     'Rebuild the recordset
End Sub
```

The first two instructions assign appropriate values to the DatabaseName and RecordSource properties of the Data control.

The `Data1.Refresh` instruction uses the `Refresh` method to open the database, and refresh the recordset.

Finally, the `Do-While` loop fills the list box with the Country Names from the first field of the Country table.

How the List Box's *Do-While* Loop Works

The `List1` code works by accessing the `Fields` Collection, which contains the set of `Field` objects that comprise the recordset. You can use the `Count` property to determine the number of items in a collection. They are ordered sequentially from zero to (`Count - 1`).

NOTE Visual Basic provides access to all the fields in the recordset through `Fields` Collection. The `Fields` Collection is an array-type mechanism which references database fields as does the `Forms` Collection for forms, and the `Controls` Collection for controls. For more information on working with Collections, see Chapter 20, "Using Object Variables."

The default collection for a recordset is `Fields`. Also, the default property for a `Field` is `Value`. So, in this case, the reference to `Data1.Recordset(0)` in the line

```
List1.AddItem Data1.Recordset(0)
```

is a shorthand version of either of these lines:

```
List1.AddItem Data1.Recordset.Fields(0).Value
```

```
List1.AddItem Data1.Recordset.Fields(0)
```

The '0'th member of the `Fields` collection is the first field in the `Recordset`. In this instance, this is the "Country Name" field. Therefore, the following two lines are equivalent as well:

```
List1.AddItem Data1.Recordset.Fields("Country Name")
```

```
List1.AddItem Data1.Recordset("Country Name")
```

The loop continues while the `EOF` property is not True. A check is made to ensure that there is an entry in the Country Name field. If so, the value of the first record is added to the list box. The loop continues, stepping through the records using the `MoveNext` method. After the loop, the `Refresh` method resets to the first record.

The *FindFirst* Method

Now that the unbound list box is functional, you might decide to further integrate it into the navigational aspects of the application. It would be useful if double-clicking the name of a country in the list would make its record the current one. This is easily accomplished with the FindFirst method.

A FindFirst, FindLast, FindNext, or FindPrevious instruction each locate a record that satisfies criteria specified as part of the instruction. Create the following List1_DblClick event procedure:

```
Sub List1_DblClick ()
    Data1.Recordset.FindFirst "[Country Name] ='" & List1.Text & "'"
End Sub
```

The right side of the FindFirst instruction (and FindLast, FindNext, and FindPrevious similarly) specifies the location criteria with a string expression. This expression conforms with the WHERE syntax used in an SQL string, except that the word "WHERE" is omitted. SQL stands for Structured Query Language, which is a standardized language for querying, updating, and managing relational databases. SQL is discussed further later in this chapter.

NOTE You can use an SQL statement, instead of a table or QueryDef, as the value of the RecordSource property. If you do, the WHERE clause identifies the specific data you want to retrieve.

You can use the Text property of the list box to determine the currently selected item, which in this case is the one the user double-clicks. If you were to specify the country name directly in the program code, the instruction might read:

```
Data1.Recordset.FindFirst "[Country Name] ='United States'"
```

NOTE Pay careful attention to the syntax and quoting used in this instruction. Surround a field name with brackets when you enter one that contains a space or punctuation in an SQL statement. An example is [Country Name]. These brackets are in addition to, not instead of, any quotes needed. Regarding the construction of the rest of the instruction, the List1.Text property evaluates to a string, which is then concatenated to the "[Country Name] ='" section on the left, and "'" on the right.

If the recordset contains more than one record that matches the criteria, FindFirst locates the first occurrence. Then, FindFirst makes that the current record. You can use FindNext to move to each occurrence in turn. However, in this case, remember that the Primary field of the Country table is Country Name. Primary fields are Unique by default, which makes duplicate values impossible.

One of the beneficial features of Visual Basic is that, as you develop an application, you can add features that refine and enhance as needed. With the addition of the List1 double-click code, the user now has two different ways of moving to a new record. Next, you use the Data control's Reposition event to synchronize the list box and Data1's arrow buttons.

The *Reposition* Event

The Reposition event occurs *after* a record becomes current; it first happens when the Data control loads, which makes the first record in the recordset the current one. Any subsequent move or Find method also triggers a Reposition. Consequently, this event procedure is a good place to continuously update the unbound list box. The goal is to have the selection reflect the current record not only when double-clicking the Country Name in the list box, but also when navigating with the Data control. Follow these steps to synchronize your unbound control:

1. Place the following module-level variable in the General Declarations section at the form level:

   ```
   Dim Loading As Integer     ' Global True/False variable
   ```

2. Add the following three lines to the Form_Load event procedure, the first preceding the initial Refresh instruction, and the other two at the end:

   ```
   Loading = True  ' Set the global variable.

   Loading = False ' Turn off global variable.
   List1.ListIndex = 0     'Set selection to first record on load
   ```

   The updated Form_Load event procedure resembles the following:

   ```
   Sub Form_Load ()
       Data1.DatabaseName = "C:\VB\COUNTRY.MDB"
       Data1.RecordSource = "Country"

       Loading = True    'Set the global variable

       Data1.Refresh     'Open database & recordset
       Do While Not Data1.Recordset.EOF
          If Not IsNull(Data1.Recordset(0)) Then   'If not empty, then
             List1.AddItem Data1.Recordset(0)      'add to the list
          End If
          Data1.Recordset.MoveNext     'Move to next record
       Loop
   ```

```
    Data1.Refresh              'Rebuild the recordset

    Loading = False            'Turn off global variable
    List1.ListIndex = 0        'Set selection to first record on load
End Sub
```

3. Create the following `Reposition` event procedure for the `Data1` control:

```
Sub Data1_Reposition ()
    Dim I As Integer
    If Loading Then Exit Sub   'If global variable is set
    For I = 0 To List1.ListCount - 1    'Check items in list box
        If List1.List(I) = Data1.Recordset("[Country Name]") Then
            List1.ListIndex = I    'Select matching item
            Exit For       'Stop looking through list
        End If
    Next I
End Sub
```

How *Reposition* Works

You might wonder why the additional code in the `Form_Load` and Declarations sections is needed. First, examine the `Reposition` procedure to see how it works. The code loops through the list box's items, comparing each to the current record's Country Name field value. When a match occurs, the `ListIndex` property is set to that item, highlighting it as the currently selected one. Then, the loop is terminated. This works well, except for the situation that occurs when the form loads.

Recall that the code for the list box is filled with a loop that steps through the records with the `MoveNext` method. After the last Country Name is reached, one more `MoveNext` is executed, making the `Recordset.EOF` property True. In other words, there is no current record, yet the `MoveNext` method triggers a `Reposition` event. When the `For-Next` loop in the `Reposition` code reaches the comparison line

```
If List1.List(I) = Data1.Recordset("[Country Name]") Then
```

an error occurs. The reason is that the current record is not valid. If you try running this application without the additional `Form_Load` and Declarations code, the program halts with a warning message: No current record.

To solve this problem, the `Loading` global variable is declared. `Form_Load` sets its value to True prior to adding items to the list box. Then, after the items are added to the list box, `Form_Load` sets the value of `Loading` to False. With this code in place, the global variable is True while the form loads, and the `Reposition` code terminates before the synchronization loop begins. In any other situation, `Loading` is False, and everything proceeds with no difficulties.

Finally, because the `Reposition` code does not execute during the `Form_Load` event, the following line is added:

```
List1.ListIndex = 0      'Set selection to first record on load
```

As the comment indicates, the list box is synchronized to the first record.

Save COUNTRY.FRM with the updated code. Run the application. You can now move from one record to another with either the arrow buttons or the list box. The selected Country Name in `List1` corresponds to the current record. Figure 28.14 shows the application open to the Great Britain record. It was opened by clicking the country name in the list box.

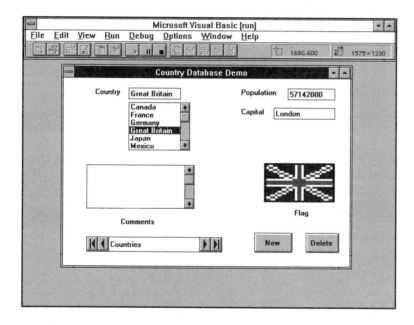

Figure 28.14.

The Great Britain record is opened.

You might wonder whether there are any other side effects associated with adding the `Reposition` event code. Indeed, there are. They become apparent only when you use the New command button to add a record you have just created, then subsequently try to erase the record with the Delete button. First of all, you need to add code to update the unbound `List1` list box when you are saving new Country data (and, therefore, a new Country Name). The Data control's `Validate` event can do this.

The *Validate* Event

You've learned that the `Reposition` event occurs *after* a record becomes the current one. In contrast, the `Validate` event occurs *prior to* completing a move to a new record; it also comes before the `Update` method. `Validate` occurs prior to a Delete, Unload, or Close operation as well. You can use the UpdateRecord method to save data without triggering a Validate event. However, in such cases, it's a good idea to write code for the Validate procedure that offers the user one last chance to determine the status (or confirm the actions) of your application before changing the stored data.

Validate is triggered by a number of different methods; you can determine what caused the event by examining one of its two arguments: Action and Save. The empty template of the Validate event procedure indicates the syntax of the two arguments:

```
Sub Data1_Validate (Action As Integer, Save As Integer)
```

The *Action* Argument

The Action argument contains a value representing one of a list of operations as Table 28.12 shows.

Table 28.12. Validate *Action* constants and values.

Constant	Value	Description
DATA_ACTIONCANCEL	0	Cancel the original Action
DATA_ACTIONMOVEFIRST	1	MoveFirst method
DATA_ACTIONMOVEPREVIOUS	2	MovePrevious method
DATA_ACTIONMOVENEXT	3	MoveNext method
DATA_ACTIONMOVELAST	4	MoveLast method
DATA_ACTIONADDNEW	5	AddNew method
DATA_ACTIONUPDATE	6	Update (not UpdateRecord)
DATA_ACTIONDELETE	7	Delete method
DATA_ACTIONFIND	8	Find method
DATA_ACTIONBOOKMARK	9	The Bookmark property has been set.
DATA_ACTIONCLOSE	10	Close method
DATA_ACTIONUNLOAD	11	The form is being unloaded.

NOTE   The CONSTANT.TXT file includes these constants and values.

The DATA_ACTIONBOOKMARK constant, with the value of 9, is passed to Validate when the Bookmark property of a record is set. Each record already has a unique bookmark when a recordset is created or opened. You can save the bookmark of the current record to a variable. After performing some other action, such as a move or Find method, you can jump back to the bookmarked record by setting the recordset's Bookmark property to the value of that variable. The movement to a new current record triggers Validate.

You can change the Action argument in your Validate event code to convert certain actions into others. Specifically, any move or AddNew method can be substituted for another of the same kind. You can completely cancel an action by setting Action to 0 (False).

The *Save* Argument

The Save argument is set to True if any of the bound controls have changed. You can examine the DataChanged property of any bound control to determine which specific data has been altered. If you want to keep any particular control from saving the new data in the database, set the DataChanged property to False. In the same way, you can set the Save argument to False to cancel, or invalidate, all data replacement. This does not cancel the action that triggered Validate, just the saving of new data. Conversely, if Save is True, and you set Action to False, the changed control's data is saved while the current record remains the same.

It is important to remember that you cannot use any methods (such as MoveNext) during the Validate event. Visual Basic generates an error if you try to do so. If allowed, it would cause infinite looping—a Move method would trigger a Validate event, which would generate the move again, and so on. As you will see in the next example, you use the Action argument to accomplish those tasks when necessary.

Using the *Validate* Event in the Sample Application

In the COUNTRY sample application, a new record is added by clicking the New button, then entering data into the bound controls. You then click one of the Data control's arrow buttons to initiate saving the record. Clicking an arrow button triggers one of the Move methods, which in turn starts the Validate event. You want not only to save the new data, but also to enter a new Country Name in the list box.

Another possible way exists to save data that you have created: a way in which you do *not* want a new name in the list. That's the situation when the user edits or changes an existing Country Name, then navigates to another record. For example, perhaps the user misspells "Japan," or wants to change "Great Britain" to "England." You don't want to create a new record. Instead, you want either to modify the old record or to confirm that the new data is entered correctly. Validate, with the help of the Data control's EditMode property, can handle these different possibilities with ease.

Create the following Validate event procedure for the Data1 control:

```
Sub Data1_Validate (Action As Integer, Save As Integer)
    Dim I As Integer

    If Save Then
        If Data1.EditMode = 2 Then
            List1.AddItem Text1.Text
            Action = 4    'DATA_ACTIONMOVELAST
        Else
            For I = 0 To List1.ListCount - 1 'Check list box items
                If List1.List(I) = Data1.Recordset(0) Then
                    List1.List(I) = Text1.Text    'Change name
                    Exit For       'Stop looking through list
                End If
            Next I
        End If
    End If
End Sub
```

How *Validate* Works

If the user has created and added a record, then clicks an arrow button to move to another, the Validate event occurs with the Action argument set to whichever Move method has been executed. Assuming that data has been entered in the new record, the Save argument is True. The Data control's EditMode property returns a value indicating the state of editing for the current record, as Table 28.13 lists.

Table 28.13. *EditMode* **property settings.**

Constant	Value	Description
DATA_EDITNONE	0	No editing in progress.
DATA_EDITMODE	1	Edit method has been invoked.
DATA_EDITADD	2	AddNew method has been invoked.

As a result, if Save is True, and Data1.EditMode is 2, the text from the Country Name bound control is added to the end of the list box. If you add a new record to a Dynaset, that record appears at the end of this object. Therefore, the list item reflects the record's position. Finally, the Action argument is converted from the Move operation that caused Validate to occur to MoveLast. This positions the current record to the newly created one at the end of the recordset.

Otherwise, Validate has occurred not because of a new record, but rather as the result of a change to an existing one. Here, the task is to update the Country Name in the list box to reflect any changes, without adding another name to it. The code loops through the list items, comparing each name to the current Country Name field value. Remember that the Validate event occurs *before* the current record is changed. Therefore, the field value is still the old text, the same as the value in the list box. When the match is found, the new text from the bound control replaces the old list item.

One other alternative exists: If the user clicks the New command button to add a new record, then navigates off it without entering any data, the Save argument is False. Thus, the new record is not saved. The Validate event is a powerful tool that serves as a kind of traffic cop in your data processing.

Clearing the List Box after Deleting

You must deal with one more side effect: cleaning up the list box after you use the Delete command button. Modify the Click procedure for the Delete command button to appear as follows:

```
Sub Command2_Click ()
   Dim I As Integer

   Dim MSGBOX_TYPE As Integer
   Dim Msg As String
   MSGBOX_TYPE = 17    'Stop icon, OK & Cancel buttons
```

```
Msg = "Are you sure you want to delete" & Chr$(10)
Msg = Msg & Text1.Text
If MsgBox(Msg, MSGBOX_TYPE, "Delete Record?") <> 1 Then Exit Sub

Data1.Recordset.Delete

For I = 0 To List1.ListCount - 1  'Check items in list box
    If List1.List(I) = List1.Text Then
        List1.RemoveItem (I)  'Remove matching item
        Exit For       'Stop looking through list
    End If
Next I
Loading = True   'Set global variable

Data1.Recordset.MoveNext
If Data1.Recordset.EOF Then Data1.Recordset.MovePrevious
Loading = False   'Turn off global variable
End Sub
```

How the *Command2_Click* Procedure Works

In the Command2_Click procedure, you use the Loading variable even though this is not actually a Form_Load situation. The global variable is used in the same way; there is no need to use more memory by declaring another variable. You remember from the section on creating the Delete button that the Delete method leaves the record that you erased Null, yet still current, and therefore invalid. This causes the same problem with the Reposition event that occurred with Form_Load: The program halts with a No current record warning. The cure is the same here: bracketing the move methods with updates to the Loading variable.

The other new code steps through the list box names, comparing each item with the current text in the Country Name bound control. When a match is found, the list item is removed.

Running the Application

Now, when you run the COUNTRY application, you can add, delete, and modify records, navigating either with the Data control's arrow buttons or the un-bound list box. As you can see, synchronizing unbound and bound controls requires a good deal of code. However, it illustrates the value and usefulness of the programming tools to which you have access, particularly the Reposition and Validate events.

Using Queries with Multiple Tables

Queries are another way to manipulate and extract data from a database. You can use a SELECT query that asks the database for a set of records matching specified criteria. Alternatively, you can make an ACTION query that performs operations on a recordset. You can create these queries using SQL (Structured Query Language). The SQL syntax used in Visual Basic and Access is similar to those used with many other software applications.

Also, facilities exist in Visual Basic for connecting directly to external databases using the appropriate SQL syntax for each. You can enter an SQL statement in the Data control's RecordSource property instead of a Table name. Alternatively, you can use a predefined QueryDef. You need either Visual Basic 3.0's Professional Edition or Microsoft Access to create QueryDefs. The discussion here concerns SQL statements you can define either at design or run time with the Standard or Professional Edition.

You can use an SQL statement to define a set of records with single or multiple tables. For example, to create a recordset with COUNTRY.MAK at run time that contains only those countries with a population greater than 100 million, you can use the following instruction:

```
Data1.RecordSource = "SELECT * FROM Country WHERE Population > 100000000"
```

The asterisk (*) indicates "all" records that satisfy the criteria. You follow this instruction with a Refresh method to re-create the recordset. The resulting recordset includes Japan, Russia, and the United States, if you've built the sample application as indicated earlier.

Adding a New Table and Field to COUNTRY.MDB

By tying together multiple tables with a query, you can greatly expand the power and efficiency of your database application. To explore this, use Data Manager to create a new table. To activate the Data Manager, choose it from the Window menu.

 NOTE The DOS program SHARE.EXE must be running in order to access a database with the Data Manager while an application is loaded. SHARE is discussed earlier in this chapter.

Choose the Open Database option from the File menu. Then, choose Access from the submenu. Now, open the COUNTRY.MDB database you created earlier. Click the New button to open the Create New Table dialog box. Name the new table "Language" (see Figure 28.15).

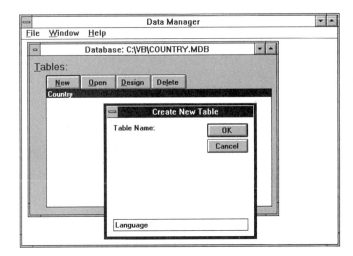

Figure 28.15.

Creating the new
Language table.

When you click OK, the Table Design window displays; click the Add button in the Fields grid to display the Add Field dialog (see Figure 28.16). Enter the first field's name **Language ID**, then click the down arrow to select the field's data type. When you choose the Long Integer type, a small check box appears labeled "Counter." Check that box to select it (see Figure 28.16).

By checking this box, you stipulate that the values for the Language ID field should be consecutive increasing integers. The value of Language ID is 1 for the first record. The value is automatically incremented by one as each new record is added. A field created with Counter makes an excellent primary key index.

Figure 28.16.

Completing the Add Field dialog.

Click OK. Click the Add button again to define another field. Name this field **Language Name**, and select the Text data type. Then, give the field a size of 20. (Notice that when you select the Text type, the Counter box does not appear. That's because only fields created with a numerical data type, (not Text), provide the option of choosing Counter.

Next, create an index for the new table as you did for the Country one. This time enter **LangID** in the Index Name text box; then, click Language ID to select it. Click Add (Asc), and check the Primary Index box (see Figure 28.17).

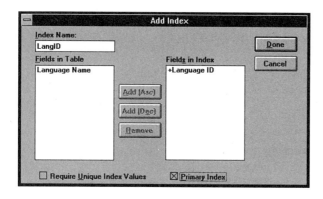

Figure 28.17.

Adding the LangID index.

Click Done to create the index. Close the Fields Design window. Click the Language item in the Fields section of the table to make sure it is selected. Then, open the Table Access window on the Language table to add the data that Table 28.14 shows. You don't have to enter the Language ID value, because it auto-increments when you save each new record's data. (This is the reason you marked the Counter check box when you defined the field type.) Figure 28.18 shows a data value that is entered.

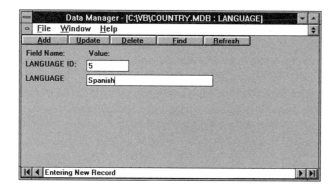

Figure 28.18.

Adding the Spanish language data value.

Table 28.14. Language table data for the COUNTRY database.

Language ID	Language Name
1	English
2	French
3	German
4	Russian
5	Spanish
6	Japanese

With the new table created and filled with data, close the Table Access window. Click the Country table, then click the Design button to open the Table Design window. As promised earlier, add an additional field named **Language ID**, and a field type of Long Integer. Do not check the Counter check box in this case, because you are about to enter the ID values manually. Figure 28.19 shows the Language ID field added to the Fields section of the Country table.

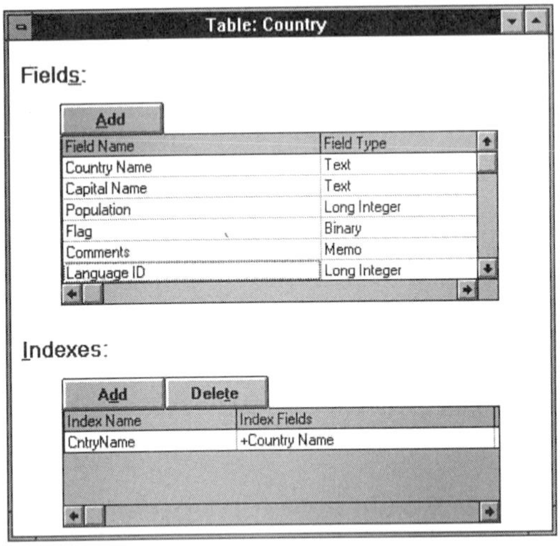

Figure 28.19.

The Language ID field is added to the Country table.

Close the Fields Design window. Then, open the Table Access window on the Country table. Add the following data that Table 28.15 shows. (Note that you need only add the Language ID field data; the first field is the existing Country Name data.) Figure 28.20 shows the Language ID value of 5 that is added to the Mexico record.

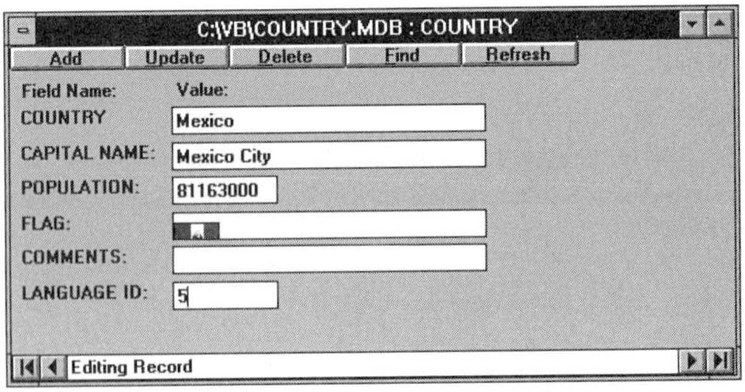

Figure 28.20.

Specifying the Language ID for Mexico.

Table 28.15. Country table additional ID field data.

Country Name (already entered)	Language ID
Canada	1
France	2
Germany	3
Great Britain	1
Japan	6
Mexico	5
Russia	4
Spain	5
United States	1

Finally, select Exit from the File menu to close the Data Manager.

Add both a Label (Label6) and a Text Box control (Text5) to the form. The text box will be made data-aware. Assign the property values that Table 28.16 shows.

Table 28.16. Design-time properties for additional controls.

Control	Property	Value
Label6	Caption	Language
	Height	255
	Left	4560
	Top	1200
	Width	855
Text5	DataSource	Data1
	Height	285
	Left	5520
	Top	1200
	Width	1455

Relating Two Tables

You might have guessed the reason for adding this new table and the additional field in the existing table. Now, you will be able to display the language for each country in your database, by *relating* information from one table to another. You establish a relationship between two tables by having fields in both tables that share a common value.

In this case, the Language ID fields are the linking fields. You use this relationship with an SQL statement to *look up* the Language Name in the Language table. You then relate this language to the appropriate country in the Country table. This is not coincidentally referred to as a *look-up table*. It serves a vital purpose in database design, by reducing the duplication of data.

The SQL-like instruction that links the fields from both tables follows. You must type the entire instruction on one line in the Form_Load event procedure, replacing the existing RecordSource property setting.

```
Data1.RecordSource = "SELECT Country.*, [Language Name] FROM Country,
➥Language, Country INNER JOIN Language ON Country.[Language ID] =
➥Language.[Language ID] Order by [Country Name]"
```

Note that you can also enter the same statement without the quotes for the RecordSource property in the Properties window.

Although this chapter cannot provide a comprehensive tutorial on SQL, here is a brief explanation of the previous instruction: it selects all the fields from the Country table, as well as the Language Table field from the Language table. (The Language ID field from the Language table is not selected.) Remember that field names with spaces need to be bracketed. An INNER JOIN operation connects the Country and Language tables. The operation combines records from the two tables whenever there are matching values in a field common to both. The Language ID fields qualify on that score; in fact, they don't need to have the same name, as long as they are of the same data type. Finally, the resulting recordset is ordered (Order) by the Country Name field, so that the records are sorted alphabetically.

NOTE The Visual Basic help system contains descriptions of the various statements in the SQL query language.

Remember that you can set the DataSource property only at design time. However, you can set the DataField property at either design time or run time. Here, you set the DataField property in the Form_Load event procedure using the following instruction:

```
Text5.DataField = "[Language Name]"    ' Set field for text box.
```

With these changes and additions, the Form_Load procedure now appears as follows:

```
Sub Form_Load ()
    Data1.DatabaseName = "C:\VB\COUNTRY.MDB"
    Data1.RecordSource = "SELECT Country.*, [Language Name] FROM Country,
    ➥Language, Country INNER JOIN Language ON Country.[Language ID] =
    ➥Language.[Language ID] Order by [Country Name]"
```

```
    Loading = True    'Set the global variable

    Data1.Refresh    'Open database & recordset

    Do While Not Data1.Recordset.EOF
        If Not IsNull(Data1.Recordset(0)) Then    'If not empty, then
            List1.AddItem Data1.Recordset(0)        'add to the list
        End If
        Data1.Recordset.MoveNext      'Move to next record
    Loop
    Data1.Refresh      'Rebuild the recordset

    Text5.DataField = "[Language Name]"   'Set field for text box
    Loading = False   'Turn off global variable
    List1.ListIndex = 0    'Set selection to first record on load
End Sub
```

Running the Application

Run the application, and navigate through the records with the Data control's arrow buttons. Each record now displays all the original data, as well as the language of each country. English is spoken in Canada, Great Britain, and the United States, while Spanish is the language of both Spain and Mexico. In these instances, the application looks up the Language Name field in the Language table, and displays the result on the form. This saves the space that normally would have been taken up by the repetition of the language text. The savings are small here. However, they can add up quickly in actual database applications.

If you try to add a new record with the application in its current state, you will encounter trouble. If you specify data for a new country, and click one of the arrow buttons to save the record, the program halts with the following warning message: Join is broken by value(s) in fields 'Language ID'. The error message describes the problem precisely. Remember that the SQL statement has created a recordset of those records from both tables in which the Language ID fields have matching values. The new record has no matching value; the reason is that there is no bound control in which to enter such a value.

However, you can add a new text box, and bind it to the ID field. To do so, use the Properties window to set the text box's DataSource property to Data1, and DataField property to Language ID. You must type the DataField property value in the Properties window, rather than select it from the drop-down list. The reason is that the SQL statement does not run until the Form_Load event procedure executes.

Now, when you run the program, you can click the new ID text box, and type one of the ID numbers that corresponds to the language for the new record's country. The record will now be saved normally. To make this more intuitive, you could automate adding the language ID in code, perhaps using another list box with language names.

Some Additional Tools

Several tools exist that help the developer to streamline and protect more complex applications, especially those that involve multiuser and data integrity issues. The next several sections discuss the following tools:

- Transaction statements
- The `UpdateRecord` and `UpdateControls` methods
- The `Error` event
- The `FieldSize`, `GetChunk`, and `AppendChunk` methods
- The `Database` Property

Transaction Statements

In many database applications, actions taken in one area of the program depend on what transpires in another section. You deal with this type of transaction every time you use a cash machine, or write a check. If one element of the transfer of funds fails (for example, not having enough money to cover the rent check), all the interim actions need to be reversed. Also, the user must be notified.

In a Visual Basic application, a *transaction* is a series of updates to a database which you want to treat as a single unit. A `BeginTrans` instruction begins a transaction. Any updates executed after `BeginTrans` can be undone by using a `Rollback` instruction. Alternatively, a `CommitTrans` instruction accepts the changes and terminates the transaction.

Your application is in *auto-commit* mode from the moment the database is opened; any changes made to your data are automatically saved to the database. That is, by default, the value of each recordset's `Transaction` property is True. If you change the value to False, you disable the recordset from processing any transactions.

Using the Transaction statements enables you to perform a number of potentially irreversible operations on a database, and display a confirmation message with a summary of those actions. At this point, the user can still cancel the changes.

UpdateRecord and *UpdateControls*

The UpdateRecord method saves the current values of bound controls to the database. UpdateRecord differs from the Update method in that the former does not trigger a Validate event. Therefore, you can use UpdateRecord in a Validate event procedure without triggering another Validate event. In this way, you avoid a recursive situation known as a *cascading event*.

The UpdateControls method works the other way around, restoring the current record's field values to the bound controls. This is useful to undo changes the user makes to data in the bound controls. Both UpdateRecord and UpdateControls perform their actions without moving from the current record. This makes them ideal for use during the Validate event to either save or cancel changes.

The *Error* Event

You are expected to provide error-handling for run time errors in your code. However, the Error event triggers when an error relating to a Data control occurs when no Visual Basic code is executing. For example, suppose the user types a database name that doesn't exist into an Open dialog box used to set the DatabaseName property. In such a case, the Error event occurs when the database is not found. You can write code in the Error event procedure that informs the user of the problem. The code might display another Open dialog box so the user can try again, rather than letting the application come to a halt.

The *FieldSize, GetChunk,* and *AppendChunk* Methods

FieldSize, GetChunk, and AppendChunk deal with large data fields that you can store in Memo and Long Binary fields. While Visual Basic string variables can be no larger than 64K, the Memo field data types can handle much greater amounts of binary data. With the technology afforded by multimedia computing, Visual Basic can now store large graphics, sound, and even video data in Memo fields.

You can determine the size of a Memo field using FieldSize, then use repeated GetChunk and AppendChunk methods to carve up the data into manageable portions. With smaller units, it's easier to copy the data from record to record, or to save the data to a disk file.

GetChunk includes an *offset* argument to access successive 64K chunks of data. Then, AppendChunk pastes each new chunk to the end of the target field. You can use FieldSize to determine the number of loop iterations needed to handle all the data in the field.

The *Database* Property

You can use the Database property not only to manage opening the databases, but also to access their structure and tables. You can navigate through the database's hierarchy to examine the internal design structure of the tables, fields, and indexes. This property is read-only at run time.

Using Visual Basic and Microsoft Access

Visual Basic 3.0 uses the Microsoft Access engine to work with databases. This "engine" is a dynamic link library that offers to program code a variety of relational database tools: transaction processing, distributed joins, data types such as BLOB (binary object), data validation, stored queries, referential integrity, multiuser access, and security features. In addition, data can be accessed and stored in a number of database formats, including Microsoft Access, Microsoft FoxPro, dBASE, Paradox, Btrieve, SQL Server, and Oracle.

If you own Microsoft Access, you will find it invaluable in learning about database design and techniques. Databases created in either Access or Visual Basic work interchangeably. You can use Access's QBE windows to interactively create complex queries, test the results, and then copy the generated SQL code into your Visual Basic application.

Figure 28.21 shows Access loaded with a sample database. This database contains information about the nine employees of a small business.

Access has an intuitive interface that makes it easy to set up complex multiuser relationships. Data integrity and field validation can be performed with built-in tools not provided with Visual Basic. It requires a substantial programming effort to create the same functionality in your Visual Basic applications.

On the other hand, compared with Access, Visual Basic has considerably more tools to manipulate forms and other screen objects. The growing library of third-party controls and accessories gives Visual Basic programmers much more flexibility in application development than they have with the more limited objects in Access. Although Visual Basic 3.0 does not ship with bound grid, combo, or list box controls as does Access, third-party developers have filled the gap with a variety of custom VBX controls.

When creating database applications, there are other advantages to working with Visual Basic and Access in tandem. The underlying Access Basic language is very similar to Visual Basic's. Porting code between Access and Visual Basic is relatively trouble-free, especially when the code is not tied to specific properties of Access controls. Even then, alternate solutions are possible.

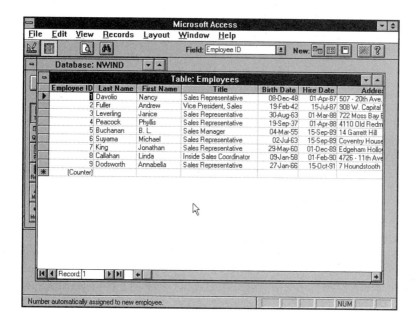

Figure 28.21

A sample database loaded into Access.

Some applications run faster in Visual Basic—particularly those with many bit-mapped graphics, such as photos in personnel databases. Many database programmers find it desirable to create a database with Access, and then develop a Visual Basic "front end" for the user to navigate through the data.

Microsoft does sell an Access Distribution Kit. This kit provides a royalty-free run-time version so that you can distribute Access applications. However, Visual Basic database applications will likely have less overhead in code size and speed than their Access counterparts. Bear in mind, though, that with Visual Basic, you will have to write code for many things that are provided automatically in Access's interface.

Developing Database Applications with the Professional Edition

While the Standard Edition of Visual Basic offers much in the way of programmability, the Professional Edition is necessary for anyone interested in developing complex database applications. The programmatic data-access layer of the Professional Edition provides tools to create new databases and modify existing database structures. The data-access layer consists of the following eight predefined objects that let you "get under the hood" and control the full functionality of the Access engine:

- The Database object
- The Table object
- The TableDef object
- The Dynaset object
- The Snapshot object
- The QueryDef object
- The Field object
- The Index object

Although you can create Database and Dynaset objects using a Data control, you are limited to the physical presence of the control on your form, regardless of whether it's visible. Additional features *not* possible with the Standard Edition include creating, opening, manipulating, and deleting the following objects: Index, QueryDef, Table, and Snapshot.

In either edition, you can view the structure of your database with these Collections: TableDefs, Fields, and Indexes. However, the Professional tools let you create and modify both the structure and data at any level. There are 144 new properties and methods associated with the data-access layer.

Three additional data-aware controls are included with the Professional Edition: Masked edit, 3D Panel, and the 3D Check box. The package also includes documentation and examples to aid in creating your own data-aware custom controls, though you'll need additional programming tools and experience to accomplish this. You'll find more code examples and sample applications that demonstrate data access techniques, including an example that uses the new Outline control, which comes only with the Professional Edition. For more about the custom controls included with the Professional Edition, see Chapter 32, "Using Custom Controls."

Also bundled is Crystal Reports 2.0 for Visual Basic, a report writer that uses the Microsoft Access 1.1 engine for data access and includes a custom control to embed reports in your application. You can design reports with a graphical WYSIWYG (What You See Is What You Get) banded report designer. This tool supports advanced features such as formulas, two-pass calculations, unlimited grouping, standard and custom mailing-label formats, bitmaps, borders, drop shadows, lines, boxes, rich text, and more. You can accomplish most of this functionality with the Standard Edition, but not easily and certainly not as quickly.

The Professional Edition fully supports ODBC, Microsoft's Open Database Connectivity standard, which uses drivers to import, attach, and export data to supported SQL databases. The Access 1.1 engine ships with ODBC drivers for Microsoft and Sybase SQL Server and Oracle Server databases. More drivers are forthcoming from Microsoft and other vendors.

You can browse the on-line help in the Standard Edition to learn all about the Professional Edition's Data Access extensions. (Both editions come with the same on-line documentation.) The Professional Edition includes additional printed documentation. However, SQL information is available *only* from the on-line help, with the exception of a limited Appendix in the Professional Edition.

If you are interested in developing multiuser, complex data-aware applications that can serve as front-ends for a variety of external and server-based databases, by all means upgrade to the Professional Edition. Even intermediate users will quickly find much to be gained by moving up.

Summary

The Data control is new with Visual Basic 3.0. This control and the bound data-aware controls work together to provide powerful tools for manipulating databases. You can develop a wide variety of data-aware applications, including easy-to-use visual front ends for existing databases. Typically, only a minimum of programming is necessary.

While the Standard Edition offers much in the way of programmability, the Professional Edition is a vital tool for anyone interested in developing serious database applications. The programmatic data-access layer gives you tools to create new databases and modify the structure of existing ones. Three more data-aware controls are included.

The Professional Edition also includes Crystal Reports 2.0, a report writer that uses the Microsoft Access 1.1 engine for data access. Crystal Reports 2.0 includes a custom control to embed reports in applications. Also included are full ODBC support, additional code examples, and expanded documentation for creating data-aware controls.

If you also own Microsoft Access, you will find it invaluable for learning about database design and techniques. Databases created in Access or Visual Basic work interchangeably.

Interacting with Other Windows Applications

PART

VI

Manipulating the Windows Environment

Visual Basic applications are citizens of the Windows environment by necessity. This environment supports multitasking, which means that several applications can run simultaneously. As such, your Visual Basic applications are not isolated programming "islands," but rather dynamic components under the Windows umbrella.

Through program code, your applications can "reach out" to this environment. Not only can you tap into the resources of Windows itself, your Visual Basic applications can manipulate other applications, and share information with them.

This chapter discusses several ways that Visual Basic applications can manipulate the resources of the Windows environment. This chapter covers the following subjects:

- Using the Clipboard
- Launching other applications
- Sending keystrokes to other applications
- Using timers to manipulate unattended applications
- Using DoEvents to improve Windows performance
- Calling procedures in Dynamic Link Libraries
- Using the Common Dialog control to create standardized dialog boxes

Using the Clipboard

The Clipboard is a Windows accessory that temporarily holds text and graphics. As long as Windows is running, the Clipboard is available throughout the Windows environment.

Many Windows applications take advantage of the Clipboard to store and retrieve data. You can copy some text or graphics from an application to the Clipboard. Later, you can paste those Clipboard contents into an entirely different Windows application, or back into the same one. For example, using Windows Paintbrush, you can create a graphics design, then copy it to the Clipboard. Next, you can paste it from the Clipboard into a document that is created with a Windows word processor.

Applications typically use an Edit menu to interact with the Clipboard. For example, the cut and paste features of Visual Basic's Edit menu utilize the Clipboard. As Table 29.1 describes, three standard Clipboard-related commands found in Edit menus are Cut, Copy, and Paste.

Table 29.1. Common Edit menu commands.	
Command	**Description**
Cut	Deletes selected text or a graphics design from an application, and places the data into the Clipboard. The Cut operation erases from the Clipboard any previous data of the same type.
Copy	Places a copy of the data in the Clipboard but, unlike Cut, does not delete the original data from the application.
Paste	Places a copy of the Clipboard contents into the application.

The Clipboard works "destructively": If you copy a text block into the Clipboard, its previous contents (text or graphics) are lost. You cannot append text to the end of what is already contained in the Clipboard. Similarly, any new graphics design you place in the Clipboard wipes out any picture or text previously there.

The Clipboard is actually an independent program which is always running while Windows is active. This program has specialized data-conversion features which can manipulate data of differing formats. For example, the Clipboard can usually accept text from an ASCII editor (such as Windows Notepad), and successfully transfer the text to a non-ASCII word processor (such as Word for Windows).

You can access the Clipboard program directly from within Windows. The Clipboard Viewer application can be found in Windows Main program group. By launching the Clipboard Viewer, you not only can view the current contents of the Clipboard, but also store the contents on disk or retrieve data from a previously-saved file.

Accessing the Clipboard from Visual Basic

Your Visual Basic applications can access the Clipboard at run time through program code. You can import text and graphics from the Clipboard, as well as copy data from your application to it.

The mechanism to access the Clipboard is the Clipboard object. The Clipboard object does not have any events or properties. However, it does have several associated methods. Table 29.2 summarizes them.

Table 29.2. Methods Associated with the *Clipboard* Object.

Method	Description
Clear	Erases the contents of the Clipboard
GetData	Retrieves a picture from the Clipboard
GetFormat	Determines if the Clipboard contains data of a specified type
GetText	Retrieves a text string from the Clipboard
SetData	Sends a picture to the Clipboard
SetText	Sends a text string to the Clipboard

The following sections describe these methods.

Erasing the Clipboard Using *Clear*

The syntax for the Clear method is straightforward:

```
Clipboard.Clear
```

This instruction deletes the current contents of the Clipboard.

Understanding the Clipboard Data Formats Recognized by Visual Basic

The remaining Clipboard methods work with data in several possible formats. To transfer data, Visual Basic must know which type of data the program is retrieving or sending. The syntax for the Clipboard methods includes a numeric parameter which describes the format of the transferred data. Table 29.3 summarizes the various data formats.

Table 29.3. Clipboard Data Formats.

Value	Format	Symbolic Constant
&HBF00	DDE data transfer	CF_LINK
1	Text	CF_TEXT
2	Standard bitmap (.BMP files)	CF_BITMAP
3	Windows metafile (.WMF files)	CF_METAFILE
8	Device-independent bitmap (.DIB files)	CF_DIB
9	Color palette	CF_PALETTE

The first column of the table indicates the numeric value that Visual Basic assigns to each data type. The third column shows the symbolic constant associated with each format. These constants are defined in the CONSTANT.TXT file. If you load CONSTANT.TXT into a module, you can use the constants in your program code rather than the literal numeric values.

Transferring Text Using *SetText* and *GetText*

The SetText method copies a text string from your Visual Basic application to the Clipboard.

```
Clipboard.SetText stringdata, dataformat
```

in which

   stringdata specifies the text to be copied to the Clipboard,

and

   dataformat specifies whether the format is &HBF00 (DDE transfer) or 1 (Text).

The *dataformat* parameter is optional.

The *stringdata* parameter can be a text literal enclosed in quotation marks, a variable of string type, or a reference to an object containing string data. If you omit the *dataformat* parameter, text format (CF_TEXT) is assumed.

For example, the following instruction places a text literal into the Clipboard.

```
Clipboard.SetText "This text is bound for the Clipboard"
```

Similarly, the following instruction places the contents of the Text1 text box in the Clipboard.

```
Clipboard.SetText Text1.Text, 1
```

To retrieve text from the Clipboard, use the GetText method.

```
Clipboard.GetText(dataformat)
```

in which

    dataformat species whether the format is &HBF00 (DDE transfer) or 1 (Text).

The *dataformat* parameter is optional.

If you omit the *dataformat* parameter, CF_TEXT is assumed. The parentheses must always be present, even if you omit *dataformat*.

Although GetText is a method, you use it in program code similar to a function. For example, the following instruction assigns the current text contents of the Clipboard to the variable MyText$:

```
MyText$ = Clipboard.GetText()
```

If the Clipboard does not contain a text string which matches the specified format (CF_LINK or CF_TEXT), the GetText method returns a null string ("").

Transferring Pictures Using *SetData* and *GetData*

The SetData method copies a graphics image from your Visual Basic application to the Clipboard. The syntax for SetData is similar to that for SetText.

```
Clipboard.SetData picturedata, dataformat
```

in which

    picturedata specifies the graphics image that is copied to the Clipboard,

continues

continued

and

dataformat species whether the format is 2 (regular bitmap), 3 (Windows metafile), 8 (device-independent bitmap), or 9 (color palette).

The *dataformat* parameter is optional.

The *picturedata* parameter typically specifies the Picture or Image property of a picture box control. If you omit the *dataformat* parameter, the SetData method automatically determines the picture format.

For example, the following instruction copies to the Clipboard the picture stored in the Picture1 picture box control:

```
Clipboard.SetData Picture1.Picture
```

If you want to explicitly specify the picture format as bitmap, and you have the CONSTANT.TXT file loaded, you can add the *dataformat* parameter in this way:

```
Clipboard.SetData Picture1.Picture, CF_BITMAP
```

You can use the LoadPicture function to specify a picture file stored on disk. For example:

```
Clipboard.SetData LoadPicture("C:\WINDOWS\CARS.BMP")
```

To retrieve a picture from the Clipboard, use the GetData method.

```
Clipboard.GetData(dataformat)
```

in which

dataformat species whether the format is 2 (regular bitmap), 3 (Windows metafile), 8 (device-independent bitmap), or 9 (color palette).

The *dataformat* parameter is optional.

If you omit the *dataformat* parameter, or specify a value of 0, Visual Basic automatically determines the appropriate format. The parentheses must always be present, even if you omit *dataformat*.

Similar to GetText, you use GetData in program code as a function. For example, the following instruction assigns the current picture in the Clipboard to the Picture property of a picture box named MyPicture.

```
MyPicture.Picture = Clipboard.GetData()
```

If the Clipboard does not contain a picture with the format specified by *dataformat*, the GetData method returns a null picture.

Determining the Format of the Clipboard Contents Using *GetFormat*

The GetFormat method determines whether the Clipboard contains data in a specified format.

```
Clipboard.GetFormat(dataformat)
```

in which

   dataformat is one of the values that Table 29.3 specifies.

The GetFormat method returns a True or False value.

For example, the following instruction retrieves text data only if the Clipboard contains a text value.

```
If Clipboard.GetFormat(1) Then MyText$ = Clipboard.GetText()
```

With CONSTANT.TXT loaded, you can specify the *dataformat* parameter with a constant. For example:

```
If Not (Clipboard.GetFormat(CF_BITMAP)) Then
   MsgBox "No bitmap available"
End If
```

ClipDemo—A Sample Application Using the Clipboard

The ClipDemo application demonstrates how you can use the Clipboard methods in a Visual Basic application. With ClipDemo, you can transfer text and graphics to and from the Clipboard.

Creating the Form for ClipDemo

To create ClipDemo, start a new project. Place a text box, picture box, and four command buttons on the form. Using the Properties window, assign the property values that Table 29.4 shows.

Table 29.4. Property values for the ClipDemo application.

Object	Property	Value
Form1	Caption	Clipboard Demonstration
	Height	5040
	Left	1035
	Top	1140
	Width	4995
Text1	MultiLine	-1 'True
	ScrollBars	2 'Vertical
	Text	(blank) 'clear contents
	Height	735
	Left	120
	Top	120
	Width	4575
Picture1	Height	1935
	Left	120
	Top	1800
	Width	4575
Command1	Name	btnCopyText
	Caption	Copy Text to Clipboard
	Height	495
	Left	120
	Top	960
	Width	2175
Command2	Name	btnViewText
	Caption	View Text in Clipboard
	Height	495
	Left	2520
	Top	960
	Width	2175

Object	Property	Value
Command3	Name	btnCopyPicture
	Caption	Copy Picture to Clipboard
	Height	495
	Left	120
	Top	3960
	Width	2295
Command4	Name	btnViewPicture
	Caption	View Picture in Clipboard
	Height	495
	Left	2520
	Top	3960
	Width	2295

Figure 29.1 shows the form's appearance at design time. As explained in the next several sections, the upper box displays text while the larger, lower box displays graphical pictures.

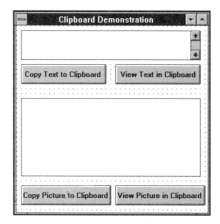

Writing the Text Box Event Procedures

At the top of the form is a multiline text box with a vertical scroll bar. When ClipDemo is running, you can move the focus to this text box, and type text directly into it.

Two command buttons are below the text box. Clicking the one to the left transfers the contents of the text box to the Clipboard. The following simple event procedure is all you need to implement this command button:

```
Sub btnCopyText_Click ()
    Clipboard.SetText Text1.Text
End Sub
```

However, you might want the procedure to check whether the text box is empty before transferring the data to the Clipboard. As currently written, clicking the command button when the text box is empty has the effect of clearing any text in the Clipboard. The following is a more elaborate form of the event procedure that you can use instead of the simpler version:

```
Sub btnCopyText_Click ()
    If Text1.Text = "" Then
        MsgBox ("The text box is empty")
    Else
        Clipboard.Clear
        Clipboard.SetText Text1.Text
    End If
End Sub
```

If the text box is empty, this procedure displays a message box warning the user of that fact. The Clipboard contents are not updated. In this procedure, the Clipboard.Clear instruction is not really necessary because any new text sent to the Clipboard replaces its previous contents. However, the instruction ensures that the Clipboard is empty before any new data is sent. This precaution avoids some remote error situations.

To transfer a copy of the Clipboard's text contents into the text box, you click the button below it that is on the right side. The following is the appropriate event procedure for this command button:

```
Sub btnViewText_Click ()
    If Clipboard.GetFormat(1) = True Then
        Text1.Text = Clipboard.GetText(1)
    Else
        MsgBox ("Clipboard does not contain any text")
    End If
End Sub
```

The `Clipboard.GetFormat(1)` method returns True if the Clipboard contains some text. In this case, the procedure uses the `GetText` method to assign a copy of the text in the Clipboard to the `Text` property of the text box. If there is no text in the Clipboard, the procedure displays a warning message box.

Writing the Event Procedures for the Picture Box

The bottom half of the form contains a picture box. You use this picture box to transfer graphics images to and from the Clipboard.

Clicking the command button to the left below the picture box transfers a copy of the its contents to the Clipboard. The following is the `Click` procedure for this command button:

```
Sub btnCopyPicture_Click ()
    Clipboard.Clear
    Clipboard.SetData Picture1.Picture
End Sub
```

Clicking the button to the right below the picture box places a copy of the current Clipboard picture, if any, into the picture box. The following is the appropriate `Click` procedure:

```
Sub btnViewPicture_Click ()
    Picture1.Picture = Clipboard.GetData()
End Sub
```

By using blank parentheses in the `GetData` method, this procedure can transfer data of any picture format (bitmap, metafile, device-independent bitmap, or color palette).

Save the form as CLIPDEMO.FRM, and the project as CLIPDEMO.MAK.

Running ClipDemo

Run ClipDemo, and experiment with transferring text and graphics to and from the Clipboard. You can open other Windows applications to copy data to the Clipboard. Or you can paste data you sent to the Clipboard using ClipDemo.

To see the current contents of the Clipboard, you can launch Windows' Clipboard Viewer application. As mentioned earlier in this chapter, this application is located, by default, in the Main program group. Clipboard Viewer displays a window which shows the contents of the Clipboard. By having this window open while you run ClipDemo, you can see what's happening in the Clipboard as you transfer data.

Follow these steps to experiment with ClipDemo:

1. Start ClipDemo, and move the application's window to the left edge of the screen, just below the Toolbar.

2. Launch the Clipboard Viewer application.

   To do so, open the Main program group from the Program Manager. Then, double-click the icon labeled Clipboard Viewer.

3. Resize the Clipboard Viewer window to about half the height of the one for ClipDemo. Move the Clipboard Viewer window to the right of the ClipDemo's, just below the Toolbar.

4. Launch the Notepad application from Windows.

   To do so, open the Accessories program group from the Program Manager. Double-click the icon labeled "Notepad."

5. Move and resize the Notepad window until it fills the screen space below the Clipboard Viewer (see Figure 29.2).

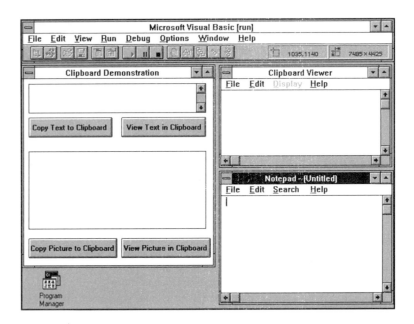

Figure 29.2.

The screen contains ClipDemo, Clipboard Viewer, and Notepad.

6. Type **Here we go** (or any other text string) in the Notepad window. Select the text that you type.

To select the text in Notepad, hold down the left mouse button when the pointer is at one end of the text. Then, drag the mouse to the other end of the text. The selected text becomes highlighted. (An alternate way to select the text is to use arrow keys to move the cursor over it while you hold down the Shift key.)

7. Choose **C**opy from Notepad's **E**dit menu. This command transfers a copy of the selected text to the Clipboard.

A copy of the selected text appears in the Clipboard Viewer window.

8. Click the View Text in Clipboard command button in the ClipDemo window.

A copy of the Clipboard text instantly appears in the text box (see Figure 29.3).

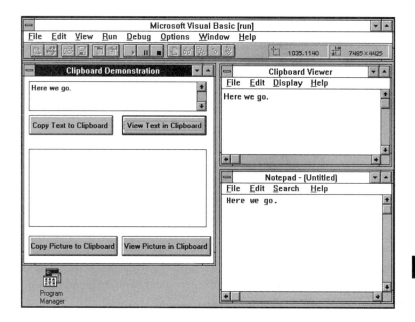

Figure 29.3.

The text box contains a copy of the Clipboard text.

9. Edit the contents of ClipDemo's text box to read **It was a very good year** (or any other text string).

10. Click the Copy Text to Clipboard command button.

As reflected in the Clipboard Viewer, the Clipboard now contains what is in the text box (see Figure 29.4).

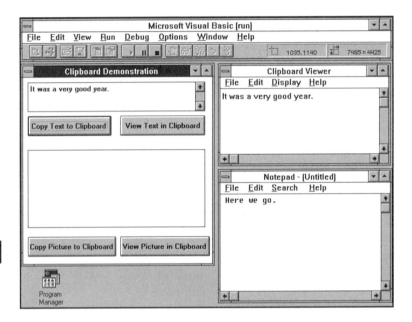

Figure 29.4.

The contents of the text box are copied to the Clipboard.

11. Close the Notepad application.

To do so, click the control-menu box in the upper left corner of the Notepad window, then choose the **C**lose option. When asked whether you want to save the text in Notepad, respond No.

Before closing Notepad, you can optionally choose **P**aste from Notepad's **E**dit menu. If you do, the text string from the Clipboard is copied into the Notepad window. This option demonstrates how the **P**aste command, found in most Windows programs, copies data from the Clipboard to the application.

12. Launch the Paintbrush application from Windows.

To do so, open the Accessories program group from the Program Manager. Double-click the icon labeled "Paintbrush."

13. Resize and move the Paintbrush window until it fills the screen space formerly occupied by the Notepad application.

14. Using Paintbrush, draw a picture in its window (see Figure 29.5).

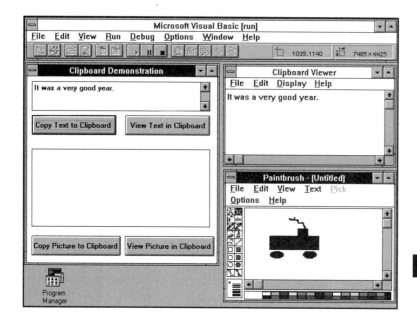

Figure 29.5.

A picture of a truck using
Paintbrush.

15. Copy the picture from Paintbrush to the Clipboard.

   To do so, first choose the Scissors tool in Paintbrush. This tool is found
   in the upper right corner of Paintbrush's Toolbox. Move the mouse
   pointer to the upper left corner of the picture. Press and hold down the
   left mouse button as you drag the mouse across the picture. You are
   creating a rectangular frame that surrounds the picture. Release the
   mouse button. To copy the picture to the Clipboard, choose the Copy
   option from the Edit menu in Paintbrush. A copy of the picture appears
   in the Clipboard Viewer window.

16. Click the View Picture in Clipboard command button in the ClipDemo
   application.

   A copy of the picture appears in the picture box (see Figure 29.6).

17. Click the Copy Text to Clipboard command button.

   The Clipboard Viewer now shows the text string.

18. Click the Copy Picture to Text command button.

   The Clipboard Viewer shows the graphics picture once again.

The preceding steps demonstrate ClipDemo. You can experiment further by
opening various applications and transferring data to and from the Clipboard
using ClipDemo and the Edit menu options in the other applications.

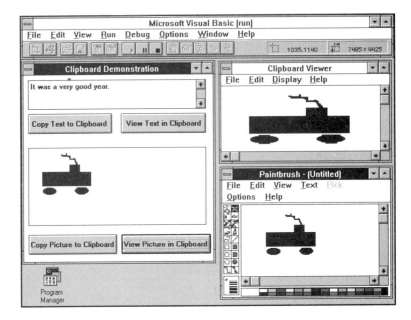

Figure 29.6.

The picture of the truck
is copied from the
Clipboard to the
picture box.

Activating Other Windows Applications

Besides DDE and OLE (which are the subjects of the next two chapters), Visual Basic provides a number of other ways to control Windows applications from your program code. You can activate any application, and send keystrokes that it can process. The following subjects are discussed in the next several sections:

- Using Shell to activate a Windows application

- Changing the focus to any loaded application

- Sending keystrokes to other applications

Using the *Shell* Function

With the Shell function, you can activate any Windows application from your program code.

```
Shell(appname, windowstyle)
```

in which

   appname is a string which specifies the name of the application you want to activate,

and

   windowstyle specifies with a numeric value the appearance of the application's window.

The *windowstyle* parameter is optional.

The *appname* parameter can specify any executable program or batch file. Valid file extensions are .EXE, .COM, and .BAT. If you don't specify a file extension, Visual Basic assumes .EXE.

Be sure that Visual Basic has access to the directory containing the executable program. The DOS PATH command provides the simplest way to ensure that the path is available. In your AUTOEXEC.BAT file, place a PATH command that specifies the subdirectory containing any shelled program.

Table 29.5 shows the valid values of the *windowstyle* parameter. With this parameter, you can specify the size of the window when the application activates. You can also specify whether its window has the focus.

Table 29.5. Values of *windowstyle*.

windowstyle Value	Meaning
1, 5, 9	Normal window size with the focus
2	Minimized window with the focus (default value)
3	Maximized window with the focus
4,8	Normal window size without the focus
6,7	Minimized window without the focus

Shell is a function, not a statement. The Shell function returns an integer value representing the task identification number for the newly-activated application. This ID number uniquely identifies the running program to Windows. Normally, you have no need for this number in your Visual Basic applications. However, as demanded by the syntax of a function, you must use Shell on the right side of an assignment instruction. For example, the following instruction starts the Windows Notepad application.

```
Dummy% = Shell("NOTEPAD.EXE")
```

The following instruction starts Paintbrush, and maximizes the application window.

```
Dummy% = Shell("PBRUSH", 3)
```

Here, the instruction takes advantage of the fact that the .EXE extension for PBRUSH.EXE is the default file extension.

You can use Shell to activate DOS commands. Suppose you want the user to be able to format a floppy disk while your Visual Basic application is running. The following instruction formats the disk in the B drive:

```
Dummy% = Shell("FORMAT.COM B:", 1)
```

Changing the Focus with *AppActivate*

With the AppActivate statement, you can move the focus to any application loaded in the Windows environment.

```
AppActivate titlestring
```

in which

> *titlestring* is a string expression which specifies the name of the application.

Set the value of *titlestring* to the name that appears in the title bar of the target application. For example, the following instruction moves the focus to the Paintbrush application:

```
AppActivate "Paintbrush"
```

Capitalization is not case-sensitive in the *titlestring* parameter. For example, in the previous instruction, "Paintbrush", "paintbrush", and "PaintBrush" all work equivalently.

AppActivate does not launch an application; you must use Shell to do that. AppActivate merely moves the focus to the specified application without affecting whether its window is normal size, minimized, or maximized.

An AppActivate instruction does not transfer program control away from the Visual Basic application. After an AppActivate instruction executes, the directives following AppActivate continue to be carried out.

The most common use of AppActivate is to move the focus to another application in preparation for sending keystrokes to it. Sending keystrokes is the subject of the next section.

Sending Keystrokes with *SendKeys*

In Chapter 23, "Responding to Keyboard Events," you learned how to use the SendKeys statement to send keystrokes to any loaded Windows application. Keystrokes sent to an application produce in it the same effect as would occur if the user typed them at the keyboard.

Recall that the basic syntax for SendKeys includes a text string which describes the keys to press. For alphanumeric keys, the string is simply the characters themselves. For example, the following instruction sends the V and B keys:

```
SendKeys "VB"
```

Keys that cannot be displayed are denoted by special keycodes enclosed in curly braces. Most of these keycodes simply spell out the name of the key. For example, {ESC} represents the Escape key, {F8} the F8 key, and {SCROLLLOCK} the Scroll Lock key.

Preceding a key name with a plus sign (+) indicates that the user must press Shift in conjunction with the key. For example, +{F9} indicates Shift+F9. Similarly, the caret (^) symbol represents the Ctrl key, while the percent sign (#) indicates Alt.

A SendKeys instruction sends the keystrokes to the application that has the focus. With AppActivate, you can give the focus to any application in preparation for sending keystrokes to it.

> SendKeys can be useful within the context of a single Visual Basic application. That is, you can send keystrokes to the same Visual Basic application that contained the SendKeys instruction. This technique is most common in self-running demo programs. To demonstrate various features of the program you can send keystrokes to mimic what a user might do from the keyboard.
>
> **T I P**

Shell, AppActivate, and SendKeys work well together to control Windows applications from your Visual Basic code. As an example of this technique, suppose you add a new command button to the ClipDemo application presented earlier in this chapter.

This command button is named btnNotepad. When the user clicks this command button, ClipDemo launches Notepad, then types text into its window. Next, ClipDemo copies this text to the Clipboard. The following is the Click procedure for this command button:

```
Sub btnNotepad_Click ()
   Dim Dummy As Integer
   Dummy = Shell("Notepad", 4)    'Launch Notepad

   btnNotepad.Enabled = False     'Disables command button
   AppActivate "Notepad - (Untitled)"     'Move focus to Notepad
   SendKeys "This is sample text", True    'Text appears in Notepad
   SendKeys "{HOME} +{END}", True    'Selects the typed text
   SendKeys "%E C", True                  'Opens Edit menu, chooses Copy
                                          'option
   AppActivate "Microsoft Visual Basic"    'Moves focus to ClipDemo
End Sub
```

The three SendKeys instructions manipulate the Notepad application. Notice the True parameter in each of these instructions. That parameter ensures that the keystrokes are processed before Visual Basic executes the following instruction.

The first SendKeys instruction types the text string "This is sample text" into the Notepad window. The next instruction mimics pressing Home, then Shift+End. The effect is to select the text in the Notepad Window.

The third SendKeys instruction mimics pressing Alt+E, then C. This instruction is equivalent to the user opening Notepad's Edit menu, then choosing the Copy option. The effect is to copy the selected text to the Clipboard.

The final instruction returns the focus to ClipDemo. You can now click the View Text in Clipboard command button to copy the Clipboard text to ClipDemo's text box. If you do, the text string This is sample text appears in the text box.

Revisiting the Timer Control

Chapter 8, "Using the Toolbox and the Common Controls," introduced the Timer control. In that chapter, you used a timer to create a digital clock. Timers can also be used to manipulate programs in the Windows environment while you are away from your computer.

For example, suppose you have a Windows program which can receive incoming faxes while your computer is unattended. The program stores received faxes in the C:\NEWFAX directory. Each fax is given a file name with the extension .FAX.

Suppose you are going out of town for several days. You want to leave your computer running so that you can receive your faxes. However, your fax-receiving program cannot manage more than 10 faxes stored at once in the \NEWFAX directory. You are expecting several faxes, so you need a way to periodically move these fax documents to a backup subdirectory.

Using a timer control, you can write a Visual Basic application that backs up your fax program. With each triggering of the timer event, the Visual Basic application renames each fax document in the C:\NEWFAX directory to avoid any duplicate file names. Then, the application moves the file to a backup directory named C:\FAXBAK.

Figure 29.7 shows how the form might appear for such a Visual Basic application. Besides the timer control, the form includes two command buttons and three list boxes: a Drive, Directory, and a File.

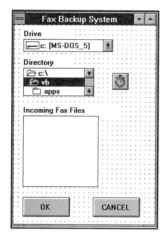

Figure 29.7.

Design-time form for the Fax Backup application.

The maximum value of a timer's Interval property is 65,535 milliseconds. Assume that, at design time, the Timer's Interval property is set to 60000 (one minute), and the Enabled property is set to False. The timer operates only when enabled. If the Enabled property is False, the timer is disabled, regardless of the value of the Interval property.

Writing the *Timer* Event Procedure

You put the code to transfer the fax files in the Timer event procedure. This procedure might resemble the following:

```
Sub Timer1_Timer ()
   Dim FaxFileName As String
   Dim FileNumber As Integer
```

```
Const MAX_INTERVALS = 15      '15 minutes

'Assume that the following two variables are declared
'globally as type Integer, and each variable is assigned a
'default value of 0 before the first Timer event triggers
'
'   FaxNumber -- The running count of the # of faxes transferred
'   NumTimerEvents -- The number of Timer events that triggered
'                     since fax documents were transferred

ChDir Dir1.Path    'Set the default path

NumTimerEvents = NumTimerEvents + 1
If NumTimerEvents >= MAX_INTERVALS Then   'Execute code each 15 minutes
   FileNumber = 0
   Do While File1.ListCount > FileNumber
      FaxFileName = Trim$(Str$(FaxNumber))
      FaxFileName = "C:\FAXBAK\FAX" & FaxFileName & ".BAK"
      FileCopy File1.List(FileNumber), FaxFileName
      FaxNumber = FaxNumber + 1
      Kill File1.List(FileNumber)
      FileNumber = FileNumber + 1
      File1.Refresh
   Loop
   NumTimerEvents = 0    'Get ready to count next 15 timer events
End If
End Sub
```

This procedure uses a trick. The transfer code needs to execute no sooner than every 15 minutes. However, as explained earlier, the maximum value of the Timer's Interval property is just over one minute. So, with Interval set to one minute, this procedure increments the value of NumTimerEvents by 1. The file transfer code doesn't execute until the fifteenth call, after 15 minutes have elapsed.

The Do-While loop does the actual transferring of the fax documents from the \NEWFAX directory to \FAXBAK. Notice that through the global FaxNumber variable, the procedure assigns an individual incrementally-increasing number for each fax document. The saved files use a naming scheme of FAX0.BAK, FAX1.BAK, FAX2.BAK, and so on. As a result, no duplicate file names can occur.

The FileCopy instruction copies the fax document to the C:\FAXBAK directory. The Kill instruction deletes the fax document from the C:\NEWFAX directory. Each time through the loop, the File1.Refresh instruction refreshes the contents of the File list box to prepare for processing the next fax document.

Running the Fax Backup Application

When you first run this application, you set both the drive and directory list boxes to point to the C:\NEWFAX directory. Figure 29.8 shows three fax documents pending in the C:\NEWFAX directory.

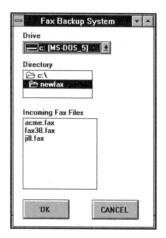

You click OK to enable the Timer. The `Click` event procedure for this command button consists entirely of the following instruction:

```
Timer1.Enabled = True
```

At this point, you can walk away from your computer knowing that all incoming faxes will be backed up to the C:\FAXBAK subdirectory.

Yielding Processor Time with *DoEvents*

Windows must oversee all the loaded applications, and assign processor time to each one in turn. This situation can be compared to a nest full of hungry baby birds. Each bird (a loaded Windows application) cries for food (CPU time). The mother bird (Windows) moves from baby to baby, feeding each one in turn.

As long as each bird in the nest cries for food, the mother feeds all the babies, no matter how much one individual bird tries to monopolize her time. Windows, however, does not work in the same manner. Once Windows yields the processor to an application, it can monopolize the CPU time.

For example, an application can contain a time-intensive mathematical calculation which proceeds unabated. This continues until the application takes specific action to temporarily yield control back to Windows. Releasing control is necessary so that Windows can process pending requests from other applications.

Most commercial Windows applications are programmed to periodically yield temporary control back to Windows when a time-intensive calculation is in progress. In fact, Windows *depends* on applications yielding such control. Otherwise, Windows can become overburdened, and fail to respond to the environment.

In general, Visual Basic applications work well within the Windows environment. Program code executes in response to system events. Between events, Windows usually has plenty of time to respond to requests from other applications. It can also usually respond to different events in the Visual Basic application.

However, if the Visual Basic code executes a lengthy CPU-intensive calculation, problems can arise. This situation occurs most often in a loop doing a time-intensive mathematical calculation. The CPU becomes exclusively devoted to finishing the calculation, and the Visual Basic application does not yield time back to Windows. As a result, Windows seems to "hang up." The system doesn't respond to mouse clicks—not only in other applications, but also to events, such as pressing a command button in the Visual Basic application.

Using *DoEvents* Instructions

Your Visual Basic applications need a way to temporarily yield control to Windows when a time-intensive calculation is in progress. Visual Basic provides DoEvents for just this purpose. DoEvents has both a statement and function syntax.

The statement syntax is simply the instruction DoEvents:

```
DoEvents
```

The function syntax returns the number of form windows opened in the Windows environment:

```
NumForms% = DoEvents()
```

If you write any time-intensive programming loops, it's good practice to intermittently use DoEvents in them. That way, Visual Basic can temporarily release control to Windows, and maintain responsiveness to its environment in general.

When Visual Basic executes a `DoEvents` instruction, program control is passed to Windows. As such, Windows can process all the pending events. These include keystrokes, mouse clicks, and processor requests generated by program code. When Windows processes every pending event, program control returns to the instruction after `DoEvents` in the Visual Basic procedure.

Be careful that you don't reinvoke a procedure containing a `DoEvents` instruction while Windows is processing `DoEvents` from the same procedure.

For example, assume your application has a command button labeled Calculate. Clicking this button invokes a procedure which executes a lengthy mathematical loop. It repeatedly uses `DoEvents` to temporarily yield control to Windows.

Suppose that you have clicked the Calculate button to execute the procedure. Then, while the procedure has temporarily yielded control, you click the button again. Windows reinvokes the procedure before the first call finishes. The results are unpredictable.

One way to avoid this problem is to have the procedure disable the Calculate button before the first `DoEvents` instruction executes. The procedure can later reactivate the command button just before terminating.

A DoEvents Example

As an example of `DoEvents`, suppose you have a `For-Next` loop that performs a tedious math calculation for values of `J%` which run from `1` to `20,000`. The loop might take more than half of a minute to complete. This is a long time by Windows standards. You should use `DoEvents` to periodically release control to Windows. For example:

```
For J% = 1 To 20000
    Rem  Math instructions go here
    If J% Mod 500 = 0 Then DoEvents
Next J%
```

This loop uses the `Mod` operator to trigger `DoEvents`. It is triggered once every 500 times through the loop. The periodic `DoEvents` calls give Windows a chance to process any pending events while the loop executes.

Programming an *Idle Loop*

For a Visual Basic application, the time between events is known as *idle time*. During idle time, Visual Basic automatically releases control to Windows. Visual Basic again requests that Windows give processor time to an application when an event occurs in it.

Occasionally, you might want to write a loop that executes only during what would otherwise be idle time. That is, the loop executes only while no other event is pending. The loop should temporarily relinquish control when any other event occurs. Such a loop is known as an *idle loop*.

Visual Basic permits you to write an idle loop only in the special Sub Main procedure. Recall from Chapter 9, "Managing Projects," that you can use Sub Main in a code module to have an application immediately start executing program instructions (so that it doesn't have to wait for events to occur on a form).

To write an idle loop, create a Sub Main procedure in any code module. Open the Project Options dialog box by choosing **P**roject from the **O**ptions menu. In the dialog box, specify Sub Main (rather than Form1) as the Start Up Form. In the Sub Main procedure, write a Do-While loop that uses DoEvents. The following is the skeletal form of the Sub Main procedure:

```
Sub Main ()
    'Use the Show method to display any form that you want visible
    Do While DoEvents()    'Always executes
        'Program instructions that should execute during idle time
    Loop
End Sub
```

Creating the Cycler Application

As an example of an application using an idle loop, consider the simple form that Figure 29.9 shows. This form contains a label and a text box. The application, named Cycler, uses an idle loop to count idle computing cycles.

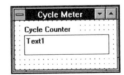

Figure 29.9.

Design-time form for the Cycler application.

To create Cycler, start a new project. Make `Cycle Meter` the caption for the form. Add a text box and a label control to the form. Make `Cycle Counter` the caption for the label. Resize the form and the controls to create a relatively small form which resembles that in Figure 29.9.

Add a code module to the project. Place the following instruction in the Declarations section of this module.

```
Global NumCycles
```

This instruction creates a global variable named `NumCycles` of data type Variant.

Create the following `Sub Main` as a General procedure in the code module.

```
Sub Main ()
    Form1.Show
    Do While DoEvents()
        NumCycles = NumCycles + 1
        Form1!Text1.Text = NumCycles
    Loop
End Sub
```

Choose **P**roject from the **O**ptions menu to open the Project Options dialog box. Change the Start Up Form option to `Sub Main`.

When you run the application, Visual Basic displays a rapidly increasing number in the text box. This number is updated each time the idle loop in `Sub Main` executes.

Look at the `Sub Main` procedure to see how it works. The procedure begins by using the `Show` method to display the form. Remember that with `Sub Main` as the start-up module, you must explicitly show any form that you want visible.

Next, the idle loop executes. Each time through the loop, the procedure increases the value of the global variable `NumCycles` by 1. The new value of `NumCycles` is then displayed in the text box.

By watching how fast the number in the text box updates, you get a good idea of Windows activity in general. When Windows does not need to process other events, the numbers increase rapidly. However, if you load other applications into Windows, and begin additional processing, updates to the text box number slow down considerably. When the other applications become idle once again, the rapid updates resume also.

You can pause Cycler to temporarily stop the numeric counter. See Figure 29.10 which shows the counter arbitrarily stopped at the value 2445.

Then, you can resume execution to again continue the idle loop. Notice that the DoEvents function used in Sub Main returns the number of form windows loaded in the Windows environment. The idle loop terminates when all form windows are unloaded, or when you end the application.

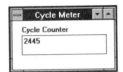

Cycler has a practical use. The application can help with capacity planning in offices which run Windows. For organizations with a large number of computers, it's expensive to purchase and maintain additional machines. By running Cycler on each of the Windows-based computers, you get a simple count that approximates the activity on each one. Office managers can use this "idle time" information to determine which computer(s) should be assigned processing responsibilities when user(s) must run new applications.

Using Dynamic Link Libraries

For most applications, Visual Basic supplies sufficient program support with its functions, statements, and other language features. Windows, however, offers more than 500 specialized procedures that are available to any application running in this environment.

These Windows procedures are called *Application Programming Interface* (API) functions. (Although the term "API functions" appears in common use, the API includes both Sub and Function procedures.) The API procedures are stored in files known as a *Dynamic Link Library* (DLL). The most important DLL files supplied with Windows are USER.EXE, KERNEL.EXE, and GDI.EXE. Third-party vendors also produce DLL files which contain customized Windows procedures.

If necessary, your Visual Basic applications can directly call the external procedures stored in dynamic link libraries. To do so, your Visual Basic application uses Declare statements to specify in which place the external procedures are stored, and define the calling syntax for them.

Benefits of a DLL

Besides providing functionality not available within Visual Basic, two significant benefits exist for using DLL files. First, Dynamic Link Libraries are available to *all* applications running under Windows. As a result, only one copy of a

DLL procedure is needed by Windows, even though many applications might use it. Individual applications do not have to store the DLL procedures. Therefore, each application's size can be smaller.

Second, modifications or performance enhancements to DLL procedures are at times supplied by Microsoft in Windows upgrades. These modifications sometimes come with DLL upgrades from other vendors, also. Windows applications that use DLLs automatically have the revised procedures available immediately after the upgrades take place in the host computer. As a result, applications benefit from changes made in the DLL. The applications themselves don't need any modifications.

Understanding Dynamic Link Libraries

Explaining the terms in Dynamic Link Library might help you better understand how these libraries work.

- *Dynamic*

  The DLL (which is an executable program) is not loaded into Windows memory until at least one application needs a procedure contained in the library. Windows knows when a particular DLL is needed by an application: The system examines its references to DLL procedures. Loading a DLL does not happen until run time, which is the reason these libraries are referred to as "dynamic."

- *Link*

  Once Windows loads the application program and the DLL, a special process known as "linking" occurs. This process connects the application program to the DLL. As a result, the application runs as though the DLL procedure was actually part of it.

- *Library*

  Libraries are similar to code modules in that both entities can contain functions and Sub procedures. Library procedures declared in code modules are globally available.

Declaring a Dynamic Link Library in a Visual Basic Application

Declare statements can appear only in the Declarations section of a form or a code module. Only the form can access the DLL procedure if it is declared in the Declaration section. If declared in a code module, the DLL procedure is available throughout the application's program code.

Once a Declare instruction associates with an application a DLL procedure, it can be invoked continually in the program code. No further reference to the Dynamic Link Library is necessary.

Using *Declare* Instructions

A Declare instruction can define a procedure as a Sub or Function. As usual, Sub procedures do not return any values. Function procedures return values of a specified data type.

The following is the basic syntax for Declare instructions. The syntax presented here does not include all possible optional arguments.

```
Declare Sub name Lib "libname" (ByVal var1 As type, ByVal var2 As type,...)
```

or

```
Declare Function name Lib "libname" (ByVal var1 As type,
➥type,...) As type ByVal var2 As
```

in which

    name specifies the name of the DLL procedure. For Function procedures, this name can optionally include a type-declaration suffix,

    libname specifies with a string literal the name of the DLL containing the declared procedure,

    ByVal specifies that the argument is passed by value.

    var1, *var2*,... specify Visual Basic variable names used as arguments to the DLL procedure,

and

    type specifies the data type of the argument variable. The final As *type* clause specifies the data type of the DLL function.

ByVal clauses are optional. For variables and function names without type-declaration suffixes, an As *type* clause specifies a data type. As *type* clauses are also optional.

For example, consider the following declaration:

```
Declare Function FlashWindow Lib "User" (ByVal hWnd As Integer,
➥bInvert as Integer)
```

This declaration indicates that a function named FlashWindow is obtained from the DLL referred to as USER.EXE (the .EXE extension is assumed by default).

This function uses two integer parameters: `hWnd` and `bInvert`. The `FlashWindow` function causes the window of a loaded Windows application to flash.

Once a declaration appears, you can use the declared procedure much as you would an ordinary Visual Basic one. For example, `FlashWindow` can be invoked in this way:

```
rVal = FlashWindow(hWnd, 1)
```

Here, the `hWnd` variable contains the handle of the application window that should be flashed. The value `1` specifies that flashing should begin. The `rVal` variable is set to indicate the prior state (flashing or not flashing) of the `hWnd` window.

Windows API Reference Sources

The Professional Edition of Visual Basic includes a file containing the `Declare` statements for most API procedures. Consult your Windows documentation for references to the API.

> Be careful whenever you use an API procedure from a DLL. Your `Declare` instruction must conform exactly to the expected syntax. Otherwise, you are quite likely to experience program hang-ups and other error conditions.

Using the Common Dialog Control

Experienced Windows users are accustomed to seeing a standard set of dialog boxes that several applications use. In particular, Save As and Open dialog boxes have a standardized appearance. Figure 29.11 shows a typical Save As dialog box.

Windows provides a set of procedures to create commonly used dialog boxes. These procedures are located in a DLL named COMMDLG.DLL. Many commercial Windows applications call this DLL to utilize the standard dialogs.

Through the Common Dialog control, Visual Basic provides an easy way to access the routines in COMMDLG.DLL. With little effort, your applications can display standardized dialog boxes for such tasks as opening and saving files, printing them, and choosing colors and fonts. As such, the Common Dialog control is a convenient feature offered by Visual Basic.

```
┌─────────────────────────────────────────────────────────────┐
│ ⊟                           Save As                           │
├─────────────────────────────────────────────────────────────┤
│ File Name:                  Directories:        ┌──────────┐  │
│ ┌──────────────┐            c:\vb\samples        │    OK    │  │
│ │ *.txt        │                                 └──────────┘  │
│ └──────────────┘            ┌─────────────┐▲    ┌──────────┐  │
│ ┌──────────────┐▲           │ 📂 vb       │█    │  Cancel  │  │
│ │              │            │ 📁 samples  │█    └──────────┘  │
│ │              │            │ 📁 calc     │█                  │
│ │              │            │ 📁 calldlls │█    ☐ Read Only   │
│ │              │            │ 📁 controls │█                  │
│ │              │            │ 📁 datactrl │                   │
│ │              │▼           │ 📁 dde      │▼                  │
│ └──────────────┘            └─────────────┘                   │
│ Save File as Type:          Drives:                           │
│ ┌──────────────┐▼           ┌─────────────┐▼                  │
│ │ Text files [*.txt] │      │ 💾 c: ms-dos_5 │                │
│ └──────────────┘            └─────────────┘                   │
└─────────────────────────────────────────────────────────────┘
```

Figure 29.11.

A typical Save As
dialog box.

Common Dialog is a custom control supplied in the Visual Basic file named
CMDIALOG.VBX. The normal installation of Visual Basic places this control in
the Toolbox. If you do not have the Common Dialog control in your Toolbox,
use the **Ad**d File option from the **F**ile menu to load the custom control into
your Visual Basic environment.

Before the release of Visual Basic 3.0, the Common Dialog control was available only with the Professional Edition. However, the Standard Edition now
includes the Common Dialog control as well.

A common dialog control appears as an icon when placed on a form at design-
time. Similar to a timer, a common dialog control cannot be sized. The control
becomes invisible when the Visual Basic application is run.

A single common dialog control can display various standard dialog boxes. At
run time, you modify certain property values to display the dialog box of your
choice.

The user can manipulate the resulting dialog box to select available options.
Your application can determine the selections by reading the appropriate
property values once the user closes the dialog box.

The default name for the first common dialog you place on a form is `CMDialog1`.
Generally, you don't need more than one common dialog control because
you can use the same one continually to display various dialog boxes as the
application demands. However, you can place more than one common dialog
on any form. Additional common dialog controls have the default names
`CMDialog2`, `CMDialog3`, and so on.

Using the *Action* Property

At run time, you display a dialog box by executing an instruction which sets
the value of the `Action` property for a common dialog control. As Table 29.6
shows, the value you specify for the `Action` property determines the type of
dialog box that displays.

Table 29.6. Values of the Action property.	
Value of Action	**Type of Dialog Box Displayed**
0	None
1	Open (File Open)
2	Save As
3	Color
4	Font
5	Print
6	Invokes Windows Help file

For example, the following instruction displays a Save As dialog box:

```
CMDialog1.Action = 2
```

When Action is 6, Visual Basic does not display a dialog box. Instead the system invokes the Windows Help utility WINHELP.EXE. For more information on WINHELP.EXE, and creating Help systems, see Chapter 33, "Adding a Help System to an Application."

You cannot specify the screen position in which Visual Basic displays the resulting dialog box. These dialog boxes are modal. The user cannot resize the boxes, but is able to move them around the screen.

Using the *Flags* Property

Dialog boxes appear in a standardized format. By modifying the value of the Flags property at run time, you can specify various customized features for the dialog boxes. Every type of dialog box defines particular numeric values of the Flags property that correspond with special features of each box. You specify a value for Flags before displaying the dialog box with the Action property.

Valid values for Flags consist of long integer numbers. The CONSTANT.TXT file defines a symbolic constant for each permissible value of Flags. You can also combine effects by adding together the appropriate Flags values.

For example, the File Open dialog box normally permits the user to select only a single file from the dialog box. However, when Flags is set to &H200&, the dialog box lets the user select multiple names from the File Name list box. As such, you allow multiple file selection by executing the following instruction:

```
CMDialog1.Flags = &H200&
```

The CONSTANT.TXT file defines the constant OFN_ALLOWMULTISELECT, which is set to the numeric value that the previous instruction shows. With CONSTANT.TXT loaded in the Visual Basic application, the following instruction also permits multiple file selection:

```
CMDialog1.Flags = OFN_ALLOWMULTISELECT
```

Visual Basic permits many values of Flags for each type of dialog box. For further information on Flags and its various values, see Chapter 32, "Using Custom Controls." Also, you can get an explanation of all the available options through the Visual Basic Help system.

Using the Open Dialog Box

The Open dialog box permits selection of a drive, directory, and name for a file that the user wants to open. Figure 29.12 shows a standard Open dialog box.

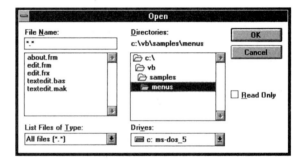

Figure 29.12.

An Open dialog box.

The default caption for the title bar is Open. You can modify this caption by specifying a value for the DialogTitle property before displaying the dialog box. For example, the following instruction displays the caption File Specification:

```
CMDialog1.DialogTitle = "File Specification"
```

Before displaying the dialog box, you can set the Filter property to specify what types of files are specified in the File list box. The syntax for the Filter property separates each description and filter with the pipe symbol (¦).

```
description1¦filter1¦description2¦filter2
```

For example, the following instruction specifies the filters *.txt and *.doc along with appropriate descriptions:

```
CMDialog1.Filter = "Text files (*.txt)¦*.txt¦Documents (*.doc)¦*.doc"
```

By default, no filter is set. If you don't specify the Filter property, the user must explicitly type a file name in the File Name edit box. The user cannot click a name from a list of files filtered to the File list box.

To display the File Open dialog box, set the `Action` property value to `1`.

After the user selects a file, and closes the dialog box, you can retrieve the selected file with the `FileName` property of the common dialog control. For example:

```
ChosenFile$ = CMDialog1.FileName
```

Using the Save As Dialog Box

The Save As dialog box works and appears very similar to the Open dialog box. The main exception is the caption in the dialog's title bar. As Figure 29.11 shows, the caption for the Save As dialog box is, naturally enough, `Save As`.

To display the Save As dialog box, set the `Action` property value to `2`. As with the Open dialog, you can retrieve the user's selected file with the `FileName` property of the common dialog control.

Using the Color Dialog Box

The Color dialog box displays a color palette. The user can select one of the predefined colors directly from this palette, or create a customized color by opening a color selection window.

To open the Color dialog box, set the value of `Action` to `3` in your program code. Figure 29.13 shows the resulting dialog box.

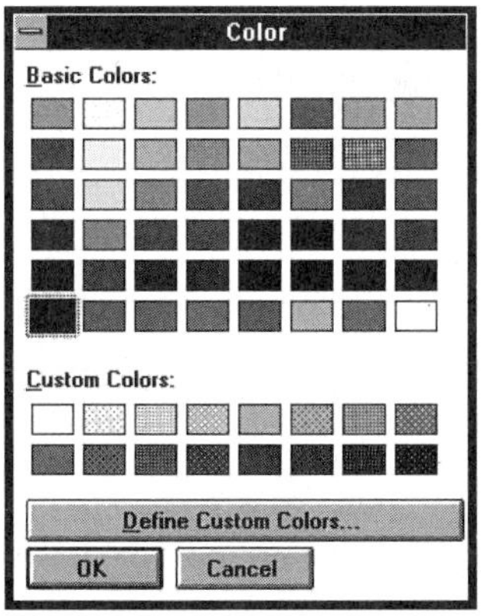

Figure 29.13.

A Color dialog box.

The user can select one of the colors presented in this palette. Alternatively, the user can click the Define Custom Colors command button to expand the dialog box to include a region which enables the selection of a customized color (see Figure 29.14).

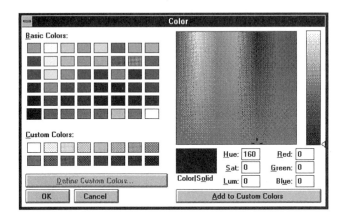

After the user chooses a color, and closes the dialog box, the Color property of the Common Dialog control indicates the selection. Suppose your application invokes the Color dialog box so that the user can choose a background color for a picture box. The following instruction assigns the selected color appropriately:

```
Picture1.BackColor = CMDialog1.Color
```

Using the Font Dialog Box

Windows supplies several fonts for use throughout the Windows environment. You can also purchase custom fonts to complement those provided by the software. With the Font dialog box, the user can choose an available font typeface and specify its various characteristics.

Before opening the Font dialog box, you must specify whether the selection consists of screen or printer fonts, or both. Use the Flags property to specify this value as &H1&, &H2&, or &H3&, respectively. The CONSTANT.TXT file defines a constant for each of these values. For example, the following instruction uses a constant from CONSTANT.TXT to specify printer fonts:

```
CMDialog1.Flags = CF_PRINTERFONTS
```

To display the Font dialog, set the value of Action to 4. Figure 29.15 shows a typical Font dialog box in use.

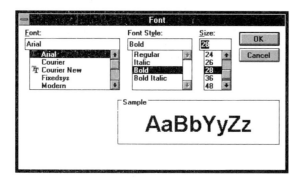

Figure 29.15.

The Font dialog box.

When the user makes the selection, and closes the dialog box, the `FontName` property of the common dialog control specifies the name of the chosen font. The `FontSize` property specifies the size of the chosen font. The `FontBold`, `FontItalic`, `FontStrikethru`, and `FontUnderline` properties indicate respectively whether the user has selected bold, italics, strikethrough, or underline attributes.

Using the Print Dialog Box

With the Print dialog box, the user can specify various options for printing output. These options include the number of pages and the quality of the print. Furthermore, the dialog box contains a Setup button which the user can click to reconfigure the default printer, or install a new one.

To display the Print dialog box, set the value of the `Action` property to 5 (see Figure 29.16).

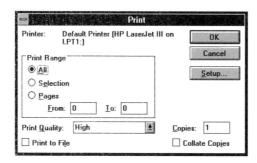

Figure 29.16.

The Print dialog box.

When the user closes the dialog box, the selected printing options are stored in property values of the common dialog control. Values of the `Copies`,

FromPage, and ToPage properties indicate how many copies to print, and the starting and the final page numbers, respectively.

However, the Print dialog box does not actually initiate printing. Your program code must do that, based on the selections that the user made. However, if the user clicks the Setup command button to reconfigure the Windows printer environment, those reconfiguration changes are implemented.

Detecting the Cancel Button

Each type of dialog box includes a Cancel button. By default, when the user clicks the Cancel button, Visual Basic aborts the selection of dialog options, and the dialog box immediately closes. Property values of the common dialog control are not updated.

You can force Visual Basic to treat the clicking of the Cancel button as an error. In your program code, you can trap the error, and execute an error handler. In this manner, you can require users to specify dialog box options by not allowing them to cancel the dialog box.

To implement this error handling, set the CancelError property of the common dialog control to True. (The default value is False.) For example, execute this instruction before invoking Action to display a dialog.

CMDialog1.CancelError = True

When CancelError is True, Visual Basic treats clicking the Cancel button as an error. You can now utilize On Error GoTo and a handler to trap this error. For example, here is the skeletal outline of a Click procedure that traps clicking the Cancel button for a Font dialog:

```
Sub Command1_Click()
    CMDialog1.CancelError = True    'Treat clicking Cancel as an error
    On Error GoTo MyErrorHandler    'Enable the error handler

    'Set Flags and other properties

    CMDialog1.Action = 4            'Activate the Font dialog

    'Treat normal return from the dialog box here
    Exit Sub

MyErrorHandler:      'Beginning of error-handler routine
    If Err = 32755 Then
        MsgBox "You must specify Font options"
```

```
      Resume
    End If
End Sub
```

Notice that 32755 is the error number Visual Basic assigns to clicking the Cancel button. In the error handler, the Err function tests for this value.

A Sample Application Using Common Dialogs

Chapter 32, "Using Custom Controls," contains a sample application which uses the Common Dialog control to display several dialogs. That chapter also contains additional information about options available with the Flags property.

Summary

In this chapter, you learned about various ways that your applications can manipulate the Windows environment. Windows provides many resources, and Visual Basic contains several tools so that your applications can tap those resources.

With the Clipboard, you can cut and paste data between your Visual Basic program and other loaded applications. Shell, AppActivate, and SendKeys let you manipulate other applications directly from program code.

Timers provide access to the system clock to initiate periodic events. With DoEvents, you can write idle loops, and also temporarily release control to Windows in the middle of CPU-intensive calculations.

With Declare statements, your applications can access Windows procedures contained in Dynamic Link Libraries. One such library contains routines that display and implement standard dialog boxes. However, Visual Basic provides the Common Dialog control as an easy way to implement those standard dialog boxes.

This chapter only begins discussing ways that Visual Basic programs can communicate with Windows and other running applications. The next two chapters explain Dynamic Data Exchange (DDE) and Object Linking and Embedding (OLE)—the most flexible and modern ways for Windows applications to share information.

Using Dynamic Data Exchange (DDE)

Before Windows, applications running under DOS were self-contained by necessity. The software developer included in the application any features that were needed. For example, if a spreadsheet required charting, the developer had to program this capability into the software.

With the introduction of Windows, the situation has changed. Windows acts as a platform for simultaneously running multiple programs on a single PC. The programs can even pass data back and forth. A spreadsheet program can pass data to a charting application which processes it, and returns a completed chart. Dynamic Data Exchange (DDE) is a process through which two or more Windows programs pass data to each other. With Visual Basic, you can now create applications that take advantage of DDE.

The main topics of this chapter include:

- Learning the Visual Basic DDE methods, events, and properties
- Developing client and server applications
- Designing DDE conversations
- Establishing automatic and manual links
- Using Paste Link to establish a DDE link at design time

Understanding DDE

The process of DDE can be compared to a conversation between two people. The exchange starts when one person asks a question of the other. The questioner stops talking, and waits for an answer.

The other person answers the question, and might wait for further queries. This back and forth exchange is *dynamic* because the conversation occurs while the two people are actively meeting face to face. (If the two people were writing letters back and forth, that "conversation" wouldn't be dynamic.) The conversation provides an exchange of data from the second person back to the first. In short, it becomes something of a dynamic data exchange.

Laying the Ground Rules

For most conversations, whether between two friends or Windows programs, there is a protocol of rules that govern just how the interchange is carried out. When two friends get together, the conversations are relaxed and informal. A conversation of this type follows few formal rules.

Establishing Protocols

However, consider a conversation between the ambassadors of two countries. Language and culture barriers between two countries can cause communication difficulties between their ambassadors. To discuss relations between the two countries, their aides must meet, and agree on how the ambassadors are to communicate. The aides must decide how to present documents, and the number of people that are to be present during the meeting. A few issues that must be decided include who sits in what place, and other similar rules.

Whether a meeting between friends, or a summit involving heads of state, conversations follow specific rules, or *protocols*. These protocols dictate how, and what, takes place from the start of the discussion to the end.

For friends, an informal and friendly protocol is appropriate. However, in the case of the two diplomats, the conversation is formal, and must rigidly follow specific rules.

Under Windows, applications running simultaneously can converse with each other. DDE establishes a formal protocol which governs just how such Windows conversations take place.

Conversation Between Applications

Consider two applications that need to exchange data. In order for the exchange to occur, both applications need to be simultaneously running in Windows. One of them must take the initiative, and begin the process of exchanging data. This application is called the *client* because it is requesting the services of the other.

The other application in this conversation is called the *server*. Its duty is to provide some kind of service to the client.

 In other literature about DDE, you might notice that the client and server are referred to as the *destination* and *source*, respectively.

Once the client (or destination) initiates the conversation with the server (or source), many types of exchange are possible. For example, the client can request data from or send it to the server, or both.

During this data exchange, once the client satisfies its needs, it tells the server that the conversation is complete. The communication link between the two applications terminates. Then, each application can resume independent work.

When two applications converse under DDE, their "conversations" follow this client/server etiquette. As such, DDE establishes a formal protocol.

A First Look at a DDE Conversation

To begin understanding DDE, notice the order in which transactions occur, and the direction the data is sent. Figure 30.1 shows how two applications might carry out a typical conversation.

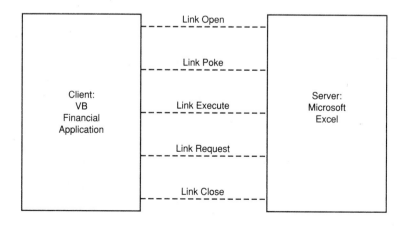

Figure 30.1.

Client/Server DDE conversation.

The figure depicts a conversation between a client and a server. The client, depicted on the left, is a financial application written using Visual Basic. The server, depicted on the right, is Excel (a commercial Windows spreadsheet program from Microsoft).

The two programs communicate using DDE commands. Windows acts as the conduit for the conversation. When the client issues a DDE command, it is passed to Windows. Then, Windows, in turn, passes the command to the server.

The conversation that Figure 30.1 depicts consists of a series of five DDE commands. These represent a few of the commands available in Visual Basic's DDE command set.

The following sections briefly describe the five commands to give you the flavor of a DDE conversation. In fact, the "command" names in the figure are actually titles of various DDE events and methods. Another section, later in the chapter, explains all DDE events, methods, and properties.

Introducing *LinkOpen*

The conversation starts when the client sends a `LinkOpen` command to the server. The server recognizes this command, and keeps track of the fact that this client wants to carry on a conversation. Once this command completes, the client is assured that the link is open, and the server is ready to provide requested services.

Introducing *LinkPoke*

The client can continue the conversation by issuing a `LinkPoke` command. `LinkPoke` sends data from the client to the server. That is, the command "pokes" data over to the server. The server accepts the data, and waits for further instructions.

Suppose, in this example, that the client application manages a portfolio of rental real estate properties. Excel contains a complex macro designed to calculate a property value based on the gross rent. With this in mind, the client sends a gross rent dollar amount to Excel using `LinkPoke`.

Introducing *LinkExecute*

The client then issues a `LinkExecute` command. This command instructs Excel to run the macro. By so doing, Excel calculates the property value based on the gross rent. After receiving this command, Excel executes the macro, and produces the present value dollar figure.

Introducing *LinkRequest*

Next, the client sends a `LinkRequest` command to Excel. This command requests that the server send data to the client. In this example, the server has just been instructed to compute a property value. Excel determines that this property value is requested, and sends a newly computed one to the client.

Introducing *LinkClose*

After sending the requested property value to the client, the server waits for further instructions. The client, however, no longer needs anything from the server, and wants to end the conversation.

By sending a `LinkClose` command to the server, the client terminates the link. The server now knows that no further DDE conversations will occur (with this client at this time).

Understanding the Visual Basic DDE Model

A Visual Basic application can act as either a server or a client in a DDE conversation. Under Windows, a single application can conduct multiple DDE conversations simultaneously. In fact, a Visual Basic application can act as a server in one conversation while performing as a client in another at the same time.

In a Visual Basic application, data links are established through forms, text boxes, labels, and picture boxes. You carry out a DDE conversation by manipulating the events, properties, and methods associated with these objects.

From the point of view of the client, the following three terms characterize a particular conversation:

Application   The conversation partner. To engage the server, the client must know the server's name. Windows maintains a name for each application. For commercial applications, consult the product's documentation to find the proper name. Microsoft Excel, for example, is simply named "Excel." Visual Basic applications use the project name (at design time), or the executable file name (at run time).

Topic   The data domain under discussion. The topic is most often a document specified as a file name. For Excel, the topic is a spreadsheet file. For a word processor, the topic is a document file. For a Visual Basic application acting as a server, the topic is specified by the value of the form's `LinkTopic` property. (The `LinkTopic` property is explained shortly.)

Item   The specific object under discussion. For Excel, the item is a range of cells. For a word processor, the item is a block of text. For a Visual Basic application, the item is the name of a specific text box, label, or picture box.

DDE Events, Methods, and Properties

As mentioned, Visual Basic establishes and carries out a DDE conversation through events, methods, and properties. The following tables introduce the DDE terms. Notice that the name of each term is prefaced with the word `Link`.

DDE Events

The following events can occur during a DDE conversation:

`LinkOpen`   Occurs on a label, text box, or picture box which acts as a client initiating a DDE conversation. The event occurs on a server's form when a client initiates the DDE conversation with it.

`LinkExecute`   Occurs on the server's form when the client sends a DDE command to the server. The client wants the server to execute the command.

`LinkNotify`   Occurs when the server changes the value of a linked data item. The server notifies the client that a new value is available. This event occurs on the client's labels, picture boxes and text boxes.

`LinkError`   Occurs on the server and the client when something fails during a DDE conversation. The event applies to forms, labels, picture boxes, and text boxes.

`LinkClose`   Occurs when either the client or the server terminates a DDE conversation. The event applies to forms, labels, picture boxes, and text boxes.

DDE Methods

The following methods act as DDE commands:

`LinkExecute`   Sends a command string to the conversation partner. The method applies to labels, picture boxes, and text boxes. It is pertinent to both servers and clients.

`LinkSend`   Sends a picture from the server to the client. This method is defined only for picture box controls.

LinkPoke   Transfers data from a client to the server. This method is defined for the client's labels, text boxes, and picture boxes.

LinkRequest   Asks the server to update the property values of a client's DDE control. This method is defined for labels, picture boxes, and text boxes.

DDE Properties

The following properties specify items important in DDE conversations:

LinkItem   Identifies the particular data (the *item*) that the server sends to the client. This property applies to labels, picture boxes, and text boxes.

LinkTopic   Used by a client's label, picture box, or text box to identify the source *application* and *topic*. When used in conjunction with LinkItem, the complete conversation is defined. This property is also used by a source's form to identify the *topic* to which it responds.

LinkMode   Identifies the type of link that is used during a DDE conversation. It lets the application determine whether the client control receives new values anytime the data changes in the source ("automatic" or "hot" link). Alternatively, LinkMode lets the application decide whether the client must explicitly request the updated values ("manual" or "cold" link). This property applies to forms, labels, picture boxes, and text boxes.

LinkTimeout   Determines how long a control waits before assuming that there is a problem with the DDE conversation. The default value is five seconds. This property applies to labels, picture boxes, and text boxes.

A Sample DDE Application— Log Calculator

Log Calculator is a simple Visual Basic application that demonstrates DDE. The application acts as a client which requests data from the server, Microsoft Excel.

You need Excel to try this application. If you don't have Excel, you can follow the general techniques without actually building the application.

Be sure that Excel is set to reference cells with the letter and number notation: for example, A1. To make sure, start Excel. Choose the **W**orkspace item from the **O**ptions menu. Find the check box labeled R1C1. You want this box to be unchecked so, if the box is checked, click the box to make it unchecked. Then exit from Excel.

The Log Calculator contains two text boxes. The user types a number into the text box labeled "Input Number." When the Calculate button is clicked, Excel computes the log of the number. The Log Calculator obtains the result from Excel and displays the value in the text box labeled "Log Value from Excel." For more information about logarithms ("logs"), see Chapter 16, "Working With Numbers."

Constructing the Form

Figure 30.2 shows how the application appears at run time.

To create the Log Calculator, start a new project. Place two of each of the following on the form: labels, text boxes, and command buttons. Using the Properties window, set the property values as Table 30.1 shows.

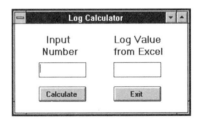

Figure 30.2.

Running the Log Calculator.

Table 30.1. Design-time property values for the Log Calculator application.

Object	Property	Value
Form1	Name	frmCalculator
	Caption	"Log Calculator"
	Height	2610
	Left	2160
	Top	2595
	Width	4530

Object	Property	Value
Label1	Alignment	2 'Center
	Caption	"Input Number"
	FontSize	12
	Height	615
	Left	480
	Top	240
	Width	1335
Label2	Caption	"Log Value from Excel"
	FontSize	12
	Height	615
	Left	2520
	Top	240
	Width	1455
Text1	Name	txtNumber
	Height	372
	Left	600
	Text	(blank) 'empty string
	Top	960
	Width	1212
Text2	Name	txtLogValue
	Height	372
	Left	2520
	MaxLength	8
	Text	(blank) 'empty string
	Top	960
	Width	1212

continues

Table 30.1. Continued

Object	Property	Value
Command1	Name	cmdCalculate
	Caption	"Calculate"
	Height	372
	Left	600
	Top	1560
	Width	1212
Command2	Name	txtLogValue
	Caption	"Exit"
	Height	372
	Left	600
	Top	1560
	Width	1212

This calculator computes the natural logarithm of a decimal number. You type a number into the Input Number text box. In code, this text box is named txtNumber.

Next, you click the Calculate command button (or, alternatively, press Tab to move the focus to it, then press Enter).

A value appears immediately in the Log Value from Excel text box. In code, this text box is named txtLogValue. Behind the scenes, a DDE conversation has taken place. The number you typed was sent to Excel, and loaded into cell A1 of the spreadsheet. (A1 is the cell in the upper left corner of the spreadsheet.) Then, Excel was requested to calculate the log of the number, and place the result in cell A2. (A2 is the cell just below A1.) Finally, the Text property of the second text box is assigned the value in cell A2.

For example, suppose you type **26** into the text box to the far left. When you click the Calculate button, the number 3.258097 (the log of 26) appears in the other text box (see Figure 30.3).

Figure 30.4 shows how the Excel application appears after this DDE conversation takes place.

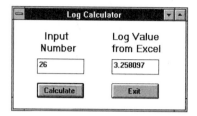

Figure 30.3.

The Log Calculator in action.

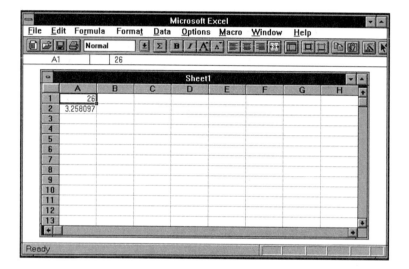

Figure 30.4.

Excel has processed the DDE conversation.

Writing the *Form_Load* Procedure

The following is the Form_Load event procedure. This procedure executes when you start the Log Calculator application.

```
Sub Form_Load ()
   Dim TaskID As Integer
   TaskID = Shell("c:\excel\excel", 6)    'Start Excel
   txtNumber.LinkTopic = "Excel¦Sheet1"

   txtNumber.Text = "=LN(A1)"     'Excel spreadsheet formula
   txtNumber.LinkItem = "R2C1"    '   goes into cell A2
   txtNumber.LinkMode = 2         'Manual DDE
   txtNumber.LinkPoke             'Initiate DDE action
   txtNumber.LinkMode = 0         'Turn DDE off

   txtNumber.Text = ""            'Clear contents of text box
```

```
      txtLogValue.LinkTopic = "Excel¦Sheet1"    'Prepare LogValue properties
      txtLogValue.LinkItem = "R2C1"
End Sub
```

The following sections examine the various instructions found in Form_Load.

Using *Shell* to Launch the Source Application

The Shell instruction launches Excel. As explained in Chapter 29, "Manipulating the Windows Environment," Shell is a function which returns the Windows task ID number of the launched application. Here, the application does not actually use TaskID but, because Shell is a function, the left hand side of the instruction must contain a variable to conform with the required syntax.

Excel is presumed to be stored in the file referred to as EXCEL.EXE in a directory named C:\EXCEL. The full path is C:\EXCEL\EXCEL.EXE. Visual Basic assumes the file extension .EXE if none is specified.

 NOTE If you have Excel stored in a different directory, specify your directory path in the Shell instruction. Also, if C:\EXCEL appears in the PATH commands of your AUTOEXEC.BAT file, you can indicate only "Excel" for the file specification.

The second argument of the Shell function is a number which tells Windows whether the launched application should have the focus. This argument also indicates whether the application should appear minimized. Table 30.2 shows the possible values for this argument.

Table 30.2. The second argument in *Shell* function.

Value	Meaning
1, 5, 9	Launch at normal size with the focus
2	Launch minimized with focus (default value)
3	Launch maximized with focus
4, 8	Launch at normal size without the focus
6, 7	Launch minimized without the focus

The Shell function itself does not prepare any specific DDE activity. Shell merely activates another application in the current Windows environment.

Using the *LinkTopic* Property

The `LinkTopic` property for the `txtNumber` text box establishes a specific DDE link. This property indicates the application and topic for the DDE conversation.

For a client control that is linking to the source, a `LinkTopic` instruction has the following syntax.

```
control.LinkTopic = application¦topic
```

in which

   control is the name of the label, picture box, or text box,

   application is the name of the source application,

and

   topic is the data group under discussion.

The following is the relevant instruction that appears in `Form_Load`:

```
txtNumber.LinkTopic = "Excel¦Sheet1"
```

The `txtNumber` text box is the client control. This instruction establishes the source application as Excel. The topic is `Sheet1`. In Excel, the start-up spreadsheet is named `Sheet1` by default. (This spreadsheet is blank when Excel starts.)

As a result, this instruction prepares the `txtNumber` control to communicate with Excel's start-up spreadsheet. The vertical bar between "`Excel`" and "`Sheet1`" is required as part of the formal command syntax.

Carrying Out a DDE Conversation

The next instruction block actually passes data from the text box to the source using DDE:

```
txtNumber.Text = "=LN(A1)"    'Excel spreadsheet formula
txtNumber.LinkItem = "R2C1"   '   goes into cell A2
txtNumber.LinkMode = 2        'Manual DDE
txtNumber.LinkPoke            'Initiate DDE action
txtNumber.LinkMode = 0        'Turn DDE off
```

The goal of this block is to put a formula into the A2 cell of Excel. The formula, expressed in Excel terms, is `=LN(A1)`. In Excel, this formula causes the A2 cell to display the logarithm of the value in the A1 cell. Once the formula is placed in A2, Excel updates its value whenever A1 changes. As a result, A2 always displays the logarithm of the value in A1.

First, the `Text` property of `txtNumber` is set to `=LN(A1)`. If the Log Calculator form was visible, you would see `=LN(A1)` displayed in the text box. Although this data has been put into the `Text` property, no DDE activity has occurred at this point.

Next, the value of `txtNumber`'s `LinkItem` property is set to `R2C1`. The `R2C1` notation is another way to designate cell A2 in Excel. (`R2C1` is shorthand for row 2, column 1). This instruction establishes that the source (Excel) will use the cell A2 in DDE conversations with the client (the Visual Basic application).

 The `LinkItem` property can specify a range of cells, as well as a single cell.

Establishing a Manual DDE Link

The `LinkMode` property determines what type of DDE link occurs. As Table 30.3 shows, you can establish manual or automatic links by setting a value for the `LinkMode` property.

Table 30.3. *LinkMode* values.

Value	Meaning
0	No DDE activity, turns off DDE (default value)
1	Automatic link
2	Manual link
3	Notify link

With an *automatic* link, the server updates the value in the client control anytime the linked source data changes. With a *manual* link, the server supplies updated data values only when the client explicitly requests them.

 Automatic links are sometimes referred to as *hot* links. Manual links are sometimes called *cold* or *warm* links.

A *Notify link* is a special type of manual link in which the server notifies the client whenever the source data changes. However, the client must request the updated values before receiving them from the server. A `LinkNotify` event occurs whenever the server changes a data value. For more information on Notify links, see "Establishing Notify Links" later in this chapter.

In the sample application, `LinkMode` is set to 2 (manual DDE). As such, the DDE data transfer does not take place until the sample application specifically requests it. (For this particular application, you could successfully use either an automatic or a manual link.)

This instruction causes Visual Basic to open the link with Excel. Anytime you change `LinkMode` to a nonzero value, Visual Basic attempts to open the link. The target application and topic are specified by the `LinkTopic` property. Although the link is now open, no data transfer has yet occurred.

Poking Data to Excel

The next instruction finally causes the DDE data transfer to take place:

```
txtNumber.LinkPoke            'Initiate DDE action
```

`LinkPoke` is a method, not a property. Visual Basic requests that the current value of `txtNumber`'s `Text` property be "poked" to Excel. As established by `LinkTopic` and `LinkItem`, the data goes into cell A2 of `Sheet1` in Excel.

`LinkPoke` works with text boxes, picture boxes, and labels. The poked value is determined by the value of a particular property of the control. The property depends on the control type: `Text` property for text boxes, `Caption` property for labels, and the `Picture` property for picture boxes.

Terminating a DDE Conversation

The following instruction temporarily ends the DDE conversation:

```
txtNumber.LinkMode = 0     'Turn DDE off
```

It's good programming practice to set `LinkMode` to 0 before changing the value of `LinkTopic` or `LinkItem`. (Later in the application, the value of `LinkItem` is changed so that instead of sending the formula to cell A2, `txtNumber` sends the target number to cell A1.)

Next, the `Text` property of `txtNumber` is set to a blank string. This instruction clears the contents of the text box in anticipation of the form becoming visible when `Form_Load` completes.

Establishing Another Conversation

The remaining two instructions in `Form_Load` establish a similar DDE conversation between Excel and the `txtLogValue` text box:

```
txtLogValue.LinkTopic = "Excel¦Sheet1"  'Prepare LogValue properties
txtLogValue.LinkItem = "R2C1"            'Cell A2
```

These instructions prepare the `txtLogValue` text box to communicate with cell A2. Notice that the values of `LinkTopic` and `LinkItem` for `txtLogValue` are the same as for `txtNumber`.

When the application runs, cell A2 will contain the natural log of the value in cell A1. (The formula you poked into A2 makes this happen.) An open DDE link between cell A2 and `txtLogValue` transfers that natural log value from Excel to the Log Calculator application.

This completes `Form_Load`. At this point, there is nothing more for the sample application or Excel to do except wait for the user to enter a new number in the form's leftmost text box.

A Few Words on Sending Formulas to Excel

The first DDE conversation in `Form_Load` sends the value `=LN(A1)` to Excel. Recall that `txtNumber.Text` was set to `=LN(A1)`, and a DDE transaction transferred this formula to cell R2C1 (A2) in Excel. Figure 30.5 shows how Excel appears after this transaction.

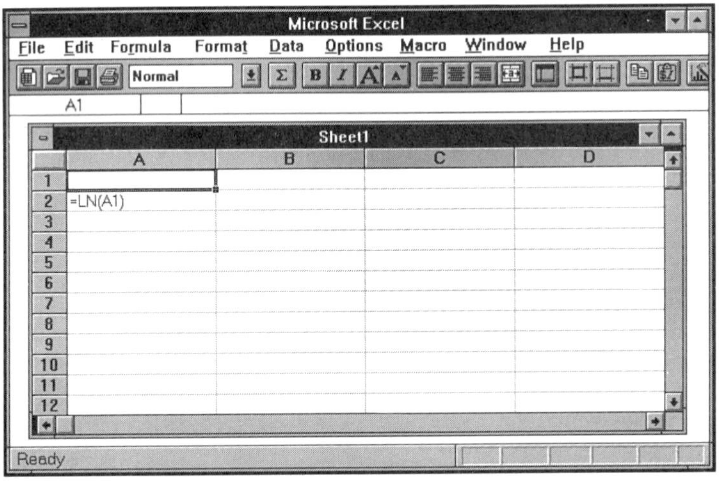

Figure 30.5.

Excel in "formula view" mode.

In the figure, Excel has been switched from the normal "data view" to "formula view."

Excel treats any value beginning with an equal sign as a formula. The formula `=LN(A1)` tells Excel to get from cell A1 (R1C1) the value, compute its natural logarithm, then store the result in cell R2C1.

This formula takes advantage of the "recalculate" feature built into Excel. By default, Excel recalculates every formula in a spreadsheet if any value changes. (You can turn off this feature if you don't want recalculation to occur automatically.)

The Log Calculator application depends on Excel's normal "recalculate" mode. As you will see, once a number is entered and transmitted to cell A1, Excel automatically calculates the log, and stores the result in cell A2.

Writing the *txtNumber_LostFocus* Event Procedure

The user of Log Calculator types a number into the Input Number text box. Then, the user clicks the Calculate button, or presses Tab to move the focus to it. In either case, the txtNumber control loses the focus.

As such, the txtNumber.LostFocus event procedure is a natural place to put the code which pokes the target number to Excel. The following is the event procedure.

```
Sub txtNumber_LostFocus ()
    txtNumber.LinkItem = "R1C1"
    txtNumber.LinkMode = 2
    txtNumber.LinkPoke
    txtNumber.LinkMode = 0
End Sub
```

The LinkItem property is changed to R1C1 in preparation for sending the number in txtNumber.Text to cell R1C1 (A1). Recall that the LinkTopic property is set to Excel¦Sheet1 by Form_Load. This value remains the same throughout the application, so there is no need to assign a value to txtNumber.LinkTopic here.

The next three instructions turn on manual DDE mode, poke the data from txtNumber.Text to cell A1, then turn off the DDE link. Keep in mind that the LostFocus event procedure triggers every time the user moves the focus away from the Input Number text box.

The Log Calculator Uses Excel's Built-In Features

The Log Calculator takes advantage of two of Excel's built-in features. First, Excel always begins operation by creating the default spreadsheet Sheet1. The Log Calculator application needs Excel only as a "computational source." Therefore, Log Calculator can rely on the fact that this spreadsheet is always available.

Second, as described earlier in the chapter, Excel automatically recalculates all the formulas on a spreadsheet if any value changes. As a result of the DDE conversation, the value in R1C1 does change. Once Excel gets this number, it places the value in R1C1, then recalculates the spreadsheet. In this example, there is only one formula to recalculate—=LN(A1).

Writing the *cmdCalculate_Click* Event Procedure

When the recalculation is complete, Excel stores the answer in cell R2C1. However, this answer has not yet been sent back to the client (the Log Calculator application).

The Log Calculator retrieves the answer when the user clicks the command button Calculate. The Click event procedure contains the necessary code.

```
Sub cmdCalculate_Click ()
    txtLogValue.LinkMode = 2
    txtLogValue.LinkRequest
    txtLogValue.LinkMode = 0
End Sub
```

Here, the DDE link is set up between the text box to the far right in the Visual Basic application and the R2C1 cell in Excel. First, LinkMode is set to 2 to establish a manual mode link for the text box labeled "Log Value from Excel." On the source side, the link was established with the final two instructions from Form_Load. The following again details those two instructions:

```
txtLogValue.LinkTopic = "Excel|Sheet1"   'Prepare LogValue properties
txtLogValue.LinkItem = "R2C1"
```

Notice that the values of the LinkItem and LinkTopic properties link the text box with the R2C1 cell from Excel.

The LinkRequest method asks the source application to update the contents of the txtLogValue text box. As with LinkPoke, LinkRequest works with both text and picture boxes, and labels. The property which gets updated depends on the control type: the Text property for text boxes, the Caption property for labels, and the Picture property for picture boxes. As a result of the LinkRequest instruction, the correct answer is transferred from Excel to the sample application.

Finally, the procedure resets the value of LinkMode to 0 in order to temporarily end the DDE conversation. The entire DDE process happens so fast that the Log Value from Excel text box seems to display the computed result as soon as you click the Calculate button.

Writing the *cmdCalculate_LostFocus* Event Procedure

To calculate the logarithm of new number, the user must type it into the Input Number text box. As such, the focus leaves the Calculate command button, and returns to the Input Number text box.

The `LostFocus` event for the command button occurs anytime the user moves the focus away from it. This event triggers when the user presses the Tab key or clicks one of the form's two text boxes:

```
Sub cmdCalculate_LostFocus ()
    txtNumber.SetFocus
    txtNumber.Text = ""
    txtLogValue.Text = ""
End Sub
```

These instructions "tidy up" the form to prepare for inputting a new number. The contents of both text boxes are cleared. Then, the focus is moved to the `txtNumber` text box. As such, the cursor in the Input Number text box blinks as it waits for the user to type a new number to begin the DDE conversation again.

Ending the Application

Clicking the Exit command button ends the Visual Basic application.

```
Sub cmdCancel_Click ()
    End
End Sub
```

Notice that this procedure closes the Log Calculator application. However, it does not terminate Excel which remains loaded in the Windows environment. You can move the focus to the Excel window, (maximizing, if necessary) and work with the spreadsheet directly.

You can save the Log Calculator form as LOGCALC.FRM, and the project as LOGCALC.MAK. This sample application was purposely kept simple so that the DDE statements and processes would be visible, and easy to understand. The following sections explore more advanced uses of DDE.

DDE Techniques and Practices

You can initiate DDE conversations in Visual Basic either at design time or run time. Only hot links can be established at design time.

Establishing an Automatic Link with Visual Basic as the Client

You can create a hot link at design time through the Edit menus of the two applications in a DDE conversation. For example, follow these steps to create an automatic design-time link with a Visual Basic application as the client, and another Windows program as the source:

1. Highlight the cell, bookmark, text block, or other item in the source application.

2. Choose the Copy option from the source application's Edit menu.

3. Switch to the Visual Basic application, and select the text box (or other desired control) by clicking the control. (You should see the sizing handles for the selected control).

4. Choose the Paste Link option from Visual Basic's Edit menu.

Notice that these steps begin with the application that has the desired data (or has it during program execution). They end with the application that needs the data.

You can test the link at design time. For example, if the server is Excel, move to the its window, and type something in the cell you highlighted when establishing the link. That value should appear immediately in the text box of the Visual Basic application.

Establishing an Automatic Link with Visual Basic as the Server

You can also make the Visual Basic application the server. The technique reverses the process used when the Visual Basic application is the client. You start with the Visual Basic application, and end with the other one (Excel, Word for Windows, etc).

In Visual Basic, only forms can be servers. (However, the data that eventually is transferred usually comes from a control.)

Follow these steps to make a Visual Basic form the server.

1. Set the value of the form's LinkMode property to 1. As explained in the next section, this value allows the Visual Basic application to act as a server.

2. In the Visual Basic application, select the text box (or other control) by clicking it.

3. Choose the Copy option from Visual Basic's Edit menu.

4. Activate the other application, and select the cell, bookmark, text block, or other target item to be the client.

5. Choose the Paste Link option from the application's Edit menu.

Using the *LinkMode* Property for Forms

The application that begins these steps becomes the source for the DDE transactions that occur during program execution. If you start with your Visual Basic application, and do this Copy/Paste Link operation, you are creating a "source link" from your application to the other one.

Before you create this link, you must change the LinkMode property of the form involved in this process. For forms, LinkMode can only have the values 0 and 1. (Recall that for controls, LinkMode can have a value from 0 to 3 which corresponds to no DDE, automatic link, manual link, and notify link respectively.)

For a form, a value of 0 (the default) means that the form does not and *will not* engage in a DDE conversation. If LinkMode is 0 at design time, the program code cannot change the value to 1 at run time.

A value of 1 (source) indicates that the form is or *will be* a source (server) in a DDE conversation. Once established as a source, any label, or text or picture box on the form can supply data to whatever client application requests it through a DDE link.

Remember that if you want a form to act as a server at run time, you must set the value of its LinkMode property to 1 (source) at design time.

Establishing Notify Links

A *Notify link* is a special type of manual link that has this added feature: The source "notifies" the destination when changes occur in the data. A notify link can help you reduce the complexity of your program code. Using this type of link, you are not required to accept the data when it becomes available (automatic link), or periodically check to see if it has changed (manual link).

You establish a notify link by setting the value of the client's LinkMode property to 3 (notify). For example, suppose the following code appears in the Log Calculator application:

```
txtLogValue.LinkMode = 3
txtLogValue.LinkTopic = "Excel¦Sheet1"
txtLogValue.LinkItem = "R3C1"       ' Source cell in Excel
```

With this code, whenever the value of cell R3C1 changes, Excel sends a message to the Visual Basic application to indicate that the linked data is updated. Visual Basic responds to this notification by triggering the text box's LinkNotify event. By writing code for the txtLogValue_LinkNotify event procedure, you can take whatever action you want when Excel notifies the Log Calculator.

Using the DDE Methods

The following sections describe the various DDE methods: `LinkExecute`, `LinkPoke, LinkRequest`, and `LinkSend`.

Using the *LinkExecute* Method

The `LinkExecute` method is available for label, text box, and picture box controls. This method sends a command string from the client application to the server using the DDE link.

> *control*.`LineExecute` *command*
>
> in which
>
> > *control* is a client's label, text box, or picture box control,
>
> and
>
> > *command* is a string expression which specifies a command recognized by the server.

The *command* must be in a form acceptable to the server application. For information on acceptable DDE commands, see your documentation for the server application.

The following program fragment illustrates how `LinkExecute` can be used during `Form_Load` to close the document with the input focus in Word for Windows.

```
Sub Form_Load()

BeginProcessing:
    On Error GoTo StartWinWord
    MyCtl.LinkMode = 0
    MyCtl.LinkTopic = "WinWord¦System"
    MyCtl.LinkMode = 2
    MyCtl.LinkExecute "[FILECLOSE 2]"    'Closes document
    Exit Sub

StartWinWord:
    If Err = 282 Then  'Application did not respond to DDE request
        hWinWord = Shell("winword.exe", 3)  'Maximized with focus
        Resume BeginProcessing
```

```
    Else
        Error Err
    End If

End Sub
```

This procedure prepares the DDE link for the `MyCtl` control. Then, `LinkExecute` sends a `FileClose` command to `WinWord` which closes whichever current file happens to be open. If `WinWord` is not running in Windows when the command is issued, the `StartWinword` error-handling routine gets control. The `Shell` function in this routine requests that Windows launch `WinWord`. Program control then routes back to the `BeginProcessing` routine in an attempt to re-establish the DDE link, and reissue the `FileClose` request.

Using the *LinkPoke* Method

The `LinkPoke` method is defined for DDE controls.

> *control*.`LinkPoke`
>
> in which
>
> > *control* is a label, text box, or picture box.

`LinkPoke`'s sole purpose is to send the contents of a client control to the item specified in the source application. `LinkPoke` is typically used to send data from one application to another when the user clicks a particular button.

The following `Click` event procedure shows an example of "poking" data from the client application to the server.

```
Sub SendButton_Click ()

BeginExecution:
    On Error GoTo OpenServer
    MyCtl.Text = "Data to be transfered"
    MyCtl.LinkTopic = "Excel¦Sheet1"
    MyCtl.LinkItem = "InputCell"
    MyCtl.LinkMode = 2
    MyCtl.LinkPoke
    MyCtl.LinkMode = 0
    Exit Sub
```

```
OpenServer:
    If Err = 282 Then      'Application did respond to DDE request
        hExcel = Shell("Excel.exe", 3)  'Maximized with focus
        Resume BeginExecution
    Else
        Error Err
    End If
End Sub
```

This event procedure triggers when the user clicks the Send button. If a DDE error occurs, Visual Basic reacts (because the program code uses the On Error instruction at the beginning of the BeginExecution routine) by transferring program flow to the OpenServer error handler. The error handler launches Excel, then transfers program control back to the BeginExecution routine.

The LinkItem property of MyCtl specifies the destination for the data sent by LinkPoke. In this case, you use a named cell rather than a row/column cell address as used in the Log Calculator.

Using the *LinkRequest* Method

The LinkRequest method is defined for DDE controls. This method "requests" data from another application, and stores the received value in the appropriate property of the control.

```
control.LinkRequest
```

in which

    control is a label, text box, or picture box.

The specific property depends on the control: the Caption property for a label, the Text property for a text box, and the Picture property for a picture box.

As illustrated in the following Click event procedure for a text box, you use LinkRequest much as you do the other DDE methods.

```
Sub Text1_Click ()

BeginExecution:

    On Error GoTo OpenApp
    Text1.LinkMode = 0    'No DDE temporarily
    Text1.LinkTopic = "Excel¦Sheet1"
```

```
    Text1.LinkItem = "R2C3"
    Text1.LinkMode = 2      'Manual DDE
    Text1.LinkRequest
    Exit Sub

OpenApp:
    If Err = 282 Then
        hExcel = Shell("Excel.exe", 3)
        Resume BeginExecution
    Else
        Error Err
    End If
End Sub
```

Using the *LinkSend* Method

The LinkSend method applies only to picture box controls.

picturebox.LinkSend

in which

picturebox is the name of a picture box control.

The LinkSend method "sends" the contents of a picture box on a Visual Basic form to another application. For example:

```
Picture1.LinkSend
```

The picture specified by the Picture property of Picture1 is sent to the application designated by LinkTopic, and to the particular location as directed by LinkItem.

Using the DDE Events

The following sections describe the various DDE events: LinkOpen, LinkError, LinkExecute, and LinkClose.

Using the *LinkOpen* Event

The LinkOpen event triggers when a DDE link is opened between your Visual Basic application and another program. The event is defined for forms, labels, and both picture and text boxes.

The event occurs for a form when another program initiates a DDE link with your Visual Basic application. The event occurs for a control when it initiates a DDE conversation with a server application.

Using the *LinkError* Event

The LinkError event occurs when there is an error in a DDE conversation. The event is defined for forms, labels, picture boxes, and text boxes.

```
Sub Form_LinkError (LinkErr As Integer)
```

or

```
Sub control_LinkError (Index As Integer, LinkErr As Integer)
```

in which

  control is the name of a label, picture box, or text box.

The Index As Integer clause appears only when the control is part of a control array.

The LinkError event triggers when an error occurs in a DDE conversation as long as no Visual Basic instruction is executing.

The LinkErr argument identifies the type of error which has occurred. This parameter is passed to the procedure, so that your event code can determine what error took place. Table 30.4 shows the meaning of the possible error numbers.

Table 30.4. *LinkErr* values for *LinkError* events.

LinkErr Value	Description of Error
1	The other application requested data in the wrong format.
6	The client application attempted to continue the DDE conversation even though the Visual Basic server application has set LinkMode to 0 (Terminate DDE).
7	All the server's DDE links are in use. (A server is limited to 128 links.)

LinkErr Value	Description of Error
8	An automatic link or a LinkRequest method failed to update the data in a destination control. Or the client unsuccessfully attempted to poke data to a control in the Visual Basic server form.
11	There is not enough memory for DDE to take place.

Using the *LinkExecute* Event

The LinkExecute event triggers when another program sends a command string to your Visual Basic application. This event is defined only for forms.

Recall that the Log Calculator application sends the command string =LN(A1) to Excel. You could send any other Excel command using this technique. For example, you could send [OPEN("*filename*")] in which *filename* is the name of a file you want Excel to open. Excel understands the OPEN command, and makes that file the active spreadsheet.

Similarly, your Visual Basic application can receive command strings from other programs. For example, you can develop an application that performs customized actions when the string DATE or TIME is received. If another application sends either of these strings, the Form_LinkExecute event procedure activates.

The received command string is passed to the Visual Basic application through an argument in the Sub procedure declaration.

```
Sub Form_LinkExecute (CmdStr As String, Cancel As Integer)
```

CmdStr is the command string sent by the other application. You can define any string values you want to be acceptable values of CmdStr. In the example just cited, DATE and TIME are acceptable commands. The client application must know which commands are meaningful to your Visual Basic application.

The value of Cancel can be set to True or False to indicate whether the Visual Basic application accepted the command string. This information is sent back to the other application. A value of False means that the command has been accepted (that is, the command string has not been canceled). A value of True means that the command string has *not* been accepted (that is, the command string has been canceled). The default value of Cancel is True.

The LinkExecute event is the only mechanism through which your Visual Basic application receives command strings from another program. If you don't write code for this procedure, your application cannot accept any DDE command strings.

Using the *LinkClose* Event

The LinkClose event occurs when either application in a DDE link terminates the conversation. The event is defined for forms, labels, text boxes, and picture boxes.

In a Visual Basic application, you can terminate a DDE link by modifying the link topic, or setting the value of the LinkMode property to 0. You often use the LinkClose event procedure to inform the user that the DDE link has been severed.

Summary

Dynamic Data Exchange (DDE) is a process used by two Windows applications to exchange data. Three types of DDE links exist: Automatic, Manual, and Notify. Typically, a client (destination) application requests data from a server (source) application.

In Visual Basic applications, forms, labels, and both text and picture boxes can participate in DDE conversations. Forms and controls can be sources of data. Only the controls can be involved in DDE conversations as clients.

Data is transferred to and from controls through a particular property in each type of control: the Caption property for a label, the Text property for a text box, and the Picture property for a picture box.

A conversation is manipulated with several DDE-related events, methods, and properties. The conversation partner and the topic are determined by the value of the LinkTopic property. For example, if Excel is the partner, the topic might be a specific spreadsheet. The LinkItem property identifies the item or subject under discussion. For Excel, the item might be a particular cell or a range of them. By setting the value of the LinkMode property, a Visual Basic application can begin or terminate a DDE link.

DDE links can be established at design time or run time. All links established at design time are automatic (hot) links.

Using Object Linking and Embedding (OLE)

*O*bject Linking and Embedding *(OLE)* permits Windows applications to work together to create compound documents. A *compound document* results when two or more applications combine to create a single document. For example, a text document created with Word for Windows might contain a spreadsheet produced with Microsoft Excel as well as a graphics chart created using Microsoft Chart.

OLE and DDE (Dynamic Data Exchange) are similar in that both technologies pass information between Windows applications. However, OLE extends the capabilities of DDE in that, instead of merely passing data values from the server to the client, OLE passes the complete graphics image of the client application. For example, when Excel uses OLE to pass the spreadsheet to the text document created with Word for Windows, it displays in row and column format, exactly as it appears in Excel.

With the OLE control, Visual Basic supports object linking and embedding. You can place onto a Visual Basic form an OLE control, then import into it a document from another application.

With Visual Basic 3.0, the OLE control has been enhanced to support the newest features of OLE technology. Not only can you link and embed documents in your Visual Basic applications, but you can take advantage of recent innovations, such as OLE automation.

Microsoft views OLE as taking an expanding role in the next several years. Windows is becoming (actually, already *is*) the standardized PC computing environment. Microsoft is pushing hard for OLE to become the standard through which Windows applications work together. By supporting recent standards in OLE, Visual Basic stands at the forefront of this technology.

This chapter introduces the OLE control in particular. It also discusses OLE technology, in general. Topics that this chapter covers include:

- Using the OLE custom control
- Understanding the differences between linking and embedding
- Creating OLE objects at design time
- Creating OLE objects at run time
- Introducing advanced OLE features, such as OLE automation and in-place activation

The Evolution of OLE 2.0

In the early days of Windows, the Clipboard provided the only way that applications could share data. You could copy information from one application to the Clipboard. Then, switch to another application, and paste the clipboard contents into it.

DDE represents the next evolutionary step. With DDE, applications directly link to each other, and can pass data back and forth. However, the receiving application merely obtains the raw data, and is entirely responsible for managing how the information is treated. This situation is similar to two individuals communicating information over the telephone. The recipient gets the raw data, but must display and manipulate the information independently.

With OLE, the connection between applications is much closer. Objects created in one application can be displayed in a number of others while still managed by the original application. In the client application, the object appears and acts just as it does in its "creator."

Microsoft is constantly adding additional capabilities to OLE as the technology for it improves. With the OLE 2.0 standards introduced in 1993, advanced features such as OLE automation are now part of this technology. With OLE automation, the client application can instruct the server to perform various actions on the OLE objects.

Visual Basic supports OLE 2.0 with the OLE custom control. Using the techniques explained throughout this chapter, you can use OLE controls to manipulate OLE objects.

Introducing Object Linking and Embedding

Although OLE stands for "Object Linking *and* Embedding," an object is never linked and embedded at the same time. A more precise description of this technology would be "Object Linking *or* Embedding."

Linked data is physically stored and maintained by the server application. The client application establishes a link to the data. However, the data does not physically exist as part of the client application. On the other hand, embedded data is physically stored in both the server and client applications.

With OLE, you can create Visual Basic applications and documents which contain various data objects that originate in other Windows applications. Such documents are often referred to as *compound documents*. The linked or embedded data that "belong" to the other applications are referred to as *OLE objects*.

Compound documents can contain objects that can be displayed or controlled by a Windows application which supports OLE. Some of these objects might include spreadsheets, word-processed text, various graphics objects (bitmaps), and sound bytes.

A typical example of a compound document is a report which contains text, spreadsheet tables of supporting numeric figures, and presentation graphs and charts. In such a report, the text is best managed by a word processor such as Microsoft Word, while the tables, charts, and graphs are handled by a spreadsheet program such as Excel.

When an object is linked, the source data is stored as a file in some other location. The data is not part of the "linked" compound document. The compound document containing the reference to this data file is "linked" to the file containing the object by this internal reference.

If the document referencing the data object is moved to another machine, the linked data object must also be moved so that the document can access the required data. For example, a document containing a link to an Excel spreadsheet has only the name of the data file. The actual spreadsheet data is not part of the compound document.

When an object is embedded in a compound document, the source data is actually stored in it, along with a reference to the server that created the data. As a result, the compound document is larger than a similar linked document. The reason is that the embedded data is stored as part of the compound document.

Understanding Concepts and Terminology Used in OLE

To enable you to better understand the concepts involved with Object Linking and Embedding, the following section explains some of the commonly used terms:

OLE Object

This object is any unit of data that is passed from one Windows application to another using OLE technology. Such a data unit is typically stored in a file which is used by one application, but managed by another. With today's Windows technology, OLE objects now include text documents, spreadsheets, charts, graphics, pictures, and audio and video data.

Linking

An OLE link places a special encoded reference in a client application to an OLE object which exists in a server application. Only one copy of the linked object exists. That copy remains in the server application. Consider a Visual Basic form which has an OLE link to a spreadsheet object. The form does not contain a copy of the spreadsheet, but rather a reference link to it. This OLE link includes the path and file name of the spreadsheet. Using OLE technology, the Visual Basic form treats the link information as a command. It is instructing the form to display the spreadsheet object.

In general, linked objects can be accessed and modified by any application containing an OLE link to them.

Embedding

Embedding operates similar to linking, except that the server data is included in the client application file in the place in which the custom OLE control is located. The client application is given a server name reference. In this way, when the data needs to be revised, the server can be activated to perform the changes. Only the application in which the embedded object appears can access it. No other applications have access to it.

Compound Document	This type of document includes references (OLE links) to data in other applications. It can also contain data (OLE embedding) created and maintained by other (server) applications. In this context, a Visual Basic form containing OLE objects acts as a compound document.
Container Application	An OLE object is linked or embedded into this application. When a Visual Basic application contains linked spreadsheet objects, it is the container application. And the Visual Basic form is the container document.
Client Application	This is the same as the Container Application.
Server Application	This application supplies the OLE object.

Introducing the Visual Basic OLE Control

Visual Basic supports object linking and embedding with the OLE control available from the Toolbox. With this control, you can link and embed OLE objects into your Visual Basic applications to create compound documents.

The OLE control is a custom control. As such, the control is not automatically built into Visual Basic. Instead, it is available from the add-on file MSOLE2.VBX. This file is included in both the Standard and Professional Editions of Visual Basic. The normal installation of Visual Basic places the OLE control in the Toolbox. The icon for the OLE control is labeled OLE 2.0. Here is a picture of the OLE control's Toolbox icon:

If your Toolbox does not contain the OLE control, either you elected not to include the custom controls when you installed Visual Basic, or you modified your AUTOLOAD.MAK file to exclude the MSOLE2.VBX file. You can add the OLE control to your Toolbox by performing the following steps:

1. Choose the Add File option from Visual Basic's **File** menu.

   The Add File dialog box opens.

2. Locate and specify the MSOLE2.VBX file.

   Most likely you find this file in the Windows SYSTEM directory. The complete file path is probably C:\WINDOWS\SYSTEM\MSOLE2.VBX. If you don't find the file there, it might be in the Visual Basic directory C:\VB\MSOLE2.VBX.

3. Click OK to close the dialog box.

You should now see the OLE control icon in the Toolbox, and the MSOLE2.VBX file listed in the Project window.

This control is capable of containing most any kind of OLE object. Besides text documents and spreadsheets, the OLE control can also contain bitmap images, graphics, vectors, voice messages, and even video clips.

Linking and Embedding at Design Time

CAUTION

To use Visual Basic's OLE control successfully, you must be running the DOS program SHARE.EXE. This program permits data and file sharing among applications. SHARE.EXE is supplied with DOS, and runs as a TSR (Terminate and Stay Resident) program. You must run SHARE.EXE before you launch Windows.

To invoke SHARE.EXE, you can type the command **SHARE** from the DOS prompt. However, a recommended method is to place a line in your AUTOEXEC.BAT file which automatically runs SHARE.EXE every time you boot your system. The following line accomplishes this:

```
C:\DOS\SHARE.EXE:
```

In the following example, you place two OLE controls on a Visual Basic form. While still in design mode, you then link (or embed) a different OLE object to each of these controls. The linked (or embedded) objects appear inside the OLE controls.

The example uses Microsoft Excel to create two OLE objects. The first object is a worksheet containing two columns of data. The second is a chart based on the worksheet numbers.

If you have Excel, you can follow the example. If not, you can skim the material to get an idea of the steps involved, and how linking and embedding works.

In this example, the Excel files are saved in a directory named C:\TESTOLE. You can create this directory on your hard drive, or save the object files in another directory that you choose.

Creating the OLE Objects with Excel

To begin the example, you must first create the two OLE objects with Excel. The directions here cannot give detailed explanations on using Excel. If you need more help on using Excel to create worksheets and charts, consult your Excel documentation or one of many independent books on the market, such as Que's *Using Excel 4 for Windows,* Special Edition.

The first task is to start Excel, and create a two-column worksheet. This worksheet represents the month-by-month sales for a fictitious business. The column on the far left contains abbreviations for the first six months of the year. The column on the far right contains the monetary sales data for each month.

Figure 31.1 shows the completed worksheet. Save this file as SALES1.XLS in the C:\TESTOLE directory. You can use a different file name. Alternatively, you can save the file in a different directory. This worksheet is the first of the two OLE objects you later place in the OLE controls.

	A	B	C	D	E	F	G	H
1	Jan	$185						
2	Feb	$220						
3	Mar	$340						
4	Apr	$195						
5	May	$110						
6	Jun	$160						
7								
8								
9								
10								
11								
12								
13								
14								

Figure 31.1.

The SALES1.XLS worksheet.

The next task is to create a chart based on the worksheet sales figures. To create it, you can use Excel's charting utility. This chart becomes the second OLE object that you eventually place in the OLE controls.

With the worksheet still loaded in the Excel environment, select the data in both columns. (That is, highlight the month names and the sales figures.) Choose the **New** option from Excel's **F**ile menu. When Excel prompts you for the type of new file that you desire, choose the Chart option.

Using the charting utility, create a 3-D bar chart, or any other chart type (see Figure 31.2). Save it as CHART1.XLC on the directory C:\TESTOLE. (You can also use an alternate file name and directory path.)

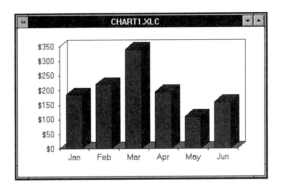

Figure 31.2.

The CHART1.XLC chart.

Linking the Worksheet to an OLE Control

Close Excel, and start Visual Basic. Double-click the OLE icon in the Toolbox to place an OLE control on the blank form. The icon for the OLE control is labeled OLE 2.0.

Visual Basic immediately displays the Insert Object dialog box. This dialog box lists all the applications and utilities in your Windows environment which can produce OLE objects. The listed applications do not have to be currently loaded. The list comes directly from a file updated and maintained by Windows. Figure 31.3 shows a typical Insert Object dialog box. The applications listed with your machine are likely to vary.

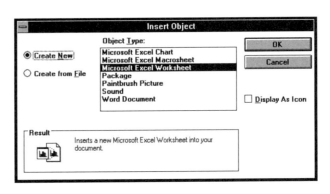

Figure 31.3.

A typical Insert Object dialog box.

Select Microsoft Excel Worksheet. This indicates that the OLE object is a worksheet created by Excel.

The dialog box contains two option buttons: one labeled Create New, and another labeled Create from File. Select the Create from File button. This choice indicates that the OLE object has already been saved as a disk file. If you select the Create New button instead, Visual Basic invokes Excel so that you can make the OLE object from scratch.

When you select Create from File, a Browse button appears in the dialog box. Click the Browse button. Visual Basic opens a Browse dialog box so that you can specify the file which contains the OLE object. Select C:\TESTOLE\SALES1.XLS as the target file. Click OK to return to the Insert Object dialog box.

Select the Link check box from the Insert Object dialog box. Doing this indicates that the OLE object is to be linked. If you don't select this check box, the OLE object is embedded instead of linked.

Click OK to close the Insert Object dialog box. An OLE control appears on the Visual Basic form. A visual image of the worksheet appears in the control.

Enlarge the form to cover most of the screen below the Toolbar. Then, using its sizing handles, enlarge the control to display the entire worksheet. Move the control near the left edge of the form. Figure 31.4 shows the result.

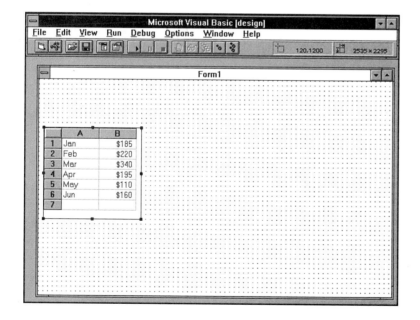

Figure 31.4.

The Excel worksheet is linked to the OLE control.

By default, Visual Basic names the first OLE control on a form as OLE1. Subsequent OLE controls are named OLE2, OLE3, and so on.

Embedding the Chart in an OLE Control

Place a second OLE control on the form. When the Insert Object dialog box appears, select Microsoft Excel Chart. Use the Create from File option to specify, using the Browse dialog box, the C:\TESTOLE\CHART1.XLC file. Indicate that the object is to be embedded by *not* selecting the Link button.

When you click OK to close the dialog box, a copy of the chart embeds in the second OLE control. Enlarge the control to display the entire chart. Then, move the chart to a position to the right of the first OLE control (see Figure 31.5).

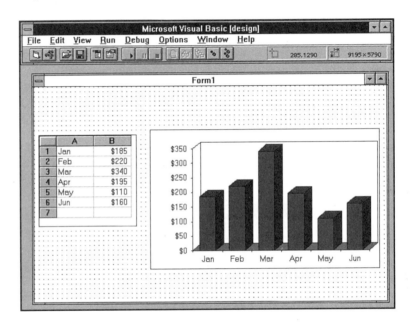

Figure 31.5.

The Excel chart is embedded in the OLE control.

Running the Application

Run the application even though no program code exists. Notice that the OLE objects are displayed on the form. Figure 31.6 shows how the form appears with a few label controls added for annotation. You can see just how easily the OLE control helps you construct compound documents.

Stop the application. Save the form as TEST1.FRM, and the project as TEST1.MAK.

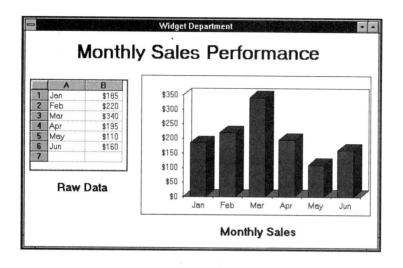

Figure 31.6.

The form becomes a compound document at run time.

Using the OLE Pop-Up Menus

Visual Basic provides a special pop-up menu system for manipulating OLE controls. These pop-up menus work at both design time and run time.

To activate a pop-up menu, you move the mouse pointer onto an OLE control. Then, you click the right mouse button. A pop-up menu appears which lists various OLE-related commands. The specific commands listed depend on the current context: whether an object is already in the control, what property values have been set, and when the operation is occurring—at design time or run time.

The Pop-Up Menus at Design Time

Figure 31.7 shows the pop-up menu which appears when you click an empty OLE control at design time.

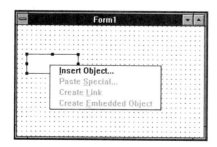

Figure 31.7.

The pop-up menu for an empty OLE control at design time.

The following includes a summary of the commands that Figure 31.7 shows:

Insert Object	Opens the Insert Object dialog box from which you can specify an OLE object to place in the control
Paste **S**pecial	Creates an OLE object from the data currently in the Windows Clipboard
Create **L**ink	Establishes an OLE link to an object which you specify with property values
Create **E**mbedded Object	Embeds an OLE object which you specify with property values

Notice that in Figure 31.7 only the Insert Object command is enabled. The other commands are grayed which indicates that they are temporarily disabled. The following sections explain how to enable these grayed commands.

Paste Special

The Paste **S**pecial command is enabled anytime a suitable OLE object is contained in the Clipboard. You can place such an object in the Clipboard directly from the server application.

To use Paste **S**pecial, first run the application containing the data you want to place in the Clipboard. From that application, you select (highlight) the data to become linked or embedded into the OLE control. Then, you use the **C**opy command from the application's **E**dit menu to place the selected data into the Clipboard.

In Visual Basic, the Paste **S**pecial command now appears enabled in the pop-up menu. When you select this command, Visual Basic opens the Paste Special dialog box. Figure 31.8 shows this dialog box when a Paintbrush Picture has previously been copied to the Clipboard.

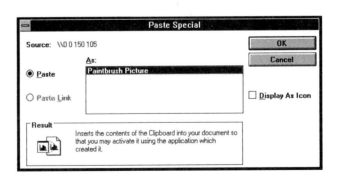

Figure 31.8.

A typical Paste Special dialog box.

In the Paste Special dialog box, you can select **Paste** to create an embedded object, or Paste **Link** to make a linked object. When you click OK, Visual Basic creates the object in the OLE control from the Clipboard data.

One advantage of using the Clipboard is that you can create an OLE object from a portion of its entire data. For example, suppose you have an Excel worksheet which contains several columns of data. Suppose that you only want to link two columns of the data to an OLE control. You can select the two columns in Excel, and copy this data to the Clipboard. Then, using Paste **S**pecial, you can create an OLE object in Visual Basic which consists only of the selected data.

Create Link

The Create Link command becomes enabled if you specify values for the `Class` and `SourceDoc` properties. In this section, these properties are described briefly. Another section, later in the chapter, discusses the two properties in more detail.

The `Class` property specifies the type of OLE object. Examples include an Excel Worksheet and chart, and a Paintbrush picture. You can see a list of the available Class values by selecting the `Class` property in the Properties window, then clicking the ellipsis (...) to the right of the settings box. Choose one of the listed values to specify the `Class` property.

The `SourceDoc` property specifies the file name for the linked object. When `Class` and `SourceDoc` are set to valid values, the Create Link command appears enabled in the OLE pop-up menu.

Create Embedded Object

To enable the Create Embedded Object command, you need only specify a valid value for the `Class` property.

For both the Create Link and the Create Embedded Object commands to appear in the pop-up menus, the value of the `OLETypeAllowed` property must be set appropriately. By default, the value of this property is 2, which enables either linked or embedded objects. However, if the value of `OLETypeAllowed` is set to 0 (linked objects only) or to 1 (embedded objects only), the pop-up menu contains only the Create Link or Create Embedded Object command, respectively.

The Pop-Up Menu When an OLE Object Is Already Present

If you click the right mouse button when the OLE control already contains an OLE object, the pop-up menu has a separate set of commands. Figure 31.9 shows the menu when the OLE control already contains an Excel worksheet.

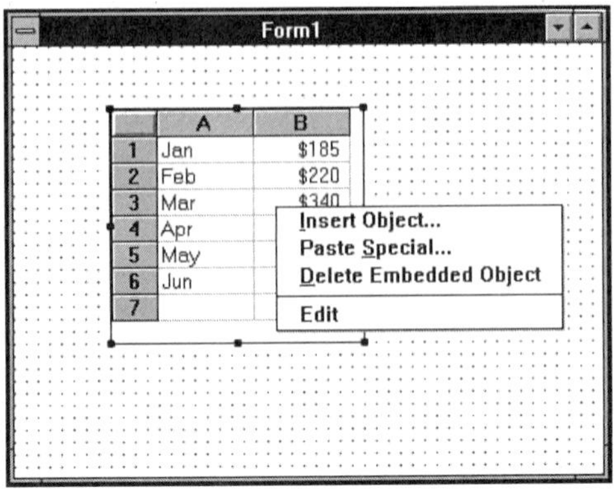

Figure 31.9.

The design-time, pop-up menu for an OLE control already containing an object.

The **D**elete Embedded Object command removes the OLE object from the control. By selecting this command, you free the OLE control to later contain a different OLE object. However, if you choose the **I**nsert Object command, you can immediately link or embed a different object into the OLE control. An OLE control can only contain one object at a time.

Commands which appear below the separator bar stem from the application which created the OLE object. As such, the commands which appear below this bar depend on what OLE actions the source application supports.

Using the Pop-Up Menus at Run Time

At run time, the pop-up menu displays only the commands stemming from the source application. As such, the listed commands correspond to those which appear below the separator bar at design time.

For example, when an Excel worksheet is the OLE object, the Edit command is the only one that appears in the pop-up menu at run time. This command lets you edit the data in the original worksheet.

You can try editing the data with the TEST1 application developed earlier. Run the application. Move the mouse pointer over the worksheet data, then click the right mouse button. A pop-up menu appears that displays only the Edit command. The menu appears on-screen near the position of the mouse pointer.

Click the Edit command on the pop-up menu. Excel is activated with a loaded worksheet labeled `Embedded Object`. This worksheet contains the data from the OLE object.

Add two more rows to the worksheet to specify data for July and August. Figure 31.10 shows the edited worksheet.

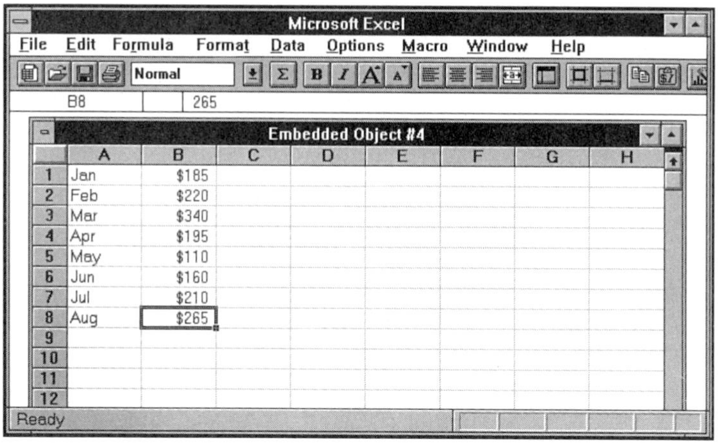

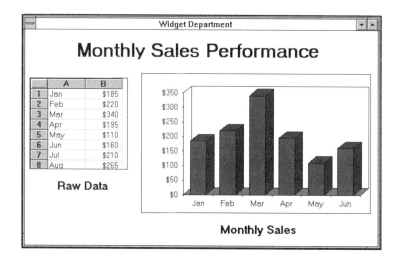

Figure 31.10.

The Excel worksheet is edited to add new data.

Open Excel's **File** menu, then select the **Update** command. Next, close Excel, and return to the Visual Basic environment. Notice that the edited data now appears in the OLE worksheet object (see Figure 31.11).

Figure 31.11.

The edited worksheet is entered in the OLE object.

The chart is not updated because it is a separate embedded object. You can, however, update the chart. To do this, you open the pop-up menu for the chart, and select Edit. Then, revise the chart.

Using the OLE Control at Run Time

At run time, you manipulate OLE controls by setting property values in your program code. Table 31.1 introduces the most important properties used when working with OLE controls at run time.

Table 31.1. Important OLE properties.

Property	Description
Class	Specifies the type of OLE object
SourceDoc	Specifies the name of the particular server document (file) that becomes an OLE object
SourceItem	For linked objects, this property specifies the range of data which becomes linked
Action	Specifies the operation that the OLE control should perform

Establishing a Link at Run Time

As a simple example of a run-time application, start a new project, and place an OLE control on the blank form. When the Insert Object dialog box appears, click Cancel. The form now contains an empty control named OLE1.

Using the Properties window, specify the control's size and location by assigning the property values that Table 31.2 shows.

Table 31.2. Design-time property values for the *OLE1* control.

Property	Value
Height	1695
Left	2280
Top	1080
Width	2775

Now, create the following Form_Load procedure:

```
Sub Form_Load ()
    OLE1.Class = "ExcelWorksheet"
    OLE1.SourceDoc = "C:\TESTOLE\SALES1.XLS"
    OLE1.SourceItem = "R1C1:R4C2"      'Use first four rows only
    OLE1.Action = 1  'Create a linked object
End Sub All numbers
```

This procedure uses the SALES1.XLS worksheet created earlier in the chapter. The `Class` property identifies the upcoming OLE object as an Excel Worksheet. The `SourceDoc` property specifies the file that contains the worksheet object.

The `SourceItem` property establishes a range of data to use for the OLE object. Recall that the SALES1.XLS file actually contains six rows of data in two columns. In this event procedure, however, you use only the first four rows of the spreadsheet when creating the OLE object.

The actual link occurs when Visual Basic executes the instruction specifying the `Action` property. By setting Action to 1, the code specifies that an OLE linked object is to be created. (Another section, later in this chapter, gives a complete list of `Action` values.)

Figure 31.12 shows the result of running this application. Notice that the worksheet appears as a linked object in the `OLE1` control. Only the first four rows of the worksheet are linked.

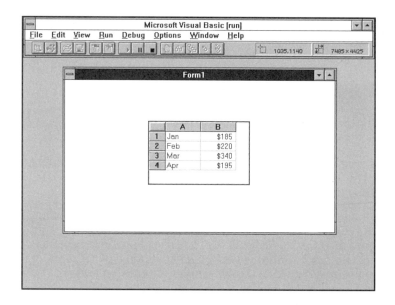

Figure 31.12.

Creating a linked object at run time.

Establishing an Embedded Object at Run Time

At run time, you can embed an object in an OLE control. You do this in the
same way you link a document at run time. For example, the following is a
Form_Load procedure which embeds the SALES1.XLS object in the OLE1 control:

```
Sub Form_Load ()
    OLE1.Class = "ExcelWorksheet"
    OLE1.SourceDoc = "C:\TESTOLE\SALES1.XLS"
    OLE1.Action = 0   'Create an embedded object
End Sub
```

Notice that the SourceItem property is not specified in this procedure. The
SourceItem property has meaning only for linked objects, not for those that are
embedded. As such, you can't specify a portion of the object file when embedding. You must specify the whole object. Also, notice that you set Action to 0
to embed an object.

You can also create an empty embedded object at run time. To do so, don't
specify any value for the SourceDoc property. Visual Basic then embeds an
empty object of the specified Class. For example, if you remove the specification of SourceDoc in the current Form_Load procedure, the resulting embedded
object is an empty worksheet.

By creating an empty embedded object when an application loads, your code
can later let the user generate the actual object at run time. To do so, you
specify various values of the Action property as described later in this chapter.

Understanding the OLE Control Properties

This section examines the various properties that are important in OLE
applications. This discussion introduces several new properties, and gives
more detailed information about others mentioned previously.

Many of the OLE properties accept values specified with integer quantities.
The CONSTANT.TXT file predefines several constants for use with such OLE
properties. By adding the CONSTANT.TXT file (or appropriate portions of
this file) to any OLE application, you can take advantage of these predefined
constants in your program code. In the ensuing discussion and data tables,
the OLE-related constants come from the CONSTANT.TXT file.

Class Property

Each Windows application that can act as an OLE server (that is, supply an OLE object) defines a set of possible class names. These class names become valid values of an OLE control's Class property. You specify a Class name with a string value.

For example, as you've seen in this chapter, Microsoft Excel for Windows supports worksheet and chart objects. These objects have the Class names ExcelWorksheet and ExcelChart, respectively. Other examples of class names are WordDocument and MSGraph for Word documents and Microsoft graphics objects, respectively.

You can determine the available Class property values for your computer system by opening the Properties window for an OLE control. Then, you select the Class property, and click the ellipsis (…) at the right end of the Settings box.

OleTypeAllowed Property

By default, an OLE control can contain either a linked or an embedded object. If your application permits the user to make an OLE object at run time, you might want to allow the creation of only one type of object. That is, you might restrict the user to creating only a linked or an embedded object. To do so, you can specify a value for the OleTypeAllowed property.

Table 31.3 shows the possible values of OleTypeAllowed.

Table 31.3. Values of the *OleTypeAllowed* property.		
Value	**Constant**	**Meaning**
0	OLE_LINKED	Linked objects only
1	OLE_EMBEDDED	Embedded objects only
2	OLE_EITHER	Either linked or embedded objects

For example, the following instruction restricts the OLE1 control to containing only linked OLE objects:

```
OLE1.OleTypeAllowed = OLE_LINKED
```

You can specify this property at design time or run time. The default value is 2.

OleType Property

The OleType property determines whether a control contains an OLE object. If so, the property indicates whether it is linked or embedded. Table 31.4 shows the values that this property can have.

Table 31.4. Values of the OleType property.

Value	Constant	Meaning
0	OLE_LINKED	OLE control contains a linked object
1	OLE_EMBEDDED	OLE control contains an embedded object
3	OLE_NONE	OLE control does not contain any object

This property is read only at run time.

SourceDoc and SourceItem Properties

As explained earlier in this chapter, the SourceDoc property specifies a file to be linked or embedded. For linked objects, the SourceItem property specifies a data range within the file.

Each application that can provide a linked object has a specific syntax for designating the SourceItem property. As you've seen for worksheet objects, you can use a cell range such as R2C5:R8C7 for the SourceItem property. In a Word for Windows document object, you can use a bookmark reference to specify the SourceItem property. Refer to the server application's documentation to determine the exact syntax required to specify a data range for OLE objects that application creates.

Once an OLE linked object is created, Visual Basic adjusts the values of the SourceItem and SourceDoc properties. At run time, Visual Basic expands the value of the SourceDoc property to include the design-time value of the SourceItem property. The value of SourceItem becomes the empty string.

For example, suppose the values of SourceDoc and SourceItem are "C:\TESTOLE\SALES1.XLS" and "R1C1:R4C2", respectively. As previously described, the program code uses the Action property to create a linked object in the OLE1 control.

If you read the values of SourceDoc and SourceItem once you have created the linked object, you find that SourceDoc is "C:\TESTOLE\SALES1.XLS!R1C1:R4C2", and `SourceItem` is the empty string. Notice that the value of `SourceDoc` uses an explanation point (!) to separate the data range (`R1C1:R4C2`) from the file specification.

Action Property

At run time, you make Visual Basic perform an OLE-related operation by assigning a value to the `Action` property for an OLE control. As such, the OLE `Action` property works similarly to a Visual Basic method. That is, when Visual Basic executes an instruction which assigns a value to the `Action` property, the system immediately performs the indicated action on the OLE control.

The `Action` property is not available at design time, and is write-only at run time. That is, your program code can only assign a value to `Action`. You can't read the current value.

The following is the general syntax for an instruction which assigns a value to `Action`:

```
formname.OLEcontrol.Action = value
```

in which

> `formname` is the name of a form,

> `OLEcontrol` is the name of an OLE control,

and

> `value` is an integer number which specifies the action to take.

The `formname` parameter is optional.

If you omit `formname`, the current form is assumed.

For example, the following instruction creates an embedded object in the OLE control named `MyOLE`:

```
MyOLE.Action = 0   'Create an embedded object
```

Nineteen possible values exist that you can assign to `Action` (the integer numbers from 0 to 18). However, some of the values are reserved for future use, and do not correspond to a specific action. Table 31.5 summarizes the OLE actions you can perform.

Table 31.5. Values of the OLE *Action* property.

Value	Constant	Meaning
0	OLE_CREATE_EMBED	Creates an embedded OLE object. The Class property must have a valid value. Also, the OleTypeAllowed property must be set to 1 (embedded) or 2 (either).
1	OLE_CREATE_LINK	Creates a linked OLE object. The Class property must have a valid value. Also, the OleTypeAllowed property must be set to 0 (linked) or 2 (either).
2		Reserved, not currently supported.
3		Reserved, not currently supported.
4	OLE_COPY	Copies the contents of the OLE object to the Clipboard. Both linked and embedded objects are supported.
5	OLE_PASTE	Copies the data from the Clipboard to the OLE control. The PasteOK property must have a value of True for the Paste operation to work.
6	OLE_UPDATE	Updates (refreshes) the contents of an OLE control by obtaining the current data from the application that created the OLE object. Then, displays that data in the OLE control.
7	OLE_ACTIVATE	Performs the action specified by the Verb property. The value of the Verb property must be previously set.
8		Reserved, not currently supported.
9	OLE_CLOSE	Closes an embedded OLE object. Then, severs the association with the application that created the object. This action is meaningless for linked objects.
10	OLE_DELETE	Deletes, or removes, the OLE object from the application.
11	OLE_SAVE_TO_FILE	Saves the OLE client object on-disk as a data file. Before this action can be taken, a binary file must be opened with an Open instruction. The FileNumber property must be set to the file number of the open binary file. (This file number can be obtained from the Open instruction). For a linked object, only the link data is saved in the file. The data is maintained by the server application. For an embedded object, the actual data is saved to the binary file.

Value	Constant	Meaning
12	OLE_READ_FROM_FILE	Obtains from a binary file data, and puts the information into the OLE control. Before this action can be taken, a binary file must be opened. Then, the FileNumber property must be set to the same file number used for opening the binary file.
13		Reserved, not currently supported.
14	OLE_INSERT_OBJ_DLG	Displays the Insert Object dialog box at run time. The user can then specify the OLE object to be linked or embedded.
15	OLE_PASTE_SPECIAL_DLG	Displays the Paste Special dialog at run time. The user can then specify the OLE object to be pasted from the Clipboard.
16		Reserved, not currently supported.
17	OLE_FETCH_VERBS	Updates the list of verbs that an OLE object supports
18	OLE_SAVE_TO_OLE1FILE	Saves the object in the file format used with the OLE Client control from previous versions of Visual Basic.

PasteOK Property

By setting the Action property to 15, Visual Basic displays the Paste Special dialog box at run time. You might want to invoke this action so that the user can specify an OLE object that should be pasted from the Clipboard.

The PasteOK property for a control indicates whether the Clipboard currently contains data that can be pasted into an OLE control. This property has a value of True or False. PasteOK is read-only at run time.

You can use the PasteOK property to verify that the Clipboard contains suitable data before setting Action to 15. For example, the following instruction opens the Paste Special dialog box as long as the Clipboard contains data that can be pasted:

```
If OLE1.PasteOK then OLE1.Action = OLE_PASTE_SPECIAL_DLG
```

UpdateOptions Property

One benefit of linked OLE objects is that the source data is managed by the server application. A client application can display the linked data without having to individually maintain the information. That way, several client applications can contain OLE links to a single data file in the server.

The UpdateOptions property is especially practical when other users might employ the server application to modify the linked data. If the OLE data is changed at the source, the OLE control must respond to that modification. Through the UpdateOptions property, you can specify how the OLE control responds when the linked data is modified.

This property is used only at run time. Table 31.6 shows the available values.

Table 31.6. Values of the *UpdateOptions* property.

Value	Constant	Meaning
0	OLE_AUTOMATIC	Automatic. The OLE object is updated whenever any modification occurs to the source data.
1	OLE_FROZEN	Frozen. The OLE object is updated whenever the source data file is saved in the server application.
2	OLE_MANUAL	Manual. The OLE object is updated only when the program code sets the Action property to 6, the update option.

By default, the value of UpdateOptions is 0 (Automatic).

AutoActivate Property

At run time, the user can potentially activate an OLE object by double-clicking the object. In this context, "activate" means that the OLE control takes a particular action defined by the server application. Typically, the action consists of activating the server application so that the user can edit and resave the data.

With the AutoActivate property, you can specify whether the user is permitted to activate the OLE object, and how to initiate this action. Table 31.7 explains the three values that the AutoActivate property can have.

Table 31.7. Values of the *AutoActivate* property.

Value	Constant	Meaning
0	OLE_ACTIVATE_MANUAL	Manual. The OLE object cannot be activated by the user. To activate the object, the program code must set the value of the control's Action property to 7.

Value	Constant	Meaning
1	OLE_ACTIVATE_GETFOCUS	GetFocus. The OLE object is activated whenever the OLE control gets the focus.
2	OLE_ACTIVATE_DOUBLECLICK	Double-click. Whenever the user double-clicks an OLE control that contains an object, the object is activated.

By default, the value of AutoActivate is 2. The following instruction disables the user from activating the object specified in the MyOLE control:

```
MyOLE.AutoActivate = OLE_ACTIVATE_MANUAL
```

Working with Verbs and Object Activation

As described previously, the server application determines the specific action taken when an OLE object is activated. Each server application defines a set of actions, called *verbs*. That application can process these verbs on the OLE objects that it creates.

Visual Basic communicates with the server application to enable the processing of various actions on an OLE object when it is created. An object can be activated by program instructions, and mouse movements that the user makes.

As explained shortly, you can manipulate the set of verbs by modifying various property values. Also, the actions that can be performed on an OLE object (that is, the list of verbs) can vary at run time. The actions depend on the current state of the OLE control, and the object it contains. For example, you can usually "edit" an OLE object. Such editing involves activating the server application to modify the OLE data object. At other times, you might be able to "play" the OLE object, for example, listening to an embedded audio track.

OLE controls support a number of properties that let you manipulate the list of verbs. The following sections discuss those properties.

AutoVerbMenu Property

As described earlier in the chapter, when you click an OLE control using the right mouse button at run time, a pop-up menu displays a list of commands that you can perform on the object. Those listed commands are the verbs supported by the object in the OLE control.

You can disable the pop-up menu by setting the value of the control's AutoVerbMenu property to False. For example, the following instruction disables the run time, pop-up menu system for the OLE control named MyOLE:

```
MyOLE.AutoVerbMenu = False
```

The default value of AutoVerbMenu is True. As such, the pop-up menu system is enabled at run time. If you don't want your users to have access to the pop-up menu system for any OLE control, set its AutoVerbMenu property to False.

Verb Property

Each OLE object supports a set of verbs determined by the server application and the Visual Basic run time context. This set of verbs is sequentially ordered by Visual Basic. The system puts them in order using index values of 1 up to the number of verbs on the list. As discussed shortly, you can determine the verbs on the list using the ObjectVerbs and ObjectVerbsCount properties.

Furthermore, each OLE control object has a default verb. This verb specifies the action that takes place when either your program code or the user activates the object. The program code activates it by setting the Action property to 7. The user activates the object by double-clicking the OLE control.

Each OLE control's Verb property specifies the default verb. For example, the following instruction sets MyOLE's default verb as the second one on that control's verb list:

```
MyOLE.Verb = 2
```

Besides values from 1 upward, the Verb property for every OLE control supports values from 0 down to -3. Table 31.8 explains this set of standardized verbs.

Table 31.8. Standardized values of the Verb property.

Value	Constant	Meaning
0	VERB_PRIMARY	Resets the default verb to be the default action for the OLE object.
-1	VERB_SHOW	Edit. Activates the object for editing. By default, the object activates within the server application. However, if the application supports in-place activation (discussed later in this chapter), the object activates inside the OLE control.
-2	VERB_OPEN	Opens the OLE object in its own application window.
-3	VERB_HIDE	If the OLE object is embedded, this option hides the server application on the Windows screen.

ObjectVerbs and *ObjectVerbsCount* Properties

The `ObjectVerbsCount` property specifies the number of verbs that the object supports. The `ObjectVerbs` property specifies the list of these verbs. Both of these properties are unavailable at design time, and are read-only at run time.

The `ObjectVerbs` property works similarly to a string array. You use an index value to access the name of any particular verb on the list. The following is the general syntax:

```
formname.OLEcontrol.ObjectVerbs(index)
```

in which

  `formname` is the name of a form,

  `OLEcontrol` is the name of the OLE control,

and

  `index` is an integer number which specifies the "array" element in the list of verbs.

The `formname` parameter is optional.

When `index` is 0, the `ObjectVerbs` property returns the default verb. Recall that the default verb specifies the action which takes place when the OLE object is activated. The same verb also appears somewhere in the `ObjectVerbs` list with an index value greater than 1.

`ObjectVerbs` is commonly used to display to the user a list of the available verbs. This list can be displayed in a menu, or other Visual Basic control. Then, the user can select one of the verbs to request a particular action on the OLE object.

For example, the following code fragment uses the `AddItem` method to place the verb list for the `MyOLE` control into a list box control named `MyList`. In this code fragment, the `VerbNum%` variable is an integer which acts as a loop counter:

```
MyOLE.Action = OLE_FETCH_VERBS    '(Action = 17)
For VerbNum% = 1 To MyOLE.ObjectVerbsCount
   MyList.AddItem MyOLE.ObjectVerbs(VerbNum%)
Next VerbNum%
```

Notice that the first instruction in this code fragment executes `Action` number 17. The list of verbs supported by an OLE object can vary according to its current state. The verb list is not automatically updated by Visual Basic. By executing `Action` number 17, you explicitly update the verb list for the OLE control. In general, you should execute this action before working with the `ObjectVerbs` and `ObjectVerbsCount` properties.

The *Updated* Event

OLE controls support a standard set of event procedures. These procedures include Click, mouse events, Resize, and keystroke-related events, such as KeyDown, and so on.

Also, OLE controls have a special event known as Updated. This event triggers whenever the data in an OLE control is modified. The following is the Sub instruction syntax of the Updated event for an OLE control named OLE1:

```
Sub OLE1_Updated(Code As Integer)
```

As Table 31.9 explains, the value of Code indicates the manner in which the data in the OLE control has been updated.

Table 31.9. *Code* values for the *Updated* event.

Value	Constant	Meaning
0	OLE_CHANGED	The data in the OLE object has changed.
1	OLE_SAVED	The server application has saved the data in the OLE object.
2	OLE_CLOSED	For a linked object only, the server application has closed the file to which the OLE control is linked.
3	OLE_RENAMED	For a linked object only, the server application has renamed the file to which the OLE control is linked.

Working with Advanced OLE Features

Microsoft is constantly expanding the capabilities of Object Linking and Embedding. In an attempt to make OLE the industry-standard protocol for data sharing among Windows applications, Microsoft is continually redefining OLE standards.

In early 1993, Microsoft released a revised set of OLE standards and conventions now known as the OLE 2.0 standards. These standards not only spelled out how Windows applications should link and embed objects with each other, but also specified several advanced OLE features, such as OLE automation and in-place activation. Furthermore, the new standards add several editing and managing features to the OLE process.

With the release of Version 3.0, Microsoft has kept Visual Basic at the forefront of the OLE technologies. Visual Basic OLE controls are now capable of supporting many of the advanced OLE 2.0 features.

At this time, most available Windows applications do not yet fully support the advanced OLE features that OLE 2.0 defines. However, buoyed by the persuasive presence of Microsoft in the Windows arena, the OLE 2.0 standards will probably gain widespread acceptance. Newer versions of Windows applications will more than likely support the OLE standards advocated by Microsoft.

Whenever you contemplate using advanced OLE features in your Visual Basic programs, you must be aware of exactly which features your targeted server applications can support. To find out, consult the documentation for your intended server applications, or contact their vendors. Remember that, with time and the technological advances it brings, the barriers between the capabilities of the Visual Basic OLE control and the OLE-supported features (that most major Windows applications offer) are likely to fade.

The following sections introduce many of the advanced OLE features supported by the OLE control. These features include the following:

- OLE Automation
- In-Place Activation
- Nested Object Support
- Property Inheritance
- Drag and Drop

Introducing OLE Automation

OLE automation is the capability of a Windows application to manipulate objects contained in other applications. Through OLE automation, one application can direct the operation of another.

In essence, a program that supports OLE automation offers objects that it creates to other applications. These receiving applications can then manipulate the objects by directing how the server acts on them. For example, a spreadsheet application that supports OLE automation might offer complete worksheets, cell ranges, or charts as objects. Other applications can access these objects and direct how the spreadsheet program manipulates them.

With Visual Basic, you can access objects offered by other applications. In your Visual Basic program code, you can execute methods and properties on those objects just as you might manipulate objects that originate in Visual Basic.

Creating OLE Automation Objects

OLE Automation is not restricted to objects which support linking and embedding. With Visual Basic, it's possible to automate objects which are not contained in OLE controls.

To do so, you declare a Visual Basic variable of type `Object`. Then, using the `Set` statement and the `CreateObject` function, you create an OLE Automation object. At that point, you can manipulate the object with properties and methods just as you do with Visual Basic objects.

For example, consider the following program fragment:

```
Dim MySheet As Object
Set MySheet = CreateObject("Excel.Worksheet")
MySheet.Row = 1
MySheet.Column = 1
MySheet.Insert = "$300"
```

The `Set` instruction creates an OLE automation object consisting of an Excel worksheet. This instruction activates Excel, and creates a worksheet object. Notice that the argument inside a `CreateObject` function uses a period to separate the application and the object type.

The remaining instructions identify the first row and column of the spreadsheet, and store the value $300 in that cell. `Row` and `Column` are automation *properties* that Excel supports; `Insert` is an automation *method* that Excel supports. To find the properties and methods supported by any OLE application, consult its documentation.

Retrieving Stored OLE Objects

The `GetObjects` function retrieves an OLE automation object that has been previously stored in a file. You can use this function in a `Set` instruction as you do the `CreateObject` function.

For example, the following code fragment declares an OLE automation object, then retrieves it from a disk file:

```
Dim MySheet As Object
Set MySheet = GetObject("C:\TESTOLE\MYSHEET.XLS")
```

Automating OLE Objects Stored in OLE Controls

So far, the discussion has focused on OLE automation with objects declared through Visual Basic variables. In such cases, the objects remain within the server application. The discussion thus far has centered on the Visual Basic application using program code to manipulate both the object and the server application.

However, if supported by the server application, you can also use OLE automation with linked and embedded objects contained in OLE controls. To do so, you use the Object property defined for OLE controls.

With the Object property, you can write code that executes the methods and properties that the OLE object supports. The Object property acts as a bridge between the object contained in the OLE control and the server application which created the object.

For example, consider an OLE control named MyOLE. It contains an OLE worksheet object. Suppose that the object supports Row, Column, and Italic properties, as well as Select and Insert methods. The following code fragment writes a text string into the cell at row 2, column 3. The fragment also makes that text italic:

```
MyOLE.Object.Row = 2
MyOLE.Object.Column = 3
MyOLE.Object.Insert = "Send money"    'Put text string in cell
MyOLE.Object.Select                   'Select the text
MyOLE.Object.Italic = True            'Turn on italics
```

Introducing In-Place Activation

In-Place Activation is a means of activating an OLE object within the boundaries of an OLE control. Directly from the OLE control in the Visual Basic application, the user can manipulate an object when it supports in-place activation. With the current OLE 2.0 standards, only embedded objects can support in-place activation.

If you set to 1 the value of the AutoActivate property of an OLE object, it is activated whenever the OLE control gets the focus. Using the OLE control, the user can edit (or perform any other supported action to) any object if it supports in-place activation.

In-place activation does not require switching to the server application to edit the object. Instead, the menus, palettes, and other controls used to edit and interact with the object temporarily replace the existing tools of the Visual Basic "container" application.

These menus and controls are used to edit the object in the same way that they are employed in the underlying server application. However, the remaining part of the Visual Basic application retains its current appearance. When the user finishes editing, and the object is deactivated, the original menus and controls in the Visual Basic application are restored. The result is that in-place activation provides a smooth transition from client to server during object editing.

Using Drag and Drop

With OLE 2.0, the user selects some data from a server application, and drags the information to a destination. Then, the user drops the data into the destination. This style of dragging data from one application to another is called *inter-window dragging*.

Two other styles are used in drag and drop: *inter-object dragging* and *dropping on icons*.

With inter-object dragging, one object can be nested within another. To move a nested object, you click it. Then, you drag it to another container. You can move nested objects among containers, or into other windows. The reverse is also true. You can drag objects to others. Then, you can drop an object into another to create a nested object.

Objects can also be dragged and dropped onto icons. The application represented by an icon obtains the object that is dropped on it. At that point, the application performs whatever actions it is programmed to do on the dropped objects.

Printing and electronic mail are examples of specialized applications that can be programmed to accept dropped objects.

Nested Object Support

With OLE 2.0, one object can be linked or embedded in another in the same compound document. For example, a graph can be linked to an embedded spreadsheet in the compound document. When you change the figures in the spreadsheet, the graph is automatically altered.

Property Inheritance

OLE objects often have their own unique properties. For example, you might create a chart object with a special drawing style and font type.

Before OLE 2.0, the properties of the chart would carry over to the application in which the chart had been embedded. However, container objects can now control the appearance of the embedded objects which they contain. OLE 2.0 matches the related properties of the container and the object. Those properties of the container replace the corresponding ones in the object.

This inheritance affects the embedded object only as long as it remains part of the container. The inherited properties are those of the container that apply at the point at which the object is embedded.

Additional Uses of OLE

Managing an OLE conversation involves specifying various properties, then using Action to activate the object or invoke some operation. You can set properties at design time, or dynamically, in program code while the program is executing.

Setting properties at design time is less flexible but does simplify the programming done later. By setting and re-setting most properties with program code, your Visual Basic applications can gain full control over OLE objects, including when and how each one is used.

Using the more advanced OLE features, such as OLE automation, you can essentially control the execution of macros in the server applications. You can, for example, create a wide variety of macros in Excel, then execute them from a Visual Basic application.

By doing so, you can make special calculations, create and manage a database, prepare customized charts, generate word-processed documents, or perform any other required task. This capability to customize your processing helps servers to work even better with client applications.

Summary

With Object Linking and Embedding, a Visual Basic program can contain data which originates in another Windows application. The Visual Basic application can display such data, referred to as an OLE object. To do this, Visual Basic uses the same format employed by the server application when the object was created. For example, a Visual Basic application can display a graphics chart exactly as it appears in the charting application.

The Visual Basic OLE control supports both linked and embedded objects. A linked object is physically stored and maintained by the server application while displayed in the OLE control. An embedded object is physically stored in both the Visual Basic and the server application.

Using the OLE control, you can not only display OLE objects, but activate them. Through various property values, you can manipulate the OLE object and its server application in program code. For example, directly from a Visual Basic application, the user can edit an OLE worksheet using the resources of the Windows spreadsheet application.

Microsoft intends to continue molding OLE to become the primary means by which Windows applications do advanced data sharing. With the Version 2.0 standards recently introduced, OLE now includes such features as OLE Automation and In-Place activation. With Visual Basic 3.0, the OLE control can now support most of the newest OLE features.

In Microsoft's long-term plans, OLE seamlessly links Windows applications together. The goal is for Windows to provide a platform in which individual applications are really just features and resources of a single operating environment. Undoubtedly, Microsoft intends to keep Visual Basic on the leading edge of that vision.

PART

VII

Using VB Professional Edition

Using Custom Controls

C ompared to the Standard Edition of Visual Basic, the Professional Edition includes additional custom controls. These controls offer you enhanced design flexibility in creating the user interfaces for your applications. The Professional Edition custom controls include Graphs, 3D controls, Spin Buttons, Masked Edit controls, Key Status controls, Picture Clip controls, Gauges, Animated buttons, Common Dialog control, and the Outline control.

The Professional Edition also contains custom controls that allow access to Serial Communications, Messaging Systems, Multimedia, and Pen Editing. Although these controls offer a great deal of power, they require computer systems configured with specialized hardware.

This chapter explains the custom controls and offers sample applications that demonstrate their uses.

The Professional Edition Desktop

When all the custom controls are loaded, the Project window and the Toolbox appear as shown in Figure 32.1. (As explained in this section, it's possible that your Toolbox may contain a different number of controls or that the controls are located in different positions within the Toolbox.) In general, the custom controls appear in the lower half of the Toolbox while the controls built-in to Visual Basic appear in the upper half.

The process of loading the custom controls activates the Windows Graphics Server, which appears as a minimized icon directly on the desktop. For more about the Windows Graphics Server, see the upcoming discussion on the Graph custom control.

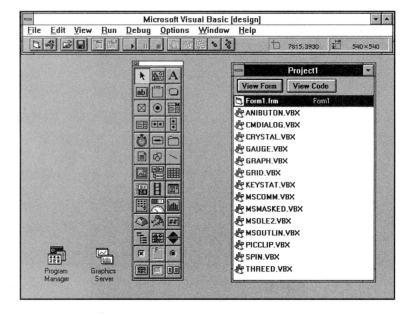

Figure 32.1.

The Project window, the Toolbox, and the Graphics Server Icon.

NOTE

The Crystal Custom Control

The Toolbox shown in Figure 32.1 includes the Crystal custom control. This control permits a Visual Basic application to print reports based on data contained in database files. The Crystal control icon depicts a printed report as a grid of small squares.

Visual Basic's SETUP program adds the Crystal control to the Toolbox whenever you install the complete version of the Professional Edition. If you do a customized installation with SETUP, you can choose whether to include the Crystal control in your Toolbox. For more about running SETUP and selecting the Crystal icon, see Chapter 1, "An Overview of Visual Basic."

The Crystal control and the Crystal Report Writer are not discussed in detail in this book. For more information, consult your Microsoft documentation.

NOTE

Installing the Specialized Custom Controls

Figure 32.1 does *not* show all the custom controls that Microsoft supplies with the Professional Edition. If you install the complete Professional Edition, or you select the Custom Controls option

while running SETUP, Visual Basic installs some custom controls which require specialized system hardware or software. However, unless your computer system has the required configuration, these controls do not appear in your Toolbox or in the Project window. The .VBX files for these files are placed in your C:\WINDOWS\SYSTEM directory.

These specialized controls are the MAPI (*M*essaging *A*pplication *P*rogram *I*nterface) controls which require the Microsoft Mail for Windows electronic mail system, the Multimedia MCI (*M*edia *C*ontrol *I*nterface) controls which require a PC equipped with multimedia hardware and software extensions, and the Pen controls which require a pen-equipped computer system running under the Microsoft Windows for Pen Computing environment. These controls are discussed briefly at the end of this chapter.

Working with .VBX Files

Custom controls are stored on disk in files named with a .VBX extension. For example, the Gauge control is stored in the file named GAUGE.VBX. The name VBX stands for *V*isual *B*asic e*X*tension. When you install Visual Basic, the SETUP program places the .VBX files in the C:\WINDOWS\SYSTEM directory.

Each .VBX file is a special type of dynamic link library (DLL) which contains one or more custom controls. The custom controls are not part of Visual Basic 3.0's standard dynamic link library: VBRUN300.DLL. Recall that the VBRUN300.DLL file contains all the non-custom controls which are built into Visual Basic.

The Project window lists all the .VBX files which are currently loaded into the Visual Basic environment. Some .VBX files contain more than one custom control. For example, the THREED.VBX file contains six different 3D controls that appear in the Toolbox (3D Check Box, 3D Command Button, 3D Frame, 3D Group Push Button, 3D Option Button, and 3D Panel).

Modifying the Custom Control Configuration

You can specify which custom controls appear in the Toolbox (and in the Project window). To modify your current configuration, choose one of the following actions:

- *To add a custom control to the Visual Basic environment at design time.* Choose the A**d**d File option from the **F**ile menu. Visual Basic opens an

Add File dialog box. Select a file with a .VBX extension. You should find such files in the C:\WINDOWS\SYSTEM directory. When the file is added into Visual Basic, you will see the file name with the .VBX extension listed in the Project window and any custom controls contained in that file will appear in the Toolbox.

■ *To remove a custom control from the Visual Basic environment at design time.* Select (highlight) the .VBX file in the Project window. Then choose the **R**emove File option from the **F**ile menu. Visual Basic deletes the .VBX file from the Project window and any custom controls associated with that file are removed from the Toolbox.

■ *To add or delete individual custom controls when starting Visual Basic.* By modifying the AUTOLOAD.MAK file, you can specify which custom controls are loaded into the Project window and the Toolbox when you start Visual Basic. The AUTOLOAD.MAK file is a text file which lists the default .VBX files loaded into the Visual Basic environment. The file is saved in your Visual Basic directory. You can modify AUTOLOAD.MAK with any text editor or word processor that works with text files. For more about AUTOLOAD.MAK and how to modify it, see Chapter 1, "An Overview of Visual Basic" and Chapter 9, "Managing Projects."

■ *To place all available custom controls into the default Visual Basic environment.* Rerun the Visual Basic SETUP program. Either select the complete installation, or select a customized installation and choose the Custom Controls and Crystal Reports options. When you now start Visual Basic, all available custom controls appear in the Toolbox with the associated .VBX files listed in the Project window.

Distributing Executable Files that Use Custom Controls

Just as with any Visual Basic application, you can create an executable (.EXE) file from an application which uses one or more custom controls. In order to successfully run such an .EXE files, the .VBX files associated with the custom controls must be present. As a result, if you distribute .EXE files to others, you must distribute the necessary .VBX files as well.

Fortunately, Microsoft grants you the right to freely distribute .VBX files along with your applications. Each user should load the .VBX files in the same directory as the .EXE file, or in a system directory specified with a PATH command in the AUTOEXEC.BAT file. Also, don't forget that you must distribute the VBRUN300.DLL file to anyone that uses an .EXE file you create with Visual Basic. For more about creating .EXE files, see Chapter 9.

Understanding the VB.LIC File

When working with the Professional Edition custom controls at design time, Visual Basic must have access to the VB.LIC file. The presence of this file indicates that Microsoft grants you license to use the Professional Edition custom controls. When you run SETUP to install the Professional Edition, the VB.LIC file is stored in the C:\WINDOWS\SYSTEM directory. As such, the file is automatically present. You normally don't have to worry about this file unless you inadvertently delete the file or move the file to a different directory.

Be aware that Microsoft does *not* grant you the right to distribute the VB.LIC file to others. This should not cause any problem because the file is not needed when running the .EXE files which you *may* distribute to others.

Creating Sample Applications

This chapter shows you how to create several sample applications that demonstrate the Professional Edition custom controls. In the first part of this chapter, the sample application graphs sales data and allows the user to change the graph parameters with the 3D controls and Spin Button. The second part of the chapter uses an application with a text box to manipulate, save, retrieve, and print the text to a file using the common dialog boxes, masked edit, and key status controls. Separate applications demonstrate the Picture Clip, Gauge, and Animated Button controls.

To begin the first sample application, GRAPH, start a new project. Using the Properties window, modify the form's property values as shown in Table 32.1.

Table 32.1. Properties for GRAPH.MAK.

Control	Property	Value
Form1	Caption	Sales Graph
	Height	5580
	Name	frmGraph
	Width	9900

The Graph Control

The Graph control provides a link with the Graphics Server to allow you to create graphs. By placing the Graph control on your form and modifying the properties, you can create 2D and 3D Bar, Line, 2D and 3D Pie, Area, Gantt, Log/Lin, Scatter, Polar, and High-Low-Close graphs. At design time, you can interactively produce various graphs drawn from data that you enter. At run time, you can change the data and modify the graph while the application is running.

The Graphics Server is a Windows application which provides support routines utilized by the Graph control. Microsoft supplies the Graphics Server as the file GSW.EXE which comes with Visual Basic. When you install the Professional Edition custom controls, the SETUP program automatically installs GSW.EXE in your C:\WINDOWS\SYSTEM directory.

Whenever the Graph control is loaded into the Toolbox, Visual Basic automatically loads the Graphics Server into the Windows environment. As a result, you see the Graphics Server icon on your desktop. (If you remove the GRAPH.VBX custom control from the Project window, Visual Basic unloads the Graphics Server from the Windows environment and the Graphics Server icon is removed from your desktop.)

Adding the Graph Control to Your Project

The Graph control is contained in the GRAPH.VBX file. In addition to GRAPH.VBX, the Graph control requires the GSW.EXE Graphics Server file and the special dynamic link library named GSWDLL.DLL. When you install the Professional Edition custom controls, SETUP automatically places these three files in your C:\WINDOWS\SYSTEM directory. However, if you distribute .EXE applications which use the Graph custom control, you must distribute the GRAPH.VBX, GSW.EXE, and GSWDLL.DLL files to your users as well.

You can add a Professional Edition custom control to your application in the same manner that you add any control to your application. You can double-click the control icon in the Toolbox, or single-click the control icon and then click and drag the mouse pointer to any desired location on the form.

For this sample application, perform the following steps:

1. Add a Graph control on the form.

   You will see a rectangular control on your form. The mouse pointer appears as an hourglass until a bar graph based on random data appears in the control. Visual Basic gives this Graph control the default name Graph1.

2. Using the Properties window, modify the following property values for the Graph control:

Height	3960
Left	3915
Name	gphSales
Top	300
Width	5595

For the graph name, there is a prefix *gph* followed by the word *Sales*. Microsoft doesn't recommend a standard prefix for the graph control. Here, *gph* is chosen because it is significantly different from the *grd* prefix used for the grid control. Now that you have changed the dimensions of the graph control, your form should look something like Figure 32.2. Because the design-time graph is based on random data, your graph will likely represent different data than the graph shown in the figure.

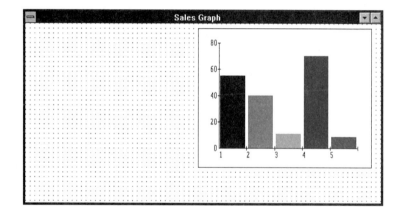

Figure 32.2.

The default graph.

Once the graph is placed and positioned on your form, you can modify the property values to start customizing the graph to your specifications.

Entering the Data

You can enter your own data for the graph by using the NumSets, NumPoints, and GraphData properties. NumSets specifies the number of data sets which appear in the graph while NumPoints indicates the number of data points in each set. For example, in the default graph, NumSets is 1 while NumPoints is 5. GraphData specifies the actual data values which appear in the graph. This property acts as a two-dimensional array with the values of NumSets and NumPoints specifying the bounds of the two dimensions. When using the Graph control, the value of NumPoints must be at least 2, and the product of NumSets and NumPoints must be less than 3800.

You can enter the graph data by modifying values in the Properties window or by writing code to specify the data at run time. For this application, you start by modifying property values at design time. Select the Graph control and then open the Properties window. Complete these steps:

1. Change the value of NumSets to 2.

2. Verify that the value of NumPoints is 5. If not, change the value to 5.

3. Select the GraphData property from the Properties window.

4. Type **10**, then press Enter.

5. Type the values for the remaining data points: **20**, **30**, **40**, **50**, **5**, **10**, **15**, **20**, and **25**. Press Enter after typing each value.

In the final two steps above, you directly entered the data which filled the GraphData array. By entering data this way, you take advantage of the Graph control's auto-increment feature. The data you entered first filled the five array values when NumSets was 1 and then filled the five values when NumSets was 2. As you enter the data, the graph changes visibly on-screen, but you cannot see a list of your data points.

Adding Titles and Labels

You can add labels and titles to your graph so that the user will better understand its contents. If, for example, you want to add descriptive labels for the data, you use the Labels and LabelText properties. The Labels property indicates whether or not the labels are displayed. The LabelText property is a string array which specifies the actual labels, one label for each value of NumPoints. If you choose to have labels, then you can enter the label text by following these steps:

1. Select the LabelText property from the Properties window.

2. Type **Reg. 1**, then press Enter.

3. Taking advantage of the default auto-increment feature, type the values for the remaining four data points: **Reg. 2**, **Reg. 3**, **Reg. 4**, and **Reg. 5**. Press Enter after typing each value.

If the labels look too crowded, you can use the LabelEvery property to modify which items will have labels. For example, if you change the LabelEvery property to 2, every other data item will have a label. You can also add a legend for the graph using the same method, except that you use the LegendText property. You can control the type of legend using the LegendStyle property.

You can also place an overall title, a y-axis title, and an x-axis title on your graph by specifying values for the GraphTitle, LeftTitle, and BottomTitle properties. For the sample application, change these properties to the following values:

Property	Value
GraphTitle	1993 Sales
LeftTitle	000
BottomTitle	Regions

Changing the Graph Type

Now that the data and the text of the graph have been modified, you can change the type and style of graph by using the GraphType and GraphStyle properties. To change the graph type and style, complete these steps:

1. Change the value of the GraphType property to 6 (Line Type).

2. Change the GraphStyle property to 6 (Lines and Sticks).

After these changes, the form should look like Figure 32.3.

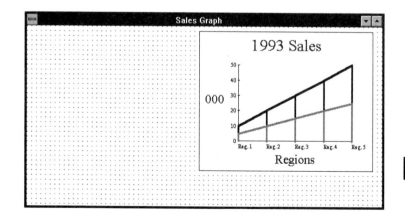

Figure 32.3.

Creating a Line-Type graph.

Additional Formatting

Additional style can be added to your graph by using some of the other properties. You modify the colors with the ColorData property and change the color set by using the Palette property. You add patterns with the PatternData or PatternLines properties. You control line thickness and symbols with the ThickLines and SymbolData properties, respectively. You can explode your pie chart pieces or accent your 3D bar charts with color by using the ExtraData property.

The way you modify the font, style, and size of the text on a graph is different from the way you modify similar properties for other controls. For a graph, the properties you use to modify font, style, and size are FontFamily, FontStyle, and FontSize. The FontFamily property offers fewer choices than the regular FontName property used with other controls. You can also designate which text items are affected with the FontUse property. This is an important consideration when you are using multiple fonts on a form; you want to keep the fonts as similar as possible.

Statistics can be placed on the graph itself using the LineStats property. Adding gridlines and controlling the x- and y-axis positioning, minimums, maximums, and tick marks can be accomplished with the GridStyle, XPosData, YPosData, YAxisStyle, XAxisMin, XAxisMax, YAxisMin, YAxisMax, Ticks, TicksEvery, and YAxisTicks properties.

Creating the Graph

As the property values are adjusted, the graph is modified on-screen to reflect the changes. You can modify the value of the DrawMode property to activate special drawing modes. To clear the graph, use a value of 1. To draw the graph, use a value of 2 ("Draw"—the default) to create a metafile graph or 3 ("Blit") to create a bitmap graph. You can make a copy of the graph with a value of 4, print the graph with a value of 5, or save the graph to a disk file with a value of 6.

With the last three settings, the property value reverts to its previous Draw or Clear state after the selected action takes place. For example, suppose the value of DrawMode is 2 and your code changes that value to 4. The application responds by sending the graph to the Print Manager for printing, and then resets the value of DrawMode to 2 in order to reproduce the on-screen graph.

Resetting the Graph

When a program is designed to graph data, you normally want to try out different graphics representations. To reset your data or your settings, use the

`DataReset` property. This property allows you to reset the values of the `GraphData`, `ColorData`, `ExtraData`, `LabelText`, `LegendText`, `PatternData`, `SymbolData`, and `XPosData` properties, either individually or all at once.

Writing Code for the Graph Control

You can modify a graph's property values with program code at runtime. You use the same method that you have been previously using for the other Visual Basic controls. You write an instruction which specifies the name of the Graph control followed by the property name, separated by a period, and then assign a value to this expression.

If you set the value of `AutoInc` to 1, you can specify values for the array-like properties with a series of consecutive assignments which incrementally points data to the array. For example, consider the following program fragment which assigns a series of values to the `GraphData` property (rather than repeatedly modifying the value of one particular array element).

```
gphSales.AutoInc = 1      'turn on auto-incrementing
gphSales.GraphData = 10
  .
  .
  .
gphSales.GraphData = 50
```

To better illustrate this concept, you are going to add some 3D custom controls to enable the user to choose the number of data sets and graph points and the type of graph displayed. You will then add code that transfers the user's choices to the graph properties.

The 3D Controls

The 3D controls are three-dimensional counterparts to standard Visual Basic controls. There is a 3D Command Button, 3D Frame, 3D Option Button, and 3D Check Box. There are also a 3D Panel, which is similar to the frame, and a 3D Group Push Button, which allows you to create a toolbar similar to the Visual Basic Toolbar.

The 3D controls give your applications more visual depth than the standard controls. To access the 3D controls, you need to have THREED.VBX loaded into your project—and you must ship it along with any executable version of your application. When THREED.VBX is in the Project window, the 3D controls are added to the Toolbox. The rest of this section introduces each 3D control and explains its individual properties.

3D Command Button

The first 3D control is the 3D Command Button. Compared to a standard command button, the 3D version offers more flexibility in designing its appearance. 3D command buttons support all the properties of standard command buttons, except that the 3D buttons do not recognize the Cancel and Default properties.

For the sample application, you will add two 3D command buttons. One button is used to graph the data, and the other prints a copy of the graph. To add these buttons, complete the following steps:

1. Place two 3D command buttons on the form. Visual Basic assigns these controls the default names Command3D1 and Command3D2.

2. Modify the following property values for these buttons:

Control	Property	Value
Command3D1	Caption	Graph Data
	Height	495
	Left	5565
	Name	cmdGraph
	Top	4485
	Width	1590
Command3D2	Caption	Print Data
	Height	495
	Left	7620
	Name	cmdPrint
	Top	4485
	Width	1590

At this point, the 3D command buttons appear like standard command buttons. You change the three-dimensional appearance of these buttons by modifying property values. For example, you can modify the BevelWidth property to adjust the depth of the button on the form; BevelWidth can be between 0 and 10.

By modifying the value of BevelWidth, you can make the 3D button appear "raised" on the form. However, the 3D controls are designed to appear best with a gray background. To change the background of the form and the graph to gray, you modify the values of the form's BackColor property and the graph's Background property. With the form, you select a color from the palette or type the desired color's hexadecimal value; with the graph, you select a color from amongst 16 predefined values.

Another way to change the appearance of the 3D Command button is to modify the Font3D property. You can raise the caption off of the button with various shading options. Font3D has these choices: No Shading, Raised Letters with Light Shading, Raised Letters with Heavy Shading, Inset Letters with Light Shading, or Inset Letters with Heavy Shading.

Follow these steps to modify the appearance of the two 3D command buttons.

1. Change the value of the BevelWidth property to 5 for both buttons.

2. Change the form's BackColor property to &H00C0C0C0& and the graph's Background property to 7—Light Gray.

3. Change the Font3D property to 1 (Raised with Light Shading) for both buttons.

You can add some definition to the outline and corners on a 3D command button with the Outline and RoundCorners properties. Each of these properties can have True or False values. For the Outline property, changing the value from False (the default) to True makes it easier to distinguish the border. When RoundCorners is True (the default value), the button appears with rounded corners while a value of False creates squared corners.

The remaining property that the 3D command buttons have but the standard command buttons do not is the ability to display a picture instead of a text caption. The Picture property supports the use of a Bitmap (*.BMP) or an Icon (*.ICO) file. You can make the value of the AutoSize property True to let the command button automatically resize to fit the graphic image. With the Picture property, 3D Command buttons can be used in conjunction with the 3D Push Buttons to create a Toolbar. This will be illustrated in the next sample program.

3D Frame

The 3D Frame can be used in the same fashion as the standard frame and shares many of the same properties. The 3D Frame provides a way to focus the user's attention and a mechanism for easily grouping controls on a form. The 3D Frame does not have BackColor and ForeColor properties because it was designed for a gray background. The 3D Frame also lacks the ClipControls property used to determine how the graphics methods work in Paint events for the standard frame.

Like the 3D command button, there are some additional properties to customize the 3D frame's appearance. In addition to Font3D, you can also adjust the alignment of the caption with the Alignment property and change the shadow color and style with the ShadowColor and ShadowStyle properties. For the GRAPH sample program, the types of graphs which the user can choose will be placed in a 3D frame. To create the frame, complete these steps:

1. Add a 3D frame control on the form and modify its property values as follows:

Property	Value
Caption	Graph Type
Height	2250
Left	75
Name	fraType
Top	2160
Width	3495

2. Change the frame's Font3D property to 1—Raised with light shading.

3. Change the frame's Alignment property to 2—Centered caption.

4. Change the frame's ShadowColor to 1—Black.

5. Change the frame's ShadowStyle to 1—Raised.

 NOTE **The Use of the 3D Properties**

It is important to use all the 3D properties consistently on your form or throughout the application. If more than one style is used on a form, it creates an inconsistent or fuzzy effect. Users will think something is wrong or, in the case of Font3D, that they need glasses.

After the 3D frame is placed on the form and the properties are set, this frame can be treated like its standard counterpart. The double-click method cannot be used for placing controls in a standard or 3D frame. For the sample application, the 3D frame will hold option buttons with which the user can choose the graph type.

3D Option Button

A 3D option button is identical to the standard option button except that the 3D version lacks BackColor and ForeColor properties and includes the Font3D property. For the sample application, you need to add six 3D option buttons. As with the standard option buttons, it is best to create a control array to minimize the coding. To complete the Graph Type selections, follow these steps:

1. Place a 3D Option Button on the fraType control (the 3D frame).

2. Change the value of the 3D option button's Alignment property to 1— Right Justify.

3. Change the button's Name property to optType.

4. Change the button's Font3D property to 1—Raised with light shading.

5. Select Copy from the Edit menu to place a copy of the option button on the Clipboard.

6. Click anywhere on the 3D frame control to select it.

7. Select Paste from the Edit menu.

8. Answer Yes when Visual Basic asks whether to create a control array.

9. Repeat steps 6 and 7 four more times to add four additional copies of the 3D option button into the optType control array. Altogether, this control array contains six option buttons, with index values ranging from 0 to 5.

10. Modify the property values of the optType control array as shown in Table 32.2

Table 32.2. optType() property values.

Control	Property	Value
optType(0)	Caption	Line
	Height	375
	Left	240
	Top	300
	Width	1005
optType(1)	Caption	2D Bar
	Height	375
	Left	240

continues

Table 32.2. Continued		
Control	**Property**	**Value**
	Top	790
	Width	1005
optType(2)	Caption	3D Bar
	Height	375
	Left	240
	Top	1300
	Width	1005
optType(3)	Caption	2D Pie
	Height	375
	Left	1800
	Top	300
	Width	1005
optType(4)	Caption	3D Pie
	Height	375
	Left	1800
	Top	790
	Width	1005
optType(5)	Caption	Area
	Height	375
	Left	1800
	Top	1300
	Width	1005

3D Check Box

A 3D check box works like the standard check box, except that the 3D version supports the Font3D property but does not support the BackColor and

ForeColor properties. Also, the Value property works a bit differently between the 3D and standard versions. A standard check box supports Value settings of 0—Unchecked, 1—Checked, and 2—Grayed (disabled). A 3D check box cannot be disabled and therefore supports the following settings for the Value property: 0—False (unchecked), and 1—True (checked).

For the sample application, a 3D check box is used to select a pie slice for explosion (if the 2D or 3D pie type is chosen). Complete the following steps to add a 3D check box inside the 3D frame:

1. Add a 3D inside the 3D frame.

2. Modify the property values for the 3D check box as follows:

Property	Value
Caption	Explode Largest Pie Slice
Font3D	1—Raised with light shading
Height	315
Left	390
Name	chkExplode
Top	1785
Value	True
Width	2970

After these changes, the form should be similar to the one shown in Figure 32.4.

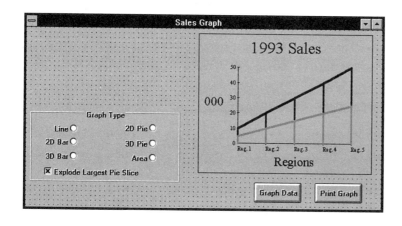

Figure 32.4.

The Sales Graph form.

3D Panel

The 3D Panel does not have a standard-control counterpart. A 3D panel can act like a frame or a label. You can use a 3D panel to catch the user's attention. The panel can be used as a frame, to hold other controls, or as a label with more flair, to fit in with the other 3D controls.

In the GRAPH application, you want to allow the user to choose how many data sets and points to graph. One way to accomplish this task is to use a label and a text box. The problem with using a label is that it cannot support a 3D font. All the other controls on the GRAPH application's form use the 3DFont property to implement raised letters with light shading. A standard label would look out of place. The panel is a valuable solution when it is combined with a text box. To implement this solution, complete the following steps:

1. Place two 3D panels on the form.

2. Modify the property values for the two 3D panels as follows:

Control	Property	Value
Panel3D1	Caption	Number of Data Sets:
	Font3D	1—Raised with Light Shading
	Height	885
	Left	100
	Name	pnlSets
	Top	135
	Width	3450
Panel3D2	Caption	Number of Data Points:
	Font3D	1—Raised with Light Shading
	Height	885
	Left	100
	Name	pnlPoints
	Top	1200
	Width	3450

A panel's appearance is controlled with special properties. A panel has beveled edges like a command button, but a panel allows you to modify the bevel as well as the border. The BevelWidth property specifies the width of the inner and outer bevels of the panel, while the BorderWidth property specifies the width of the border around the bevel area. Both of these properties can have values from 0 to 30. You can also modify the styles of the inner and outer bevels with the BevelInner and BevelOuter properties, respectively. You can choose from an inset, raised, or no bevel to create different effects.

The panel has the Outline, RoundedCorners, and ShadowColor properties. It also has four properties which change the background colors. The value of the FloodColor property specifies the background color inside the bevel area. The FloodType, FloodPercent, and FloodShowPct properties allow you to create a visual gauge. FloodType determines whether the panel will display a gauge and, if so, how color will be used as a status indicator for the gauge. The value of FloodType can be 0—no gauge (the caption, if any, is displayed), 1—left to right (panel is painted in a color which moves from the left inner bevel to the right bevel as the value of FloodPercent increases), 2—right to left, 3—top to bottom (the flood color fills from the top inner bevel downward), 4—bottom to top, or 5—widening circle (the flood color fills in an enlarging circle starting from the center of the panel). FloodPercent is a run-time only property which specifies the percentage of the painted area to fill. FloodShowPct determines whether the panel displays a gauge at all: True means that the value of FloodPercent determines the amount of the filled color, while False means that the current value of FloodPercent is not displayed as a gauge.

By specifying the Caption property for a panel, you create a kind of 3D label. The placement of the caption inside the panel can be changed with the Alignment property. A panel offers several alignment choices. You can align the caption to the left, right, or center, but you can also adjust the vertical alignment to the top, middle, or bottom.

In addition to the Alignment property, the AutoSize property allows you to control the size of the panel based on the caption or any controls placed in the panel. You can set the value of AutoSize to 0—no autosizing (the default), 1—autosize the panel width to the size of the caption, 2—autosize the panel height to the size of the caption, or 3—autosize a control placed inside the panel to fit exactly within the panel.

For the sample application, the two panels will allow the user to choose the data sets and points. To accomplish this task, you must place a text box inside each panel. To complete the panels for the GRAPH application, modify the property values of *both* panels as follows:

1. Change the value of Alignment to 1—left justify, middle.

2. Change the values of BevelInner and BevelOuter to 1—Inset.

3. Change the values of BevelWidth and BorderWidth to 4.

4. Place a text box inside each panel. The Text1 control goes in the pnlSets panel while the Text2 control goes in the pnlPoints panel.

5. Modify the text box properties as follows:

Control	Property	Value
Text1	Height	360
	Left	2430
	Name	txtSets
	Text	4
	Top	240
	Width	420
Text2	Height	360
	Left	2430
	Name	txtPoints
	Top	225
	Text	4
	Width	420

After these steps are completed, the form should look like Figure 32.5.

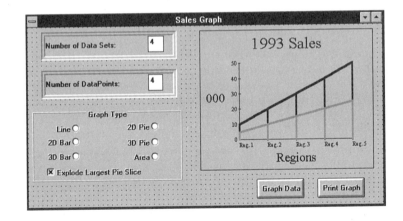

3D Push Button

The 3D Group Push Button, or simply 3D Push Button, is the last of the 3D controls. It is designed to let you create toolbars similar to the Visual Basic Toolbar. A 3D push button appears to be either up (raised from the form) or down (pushed in to the form). The up or down state of a push button changes each time you click it. A push button can function as part of a group (like an option button), or alone as a toggle (like a check box).

The operation and appearance of a push button are controlled with properties. The value of the GroupNumber property indicates whether a push button acts independently (like a check box) or as part of a group of controls (like an option button). By default, the value of GroupNumber is 1. This means that the push button is part of the first group of push buttons. It can be turned on with a mouse click and turned off when one of the other push buttons in that group is activated.

Two push buttons are in the same group when the values of their GroupNumbers properties are the same. The maximum value of GroupNumbers is 99, which means that you can have up to 99 different groups on each form. You can set the value of GroupNumbers to 0 to make a push button independent from all others. The state of a push button with GroupNumbers set to 0 does not depend on the state of any other push button.

The GroupAllowAllUp property specifies whether one button in a group must be depressed at all times, or whether all the buttons can be turned off at the same time. If this property is set to True, all the buttons may be up at the same time.

In addition to the Autosize, BevelWidth, Outline, and RoundedCorners properties which affect a push button's appearance, you can specify a bitmapped graphic image to display inside the button. There are four properties that manipulate the picture shown in a push button. When a user clicks a push button, the picture can change according to the state of the button. You can use the PictureUp, PictureDn, and PictureDisabled properties to indicate different graphic images when the button is in the up, down, and disabled state, respectively; use PictureDnChange to specify what happens to the PictureUp bitmap when the push button is clicked.

The PictureDnChange property has meaning when a PictureUp bitmap, but no PictureDn bitmap, is specified. In this case, the value of PictureDnChange determines how the PictureUp bitmap is modified when the push button is clicked. If the value of PictureDnChange is 0, no modification takes place; that is, the PictureUp bitmap displays whether the button is up or down. If the value of PictureDnChange is 1 (the default), the PictureUp graphic image is dithered when the button is clicked. A value of 2 means that the graphic image is inverted. *Dithering* is the process of changing every other pixel with the BackColor color to white. The effect is to make the bitmapped image appear as if it is on lighter gray background.

The most common use of push buttons is to create toolbars. A toolbar provides quick access to menu options. In the next sample application, you create just such a toolbar.

The Spin Button

The Spin Button control is a button that is separated into two halves. The user can click the top or bottom half to increment or decrement a counter. That counter could be implemented on-screen with a text box or a label standard control.

To access the Spin control, you need to have SPIN.VBX loaded into your project. You must ship that file along with any executable version of your application.

The GRAPH application can utilize spin buttons. The application has two text boxes used to change the number of data sets and points. The user may not know how many sets and points are possible. The addition of a spin button alongside each text box allows the user to click the value up or down to arrive at the number desired.

As with other controls, the appearance of a spin button is specified with property values. The SpinOrientation property determines whether the spin control is aligned horizontally or vertically. The BorderColor and BorderThickness properties specify the color and thickness of the border. The TdThickness, LightColor, and ShadeColor properties control the thickness of the margin and the upper and lower margin colors. You can add a shadow with the ShadowBackColor, ShadowForecolor, and ShadowThickness properties. With the Delay property, you can indicate how long the control pauses before registering the effect of a click.

In addition to the appearance factors, you must add code to tell the program what to do if the user clicks on the upper or lower half of a spin button. This code goes in the SpinUp and SpinDown event procedures, respectively. For the GRAPH application, you will add this code in the next section. First, follow these steps to add spin buttons to the GRAPH application:

1. Add one spin button in each panel—to the right of the text box. Visual Basic names these spin buttons Spin1 and Spin2, respectively.

2. Change the property values for these spin buttons as follows:

Control	Property	Value
Spin1	Height	390
	Left	3000
	Name	spnSets
	Top	195
	Width	300
Spin2	Height	390
	Left	3000
	Name	spnPoints
	Top	270
	Width	300

The user interface is complete for the GRAPH application and should appear like the form shown in Figure 32.6.

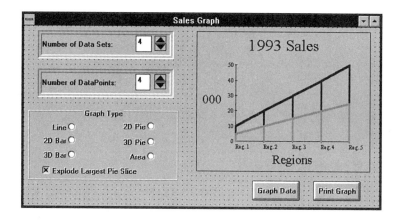

Figure 32.6.

The Completed Sales
Graph form.

Adding Code for the GRAPH Application

The interface is complete, but to generate the graph, you must add code that modifies the graph properties at run time. Before adding code, you need to reset some of the properties that were changed interactively by completing the following steps:

1. Select gphSales (the graph control) and open the Properties window.

2. Change the value of DataReset to 9—All Data.

3. Change the value of GraphStyle to 0—Default graph.

4. Change the value of DrawMode to 1—Clear.

To add code for the custom controls in Visual Basic's Professional Edition, as with the standard controls, you need to access the Code window for that control and event procedure. You then add your code between the Sub and End Sub statements. For the GRAPH application, code needs to be added to change the graph settings for data sets and points, to change the graph type, to generate the graph, and to print the graph.

Coding for the Data Sets and Points

To properly implement the data sets and points, you must code the Change events for the two text boxes. Inside those event procedures, the Text properties are converted to integer values, and the resulting numbers are assigned to the NumSets and NumPoints properties. Also, a warning message is displayed if the user types an invalid number into one of the text boxes. Create the following event procedures:

```
Sub txtSets_Change ()
    If CInt(txtSets.Text) >= 1 And CInt(txtSets.Text) <= 4 Then
        gphSales.NumSets = CInt(txtSets.Text)
    Else
        Msg$ = "You have entered an invalid number of sets."
        MsgBox Msg$
        txtSets.Text = "4"
    End If
End Sub

Sub txtPoints_Change ()
    If CInt(txtPoints.Text) >= 2 And CInt(txtPoints.Text) <= 4 Then
        gphSales.NumPoints = CInt(txtPoints.Text)
    Else
        Msg$ = "You have entered an invalid number of points."
        MsgBox Msg$
        txtPoints.Text = "4"
    End If
End Sub
```

Coding the Spin Buttons

The contents of the text boxes must also be modified when the user clicks on the upper or lower portion of one of the spin buttons. The necessary code goes into the SpinUp and SpinDown event procedures for each spin button. These procedures increment or decrement the Text property of the associated text box. The code also must designate the lowest value or the highest value when the value in the text box hits the upper and lower limits permitted for this application. Create the following event procedures:

```
Sub spnSets_SpinUp ()
    If CInt(txtSets.Text) = 4 Then
        txtSets.Text = 1
```

```
        Else
            txtSets.Text = Str$(CInt(txtSets.Text) + 1)
        End If
    End Sub

    Sub spnSets_SpinDown ()
        If CInt(txtSets.Text) = 1 Then
            txtSets.Text = 4
        Else
            txtSets.Text = Str$(CInt(txtSets.Text) — 1)
        End If
    End Sub

    Sub spnPoints_SpinUp ()
        If CInt(txtPoints.Text) = 4 Then
            txtPoints.Text = 2
        Else
            txtPoints.Text = Str$(CInt(txtPoints.Text) + 1)
        End If
    End Sub

    Sub spnPoints_SpinDown ()
        If CInt(txtPoints.Text) = 2 Then
            txtPoints.Text = 4
        Else
            txtPoints.Text = Str$(CInt(txtPoints.Text) — 1)
        End If
    End Sub
```

Coding the Type Options

After the user chooses the number of data sets and points, the user then
selects a graph type and chooses whether to explode the largest pie slice
(if 2D or 3D pie chart is selected). This is accomplished with code for the 3D
option button array. Create the following Click procedure:

```
Sub OptType_Click (Index As Integer, Value As Integer)
    Select Case Index
        Case 0
            gphSales.GraphType = 6    ' Line
            chkExplode.Visible = False
```

```
        Case 1
            gphSales.GraphType = 3    ' 2D Bar
            chkExplode.Visible = False
        Case 2
            gphSales.GraphType = 4    ' 3D Bar
            chkExplode.Visible = False
        Case 3
            gphSales.GraphType = 1    ' 2D Pie
            txtSets.Text = "1"
            chkExplode.Visible = True
        Case 4
            gphSales.GraphType = 2    ' 3D Pie
            txtSets.Text = "1"
            chkExplode.Visible = True
        Case 5
            gphSales.GraphType = 8    ' Area
            chkExplode.Visible = False
    End Select
End Sub
```

Coding for Graphing and Printing

Once the number of data sets and points and the graph type is selected, graph must be generated. To produce the graph, you must add code to reset the data before each graph operation, to add the labels, to add any legends, and to write the actual graph data. When this data is specified, the code changes the value of the DrawMode property to actually draw the graph. For the Print command button, you must change the value of DrawMode to activate Print mode. Create the following event procedures:

```
Sub cmdGraph_Click ()
    gphSales.DataReset = 1     'Reset the Data
    gphSales.DataReset = 3     'Reset the ExtraData
    gphSales.DataReset = 4     'Reset the Labels
    gphSales.DataReset = 5     'Reset the Legends

    gphSales.AutoInc = 1
    For i% = 1 To CInt(txtPoints.Text)
        gphSales.LabelText = "Region" + Str$(i%)
    Next i%
```

```
        gphSales.AutoInc = 1
        If CInt(txtSets.Text) <> 1 Then
            For i% = 1 To CInt(txtSets.Text)
                Select Case i%
                    Case 1
                        gphSales.LegendText = "1st Qtr"
                    Case 2
                        gphSales.LegendText = "2nd Qtr"
                    Case 3
                        gphSales.LegendText = "3rd Qtr"
                    Case 4
                        gphSales.LegendText = "4th Qtr"
                End Select
            Next i%
        End If

        gphSales.AutoInc = 1
        For s% = 1 To CInt(txtSets.Text)
            For p% = 1 To CInt(txtPoints.Text)
                gphSales.GraphData = s% * p% + 10
            Next p%
        Next s%

        If OptType(3).Value = True Or OptType(4).Value = True Then
            If chkExplode = True Then
                gphSales.ThisSet = 1
                gphSales.ThisPoint = CInt(txtPoints.Text)
                gphSales.ExtraData = 1
            End If
        End If
        gphSales.DrawMode = 2
End Sub

Sub cmdPrint_Click ()
    gphSales.DrawMode = 5
End Sub
```

The application is now ready to run. Start it and then click the Graph Data button. The result is the graph shown in Figure 32.7. Experiment with producing different graph types and with printing a graph. Then stop the application. Save the form as GRAPH.FRM and the application as GRAPH.MAK.

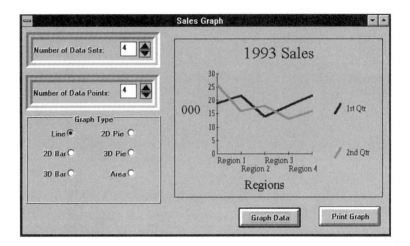

Masked Edit

The Masked Edit control serves as a possible replacement for a text box, allowing greater screening and manipulation of user input. To illustrate the Masked Edit control (and other custom controls), a second sample application will be created. This application works with phone numbers.

Setting Up the Application

To create the phone numbers example, follow these steps:

1. Access the **File** menu and select **New Project**.

2. Using the Menu Design window, create an &File menu named mnuFile. Create the following submenus under this File menu: &Open, &Save, Save &As, &Print, and E&xit. Name these submenu options mnuFileOpen, mnuFileSave, mnuFileSaveAs, mnuFilePrint, and mnuFileExit respectively.

3. Place a separator bar between the &Print and E&xit menus. Name this separator bar mnuSep1.

4. Create an &Options main menu named mnuOpt. Create the following submenus under this Options menu: &Attributes and &Color. Name these submenus mnuOptAttr and mnuOptColor respectively.

5. Add the following submenu options to the Attributes menu: &Bold, &Italic, and &Underline. Name these submenus mnuOptAttrBold, mnuOptAttrItalic, and mnuOptAttrUnderline respectively.

6. Set the `Checked` property for the `&Bold` submenu.

7. Add two labels and a text box to the form: `Label1`, `Label2`, and `Text1`.

8. Modify various property values as shown in Table 32.3

Table 32.3. Application properties.

Control	Property	Value
Form1	Caption	Phone Numbers
	Height	3045
	Name	frmPhone
	Width	7485
Label1	Caption	Name:
	Height	255
	Left	600
	Name	lblName
	Top	1000
	Width	855
Label2	Caption	Telephone Number:
	Height	255
	Left	5160
	Name	lblPhone
	Top	1000
	Width	1815
Text1	Height	450
	Left	600
	Name	txtName
	Top	1320
	Width	3650
	Text	(blank) 'clear contents of text box

After these changes have been made, the form should resemble the one shown in Figure 32.8 and the menus should resemble those shown in Figure 32.9.

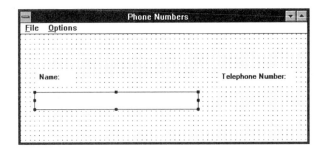

Figure 32.8.

The Phone Numbers Form.

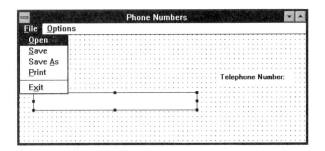

Figure 32.9.

The **F**ile and **O**ptions
menus.

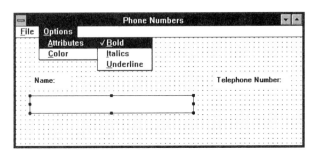

8. Create the following Click procedures for the **S**ave menu, E**x**it menu, and attribute menus:

```
Sub mnuFileExit_Click ()
    End
End Sub

Sub mnuFileSave_Click ()
    If PhoneFile <> "" Then
        MsgBox "File has been saved as " + PhoneFile
        Open PhoneFile For Output As #1
        Print #1, RepName
```

```
        Print #1, Number
        Close #1
    Else
        mnuFileSaveAs_Click
    End If
End Sub

Sub mnuOptAttrBold_Click ()
    mnuOptAttrBold.Checked = Not mnuOptAttrBold.Checked
    If mnuOptAttrBold.Checked = True Then
        txtName.FontBold = True
    Else
        txtName.FontBold = False
    End If
End Sub

Sub mnuOptAttrItalic_Click ()
    mnuOptAttrItalic.Checked = Not mnuOptAttrItalic.Checked
    If mnuOptAttrItalic.Checked = True Then
        txtName.FontItalic = True
    Else
        txtName.FontItalic = False
    End If
End Sub

Sub mnuOptAttrUnderline_Click ()
    mnuOptAttrUnderline.Checked = Not mnuOptAttrUnderline.Checked
    If mnuOptAttrUnderline.Checked = True Then
        txtName.FontUnderline = True
    Else
        txtName.FontUnderline = False
    End If
End Sub
```

Adding the Masked Edit Control

For purposes of manipulating user input, a masked edit control offers greater flexibility than a text box. Masked edit is especially valuable for numeric input. The sample application has a text box for the user to type a name but it still needs a place for the user to type the telephone number. Another text box could be used, but that would require the user to determine the correct format for the number and might needlessly result in the user typing excess information. Using a masked edit control instead of the text box gives you an opportunity to solve the user's dilemma and more easily screen the input.

To access the Masked Edit control, the application must have the MSMASKED.VBX file included in the project. With this file included, a masked edit control can be placed on a form in the same manner as a text box. A masked edit control looks like a text box—without the text. For this application, once a masked edit control is placed on the form, you set property values so that the control guides the user toward entering the required information.

The first step is to change the value of the Mask property to create a template for the user to complete. You specify this input mask with a string code similar to those used with the Format function, except that with Mask you can specify alphanumeric input with the *A* character. The maximum number of characters that the user can type in a masked edit control is specified by the MaxLength property.

The value of the Format property can be modified if you want to display the control's text in a different format than was used for the Mask. That is, the Format property determines the appearance of the typed information after the user has entered it.

You can also specify what happens as the user types information while the masked edit control has the focus. When no data has been entered, the empty data slots are indicated by an underline. As data is entered, the FontUnderline property determines whether the underline disappears. The default is False, which causes the underline to disappear.

You also can specify what happens when information is added, cut, or copied. The AutoTab property determines whether the focus shifts to the next tab stop after the information has been entered. This property is very useful for the speed typist. The HideSelection property can hide the display of information in the masked edit control when it loses the focus.

You can eliminate a keystroke for the user by shifting the focus automatically. You can also control what happens to the literal characters when the information is cut or copied to the Clipboard with the ClipMode property. By default, the value is True, and the literals are cut or copied with the numbers.

When you want to assign the information to another control or variable, you can use the FormattedText property or the FormattedText property. The Text property assigns the entire string including literals and underscores that are part of the input mask, while the FormattedText property assigns the string without the literals. The FormattedText property can be read at run time, but you cannot assign it a new value in program code.

If you want to cut or copy only the selected or highlighted information in the masked edit control, you can use the SelText property (just like a text box). You can use the ClipText property to get only the selected text (without the literal characters).

For the sample application, a masked edit control provides an entry area for the telephone number. Complete these steps to add a masked edit control to the form:

1. Place a masked edit control on the form.

2. Modify property values for the masked edit control as follows:

Property	Value
Height	450
Left	5160
Mask	(###) ### - ####
MaxLength	16
Name	mskPhone
Top	1320
Width	2055

The form should now appear as shown in Figure 32.10.

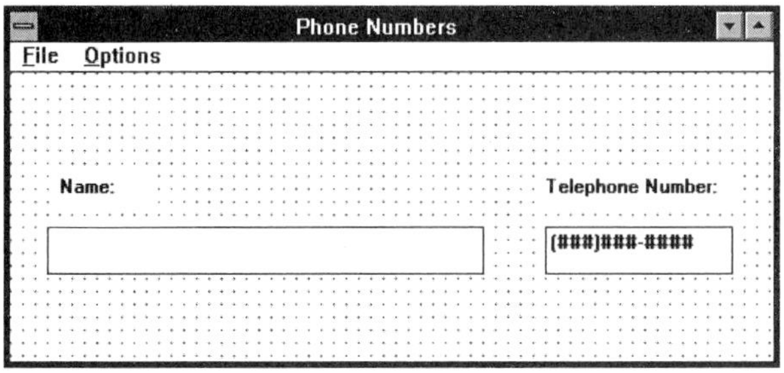

Figure 32.10.

A masked edit control is added.

The Common Dialog Control

Now that the user interface is in place, you need to add code to complete the task of implementing the menu items. The Common Dialog control offers a convenient way to accomplish this task. For further discussion of this control, see Chapter 29, "Manipulating the Windows Environment."

Recall that before the release of Visual Basic 3.0, the Common Dialog custom control was available only with the Professional Edition of Visual Basic. However, with Version 3.0, the Common Dialog control is now provided with the Standard Edition as well.

A common dialog control can be placed on a form to access the standard Open, Save, Print, Help, Color, and Font dialog boxes. To use this control, the CMDIALOG.VBX file must be included in the project. When a common dialog control is placed on the form, you can access all these standard dialog boxes by modifying various property values.

For the sample application, a common dialog control is used to access the Open, Save, Print, and Color dialog boxes. Accessing Help is discussed in Chapter 33, "Adding a Help System to an Application."

For the sample application, the information on the form will be saved to a sequential file. The first step is to place a common dialog control on the form as shown in Figure 32.11. In the figure, notice that the control is placed near the lower right corner of the form.

Adding the CONSTANT.TXT File

The CONSTANT.TXT file defines a number of constants useful when coding the event procedures for the common dialog control. Follow these steps to add a code module to the application and to place a copy of CONSTANT.TXT into that code module.

1. Choose the **Add** File option from the **File** menu.

2. When the Add File dialog box appears, specify the CONSTANT.TXT file. This file should be located in your Visual Basic directory. The complete path is likely to be C:\VB\CONSTANT.TXT.

3. Click the OK button to close the Add File dialog box.

You now have a copy of CONSTANT.TXT loaded into your project as a code module. Notice that CONSTANT.TXT is listed in the Project window. You can view the contents of the file by selecting (highlighting) CONSTANT.TXT in the Project window and then clicking the View Code button. The section of constants relevant to the Common Dialog control begins with the following lines:

```
'Common Dialog Control
'--------------------
'Action Property
Global Const DLG_FILE_OPEN = 1
Global Const DLG_FILE_SAVE = 2
  .
  .
```

Coding the Form's General Declarations

The sample application uses some form-level string variables in conjunction with the common dialog control. Add the following lines to the general declarations section of the form:

```
Dim Number As String * 16
Dim RepName As String
Dim PhoneFile As String
```

Coding the Change Event Procedures

The masked edit control mskPhone and the text box control txtName must update the values of the Number and RepName string variables, respectively, whenever the user types new data into the controls. To update these values, create the following Change event procedures:

```
Sub mskPhone_Change ()
    Number = mskPhone.Text
End Sub

Sub txtName_Change ()
    RepName = txtName.Text
End Sub
```

Creating the File Save Dialog Box

The common dialog control is used to implement several of the sample application's menu options. The first menu option to tackle is the Save operation. The application's **F**ile menu contains a **S**ave and a Save **As** option.

The Save **As** option lets you specify a file name when saving the data on disk. The **S**ave option updates an existing file assuming that the data has been saved previously. If the data has not been saved previously, the **S**ave option automatically invokes Save **As**. The common dialog control accesses the standard Windows' Save dialog box to implement these menu options.

With the Common Dialog control, you have to set up the properties for a dialog box, activate the dialog box, and act on the results, as well as take care of some basic error checking. The code for mnuFileSaveAs_Click procedure is shown below. Add this procedure to the sample application.

```
Sub mnuFileSaveAs_Click ()
    On Error Resume Next
```

```
'Set the dialog properties
CMDialog1.CancelError = True
CMDialog1.DefaultExt = "PHN"
CMDialog1.Filter = "Phone Files(*.PHN)|*.PHN"
CMDialog1.Flags = OFN_PATHMUSTEXIST Or OFN_OVERWRITEPROMPT Or
➥OFN_SHOWHELP

'Access the Save As dialog box
CMDialog1.Action = 2
'Store the filename to a variable
If Err = 32755 Then  'Cancel is selected
    Exit Sub
Else
    PhoneFile = CMDialog1.Filename
End If

'Save the data to the file
Open PhoneFile For Output As #1
Print #1, RepName
Print #1, Number
Close #1
frmPhone.Caption = frmPhone.Caption & " - " & PhoneFile
End Sub
```

The instruction which assigns a value to the Flags property uses several constant names that begin with OFN. These are references to constants defined in CONSTANT.TXT. The constants in that file typically consist of all uppercase letters. Similar constant names appear in the program code throughout the remainder of this chapter.

The On Error Resume Next instruction enables error checking while this procedure executes. If an error occurs, this instruction forces the code to continue executing.

The next several lines specify various property values for the Save dialog box. The CancelError property controls what happens if the user clicks the Cancel button while the dialog box is displayed. The value of True causes an error condition to occur if the Cancel button is selected. If this happens, the error is intercepted and processed in the instruction that begins If Err = 32755.

The DefaultExt property specifies the extension to be used for the file if the user fails to type an extension. The Filter property specifies the list of file types and extensions listed in the file type list. The sample code shows one file type, but you can specify more than one by separating each type and extension with the vertical bar character (|).

The `Flags` property is the last property that needs to be set before the dialog box is accessed. Values for this property can be assigned using constants defined in the CONSTANT.TXT file which you have loaded into the code module.

The `Flags` property for the Save dialog box has 13 possible values. These values are defined in CONSTANT.TXT and listed in Table 32.4. You only have to specify the values that you want to use. You can combine two or more values by using the `Or` operator as demonstrated in the code for the `mnuFileSaveAs_Click` procedure.

Table 32.4. *Flags* property values for the Save As dialog box.

Value	Definition
OFN_ALLOWMULTISELECT	Allows the user to choose more than one file from the file list.
OFN_CREATEPROMPT	Asks the user whether to create a file that does not exist.
OFN_EXTENSIONDIFFERENT	Indicates if the chosen file has a different extension than the default.
OFN_FILEMUSTEXIST	Forces the user to enter a file name that already exists.
OFN_HIDEREADONLY	Hides the read-only check box.
OFN_NOCHANGEDIR	Does not allow the user to switch to another directory.
OFN_NOREADONLYRETURN	Forces the file to be opened without the Read-only bit set.
OFN_NOVALIDATE	Will not validate the file name entered by the user for invalid characters.
OFN_OVERWRITEPROMPT	Prompts the user if the file name chosen already exists and the action overwrites the contents.
OFN_PATHMUSTEXIST	Allows the user to enter only valid pathnames.
OFN_READONLY	Forces the chosen file to open with the Read-only bit set to prevent editing changes.
OFN_SHAREAWARE	Causes the dialog box to ignore the sharing violation errors.
OFN_SHOWHELP	Places the Help command button on the dialog box.

After the properties are set, the Save As dialog box needs to be activated. This is accomplished by assigning a value of 2 to the `Action` property. (Other values of Action activate other dialog boxes.) The common dialog control handles all the processing when the dialog box is open. When the user selects the OK or Cancel buttons, the dialog box closes and execution returns back to the application. You must add code to deal with each of these cases.

When the value of the `CancelError` property is set to True, selecting the Cancel button generates runtime error 32755. At that point, the code for saving the file should not be processed. To eliminate the processing, an `Exit Sub` instruction is used.

When the user clicks the OK button, the dialog box closes. The common dialog control assigns values for the `FileName` and `FileTitle` properties. `FileName` specifies the file name including the complete path; `FileTitle` is the file name without the path. You can choose which one you want to use. In this application, the value of the `FileName` property is assigned to the form-level string variable `PhoneFile`.

The remaining instructions save the name and phone number data entered by the user. The data is saved on a sequential disk file using the file name specified by the user in the Save dialog box.

Creating the File Open Dialog Box

The next menu option for which you need to add code is the **O**pen option on the File menu. The same `CMDialog1` control used for the previous procedure is also used for this procedure. The properties that control the Open dialog box are the same as those properties that control the Save dialog box.

You assign a value of 1 to the `Action` property to activate the Open dialog box. When the user specifies a file name in the dialog box, the code can determine this file name with the `FileName` or `FileTitle` properties. For the sample application, create the following event procedure:

```
Sub mnuFileOpen_Click ()
    On Error Resume Next
    'Set the dialog properties
    CMDialog1.CancelError = True
    CMDialog1.DefaultExt = "PHN"
    CMDialog1.Filter = "Phone Files(*.PHN)¦*.PHN"
    CMDialog1.Flags = OFN_SHOWHELP Or OFN_FILEMUSTEXIST

    'Access the Open dialog box
    CMDialog1.Action = 1
    'Store the filename to a variable
```

```
    If Err = 32755 Then
        Exit Sub
    Else
        PhoneFile = CMDialog1.Filename
    End If

    'Get the data from the file
    Open PhoneFile For Input As #1
    Line Input #1, RepName
    Line Input #1, Number
    Close #1

    txtName.Text = RepName
    mskPhone.Text = Number
    frmPhone.Caption = frmPhone.Caption & " - " & PhoneFile
End Sub
```

Creating the Print Dialog Box

The Common Dialog control has assisted you with the file operations, and it can assist with printing as well. Rather than designing and programming your own Print dialog box, you can access the standard Windows' Print dialog box with the common dialog control.

You use the Print dialog box much as you do the other dialog boxes available with the common dialog control. You must specify property values, assign 5 to the Action property, and then act on the results.

You can specify several attributes of the Print dialog box with the Flags property. You can choose from among the 16 values listed in Table 32.5.

Table 32.5. *Flags* property values for the Print dialog box.

Value	Definition
PD_ALLPAGES	Specifies the All Pages button.
PD_COLLATE	Specifies use of the Collate check box.
PD_DISABLEPRINTTOFILE	Disables the Print to File check box.
PD_HIDEPRINTTOFILE	Makes the Print to File check box invisible.
PD_NOPAGENUMS	Disables the capability to select a number of pages to print.

continues

Table 32.5. Continued

Value	Definition
PD_NOSELECTION	Disables the Selection option button.
PD_NOWARNING	Does not display a warning message if there is no default printer.
PD_PAGENUMS	Specifies the use of the Pages button choice.
PD_PRINTSETUP	Displays the Printer SetUp dialog box instead of the Print dialog box.
PD_PRINTTOFILE	Allows the user to print to a file.
PD_RETURNDC	Returns a device context for the printer in the dialog box.
PD_RETURNDEFAULT	Displays the default printer.
PD_RETURNIC	Returns information about the printer without creating the device context.
PD_SELECTION	Enables the Selection option button
PD_SHOWHELP.	Displays the Help button in the dialog box.
PD_USEDEVMODECOPIES	Prevents the use of the copies text box if the printer cannot support multiple copies.

If the user will be able to specify a number of pages to print, you can specify the minimum and maximum page numbers to print using the Min and Max properties. You can also allow the user to change the default printer by setting the value of the PrinterDefault property to True.

After the other property values are specified, the Print dialog box is accessed by specifying a value of 5 for the Action property. When the user has made selections in the dialog box, the choices are returned with the Copies, FromPage, ToPage, and hDC properties.

Copies returns the number of copies specified, ToPage and FromPage return the page numbers to print (based on the Page selection choices), and hDC identifies the selected printer within the Windows environment.

These properties can be assigned to variables or used directly to print the output. The hDC property is only necessary if you are going to let the user choose a printer that isn't the default. This will require some additional programming using the Microsoft Windows Software Developer's Kit.

For the sample application, the code for the Print option is as follows:

```
Sub mnuFilePrint_Click ()
    On Error Resume Next
    ' Set the CMDialog parameters
```

```
    CMDialog1.CancelError = True
    CMDialog1.Flags = PD_ALLPAGES Or PD_DISABLEPRINTTOFILE Or
    ➥PD_NOPAGENUMS Or PD_SHOWHELP
    CMDialog1.Min = 1
    CMDialog1.Max = 9999

    'Access the Print Dialog Box
    CMDialog1.Action = 5
    If Err = 32755 Then Exit Sub

    'Store dialog properties in variables
    Copies% = CMDialog1.Copies

    'Send the output to the printer
    For i% = 1 To Copies%
        Printer.Print "Name"; Tab(50); "Telephone Number"
        Printer.Print txtName.Text; Tab(50); Number
        Printer.NewPage
    Next i%
    Printer.EndDoc
End Sub
```

Creating the Color Dialog Box

For the sample application, the Options menu allows you to change the
Background Color for the form. Once again, using the common dialog control
is more efficient that creating your own Color dialog box.

The process is the same as you have been using. By taking advantage of the
existing common dialog control, you assign a value to the Flags property,
activate the dialog box, and use returned property values to modify the
background color. Create the following event procedure:

```
Sub mnuOptColor_Click ()
    On Error Resume Next
    ' Set up the properties
    CMDialog1.CancelError = True
    CMDialog1.Flags = CC_FULLOPEN Or CC_RGBINIT Or CC_SHOWHELP

    'Access the dialog
    CMDialog1.Action = 3   'Color dialog box
    If Err = 32755 Then Exit Sub
```

```
                    'Apply the choices
                    frmPhone.BackColor = CMDialog1.Color
                    lblName.BackColor = CMDialog1.Color
                    lblPhone.BackColor = CMDialog1.Color
                    txtName.BackColor = CMDialog1.Color
                    mskPhone.BackColor = CMDialog1.Color
                End Sub
```

For the Color dialog box, the Flags property has four possible values: CC_RGBINIT sets the initial color value which appears in the dialog box; CC_FULLOPEN and CC_PREVENTFULLOPEN determine whether the user will see the custom color portion when the Color dialog box opens; and CC_SHOWHELP adds the Help button to the dialog.

Creating the Font Dialog Box

The Common Dialog control also provides access to the standard Windows Font dialog box. This dialog box permits the selection of both screen fonts and printer fonts. You access this dialog box by specifying a value of 4 for the Action property.

The Font dialog box is not used in the sample application. For more information about using Font dialog boxes, see Chapter 29, "Manipulating the Windows Environment."

Creating a Toolbar

You have just written code for the sample application to activate the various menu options. However, power users often want to use the keyboard to quickly execute commands and avoid the menu system altogether. With the Menu Design window, you can give power users access keys and shortcut key combinations.

Another way to let power users bypass the menus is to provide a toolbar. A toolbar contains a series of buttons which display various icons. When the user clicks one of the buttons on a toolbar, the associated menu command is immediately executed.

You can build a toolbar for the sample application using a 3D panel, command buttons, and push buttons. The graphic images displayed in the toolbar can be icons when command buttons are used or bitmaps for the push buttons. The graphics used for this application's toolbar will be standard graphics that ship with the Professional Edition of Visual Basic.

In the sample application, the File menu has an **O**pen submenu and the Options menu has various attribute submenus. Such items often have toolbar buttons.

A command-type item, such as the Open command, is best represented in the toolbar with a 3D command button. That's because these buttons provide a pleasant 3D effect and they automatically release after being selected.

An attribute-type item can be well represented with a 3D push button because such a button can toggle between an up and down state. As the user turns an attribute on and off, the associated 3D push button visually indicates the current state.

To add a toolbar to the sample application, follow these steps:

1. Add a 3D panel to the form and modify its property values as follows:

Property	Value
Align	1 'Align Top
BevelInner	1 'Inset
BevelOuter	1 'Inset
BevelWidth	2
BorderWidth	2
Caption	(blank) 'remove existing text
Height	735
Width	7365

2. Add a 3D command button to the panel and modify its property values as follows:

Property	Value
BevelWidth	3
Caption	(blank) 'remove existing text
Height	495
Left	240
Name	cmdOpen
Picture	Icon = Folder02.ICO from C:\VB\ICONS\OFFICE
Top	100
Width	615

3. Add a 3D push button to the panel and modify its property values as follows:

Property	Value
GroupNumber	0
Height	450
Left	2040
Name	pshAttr
Top	150
Width	450

4. Copy the push button to the Clipboard.

5. Paste two more push buttons on to the panel, creating a control array.

6. Modify the property values for the control array as follows:

Control	Property	Value
pshAttr(0)	Left	2040
	PictureUp	Bitmap BLD-UP.BMP *
	Top	150
pshAttr(1)	Left	2520
	PictureUp	Bitmap ITL-UP.BMP *
	Top	150
pshAttr(2)	Left	3000
	PictureUp	Bitmap ULIN-UP.BMP *
	Top	150

*All of the bitmap files are located in the C:\VB\BITMAPS\TOOLBAR3 directory.

7. Create the following two event procedures:

```
Sub cmdOpen_Click
    mnuFileOpen_Click
End Sub
```

```
Sub pshAttr_Click (Index As Integer, Value As Integer)
    Select Case Index
        Case 0
            mnuOptAttrBold_Click
        Case 1
            mnuOptAttrItalic_Click
        Case 2
            mnuOptAttrUnderline_Click
    End Select
End Sub
```

The Key Status Control

Another addition to the toolbar that is valuable to the touch typist is an on-screen key status toggle indicator for the NumLock, CapsLock, ScrollLock, and the Insert keys. The Key Status control not only provides on-screen information about those keys, but the user also can modify the state of the keys by clicking the Key Status control.

To use the Key Status control, the KEYSTAT.VBX file must be added to the project file. After that addition, the control can be placed on the form and the `Style` property adjusted to indicate which key's status is displayed on screen. You can also modify the size of the key status button using the `Height` and `Width` properties when the `AutoSize` property is set to False.

In order to display the current state of a key, the application must periodically check the status of that key. You can adjust the time interval used to check the key by modifying the value of the `TimerInterval` property. The `Value` property indicates the status of the key specified by the `Style` property. When `Value` is True, the key status is on (pressed); when `Value` is False, the key status is off.

For the sample application, a touch typist might want to use the numeric keypad to enter the telephone number. A key status button for the NumLock key would be valuable. To place a NumLock status indicator on the toolbar panel, complete these steps:

1. Place a key status control on the panel.

2. Modify the following property values for the key status control:

Property	Value
Left	6840
Name	kysNumLock
Style	1 'NumLock

When this button is added to the application, the toolbar should look like Figure 32.12.

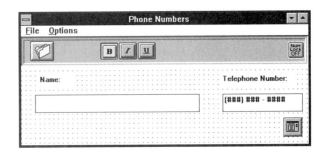

The Picture Clip Control

The Picture Clip control provides a way to cut down some of the overhead associated with many bitmaps stored in one application. For the sample application, each push button has a separate bitmap file. Each of those files becomes part of the executable file when you compile the project.

With a picture clip control, all the bitmaps can be combined into a single bitmap and referenced as one file.

Creating the Bitmap

A picture clip control allows you to specify the area to clip by giving clip positions or by using the `GraphicCell` property, which takes the height and width and divides by the number of rows and columns. For the toolbar in the sample application, you can use the `GraphicCell` method because each bitmap is the same size.

You need a single bitmap file which contains the three individual bitmap files. The new bitmap can have one row and three columns. One way to create the new bitmap is with the Windows Paintbrush application. To prepare the toolbar bitmap, complete these steps:

1. Start two copies of the Paintbrush program.

2. Access the Open dialog box in the second copy.

   To do so, choose the **O**pen option from the **F**ile menu.

3. Select the first bitmap C:\VB\BITMAPS\TOOLBAR3\BLD-UP.BMP but don't press Enter or click the OK button.

4. Select the Info... button in the Open dialog box.

   The image statistics appear in a window. Notice that the width is 24 and the height is 22.

5. Click OK to close the Picture Information window.

6. Click OK in the Open dialog box to open the file.

7. Select the first copy of Paintbrush.

8. Open the **O**ptions menu and select Image Attributes.

9. In the Units box, select "pels".

10. Change the Width to 72 and Height to 22 for a one-row, three-column cell map. Click OK.

    You must change the Image Size before you complete any artwork. Once you have modified the image, you cannot resize it. You must start over.

11. Select the second copy of Paintbrush.

12. Select the Scissors tool (the first one on the left) and draw a dotted outline around the picture.

    This task is best accomplished by placing the crosshair on the top-left corner, going to the right past the border, and then down past the bottom right border and to the left and to the top to complete the square. Using this method ensures that you get the whole image.

13. Choose the **C**opy option from the **E**dit menu to put a copy of the image in the Clipboard.

14. Select the first copy of Paintbrush and paste the image from the Clipboard.

15. Select the second copy of Paintbrush and open the second bitmap: C:\VB\BITMAPS\TOOLBAR3\ITL-UP.BMP.

16. Repeat steps 10 through 12.

17. Click and drag the pasted bitmap to the right of the first.

18. Repeat steps 13 through 15 for the third bitmap, C:\VB\BITMAPS\TOOLBAR3\ULIN-UP.BMP, but move it to the far right of the image.

19. Close the second copy of Paintbrush.

20. Save the new bitmap as JOIN.BMP.

21. Close the remaining copy of Paintbrush.

The new bitmap should look like the one in Figure 32.13.

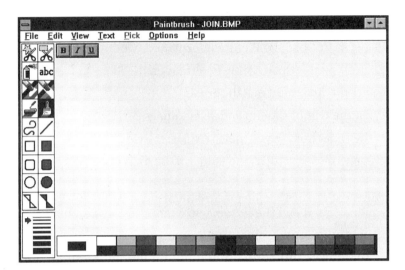

Figure 32.13.

The combined bitmap.

Adding the Picture Clip Control

After the combined bitmap is prepared, the application has to be modified to use a picture clip control. You must remove the earlier bitmaps you specified for each push button with `PictureUp` properties, extend the lower border of the form to accommodate the picture clip control, and add the code to reference the picture clip. Be sure that the PICCLIP.VBX file is loaded into the project before completing these steps:

1. Select the first (Bold) push button.

2. In the Properties Window, select the `PictureUp` property, double-click the entry line in the Settings box, and choose the **D**elete option from the **E**dit menu.

3. Repeat steps 1 and 2 for the other two push buttons (Italic and Underline).

4. Adjust the form's height to 5000.

5. Place a picture clip control on-screen at the bottom of the form.

6. Assign a value of 3 to the `Cols` property and a value of 1 to the `Rows` property.

7. Assign the JOIN.BMP file to the `Picture` property.

8. Add the following code to the `Form_Load` procedure to load the `GraphicCell` property information into each push button:

```
pshAttr(0).PictureUp = PicClip1.GraphicCell(0)
pshAttr(1).PictureUp = PicClip1.GraphicCell(1)
pshAttr(2).PictureUp = PicClip1.GraphicCell(2)
```

9. Make the form's height 3045. The picture clip control will be clipped from the visual portion of the form.

You can specify the portion of a bitmap using the ClipHeight, ClipWidth, ClipX, and ClipY properties of the Picture Clip control. You can specify a target size with the StretchX and StretchY properties if the bitmap sections are not a uniform size.

The bitmaps used for this sample application came from the standard set shipped with Visual Basic. The set includes the bitmaps for shapes, attributes, buttons, cameras, justification, tabs, and much more.

Running the Sample Application

Save the form as PHONE.FRM and the application as PHONE.MAK. Try running the application. You can type a name in the text box and a phone number in the masked edit control.

Select various menu options. Save the data to a file and then later open a saved file to restore the saved data. Try clicking the toolbar buttons to see the effects. Stop the application.

The Gauge

The Gauge control allows you to provide the user with clues on the progress of a task. For example, a gauge is often used to indicate what percentage of a task has been completed. To work with a gauge, you add the control to the form, set property values to specify the control's behavior, and create code to run it.

The Autosize, Height, and Width properties control the size of the gauge. The type of gauge is set with the Style property, with a choice of Horizontal Bar, Vertical Bar, SemiCircle, or Full Circle gauges.

The BackColor and ForeColor properties control the color of the gauge unless the Picture property is set; then color is controlled by the bitmap. The placement of the beginning fill area is specified with the InnerTop, InnerLeft, InnerRight, and InnerBottom properties. These properties are measured in pixels from the control's top, left, right, and bottom edges.

As with the scroll bars, you also have to set the Min and Max properties for the gauge scale. With the semicircle and full circle styles, you can control the width of the needle (in pixels) by using the NeedleWidth property.

The Value property specifies the placement of the needle or the level of the fill region during run time. You need to write code to change this property value. Follow these steps to create a sample application with a counter that increments the gauge to a value of 30 and then changes the text in a label:

1. Create a new project named GAUGE.MAK with one form named GAUGE.FRM.

2. Place a label, a timer, and a gauge on the form named as follows: Label1, Timer1, and Gauge1.

3. Assign the property values shown in Table 32.6.

Table 32.6. Property values for the GAUGE application.

Control	Property	Value
Form1	Caption	Gauge Example
	Height	4320
	Width	6420
Label1	Alignment	2 'Center
	Caption	In Progress
	Height	195
	Left	1950
	Top	2640
	Width	2415
Timer1	Interval	1000
	Left	5400
	Top	120
Gauge1	Autosize	False
	Height	1335
	InnerBottom	50

Control	Property	Value
Gauge 1	Left	2040
	Max	30
	NeedleWidth	2
	Picture	Bitmap C:\VB\BITMAPS\GAUGE\SEMICIRC.BMP
	Style	2
	Top	480
	Width	2055

4. Create the following Timer event procedure:

```
Sub Timer1_Timer ()
    Gauge1.Value = Gauge1.Value + 1
    If Gauge1.Value = 30 Then
        Label1.Caption = "Process is finished"
        Timer1.Enabled = False
    End If
End Sub
```

5. Run the application and watch the needle change with each second and the label change when the count is complete.

The Animated Button

The Animated Button control enables you to create a button that appears to change when selected. You can also use it to create a visual signpost to register a program's progress. This control can display a series of pictures sequentially. The result is animation, like a cartoon.

The current sample application uses a gauge to act as a counter for 30 seconds. An animated button can be added to this application to start the timer. The button shows a stoplight at the beginning. After the user clicks the button to start, the stoplight changes to green; at the halfway mark, the light changes to yellow. The button changes to red when the gauge is finished.

To create an animated button, you have to place the control on the form, determine what type of animation is required, set the button's appearance, plan the graphics, and create code to increment the counter to create the animation.

Adding the Control and Setting Its Type

The first step is to place the control on the form and determine the animation type by completing the following steps:

1. Verify that the ANIBUTON.VBX file is loaded into the project and place an animated button on the form. Visual Basic assigns the default name AniButton1 to this control.

2. Assign the following property values to the animated button:

Property	Value
Caption	Click to Begin
Cycle	1--By Frame
Height	735
Left	4560
Top	3000
Width	1215

The Cycle property indicates the animation type. With a value of 0, the animation is set to happen with one mouse click. This means that the first half of the frames appears when the mouse button is depressed and the second half appears when it is released. A value of 1 means that each frame is shown one at a time. A value of 2 shows half of the frames the first time the animated button is selected (clicked), and the remaining frames the second time the button is selected.

Setting the Animated Button's Appearance

Animated buttons have some special properties that specify the appearance of the buttons. When the value of ClearFirst is True, the button is cleared between the display of each frame. The HideFocusBox property specifies whether a gray outline appears around the button when it has been selected. With graphics, it is best to set ClearFirst to True to clean up the image.

The operation of the button can be changed with the ClickFilter and Speed properties. ClickFilter determines where in the button area a mouse click will be recognized. The Speed property specifies the delay time, in milliseconds, between the display of each frame.Microsoft recommends that you use a value less than 100 to minimize the impact on performance.

You can specify the placement of both the text and graphics with the PictDrawMode and TextPosition properties, or by specifying the individual X and Y positions with the PictureXPos, PictureYPos, TextXPos, and TextYPos properties.

Planning the Graphics

The animation is created by assigning graphics images to frames that will run in a sequence. Two properties control this process. The Frame property keeps track of which frame has the focus, and the Picture property keeps track of which graphics file is in the frame.

The Animated Button has a Select Frame graphic dialog box system to facilitate the process of specifying the graphics images. To create the graphics sequence for the sample application, complete these steps:

1. Select the Frame property and click the ellipsis in the Settings box. The Select Frame dialog box appears, as shown in Figure 32.14.

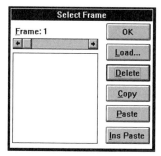

2. Select the Load... button. The Load Picture dialog box appears.
3. Select the C:\VB\ICONS\TRAFFIC\TRFFC09.ICO file.
4. Select the Replace button.
5. Click the right arrow of the scroll bar to work with Frame 2.
6. Repeat steps 2 through 4 for C:\VB\ICONS\TRAFFIC\TRFFC10A.ICO.
7. Click the right arrow of the scroll bar to work with Frame 3.
8. Repeat steps 2 through 4 for C:\VB\ICONS\TRAFFIC\TRFFC10B.ICO.
9. Click the right arrow to work with Frame 4.
10. Repeat steps 2 through 4 forC:\VB\ICONS\TRAFFIC\TRFFC10C.ICO.
11. Click OK.

The Select Frame dialog box allows you to view the frames using the scroll bar, delete frames, and copy frames, as well as paste a graphic on the Clipboard replacing the existing graphic for that frame or, with insert paste, place the graphic on the Clipboard in a new frame in front of the selected frame. Once the graphics are set, you need to add code to control the animation.

Although the appearance of the animated button and the selected graphics are stored in the application by default, you can also store this information in a separate file. That file has a .CCB extension, and you have to use the CCBfileLoad and CCBfileSave properties to indicate which file to access for the information.

Using the Properties window, set the value of the animated button's TextPosition property to 4. As a result, the text caption moves below the stoplight picture.

Creating the Animation

With the animated button, the process of changing the frame can be controlled with the mouse or with code. With the multistate cycle, the frames can be changed with the Value property. With the other cycle settings, the mouse normally controls the frame switch, but if you want to switch it with code, the SpecialOp property must be used. The multistate cycle was selected for the sample button; therefore, the Value property will be used to finish this application. Create the following two event procedures (you will be modifying the old Timer1_Timer procedure):

```
Sub AniButton1_Click ()
    AniButton1.Caption = ""
    Timer1.Enabled = True
End Sub

Sub Timer1_Timer ()
    Gauge1.Value = Gauge1.Value + 1
    If Gauge1.Value = 15 Then AniButton1.Value = 3
    If Gauge1.Value = 30 Then
        Label1.Caption = "Process is finished"
        Timer1.Enabled = False
        AniButton1.Value = 4
        AniButton1.Caption = "Done"
    End If
End Sub
```

Using the Properties window, set the value of the timer's Enabled property to False. The application is now complete and should appear as shown in Figure 32.15. Save the updated version of the application. Then start the application and click the stoplight. Watch the stoplight as the gauge reaches the halfway mark and as it finishes. Animated buttons can add a little life to your applications.

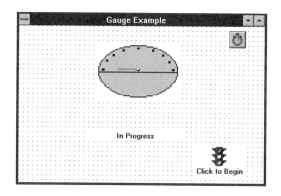

Figure 32.15.

The animated stoplight is added to the GAUGE application.

The Outline Control

The Outline control enables you to create hierarchical lists. Outline's operation and appearance are similar to the other list controls, but the listed items can be indented to various levels to show subordinate items. You can use the Outline control to create a specialized file list or a structured selection area like a "to do" list.

To illustrate this control, you create a sample application that tracks a list of things to do. To begin this project, complete the following steps:

1. Create a new project named OUTLINE.MAK with one form named OUTLINE.FRM.

2. Verify that the MSOUTLIN.VBX file is loaded into the project and place an outline control on the form.

   Visual Basic assigns the default name Outline1 to this control.

3. Place two command buttons on the form: Command1 and Command2.

4. Assign the property values shown in Table 32.7.

Table 32.7. Property values for OUTLINE.FRM.

Control	Property	Setting
Form1	Caption	Things To Do
	Height	4470
	Width	3390

continues

Table 32.7. Continued

Control	Property	Setting
Command1	Caption	&Add
	Left	240
	Name	cmdAdd
	Top	3480
Command2	Caption	&Delete
	Left	1800
	Name	cmdDelete
	Top	3480
Outline1	FontSize	9.75
	Height	3135
	Left	240
	Name	outToDo
	Top	120
	Width	2775

These steps are the base for the Things To Do list. When you place the Outline control on the form, you can set up many of the same properties that you can use with the List control. Notice that instead of getting the control name in the control at first, you get an outline tree. A list can only be added at run time.

Adding a List

The outline tree is visible because items cannot be added to the control at design time. You have to write code to place items in the list using the AddItem method—like a list control. With an application involving any list, you normally want to have the list visible when the application begins. For the To Do list, you can begin with a set of categories for the activities. To begin with the categories, create the following Form_Load procedure:

```
Sub Form_Load ()
    outToDo.AddItem "Memos"
    outToDo.AddItem "Requests"
    outToDo.AddItem "Correspondence"
    outToDo.AddItem "Telephone Calls"
End Sub
```

This procedure loads the categories when the user starts the application.

Adding Items

This application allows you to add or delete items from the list. You need to add code to control those operations. To minimize the code to accomplish those tasks, use the MsgBox and InputBox functions to communicate with the user. To use these functions, define five constants by adding the following lines to the General Declarations section for the form:

```
Const MB_YESNOCANCEL = 3 'Display Yes, No, and Cancel buttons.
Const MB_ICONQUESTION = 32 'Displays the question mark icon.
Const IDCANCEL = 2 'Cancel button selected.
Const IDYES = 6     'Yes button selected.
Const IDNO = 7      'No button selected.
```

Now you can add the code for the operation of the Add command button. With an outline control, you can add items to the list as a new item or as a subitem of one of the items that already exists. This is controlled with the ListIndex property of the Outline control.

The code for this application uses an If-Then-Else structure to see if a ListIndex value other than the default of -1 is present. If there is such a ListIndex property, the code uses the InputBox function to prompt the user to supply the new item. It also uses the Expand property of the outline control to show the sublevels for that category.

If the value of ListIndex is -1, a message box appears to ask whether the user wants to create a new project. Based on that answer, the program prompts for the information or it waits for the user to choose a category. To implement the Add button, create the following Click procedure:

```
Sub cmdAdd_Click ()
    If outToDo.ListIndex <> -1 Then
        Msg$ = "Please enter the Item Information?"
        Item$ = InputBox$(Msg$, "Item Information")
        outToDo.AddItem Item$
        outToDo.Expand(outToDo.ListIndex) = True
        outToDo.ListIndex = -1
    Else
```

```
            Msg$ = "Do you wish to create a new project?"
            Temp% = MsgBox(Msg$, MB_ICONQUESTION + MB_YESNOCANCEL,
            ➥"New Project")
            Select Case Temp%
                Case IDYES
                    Msg$ = "Please enter the Item information?"
                    Item$ = InputBox$(Msg$, "Item Information")
                    outToDo.AddItem Item$
                Case IDNO
                    Msg$ = "Please select a category?"
                    MsgBox Msg$, MB_ICONQUESTION, "Category"
                Case IDCANCEL
            End Select
        End If
End Sub
```

Deleting Items

The other command button on the form, labeled Delete, allows the user to delete items from the list. The user can select this button when an item is selected or when nothing is selected. Code must be added to accommodate both cases.

An If-Then-Else block can be used to test whether an outline control's ListIndex property is -1—and take the appropriate action depending on the result. If the value is -1, you need to prompt the user to select the item to delete. If the choice has a valid number, the item needs to be eliminated from the list. This is accomplished with the RemoveItem method. Create the following Click procedure:

```
Sub cmdDelete_Click ()
    If outToDo.ListIndex = -1 Then
        Msg$ = "Please select an Item?"
        MsgBox Msg$, MB_ICONQUESTION, "Delete Item"
    Else
        Msg$ = "Are you sure you want to delete this item."
        Temp% = MsgBox(Msg$, MB_ICONQUESTION + MB_YESNOCANCEL, "Delete
        ➥Item")
        Select Case Temp%
            Case IDYES
                outToDo.RemoveItem outToDo.ListIndex
```

```
        Case IDNO
        Case IDCANCEL
      End Select
    End If
End Sub
```

Adding Extra Features

You have now set up the operations of the Things To Do list, but you can still add several things to make the application easier to use. The first thing that needs to be added is the capability to change the appearance of an item on the list when the user clicks it. An outline control allows the user to choose how much or little of the list can be viewed when an item is clicked. You can do this by using the Expand property. Create the following Click procedure to allow the user to change the view of items:

```
Sub outToDo_Click ()
    Item% = outToDo.ListIndex
    outToDo.Expand(Item%) = Not outToDo.Expand(Item%)
End Sub
```

Once this code is added, the user will be able to change the view by clicking on a particular item. When an item is collapsed, the sublevels will not be visible.

The Outline control has some additional properties that can change the visible appearance of the list. Style is one such property. You can choose from text only; picture and text; plus/minus and text; plus/minus, picture, and text; tree lines and text; or tree lines, picture, and text.

For this example, choose plus/minus, picture, and text. Then test the application. Follow these steps:

1. Set the value of the outline control's Style property to 3 (plus/minus, picture, and text).

2. Run the application.

3. Click Telephone Calls.

4. Click the Add button to display the Input box for the new item.

5. Type **David** and press Enter.

6. Look at the Telephone Calls category. You see a new subitem as shown in Figure 32.16.

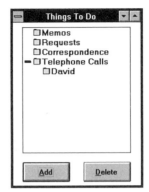

Figure 32.16.

The Things to Do outline.

7. Click the Delete button without first selecting a category.

   A message box opens asking you to first select an item.

8. Click OK to close the message box.

9. Stop the application.

10. Choose **S**ave File from the File menu to save the modifications to the form.

The Outline control is very versatile. You can customize the appearance of an outline with various properties. You can change the displayed pictures by modifying values of the PictureClosed, PictureOpen, PictureLeaf, PictureMinus, PicturePlus, and PictureType properties.

You can also get additional information from the outline by using the TopIndex property, which returns the index number of the first visible item. The List property returns the string of the item text. You also have the FullPath property to see the hierarchy for an item, the PathSeparator property to determine how the items are separated when shown with the FullPath property, and the Indent property to show the level of indention. You can also check an item's status with the HasSubItems and IsItemVisible properties.

Other Professional Edition Controls

Four other custom control .VBX files ship with the Professional Edition of Visual Basic 3.0: the Communications control, the Messaging Application Programming Interface (MAPI) controls, the Multimedia (MCI) control, and the Pen Edit controls.

These controls are all dependent on some type of computer hardware and, in two cases, special versions of Microsoft Windows 3.1. Descriptions of these controls (in the next four sections) include their VBX files, hardware and software requirements, and information on their functionality. For additional information, refer to the Microsoft documentation.

The Communications Control

The Communications control provides a way for your application to transmit and receive data through a serial port. There are properties to control the settings for that port as well as the OnComm event to respond to any changes to the CommEvent property.

The MSCOMM.VBX file must be added to the project before you can access this control; then, the control can be placed on your form like any other control. Your computer system must have a serial port to use the Communications control.

The Communications control has properties to break a serial connection, to detect a carrier and query the current state; to set the communication identification; to control the comport selection; to specify serial port settings including handshake, baud rate, parity, data bits, and stop bits; to establish and manage a transmission buffer; as well as determine the state of the port and solve parity problems.

MAPI Controls

The Messaging Application Programming Interface (MAPI) controls allow the addition of mail processing functions to a Visual Basic application. Your computer system must be running the Microsoft Mail electronic mail system or compatible Windows messaging software.

The MAPI controls require the addition of the MSMAPI.VBX file to the project. If you try to load the VBX file and you don't have a compliant system, you get the error message shown in Figure 32.17, followed by a Visual Basic error message indicating that the file could not be added to the project.

Figure 32.17.

The MAPI error message.

Two MAPI controls exist. The MAPI Session control directs the logon/logoff procedures to and from the Mail system and provides mail downloading.

The MAPI Messages control directs the activities needed to work with the messaging system, including the standard message handling, OLE attachment capability, and address book functionality.

Multimedia MCI Control

The Multimedia Media Control Interface (MCI) control operates MCI-compliant devices like CD-ROM, videotape recorders, and so on.

The Multimedia MCI controls require the MCI.VBX file and the Microsoft Windows 3.1, Multimedia version that provides the MCI services and MCI compliant hardware.

The Multimedia control provides buttons that resemble, in appearance as well as function, those on a videotape recorder. The buttons are Prev, Next, Play, Pause, Back, Step, Stop, Record, and Eject. Microsoft has several publications offering programming information and support for multimedia.

Pen Edit Controls

Four controls support pen-aware applications. The first two controls, BEdit and HEdit, are modified text boxes that allow for directed input from the pen. BEdit (Boxed Edit) provides combs or boxes to direct the user to place one character per marked area, and HEdit supports free form entry. The third control is the Pen Ink on Bitmap control. This control allows the user to mark up a bitmap with the pen and save the annotations either as the bitmap, as compressed ink, or as a combined ink and bitmap file. The fourth control provides access to the Pen On-Screen Keyboard.

All the pen controls require the PENCTRLS.VBX file added to the Visual Basic project. They require Microsoft Windows 3.1 for Pen Computing and compliant pen computing hardware. If the pen computing software and hardware are missing, the program generates an error message similar to the one generated for the MAPI system.

Summary

The Professional Edition of Visual Basic includes several custom controls not found in the Standard Edition. These controls offer increased functionality and they make some programming tasks easier. This chapter explored the functionality, property values, and event procedures associated with these controls.

The Graph control permits you to interactively design graphs directly on your forms. This control can produce several types of graphs including bar graphs, line graphs, pie charts, Gantt charts, and scatter graphs.

The 3D controls offers three-dimensional counterparts to standard Visual Basic controls. The 3D controls include a 3D Command Button, 3D Frame, 3D Option Button, and 3D Check Box.

Other Professional Edition custom controls include spin buttons, which you can click to increment or decrement numerical values; masked edit controls, which act like text boxes with formatting capability; key status controls, which display the values of NumLock and other special keys; gauges, which display user-defined gauges; animated buttons, which display a series of graphics images, and outline controls, which display hierarchical lists.

To access these custom controls, you must have the appropriate .VBX library files from the C:\WINDOWS\SYSTEM directory loaded into your application. In some cases, a custom control requires specialized software or hardware. Once these requirements are met, the controls can be added to forms just like any other control. You can adjust property values to tailor custom controls to your application and write code to take advantage of their functionality.

Adding a Help System to an Application

A s your applications become more complex, it becomes necessary to provide online assistance. Users of Windows applications expect to get such assistance from a Help menu, or by pressing F1. Most commercial applications include online help in addition to (sometimes instead of) the printed documentation.

For relatively simple Visual Basic applications, you can provide online help using nothing more than a few message boxes and/or customized forms. For more sophisticated applications, however, this approach is no longer satisfactory. A considerable programming effort is required to display volumes of information in separate windows. Besides, users will expect the kind of menu-driven help system available in commercial applications.

Windows includes an application named WinHelp (WINHELP.EXE). This application, sometimes called the Windows Help Engine, supports multiple-fonts, colors, keyword searching, and the many other familiar features prevalent in the Help systems of today's commercial Windows applications.

To activate its Help system, a Windows application can directly invoke WinHelp. WinHelp requires that an application's particular Help information be compiled into a specialized format and saved as a disk file.

The Professional Edition of Visual Basic includes a Help Compiler (HC31.EXE) which creates help files in the format required by WinHelp. Once a help file is created for a particular application, the program can invoke WinHelp, which in turn uses the help file.

With the aid of the Help Compiler, you can easily create a full-featured Help system for any Visual Basic application. Such a Help system can let the users of your application access a table of contents, browse through the topics, search for particular information, jump to related subjects, and view helpful graphics.

This chapter shows you how to use the Help Compiler to add a Help system to an application. The following topics are discussed:

- Preparing to create a Help system
- Planning your online Help system
- Gathering information
- Tracking the Help information
- Programming your application to access the Help system
- Creating the Help text
- Entering the Help codes in the text
- Creating the Help file
- Using additional tools to refine your Help system

Preparing to Create a Help System

When you install the Professional Edition of Visual Basic, the SETUP program places the Help Compiler in the HC subdirectory of your Visual Basic directory. The complete path is C:\VB\HC\HC31.EXE. The HC directory also contains support files used by the Help Compiler.

NOTE **Installing the Help Compiler**

If you did a complete installation of the Professional Edition, the SETUP program automatically installs the Help Compiler and its associated files. However, if you selected a custom installation of Visual Basic, and did not select the Help Compiler option, the SETUP program does *not* create the HC directory. In such a case, you can rerun SETUP to install the Help Compiler. For information about running SETUP and installing Visual Basic, see Chapter 1, "An Overview of Visual Basic."

In addition to the Help Compiler, you need access to some other software tools when creating a Help system. These other tools include

- A word processing program that supports the *Rich Text Format (RTF)*
- DOS
- A graphics package (optional)

Creating the Getaways Application

In this chapter you create a sample application that includes a Help system. The application, named Getaways, processes orders for vacation tours. The user enters a traveler's name, selects a tour choice, and prints the resulting order form.

Designing the Form for the Getaways Application

To begin the sample application, follow these steps:

1. Open the Windows File Manager, and highlight the root directory, normally C:.
2. Select the Create Directory option from the File Manager's File menu.
3. Type **getaway** in the Create Directory dialog box, then press Enter.
4. Close the File Manager (choose the Exit option from the File menu).
5. In Visual Basic, select New Project from the File menu.
6. Place a label on the form: Label1.
7. Place a text box on the form: Text1.
8. Place a frame on the form: Frame1.
9. Place two option buttons inside the frame: Option1 and Option2.
10. Using the Properties window, assign the property values that Table 33.1 shows.

    The option buttons become a control array named optVacation.

Table 33.1. Properties for the Getaways controls.

Control	Property	Value
Form1	Caption	Vacation Getaways
	Height	2835
	Left	1420
	Top	1245
	Width	5850
Label1	Caption	Name:
	Name	lblName
	Height	255
	Left	240
	Top	480
	Width	615
Text1	Text	(empty string)
	Name	txtname
	Height	495
	Left	1080
	Top	360
	Width	4455
Frame1	Caption	Vacation Package
	Name	fraPackage
	Height	855
	Left	240
	Top	1080
	Width	5295
Option1	Caption	Alaska
	Name	optVacation
	Height	255
	Index	0
	Left	720
	Top	360
	Value	True
	Width	975
Option2	Caption	Caribbean
	Name	optVacation
	Index	1
	Height	255
	Left	3120
	Top	360
	Width	1215

11. Access the Menu Design Window. If you need some additional instructions for creating a menu, please refer to Chapter 24, "Designing Custom Menus."

12. Create a File menu with &File as the caption, and mnuFile as the name.

13. Create a second-level item under the File menu using &Print as the caption, and mnuPrint as the name. Assign Ctrl+P as the shortcut key.

14. Create another second-level item under the File menu using E&xit as the caption, and mnuExit as the name.

15. Click OK to close the Menu Design Window.

Your form should resemble the one in Figure 33.1.

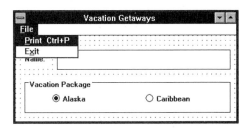

Figure 33.1.

The Vacation Getaways form.

Coding Event Procedures for the Print and Exit Menu Options

Create the following Click procedures for the Exit and Print menu items:

```
Sub mnuExit_Click ()
    End
End Sub

Sub mnuPrint_Click ()
    PrintForm
End Sub
```

Save the form as GETAWAY.FRM in the GETAWAY directory, C:\GETAWAY\GETAWAY.FRM. Save the project as GETAWAY.MAK in the same GETAWAY directory.

Planning Your Online Help System

The first step in planning an online Help system is determining the level of help your users require. To do so, you must determine who your users will be, and understand how sophisticated they are. Next, you must think about the contents and structure of the Help topics, and the various options you want to provide. The following sections help you make these determinations.

Determining Your Audience

One way to determine the audience for your application, and what level of support these users require, is to ask yourself the following questions:

■ *Who is using this application?*

Brainstorming is a reliable method of determining who will use the application: you want to list frequent users, as well as occasional ones. The sample application is designed for a travel agency. The travel agents would be the obvious user group; however, receptionists, and possibly part-time employees might use this application occasionally.

■ *What is the user's experience with computers?*

When you start planning the Help system, you make an assessment of the user's computer experience. If you have more than one type of user, make an assessment for each category.

For the sample application, the expected experience level of the users is mixed. Travel agents use computers to book travel arrangements. Receptionists have some computer experience from writing reports and letters. They do not, however, use computers to book travel arrangements. Part-time employees might have no experience with computers.

■ *For what type of work does the user need the computer?*

If the user base is familiar with using computers, you must decide whether their previous work and expected skill levels are applicable to your application. If their previous type of work is similar, you can expect the users to be able to master your application quickly, without needing much assistance from the Help system.

The travel agents probably will be able to use Getaways without much assistance from the Help system. They are familiar with using the computer as well as with the vacations offered in the application. The receptionists probably require more help to master the application. They might need some explanation of the specific vacation packages.

What Type of Help Is Needed

After you answer the preceding questions, you are ready to determine what kind of help the users need. Microsoft recommends that you categorize the user group into four groups. Each of these groups requires different levels of Help support. The following list defines the categories Microsoft recommends, and discusses the level of help required by each:

Computer Novice	The computer novice has no experience with computers. Novice users, such as part-time employees, often need to overcome some computer anxiety.
	Such users require a step-by-step approach for help. Definitions of key terms often are included to enable the user to explore without searching elsewhere for terms. Help can include mouse instructions that indicate in which place to point and click.
Application Novice	The application novice has some experience with computers, but not with your type of application. The receptionist falls into this category.
	These users benefit from a step-by-step approach to help. The purpose of the Help system is to acquaint users with application features that are unfamiliar, enabling them to use Help as a reference to jog their memories.
Application Intermediate	The intermediate has some experience with computer applications such as Getaways. Some of the travel agents fall into this category.
	The application intermediate user employs Help as a reference for unfamiliar details. The step-by-step approach slows down this user.
Application Expert	The expert has extensive experience with computer applications and software upgrades. Some of the travel agents fall into this category as well.
	This user employs the Help system to verify old methods of operation, and locate new features and procedures. Most experts find online Help quite useful. Locating information using online systems is quicker than searching through printed manuals.

With respect to the sample application, there is a wide range of users from all levels. This is a common situation. Certainly, most applications support more than one level of user.

To provide multiple levels of Help support, you can choose from several methods. The first method involves the selection and arrangement of the Help information.

The Contents of the Help System

After you determine the audience, you need to plan the *contents of the Help system*. A Help system for an application contains several components: the Help menu and the topics that appear on the Contents screen.

The *Contents* screen provides the user with an overview of the information contained within the Help system. From this screen, the user can choose a topic and receive help directly.

The following sections show you how to implement the various components of a Help system.

The Help Menu

In most commercial applications, the user expects to find assistance from a main menu item labeled Help. Microsoft recommends that the Help menu appear on the right end of the menu bar, and that the access key be **H**. A Help menu can contain a variety of options.

The standard items on the Help menu are *Contents*, *Search*, and *About.* The Help menu also should include the *Index*, *Keyboard Guide,* and *How to Use Help Menu* items. These menu items have the following purposes:

Contents	Displays the table of contents for the Help file. This option enables the user to make choices about what topic to view. Contents generally appears as the first option on the Help menu. This option should not be displaced from the Search and Index options (if included) by a separator bar.
Search	Displays the WinHelp Search dialog box. This option lets the user enter a keyword and get help on that topic. Search generally appears as the second option on the Help menu.
About	Displays the About dialog box. This dialog box contains fundamental information about the application—such as the author and the copyright notice. About should be the last option in the Help menu. A separator bar places About apart from the rest of the menu options.
Index	Displays an alphabetized list of help topics. If included, Index should be the third option on the Help menu.
Keyboard Guide	Displays a list of keystrokes specific to the application, such as the Ctrl+P shortcut key for Print option.
How to Use Help	Accesses the Microsoft Windows instructions for using the Help window.

The three optional items (About, Index, and Keyboard Guide) are the most common additions to a Help menu. However, you can include any other menu items as you see fit.

Figure 33.2 shows the Visual Basic design environment with the Help menu opened. In addition to the standard **C**ontents, **S**earch, and **A**bout options, this Help menu includes options for **O**btaining Technical Support and **L**earning Microsoft Visual Basic.

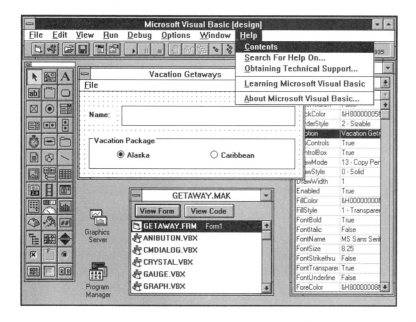

Figure 33.2.

The Visual Basic Help menu.

The Getaways application is relatively simple. Therefore, its Help menu contains the three standard items along with the recommended optional items: Index and How to Use Help. The other recommended item, Keyboard Guide, is omitted because Getaways contains only one shortcut key. (Of course, you can add Keyboard Guide if you so desire.)

The Contents Screen

The Contents screen appears when the user selects the Contents option from the Help menu. This screen lists the available Help topics. You can list the topics on-screen in any order. If you plan to include an index, showing the topics in alphabetical order is repetitious. Instead, you might arrange the topics in categories appropriate for different skill levels, or arrange them by commands or procedures.

The Visual Basic Help Contents screen separates the topics into three categories: *How To*, *Building*, and *Reference*. Microsoft recommends that you limit the number of topics on a Contents screen to 15 or less. You may need to use sublevel content screens. Microsoft also recommends that you try to limit the number of sublevels to three or less. Users sometimes become frustrated if they need to access more than three screens to retrieve information.

The Help menu for the Getaways application contains both Contents and Index menu options. Because the Index topics are arranged alphabetically, it's useful to organize the Contents screen into categories.

A common content organization is to provide procedural help for the novice users, and reference assistance for the more experienced ones. On the Contents screen, you can include a How to Use Vacation Getaways section that contains the following topics for novice users: "Enter the Travel Data," "Print the Vacation Order," and "Exit Vacation Getaways."

For the experienced users, a Reference section might follow the How To category. This section could include "File Menu," "Name Prompt," and "Vacation Package" topics for use with the Alaskan and Caribbean tours.

Help Topic Structure

After you decide what kind of information you want to appear on the Contents screen, you need to determine the following:

- What topics do you want to include, and how are they to be associated with those of the Contents screen?
- How is the user to search through the Help information?
- What is the best way to organize the material logically for browsing?
- Do you want to provide context-sensitive help when the user presses F1?

The Topic Hierarchy

After planning the Contents screen, you need to determine the hierarchy of topics. From the Contents screen, the user can choose to use either the How To or Reference section. This constitutes the first level in the Help system.

Under the How To section, the step-by-step instruction topics enable the user to choose what to explore first. All the options, such as entering data, printing the request, and exiting the application, lead to different topic screens that contain the information for that task. No levels exist below the instruction topics.

With the Reference section, the topics enable the user to quickly locate a subject of interest. The three topics, File Menu, Name Prompt, and Vacation Package, are visible on the Contents screen. The Name Prompt and Vacation Package options lead directly to screens which provide the appropriate information. The File Menu option, however, leads to a secondary screen which lists the Print and Exit options. From that screen, the user can choose Print or Exit to get specific information about either of those two options.

A well-designed outline can make the job of creating text for the topics much easier. Such an outline should display the hierarchical relationship between the topics. When determining the hierarchy, you might find that a flowchart, similar to the one in Figure 33.3, can be helpful. In this figure, each rectangle corresponds to one screen in the Help system.

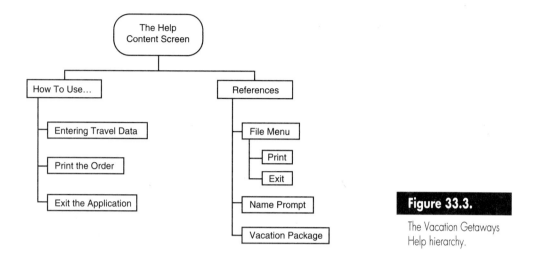

Figure 33.3.

The Vacation Getaways
Help hierarchy.

Search Provisions

After you set up the hierarchy, you must determine the way in which you want the user to search for information in the Help file. Most experienced users have an idea of what information they need. They often prefer to search for the exact piece of information rather than read through a Contents screen, or Index.

To plan the search provisions, you need to look at the topics and determine specific words for which the user might search. These words (or word phrases) are called *keywords*. One of the topics, for example, is the Exit command. Exit is the obvious choice for a keyword; however, other users might search for Quit or End. Brainstorming also can be a valuable tool when you are at this stage. You might want to use the keywords in Table 33.2 for the Getaways application.

Table 33.2. Getaways keywords.	
Topic	**Keywords**
Enter the Travel Data	Entering Travel Data, Name Prompt, Vacation Package
Print the Vacation Order	Print, Printing, Output
Exit Vacation Getaways	Exit, End, Quit
File Menu	Menus, File Menu, Commands
Print Command	Menus, File Menu, Commands, Print

continues

Table 33.2. Continued

Topic	Keywords
Exit Command	Menus, File Menu, Commands, Exit, End, Quit
Name Prompt	Name Prompt, Client, Entering Travel Data
Vacation Package	Vacation Package, Tours, Alaska, Caribbean

Browse Sequence

Some users prefer to read through documentation from beginning to end. You can provide this capability in the Help system by planning a *browse sequence*. The browse sequence is the order in which topics appear when the user clicks the arrow buttons in the Help window—similar to turning the pages in a book. You can have more than one browse sequence.

To set up this sequence, you must plan a browse sequence code for each topic that should be included. The browse sequence codes can include a group string, but must contain an order number. The browse group string is first. It indicates the name of a browse sequence. If only one browse list exists, you can omit the group string.

The order number indicates the sequence of the topics as the user clicks the right-arrow button in the Help window. The numbers must be sequential, but do not need to be consecutive. Microsoft recommends that you number each topic using multiples of five to give you four extra numbers. This makes updating the Help text file easier when you need to add additional topics to the Help system.

When planning the browse sequence, think of the way in which the topics might be organized in a book. With the Getaways application, you could have one sequence that begins with the How To section, and another for the Reference section. This would enable both the novice and experienced users to page through the Help file. This resembles the Help system's Contents screen because it was designed for both types of users. For the Getaways application, only the browse sequence for the How To section will be implemented.

The following order numbers will be used when you enter the help codes (see the section titled "Entering Help Codes" later in this chapter):

Contents	005
Enter the Travel Data	010
Name Prompt	015
Vacation Package	020

Print the Vacation Order	025
Exit Vacation Getaways	030
Index	035

You do not have to include every topic in the browse sequence. In the preceding sequence, File Menu, Print Command, and Exit Command are not included. The topics in this Help file are designed to meet the needs of several types of users.

The File Menu topic is a submenu. There is no reason to include a submenu screen in the browse sequence—it would force the user to click twice to get to relevant information.

When the Contents screen was planned, there were two types of users in mind. Each command, such as Print and Exit, is covered in two places on the Help Contents screen. A user can choose `Print the Vacation Order` and `Exit Vacation Getaways`, or alternatively, the `Print`, then the `Exit` commands from the File menu. The information is covered twice to accommodate both types of users. For experienced users, it is covered in a very concise manner, so they can do a quick overview. For the novice users, the information is covered in a greater detail; it includes step-by-step instructions.

Context Sensitivity

The last decision you need to make for the topic hierarchy is whether the user can directly access help for the item with the focus by pressing F1. This functionality is called *context-sensitive help*. If not implemented, the user must locate the relevant help by searching through the topics on the Contents screen.

For example, suppose the user wants help on the Alaska option button. If context-sensitive help is implemented, the user can simply move the focus to this button and then press F1. That's quite a time-saver compared to navigating through the screens of the Help system.

Context-sensitive help is one of the most beneficial features you can add to a Help system. You may have noticed how convenient it is with Visual Basic and other Windows applications. To add context-sensitive help to Getaways, you must do some additional planning and programming.

For the Help system features discussed thus far, the implementation involves writing the Help text. To implement context-sensitive help, however, you also must do additional programming along with the Help access. These programming tasks are discussed later in this chapter.

Providing context-sensitive help requires that you plan a unique context string for each sensitive topic. Table 33.3 shows appropriate context strings for the "Entering Help Codes" and "Creating the Help Project File" sections of Getaways:

Table 33.3. Help context strings.	
Topic	**Context string**
File Menu	FILE_MENU
Print Command	PRINT
Exit Command	EXIT
Contents	CONTENTS
Index	INDEX
Name Prompt	NAME_PROMPT
Vacation Package	PACKAGE
Entering The Travel Data	ENTERING
Printing The Order	PRINTING
Exiting Vacation Getaways	EXITING

The Help Topic File Structure

All the Help system information is created in word-processed files. These files contain the information about which screens are included in the Help system, the browse sequence, the context-sensitive links, as well as the topic text. As you write the text, you can place all the topics in one file, or separate the information into more than one. The Visual Basic Help Compiler can deal with multiple source files.

In the word-processed file, the Contents screen, Index, and each individual topic are separated by page breaks. If your application is complex, and you are managing many topics, you might find it helpful to create separate documents for each category of your Contents screen. Some applications are so large that a separate document is used for each menu. Even if you use multiple documents, the Contents screen and the Index go together in one document.

If you were to expand the Getaways application, you might have one document for the Contents and Index, a second for the How To topics, and a third for the Reference material (see Figure 33.4). The Getaways application as developed here contains only a few topics, so one document file is sufficient.

After you decide how many files you want to use, it is helpful to choose meaningful file names, especially if more than one person is going to work with them. If you are going to have more than one file, you should ensure that the file names are easy to identify. They should support a numbering system. You might, for example, want to assign GAWAY01 as the file name for the sample application. This enables the file number to grow as the size of the application increases, and the Help system requires more topics.

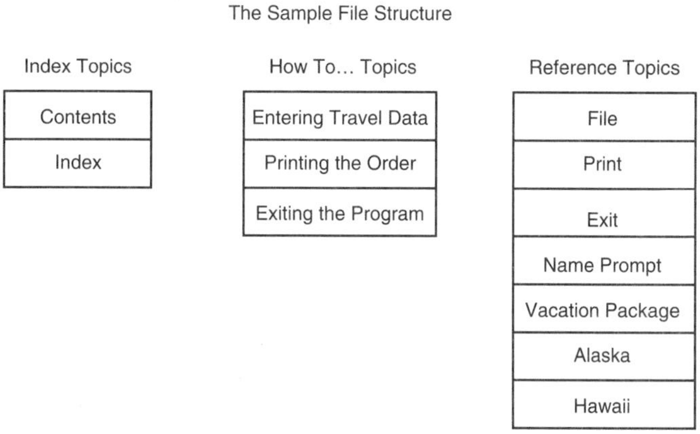

The Sample File Structure

Index Topics	How To... Topics	Reference Topics
Contents	Entering Travel Data	File
Index	Printing the Order	Print
	Exiting the Program	Exit
		Name Prompt
		Vacation Package
		Alaska
		Hawaii

Figure 33.4.

A sample file structure.

The Help Topic Format

After you determine the topics you want to include, and their desired arrangement, you need to decide how you want them to appear to the user. Determining this appearance combines the text and screen design tools. The appearance of the text affects the way the user receives your messages. In addition to writing style, you need to choose fonts, point sizes, highlighting, placement, and color.

Fonts, and Point Sizes

The first choice you need to make when designing the Help screens is to determine how you want the text to appear to the user. This choice is similar to choosing the font and its size for the captions (or text) of various controls. Microsoft recommends that you use one of the standard fonts and sizes that come with Windows 3.1. Three types of fonts are included: bitmap, TrueType, and vector. Both bitmap and vector fonts ship with Windows; however, True-Type fonts are sold separately. Table 33.4 lists the Windows fonts and sizes.

Table 33.4. Microsoft Windows 3.1 screen fonts and sizes.

Bitmap Fonts

Courier (10, 12, and 15 pts)

MS San Serif (8, 10, 12, 14, 18, and 24 pts)

MS Serif (8, 10, 12, 14, 18, and 24 pts)

Symbol (8, 10, 12, 14, 18, and 24 pts)

continues

Table 33.4. Continued
Vector Fonts
Modern
Roman
Script
TrueType Fonts
Arial*
Courier New*
Times New Roman*
Symbol
Wingdings

Including Normal, Bold, Italic, and Bold-Italic attributes

When choosing a font to use for the Help text, select a type style that you are confident most, if not all, users will have loaded. The TrueType fonts that come with Windows have more flair than the standard styles; however, you need to be sure that the users have the TrueType fonts loaded in their systems. If WinHelp cannot locate the selected font, the Windows help engine displays the text in the font that most closely matches the original.

When deciding on fonts, you might find it helpful to examine the Help systems for existing applications. Many applications use MS San Serif, which offers a wide range of point sizes. Although you can use multiple fonts in a Help system, it is generally recommended that you use no more than two fonts in the Help text file. Multiple fonts often produce confusing, hard-to-read screens.

After a font is selected, you have to choose a character or point size for the text. Your Help system has different categories of text: topic titles, subtitles, and the general information. When you choose point sizes, use a given size consistently. For example, if you decide you want the text to be 12 points, subtitles 14 points, and titles 18 points, you should not vary from these conventions. If you have more categories, decide on one point size for each.

Typefaces

You also can accent text using typefaces, such as bold, italic, capitalization, small caps, subscript, superscript, and so on. However, it is best to use them sparingly and consistently. Boldfacing titles and subtitles is a common way to make text stand out.

The Help Compiler reserves the underline, double underline, and strikethrough typefaces for specific purposes in the text file. Therefore, it is best that you do not use these typefaces in your text. (Underline, double underline, and strikethrough text are explained in the section titled "Entering Help Codes," later in this chapter.)

Spatial Arrangement

When you create the text file, you need to pay special attention to the amount of space you leave around the information. Information appears more crowded on-screen. Microsoft states that if the relationship between the text and the surrounding space is 50/50, the user perceives it as 60/40.

Language Level

The level of the language you use in the Help text also is important. When you define your audience, you determine their level of competence in using computers and applications. You need to write to that level. Novices appreciate a step-by-step approach, including where to point and click. Advanced users prefer an "only the facts" approach.

Color

Adding color is another way to emphasize your text. Microsoft recommends that you use color to group items together rather than for emphasis. For example, you can make the titles blue to separate them from the body of the text.

When you contemplate using color accent, you need to consider the following:

- Do any users have laptops?
- Are any users color-blind?
- What colors should I use?

Microsoft provides the following general recommendations for using color:

- Design the colors to make a pleasing appearance on a VGA screen.
- To avoid eyestrain, avoid bright or complimentary colors, and light colors on a similar-colored background.
- Do not use green—it is reserved for specific purposes in the Help text file.

Defining the Help Text's Appearance

The choices you make enable you to present a clear, concise message without confusing the user. Changing fonts, point size, and typefaces at random, and squeezing too much information on-screen, can irritate the operator, and make the Help system difficult to use.

The Getaways application uses the MS San Serif font with 12-, 14-, and 18-point sizes for text, subtitles, and titles, respectively. The titles and subtitles are boldfaced, with black as the only text color.

Tracking Help Information

The planning stages of the Help system generate a substantial amount of information. Microsoft recommends that you keep track of this information in written form so that you can use it as a reference, without having to rely on memory. You can use a Help tracker file to keep a record of all the topic information.

The Help tracker file can be a word-processor document or a spreadsheet. It should have four columns: Title, Help Context ID, Browse Code, and Keywords. You can refer to this file as you create your text. Figure 33.5 shows a sample Help Tracker file created with Microsoft Word for Windows.

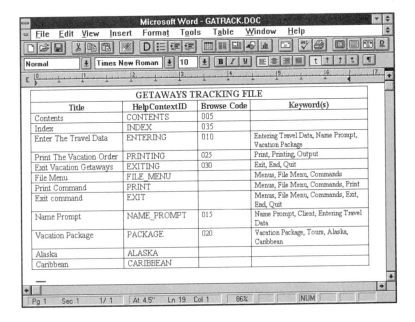

Figure 33.5.

The Getaways Tracking File.

Gathering Help Information

Gathering the information for your Help system is the second step of the development process. This can be an ongoing part of the process, depending on your application development cycle. This step can include step-by-step instructions for using the application, definitions of different windows and controls, tips for advanced users, warnings and error messages, and helpful graphics.

The information can come from a variety of sources, depending on the size of the development effort. Resources can include application design documents, programming notes, testing results, user documentation, your experimentation, and your users.

Programming Help System Access

You determined in the planning stage what you wanted in the Help system. Preparing your application to access the Help system is the next step. You need to add the Help menu to the application, and specify the file containing the Help text. You must assign the HelpContextID properties for the context-sensitive help.

Furthermore, you must set up the call to WinHelp. This requires writing program code to access WinHelp and to release the Help engine when the user closes the Help system.

Adding the Help Menu

Adding the Help menu is similar to adding any menu. You use the Menu Design Window. The Getaways application contains a Help menu that includes Contents, Index, Search, About, Keyboard Help, and How to Use Help. To complete the Help menu, follow these steps (if you need some additional instructions for creating a menu, please refer to Chapter 24, "Designing Custom Menus"):

1. Open the Menu Design Window.

2. Click the E&xit menu option, then click the Next button to get a new menu item.

3. Create the main menu title using &Help as the caption, and mnuHelp as the name. Then, press Enter.

4. Create the Help submenu using the parameters in Table 33.5.

Table 33.5. The Help submenu.

Item	Caption	Name
Contents	&Contents...	mnuHelpContents
Index	&Index...	mnuHelpIndex
Search	&Search...	mnuHelpSearch
Separator		SepBar1
How to Use Help	&How to Use Help...	mnuHelpOnHelp
Separator		SepBar2
About Vacation Getaways	&About Vacation Getaways...	mnuHelpAbout

The Help menu should resemble the one in Figure 33.6.

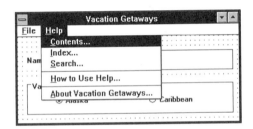

Figure 33.6.

The Getaways Help menu.

Specifying the Help File

In addition to completing the Help menu, you must specify the file name for the Help system that your application is to use. When WinHelp is accessed, it looks at the specified file for the Help information. To specify the Help file you want WinHelp to access, complete these steps:

1. Select **Project** from the **Options** menu.

2. Click Help file.

3. Type **c:\getaway\getaway.hlp**.

4. Click OK to close the Project Options dialog box.

Declaring the *WinHelp* Function

Your program will use the WinHelp function of the Windows *application pro-gramming interface (API)* user library to provide a Windows-consistent Help system. Before you can use this function, you must declare it in a separate module of your Visual Basic application. You also need to define any constants used by the function. Follow these steps to create the module, and then add the declaration statement:

1. Choose the New **M**odule option from the **F**ile menu.

    A new module is created. The code window opens and displays the General Declarations section for this module.

2. Add the following lines of code. (Note that most of these constants are defined in CONSTANT.TXT. If you wish, you can cut and paste the appropriate declarations from CONSTANT.TXT to this new module.)

```
'Help Constants
Global Const HELP_CONTEXT = &H1          'Display topic in Topic
Global Const HELP_QUIT = &H2             'Terminate help
Global Const HELP_INDEX = &H3            'Display index
Global Const HELP_CONTENTS = &H3
Global Const HELP_HELPONHELP = &H4       'Display help on using help
Global Const HELP_SETINDEX = &H5         'Set the current Index
➥for multi index help
Global Const HELP_SETCONTENTS = &H5
Global Const HELP_CONTEXTPOPUP = &H8
Global Const HELP_FORCEFILE = &H9
Global Const HELP_KEY = &H101            'Display keyword
➥topic in search
Global Const HELP_COMMAND = &H102
Global Const HELP_PARTIALKEY = &H105     'Call the search
➥engine in WinHelp

' Declare the Help Function
Declare Function WinHelp Lib "User" (ByVal hWnd As Integer,
ByVal lpHelpFile As String, ByVal wCommand As Integer,
ByVal dwData As Any) As Integer
```

The preceding Declare Function declaration specifies that you want this application to use the WinHelp function, located in the User library. Your application passes four parameters to the function: hWnd and wCommand as integers, lpHelpFile as a string, and dwData as the Any data type. These four parameters are each passed by value.

The hWnd parameter identifies your application as the one requesting WinHelp. The lpHelpFile indicates the path and file name of the Help file. The wCmd parameter indicates what action you want to take in WinHelp, such as Search or Quit. The dwData parameter communicates the requested topic in the Help file. These parameters are discussed in detail later in this chapter.

3. Choose the **S**ave File option from the File menu. When the Save File As dialog box opens, save the module as GETAWAY.BAS.

Assigning *HelpContextID*

You also need to specify the Help Context numbers using the HelpContextID property. You need to assign a number to those controls that need a context-sensitive response. When you are assigning the HelpContextID property, you will not be able to do so for the five types of controls that cannot get the focus: Line, Shape, Image, Label, and Timer. You use the Properties window to set HelpContextID property values for forms and controls.

> **T I P**
>
> Do not number the controls in consecutive order. If you leave gaps in the numbering system, you can later insert new controls. You also can keep the HelpContextID numbers in sequence with the others on that menu or in that dialog box. One way of assigning the numbers is to start with the left menu title. You begin with 5 and assign numbers in multiples of five.

You use the Menu Design window to assign HelpContextID values for the menu items. You use the Properties window for other controls. Assign the following for the Getaways application's HelpContextID:

File Menu	5
Print	10
Exit	15
txtName	20
fraPackage	25
optVacation(0)	25
optVacation(1)	25

Visual Basic automatically includes support for F1 as the context-sensitive help key. When your application has HelpContextID values assigned, pressing F1 at run time launches WinHelp, and displays the appropriate context-sensitive help topic.

Programming the *WinHelp* Access

Although you don't need to program F1 support, you must add code to access the Help system for the Help menu commands. To access the WinHelp function, set up the command as you would for any other function. Then, pass to the command the necessary parameters.

1. Open the Code window for GETAWAY.BAS, and add the following line of code in the General Declarations procedure:

   ```
   Global HelpFile As String
   ```

2. Open the Code Window for GETAWAY.FRM, and add the following line of code to the Form_Load procedure:

   ```
   HelpFile = App.HelpFile
   ```

The Contents Command

The first command that uses WinHelp is the Contents... option on Getaways' Help menu. When the user selects Contents, the Help window should appear, and display Contents. To implement this command, add the following line of code to the mnuHelpContents_Click procedure:

```
Temp% = WinHelp(hWnd, HelpFile, HELP_INDEX, CLng(0))
```

When the WinHelp function is called, HELP_INDEX is the wCommand that opens the Help window to the Contents topic. You need to include the null parameter Clng(0).

The Index Command

Index... is the second option on the Help menu. When the user selects Index, the Help window appears, and displays the index. Index is one of the topics in the Getaways Help file. Add this line to the mnuHelpIndex_Click procedure:

```
Temp% = WinHelp(hWnd, HelpFile, HELP_CONTEXT, CLng(30))
```

The wCommand is HELP_CONTEXT, which uses the dwData parameter. This parameter must have the context string, which is 30 for the Index topic as a long integer.

The Search Command

To provide the search function without having to access the Help window first, Visual Basic 3.0 has two functions: HELP_KEY, and HELP_PARTIALKEY. HELP_KEY searches for a specific string. Although not documented in the Help Compiler

Guide, HELP_PARTIALKEY is more valuable because it opens the Search dialog box at a specified location, and enables the user to experiment with different keywords. The dwData parameter acts as a long pointer for the search string for both commands. To access the Search dialog box without passing a search string, use a null pointer, as in the following command, which you must add to the mnuHelpSearch_Click procedure:

```
Temp% = WinHelp(hWnd, HelpFile, HELP_PARTIALKEY, CLng(0))
```

For more information on HELP_PARTIALKEY, refer to the online Win SDK Help file installed with Visual Basic 3.0, Professional Edition.

The How to Use Help Command

The fourth command on the Help menu is How to Use Help. This option accesses the Help window that contains the Microsoft information for using Help systems. You use the HELP_HELPONHELP command to assign to dwData the null value. To do this, add the following line of code to the mnuHelpHowTo_Click procedure:

```
Temp% = WinHelp(hWnd, HelpFile, HELP_HELPONHELP, CLng(0))
```

The About Getaways Travel Command

When you select the About command from the Help menu, another window with information about the program appears. It shows the program's title, developers, and copyright information. You can design a form for this purpose, or include a MsgBox. The following lines of code add a simple message box with the title, development, and chapter information on separate lines:

```
Title$ = "Vacation Getaways, Version 1.0"
CRLF$ = Chr$(10) + Chr$(13)
Dev$ = "Developed for Using Visual Basic 3.0"
Chp$ = "Chapter 35, Adding A Help System"
Message$ = Title$ & CRLF$ & Dev$ & CRLF$ & Chp$
MsgBox Message$
```

Place these code lines in the mnuHelpAbout_Click event procedure.

Programming the Release *WinHelp*

The last Help command for the Getaways Travel application you need to add is HELP_QUIT. This command notifies Windows that your application has finished with the WinHelp function, and does not need to access it again. Normally, this command is issued prior to the End instruction. The command ignores the dwData parameter, and needs a null parameter to act as a placeholder. To release WinHelp, add the following line of code to the mnuExit_Click procedure, just before the End statement:

```
Temp% = WinHelp(hWnd, HelpFile, HELP_QUIT, CLng(0))
```

The Help menu code and the addition to the Exit command illustrate how to use six of the eight WinHelp commands. You also can point to a multiple keyword list to set a new Index (Contents) topic. For more information on the WinHelp commands, refer to Microsoft's Help Compiler Reference Guide, or get online help for the Win SDK.

Creating the Help Text

The preceding section discusses the steps necessary to access WinHelp through the application's program code. In addition to programming the WinHelp access, you need to create the Help file. The next section discusses how to create the Help text file.

You create the Help file with a suitable word processor. With this word processor, you create one or more files containing the help text and Help codes.

Choosing a Word Processing Program

You use a word processor to create a Help file. The word processing program must have the following features:

- Capability to save the file in a Rich Text Format (RTF)
- Underlining
- Double underlining or strikethrough
- Hidden text attributes
- User-defined footnotes (sometimes called *custom footnotes*)

You can choose from several word processing programs, including the following:

- Microsoft Word for Windows, Version 1.0 or later
- Microsoft Word MS-DOS Series, Version 5.0 or later
- Microsoft Word Macintosh Series, Version 3.0 or 4.0

You can use the word processing program of your choice provided that it contains the required features. Microsoft recommends, however, that you write a sample text file, and test it with the Help Compiler to ensure that it creates a working Help file.

Entering the Text

After you select a word processing program, you are ready to begin creating the Help text. This chapter is not designed to teach you how to generate the text for every possible word processing program. The examples that this chapter shows are generated in Microsoft Word for Windows 2.0.

All topics, as planned, are in one file. You now need to create the text for the Contents screen, the Index, and each topic. Each topic, in general, will have a title with the text spaced as you expect to see it on-screen. Each also will be separated by a hard page break. The typing for this example has been minimized as much as possible. When text is excluded, it is indicated by ellipsis(...).

Setting Up the Text File

You first need to start your word processing program, and create a new document. The first page of the new document is the Contents screen. You might want to save it with the file name GAWAY01, and accept the word processing program's default file extension.

In the planning stage, you chose the MS San Serif font. You should select that font. MS San Serif is a font for a screen rather than for a printer; therefore, it might not appear in the font list. If it does not appear in the list, choose a similar font, such as Helvetica. You can set up the Help project file to remap, or treat that font as MS San Serif later.

Creating the Contents Screen

You now are ready to enter text for the Contents screen. Any change in point size or formatting information appears in parentheses in front of the text it affects. Enter the following text, beginning at the top of the new document file:

```
(18 point)Vacation Getaways Help
(carriage return)
(12 point)The Vacation Getaways application is to allow
➥you to ... To learn how to use Help, press F1, or select Using Help from
➥the Help menu.
(carriage return)
(carriage return)
(14 point)How to Use Vacation Getaways
(carriage return)
(12 point)Enter the Travel Data
Print the Vacation Order
Exit Vacation Getaways
```

```
(carriage return)
(carriage return)
(14 point)References:
(carriage return)
(12 point)File Menu
Name Prompt
Vacation Package
(hard page break)
```

The preceding lines compose the Contents or first screen of the Help text file. As discussed in the plan, the title is followed by the two types of help: the How To and Reference sections. To provide extra white space, the How To and Reference sections are separated by several paragraph breaks.

A brief introduction precedes the topic sections. The second sentence, "To learn how to use Help, press F1, or select Using Help from the Help menu," is a standard one that enables the user to select the correct menu from the Help window. The first page should be similar to the one that Figure 33.7 shows.

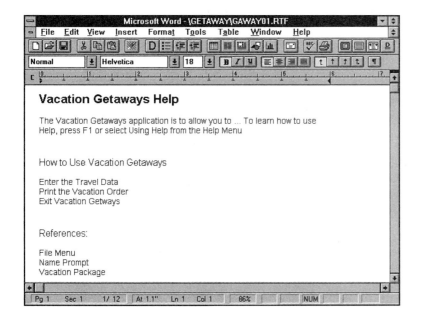

Figure 33.7.

The Contents topic.

Creating the Index Screen

The Index is the second page in the document. The Index is a list of the topics in alphabetical order. The title appears at the beginning followed by the topics in a list. To provide extra white space, separate the topics using a paragraph mark. Enter the following text:

```
(18 point)Vacation Getaways Help Index
(carriage return)
(12 point)Enter the Travel Data
Exit Command
File Menu
Name Prompt
Print Command
Vacation Package Choice
(hard page break)
```

The Index page should be similar to the one shown in Figure 33.8.

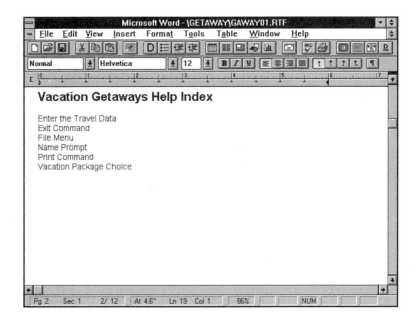

Creating Topic Screens

Creating the remainder of the topics screens is just a matter of entering the text. Enter the following text:

```
(18 point)Entering Travel Data
(carriage return)
(12 point)When the client calls, you can use ...
(carriage return)
To enter data:
(carriage return)
1.     Type the client's name.
(carriage return)
```

2.   Click on the desired package in Vacation Package.
(carriage return)
After completing these steps, you are ready to print the vacation order
(hard page break)
(18 point)Printing Your Vacation Order
(carriage return)
(12 point)To print the order, follow these steps:
(carriage return)
1.   Click on the File Menu.
(carriage return)
2.   Click on the Print option.
(carriage return)
As the application prints ... and you are ready to exit the program.
(hard page break)
(18 point)Exiting the Program
(carriage return)
(12 point)When you want to exit, complete the following steps:
(carriage return)
1.   Click on the File Menu.
(carriage return)
2.   Click on the Exit command.
(hard page break)
(18 point)The File Menu
(carriage return)
(12 point)Print Command
Exit Command
(hard page break)
(18 point)The Print Command
(carriage return)
(12 point)The Print command allows you to print the vacation order.
(hard page break)
(18 point)The Exit Command
(carriage return)
(12 point)The Exit command allows you end the application.
(hard page break)
(18 point)The Name Prompt
(carriage return)
(12 point)The name prompt is used to enter the client's name.
(carriage return)
(18 point)The Vacation Package
(carriage return)
(12 point)Vacation Package allows you to choose the tour package from:
(carriage return)
Alaskan Tour

```
Caribbean Tour
(hard page break)
(18 point)The Alaskan Tour
(carriage return)
(12 point)The Alaskan tour...
(hard page break)
(18 point)The Caribbean Tour
(carriage return)
(12 point)The Caribbean tour...
```

Entering Help Codes

In the preceding section, you created the text for the Help system. The next step is to add help codes which enable you to program the type of support planned, such as browsing, and so on.

You also need to program Help *jumps* and *definitions*. To the user, a jump appears in a Help window as an underlined text string. On color monitors, these jump strings are green. When the user places the mouse pointer over a jump string, the pointer shape changes from an arrow to a small pointing hand. Anytime the pointer has the hand shape, the user can access help for that topic by clicking the left mouse button.

A *definition* string appears with a dotted underline. Such strings appear green on color monitors. When you click a definition string, a pop-up window appears which contains a definition of the term. Clicking outside the pop-up window closes it.

Although entering Help codes is a separate step in this book, you can add the codes as you type the text. That way, you don't need an extra step. Instead, you could enter the codes after you create the text. You need to see which method works best for you.

You place the context strings, keywords, titles, browse sequences, and build tags in the text file by employing user-defined footnotes. These footnotes contain two parts: the footnote reference character and the text. You can specify with user-defined footnotes that the reference character appears in the body text, and with the footnote text.

In the word-processed document file, jumps are coded with the double underline, and definitions are added (and indicated) by underline or strikethrough. Both are directed to the jump topic using the context string as hidden text.

The Context String

The context string, which is the identifier for each topic that enables jumps, definitions, and context-sensitivity, is the first code you add to the text file. The context string is placed in the text file employing a user-defined footnote. A pound sign (#) is the reference character for a footnote. Each topic must have a context string. To add a context string to the Contents topic, type **Contents** to the left of "Vacation Getaways Help" as the footnote text. Then, add the pound sign (#) as the footnote reference character (see Figure 33.9).

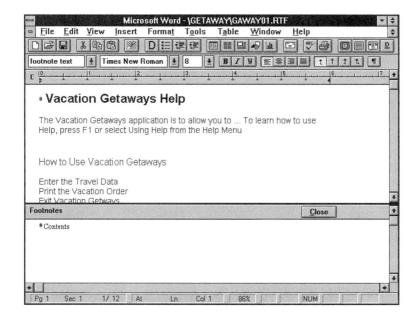

Figure 33.9.

The Contents topic context string.

You need to add context strings for each topic of the Getaways application. You can find the appropriate context strings in the HelpContextID column of the Help tracker file you created earlier in this chapter (refer to Figure 33.5).

To add the context strings, you use the same footnote technique you just used for the Contents context string. Use the following context strings:

Topic	Context String
Vacation Getaways Index	INDEX
Entering The Travel Data	ENTERING
Printing The Order	PRINTING

continues

Topic	Context String
Exiting Vacation Getaways	EXITING
The File Menu	FILE_MENU
The Print Command	PRINT
The Exit Command	EXIT
The Name Prompt	NAME_PROMPT
The Vacation Package	PACKAGE
The Alaskan Tour	ALASKA
The Caribbean Tour	CARIBBEAN

The Keyword and Title

The Help system plan should enable Getaways Travel to have search capabilities. To provide these capabilities, you add *keywords*. Keywords are strings the user can type to access a particular topic. You need to add titles so that the topics can appear in the search list. You need to provide keywords and titles only for those topics that the user can search.

You add keywords and titles with user-defined footnotes. You employ an uppercase κ as the footnote reference character, and separate keywords in the footnote text with semicolons (;). You use a dollar sign ($) as a footnote indicator for the title. The first topic from the tracker file which needs a title and keyword is "Enter The Travel Data." To add a title and keyword, follow these steps:

1. Position the cursor to the left of the "Enter The Travel Data" topic title.

2. Add the footnote with the dollar sign ($) reference character.

3. To enter the footnote text, type **Entering Travel Data**.

4. Add the footnote with a (κ) reference character.

5. Type the keywords for the footnote text: **Entering Travel Data;Name Prompt;Vacation Package**. These keywords are listed in the tracker file.

    The result should be similar to that shown in Figure 33.10.

Several other topics require keywords and titles. Repeat the preceding steps for the topics that Table 33.6 lists.

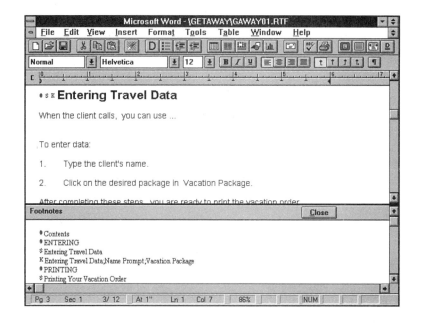

Figure 33.10.

The Entering Travel Data topic with title and keyword footnotes.

Table 33.6. Titles and keywords.

Topic (Title)	Keywords
Printing Your Vacation Order	Print;Printing;Output
Exiting The Program	Exit;End;Quit
The File Menu	Menus;File Menu;Commands
The Print Command	Menus;File Menu;Commands, Print
The Exit Command	Menus;File
	Menu;Commands;Exit;End;Quit
The Name Prompt	Name Prompt;Client;Entering Travel
	Data
The Vacation Package	Vacation Package;Tours;Alaska;Caribbean

You can create a multiple keyword table if you want to have more than one list for specialized searches. This is helpful if you want to have certain search parameters when Help is invoked from different locations in the application. It is important to specify a topic when using a multiple keyword list: WinHelp only displays the search topic without the search dialog box. You also need to specify the topics with a footnote reference character other than κ. When you create the Help project file, you specify the character in MULTIKEY option. For more information, refer to the reference manual.

The Browse Sequence

Getaways Travel also has browse sequences that enable the user to begin at one topic and read to its end. The browse sequence uses the plus sign (+) as the footnote reference character. If more than one browse sequence exists for the order number, the footnote text has a browse group. The group and order number are separated by a colon (:). To add the browse sequence for the Contents screen, follow these steps:

1. Position the cursor to the left of the "Contents" topic title, and add the footnote with the plus sign (+) reference character.

2. Type **005** as the footnote text.

   Repeat the preceding steps for the following topics:

Topic	Browse Code
Enter the Travel Data	010
Name Prompt	015
Vacation Package	020
Print the Vacation Order	025
Exit Vacation Getaways	030
Index	035

The Build Tag

The last code you can optionally place in the text file with user-defined foot-notes is a *build tag*. A build tag is a string associated with a topic. The tag indicates whether that topic should be compiled into the next build of the compiled Help file.

The build tag enables you to choose which topics to compile into the Help file. This is useful if you want to create a test Help file for application debugging purposes. The tag can also aid you in minimizing the size of this type of file by providing separate Help files for novice and experienced users.

The build tags enable you to have one set of Help text files, and still support separate files of this type. This is often used if you want to have one Help file for novice users, and another for experienced operators. You can also use build tags if you want to have a smaller version of the Help file to test the calls to the `WinHelp` function without the overhead of all the topics.

The build tag footnote reference character is the asterisk (*). The footnote text consists of each build tag separated by a colon (:). To create a valid build tag footnote reference mark, you must place it to the left of the topic, in front of the other footnotes.

The Help compiler always includes any topic that does not have a build-tag footnote. As explained later in this chapter, if a build tag is present, the compiler includes or excludes the topic depending on the information specified in the BUILD option of the document file.

Follow these steps to try a build tag for the sample application. This build tag excludes from the Contents screen the topic named Live during test builds of the Help file, but includes that topic when compiling the final (production) version of the application.

1. Position the cursor to the left of the topic title "Vacation Getaways Help," in front of the pound and plus signs.

2. Create a footnote and type the asterisk (*) reference character.

3. Type **LIVE:TEST** for the footnote text.

The Jump

You now need to tie the topics together by coding in a *jump*. As the text file currently stands, WINHELP can access each topic individually. However, it cannot branch from one topic to another.

To code in the jump, assign the double underline attribute to the jump text string. Then, add the context string for the jump topic using the hidden text attribute. You need to add jumps to the Getaways' Contents topic. All the topics on the Contents screen need to have jumps to their respective screens. Add the jump for entering the travel data first by following these steps:

1. Highlight Enter the Travel Data, and apply double underline or strikethrough.

2. Position the cursor at the end of Data, then turn on the hidden text attribute. Next, type **ENTERING** for the context string of that topic.

Repeat the preceding steps for the other topics in Contents, and those on the Index and the File menu. The Contents topic might appear similar to Figure 33.11 when you have completed the jumps.

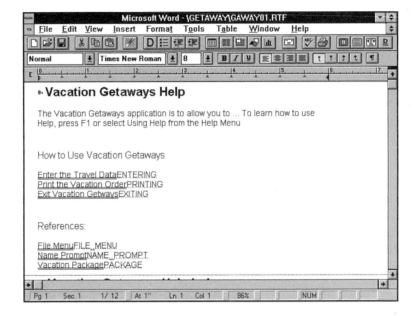

Figure 33.11.

The completed Contents topic.

You do not need to reserve jumps for Contents and Index topics. They are often used to indicate additional available information. To include an additional jump to the Vacation Package of the Entering Travel Data topic, follow these steps:

1. Highlight "Vacation Package" in Step 2 of the Entering Travel Data topic, and apply the double underline or strikethrough attribute.

2. Position the cursor at the end of the word "Package," then turn on the hidden text attribute. Next, type **PACKAGE** for the context string of that topic.

Adding the Definition

The last code you add to the text file is a *definition.* The user can click a word to see if it has a definition. If the word does, a pop-up box appears with a short definition of the term.

To code a definition, highlight the text string you want to define, then turn on the underline attribute. Next, add for the definition the context string as hidden text. To code the definitions for packages that define tours, follow these steps:

1. Highlight Alaskan Tour, then apply the underline attribute.

2. Position the cursor at the end of "Tour," then turn on the hidden text attribute. Next, type **ALASKA** as the context string for that topic.

3. To code a definition for the Caribbean tour, repeat the preceding steps using CARIBBEAN instead of ALASKA.

The basic Help text file is created after you enter the codes. Save the file in the Rich Text Format (RTF). To add emphasis to the Help file, however, you can add graphics before saving the file.

Adding Graphics for Greater Impact

Adding graphics to the Help file can focus the user's attention. However, as with any stylized effect, you want to use graphics sparingly and consistently. You can include bitmap, metafile, hypergraphic, and multiple resolution bitmap graphics in your file.

You add graphics by following two steps: You can create your own graphics, or select them from a clip art collection. Then, you have to include them in your Help text file. This section examines how to create different graphics types that are available, and include them in the Help file.

Creating Graphics

Graphics can be artwork, logos, graphics icons, or screen captures. A screen capture is similar to a snapshot of the current screen or window. Regardless of the content, you have to make sure that the type of graphics you want is in one of the accepted formats. Visual Basic's Help Compiler can work with bitmaps, metafiles, hypergraphics, and multiple resolution bitmaps. Each of these is described in the sections that follow.

Creating Bitmaps

Bitmaps are constructed with a pattern of pixels. These raster graphics often are referred to as *paint* files. One package that can create bitmap files is the Microsoft Paintbrush application that ships with Windows.

A common use for graphics is to insert a picture of the window described in a topic. Inserting a picture into a Help file is a three-step process. The first step is to capture or move a snapshot of a window to the Windows Clipboard. After you have captured the window to the Clipboard, you must paste it into Microsoft Paintbrush using its Edit menu. The last step is to save it as a bitmap file. To create a screen-captured bitmap file for the Entering Travel Data topic, follow these steps:

1. Launch the sample application.

2. Select the Getaways Travel window, then press Alt+Print Screen. This places a picture of the window on the Clipboard.

3. Quit the sample application, then launch Microsoft Paintbrush.

4. Select Image Attributes from the Options menu to open the dialog box.

5. Change the Width to 4.5, and the Height to 2.5. Next, select the Colors option button.

   Doing this adjusts the dimensions so that they are slightly larger than the window, and ensures that you are working in color. Color graphics appear best on-screen.

6. Select Paste from the Edit menu. A picture of the Vacation Getaways window appears.

7. Select Save from the File menu, and save the file in the GETAWAY directory as GETAWAY.BMP.

For more information on capturing screens, refer to your Windows 3.1 manual, Chapter 2, "Application Basics."

Creating Metafiles

Unlike bitmaps, *metafiles*, commonly known as *vector graphics*, are constructed with code. You can create metafiles with most graphics packages. Microsoft recommends CorelDRAW! and Micrografx Designer. If you are using another drawing package, you might want to create a sample graphics image, and open it in Visual Basic's Hot Spot Editor to make sure it is a true Microsoft metafile.

Creating Hypergraphics

Hypergraphics or *Hot Spots* are bitmaps or metafiles that are modified to include areas a user can activate with the mouse using Visual Basic's Hot Spot Editor. The Visual Basic Help Contents screen uses hypergraphics in conjunction with jump text to enable the user to jump to the Help topic by clicking the text or graphics.

 Creating hot spot graphics is an operation in itself. For more information on how to use the Hot Spot Editor, SHED.EXE, please refer to Chapter 4, "Creating Graphics for Help," in the Help Compiler Guide section of the *Professional Features Book 1* manual.

Creating Multiple Resolution Bitmaps

Multiple Resolution Bitmaps (MRB) are files that contain a combined image. The MRB files enable you to use one graphics file for different monitor resolutions.

The Vacation Getaways window, for example, was captured in VGA video resolution. If you display this image on a non-VGA monitor, the figure appears different from the original captured image. If you know that users of the Getaways application use different monitors, you can capture the screen using different resolutions, and compile the versions into one MRB file.

In the Help text, you can reference the combined MRB file instead of creating for each video resolution four different versions of Help. If you think that you need MRB graphics, refer to Chapter 4, "Creating Graphics for Help," in the Help Compiler Guide section of the *Professional Features Book 1* manual.

Including Graphics

After you create the graphics, you add them to the Help text file. You can add graphics to the Help system in two ways: use a code in the text to refer to the graphics file, or integrate the graphics directly into the text using the Windows Clipboard.

Graphics By Reference

Including graphics by reference means that you put a line of text in the document file which indicates where the graphics should appear and the name of the file which contains the image. This takes up less space on the hard drive than putting the actual graphics in the Help file. Furthermore, it becomes easier to change the graphics because the images are located in independent files rather than being contained in the Help text file.

When a set of graphics is included by reference, you put a code for the placement of the graphics on-screen. To do this, you use one of the following three codes: bmc, bml, and bmr. The bmc code indicates that the graphics are separate from the text. With the command on a separate line, the text appears above and below the graphics.

To align the graphics with the left margin, and wrap the text to the right, use bml. bmr aligns the graphics at the right margin, and wraps the text to the left. Using bmr is useful when you want graphics to appear on one side of a paragraph. To align to the left or right of a paragraph, you use the format of the command followed by the file name. However, the command is at the beginning of the line with the text of the paragraph immediately following, with no spaces.

You also can add graphics as a character, which is useful with Hot Spots. The command for inserting graphics by reference uses bmc followed by the text string to appear next to the graphics on the same line. This creates the appearance that is illustrated in the Visual Basic Help Contents screen. The Hot Spot graphics are followed by the jump text. To access the correct topic, click only the graphics or the text.

The graphics for the Getaways Travel need to appear with the Entering Travel Data topic, on the line preceding To enter data:. To add the graphics, follow these steps:

1. Position the text cursor on the line preceding To enter data:, and press Enter.

2. Type {bmc GETAWAY.BMP}.

   This command on a line by itself inserts the graphics during the Help compile, so that the text of this screen begins on the next line. The screen should resemble the one in Figure 33.12.

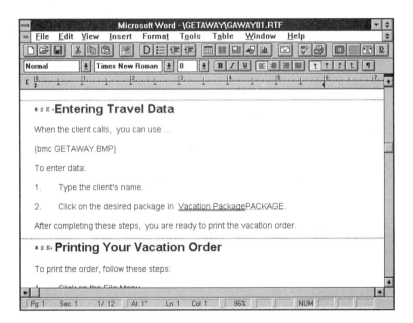

Figure 33.12.

The graphics reference.

Integrated Graphics

You also can include graphics designs by importing them from the Windows Clipboard into the Help text file. Microsoft Word for Windows is currently the only word processor that supports this method.

Processing visible graphics designs takes a little longer than including them by reference, so you might notice a slight speed loss when viewing the help at run time.

To import the graphics into the Entering Travel Data topic, follow these steps:

1. Place the image on the Windows Clipboard.

2. Open the Help text file.

3. Position the cursor on the line preceding `To enter data:`, and press Enter.

4. Select **P**aste from the **E**dit menu. The screen should appear as shown in Figure 33.13.

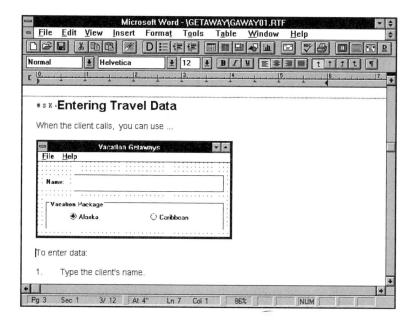

Figure 33.13.

The imported graphics.

Advantages and Disadvantages of Integrating Graphics

Both methods of integrating graphics have advantages and disadvantages. Table 33.7 compares the two methods.

Table 33.7. Graphic integration methods.

Feature	By Reference	Imported
Word Processing program	Your choice	Word for Windows
Location Control	Separate Line, Aligned with the left or right margin, or treated as a character	Imported to what place?
Text Wrap	None, Left, or Right	None
Support Hot Spots	Yes	No
Modify Graphics	Modify the graphics file.	Make changes to the graphics. Copy the new image to the Clipboard. Delete the original, and paste the new one in its place.
Multiple References	Yes	Import the graphics at each location.

Additional Ways to Refine Your Help System

In addition to adding graphics, Visual Basic provides two more ways to add functionality to your Help system. You can add a *nonscrolling region* to keep the topic title visible as the user scrolls through a topic. You can also program Help macros that enable you to control the WinHelp function more extensively.

Nonscrolling Regions

Visual Basic enables you to define a section of text to act as a topic header. If the topic is too large to fit in the Help window, the user can scroll through the text while the header remains on-screen. To set up this nonscrolling header region, use the Keep With Next function. If the "Printing Your Vacation Order" topic was longer, and required a header, you could add one by following these steps (the nonscrolling region must be at the beginning of the topic):

1. Position the cursor on the first line of the "Printing Your Vacation Order" topic.

2. Format the text with the Keep with Next function on your word processor.

3. Position the cursor on the last line in this topic, and press Enter 20 times.

4. Type **The last line**.

5. Save the file in the RTF format as **GETAWAY.RTF**.

After you compile the Help file, the title "Printing Your Vacation Order" remains on-screen as you scroll through the topic.

Help Macros

Visual Basic also enables you to access more of the functionality of WinHelp and other Windows functions by creating macros. Macros can assist you in changing the way the Help window appears and operates.

You can add, change, or delete buttons and menus during the user's access of specific topics with the Help Macro Language. You can program the Help function to jump to particular locations in the Help file, enable the user to run other Windows applications, and many other features.

You need to be familiar with one macro in particular for the Getaways application. To place the browse buttons in the Help window, you use the BrowseButtons() command, which is outlined later in this chapter. For more information about macros and macro language, please refer to Chapter 5, "Creating Help Macros," in the Help Compiler Guide section of the *Professional Features Book 1* manual.

Creating the Help File

After you create the Help text file and add the special effects, you need to write the Help file. The WinHelp function uses this file during the operation of your application to provide help. You have to write instructions for the Help compiler to create this Help file. You have to create these instructions in a Help project file. Then, the Help project file has to be compiled into the Help file. The last step is to debug and test a Help file.

Creating the Help Project File

To create the Help file, you need to write the *Help project file*. It communicates the files and parameters that go into the Help file.

You can create the Help project file in any text editor that enables you to save text as unformatted ASCII. The example presented here uses the Windows Notepad utility. The Help project file can contain a maximum of nine sections, including Options, Files, Build Tags, Config, Bitmaps, Map, Alias, Windows, and Baggage.

To begin the Help project file for the Getaways applications, start Windows Notepad. Save the new document in the GETAWAY directory as **GETAWAY.HPJ**. (The project file always has an extension of .HPJ.)

The Options Section

The Options section enables you to specify preferences that control the construction of the Help file during the compile process. This is optional. However, if you use any of the settings, they must appear as the first section in the Help project file.

To begin with the identification tag, type **[OPTIONS]** in the file on a line by itself. (You must specify each option on a line by itself.) Seventeen options are available in this section, and can appear in any order; however, Getaways Travel uses only eight of these options.

COMPRESS sets the level of data compression to control the size of the Help file. NO compiles the Help file without minimizing the size. MEDIUM compresses the file approximately forty percent, and HIGH does so approximately fifty percent. To implement compression, type

```
COMPRESS = HIGH
```

CONTENTS enables you to specify the topic context string for the opening Help topic. If you do not set this option, the first topic from the initial file in the FILES section is used. To specify the topic context string, type

```
CONTENTS = CONTENTS
```

COPYRIGHT enables you to specify that a string of 35 to 75 characters appears following the Microsoft Help copyright in the Help About box. To add the Getaways copyright, type

```
COPYRIGHT = Getaways Travel Help File, Version 1.0
```

ERRORLOG enables you to specify an error log file for any problems that arise during the compilation. You can include a path, or it is created in the directory with the compiler as a default. To do this, type

```
ERRORLOG = C:\GETAWAY\GAERROR.LOG
```

OLDKEYPHRASE enables you to specify whether the compile uses an older version of the keyphrase file. During the compilation, the program searches the text file for keywords, and writes them to a file with a PH extension. Use this parameter to instruct the compiler to ignore the existing file, and create a new one. To do this, type

```
OLDKEYPHRASE = FALSE
```

REPORT enables you to specify that error messages appear on-screen. This option is helpful because it displays the stages of the compiling process on-screen, as they happen. Tracking the process of the routine without this option is difficult because only the blinking cursor appears. To specify visual error messages, type

```
REPORT = ON
```

ROOT enables you specify a directory in which the data files are located. To specify GETAWAY as the default root directory, type

```
ROOT = C:\GETAWAY
```

TITLE enables you to specify the string you want to appear in the title bar of the Help window. You can, for example, add the word "Help" to the title of the main application window. To do this, type

```
TITLE = Getaways Travel Help
```

WARNING enables you to specify the types of error messages you want to appear on-screen or place in the error log, or both. You can set this option to 1 for only severe errors, 2 for intermediate problems, or 3 to view all errors. To view all errors, type

```
WARNING = 3
```

The following is an overview of the remaining options:

BMROOT	Identifies a separate directory for the bitmap files
BUILD	Specifies the build tags to use
FORCEFONT	Designates a font, regardless of those specified in the document
ICON	Identifies the .ICO file to use as the Help window's icon when this window is minimized
LANGUAGE	Identifies the language to use for sorting keywords (English is the default)
MAPFONTSIZE	Designates point sizes to use when certain ones are specified in the document
OPTCDROM	Specifies additional optimization parameters for Help files for use with CD-ROM

For more information, refer to Chapter 6, "Building the Help Files," in the Help Compiler Guide section of the *Professional Features Book 1* manual.

The *Files* Section

The project file requires the `files` section. This section specifies one or more text files that are used to create the Help file. The section header is `[FILES]` on one line, with each file listed on a separate line. The Getaways Travel section contains the following:

```
[FILES]
GAWAY01.RTF    ;RTF version of GAWAY01.DOC, the help text file.
```

If you have more than one file, and have not specified the `OPTIONS CONTENT` parameter, place the file with the Contents topic first. If you have many files, you can include them in a text file. For more information on including files in a text file, see the Help Compiler Guide in the *Professional Features Book 1* manual.

The *Config* Section

The `CONFIG` section enables you to customize Help using specialized macros. If you plan browse sequences, add the following macro command to place the buttons on the Help window button bar:

```
[CONFIG]
BrowseButtons()
```

The *Map* Section

The `MAP` section matches the `HelpContextID`'s with the topic context strings. The section begins with the `[MAPS]` header on one line, followed by each context string with its corresponding `HelpContextID` number.

```
[MAP]
CONTENTS       1
FILE_MENU      5
PRINT          10
EXIT           15
NAME_PROMPT    20
PACKAGE        25
INDEX          30
```

The *BITMAPS* Section

The `BITMAPS` section specifies the name of the bitmaps referenced in the Help text file. It is organized similar to the `[FILES]` section with the section header,

[BITMAPS], on one line. The bitmap files are on separate lines. These files can include a path, or you can specify the bitmap path in the [OPTIONS] section. The Getaways Travel application contains the following bitmap section:

```
[BITMAPS]
C:\GETAWAY\GETAWAY.BMP
```

BUILDTAGS, ALIAS, WINDOW, and BAGGAGE

You also can include in the project file the BUILDTAGS, ALIAS, WINDOW, and BAGGAGE sections.

Include the BUILDTAGS section only if you specified build tags in your text file. The section header [BUILDTAGS] is on one line followed by each build-tag string on a line by itself. If you had included the tags for the test build in the text file, they appear as follows in the project file:

```
[BUILDTAGS]
TEST        ;A build for testing use only
LIVE        ;The complete build for distribution to users
```

ALIAS enables you to remap context strings to others. This is beneficial when you create a text file, then revise it to replace a topic. Rather than locating the place in other topics in which the old one is referenced, you can assign the old context string to the new one:

```
[ALIAS]
old_context_string = new_context_string
```

WINDOWS enables you to specify the position and size settings of the Help window. If you do not use this section, the Help window opens in the default position.

BAGGAGE enables you to list any files you want to store in the Help file. MS-DOS cannot reference files on a CD-ROM; however, the WinHelp file system can. You usually use this section to accommodate multimedia references on CD-ROM. You can also use it while preparing Help for the Multimedia version of Microsoft Windows.

For more information on BUILDTAGS, ALIAS, WINDOW, and BAGGAGE, refer to the Help Compiler Guide.

Compiling the Help File

After you create the text and project files, you are ready to compile the Help file. To compile the Help file for Getaways Travel, follow these steps:

1. Begin at the DOS command prompt. (This can be from the DOS prompt icon in the Main Group in Windows, or directly from the DOS prompt outside of Windows.)

2. To begin the compiling process, type **hc31 getaway.hpj**. (The HC31.EXE file must be in the current directory or in a path specified with a PATH command in your AUTOEXEC.BAT file.) When the DOS prompt returns, you are ready to debug the Help file.

The output of the Help Compiler is a file named GETAWAY.HLP. This is the Help file to be used within the application. The Help Compiler creates a file with the same root name as the input project file, but with a .HLP extension.

T I P   If your compilation uses a large number of topic files, it can take several hours to compile the Help file. Therefore, you might consider running HC31 at night, after your normal working hours. If you do, to track the compiling errors, be sure that the project file uses the ERRORLOG parameter in the OPTIONS section.

It's also possible to run HC31 in the background under the control of Windows. To do so, initiate the Help compiler from the command line in Windows. Then change your Windows settings to place the task in background mode. You can then run other Windows applications, including Visual Basic, in the foreground. For more about running applications in the background, consult your Windows documentation.

Debugging and Testing the Help File

After you compile the Help file, you need to debug and test it. The debugging process involves resolving any errors that occurred during the compile process.

Testing involves two steps. You need to test the Help file to see if the topics display as you expect, and you need to see if your program will work with the Help file.

The following sections explain the debugging and testing of the Help file.

Debugging the Help File

After you compile the Help file, you debug it to correct any errors. First, view the GAERROR.LOG error log generated during compilation. You can do this by using Windows Notepad (see Figure 33.14).

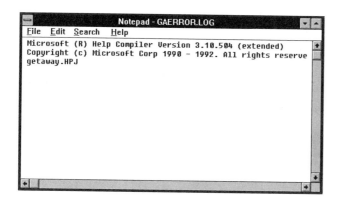

Figure 33.14.

The error log.

This file shows the steps of the compile process, and indicates any errors. They appear below the name of the project file. Each lists the error message number, the line in the file that caused the error, and a brief description of it. If errors are preceded by WARNING, you cannot open or test the resulting Help file.

Many error messages can appear. For more information, refer to the Help Compiler Guide, or open the Help Reference file that comes with Visual Basic. **T I P**

You must correct each line that generates an error. It can be something as simple as a typographical error, or as complex as an incorrect command or cross-reference. After you correct the errors, repeat the compile process.

Testing the Help File

After you compile and debug the Help file, you need to test it to ensure that it operates properly. Follow these steps to run the WinHelp application and check the GETAWAY.HLP file:

1. Using the Windows Program Manager, choose the **R**un option from the File menu.

   The Run dialog box opens.

2. In the dialog box, type the file name **c:\windows\winhelp.exe**.

3. Click the OK button to accept the file name and close the dialog box.

   Windows launches the WinHelp application.

4. Choose the **O**pen option from WinHelp's **F**ile menu.

    The Open dialog box appears.

5. In the dialog box, type the file name **c:\getaway\getaway.hlp**.

    WinHelp loads the Getaways help file for viewing (see Figure 33.15).

Figure 33.15.

The Getaways Travel
Help file.

6. Verify the text, jumps, browse sequences, definitions, search keywords, graphics, title, and copyright information. (You can check all the Help features except for the context-sensitive access and Index.)

Accessing the Help window from the Program Manager enables you to concentrate on the Help file without worrying about the host application. After you verify the Help file, close the WinHelp application by selecting **E**xit from the File menu. Now it's time to test the Help file with the actual application.

Testing an Application's Help System

After you test the Help file to ensure that it appears and behaves as expected, make sure the application calls it correctly. To do this, follow these steps:

1. Launch the application.

2. Test the Help menu options to see if the correct window is opened with the corresponding topic.

3. Test Search to make sure the keyword pulls up the correct topic.

4. Give each control the focus, and press F1 for each one that has a
   `HelpContextID`.

   The Help window should open with that control's Help topic.

5. Exit the application while the Help window is open. Help should close,
   along with the application.

Summary

Visual Basic provides tools to create a Help system that works with `WinHelp`,
the Windows Help Utility. With Visual Basic, you can design a conventional
Windows Help system for each of your applications.

Your system can enable the user to search for a topic, and browse through the
various help screens. It also helps the user to jump to topics of interest, and
use F1 to access the specific help screen for the control that has the focus.
You also can include graphics, Hot Spots, and macros to provide a more
sophisticated Help system.

To create the Help system, you need to plan the type of support you want to
provide, then program your application to access the Help file. You need to
write the Help text, and its project file. After you have done this, you compile
the Help file, debug any errors, and test the Help system.

Reference

Reserved Words

This appendix lists the keywords found in the Standard Edition of Visual Basic 3.0. You should avoid using any of these words as variable names, control names, or other user-created identifiers.

For most of these words, you *can't* use the word as a variable name. If you do, an error results. However, Visual Basic does allow you to use *some* of these words as variable names. Nevertheless, it's good programming practice to name your variables with words that don't appear on this list. Reading and debugging your programs will be easier.

Abs	AppActivate	Beep
Access	Apend	BeginTrans
AddItem	AppendChunk	Binary
AddNew	Arrange	ByVal
Alias	As	Call
And	Asc	Case
Any	Atn	CCur
App	Base	Cdbl

ChDir	Cos	DateValue
ChDrive	CreateDatabase	Day
Choose	CreateDynaset	DDB
Chr	CreateObject	Debug
Chr$	CreateQueryDef	Declare
CInt	CreateSnapshot	DefCur
Circle	CSng	DefDbl
Clear	CStr	DefInt
Clipboard	CurDir	DefLng
CLng	CurDir$	DefSng
Clone	Currency	DefStr
Close	CVar	DefVar
Cls	CVDate	Delete
Command	Data	DeleteQueryDef
Command$	Database	Dim
CommitTrans	Date	Dir
CompactDatabase	Date$	Dir$
Compare	DateAdd	Do
Const	DateDiff	DoEvents
Control	DatePart	Double
Controls	DateSerial	Drag

Dynaset	Field	Get
Edit	Fields	GetAttr
Else	FieldSize	GetChunk
ElseIf	FileAttr	GetData
End	FileCopy	GetFormat
EndDoc	FileDateTime	GetObject
EndIf	FileLen	GetText
Environ$	FindFirst	Global
EOF	FindLast	GoSub
Eqv	FindNext	GoTo
Erase	FindPrevious	Hex
Erf	Fix	Hex$
Err	For	Hide
Error	Form	Hour
Error$	Format	If
Execute	Format$	Iif
ExecuteSQL	Forms	Imp
Exit	FreeFile	Indexes
Exp	FreeLocks	Input
Explicit	Function	Input$
False	FV	InputBox

InputBox$	Line	Me
InStr	LinkExecute	Mid
Int	LinkPoke	Mid$
Integer	LinkRequest	Minute
Ipmt	LinkSend	MIRR
IRR	ListFields	MkDir
Is	ListIndexes	Mod
IsDate	ListParameters	Month
IsEmpty	ListTables	Move
IsNull	Load	MoveFirst
IsNumeric	LoadPicture	MoveLast
Kill	Loc	MoveNext
LBound	Local	MovePrevious
LCase	Lock	MoveRelative
LCase$	LOF	MsgBox
Left	Log	Name
Left$	Long	New
Len	Loop	NewPage
Let	LSet	Next
Lib	LTrim	NextBlock
Like	LTrim$	Not

Nothing	Printer	RGB
Now	PrintForm	Right
NPer	Private	Right$
NPV	PSet	RmDir
Null	Put	Rnd
Oct	PV	Rollback
Oct$	QBColor	RSet
On	QueryDef	RTrim
Open	Random	RTrim$
OpenDatabase	Randomize	SavePicture
OpenQueryDef	Rate	Scale
OpenTable	Read	Screen
Option	ReDim	Second
Or	Refresh	Seek
Output	RegisterDatabase	Select
Partition	Rem	SendKeys
Pmt	RemoveItem	Set
Point	RepairDatabase	SetAttr
PopupMenu	Reset	SetData
PPmt	Restore	SetDataAccessOption
Preserve	Resume	SetDefaultWorkspace
Print	Return	SetFocus

SetText	Switch	TypeOf
Sgn	SYD	UBound
Shared	System	UCase
Shell	Tab	UCase$
Show	Table	Unload
Sin	TableDef	Unlock
Single	TableDefs	Until
SLN	Tan	Update
Snapshot	Text	UpdateControls
Space	TextHeight	UpdateRecord
Space$	TextWidth	Using
Spc	Then	Val
Sqr	Time	Variant
Static	Time$	VarType
Step	Timer	Weekday
Stop	TimeSerial	Wend
Str	TimeValue	While
Str$	To	Width
StrComp	Trim	Write
String	Trim$	Xor
String$	True	Year
Sub	Type	ZOrder

ANSI Code Chart

The following table lists the values that represent alphanumeric characters for the Visual Basic interpreter. The table shows the basis of the character code of the American National Standards Institute (ANSI). This code has been adapted by Microsoft for use with Microsoft Windo ws, so it contains some elements of the all-encompassing ANSI code as well as some elements of ASCII (American Standard Code for Information Interchange) on which the ANSI code is partly based. This table assumes you have installed the English code table for your copy of MS-DOS.

Character	Hex code	ANSI code
Backspace	&H08	8
Tab	&H09	9
Line feed	&H0A	10
Carriage return	&H0D	13
Space	&H20	32
!	&H21	33
"	&H22	34
#	&H23	35
$	&H24	36
%	&H25	37
&	&H26	38
'	&H27	39

Character	Hex code	ANSI code
(	&H28	40
)	&H29	41
*	&H2A	42
+	&H2B	43
,	&H2C	44
-	&H2D	45
.	&H2E	46
/	&H2F	47
0	&H30	48
1	&H31	49
2	&H32	50
3	&H33	51
4	&H34	52
5	&H35	53
6	&H36	54
7	&H37	55
8	&H38	56
9	&H39	57
:	&H3A	58
;	&H3B	59
<	&H3C	60
=	&H3D	61
>	&H3E	62
?	&H3F	63
@	&H40	64
A	&H41	65
B	&H42	66
C	&H43	67
D	&H44	68
E	&H45	69
F	&H46	70
G	&H47	71

Character	Hex code	ANSI code
H	&H48	72
I	&H49	73
J	&H4A	74
K	&H4B	75
L	&H4C	76
M	&H4D	77
N	&H4E	78
O	&H4F	79
P	&H50	80
Q	&H51	81
R	&H52	82
S	&H53	83
T	&H54	84
U	&H55	85
V	&H56	86
W	&H57	87
X	&H58	88
Y	&H59	89
Z	&H5A	90
[	&H5B	91
\	&H5C	92
]	&H5D	93
^	&H5E	94
_	&H5F	95
`	&H60	96
a	&H61	97
b	&H62	98
c	&H63	99
d	&H64	100
e	&H65	101
f	&H66	102
g	&H67	103

Character	Hex code	ANSI code
h	&H68	104
i	&H69	105
j	&H6A	106
k	&H6B	107
l	&H6C	108
m	&H6D	109
n	&H6E	110
o	&H6F	111
p	&H70	112
q	&H71	113
r	&H72	114
s	&H73	115
t	&H74	116
u	&H75	117
v	&H76	118
w	&H77	119
x	&H78	120
y	&H79	121
z	&H7A	122
{	&H7B	123
		&H7C	124
}	&H7D	125
~	&H7E	126
'	&H91	145
'	&H92	146
"	&H93	147
"	&H94	148
°	&H95	149
–	&H96	150
—	&H97	151
Space	&HA0	160
¡	&HA1	161

Character	Hex code	ANSI code
¢	&HA2	162
£	&HA3	163
⊗	&HA4	164
¥	&HA5	165
¦	&HA6	166
§	&HA7	167
¨	&HA8	168
©	&HA9	169
ª	&HAA	170
«	&HAB	171
¬	&HAC	172
-	&HAD	173
®	&HAE	174
‾	&HAF	175
°	&HB0	176
±	&HB1	177
²	&HB2	178
³	&HB3	179
´	&HB4	180
µ	&HB5	181
¶	&HB6	182
•	&HB7	183
¹	&HB8	184
‾	&HB9	185
º	&HBA	186
»	&HBB	187
¼	&HBC	188
½	&HBD	189
¾	&HBE	190
¿	&HBF	191
À	&HC0	192
Á	&HC1	193

Character	Hex code	ANSI code
Â	&HC2	194
Ã	&HC3	195
Ä	&HC4	196
Å	&HC5	197
Æ	&HC6	198
Ç	&HC7	199
È	&HC8	200
É	&HC9	201
Ê	&HCA	202
Ë	&HCB	203
Ì	&HCC	204
Í	&HCD	205
Î	&HCE	206
Ï	&HCF	207
Ð	&HD0	208
Ñ	&HD1	209
Ò	&HD2	210
Ó	&HD3	211
Ô	&HD4	212
Õ	&HD5	213
Ö	&HD6	214
X	&HD7	215
Ø	&HD8	216
Ù	&HD9	217
Ú	&HDA	218
Û	&HDB	219
Ü	&HDC	220
Ý	&HDD	221
Þ	&HDE	222
ß	&HDF	223
à	&HE0	224
á	&HE1	225

Character	Hex code	ANSI code
â	&HE2	226
ã	&HE3	227
ä	&HE4	228
å	&HE5	229
æ	&HE6	230
ç	&HE7	231
è	&HE8	232
é	&HE9	233
ê	&HEA	234
ë	&HEB	235
ì	&HEC	236
í	&HED	237
î	&HEE	238
ï	&HEF	239
ð	&HF0	240
ñ	&HF1	241
ò	&HF2	242
ó	&HF3	243
ô	&HF4	244
õ	&HF5	245
ö	&HF6	246
÷	&HF7	247
ø	&HF8	248
ù	&HF9	249
ú	&HFA	250
û	&HFB	251
ü	&HFC	252
ý	&HFD	253
ρ	&HFE	254
ÿ	&HFF	255

The _KeyPress event is recognized whenever a standard ANSI character—not including function keys or control keys—is pressed once on the keyboard. The returned value will be one of those listed in the preceding table. By contrast, a key code is recognized continually by the _KeyUp and _KeyDown events *while* a key on your keyboard is being pressed. This key may be one of those in the preceding ANSI table, although it may also be a key that is not represented by the ANSI code, such as the Ctrl key or Print Screen. These other keys are listed within the CONSTANT.TXT file supplied with your copy of Visual Basic as declarations of constants that can be attached to the global module of your VB application.

Symbols

A

O

P

Learning is Easy with Easy Books from Que!

Que's Easy Series offers a revolutionary concept in computer training. The friendly, 4-color interior, easy format, and simple explanations guarantee success for even the most intimidated computer user!

Easy WordPerfect 6
Version 6

$16.95 USA
1-56529-087-9, 256 pp., 8 x 10

Easy DOS, 2nd Edition
Through Version 6

$16.95 USA
1-56529-095-x, 200 pp., 8 x 10

Easy 1-2-3, 2nd Edition
Releases 2.4

$19.95 USA
1-56529-022-4, 224 pp., 8 x 10

Easy Macintosh
All Macintosh Computers

$19.95 USA
0-88022-819-9, 200 pp., 8 x 10

Easy Quattro Pro
Version 4

$19.95 USA
0-88022-798-2, 200 pp., 8 x

Easy Word for Windows
Versions 1 & 2

$19.95 USA
0-88022-922-5, 224 pp., 8 x 10

Easy Quattro Pro for Windows
Version 5.1 for Windows

$19.95 USA
0-88022-993-4, 224 pp., 8 x 10

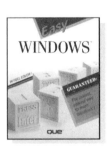

Easy Windows
Version 3.1

$19.95 USA
0-88022-985-3, 200 pp., 8 x 10

Easy WordPerfect for Windows
Version 5.2 for Windows

$19.95 USA
0-88022-126-3, 208 pp., 8 x

 To Order, Call: (800) 428-5331 OR (317) 573-2500